The Psychological Testing Enterprise: An Introduction

Tim B. Rogers

The University of Calgary

Brooks/Cole Publishing Company

Pacific Grove, California

ITP™ The trademark ITP is used under license.

Brooks/Cole Publishing Company
A Division of Wadsworth, Inc.

Printed in the United States of America

10 9 8 7 6 5 4 3 2

Library of Congress Cataloging-in-Publication Data

Rogers, Timothy B., [date]
   The psychological testing enterprise: an introduction / Tim B. Rogers.
       p.   cm.
   Includes bibliographical references and index.
   ISBN 0-534-21648-X
   1. Psychological tests.   I. Title.
BF176.R63   1994   94-25008
150′.28′7--dc20   CIP

Sponsoring Editors: Jim Brace-Thompson, Kenneth King
Marketing Representative: Rachel Leitch
Editorial Associate: Cathleen S. Collins
Production Editor: George Calmenson/The Book Company
Production Coordinator: Joan Marsh
Manuscript Editor: Betty Duncan
Permissions Editor: Cathleen S. Collins
Interior Design: Wendy Calmenson/The Book Company
Cover Design: Sharon L. Kinghan
Cover Photo: Lee Hocker
Interior Illustration: Impact Publications
Photo Researcher: Diana Mara Henry
Typesetting: Impact Publications
Cover Printing: Phoenix Color Corporation
Printing and Binding: Arcata Graphics/Fairfield

Preface

The Psychological Testing Enterprise: An Introduction is a student-oriented text crafted to provide deep understandings of the social and scientific character of psychological testing. This is accomplished by organizing the curriculum in a novel and creative way—one that facilitates the student's grasp of the material and one that also renders the material readable and interesting.

The Enterprise starts out by providing a snapshot of testing today, wherein its importance as contemporary social *and* scientific practice is articulated. Focus then shifts, with the remainder of the book exploring *why* testing has emerged as it has within our culture.

This is accomplished by first examining the social, mathematical, and philosophical foundations of testing. After exploring test-like practices in several cultures, some basic mathematical ideas such as the normal curve and correlation are presented in their historical context to embellish the importance of the quantitative worldview in our own culture. The antecedents of conceptual issues such as the nature-nurture controversy, to which testing is strongly wed, are also sketched out.

With the foundations for the emergence of testing laid, discussion then turns to the pioneer era during which the notions of reliability, IQ, and criterion-related validity emerged. Seeing the evolution of these critical ideas and tests in the context in which they actually occurred is not only an interesting story in its own right, but also provides students with insights into why these concepts emerged as they did.

The next part of the text deals with numerous variations on the earlier foundational ideas. The philosophical and technological innovations associated with tests like the MMPI are presented, and the manner in which factor analysis emerged as a method to resolve problems with the global view of intelligence is also sketched out. Variations such as content validity, internal consistency measures of reliability, and item analysis are also presented as solutions to specific problems being faced by the rapidly-growing testing enterprise.

The modern era of testing is discussed in light of the professionalization of psychology which occurred after World War Two. The introduction of construct validity is treated as an outgrowth of this institutionalization, and thereby becomes clearly understandable to students. The emergence of a strong antitest movement in the 1960s is then documented and its impact upon contemporary testing practice demonstrated. The continual interplay between professional, scientific, and social factors in this part of the text brings the true nature of the testing enterprise into fascinating focus.

To provide a sense of the current status of testing, four domains of contemporary testing practice are then discussed: intelligence, personality, behavioral assessment, and neuropsychological testing. These four chapters, while not exhausting the areas in which testing is currently active, provide students with a wide-ranging set of exemplars of the manner in which the contemporary testing enterprise conducts its day-to-day business.

The final section of the text looks at some of the emerging ideas in testing such as meta-analysis and the unitary vision of validity. Additionally, a framework is provided which gives students a means of deciding, for themselves, their personal positions on the critical tensions of testing such as the conflicts between the individual and institution, nature and nurture, science and art, as well as the positivist program and possible alternatives.

The Psychological Testing Enterprise, then, provides a provocative, stimulating, and readable presentation of testing in our culture. It provides students with the background necessary to deal with testing as it touches their lives. It also provides sophisticated understandings of specific methodological techniques, as well as discussions of the details of many of the classic tests. And, as an added bonus, it provides students with the intellectual tools to be able to evaluate testing and its practices for themselves.

Several other features of *The Enterprise* add to the student-oriented nature of the book. Included here are detailed chapter-end glossaries that define critical terms, carefully chosen suggested further readings that can be used to explore various topics in greater depth, and sets of discussion questions designed to allow students to apply their newfound knowledge to new problems and situations. Appendices and discussions of how to discover information about tests are also provided as well as a number of resources such as detailed discussions of ethics, technical aspects of tests, and an annotated listing of major psychological assessment instruments that includes information about the location of reviews and evaluative commentaries. In all *The Enterprise* is an unparalleled information package for students.

An additional feature of *The Enterprise* is a *Student Study Guide* of high quality that has been developed in consultation with several cohorts of students using early drafts of the text. This supplement has been carefully designed to provide students with a number of diverse activities that allows them to test themselves and to develop their understandings of the materials. Based upon the creative suggestions of many undergraduate students, the *Guide* contains properly formatted study materials, detailed content outlines, self-quizzes, and a series of crossword puzzles—all oriented toward facilitating student understanding and interest in the curriculum.

The Psychological Testing Enterprise is the first text to provide an alternative to the more or less standard handbook format that currently dominates the field. All the materials covered in the traditional text can be found in *The Enterprise*, with the added bonus of clear and fascinating presentations of the interactions between these and the society in which they are practiced. As such, this text emerges as the first to explicitly place testing into its social context. From this, students are able to draw significant understandings of testing and the manners in which it touches their lives. This text empowers them with the tools that will allow them to take control of this important component of their lived cultural experience.

The Enterprise arose out of a number of tensions associated with teaching tests and measurements. Foremost here was consistent student commentary indicating that the traditional texts took too much for granted and did not explicate the "whys" of contemporary testing practices. To be sure, these handbook-style texts were rife with information, but, to students, they were mute about the genesis of the ideas and practices. As well, becasue of the taken-for-granted nature of these traditional texts, student motivation to read the material began to flag. As I began to react to these concerns in my lectures I soon found that I was fighting the available texts. It was almost impossible to address these student concerns while remaining faithful to the organizational and conceptual schemata underlying the handbook-style text. *The Enterprise* addresses these concerns. Taking a contextual/chronological approach to instructing the material rendered the "whys" extremely visible. Additionally, it was possible to create a text that students enjoyed reading because it told a coherent story about testing and our culture. An added bonus of this orientation is the manner in which the text offers an explicit framework for addressing questions of value and worth of the testing enterprise in our culture—something that, as instructors, we have an obligation to impart to our students.

Because of this orientation, *The Enterprise* brings numerous advantages to instructors. With a book that has been crafted to address student concerns, many of the traditional problems of teaching in this field are resolved. With students gaining a sense of the entire field from the text, the instructors can focus on whatever aspect of the course curriculum they feel is most important—knowing that the basics will be covered by student reading. This provides instructors with unparalleled freedom in designing their course. The carefully designed *Instructor's Manual* contains a discussion of several course design options that emerge once this freedom has been attained. Additionally, the *Manual* contains the expected pool of multiple-choice questions, annotated references to provide alternative materials for in-class presentations, as well as some visual support in the form of photocopy-ready overhead and xerox masters.

So here you have it—a new and exciting package of materials for teaching and studying a course in tests and measurements. If the reactions of the students who have already used early drafts are any indication, there can be little doubt that it will enhance and strengthen the teaching and learning of this material.

Thanks

This book was conceived well over a decade ago in response to a number of tensions surrounding the teaching of tests and measurements. Since that time, it has been painstakingly poked and prodded by many individuals whose cooperative efforts lie at its heart. I offer sincere thanks to all these people, and my hope that the final product is at least a pale imitation of the collective wisdom and effort they contributed.

The numerous students—especially those who served as guinea pigs for draft versions of the emerging work—were a constant source of inspiration and expertise. I hope I have done justice to their numerous comments and exceptional creativity. I'm only sorry that space does not permit listing of their names as a small token of acknowledgement of their critical contributions.

My colleagues—especially those who, no doubt, came to rue my frequent visits scouring for source materials—were equally important to the realization of this text. Again, there are a tremendous number of individuals involved here and I cannot mention them all. But I would like to formally acknowledge the tremendous help provided by: June Adam, Brian Bland, Ed Boyd, Tom Briggs, Charles Costello, Kurt Danziger, Jerry Devins, Keith Dobson, Jos Eggermont, John Ellard, Jerry Ells, Doug Francis, Dave Gibson, Chris Green, Gustav Habermann, Bat-ami Klejner, Don Kline, Bryan Kolb, Candice Konnert, Marvin MacDonald, Eric Mash, John Mills, Lary Mosley, Valerie Pruegger, Lorraine Radtke, Patty Rogers, Brian Rusted, Bob Sainsbury, Nancy Johnson Smith, Hank Stam, Lorne Sulsky, Barre Toelken, and Charles Tolman. Whether providing some source materials or just discussing an issue and providing new understandings, the input of these colleagues, and many others, was an essential aspect of the emergence of the text. Additionally the collective expertise of the many reviewers who have toiled over various revisions of this text have made a significant contribution to the final product. I wish to thank: Michael Botwin, California State University—Fresno; George Domino, University of Arizona; Eric Dubow, Bowling Green State University; Valerie Greaud Folk, Educational Testing Service; Timothy Hartshorne, Central Michigan University; Richard Hudiburg, University of North Alabama; Charles Krauskopf, Ohio State University; Marvin MacDonald, Augustana University College; Richard Rankin, University of Oregon; Garnett Stokes, University of Georgia; Robert Strahan, Iowa State University. Some of the research that was conducted to permit "telling testing's tale" was supported by grants from the Social Sciences and Humanities Research Council of Canada.

And then there is the tremendous production and editorial staff who put their hearts and souls into this book. Again the list is too long to be complete, but I would especially like to acknowledge the support of Ken King of Wadsworth, the editor who originally championed this work. His support has been well-extended by Jim Brace-Thompson of Brooks/Cole and the fine crew including, among others, George and Wendy Calmenson, Cat Collins, Betty Duncan, Diana Henry, and Joan Marsh. Much of what you hold in your hands is due to their exceptional effort and skill. Additionally the secretarial and organizational skills of Alison Wiigs here in the Department of Psychology at the University of Calgary were a tremendous help.

Finally there are those who provided the day-to-day support as the project was realized. The light of intellectual curiosity that burns so strongly in the eyes of my son and daughter, Ben and Lisa, was a constant reminder of the real reason for spending a decade preparing this book. And whether I came home grumpy because a chapter hadn't "worked" or elated because it had, my wife Patty was always there to offer counsel and support. Her kindness and love are so much a part of this book that it is dedicated to her.

Brief Contents

Contents

PART II   FOUNDATIONS   79

Chapter 3   Social Foundations of Testing: A Multicultural Perspective   81

PART IV   THE GOLDEN AGE   277

Chapter 9   Spreading the Word: Operationism and the MMPI   279

PART V   THE MODERN ERA

Chapter 12   On Becoming a Profession: Ethics, Training, and Standards

Part I

Introductory Considerations

The first part of *The Psychological Testing Enterprise: An Introduction* sets the stage for the story that will follow. It provides you with a sense of the orientation taken in this book, as well as an outline of the subject matter that will be covered.

The Enterprise starts out by outlining the basic approach used to present psychological testing. This involves the notion of narrative in which the materials of testing are organized so that they tell a coherent story. As outlined in Chapter 1, this approach provides a particularly effective way of structuring the incredibly complex domain of psychological testing.

Chapter 2 presents a brief sketch of the testing enterprise as it exists today. The goal here is to give you a sense of where our story is going. It serves to frame the organizational schema that underlies the text by providing a sense of the end point of our journey through the evolution of psychological testing in North American society.

Chapter 1

Telling the Story of Testing

In This Chapter

Inside/Outside

The Narrative Approach

A Contextual Orientation

An Alternative to Narratives: Propositions

Some Thoughts on History

Goals of the Text

CLOSE UP | **A Summer Job**

Feeling a strange sense of nervousness and excitement, I approached the office building of the phone company for the first day of my job as an installer. I had been lucky enough to land a summer job in a rural vacation district, which involved apprenticing with an experienced hand and then being sent out on my own. As I entered the building, I took a deep breath—trying my best to make a good impression. After filling in what seemed to be an endless number of forms, I was eventually introduced to my mentor, Peter Trudel, a longtime resident of the small town to which I had been assigned. He was most cordial, and we eventually struck up a good working friendship.

But things were not quite so simple when we ended up in a restaurant for lunch. Many other phone company workers were there, as well as a number of others, all of whom seemed to know Peter and each other quite well. All of a sudden, I felt as if I didn't belong. Everyone was polite, but I felt excluded from the group. They used expressions and phrases that I didn't understand. I didn't find their jokes particularly funny, even though they were well received by the crowd. It was even hard to predict when they were going to laugh. The stories, which echoed around the table, contained so many names and obscure references that I could barely follow them. I even found the food a bit strange, having different spices than I was used to. Everyone seemed to share "code" words, which meant something entirely different to them than they did to me. After 15 minutes, I found myself totally isolated from the group—the city boy sitting there wondering what I had done wrong. I had absolutely no sense of how these people were seeing the world—I was a true outsider.

INSIDE/OUTSIDE

I expect that everyone has had similar experiences of being excluded. Be it a work setting, a social gathering, or summer camp, almost all of us have experienced this sense of being an outsider. And it is a frightening thing. All of a sudden, the social communication on which we rely so heavily is no longer there. Like being in a state of suspended animation, our only sense of understanding comes from something from the past.

We also have been in situations where we are the insiders. There are places where we understand all of the code words, know all of the jargon and esoteric references, find the jokes funny, relish the food, and have effective social networks. Be it at home around the dinner table, with a group of chums at the pub, or at work during a meeting, we all belong to specific groups for which we have a sense of the world as the group perceives it.

Emic Versus Etic Understanding

For some time now, social scientists have recognized this insider/outsider distinction. Special words have been coined to denote these differences, particularly when it comes to studying groups. **Emic understanding** of a group is that which comes from insiders—members of the group. Techniques such as participant observation are oriented toward discovering these kinds of understandings, which typically involve rich and detailed analyses of the world as experienced by a group member. Emic understanding functions to lay out the way the world is perceived by group members, focusing on the rich nuance of meanings and significances as experienced by the group members. **Etic understanding**, on the other hand, is that which the outsider looking in discovers. Offering a promise of objectivity, etic understanding reflects the group's activities from the perspective of another group—seeing the collective as an outsider would. Both types of understandings have their strengths and weaknesses, and both can provide very useful insight. Neither is superior to the other; they are just two types of understandings that have their time and place in understanding of people and groups.

For our purposes, the emic/etic distinction helps us understand the manner in which this text is put together. At this point in your career, as a student, you are an outsider to the field of psychological testing. In the same sense that I was excluded from Peter Trudel's world, so too are you an outsider to the domain of psychological tests. If you sat in on a conversation between me and a colleague, you would, no doubt, experience many of the same things I did during the initial days at my summer job. There would be code words you would not fully understand, stories that you would have difficulty appreciating, jokes that would not be funny, and esoteric references that would not mean a thing to you. In total, there would be a perspective of the world that you might not fully appreciate, and perhaps with which you might disagree. As a student beginning the exploration of the domain of psychological testing, you are an outsider.

A problem emerges when we realize that I am an insider by virtue of years of graduate-level training, research, and experience with tests. In a very real sense, this means that I have a different worldview from yours. My years of experience with this domain have given me a specific way of approaching problems, a definite set of values, some strong beliefs, and specific knowledge, all of which have combined to create a specific way of constructing the world. This means that we, almost literally, see the world of psychological tests through different eyes—mine being emic, yours being etic.

The problem for the textbook writer, then, is to develop a means of facilitating your gradual transition from being an outsider to gaining a sense of the insider's world. In this text, I am an informant, trying to develop a route for you to follow to uncover the inside experience of a specific group—in this case, the group of scholars, test developers, researchers, and businesspeople who are involved in the domain of psychological testing. Developing this route is not easy, particularly when I have been an indoctrinated member of the in-group for many years. Herein lies the challenge of developing an effective textbook.

The Importance of Talk

How can we infiltrate the in-group? Perhaps the best place to start is to consider how we do this in real life. Returning to my summer-job experience, what allowed me to feel at least a sense of belonging by the time I left? Perhaps you can recall a specific set of experiences that led you to the inner circle of a group of which you are now a member. For me, the singularly, most important aspect of this transition from out- to in-group is **talk**. It is through conversations with group members that entrance into the group occurs. These conversations typically converge on common grounds, which are shared with group members, and act as a necessary prerequisite to eventual acceptance. For example, I finally began to establish contact with the summer-job group when we began to talk about sports, for there was a shared set of experiences. It was possible to talk about favorite players and teams in hockey, baseball, and football. Similarly, stories of encounters with wildlife, which I had had in other summer jobs, provided a starting place for us to swap tales and get to know each other. Through these stories, I began to feel how these folks "worked," and they began to get a sense of me as well. I started to understand the history of the workers in the small town. I began to comprehend their special lingo and jargon. Names and references, which I had not previously understood, soon became clear. Before long, I recognized the humor in the jokes and was participating along with the group members. Indeed, it was through the narratives—our conversations and stories—that I eventually gained entry into this group.

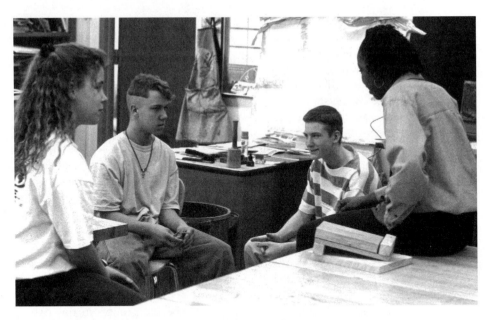

Talk is an important way of gaining entry to social groups.

THE NARRATIVE APPROACH

How does this translate to textbook writing and helping you move from the out- to the in-group? The most effective way of achieving this goal is to use **narratives**—presentations that situate the specific ideas, events, and people in a temporal order. The most natural way of helping you gain a sense of the in-group associated with psychological testing is to present stories that will begin to shape your understanding of the field. This book can be seen as a narrative about testing; it tells of the manner in which the field developed, the sources of various concepts, the strengths and weaknesses of various ideas, the reasons why a particular approach was taken over another, and a wide range of other understandings—thereby providing you with an understanding of the inner workings of the field.

The narrative approach involves creating an intellectual history that presents ideas of the testing field in the **contexts** in which they emerged. The link between sections, like a tale, is chronological, and the vehicles of communication are very much those of a storyteller. This presentation is both novel and exciting for a testing text—promising an insightful and rich understanding of an exceedingly important aspect of our current social fabric.

Plots and Subplots

The story of psychological testing is a very complex one. It involves an intricate interplay between social forces, developments in the discipline of psychology, some important ideas from philosophy, a considerable amount of business entrepreneurship, and even mathematics. Organizing all of this material is a particularly difficult task because developments in each of these subfields, and the interactions between them, have had profound impact on the testing field. To deal with this complexity, this text has adopted a fundamental metaphor that guides the story as it unfolds. This metaphor casts the testing field as having emerged from the interactions among five different sources or what might be considered **narrative strands.** For convenience we will call these social, psychology, philosophy, business, and mathematics. The emergence of the contemporary testing field is constructed in this text as a complex interaction between these five narrative strands, and the story of testing requires that all five be considered. Let's first look at the five narrative strands separately:

1. *Social.* A number of important events in society have affected the development of testing. Events such as the Great Depression, previous social policies favoring **eugenics,** or "selective breeding," and contemporary views about equal opportunity have had a profound impact on testing. These events emerge as highly significant aspects of the overall story, influencing in many and varied ways the development of tests and their use within our culture.

2. *Psychology.* Many important developments in the discipline of psychology, considered generally, have influenced testing. Included here are the adoption of specific ethical codes to enhance professionalism and the **cognitive revolution,** which has had a profound effect on how testers conceptualize the idea of intelligence. We will examine these and many other developments within the science of behavior, and we will explore the manner in which they affected the testing field.

3. *Philosophy.* Philosophers of the sciences and social sciences have, over time, provided a number of important ideas that have captured the essence of the procedures and thinking underlying psychological testing. Ideas such as **operationism,** construct validity, and investigative practices are central here and represent an essential aspect of the testing field. We will explore the relevance of these and many other philosophical positions.

4. *Business.* Testing is big business. Tests are expensive, and we use them extensively throughout our culture; hence, economic considerations and business practices are an integral part of the overall story of contemporary testing. Indeed, the title of this text, *The Psychological Testing Enterprise,* was selected to highlight the importance of these concerns in the contemporary domain.

5. *Mathematics.* The basic view of measurements revealed in tests involves the translation of psychological characteristics into numbers (more about this in Chapter 2). This fundamental beginning signals that mathematical procedures to deal with the numbers will have an important place in our story. To the extent that the testing procedures culminate in numbers and the testing field wants to use these numbers to facilitate making important social decisions, mathematics will inevitably be a significant part of the field.

A full understanding of the testing enterprise demands consideration of each of these five narrative strands. More important than the five separate strands, however, is the manner in which they interact with each other to produce a highly complex and fascinating field of inquiry. For example, social reactions against intelligence (IQ) testing in the late 1960s forced a major change in both the theories and tests of this idea. Developments in mathematics also had a profound effect on the nature of tests, particularly those purporting to measure intelligence. These and many other aspects of the testing enterprise can only be understood by considering the five strands and the manners in which they have interacted with each other.

Considering the five narrative strands and their interactions suggests that it is appropriate to view the overall testing enterprise as a colorful, braided belt, with the five strands being woven together. Indeed, the cover of the text reflects this metaphor. To be sure, some understanding of the individual strands is necessary, but the manner in which they are interwoven captures the essence of the belt. The color, texture, and impact all arrive by considering the total enterprise, not the woven strands examined separately. Too much focus on an individual strand detracts from some important issues that emerge from an examination of the total enterprise.

A "Road Map" for the Text

Table 1-1 presents the overall story line that emerges when the psychological testing enterprise is organized into a narrative frame. The five narrative strands are shown at the top of each column, and the important dates are in the leftmost column to indicate the chronological unfolding of the story. The substance of the chapters that follow are drawn from this "road map."

This road map may seem overwhelming, containing many unfamiliar ideas and references, but it gives you a sense of the overall picture that emerges when the field is arranged in a narrative framework. Refer to this table as you work your way through the text because it will help you keep things in place as the amount of information increases.

Table 1-1   A road map for the text

	Social	Psychology	Philosophy	Business	Mathematics
Dawn of civilization	Organized groups			Dedication of resources for social decision making	
2200 B.C.	Chinese civil service exams				
500 B.C.	Greece (for example, Hippocrates)				
A.D. 500	The Dark Ages				
1219	Formal exams in universities				
1540	Written exams in universities				
1599	Rules for written examinations published by Jesuits				
1679		Hooke proposes measuring visual acuity			
					Newton's *Principa*
1690		Locke's *Essay on Human Understanding*			
1700	End of medieval world order	Dawn of modern Western science			
1708		De Piles proposes measuring aesthetics			
1711		Thomasius proposes measuring personality			
1738		Von Wolff's *Perfection and Imperfection*			
1750		Caldenius proposes the use of reaction-time measures			
1781		Bonnet introduces digit span as a measure of memory			
1785		Reid's *Essays on the Intellectual Powers of Man*			

continued

Table 1-1 A road map for the text (*continued*)

	Social	Psychology	Philosophy	Business	Mathematics
1816					Bessell and the personal equation
1820					The normal curve, standard deviation, z scores
1825					Quetelet and *l'homme moyen*
1830	de Tocqueville describes Americans' tendency to count and calculate		Lyell formulates geological time		
1833	Competitive civil service exams in England				
1843			Mill's *System of Logic*		
1858	Victorian sense of self		Darwin's *Origin of Species*		
1865		Galton proposes first IQ test			
1869		Galton's *Hereditary Genius*			
1870	Competitive civil service exams in the United States				
1872		Darwin's *Expression of Emotions*			
1879		Wundt's laboratory established			

Table 1-1   A road map for the text (*continued*)

	Social	Psychology	Philosophy	Business	Mathematics
1883		Galton's *Inquiries into the Human Faculty*—questionnaire invented			
1884				Galton's Kensington laboratory	
1885	Progressive Era	The "new" psychology (for example, James)			
1890		Cattell's 10 basic tests			
1891		Boulton's use of the test-criterion method			
1896					Pearson product-moment correlation
1898				Cattell's *Desiderata for Mental Tests*	
1900				College Entrance Examination Board in the United States	
1903		Wissler and the demise of faculty psychology	Einstein's special theory of relativity		
1904		Thorndike's *Mental and Social Measurements*			Spearman and his mathematical two-factor theory of intelligence
1905	Major growth in education			Binet's first IQ test	

continued

Table 1-1   A road map for the text (*continued*)

	Social	Psychology	Philosophy	Business	Mathematics
1907					Introduction of the reliability coefficient
1908				Mental age in Binet's second test	
				Goddard's first translation of Binet's scale	
1911				Binet's third revision	
1912				Terman and Childs translate the Binet scale	
1913		Watson and behaviorism			
1914	World War I begins	Stern and the mental quotient			
1915		First published multiple-choice items (Kansas Silent Reading Test)	Stenquist Test of Mechanical Ability		
1916				Stanford–Binet test revised	
1917	The United States enters World War I	Yerkes's army committee formed		Army Alpha and Beta	
1918	World War I ends			Army testing program canceled	
1919	Major influx of immigrants from Europe	Woodworth's Personal Data Sheet		Seashore Measures of Musical Talent	
		Thurstone's work in selecting telegraphers			

Table 1-1   A road map for the text (*continued*)

	Social	Psychology	Philosophy	Business	Mathematics
1921	Postwar immigration debate	Formal emergence of validity (NADER)		First publication of Rorschach's inkblots in Germany	
		Yerkes publishes army data		The Psychological Corporation, the first major test publisher is founded	
		Conferences trying (unsuccessfully) to develop a consensual definition of intelligence			
1922	Lippman's attack on testing	Terman's response to Lippman		Downey Will Temperament Tests (DWTT)	
1923	The Roaring 20s	Boring's "IQ is what IQ tests test"	Received view of logical positivism (Carnap)		
			Brigham's *Study of American Intelligence*		
1924	Passage of Restrictive Immigration Act	Measurement without definition		Rorschach introduced to the United States	
1926				Scholastic Aptitude Test (SAT)	
1927			Bridgman's *Logic of Modern Physics* (operationism)	Strong Vocational Interest Blank (SVIB)	Spearman offers mathematical proof of *g*

continued

Table 1-1   A road map for the text (*continued*)

	Social	Psychology	Philosophy	Business	Mathematics
				Gessell test of physical/motor development	
1929	Stock market crashes				
1930	The Great Depression	Introduction of content (curricular) validity			
1931				Bernreuter Personality Inventory	
1932		Psychiatrist May's attack of psychology		Metropolitan Achievement Test	
1934		Spreading dissatisfaction with personality tests			
1935		Stevens introduces operationism		Murray's Thematic Apperception Test (TAT)	
1937		Stanford–Binet test revised			KR20 measure of internal consistency
1938		Thurstone's *Primary Mental Abilities*		Raven Progressive Matrices	Factor analysis
		Skinner's operant conditioning		Bender Visual Motor Gestalt Test	
		Murray's *Explorations in Personality*		First *Mental Measurements Yearbook* (*MMY*)	
1939	World War II begins			Wechsler–Bellevue Intelligence Test	Taylor–Russell tables

Table 1-1   A road map for the text (*continued*)

	Social	Psychology	Philosophy	Business	Mathematics
				Army General Classification Test	
				Kuder Preference Record	
1940		Thomson's critique of *g*		*Second MMY*	
1941				Pilot Aptitude Score (PAS)	
1943	Increasing return of veterans	Burt's first publication of twins-reared-apart data		Minnesota Multiphasic Personality Inventory (MMPI)	
1944			Isreal and Goldsteins's critique of operationism		
1945	World War II ends	Special issue of *Psychological Bulletin* on operationism			
1946		Jenkins's *Validity for What?*			
1947		Mosier's critique of face validity		Differential Aptitude Test Battery (DATB)	
		Halstead's work on biological intelligence			
1949				Wechsler Intelligence Scales for Children (WISC)	
				Third MMY	

continued

Table 1-1   A road map for the text (*continued*)

	Social	Psychology	Philosophy	Business	Mathematics
1950		APA ethical standards for for the distribution of tests		Increased popularity of TAT	Gulliksen's *Theory of Mental Tests*
1951					Cronbach's coefficient alpha
1952	Discovery of drugs that suppress psychotic symptoms	APA ethical code adopted Rod and Frame test			
1953				*Fourth MMY*	
1954		Construct validity introduced		APA technical recommendations for tests	
1955		Cronbach and Meehl's detailed presentation of construct validity Meehl and Rosen's base-rate paper		Wechsler Adult Intelligence Scale (WAIS)	
1956	Whyte's *Organization Man*	MIT conference said to have started the cognitive revolution		Halstead–Reitan Neuropsychological Test Battery	
1957		Cronbach's two-disciplines paper Loevinger's monograph on construct validity		In-Basket Test California Psychological Inventory (CPI)	Tyron's mathematical integration of the methods of estimating reliability

Table 1-1   A road map for the text (*continued*)

	Social	Psychology	Philosophy	Business	Mathematics
1958		APA ethical code revised		Barnum effect demonstrated	
1959	Test burning in Texas	Multimethod/ multitrait matrix	Popper's *Logic of Scientific Discovery*	*Fifth MMY*	
1960				Stanford–Binet test revised	
1962		Response style-content debate	Kuhn's *Scientific Revolutions*		Higher-order factor analysis applied to intelligence debate
1963	Kennedy's mental-health plan *Myart v. Motorola*	Royce's application of factor analysis to logical positivism		Strong Vocational Interest Blank (SVIB) revised	
1964	Civil Rights Act and Tower Amendment			Hain system for scoring the Bender as a neuro-psychological test	
1965	Congressional and Senate hearings into testing	Criterion-referenced testing		*Sixth MMY*	Cronbach and Gleser's *Tests and Personnel Decisions*
1966		Burt publishes more twin data ($n = 53$)		Revised APA recommendations for tests	
1967		Guilford's *Structure of Intellect* Neisser's *Cognitive Psychology*		Personality Research Form (PRF)	

continued

Table 1-1   A road map for the text (*continued*)

	Social	Psychology	Philosophy	Business	Mathematics
1968		Wesman's *Intelligent Testing* Mischel's critique of personality assessment		Wechsler Preschool and Primary Scale of Intelligence (WPPSI)	Lord and Novick's *Statistical Theory of Mental Test Scores*
1969	Public outcry against Jensen	Jensen's "Boosting IQ" paper Bandura's *Social Learning Theory*		Sixteen Personality Factor Questionnaire (16PF)	
1971	Hernstein's *Atlantic Monthly* article				
1972		Goldfreid and Kent discuss behavioral assessment		Matarazzo's WAIS analysis Stanford–Binet test revised *Seventh MMY*	Generalizability theory
1973		McClelland's *Testing for Competence*			
1974	Family Education Rights and Privacy Act	Kamin's *Science and Politics of IQ* Bem and Allen's consistency paper		WISC–R Revised APA recommendations for tests Strong–Campbell Interest Inventory	

Table 1-1 A road map for the text (*continued*)

	Social	Psychology	Philosophy	Business	Mathematics
				Halstead–Reitan Neuropsychological Test Battery revised	
1975	Public Law 94-142	Increased movement toward learning disabilities	Salmon's treatise on auxiliary hypotheses	Eysenck Personality Inventory	
1976	Burt controversy erupts				
1977		Sternberg's componential theory of intelligence		Jackson Vocational Interest Survey	
1978		Meehl's critique of soft psychology		*Eighth MMY*	
1979	*Larry P.* case banning testing in California	Epstein's aggregation argument			Validity generalization
1980	Reagan elected president of the United States	Messick's assessment of validity		Guion's *Holy Trinity* Assessment centers	
1981	Hinkley tries to assassinate Reagan	APA ethical code revised		WAIS–R	
1983				Kaufman Assessment Battery for Children (K-ABC) Millon Clinical Multiaxial Inventory (MCMI)	

continued

Table 1-1   A road map for the text (*continued*)

	Social	Psychology	Philosophy	Business	Mathematics
1985	Increasing search for physical explanations of behavior		Serlin and Lapsley's *good-enough principle*	*Ninth MMY*	
1986	Public Law 99–475	Jackson's advantages of computerized tests Landy's construct validity as hypothesis testing		Stanford–Binet test revised	
1987				*Diagnostic and Statistical Manual of Mental Disorders* (3rd ed.; revised) (*DSM III–R*)	
1988		Sternberg's *Triarchic Mind* Messick's consequential basis of test use		MCMI II	
1989				*Tenth MMY* MMPI II	
1990		Just's cognitive analysis of the *Raven* Cognitive evaluation of ADHD (Posner et al.)	Meehl's *Lakatosian Defense*	WPPSI–R Connors's attention deficit hyperactivity disorder (ADHD) scales	
1991			Sampson's *Experiential Democracy*	WISC III	

A CONTEXTUAL ORIENTATION

Several strategies were employed to develop the narrative of this highly complex story of testing. For one, the text embraces a **contextual orientation**. The basic idea here is that the testing enterprise evolved in response to a number of forces that created a specific context demanding action. For example, the first major use of IQ tests in the United States was during World War I when it was necessary to make many fast decisions about who was not fit to serve in a combat unit. The concern for efficiency that characterizes contemporary testing, then, evolved in response to specific contextual factors some time ago (for example, global conflict, need for speed and economy). Whether this value is relevant in today's testing enterprise is an interesting question. This example hints at the manner in which a contextual approach sheds insight into how tests are developed and marketed.

The contextual factors that shaped the testing enterprise were many and varied—important developments in the philosophy of science, political factors favoring particular views of humanity, technological developments, social policies favoring equal opportunity, and business practices, to name a few. The story that follows brings these contextual factors into focus and provides a provocative view of the evolution and present status of the testing enterprise.

Presenting the five narrative strands in concert with each other is a daunting challenge. We will accomplish this by taking a chronological approach to the analysis of the testing enterprise. We will examine the developments in the testing field as they unfolded—embedded in the social/historical context in which they emerged. We will then consider the various contextual factors at play at a specific time, followed by discussion of the proposed solutions. The next major contextual change and the impact it had on the field then follows, and so on. Thus, instead of presenting all mathematical propositions in a section at the start of the book, they are given when they were introduced. This permits us to examine their implications at the time they were proposed and to determine their relevance after the original context that spawned them had changed. Contextual factors associated with the social, business, and philosophical strands in our story are also treated in the same way. They are introduced when they occur, not in separate sections. The total effect is to present a fascinating but complex story that shows incredible interactions between various aspects of our contemporary society.

AN ALTERNATIVE TO NARRATIVES: PROPOSITIONS

The jury is still out on this approach to writing textbooks. Not a panacea by any means, it has its problems as well as its strong points. It seems reasonable, then, to consider in a bit more detail the strengths and weaknesses of narrative approaches and the assumptions that this orientation implies.

In order to proceed, identifying a major alternative to the narrative approach is necessary. Narratives are constructed sequences of events with a temporal dimension. Typically told from a first- or third-person perspective, they are oriented toward an agent or actor, and linkages between events are made in terms of chronological order. In contrast to this, we can consider **propositions**, which focus on ideas and concepts devoid of this temporal dimension. Table 1-2 illustrates these points.

The traditional approach to teaching Euclidean geometry is an excellent example of a propositional format. In this case, various theorems are presented, elaborated into a logical set of corollaries, and applied to the solution of specific problems. In such a format, there is no concern with time, no person reference, and no target agent or actor because the text is oriented toward the subject matter and linkages relate to logical, not chronological, order. The order in which material is presented is important in the geometry example, but the linkages are from simple-to-complex *subject matter*—not the order in which Euclid conceived them. Thus, propositional frames emerge as alternatives to narratives as a means of constructing knowledge.

There is more than organizational format underlying this distinction between narrative and propositional formats. Going back as far as Plato, we find a distinction between mythos and logos. **Mythos** is thought to be the crude discourse of ordinary language, including the narrative. The purportedly higher form of discourse, **logos**, involves technical and philosophical discourse designed to replace the primitive concrete language of oral memory. With the advent of empiricism, scientific discourse, and its inherent logos, was elevated even further over mythos and over the rational varieties of logos. With this came the implication that Truth was associated with the higher forms of logos, and the lower forms of discourse—particularly fairytales and stories (that is, narratives)—were somehow suspect. Thus, the propositional/narrative distinction relates to some very fundamental ideas about the nature of Truth because they arose from two entirely different theories of knowledge.

The rise of the propositional view, with all of its inherent logos, has been taken more or less for granted within the official proceedings of psychology. Generations of

Table 1-2 Narrative and propositional formats

Narrative	Propositional
Told using either a first- or third-person perspective	Does not require person reference
Oriented toward an agent or actor	Oriented toward the subject matter
Time is important	Time not a focus
Linkages achieved using chronological order	Linkages achieved by logical order
Derives from *mythos*	Derives from *logos*
Root metaphor is contextualism (Pepper, 1942)	Root metaphor is mechanism (Pepper, 1942)

SOURCE: Based on Kent (1984).

psychologists have attempted to emulate the theories of knowledge handed to us by our colleagues in the hard or natural sciences. In so doing, propositional frames have become the unconscious way of organizing material and communicating what Danziger (1990) calls our **investigative practices** to would-be entrants to the discipline. Inspection of almost all textbooks in psychology, in general, and psychological testing, in particular, reveals that they are organized in a fundamentally propositional manner. In testing, almost all texts begin with sections on logical and mathematical concepts—treating them independently of the other aspects of the field. This commits the writer to a propositional framework. The proposition has indeed become the fundamental building block of the majority of the discourse within psychology.

An Example: Validity

An example will help here. Let's examine an important concept from the testing field, using a propositional perspective to illustrate how this approach to presenting ideas works. **Validity** is the most important concept in the field of psychological testing. Defined by the American Psychological Association (APA) as the "appropriateness, meaningfulness, and usefulness of the specific inferences made from test scores" (APA, 1985, p. 9), this term lies at the heart of the investigative practices of the testing field. Whether talking about abilities, personality, aptitudes, psychopathology, achievement inventories, or interests, psychological tests are constantly held up to the critical scrutiny demanded by validity. Virtually every contemporary text in psychological testing has a chapter dedicated to the concept, and the *Standards for Educational and Psychological Tests* states that: "validity is the most important consideration in test evaluation" (APA, 1985, p. 9). It is impossible to find a more important concept within the testing field. The following Close Up presents the idea of validity in a propositional framework.

CLOSE UP | **A Propositional Treatment of Validity**

Validity is the extent to which a test actually measures what it purports to measure. Thus, a valid IQ test is one that actually measures intelligence. The fundamental concern of validity is what a given test measures and how well it does it. All procedures for establishing the validity of a test involve, at one level or another, the establishment of relationships between test performance and other independently observable facts. For example, an IQ test can be validated by demonstrating a relationship between test scores and independent estimates of intelligence such as ratings given by teachers who know the students who were tested.

Validity is divided into three principal subcategories that relate to the kinds of evidence presented. **Content validity** is concerned with whether the test is a representative sample of the entire domain that the test purports to measure. For example, asking if an IQ test is a fair sample of all possible intelligent behaviors is tantamount to asking about a test's content validity. Determination of this form of validity involves a careful inspection of the actual test materials against the domain of all possible ramifications of the notion being tested. This is not a simple task because, even in relatively simple domains, the specification of the *content universe* is very time-consuming and involves making many exclusionary judgments. Yet, a number of strategies for developing content validity have evolved in the literature, and it is possible to develop a strong case for this type of validity if the proper research and methodologies are used.

Criterion-related validity is concerned with the effectiveness of a test in forecasting an individual's performance in other activities. For example, asking whether an IQ test predicts grades in school is a criterion-related validity question. The "other activity" referred to in this definition is typically called a **criterion**, which is a direct and independent measure of something that the test was designed to measure. Common criteria used in validity studies for IQ tests are academic achievement such as grade point average, teacher ratings, and level of education attained.

Criteria vary in the time frame between the test and criterion. If a test is being used to predict criterion status at the time of testing, **concurrent validity** is being assessed. Tests that are used to provide diagnoses of present states (for example, testing to determine if George is depressed right now) would be evaluated in terms of their concurrent validity. If, on the other hand, a test is being used to make forecasts about criterion performance in the future, a test's **predictive validity** is being assessed; an example would be using IQ tests to predict grades at the end of the coming term. Much of the research intended to validate tests is concerned with criterion-related validity, making it the most popular of the three subcategories of validity.

The third subcategory of validity is concerned with the extent to which a test is a measure of a theoretical construct or a trait. Called **construct validity**, concern here relates to whether a given test is an effective measure of a theoretical idea that is thought to drive test performance. Thus, an IQ test would have construct validity to the extent that it represented an effective measure of an explicit and valid theory of intellect. Any data throwing light on the nature of the theoretical entity thought to underly test performance are considered important to the establishment of this type of validity. Included here are relationships with other tests thought to measure similar (or dissimilar) constructs, analyses of the internal structure of the test that indicate the numbers of separate entities being measured, and experiments intended to put the theory to test. Clearly, a valid theory is a prerequisite of the demonstration of the construct validity of a test.

The conceptual apparatus attending the question of whether a test measures what it purports to measure—that is, its validity—is very complex. The kinds of evidence required to validate a test are astounding, demanding the need for considerable hard and sophisticated research and data collection to establish its validity.

This short, propositional presentation of validity provides the fundamental idea that members of the psychological testing enterprise use to determine whether a particular test is a good one. It is the essential evaluative criterion used in the field. Another idea that relates to the extent to which a test produces consistent or error-free results, called **reliability,** is also part of this decision-making process, but validity is clearly the most important idea.

Now we turn to how we might use the narrative frame to present this same material. As indicated earlier, the narrative frame involves placing the notion of validity into temporal context, telling the story of validity—the manner in which it evolved—as an alternative to the propositional frame. The following Close Up provides the narrative presentation.

CLOSE UP   A Narrative Treatment of Validity

When tests were introduced to North America, around 1900, one of the first questions asked was how to decide if a particular instrument was good or not. The first solution that emerged involved using the test to predict nontest behavior. Thus, by 1915 IQ tests were administered to students, and their scores compared with teacher ratings of intelligence, with substantial relationships between them being used to indicate that the test was effective. In this example, teacher ratings were called criteria, and this method of establishing test-score meaning became known as the **test-criterion method**. If a test was effective in forecasting future performance, it was said to have **prognostic value**, whereas tests that were good reflections of current status were said to have **diagnostic value**.

With some particularly successful demonstrations of usefulness during World War I, tests became popular, with many researchers and test developers becoming involved in the field. Testing became the most important demonstration of the practical worth of the emerging discipline of psychology. By 1921 there were so many tests available that issues of distinguishing good from bad tests became critical. In response to this, the National Association of the Directors of Educational Research introduced the term *validity*, defined as the extent to which a test measures what it purports to measure. The only way of establishing validity, at this time, was using the test-criterion method, with the terms *concurrent validity* and *predictive validity* replacing the older ideas of diagnostic value and prognostic value, respectively. Because of the use of the test-criterion method, these two approaches became known as criterion-related validity. Even today, much of the validity evidence presented in the literature is concerned with criterion-related validity. Perhaps because of its head start in the validity game, it is the most popular approach.

As the areas in which tests were being used expanded during the 1920s, it became clear that the test-criterion method alone was not sufficient. Particularly for standardized tests of academic achievement such as spelling and reading, it was necessary to pay attention to how well a given test represented a specified subject curriculum. The term **curricular validity** was introduced in the early 1930s to serve this purpose. Subsequently renamed content validity, this aspect of evaluating tests involved determining whether the items in a test were a representative sample of all possible questions that could be asked of this domain of content. Determining this form of validity is complex because it demands that all possible ramifications of whatever is being measured be documented and that the test be representative of this larger set. This was particularly difficult when the notion of content validity was generalized to other domains, resulting in the development of many sophisticated approaches and strategies.

The final chapter in this narrative of validity did not emerge until 1954. To this point, the field of testing had avoided the necessity of clearly defining what a given test measured. For example, an IQ test could be validated by establishing relationships with relevant criteria such as academic achievement, education attained, or teacher ratings, without ever explicitly defining what intelligence was. Indeed, the rhetoric of the time suggested that intelligence was what the intelligence tests test—thereby obviating the need to define intelligence! On both philosophical and practical grounds, it evolved that an explicit definition of whatever underlay test scores must be included in the validation process—test developers must define what it was their tests tested and provide evidence to demonstrate that this was true. This newest form of validity was called construct validity. Test developers could use any of a number of methods—detailed studies of the relationships between tests and criteria, analyses of the internal aspects of a test, experiments, and a wide range of other methodologies—to establish this form of validity.

The conceptual apparatus attending the question of whether a test measures what it purports to measure—that is, its validity—is very complex. The kinds of evidence required to validate a test is astounding, demanding the need for considerable hard and sophisticated research and data collection to establish its validity.

Notice how the narrative treatment locates the very source of the idea of validity and its subtypes. This locating provides you with a ready-made memory aid. Simply by knowing the sequence of events, reconstructing the actual substance of the ideas becomes possible. For example, knowing that tests were expanded to include educational curricula and that the test-criterion method was the only method for establishing validity allows you to generate the substance of the idea of content validity as a solution to this particular problem. It is here, in the provision of a chronological and contextual framework, that the narrative approach is particularly effective.

Both the narrative and propositional treatments of validity contain much of the same basic information, although the manner in which the material must be presented dictates some variation. The narrative passage contains more facts by virtue of the dates and chronological information that were necessary to make the story coherent. Both presentations of validity are of comparable length, indicating that using the narrative framework without requiring more space is possible. However, both presentations are very short and do not contain a great deal of detail—neither would suffice as complete presentations of the concept of validity—yet the two presentations do indicate the fundamental differences between these two formats.

Let's examine some of the differences between these two approaches. Several students, who have used earlier drafts of this text, suggested that the propositional version may be easier to memorize because it is already in point form. Working your way through the propositional version with a highlighter pen and abstracting the fundamental structure of validity is a relatively simple task. This being the case, memory should be better for the propositional version. We have done some research on this important issue. Two passages drawn from Chapters 3 and 4 of this book[1] were rendered in both propositional and narrative frames by Ann Naylor, an honors student in our program. She had students read one version[2] and examined their memory for the materials both in terms of recall for details and their ability to paraphrase the passage. The graphs shown in Figure 1-1 illustrate the results of this study. In all cases, the narrative approach provides at least comparable, if not better, memory performance regardless of type of question asked. It appears as though the narrative approach, by virtue of its chronological and storied nature, functions to help memory to some degree.

---

[1]Passage A was the Vision Quest (see Chapter 3), and passage B was the celebrated astronomy incident (see Chapter 4) that demonstrated individual differences in vigilance reaction times.

[2]Students were randomly assigned to one of the two presentation modes to minimize the possibility that those with better memories ended up in one group.

Figure 1-1 Memory for narrative and propositional passages as a function of type of question asked: (a) text passage A (the Vision Quest) and (b) text passage B (the astronomy incident).

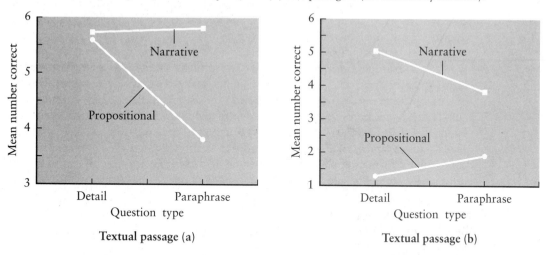

These data do not "prove" the superiority of narrative organization. Problems of selectivity, student sampling, and content validity make drawing a strong conclusion inadvisable. They are cited here only as demonstration of how the narrative can, in several places, yield a memory advantage, which propositional frames do not automatically guarantee.

Another difference between the two renderings of validity is that the narrative version, by virtue of its informality and storied nature, does not appear as serious or "scientific" as the propositional passage. Here we run into the prejudice against mythos mentioned earlier. Within the confines of the scientific establishment, narrative presentations are definitely seen as less reliable and less worthy of consideration. This approach to knowledge cannot be denied and appears to suggest a major problem for this book.

However, if we recall the goal of the book, it becomes evident that this is not really a problem. *The Psychological Testing Enterprise* (hereafter called *The Enterprise*) is intended to bring you, the outsider, into closer proximity to the inner, scientific world of psychological testing. The text is not intended to be a compendium of how these scientists view their world but has been carefully designed to allow you, the student outsider, to gain a degree of understanding of this community. The use of narrative, then, is to bring you closer to the domain of the scientific aspects of psychological testing. You will gain a firm understanding of this world that you can render in propositional format should the need arise. Glossaries and discussion questions, presented at the end of each chapter, will allow you to test your knowledge of the ideas covered in the section. Your understanding of key terms such as *validity* and *reliability* will be extensive and comparable to that attained using a propositional format, as will your knowledge of specific tests and methods used in the field. An additional bonus will be learning about the history of the field. In all, the use of a narrative approach does not threaten or compromise the scientific logos; it strengthens it. By using narrative, the scientific logos of the field is rendered accessible to outsiders in a way that etic-to-emic understandings are attained in day-to-day life.

Perhaps the major gain from a narrative orientation is the manner in which it gives you knowledge to ask what my students call the "why questions." These are queries about the reasons underlying the choice of specific methodologies and approaches, which are often very difficult to extract from a propositional framework. For example, in the propositional treatment of validity, construct validity seems to come "out of the blue." There is no clear reason why it emerged. Because of this, appreciating the importance and significance of this idea is exceedingly difficult (which, incidentally, is probably one of the most important in the field—see Chapter 13). In contrast, the narrative frame clearly locates the evolution of construct validity and provides an indication of both its genesis and importance. This contextual information sheds light on some of these immensely complex why questions and thereby provides one of the major advantages of narrative organization.

As you work your way through the text, you will find that it gradually begins to assume a more propositional character. This is to be expected because the further along you read in the text, the more emic your understanding will become—technical jargon and the in-group worldview will become familiar. Toward the end of the text, you will have, through the process of talk and narrative, become sufficiently familiar with the inner workings of the field to deal with it in an effective emic manner.

Getting to the emic end state will be more fun with a narrative frame. The transition from etic to emic is achieved by using the devices of the storyteller—resulting in a readable and engaging text that flows from one section to the next, as well as providing color and background material. This stands in stark contrast to propositional presentations, which can be very difficult and boring reading. The story itself, which tells of the emergence of the new discipline of psychology and the manner in which psychological tests were and still are a significant part of this ongoing evolution, is an intrinsically interesting story. The social factors that shaped this evolution, the residue of old ideas still propagated in the methodology, the conflicts between and among various factions in the field, the rhetoric for selling the product, and a myriad of other deeply human issues are the substance of what follows; all combine to create a rich and vibrant story of a highly significant practice within our culture—psychological testing.[3]

CLOSE UP   **But I'm Irish...**

When I was working with Ken King, the editor who originally accepted this book, he reacted to my proposed use of narrative by saying, "But I'm Irish—if I want to tell a good story, I lie." This, of course, took me back a bit because the comment implied that storytelling and truth do not necessarily overlap, and this poses problems for a textbook.

---

[3]The term *narrative* is being used in two ways here. First, there is narrative-as-talk, which has been proposed as a major vehicle for coming to know the in-group and to develop emic understanding. Second, there is narrative-as-history because chronological/narrative organization is an important part of any historical analysis. Both uses are intended.

This is an important point: One difficulty with narratives is that sometimes the desire to tell a good story can tempt one to deviate from the "facts." In the context of *The Enterprise*, however, this is not a real problem because verifying the facts in the extensive technical and historical literatures surrounding the field is possible. Indeed, throughout the book, considerable effort has gone into providing backup references for the points being made. These can readily be consulted if there is some concern about the veracity of an incident within the story. The overall story, embedded as it is in a chronological framework, is equally verifiable by reference to the dates involved. So whether I am Irish or not, *The Enterprise* is a good story, but this goodness has not been purchased at the expense of the reality of the chronicled events.[4]

SOME THOUGHTS ON HISTORY

The Enterprise is a narrative, telling the story of the community of scholars, researchers, test developers, and marketers involved with psychological testing. In one sense, it is a history of the field; however, it is not a history in the traditional sense. A proper history is complete and thorough, based on primary materials such as letters between principal characters, as well as the formal proceedings of the field. The text does not qualify as a proper history in this sense because it is not thorough and complete. It is *not* a compendium, or handbook, of psychological testing. You will not find lists of "every intelligence test ever published" or even a collection of the "top-ten personality inventories" in the chapters that follow. Nor will you find exhaustive reviews of the literature dealing with specific domains of testing. Indeed, some revered pioneers of the testing field have not been mentioned, mainly because of the incredible size and growth rate of the literature in the field. Writing a complete book in this field has become an impossible task because of its size. Hence, there was selectivity in the materials presented in this book. I acknowledge these biases but can explicitly tell you of the concerns that directed the selections.

The overriding concern in deciding what to include was the extent to which the materials illustrate the content of a specific section of the book. You will find discussion of the basic issues underlying the emergence of specific and important tests. A number of highly important measurement devices are presented in detail, as are several others that relate to the evolving story line. Appendix C contains information about other important tests. Throughout the text, you will be shown how to find information about tests that are not mentioned, should you want to explore a specific domain more fully than is done here. You will be referred to exhaustive literature reviews, should you want to follow up on the domain of concern. Thus, the text is a selective beginning, or introduction, to the narrative of psychological testing and is therefore not a traditional history.

The text, however, is a history in another sense. Forman (1991) suggests a distinction between two different approaches to history of science. Of note for our

---

[4]Determination of the "goodness" of a story is a complex topic. For explicit discussions of this issue and some suggested solutions for a psychological context, see Sarbin (1986), Landau (1986), and Steele (1986).

purposes is what he calls **critical history.** This form of history recognizes that scientific knowledge has a social component, being, in part the product of a series of social practices of a given scientific community. To the extent that *The Enterprise* brings consideration of social issues and their representation within the community associated with testing into focus, it can be seen as a critical history in Forman's sense. It should be mentioned here that the term *critical* does not only relate to its negative sense but also to examining the positive consequences of particular practices.

My personal perspective is that, like it or not, testing is a significant aspect of the **lived cultural experience** of the vast majority of North American students (more about this in Chapter 2). Like any practice within a culture, it has its good points and bad points. It serves the interests of society over the individual in a number of cases and is thereby a potential threat to individual freedom. But testing can be of great use to individuals by providing access to opportunities that might otherwise be denied them. Because of this, my orientation toward tests, and that presented in this book, is one of caution where focus is on determining the strengths and weaknesses of this aspect of our cultural activity. I am not a "cheerleader" for tests—blindly supporting their use in any and all social contexts. Nor am I a rabid "antitester," feeling that any use of tests is tantamount to personal oppression. The well-conceived and morally considered use of psychological tests can, under some circumstances, be of great advantage to all parties concerned. But

Testing is very much a part of our lived cultural experience.

tests can also create great injustices and be used to promote morally repugnant goals. These two extremes suggest a love/hate relationship between individuals and psychological tests, which will be woven throughout the story that follows. When doubt about a particular testing application surfaces, I side with the potential victim of testing practice, arguing that testing practice must be clearly and explicitly justified by its proponents before considering the practice to be justifiable. I am, then, a healthy skeptic about testing. The use of tests *must* be clearly and rationally defended by the parties responsible for their administration and interpretation. *The Enterprise* has been carefully constructed to give you the background to become a healthy skeptic regarding psychological testing.

The major challenge of understanding and dealing with this field, then, is to develop a conceptual and knowledge base that will allow you, the student and potential benefactor or victim of testing, to examine any specific use of this technology and to give you the background to make a personal decision about the appropriateness of any given application.

GOALS OF THE TEXT

A complicating factor in this picture is that the situations in which tests are used are about as varied as imagination allows (this will be discussed in detail in Chapter 2). Thus, anticipating every possible scenario regarding the tests you might encounter is impossible. It follows that the optimal strategy for introducing this field is to present the ideas and technology, which has emerged from tests, in a way that allows you to *derive* the value implications inherent in a specific application of tests. The narrative approach is particularly effective here because it provides a conceptual backbone that can be used to extrapolate the important aspects of a given situation. For example, understanding the origin and character of the notion of validity allows you to ask the correct questions about whether a specific test has been used appropriately, as well as to query the fundamental notion of validity itself. Knowing the history and implications of how a specific test was constructed allows you to make an informed evaluation of its use in a specific situation. Recognizing the manner in which a given test construes personal information provides the context for you to evaluate its use. This contextual information can be gleaned from knowing the historical background of the field, which is the substance of the text that follows.

Following from this argument, the fundamental goal of *The Enterprise* is to provide you with enough information and understanding to be able to deal with psychological tests in an intelligent and informed way. Whether it is you, a friend, or your children who have been touched in one way or another by tests, this text has been explicitly written to empower you with enough information to make an individual decision about whether an encounter with tests has been beneficial. The goal is to give you sufficient power, in an environment populated by numerous experts, to evaluate the appropriateness of tests—*for yourself.*

Glossary

cognitive revolution Occurring in psychology in the 1960s, a shift in thinking that brought studies of the processes of thinking under intense scrutiny. It used experimental methods and a metaphor that viewed the human as an information-processing computer. (This idea will be discussed in more detail in Chapter 15.)

concurrent validity One of two subtypes of criterion-related validity that focuses on the extent to which a test is an effective measure of criterion status when the criterion and the test are established at the same time. An example is using tests to provide diagnoses.

construct validity One of a number of subtypes of validity that focuses on the extent to which a given psychological test is an effective measure of an explicit theory of test performance. (This idea will be discussed in more detail in Chapters 2 and 13.)

content validity One of a number of subtypes of validity that focuses on the extent to which the items in a test fairly represent the entire domain of the entity being measured by a test. (This concept will be discussed in greater detail in Chapter 11.)

context The parts of a discourse that surround a passage and can help one understand the meaning of that passage. As used here, context refers to the social/historical events and ideas that shaped the evolution of the psychological testing enterprise.

contextual orientation The development of a narrative that uses context to help flesh out the meanings inherent in the story.

criterion-related validity One of a number of subtypes of validity that focuses on the extent to which test scores are related to specific criteria. (This concept will be discussed in greater detail in Chapter 8.)

criterion A direct and independent measure of something that a psychological test is thought to measure. For example, teacher ratings of intelligence would be criteria for an intelligence test. (This concept will be discussed in more detail in Chapters 6 and 8.)

critical history In examining science, a type of history that focuses on the social component of knowledge, recognizing that such knowledge is the result of a series of social practices within a specific scientific community.

curricular validity An earlier term for content validity.

diagnostic value An earlier term for concurrent validity.

emic understanding Comprehension of a functioning social group that is derived from a member of the group, providing the insider's perspective.

etic understanding Comprehension of a functioning social group that is derived by examining the group from the outside, providing a sense of the group as it is seen by others.

eugenics The science of trying to improve a human social group by practicing selective breeding. (This idea will be discussed more fully in Chapter 5.)

investigative practices The methods and their underlying assumptions that characterize the day-to-day workings within a specific scientific field. (These practices will be discussed in more detail in Chapter 20.)

lived cultural experience Real-life events and occasions that are commonly encountered by members of specific cultural groups.

logos From Plato, technical, logical, and philosophical discourse that was designed to replace mythos. Two forms of logos are verbal forms, such as those typically practiced in philosophy, and scientific forms, which incorporate empirical data into the discourse.

mythos The "crude" discourse of ordinary language and conversation that involves the primitive concrete language of oral memory. It derives from Plato and contrasts with logos.

narrative As used here, (1) presentations that situate specific ideas, events, and people in a temporal order, organizing a domain (like psychological testing) into a coherent story and helping to elaborate the meanings inherent in the domain; and (2) an essential component of historical analysis wherein a domain of information is arranged into a chronological sequence.

narrative strand One of several subplots within a grander narrative. In the text, five narrative strands were identified: social, psychology, philosophy, business, and mathematics.

operationism A 1930s philosophical position from physics, which was borrowed (and changed) by psychologists. This view suggests that the meaning of a theoretical entity is totally contained in the the procedures (operations) used to measure the entity. (This idea will be discussed more fully in Chapter 9.)

predictive validity One of two subtypes of criterion-related validity that focuses on the extent to which a test is an effective measure of criterion status when the goal is to forecast a criterion by the use of a test. An example is using an IQ test to predict grades at the end of term.

prognostic value An earlier term for predictive validity.

proposition A means of organizing ideas that focus on logical relationships inherent in the material itself rather than consideration of temporal order, as is done with a narrative frame.

reliability The extent to which a test provides consistent or error-free measurements. (This concept will be discussed in more detail in Chapters 6, 11, and 19.)

talk As used here, conversations between would-be entrants into a group and group members in which common grounds and eventual common understandings are established. Talk is viewed as the primary way in which a person gains entry into a social group.

test-criterion method An approach to establishing test-score meaning that involves examining the relationships between test scores and criteria thought to represent the entity the test measures. (This idea will be discussed more fully in Chapters 6, 8, and 19.)

validity The extent to which a test measures what it purports to measure. A more contemporary view defines it as the "appropriateness, meaningfulness, and usefulness of the specific inferences made from test scores" (APA, 1985, p. 9). It is divided into a number of subtypes including criterion-related, content, and construct validity. (This concept will be discussed in greater detail in Chapters 2, 8, 13, and 19.)

Suggested Further Reading

Bruner, J. (1986). *Actual minds, possible worlds*. Cambridge Mass.: Harvard University Press.

> This very timely book explores the utility of a narrative framework for developing an understanding of the human mind. Multidisciplinary in scope, this book presents coherent and exciting arguments about the differences between scientific and narrative accounts.

Danziger, K. (1990). *Constructing the subject: Historical origins of psychological research*. Cambridge, Eng.: Cambridge University Press.

> This book is a lively and telling demonstration of the manner in which historical analysis can inform us of the strengths and weaknesses of the approaches we take to constructing psychological knowledge—what we called the why questions in the text. Danziger traces the manner in which the nature of the relationship between the experimenter and the subject has changed over time and demonstrates how the eventual choice of the current model frames and constrains the attained knowledge. *The Enterprise*, by virtue of its narrative framework, shares some of the ideas so aptly articulated by Danziger. The historically oriented psychological student will not be able to put this book down once begun.

Parker, I. (1992). *Discourse dynamics: Critical analysis for social and individual psychology*. London: Routledge.

> The importance of talk, as discussed in the chapter, is particularly well articulated in an emerging domain of research called *discourse analysis*. Although there are a number of highly readable presentations of this field, Parker's book provides the reader with a strong version of the manner in which discourse analysis can shape the way we approach doing psychology. His application of this technique to both cultures and individuals particularly illuminates some of the underlying ideas that have led to the choice of the narrative framework for constructing *The Enterprise*.

Sarbin, T. R. (Ed.). (1986). *Narrative psychology: The storied nature of human conduct*. New York: Praeger.

> This edited volume offers an excellent set of articles about the manner in which the concept of narrative is slowly infiltrating various corners of the discipline of psychology. The first part of the book deals with the narrative in science, which is very close to the application discussed in this chapter. The remaining sections deal with narrative competency and issues of how the self is defined in terms of the performance of narratives.

Wainer, H. I., & Braun, H. I. (Eds.). (1988). *Test validity*. Hillsdale, N.J.: Erlbaum.

> The basic notion of validity is exceedingly complex, including a number of very diverse and complex topics. Although most of these topics are presented as part of the narrative that follows, a contemporary reference source may be useful here. This edited volume offers the knowledgeable reader a glimpse of the current state-of-the-art thinking about this concept. Historical and epistemic issues are discussed, some of the changes that are occurring are noted, and a series of sophisticated methodological and statistical innovations are presented.

Discussion Questions

1. Discuss the implications of the emic/etic distinction as it applies to learning about science.

2. List the advantages and disadvantages of emic versus etic understandings.

3. Why is talk important?

4. Define the narrative approach to presenting material. Evaluate its strengths and weaknesses.

5. List and briefly define the five narrative strands used in the text.

6. From your life experience, give two examples where it was necessary to understand context before proper understanding of the experience was possible. Explain how context mediated the interpretation of these events.

7. Compare and contrast narratives and propositions.

8. Draw a schematic chart that represents the various types of validity discussed in the chapter.

9. Sketch out the story line of validity that underlies the narrative presentation of validity.

10. Do you think that narrative or propositional frames produce better memory? Why?

11. Prepare an argument to defend the contention that narratives can be as truthful or faithful to the facts as propositions.

12. Compare and contrast traditional and critical histories

Chapter 2

The Psychological Testing Enterprise Today

In This Chapter

CLOSE UP   **Tests in Action**

I was mad—hopping mad—about as angry as I had ever been.

I had been chatting with a chum who had returned from a long session with Mr. Hunter, the guidance counselor, and what I heard made me boil. Jack and I were just two of many high school students who had been put through a process of being told what we could do with our lives, and what Jack heard was not good news.

We were walking down the rather sterile high school hallway, lined with lockers, glinting terrazzo floor, bland fluorescent lighting, and he turned to me and said "You know what that jerk Hunter said to me just now?"

"No," I replied, sensing something was up.

"That moron said that there was no way I was ever going to be able to go to university."

After a stunned delay, I said "What?"

"Yeah," Jack yelled, with a slight shake in his voice. "He said that I don't have the ability to go beyond high school. He said that I was too stupid to do anything but go to tech school." After a pause, the loudness in his voice subsiding, his face darkening, he said "I just don't know what to think—what am I going to do?"

I looked over at my friend and could see that Hunter's comments had cut very deeply. In all of my dealings with Jack, I never had any doubt that he would go on with the rest of us to university. Sure, he was a bit loud and played on the line for the football team—and sure, we always chided him and his large teammates as the "big, dumb linemen"—but it never occurred to me that these jibes might be true. As far as I was concerned, Jack was bright and articulate; there was no doubt he would go on—something was wrong somewhere.

I asked tentatively, "How did Hunter come up with this revelation?"

With contempt that defies description, he replied "He gave me a bunch of those tests—you know, the kind that you have to answer as fast as you can. There were a bunch of questions where I had to spot spelling mistakes, and more where I had to add up a bunch of numbers—all that stuff. . . ." His voice trailed off, and I could see the pain clearly spread across his face.

"So how can he figure you shouldn't go to university from those things?" I asked.

"Darned if I know," Jack answered. "Hunter just sat me down, showed me a bunch of numbers, and then told me I should apply to a trade school for next year. Geez, Tim, I don't want to go to trade school—I'd die."

"But didn't he talk at all with you about what you wanted to do?" I asked.

"No."

"Didn't he ask about the things you do well in?"

"No . . . no . . . no. He just pointed at this piece of paper and told me I wasn't smart enough," Jack replied, the anger coming back into his voice.

I can still see the pain and anger etched across his face on that day in grade 12. It made me angry—very angry—because of the inhumanity of it all. These hard, cold "facts" reflected in the test scores were being used to try to cut someone off from doing what he wanted to do. They were being used to support a plan of action that was wrongheaded and highly dehumanizing. Boy, I was angry. . .

One interpretation of this story is that the guidance counselor was just telling Jack the truth—and, as we all know, the truth hurts. Maybe he was stupid and should not have gone on to university. Were it not for the fact that he easily earned his Ph.D. degree and is presently holding a prestigious post at an eminent eastern university, I might agree with this interpretation. Jack did go on, and he did exceedingly well, being a celebrated member of the academic community. The guidance counselor was wrong, very wrong. The tests were wrong, very wrong. The whole thing was wrong, very wrong.

But there are other stories, too. After an abortive attempt in first-year architecture, I found myself trying to figure out what I might do with the rest of my life. My self-confidence was at a low ebb, and I was earnestly searching for some kind of inspiration about what to do.

I ended up seeing a counselor who made me take what I believe were the same tests my friend Jack had taken about 2 years earlier. He, too, showed me a bunch of figures and profiles and slowly explained to me that I probably could do just about anything I wanted to do. He was not much help in directing me to specific areas that I could study, but he did give my self-confidence a much-needed boost. I finished my undergraduate work in mathematics, one of the areas that had been identified as a strength in the tests. So, it isn't all bad. There are times when these things called *tests* can be useful, but at times they can be very bad.

These tests have become so much a part of our lives that any educated person *must* have an intelligent knowledge of how they work, what they can and cannot do, how they can be misused, and their limitations. Without the ability to appraise the strengths and weaknesses of these instruments, we are forced to defer to various "experts." If the decisions being made were trivial, this might not be a problem, but psychological tests are very important parts of very important decisions. Survival in our culture virtually demands a fair knowledge of testing. Without knowledge of the foibles of tests, stories like Jack's could have very sad endings, and it could happen to you or your family or friends. Without an understanding of the kinds of things tests can do well, their potential for helping people through trying times will be lessened.

A SNAPSHOT OF THE PSYCHOLOGICAL TESTING ENTERPRISE

As recent as 1915, the concept of a psychological test was unknown to the North American public. These devices have now become a significant part of our **lived cultural experience**. They are embedded into the very fabric of our society in so many diverse ways and in so many different situations that it is almost impossible to document them all. In this chapter, you will gain a sense of the nature and extent of psychological tests as they exist in our contemporary context. Once we have a sense of tests used today, we can begin our long narrative journey to discover their source and character.

In this chapter, we can produce only a static snapshot of a vibrant and dynamic field, freezing in time the incredibly active and complex domain of psychological testing. Like any photograph, it will select out certain aspects of the environment and not attend to others. What follows, however, will provide a general view that will frame our narrative in later chapters. We will begin by defining psychological tests and exploring some of the implications of this definition. Then, with the help of a number of students who have used this book as a text, we will explore the situations in which one finds psychological tests being used. We will discuss the diversity of these instruments, both in terms of what they purport to measure and the actual tests themselves, to provide a sense of the breadth of the testing field. Next we will examine some basic issues regarding measurement and quantification, followed by a brief discussion of the characteristics of a good test. Finally, we will explore a diversity of opinions about the costs and benefits of testing as they are experienced in contemporary society. Taken together, these sections offer an interesting snapshot of testing today. They begin to define the end point of the narrative that will follow in the next chapters.

DEFINITIONAL CONSIDERATIONS

> **psychological** (adjective): of or relating to psychology, the science of mind and behavior
>
> **test** (noun): a critical examination, observation, or evaluation[1]

In a sense, psychological tests are so much a part of our way of life that it seems somewhat unnecessary to devote time to defining them. It is almost impossible for anyone in our society to escape "testing" in one form or another, and most of us are pretty certain that we can identify a test when we run into it. But this ability to spot a test may be a bit more of an illusion than we might first expect. For example, has it occurred to you that every time you reach for your favorite brand of soap on a supermarket shelf you are, in a very real sense, being tested? The impact of media messages (for example, advertising) on your consuming behavior is being monitored and tested through your product choices. Or perhaps you have not realized that your deciding to watch public television is a kind of test, wherein, not unlike a test of occupational preference, your choices are being polled. Responses of strangers to your presence involve all kinds of tests, wherein the results of certain kinds of evaluations (for example, intuitive assessments of your clothing style) dictate the manner in which you are treated. Each of these situations, and many others, suggests that our way of life is virtually saturated with various kinds of tests. Some of these are very informal or intuitive, whereas others are highly formalized and structured, but they all involve testing of one kind or another and all culminate in important social decisions.

Not all the tests described so far are properly described as psychological tests. What are the properties that allow us to use the adjective *psychological* to describe a test? What attributes define the subset of tests in our culture that are appropriately described as *psychological*? And what makes one kind of test psychological and another kind something else? The answers to these questions appear to rest in the structured and objective nature of psychological tests; to derive this, we must examine the standard definitions.

Let's look at some examples first. If I were to show you this matrix:

A	B	C
D	E	F
G	H	?

and ask you which of A, C, E, G, I, K, or M ought to replace the ? in the lower-right corner, you would probably come up with the letter *I* fairly easily.[2]

You might not have much more trouble choosing which of 1, 9, 25, 49, 81, 121, or 254 ought to replace the ? in this matrix:

---

[1]These definitions are drawn from Gove (1965).

[2]The correct answer is *I* because the matrix has been constructed with letters in alphabetic order, starting in the upper-left corner and moving in the order associated with reading in our culture.

$$
\begin{array}{ccc}
1 & 4 & 9 \\
16 & 25 & 36 \\
49 & 64 & ?^3
\end{array}
$$

Perhaps, though, you might find the matrix in Figure 2-1 a bit harder.[4]

Figure 2-1   The Imaginary Matrix Quiz.

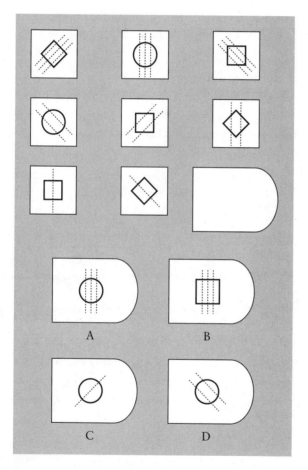

---

[3]The correct answer is 81 because, instead of letters as in the first example, this matrix has been made up of squaring incrementing numbers starting with 1 in the upper-left corner and proceeding as we would if we were reading the matrix. As well, 81 can be attained by adding consecutive odd numbers (starting with 3), working from left to right.

[4]Detection of any two of four relationships in the figure leads to these solutions: (a) Every row and column should have a circle; thus, the correct answer is a circle—either C or D. (b) The bottom row should have only one line through it, making C the correct answer. (c) Every column should contain, in order from the top, 3, 2, and 1 lines through it, making C the correct answer. (d) Every row and column should contain lines oriented up and down, left-to-right upward, and right-to-left upward. The bottom right should be left-to-right upward, making C the correct answer.

Imagine, if you will, a set of problems like these, arranged with the easiest one first, followed by the next easiest, through to the most difficult as the last problem. Also assume that each problem has only one correct answer. We could ask people to solve the problems and count up the number of times they gave the correct answer. This number, presumably, would represent some aspect of a person's performance on this set of problems, with higher numbers representing better performance.

A Ten-Word Definition

The **Imaginary Matrix Quiz**[5] demonstrates the fundamental nature of the psychological test. The following points are worth noting in this example:

1. There is very little subjectivity involved in determining a correct answer because a clear, unambiguous criterion of correctness is available.
2. Every person who takes the quiz is presented with exactly the same stimulus materials and instructions.
3. The scoring procedure (counting up the number of correct answers) is rigorous and consistent, in that two scorers will end up with the same result.
4. Scoring the quiz results in a number.
5. The behaviors required on the quiz are a sample from a potentially infinite number of possible behaviors.

These five points represent the essential characteristics of the psychological test as it is discussed in the contemporary literature. Specifically, a **psychological test** is defined as an objective and standardized measure of a sample of behavior. In a very broad sense, the Imaginary Matrix Quiz is all of the following:

Objective: The test result is clearly observable and verifiable by any number of people.

Standardized: Everyone is presented with the same stimuli and instructions, and the scoring procedures are standardized by being rigorous and consistent.

A measure: The result of the test is expressed as a number.

A sample of behavior: Only a subset of possible behaviors is included in the quiz.

The imaginary matrix quiz therefore qualifies as a psychological test by our definition.

This definition allows us to differentiate various types of tests as either psychological or something else. The intuitive tests made by salespeople trying to size up customers as potential buyers are clearly not psychological tests by this definition. They are neither objective nor standardized. There may be important psychological information embedded in these decision-making processes, but the actual test does not conform to the technical definition. The choice to watch public television does

---

[5]In actuality this test is not as imaginary as you might expect because the items are based on the Raven Progressive Matrices (see Chapter 10)—a test touted to be a good measure of general intelligence.

not fit with our definition either because the stimulus situation leading to the behavior is not known; it is therefore not a standardized situation. However, under conditions of equal exposure to advertising, product purchasing can conform to the definition of a psychological test; it fulfills all of the criteria, particularly if the "test" is carried out in the same store, with the same configuration of products on the shelves. This definition provides a rule or set of criteria for deciding which of the myriad of tests in our culture can be considered psychological.

Of course, there is considerable room for debate about whether a given test conforms to the suggested criteria. The product-preference example could be faulted by arguing that time of day is an important variable, suggesting that the situation is not as standardized as we might like. There are also a number of possible contingencies relating to pricing and previous history in product selection. Even the Imaginary Matrix Quiz might fail to qualify if it could be demonstrated that lighting conditions, time of day, and/or the presence of other people affect the standardized nature of the test. In fact, a strict application of the definition would render the domain of psychological tests quite small—perhaps even nonexistent. In practice, the goal is to try to establish acceptable limits of variation in the standardized, objective, measurement, and sampling characteristics of a given test.

Typically, the notion of objectivity is intended to apply to more than the test-scoring and -administration procedures. The manner in which the test was developed should also be based on empirical **data**, thereby making it objective as well. For example, in the Imaginary Matrix Quiz, empirical data should have gone into the establishment of the order in which the problems were administered. Each item ought to have been administered to a number of people, and this empirical evidence should be used to estimate the difficulty of each item in order to establish the presentation order. Rather than rely on intuitive estimates of item difficulty (for example, a "gut" reaction that one item seems harder than another), the test construction should also incorporate as much objectivity as possible—the more the better.

In summary, the psychological test is an objective and standardized measure of a sample of behavior. This definition serves to distinguish these kinds of tests from the millions of other types of tests that confront us in our day-to-day lives. In addition, our ten-word definition suggests that a schema might prove useful in deciding whether one test is better than another. Presumably, a better test would conform more closely to the definition.

Although this definition is consistent and seemingly straightforward, there are a number of exceedingly important assumptions embedded in our ten words; these need to be understood if we are to develop an intelligent and informed view of the field of psychological testing. The inclusion of the words *objective* and *standardized*, and the specialized meanings accorded them, is not accidental. Neither was the choice of the phrase *sample of behavior* coincidental, nor was it happenstance that the entire definition is based on a particular and specific conception of measurement. In a very real sense, the foundational definition of the test, as articulated in contemporary psychology, is derived from a number of long and illustrious traditions in the discipline of **psychology** and well beyond. Each tradition brings with it a series of assumptions about how best to study human beings, and these are firmly embedded in our deceptively simple, ten-word definition.

I'M AN AMERICAN, I WAS BORN TO BE TESTED

It is almost impossible in our culture to have escaped having been assessed by a psychological test. Hanson (1993) begins a provocative review of testing in North America by stating, "America is awash in tests. Some nursery schools require the toddlers who would attend them to pass an entrance examination. That is just the beginning of a torrent of tests that will probe every corner of their nature and behavior for the rest of their lives" (p. 1). He also told the story of a student who was planning to attend graduate school after working for several years. When asked if she was nervous about having to write an entrance examination, she responded "Well, I'm an American. I was born to be tested." Clearly, tests are part-and-parcel of our everyday lives.

Testing Frequency

One index of this can be gathered by asking university students the number of significant encounters with tests that they can recall. Figure 2-2 shows the results for 174 university students.[6] These data underestimate the number of encounters because students were asked to report only those times they viewed as significant and to restrict themselves to published and professionally printed tests. There would have been many more encounters if these conditions had not been imposed. Considering educational tests alone, the numbers of encounters would have skyrocketed because Medina and Neill (1990) estimate that between two and one-half and five standardized tests are administered to each student in the American school system per year! Despite the built-in underestimation of the data in Figure 2-2, testing is a meaningful aspect of university students' lives. The technological devices called psychological tests are encountered with considerable frequency and represent a significant aspect of our lived cultural experiences.

Testing Settings

Where are you most likely to encounter tests? Figure 2-3 shows the settings where the 174 students have had "close encounters of the testing kind." Most test encounters experienced by university students occur in three places: in school, at work, or as part of some kind of clinical or service program. Within each of these settings, the uses of tests are exceedingly diverse and varied. These data relate to a very specific group of respondents—university students—and no attempt should be made to generalize these results to other segments of the North American population.

Educational settings. As might be expected from the amount of time spent in school, the vast majority of student encounters with tests (a full 71%) have

---

[6]These data are likely to be highly specific to the situation in which they were collected and are likely to vary significantly depending on the context in which the test is being used. Collection of local data as part of the classroom experience is recommended to make the data appear less "exotic" and more part of local students' concerns.

Figure 2-2 Numbers of significant "close encounters of the testing kind" reported by university students (*n* = 174).

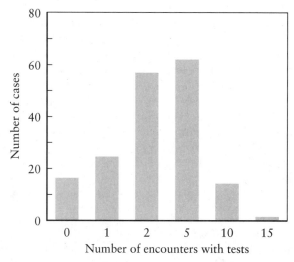

Figure 2-3 Relative frequencies of settings in which students have had significant encounters with psychological tests (*n* = 174).

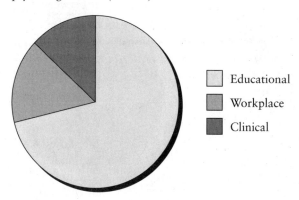

occurred in schools. Included here are tests related to measuring **academic achievement,** examinations taken when applying for admission, IQ tests, certification tests to indicate mastery of a particular aspect of curriculum, inventories used to assess vocational interests and abilities with the goal of career counseling, and a variety of other applications.

In our sample of 174 university students, their significant encounters with testing occurred at all levels of the educational system. As shown in Figure 2-4, significant numbers of incidents were reported from the elementary, junior and senior high school, and university levels.

Figure 2-4   Proportions of significant encounters with tests reported by university students at various levels of the educational system (*n* = 174).

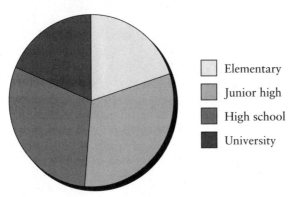

Elementary

Junior high

High school

University

In virtually all of these situations, tests alone do *not* make decisions about admissibility, certification, or vocational directions. Rather, inventories are typically only part of the decision-making process. They provide useful data that can be used effectively with other sources of information (for example, interviews, demographic considerations, letters of references, statements by the person tested). Tests are best viewed as adjuncts to educational decision making.

The workplace. The second most likely setting where you are apt to encounter tests is at work (16% of the recalled incidents in our sample of 174 students). These instruments are often used when decisions involve hiring, placement into specific jobs, promotion, workplace evaluation, training, and retraining. Figure 2-5 indicates the relative frequencies of these types of testing situations found within the workplace.

Hiring and promotion are typically the most important uses of tests in the workplace. In almost all of these employment situations, tests provide measures of the knowledge, personal characteristics, or skills that are demanded by the job of concern. They emerge as particularly powerful tools for these tasks. As we observed in educational settings, workplace tests are only one component of the decision-making processes with other considerations (for example, personal and attitudinal attributes, work history) being factored into eventual decisions.

Clinical settings. If you have encountered some kind of trouble and have sought professional help, the clinical setting is the third most likely place where you are likely to find tests. This might occur in clinics (both inpatient and outpatient), hospitals, the office of a private practitioner, or other types of institutions. Many programs in this immense field of clinical practice use tests as indicators of the kinds of problems being experienced (**diagnosis**), as predictors of how treatment might proceed (**prognosis**), as monitors of how treatment is progressing, and as measures of whether recovery has been achieved. Tests might also be used when a clinician is searching for nonobvious clues to a patient's maladjustment, as part of a program to detect learning difficulties, in the evaluation of the effectiveness of a treatment

Figure 2-5   Relative proportions of various situations in which students recall being tested in the workplace (*n* = 174).

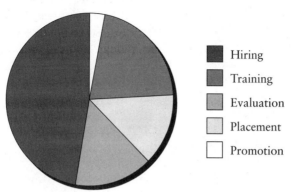

- ■ Hiring
- ■ Training
- ■ Evaluation
- □ Placement
- □ Promotion

program, in the context of an investigation to determine the nature of an insurance claim, in the courts to determine competency to stand trial, and in a prison to provide an opinion of rehabilitation. In this highly complex field, the uses to which tests are put are as varied as the creativity of the individuals involved. As mentioned before, tests are seldom used alone; they are but one component of complex information that is used to make a clinical decision.

Counseling. A fourth setting in which tests are likely to be encountered is in the field of **counseling**. This application of testing, which can occur almost anywhere, has the basic goal of helping the person being tested achieve a better adjusted or more productive life. To achieve this goal, a counselor might administer tests intended to measure a wide variety of psychological concerns such as interests, attitudes, values, academic skills, abilities, and/or personal characteristics. Typically, clients are the principal recipients of the results because the entire endeavor is conducted for their benefit. Thus, in the counseling context, test results must be presented to the client in a way that they can interpret and understand. This requires a properly trained counselor. The client and counselor must also spend considerable time discussing test results and actions that may emerge from their discussions.

Counseling did not emerge in our survey of 174 students (see Figure 2-3) because they placed counseling applications into the other three settings (educational, workplace, clinical). For example, vocational counseling was encountered in school, at work, and in clinical settings by various students. When we examined the recalled experiences in more detail, tests of vocational interest and ability, which are clearly part of the counseling enterprise, emerged as the most significant. It appears that although our students did not draw a sharp distinction between counseling and the other three settings, their responses clearly indicated the importance of this fourth setting.[7]

---

[7]Here is a good example of emic/etic differences (see Chapter 1). Students did not consider counseling settings in their responses, whereas almost all dissertations about tests written by experts do. The fourth category of settings has been added because the "insiders" have found this distinction useful.

Summary

We are most likely to encounter tests in four major settings: in school, at work, in clinical situations, and as part of a counseling program. Each of these settings refers to the person who is tested with different terms. The words *student*, *employee*, *patient*, and *client* are typically used to refer to those tested in the educational, workplace, clinical, and counseling settings, respectively. There are other testing situations, but these do appear to cover the majority of contexts.[8]

TESTING VERSUS ASSESSMENT

Of note in all four settings is the fact that tests rarely, if ever, are used alone. Almost always they are but one component of a complex bundle of information that goes into making important human decisions. This observation helps us formulate an important distinction within the testing enterprise (for detailed discussion, see Matarazzo, 1990). In the following sections, we will talk about psychological **testing** when we discuss the technical aspects of tests—whether they measure what they are supposed to, whether they produce consistent results, and so on. The manner in which tests are used to make decisions in concert with other sources of information will be considered psychological **assessment**. This latter and more complex topic involves the domain of making psychological judgments about specific individuals. Psychological assessment can and typically does involve testing, but it is concerned with the kinds of statements that can be made about students, employees, patients, and clients. Some of these statements are test-based, whereas others may draw on the expertise of the professional or on a myriad of other sources. Psychological assessment is concerned with the complex interplay between the client, the professional, and the context in which the information is being collected, as well as that to which it is being applied. The goal of this text is to provide you with sufficient background to permit evaluation of psychological assessment, but one of the prerequisites of this is to gain sufficient knowledge about psychological testing to permit an informed opinion about assessment. To achieve this, looking a little more closely at the nature of psychological tests themselves is necessary.

THE DIVERSITY OF TESTS

As you might expect from the varied settings in which we encounter them, a tremendous number of tests are available. All can be labeled *psychological* by our ten-word definition given earlier. The most recent version of the *Mental*

---

[8]The questionnaire explicitly asked students not to consider research projects in which they had encountered tests. Such settings would emerge as a fifth category. However, research applications rarely have important, direct social implications for those tested, so they have not been considered here.

Measurements Yearbook (Kramer & Conoley, 1992), one of the major reference sources for tests, gives an indication of the vast numbers of tests available. This book presented 477 new or significantly revised instruments since its last publication in 1989. This may not seem like a large number, but this is a publication rate of over 100 per year, or 3 every week. Most of these tests are the result of thousands of hours of research and development, giving you a glimpse of the massive nature of the psychological testing enterprise. It should be noted, as well, that many more tests are in circulation, being either in the developmental stages or used exclusively for research, which means that they typically are not listed in the *Yearbook*. When you add the hundreds of thousands of examinations that are created daily in schools and universities, the number of tests in our culture is truly astounding. The amount of psychological testing that is conducted is remarkable.

What Is Measured

Tests come in all shapes and sizes. They can range from simple one-item questions relating to opinions on various issues to long and elaborate batteries of examinations that may take days to answer. They deal with a great diversity of content areas: measurements of vocational preference, intelligence, personality, school performance, and employee satisfaction, to name a few. Table 2-1 presents the categories into which the 396 new tests from the *Tenth Mental Measurements Yearbook* can be sorted.

Clearly, the instruments being published currently represent a tremendous variety of concerns covering the psychological "waterfront." **Vocational tests**, which are the purview of the counseling setting, are concerned with any and all measures that help clients select proper occupational paths. Included here are measures of stated interests (preferences for specific activities), **abilities** (the power to perform an act before or after training), and **aptitudes** (the ability to acquire knowledge or skill). Measures of school subjects are standardized tests that provide indices of the extent to which specific curriculum units (for example, grade 10 mathematics) have

Table 2-1 Major categories of new or significantly revised tests in the *Tenth Mental Measurements Yearbook*

Category	Number of Tests	Percentage
Vocational	100	25.3
School subjects	96	24.2
Personality	72	18.2
Miscellaneous	47	11.8
Developmental	31	7.8
Intelligence and scholastic aptitude	28	7.1
Speech and hearing	22	5.6
Total	396	100.0

SOURCE: Conoley and Kramer (1989).

been mastered. These will be found, for the most part, in the educational setting and are sometimes called **achievement tests**. Performance on these tests is a combination of individual variables and the schooling students have received. **Personality tests** are concerned with measurement of the "stable factors that make one person's behavior consistent from one time to another or different from the behavior other people would manifest in comparable situations" (Hampson, 1988, p. 1). Such tests will be found in all four settings outlined in the previous section and often focus on individual characteristics in thought, feeling, or behavior, known as **traits**. Tests intended to identify **psychopathology** are also included in this category. The miscellaneous tests in Table 2-1 incorporate a wide range of topics including specific workplace abilities and neuropsychological batteries (instruments intended to measure brain/behavior relationships). **Developmental tests** provide measures of the manner in which various psychological phenomena unfold with the passage of time. Such tests, which are used in all four settings, can relate to psychological growth across the entire life span, from infancy to old age. **Intelligence tests** provide numerical indices of the kinds of skills required to perform well in school settings, or what might be called **scholastic aptitude**. They can be found in most of the four settings, with especial frequency in the educational and clinical spheres. They can also relate to all ages, although emphasis tends to be placed on the younger end of the spectrum. Speech and hearing tests quantify the manner in which basic psychological processes attending language are functioning and, for the most part, are employed in educational and clinical settings.

A Cubic Organizational Model

The categories listed in Table 2-1 are fairly general; many instruments would escape classification by this rather crude categorization system. However, it does provide us with a sense of the breadth of the psychological testing enterprise. Within each of these domains, there is tremendous variability in the nature of the tests themselves. Some involve complex written stimuli, whereas others consist of simple pictures. Some provide specific answers from which respondents choose, and others leave the response format open-ended. Some require finding correct answers, whereas others solicit opinion or preference judgments. A helpful way of organizing this complex world of psychological tests emerges if we consider three aspects of the tests themselves. Tests vary in the **stimulus** that is presented to the person being tested. They vary in the **response format** that test takers can use to indicate their answers, and they have different **task demands**. Considered in concert, these three aspects of tests give us a classification system that helps systematize the variability seen in this field. Additionally, examining this system introduces us to some important concepts and vocabulary that are part of the testing enterprise.

Test stimuli. For a test to function as a sample of **behavior**, some kind of environmental event or stimulus must trigger the performance of a specific act. In testing, this stimulus is called the **test item**. It may be a simple picture (see Figure 2-1, the

Imaginary Matrix Quiz), a multiple-choice item on a test, or a question asked by an interviewer. Typically, quite a few items are in a given test, and they represent the environmental aspect of the test itself—that is, what the respondent sees or hears while being tested.

Considerable variety exists in the test **items** used in contemporary testing. Figure 2-6 (page 52) shows five possibilities drawn from the field. Although these samples do not cover all possible item types, they do give a sense of the variety that can be found. Distinguishing between **semantic items**, which are related to the verbal processing system, is possible. Reading, comprehension of the spoken or written word, and an understanding of vocabulary and grammar are all required to process such items. They can vary in complexity, ranging from simple spelling tasks, such as in Figure 2-6(d), to complex questions of the type asked on an oral examination in graduate school.

Pictorial items, which contrast with semantic items, are actual physical objects or pictures. Pictorial items relate to actual, concrete objects either in reality or as representations of them. Pictorial items can vary in specificity, being as precise as those in the Imaginary Matrix Quiz (see Figure 2-1), or involve very vague and abstract things such as inkblots or pictures of clouds. The operational feature of this type of item is the manner in which the stimulus itself either is or represents a concrete object and is not fundamentally semantic in nature.

By considering the type of test item used, placing almost all tests into two classes is possible. Some use words, and others use pictures or objects. The importance of this distinction emerges because, as research in cognitive psychology has made clear, pictures and words are processed differently (Paivio, 1971). In the context of psychological testing, different aspects of psychological ability or predisposition will be tapped, depending on the nature of the test item. In the domain of IQ testing, many contemporary instruments indeed reflect the semantic/pictorial distinction in the scores that are generated (see Chapters 10 and 16). Semantic/pictorial items may sometimes be mixed[9]; for our present purposes, however, this simple twofold category provides a beginning in describing the domain of psychological tests.

Response format. Besides the stimulus, tests vary in the manner in which they permit respondents to indicate their answers. In very broad terms, the major possibility here is that the test designer may or may not provide alternatives.

In the first case, the test designer may provide alternatives from which the respondent chooses. The person taking the test simply indicates which of the provided alternatives is most appropriate. True/false questions and multiple-choice items are the most frequent approaches, but there is a wide variety of possibilities. These approaches are collectively known as **structured response formats**; thus, structured personality assessment would involve measurement of traits using some version of a forced-choice strategy.

---

[9]For example, some multiple-choice items, which are semantic, incorporate pictures as part of the question. Such items remain, at root, semantic.

Figure 2-6 Sample test questions showing the diversity of stimuli used for psychological test items.

(a) *Objects*: Respondents are required to reassemble the mechanical items presented in pieces:

(b) *Pictures*: Respondents are required to indicate which of A, B, or C reflects the same relationship with 3 as pictured in 1 and 2. (ANSWERS: B, A, and A)

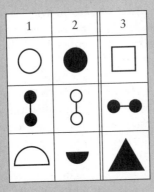

(c) *Symbols*: Respondents are required to place the following in alphabetic order:

D   P   G   L   C

(d) *Words*: Respondents are required to indicate which of the following words are spelled correctly:

potatoe
clandestine
accomodate

(e) *Sentences or Paragraphs*: Respondents must determine if the conclusion at the right is justified from the three premises on the left:

All hurdlers are swimmers
All swimmers are golfers   No boxers are swimmers
No swimmers are boxers

Figure 2-7 Samples of structured formats.

(a) *Dichotomous* (circle the best answer):
  I prefer to be alone   true   false
  I prefer to be alone   yes   no
  I prefer to be alone   agree   disagree

(b) *Likert Scale* (circle the number corresponding to your answer):

	Strongly agree			Strongly disagree		
I prefer to be alone	1	2	3	4	5	

	Strongly agree			Neutral		Strongly disagree
I prefer to be alone	1	2	3	4	5	6	7

(c) *Multiple choice* (indicate the best answer):
  On most days I
  a. Like to be with other people all of the time.
  b. Like to be with other people most of the time.
  c. Don't have strong opinions about being with other people.
  d. Prefer to be by myself most of the time.
  e. Prefer to be by myself all of the time.

(d) *Forced Choice* (indicate the best answer):
  a. I would prefer to be alone.
  b. I would prefer to be with other people.

(e) *Graphic scale* (mark the scale at the place that best represents how you feel. Scoring involves measuring the distance from the end of the line to the mark):
  I would prefer to be alone:
  Always ——————————————————————— Never

(f) *Check List* (check the words that best describe how you would like to be right now):
  ——— Happy
  ——— Alone
  ——— With friends

There is considerable variability in the number and nature of response alternatives that appear in contemporary psychological tests. Figure 2-7 provides examples of the manner in which a question can be rendered into a variety of structured formats. Figure 2-7 does not exhaust all possible structured formats that can be used. Indeed, considerable creativity has been shown in developing novel formats. However, these examples do indicate the more frequent types of approaches that you will find in the contemporary field. The major advantage of these formats is that they are readily translated into numbers, simply by assigning numerical values to the various response options. On the down side, they do sometimes seem to put words into the mouths of those taking tests, restricting their freedom to communicate their opinions or answers.

Open-ended response formats stand in direct contrast to structured approaches. Preselected alternatives are not provided, but freewheeling answers are allowed.

Testing can take a wide variety of formats such as the structured approach shown here.

The typical essay question on an exam or a person's answers in an interview are examples of this **unstructured format response.**[10] These formats are not popular in the testing field because they entail considerable interpretive work to make sense of the results, often a difficult task. Hence, unstructured formats tend to be more time-consuming than structured ones. They do have the benefit of providing an opportunity to hear the respondent's "voice," though, and are particularly effective in certain types of situations despite the difficulties associated with them.

Combining considerations of test-item type and response format provides a 2×2 matrix that can be used to locate a specific test. For example, the Imaginary Matrix Quiz (Figure 2-1) is pictorial *and* structured. Figure 2-8 provides examples of the types of tests that might appear in each of the four cells of this classification matrix.

Task demands. So far we have examined the stimulus and the response aspects of tests. What we have not discussed is the operations that respondents must apply to the test item to generate the response. It is here that we encounter the greatest variability in tests. Virtually every kind of problem-solving skill has been used—ranging from recognizing silhouettes to solving complex sets of nuclear fission equations. Additionally, a wide variety of requests for opinions and preferences on incredibly diverse topics has become part of the testing repertoire. To describe the types of task

---

[10]Some tests simply ask the respondent to point to some aspect of the stimulus to indicate the answer. For our purposes, these will be considered unstructured tests in that the respondent can point to any of a number of unspecified (that is, unstructured) alternatives.

Figure 2-8 Examples of various psychological test items as a function of item type and response format.

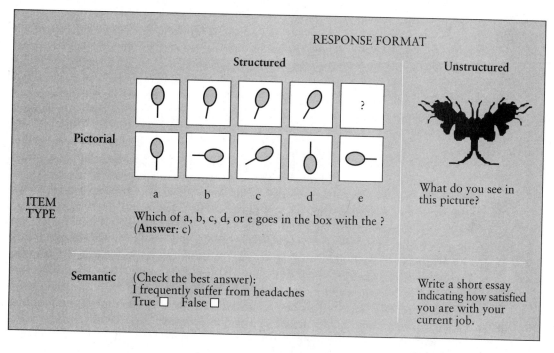

demands shown in psychological testing would require a virtually complete compendium of possible cognitive tasks that humans can perform.[11]

For our introductory purposes, sorting tests into two types of task demand will help us grasp the breadth of the domain. One class of test is characterized by there being a correct answer. Examples here include standard university examinations, most IQ tests, and a wide range of achievement tests such as those required for entry into law school. In the testing enterprise, such tests are typically called **objective tests** because both the correctness of the answer and the respondents' replies can be verified by outside observers.[12] In such cases, items are scored by deciding whether or not the respondent has provided the correct answer.

The second class of task demand embedded in tests is the instrument that asks respondents for statements of personal opinion or preference. In this case, there is no correct answer; the search is for an expression of attitude or personality. Such

---

[11]In Chapter 15, we will encounter Guilford's Structure of Intellect model, which has attempted to develop such a compendium in the context of testing. The classification scheme presented here is based, in part, on Guilford's ideas.

[12]It is perhaps unfortunate that the word *objective* is used in two senses within this book: (a) as part of the definition of a test and (b) as a subtype of test. Although both uses of the word refer to the possibility of intersubjective observability and verifiability, the dual use can create some confusion. The only solution here would be to coin a new term (for example, *factual* for tests with correct answers), but this would put you at a disadvantage because the literature in the field uses the word both ways.

tests, which we will call **voluntary tests**[13] indicate that any answer is acceptable. The respondent must agree to provide the required information, acting as a volunteer to generate the test responses. Entire areas of testing, such as personality and attitude assessment, are based almost exclusively on voluntary testing. Typically, voluntary tests search for idiosyncratic ideas or personal description. In most contexts, voluntary instruments are not called *tests* but use such terms as *inventories* or *forms* because they are not tests in the objective sense. Voluntary instruments do not have an external criterion against which it is possible to determine if a response is correct, indicating that a degree of interpretation is typically necessary to generate a score for them.

A Three-Dimensional Matrix

We can now merge our three categories to provide a classification scheme that hints of the breadth and complexity of the domain of psychological tests. Figure 2-9 shows this as a three-dimensional matrix, which has eight categories. Table 2-2 shows this same system along with brief descriptions of sample tests that could fall into the eight categories.

Examples of each category of tests can be found in the literature, and the variety within each category is extensive. For the most part, the choice of test category is guided by careful attention to the goals of the instrument. Some psychological ideas are readily accessed using specific test types. For example, tests of first-language ability and academic achievement are easily framed with semantic content, whereas tests relating to constructs such as mechanical ability are readily addressed using pictorial items. Measures of personality, attitude, predisposition, and preference are almost always voluntary, whereas measures of ability, aptitude, knowledge, and accomplishments are typically objective. Unstructured formats often emerge in cases where the richness of individual voices is an important part of the domain of interest, such as clinical psychology where the patient's articulations are particularly salient. Unstructured approaches can also be found in areas where it is not entirely clear what kinds of responses might be elicited. On the other hand, structured approaches are valuable when potential reactions to specific item content are limited and when issues of cost are paramount.

The testing enterprise shows a definite preference for some of the categories in Figure 2-9. This emerges when we examine the numbers of tests in each cell. In general, the most popular categories of tests show a definite bias toward structured tests (both voluntary and objective) that involve verbal processing. This is not particularly surprising because our culture has a bias toward verbal thinking. The relative ease of translating structured tests to numbers also makes them convenient and cost-effective. Additionally, as revealed in our ten-word definition of a psychological test, structured and objective tests are likely to be preferred because they conform more readily to the desiderata implied by the definition.

---

[13]This term, as well as the dichotomy underlying response format, has been drawn from Campbell (1958). He suggests another dichotomy, direct *versus* indirect tests—with indirect instruments being those where the respondent is not aware of (or duped about) what is being measured. The frequency of indirect assessment is sufficiently low to omit it from this rudimentary classification system.

Figure 2-9 The three-dimensional matrix that emerges when considering item type, response format, and task demand.

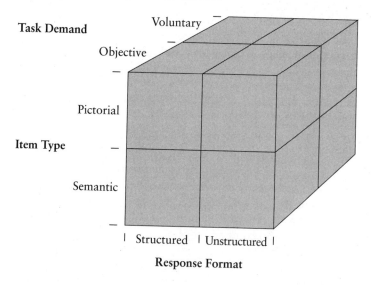

Table 2-2 Test types from ther merger of item type, response format, and task demand

Task Demand	Response Format	Item Type	Example
Objective	Structured	Pictorial	The Imaginary Matrix Quiz (see Figure 2-1)
Objective	Structured	Semantic	Multiple-choice questions on an examination
Objective	Unstructured	Pictorial	Asking respondents to describe the functions of pictured objects such as crochet hooks or tin snips
Objective	Unstructured	Semantic	Essay questions on an examination (for example, "What were the causes of the French revolution?")
Voluntary	Structured	Pictorial	A multiple-choice test in which respondents are asked to select which alternative describes what they see in ambiguous pictures
Voluntary	Structured	Semantic	A personality inventory wherein respondents answer true or false to a set of first-person singular sentences (for example, "I enjoy helping other people")
Voluntary	Unstructured	Pictorial	Asking respondents to tell a story about a pictured scene
Voluntary	Unstructured	Semantic	A sentence completion task where respondents are asked to finish sentences (for example, "Most of the time I feel _____")

The three-dimensional matrix shown in Figure 2-9 provides a sense of the range of tests that have been developed to reflect the definition of a psychological test as an objective and standardized measure of a sample of behavior. We now have a sense of the boundary conditions implied by this definition and a glimpse of the nature of technological devices that have been developed as part of the psychological testing enterprise.

TESTS AND NUMBERS

Our discussion thus far has argued that a psychological test should culminate in a number. In practice, most structured instruments are quantified by administering a set of items to respondents. The answers are then scored with reference to some preset criterion, such as an answer key, and the number of items that a person answered correctly in the keyed direction is tabulated. This sum, typically called a **raw score**, is the numerical component of our definition of a psychological test. For example, your raw score for our Imaginary Matrix Quiz, should it contain 20 items, would be the number of items you answered correctly, using a predetermined answer key to determine correctness. The obtained raw score could range between 0 and 20. Although there are many other complex and involved ways of deriving raw scores, particularly with unstructured tests, adding up the number of items answered relative to a predetermined key is by far the major strategy used in deriving a numerical value from a psychological test. More is involved, however, because at least three different levels of meaning can be accorded a number from a test. These levels relate to the manner in which a test was developed and place limits on the meanings that can be assigned to them.

The Nominal Scale

Some tests, which can legitimately be considered psychological by our definition, do not actually culminate in a number. A test may place persons into particular categories rather than assign them numbers. For example, some neuropsychological screening tests assign a person to either a normal or test-positive category, with the latter result indicating the need for further investigation. Such tests can be likened to blood tests where positive results either confirm a diagnosis or suggest further investigatory procedures. Thus, measurement devices can result in either a numerical or a categorical result. Whether a test culminates in a number or a category assignment is a joint function of the uses of the test and the manner in which the test was developed. Both approaches are considered measures in the sense expected in our definition.

Nominal scales are the simplest form of measurement scales and place those tested into specific categories. These scales are called *nominal* because they only provide a *name* for the slot into which our test places the respondent. Dividing a group of people into "female" and "male" represents the assumption of a nominal scale. Our Imaginary Matrix Quiz could be considered nominal if we placed everyone who obtained a raw score above 15 into a category called "superior" and the remainder in a group called "average," thus using the test to assign respondents to specific categories or slots.

Typically, the only legitimate inferences that can be drawn from nominal data relate to the frequencies and proportions of cases falling into each category. For example, indicating that 53% of the class was classified as "superior" using the Imaginary Matrix Quiz and our cutoff score of 15 would be acceptable, assuming the test was nominal. As well, summary statements of the proportions of patients testing positive on a specific test are legitimate with nominal scales.

Confusion can arise with this type of scale because numbers are sometimes used to describe the categories. For example, the **Diagnostic and Statistical Manual of Mental Disorders** (American Psychiatric Association, 1987) provides each diagnostic "slot" with a reference number. In this manual (usually referred to as *DSM III–R*), anorexia nervosa, a disorder in which a person does not eat properly, is coded as 307.10. The general mood disruption of depression is coded 311.00. It would clearly be inappropriate to do mathematical manipulations on the numbers themselves for at least two reasons: (1) One cannot suggest that a person suffering from anorexia nervosa is less sick than a depressed patient by virtue of the diagnostic category being a lower number and (2) the difference between the two category numbers is not a meaningful index of some psychological difference between two patients. The category numbers are best considered arbitrary and serve only as convenient shorthands for representing the complex domain of types of mental disorders. The major limiting characteristic of nominal scales is that not much can be done with the numbers except count the frequencies of occurrence.

The Ordinal Scale

Most structured tests culminate in a number—that is, they generate a raw score by some kind of standardized procedure. The numbers obtained by this process can have, under varying conditions, radically different properties. The **ordinal scale** is the simplest form of numerical scale because it conveys information only about the rank ordering of those who have taken the test. Thus, if you obtain a raw score of 17 on the Imaginary Matrix Quiz and your neighbor scores 9, all we can say, from the perspective of an ordinal scale, is that you rank higher than your neighbor on that test. We would not be willing to make any statements about the size of the difference between the two of you—only your relative positions.

Another example of ordinal scales can be found in a subcomponent of the *DSM III–R*. There is actually some ordinal information *within* several diagnostic categories. For example, the last digit in the general category of mood disorders represents the current state of the problem with respect to the following ordinal scale:

1 = Mild

2 = Moderate

3 = Severe without psychotic features

4 = Severe with psychotic features

Thus, a person who is experiencing a mild, single-episode depression would be assigned the *DSM* III–R number of 296.21, with the 1 representing the "mild" aspect of the diagnosis. A person with the same disorder but classified as "severe without psychotic features" would obtain the number 296.23, where the 3 indicates severity. In this case, it is reasonable to assume that, within the 296.2x category, some ordinal information is conveyed.[14] In the *DSM* III–R then, the category systems are nominal, and the fifth digits of some classifications are ordinal within a given diagnostic category. However, the ordinal information relates only to the relative positions of the patients classified in this manner. No statements about the actual size of the differences between two persons in this category are warranted. To make these kinds of statements, it is necessary to move on to the next level of measurement.

The Interval Scale

A more complex type of scale makes further assumptions regarding the distances between the numbers. **Interval scales** assume that the psychological distances between the numbers are equal across the entire scale. If we treated our Imaginary Matrix Quiz as though it was an interval scale, we would be assuming that the distance between raw scores of, say, 9 and 11 was equal to the distance between 16 and 18. In other words, a two-item difference in scale scores represents the same psychological difference, no matter where on the scale the two-point difference occurs. The only way in which we could justify this assumption would be to demonstrate that each unit of our scale has comparable psychological meaning. Without going into the technical details, it should be clear that the justification of intervality is relatively complex and demanding.[15]

There is some debate within the psychological testing enterprise about whether psychological test scores reveal ordinal or interval scales. Most people in the testing field treat their scales as though they were interval.[16] But others, like Kerlinger (1973), suggest that most psychological testing scales are fundamentally ordinal, justifying only statements about the relative positions of respondents. Examination of our example, the Imaginary Matrix Quiz, suggests that the raw score has at least some interval properties. Perhaps, most test scores fall somewhere between the two extremes represented by the ordinal and interval levels of measurement. The salient point in this argument is the extent to which the obtained scales provide useful indicators of important psychological concerns, and perhaps debates about the

---

[14]The ordinal nature of the fifth digit in this category is compromised somewhat by the use of the digits 5 and 6 to indicate partial and full remission, respectively.

[15]It should be noted at this point that there is a fourth level of measurement called a **ratio scale**. This level assumes intervality and adds the assumption of an absolute zero. Only with a ratio scale is it possible to make inferences about a person possessing twice as much of a given characteristic by virtue of obtaining twice the score. Ratio scales have not been presented here because nontrivial examples do not appear to be in the testing literature.

[16]While beyond our present scope, it turns out that you need at least an interval scale to conduct certain kinds of statistical operations, such as calculating a Pearson product-moment correlation coefficient, on raw scores. Thus, by using these techniques, the assumption of intervality has been made.

level of measurement underlying our numbers are not necessary. This is a point we will examine after we have gained some specific technical knowledge about test construction and interpretation. For the time being, it is important to note the distinction between categorical (that is, nominal) and numerical (that is, ordinal and interval) scales. Recognizing the issues attending the differences between ordinal and interval levels is also critical because they relate to the meaning attributed to the numbers that are obtained from a psychological test.

RECOGNIZING A GOOD TEST

Continuing with our snapshot of the contemporary testing enterprise, we can now ask how we can know the "goodness" or "badness" of a given test. This is a particularly complex issue, but the field provides a useful framework that can help us make these most important judgments. You will be introduced to this framework in the following section. It will acquaint you with some important ideas that will be discussed in considerably more detail later on, thereby serving to foreshadow some of what follows. In a sense, this section of the text provides you with a glimpse of the ideas that will emerge as the "principal players" in the following narrative, sharpening focus on the important evaluative themes and concepts that have emerged in the field.

As indicated earlier, the closer a given test is to our ten-word definition of psychological tests (as objective and standardized measures of a sample of behavior), the more likely it is to be viewed as "good" by members of the field. But how do we determine this? Do we just argue about which test is more "standardized"? No, because opinions and debate usually result in more problems than supported claims. Hence, intuitions, personal biases, and the like are not influential. The contemporary field demands **empirical evidence** and strong, documentable argumentation to demonstrate the goodness of a test. This may be in the form of the presentation of empirical data that confirm various assertions, or it may emerge as detailed demonstrations of the characteristics of a given test. Most important, assertions about the goodness of a test must be supported by empirical data. This is most readily accomplished by reference to two especially important terms—reliability and validity.

Reliability

As employed in the testing field, **reliability** relates to the consistency of scores when respondents are retested with the same test or an equivalent form. If scores show very little change across testings—being free of error, "noise," or slippage—the test is said to be reliable, and a degree of confidence can be placed in the test results. On the other hand, if test scores show a great deal of variation when administered to the same respondents on several occasions, they are interpreted as being unreliable, and grave concerns about error, noise, and slippage are entertained. Confidence in the quality of the test data also declines if unreliability is observed because interpretations of the scores are problematic.

Notice how reliability is defined in terms that permit **empirical** determination of its presence or absence. By testing the same group of respondents twice, an empirical estimate of reliability is obtained, thus moving discourse onto the observable plane. Perhaps one of the greatest assets of the concept of reliability is that it helps us frame our concerns about the goodness of a specific test in empirical terms. Tests whose objectivity, standardization, measurement properties, and sampling characteristics are poor will more than likely demonstrate unreliability.

The demonstration of reliability is not as simple as it first appears; there are a number of different ways to estimate it (see Chapters 6, 11, and 19). Because of this, it is important to be aware of the type of reliability being presented and to be familiar with the strengths and weaknesses of the version being reported. The nature of the sample that has been used to demonstrate reliability and its similarity to the group on which the test is being used are also very important. All this indicates the need for presenting substantial detail when making a claim of test reliability.

Validity

The fundamental concern of **validity** is the extent to which a test measures what it purports to measure.[17] A valid test of aggression is one that *actually* measures aggression. A test that claims to measure spatial ability but actually measures something else (for example, general intelligence) is an invalid test of spatial ability. Thus, whereas reliability is concerned with the consistency of a test measurement, validity is concerned with what it actually measures. It addresses fundamental questions about the meaning of the test scores: What inferences can legitimately be drawn from a particular test score? What does a given test score mean?

There are a number of different ways of establishing test validity. Each focuses on providing an empirical argument by presenting hard evidence to support a claim of validity. The simplest method of demonstrating validity involves administering a test to a group of respondents on whom you have an independent measure of their status on the characteristic the test measures. For example, if you are validating a test of mathematical ability, you might use grades in mathematics as your independent estimate of this ability. A validity study would involve administering the math ability test to a group of students for whom you have access to their grades. If the test is closely associated with the independent measure (for example, a strong relationship between math ability test scores and grades), evidence of the test's validity has been provided. However, if the test results and the independent measure are not closely associated with each other (for example, a weak or nonexistent relation between math ability test scores and grades), a claim for validity cannot be sustained.

As with reliability, notice the manner in which the concept of validity serves to frame questions about the goodness of a test in a way that forces the provision of empirical evidence, thereby moving discourse about validity onto an observable plane. However, the demonstration of validity is not as simple as it might appear here. There are a number of important subtypes of validity, and it is important that

---

[17]Two introductory expositions on validity are presented in Chapter 1. Besides this brief presentation, you might want to review these to "triangulate" your understanding of this most important idea.

all of these be established—not just one subtype. The strengths and weaknesses of these various forms of validity must also be taken into account. Validity studies must also clearly specify the type of validity being demonstrated, and details of sample size, representativeness, and relevance to the group on whom the test is being used must be provided—else the claim for validity should not be accepted. (These aspects will be discussed in detail in Chapters 8, 11, 13, and 19.)

These two concerns, reliability and validity, are the two most important issues when it comes to determining the goodness of a test. Both demand empirical evidence, and both must be present before a test is accepted for use in a specific situation. They represent the critical concerns when the technical issues of testing (as opposed to assessment) are under investigation.

Utility and Assessment

When a test is used in a specific situation, concern shifts to issues of assessment. Deciding if a specific test application is good becomes much more complex here, demanding considerations that supersede reliability and validity. This follows because a perfectly reliable and valid test used in the wrong way could produce an assessment disaster. Unreliable or invalid tests, even if used properly, can also cause significant assessment problems. Reliability and validity are necessary but not sufficient conditions for good assessment, indicating a need for something else in our repertoire of evaluative concepts to accommodate assessment. This has emerged in the field under the generic label of **utility**. This concept relates to the benefits and costs associated with the use of the test in a specific situation. To demonstrate utility, the benefits must outweigh the costs, which is a complex issue.

Benefits relate to the overall social context of the assessment and are a function of the particular situation in which the test is being used. Providing unique information that could not be gained otherwise (for example, providing a comparison of a person's test performance with a larger sample) is a typical assessment benefit that accrues from the use of tests. Another benefit is the manner in which the use of a test can be significantly lower in cost than a more complex approach like an interview, thus making funds available for other activities such as therapy. It is also important to consider psychological benefits attributable to tests, such as gaining access to elite educational programs or gaining a much-needed boost in self-esteem.

Costs involve the expenses of purchasing, administering, and interpreting tests, including the salaries of those involved, overhead, and the like. Costs must also take into account the extent to which the test and its interpretation might cause harm to the test taker. The story of Jack at the beginning of this chapter is one such cost. Putting a dollar value on such costs, however, is very difficult, making the fair determination of costs a challenging task.

The situation specificity of test benefits and costs makes it impossible to provide an exhaustive list of each. They require elaboration in specific situations. An additional problem is the frequent occurrence of unintended or unanticipated benefits and/or costs that make demonstration of utility difficult. Costs and benefits are a function of whose pocketbook and whose welfare is being considered, and the documentation of utility of an assessment application is complex.

Perhaps the simplest utility analysis for assessment is to pose the Hamletian query: "To test or not to test ... that is the question." The questioner is forced to compare the utility of two situations—one in which the test is used and one in which it is not. In a proper utility analysis, data should demonstrate conclusively that the former alternative (to test) provides more benefits and/or costs less than the former (not to test). The comparison of costs and benefits is difficult because the two are seldom articulated using the same metric, which can result in an attempt to compare apples and oranges.

In response to some of these difficulties, several interesting technologies of establishing benefits, costs, and utility have been proposed (see Chapters 11 and 14). Although these techniques have not solved the value problems inherent in establishing utility, they have provided a framework for approaching this most complex topic. As with reliability and validity, the proof of utility for testing resides with the test user, and this should be accomplished using empirical data.

In summary, the notions of reliability, validity, and utility have been proposed as contemporary answers to the most important question "How would you know a good test if you saw one?" Each of these ideas forces consideration of empirical evidence to establish their respective claims, and each frames the fundamental evaluative question in a different manner. The evolution of these ideas and details of the ways in which they are applied are a very significant part of the narrative of testing that appears in the following chapters. These basic evaluative concepts are the foundation of the worldview held by those involved in the testing enterprise. As such, they are of critical importance for an informed view of the field.

STAKEHOLDERS IN THE TESTING ENTERPRISE

Thus far we have seen that testing is a massive and complex area of contemporary human endeavor. The variety of tests, the numbers of settings in which we encounter them, the sophisticated measurement considerations that underlie them, the manner in which they are evaluated, and the sheer number of tests that are administered on a day-to-day basis in our culture all underscore the significance of this enterprise. Not surprisingly, there is a tremendous variety of reactions to this aspect of our lived cultural experience. Testing is many things to many people. To some, it is a way of making a living, to others an opportunity to apply scientific knowledge. Some see testing as a necessary evil associated with the need to make decisions on a mass scale, whereas others perceive it as an invasion of their privacy. Reactions to testing range from rave reviews to devastating critical appraisals.

One way of providing some structure to this diversity of opinion is to consider the groups of people who have vested interests in the testing enterprise. Such groups are called **stakeholders** (Bryk, 1983) by virtue of their having a stake, or vested interest, of one kind or another, in testing. Four stakeholder groups seem particularly salient for our purposes: test takers, test users, test makers, and society in general. The value accorded testing will vary as a function of stakeholder group, being dictated by the degree of involvement in and experiences with psychological tests. There will also be disagreements within the various stakeholder groups, which signal important concerns. To provide a picture of the variety of opinions about testing in contemporary society, we will discuss each group in the pages that follow.

Test Takers

For most of you, your encounters with testing have occurred when you have had to sit down and fill out a test. Here you are a member of the test-taker stakeholder group. As indicated in Figures 2-2 and 2-3, on average, members of this group have had a number of significant testing encounters in a number of different settings.

When asked in our survey, students indicated that a number of benefits emerged from their testing encounters, including the following:

1. The discovery of new career and educational choices attending the use of vocational tests
2. Increased self-understanding and insight
3. Enhanced self-confidence
4. Successful outcomes such as getting a job in a competitive situation
5. Documentation and confirmation of personal strengths
6. Persuasion to pursue higher goals such as going to university
7. A variety of intrinsic benefits such as finding the experience interesting, challenging, and a good brain workout

This list suggests that testing can provide a number of significant benefits to the test-taker stakeholder group.

But there is a down side to testing as well. Two classes of concerns emerged in our student responses. The first related to generic concerns about psychological assessment and the uses to which the tests were being put. The second set of worries was associated with more technical aspects of the tests themselves.

The student group indicated the following worries concerning assessment:

1. Test results were thought to be taken too seriously and either could or did create negative outcomes such as being labeled as "dumb" or not being admitted to medical school.
2. Test results were in such great disagreement with expectation that major conflict and concern was created.
3. Tests gave incorrect advice such as indicating a course of action that later turned out to be inappropriate.
4. Tests can be very unfair to particular classes of people such as those for whom English is a second language.
5. Tests and the interpretations and labels they engender create undue anxiety, stress, and unrest.

6. Test results were not discussed with the respondent, creating unnecessary stress and concern about something being wrong.

7. Respondents were not told why testing was being undertaken, creating a sense of "there must be something wrong with me."

8. Aspects of the test itself made the experience appear to be useless. For example, some found it exceedingly difficult to answer questions truthfully because they were unsure of the context from which they were supposed to be answering. Tricky, ambiguous, or inadequate response alternatives also made the testing quite difficult and seemingly useless.

These are not complete lists of benefits and concerns associated with testing. This list is presented to provide a sense of the concerns and worries voiced by a subgroup of a stakeholder group—university students—and are not intended as a complete compendium. Presumably, more benefits and concerns would emerge if the sample were extended.

A basic issue for test takers is the number of important factors that can affect the outcome of the testing event. If you are not feeling well at the time of testing, are poorly prepared, or are in an argumentative mood, the obtained results will likely be inaccurate. Some test takers experience test anxiety, feelings of uneasiness and discomfort associated with the testing encounter itself, which affects performance. Your strategy of handling questions when you are uncertain of your answer (for example, guessing habits, sense of being able to "beat the odds") also adds noise to the measurement process and detracts from its utility. Fatigue, a hangover, prior coaching, the presence of physical pain, and a wide range of other transient factors play a role in shaping the eventual numerical result of the test experience. Almost all test takers are aware of these factors and realize that they have a degree of control over the outcome of the testing event. This is particularly true for voluntary tests such as personality inventories, but it also holds for objective tests, albeit it to a lesser degree. All of this translates into the understanding, within this stakeholder group, that those being tested have significant control over the testing event. The test taker can easily withdraw cooperation and thereby invalidate the obtained result. It follows that test-taker cooperation is an absolutely necessary and integral part of the testing event. In some settings, this cooperation is given freely (for example, vocational counseling sessions), whereas in others it is coerced (for example, "take this test or your application file will be incomplete and you won't be considered"). Many worries about tests stem from the perception that cooperation is being coerced and that the test taker does not have freedom of choice. Test takers, however, do have the choice of refusing to participate in the event, and any testing event is the result of a cooperative endeavor between the persons taking and administering the test.

It seems clear that the test-taker group has an ambivalent attitude toward tests. These devices undoubtedly serve group needs in some instances. However, these benefits contrast with some real human concerns. Issues of cooperation are also important. An incredibly complex cost/benefit equation demands careful and informed consideration of both the pluses and minuses of testing. The major goal of this book is to provide you with sufficient information and knowledge to permit you to align yourself on the cost or the benefit side of this equation.

Test Users

This stakeholder group is represented by myriad professionals who use tests as part of their day-to-day activities. Be they educators, industrial psychologists, clinicians, counselors, research scientists, or any of a wide range of other service communities, test users have adopted these instruments as tools they use in the execution of their jobs. For the most part, these professionals have (or should have) received significant training in the administration, scoring, and interpretation of the tests they use.[18]

Members of this stakeholder group have, in general, a positive view of tests because these instruments are an integral part of their professional toolboxes. It is almost impossible to value tests negatively and then use them. Hence, most public discourse in the test-user community is clearly supportive of tests. However, by virtue of their experience and training, test users have developed an excellent sense of the limitations of these devices. This information is usually embedded in the confines of the profession by virtue of being available only to those who know what to look for and where to find it. This indicates that there is some significant knowledge within the test-user community that could, under some conditions, be considered negative toward tests. Like the test-taker group, there is a degree of ambivalence toward tests in the test-user group. On average, however, this group sees the benefits of tests far outweighing the potential problems and concerns.

A major concern within the test-user group is proper administration, scoring, and interpretation of tests. Like all tools, tests come with detailed instructions. These are in the form of a **test manual**, which should provide all the information necessary to correctly use the instrument. Included here is a standardized set of procedures that must be used in administration, scoring, and interpretation.[19] Failure to adhere to any component of these instructions defeats the purpose of the test—no matter how well designed it is.

This need to follow instructions properly is so strongly embedded within the test-user group that it has become a matter of ethics within the community.[20] The issue of ensuring that test takers do not have an opportunity to see the test prior to administration is also important here, as are the test users' obligations to ensure that testing conditions are optimal. All these strictures to the test user are driven by the need to maximize the standardized nature of the testing event. Any conditions that result in one person being tested differently from another compromises the rigor of the testing event and confounds any comparisons that the test user might want to make. Hence, there is great concern about procedure and consistency within the test-user community.

---

[18]All professional groups involved with testing have developed associations that provide counsel and regulations regarding the use of tests. For psychology, the major body is the American Psychological Association whose recommendations, guidelines, and standards for testing will be discussed in detail in Chapter 12.

[19]The American Psychological Association has provided a set of detailed guidelines regarding the information that must be included in the manual. These guidelines will be discussed in detail in Chapter 12.

[20]Ethics is much more than "getting instructions right," but adherence to proper procedure is a component of ethical behavior within the profession. The American Psychological Association has taken the lead in developing ethical codes not only for psychologists in general but also for the test-user community. These codes will be discussed in detail in Chapter 12.

One particularly important aspect of the test user's world is **rapport**, which relates to the working relationship between the examiner and the person being tested. Good rapport occurs when cooperation is attained and the test takers can perform at their optimum. Bad rapport is associated with situations where respondents cannot perform at their best because of a poor relationship with the administrator.

Given the importance of test-taker cooperation outlined in the previous section, it is crucial that effective rapport be established. In some cases, a short chat prior to testing is sufficient; in other cases, much more is required. For example, a test-anxious client may require considerable coaxing to begin the test, or an exceedingly shy child may require considerable prompting in order to articulate a correct answer. The problem here is that such coaxing and prompting may violate the standardization of the test. For example, if one child is prompted regularly and another is not, then any comparison of their test results is unfair. The issue of rapport, then, emerges as a delicate balance between the need to establish test-taker cooperation on the one hand and standardization on the other. Although some test manuals provide explicit procedures for handling this issue, many do not, leaving considerable room for variability within the test-user community.[21]

Like any tool, users evaluate tests in terms of the effectiveness with which they do the job for which they are designed and the costs inherent in acquiring and using them. A highly specialized vocabulary and set of concepts have evolved and are used to help test users make these kinds of decisions. One of the goals of this book is to provide you with sufficient understanding of this vocabulary and conceptual schema to allow you to understand, or at least query, the reasons why specific tests are used in specific situations. In a sense, the text will allow you to see the world as the test user does and thereby understand the concerns of this stakeholder group. Such knowledge gives you the power to evaluate the suitability and appropriateness of a particular test in a particular situation.

Test Makers

The third stakeholder group is made up of those people who create and distribute the tests. They can include actual test designers and developers, publishers, marketers, salespersons, sponsors, and, under some circumstances, test users. As noted earlier (see Table 2-1), this is a very busy group who releases new and significantly revised tests at a significant pace. The variety of tests being introduced, combined with the older ones that are still available, indicates an incredibly large corpus of materials attributed to this group.

Test makers' levels of activity indicate that they are continually reacting to the needs of the professional communities that use tests, attempting to provide them with devices that satisfy their varied needs. This reactivity demonstrates that the test-maker stakeholder group is dedicated to servicing the continually changing needs of the professionals who use their products.

---

[21]The Wechsler series of IQ tests discussed in Chapter 10 offer such guidelines that provide the administrator with a set of acceptable prompts.

Rapport, the relationship between the test taker and the test administrator, is very important when optimal levels of performance are being measured.

Current activities of the test-maker group are dictated in large measure by the same set of standards for tests that bind the test-user group. Of particular note is the American Psychological Association's ***Standards for Educational and Psychological Testing*** (APA, 1985), which contains a set of guidelines for proper test development and evaluation.[22] Having evolved over the past 40 years, this document provides a particularly important set of recommendations regarding the manners in which test developers ought to proceed.

The test maker's value orientation toward tests is clearly positive. Although considerable attention is paid to developing the best possible instrument, it remains that a significant aspect of the group's activities involves convincing users to adopt the instrument they have developed. Yet there is some ambivalence toward tests in this stakeholder group. The product offered the test users should meet the best possible standards. This being the case, the test-maker community places considerable emphasis on standards and product quality. Inherent in these concerns is the argument that tests failing to live up to standards are not to be endorsed—that is, test makers negatively value such tests. Thus, we find considerable emphasis on standards and quality within this stakeholder group, all oriented toward providing the best possible product to users.

---

[22]These standards are discussed in detail in Chapter 12 and are presented in Appendix D.

There is a significant fiscal aspect to this stakeholder group, which must not be overlooked. The amounts of money involved are rather large. To quote from Cohen et al. (1988),

> Test publishers do not publicize their earnings, and exact, up-to-date figures are hard to come by. However, to provide the reader with an idea of the extent to which psychological and educational testing is indeed "big business," consider a sampling of the revenues earned by just a few of the many psychological and educational test publishers in the mid-1970s. Kohn (1975) reported that one test publisher, Harcourt Brace Jovanovich, had approximately $21 million in sales in 1974. For the same year Kohn reported that the measurement and guidance division of Houghton Mifflin recorded sales of approximately $5.5 million, the American College Testing Program had sales of approximately $11 million, and Educational Testing Service had sales of approximately $54 million. [p. 17]

These figures, particularly if they were adjusted to dollar values for the current year, indicate a considerable amount of vested (and invested) interest in the testing enterprise. There is a large and financially powerful corporate presence in the testing enterprise that must be factored into any evaluation of this aspect of our culture. Given this situation, the need for individuals to be aware of the strengths and weaknesses of testing is amplified.

Society

The final stakeholder group to be considered here is society in general. The questions we have to ask here are: "To what extent does the testing enterprise contribute to the smooth and effective functioning of our culture?" "Do tests do more good than harm?" "Do the costs of these activities outweigh the benefits?" "If tests are problematic, is there anything else that is better, or would an alternative approach create as many problems?" These are clearly very heady questions that will require some significant thought and analysis before it is possible to answer them. At this point in our knowledge of the field, we are not ready to attempt answers—there is an important prerequisite we need before proceeding. Specifically, we have to gain a certain amount of detailed, technical knowledge about tests themselves—what they are, where they came from, how they work— before proceeding. If we fail to learn about the testing enterprise from the inside, our evaluations of its utility will be invalid because we will not have considered the problem from the varying perspectives of all the stakeholders involved in this great social experiment.

Summary

We now turn our attention to the task of becoming familiar with the inner workings of the psychological testing enterprise. As indicated in Chapter 1, we will accomplish this by examining a narrative account of the manner in which the enterprise evolved to occupy such a significant place in our society. What we have accomplished in this chapter is a snapshot of the testing field today, which acts as a target for our narrative. It has given us a sense where our story will end—foreshadowing the story that follows. We have examined the foundational definition of a psychological test, discovered the settings in which tests are likely to be found, seen the tremendous diversity of the tests themselves, learned some basic ideas about quantification, seen the evaluative schemata used in the field, and encountered a wide range of opinions about tests related to the stakeholders in the field. Here we have found a large, vibrant, and active enterprise with the stated concerns of helping society work more effectively. Determining the success of this enterprise in fulfilling its stated goals is the challenge for you to work out—for yourself—as we proceed through the following chapters.

Glossary

ability The power to perform an act before or after training.

academic achievement Success in school settings based on indicators such as grades or performance on standardized tests designed to assess mastery of specific curriculum units.

achievement test An instrument that measures the extent to which specific curriculum units have been mastered.

aptitude The natural ability to acquire relatively general or special types of knowledge or skills.

assessment In contrast to testing, the use of tests to make psychological judgments about specific individuals.

behavior A person's overt act that can be reliably observed by an outsider.

counseling A branch of the psychological service professions that is concerned with helping persons achieve a better adjusted and more productive life.

data Empirical observations.

developmental test A test designed to measure the manner in which specific behaviors unfold as a passage of time. Most of these tests are designed for infants and toddlers, to track the sequence and timing of their growth.

diagnosis A statement of the present status of an individual. When used for diagnosis, psychological tests attempt to predict the current state of the individual being tested.

Diagnostic and Statistical Manual of Mental Disorders (DSM) An important reference work that defines each psychiatric diagnosis and provides a category number to enhance standardization among service professionals.

empirical Of and relating to the senses.

empirical evidence Systematically gathered sets of observations relevant to a specific question.

Imaginary Matrix Quiz A fictional psychological test that demonstrates various aspects of the ten-word definition of a psychological test.

intelligence test A test designed to provide indexes of cognitive status. Most intelligence tests are good predictors of academic achievement. (See Chapter 15.)

interval scale A numerical measurement outcome that conveys information about relative position, as well as permitting some inferences about the sizes of differences between numerical values.

item As used here, the unit stimulus of a test that is presented to the test taker, such as the question presented in Figure 2-8.

lived cultural experience Events encountered by a vast majority of the members of a given social group that become a significant, shared aspect of membership in the group.

measure In this context, the output of a psychological test as either a number or a categorical statement. Psychological measures can exist at three different measurement levels: nominal, ordinal, and interval.

Mental Measurements Yearbook An important reference source that provides information about and reviews of all published psychological tests.

nominal scale A measurement outcome that culminates in placing the individual into a category.

objective Belonging to the world of sensory perception and being intersubjectively observable and verifiable, especially by scientific methods. Objective is used in two ways in the chapter: (a) as a component of the definition of a test and (b) as a label to describe a subtype of test item for which there is a correct response.

objective test An instrument for which there is a correct answer (or answers) for each item; contrasts with a voluntary test for which there is no correct answer(s).

ordinal scale A numerical measurement outcome that conveys information only about relative position or ranking.

personality test An instrument used to measure the "stable factors that make one person's behavior consistent from one time to another or different from the behavior other people would manifest in comparable situations" (Hampson, 1988, p. 1).

pictorial item A test item that is an actual, concrete object or graphic representation of it.

prognosis A statement of the anticipated or predicted status of an individual. When used for prognosis, psychological tests attempt to predict the future state of the individual being tested.

psychological test An objective and standardized measure of a sample of behavior.

psychology The scientific study of behavior and mental processes.

psychopathology The study of mental functions and processes under conditions brought about by disorder or disease.

rapport The working relationship between the test giver and the test taker in a specific testing situation.

ratio scale A numerical measurement outcome that contains all characteristics of an interval scale and includes an absolute zero. Such scales are not typically found in psychological test data.

raw score The actual number that is gathered from any observational process such as the administration of a psychological test. In many cases, the raw score is generated by counting up the number of times a respondent answers items correctly or in the direction of a predetermined scoring key.

reliability The extent to which a test provides consistent or error-free measurements. (This concept will be discussed in more detail in Chapters 6, 11, and 19.)

response format The manner in which the potential answers to a psychological test item can be answered.

sample of behavior A selected portion or component of the overt actions of specific persons.

scholastic aptitude The natural ability to acquire general or specific academic skills or knowledge.

semantic item A test item that demands the use of an active, verbal processing system to generate an answer.

stakeholder A person in a group who has a common, vested interest in a specific social program or activity.

standardized The property of psychological tests in which everyone taking the test is treated in exactly the same way (for example, presented with the same stimuli, in the same order; hears the same instructions) and includes the procedures for scoring and interpreting the test—everyone must be treated in exactly the same way.

Standards for Educational and Psychological Testing A set of guidelines for proper test development and evaluation. (These standards will be covered in more detail in Chapter 12.)

stimulus Any energy change that excites a receptor. Typically refers to any object or event that elicits a given effect. In the present case, the test item was defined as the fundamental stimulus for a psychological test.

structured response format Any psychological test in which the tester provides all possible (or acceptable) response options for the respondent, who must choose the best answer from among the provided alternatives.

task demand The cognitive activity that must be enacted in order to answer an item in a psychological test.

test "A critical examination, observation, or evaluation" (Gove, 1965).

testing In contrast to assessment, the technical aspects of psychological instruments such as validity and reliability.

test item The stimulus that the test taker sees while being tested.

test manual A technical document, which accompanies a psychological test, containing information about the administration, scoring, and interpretation of the test. (This will be discussed in more detail in Chapter 12.)

trait Individual characteristics in thought, feeling, or behavior. Typically, traits are the fundamental building blocks for the study of personality.

unstructured response format Any psychological test in which open-ended responses are permitted.

utility As used here, the costs and benefits associated with the use of tests in a specific assessment situation.

validity The traditional notion of validity refers to the extent to which a test measures what it purports to measure. A more contemporary view defines it as the "appropriateness, meaningfulness, and usefulness of the specific inferences made from test scores" (APA, 1985). It is divided into a number of subtypes including criterion-related, content, and construct validity. This concept is discussed in greater detail in Chapters 8, 11, 13, and 19.

vocational test A psychological test that is used to help select optimal educational and occupational paths.

voluntary test An instrument for which there is no correct answer. Tests of preference, personality, and attitude are typically considered to be voluntary tests.

Suggested Further Reading

Carmines, E. G., & Zeller, R. A. (1979). *Reliability and validity assessment.* Newbury Park, Calif.: Sage.

> This book is a good source if you want to find out more about the foundational concepts of reliability and validity. It is fine introductory treatment of these two topics, providing many good examples and details.

Gladding, S. T. (1992). *Counseling: A comprehensive profession* (2nd ed.). New York: Merrill.

> As indicated in the chapter, counseling was not one of the settings in which students indicated they had encountered tests, suggesting that this field is not part of their active considerations. This is due, in part, to the diversity of settings in which counseling is practiced. Gladding's book provides a good overview of the counseling field and allows the reader to determine the activities of this profession. Of particular note is Chapter 21, which explicitly discusses the use of tests in counseling.

Gould, S. J. (1981). *The mismeasure of man.* New York: Norton.

> This book presents a very well-developed antitest argument. Aspects of the history of testing as well as some of the more modern ideas are clearly analyzed, and a number of important conclusions are developed. This is very important reading for anyone who wishes to attain a balanced view of the costs and benefits of the testing enterprise.

Guba, E. G., & Lincoln, Y. S. (1989). *Fourth generation evaluation.* Newbury Park, Calif.: Sage.

> This provocative book provides detailed information about the idea of stakeholders. Of particular interest is the manner in which these authors argue about the importance of considering *all* potential stakeholders when making evaluative judgments. They indicate that some of the more traditional methodologies that have stemmed from contemporary testing encounter difficulties when the real-life problems of making important social decisions are at the forefront of one's concerns.

Hanson, F. A. (1993). *Testing testing: Social consequences of the examined life.* Berkeley: University of California Press.

> This is another important book that develops a series of antitest arguments. One of the most interesting theses is that tests actually create or construct the entities they purport to measure. The idea of intelligence, then, as you think about it, has actually

been created by the tests, making it a "fiction" rather than a "reality." *The Enterprise* will provide you with sufficient background to help you decide if this is a justifiable argument.

Kolb, B., & Whishaw, I. Q. (1990). *Fundamentals of human neuropsychology* (3rd ed.). New York: Freeman.

This book provides some detailed information about the manner in which tests are involved in the detection of problems associated with trauma to the central nervous system. Part 7, "Applied Human Neuropsychology," is particularly informative regarding the use of tests to facilitate neurosurgical cases, learning disabilities, psychiatric disorders, and head trauma. Chapter 31 provides some background on testing procedures.

Landy, F. J. (1989). *The psychology of work behavior* (4th ed.). Pacific Grove, Calif.: Brooks/Cole.

The manner in which tests are used in industry is well presented in this book. If you want to gain a sense of the place of testing in the contemporary workplace, this is a good place to start. Of particular note is a chapter on tests and testing techniques (Chapter 6), as well as several others on prediction, performance appraisal, and interviews.

Leahey, T. H. (1992). *A history of psychology: Main currents in psychological thought* (3rd ed.). Englewood Cliffs, N.J.: Prentice Hall.

The notions of objectivity, standardization, measurement, and behavior samples inherent in the definition of the psychological test are drawn from a long and illustrious history within the discipline. Leahey's history provides a highly readable and understandable account of the evolution of psychology, providing access to much wider contextual information than it is possible to provide in this text. Chapter 12, entitled "Psychology Takes Off" demonstrates clearly the manner in which tests were instrumental in establishing psychology as a viable academic discipline in North America.

Matarazzo, J. D. (1990). Psychological assessment versus psychological testing: Validation from Binet to the school, clinic, and courtroom. *American Psychologist, 45,* 999–1017.

The first section of this article is good background on the distinction between assessment and testing drawn in this chapter. The latter part of Matarazzo's presentation reveals some of the problems that are being encountered as the use of tests is moving increasingly into potentially controversial and confrontational settings such as the courtroom.

McLoughlin, J. A., & Lewis, R. B. (1992). *Assessing special students* (3rd ed.). Columbus, Ohio: Merrill.

This book presents a wide variety of contextual materials relating to the use of tests in education. It covers many and varied applications of various assessment tools in the contemporary school system, providing a useful overview of this domain of testing in our culture.

Neitzel, M. T., Bernstein, D. A., & Milich, R. (1991). *Introduction to clinical psychology* (3rd ed.). Englewood Cliffs, N.J.: Prentice Hall.

The contemporary field of clinical psychology is summarized in this book. Of particular note is Chapter 5, "Testing in Clinical Psychology," which outlines some of the testing methods currently in use in the field.

Stevens, S. S. (1951). *Handbook of experimental psychology.* New York: Wiley.

On pages 23–30, you will find the authoritative treatment of the characteristics of nominal, ordinal, interval, and ratio scales. It should be noted that several authors (for example, Torgerson, 1958) have challenged this system of categorizing levels of measurement. The material in Stevens preceding his presentation of scale types provides useful background on the manner in which psychologists have conceptualized measurement. It is useful reading because it provides a context for understanding the assumptions that have gone into framing the contemporary approaches to measurement.

Discussion Questions

1. Take a moment to think about the most important encounter you have had with psychological tests. List both the benefits and the concerns of this encounter. On balance, do you feel it was good for you? Why, or why not?

2. Develop a list of important lived cultural experiences that you think your class-mates have shared. Compare your list with your classmates' lists to determine if the experience and your interpretations of them are indeed shared.

3. Discuss the ten-word definition of a psychological test, with respect to an examination you have recently taken. Was it a psychological test in the sense discussed in the text? Why, or why not?

4. With respect to your experience in other courses, indicate the manner in which a seemingly simple definition of subject matter (like our ten words) in actuality articulates "goodness" or "badness" judgments (as our definition of the psychological test did).

5. How many significant encounters with tests can you recall? Where did they take place? In what ways do your memories agree or disagree with the data from the university students presented in the chapter?

6. Clearly indicate the differences between testing and assessment. Suggest two real-life situations that demonstrate these differences.

7. List the major categories of tests derived from the *Mental Measurement Yearbook.* Suggest a specific example of each type of test based, if possible, on your personal experience.

8. Do you think IQ tests are the same thing as measures of scholastic aptitude? What aspect of your understanding of the notion of intelligence has led you to your answer?

9. Why is the semantic/pictorial distinction among types of test items important?

10. Design six different structured response formats to test someone's knowledge of the outcome of the last presidential election.

11. Outline the strengths and weaknesses of structured versus unstructured response formats.

12. In what sense are *voluntary* tests voluntary?

13. Using the format in Table 2-2, indicate eight different sample items that could be used to evaluate your knowledge of and reactions to this chapter.

14. Indicate separate situations in which it would be most appropriate to use nominal, ordinal, and interval levels of measurement.

15. Discuss the core idea that unites the disparate evaluative criteria of reliability, validity, and utility as they are used in the testing enterprise.

16. Clearly define and differentiate between *validity*, *reliability*, and *utility*.

17. Some have argued that reliability is a necessary but not sufficient condition for the demonstration of validity. Why do you think this might be so?

18. Discuss the relationship between validity and utility.

19. Of the four stakeholders in the testing enterprise listed in the chapter, who is likely to have the most negative opinion? Why?

20. Can you think of any other stakeholder groups in testing who have not been mentioned in the chapter? Should they have been included? Why, or why not?

21. Suggest as many additions as you can to the lists of benefits and worries about testing presented in the chapter.

22. What are the major implications of the observation that testing involves a cooperative relationship between the tester and person being tested?

23. Prepare a list of everything you think should be included in a test manual if a test is to be used properly. (You might care to file this list away and compare it with the actual suggestions presented in Chapter 12.)

24. Define *rapport* and suggest at least ten factors that might affect it negatively.

25. In what ways do you think the vested interests of the test makers might affect their marketing of and opinions about tests?

26. In your view, are psychological tests as important to your age group as they were for your parents? Can you think of any reasons why this might be the case?

Part II

Foundations

Psychological testing is the outcome of a number of important developments that transpired well before the invention of the first formalized test, which occurred about 1900. The manifestation of tests in our culture is the result of a long, extensive evolutionary process, which, in some senses, can be traced as far back as the emergence of our species. This part of the text outlines these foundational concerns to provide you with the intellectual background of this aspect of modern technology.

Chapter 3 places testing into a broad social context. Viewed as a social practice with the objective of placing individuals into the best possible roles within a society, the goals that testing serve in our culture can be seen as an integral part of all organized societies. To illustrate this point, Chapter 3 provides several examples of testlike applications from other cultural contexts. Such comparisons give us a vantage point to view the role of tests in our own, specific situation.

Science, especially with its emphasis on mathematics and quantification, is one of the hallmarks of our contemporary cultural system. Its products and methods are celebrated in every nook and cranny of North American life. Testing has not been immune from this influence and can be seen as one of the most interesting applications of mathematical and quantitative approaches to social decision making. To appreciate this, though, we have to examine the genesis of this fascination with numbers that is so prevalent in our culture. To do this, Chapter 4 traces the emergence of mathematics as it relates to testing. It documents the evolution of the quantitative worldview, which is the bedrock of science. In a broad overview, we see the emergence of the importance of numbers in our own world and come to appreciate the manner in which this worldview undergirds the entire psychological testing enterprise.

Chapter 5 traces some of the philosophical issues that have become infused into the contemporary testing field. Here we encounter some long-standing debates such as the differential roles of nature and nurture in explaining human behavior, coming to understand that these issues predated the invention of tests—even though they continue to be important in the field. This chapter also introduces some of the mathematical techniques that were created in the service of these philosophical issues (for example, the correlation coefficient).

These foundations provide important contextual information that allows us to fully appreciate contemporary testing practice. Seen as the result of a complex interplay between social, scientific, and philosophical issues, we begin to understand the central place of psychological testing in our day-to-day lives. Furthermore, we gain an appreciation of the long-standing historical and social factors that forged the shape of current testing practice.

Chapter 3

Social Foundations of Testing
A Multicultural Perspective

TESTING AND SOCIETY

Psychological testing is social practice. Involving a technology that has evolved to serve specific social needs, psychological testing is a reflection of the society in which it is practiced. This implies, among other things, that it is instructive to examine several aspects of society and social groups to develop a framework that we can use to embellish the nature and function of tests in our culture. Such considerations will help us elaborate the social strand of our narrative of testing.

Studying cultures, however, can be problematic, particularly when the goal is to understand our own. We have blind spots, and we have great difficulty seeing and understanding certain aspects of our own social behaviors. In a sense, we are too familiar with our own world, sometimes unable to reflect on it with accuracy

81

and insight. This brings us close to the emic/etic distinction drawn earlier—wherein emic understandings can, under some circumstances, exclude significant aspects that are clearly visible from an etic perspective. It is here that a comparative approach to studying cultures can be particularly informative. By examining test-related practices in other social groups, it is possible to develop a perspective that can then be turned onto our own social groupings to great analytic advantage. This is the true value of a multicultural view; it provides a highly effective arena for examining our own social practices and the manners in which they affect our own day-to-day lives.

CLOSE UP   The Snowball Fight

Although it wasn't a particularly significant triumph in the grand scheme of the world, I do recollect, with some pride, the giant snowball fight we had one bright February day. The snow was perfect. The late winter sun had created a texture that was ideal for the young band of play soldiers to try out their strategic powers as two groups of about 15 children each squared off for the great battle. The enemy was from the bordering neighborhood and was, on average, older and bigger, but we had moxie.

By midafternoon the battle had degenerated into long-distance bombardment, and excepting an all-out charge against the other's well-stocked fortress, things appeared to be at an impasse. Because we were younger and smaller, we feared that they might charge us—a rout could be at hand.

Desperately seeking some way of gaining an advantage, we began to scheme. Before long we were asking each other what kinds of things we could each do well that we might incorporate into the evolving battle plan. After some intense discussion, we discovered that four of us were very familiar with the surrounding terrain, particularly the access routes to various garage roofs just behind the enemy fort. Soon we were divided into runners, climbers, and throwers, and our great plan was launched with youthful enthusiasm. The runners, who were our bigger members, worked their way into some trees just off from our fortress, drawing fire and acting as a diversion for the climbers who slipped off the battlefield unnoticed. The climbers, knowledgeable of the local terrain, circled around to Patterson's place, which provided access to the garage roof. The rest of us, the throwers, waited patiently in the fort, building up an impressive arsenal of snowballs.

Before long we saw the black-and-red toque of Alex Piggot, our "head climber," pop over the garage roof behind the enemy fortress, then Donny Wilson's grin, then Sarah Church, and finally the guy from the big house by the school. Sitting astraddle the roof, which provided an infinite supply of perfect snowball snow, these four let loose a ferocious barrage at the unprotected backside of the enemy fort, forcing them to vacate their shelter. Then we had them. Caught in a three-way cross fire between our runners, throwers, and climbers (who immediately occupied the recently vacated fortress), the enemy was forced to capitulate—we had won the day! There was great joy and glee...

Looking back at this vignette of growing up makes me wonder how often this kind of story has been played out before. How often have groups of younger and smaller adversaries prevailed? My guess is millions of times. This is in fact a very old story. My snowball fight was set in urban North America, but the structure and plot of this story go back to the beginning of our species. If we look at the evolution of ourselves, *Homo sapiens*, we can readily envisage reenactment after reenactment of this fundamental story. Strange, small apelike creatures such as *Australopithicus* and *Pithecanthropus* were very often victorious against larger foes; the evolution of our species is testimony to the frequency with which this basic story actually occurred.

In this chapter, we will examine some fundamental aspects of social groupings. We will discuss the manner in which role assigment strengthens social groups. Then we will look at testlike procedures in four distinct contexts: a relatively simple social structure associated with the Ojibway, a tribe of North American indigenous people; a sophisticated selection system in pre–20th century China; the emergence of several typologies in ancient Greek culture; and the use of examinations in the early university system. Each example provides understandings that will help us create an appropriate social framework for the development of our narrative of testing.

SOCIAL SYSTEMS TO SUSTAIN SOCIAL ACTION

One fundamental factor in the emergence of our species was the development of **social systems**. Once an even rudimentary social system was in place, its advantages became legion. Assigning individuals to specific roles became possible: The accomplished hunters could hunt, the good cooks could cook, the effective spiritualists could interpret nature, the strong warriors could war, and weaker group members could be assigned to less physically demanding tasks. This strategy, assigning persons to the roles that best fit their skills and strengths, fortified a given group because members did not need to be jacks-of-all-trades but could focus on their strengths. A social system permitted the group to become more than the sum of its parts. The effective **role assignment** of group members to positions within the society can be seen as a particularly important aspect of the emergence of our species.

The snowball-fight story is simply a variant of this age-old narrative. A group of younger children banded and formed a short-lived social structure in which persons were assigned to specific roles. Each child was given a job that fit his or her individual effectiveness, as well as that of the group. The runners were the bigger members who could sustain the diversion and absorb an attack from the enemy, and the climbers were familiar with the terrain. Once created, the social system sustained a plan of action that resulted in victory for the smaller group.

A variant of this story can be drawn from the hunting practices of some civilizations, where beaters drive game toward the accomplished marksmen. Clearly, the emergence of role diversification within a group has untold implications for the strength of the collective and its membership. The robustness of a social group can indeed be attributed, in no small measure, to the effectiveness with which role assignments are carried out.

The development of social systems, however, is not the singular or most important factor in the emergence of our species and its complex social networks. Although somewhat speculative, the emergence of social systems can be seen as the result of a very complex set of precursors. According to Washburn (1960), the critically important behaviors were bipedal locomotion and the use of tools. **Bipedalism** freed the hands for carrying tools and weapons, thus leading to skill in **tool use**. Weapons were slowly improved, particularly as the species moved to become meat eaters to adapt to dwindling vegetation. This led to hunting, which resulted in the formation of groups and the development of social systems and, eventually, to all of the behaviors (as well as many more) associated with group membership.

Thus, although not the first or only innovation to provide an advantage for our evolutionary ancestors, role diversification was clearly an important factor. As we evolved, the size of the human brain enlarged along with the complexity of various social networks, emerging finally with *Homo sapiens* who are capable of existing in immensely complex social systems. Through all of this, the need for the effective assignment of group members to socially useful roles has remained constant.

This aspect of culture had one major implication: For the society to function well, there must be effective means of assigning individuals to specific duties. A mechanism was needed that ensured the fittest individual assumed the duties of a specified role within the culture. This decision was not insignificant for society because effective role assignment is a necessary prerequisite for the smooth and efficient functioning of the group. Having an ineffective person in a role can be highly disruptive, and having an excellent individual in the right position can produce great gains for the social group. Thus, the assignment of specific persons to specific roles, in the best interests of the social group, emerges as an important component of social structure.

Most collectives dedicate a proportion of their resources to making these important decisions about who should be assigned where. That is, the society turns on itself and uses whatever resources it has at its command to make determinations about who would be the best warrior, gardener, scout, or teacher or whatever activities were demanded by the group. These decisions are made with the overall interests of the group in mind, using the group's resources to make what is viewed as the "best" decision.

Differences in the manner in which these decisions have been made in social groups are about as varied as the groups themselves. Hunting groups would use tests of hunting prowess (or its potential) to admit young men into their hunter class. In societies where literary skills were demanded, tests of literary ability would be used to assign group members to the class of teacher or scholar. Groups in which eye/hand coordination was important—say, for archery—would use assessments of this ability to determine who ought to be trained as archers. In a society where information exchange was fundamentally oral, storytelling skills would be the subject of role assignment. Functional societies would tailor their role-assignment decision making to the required tasks of the society, using the skills and knowledge of the society.

ROLE ASSIGNMENTS AS SOCIAL DECISION MAKING

All of this sounds rather impersonal—we have forgotten the people in this analysis. After all, we are dealing with human lives here. It is rather easy to forget or ignore the impact these tests have on the people involved, whether in an ancient culture or in today's information-laden society. Role assignments often have considerable significance for both the assignor and the assignee, meaning that they are highly value-laden and immensely important lived cultural experiences for everyone involved.

THE VISION QUEST

An example that helps demonstrate the human quality of such tests comes from the **Ojibway** culture. In this North American indigenous group, young men went through a process called *Waussaeyuabindumowin*, or the **Vision Quest**. They had to spend 4 days in the wilderness and have an encounter with the spirit world. The tribal elders interpreted the young man's visions and used the results of this interpretation to select his social role. Because the Ojibway culture was highly spiritual, this was the focal quality of the experience and the subsequent interpretations. The following Close Up (based on Johnson, 1982) tells of the Vision Quest of 14-year-old Mishi-Waub-Kaikaik. Kitchie Manitou is the Great Spirit who presides over all of nature, and Weendigoes are frightening, fictional monsters in the lore of the Ojibway. Before reading this narrative, try to remember how you felt about unknown things when you were 14 years old and what kind of experience this would have been for you.

CLOSE UP   ### The Vision Quest of Mishi-Waub-Kaikaik

The principal player in our Ojibway drama is a 14-year-old lad by the name of Mishi-Waub-Kaikaik. The elders had deemed that he was ready to embark on what, for him, would be the most significant event in his young life—the Vision Quest. For over 8 years, he had been tutored by his father and grandfather about this solemn event, known as the *Waussaeyuabindumowin*. He understood its meaning and what he was going to have to do, but how would he do?

Mishi's arms and legs were blackened with ash in preparation for the journey to the Place of Visions. He embarked on this great journey with his father, and after a lengthy walk they came to a small meadow circled by tall pine trees. There was an unnatural, mystical feeling here. The elders said that it belonged to the spirits—only those on a Vision Quest were permitted to walk on this sacred ground.

Mishi's father placed an offering of tobacco in the center of the circle and uttered an incantation intended to bring good visions to his son. They built a small lean-to, and then Mishi's father left, indicating that he would return in 4 days. Mishi was alone for the first time in his life; a strange feeling of desolation overcame him as he saw his father's form disappear through the pines.

The sense of uneasiness remained for the rest of the afternoon as he inspected every nook and cranny of his small, strange world. As night time closed in, all he could see was the tall black forms of the pine trees and the bright stars beyond. His mind began to drift back to the past where he found a sense of familiarity. Yet the sounds, which he recognized, still frightened him as his world darkened. A flutter of wings sent a chill down his spine. He remembered the old tales of the Weendigoes—fierce beasts that waited to grab unsuspecting hunters. A feeling of dread crept over the lad and consumed his whole being.

Only with the graying sky of dawn did this fear subside—he had lived through the first test of his manhood! His spirit soared into vast regions of his soul where there appeared to be no sense of time, no dimension. He moved freely between the past and future in a way he had never experienced before.

The sun was high in the sky before he returned to the present. He stretched out his legs and walked around his small, circular world. Time stood still, and yet soon the sky was darkening again, revealing the black outlines of the pine trees and the stars beyond. Strangely, the noises of the forest no longer frightened Mishi. Hunger and cold swept in on the 14-year-old, creating a night of intense discomfort. Again, dawn provided relief, and Mishi began to understand that he must not let the desires of his body drive out the spirit—he must prepare himself to receive the spirits from the great Manitou. As a harbinger of the visions to come, a great eagle crested across the blue sky. He was ready.

Over the next days, Mishi experienced three visions. In the first, he was escorted to the lodges of the three stars named Fisher, Morning, and Evening. He heard the incantations of the sky spirits in a tongue that he did not understand but that was strangely familiar. His second dream involved an encounter with the dreaded Weendigoe. Chased by these dreaded creatures, he used his friendship with the animals to fashion a cunning escape. In the third vision, he encountered a group of lost people who had left their homeland because it was so poor. Mishi led them on a journey to other regions, after which they realized that their home was not as bad as they had thought and they returned happy to their lands.

Mishi awoke from this last dream to find his father beside him offering some meat, corn, and water. They walked home slowly, and he told his father that he felt he had had a dream; his father only nodded.

Upon arrival at the village, Mishi was taken to the Cheengwun, the elders, who would interpret his dreams. When Mishi told his stories, the Cheengwun confirmed that they were visions and that Mishi need not go out again. His visions turned out to be true because they told of the life he would lead. The chanting sky spirits signified the gift of prophecy, and Mishi eventually became a member of the Midewewin, the fortune-tellers of the tribe. His ability to commune with the animals in his second vision signified the gift of an understanding nature, which would serve him well throughout his life. The third vision, which involved the lost people, signified the gift of leadership, and eventually Mishi was chief of his tribe for more than 20 years. The visions directed Mishi-Waub-Kaikaik through his entire life, emerging as an integral part of the manner in which he contributed to his tribal community.

Functions of the Vision Quest

Four fundamental characteristics of the Vision Quest demonstrate that it was part of the social role assignment in the Ojibway culture. First, there was the clear test of self-mastery brought on by having to go without food for 4 days. In the area of

Lake Superior, the main home of the tribe, food was not particularly easy to come by during the winter, so demonstration of surviving a fast—albeit a rather short one—was clearly a significant group-related activity. Demonstrating this skill was important for a would-be group member.

A second aspect of *Waussaeyuabindumowin* was the demonstration of survival skill. Perhaps you can empathize with the stress of spending 4 days alone in the bush. Even if well prepared, for a 14-year-old to spend 4 days without human contact is a trying task that requires a considerable amount of inner strength to endure. The Vision Quest ritual had incorporated this test of survival skill, the amount of inner strength a boy had, because it was clearly deemed as important for the social group.

Third, the Vision Quest required a demonstrated contact with the spirit world. This was evaluated in terms of the report that the boy made to the elders (the Cheengwun) on his return from the Quest. For Mishi-Waub-Kaikaik, the verdict was positive because the elders declared that he indeed had a vision and contacted the spirit world. In a social context where spiritual explanations are highly prized, contact with the spirits is particularly important. Failure to report a dream or vision during the Quest would seriously question a boy's readiness for entry into the tribe. This was perhaps the most important test in the Vision Quest because of the importance of spirituality in the culture. Verified contact with the gods was critical.

Although not made clear in the Close Up, a fourth component of the quest is important. Specifically, Mishi must have shown considerable skill in describing his dreams in order for the elders to determine that he had experienced visions. The young boy must have learned the tribe's storytelling skills and rhetorical devices very well in order to gain the positive evaluation of the older members of the community. If his reportage of the dreams had been poor—by the Cheengwun's criteria—he probably would not have passed as well as he did. The *Waussaeyuabindumowin*, then, also involved a test of communication skills within the tribe. The boy's ability to construct and perform a story based on his dreams was an incredibly important component of the Vision Quest.

Mishi passed all four components of the test.

Waussaeyuabindumowin, however, went even further. The content of the visions was interpreted and affected even greater aspects of the social decision making of the tribe. The trek across the waters and plains (the third vision) symbolized leadership, and Mishi was subsequently made a chief. Although he was not made a leader the next day, the Quest did serve to identify Mishi as a potential chief, suggesting that some societal resources would be well spent in tutoring him to become prepared to assume this role. *Waussaeyuabindumowin* was a vehicle for facilitating perhaps the most important societal decision of all—the selection of a leader. As well, Mishi's encounter with the sky spirits and deities was interpreted as his having the gift of prophecy. This resulted in his becoming a member of the Midewewin, which gave him the right to conduct a number of important rituals.

Thus, incorporated in the seemingly simple ritual of the Vision Quest, we find a number of important social decisions being made. The Vision Quest ritual included demonstrations of self-mastery, inner strength, contact with the spirit world, and storytelling ability. In addition, aspects of the visions were used to assign the young man to his role within the tribe—in Mishi's case as a priest and eventually as a chief. Because of the number of socially critical attributes that are considered, the effectiveness of the Quest as a means of social decision making is impressive. Thinking of a more appropriate strategy is difficult when you realize the nature of the Ojibway culture and geographic context in which it evolved. The *Waussaeyuabindumowin* was a masterpiece of social planning, incorporating the demonstration of a large number of exceedingly important characteristics—all in the interests of assigning group members to effective positions, positions that would have best served the long-term interests of the group.

Faking and Subjectivity

You may feel a bit uneasy about this rave review of the *Waussaeyuabindumowin*. Some aspects of the ritual seem eminently vulnerable to **faking**. For example, the candidate could have been tutored in storytelling prior to the quest. A concerned father could have imparted various hints to his child that would have shaped the eventual interpretation the boy placed on his dreams and the manner in which he chose to tell them to the elders. The candidate could have just as easily fabricated the entire vision as actually experienced it. If the candidate wished to become a Midewewin, he could have made up a vision about contacting the deities and spirits. Yes, the Vision Quest could have been easily faked.

The Vision Quest was also very **subjective**. One place where this is clear is the role of the Cheengwun in interpreting the dreams. It is doubtful that a given vision would be interpreted the same way on different occasions because of the private and nonobjective manner in which the dreams are construed. The validation of the visions was definitely at the whim of the tribal elders. This brings us to question the fairness of the ritual because any elder wishing to keep a young man "down" (in a social sense) could have undermined his chances by arguing against the validity of his dreams. In fact, it could be argued that the *Waussaeyuabindumowin* is a device of social control, wherein the elders promoted those they wished by using the ritual. The Vision Quest, then, can be seen as simply a convenient way for the elders to have advanced their own personal positions.

Both the vulnerability to faking and subjective interpretation of the dreams appear to suggest that the *Waussaeyuabindumowin* was not a useful device. However, such an evaluation assumes the importance of "objectivity" and "not faking." These are salient values in our 20th-century culture, but they may not be the least bit appropriate to 18th-century Ojibway. In other words, evaluating an 18th-century testing ritual from our 20th-century perspective is very unfair, perhaps even more unfair than the unfairness suggested in the Vision Quest itself. Using one's own values to evaluate the utility of the cultural practices of other groups is called **ethnocentrism**. Concern with objectivity and faking are our values and do not necessarily apply to other cultures. Hence, using these notions to evaluate the Vision Quest is an example of ethnocentrism. We must keep this concept close at hand as we work our way through the psychological testing enterprise, particularly when we begin to consider the use of psychological tests in cultural contexts other than the ones in which they were designed.

The Vision Quest and Social Negotiation

Rather than criticize the Vision Quest ritual from a modern perspective, it seems more appropriate to consider its functions openly. To be sure, there was room for cheating and power mongering within the ritual, but you have to ask to what end such activities are being directed. Simply put, the entire exercise was directed toward enhancement of the social good—despite its weaknesses.

If a boy had been tutored in storytelling and he could have "pulled it off" in his conversations with the Cheengwun, he was still suitable to be admitted as a high-status member of the group. He had demonstrated the requisite skills and could have made his appropriate contribution to the group. Tutored or not, the good performance of storytelling in the Ojibway culture was a valued skill, and those possessing it deserved a place of value within the group.

If the elders had decided to keep a young candidate down by refusing to validate his dreams, they were doing so using their view of the social good. You might argue that the elders' view was out of touch with the important issues, but in the Ojibway culture the elders' view was revered and accepted. It was the best view around and was incorporated rather effectively into the *Waussaeyuabindumowin* by maintaining the subjective nature of dream validation. If, in the eyes of the elders, a young man was unsuitable to the role of spirit medium (perhaps he was too aggressive), the elders could reject him and channel him to another role because of the latitude permitted in the Quest. Thus, subjectivity can be seen as a strength of the ritual, not a weakness. It allowed the elders to make social decisions using their wisdom and experience. By being subjective, the Vision Quest took advantage of the utility of the most important social information in the culture—the wisdom of the elders.

This leads us to an alternative interpretation of the *Waussaeyuabindumowin*. In a very real sense, the ritual was a **social negotiation**. By the time the young man was 14 years old, he probably had some idea about the kinds of things he wanted to do in the tribe. The ritual provided him with an opportunity to negotiate with the elders to try to achieve this end. If he aspired to becoming a spiritual medium, he could through his dreams and storytelling enter into an exchange with the elders. He told them of his goals and awaited, with respect, their decision. If the elders had felt that he would make a better warrior/hunter than spiritual medium, they would have similarly entered into negotiation. They might have suggested alternative interpretations of the dreams that would be part of a rhetoric intended to convince the candidate of his future place in the society. In this sense, the Vision Quest was a cooperative endeavor between the elders and the young man. Both were willingly entering into a dialog about role assignment.

The *Waussaeyuabindumowin*, then, was a rather sophisticated mechanism of social decision making. It facilitated contact with the prevailing cultural resources (that is, the elders) and provided a means of entering into a negotiation process about role assignment within the culture. This is a far cry from a cursory analysis that appeared to suggest that vulnerability to faking and subjectivity is a weakness. In fact, they were major strengths of the process, and their removal would have resulted in the ritual becoming considerably less effective.

The Ojibway example indicates the level of complexity in social decision making. The culture supporting the *Waussaeyuabindumowin* was relatively simple and small in comparison to many other groups. What happens to these kinds of processes when a culture becomes much more complex? The intricacy of the analyses and understandings will increase geometrically, with the layers of complexity associated with more modern cultures. Even a peripheral glance at the manner in which role assignments are made in larger and more complicated societies readily demonstrates this.

THE CHINESE EXAMPLE

A particularly interesting example comes from early China. What is notable about this culture was the lack of an hereditary ruling class, in combination with an incredibly stable government structure. An intricate system of social decision making evolved in this setting, which begins to signal how cultural complexity affects role assignment. The Chinese civil service exams started very simply with a procedure for testing government employees every 3 years. It evolved into an intriguingly modern approach.

The story begins almost two centuries before the birth of Christ:

> For more than 3,000 years an elaborate system of competitive examinations was used to select personnel for government positions in China, which, unlike European countries, had no hereditary ruling class. Origins of the system go back to 2200 B.C., when the Chinese emperor examined his officials every third year to determine their fitness for continuing in office. After three examinations, officials were either promoted or dismissed. [DuBois, 1970, p. 3]

Unfortunately, sources do not provide us with details about the nature of the testings, but judging the activities associated with adequate performance as a government official were likely used.

The system changed about 1000 years later, and some details are available: "In 1115 B.C., candidates for government posts were examined for their proficiency in the 'six arts': music, archery, horsemanship, writing, arithmetic, and the rites and ceremonies of public and private life" (DuBois, 1970, p. 3). The relevance of music, archery, and horsemanship for service as a government official may not be clear, but the other three arts (writing, arithmetic, and protocol) were immediately tied into the social roles played by jobholders. Again, we see a fine example of important social functions being tested and decisions about placement being based on these assessments.

The Chinese system changed again and provides us with an example of the increasing complexity incorporated into the procedures and the manner in which changing social needs were reflected in the changes:

> Later, under the Han dynasty (202 B.C.–200 A.D.), written examinations were introduced in the "five studies," civil law, military affairs, agriculture, revenue, and

Hundreds of individual civil service examination rooms at Nanking, China.

the geography of the Empire. Local authorities were under instructions from the Emperor to seek out and recommend capable individuals of high moral standards to take the examinations and to qualify for an appointment. [DuBois, 1970, p. 4]

The subjects in the testing program were now clearly related to the prevailing social agenda, with law, military affairs, agriculture, revenue, and geography making up the attributes employed in the assignment decisions. Note the inclusion of "high moral standards" as part of the assessment process, returning to some of the subjective aspects of the Vision Quest discussed earlier.

The actual assessment process was remarkably sophisticated:

Through the centuries, the examination system underwent many changes, taking final form about the year 1370 A.D. Proficiency in remembering and interpreting the Confucian classics was emphasized. A man aspiring to high public office was required to pass three competitive examinations. The first, given annually in the chief city of the district in which the candidate lived, required a day and a night in a small isolated booth, where the candidate wrote a poem and composed an essay or two on assigned themes. Work was judged by beauty of penmanship and grace of diction; the percentage passing is reported to have been 1 per cent to 7 per cent.

Every three years competitors successful in the district examinations assembled in the provincial capitals for three sessions of three days and three nights each. Compositions in prose and verse revealed extent of reading and depth of scholarship. At this level, penmanship did not count, since a bureau of examination copyists (established in 1015 A.D.) reproduced the papers in another hand before they were evaluated by two independent readers, with a third reader to receive and reconcile the sealed grades. Successful candidates (reported as 1 per cent to 10 per cent) were considered "promoted scholars" and were admitted to the examinations given the following spring in Peking, the capital of the Empire. Here perhaps 3 per cent became mandarins, eligible for public office. [DuBois, 1970, p. 4]

Note the sophistication of this system. Although focusing on classical scholarship, the system resembled contemporary "hurdle" approaches to sequential testing. The first hurdle (the city exam) focused on literary skills (composition and penmanship), acting as a basic screen for literacy. The second hurdle (the district exam) explored depth of knowledge and scholarship. Once evaluated as literate and possessing sufficient depth of knowledge (labeled as promoted scholars), the candidates were allowed to take the third hurdle (the Peking exam). This was a wonderfully intricate system that rivals many contemporary applications.

The success rates for the exams reveal a large number of rejections. The upper limits of acceptance rates from the three hurdles were .07 for the city exam, .10 for the district exam, and .03 for the Peking exam. The probability of passing the Peking exam is .00021 (that is, $.07 \times .10 \times .03$). Only 2 of every 10,000 candidates were successful, indicating a very rigorous selection procedure.

It is particularly noteworthy that this system developed in a culture that had no formal schooling system. In essence, the testing system served fundamentally the same needs as contemporary educational systems do:

> During the centuries the civil service system was in use, China had no universities or public school system. Nevertheless, demonstrated knowledge led to public honor and responsibility. The system, emphasizing classical scholarship, was important in the high degree of stability attained by the Chinese empire, which was more or less isolated from outside influences. [Dubois, 1970, p. 5]

The Chinese testing program evolved independently of Western influences and emerged as a particularly strong monument to the cultural sophistication of the Chinese (whose culture, incidentally, has invented and sustained many aspects of modern technology). It provides a hint about the manner in which complex societies have chosen to handle social role-assignment decisions.

Of course, these kinds of social decision-making programs change with the society in which they exist. In China, increasing contact with the Western world began to indicate that a system built on classical scholarship was not adequate: "After the Chinese came in contact with the West, the need for skills other than classical scholarship became apparent. In 1905 the examination system was abolished so that formal university training in science and other areas of modern knowledge would be accepted by Chinese aspiring to office" (Dubois, 1970, p. 5).

When we look at role-assignment practices in more complex cultures than the Ojibway, we begin to see some interesting developments. The complexity of the testing exercise grows with larger societies. Reflected in the three-tiered hurdle system, the process had taken on a radically different texture compared with the Vision Quest. More impersonal and probably more economically efficient, the larger system begins to provide less and less room for the kind of social negotiation noted in the smaller context. The selection process itself also becomes more specialized because the only decision being accommodated by the complex Chinese system was whether or not a person ought to be admitted as a government official. Recall that, in the smaller system, decisions about where in the total society an individual ought to be placed were also made—the Vision Quest was not simply a test of fitness for admission to the Midewewin but also incorporated decisions about other roles an individual could possibly occupy. Thus, in more complex societies, the role-assignment process itself becomes more specialized, as revealed in the Chinese example.

THE GREEKS

The increasing complexity of social systems and their associated role-assignment processes is particularly evident in large, multilayered cultures such as existed in Greece prior to the birth of Christ. A number of complicated social structures emerged along with a number of ideas that began to shape the eventual emergence of modern-day psychological testing. Most noteworthy here was the Greeks' use of mathematics to solve social problems. Here we find the genesis of a critical aspect of the psychological testing enterprise. The following Close Up provides one narrative of how simple arithmetic helped resolve an important social difficulty.

CLOSE UP   **The Ladders of Plateia**

Picture this: Your country has been fighting with the Spartans for over 5 years. As part of the great Peloponnesian War, the enemy has just laid siege to your hometown Plateia. To add insult to injury, the Spartans have built an exceedingly high wall around your entire city to ensure that no one escapes the siege—no doors, no way out. It would appear that these Spartans don't fool around when it comes to laying siege.

Local entertainments were a bit boring one night, so a group of the younger men decided to breach the wall and look around outside. However, they ran into a problem when they started to build the ladders necessary to get over the wall. How long should the ladders be? As described by the historian Thucydides, they used a novel trick to determine the required length of the ladders. They assembled a large number of people at the point in the wall they intended to climb and had each of them count the numbers of rows of bricks. As you might expect, the numbers obtained varied somewhat between observers. Each person repeated their counting a number of times, yet the numbers of rows were still not the same for everyone. Whose count should they use to determine the proper ladder length? As a solution to the problem, they selected the number that most people counted (now called the **mode**). They then multiplied this number by the thickness of the bricks (and one layer of mortar) to determine the required length. This technique was successful in building the ladders and the Plateians were able to scale the wall.

This story (based on Ramul, 1963) can be seen as symbolizing an exceedingly important development in the eventual emergence of modern psychological testing. The systematic application of a simple statistical procedure (that is, calculating the mode of perceptual judgments) yielded a solution to an exceedingly pressing social problem. The possibility of using mathematics to solve social problems had been born. Will it be long, you might ask, before this new mathematical tool of social problem solving would be applied to role-assignment decisions? Before we can point to clear examples of using mathematics for role assignment, several other things had to happen, a number of which occurred during the time of Greek civilization.

A necessary first step in this long process involved developing a state of mind that embraced the notion of dealing with human beings in quantitative ways. If we could not somehow transpose aspects of individuals into numbers, we would not be able to apply mathematical techniques. What was needed was a mind-set that facilitated a quantitative orientation toward the human.

One of the first indications that this mind-set was emerging can be found in some early Greek efforts to develop theories of how the body functioned. The famous Greek physician Hippocrates advanced one such theory around 500 B.C. He suggested that it was possible to divide people into two categories based on an assessment of body type. The first, *habitus apoplecticus*, was described as volatile and hyperactive, characterized by quickness of movement and a number of other physical qualities. The label itself was not as important as its correlation with an expected disease pattern. Hippocrates indicated that *habitus apoplecticus* was prone to heart problems, thereby giving the physician a useful diagnostic (and potentially preventive) tool. The second body type in Hippocrates' scheme was *habitus phthicus*, who presented a sickly and weak appearance. The attending disease pattern focused on respiratory ailments such as asthma and a tendency toward wheeziness. This twofold classification system, based on the physician's reading of a person's body type, emerged as an important tool for the physician. It demonstrates the manner in which testing, albeit a rather subjective variety, was adapted to a specific socially valued activity—medicine.

As the fledgling discipline of medicine flourished under the Greeks, so too did the sophistication of the classification schemata. Before long it became clear that numerous aspects of disease came from within the patient and that some kind of manner of relating external symptomatology to internal states was needed. The eminent physician Galen provided one such system. He theorized that there were four basic chemicals (or what were called **humors**) in the body (Table 3-1). The symptomatology shown by a person, particularly when ill, was thought to be a function of the relative balance of these four humors. Behavior, then, was seen as a matter of chemical balance within the body. Like Hippocrates' system, the importance here is that there is a relationship between some observable entity (that is, the overabundance of a specific humor) and some expected disease pattern (that is, the symptoms associated with the humor).

Galen's is a wonderful system. The words he coined to describe the humors remain active in our language and form part of the lexicon we have to describe different people. As well, the foundational idea underlying Galen's system drives contemporary approaches in neurochemistry. Although the specific chemicals he

Table 3-1 The four humors postulated by Galen

Humor	Type	Symptoms
Blood	Sanguine	Optimism, changeableness, freedom from load, activity, and shallow emotions
Yellow bile	Choleric	Quick, intense, emotional response
Mucus	Phlegmatic	Sluggish, emotionally cold
Black bile	Melancholic	Depressed, down, and blue

postulated, as well as their locus of activity, did not hold up under contemporary research, the fundamental idea has indeed survived. Had Galen known about dopamine or gamma aminobutyric acid, he certainly would have been several millennia ahead of his time in his assertion of the relationship between chemicals in the body and various diseases.

Thus, within the medical institution in Greek culture, we find the emergence of particular types of assessments. In very basic terms, these assessments involve taking a sample of some aspect of observable behavior and using this to make some kind of assertion about the underlying cause of a specific disorder. These "tests" are very similar to those described earlier for the Ojibway and Chinese. In all cases, the activity involves using some kind of publicly observable entity (the telling of dreams, performance on a test of geography, or assessment of bodily fluids) and using these to make decisions that are valued within the society in which the test is being conducted. What appears to be changing between these examples is the complexity of the society in which they are being applied as well as the social needs that the assessments are serving. In addition, a kind of quantitative orientation is emerging that sets the scene for the possibility of mathematical manipulation of the observable indicators used to make the important social decisions.

UNIVERSITY EXAMINATIONS: BRINGING IT CLOSER TO HOME

Another important aspect of the increasing complexity of social systems was the eventual emergence of institutions of formal learning such as universities. These institutions developed over time to serve the socially critical role of passing on generations of knowledge in a way that made it accessible to members of the society. Not everyone in the society was qualified to do this, and a decision-making mechanism was needed to determine who ought and ought not continue in the institution.

The solution that evolved is not that different from the Ojibway and Chinese examples. What was required was the performance of a specific act related to the desired role. If properly measured, this performance could then be used to make the social decisions regarding suitability for further education. In the case of the

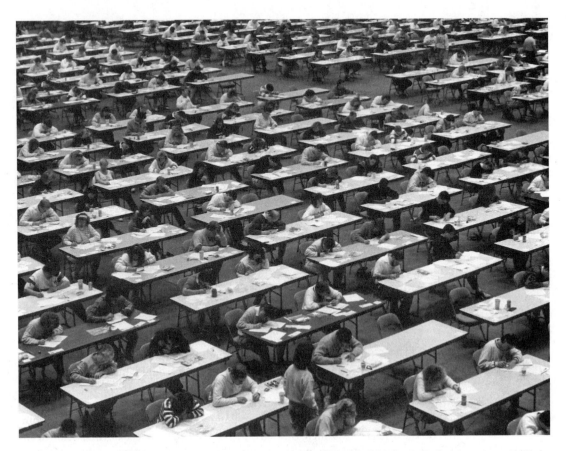

It is unlikely that the academics who invented the university examination circa 1250 AD envisioned the eventual form the activity would take.

university, the ability involved the extent to which candidates could demonstrate mastery of the content being studied. You guessed it—enter the dreaded **university examination**.

As far as we can tell, there were no examinations of the kind we have come to know (and love) in earlier schools. Greek and Roman institutions of learning or the monastery schools of medieval Europe did not, according to the historical record, have formal examinations. However, as the university system became more complex, oral examinations began to emerge. The law faculty of the University of Bologna had a competence test in 1219. In 1257 formal examinations were introduced in the institution that was the forerunner of La Sorbonne in Paris. Louvain University had competitive examinations as early as 1441 in which candidates were arranged in four classes: *rigorosi* (honor men), *transibles* (satisfactory), *gratiosi* (charity passes), and failures. Oxford University introduced oral examinations for both the B.A. and M.A. degrees in 1636.

Written exams followed the introduction of paper. The first documented, systematic application was with the Jesuit Order founded in 1540. Placement and instruction were evaluated in a written format. The British university system waited a while before moving to written exams, with 1803 being the date of the earliest written examinations at Oxford. The acceptability of this format increased like wildfire:

> By the middle of the nineteenth century, written examinations had been recognized in England, on the Continent, and in the United States as an appropriate basis for important decisions: who should be awarded degrees; who should be permitted to exercise a profession, such as law or teaching or medicine; and who should serve in a government post. [DuBois, 1970, p. 10]

By 1850 most of the evaluation decisions being made in the university context were in the form of written examinations, whereby the candidate had to demonstrate mastery of the content associated with the instruction. These exams spread to professional training institutions, which (like medicine) were often associated with universities, as well. The civil service also adopted them to determine who should hold nonelected government positions.

The important point here is that the fundamental idea of the examination is not that different from the kinds of tests discussed earlier. Not unlike Mishi in his Vision Quest or the aspiring Chinese bureaucrat, the degree candidate was put in a situation that permitted the demonstration of socially valued behaviors. In the case of the university, these behaviors related to a recapitulation, at one level or another, of the content that had been instructed. Failure to demonstrate the expected performance resulted in the individual being assigned a lower-status role within the overall culture. The university emerged as an institution that had a major responsibility in social role assignment, with the examination being one of the major tools used to make the important social decisions.

The nature of the output from the exams could also be used to point in which direction the candidates ought to direct their efforts. Not unlike the interpretations of Mishi's dreams, a candidate showing exceptional ability in, say, politics would be directed toward advanced study in that subject. The university examination, which had gained such immediate acceptance, can be seen as a simple variant of the type of test that was in evidence in less complicated social structures—the form, function, and importance are fundamentally the same. By consolidating social decision making such as role assignment in the university, the breadth of decisions possible was radically increased. Not only could the institution serve to decide which of its candidates deserved a high-status position (that is, a degree), but the university could also be used to stream candidates toward the skills that best fit their strengths.

It is worth noting the manner in which **technology** affected the development of the university examination. The emergence of the written exam can be traced directly to the introduction of paper—perhaps one of the most important technological advances ever. A society, no matter how complex, will use whatever resources it has available—technological, conceptual, and political—to enhance the utility of the social decision-making process. This suggests an interesting interaction between technology and social decision making, which deserves recall when we examine modern approaches to testing. (Not surprisingly, the computer is emerging as an important aspect of modern social decision-making procedures.)

TESTS AS MIRRORS OF CULTURE

In each of the preceding examples, the tests have a tendency to reflect the culture in which they were practiced. The Ojibway example emphasized spirituality, which was an important component of the tribal ethos. Classical scholarship was the important variable in the Chinese example because the culture was devoid of formal training institutions for literacy. The Greek medical tests incorporated contemporary theories of disease and physiology. In the case of the university examination, the form of the test mirrored the prevailing popularity of written communication. The emergence of the printing press, which rendered communication both permanent and relatively inexpensive, placed a tremendous emphasis on written forms of communication. It offered a remedy for the frailty of human memory, and soon the written word was viewed as "true" knowledge. The university examination processes focused on a demonstration of the manner in which the candidate could work in the written medium, which was considered to be the most important component of knowledge at the time when examinations were introduced.

In a very real sense, the types of tests developed by a society to make role assignments are **mirrors of the culture** itself. Prevailing technology, communication forms, ideas, and values are all incorporated into the system to form an assessment procedure that serves the social need. Although probably oversimplified, the following statement may well be tenable: "Show me the way in which a society decides social roles for its young people, and I'll show you the fundamental nature of that society." Testing procedures inform us of society, and society informs us of testing procedures. The two are inexorably wrapped up in each other, and any effort to discuss one without the other is bound to be less than acceptable. The meaning of a testing procedure cannot be properly understood without a thorough knowledge of the social context that the procedure has evolved to serve.

The fundamental argument here is that the psychological testing enterprise, as described in Chapter 2, serves exactly the same goals as the testing systems described for other cultures. The Vision Quest, the Chinese civil service exams, tests within early Greek medicine, and university examinations all emerged within specific social contexts to serve specific social functions—most notably, role assignment within the collective. Psychological testing has evolved for exactly the same reasons in our culture, and it is no different from the examples presented in this chapter. Seeing examples in other contexts provides us with a lever for beginning to see our own cultural practices in a similar light. And here lies a particularly exciting possibility for our journey through the evolution of the psychological testing enterprise. Not only do we come to know something about testing, but we also can gain some insight into our own culture through this knowledge.

Summary

This chapter started out by demonstrating the manner in which social decision-making processes are an integral part of virtually every culture. In the Ojibway example (the Vision Quest), we saw a prototypical example of a ritual that provided very useful information to aid in role-assignment decisions. The Chinese civil service system saw this social function extrapolated to a much larger and complex society. The Greeks introduced the development of a specific mind-set to use numbers and several novel ways of categorizing individuals. Finally, the evolution of university examinations showed role assignments being conducted in an important institutional context. The university examination example also indicated the manner in which available technology is adapted to social decision making. These examples demonstrate the diversity of mechanisms that various cultures have developed for making these kinds of important decisions. Tests are mirrors of culture—reflecting the very heart of the inner workings of a specific social group. This being the case, coming to understand psychological tests in our society—which is the goal of this text—is to examine our own culture.

In the next chapter, we will begin to investigate this possibility by looking at the genesis of the major intellectual movement that characterizes our current culture—specifically, the scientific worldview. By seeing the manner in which this particular perspective evolved, we can see how the foundation of the contemporary psychological testing enterprise was laid.

Glossary

bipedalism Walking on the two hind legs is seen as a particularly important development in the evolution of the human species.

ethnocentrism Evaluating the practices of one culture, using the value system of one's own.

faking Intentional efforts to fabricate a specific, desired result. In the testing domain, faking is seen as undesirable, whereas in other situations (for example, the Ojibway Vision Quest) it does not seem as problematic.

habitus apoplecticus One of two types within Hippocrates' typology of people characterized as being volatile and hyperactive, with quickness of movement.

habitus phthicus One of two types within Hippocrates' typology of people characterized as sickly and weak, with a tendency toward wheeziness.

humor Chemicals in Galen's typology, each with an associated psychological characteristic. (See Table 3-1.)

mirror of culture A practice that provides a sense of the inner workings of a particular society. In the present context, tests are particularly useful mirrors because they provide a direct indicator of the aspects of social activity seen as important by that society.

mode The most frequently occurring observation in a given set.

Ojibway A subgroup of the Cree nation who resided around Lake Superior.

role assignment Making social decisions about which individuals will serve what functions within varying social systems. Psychological tests are useful devices for doing this within our culture.

social negotiation The act of two parties entering into dialog about various aspects of a particular social system. In the present context, the Vision Quest was a vehicle for a would-be applicant to negotiate with those in power for entrance into a specific social role.

social system Various groupings into which a society is organized to facilitate conducting the business of the society. In the present context, the assignment of individuals to various roles within the social systems was seen to be particularly important, with psychological tests evolving to serve this function within our contemporary society.

subjective An element of human knowledge involving the use of personal opinion such that the same result may or may not be obtained by different individuals.

technology Tools that facilitate work in a particular activity. In the present context, it was suggested that a culture's available technology is adapted to help serve the functions demanded of role assignment (for example, paper and university exams).

tool use The adaptation of various aspects of the environment to help with doing work and seen as a particularly important aspect of the evolution of our species.

university examination A device used to determine the readiness of a university student to progress on to the next level of complexity within a particular subject. These examinations evolved in concert with the modern university system (starting around 1300) and serve role-assignment functions within contemporary society.

Vision Quest A ritual of the Ojibway in which a young man spent several days alone in the wilderness. It functioned as a role-assignment device by virtue of providing the tribal elders with indications of the self-mastery, survival skills, contact with the spiritual world, and storytelling abilities of the would-be tribal adult. The results of these tests were used to assign youngsters to social roles to which they were best suited.

Suggested Further Reading

Caplan, A. L. (Ed.) (1978). *The sociobiology debate: Readings on the ethical and scientific issues concerning sociobiology.* New York: Harper & Row.

This chapter of *The Enterprise* was written with several things taken for granted. One is that the mechanistic examination of human nature, using the instruments of conventional biology, is an acceptable way of understanding development of ourselves and our cultures. I recognize that this statement, in and of itself, is controversial and hence refer you to some sources that address the attending disagreements. Although somewhat dated, Caplan's edited book provides a fine basis for understanding the important foundational controversies in this field, thereby providing a wider context in which to understand the underlying issues. *See also* Milton (1992) below.

Clagett, M. (1957). *Greek science in antiquity.* London: Abelard-Schuman.

This book provides a good glimpse of the Greek contributions to science. Because we could discuss only a few aspects of the astounding developments that occurred during this time, I recommend Clagett's book to round out this picture.

DuBois, P. H. (1970). *A history of psychological testing.* Boston: Allyn and Bacon.

This short history provides useful background and elaboration of the Chinese civil service selection system and university examinations. In addition, this is a good read if you want to get a sense of the history of the emergence of testing as seen from the emic perspective. This book remains as the only insider's history dedicated specifically to psychological testing.

Gould, S. J. (1977). *Ever since Darwin*. New York: Norton.

This is a readable treatise on evolutionary theory, which frames most of the chapter, albeit at a different level of analysis from that used by Gould. Darwinian thought has been poked, prodded, pulled apart, and perverted by many authors. Gould's presentation brings the reader close to the original intent and provides a provocative discussion of a wide range of implications drawn from the fundamental theory.

Hergenhahn, B. R. (1992). *An introduction to the history of psychology* (2nd ed.). Belmont, Calif.: Wadsworth.

The brief presentation of ancient Greek culture in the text hardly begins to touch on the numerous important contributions of this civilization. Chapter 2 of Hergenhahn's book provides an overview of the major contributions of Greeks to contemporary psychology. It provides some detailed context into which it is possible to place the snippets about Hippocrates and Galen presented here.

Johnson, B. (1982). *Ojibway ceremonies*. Toronto: McClelland and Stewart.

This highly readable primer provides a glimpse into the Ojibway traditions, which were briefly sketched in the chapter. A number of other Ojibway rituals are described in detail, and what emerges is a rich description of these various rites. Johnston was educated in Ojibway reserve schools and, after obtaining a university education, was employed by the Royal Ontario Museum. This presentation, then, is a combination of emic and etic perspectives.

Milton, R. (1992). *The facts of life: Shattering the myth of Darwinism*. London: Fourth Estate.

This provocative book is a contemporary treatise on the emerging difficulties being encountered by a strong evolutionary perspective. To the extent that a variation of this perspective was assumed in the chapter, this book presents a counterargument that deserves consideration. It presents the ongoing debates in a provocative and interesting manner, making good reading for anyone who wants to gain a sense of the place of Darwin's thought in today's world. *See also* Caplan (1978) above.

Discussion Questions

1. Describe a situation from your own experience in which assigning persons to specific roles resulted in gaining a sought-after goal. How was role assignment carried out in this situation? To what extent was the outcome determined by the role-assignment procedures?

2. Briefly describe two examples from cultures other than your own or those mentioned in the text in which group organization facilitated group goal attainment.

3. Prepare an argument to indicate that some selection factor other than bipedalism was more important in the eventual evolution of our species.

4. Consider a work group of which you have been a member (for example, a sports team, a unit on the job, a volunteer group) and describe the processes that were used to assign members to specific roles. Discuss whether these procedures were mirrors of the overall goals of the group.

5. What ritual from your own culture is most closely associated with the Vision Quest? Indicate why you feel this is so.

6. Discuss why storytelling ability was an important aspect of the Vision Quest.

7. Outline the advantages and disadvantages of subjectivity of the kind that emerged in the elders' interpretations of the visions in the *Waussaeyuabindumowin*.

8. Based on your own experience, outline a clear example of ethnocentrism. Briefly discuss the moral implications of this particular example.

9. In the psychological testing field, there is considerable concern about coaching, surfacing in the form of arguments about the possibility that persons who have had a chance to practice on the tests will have an unfair advantage over those who have not. Discuss this issue with respect to the notions of social negotiation presented in the chapter.

10. Draw flowcharts to represent each of the three Chinese civil service examination systems discussed in the chapter.

11. List as many reasons as you can why the Chinese civil service examination system was abandoned.

12. Describe a contemporary situation in which you might be able to adapt the wisdom of the Plateians to solve a specific problem.

13. Both Galen's and Hippocrates' systems were typologies. What level of measurement would be relevant here? Why? Can you think of a way in which Galen's system could be adapted to incorporate another level of measurement?

14. Briefly outline the history of examinations in universities.

15. Describe an example other than the one in the text (written exams and the invention of paper) that demonstrates the manner in which available technology was adapted to role-assignment decision making.

16. List all the functions that contemporary university examinations serve. What does this list tell us about universities and the culture that sponsors them?

17. If psychological tests are mirrors of our own culture, what does the popularity of "intelligence tests" tell us about ourselves?

18. In Chapter 2, we defined the psychological test as "an objective and standardized measure of a sample of behavior." Considering the argument that tests reflect culture, what does this definition tell us about our own social/cultural groups?

Chapter 4

Mathematical Foundations of Testing
The Quantitative Worldview

In This Chapter

The Changing Worldview

Bessel and the Personal Equation

The Normal Curve

Adolph Quetelet and *L'Homme Moyen*

The Idea of Variance

The *z* Score

Counting and Measuring: Part of Our Way of Life

Summary

THE CHANGING WORLDVIEW

After the fall of the Roman Empire, the Western world entered what has become known as the Dark Ages. Government structure collapsed, and the flame of intellectual inquiry was almost extinguished as region after region of Europe became dominated by various warring tribes. Except in the excluded confines of monasteries, life of the time was driven by a view of the world as a magical and fearful place. However, around 1600 things began to change. A storehouse of old Greek writings was discovered in Toledo, Spain, and slowly but surely the Western world emerged from the Dark Ages and its medieval **worldview:**

By 1700 the medieval world order was finished. Three dates seem especially por-
tentous. In 1686 a popular French writer, Fontenelle, brought science to the literate
public of France, dazzling his readers. Although humans were reduced to a
mechanical speck in a mechanical universe, knowing this secret was uplifting.
Science and mathematics became all the rage. In 1687 Newton's *Principa
Mathematica Philosophiae Naturalis* appeared, the triumph of the mathematical
view of the world-machine. Soon natural law would be extended to human beings
and governments with revolutionary impact. In 1688 came England's Glorious
Revolution, the peaceful deposition of James II and the installation of William of
Orange. In this revolution was born the modern liberal state: Kings are not divinely
appointed agents whose will is absolute law. They are instruments of the people,
replaceable at the people's will.... Reason had prevailed over tradition and faith.
[Leahey, 1992, p. 104]

The evolving complexity of Western societies brought a truly astounding revolution. Prior to 1600, the medieval scholar saw the world as a rather mysterious
place—"organized in a grand hierarchy from God to human to material world, in
which each event had a special meaning" (Leahey, 1992, p. 88). Between roughly
1600 and 1700, this perspective was challenged, banished, and replaced by another. This new view was empirical, quantitative, mathematical, and mechanical—
the **scientific revolution** had begun. In the next century (the Age of Enlightenment),
this new view of the world was refined and eventually applied to human affairs
with revolutionary consequences.

The Concept of Self

As an example of this new worldview, it is interesting to examine changes in the
concept of **self** as this critical phase in the development of our species unfolded.
Prior to 1600, the concept of selfhood was very unlike contemporary views, with
personal identity being defined by society (see Baumeister, 1987). The number of
English surnames relating to occupations (for example, Smith) is a residual of this.
Self-definition emphasized the Christian values of morality and virtue, with criteria
of personal goodness being fixed by society in terms of honor, glory, and reputation. Salvation was the ultimate fulfillment of a person's time on earth. Of particular note was the manner in which the public and private self were considered to be
one and the same—people were no more than their public images. Indeed, there
was very little emphasis on personal needs and desires; society was preeminent in
the determination of personal identification. Personal needs were submerged into
the public common good.

The astounding changes wrought by the reawakening of the intellectual spirit,
which began around 1600, soon challenged this socially driven identity process.
Baumeister (1987) outlines the several phases this process went through, leading to
a stage called Victorian, which occurred in the latter half of the 1800s. In this
period, the concept of the "rugged individual" was well embedded in social practice. People placed considerable emphasis on self-reliance, and any sense of fulfillment had emerged as a deeply personal, private affair. The criteria of fulfillment
were now individual rather than social. Aided and abetted by the emergence of the

concept of property and ownership, firm self/other boundaries had been drawn by the Victorian era.

This change was truly remarkable. In a period of just over 200 years, the entire concept of the person had undergone a revolutionary change. From a totally socially embedded view, the person as self-ish, self-contained, and having personal worth beyond social definition had emerged. For our purposes, this change was important because it signaled the direction that social decision making took. Because individuals were now entities unto themselves, social decision making had to emphasize the manner in which private beings could be brought safely into social roles. Thus, emphasis was on **individual differences** and the manner in which these could be reconciled to the social need. Indeed, this is the fundamental challenge that was addressed by the psychological testing enterprise. Without the emergence of a self-contained vision of personhood, the contemporary domain of psychological testing would not have emerged in its modern form.

Such a profound change in the manner in which the world was interpreted led to many changes in social organization. For example, as society began to shift from an ecclesiastical to a secular view, a need developed for institutions that would care for indigent, sick, and deviant members, leading to the development of many different social institutions (see Grob, 1966b). The emergence of the hospital, and its eventual acceptance of mental patients, was driven by these important social changes (see Sharma, 1970). The issues of role assignment, perhaps seen relatively clearly in the context of simpler cultures, became immensely complicated because of these transitions. For our particular purposes, the scientific view provided a fresh set of resources that could be applied to the problem of social decision making in this new context. The emerging doctrine of empiricism and science provided an incredibly powerful set of tools that could be used to facilitate the types of decision-making processes described in Chapter 3. Soon it would be possible to make social role-assignment decisions using scientific procedures.

The dominant culture, however, did not quickly adapt science to these social tasks, but the manner in which this eventually came to pass is particularly interesting. The scientific revolution was not instantaneous. The worldview of Europeans was not transformed into an empirical and mechanistic one overnight. The matter of ridding the intellectual house of all references to spiritual, mystical, and nonempirical influences was a long-term project, which was realized only through the slow and laborious efforts of thinkers such as Bacon, Descartes, Hobbes, Locke, Hume, and Kant. For example, Francis Bacon envisioned, with prescient clarity, the extensive role that the new scientific orientation would play. He argued the need for organized research and systematic data collection, which could then be applied to "the relief of man's estate."

For our purposes, the most important idea to emerge from this evolutionary process was the basic belief in the possibility of **positive knowledge**. The fundamental core of the emerging scientific view was the staunch assertion that it was possible to gather absolutely true, incontrovertible knowledge through the senses. This position, which stands in stark contrast to the earlier magical worldviews, places emphasis on the quest for absolute knowledge. In time this basic position became known as **positivism**, which is the generic philosophical position that underlies the psychological testing enterprise—even to this day. Positivism endorses the possibility of positive knowledge.

The emergence of a positivistic view of testing and social decision making, however, was long and drawn out over several centuries of important developments. Perhaps because of its complexity, mental life was one of the last topics to be tackled, particularly in terms of trying to quantify any aspect of it: "Until about a century ago, the whole idea of measuring any aspect of human mental life was unthinkable. Mind was generally held to be an order of reality to which figures were just not applicable" (Tyler, 1965, p. 8). Table 4-1 presents the time frame when discussions of the quantification of various mental phenomena emerged. As can be seen, significant discussion began to emerge in the mid-1700s.

These early psychological measurement projects provide some interesting insight into the way scholars were thinking as the foundations of the quantitative worldview were being laid. The following Close Up provides some details of the work done by Christian Thomasius (1655–1728), a famous German lawyer and philosopher.

Table 4-1   Emergence of discussions about measuring mental phenomena

Date	Entity	Whom
1679	Visual acuity	Hooke
1708	Aesthetics: composition, drawing, coloring, expression	De Piles
1711	Personality: reasonable love, hedonism, ambition, voluptuousness	Thomasius
1734	Mental powers	Hagen
1738	Perfection and imperfection	von Wolff
1740	Duration of visual sensation	Segner
1749	Moral certitude	Buffon
1750	Reaction time—completed thoughts	Chaldenius
1760	Literary merit: critical disposition, pathetic disposition, dramatic disposition, fortuitous disposition, taste, coloring, versification, moral, general value	Anonymous
1781	Memory—digit span	Bonnet
1786	Possibility of measuring psychological magnitudes	Mendelssohn
1816	Simple reaction time	Bessel
1825	Statistics applied to human physical measures	Quetelet

SOURCE: Ramul (1960).

Personality, Passions, and Persuasion

Thomasius argued that all of the "inclinations of the human mind" were derived from four main sources that he called **passions**. These were reasonable love, hedonism, ambition, and voluptuousness. He argued that all persons are composed of these main passions, sharing in all of them. However, at a particular point, one of them is dominant. Thus, each person's mind can be known on the basis of the dominant passion as well as on the manner in which the other three are blended with each other.

Things get interesting, as far as psychological testing is concerned, in Thomasius's argument: The strength of each passion can be expressed by means of definite numbers, and understanding the human mind has the same character as a simple mathematical problem. He proposed a 60-point scale, the units of which he called **degrees**. The dominant passion always received 60 degrees in his system, and the weakest typically received 5 degrees. The other two obtained figures between 5 and 60 degrees. Thomasius assigned the degrees for each passion on the basis of the individual's past actions, indicating that tests had yet to develop. The stage, however, was clearly set for the emergence of assessment instruments.

Thomasius used this system to explain various aspects of human activity. For example, he analyzed a famous incident in which a Cardinal Mazarin (60 degrees of ambition, 50 of voluptuousness, 20–30 of reasonable love, and 5–10 of greed) outnegotiated a Spaniard, Haro (60 degrees of greed, 50–55 of ambition, 10–20 of voluptuousness, and 5 of reasonable love), while the terms of the Treaty of the Pyrenees were being forged. Apparently, the combination of greater ambition and voluptuousness and lesser greed for money carried the day during this incident, explaining why "Mazarin succeeded in extorting everything from what was usually a very cunning and dissembling Haro and gained the upper hand over him" (quoted in Ramul, 1963, p. 657).

Although we may wish to quibble with the basic variables that Thomasius used (his passions), it seems clear that the style of thinking, stimulated in no small manner by the acceptance of a **quantitative** approach, is remarkably similar to contemporary orientations (see, for example, Chapter 16). Thomasius is a fine example of how the adoption of a quantitative worldview shapes and structures the kinds of ideas and theories that emerge.

Further evidence of the beginnings of the psychological testing enterprise can be found in the writings of several 17th-century writer/mathematicians. Christian von Wolff, in his *Psychologia Empirica* (1738), argued that elements such as perfection and imperfection ought to be as measurable as any other. In 1786 Moses Mendelssohn discussed the possibility of a *mathesis intensorum*—the mathematical measurement of psychological magnitudes.

Gottlieb Friedrich Hagen, who in 1734 defended the utility of a mathematical approach to psychological phenomena, presented perhaps the best argued position. He suggested that, in order to make comparisons between the powers of different persons, all such powers must be dealt with using a common denominator. He recommended that the unit of measurement should be smaller than the power being dealt with, providing several interesting examples such as "number of ideas one can think about," "judgment," and "perfection."

Several other thinkers such as Johann Gottlieb Kruger and Christian Albrecht Korber joined in, creating an active discussion about the possibility of developing a science of psychological measurement. Interestingly, these thinkers never tried out their ideas by gathering any real measurements—rather, they were theorists.

BESSEL AND THE PERSONAL EQUATION

The first hint of the basic ideas being applied occurred in an observatory in Greenwich, England, toward the end of the 1700s. In those times, scientists such as Maskelyne, the astronomer royal at the Greenwich Observatory, used what was called the **eye-and-ear method** when telescopically observing a star crossing a specific point. The field of view in the telescope was divided by two vertical parallel lines, and the observational problem simply involved relating the time at which a given star was between the two lines by using a series of tones that pulsed at a rate of 10 per second. These observations were the bedrock of the emerging science of astronomy and were used, among other things, to calibrate the master clock, which was the definitive timepiece for the entire Western world.

The astronomer royal of Greenwich hired a new assistant named Kinnebrook in 1794. In August of the next year, Maskelyne found that the assistant's recorded times were about .5 second later than his. This error was pointed out to Kinnebrook, along with instructions to correct it. However, things got worse, and by January 1796 the error had grown to .8 of a second. This was no laughing matter because of the importance of the observational data for calibrations. In the face of Kinnebrook's inability to correct the error, he was dismissed, with Maskelyne stating that the assistant had fallen "into some irregular and confused method of his own" in making the stellar transit observations.

It wasn't until 1816 that Bessel, the head of a new observatory at Konigsberg, became aware of the Kinnebrook–Maskelyne incident when reading a history of the Greenwich Observatory. He reasoned that Kinnebrook must have tried to correct his error and that perhaps the "errors" were involuntary mistakes. Prompted by curiosity and some recently acquired knowledge of emerging concepts in probability theory, Bessel constructed a trial to determine if it might be possible that differences of the magnitude observed between the Greenwich astronomer royal and his assistant could be found between other observers. He recruited an astronomer named Walbeck, and the two of them observed a number of stars over five nights. On the average, Bessel was 1.041 seconds faster than Walbeck, but with little variability around the average. Both were trained observers, and the magnitude of the differences was astounding. The two astronomers examined their technique very carefully, and Bessel subsequently recorded "We ended the observations with the conviction that it would be impossible for either to observe differently, even by only a single tenth of a second" (Boring, 1957, p. 136). These observations represented real differences between the two scientists. This event is often cited as the first time the new scientific approach had been applied (successfully) to the study of individual differences. It heralded a whole new way of construing the individual, which was to have profound effects on the manner in which various social decisions, such

Carl Friedrich Gauss

as role assignment, would eventually be made. The foundations for the contemporary conceptions of psychological testing had been laid.[1]

The most immediate application of Bessel's findings about individual differences in observation time was to develop corrections to adjust for these anomalies; this correction was called the **personal equation**. Considerable research ensued in which various new measurement technologies were developed, and the whole idea of individual corrections became accepted in the field.

As Bessel was pursuing the personal equation, a child prodigy by the name of Carl Friedrich Gauss was developing the foundations of contemporary probability theory.

CLOSE UP | Carl Friedrich Gauss, Child Prodigy

The late K. D. C. Haley, a mathematics professor at Acadia University in Nova Scotia, told an interesting story about Gauss. Apparently, the young boy was a bit difficult to handle in class because he always finished his work before everyone else and was continually demanding attention. In one such situation, the exasperated teacher tried to quiet him by telling him to add up the numbers between 1 and 100, assuming this task would take a fair amount of time.

The young Gauss responded almost immediately: "5050!"

In shock the teacher demanded "How did you do that? Did you have it memorized?"

---

[1]This story is told as *symbolizing* the emerging concern with individual differences. It should not be interpreted as suggesting that, somehow, Bessel "discovered" individual differences. Rather, the emergence of this concern was the confluence of many and varied factors associated with the movement toward a quantitative worldview.

"No," responded the child, "I simply noted that the sum of the first and last numbers in the series, 1 and 100, is 101. But so is the sum of the second and second last numbers, 2 and 99, equal to 101, and so on. There are 50 such pairs, so the answer is 50 times 101, which is 5050."

Not bad for a kid, eh?

THE NORMAL CURVE

In the mid-1780s, Gauss, along with some of his contemporaries such as Laplace, eventually described the mathematical properties of the **normal curve**.[2] This mathematical function has the very distinctive shape shown in Figure 4-1. The mathematical properties of the bell-shaped curve were of particular importance for the psychological testing enterprise. The initial understanding of this manner of relating two variables to each other (labeled x and y in Figure 4-1), however, were worked out by mathematicians such as Gauss and Laplace whose concerns were strictly mathematical. Let's look at this interesting mathematical distribution.

Suppose you rob the piggy bank and find nine shiny new coins in it. You throw these coins up in the air and count the number of heads showing when they land. Perhaps there are four heads and five tails. Then you do it again, and again, and again ... up to a total of 512 times, counting the number of heads that turn up with each nine-coin toss. After having done this, you tally the number of times you observe varying numbers of heads. If your tosses and the coins are fair, you will likely obtain numbers that bear a striking similarity to the normal curve. The most frequent result of your coin tosses will be four or five heads. Slightly less often you will find either three or six heads, followed by even less frequent observations for two and eight heads. Finally, in the 512 tosses, you might observe one case where all coins come up as heads and another of all tails. As Figure 4-2 shows, the relationship between number of heads and frequency of observation will look very much like the normal curve. In Figure 4-2, the curve has been smoothed out to indicate the extent to which this coin-toss experiment would generate data that are very much like the normal curve.

The Arithmetic Mean

Figure 4-3 illustrates a general version of the normal curve, showing some of its mathematical properties. The highest point of the curve is labeled the **apex**. In this figure, a perpendicular line drops down from the apex to the horizontal axis. This line is called a **projection**. Notice how the intersection of this projection with the horizontal axis defines the midpoint of the axis itself. Mathematicians verified that this midpoint can be estimated directly from observations as the arithmetic **mean**, or average. This is calculated by summing all observations and dividing by the

---

[2]Originally, the normal curve was referred to as the Laplace–Gaussian curve and was only later on labeled by its current name. Interestingly, it was renamed by Karl Pearson, a scholar who was to have significant impact on testing. More about this later. (We will discuss this in Chapters 6 and 10.)

Figure 4-1   The normal curve.

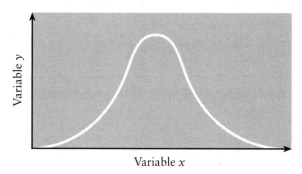

Figure 4-2   The histogram and normal curve for expected frequencies of heads in tossing nine coins 512 times.

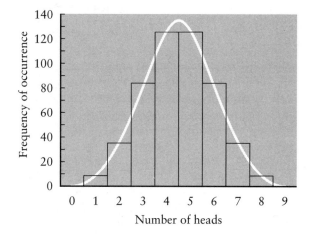

Figure 4-3   A normal curve showing the apex and the manner in which a projection from the apex defines the center of the horizontal axis.

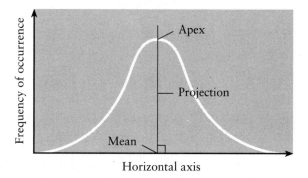

Table 4-2	Calculating the arithmetic mean, or average, of height from a sample of ten people

Person	Height (inches)
1	67
2	68
3	68
4	68
5	71
6	63
7	73
8	70
9	68
10	65
Sum	681

Arithmetic average, or
mean $= \frac{681}{10} = 68.1$ inches

Table 4-3	Calculating the median height from a sample of ten people

Person	Height (inches)
6	63
10	65
1	67
2	68
4	68
Median	
9	68
3	68
8	70
5	71
7	72

Median = 68 inches

number of observations. Table 4-2 shows an example of calculating the mean from a set of observations. The equation for estimating the mean is the following:

$$M_x = \frac{\sum\limits_{i=1}^{n} x_i}{n}$$

(4-1)

where

M_x = the mean of x

n = the number of observations

x_i = person i's value on x

$\sum\limits_{i=1}^{n} x_i$ = the sum of all n values of x

Equation 4-1 is just another way of summarizing the procedure described above. Using Σ (sigma) to denote adding up the n values of x is a convenient shorthand.

With a true normal curve, we can estimate, in several ways other than the arithmetic mean, the point where the perpendicular from the apex intersects the horizontal axis. The **mode** is the most frequently occurring observation in a set. In the data presented in Table 4-2, the mode is 68 because there are four cases of this height (persons 2, 3, 4, and 9). The **median**, the middle score in a distribution, is calculated by ranking the observations and marking the midpoint. Table 4-3 shows how the median, which turned out to be 68 inches for the data in Table 4-2, is determined.

Collectively, the mean, median, and mode are called **measures of central tendency** because they reflect, in varying ways, the middle of the set of observations.

Notice how, in Figure 4-3, the projection from the apex divides the area under the curve in half such that 50% of the observations fall below the mean, while 50% fall above it.

The Point of Inflection

If you laid out a big normal curve on a parking lot and drove your car along it, starting at one end, a bit more than halfway before you reached the apex something interesting would happen. There would come a point—ever so briefly—when you would be driving straight. Most of the time you would be turning either left or right, but for an instant, in the shift from a left to a right turn (or vice versa), your steering wheel would be directing your wheels straight ahead. The place at which this happens is called the **point of inflection**. In a true normal curve, there are two of these—one below and one above the mean. If you drop a projection from the point of inflection down to the horizontal axis, you will divide the curve into three segments, which are labeled A, B, and C in Figure 4-4.

In a true normal curve, roughly two-thirds of the area will fall into the middle segment (the one labeled B). Thus, one-third of the area will fall in segments A and C. Because the curve is symmetric, one-sixth of the area will fall into A, and one-sixth will fall into C. The distance between the projections from the points of inflection onto the horizontal axis appears to be important because it contains a specified percentage of the area under the curve (two-thirds of it). All of this follows directly from the mathematical characteristics of the normal curve.

Mathematicians derived these properties of the normal curve, with virtually no concern for the manner in which they might describe nature. The properties were presented as a nicely consistent set of mathematical propositions about a specific statistical distribution. However, in an age that revered a mathematical interpretation of the world, we might expect that it would not be long before scholars began to explore the possibility that aspects of human mental life might be usefully described using mathematical distributions such as the normal curve.

Figure 4-4 A normal curve showing the points of inflection and the manner in which projections from them divide the area of the normal curve into three segments.

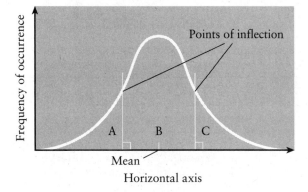

ADOLPH QUETELET AND L'HOMME MOYEN

Adolph Quetelet, an astronomer and statistician in Belgium, was among the first to apply the normal distribution and its attending mathematical properties to social and biological data. Around 1825 he demonstrated that the heights of French army conscripts, as well as many other anthropomorphic measures, could be described using the normal curve. Figure 4-5 shows the type of distributions he obtained. In this case, the horizontal axis represents height, and the vertical axis represents the number of individuals who obtained a given height. Such graphical representations of data are known as **frequency distributions**.

Notice how both the male and female curves in Figure 4-5 are remarkably normal in shape, even though there is a difference in the means and one distribution is taller than the other. It turns out that an incredible array of biological observations can be effectively described with the normal curve—a highly convenient and

Figure 4-5   Frequency distributions of heights of males and females.

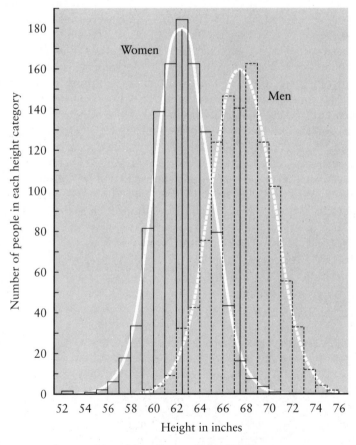

SOURCE: Adapted from Pearson & Lee (1903)

Figure 4-6   Frequency distribution of the number of correct answers to an 11-question vocabulary test (*n* = 566 university students).

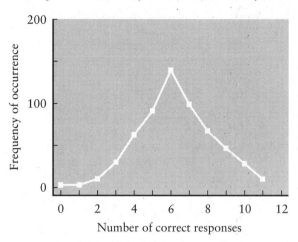

Adolph Quetelet

important finding for the testing enterprise. As an example, Figure 4-6 is a frequency distribution of the number of correct answers given to an 11-question vocabulary test by a sample of 566 university students. Notice how remarkably normal this distribution is, indicating that the normal curve appears to occur in sets of psychological observations.

Quetelet interpreted the frequent finding that the normal curve described biological data as indicating that there is an ideal observation—namely, the mean. Observations that deviate from the average can be thought to have "missed" this ideal. In other words, deviations from the average are *error*. Quetelet demonstrated that these errors can be described mathematically by the normal distribution. He posited the concept of *l'homme moyen* in which the average man is seen as nature's ideal and deviations from this are nature's mistakes. This was supported by the empirical observation that the mean is the most frequent value and large errors are infrequent.

Although we might wish to quibble with Quetelet's concept of *l'homme moyen*,[3] we cannot argue with the incredible importance of his application of mathematical principles to biological and social data. The powerful and revered tools of mathematics (which, for example, had untold impact on the problems of astronomy) were now being brought to bear on human issues. This was a truly astounding achievement and resulted in Quetelet being considered the founder of modern statistics and, by some, the founder of modern sociology as well.

---

[3]In today's context, deviation from the average (that is, being exceptional in one way or another) seems to be *valued*, not a sign of a mistake: Exceptional athletes are rewarded, exceptional intellects gain great recognition, exceptional entrepreneurs gain riches, and so on. Thus, Quetelet's interpretation does not appear to be appropriate to the current cultural context.

THE IDEA OF VARIANCE

One implication of Quetelet's ideas is that the distance of an observation from the mean is a useful characteristic. What was needed was a statistic that would somehow represent the average size of the deviation that each observation showed from the mean. This would be very useful in describing the characteristics of various distributions and would permit comparisons between various types of measurements.

Perhaps the most obvious way to develop a statistic conveying the average deviation from the mean would be to subtract each observation from the average, add up all of these, and divide by the number of observations—this would literally be the average deviation.[4] A problem emerges, however, in that such a procedure would always produce a value of 0 because the mean has been calculated to represent the measure of central tendency in a distribution (Table 4-4).

The Standard Deviation

Squaring the deviation to eliminate the plus and minus signs is a way to avoid producing a value of 0. The statistic representing deviation from the mean involves subtracting each observation from the mean, squaring them, summing them, and dividing this sum by the number of observations. This statistic is called the **variance**. The square root of the variance (taken to compensate for the fact that you squared them in the first place) is called the **standard deviation** (SD). The standard deviation is an estimate of the average deviation from the mean in a normal distribution. Table 4-5 shows an example of the calculation of the variance and standard deviation. Equation 4-2 is the mathematical equation for calculating the standard deviation.

$$SD_x = \sqrt{\frac{\sum_{i=1}^{n} (x_i - M_x)^2}{n}} \tag{4-2}$$

where

$$SD_x = \text{the standard deviation of variable } x$$
$$x_i = \text{person } i\text{'s score on } x$$
$$M_x = \text{the mean of } x$$
$$n = \text{the number of values of } x \text{ (or } n-1 \text{ if } n \text{ is less than 30)}$$
$$\sum_{i=1}^{n} (x_i - M_x)^2 = \text{the sum of all } n \text{ values of the squared deviation from the mean}$$

---

[4]Another approach here would be simply to estimate the *range* of the distribution by subtracting the smallest from the largest observation. However, this method is highly susceptible to fluctuations associated with the occurrence of one abnormal observation, or *outlier*.

Table 4-4 The average deviation of observations from the mean equals 0

Subject	Height (inches)	Height – Mean
1	67	$67 - 68.1 = -1.1$
2	68	$68 - 68.1 = -0.1$
3	68	$68 - 68.1 = -0.1$
4	68	$68 - 68.1 = -0.1$
5	71	$71 - 68.1 = +2.9$
6	63	$63 - 68.1 = -5.1$
7	73	$73 - 68.1 = +4.9$
8	70	$70 - 68.1 = +1.9$
9	68	$68 - 68.1 = -0.1$
10	65	$65 - 68.1 = -3.1$
Sum	681	0.0

Average deviation = $\frac{0}{10}$ = 0.0

Table 4-5 Calculating the variance and standard deviation

Subject	Height (inches)	Height – Mean	(Height–mean)^2
1	67	$67 - 68.1 = -1.10$	1.21
2	68	$68 - 68.1 = -0.10$	.01
3	68	$68 - 68.1 = -0.10$	.01
4	68	$68 - 68.1 = -0.10$	.01
5	71	$71 - 68.1 = +2.90$	8.41
6	63	$63 - 68.1 = -5.10$	26.01
7	73	$73 - 68.1 = +4.90$	24.01
8	70	$70 - 68.1 = +1.90$	3.61
9	68	$68 - 68.1 = -0.10$	.01
10	65	$65 - 68.1 = -3.10$	9.61
Sum	681	0.00	72.90

Mean = $\frac{681}{10}$ = 68.1

Variance = $\frac{72.90^*}{9}$ = 8.10

Standard deviation = square root of variance = 2.85

*Because this is a small sample, the variance is calculated by dividing the sum of the squared deviations from the mean by $n-1$ observations, which is 9 in this case. If n is greater than 30, the sum is divided by n.

In samples with a small number of observations (say, less than 30 data points), calculate the variance by dividing by the number of observations *minus* 1, to provide a better estimate of the exact place where the projection from the point of inflection intersects the horizontal axis. With larger samples, this correction is not necessary, so the sum of the squared deviations is divided by *n*. Almost all psychological data involve the selection of a (hopefully representative) number of individuals from the total set of possible individuals that could be considered. This grand set of individuals is called the **population**, and the smaller selected set is called a **sample**. If dealing with the population, the standard deviation would be calculated by dividing by *n*, as it is with a larger sample. It is only in the small-sample case (that is, $n < 30$) that the variance is calculated by dividing by $n - 1$. Large values of the standard deviation suggest a flat, spread-out distribution, and small standard deviations describe steep, or peaked-shaped, distributions (Figure 4-7).

Figures 4-5 and 4-7 reveal that the normal curve can take a number of different shapes as a function of the mean of the distribution and its standard deviation. They can be stretched out (large standard deviation) or very high and peaked (small standard deviation), or they can be located along the horizontal axis in any number of different ways (pending the mean). Indeed, an infinite number of normal curves is possible. What unites all of them is the characteristic bell shape of the curve and the mathematical function that characterizes the normal curve describes the observed frequency distribution.

Of particular importance here is the manner in which mathematicians demonstrated an interesting relationship between the standard deviation and the point of inflection. It turns out that the distance on the horizontal axis between the mean and the perpendicular projection from the point of inflection *equals* the standard deviation. What a wonderfully convenient finding. The projection of the point of inflection and standard deviation are basically one and the same thing, as shown in Figure 4-8.

Recall that two-thirds of the cases fall between the lines defined by the point of inflection (see Figure 4-4). Knowing that this point and the standard deviation are the same means that, in a normal distribution, roughly two-thirds of the cases fall between ±1 SD from the mean. Figure 4-9 illustrates this, but with a bit more precision than in Figure 4-4. The percentages noted in Figure 4-9 are drawn from standard tables of areas under the normal curve. As can be seen, 68.26% of the cases fall within 1 SD of the mean, not exactly two-thirds as indicated earlier. By extending the standard deviations along the axis, 2.14% of the area under the curve falls 2 SDs above the mean and an equal percentage 2 SDs below it (see Figure 4-9).

This finding has a number of implications, particularly with frequency distributions where the area under the curve represents the number of cases being described. In this case, we can now link individual observations to a person's group standing if we know the mean and standard deviation of the distribution. For example, let's assume that we measured the heights of 1000 university students and found a mean of 67.6 inches and a standard deviation of 3.4 inches. A person who is 71 inches tall falls 1 SD above the mean ($71 - 67.6 = 3.4$ inches $= 1$ SD). If height is normally distributed, it follows that our 71-inch-tall person is taller than 83.99% of all other people. This follows from Figure 4-9 because we can see that the observation that falls 1 SD above the mean is greater than

Figure 4-7 Normal curves for distributions of differing standard deviations.

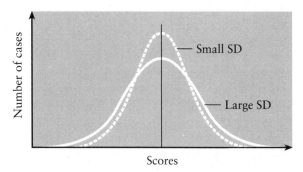

Figure 4-8 A normal curve showing the relationship between points of inflection and the standard deviation.

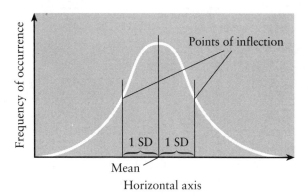

Figure 4-9 The normal curve divided into standard deviations, showing the percentages of cases falling within each standard deviation from the mean.

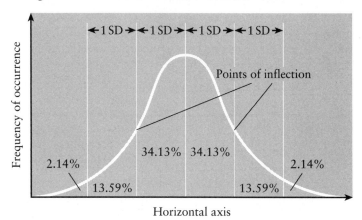

Figure 4-10 The group standing for a person who is 71 inches tall, assuming height is normally distributed with a mean of 67.6 inches and a standard deviation of 3.4 inches.

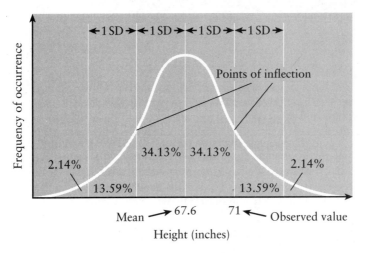

2.14% + 13.59% + 34.13% + 34.13% = 83.99% of all other observations. Figure 4-10 illustrates this for the 71-inch-tall individual.

As you can see, our 71-inch-tall person is taller than 83.99% of all persons measured. In a room containing 100 individuals from the same population as those on whom Figure 4-10 is based, the 71-inch-tall person would be taller than 83 of those in the room. A convenient way of describing this is to suggest that our 71-inch-person falls in the 84th percentile of height, where **percentile** represents the group standing of the individual on the measure in terms of how many persons would attain lower measurement values. Thus, relating a single observation to percentile is possible simply by knowing the mean and standard deviation of the distribution.

This can be generalized. For example, persons who are 60.8 inches tall fall in the 2nd percentile because they would be 2 SDs *below* the mean (60.8 − 67.6 = −6.8 = −2 SDs). All we have to know is the mean and standard deviation of a distribution, and we can make a statement about the percentile in which a specific observation falls. This is an incredibly convenient characteristic of the normal curve because we can now roughly equate our individual observations with a comparative statement (that is, percentiles) knowing only the mean and standard deviation of the underlying distribution.

THE *z* SCORE

This relationship between an observation and its percentile can be extended with a considerable degree of precision. For example, what if a person falls 0.5 SD above the mean? Can we make any statements about this person's percentile? Happily, we can. Again, because of the mathematical properties of the normal curve, an individual who is 0.5 SD above the mean on a normal curve falls in the 69th percentile of the distribution by *mathematical definition*. That is, the nature of the normal curve dictates that a person who scores 0.5 SD above the mean *must* fall in the 69th percentile. In fact, we can develop a table (based on the mathematics of the curve) that tells us exactly the percentile a person's score occupies as a function of the distance it is away from the mean. This distance must be expressed in standard deviations. Table 4-6 presents a rough version of this relationship.[5] In this table, an observation that is 0.5 SD above the mean (expressed as +0.5) falls in the 69th percentile.

Here are several simple examples to help you understand how this works. If the mean score of female undergraduate students on an ability test is 163, with 5 SDs, what is the percentile of a person who scores 165.5? To figure this out, simply calculate how many standard deviations the observed score is away from the mean. In this case, the person scored 2.5 higher than the mean (165.5 – 163 = 2.5). The figure 2.5 is 0.5 SD because SD = 5 (2.5/5 = +0.5). The percentile value for +.05 is 69 from Table 4-6, which is the percentile value for a person who scored 165.5 on the ability test. That is, the person who scored 165.5 is in the 69th percentile of the ability measure—such that she scored higher than 68 of her colleagues. Here are several other examples to help ensure that you have understood this idea: What is the percentile of a person who scored 153?[6] What score must a person obtain to be in the 95th percentile?[7]

In generic form, the number of standard deviations an observation is from the mean is called a **z score**. It expresses the distance in standard deviations that a given observation is from the mean. It can be calculated as

$$z_i = \frac{x_i - M_x}{SD_x}$$

(4-3)

where

z_i = the **standardized score** of person *i* on *x* (that is, the number of standard deviations that person's score is away from the mean)

x_i = person *i*'s score on *x*

M_x = the mean of *x*

SD_x = the standard deviation of *x*

---

[5]This table is only approximate, provided to give you an understanding of the underlying concepts. A much more detailed table is presented in Appendix A.

[6]This observation is 10 *below* the mean (153 – 163 = –10). Because this is 2.0 SDs, reading from the table tells us that person is in the 2nd percentile.

[7]If a person falls in the 95th percentile, the table tells us that she scored 1.6 SDs *above* the mean. Now, 1.6 × 5 = 8, indicating that a person who is 1.6 SDs above the mean must have scored 8 above it; this is 171 (163 + 8 = 171). Therefore, a person who scores 171 is in the 95th percentile.

Table 4-6   The relationship between the number of standard deviations an
observation is from the mean and the percentile of the observation
in a normal curve

Number of Standard Deviations from the Mean	Percentile	Number of Standard Deviations from the Mean	Percentile
−2.0	02	+0.1	54
−1.9	03	+0.2	58
−1.8	04	+0.3	62
−1.7	04	+0.4	66
−1.6	05	+0.5	69
−1.5	07	+0.6	73
−1.4	08	+0.7	76
−1.3	10	+0.8	79
−1.2	12	+0.9	82
−1.1	14	+1.0	84
−1.0	16	+1.1	86
−0.9	18	+1.2	88
−0.8	21	+1.3	90
−0.7	24	+1.4	92
−0.6	27	+1.5	93
−0.5	31	+1.6	95
−0.4	34	+1.7	96
−0.3	38	+1.8	96
−0.2	42	+1.9	97
−0.1	46	+2.0	98
0.0	50		

The utility of the z score is that it allows immediate translation from specific observations to more easily understood statistics such as percentiles, using Table 4-6. All that you need to know is the mean and standard deviation of the distribution. This aspect of the normal curve made it exceedingly useful as the testing enterprise evolved from its earlier beginnings. Appendix A presents a much more detailed table of values for the normal curve at varying z scores. Instructions on how to use this table are given there.

CLOSE UP   **Some Technical Aspects of Normal and Nonnormal Curves**

To the extent that testers want to use the tremendously convenient characteristics of the normal curve, it becomes important to ensure that a given frequency distribution conforms, within limits, to the mathematical function that Gauss gave us. This can be a bit problematic because considerable variation exists within the family of normal curves. We have already seen this in Figure 4-7 in which larger standard deviations have the effect of stretching out the curve. However, even more subtle variation within normality can occur. Known as **kurtosis**, this refers to the steepness of the curve—with some normal curves being quite stunted or flattened, whereas others are relatively tall and skinny such as those shown in Figure 4-5. Figure 4-11 shows these variations, with tall, skinny curves being called **leptokurtic** and short, fat ones being called **platykurtic**. Normal curves in the middle range are given the prefix *meso-* (middle) and are thereby referred to as **mesokurtic**. There are methods of estimating kurtosis (see Ghiselli, Campbell, & Zedeck, 1981, pp. 48–49), but we need not concern ourselves with these at this point. The main point is to recognize that a wide variety of different-shaped functions can be accommodated within the set of curves described as normal. All of these, however, show the characteristics of being symmetric about the mean and **asymptotic** from the mean out to the extremes, showing a point of inflection (change of acceleration) part way out toward the scale ends.

Deviations from normality. As you might expect, Mother Nature has a tendency to throw curves on occasion. Many distributions of observations found in the real world are normal, but quite a few are not. Figure 4-12 (page 124) shows some of the different-shaped frequency distributions that can be found. A **skewed distribution** is one in which individuals fall disproportionately at either the low end (positively skewed) or the high end (negatively skewed) of the scale.[8] Deviations from normality, such as those illustrated in Figure 4-12, are problematic if concepts such as *z* scores, which presume normality, are to be used. Nonnormality poses problems of interpretation and meaning associated with the observations.

The most intuitively obvious means of assessing normality is to draw the frequency distribution and "eyeball" it to determine how normal it looks. This is not really an acceptable approach because it lacks the objectivity expected of properly scientific procedures. One simple way of objectively telling whether a given distribution is approximately normal is to determine if all three measures of central tendency (the mode, median, and mean) are equal. If they are not, the evidence suggests that the distribution is not symmetric, therefore not normal. However, several types of nonnormal distributions (**rectangular, J-shaped,** and **bimodal** in

Figure 4-11

Normal curves of varying kurtosis.

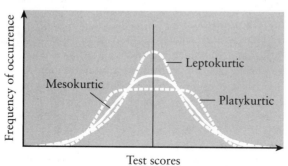

---

[8]For formulas concerning the estimation of skewness, see Ghiselli et al., 1981, pp. 47–48.

Figure 4-12 Various forms of nonnormal frequency distributions.

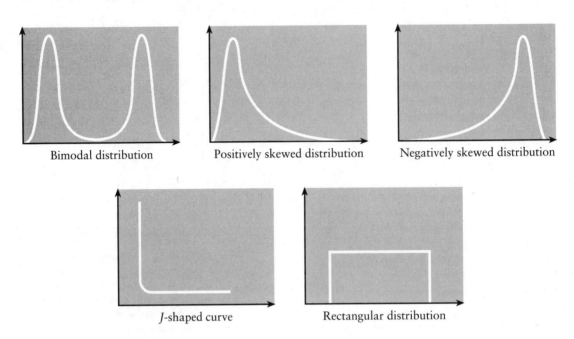

Bimodal distribution Positively skewed distribution Negatively skewed distribution

J-shaped curve Rectangular distribution

Figure 4-12) would pass this rough test and perhaps lead to a premature conclusion of normality. Sophisticated curve-fitting procedures are available to assess normality (for example, the Shapiro–Wilks test: Conover, 1980), but these are beyond the scope of this text.

Several procedures are available in the event that a distribution emerges as nonnormal. It is possible to perform mathematical transformations to the scores so that they conform to the expected normal shape (for example, see Ghiselli et al., 1981, pp. 68–69). Such transformed variables are called **normalized standard scores**. As well, when constructing a test, we can carefully select items to optimize the possibility that the obtained test-score distributions will be normal. For example, selecting some very easy and some very difficult items on an objective test will help minimize the possibility of a skewed distribution. These procedures have the benefit of preserving the utility of methods such as z scores, but they do create the obligation to clearly communicate the exact procedures that were used to modify the test scores.

The normal curve, and its attending mathematical conveniences such as z scores, emerged as particularly important developments in the prehistory of the psychological testing enterprise. Unknown to its creators such as Gauss and Laplace, this mathematical function was going to emerge as a central concept in both the description of biological observations (as noted by Quetelet) and, later on, the measurement of psychological variables. The mathematics were in place; all that was required was the right combination of social and intellectual factors, and the normal curve would become a central player in the emergence of the psychological test.

COUNTING AND MEASURING: PART OF OUR WAY OF LIFE

The movement toward a mathematical and quantitative worldview did not happen in a vacuum. When the young Frenchman Alexis de Tocqueville visited the United States in 1830, he was struck by the amount of arithmetic that he encountered. He described Americans as "always calculating to improve their lot" (cited in Cohen, 1982, p. 3). Yet a mere century earlier, evidence of such extensive **numeracy** was not evident. Some interesting things had apparently happened prior to this time, which led to the social context being primed and willing to accept quantification. People, in general, appeared to have a strong urge to measure and to count—quantification had become a part of the cultural and social landscape.

Changes in the world of commerce had tremendous effects on this movement toward quantification. Around 1600 the needs to be able to navigate a ship in order to explore new territory, to effectively aim a gun and hit the target, and to document cargo in ships all conspired to create a class of "counters." Before long, under the leadership of the likes of Sir William Perry and his political arithmetic, the disparate domains of quantification, economic thought, and empiricism were linked, with each feeding on the other to create a context in which counting and measuring were valued and necessary activities. In other words, the movement toward quantification was not restricted to the ivory towers of universities but had its genesis in the day-to-day activities of commerce that were shaping the world. Once centralized government was established, overseas trade became economically viable, and capitalism arose as a guiding economic dogma, the quantitative worldview had become part of the lived cultural experience of everyone in the European and North American worlds. People became infatuated with numbers. Counting and measuring provided satisfaction because they signaled certainty. Statistical knowledge became deeply gratifying because it was presumed to reveal an objective and unimpeachable truth. Counting and measuring became ends in themselves. Indeed, it emerged that, if used properly, numbers could create or capture political power. By the mid-1800s, the quantitative worldview had been firmly established in both Europe and North America.

CLOSE UP | What's Counted Is What Counts

The quantitative worldview brings a number of advantages. For example, we can settle some disputes, such as the rise or fall of specific social problems, by referring to actual numbers. The objectivity inherent in properly counted and measured empirical observations is difficult to deny. As well, large-scale counting, such as census taking or national-level statistics regarding various diseases and social ills, provides a wider window of observation than do nonquantitative approaches. In all, numbers appear to constitute an unassailable bedrock of positivist truth and are thus essential to the proper functioning of our most cherished institutions—including governments.

However, there is more here than meets the eye. The very act of deciding what to count or measure is itself a value statement. Whereas the numbers obtained may be objective, the actual decision about what to measure is not. For example, Cohen (1982) notes that prostitution was as widely practiced in America as it was every-where else in the mid-1850s—yet it was not counted or enumerated. Calculating prostitution rates was instituted only after a group of moral reformers became con-cerned. That is, the decision to quantify prostitution was born of a specific value concern—namely, the elimination of the practice. The numbers then became rhetoric for the implementation of a specific political/social practice. In the prosti-tution debate, the objectivity of the empirical indicators made counterargument very difficult. Cohen also points out that antislavery and protemperance move-ments were highly facilitated by the decision to count specific, previously uncount-ed aspects of social practice. Only when something becomes particularly important does it merit being counted or quantified, and herein lies the value-laden nature of numbers, despite their apparent value-neutral status as agents of positivist truth.[9]

The point here is that we must lay bare the historical roots of any particular instance of quantification to determine where, in the system, the value positions have been inserted. Nowhere is this more important than in the discourse in subse-quent chapters when concern shifts to examining psychological tests as agents of social practice and decision making. The narrative and historical approach employed in this text aids in the awareness of these considerations.

By the mid-1800s, the quantitative worldview had won the day. The power and strength of rendering argument in the form of numbers and counted categories were undeniable. Scientists, politicians, reformers, businesspeople, economists, and almost all other powerful members of the culture had been converted to a special kind of numeracy that placed truth based on counted and measured entities ahead of all other forms. The positivist, empirical approach had been so strongly wed to this quantitative worldview that its utility was unconsciously accepted as part-and-parcel of the apparent "only" way to proceed. Could it be long before procedures to render things psychological into numbers would become the order of the day?

Summary

In this chapter, we explored some of the antecedent developments in the creation of our cultural worldview that places considerable emphasis on the quantitative. The emergence of positivism was seen as an important factor, as was the "discov-ery" of individual differences and the desire to measure certain complex human characteristics. Some mathematical notions such as the mean, standard deviation, and a set of ideas related to the normal curve were introduced, and the manner in

---

[9]It should be noted that not only the decision about what to count but also the labels and categories that are used constitute value judgments, or what Cohen (1982) calls *a priori assumptions*.

which these were pressed into the service of the emerging quantitative worldview was articulated.

It should be noted at this point that the quantitative worldview is not necessarily *correct*. It represents a way of thinking that has become an almost unconscious way of looking at things within our cultural framework. This view has yielded many important and significant discoveries, but at root it is but one set of lenses through which it is possible to view the world. To assume that the quantitative is the only possible worldview would be yet another example of ethnocentrism. In cultural contexts that do not share our specific worldview, emphasis might be placed on the nuance of quality rather than on number. So too might alternative worldviews emphasize nonlinear (say, circular) motifs in contrast to the linear ideas that are at the heart of our quantitative-oriented views of time and space (see Toelken, 1979). It is important to bear this in mind as we proceed because there is an unfortunate tendency to forget this aspect of our worldview and assume that it applies to everyone—thereby cutting off important discourse and dialog.

The relationship between this quantitative worldview and other issues in social development, such as economics, was presented in this chapter. What remains now is for us to explore some issues that led to the actual emergence of psychological testing, in the form it did, as an important component of social decision making in our culture. We now turn to this fascinating topic.

Glossary

apex The highest point of a normal curve. A perpendicular projection from the apex to the horizontal axis locates the arithmetic mean of the distribution. (See Figure 4-3.)

asymptotic A type of curve that flattens out and slowly converges with an axis. Such curves, technically, never reach the axis but get continually closer to it. Both ends of the normal curve are said to be asymptotic with the horizontal axis.

bimodal distribution A frequency distribution that shows two definite humps. (See Figure 4-12.)

degree As used here, the unit of measurement suggested by Christian Thomasius to underly the assessment of his "passions." He suggested that passions could vary in amount between 5 and 60 degrees.

eye-and-ear method A particular technique of observing stars and documenting their locations at a specific time. The technique involved determining exactly when a given star appeared between two vertical sight lines on the telescope by reference to a series of pulsing tones.

frequency distribution A graphical representation of a set of numbers where the number of times each digit within the set is counted and mapped into a two-dimensional space with the axes being the number of observations and observation value (see Figure 4-5). In the present context, discussion focused on the manner in which the normal curve can be used to describe such distributions of biological and psychological data.

individual differences A generic term that relates to any analysis focusing on the manners in which persons within a given context vary from each other. In contemporary psychology, individual differences are typically studies that use various test-based measurements to determine the similarities, or lack thereof, between and among sets of persons.

J-shaped distribution A distribution indicating that large numbers of observations are at the extreme end of the horizontal axis. (See Figure 4-12.)

kurtosis An index that reflects the steepness or fatness of a normal curve.

leptokurtic A normal curve that is quite sharp or steep. (See Figure 4-11.)

l'homme moyen **(the average man)** Adolph Quetelet's theoretical idea that the average of a set of biological observations was the ideal and that deviations from this average were anomalous with larger deviations being less frequent.

mean A measure of central tendency, the arithmetic average of a set of numbers. (See Equation 4-1.)

measures of central tendency A family of indices that, in varying ways, conveys the midpoint of a distribution of numbers. In the text, the mean, mode, and median are discussed as measures of central tendency.

median A measure of central tendency, the middle score in a distribution. (See Table 4-3.)

mesokurtic A normal curve that is in the middle range of sharpness or steepness. (See Figure 4-11.)

mode A measure of central tendency, the most frequently occurring observation from among a set.

normal curve A bell-shaped mathematical function that serves to describe many probability functions. Of particular note is the manner in which this function serves to describe frequency distributions of empirical observations from nature such as adult height. The mean, or average, of a set of observations occurs at the apex of this curve, whereas the standard deviation occurs at the point of inflection.

normalized standard score A z score based on observations that have been mathematically transformed to render the underlying distribution a normal shape.

numeracy Analogous to literacy with words, the capacity to deal, perform calculations, and communicate with numbers. In the present context, numeracy was seen as a result of the scientific worldview.

passions As used in this chapter, the four main sources of human personality (reasonable love, voluptuousness, ambition, and greed) suggested by Christian Thomasius.

percentile An index of the relative placement of an observation within a larger set. For example, the percentile gives an indication of what percentage of people within the set of observations would obtain a lower score than the observation with which you are concerned.

personal equation Coined by Bessel, this idea relates to the possibility of mathematically adjusting perceptual response times for individual variations in the speed of perception. This notion was important for the development of a reliable observational base for astronomy.

platykurtic A normal curve that is quite stunted or flat. (See Figure 4-11.)

point of inflection The place on a normal curve where the curve changes from a negative to a positive acceleration (or vice versa). There are two points of inflection on a normal curve, and perpendicular projections from them to the horizontal axis are located ±1 SD from the mean and encompass (roughly) two-thirds of the cases described in a frequency distribution. (See Figure 4-4.)

population The complete set of individuals belonging to a category of interest to a scientist.

positive knowledge Knowledge that is absolutely true and incontrovertible. The only source of such knowledge was thought to be via the senses.

positivism An evolving family of philosophical positions based on the assertion of the possibility of positive knowledge.

projection A line drawn to an axis of a graph and that intersects the axis at a 90-dgree, or right, angle.

quantitative Having to do with translation of important phenomena to numbers.

rectangular distribution A frequency distribution in which there is an equal number of all values, thus creating a rectangular shape (see Figure 4-12). Percentiles are rectangular distributions.

sample A selected group of individuals from a population. In the chapter, a small sample was defined as one with less than 30 individuals.

scientific revolution The change in worldview that began in the 1600s, culminating in the valuing of empirical, mathematical, and mechanical explanations of the universe.

self The psychological conceptualization that people have about their own person and personality. In the present context, changes in the visions of self over historical time were discussed to demonstrate the manner in which the self as an autonomous individual was necessary for the development of the field of individual differences.

skewed distribution The degree to which a frequency distribution is nonsymmetric, with positive skew reflecting a collection of observations at the left of the horizontal axis and negative skew showing an aggregation of observations to the right. (See Figure 4-12.)

standard deviation An index of the spread around the mean of a set of numbers. It is coincidental with the perpendicular projection from the point of inflection of a normal curve to the horizontal axis. (See Equation 4-2 for calculation.)

standardized score *See z score.*

variance An index of the spread around the mean of a set of observations. Larger values suggest more spread-out distributions. Technically, the variance is the square of the standard deviation.

worldview The culturally determined lenses through which a person sees the environment. Adapted from anthropology, this concept involves a wide range of deep-seated propensities for interpreting external events in specific ways. In the present context, the scientific revolution was suggested to have brought about a change toward a quantitative worldview.

z score A means of transforming an observation to take into account the mean and standard deviation of the distribution from which it comes. The *z* score indicates the number of standard deviations an observation is from the mean. (See Equation 4-3 for calculation and Table 4-6 for the percentiles associated with various *z* scores.)

Suggested Further Reading

Anderson, D. R., Sweeney, D. J., & Williams, T. A. (1991). *Introduction to statistics: Concepts and applications* (2nd ed.). New York: West.

> The section on the normal curve (pp. 185–203) is very readable and provides a more mathematical presentation than was offered in this chapter of *The Enterprise*. It is a good introduction to the normal curve as the mathematician sees it.

Cohen, P. C. (1982). *A calculating people: The spread of numeracy in early America*. Chicago: University of Chicago Press.

> This wonderful book presents the fascinating story of the development of numeracy in our culture. Its narrative starts before the scientific revolution and tracks the development of counting and quantification through to the late 1800s in the United States. It provides wonderful examples of the manners in which numbers have come to take a very important place in contemporary lived cultural experience.

Jacob, M. C. (1988). *The cultural meaning of the scientific revolution*. New York: Knopf.

> This is a fine example of the more contemporary approach to the history of science. Compared to Lindsay (1951) (listed below), this book is much more interpretive by placing the changes inherent in the emergence of science into cultural context. Additionally, this book is a "good read," providing a number of fine examples and arguments of relevance to the transitions discussed in this chapter.

Lindsay, J. (Ed.) (1951). *A short history of science*. Garden City, N.Y.: Doubleday Anchor.

> The history of science is a very extensive domain, with myriad books being available on your library shelves. This area has changed over the years as well, with more interpretive approaches emerging in the last several decades (for example, see Jacob, 1988, above). Lindsay's edited volume provides a collection of classic articles from the older, less critical approach to the history of science. These essays cover the periods discussed in this chapter and provide a considerable amount of additional information, particularly in terms of other major players and ideas in the evolution of the scientific worldview.

Toelken, B. (1979). *The dynamics of folklore*. Boston: Houghton Mifflin.

> Chapter 7 of this book provides a highly readable and intriguing discussion of the notion of worldview. It presents the European/American view (what I've called quantitative), along with several others such as the Navajo. The manners in which worldview is reflected in day-to-day activities and how it can be used to differentiate among cultures are highlighted in this treatise.

Discussion Questions

1. Describe an incident from your youth in which you enacted the medieval world-view by attributing something to "magical" or "mysterious" forces. Can you now reinterpret this event from a more modern perspective?

2. Discuss why the development of a view of personhood that embodies firm self/other boundaries was a necessary prerequisite of the emergence of technologies such as the IQ test.

3. Would contemporary feminist thought be willing to accede to Baumeister's idea that there is a single notion of self reflected in firm self/other boundaries and the like? What are the implications of this for Baumeister's idea of the evolution of self?

4. Sketch out the manner in which hospitals and allied institutions evolved and suggest some of the implications these developments had for contemporary health-care delivery systems.

5. Define and give an example of positive knowledge. What are the advantages and disadvantages of this idea?

6. Refer to Table 4-1 and discuss several critical factors that affected the order in which measurement of various aspects mental phenomena evolved.

7. Write a short screenplay or script that captures the essence of the Maskelyne–Kinnebrook incident.

8. Design an experiment, which could have been conducted by Bessel, regarding vigilance reaction times that would have improved the quality of the reported data.

9. List as many examples as possible of personal equations from your daily experiences (for example, golfer's handicap).

10. In statistics the central limit theorem states that the means of samples from distributions of any shape are normally distributed. How does this help us explain the frequent appearance of normal distributions in nature? What does it tell us about normally distributed phenomena?

11. Recalling the levels of measurement discussed in Chapter 2, indicate which measures of central tendency are appropriate to which level. Discuss the implications of this, regarding inferences that can be made from various levels of measurement.

12. Discuss whether the calculation of the mean of a distribution of scores that relate to people eliminates individual differences.

13. Draw frequency distributions that would emerge if all possible combinations of the mean, median, and mode were not equal to each other.

14. Draw a distribution that has four points of inflection. What are the implications of this for the calculation of the standard deviation?

15. Demonstrate the fact that the area under the normal curve in a frequency distribution relates to the number of individuals used in generating the frequency distribution.

16. Provide a detailed critique of Adolph Quetelet's notion of *l'homme moyen*.

17. Invent a way other than the standard deviation to express the variability of a distribution about the mean. What are the strengths and weaknesses of your statistic compared to the standard deviation?

18. What shape is the frequency distribution for percentiles? Because it is nonnormal, what difficulties does this create for the interpretation of scores rendered as percentiles?

19. If an IQ test has a mean of 100 and a standard deviation of 15, what are the percentiles of students who obtained the following scores: 75, 182, 109, 88, and 120?

20. Write a short description of the z score that would clearly communicate the meaning of percentiles to the parent of a child who has just been tested on an achievement test (say, mathematics) and who received a score of –1.25. (Assume the parent has no formal training in testing.)

21. Define *kurtosis* and draw sample curves of the three classes of kurtosis mentioned in the text.

22. Provide an argument showing that the quest for positive truth had its genesis in the day-to-day practices of people rather than having been driven by academic concerns.

23. Describe and evaluate two specific examples from your own experience that indicate the act of deciding to count something is a value judgment.

24. Debate the assertion that quantitative methods are just as value-laden as qualitative ones, with the only difference being where in the process the value judgments are enacted.

Chapter 5

Psychological and Philosophical Foundations of Testing
On the Origin of Differences

EARLY INFLUENCES

Thus far, the mathematical/scientific approach to individual differences has been mostly descriptive. That is, we have focused on using various mathematical techniques to provide summaries of this aspect of nature. An important step in the scientific process is the exploration of the reasons underlying the various phenomena that have been observed. For example, it was when Charles Darwin published

133

his *Origin of Species* in 1859 that biology exploded as a major science. This important dissertation provided a set of possible causal explanations of variation in the animal kingdom, with ideas stimulating major growth in the biological sciences. Until this time, scholars had described aspects of the variation between individuals, but very little had been said about the sources of these differences—where do individual differences come from?

It turns out that philosophers and politicians had been pursuing this problem for quite some time. Although the style of articulation and the arguments used were different from what we might expect today, there had been considerable debate about this topic in a number of different settings. These early debates were clear precursors of several of the most important issues to loom as critical in the modern psychological testing enterprise.

During this intriguing time, no clear distinction was drawn between what we today call philosophy and psychology. Psychology as an independent, scientifically oriented discipline had yet to emerge.[1] This suggests, among other things, that the contributions of the two disciplines were inexorably intertwined when the foundations for psychological testing were being laid. There is, then, an important body of thought and opinion that has been inherited from the earlier times when psychology and philosophy were one and the same thing. Paying attention to these differences is an exceedingly important part of being able to fully understand contemporary testing practice. In a very real sense, we, as students of psychology, ignore history and philosophy at our peril when it comes to understanding testing.

Let's now examine two grand intellectual traditions that were instrumental in the emergence of the psychological test: the associationistic and the commonsense views. Each conceptualized the origin of individual differences in fundamentally different ways, and the resolution of the attending debate was of great consequence to the manner in which tests eventually emerged.

THE ASSOCIATIONISTIC TRADITION

The emergence of dissimilar and conflicting views on the origins of individual differences can be traced to variations in philosophical positions that evolved in concert with the emergence of science. One of the fundamental schools of thought is well revealed in John Locke's classic *Essay on Human Understanding* (Locke, 1690/1975). This calm, unpretentious, and reasonable work dismissed all speculation and directed attention toward the process of knowledge. How was it obtained? What were its limitations? In answer to these queries, Locke suggested that all knowledge was derived from experience, observation, and reflection. At the start,

---

[1] It was not until, roughly, the beginning of the 20th century that psychology as we know it emerged in its present institutional form as an independent department or discipline.

the mind was like white paper with nothing written on it—what he called a *tabula rasa*. Experience was written on this blank slate, and knowledge emerged through this process. According to Locke, there was no need to postulate any kind of inner, or intrinsic, knowledge; all that was important was derived from experience.

From this simple beginning, an elaborate philosophical position developed that emphasized the manner in which various experiences become associated with each other and the manner in which these associations combine to create ideas, thoughts, and knowledge. A school of thought called **associationism** emerged to serve this role and was advanced under the agency of Locke and subsequently by a number of highly influential British philosophers (for example, Berkeley, Hume, Hartley, and James Mill). Approaches to education, politics, and morality followed from the basic associationistic position, which emphasized the impact of experience on the formation of the human mind. For example, it follows from an associationistic position, with its *tabula rasa*, that the optimal educational system should be designed to maximize experience. This school of philosophical and political thought became known as the **empiricist tradition** because the emphasis was on experience gathered through the senses in determining the nature of mind.

These associationistic, or empiricist, positions brought with them a way of explaining the origin of human individual differences. If the human mind was strictly a function of experience, then differences in people must similarly be a function of experience. That is, the associationistic position predisposes adherents to consider that human individual differences are a function of the environment. This does not deny the possibility of native differences between people but does suggest that environmental conditions are at the forefront of individual differences. This is the first of two positions on the origin of individual differences that have had a profound effect on contemporary psychological testing.

THE COMMONSENSE TRADITION

Locke and the associationistic/empiricist school that followed him did not go unchallenged. Wholesale attacks on this position were launched from Germany (for example, Leibnitz, then Kant), Italy (for example, Vico), and France (for example, the so-called romantic movement; for discussion, see Hearnshaw, 1987). For our purposes, yet another assault on associationism/empiricism warrants mention. Scotsman Thomas Reid formulated a position, known as the **commonsense tradition**, that questioned some of the tenets of associationism and in so doing forged the basis of an alternative view of the origin of individual differences.

Reid argued that commonsense beliefs, not abstract associations, should be the starting point for the development of a philosophy of mind. These beliefs included the existence of an objective material world and our capacity to have direct awareness of this world. Equally important was the belief in the identity of the self and the existence of other persons. Obviously, these are commonsense beliefs in the broadest sense of the term because they seem so plausible, even today. Philosophers in general and the associationists in particular had argued that these kinds of beliefs were not adequate for building a workable psychology. For example, Locke suggested that the experience of reality was indirect—being mediated by a series of **ideas** that were built up from associations. Reid said that direct experience of reality was not only possible but was the foundation of day-to-day experience.

For our purposes, the major aspect of Reid's position was his description of the human mind at birth. He suggested that our psyche was equipped, from the start, with innate intuitions and instincts: "All reasoning must be from first principles, and these are part of our constitution" (Reid,1785/1941, p. 130). In contrast to Locke then, Reid placed some capacities into the human mind at birth—characteristics that he called **constitutional factors**. If we extrapolate this position to an explanation of individual differences, we would immediately begin to consider native, or innate, characteristics. That is, adopting Reid's position predisposes us to begin to look for inborn differences between people. This is the foundation of a second major view of individual differences—one that is still part of contemporary psychological testing.

Reid also anticipated an important development that would shape modern views of individual differences in no small way. He emphasized that our species had been an irrational animal for some time before becoming rational. This style of thinking is reminiscent of Darwin's evolutionary theory, which did not emerge for another 60 years. Reid further argued that these rational, constitutional higher powers matured only gradually and that this maturation was "much aided by proper culture" (Reid, 1788/1846, p. 595). Thus, Reid's was not a totally innate position—he left room for environmental influences in the emergence of psychological powers. However, his position was clear not only in its emphasis on inborn influences but also in its rejection of the associationistic position.

As early as 1790, we begin to see a bifurcation of theories of the origin of individual differences. One emphasized environmental experience, whereas the other considered innate attributes of the human mind. However, to this point, the debate had not emerged in exactly the same form as it would take in more modern years. Time was needed for the emergence of a psychological climate that cast the person as a self-contained individual. In addition, time was needed to provide the mathematical tools for the development of psychological testing. It appears that all of these influences converged in England during a period known as the Victorian era. By this time, the Locke–Reid debate about the origin of individual differences had begun to solidify. As we saw in Chapter 4, a view of self, replete with firm self/other boundaries, emerged at this time. A number of mathematical tools, which allowed for the application of the quantitative worldview to the complexities of human behavior (see Chapter 4), were also becoming available. As an added force, the theory of evolution emerged during this time. This confluence of factors is best noted in an examination of the thinking of two Victorian scholars whose intellectual roots go back to the original arguments between the associationistic and commonsense views—John Stuart Mill, an associationist/environmentalist, and Francis Galton, who extended the commonsense view in highly significant ways.

JOHN STUART MILL

By the Victorian era, the associationistic position had evolved considerably. The vehemence of extolling the impact of environmental influences on the intellect had increased. John Stuart Mill, sometimes known as the "patron saint of liberty," was perhaps the strongest advocate of this environmental position, and it is to his version of associationism and environmentalism that we now turn.

A strong case can be made that Mill's advocacy for an environmental explanation of individual differences stems from his upbringing (see Fancher, 1985, Chapter 1). The son of a highly respected philosopher, James Mill, John was highly precocious as a youngster. As early as the age of 8, he had read a goodly proportion of the Greek classics—in Greek! His father was his teacher and, by all accounts, an exacting taskmaster. By the time John was 16 years old, he was acting as a critic for his father's books.

John viewed this experiment in home education as a success because, as he concluded in midlife, "Through the early training bestowed on me by my father, I started, I may fairly say, with an advantage of a quarter of a century over my contemporaries" (Mill, 1909/1971, p. 20). He came to believe that virtually anyone could be taught anything if the conditions were correct. He was so convinced of the environmental influence that he stated

> If I had been by nature extremely quick of apprehension, or had possessed a very accurate and retentive memory, the trial would not have been conclusive; but in all these natural gifts I am rather below than above par. What I could do, could assuredly be done by any boy or girl of average capacity and healthy physical constitution. (Mill, 1909/1971, pp. 19–20)

Led by his early educational experiences and his interpretation that his accomplishments were part-and-parcel of this environmental advantage, Mill emerged as a strong proponent of the associationistic position. In his capable hands, this position emerged not only as a systematic philosophy/psychology but also as an important political doctrine.

Mill's Associationism

Mill clearly advocated the *tabula rasa* position of John Locke, emphasizing the capacity for receiving and recording the impressions of events:

> Whenever any state of consciousness has once been excited in us, no matter by what cause; an inferior degree of the same state of consciousness, a state of consciousness resembling the former, but inferior in intensity, is capable of being reproduced in us, without the presence of any such cause as excited it at first. Thus, if we have once seen or touched an object, we can afterwards think of the object though it is absent from sight or from touch. (Mill, 1843/1973, p. 825)

For Mill, the basic building block of the human mind was the **idea**. Every psychological event has an associated idea, and these ideas can be called into consciousness

John Stuart Mill (1806–1873).

independently of the actual event. Mill's concern was the manner in which these ideas flowed through consciousness and the nature of the linkages between them.

According to the extant associationistic view, ideas could become associated in three ways:

1. Similar ideas would be linked to each other.
2. Ideas that occurred closely in time became associated with each other.
3. Stronger or more intense ideas would become established more strongly.

Mill added to this theory when he suggested that two or three single ideas could become so strongly established they formed a **complex idea**, where the union of the basic ideas served as if it was a single idea. These complex ideas were thought to be more than the sum of constituent parts, creating a unique psychological notion. An even stronger version of the possibility of simple ideas emerging into complex cognitions can be found in Mill's notion of **mental chemistry** in which complex ideas may form and take on new properties that are independent of the original constituent ideas. Mill, then, extended the current associationism by suggesting a series of notions (for example, complex ideas, mental chemistry) that allowed for the construction of psychologically meaningful complexity from basic units (that is, ideas).

Mill argued that this version of associationism could account for many of the ideas that others regarded as innate, or constitutional (for example, contemporary followers of the commonsense school, such as William Hamilton). Although Mill did not deny the existence of innate factors, he argued that it was necessary to push associationism as far as possible before relying on explanations involving innate attributes of the human mind. He called the part of the mind that could not be explained by associationism the **residuum**. He was convinced that the vigorous and expert application of an associationistic position would render the residuum much smaller than people expected.

Mill and Individual Differences

Mill's approach to individual differences flowed directly from his associationistic psychology. He argued that particularly intense experiences in childhood would lead to the formation of particularly strong associations among various ideas and that these would predispose an individual to specific types of activities. In other words, individual differences are attributable to environmental differences among people.

The residuum of activities not attributable to environmental factors would, according to Mill, be minimal, thereby arguing for the inappropriateness of innate explanations: "It is certain that, in human beings, at least, differences in education and outward circumstances are capable of affording an adequate explanation of by far the greatest portion of character" (Mill, 1843/1973, p. 859). He actually proposed a new science, **ethology**, whose basic function would be to explain individual differences on the basis of associationistic principles.

As you might expect from the foregoing, Mill did not deny innate differences between people. However, he was concerned that constitutional explanations were deeply problematic, particularly in the manner in which they condoned unsophisticated and politically convenient rationalizations of certain practices: "Of all vulgar modes of escaping from the consideration of the social and moral influences on the human mind, the most vulgar is that attributing the diversities of human conduct and character to inherent original natural differences" (Mill, 1848/1978, p. 319).

The following quotation begins to signal the *moral* importance of this debate over innate versus environmental precursors of individual differences:

> The prevailing tendency to regard all the marked distinctions of human nature as innate, and in the main indelible, and to ignore the irresistible proofs that by far the greater part of those differences, whether between individuals, races, or sexes, are such as not only might, but naturally would be produced by differences in circumstances, is one of the chief hindrances to the rational treatment of great social questions, and one of the greatest stumbling blocks to human improvement. (Mill, 1909/1971, p. 162)

According to Mill, the fundamental problem with explanations focusing on innate factors is that they allow politicians to rationalize bad treatment of the disadvantaged. After all, a constitutionalist might argue, if a group of people—say, slaves in the United States—are in a powerless position, it is because they are innately inferior. Thus, efforts directed toward changing the position of this group are not necessary. To rebut this line of argument, Mill argued that politicians have a moral obligation to accept the environmentalist explanation.

This discussion of John Stuart Mill reveals that the associationistic position is more than a simple psychology of ideas. When taken to its logical conclusion, this basic environmentalist position establishes a particular moral and political agenda for its advocate. This is no ordinary, dry, paltry philosophy. Rather, Mill's position represents a strong exhortation to political action. Mill spent a good deal of his life arguing for his liberal view when he wrote papers dealing with sensitive topics such as the degradation of the Irish peasants and Black slaves in the United States and Jamaica. He also introduced Britain's first women's suffrage bill to Parliament in 1866.

In summary, John Stuart Mill elaborated the associationistic view of psychology during the Victorian era into a strong moral, political, and scientific position.

He provided a viable alternative to the commonsense views, which were slowly but surely gaining greater popularity. Indeed, the innate position was about to receive a very important boost, which would bring it into ascendance over the more environmental perspective. Mill was only 25 years old, just beginning to work out the details of his position, when a relatively unknown biologist by the name of Charles Darwin sailed away on the HMS *Beagle* for a trip around the world that would change the entire face of science in a deeply profound and significant manner.

CHARLES DARWIN AND NATURAL SELECTION

Recall that Thomas Reid suggested that our species had somehow emerged from a less developed form, indicating some kind of continuity from older species to the human. He was not alone in this assertion. For example, a number of earlier theorists such as Leibnitz and Lamarck had speculated that the human had descended from lower species. Indeed, Monboddo (1773) boldly suggested that man was related to the orangutan! For the most part, these views were considered to be on the fringe of respectability partly because there was no supporting evidence and partly because such views challenged prevailing religious dogma. Another problem was the uncountable number of years it would have taken for any kind of evolutionary process to have occurred. The received wisdom of the time viewed the human species to be but several thousand years old or, at the most, 75,000. There was simply not enough time for an evolutionary scheme to have been played out.

The first of these obstacles to be cleared away was the issue of time. Geologist Charles Lyell (1797–1875) redefined the entire concept of geological intervals in his discussion of millions of years for the emergence of aspects of the earth's surface. It has been argued that this reconceptualization of time has been one of the most profound in history (see Toulmin & Goodfield, 1965), paving the way for an evolutionary perspective.

The next obstacle to be removed was the collection of substantive data to support an evolutionary position, and this is where Darwin's 1831–1836 voyage on the HMS *Beagle* emerged as critical. Within 6 years of this voyage Darwin had sketched out his theory of evolution, eventuating in its publication.

The theory essentially focused on explaining the origin of biological variation. In cases of competition for resources or environmental change, the fittest members of the species survived. Successful individuals were more likely to procreate, meaning that adaptations and variations would be transmitted through inheritance. This is the process termed natural selection. The masses of data that Darwin cited to verify this position were impressive, and a true revolution in human thought had begun. An explanation of the origin of biological variation was now available.

Darwin himself applied his theory to the human case in his works *The Descent of Man* (Darwin, 1871) and *The Expression of the Emotions in Man and Animals* (Darwin, 1872). However, it was Darwin's second cousin, **Francis Galton**, who adapted the theory to the human in a way that was to have a profound effect on the emergence of psychological testing.

FRANCIS GALTON: HEREDITARIAN

Galton's ideas can be seen to have been shaped by the commonsense tradition out-lined earlier (see Hearnshaw, 1987, p. 93; Robinson, 1981, p. 241). Although believing in the innate nature of certain aspects of human capacity, Galton had a major advantage over his earlier contemporaries—namely, Darwin's revolutionary evolutionary ideas were available to him. Because of this, Galton was able to advance a much stronger version of the hereditarian hypothesis than had been pos-sible earlier. The story of Galton and his elaboration of the constitutional hypothe-sis is probably the most significant narrative in the emergence of the psychological testing enterprise as we know it today. Not only did he provide a foundational philosophical position for the enterprise, but he also pioneered several mathemati-cal and conceptual techniques that are still with us in the 1990s (for biographical details, see Forrest, 1974; Galton, 1908).

Not unlike John Stuart Mill, Galton's advocacy for a constitutional view stemmed from his early upbringing (see Fancher, 1985, Chapter 1). The youngest child of a wealthy and distinguished British family, he was pampered, particularly by his older sister Adele, who tutored him throughout his youth. By the age of 2½ years, Francis was reading, at age 3 years he was writing, and by age 4 years he was learning Latin and French. This precociousness continued, culminating in his clear expectation that he would earn great academic honors when he entered university.

Sadly, Galton's early promise was not realized in his formal schooling. He could not achieve honors in the boarding schools to which he was sent. The lack of rigor in his early training did not prepare Francis to compete with his contempo-raries. He was unsuccessful in winning competitions in forensic medicine and mathematics at university and emerged as what we might call a "B student" these days. Despite such laudatory accomplishments as a child (Cambridge University was brutally competitive), the young Galton was devastated and suffered a major emotional breakdown, which forced him to withdraw from honors and pursue an ordinary degree.

After this he went through the motions of studying medicine but withdrew when his father died in 1844, leaving him a substantial inheritance. These educa-tional experiences forged a belief in Galton that hereditary factors were responsible for his perceived failure. He had had the best of environments and educational opportunities, yet he was unable to succeed at his expected level of achievement. The young Francis began to believe that innate, or inborn, factors were responsible for his failures.

For several years following his withdrawal from medicine, Galton lived the life of the idle rich. During this time, he noted the considerable popular press sur-rounding the escapades of African explorers such as Stanley and Livingston. The unhappy Francis was eventually attracted to geographic exploration because he had the money and the time to become involved in this high-status activity. In 1850 he spent 2 years mapping in Africa, returning to become an accepted member of the Royal Geographical Society.

His time in Africa, during which he became interested in the "human side of geography," was very important. He became convinced that most Africans were

Francis Galton (1822–1911).

intellectually and morally incapable of adapting positively to Western civilization. In keeping with his interpretations of his academic misfortunes, he began to believe that this too was hereditary. Slowly but surely, Galton was converging on a view of humanity that strongly favored the innate side of the coin. It was at this point in his life that Darwin's insights became part of the British intellectual scene.

Galton's Case for Mental Heredity

Galton's extrapolation of evolutionary theory to humans was much bolder than Darwin's. Rather than limit considerations to emotional expression, Galton went to the fullest extent and suggested that almost all human individual differences might be inheritable—even psychological attributes such as intellect, morality, and character. Although his Scottish intellectual antecedents had suggested that such differences might be innate, Galton added the supposition that these were inheritable as well. With this jump, Galton was in the position to argue that differences among individuals *and* ethnic groups could be explained on hereditary grounds. This being the case, it might be possible to intervene in one way or another and actually speed up the evolutionary process to produce a superior breed of human being! Galton proposed a new science, **eugenics**, which was concerned with improving human stock to create just such a superior race.

Before developing his eugenics program, Galton had to collect data to prove the inheritability of psychological qualities. He addressed this issue in three distinct ways. First, he examined prevailing "national characters" (Galton, 1865). He noted the stereotypical Victorian images of various races such as the "typical West African negro" and analyzed these in ways that he felt supported his hereditarian hypothesis. For example, he viewed Americans as developing according to his view:

Whenever, during the last ten or twelve generations, a political or religious party has suffered defeat, its prominent members, whether they were the best, or only the noisiest, have been apt to emigrate to America as refuges from persecution. Men fled to America for conscience' sake, and for that of unappreciated patriotism. Every scheming knave, and every brutal ruffian, who feared the arm of the law, also turned his eyes in the same direction.... If we estimate the moral nature of Americans from their present social state, we shall find it to be just what we might have expected from such a parentage. They are enterprising, defiant and touchy; impatient of authority; furious politicians; very tolerant of fraud and violence; possessing much high and generous spirit, and some true religious feeling, but strongly addicted to cant.[2] [footnote added] [Galton, 1865, p. 321]

He argued that the open educational system of America (contrasted to the closed, elite system in Britain) had failed to produce very many distinctive products:

America most certainly does not beat us in first-class works of literature, philosophy, or art.... The Americans have an immense amount of the newspaper-article-writer or of the member-of-congress stamp of ability; but the number of their really eminent authors is more limited even than with us. [Galton, 1865, p. 320]

Taken in total, Galton felt that his analyses of national character supported his hereditarian hypothesis.

Galton's second line of attack was to examine the family trees of particularly talented individuals (Galton, 1869/1972). He selected a sample of eminent people by consulting the equivalent of "Who's Who." Throwing out those who had attained **eminence** because of birthright (for example, members of the aristocracy), Galton determined that roughly 1 in 4000 people would turn up on his list of eminent people. He then examined the family trees of his list and found that 1 in 10 had at least one close relative in his eminent category. If hereditary factors were not in place, he argued, this proportion should have been .004, not the .10 he found. This significant difference in occurrence rates was interpreted as additional support for his hereditarian hypothesis.

A third line of evidence for the hereditarian hypothesis was advanced by his **twin studies** (Galton, 1875). Biologically, there are two types of twins: Those who develop from two separate fertilized ova at conception (called fraternal, or *dizygotic*) and those who follow from one fertilized egg (called identical, or *monozygotic*). Monozygotic twins are genetically identical, whereas dizygotic twins are not. Galton reasoned that, in terms of psychological characteristics, monozygotic twins should be more similar than dizygotic twins if his hereditarian hypothesis was correct. He solicited case histories of twins and divided them into two categories: those showing remarkable similarity and those showing divergence. He reasoned that members of the first group were identical twins, therefore providing support for his view.

By the time Galton had mustered these three lines of evidence, he was convinced that his hereditarian hypothesis was correct. In hindsight, it should be noted that he did *not* have any substantive proof of his hypothesis at this point. The analyses of national character were based on nonsubstantive, anecdotal evidence. The finding of

---

[2]*Cant* refers to the use of colloquial speech, described as conventional, trite, and voicing unconsidered opinions.

talent in various families could just as easily have been due to environmental or social-status factors as it was to heredity. Galton also failed to provide any direct evidence that the twins he classified as monozygotic were in fact identical.[3] His reasoning with the twin studies was circular, using similarity of psychological characteristics to classify twins and then using this classification to explain psychological similarity. However, with respect to the then-current criteria of scientific evidence, Galton did present a strong case for the hereditarian hypothesis.

Not unlike John Stuart Mill, Galton advanced his hereditarian hypothesis as an alternative view to the adversarial perspective. The vehemence of his antienvironmentalist rhetoric is revealed in this quotation:

> I have no patience with the hypothesis occasionally expressed, and often implied, especially in tales written to teach children to be good, that babies are born pretty much alike.... It is the most unqualified way that I object to pretensions of natural equality. The experiences of the nursery, the school, the University, and of professional careers, are a chain of proofs to the contrary. [Galton, 1869/1972, p. 56]

Clearly, Galton was convinced of the correctness of his position and was advancing his hereditarian views with considerable rigor and enthusiasm.

THE NATURE/NURTURE CONTROVERSY

By 1870 two great intellectual traditions, the Locke/associationistic/Mill view and the Reid/commonsense/Galton perspective, appeared to be on a crash course. Two radically different views of humanity were emerging—one emphasizing the environmental shaping of individual differences (Mill) and the other emphasizing innate, or constitutional, factors (Galton). Each tradition had its own specific type of evidence demonstrating its worth, each had its own social and political agenda, and each had its own proposed science—ethology for the environmentalists, eugenics for the hereditarians. At root, however, each was basically a value position because substantive evidence in favor of either position was not available.

Galton coined the catchy idiom **nature/nurture** to characterize this debate. The Mill tradition with its environmental emphasis took the nurture side of the controversy. Galton, with his emphasis on heritability of psychological characteristics, was the major spokesperson for the nature side of this great dispute.

Formulating both strong and weak versions of the nature/nurture positions is possible. A weak version of the nature hypothesis would argue that some—perhaps most—psychological characteristics were heritable. It would not deny the impact of environment but would argue that the most profitable place to start investigation would be upon heredity. Reid's original commonsense views would be classified as a weak version of the nature argument. A strong version of the nature position, called **biological determinism** by some, would argue that heritable factors place limits on the levels of achievement possible for an individual or a cultural group

---

[3]Galton did not have the advantage of the techniques of **karotyping**, which allows precise categorization of twin types.

HERMAN®

"I taught him everything I know and
he's still stupid."

HERMAN cartoon © 1990, 1991 Jim Unger. Reprinted with
permission of Universal Press Syndicate. All rights reserved.

(for elaboration and evaluation, see Gould, 1981). Emphasis would be on the proposition that no amount of environmental modification would have a positive impact on a poorly achieving individual or cultural group. Galton's position, as articulated around 1870, was significantly stronger than Reid's.

Mill's was a weak version of the nurture hypothesis because he left room for innate factors in his position in the form of the residuum. He argued that the proper manipulation of the environment would render the residuum relatively small, but he never denied the possibility of heritable characteristics. He did, however, argue for a strong version of the nurture hypothesis on moral grounds, because he felt that the social consequences of the nature position were potentially so negative that politicians must adopt a strong nurture view if they were to improve the lot of the world. A strong version of the nurture argument could be considered an **environmental determinism** in that it would imply that there are limits to human achievement set by the environmental conditions in which the individual is reared.

The foregoing analysis of the development of the nature/nurture controversy from the Locke–Reid debate (perhaps going as far back as Bacon and Descartes) reveals that this controversy had its genesis in one of the earliest attempts to conceptualize humanity from a scientific or positivist perspective. This is important to remember as we work our way through the more modern versions of the nature/nurture debacle. As will be discussed later, it may well be that the controversy itself is an artifact of the manner in which these earlier thinkers chose to conceptualize the human being in the first place.

Another point worth remembering is the strong **ideology** surrounding positions on the nature/nurture dialogue. From its very beginning, this debate was characterized by deep and significant opinions about the best way to organize society. The environmentalists argued for political systems that optimized opportunity for the individual. This ideological position is highly compatible with the founding aspirations of America and contemporary concerns about equal opportunity. The hereditarians felt that political systems should emphasize the maximization of inborn worth. If resources are limited, they should be expended on the most deserving members of the society—those with the inherited capacities to make maximal contributions to the common good. Thus, this confrontation between nature and nurture we see being played out in the psychological testing enterprise during its infancy is more than an academic debate about esoteric models of man. Rather, it is a recapitulation of a broad-based and highly significant social controversy that has astounding implications for the manner in which we ought to organize ourselves. The manner in which society both shaped and was shaped by this discourse is of no small moment for an understanding of the psychological testing enterprise. Without a deep understanding of this ideological aspect of the nature/nurture controversy, much of what has emerged in contemporary psychological testing is almost impossible to understand.

If newspaper polls had been popular in Britain around the 1880s when Galton was formulating his view, the nature side of the controversy would have won out. Not only was this view consonant with the most trendy scientific ideas of the time (for example, Darwin-based analyses, called by some **functionalism**), but the perspective was also congenial to the prevailing social climate. The British Empire was at the height of its power, being lord over great regions of the world. From this domination came a sense of moral and intellectual superiority, which was reinforced by the nature position. The disadvantaged peoples over whom Britain held power were constant testimony to the superiority of the overlords. The inability of the conquered people to attain the intellectual and cultural heights of their conquerors, despite British attempts to structure the environment appropriately, seemed ample evidence that the differences were heritable, not environmental. A stronger version of the nature perspective fit very nicely with the social climate of the times and, as such, was the predominant view of the time.

THE FIRST CALL FOR INTELLIGENCE TESTS

With data in hand and his strongish version of the hereditarian hypothesis gaining increasing popularity, Galton was in the position to bring his social plan, eugenics, to fruition. He determined that such a program should start with the identification of people who had made a worthwhile contribution to society. These eminent people would be encouraged to mate with each other, and the overall human stock would be vastly improved. Galton's was what we might call a *positive* eugenics scheme because his emphasis was on encouraging these eminent people to mate with each other as opposed to discouraging (or preventing) less eminent members from mating.[4]

---

[4]A *negative* eugenics program would emphasize *inhibiting* the mating of socially undesirable individuals. For now, Galton's was predominantly a positive program in that he never advocated anything but an educational program to discourage breeding among the less desirable elements.

One problem, however, emerged. In most societies, a person's eminence was not known until quite late in life—well past childbearing age. To solve this problem, Galton needed a means of determining which members of society were most likely to emerge as eminent in later life. He considered the development of a series of examinations for young adults in which their *natural ability* was assessed. Those with high scores would be encouraged to intermarry. The following extended quotation gives a sense of this line of reasoning:

> Let us then, give reins to our fancy, and imagine a Utopia...in which a system of competitive examinations...had been so developed as to embrace every important quality of mind and body, and where a considerable sum was allotted to the endowment of such marriages as promised to yield children who would grow into eminent servants of the State. We may picture to ourselves an annual ceremony in that Utopia, in which the Senior Trustee of the Endowment Fund would address ten deeply-blushing young men, all of twenty-five years old, in the following terms:—"Gentlemen I have to announce the results of a public examination, conducted on established principles; which show that you occupy the foremost places in your year, in respect to those qualities of talent, character, and bodily vigour which are proved, on the whole, to do most honour and best service to our race. An examination has also been conducted on established principles among all the young ladies of this country who are now of the age of twenty-one, and I need hardly remind you, that this examination takes note of grace, beauty, health, good-temper, accomplished housewifery, and disengaged affections, in addition to the noble qualities of heart and brain. By a careful investigation of the marks you have severally obtained,...we have been enabled to select ten of [the young ladies'] names with the special reference to your individual qualities. It appears that marriages between you and these ten ladies, according to the list I hold in my hand, would offer the probability of unusual happiness to yourselves, and, what is of paramount interest to the State, would probably result in an extraordinarily talented issue. Under these circumstances, if any or all of these marriages should be agreed upon, the Sovereign herself will give away the brides, at a high and solemn festival, six months hence, in Westminster Abbey. We, on our part, are prepared, in each case, to assign 5,000£ as a wedding-present, and to defray the cost of maintaining and educating your children, out of the ample funds entrusted to our disposal by the state." [Galton, 1865, p. 165]

Although this excerpt does have an air of fancifulness, it is highly serious in its intent to outline the virtues of a eugenics plan. Of particular note is the emergence of what sounds suspiciously like *intelligence tests*, although Galton does not use that particular name for them. These examinations would be used to predict eminence and thereby facilitate social decision making. For our purposes, it is important to note that we have the first call for intelligence tests being voiced in a specific social context as a specific way of solving important social decision-making problems from a specific ideological perspective. Not unlike the case histories outlined in Chapter 3, the prototypical intelligence test is being advocated as a means of social decision making. The major difference between the British example and those discussed earlier is the emergence of a scientific rationalization for the recommended procedure. Not unlike the Ojibway or the Chinese, prevailing social resources (that is, science) are being recommended for the solution of pressing social problems in the British context. The convergence of the mathematical techniques pioneered by the likes of Gauss, Quetelet, and Laplace; the prevailing social climate; a view of the person as a self-contained individual; and the long tradition of thinking embedded in the nature/nurture debate—all came together in Britain of the late 1800s to create the first call for psychological tests. The manner in which this call was answered set the foundations for the psychological testing enterprise as it exists today.

GALTON'S EFFORTS TO DEVELOP TESTS

The next step Galton took to enact his eugenics program was the development of a battery of tests, which he hoped would serve the role of predicting eminence. As part of the 1884 International Health Exhibition in London he opened a laboratory where visitors could have themselves measured. Figure 5-1 presents the announcement of this exhibit, which can be seen as the first advertisement for psychological tests. The next to last paragraph in this announcement, which indicates that those wishing to be listed in the registry had to pay a fee, is a clear indication of Galton's

Figure 5-1   An announcement of Galton's laboratory at the International Health Exhibition in 1884.

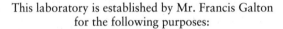

This laboratory is established by Mr. Francis Galton
for the following purposes:

1. For the use of those who desire to be accurately measured in many ways, either to obtain timely warning of remediable faults in development, or to learn their powers.
2. For keeping a methodological register of the principal measurements of each person, of which he may at any future time obtain a copy under reasonable restrictions. His initials and date of birth will be entered in the register, but not his name. The names are indexed in a separate book.
3. For supplying information on the methods, practice, and uses of human measurement.
4. For anthropometric experiment and research, and for obtaining data for statistical discussion.

Charges for making the principal measurements: Three pence each, to those who are already on the Register. Four pence each, to those who are not; one page of the register will thence forward be assigned to them, and a few extra measurements will be made chiefly for future identification.

The superintendent is charged with the control of the laboratory and with determining in each case, which, if any, of the extra measurements may be made, and under what conditions.

(SOURCE: DuBois, 1970, p. 13.)

entrepreneurial spirit. In a sense, this aspect of the anthropometric lab[5] can be seen as the beginning of the business strand of our story wherein the services of those with the tests is seen as financially significant. All the scales invented by Galton culminated in a specific number representing the status of the person on the variable of concern. He developed relatively simple means of measuring the following variables:

Height

Sitting height

Arm span

Weight

Breathing capacity

Strength of pull

Strength of squeeze

Swiftness of blow

Keenness of sight

Memory of form

Color discrimination

Steadiness of hand

A sense of the man and his approach to the practical problems of developing appropriate measurement devices are revealed in this description of the development of an effective means of measuring swiftness of blow:

> It is by no means easy to select suitable instruments for such a purpose. They must be strong, easily legible, and very simple, the stupidity and wrong-headedness of many men and women being so great as to be scarcely credible. I used at first the instrument commonly employed for testing the force of a blow. It was a stout deal[6] [footnote added] rod running freely in a tube, with a buffer at one end to be hit with the fist and pressing against a spring at the other. An index was pushed by the rod as far as it entered the tube in opposition to the spring. I found no difficulty whatever in testing myself with it, but before long a man had punched it so much on one side, instead of hitting straight out, that he broke the stout deal rod. It was replaced by an oaken one, but this too was broken, and some wrists were sprained. [Galton, 1908, p. 246]

After the measurement techniques had been fine-tuned, Galton's exhibition became part of the Health Exposition. After the exhibition closed, Galton moved his laboratory to the Science Museum at South Kensington and continued his fledgling measurement business. All told, he gathered assessments on 9337 individuals from ages 5 through 80 years.

In hindsight, it seems a bit odd that Galton decided to focus on so many physical measurements in his battery. After all, his underlying motivation was to develop

---

[5]**Anthropometry** is the study of human body measurements. Galton called his 1884 exhibit an Anthropometric Laboratory.

[6]*Deal* is a general term for a softwood such as fir or pine.

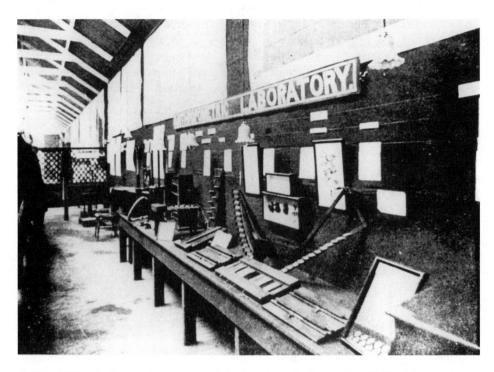

Francis Galton's first anthropometric laboratory at the International Health Exhibition, South Kensington, 1884–1885.

a means of predicting eminence to advance eugenics. You might readily query the utility of measurements of weight and hand steadiness as predictors of future social contribution. Brown and Langer (1990) suggest that the prevailing view was that the manner in which perceptual input was organized was a good indication of an organism's chances of survival, hence the sensory tasks seemed an appropriate choice to Galton. As well, Galton had absolutely no idea of whether or not such physical measurements would suffice for his needs. He was a true pioneer, and there was no previous research that he could use to decide how to proceed. His choice of the previously listed variables was, for the times, sophisticated because they would at the very least produce consistent and relatively error-free measurements.

A MEASURE OF RELATEDNESS: THE CORRELATION COEFFICIENT

With 9337 individuals in his register, each having a minimum of 13 measurements (most had 17), Galton had a considerable challenge in trying to summarize his findings. To establish the nature of the data, he needed a means of determining possible

Table 5-1   Some hypothetical data from Galton's registry

Person	Strength of Pull (SP) (pounds)	Strength of Squeeze (SS) (pounds)	Swiftness of Blow (SB) (inches)	Steadiness of Hand (SH) (seconds)	Memory of Form (MF) (errors)
1	50	31	5.1	10	5
2	60	37	6.2	4	4
3	20	16	1.9	10	8
4	30	34	3.0	9	6
5	40	30	4.0	7	6
6	50	22	4.1	5	4
7	50	37	6.0	1	6
8	30	19	2.1	6	5
9	30	25	3.9	2	7
10	70	22	7.0	9	4
11	20	25	2.9	0	7
12	70	31	6.2	3	3

relationships among the various measurements. For example, to provide a stronger test of his hereditarian hypothesis, it would be helpful if he could demonstrate that the degree of similarity of measurements between genetically similar individuals (for example, brothers and sisters) was greater than between unrelated persons (for example, husbands and wives). As well, his theory predicts that measures such as those gathered in Kensington for identical twins should be more highly related than those for siblings. A means of actually testing this prediction would be useful, and, with his characteristic flair and enthusiasm, Galton set out to invent one.

As he was pursuing his work, measures of relatedness of two variables had not received a great deal of attention in scientific circles. Most of the previous scientific work involved relatively straightforward mathematical relationships such as the fairly simple association between time and the speed of a falling body. In the emerging fields of biological and psychological measurements, however, matters were not quite so simple; relationships were often not perfect. For example, tall fathers might tend to have tall sons, but this was not always the case. Thus, there was need for a means of establishing relationships when they were not perfect—a measure of the *degree* of relatedness was what was needed.

Let's examine a small piece of Galton's data to explore how he proceeded. Table 5-1 presents a set of measurements for 12 hypothetical people on the following tasks:

1. Strength of pull (SP) is the number of pounds respondents could pull toward themselves.

2. Strength of squeeze (SS) is the number of pounds of pressure that respondents could generate by closing their strong hand.

3. Swiftness of blow (SB) is the length of travel in inches of the deal rod in the spring-loaded tube described earlier.

4. Steadiness of hand (SH) is the number of seconds respondents could hold a fat knitting needle in a ¼-inch hole without touching the sides.

5. Memory of form (MF) is the number of errors made in a recognition test for abstract forms.

Figure 5-2 is a graphical representation of the SP and SS data. Each person in Table 5-1 is represented by a point in the figure; thus, there are 12 points in Figure 5-2, one for each person. The position of each person's point in the space of the figure is dictated by their measures on SP and SS. The points are determined by

Figure 5-2 A graphical representation of the relationship between strength of pull (SP) and strength of squeeze (SS), in pounds.

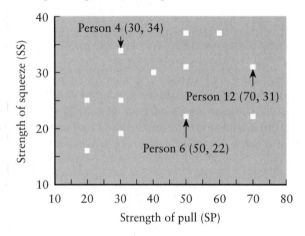

Figure 5-3 Demonstration of how a person's two scores are represented as a point in the space created by the two variables.

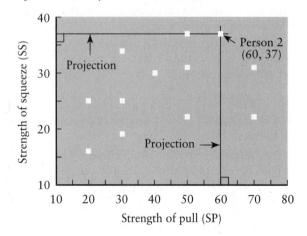

where the projections[7] drawn from the score values intersect. For example, as shown in Figure 5-3, person 2's point is located at the intersection of the projections from 60 on the SP **variable** and 37 on the SS score. The 60 and 37 are person 2's scores on SP and SS, respectively (see Table 5-1). Thus, each person's score is represented as a point in the two-dimensional space marked by the two measurement variables. This format of representing data is called a **scatter plot**.

Galton began to inspect the scatter plots of the large numbers of observations in his registry. He began to notice some interesting differences in the manner in which the data points were distributed within the two-dimensional space. Three examples of the kinds of scatter plots he found, based on our 12 respondents from Table 5-1, are shown in Figure 5-4.

Figure 5-4   Various scatter plots of data in Table 5-1: (a) strength of pull (SP) and strength of squeeze (SS); (b) strength of pull (SP) and swiftness of blow (SB); (c) strength of pull (SP) and steadiness of hand (SH).

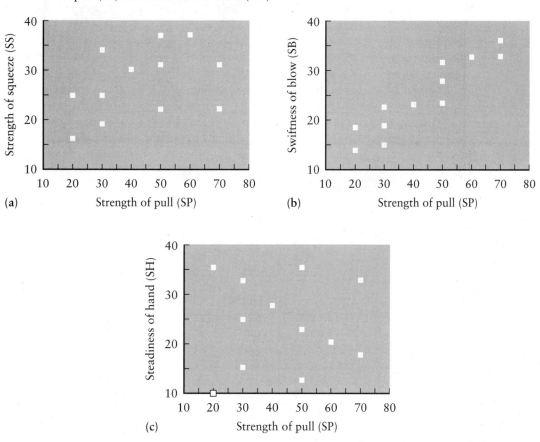

(a)   Strength of pull (SP)

(b)   Strength of pull (SP)

(c)   Strength of pull (SP)

---

[7]Recall that a projection is a line dropped from a point to an axis at a right angle, or 90-degree angle, to the axis.

In comparison with Figure 5-4(a), which is the same plot presented in Figures 5-2 and 5-3, the points in Figure 5-4(b) are more tightly clustered. The points in this middle scatter plot appear to be lining up along a straight line, which runs from the point where the axes intersect out to the edge of the space, at a 45-degree angle. Figure 5-4(b) shows a much more systematic **linear relationship** between the two variables than do either Figure 5-4(a) or 5-4(c). It does not seem unreasonable to suggest that the two variables in Figure 5-4(b) are more related to each other than are the others. Indeed, Galton reached this same conclusion. All he needed to develop was a method of expressing it mathematically.

After several unsuccessful attempts, Galton solicited the help of **Karl Pearson,** an eminent mathematician and fellow eugenicist. The eventual solution to the problem was presented in Pearson (1896). One of the first difficulties to be dealt with was the problem of metric; it appeared to be sensible to convert both variables to some kind of common unit of analysis to facilitate comparison between them. Fortunately, there already was a way of dealing with this in the form of the z score (see Equation 4-3). Why not convert the scores on both variables to z scores so they are more readily comparable? Table 5-2 shows the z scores for the data from Table 5-1, based on Equations 4-1 to 4-3.

Transforming the observations to z scores does not affect the manner in which the points are distributed in the two-dimensional space. This is demonstrated in Figure 5-5, which is a scatter plot of the z scores for strength of pull (zSP) and swiftness of blow (zSB). Notice that the distribution of dots is exactly the same as shown in Figure 5-4(b), which is the scatter plot of the nontransformed scores.

If we examine the z scores for the SP and SB variables in Table 5-2, we notice something interesting—namely, the signs of the z scores appear to match up. That

Table 5-2 z Scores for the data from Table 5-1

		SP	SS	SB	SH	MF
Mean		43.33	27.42	4.37	5.50	5.42
SD		17.75	6.95	1.72	3.55	1.50
Person	1	0.38	0.52	0.43	1.27	−0.28
	2	0.94	1.38	1.07	−0.42	−0.94
	3	−1.31	−1.64	−1.43	1.27	1.72
	4	−0.75	0.95	−0.80	0.99	0.39
	5	−0.19	0.37	−0.21	0.42	0.39
	6	0.38	−0.78	−0.16	−0.14	−0.94
	7	0.38	1.38	0.95	−1.27	0.39
	8	−0.75	−1.21	−1.32	0.14	−0.28
	9	−0.75	−0.35	−0.27	−0.99	1.05
	10	1.50	−0.78	1.53	0.99	−0.94
	11	−1.31	−0.35	−0.85	−1.55	1.05
	12	1.50	0.52	1.07	−0.70	−1.61

Figure 5-5   Scatter plot of the z scores for strength of pull (zSP) and swiftness of blow (zSB).

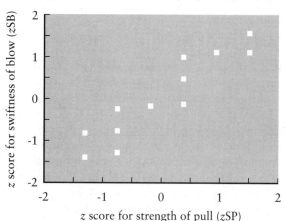

Figure 5-6   Scatter plot between the z scores for strength of pull (zSP) and swiftness of blow (zSB), with projections from the means.

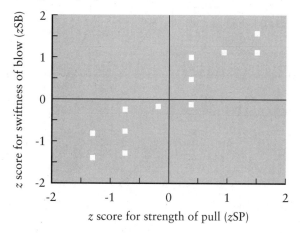

is, for SP and SB in Table 5-2, persons obtaining positive z scores on SP also tend to obtain positive z scores on SB. This means that persons who score above the mean on one variable (because their z score is positive) also tend to score above the mean on the other. Conversely, those who score below the mean on one test (hence have negative z scores) also tend to score below the mean on the other. The only exception to this in Table 5-2 for SP and SB is person 6. This pattern is demonstrated in Figure 5-6, which is the scatter plot divided into four quadrants by running projections from the means of the two variables. Notice how all but one point falls in either the upper-right or lower-left quadrants.

Recall that this scatterplot appears to demonstrate a stronger relationship than those in Figure 5-4(a) and 5-4(c). It could be possible that the number of times the signs match is the measure of relatedness for which Galton was searching. According to Figure 5-4(a) and 5-4(c), SP and SH do not appear to be very well related; this is reflected in the number of times the z scores match because 8 of the 12 pairs of z scores have different signs (or appear in the upper-left and lower-right quadrants).

Pearson went beyond this simple counting the number of times the signs matched and noticed that, in cases of highly related variables, the sizes of the z scores were also important. Persons who scored extremely high on one variable (that is, those who had very high z scores) also tended to have extremely high z scores on the other. Similarly, extreme low scorers tended to get very negative z scores on both variables. To the extent that this did not happen, the degree of relatedness of the two variables was diminished. Inspection of the scatterplots in Figure 5-4, comparing the stronger relationship in 5-4(b) with the others, indicates that this is a reasonable observation. This prompted Pearson to suggest that the best index of the relatedness of two variables emerges if you multiply the z scores for each person and then add them up. By so doing, the matching signs *and* the information inherent in the size of the z scores are preserved because higher z scores multiplied with each other would produce geometrically higher values. This product of the two z scores is called a **cross product**. The obtained sum of cross

Table 5-3   Calculating the correlation between SP and SB for the data in Table 5-1

Person	z Scores for Strength of Pull (zSP)	z Scores for Swiftness of Blow (zSB)	Cross products (zSP × zSB)
1	0.38	0.43	0.16
2	0.94	1.07	1.01
3	−1.31	−1.43	1.87
4	−0.75	−0.80	0.60
5	−0.19	−0.21	0.04
6	0.38	−0.16	−0.06
7	0.38	0.95	0.36
8	−0.75	−1.32	0.99
9	−0.75	−0.27	0.20
10	1.50	1.53	2.30
11	−1.31	−0.85	1.11
12	1.50	1.07	1.61
Sum			10.19

Pearson product-moment correlation $= \frac{10.19}{11} = .93^*$

*As before, with small samples it is appropriate to divide by $n-1$ to provide a more accurate estimate of the correlation. If $n > 30$, divide by n.

products would be an index of the relatedness of the two variables. Only one thing remained, and that was to realize that the size of the sum was a function of the number of cross products that made it up. Therefore, it was necessary to divide the sum by the number of cross products involved, calculating the average cross product of the z scores. This statistic became known as the **Pearson product-moment correlation** and emerged as the answer to Galton's quest for a measure of relatedness. The term *product* refers to the multiplication inherent in calculating the cross product, and the term *moment* was used to indicate that the scores were standardized about the first **moment,** or mean, of the distribution.

Table 5-3 shows the manner in which the Pearson product-moment correlation is calculated for the SP and SB data from Table 5-1. In English this number, which is Pearson's product-moment **correlation coefficient,** is the average cross product between z scores of two variables.

The mathematical formula for calculating the product-moment correlation is as follows:

$$r_{xy} = \frac{\sum_{i=1}^{n} zx_i \cdot zy_i}{n} \qquad (5\text{-}1)$$

where

$$r_{xy} = \text{the correlation between variables } x \text{ and } y$$
$$zx_i = \text{the z score obtained by person } i \text{ on test } x$$
$$zy_i = \text{the z score obtained by person } i \text{ on test } y$$
$$n = \text{the number of pairs of observations } (n-1 \text{ if } n < 30)$$
$$\sum_{i=1}^{n} zx_i \cdot zy_i = \text{the sum of the } n \text{ z-score cross products}$$

Equation 5-1 is simply a shorthand way of representing the procedures outlined in Table 5-2.

The manner in which this statistic reflects the degree of relationship is revealed by calculating the correlation for the variables shown in Figure 5-4. The correlation between strength of squeeze (SS) and strength of pull (SP) was found to be .39, whereas a correlation of .01 was found between strength of pull (SP) and steadiness of hand (SH). The absolute value of the correlation reflects the strength of the relationship, with higher values indicating stronger relationships.

It is mathematically impossible for the value of the correlation to exceed 1.00, so a correlation of 1 indicates a perfect relationship between two variables. There is no systematic relationship between two sets of observations if the obtained correlation is 0. Values in between 1 and 0 reflect the size of the relationship between the two scores—exactly what Galton was looking for.

But there is more to this. The alignment of signs in the calculation of the average cross product is important as well. For example, consider the scatter plot between strength of pull and memory of form of the data shown in Table 5-1. Figure 5-7 presents this plot for the z scores. In this case, 10 of the 12 scores appear in the upper-left and lower-right quadrants, suggesting that most people score low on one variable and high on the other, or vice versa. When calculating the cross products, negative z scores are multiplied with positive ones so that, on average, the cross-product product would carry a negative sign. This is reflected in the calculation of the correlation between these two variables, as shown in Table 5-4.

Notice how almost all the cross products carry negative signs, reflected strongly in the obtained sum of −9.60. Here we have a case where the absolute value of the correlation is high, but it has a negative sign. The minus sign indicates an inverse relationship between the two variables, with high scores on one being associated with low scores on the other and vice versa. The high absolute value indicates the strength of the relationship, albeit in the negative direction. The lowest possible correlation is −1.00, which represents the strongest possible negative relationship, with the absolute value of the correlation reflecting the strength of the association between the two variables.

In summary then, there are two components to consider in the Pearson product-moment correlation: strength and direction. Strength is indexed by the absolute value of the statistic, whereas direction is communicated by the sign. Notice how all of this follows from the manner in which cross products of z scores are calcu-

Figure 5-7   Scatter plot of the z scores for strength of pull (zSP) and memory of form (zMF).

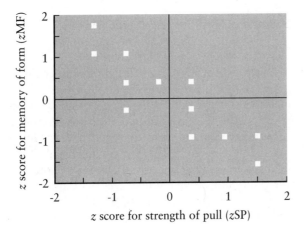

lated. Figure 5-8 (page 160) shows a series of scatter plots that reflect varying degrees of relationship, both negative and positive.

Galton and Pearson were quick to apply the newly invented correlation to the registry data. In many cases, they used observations on pairs of people of varying kinship to calculate the statistic. The data appeared to be compatible with the hereditarian theory. For example, Pearson (1896) reported the correlations shown in Table 5-5 (page 161) as indicating support for his theoretical position on nature and nurture. It was found that the degree of relationship between heights of husbands and wives, who have no genetic relationship to each other, was less meaningful than the relationships of heights between genetically related parent/child pairs. These kinds of data and analyses (and many more presented by Pearson and Galton) were used to argue for the scientific viability of the hereditarian hypothesis. The invention of the correlation coefficient provided the hereditarian cause with a highly sophisticated technique for exploring the validity of its claims.

Table 5-4   Calculating the correlation between SP and MF for the data in Table 5-1

Person	z Score for Strength of Pull (zSP)	z Score for Memory of Form (zMF)	Cross products (zSP × zMF)
1	0.38	−0.28	−0.11
2	0.94	−0.94	−0.88
3	−1.31	1.72	−2.25
4	−0.75	0.39	−0.29
5	−0.19	0.39	−0.07
6	0.38	−0.94	−0.36
7	0.38	0.39	0.15
8	−0.75	−0.28	0.21
9	−0.75	1.05	−0.79
10	1.50	−0.94	−1.41
11	−1.31	1.05	−1.38
12	1.50	−1.61	−2.42
Sum			−9.60

Pearson product-moment correlation $= \frac{-9.60}{11} = -.87^*$

*As before, with small samples it is appropriate to divide by $n-1$ to provide a more accurate estimate of the correlation. If $n > 30$, divide by n.

Figure 5-8   Scatter plots for varying sizes of correlations, both positive and negative.

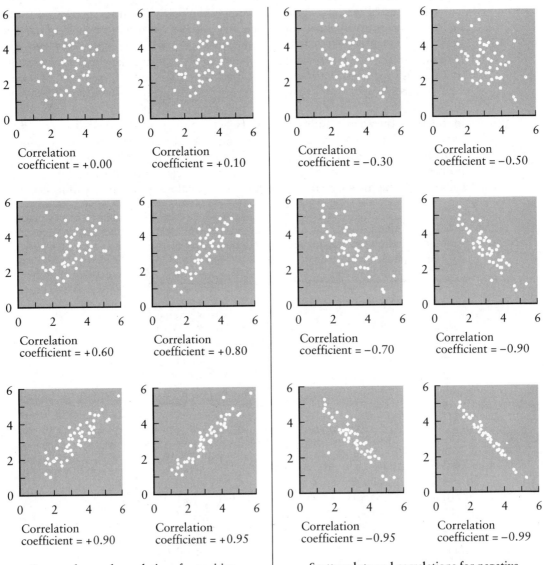

Scatter plots and correlations for positive values of *r*.

Scatter plots and correlations for negative values of *r*.

Table 5-5 A sample of correlation data for standing height

Class	Number of Pairs	Correlation Coefficient
Husbands and wives	200	.09
Fathers and sons	483	.40
Fathers and daughters	452	.36
Mothers and sons	483	.30
Mothers and daughters	452	.28

SOURCE: Pearson (1896, p. 270).

THE REGRESSION LINE

Another thing that Galton noticed in his scatter plots was the manner in which it was possible to place a straight line through the center of the points. This line would pass through the means of the scales but may or may not fall on specific points. It would pass through the middle of the mass created by the dots. Figure 5-9 shows the scatter plot for the z scores of the strength of pull and strength of squeeze from Table 5-1, with this middle line added. Notice how it passes through the intersect of the the means of the scores. Technically, the middle line is called the **regression line**. It is located to minimize the squared distances between the line and the specific points and is thus the best fit straight line for the scatter plot. It is a mathematical convenience that there is a close relationship between the correlation and the tiltedness, or **slope**, of the regression line when the plot is based on z

Figure 5-9 Scatter plot of the z scores for strength of squeeze (zSS) and strength of pull (zSP), with the middle line inserted.

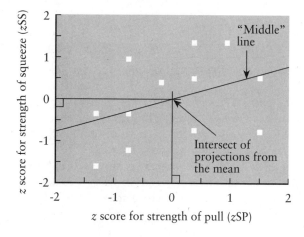

Figure 5-10 Scatter plots with regression lines demonstrating the manner in which the slope of the regression line is associated with the value of the correlation.

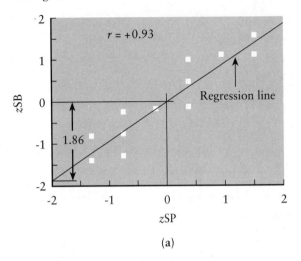

(a)

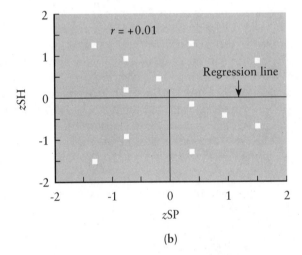

(b)

scores. For **positive correlations**, the regression line runs very close to 45 degrees, whereas the regression line runs perfectly horizontal for zero correlations. This is shown in Figure 5-10, which shows two scatter plots: (a) between z scores for strength of pull (zSP) and swiftness of blow (zSB), for which the calculated correlation (r) is .93; and (b) between z scores for strength of pull (zSP) and steadiness of hand (zSH), for which the calculated correlation (r) is .01.

Notice how the regression line for the high (positive) correlation (a) is almost at 45 degrees from the horizontal. If the correlation was 1.00, the line would be at 45 degrees. The regression line for the zero correlation (b) is almost exactly hori-

Figure 5-11 Scatter plot with regression line of z scores for strength of pull (zSP) and memory of form (zMF).

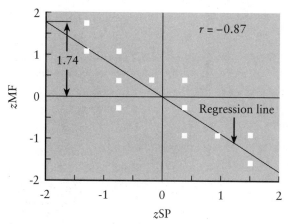

zontal and would be perfectly so if the correlation was equal to 0.00. Correlations between these two extremes would produce regression lines with slopes between 0 and 45 degrees, with the slope being dictated by the size of the correlation.

The slope of a straight line can be empirically estimated by dividing the **rise** (the number of units the line moves up or down) by the **run** (the number of units across for which the rise has been calculated). In the case of the scatter plot in Figure 5-10(a), the line rises 1.86 units for every 2 units one moves across. This can be read from the place in which the regression passes through the vertical axis where $z = -2$. The slope of the regression line, then, is 1.86/2.00 (rise/run) = .93. This is the value of the correlation between the two variables calculated using Equation 5-1. Similarly, the slope for Figure 5-10(b) is .02/2.0 = .01—again the correlation derived from Equation 5-1. In other words, *the slope of the regression line equals the correlation coefficient when the scatter plot is based on z scores.* Because the regression line passes through the means, it becomes possible to locate the regression line knowing only the correlation.

Exactly the same finding holds for **negative correlations** except that the slope of the regression line is negative as the line goes down (that is, shows "negative" rise) as one moves across. This is shown in Figure 5-11 where the correlation between zSP and zMF was calculated to be −.87 using Equation 5-1. For this line, the rise over 2 units is −1.74; thus, the slope of the regression line is −1.74/2.00 = −.87.

This property of the correlation makes it particularly useful for making *predictive statements.* Figure 5-12 is our original scatter plot between SS and SP, with the regression line added per Figure 5-9. We can use this line to predict a person's status on one variable from knowledge of the other. This is particularly handy if we know a group of persons' scores on one test but do not have information about their status on another. It could have happened, for instance, that Galton forgot to

Figure 5-12 Scatter plot of the *z* scores for strength of pull (*z*SP) and strength of squeeze (*z*SS), demonstrating how it is possible to predict one score from the other.

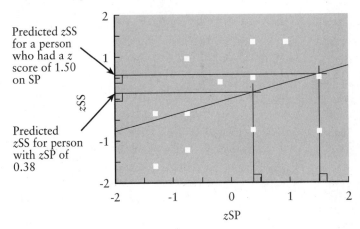

measure SS for a group of his registrants, but he wanted to make a best guess about what scores they would have obtained if he had done so. The manner in which this is done uses the regression line where we make our best guess about a person's SS score by projecting a line from the known SP score. The place where this projection intersects the regression line is then projected over to the SS axis to determine our best guess. In Figure 5-12, the best guess of SS for respondents with an SP of 0.38 is 0.12; similarly, an SP of 1.50 predicts an SS of 0.54. Using the regression line, it is possible to generate estimates of SP scores for all possible values of SS.

Of course, our guesses will, for the most part, never be perfect. A critical aspect of the correlation is that the absolute size of the statistic is an index of how good our predicted scores will be. If the correlation is high, our predicted scores will be good estimates. If the correlation is low or 0, our predicted scores will approximate random guesses. Thus, the absolute size of the correlation reveals how well we can predict one variable from another. This is an immensely convenient index because it allows us to summarize the degree of relationship between variables clearly and succinctly.

CLOSE UP   **Several Correlational Caveats**

The correlation is a wonderfully convenient statistic, which has had astounding impact on the testing enterprise. However, several limitations to this concept must be kept in mind.

Causality. If we took square miles on the North American continent as our unit of analysis and within each unit counted the number of churches and the number of alcoholics in each unit, we might be surprised to find that there was a relatively high correlation between them. Upon finding this statistic, we could be tempted to make some suggestions such as alcoholism causes people to turn to the church or, more ominously, that going to church creates alcoholics. These inferences would be incorrect because we cannot infer cause from the correlation. It is simply a description of the relationship between variables, making no claim to explain why the relationship might exist. In the alcoholic/church example, causal inferences are silly because there is a third overriding factor, population density, that has created the correlation. In wilderness areas, the numbers of churches and the number of alcoholics are nil because there is nobody around. In cities there many of each in every square mile. This would create a set of numbers that, when analyzed by Equation 5-1, would produce a positive correlation. Clearly, trying to link alcoholics with the church would be inappropriate, reflecting the need to decry any effort to infer cause from correlational data. Causality is a very complex notion, and no statistic has the power to establish it. The context in which the statistic is used is the critical factor. Suffice to say, Galton's use of the correlation did nothing to establish the causal status of genetic factors in his registry.

Nonlinearity. The correlation is based on the idea that the best way of describing the relationship between two variables is using a straight line. There are some instances where variables are related in other ways, and exclusive use of the correlation would mask these. For example, a situation might arise where being ambitious leads to enhanced performance in school—but only up to a certain point. Perhaps, if people become too ambitious, their performances decrease. This would emerge as a **nonlinear relationship**, such as the one shown in Figure 5-13, if we measured ambition and school performance. If we calculated a Pearson product-moment correlation between these two variables, the result would be relatively low, and we might infer that there is no meaningful relationship between the variables when in reality there really is one—it just doesn't happen to be linear. Any situation in which there is apt to be an optimal level of performance associated with a given variable is likely to produce nonlinear relationships. Computer programs and statistical techniques are available that permit testing for linearity and nonlinearity (for example, Draper & Smith, 1981, pp. 465–474).

Twisted pears and related phenomena. Sometimes scatter plots demonstrate **twisted-pear** patterns, which are particularly interesting. Figure 5-14(a) provides an example. A correlation calculated on these data would yield a relatively low value,

Figure 5-13
A hypothetical nonlinear relationship.

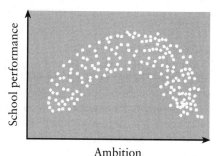

Figure 5-14

Demonstration of the twisted-pear relationship.

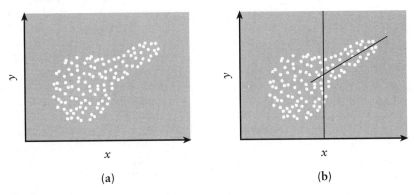

suggesting that making substantive predictions from one variable to the other is not possible. However, this is not exactly true. If, as shown in Figure 5-14(b), the scatter plot is divided into two parts, it turns out that it is possible to make accurate predictions for those who scored high on variable x. For low scorers on x, predictions would be random. This indicates again that you should exercise considerable caution in dealing with correlations because the simple statistic might lead to missing some interesting information.

Normality. As indicated earlier, one assumption underlying the calculation of z scores is that the distribution of scores should be at least approximately normal. In the case of calculating the correlation, *both* variables should be normal—an assumption that masquerades under the impressive name of **homoscedasticity**. Major deviations away from this property create all kinds of aberrations in the accuracy with which a correlation coefficient adequately reflects the relationship between the two variables.

Varieties of correlation. The Pearson product-moment correlation has been derived assuming (at least) interval properties of the scales being used. When these assumptions cannot be met, several other indices of degree of relationship can be used. Included here are (1) **Spearman's rho**, which is used for rank-order (ordinal) data; (2) **biserial correlation**, which is used when one of two continuous variables has been divided into two categories; (3) **point-biserial correlation**, which is used when correlating one continuous with one truly dichotomous variable; and (4) **phi coefficient**, which is used when correlating two truly dichotomous variables with each other (see Ghiselli, Campbell, & Zedeck, 1981, pp. 115–126 for details).

Summary. The Pearson product-moment correlation is an incredibly useful statistic. However, temper its use with considerable caution and care. Resist the temptation of inferring cause, as well as other issues that can lead to the correlation obscuring the existence of substantive and interesting relationships. Additionally, to ensure that the proper technique of calculating the statistic is used, carefully consider the nature of the scales being used. Thus, the correlation, although useful, must also be treated with considerable caution.

GALTON AND THE QUESTIONNAIRE

Another aspect of Galton's contributions to the testing field involved some pioneer work in using **questionnaires**. Galton had developed a considerable interest in the manner in which people used mental imagery in the solution of problems. He believed that some people were very adept at manipulating mental images (pictures in the mind's eye). Others had difficulty understanding what was meant by the term *mental images* and appeared to have had virtually no experience with them. To explore this phenomenon and document the extent of individual differences, Galton developed what appears to have been the first questionnaire. It involved having the respondent visualize a recent scene such as the breakfast table in the morning and then asking questions about the vividness of the images reported. A copy of the original questionnaire is reproduced here. Although this questionnaire does not contain the kinds of structured response alternatives we have come to expect, it is clearly a viable self-report questionnaire. This remarkable man Galton had, indeed, laid the foundations for modern psychological testing.

It is also noteworthy that this chapter, which deals with the philosophical/psychological antecedents of testing, concludes with a highly mathematical presentation of correlation. This is an excellent example of the manner in which the various strands of the narrative of testing interact with each other. The quantitative mindset documented in Chapter 4 was so firmly embedded in Galton's way of thinking that his solution to a psychological problem emerged as clearly mathematical. Galton's approach to measurement, which culminated in discrete observations on specific variables, was not only a reflection of the quantitative worldview but also his quest for a measure of relatedness. By the end of the 19th century, quantitative approaches to psychological problems, especially those involving tests, had become expected and normative. It is against this backdrop that the modern era of psychological testing began its evolution.

The foregoing indicates the substantial nature of Galton's contributions. He pioneered work in the following areas of direct relevance to the study of individual differences:

1. Development of some of the first measures of intellective performance
2. Research attempting to establish the hereditary nature of intellective functioning
3. Pioneering and eventually stimulating the development of the correlation coefficient
4. The use of twins to test genetic hypotheses in humans
5. Invention of the questionnaire
6. Development of the first, large-scale human measurement program

In addition, Galton established the utility of fingerprinting as a means of unique identification of individuals. He also created a legacy in the form of a faculty

Questions on Visualizing, etc.

E—QUESTIONS ON VISUALIZING AND OTHER ALLIED FACULTIES.

The object of these Questions is to elicit the degree in which different persons possess the power of seeing images in their mind's eye, and of reviving past sensations.

From inquiries I have already made, it appears that remarkable variations exist both in the strength and in the quality of these faculties, and it is highly probable that a statistical inquiry into them will throw light upon more than one psychological problem.

Before addressing yourself to any of the Questions on the opposite page, think of some definite object—and consider carefully the picture that rises before your mind's eye.

1. *Illumination.*—Is the image dim or fairly clear? Is its brightness comparable to that of the actual scene?

2. *Definition.*—Are all the objects pretty well defined at the same time, or is the place of sharpest definition at any one moment more contracted than it is in the real scene?

3. *Colouring.*—Are the colours of the china, of the toast, bread crust, mustard, meat, parsley, or whatever may have been on the table, quite distinct and natural?

4. *Extent of field of view.*—Call up the image of some panoramic view (the walls of your room might suffice), can you force yourself to see mentally a wider range of it than could be taken in by any single glance of the eyes? Can you mentally see more than three faces of a die, or more than one hemisphere of a globe at the same instant of time?

5. *Distance of images.*—Where do mental images appear to be situated? within the head, within the eye-ball, just in front of the eyes, or at a distance corresponding to reality? Can you project an image upon a piece of paper?

6. *Command over images.*—Can you retain a mental picture steadily before the eyes? When you do so, does it grow brighter or dimmer? When the act of retaining it becomes wearisome, in what part of the head or eye-ball is the fatigue felt?

7. *Persons.*—Can you recall with distinctness the features of all near relations and many other people? Can you at will cause your mental image of any or most of them to sit, stand, or turn slowly round? Can you deliberately seat the image of a well-known person in a chair and see it with enough distinctness to enable you to sketch it leisurely (supposing yourself able to draw)?

8. *Scenery.*—Do you preserve the recollection of scenery with much precision of detail, and do you find pleasure in dwelling on it? Can you easily form mental pictures from the descriptions of scenery that are so frequently met with in novels and books of travel?

9. *Comparison with reality.*—What difference do you perceive between a very vivid mental picture called up in the dark, and a real scene? Have you ever mistaken a mental image for a reality when in health and wide awake?

10. *Numerals and dates.*—Are these invariably associated in your mind with any peculiar mental imagery, whether of written or printed figures, diagrams, or colours? If so, explain fully, and say if you can account for the associations?

11. *Specialities.*—If you happen to have special aptitudes for mechanics, mathematics (either geometry of three dimensions or pure analysis), mental arithmetic,

Galton's original Breakfast Table Questionnaire.

or chess-playing blindfold, please explain fully how far your processes depend on the use of visual images, and how far otherwise?

12. Call up before your imagination the objects specified in the six following paragraphs, numbered A to F, and consider carefully whether your mental representation of them generally, is in each group very faint, faint, fair, good, or vivid and comparable to the actual sensation:—

A. *Light and colour.*—An evenly clouded sky (omitting all landscape), first bright, then gloomy. A thick surrounding haze, first white, then successively blue, yellow, green, and red.

B. *Sound.*—The beat of rain against the window panes, the crack of a whip, a church bell, the hum of bees, the whistle of a railway, the clinking of tea-spoons and saucers, the slam of a door.

C. Smells.—Tar, roses, an oil-lamp blown out, hay, violets, a fur coat, gas, tobacco.

D. Tastes.—Salt, sugar, lemon juice, raisins, chocolate, currant jelly.

E. Touch.—Velvet, silk, soap, gum, sand, dough, a crisp dead leaf, the prick of a pin.

F. Other sensations.—Heat, hunger, cold, thirst, fatigue, fever, drowsiness, a bad cold.

13. *Music.*—Have you any aptitude for mentally recalling music, or for imagining it?

14. *At different ages.*—Do you recollect what your powers of visualizing, etc., were in childhood? Have they varied much within your recollection?

General remarks.—Supplementary information written here, or on a separate piece of paper, will be acceptable.

Galton's original Breakfast Table Questionnaire (continued).

(Source: Galton, 1883, pp. 255–256.)

position that enabled mathematicians such as Karl Pearson and Ronald Fisher to make important contributions later on. This is an incredibly long line of accomplishments to have stemmed from one man. In fact, Galton's influence was so pervasive in the field that many people also bought into his radically hereditarian stance when they adopted his methodologies. In a sense, Galton's methodological contributions were so intertwined with his eugenic position that it became very difficult to do work in the field and not be considered an hereditarian. Although this may have been an acceptable position at the turn of the century, events such as World War II have convinced most educated people that an eugenic stance such as Galton's is not tenable. Many of the difficulties the testing movement has encountered over its history—particularly in the domain of the nature/nurture controversy—stem from the unthinking acceptance of the philosophical positions embedded in Galton's early work. The manner in which these were played out as the newly emerging field of psychological testing developed is a particularly interesting story, to which we now turn.

Summary

We began our discussion of the psychological/philosophical foundations of testing by examining two grand intellectual traditions: the British associationists and the Scottish commonsense movement. The manner in which these two traditions tackled the thorny questions of the origins of individual differences were seen as particularly important to the development of tests and testing. Associationists were on the environmental side of the nature/nurture controversy, whereas ascendants of the commonsense view, with a smattering of Darwinism, took the side of heredity. Indeed, it was the genius of one man from the hereditary perspective, Francis Galton, that was responsible for laying the foundations of testing as a scientific enterprise. His work on the hereditary aspects of intellective behavior, his involvement in the invention of the correlation coefficient, and his call for intelligence tests to service his eugenics program were all highly instrumental in shaping the manner in which tests would eventually emerge. By the time Galton's work had been presented, the foundations of the modern field of psychological testing had been laid. What remained was for a number of other pioneers, particularly in North America, to grab onto Galton's ideas and shape them to fit the current social and cultural context.

Glossary

anthropometry The study of human body measurements.

associationism An early British school of psychology that emphasized all human knowledge is acquired through the senses. Life starts as a blank slate (*tabula rasa*), and knowledge is written on this slate by virtue of experience. Known variously as British empiricism and championed by the likes of James and John Stuart Mill, associationism was a major school of thought throughout the formative years of formalized psychology.

biological determinism A strong version of the nature side of the nature/nurture debate that argues heritable factors place limits on the potential levels of accomplishment for individuals or cultural groups.

biserial correlation An index of correlation that is used when one of two continuous variables has been divided into two categories.

commonsense tradition An early school of psychology that emphasized the existence of constitutional factors in the acquisition of knowledge. Championed by the likes of Thomas Reid around 1785, this position was adamant in its disagreement with associationism, particularly in its assertion that it was possible to have direct, nonmediated knowledge of the world.

complex idea The combined effect of several strong ideas that have somehow become bound together.

constitutional factor An aspect of psychological makeup that can be attributed to inherited or genetic sources.

correlation coefficient An index of the degree of relationship between two sets of numbers. Developed by Karl Pearson, values approximating 1 demonstrate meaningful relationships between the variables, while the sign of the coefficient reveals whether there is a negative or positive relationship. It is the average cross product of the z scores of the two variables. (See Equation 5-1 for calculation details.)

cross product The result obtained when multiplying two sets of numbers together. Typically, the sets are arranged in rows (or vectors), and the multiplication is done *across* the rows, thus explaining the word *cross*. In the context of calculating the correlation, the product of two z scores is referred to as the cross product.

eminence A term used by Francis Galton to reflect the desirable characteristics of people that should be enhanced in an eugenics scheme. Because eminence was seen to emerge only later in life, the first call for intelligence tests was advanced under the banner of having to identify eminence before it emerged, while a couple was still able to bear children.

empiricist tradition The family of philosophical/psychological positions that assumed all knowledge was obtained via the senses. Associationism was a version of empiricism.

environmental determinism A strong version of the nurture side of the nature/nurture debate that argues there are limits to human achievement set by the environmental conditions in which the individual is reared.

ethology A science proposed by John Stuart Mill that would involve the application of associationism to the study of individual differences.

eugenics The science of enhancing the human race by selective breeding. Positive eugenics schemes encourage able individuals to mate with each other whereas negative schemes discourage mating among less able individuals. Francis Galton was a strong supporter of eugenics and thought to be the originator of the movement.

functionalism A school of psychological thought that places emphasis on the activities and goals of an organism in contrast to, say, the structure of its behavior. Thought that embraces a Darwinian perspective is described as functional.

Galton, Francis The grandfather of psychological testing by virtue of his articulating the need for intelligence tests, stimulation of the development of the correlation coefficient by Karl Pearson, initiation of the first systematic testing program, and invention of the questionnaire. A strong hereditarian, Galton's influence on current testing practices is difficult to overestimate.

homoscedasticity The expected state of affairs if both variables in a scatter plot are normally distributed. Deviation from this property causes the correlation to be an inaccurate estimate of the relationship between the two variables.

idea An integral part of associationism. All knowledge of the world was thought to be mediated by ideas acting on the various empirical sources of information from the world.

ideology The integrated assertions, theories, and aims that constitute a sociopolitical program.

karotyping A complex process that permits the definitive classification of twins as either fraternal or identical.

linear relationship A systematic relationship between two variables that can be described by a straight line. The Pearson product-moment correlation tests for a linear relationship.

mental chemistry The formation of complex ideas that take on properties that are above and beyond those of the constituent ideas making them up.

moment In the present context, this term was used in its technical sense of relating to the mean of a distribution. The term is used in the full name of Pearson's index of correlation to indicate that the scores are standardized about the mean—that is, the mean has been set to 0 by a transformation to z scores. In statistics the first moment is the mean, the second moment is the variance, and the third moment is kurtosis.

nature/nurture controversy A term coined by Francis Galton to describe the conflict between those who felt hereditarian (nature) factors were more important in explaining human behavior and those who favored environmental (nurture) explanations.

negative correlation Where a high score on one variable is associated with a low score on the other, or vice versa. This could be described as an inverse relationship between the two variables and is revealed by a negative value of the correlation coefficient.

nonlinear relationship A systematic relationship between two variables that cannot be described by a straight line. (See Figure 5-13.)

Pearson, Karl A statistician who elaborated Francis Galton's ideas regarding the relationship between two sets of numbers into the Pearson product-moment correlation coefficient. Like Galton's, Pearson's work was in the service of advancing an eugenics scheme.

Pearson product-moment correlation *See* correlation coefficient.

phi coefficient An index of correlation for use when both variables are dichotomous.

point-biserial correlation An index of correlation for use when correlating one continuous variable with one dichotomous variable.

positive correlation Where a high score on one variable is associated with a high score on the other and a low score is associated with a low score. This could be characterized as a direct relationship between the two variables and is revealed by a positive value of the correlation coefficient.

questionnaire A set of questions intended to gain information from respondents who fill in their answers. Francis Galton is credited with inventing the questionnaire.

regression line A straight line located on a scatter plot to minimize the squared distances between the line and all points in the plot. This line, which can be characterized as the best-fit straight line for the two-dimensional space, can be used to make predictions about a person's status on one variable from another. (See Figure 5-10.)

residuum That which is left after all forces of associationism have been removed. In the case of individual differences, the residuum is that which is left after all environmental influences are removed. John Stuart Mill argued that the residuum is very small.

rise The change in vertical distance shown by a line for a given distance. It is used in calculating the slope of a line.

run The length in the horizontal plane over which the rise is calculated. It is used to calculate the slope of a line.

scatter plot A graphical means of displaying the relationship between two variables, by locating each individual in the two-dimensional space marked by the two variables.

slope The deviation of a line in the horizontal plane. It is calculated by dividing the rise by the run. The slope of the regression line equals the correlation coefficient for a regression line fitted in a scatter plot of z scores.

Spearman's rho A measure of correlation for use with ranked (ordinal) data.

tabula rasa An important aspect of the associationistic position used to convey the idea that everyone starts out with no information at birth (a blank slate) and that everything one knows is acquired via the senses and written on the blank slate.

twin studies Pioneered by Francis Galton as a way of determining the extent of genetic differences in humans. Twins with identical genes (monozygotic) should be more similar than twins without identical genes (dizygotic) if the hereditarian perspective is correct. Estimating the amount of genetic variation involved from the sizes of the differences between the two types of twins should also be possible.

twisted pear A scatter plot that looks a bit like a pear. Such plots suggest that it might be possible to make good predictions within a specific range of the predictor. (See Figure 5-14.)

variable A set of numbers or raw scores reflecting one characteristic assessed over a group of individuals.

Suggested Further Reading

Forrest, D. W. (1974). *Francis Galton: The life and work of a Victorian genius.* London: Paul Elek.

> Of the several biographical works on Galton (including a two-volume opus by Karl Pearson), this one is the most accessible. It provides a detailed and thorough overview of the manner in which Galton's thought emerged. It is recommended for students wanting to explore even more fully the contributions of this man.

Fancher, R. E. (1985). *The intelligence men: Makers of the IQ controversy.* New York: Norton.

> This highly readable book provides background for a number of the arguments advanced in this chapter of *The Enterprise.* The first chapter provides a fine overview of the nature/nurture controversy, including some biographical work on John Stuart Mill and Francis Galton, which suggests why each man took the position they did. The conclusion provides a discussion of the contemporary status of the nature/nurture controversy for those who want to see how this debate has played out before we get to it later in the text.

Galton, F. (1908). *Memories of my life.* New York: Ams Press.

> Reading any of Galton's books cited in this chapter will provide a sense of the intellect of this pioneer of the testing movement. In this book, Galton looks back over his career and indicates the contributions that he felt were important. It provides a delightful glimpse into the character of this man, which could only be obtained through Galton's own writing.

Ghiselli, E. E., Campbell, J. P., & Zedeck, S. (1981). *Measurement theory for the behavioral sciences.* New York: Freeman.

> This book provides more detail regarding correlation (Chapter 5) and regression (Chapter 6) than is presented here. While considerably more mathematical than the presentations in *The Enterprise*, this book provides very clear presentations of the techniques. It is recommended especially for those who want more mathematical details regarding these concepts.

Hearnshaw, L. S. (1987). *The shaping of modern psychology.* London: Routledge and Kegan.

> This book provides considerable background on the early British empiricist/association-istic and commonsense movements. It sketches out these and other competing movements in much more detail than is presented here, making it an excellent source for understanding the broader intellectual context in which these traditions flourished.

Discussion Questions

1. Discuss the strengths and weaknesses of the associationistic and commonsense traditions as articulated around 1780.

2. In what way did the concept of "direct experience of reality" differentiate John Locke from Thomas Reid?

3. Discuss the manner in which John Stuart Mill's philosophical position led him to champion the causes of the disadvantaged.

4. If you are familiar with current views about how the brain is organized (for example, Hebb's ideas or connectionism) compare and contrast Mill's ideas of associationism, complex ideas, and mental chemistry.

5. If Francis Galton had a residuum, what would be in it?

6. One of the major contemporary controversies in the domain of personality psychology is the extent to which behavior is a function of the situation in which it occurs or the personal characteristics of the behaver. Indicate why or why not you think this controversy can be traced to the bifurcation between associationistic and commonsense traditions discussed in the text.

7. Discuss the possibility of adapting Darwinesque or functional reasoning to embellish the associationistic or environmental position such as that held by Mill.

8. Briefly describe and then evaluate Galton's case for the heritability of mental characteristics.

9. Critically evaluate both positive and negative eugenics schemes.

10. Discuss the moral implications of both biological and environmental determinism.

11. Select two contemporary politicians and discuss their ideological positions with respect to the Mill–Galton differences presented in the text.

12. Outline why Galton found himself calling for what today we call intelligence tests. Evaluate his actions to bring this about.

13. What aspects of Galton's anthropometric laboratory can be cited as belonging to the business strand of our narrative of testing? Do you think this was important to the development of the testing enterprise? Why, or why not?

14. Indicate why or why not you think that Galton was justified in assuming interval properties for the scales that he used in his registry.

15. Draw the scatter plot between swiftness of blow (SB) and steadiness of hand (SH) from the z scores in Table 5-2. Calculate the correlation between SB and SH and locate the regression line on the scatter plot. Calculate the slope of the regression line. What is the predicted value of SH for a person who scores in the 83rd percentile of SB?

16. Generate two examples each of highly positive, highly negative, and zero correlations. Draw scatter plots to verify your examples.

17. In the text, it was suggested that the number of times the signs of the z scores matched (that is, fell in the upper-right or lower-left quadrants as in Figure 5-6) might serve as a crude index of the relatedness of two variables. What are the weaknesses of this index? Can you think of a case in which this might be an appropriate index?

18. If you have taken any trigonometry, derive an alternative representation of the correlation coefficient. Can you think of any contexts in which this way of representing the correlation might prove helpful?

19. Explain why it is necessary to convert the scores to z scores before it is possible to claim that the correlation equals the slope of the regression line.

20. If you draw the proper regression line onto a scatter plot of two variables—say, x and y—and then proceed to generate a set of predicted values of y following the procedures presented in the text, what will be the correlation between x and the predicted y scores? Why? Will this correlation change as a function of the correlation between the original x and y?

21. Generate two examples that indicate the folly of inferring causality from a correlation. Clearly explain why this is the case.

22. Draw scatter plots for three realistic instances of nonlinear relationships of psychological data. Indicate the manner in which the Pearson product-moment correlation would underestimate the degree of relatedness of the two variables.

23. List the creative contributions that Galton made not only to testing but also to other aspects of the study of humans. Which of these do you think is, today, the most important? Why?

24. In what sense do you think that Galton's ideology is reflected in the apparently neutral techniques associated with the calculation of the correlation coefficient?

25. Critically evaluate Galton and Karl Pearson's attempt to use the correlation to establish the genetic cause of human individual differences.

Part III

The Pioneer Era

By the time Francis Galton had suggested the social need for intelligence tests, the stage was set for the rapid creation of the contemporary testing enterprise. This part of the text documents the explosive development of the field between, roughly, 1900 and 1930—the period during which the basic fabric of contemporary testing practice was created.

Chapter 6 chronicles the context that shaped the emergence of the modern intelligence test, as well as the early tests themselves. This chapter also presents the evolution of the notion of reliability as it relates to the consistency of a given test score for an individual. Taken together, these two concepts were the primary driving ideas behind the appearance of psychological testing, setting the stage for a number of critical developments.

Social events, as well, had a profound effect on the emergence of testing. Chapter 7 documents the impact of World War I on the neophyte testing industry. Tests were applied to a wide range of social problems during the war, and their apparent successes resulted in increasing public awareness of these new technological devices. Several significant concerns about testing, however, surfaced during this time, signaling the beginning of what has become a long-standing love/hate relationship between society and testing.

The most important development during the pioneer era was the emergence of the generic notion of *validity*. Defined as "the extent to which a test measures what it purports to measure," validity has become the single-most important criterion for determining the goodness of a test. Chapter 8 provides detailed information about this idea, the manners in which it was originally assessed, and its genesis.

The topics introduced during this critical time in the development of testing—especially reliability, intelligence, and validity—define the very fabric of testing as it exists today. Although some of the labels may have changed since the mid-1920s, the fundamental ideas forged during these pioneer days establish the basic heart of the psychological testing enterprise.

Chapter 6

Reliability and Intelligence Tests
Two Critical Developments

BACKDROP

In the previous chapters, we traced the developments leading to the emergence of psychological testing as they unfolded in Britain. In addition to this, other very important seeds were being planted in other parts of Europe. As early as 1862, Wilhelm Wundt envisaged the possibility of experimental psychology as a distinct scientific discipline. In 1879 he established the Psychological Institute in Leipzig, Germany, which soon became the focal point for the emergence of the institutional component of psychology. Psychology, as we know it today, was on the verge of becoming a bona fide academic discipline.

A full-blown scientific approach to psychology ran into some difficulties during this period in its development. According to the ideology of the time, the fundamental goal of a true science was the generation of mechanistic, material explanations. Yet day-to-day life and the meanings attributed to our presence on the planet seem to be much more than mechanical or material. An apparent fuzziness to psychological being appears to evade a strictly mechanical account. Perhaps, it was considered, a completely mechanical, scientific psychology would be missing the point, deflecting the investigator from the study of the very thing that makes humans special. In light of this, an undercurrent of resistance to the emerging scientific psychology surfaced. It suggested there must be more than a mechanistic answer. At the extreme, this opposition emerged in a series of idealistic positions attempting to justify the existence of spiritualistic (or at least nonmechanical) factors as part of the psyche. These arguments were clearly at variance with the prevailing scientific dogma, and many debates and conflicts arose. Many scholars found themselves in the uncomfortable situation of holding to one position (that is, **materialism**) at work and another (that is, **idealism**) at home. An escape from this conflict was needed.

THE NEW PSYCHOLOGY

At the start of the 20th century, a **new psychology** which provided exactly the escape needed by many scholars of the time, arose in the United States. This new offering provided an opportunity to resolve personal conflicts concerning science and religion, materialism and spiritualism, as well as determinism and free will.

The biography of William James, generally considered to be the father of modern American psychology, is particularly illustrative of how the new psychology emerged and the solutions it offered its proponents (see Bjork, 1983). James abandoned his early study of art and adopted the mantle of scientific inquiry around 1860. As the implications of the mechanistic position became clear to him, James became severely depressed. The idea of a completely determined world in which free will and moral responsibility had no place was cause for much distress. He had a great fear that "not a wiggle of our will happens save as a result of physical laws" (cited in Leary, 1987, p. 317). Equally depressing, though, was the possibility of giving up the opportunity of becoming a scientist. To use the current vernacular, James, as well as many of his scholarly colleagues, was between a rock and a hard place.

James, however, found a solution: He defined the discipline as a science dealing with the operations of the mind. This solved his dilemma because constructs such as free will and moral responsibility were operations of the mind and thereby amenable to scientific study. Over time James developed "a scientific outlook that sported a 'crack' for freedom and hence for meaning in life" (cited in Leary, 1987, p. 317). Lying somewhere between the "seductive" extremes of idealism and materialism, the new psychology left room for both religious feeling and scientific interests. By using the latter to study the former, idealistic constructs such as free will were salvaged from scientific banishment. The dilemma had been resolved!

James fine-tuned his new ideas as a lecturer at Harvard, and his views became immensely popular. Students petitioned the university to have James's lectures repeated for the general student body. The new American psychology, which clearly contains the blueprint of the contemporary discipline, had been laid. This position (1) offered a compromise between the materialistic and idealistic extremes, (2) reified the extant strength of the scientific view, and (3), perhaps most importantly, was immensely popular with students and eventually with faculty.

JAMES McKEEN CATTELL

Although James's views did not directly affect the emerging field of psychological testing, they are demonstrative of the transitions being experienced by the emerging discipline of psychology. The eventual synthesis of this development in the field of testing occurred in the scholarly achievements of another American, **James McKeen Cattell**.

After earning an undergraduate degree at Lafayette College, Cattell went abroad to study in 1880. In 1883 he worked with Wundt in Leipzig and was very successful, publishing a large number of studies of human reaction time. Of particular interest to this young American was the possibility of using reaction time as a means of measuring individual differences. He found some small but consistent individual differences in his data, which interested him considerably. Wundt attempted to discourage Cattell from considering the individual level of analysis because the quest of the emerging psychology was the discovery of general rules or

James McKeen Cattell (1860–1944).

laws that applied to everyone. Cattell held onto this interest, bringing it to fruition several years after obtaining his doctorate under Wundt in 1886.

Cattell spent 2 years at Cambridge where he encountered Galton's work. In 1888 he was appointed professor of psychology at the University of Pennsylvania where he stayed for 3 years before moving to Columbia University. He established a psychological laboratory, which he administered for 26 years. This laboratory continued the great tradition introduced by Galton in its quest for a workable approach to human measurement.

Cattell's Ten Basic Tests

In a landmark paper, Cattell (1890) coined the term **mental test** and presented the details of his ongoing research project. His program consisted of a basic set of ten mental tests intended for the general public, as well as an extended battery of 50 for use with university students. Cattell's ten basic mental tests, which are listed in Table 6-1, were highly concerned with sensory and physiological

Table 6-1   Cattell's ten basic tests

Test	Description
Dynamometer Strength	The measure of the strength of the respondent's hand squeeze.
Movement Speed	The time required for the respondent to move a hand through a distance of 50 cm, starting from rest.
Two-Point Discrimination Threshold	The distance between two caliper points that the respondent could discriminate as two distinctive points.
Pressure-Pain Threshold	The force required on a rubber-tipped needle before the respondent reported pain.
Just-Noticeable-Difference Threshold for Weights	The weight difference required for the respondent to discriminate boxes of varying weights.
Reaction Time	The measure of the respondent's reaction time to an auditory tone.
Color Naming	The respondent had to name a series of color patches as rapidly as possible, and total time was recorded.
Size Estimation	The respondent had to place a sliding line as close as possible to the middle of a 50-cm-long piece of wood.
Time Judgment	The respondent had to estimate 10 seconds of elapsed time.
Memory for Letters	The number of letters the respondent could recall after hearing a random list.

SOURCE: Cattell (1890).

processes, indicating Galton's influence. The tests were also represented on interval scales such as weight, time, and length. In fact, Galton commented on Cattell's set of ten tests:

> One of the most important objects of measurement is hardly if at all alluded to here and should be emphasized. It is to obtain a general knowledge of the capacities of a man by sinking shafts, as it were, at a few critical points. In order to ascertain the best points for the purpose, the sets of measures [Cattell's] should be compared with an independent estimate of the man's powers. We thus may learn which of the measures are the most instructive. [Cattell, 1890, p. 139]

This is a particularly important passage because it presages the manner in which the testing field would eventually develop. What Galton had suggested was the generic methodology for the establishment of validity—namely, correlating a test with a specific criterion and using the size of the correlation to make inferences about the meaning of the test score.

Immediately following the publication of the 1890 paper, an increasing number of investigators enthusiastically endorsed mental testing, and laboratories and extensive databases began to appear in many American universities—all guided by Cattell's fundamental assumptions. Cattell thought that complex mental events were simply the sum of the simpler kinds of processes (then called *faculties*). In other words, knowing an individual's status on a series of fundamental faculties, one ought to be able to construct a model of how the person would perform on a more complex test that involved the combining of these basic attributes.

In an American Psychological Association (APA) symposium on testing just prior to the turn of the century, Jastrow, Baldwin, and Cattell (1898) offered a set of general desiderata for mental tests, which are summarized in Table 6-2. This list appears to be the first published compendium of the characteristics of the ideal mental test. Notice that there is concern that the tasks have practical relevance (item 3 in Table 6-2) and that persons with special experience should not be advantaged (item 4). According to Cattell's list, tests should be simple, short, and inexpensive (items 5–7). Clarity about the attribute being measured is recommended (item 2) and only one thing should be measured at a time (item 1). This is a very

---

Table 6-2 Desiderata for mental tests

1. Tests should measure a single attribute rather than many at once.
2. One must be clear about what is being tested (pilot data is recommended).
3. All assessment must be related to activities of daily life.
4. Efficiency on the test must not be determined by experience (the use of "sense impressions unfamiliar to all" is recommended).
5. Tests should be simple, easy, and intelligible.
6. Tests should be as short as possible.
7. Testing should involve simple apparatus that is cheap and efficient.

SOURCE: Jastrow, Baldwin, and Cattell (1898, pp. 173–174).

useful list because it clearly articulates the form expected of tests as they are being pioneered. The pragmatic emphasis and concern for cost and simplicity reflect prevailing values of the time.

FACULTY PSYCHOLOGY FALTERS

Matters did not go as well as the researchers would have liked. Rather than unlocking the secrets of the operations of the mind, these mental tests faltered, and soon researchers began to question their usefulness. One of Cattell's graduate students, Clark Wissler, conducted a study representative of the disillusionment felt in the field of **faculty psychology**. He obtained mental-test scores and academic grades for more than 300 university and college students (Wissler, 1903). This study was also one of the first to use Pearson's (1896) new method of calculating the correlation coefficient.

Wissler's results were devastating to the idea that you could explain complex events from a knowledge of basic faculties. For example, class standing correlated –.02 with reaction time, .02 with color naming, –.08 with dynamometer strength, and .16 with memory for letters. This last correlation was the highest obtained for the entire matrix of interrelationships between the ten basic tests and the academic-performance measures. In addition, correlations between the tests themselves were disappointingly low and in seemingly random directions. The only reasonable relationships were obtained within the academic courses, which showed a range from .30 (literature and French) to .75 (Latin and Greek). The upshot of this study was the realization that only academic performance predicts academic performance. The idea of faculties, as measured by the ten basic tests, had been put to an empirical test and failed miserably. The practical usefulness of the tests themselves was also questioned by this finding, indicating that the neophyte testing enterprise was running into significant difficulty.

CLOSE UP   **Whatever Exists, Exists in Some Amount, and Anything That Exists in Amount Can Be Measured**

The forward advance of testing was not to be stopped by findings such as Wissler's. A number of highly creative and energetic psychologists were beginning to pave the way for the eventual emergence of tests. Perhaps the most important of these psychologists was **Edward L. Thorndike**, who was to become one of the most influential figures in the eventual adoption of tests into the educational system.

Influenced by the views of James and Cattell in his earlier education, Thorndike earned his Ph.D. degree at Columbia University in New York City. His doctoral thesis became a classic in studying associationism in animals and was eventually published under the title *Animal Intelligence* (Thorndike, 1898). After graduation he was forced to shift his interests toward education because job opportunities in animal psychology were rare. After several years in Cleveland, he returned to Columbia University and became part of the growing Teachers College.

From the first of his many books (for details, see Joncich, 1968), his integration of the quantitative, positivist perspective into education was clear:

Edward Lee Thorndike (1874–1949).

> The chief duty of serious students of the theory of education to-day is to form the habit of inductive study and learn the logic of statistics. Long after every statement about mental growth made in this book has been superseded by a truer one the method which it tries to illustrate will still be profitable and the ideals of accuracy and honesty in statistical procedure by which I hope it has been guided will still be honored. [Thorndike, 1900, p. 164]

You can gain a sense of the manner in which Thorndike accords the *methodology* of psychology ascendance over the content from this quote. His popular text in educational psychology was even more explicit: "We conquer the facts of nature when we observe and experiment upon them. When we measure them we have made them our servants" (Thorndike, 1903, p. 164). In 1904 he published a text, *Mental and Social Measurements*, that presented, among other things, the subtleties of the Pearson product-moment correlation to the growing numbers of teachers and administrators interested in testing (Thorndike, 1904). He also discussed current thoughts about measures of central tendency, variability, the normal curve, and the measurement of change.

Until his death in 1949, Thorndike proferred many diverse contributions. Included here were researches into heredity and individualism, a comprehensive theory of learning, many textbooks, and even some preliminary work on teaching machines. Throughout all of this, he was a constant advocate of quantification. His most famous quotation was uttered during the opening exercises for Columbia University in 1921, when he said "Whatever exists, exists in some amount," thereby equating the quantitative worldview with the very idea of existence. Shortly thereafter, another educational psychologist, William McCall, added "Anything which exists in amount can be measured" (1922, pp. 3–4), thereby completing the equation of measurability with existence—a truly astounding epigram that captures the zeal and enthusiasm of the emerging field of educational psychology and testing during this pioneer era.

THE EMERGENCE OF RELIABILITY

The failure of faculty psychology created a number of problems for the emerging testers, however, it was not without its gains. Attempts to make sense of the failure to document test-criterion correlations in studies such as Wissler's forced greater attention to certain aspects of measurement. In this regard, a British scholar, Charles Spearman, is particularly noteworthy.

Spearman pointed out that the inconclusive results in work such as Wissler's could be due to **errors of observation.** He argued that the correlations between tests and other criteria could be seriously lowered because errors had a dramatic effect on the correlations and that the results of studies such as Wissler's were misleading.

In attempting to argue this position, Spearman suggested that a particular test ought to be administered twice. It would then be possible to generate a correlation of the test with itself. That is, the researcher could calculate a correlation between the first and second set of scores using exactly the same methods presented in Chapter 5—the only difference being that the two observations for each person were his or her scores on two successive administrations of the same test, rather than on two different variables. Spearman reasoned that if there were no errors of measurement, the correlation ought to be perfect. That is, in the error-free case, it should be possible to make a perfect prediction about the score a person would obtain on the second testing knowing only the first-session score. If the correlation was less than 1.00, there is clear evidence of measurement error. The correlation of a test with itself, calculated over two administrations of the test, provides an index of the degree of error in the tests with values approximating 1.00, suggesting very little error in the score.

Charles Spearman

Table 6-3   Hypothetical data to indicate Spearman's ideas about errors of observation

Respondent	PPT1	PPT2	Random Number (ran)	PPT1 +ran	PPT1 +(5·ran)	PPT1 +(10·ran)
1	5	6	−0.036	4.964	4.820	4.640
2	6	7	0.523	6.523	8.615	11.230
3	2	3	−0.066	1.934	1.670	1.340
4	4	5	0.328	4.328	5.640	7.280
5	4	5	−0.696	3.304	0.520	0.000*
6	5	6	0.230	5.230	6.150	7.300
7	5	6	−0.015	4.985	4.925	4.850
8	3	4	0.445	3.455	5.275	7.550
9	3	4	−0.220	2.780	1.900	0.800
10	8	9	0.361	8.361	9.805	11.610
11	2	3	−0.976	1.024	0.000*	0.000*
12	7	8	0.207	7.207	8.035	1.035
13	6	7	−0.359	5.641	4.205	0.000*
14	2	3	0.253	2.253	3.265	1.265
15	8	9	−0.444	7.556	5.780	0.000*

*Negative values were set to 0 because a nonpositive PPT is impossible.

To demonstrate this, Table 6-3 presents some hypothetical data from Cattell's laboratory. The data presented are for pressure pain threshold (PPT)—the number of pounds of pressure, from a thumbscrewlike device, a respondent would tolerate before experiencing pain. The second column of this table presents the data for session 1 (PPT1). The third column presents data from a second session where the same 15 respondents agreed to take the test again (PPT2). This can be considered a **test/retest design**. These two data columns are not identical to each other, but they do appear to be related.

If we follow the procedures from Chapter 5 and calculate the correlation between PPT1 and PPT2, we find a result of 1.00. This means that we can make a perfect prediction about PPT2, given a person's score on PPT1 (or vice versa). This is the case of error-free measurement. If you look closely at PPT2, you will see that the data were generated simply by adding the constant 1 to each value of PPT1.[1] Perhaps, in this case, the respondents' pain tolerances increased for the second testing session but at an equal rate for all respondents. Under these conditions, Spearman would conclude that there were absolutely no errors of observation in the data.

Deviations from 1.00 occur if error is added. For example, the fifth column of Table 6-3 (labeled PPT1 + ran) was constructed by adding a small amount of random error to PPT1. In this case, the correlation with PPT1 is .98, indicating that our value has dropped from a perfect relationship—although it is still pretty high.

---

[1]Of course, it is not possible to know what constants might be involved with real data. A constant has been added here just to give you a sense of how data might look in the unlikely situation of perfectly consistent or error-free observation.

What happens if we add a bit more error? To answer this question, the random number is multiplied by 5 and added to PPT1 in the next column, and any negative values set equal to 0 [labeled PPT1 + (5 · ran)]. The obtained correlation with PPT1 is .77, indicating that the increased error has resulted in the correlation dropping a fair distance from 1.00. Finally, the random error is multiplied by 10 and added to PPT1 [labeled PPT1 + (10 · ran)], and the resulting correlation between PPT1 and this high-error score is .55. This demonstration indicates that the more error that is added to the second measurement, the lower the correlation between the two scores becomes—which was Spearman's fundamental point. The size of the test/retest correlation, then, is an index of the extent to which errors of observation are involved, with values approximating 1.00 indicating the absence of errors.[2]

Spearman called this test/retest index of consistency, or error-freeness, the **reliability** of a measure. Perfectly reliable measures show test/retest correlations of 1.00, whereas lower values indicate the presence of observational errors: the lower the correlation, the greater the amount of error in the score. Reliability, then, is the consistency of a given score, and Spearman provided one way of measuring this—the test/retest correlation. In later times, this became known as **test/retest reliability**.

CLOSE UP | **Correction for Attenuation**

As you might expect, reliability is typically less than 1.00. Spearman argued that this was the reason why the correlations of tests with other variables were lower than expected, thereby explaining results such as those found by Wissler. He provided a mathematical rationalization of his argument in terms of a concept he called **correction for attenuation**. He suggested that any observed test-criterion correlation was only an estimate of the "true" correlation and that reliability was an important aspect of the accuracy of this estimate. Equation 6-1 shows the general form of this notion for the correlation between two variables, x and y:

$$R_{xy} = \frac{r_{xy}}{\sqrt{r_{xx} \times r_{yy}}} \qquad (6\text{-}1)$$

where

R_{xy} = the true correlation between x and y, described as "corrected for attenuation"

r_{xy} = the observed correlation between x and y

r_{xx} = the (test/retest) reliability of x

r_{yy} = the (test/retest) reliability of y

---

[2]In practice, gaining an estimate of the amount of error in a specific score, as suggested in Table 5-3, is never possible. This has been presented here to demonstrate the idea that increased error reduces the test-retest correlation, not to convey the way things are actually done in the field. Techniques that incorporate random fluctuations into a mathematical formulation to explore its properties are called **Monte Carlo simulations**.

Any true correlation (R_{xy}) is a function of the observed correlation (r_{xy}), divided by the square root of the product of the reliabilities of the two variables making up the correlation.

An observed test-criterion correlation equals the true correlation value if and only if both x and y are perfectly reliable. That is, the only case where the true correlation between x and y equals the observed (empirically derived) correlation is in the unlikely case that both x and y are perfectly reliable. Equation 6-2 expresses this in mathematical terms:

$$R_{xy} = \frac{r_{xy}}{\sqrt{r_{xx} \times r_{yy}}} = \frac{r_{xy}}{\sqrt{1.00 \times 1.00}} = r_{xy} \qquad (6\text{-}2)$$

In cases where the reliabilities of the two measures are less than 1.00, the effect of unreliability is quite marked. For example, in Wissler's data the correlation between class standing (x) and memory for letters (y) was .16. If both measures had reliabilities of .8, the best guess for the value of the true correlation is .20 [that is, .16/(.8) from Equation 6-1]. If the reliabilities were .5, the best guess of the true value would be .32 [that is, .16/(.5) from Equation 6-1]. In postulating the notion of correction for attenuation, Spearman argued that measurement errors cumulate geometrically because the reliabilities of the two measurements depart from unity. Thus, the size of virtually all test-criterion correlations, such as those observed by Wissler, are severely limited by the reliabilities of the two measures. This cumulative effect of test error was thought to be one of the reasons why Wissler (and others) failed to demonstrate high test-criterion correlations.

Spearman suggested that variations in the manner in which tests were administered, differing conditions of the day of testing, and a host of other factors contribute to the lowering of reliability estimates. In 1907 he introduced the notion of reliability to the emerging testing field, and it was soon adopted as a foundational concept. To understand the size of obtained correlations, it became necessary to have information about the reliability, or error-freeness, of the measures being correlated.

The issue of how long to wait between administrations for the calculation of test/retest reliability is problematic. If the two tests are administered too close together, memory for specific answers could artificially inflate the test/retest correlation. On the other hand, waiting too long between administrations could decrease the correlation because those tested may actually grow or change on the variable being measured. The nature of what is being measured will, for the most part, dictate how long it is possible to wait between administrations, with normal practice suggesting that an interval of a few weeks is sufficient.

The test/retest approach to estimating reliability has some inherent limitations. For example, in a series of tests such as Cattell's, respondents might benefit differentially from practice, with some showing greater gains than others on the second administrations. This would lower the test/retest correlation inappropriately, indicating that this approach to estimating reliability is problematic. Other limitations of the test/retest approach appear when testing is extended to deal with other domains. Several examples are the following:

1. Tests of ideas, which by definition change as a function of time (for example, depression), are problematic. Here the respondent may show genuine change between test administrations, thereby artificially reducing the size of the test/retest correlation.

2. In some situations, memory for answers given during the first administration of the test may affect performance on the second administration, thereby inappropriately inflating the size of the test/retest correlation. This may have drastic effects on test/retest correlations if the test is short or the items are particularly memorable.

3. The second administration of very long tests, which may be boring to the respondent, poses problems because motivation to cooperate and pay attention could diminish on the second administration, thereby reducing test/retest estimates of reliability.

These three situations indicate that, although useful, the test/retest approach to establishing reliability has a number of significant limitations. Some of the solutions to these problems will be discussed when the idea of reliability is elaborated (Chapters 8 and 11).

The introduction of reliability and the test/retest approach to estimating it did not prevent the decline of faculty psychology—it continued to lose credibility within the psychological community. However, the notion of reliability did contribute to a framework that eventually supported some very critical developments to follow. Reliability has become one of the two most important concepts used today to determine if a test is a good one or not. Of note here is that the fundamental idea of reliability depended on the availability of the correlation coefficient. If Pearson's statistic had not been available, the notion of reliability and its estimation in the test/retest design would not have likely emerged, at least in the form it did. The introduction of reliability and its use of the correlation coefficient were advanced initially to solve a specific problem being faced by the adherents of faculty psychology.

AFTER FACULTY PSYCHOLOGY

While the failure of faculty psychology was being played out, the new discipline was evolving. A considerable amount of persuasion and "arm twisting" was evident in the messages being sent out as the new psychology established itself. These approaches to convincing others to accept a particular position, called rhetoric, were strong during this period. Leary (1987) outlines a number of strategies used by psychology's pioneers. These included (1) personal advocacy of a number of early psychologists, including James and Cattell; (2) the active debunking of alternative views; and (3) the gradual appropriation of a wide range of phenomena under the umbrella of the new science. Once the groundwork for the new psychology had been laid, Leary suggests that:

> ... they were now ready to perform for the public, and especially for the administrators, officials, and various interest groups who could provide support

for the New Psychology. But to win positive reviews they had to keep in mind that actions speak louder than words—that their new language would be more persuasive if presented within the context of dramatic action. [Leary, 1987, p. 322]

Describing the years between 1904 and 1917, Camfield (1973) suggests that the need went beyond the necessity to talk about potential achievements: "... they were less content to base their appeal for general social approval upon the promise of ultimate scientific achievements and increasingly anxious to render their science of practical value" (p. 71). In this context, the failure of the mental-test movement, as revealed in research such as Wissler's, was particularly untimely. Most practitioners of the day were well aware of the potential power that the discipline could gain if it were possible to measure aspects of mental life and use these to serve various social ends. That the first attempt to do this (faculty psychology) had failed was cause for great concern within the emerging field.

It also happened that the social conditions of the times created a domain where the possibility of dramatic action was greatly enhanced. The **Progressive Era** was under way in the United States, and the application of scientific technology to human problems became accepted and sought after. Education was a particularly appropriate domain in which the new psychology could demonstrate its utility. For example, there was a sevenfold increase in the number of students in primary and secondary schools between 1880 and 1920, indicating the extent of the social need to which psychology could address itself. In addition, the United States was in the throes of a significant wave of immigration, particularly from Europe. In the decade following 1905, over 10 million immigrants arrived on U.S. shores. This represents a full 10% of the 1914 population (Burgess, 1960). The problems of educational placement and aspects of the social reaction to these new arrivals also prepared the way for the eventual demonstration of psychology's usefulness.

THE FRENCH CONNECTION: ALFRED BINET

The increase in education and the immigrant population created a context that was ripe for the new discipline to demonstrate its social worth. All that was needed was some sort of breakthrough that would catapult the new psychology into the vortex of these pressing social problems, rescuing it from the failure of faculty psychology. The breakthrough did come but from an unexpected source. The seeds were sown in France under the creativity and advocacy of the psychologist **Alfred Binet**. His work and its adaptation to the American context emerged as psychology's most dramatic action—a breakthrough that indeed put the new discipline on the map.

Binet was a psychologist of prodigious interests, becoming involved in a wide range of issues throughout his career (see Wolf, 1973, for a biography). His most enduring contribution involved the design of a technology for differentiating between normal and slow students in the classroom situation. The goal of this effort was to identify students who were having difficulties with learning and moving them to special classes, thus providing them with necessary remedial help and relieving the regular classrooms of these slower students. Binet's solution, although

Alfred Binet (1857–1911).

simple, was brilliant and was the answer for which the postfaculty psychologists in North America were looking. He sampled carefully from the kinds of activities necessary for adequate performance in school, such as being able to point to objects in pictures, follow commands, do simple arithmetic, generate rhymes, and give a précis of the main themes of a read passage. Each activity was rendered as a brief test in which pupils were given the opportunity to demonstrate whether they could perform the task. Some tests were simple tasks that involved only one activity (for example, copying a square), whereas others involved multiple trials of the same task (answering a series of comprehension questions). In the latter case, a preset number of trials had to be answered correctly before credit was given for the task. Regardless of the number of trials involved, each task was called a **subtest**, which was scored as either correct or incorrect.

Once he had established these tasks, Binet administered them to children of varying ages. He then used these data to assign the various tasks to age levels. To demonstrate how he proceeded with this, Table 6-4 presents some hypothetical data of the kind generated by Binet.

In the Copies a Square subtest, pupils were shown a predrawn square and asked to copy it with a pencil onto a piece of paper. If the child's drawing was accurate, it was scored as correct. As shown in the first column of Table 6-4, this task was presented to groups of children between the ages 3 and 15 years, and the data presented in the second column represent the percentage of each age group that got the subtest correct. Binet looked for subtests that showed a relatively regular increase in proportion correct as a function of age, such as the data shown for Copies a Square. He then classified the subtest at a specific age by adopting the cri-

Table 6-4   Data of the type used by Binet to assign various subtests to age groups.*

Age (years)	Copies a Square	Counts 20 to 0	Names 60 Words
3	3	0	0
4	34	2	0
5	69†	4	0
6	88	33	12
7	95	44	3
8	98	79†	16
9	100	82	29
10	100	92	34
11	100	98	47
12	100	100	72†
13	100	100	89
14	100	100	92
15	100	100	94

*Data points are the percentage of a specific age who got the subtest correct.
†Age at which the subtest was classified.

terion that between two-thirds and three-quarters of the pupils at that age should be able to pass the subtest. The Copies a Square subtest was classified as being at the 5-year-old level by this criterion. The majority of 4-year-old students got the item incorrect, whereas the majority of 6-year-olds got it correct. Thus, the average 5-year-old would pass this subtest.

The Counts 20 to 0 subtest in Table 6-4 involved asking students to count backward from 20 in steps of 1 (20, 19, 18, 17 ... 0). The data suggested that this was an 8-year-old's task, using Binet's criterion. Pupils were also asked to list 60 different words in 3 minutes, which is the Names 60 Words subtest in Table 6-4. Those who could do this were scored as correct. The data indicated that this was a 12-year-old's task.

Figure 6-1 represents graphically the data from Table 6-4. Notice how each subtest shows a definite graduation from low to high percentages of pupils getting the subtests correct (with some minor exceptions). This form of representation has since become known as an **item-operating characteristic**; this provides a rapid glimpse of the manner in which a given subtest is performing as a function of a variable of interest, which in the case of Figure 6-1 is age. A horizontal line drawn from 75% on the vertical axis will intersect with the item-operating characteristic curves at (roughly) the age at which the subtest would be classified by Binet's criterion.

In Binet's groundbreaking work, he developed a set of subtests for the entire age range. There would be a set of subtests that 9-year-olds could pass, whereas 8-year-olds could not and so on. When these subtests were administered to a new set of pupils, there would be some overlap, such that very bright 8-year-olds would be

Figure 6-1   Graphical representation of the data from Table 6-4. The vertical lines represent the age levels at which the subtest was classified.

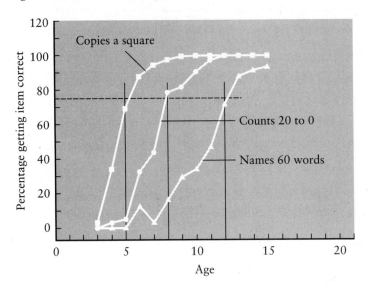

successful on some of the 9-year-olds' tests. Dull 8-year-olds might have difficulty with the 7-year-olds' items and so on.

As you might expect, a tremendous amount of work was necessary to complete this set of subtests. The actual design and refinement of the subtests was very time-consuming. During Binet's lifetime, three forms of the subtests were published—in 1905, 1908, and 1911, the year of his death. The 1911 scale consisted of 54 tests, with the easiest being within the scope of a normal 3-year-old and the most difficult supposedly taxing the intelligence of a normal adult. Binet assumed that a mental age of 16 years represented the peak of intellectual performance.

The 1911 Binet Scale

The 54 subtests selected by Binet for his 1911 revision were arranged in ascending order of difficulty as a result of trying them out on 200 children, ages 3 to 15 years, who were judged to be normal. This set of subtests, which has since become known as **scale**, consisted of five tests for each age, 3 through 10 years, except for age 4, which only had four tests. Ages 12, 15, and adult were assigned five tests each. Table 6-5 presents a list of the tests by age level as arranged by Binet in 1911.

As Table 6-5 shows, the 1911 scale covered a wide range of school-like activities from the very young preschool level up to some of the abilities we might expect of today's high school students. After the subtests were administered, an estimate of the intellectual age of the child was made by noting the level at which the pupil appeared to be functioning. For example, children who passed all of the subtests for 11-year-olds but were unsuccessful with those assigned to the 12-year-old level would be functioning *intellectually* at the 11-year-old level. The age at which children were functioning intellectually became known as the **mental age**.

Table 6-5   List of tests by ages as arranged by Binet in 1911

Age	Test
3	1. Points to nose, eyes, and mouth. 2. Repeats two digits. 3. Enumerates objects in a picture. 4. Gives family name. 5. Repeats a sentence of six syllables.
4	1. Gives his sex. 2. Names key, knife, and penny. 3. Repeats three digits. 4. Compares two lines.
5	1. Compares two weights. 2. Copies a square. 3. Repeats a sentence of ten syllables. 4. Counts 4 sous.* 5. Unites the halves of a divided triangle.
6	1. Distinguishes between morning and afternoon. 2. Defines familiar words in terms of use. 3. Copies a diamond. 4. Counts 13 sous. 5. Distinguishes pictures of ugly and pretty faces.
7	1. Shows right hand and left ear. 2. Describes a picture. 3. Executes three commissions, given simultaneously. 4. Counts the value of 6 sous, 3 of which are double. 5. Names four cardinal colors.
8	1. Compares two objects from memory. 2. Counts from 20 to 0. 3. Notes omissions from pictures. 4. Gives day and date. 5. Repeats five digits.
9	1. Gives change from 20 sous. 2. Defines familiar words in more general terms than simply specifying their size. 3. Recognizes all the pieces of money. 4. Names the months of the year, in order. 5. Answers easy "comprehension questions."
10	1. Arranges five blocks in order of weight. 2. Copies drawings from memory. 3. Criticizes absurd statements. 4. Answers difficult "comprehension questions." 5. Uses three given words in not more than two sentences.
12	1. Resists suggestion. 2. Composes one sentence containing three given words. 3. Names 60 words in 3 minutes.

continued

Table 6-5   List of tests by ages as arranged by Binet in 1911 (*continued*)

Age	Test
	4. Defines certain abstract words.
	5. Discovers the sense of a disarranged sentence.
15	1. Repeats seven digits.
	2. Finds three rhymes for a given word.
	3. Repeats a sentence of 26 syllables.
	4. Interprets pictures.
	5. Interprets given facts.
Adult	1. Solves a paper-cutting test.
	2. Rearranges a triangle in imagination.
	3. Gives differences between pairs of abstract terms.
	4. Gives three differences between a president and a king.
	5. Gives the main thought of a selection that had been read.

*The sou is the French equivalent of our penny.

Source: Adapted from Terman (1916, pp. 37–39).

In discussing the meaning of performance on his scale, Binet noted that children whose mental age was equal to their chronological age were *regular* in intelligence, whereas children whose mental age was lower than their chronological age were *retarded*[3] and those whose mental age was higher than their chronological age were *advanced*. Retarded students, by this reasoning, were identified by Binet's scale as those who should be routed to special classes.

Administrating the test involved making a guess about the effective mental age of the pupil and starting testing with subtests just below this age, continuing with successively more difficult subtests until performance indicated the child's mental age had been surpassed. With this style of administration, all children do not take all of the subtests; they take only those that are relevant to making a determination of their mental age. Such subtests have been called **Binet-type subtests** because each subtest is classified in terms of a specific age at which the test should be passed. The Binet scale is a marvel of effective problem solving, and it laid the groundwork for the contemporary intelligence test.

Binet's Caveats

A caveat is a caution, or warning, and Binet imposed four of these on his test. He was quite clear about the limits that should be placed on his tests. He argued strongly that (1) the scores on the test are merely for practical decisions; (2) the scores do not support any theory of intellect because none had been proposed; (3) the scores were simply to identify mildly retarded children and were not intended

---

[3]The word *retarded*, as used here, is a transliteration of the French *retardé*, which means late.

to differentiate within the normal range of abilities; and (4) in all uses of the tests, emphasis should be on improvement through special training (for a discussion, see Gould, 1981, p. 155).

There can be little doubt that Binet's scale was the precursor to the contemporary intelligence test. What was most important about this achievement was that Binet was able to solve the riddle of measurement where Cattell and the faculty psychologists had failed. Rather than base his observations on basic sensory processes, Binet chose tasks that bore a relatively direct relationship to the domain he was trying to predict, what he called **higher mental processes**. That is, because Binet was concerned with school performance, he chose his test items to directly reflect the kinds of activities that are necessary to perform well in school. He solved the problem experienced by the early mental testers by making his test items as closely related as he could to the areas in which he was trying to make his predictions.

Binet's invention was clearly a good one as far as administrators and educators were concerned—it solved some very real problems for them. Whether the Binet was equally beneficial to other stakeholders—particularly test takers—remains to be seen. At the time, the acceptance of the test was driven, in no small way, by the manner in which it served the needs of the educational institutions, and test-taker concerns were not highlighted.

THE BINET COMES TO AMERICA

The tests developed by Binet were the breakthrough that the American testers were seeking, and its adoption in the United States was rapid. Henry H. Goddard (1908) published the first English-language version of Binet's test. Shortly thereafter, Kuhlmann (1911) published another version. However, the most influential translation was presented by Louis M. Terman and H. G. Childs (1912). In describing the ideal test, Terman and Childs (1912) indicated that "It should ascertain as far as possible the native intellectual endowment of each pupil, and it should undertake to establish with reference to acceptable standards his exact pedagogical status" (p. 61). The adaptation involved using translations of Binet's items, classified from an age level of 3 through 15 years, plus an adult level. The median number of tests per age level was six, with a range of five through eight. The Americanized version was based on the responses of 396 children who were tested in "hallways or vacant rooms of the various school buildings, practically free from distractions" (Terman & Childs, 1912, p. 65). Not all children were administered all subtests, with, in general, testing beginning with the subtests classified "a year below the S's chronological age" (p. 65). Following the procedures pioneered by Binet, these data were used to assign the various subtests to specific age levels for the American sample.

Terman and Childs (1912) also added several new tests to the Binet battery. Included here were (1) a "fables" subtest, which involved writing down what one thought a story was intended to teach; (2) a completion subtest, which involved filling in the blanks in a piece of prose; (3) a test of practical judgment, which involved drawing the most effective pattern one could use to find a ball lost in a

Louis Madison Terman (1877–1956).

circular field; and (4) a vocabulary subtest. This last subtest involved asking the definitions of 100 words chosen, more or less randomly, from the dictionary. This test was classified from age-level 6 through 13 years, pending the score obtained by the respondent. Table 6-6 presents these classifications.

This new vocabulary subtest is a departure from Binet's original approach. In the 1911 Binet, vocabulary items were classified by age and distributed throughout the entire test, thus, scattered throughout the test were a number of subtests that dealt with vocabulary skills, each tailored to a specific age level (see Table 6-5). In the Terman and Childs test (1912), a grand series of words was selected, and these were administered in one subtest, with mental age being a function of how many words the child got correct. In a sense, Terman's vocabulary subtest has emerged as a "supersubtest," applying to all age groups rather than being divided up into age-related smaller subtests.[4]

Terman and Childs (1912) readily acknowledged the difficulties inherent in scoring the various subtests. With reference to the vocabulary subtests, they indicated that:

> In scoring, full credit was allowed for one correct meaning given, and half credit for a definition which was partially correct.... The difficulty comes in deciding when a meaning is "correct," since definitions may be of all grades of excellence. Individual differences in E's [testers] will inevitably appear here, and in order to

---

[4]In subsequent revisions, Terman recommended that only those words that are useful in determining mental age should be presented to the respondents, meaning that younger children would not necessarily experience all the harder words. Yet this remains as different from Binet-type subtests because the vocabulary test was not assigned to a specific age level but cut across all of them.

Table 6-6   Year-level assignments of Terman and Child's (1912) vocabulary subtest

Year Level	Percentage Correct
6	12
7	14
8	18
9	23
10	26
11	30
12	36
13	42

> minimize them it may be necessary ultimately to indicate definitely for each word what definition is acceptable, what deserve half credit, what none.... Whatever standard of excellence is accepted it is bound to be more or less arbitrary. [Terman, 1916, p. 207]

Subsequent revision of Terman's test took this advice seriously, with full appendices of acceptable responses being provided to those who used the test.

The test resulted in a number that Terman called the **test age**, defined as follows: "... S's test age was computed by assigning him to the lowest year in which he passed all the tests, or all but one, and then crediting him with a half year additional for each three tests satisfactorily passed beyond this" (Terman & Childs, 1912, p. 67). Terman and Childs concluded by indicating that the "Binet scale requires radical revision to make it at all suitable to conditions in this country" (p. 277). Suggestions of a number of refinements such as cleaning up the credit-assignment process were followed by an optimistic conclusion regarding the utility of the tests in the American context:

> In spite of the numerous imperfections and inadequacies of the Binet scale above mentioned, our experience in the work of applying it has given us a most favorable opinion of the practical value of the series when it has been refined and extended, an impression which grows upon us as the work continues. [p. 286]

They go on to suggest that the test is a much better classificatory system than the teacher: "By its use it is possible for the clinical psychologist to submit, after a 40-minute diagnostication, a more reliable estimate of a child's intelligence in relation to normal children of his age than most teachers can offer after a year of daily contact" (p. 286). Can it be long, they wondered, before "it will become a matter of course to apply serial mental tests in public schools to all pupils?" (p. 287). The enthusiasm of the emerging testing movement is aptly captured in Terman and Child's (1912) reference to John Stuart Mill, the champion of the nurture side of the nature/nurture controversy: "With the accumulation of positive experimental data on so many aspects of individual mentality, it would seem that John Stuart

Mill's suggestion looking toward a science of human character, ethology, as he called it, is on the verge of realization" (p. 287). Clearly, the intelligence test was well on its way to inserting itself into the very fabric of American society.

THE BINET AFTER LEWIS TERMAN AND H. G. CHILDS

Four years after the original publication, Terman (1916) published the first revision to be marketed as a test. It was based on the same fundamental idea as the earlier version, but some of the subtests had changed drastically. Because Terman's home institution, Stanford University, had been most helpful in the development of the test, it became known as the **Stanford–Binet Intelligence Test.** The various subtests were tried out on a sample of roughly 2300 California children who were tested between 1910 and 1914. The subtests of the 1916 Stanford–Binet, which are presented in Table 6-7, were developed from this impressive data set. Almost all of the revised subtests had multiple items. It is interesting to compare this set with Binet's original subtests (see Table 6-5) and to note the types of tasks that have gone into this instrument, which emerged as the classic of all individual intelligence tests.

Terman (1916) provided detailed instructions about the administration of the test. He indicated the need to obtain the complete attention of the child being tested, recommending that testing be done in a quiet room out of contact with other pupils.

Testing materials for the 1986 Fourth Edition of the Stanford–Binet Intelligence Test

Table 6-7   Subtests from the 1916 Stanford–Binet

Age	Subtests
3	1. Point to parts of the body (for example, "Put your finger on your nose.").
	2. Name familiar objects (for example, answering "What is this?" upon being shown a pocketknife).
	3. Enumerate objects in pictures (for example, naming all the objects in a picture).
	4. Give sex (for example, "Are you a little girl or a little boy?").
	5. Give family name ("What is your name?").
	6. Repeat six to seven syllables (for example, repeat "In summer the sun is hot.").
4	1. Compare lines (for example, "Tell which of two lines is longer.").
	2. Discriminate lines (finding a given form in a mixed set of various shapes).
	3. Count four pennies.
	4. Copy a square.
	5. Comprehension, first degree (for example, "What must you do when you are sleepy?").
	6. Repeat four digits.
5	1. Compare weights (a psychophysical task with wooden blocks of varying weights).
	2. Name colors (using a set of cards).
	3. Aesthetic comparison (judging which of two pictures is the most pretty).
	4. Give definitions in the use of terms (for example, "Use the word *chair* in a sentence.").
	5. The game of patience (a paperboard task where the child has to show how a cut-up card can be assembled to look like the original shape).
	6. Three commissions (must follow a set of instructions). Alternate: Give age.
6	1. Distinguish right from left.
	2. Find omissions in pictures.
	3. Count 13 pennies.
	4. Comprehension, second degree (for example, "What's the thing to do if you find that your house is on fire?").
	5. Name four coins (penny, nickel, dime, quarter).
	6. Repeat 16 to 18 syllables (for example, repeat "Walter had a fine time on his vacation; he went fishing every day."). Alternate: Distinguish forenoon and afternoon (for example, "Is it afternoon or morning?").
7	1. Give the number of fingers.
	2. Describe pictures.
	3. Repeat five digits (must get one of three sequences correct).
	4. Tie a bow knot (allowed 1 minute).
	5. Give differences from memory (for example, "What is the difference between a fly and a butterfly?").

continued

Table 6-7   Subtests from the 1916 Stanford–Binet *(continued)*

Age	Subtests

| | 6. Copy a diamond. |

Age   **Subtests**

        6. Copy a diamond.
           Alternate 1: Name the days of the week.
           Alternate 2: Repeat three digits reversed.

8   1. The ball-and-field test (for example, "Draw the path you would use if you had to find a ball in a field.").
      2. Count backward from 20 to 1.
      3. Comprehension, third degree (for example, "What's the thing for you to do when you notice on your way to school that you are in danger of being tardy?").
      4. Give similarities; two things (for example, "How are *wood* and *coal* alike?").
      5. Give definitions superior to use (for example, "What is a balloon?").
      6. Vocabulary (20 definitions) (for example, "What does *roar* mean?").
         Alternate 1: Name six coins (those in 6-5, plus a half-dollar and a dollar).
         Alternate 2: Write from dictation (for example, write "See the little boy.").

9   1. Give the date.
      2. Arrange five weights (same stimuli as 5-1).
      3. Make change (for example, "If I bought 12 cents worth and gave the storekeeper 15 cents, how much would I get back?").
      4. Repeat four digits reversed.
      5. Use three words in a sentence (for example, "Put the words *work*, *money*, and *men* into one sentence.").
      6. Find rhymes (for example, "Name all the words you can that rhyme with *day*.").
         Alternate 1: Name the months.
         Alternate 2: Count the value of stamps.

10   1. Vocabulary (30 definitions).
      2. Detect absurdities (for example, "What is foolish about 'Yesterday the police found the body of a girl cut into 18 pieces; they believe that she killed herself.' ").
      3. Draw designs from memory.
      4. Read for eight memories (for example, reads a short newspaper story aloud and is asked to remember specific details).
      5. Comprehension, fourth degree (for example, "What ought you to do before beginning something very important?").
      6. Name 60 words (3-minute time limit).
         Alternate 1: Repeat six digits.
         Alternate 2: Repeat 20 to 22 syllables.
         Alternate 3: Construct a puzzle (assemble a group of smaller rectangles to make a larger one).

12   1. Vocabulary (40 definitions).
      2. Define abstract words (for example, "What is *pity*?").
      3. The ball-and-field test (same as 8-1 but must demonstrate "superior" plan, which is carefully defined in the manual).

Table 6-7   Subtests from the 1916 Stanford–Binet *(continued)*

Age	Subtests
	4. Dissect sentences (for example, arrange this to a proper sentence: "To asked paper my teacher correct my I.").
	5. Interpret fables (must extract the moral of simple stories).
	6. Repeat five digits reversed.
	7. Interpret pictures (using same pictures as 3-3 and 7-2, asking "Can you tell me what this picture is about?" A superior interpretation of three of four pictures is expected.).
	8. Give similarities of three things (for example, "How are wool, cotton, and leather the same?").
13	1 Vocabulary (50 definitions).
	2. Induction test: find a rule (for example, fold a paper in four, nip off a corner, and ask how many holes there will be when it is opened up).
	3. Give differences between a president and a king.
	4. Problem questions (for example, "My neighbor has been having queer visitors. First a doctor came to his house, then a lawyer, then a minister. What do you think happened here?").
	5. Arithmetic reasoning (for example, "If two pencils cost 5 cents, how many pencils can you buy for 50 cents?").
	6. Reverse the hands of clock (gives a specific time and then asks what time it would be if the hands were interchanged). Alternate: Repeat seven digits.
Average adult	1. Vocabulary (65 definitions).
	2. Interpret fables (More of 12-5).
	3. Differentiates between abstract terms (for example, "What is the difference between *evolution* and *revolution*?").
	4. Problem of enclosed boxes (for example, "How many boxes are there in a big box with two smaller ones in it, each of which has a yet smaller box in it?").
	5. Repeat six digits reversed.
	6. Use a code (teaches a word-scrambling code and then asks for the person to use it). Alternate 1: Repeat 28 syllables. Alternate 2: Comprehend physical relations (a series of basic physics problems).
Superior adult	1. Vocabulary (75 definitions).
	2. Binet's paper-cutting test (more complex version of 13-2).
	3. Repeat eight digits.
	4. Repeat thought of passage.
	5. Repeat seven digits reversed.
	6. Ingenuity test (asks how to get a specific quantity of water with several different sizes of jugs).

*There was no 11-year-old group in Terman (1916).

SOURCE: Adapted from Terman (1916).

Recommendations about developing good rapport and keeping the child encouraged were also presented. Warnings about coaxing and discussions of the importance of "adhering to the formula" (for example, following the documented standardized procedure) were given. **Alternate tests** were to be used if, for some reason, standardization was violated during administration of one of the regular subtests (for example, an interruption). A maximal administration time of 30 minutes was recommended for 3- to 6-year-olds, with an extension to 90 minutes for adults.

The examination started with the subtests classified "just below the child's age" (Terman, p. 129). Thus, testing for a normal-seeming 8-year-old child would begin with the age 7 set. If the child passed five of the six tests at this level, testing would proceed to successively older levels until an age range was encountered in which the child failed five of the six subtests. If the child failed more than one test in the starting set, the examiner would move downward through the sets until an age level was found in which the child passed five of the six subtests.

Detailed answer keys were provided for each subtest, with a list of acceptable answers provided for the more open-ended questions. An extended list of remarks and comments on typical answers was offered for each subtest. All subtests also had a specific number of items that the child must get correct to be assigned a "pass." Thus, each subtest culminated in either a pass or fail categorization.

Mental age was calculated by assuming that each subtest within an age level counted for 2 months (there are six subtests per level).[5] The child's **basal age** was defined as the age below which no subtests were administered and below which it was assumed that the child would pass all the subtests. Table 6-8 outlines an example of the manner in which mental age would be calculated for an 8-year-old who took the Stanford–Binet. As Table 6-8 shows, testing began with the age 7 tests, and the child passed five of these. This permitted the test administrator to assume that the child would have passed all of the items classified as younger than age 7. The child then passed all six age 8 tests, plus three in 9 and one in 10. This latter result permitted the administrator to stop the testing process. Totaling the number of months for which the child gained credit resulted in assigning a mental age of 8 years and 6 months. The mental performance of the child in Table 6-8 is interpreted to be the equivalent of an 8½-year-old.

The Intelligence Quotient

Terman (1916) implemented a further transformation of this mental age. Based on some earlier work by Stern (1914), Terman suggested that mental age could be divided by chronological age to provide an index of the relative position of the child. Values greater than 1 would indicate children who were ahead of their age in mental development, whereas numbers lower than 1 would indicate children who were behind. In the example of the child in Table 6-8 who was 8 years old, this index would be 8.5/8 = 1.06, indicating a slight advance of mental over chronological age. The decimal places were seen as clumsy, so Terman determined to multi-

---

[5]Because of the missing age 11 level, the number of age 12 tests was increased to eight, and these were counted as 3 months each.

Table 6-8 Calculating the mental age of an 8-year-old child who was administered the Stanford–Binet

Age Level	Number of Subtests Passed	Number of Months Credit
Basal Age		72
7	5	10*
8	6	12
9	3	6
10	1	2
Total		102

Mental age = total months = 102 months = 8 years, 6 months

*Testing started at this level.

ply this index by 100. Our 8-year-old now obtains an index of 106. Because this transformation involved dividing the mental age by the chronological age, it was described as a quotient. Because it was thought to reflect the intelligence of the child, Terman called it the **intelligence quotient**, which was shortened to IQ. Equation 6-3 shows the general form of this version of the IQ (called the **ratio IQ** in later years):

$$\text{IQ} = \frac{\text{MA}}{\text{CA}} \times 100$$

(6-3)

where

MA = mental age as estimated from the Stanford–Binet

CA = chronological age at time of testing

Children who were performing mentally at exactly their chronological age would receive IQs of 100. Thus, the average IQ is 100. Persons scoring higher than 100 would be mentally ahead of their chronological years, with the size of the value above 100 varying with the extent of advancement. That is, children with IQs of 120 were considered to be more advanced (ahead of their chronological years) than those receiving IQs of 105. IQs less than 100 reveal mental development that was slower than chronological years, with the size of the value below 100 revealing the extent of this slowness. Table 6-9 provides the descriptive labels of various IQ scores provided by Terman (1916).

The concept of **feebleminded** was unique to the time when the Stanford–Binet was developed. According to Terman (1916), "A feeble-minded person is one who is incapable, because of mental defect existing from birth or from an early age, (a) of competing on equal terms with his normal fellows; or (b) of managing himself

Table 6-9   Descriptive labels for various ranges of IQ scores

IQ	Classification
Above 140	Near genius or genius
120–140	Very superior intelligence
110–120	Superior intelligence
90–110	Normal, or average, intelligence
80–90	Dullness, rarely classifiable as feeblemindedness
70–80	Borderline deficiency, sometimes classifiable as dullness, often as feeblemindedness
Below 70	Definite feeblemindedness

SOURCE: Adapted from Terman (1916, p. 79).

or his affairs with ordinary prudence" (p. 80). Feebleminded persons caused considerable consternation within the United States during this time because the expenses (both fiscal and social) of maintaining these individuals were considerable. When fanned by the perception that a higher proportion of immigrants appeared to fall in the category of feebleminded, the availability of an instant "thermometer" to measure this characteristic was indeed a welcome invention.

Terman (1916) provided some extensive data analyses to establish the utility of his test. Based on 1000 respondents, he demonstrated that IQ was normally distributed (p. 66) and that there were no gender differences in Stanford–Binet scores (p. 69). The correlation between IQ and teachers' estimates of intelligence (using a 6-point rating scale) was .48, prompting him to conclude that "this [$r = .48$] is about what others have found, and is both high enough and low enough to be significant. That it is moderately high in so far corroborates the tests. That it is not higher means that either the teachers or the tests have made a good many mistakes" (p. 75).

Terman was also quick to point out that the test was reliable. In the 1916 manual, he cited evidence that IQs deviated, on average, only 4% on retesting, with a maximal change of 8% (Terman, 1916, p. 113). He also cited an empirical study, based on the responses of 83 normal children tested 1 year apart, in which the test/retest reliability was found to be .95 (p. 113), prompting him to suggest that the test could be used "with little danger of serious inaccuracy" (p. 114).

In all, Terman presented a variety of data that were interpreted as proof of IQ testing having substantial applied benefit. He argued strongly for the importance of intelligence testing in the following domains: (1) retarded children in the schools, (2) delinquents (to determine if their antisocial behavior was due to intellectual or social factors), (3) superior children to identify those deserving of greater educational benefits, (4) comparison of schools, and (5) vocational fitness.

The Stanford–Binet was undoubtedly the most significant psychological test in North America in the early 20th century. It set the tone for the generations of tests that would follow. Figure 6-2 shows the evolutionary sequence of the test both

Figure 6-2   The evolution of the Stanford–Binet.

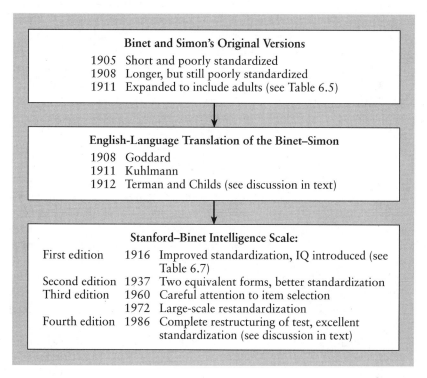

Binet and Simon's Original Versions

1905   Short and poorly standardized
1908   Longer, but still poorly standardized
1911   Expanded to include adults (see Table 6.5)

English-Language Translation of the Binet–Simon

1908   Goddard
1911   Kuhlmann
1912   Terman and Childs (see discussion in text)

Stanford–Binet Intelligence Scale:

First edition   1916   Improved standardization, IQ introduced (see Table 6.7)
Second edition   1937   Two equivalent forms, better standardization
Third edition   1960   Careful attention to item selection
                 1972   Large-scale restandardization
Fourth edition   1986   Complete restructuring of test, excellent standardization (see discussion in text)

prior to and after the original Stanford–Binet. Subsequent revisions of the scale have smoothed the rough spots (for example, the missing age 11 group was added in 1937; entry level was established by a vocabulary test in 1986; stimuli have been updated continuously) and extended the size of the groups on which test-score comparisons are made. Up to and including a major restandardization in 1972, the basic tenets of the original test remained in place, with the revisions representing improvements on the original scale. The 1986 fourth revision deviated from the historical tradition, with restructuring into 15 subtests and the introduction of a much more complex set of scores (see Thorndike, Hagen, & Sattler, 1986).

The original Stanford–Binet was a truly remarkable pioneering development, bringing together all other emerging factors outlined in earlier chapters. Under the advocacy of Louis Terman and a coterie of other pioneer researchers, the psychological testing enterprise had forged its place in the cultural and scientific heart of the United States. More than any other single date, 1916 emerges as the beginning of the testing enterprise in North America, for it was then that the emerging discipline of psychology was able to demonstrate clearly and concisely that it could deliver on its promise of social worth. Psychology was about to be "put on the map" of the United States.

Several criteria, however, were lost in the American adaptation of Binet's test. Recall that Binet placed a number of caveats on the use of his method. Of particular note was his assertion that the test was only appropriate for "mildly retarded children" and not expected to differentiate within the normal range. Additionally, he argued that all use of the test should be oriented toward remediation. As Table 6-9 shows, Terman (1916) ignored these caveats. He argued that his test discriminated appropriately all the way up to genius ratings. Using what might be considered a transliteration of Binet's original test (as seen in a comparison of Tables 6-5 and 6-7), Terman added a series of assumptions about the nature of intelligence and its testing. It will prove interesting to examine the manner in which these assumptions had impact on the testing enterprise as it began to flourish.

Summary

In this chapter, we started out exploring the manner in which psychology began to develop in North America. The emergence of a new psychology under the guidance of William James set the stage for James McKeen Cattell to introduce the mental-test movement. Conditions were primed for the young upstart discipline of psychology to demonstrate its practical value. While the prevailing ideas of faculty psychology were challenged, the movement toward a quantitative worldview was championed by a number of important pioneers, including Edward Thorndike in education.

The seminal concept of reliability was developed and embellished by Charles Spearman to provide the beginning of a systematic approach to testing. All that was needed was the creation of a methodology of intellectual assessment which was provided by Alfred Binet. Louis Terman's adaptation of Binet's test became the standard of intelligence testing in North America. It was published in a number of versions as early as 1912, culminating in the Stanford–Binet Test of Intelligence published in 1916. By the mid-1910s, testing had become a significant component of the emerging discipline of psychology, and the testing enterprise was on its way.

Glossary

alternate test An auxiliary subtest in the Stanford–Binet that was to be used in the event that administration of one of the regular subtests was faulty.

basal age In administering the Stanford–Binet, the age below which no testing is conducted and for which credit is assumed for all items associated with lower ages.

Binet, Alfred A French psychologist who was involved in many aspects of psychology but whose most enduring contribution was the development of the first test of intelligence around 1904. Designed to detect slow pupils who could then be placed into special classes, Binet's test began the testing enterprise as we know it today.

Binet-type subtest A variety of subtest developed by Alfred Binet in which a given task was assigned to a specific age group on the basis of performance of children of varying ages.

Cattell, James McKeen A pioneer in testing in the United States who coined the term *mental test* and was highly influential in the emergence of testing programs in America.

correction for attenuation A method of determining what the correlation would be between two variables if both were perfectly reliable. (See Equation 6-1.)

error of observation A variability in the results of measurements that can be attributed to factors other than the "true" or "real" value of the observation. Factors such as respondents not paying attention, fatigue, scoring errors, and numerous other problems can contribute to the size of such errors.

faculty psychology A turn-of-the-century version of psychology that thought complex mental events were simply the sum of simpler kinds of processes, called faculties, which were typically measured using simple perceptual or sensory tasks. Empirical research was not kind to this position, which has since been abandoned.

feebleminded A term from the early 1900s describing a person experiencing severe mental defects that existed from birth or an early age. Lewis Terman identified a Stanford–Binet IQ of less than 70 as indicative of feeblemindedness.

higher mental processes A term used by Alfred Binet to refer to the more complicated aspects of human cognitive functioning involved in tasks such as learning. When Binet determined to estimate higher mental processes directly, rather than measuring faculties and trying to generate composite scores, a major breakthrough for testing occurred.

idealism A philosophical position that accepts the possibility of nonmechanistic or nonmaterial agents as part of the system.

intelligence quotient (IQ) An index of the measured intelligence of an individual, which has an average value of 100. There are several types of IQ scores, with the earlier work using the ratio IQ calculated by Equation 6-3.

item-operating characteristic A graphical representation of data of the type used by Alfred Binet and Lewis Terman to assign specific subtests to specific age groups. It involves plotting performance on an item or subtest as a function of an underlying variable of interest, such as age in the Binet case.

materialism As used here, a philosophical position that seeks mechanistic, scientific explanations of human conduct. More technically, materialism espouses the existence of reality in the matter of the external world rather than attributing it to the inner workings of the perceiver's mind and is thus associated (but not necessarily constrained by) mechanistic positions.

mental age The current age at which an individual is functioning cognitively. This is the primary output of tests such as the Stanford–Binet but is often transformed into a quotient such as the ratio IQ.

mental test A term coined by James McKeen Cattell in 1890 to refer to the types of sensory/perceptual tests that he borrowed from Francis Galton and pioneered as part of the faculty psychology of turn-of-the-century American psychology.

Monte Carlo simulation A technique for exploring the characteristics of mathematical formulations by introducing random numbers and distributions to demonstrate how the function behaves under varying conditions. The demonstration of the effect of varying amounts of observational error on the test/retest correlation shown in Table 6-3 is an example of this approach.

new psychology An Americanized psychology, associated with William James, that proposed using the methods of science to study the operations of the mind.

Progressive Era A period of U.S. history around 1900 when great emphasis was placed on using the results of science to reform and improve society.

ratio IQ The quotient obtained by dividing mental age by chronological age multiplied by 100. This version of IQ was used in the original Stanford–Binet.

reliability The extent to which a test produces consistent or error-free results. Initially, estimates of reliability were obtained by correlating results of a test given on two occasions. High-positive correlations indicated reliability. Since its introduction in 1907, this form of reliability has become known as test/retest reliability.

scale As used here, a collection of subtests that is used to assign individuals a mental age or intelligence quotient.

Stanford–Binet Intelligence Test Originally published in 1916 and subsequently revised three times (see Figure 6-2), this reworking of Alfred Binet's original test is the progenitor of all American intelligence tests. The fourth edition is significantly different from its precursors in terms of structure and scores that are obtained.

subtest As used here, one of the tasks used in Alfred Binet's tests and subsequently in the Stanford–Binet. Subtests may vary in the number of trials or items that make them up but are defined by their culmination in a pass or fail score determined by reference to specific, predetermined criteria.

test age An earlier name used by Lewis Terman for what he eventually called mental age.

test/retest design An approach to gathering data in which persons are subjected to the same treatment or scale on two successive occasions.

test/retest reliability An estimate of reliability gained by administering the same test to a person on two separate occasions and calculating the correlation between the two administrations. High-positive test/retest correlations are indicative of high reliability.

Thorndike, Edward L. An early American educational psychologist who championed the quantitative worldview and demonstrated its effectiveness for the solution of many pressing problems in the U.S. educational system.

Suggested Further Reading

Joncich, G. (1968). *The sane positivist: A biography of Edward L. Thorndike.* Middletown, Conn.: Wesleyan University Press.

> This is a highly readable presentation of Thorndike's career and provides a wealth of background information. By the time you have read it, you will feel that you know this important pioneer of the testing enterprise.

Minton, H. L. (1988). *Lewis M. Terman: Pioneer in psychological testing.* New York: New York University Press.

> This biography of Terman is almost required reading for anyone who wants to get to know the man who forged such an important place for the intelligence test in North American society. It covers his life from beginning to end and provides the reader with a compassionate view of this man who, in some circles, has not received an overly sympathetic press. The list of his published works (pp. 323–336) is not only

notable because of its length but also provides access to the diversity and breadth of his scholarship.

Sokal, M. M. (1981). *An education in psychology: James McKeen Cattell's journal and letters from Germany and England 1880–1888*. Cambridge, Mass.: MIT Press.

This book provides a rich glimpse into Cattello's formative years by exploring various personal documents written while he was in Germany and England. It provides an exceedingly rich sense of this man who was so influential in the emergence of testing in North America—and is great reading to boot!

Sokal, M. M. (Ed.). (1987). *Psychological testing and American society*. New Brunswick, N.J.: Rutgers University Press.

This edited volume contains some excellent chapters dealing with aspects of the development of testing discussed in this chapter of *The Enterprise*. Of particular note are discussions of the Cattell tradition (Chapter 2), Goddard and testing (Chapter 3), and Terman (Chapter 5). Compared with *The Enterprise*, much greater detail and more context is provided in these presentations and is recommended for the reader who wants to gain a stronger sense of these times.

Terman, L. M. (1916). *The measurement of intelligence*. Boston: Houghton Mifflin.

In many cases, detailed information about specific tests is not readily available because the profession has determined that the content of the tests should be protected. This presentation of the original Stanford–Binet is available in many libraries and contains a great amount of detail about both the test and the rationales that Terman adopted in developing it. It provides an interesting snapshot of the development of this progenitor of all individual tests of intelligence.

Thorndike, E. L. (1904). *Mental and social measurements*. New York: Science Press.

Reading some of the original Thorndike is interesting if you want to extend your understanding of his critical contribution to the testing enterprise. This book was developed to introduce education students to the wonders of statistical manipulation of various kinds of measurement data, with particular emphasis on correlation. It is interesting to examine the manner in which Thorndike presents the fundamental mathematical ideas of the time and how he presages some of the developments that will follow (for example, true score-test theory as discussed in Chapter 11 of *The Enterprise*).

Wolf, T. (1973). *Alfred Binet*. Chicago: University of Chicago Press.

This is a wonderful biography of Binet. It provides a detailed account of his frustrations as a scholar (he never held a bona fide academic post) and accounts of his other contributions to psychology. Chapters 4 and 5, which deal with his approach to intelligence testing, provide much more detail than it was possible to provide here.

Discussion Questions

1. With reference to a recent experience you have had, indicate how there appears to be a conflict between a mechanistic and an idealistic approach to explaining psychological phenomena.

2. Describe and evaluate William James's solution to the dilemma he faced between idealism and mechanism.

3. Debate whether you think James's solution to the problems being faced by psychology in the early 1900s is relevant to the contemporary social context.

4. Speculate about the possible reasons why James McKeen Cattell held tenaciously to the notion of individual differences in reaction time when his mentor Wilhelm Wundt actively discouraged him from doing so.

5. In what senses are the notions of faculties different from the cognitive structures such as representations and various types of memory being studied by contemporary cognitive psychologists?

6. Imagine you are at the American Psychological Association meetings of 1898 at which Jastrow, Baldwin, and Cattell presented their desiderata of tests and you have been charged with the responsibility of criticizing their ideas. What aspects of their list would you attack? How would you do it? Why?

7. With reference to people who you know, discuss the usefulness of the fundamental tenet of faculty psychology that suggested there should be a relationship between performance on tests such as Cattell's and academic performance.

8. The Thorndike–McCall epigram reads: "Whatever exists, exists in some amount," and "anything which exists in amount can be measured." Does it follow from this that if something cannot be measured, it does not exist? Why, or why not? What are the implications of this?

9. Prepare a list of all possible sources of error of observation that could affect the Stanford–Binet.

10. Using your list from Question 9, discuss which of these might artificially inflate or deflate a test/retest estimate of the reliability of the test.

11. Using your list from Question 9 and your discussion in Question 10, discuss how it might be necessary to improve on the test/retest approach to take into account these sources of artificiality.

12. Outline a method like the one demonstrated in Table 6-3 that could be used to draw a graph that precisely relates the amount of error to the size of the test/retest correlation.

13. Critique the notion of correction for attenuation with respect to the possibility that it could lead to exaggerated claims about the effectiveness of a given test.

14. Why do you think that psychologists spend much more time discussing ideas such as reliability of measurement than their colleagues in the hard or natural sciences do?

15. Predict what might happen when the extensive immigration to the United States in the early 20th century is combined with the eugenics agenda of many of the early testers.

16. In what ways do Clark Wissler's data, which were disappointing to faculty psychology, hint at the eventual solution to the dilemma of predicting higher mental functioning proposed by Alfred Binet?

17. Evaluate Binet's criterion that a given subtest must be passed by between two-thirds and three-quarters of the pupils of a given age before it is assigned to that age level.

18. In Binet-type scales, almost all of the item-operating characteristics show an increase in performance with increasing age. What would be the implications of finding an item-operating characteristic in which performance declined after a specific age? How might you use such a subtest in a Binet-type scale?

19. It can be argued that a step function (a curve that goes from 0% to 100% correct at a specific age) is the best possible item-operating characteristic curve for a Binet-type item. Do you agree with this? Why, or why not?

20. What types of school tasks required in today's classrooms appear to have been omitted from the Binet as listed in Table 6-5? What are the implications of this?

21. Clearly distinguish between Binet-type and vocabulary scale introduced in Terman (1916), indicating the strengths and weaknesses of each.

22. Outline Binet's caveats. Suggest some of the implications that emerge from the observation that U.S. adaptations of the test tended to ignore them.

23. In the original Stanford–Binet, Lewis Terman acknowledged that there was an inevitable arbitrary element to the scoring of his subtests, such as the vocabulary items. Discuss the implications of this with respect to the fact that important social decisions may be made on the basis of performance on such tests.

24. Based on the data in the following table, what is the IQ of a 6½-year-old child who performed on the Stanford–Binet? How would Terman have interpreted this score?

Age Level	Number of Subtests Passed	Number of Months Credit
Basal Age		48
5	6	12 (testing started at this level)
6	5	10
7	5	10
8	6	12
9	4	8
10	0	0

25. One of the later empirical results with the Stanford–Binet was the finding that, although the mean IQ did appear to be 100 at various ages, the standard deviation tended to vary for the different age groups. What kinds of problems does this suggest when efforts are made to use IQs to relate performance to percentiles? Can you suggest a way in which this might be resolved?

26. Discuss ways in which you think that the presence of mass media such as television in our social context might affect the utility of instruments like the Stanford–Binet, which were developed before these were available.

27. Given the way in which the Stanford–Binet was developed, what do you think this test will best predict? Discuss your answer with respect to the limitations it poses on the meaning of the idea of intelligence.

Chapter 7

Putting Psychology on the Map
Testing and World War I

In This Chapter

CONNECTING PSYCHOLOGY WITH LIFE

Lewis Terman opened his doctoral dissertation by stating "One of the most serious problems confronting psychology is that of connecting itself with life" (Terman, 1906). The new psychology had experienced moderate growth around this time with the establishment of university laboratories, journals, a growing professional organization, an expanded profile of research productivity, and graduate education. But all was not tranquil in the halls of the psychology departments—many disagreements resounded. Academicians argued about the definition of their subject matter (mind versus consciousness versus behavior), the goals of the new science (understanding mind versus control of behavior), proper methods of study (**introspection** versus objective procedures), to name but a few. Although attempts were made to maintain a united front when dealing with the public, the internal strife had the effect of slowing the growth and accomplishments of the discipline. In fact, progress was so slow that concern was emerging for the long-term survival

215

of the discipline (for a discussion, see Camfield, 1973). Beneath the rhetoric celebrating psychology's academic successes, there was an undercurrent of doubt and frustration—would the new psychology take its place with the other established disciplines, or was it just a flash in the pan? John B. Watson suggested that psychology had "failed signally... during the fifty-odd years of its existence as an experimental discipline to make its place in the world as an undisputed natural science" (Watson, 1913, p. 164).

ROBERT YERKES AND THE WORLD WAR I TESTING PROGRAM

While the Stanford–Binet and related tests were making some headway in educational circles, it was not until the emerging testing enterprise became involved in World War I that testing really came into use. The outbreak of this war provided an important opportunity for the self-doubting discipline to begin demonstrating to itself, its colleagues, and society in general that it was indeed ready to make significant contributions. World War I, "the war to end all wars," was going to be fought on a scale so massive that even the most imaginative futurist could not have predicted the numbers of people involved. Even as the United States prepared to enter the conflict, it was clear that large-scale mobilizations of millions of men—more than ever before—were going to be required. Because of this and the emergence of increased technology, the problem of assigning soldiers to roles was going to become an increasingly important issue. Perhaps, some aspiring psychologists thought, it might be possible to adapt the emerging testing technology to this situation.

Almost on the day the war was declared, a number of psychologists went to work, forming numerous committees on war-related topics. Most of these never really got started, but the **Committee on Methods of Psychological Examining of Recruits**, quickly organized under the prodding of Robert Yerkes, did. This effort eventuated in a massive project that was instrumental in establishing the discipline in general and psychological testing in particular as part of the academy and of the American way of life.

Robert Mearns Yerkes was born into a rural Pennsylvania farming family. Expecting to train in medicine, he earned an undergraduate degree at the local Ursinis College. Upon graduation he was unexpectedly offered an opportunity to study biology at Harvard where he became especially interested in animal behavior. He grew so interested in this field that he abandoned his medical plans and earned a Ph.D. in psychology in 1902, being appointed to Harvard's faculty shortly thereafter. While at Harvard, he came into contact with the teachings of Hugo Munsterberg, a recent immigrant from Germany who was considered the leader of applied psychology, and Charles Davenport, leader of the American eugenics movement. The young Yerkes was "converted" by Davenport and soon became an outspoken supporter of the eugenics movement as it emerged in the United States (Fancher, 1985, pp. 390–391). He also came into contact with intelligence tests while moonlighting as research director at a psychiatric hospital.

Prewar Developments

Although his primary passion was for comparative psychology, the Harvard administration encouraged Yerkes to pursue educational applications, particularly if he wished to receive his professorship. As part of his efforts along these lines, Yerkes constructed a **point scale** of intelligence that did not require the concept of mental age (see Yerkes, 1917; Yerkes, Bridges, & Hardwick, 1915). Not unlike Terman's new vocabulary subtest, this was accomplished by administering the same series of questions to all respondents. However, Yerkes's scale was not scored in terms of mental age but in terms of the numbers of questions that the respondent got correct. The scale got its name because of the practice of assigning 1 point for each correct answer. A number of different questions were required for such a scale, and these became known as **test items**. Although not part of the original design, a major advantage of the point-scale method was that it could be administered to groups of people at the same time, resulting in considerable savings of money relative to Binet-type scales, which required individual administration. In this sense, it was well adapted to the challenges brought on by the massive war, which was about to erupt. The creation of the point scale was a highly influential contribution to the testing enterprise (see Dubois, 1970). It provided a basic methodological approach to measurement that remains with us to this day.

Just prior to the war, another piece of the puzzle fell into place. Even in a point-scale format, the great amount of idiosyncrasy shown in responses to items of the type found in the current intelligence scales forced test scorers to adopt various forms of arbitrary and sometimes indefensible criteria of correctness. As well, the expenses inherent in having to read and categorize responses were considerable. In terms we learned in Chapter 2, at this point in the evolution of the testing enterprise, response formats were almost always unstructured—leading to all kinds of standardization and financial problems. What was needed was some way of simplifying procedures to get rid of the arbitrariness and to reduce costs. And, as you might have guessed, enter the **multiple-choice item**.

A question could be presented with a series of possible answers, only one of which was correct. Respondents simply had to select which of the answers was correct, thereby eliminating considerable grading time and subjective guesses regarding correctness for scorers—a brilliant solution! Tests could readily be scored by the use of a stencil or an answer key. The structured response format was born. According to Samuelson (1987), the first published multiple-choice question appeared in 1915 in the context of Frederick J. Kelly's **Kansas Silent Reading Test**. Figure 7-1 shows the first page of this test. This invention, which was apparently introduced to Yerkes's committee by a young psychologist, Arthur Otis, was essential in the design of the testing program that Yerkes was about to initiate.

Yerkes's major opportunity to apply his emerging sophistication in testing came when the United States decided to enter World War I. By May 1917, shortly after the outbreak of the war, Yerkes had assembled a group of test specialists, which was the "Who's Who" of contemporary testing, including Goddard and Terman. The primary goal of this committee was to develop a test that would help the Army eliminate feebleminded recruits.

Figure 7-1   Front page of the Kansas Silent Reading Test, 1915, showing the first published multiple-choice item.

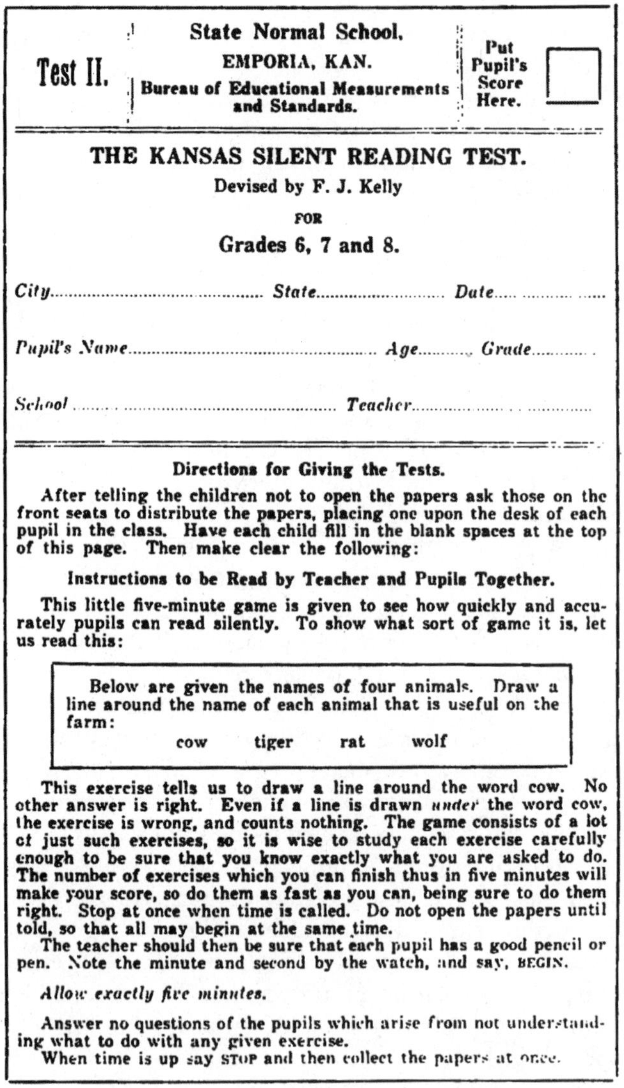

State Normal School,
EMPORIA, KAN.

Test II.
Bureau of Educational Measurements
and Standards.

Put Pupil's Score Here.

THE KANSAS SILENT READING TEST.
Devised by F. J. Kelly
FOR
Grades 6, 7 and 8.

City.............................. State.................... Date..............

Pupil's Name... Age......., Grade..........

School....................................... Teacher.......................

Directions for Giving the Tests.

After telling the children not to open the papers ask those on the front seats to distribute the papers, placing one upon the desk of each pupil in the class. Have each child fill in the blank spaces at the top of this page. Then make clear the following:

Instructions to be Read by Teacher and Pupils Together.

This little five-minute game is given to see how quickly and accurately pupils can read silently. To show what sort of game it is, let us read this:

> Below are given the names of four animals. Draw a line around the name of each animal that is useful on the farm:
>
> cow   tiger   rat   wolf

This exercise tells us to draw a line around the word cow. No other answer is right. Even if a line is drawn *under* the word cow, the exercise is wrong, and counts nothing. The game consists of a lot of just such exercises, so it is wise to study each exercise carefully enough to be sure that you know exactly what you are asked to do. The number of exercises which you can finish thus in five minutes will make your score, so do them as fast as you can, being sure to do them right. Stop at once when time is called. Do not open the papers until told, so that all may begin at the same time.

The teacher should then be sure that each pupil has a good pencil or pen. Note the minute and second by the watch, and say, BEGIN.

Allow exactly five minutes.

Answer no questions of the pupils which arise from not understanding what to do with any given exercise.

When time is up say STOP and then collect the papers at once.

The Army Alpha and Beta

Because individual testing would be too time-consuming given the numbers of recruits involved, a group administration test was developed based on Yerkes' point method and Kelly's multiple-choice format. The eventual product of this process was the **Army Alpha** (for literates) and the **Army Beta** (for illiterates), which were both designed to measure "native ability rather than the results of school training" (for details, see Kelves, 1968). The Alpha was a paper-and-pencil scale that had eight separate subtests (Table 7-1).

Each subtest had multiple items, many of which were in the multiple-choice format. A time limit was imposed on each subtest, and each correct answer received one point, with a total of 212 possible. **Letter Ratings** and mental ages were assigned to each recruit per the entries in Table 7-2. This table was based on formulas derived from a sample of 350 men who had taken both the Alpha and the Stanford–Binet.

Table 7-1   Subtests from the Army Alpha

Subtest	Description
Directions	Measures auditory span of attention to determine if the respondent can keep several things in mind at one time. *Example*: Upon presenting a vertical line of six circles, the test administrator says "Attention. Look at the circles. When I say 'Go,' but not before, make a cross in the third circle. 'Go!'"
Arithmetic	A series of arithmetic problems. *Example*: A ship has provision to last her crew of 600 men for 6 months. How long would it last 800 men?
Common Sense	A test of common sense. *Example*: The reason that many birds sing in the spring is: (a) to let us know spring is here. (b) to attract their mates. (c) to exercise their voices.

Same or Opposites	A test of semantic relationships. *Examples*:
	    Shrill-sharp: same or opposite
	    Altruistic-egotistic: same or opposite

Rearrangement	The ability to arrange words into meaningful sentences. *Example*: Make a sentence out of these words: inflict men pain needless cruel sometimes.
Ingenuity	Discovery of a relationship and the extension of this relationship to find a correct answer. *Example*: 1, 4, 9, 16, 25, 36, ?, ?
Relationships	The ability to solve analogies. *Example*: "Ocean" is to "pond" as "lake" is to: (a) "puddle" (b) "sea" (c) "continent"
Information	A test of knowledge. *Examples*: The thyroid is in the: The Leghorn is a kind of: (a) shoulder. (a) cow. (b) neck. (b) horse. (c) abdomen. (c) fowl. (d) head. (d) granite.

Source: Yerkes (1921).

Table 7-2   Determining the relationships
among Letter Rating, Alpha score,
and mental age

Letter Rating	Score Range	Mental Ages
A	135–212	18 and over
B	105–134	16.5–17.9
C+	75–104	15.0–16.4
C	45–74	13.0–14.9
C–	25–44	11.0–12.9
D	15–24	9.5–10.9
E and D–	0–14	0.0–9.4

SOURCE: Yerkes (1921).

In general terms, the Alpha appeared to be successful in fulfilling its stated goals of (1) aiding in segregating and eliminating the mentally incompetent (variously defined throughout the program, typically including the E, D, and D– categories); (2) classifying men according to mental ability, and (3) assisting in the selection of competent men for responsible positions.

The Army Beta, intended for those who could not read, involved many of the same tasks as the Alpha but used geometric figures instead of words. For example, the Ingenuity Test involved solving series of X's and O's rather than numbers that were used on the Alpha. Instructions were given mostly by pantomime. A brief literacy test was given to all recruits prior to testing to determine if they should receive the Alpha or the Beta.

An Apparent Success

The army testing program, which emerged a mere 4 months after preliminary testing, was soon the flagship of a massive testing effort in the armed services. According to Yerkes (1921), over 1 million men were examined. Using the results of the test, 7800 men were recommended for immediate discharge because of mental inferiority; for similar reasons, 10,014 men were recommended for postings to labor and development battalions. In addition, outfits with lower average test scores were improved using systematic assignments. It was also found that outcome of officer training could be predicted by Alpha scores. The overall impact of the testing program was subsequently described as follows: "Altogether, it had been shown that the application of large scale psychological testing could result in a huge increase in the efficiency of an organization like the Army and produce savings of millions of dollars to the government" (Samuelson, 1977, p. 277). By the end of the war there were examination units in 35 army camps, staffed with 120 officers and 350 enlisted men—a truly incredible accomplishment. The testing program spoke well for the future of psychologists in the military and also gave the discipline a remarkably strong demonstration of its practical worth.

Administering group examination Alpha.

Administering group examination Beta.

The impact of this testing program was not lost on the public. Although there was some concern about the technical aspects of the tests, the apparent utility of testing in the war effort had done wonders for psychology's public image: "Before the World War, the average intelligent layman probably had little confidence in the value or use of mental tests. After the War, he believed that psychologists had devised a simple and relatively perfect method of measuring intelligence" (Freeman, 1939).

There were other accomplishments for psychologists during the war, but it is clear that the testing effort was the most significant:

> Other aspects of psychologists' participation in World War I, such as personnel services and participation in training programs, led to a public recognition of the potential of psychology as a servant of society, and it was a period of great optimism among psychologists. Intelligence tests were adopted in schools and colleges, and they came to be widely used in business and industry. [Hilgard, 1987, p. 467]

According to Cattell, these developments had put psychology "on the map of the United States" (Cattell, 1922). Terman (1924) suggested that the World War I testing program had provided the opportunity for the new discipline to connect scientific psychology to life and to bring it "down from the clouds and make it useful to men" (pp. 105–106). Psychology had finally delivered on its promise of dramatic action to solve some of the problems of American society.

OTHER APPLICATIONS OF TESTING DURING THE WAR

The intelligence test received most of the glory stemming from the World War I experience, but three other types of testing were also initiated during this time. Not as heralded as the intelligence testing program, they had a significant impact in the years to follow. In all three cases, the foundations for contemporary areas of psychological testing were laid during this time.

Robert Woodworth and Structured Personality Assessment

Galton devised the questionnaire for use as a tool in psychological research to investigate imagery, but it was **Robert S. Woodworth** who, during World War I, applied the technique to the study of emotional stability. In so doing, he invented what was at first called a *personal data questionary*—the lineal ancestor of all subsequent personality inventories, schedules, and questionnaires.

Shell shock was the presenting problem for Woodworth. In contemporary terms, this might be considered burnout, acute stress response, or posttraumatic stress reaction to the combat situation. Soldiers suffering from this problem show all kinds of emotional difficulties (for example, acute fear response, withdrawal, desertion), culminating in degraded performance in the field. In World War I, this problem was felt to be as significant as low intelligence in the development of effective fighting units.

Woodworth approached the problem of predicting shell shock by examining early symptoms of neurotic tendency. He thought it might be possible to predict who would suffer from this problem by assessing a wide range of responses associated with neurosis. Woodworth collected all the descriptions of neurotic behavior he could find in the psychiatric literature and formulated them into a questionnaire. For example, if the psychiatric literature revealed that patients classified as neurotics tended to suffer from frequent headaches, Woodworth created the item "Do you have a great many bad headaches?" Respondents would simply check a yes or a no response. Table 7-3 provides several sample items from the eventual 116 items that made up the **Personal Data Sheet**. This questionnaire was administered to thousands of recruits and to small groups of abnormal subjects. Woodworth (1919) reported that the average college student reported about 10 symptoms on this questionnaire, whereas the typical neurotic at Camp Upton reported over 40. Returned shell shock cases at the Plattsburgh Reconstruction Hospital reported about 30 symptoms. Detailed analyses to determine if the instrument actually predicted shell shock were not conducted because the war ended before sufficient data had been gathered.

Woodworth's application of the emerging testing technology to problems of emotional stability was truly creative. Although it did not greatly affect the war effort, it was responsible for setting the pattern for assessing psychological predispositions using **self-report questionnaires**—an approach that is with us today.

Job Skills and Aptitudes

Just prior to the war, Hugo Munsterberg (1913) suggested that psychologists could be very useful in finding men whose attributes best fit them for specific jobs. Although formalized assessment procedures were not immediately available, Munsterberg did foresee a time when the new discipline could make a significant contribution to placement decisions.

Table 7-3   Sample items from Woodworth's Personal Data Sheet

1. Do you usually feel well and strong?
11. Do you feel well rested in the morning?
21. Do you ever feel an awful pressure in or about the head?
31. Were you happy when you were 14 to 18 years old?
41. Do you know of anybody who is trying to do you harm?
51. Have you hurt yourself by self-abuse?
61. Are you troubled with the idea that people are watching you on the street?
71. Can you do good work while people are looking on?
81. Do you find it difficult to pass urine in the presence of others?
91. Is it easy to make you laugh?
101. Did you ever have heart disease?
111. Has any of your family had a drug habit?

SOURCE: DuBois (1970, pp. 160–163).

Before long, stimulated in part by the war, isolated instances of tests and job samples being used to make job placements were being reported. Included here were tests to select telephone operators (McComas, 1914), salesmen (Lynch, 1968; see von Mayrhauser, 1987 for details regarding a conflict between Scott and Yerkes related to the war effort), telegraphers (Jones, 1917; Thurstone, 1919), and typist/stenographers (Rogers, 1917). These were precursors to the aptitude-testing programs that were soon to evolve in the business world.

The Germans were busy too. For example, they developed tests to select chauffeurs during the war (see Moede, 1926). By 1916 there were 14 centers engaged in both military and civilian chauffeur selection. Large-scale testing programs for the selection of railroad engineers were in place for the Saxon Railway Company and the Greater Berlin Tramway (see Horrocks, 1964).

Although the results of these programs were not spectacular, they did lay the foundation for important extensions of the psychological testing enterprise. The war experience had demonstrated the feasibility of using tests to facilitate placement decisions, and it was strictly a matter of imagination and time before new and important areas for this emerging technology could be found. As the war ended, excitement about the limitless potential of these tests was on the rise. The modern era of psychological assessment was beginning.

Measurement of Abilities

Measurement of the intelligence of illiterate recruits was one of the primary concerns of the army testing program. In its early deliberations related to this issue, the committee considered the **Stenquist Construction Test**. This instrument involved presenting the respondent with a series of common objects such as a doorbell, clothespin (spring type), and mousetrap. These objects were in pieces when

The Stenquist Skill Test

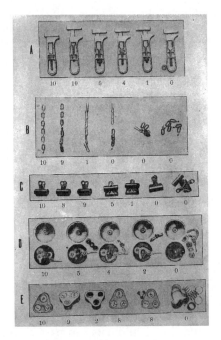

Several items in the Stenquist Skill Test

presented to the respondent, and the challenge was to assemble them properly. The respondent was allowed 30 minutes to put the objects back together. Scores reflected the extent to which the respondent was able to assemble the objects successfully.

The Stenquist was administered to 14,610 recruits in an initial experiment to determine its suitability as a measure of intelligence (Yerkes, 1921). Correlations between this test and the Alpha were disappointingly low, being in the range of .50. The relationship with officer's ratings of intelligence was even lower ($.20 < r < .30$). In the final analysis, the Stenquist Test was dropped because it did not appear to be an adequate measure of intelligence[1] and the Army Beta was developed to serve this function.

Regardless of its failure in the military context, this experimentation with the Stenquist can be seen as one of the first efforts to bring a general ability measure into a prediction situation. Indeed, shortly after the war, the Stenquist was published as an ability test (Stenquist, 1923). The operating hypothesis of the instrument was that a person who could recognize the functions of the disassembled objects and reassemble them possessed mechanical ability. Presumably, respondents with this ability would have sought out greater experience with such objects, and this learning would be reflected in their scores. Toops (1923) adapted the test

---

[1]While not mentioned in Yerkes (1921), it appears likely that the expense of administration was a factor here as well. The Stenquist required considerable individual attention during administration.

for women, using tasks such as bead stringing, cross-stitching, and tape sewing,[2] and the concept of an ability test was established.

Summary

World War I provided an opportunity for the psychological testing enterprise to demonstrate its potential contribution in a number of ways. Besides the army intelligence-testing program, pioneering developments in personality, aptitude, and ability measurement were put into place. This was an incredibly important time for the emerging industry because the foundations for future practice had been laid. The methods and ideas enacted during this period were highly instrumental in forging the directions that the enterprise was to take in its future efforts to demonstrate its practical worth.

NEGATIVE REACTIONS TO TESTING

Although the rhetoric of the testing enterprise following World War I was clear in indicating its successes, there was a sense that things did not go as well as advertised. A hint of this emerges from an inspection of the World War I army experience. In retrospect it would seem that the army program was, at best, marginally successful. For example, the program resulted in recommending 7,800 recruits for immediate discharge because of mental deficiency. This represents a .005 rejection rate (7,800/1,726,966 = .005), which is very low. With so few people being recommended for discharge, it is very difficult to justify the costs of the testing program. Also, available archival records do not explicitly state that the 7,800 men identified by the program were in fact discharged. Thus, if considered in what today are called bottom-line terms, the program probably could not have justified its existence on fiscal grounds.

Soldiers' Reactions to the Testing Program

The soldiers themselves were not particularly impressed with the testing program. This is revealed by an examination of the newsletters that were in circulation in various army camps while the testing was going on. For example, *Camplife Chickamunga* published the following song parody that was sung to the tune of Chopin's "Funeral March":

> **March of the Psychos**[3]
> The valiant, bespectacled psychos are we
> Prepared to assign every man his degree.

---

[2]This selection of tasks for women is a fairly transparent indicator of their status in the early 1920s and is presented for only historical interest, not as a statement of current practice.

[3]From Brown (1985).

Add the place he's best fitted for in the armee
By psychologee, psychologee.

Bill Kaiser will shake in his throne 'cross the sea
When he feels the earthquake of our efficiency.
Pencils up! Forward march! To the great victory
Of Psychologee in the Army.

Another indication of the soldiers' discontent with the testing program is shown in a cartoon from *The Camp Sherman News*. Although the song and cartoon are only two examples, they are indicative of discomfort within the enlisted ranks. The respondents obviously had some second thoughts about the army testing program.

Perhaps it comes as no surprise, then, to find that the testing program was canceled outright as soon as the war was over. It must be assumed that the army would have kept the program intact if it was serving their needs, but it was not (see Samuelson, 1979, for a detailed discussion).

From *The Camp Sherman News*, 1918.

POSTWAR INTERPRETATIONS OF THE ARMY DATA

More critical problems, however, were looming on the horizon. Once the army data had been gathered and the practical issues had been settled, several researchers began to interpret the results of this massive data set. These interpretations, and the debate they produced, brought the fledgling testing enterprise into full contact with a number of highly significant issues. Not the least of these was our old friend the nature/nurture controversy.

Average Mental Age of Recruits

Recall that Terman (1916) established that persons obtaining IQs less than 70 were typically considered to be feebleminded (see Table 6-9). Eighteen-year-olds with mental ages of 12 years or less would have maximal IQs of 67 [from Equation 6-3: $IQ = (12/18) \times 100 = 67$] and would thereby be considered feebleminded by this definition. Indeed, the mental age of 12 years in an adult became the standard definition of feeblemindedness. Considerable alarm was voiced when it was noted that the average mental age for the soldiers in the army sample was 13.08 years (Yerkes, 1921)—just 1 year above the criterion for feeblemindedness. Popular writers began to ask if it was possible that the average American was but 1 year from being feebleminded, and a general alarm about the state of the American intellect was sounded (for example, see Cannon, 1922; Popenoe, 1921). This interpretation was compatible with the eugenics agenda because it could be (and was) cited as support for a program of population control based on intellectual ability.

Black/White Differences

A second interpretation of the army data fed into the prevailing White views of Black people. Figure 7-2 shows the distributions of Black and White mental ages. In this subsample, the mean mental ages for White and Black draftees were 13.46 and 9.98 years, respectively. The average Black draftee was 2 years *below* the cutoff for feeblemindedness. These kinds of data were grist for the racist mill.

Data on Country of Origin

A third point that caused considerable discussion was the manner in which country of birth was related to intelligence scores. Table 7-4 presents the percentages of foreign-born recruits who were classified as D, D–, or E, which were the categories suspected of significant mental deficit. These data were frequently cited in the context of a postwar debate about the desirability of restricting immigration to the United States. Activists favoring this option were quick to point out that immigrants from northern European countries were less frequently classified in the deficit group than were those from the more southern countries. This supported the **Nordic doctrine**, which suggested that the more northerly European countries were somehow superior to the others. Perhaps the strongest rhetoric for this interpretation of the army data was voiced in Brigham (1923). Yerkes, because of his

Figure 7-2 Distribution of mental ages of a sample of White ($n = 93,965$) and Black ($n = 18,892$) draftees.

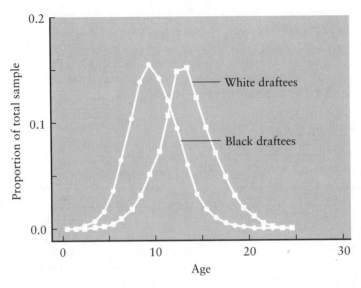

(SOURCE: Data from Yerkes, 1921, p. 654.)

Table 7-4 Percentage of foreign-born recruits classified as D, D–, or E*

Country of Birth	Percentage
England	8.7
Holland	9.2
Denmark	13.4
Scotland	13.6
Germany	15.0
Sweden	19.4
Canada	19.5
Belgium	24.0
United States (White draft)	24.1
Norway	25.6
Austria	37.5
Ireland	39.4
Turkey	42.0
Greece	43.6
Russia	60.4
Italy	63.4
Poland	69.9

*$n = 94,004$.

SOURCE: Yerkes (1921, p. 698).

eugenic conversion, became actively involved in promoting the cause, actually writing legislators when new immigration laws were being drafted.[4]

These three interpretations of the army data were publicized not only by politicians and activists but also became part of the ongoing academic debate within psychology. The academicians were more cautious than the publicists, urging the need for more research and the like, but these data were presented and discussed as scientifically valid facts. Within 10 years of its birth in the United States, the testing enterprise was enmeshed in a very vociferous debate with highly meaningful implications for social policy.

In retrospect, this use of testing to buttress eugenic and restrictive immigration arguments seems a bit implausible. How, you might ask, is it possible for intelligent people such as Yerkes to became actively involved in pushing for eugenics and restrictive legislation? Were they racists or just another example of science gone wrong? The answer to this question is not as simple as you might think because of the climate of the times. The United States of the late 1910s and early 1920s was an interesting place: "The country, marked by industrial and sociopolitical upheavals, was gripped with the fear that the 'masses' would revolt and bring about a 'Russian Revolution' right at home" (Pastore, 1978, p. 316).

The immigration of significant numbers of people from the exact geographic regions affected by the feared revolution was a true social problem in postwar America. Subtleties of geography and political affiliation (most Russian immigrants were fleeing the revolution) were lost, creating a generalized apprehension of non–English speaking "foreigners." This created a sociopolitical context that was ripe for both eugenic arguments and discourse about restrictive immigrant legislation. Testing played well in these debates: "Psychologists in the intelligence test movement interpreted and publicized the results of tests, especially those of the Army tests, in antidemocratic ways and advocated a quasi-caste system in their prescriptions for the reformation of society. Racial ideology, with a predilection for Nordic doctrine, was much in evidence" (Pastore, 1978, p. 316). Evans and Waites (1981) assert that the original attraction of IQ testing was for eugenicists who wanted to impose a program of racial "improvement": "Thus in the heyday of eugenics, high intelligence, or 'civic worth,' was considered to encompass all forms of moral and political wisdom, and low intelligence was considered to be the cause of all forms of moral turpitude and degeneracy, which eugenicists sought to eliminate" (p. 188). Low intelligence and its identification became an important issue not only for the testers but also for the future of American society. In this sense, the eugenics aspect of early testing can be seen as part of an attempt to solve what were perceived as significant contemporary social problems. When we recall that the basic tenets of the methodology of testing derived by Galton were sired from a similar perspective, it comes as very little surprise to find that the testing enterprise came out, rather strongly, in favor of eugenics and related social policies.

---

[4]Whether Yerkes's letter had an impact on the eventual passage of the Immigration Act of 1924, which imposed a quota favoring northern Europeans, is not certain. For a review, see Snyderman and Herrnstein (1983). However, Yerkes's intentions were most clear in his advocacy for **restrictive immigrant legislation.**

REPUDIATING THE "SCIENTIFIC" DATA

The eugenicists were not the only sociopolitical force in postwar America. Indeed, the very founding principles of the United States, which are closer to Mill's egalitarian views than those being espoused by the testers, were being assailed. Shortly after the publicization of the army test data interpretations, a grand debate began.

Walter Lippmann's Critique

Journalist Walter Lippmann was the most visible critic of the suggested interpretations of the army data. In a series of five articles in the *New Republic* and one blockbuster in the *Century* magazine, he severely criticized the assumptions, results, and applications of intelligence tests (for reviews, see Cronbach, 1975; Haney, 1981; Pastore, 1978). Table 7-5 summarizes the essential points raised by Lippmann. Of note in this critical appraisal is the assertion that the general notion of intelligence tests has considerable potential benefit (points 2 and 5 in Table 7-5). This indicates that Lippmann's critique is not a wholesale rejection of testing; rather, it is an evaluation of testing as currently practiced. As well, Lippmann clearly indicated the newness of the enterprise in the suggestion of the need for much more work before specific assertions could be made (points 2 and 4). In point 3, in Lippmann identified three key assumptions or value positions that clearly reflect the hereditarian position of the testing enterprise.[5] By suggesting that these values be "purged" from the enterprise, Lippmann's position is a clear reflection of an environmental perspective, coming down firmly on the nurture side of the nature/nurture controversy.

Terman (1922) attempted to rebut Lippmann's commentary, but unfortunately he adopted a somewhat sarcastic and demeaning attitude. He was no match for Lippmann and fared very poorly in the interchange (see Cronbach, 1975, p. 10; Pastore, 1978, p. 323). This debate between Terman and Lippmann certainly did not really resolve any of the important issues. However, the event clearly signaled that the psychological testing enterprise was going to run into some pretty heavy weather if it persisted in strong hereditarian views.

One particularly interesting point raised by Lippmann was his observation of a contradiction in the arguments being offered by the testers. The Stanford–Binet was based on a normative mental age of 16 years for adults. How is it possible, Lippmann asked, that the army data average was 13 years? Do we now have two averages? Which one is right? Because the conversions from Alpha scores to mental

---

[5]There is a controversy in the historical literature about the nature of Lippmann's contribution, with some suggestions his attack was journalistic sensationalism (for example, Cronbach, 1975, labeled Lippmann a "yellow journalist") and others arguing that it was not (for example, Pastore, 1975). Despite this, it remains that Lippmann's was a substantial and highly public critical appraisal of testing that warranted careful consideration by all parties concerned.

Table 7-5   Summary of Lippmann's critique of intelligence testing

1. The statement that the intelligence of the American nation has been measured by the army tests has no foundation.

2. There is reason to hope that intelligence testing may be of some practical benefit.

3. This benefit is in great danger of being offset by dangerous abuse if the claims of intelligence testers are not purged of certain fundamental assumptions, which include that
   a. the intelligence test measures "intelligence."
   b. "intelligence" is fixed by heredity.
   c. intelligence tests reveal and measure heredity.

4. Efforts to develop a universal test on these assumptions may be feasible in the future, but any claims that it has already been accomplished are unwarranted.

5. The potential for abuse of a testing program stemming from the above assumptions is considerable. (Recommends the development of specific tests for specific skills.)

SOURCE: Lippmann (1922).

ages were accomplished by reference to the Stanford–Binet, there is certainly a major problem here. In discussing this issue, Freeman (1922), a psychologist with considerable involvement in testing, agreed with Lippmann and stated "If you accept the finding that the average adult has a mental age of 13+ years you cannot at the same time hold that the mental age of the average adult is 16 years—which is involved in the acceptance of the Stanford–Binet scale of norms" (p. 442). The upshot of this aspect of the Alpha data was the eventual realization that the Stanford–Binet was not appropriate to the measurement of adult intelligence. It follows that any effort to equate adult tests such as the Alpha with the Stanford–Binet was ill advised and inappropriate. Thus, the finding of an average mental age of 13 years for Americans was the result of poorly conceived analyses, not the scientific fact touted by the publicists.

Problems with the Beta

A second aspect of the interpretations of the army data subsequently came under attack as well. The data pictured in Figure 7-2 (page 228), indicating a 3-year difference between the mental ages of Black and White draftees, were called into question. Four major points render the interpretations of these data equivocal.

1. The conversion of Alpha and Beta scores to mental ages is problematic; thus, the Black/White comparison is questionable.

2. The army testers did not follow policy in that low scorers on the Beta were supposed to be tested individually to determine if their deficit was a function of the testing. This policy was hardly ever followed (see Samuelson, 1977, pp. 279–280), leaving open the possibility that the observed

performance differences were due to aspects of the test and testing. Because a much higher proportion of Blacks received the Beta, this failure to adhere to policy had a greater effect on them, reducing the overall estimate of Black mental age.

3. This second point seems plausible because there was concern within the army testing group that the Beta did not have the degree of reliability and interscale correlations that were expected (Wood, 1919). It would appear that the Beta was not a great test, and the fact that Blacks were most often subjected to it contributed to the size of the Black/White difference in mental age shown in Figure 7-2 (page 228).

4. Perhaps the most important observation is that the instructions for the Beta were incomprehensible—even to literate recruits:

> For the sake of making the results from the various camps comparable, the examiners were ordered to follow a certain detailed and specific series of ballet antics, which had not only the merit of being perfectly incomprehensible and unrelated to mental testing, but also lent a highly confusing and distracting mystical atmosphere to the whole performance, effectually preventing all approach to the attitude in which a subject should be while having his soul tested. Fairly good results were obtained whenever these orders were disobeyed. [Wood, 1919]

> Evidence suggested that recruits were so mystified by the Beta instructions that it was almost impossible to maintain attention (Yerkes, 1921, p. 705). Thus, recruits who took the Beta were severely disadvantaged because the instructions were vague and for the most part incomprehensible. Because a higher proportion of Blacks took the Beta, this aspect of the test undoubtedly contributed to the size of the Black/White difference noted in Yerkes (1921).

In sum, it is clear that the Beta was not a good test, both in terms of its internal properties and the manner in which it was administered. It follows that any inferences made from this test must be rejected. Despite its problems, however, some aspects of the Beta have survived. For example, some contemporary intelligence tests contain subtests that were adapted from the Beta. These adaptations have been modified and changed sufficiently to rebut any assertions that they are as flawed as the Beta was.

The Nordic Doctrine

The third aspect of the army data relating to northern European immigrants performing better than southern European immigrants (see Table 7-4, page 228) did not come under the same scrutiny as did the previous two points. The Nordic doctrine remained part of the intellectual climate of the postwar era. In retrospect it is easy to see how virtually all the points outlined earlier could have been applied to this interpretation as well, particularly as non–English speaking immigrants would most likely have been tested with the Beta. It took the horrors of World War II, wrought under the banner of the "final solution," to really convince people of the unacceptability of the Nordic doctrine.

Summary

The three major interpretations of the army data outlined above (average mental age of 13, Black/White differences, intraimmigrant differences) were all found to be invalid. During the process of evaluating these ideas, the testing enterprise ran into its first major argument with American society. The prohereditarian perspective inherent in the data-collection and interpretation practices of the testing enterprise had not been supported. Very simply, *the army testing data did not provide any conclusive evidence in favor of a strong version of the hereditarian view*, which is a prerequisite for the enactment of the social policies that lay at the heart of the data interpretations. When considered along with the army's cancellation of the program, it appears that the entire exercise was a failure from a social perspective.[6] Historian James Reed (1987) captures the fundamental lesson learned from the army testing program:

> In retrospect, Yerkes's greatest coup as a scientific bureaucrat and promoter was not in getting the Surgeon General to find a place for psychologists in the army,...nor in writing tests, recruiting several hundred officers and technicians, and administering examinations to over 1.7 million individuals.... His most remarkable achievement was the myth that the army testing program had been a great practical success and that it provided a "goldmine" of data on the heritability of intelligence. [p. 84]

It would appear that history has not been kind to the army testing program, despite some recent suggestions to the contrary (for example, see Eysenck, 1979, pp. 81–84).

The entire program was not a failure, particularly if examined from the point of view of the emerging discipline of psychology. The army testing program did make a significant contribution to the methodology and theory of testing. The technology of group measurement of intelligence for adults, including the refinement of structured response alternatives, had taken place during this time. The adaptation of testing to masses of persons had been demonstrated as a potentially cost-effective way of making social decisions. The substantive results of the program were questioned and eventually were shown to be false, but such is the life of a science. The war made a significant contribution to the development of the discipline of psychology by providing a highly public forum in which the young discipline could demonstrate its practical worth. Without doubt, by 1920 psychology had been placed squarely "on the map." The promise of practical benefits had been realized through testing, even though the substantive results of the exercise had not. With its establishment in education and the military, dealing with ideas ranging from intelligence, abilities, and aptitudes through to personality, the testing enterprise was primed for major and significant development as the postwar period of prosperity, known as the Roaring 20s, got underway.

---

[6]Interestingly, most of the major players in the eugenics debate (for example, Brigham) subsequently retracted their views and accepted less hereditarian perspectives.

Summary

In this chapter, we focused on the manner in which the psychological testing enterprise was able to establish itself as a potential contributor to social affairs during World War I. The adaptation of prewar developments such as the point scale and multiple-choice format was shown in the context of a massive effort to test the intellectual capacity of all recruits into the U.S. Army. Two tests, the Alpha and Beta, were administered to over 7 million men. Testing ideas were also generalized to a number of other areas such as personality, aptitude, and ability measurement during this time. The apparent successes of the mental-testing program were challenged by exploring what really happened immediately after the war, with attempts to use the army data to support the eugenics agenda being severely criticized and eventually rejected. The lessons in testing technology garnered from this experience, though, were of great benefit to the emerging psychological testing enterprise.

Glossary

Army Alpha A test consisting of eight subscales and 212 items, the Alpha was the flagship of the army testing program during World War I. Said to be a measure of intelligence, it was intended for recruits who could read and write. The results stimulated considerable research and debate in the postwar period.

Army Beta A version of the Army Alpha developed for illiterate recruits. It involved pictorial stimuli, and instructions were given in pantomime. Its questionable quality led to severe criticism of attempts to use the Beta data to make social policy.

Committee on Methods of Psychological Examining of Recruits A committee formed at the beginning of World War I to develop intelligence testing of army recruits. Chaired by Robert Yerkes, it consisted of the "Who's Who" of the emerging testing domain.

introspection A methodology in early experimental psychology where research participants would attempt to describe what was happening as they were involved in various psychological activities. This looking inward was seen as the primary method for gaining a sense of the psychological contents of the mind and was rejected by researchers wanting to pursue an objective, experimental approach.

Kansas Silent Reading Test A 1915 test, developed by Frederick J. Kelly, that contained the first published multiple-choice item.

Letter Ratings Obtained from the Army Alpha and Beta, one of the scores that was calculated by comparing an individual's number of correct items to a table. (See Table 7-2.)

multiple-choice item A structured test format in which a question is asked and a series of possibly correct answers provided, only one of which is correct. The respondent's task is to select which alternative answer is the correct one. Incorrect alternatives are called *distractors*. The first published multiple-choice item was on a reading test in 1915.

Nordic doctrine The belief that Europeans from the north were superior to those from the south or east. The army data were (inappropriately) interpreted as support for this position.

Personal Data Sheet Robert Woodworth's pioneering self-report questionnaire developed to predict shell shock. It consisted of 116 items that were answered either yes or no. (See Table 7-3.)

point scale An approach to testing that involves administering a complete set of items to all respondents and using the number of items answered correctly as the raw score. So-named because of the practice of assigning 1 point for each correct answer. This contrasts with Binet types of subtests that are administered only to some respondents. Developed by Robert Yerkes, the point scale can be administered to groups of respondents.

restrictive immigrant legislation Laws passed to impose quotas on the numbers of people from various countries who would be allowed into the U. S. The eugenicists (including Robert Yerkes) were very active in campaigning for these laws, which were passed in 1924.

self-report questionnaire A structured inventory in which respondents provide answers to a series of questions (items). These have become the norm in the area of personality assessment.

shell shock An acute stress response encountered in the trenches during World War I. Robert Woodworth developed his Personal Data Sheet to try and predict which recruits were prone to this reaction.

Stenquist Construction Test A test of mechanical ability that involves assembling common mechanical items from their constituent parts. Thought to be the first ability test, the Stenquist was tested during World War I and subsequently used in industrial applications.

test item One of the questions that appears on a point scale. The item evolved to become the fundamental unit of analysis of the testing field once point scales became the norm.

Woodworth, Robert S. The psychologist who developed the first self-report personality inventory during World War I.

Yerkes, Robert Mearns An American psychologist who, in addition to being an eminent comparative psychologist, invented the point scale and directed the army testing program during World War I.

Suggested Further Reading

Lippmann, W. (1922). The mental age of Americans. *New Republic, 32,* 213–215; The mystery of the "A" men. *New Republic, 32,* 246–248; The reliability of intelligence tests. *New Republic, 32,* 275–277; The abuse of tests. *New Republic, 32,* 297–298; Tests of hereditary intelligence. *New Republic, 32,* 328–330; A future for tests. *New Republic, 33,* 9–11.

These short classic articles are great reading if you want to gain a sense of the debate between testers and journalists as described in the chapter. Not only do they give a feel for the times, but many of the points raised by Lippmann are relevant today. They are fine primary material.

Samuelson, F. (1979). Putting psychology on the map: Ideology and intelligence testing. In A. R. Buss (Ed.), *Psychology in social context*. New York: Irvington.

This detailed chapter presents considerable information about the manner in which the army testing program and other aspects of the testing enterprise were used to promote specific ideologial positions. It presents some of the material from the latter part of this chapter of *The Enterprise* in considerably greater detail.

Sokal, M. M. (Ed.). (1987). *Psychological testing and American society*. New Brunswick, N.J.: Rutgers University Press.

This edited volume contains some excellent source material. Of particular note are discussions of Yerkes's program (Chapter 4), multiple-choice items (Chapter 6), and the clash between Yerkes and Scott regarding how to best help the military (Chapter 7).

Yerkes, R. M. (Ed.). (1921). Psychological examining in the United States Army. *Memoirs of the National Academy of Sciences*, 15, 1–890.

This impressive volume contains thousands of analyses of the army test data, some interesting commentary by Yerkes, and a series of great photographs. It also has copies of the various forms of the tests that were used. For anyone interested in the army testing program, it is required reading. The massive nature of the program and the assumptions made by the researchers literally jump off the pages. This is a time where reading primary sources is particularly important and revealing.

Discussion Questions

1. Prepare a debate presentation in which you have to defend the tenets of introspection against a hard-headed scientist who wants all data to be objective.

2. What aspects of James McKeen Cattell's desiderata for tests (Chapter 6) presage the effectiveness of the testing enterprise in dealing with the masses of recruits in World War I? What new desiderata would you add to this list on the basis of the army experience?

3. Compare and contrast point and Binet-type scales. Why do you think point scales became the most popular?

4. From your own personal experiences with testing, outline whether you agree with Dubois who suggested that the invention of the test item was the most important invention of the early testing enterprise.

5. Outline the pragmatic benefits of structured versus unstructured response formats.

6. Multiple-choice items are so much a part of our way of life that it is difficult to realize that they haven't been around since time immemorial. In your view, was the emergence of this approach to measurement in 1915 late or early relative to other events in the testing enterprise. Why?

7. Critique Robert Yerkes's contention that the Army Alpha measured "native ability rather than the results of school training."

8. List the stated goals of the Alpha. Were they realized? (Be sure to clarify the stakeholder to whom you are referring in your answer.)

9. Outline the problems that would be inevitable in attempting to design a test like the Beta which is a nonwritten version of a verbal test (the Alpha).

10. Write a press release of the type that Yerkes might have prepared to promote the success of his testing program.

11. Of the four major testing developments during the war (intelligence, personality, aptitude, and ability testing), which was the most important? Why?

12. Supposing the war had lasted longer than it did, suggest a method that Robert Woodworth might have used to prove that his Personal Data Sheet actually worked in predicting shell shock.

13. Discuss the strengths and weaknesses of using a measure of general intelligence (for example, like the Alpha) versus a specific job-related measure (for example, Thurstone's tests of telegraphic ability) for the placement of recruits into specific jobs in the military.

14. Critically evaluate the Stenquist Skill Test.

15. Briefly describe the negative reactions to Yerkes's program from the perspective of the soldiers, the army, "pure" psychologists, and the intelligent layperson.

16. Outline the reasoning and data behind the three major postwar interpretations of the army data.

17. Sketch out the manner in which you might debate with a tester who asserted that the mental age of the average American was just 1 year higher than feebleminded.

18. Critically evaluate the data presented in Figure 7-2.

19. Develop an explanation of the country-of-origin Alpha data that incorporates the nature of the languages involved in the groups listed in Table 7-4.

20. If you were teaching the material in this chapter and were forced to take sides with either Lewis Terman, as defending the Alpha data, or Walter Lippmann, as challenging it, which side would you take? Why?

21. Carefully argue the contribution the army data made to clarifying the nature/nurture question.

22. List all the benefits *for psychology* that accrued from the army testing program. In your view, which was the most important? Why?

Chapter 8

Criterion-Related Validity

WHAT MAKES A TEST GOOD?

In this chapter, we will explore the manner in which the emerging community of scholars and researchers surrounding psychological testing began to negotiate among themselves a series of criteria regarding what constitutes a good test. During this time, a number of research practices, which constitute the very essence of today's testing enterprise, were developed, and we will discuss these as well. This process of developing evaluative criteria for tests is critically important for an informed understanding of the fundamental nature of the testing practice. In this chapter in our narrative of testing, we get a glimpse of the very heart of the emerging enterprise.

The evolution of standards of excellence for tests is a highly social enterprise. The criteria that eventually emerged were not "given of God"—they were not intuitively obvious ideas that rang with clarion clarity when first suggested. Rather, they were the result of long and arduous negotiation within the young testing community. They were debated, tried out, rejected, or accepted, much in the same way that a scientific theory is. The eventual outcome of this process provided researchers with a unique way of seeing the world—what we have earlier called a worldview—which is an accepted and expected part of belonging to the community of testers. These criteria represented a marriage of theory and practice within this new and developing field. Methods drove the criteria of excellence and vice versa. To be aware of this is important because the eventual ideas that did emerge have had a profound impact on the character of the testing enterprise.

The first development in this negotiation of criteria of excellence can be seen in Jastrow, Baldwin, and Cattell's (1898) *desiderata* of mental tests presented in Chapter 6 (see Table 6-2, page 183). Emphasis here was on simplicity and cost efficiency. Shortly thereafter, researchers dealing with tests began to apply the standard of **trustworthiness**. It was thought that trustworthy tests provided faithful representations of the real world in the generated output. This concept, though, did not provide the kinds of methodological prescriptions that the emerging field needed. There were no established ways of establishing trustworthiness at this point.

The next development came in 1907 when Spearman introduced the idea of reliability, which reflected the degree of error-freeness in a score (see Chapter 6). In a sense, Spearman's idea divided the notion of trustworthiness into two segments by attributing the consistency of a score to the idea of reliability—leaving the other part undefined—at least for a while. Spearman's idea also came with a ready-made method of measurement—the test/retest correlation. But what about the other part of trustworthiness not captured by the idea of reliability? Certainly, there was more than reliability involved, for a test could be perfectly reliable but not measure what it is supposed to—making it highly untrustworthy. For example, if a highly reliable intelligence test only measured socioeconomic status of the family in which a child was reared, suggestions that it was a good test of intelligence would be questionable. Something was needed besides reliability to capture the essential nature of the good test. But what was this other component, and how could it be measured?

The first candidate to vie for this position of evaluative excellence was the idea of **value**, defined as the quality of a test performing as expected. The major gain of this notion over trustworthiness was that it became possible to measure a test's value by a clever adaptation of the correlation coefficient.

The Test-Criterion Method

Prior to and during World War I, psychologists used the correlation coefficient to establish the value of a test in a deceptively simple way. A test would be administered to a group of respondents, *and* some other measure would also be gathered on the same respondents. This second measure, deemed to be an independent estimate of whatever the test measured, was called a **criterion**. The establishment of test value involved calculating the correlation between the test and criterion scores; if it was high enough, the value of the test had been established. For example, teacher ratings of student intelligence might be gathered by the test developer and used as a criterion measure for an intelligence test. A high correlation between an intelligence test and the criterion measure of teacher ratings would be evidence that the test and teacher ratings were measuring the same thing. Such findings were interpreted as demonstrating the value of the test, thereby showing that it was a better intelligence test. A low or zero correlation would be evidence that the test did not predict the criterion and would call the value of the test into question.[1]

This approach to evaluating tests was in evidence even before Pearson introduced the product-moment correlation. For example, Boulton (1891) used this method with a digit-span task. To determine if memory performance was related to "intellectual acuteness of the pupils," Boulton had teachers rate the pupils' schoolwork as either good, fair, or poor. This was his criterion measure. He then divided memory-test performance into three categories from poor to good using his test. A 3×3 contingency table, which contained the percentages of pupils falling in each of the nine possible cells, was then constructed. This table demonstrated a positive relationship between the test and criterion scores, thereby establishing that the test scores measure "intellectual acuteness." Boulton's study is an excellent example of a **test-criterion method** and the manner in which it was used to establish test-score meaning.

Here's another example that incorporates the correlation coefficient. The Stanford–Binet correlates .48 with teacher ratings (see Chapter 6). This result provides one piece of evidence for the value of the Stanford–Binet because there is a clear relationship between the teachers' estimates and the test scores. In a sense, the test could be used as a substitute for teacher ratings, thus indicating that it has value as a measure of intelligence. If Stanford–Binet scores could also be shown to be substantially related to whether pupils passed a given grade, with lower scorers failing more frequently, yet another piece of evidence for the value of the tests would have been provided. In essence, the method involved determining the degree of relationship between test scores and relevant criteria, using (typically) the correlation coefficient as a means of testing the degree of relationship.

As early as 1910, the test-criterion method had emerged as the preeminent means of establishing test value. In practice, a number of researchers noted that the time frame of the criterion could vary. For example, a criterion could be measured at the same time as the test was given. The test-criterion correlation, in this case, is concerned with whether the test can predict the present status of the individuals involved. This idea became known as **diagnostic value** because it related to making concurrent statements about the status of those tested. Both testing and teacher ratings taken at the beginning of an academic term would be an example of this orientation.

On the other hand, collecting criteria a significant amount of time *after* the test had been administered is also possible. In this case, the concern would be to try to use the test to predict something that will happen in the future. This approach became known as examining the **prognostic value** of a test. Using Stanford–Binet scores to predict the grades that pupils will receive at the end of the coming term would be an example of this approach. Thus, the establishment of test value could occur in two ways, prognostic value and diagnostic value, with the time frame of the criterion determining which was being used.

---

[1]The prescient quote by Francis Galton in 1890 in which he indicated that the best means of establishing test meaning involved using "independent estimates of a man's powers" (see Chapter 6) can be cited as one of the very first descriptions of the test-criterion method.

In both of these approaches to establishing test value, the original correlations would be calculated using a relevant sample of respondents. The operating assumption was that these results would generalize to a new group of similar respondents. That is, the test user could assume that the same types of relationships would obtain for a second group of respondents if they were similar to those on whom the original correlation had been calculated. Here a major gain emerges for this technology. Once the prognostic or diagnostic value of a test has been established, test users can employ the test confident that the original relationships hold for their new respondents. This provides the test with considerable usefulness and cost effectiveness because gathering criterion measures on the second sample (if the correlations are sufficiently high to permit an accurate prediction) is not necessary. The test with demonstrated value can then be used to predict criterion status in the absence of criterion measures for the second group of respondents.

By 1915 the testing literature was rife with references to prognostic and diagnostic value. The correlational technology of establishing these aspects of test value had become accepted practice, as had the notion of value emerged to become the second component of trustworthiness, coexisting easily with Spearman's ideas of reliability. At this point, the criteria of excellence for new tests were readily captured in the dual ideas of reliability and value, with the latter being broken down into subcategories of prognostic and diagnostic.

MEASUREMENT WITHOUT DEFINITION

The army experience and social reaction to it had a profound effect on the approach to establishing criteria of excellence for tests. Perhaps in its haste to be of help to society and perhaps because of something inherent in tests themselves, a specific and very important intellectual tradition had emerged. This tradition placed major value on the pragmatic and applied applications of the instruments and deemphasized the importance of knowing what a test was measuring. Indeed, it can be argued that the problems surrounding the interpretations of the army data were very much due to the failure of the testers to clarify exactly what the tests were measuring. If there had been explicit and scientifically verified statements about the manner in which intelligence tests were thought to reveal "native intelligence," many of the problems would have been avoided. These beliefs of the testers were not voiced explicitly but were assumed because explicit consideration of what the test was measuring was not demanded. No prevailing intellectual traditions forced testers to clearly stipulate the boundary conditions on what it was that their tests measured. For example, detailed consideration of exactly what intelligence tests were measuring, or even what intelligence was, was not at the forefront of thinking as the testing enterprise entered the postwar era.

An early example of this tradition can be found in a paper by Otis (1916), entitled "Some Logical Aspects of the Binet Scale." In this essay, Otis offers what appears to be a sophisticated treatment of the underlying nature of intelligence. He includes a number of fine mathematical figures and arguments that provide a sense of sophistication about the level of understanding of this complex idea. The substance of his argument, however, condenses to three questions that should be answered in the affirmative if a test was to be considered a measure of intelligence:

1. Do the percents of children at succeeding ages who pass the test[2] increase with age?
2. Do those who pass it also exceed those who do not, in the number of other tests passed?
3. Are those who pass the test generally conceded to be more intelligent than those who do not? [Otis, 1916, p. 169]

These criteria suggest that performance on the test ought to correlate with age and conform to a nonexistent, consensual concept of intelligence. Although such criteria appear to provide purchase on the nature of intelligence, they fail to provide an explicit definition of exactly what the test is supposed to measure. This is an example of **measurement without definition.** The test may be measuring something—and it may be measuring it reliably and have demonstrated value—but whatever is being measured has not been explicitly articulated.

This issue came to the fore in the postwar era when major researchers in the field convened for a symposium on intelligence testing (Rugg, 1921).[3] They discussed their definitions of intelligence, and the outcome of the proceedings was a clear indication that there was little or no agreement about the definition of the entity the tests were measuring. A review of the symposium stated bluntly that "there is very great disagreement concerning the concept of intelligence, but rather striking agreement as to the methods of measurement" (Poffenberger, 1921, p. 426). It is somewhat strange that dramatic and massive efforts such as the army testing program could be initiated and sustained by an idea (that is, intelligence) that was undefined. Driven by the pragmatic utility of tests and the desire to contribute to American society, the psychological testing movement launched a program that had a very deep weakness: There was no agreement about the meaning of the fundamental idea on which the program was based. The tests provided the emerging discipline with a powerful new tool with which to demonstrate its potential contribution to mainstream North American life, rendering the method more important than the underlying meaning. The research activity surrounding intelligence testing was fundamentally method-driven, sustained by the pragmatic utility of the tests themselves. The instruments were available and clearly useful, but there was absolutely no consensus about what they measured.

It might be argued that measurement without definition is a necessary first step in the development of any technology. For example, some contemporary technologies involve the use of ground-piercing radar to gain a sense of the underlying substrata of various landforms. This technology has tremendous practical import

---

[2]Otis is using the word *test* in this quotation to mean what we call a *subtest*.

[3]In fact, there were *three* major symposia on intelligence, one in the United States, one in Britain, and one sponsored by the International Congress of Psychology. The comments herein apply to all three symposia (see Spearman, 1927, pp. 8–11).

for environmental studies because it is noninvasive and inexpensive. When the first experiments were conducted with this technology, researchers did not know exactly what they were seeing. They were indeed involved in measurement without definition because they had no idea of the relationship between the output of their computers and what was occurring beneath the earth's surface. Perhaps this is the way that measurement technology is developed, and a situation involving measurement without definition, such as we see in the 1920s testing enterprise, should not give us pause.

In the ground-piercing radar context, as in most hard sciences, the first order of business was to find out exactly what the measurement technology was "seeing"—that is, to find out *what* was being measured. Only then will the technique be released for general use. It is here that the early testing enterprise deviates significantly from the practice in most other sciences. With the pragmatic bent of the early testers and the test-criterion method in hand, the tradition of measurement without definition was maintained well past the period expected in other sciences (see, for example, Chapter 15). Perhaps because of the difficulty of defining concepts such as intelligence, the idea of metaphysical debates about what it was tests measured were often considered to be useless philosophical discussions. The intellectual traditions of the time conspired against detailed and thorough examination of exactly what it was that the tests were measuring.

THE EMERGENCE OF VALIDITY

The failure to develop a consensual definition of intelligence was exacerbated by increasing concerns within the discipline about its status as a science. In its movement toward professionalization, psychologists "became increasingly concerned with their reputation as a science" (Camfield, 1973, p. 73). Frustrated by the presence of widespread differences within the discipline, psychologists continually searched for scientific legitimacy and offered considerable debate about the appropriate methodology to achieve this. The inability to define intelligence was not congenial to the desire for scientific legitimacy and prompted considerable activity trying to resolve the issue.

The tremendous numbers of new tests and researchers streaming into the enterprise after the war added fuel to this problem. Tests for measuring almost everything you could think of began to emerge. Indeed, 40% of the psychologists listed in the 1923 APA yearbook were listed as doing research in the field of tests (Terman, 1924). Testing had caught on within the discipline. However, this created a situation in which it was necessary to develop explicit criteria for evaluating tests. Jordan (1923) articulated this issue with considerable flourish:

> Now as long as there was only one claimant to the papal throne of Saint Peter the people were not unwilling to believe that the Pope was the one divinely appointed, but when after the "Babylonian Captivity" there were several claimants to this throne the power of the Pope suffered because the people began to wonder which

one, if any, was the real pope. So here, when instruments varying in their results claim to measure intelligence it becomes necessary to make a careful study of each group test and of each sub-test in order to discover if possible which is the best measure of intelligence. [p. 348]

Jordan suggested that there was now a critical need for criteria that would allow users to select which of the "pretenders to the throne" was the best. An additional concern was the fear that some of the many emerging tests may be forwarded by charlatans more interested in capitalizing on the current popularity than contributing to psychology. A set of criteria to provide some kind of control of the burgeoning testing enterprise was clearly necessary.

It was into this context that a new word was introduced and eventually accepted as the preeminent criterion of the goodness of a psychological test. This is the concept of **validity**, which emerged in the early 1920s as a solution to these pressing problems. *A test is said to have validity if it measures what it purports to measure.* This new concept provided the testing enterprise with a powerful and explicit evaluative criterion that could be used to sift out unacceptable tests—that is, those that are invalid. The test-criterion method became the primary way of establishing the validity of a test and helped contribute to the scientific appearance of the enterprise in its clear presentation of an empirical means of determining this aspect of a test. In all, validity emerged as a remarkably effective solution to most of the problems being experienced by the testing field in the early 1920s.

CLOSE UP   **The Negotiation of Validity**

Trying to piece together exactly how validity emerged in the testing enterprise is like an archaeologist trying to construct a dinosaur from a few bones. Much of the critical information is not readily available and has to be filled in by guesswork. Perhaps this explains why it is almost impossible to find an analysis of the emergence of validity in the historical work. If you read the trade literature, it seems the idea just came out from nowhere, but it did not—it emerged as the result of a negotiated consensus in the field.

One place where we can start is a careful examination of the published literature of the time. This approach, though only part of the puzzle, reveals an interesting story of how validity slowly but surely became the most important evaluative criterion in the testing enterprise.

There are several mentions of the word *validity* in the early literature of this time (for example, Healy, 1914; Norsworthy, 1908).[4] Upon close reading, however, these authors were not discussing the specialized concept of validity that emerged later on. Conversely, those using the test-criterion method did not employ the word *validity* (for example, Abelson, 1911; Fernald, 1912; Miner, 1914).

One of the first clear uses of the technical concept of validity occurred in Starch (1915b). Regarding the possibility that reading tests may tap expressive abilities, he indicated that "in order to determine from a different angle the *validity* [italics added] of these reading tests, *a comparison was made between the*

---

[4]In this Close Up, complete sets of references are not provided; the citations are for typical examples. For details, see Rogers and Rogers, 1990.

efficiency in reading as shown by the tests and the efficiency as indicated by the marks assigned by the teachers [italics added] (p. 12). Yet Starch's use of the word *validity* was inconsistent because he did not use it in a number of other papers published about this time (for example, Starch, 1915a, 1915c, 1916). A hint of a relationship between test-criterion methodology and validity can also be found in Terman (1916), but, as with Starch, this was not consistent.

Not many occurrences of the word *validity* appeared in wartime, but during the immediate postwar period, there was increasing but cautious use of the word in association with the test-criterion method. For example, a number of authors began to use the term but in quotation marks, signaling a self-conscious use (for example, Maxfield, 1918; Otis, 1918; Pressey & Pressey, 1923).

The year 1921 emerges as pivotal in the emergence of validity as part of the institutional proceedings of the testing field. This is when the idea gained clear acceptance. The Standardization Committee of the National Association of Directors of Educational Research polled its members about the desirability of publishing an official list of terms and procedures. The results of this survey were announced in Courtis (1921). Of particular note is this statement: "Two of the most important types of problems in measurement are those connected with the *determination of what a test measures* [italics added], and of how consistently it measures. The first should be called the problem of *validity* [italics added], the second, the problem of reliability" (p. 80). This is the first institutional definition of validity. The Standardization Committee also indicated clearly that the test-criterion correlations were the principal means of establishing a test's validity: "Members are urged to devise and publish means of determining the *relation between the scores made in a test and other measures of the same ability* [italics added]: in other words, to try to solve the problem of determining the *validity* [italics added] of a test" (p. 80). These recommendations are clear evidence that validity had emerged as a self-conscious term within the discipline by 1921 and that the test-criterion method was the means by which this idea could be made explicit. What remained was for the term to gain consensual usage.

The Standardization Committee offered their recommendations in a rather tentative manner because there was an expressed concern that standardization may be premature. The report indicated that adoption of these terms would be deferred until the next annual meeting. A reading of the subsequent proceedings of the association, which was undergoing some reconsideration of its mandate during 1922 and 1923, revealed no follow-up discussions of the committee report. In 1922 a series of new committees was formed (for example, publications policy, relationship to other associations), which subsequently reported back to the annual meeting. The Standardization Committee, along with its definition of validity, appears to have vanished.

By the end of 1921, though, the frequency of use of the word *validity* was on a clear upswing, with many authors beginning to use it. Slowly but surely, *validity* crept into the active vocabularies of workers in the field. This trend continued for the next several years, with the literature showing a growing number of substantive applications of the concept. There was also increased frequency of use in article titles and eventually in textbooks. Of particular note is the finding that the introduction of the word *validity* cannot in fairness be attributed to one particular individual, but was the result of a negotiated consensus within the field.

This summary of the manner in which *validity* was used in the literature during the critical time of its emergence does not provide the full picture. However, we can sense how the term was used very tentatively at first, how it became accepted through the efforts of the Standardization Committee in 1921, and how the idea emerged in response to a number of very important influences.

Of all the concepts that have evolved in the testing enterprise, past and present, validity is clearly the most important and significant because it addresses explicitly the issue of what tests measure. By incorporating the test-criterion method as the only way of determining test validity, this new term not only provided a useful idea but also strengthened extant practice. By early 1922, this idea had become firmly entrenched in the testing enterprise.

An Effective Solution

Validity provided an explicit means of evaluating tests during a time when new instruments were being published almost daily. A particularly good example of how validity helped serve the need for control comes from an examination of a test, published by June Downey, intended to measure **temperament**.

The **Downey Will Temperament Test** (DWTT) derived from a general movement that was exploring the assessment of nonintellective factors in individual differences. The DWTT involved the basic proposition that certain skilled motor performances (for example, speech and handwriting) could be used as indicators of specific types of individuals. The basic dimension thought to underlie the tests was marked at one end by individuals whose activity is free, forceful, and explosive and at the other end by persons whose energy is limited and inhibited. The test involved 12 subtests such as speed of handwriting, changes in handwriting under distraction, and exactness of copying another signature. The scoring, as described by Downey (1922), is somewhat subjective.

Several papers published in the literature were beginning to suggest a number of problems for this test; included here were several critical reviews and some disappointing data (for example, Meier, 1923; Ruch & Del Manzo, 1923). The weight of opinion appeared to be lining up against the DWTT, but it remained for Mark May (1925) to make the final case for its abandonment (for biographical details of May, see May, 1978). In what was one of the most complete applications of the emerging notion of validity to a specific test, May demolished the DWTT, using constant reference to validity throughout. In a section entitled "Validation by Checking Against Ratings," he outlined a number of test-criterion studies: "The results of all these attempts at validation by the rating method are uniformly ambiguous. . . . Other kinds of tests have been validated by this method" (p. 39). Equally problematic points were raised in sections entitled "Correlations with Other Tests," "Validation by Identification of Profiles," "Validation by Differentiation," and "Validation by Testing the Prognostic Value of These Tests." Another section explored the relation between the DWTT and intelligence. Each section clearly used validity as a means of debunking a specific test. As you might expect, May's final evaluation was not positive: "Whatever else they [the DWTT subtests] measure, they do not measure traits" (p. 50).

This discussion of the DWTT indicates that the emerging notion of validity, very early in its career, began to earn its keep as a means of evaluating tests. As an apparently neutral language for judging the value of a mental test, validity provided a means for making decisions about which of the many evolving tests warranted continuation and, perhaps more important, which ones should be dropped from further consideration. In a context where scientific legitimacy was important and the probability of charlatans abusing the emerging technology was high, validity provided a very important and powerful evaluative criterion. May's application of the idea can be seen as a particularly effective exemplar of how validity works.

Recall that the notion of validity was a renaming of a procedural approach that had been with the testing enterprise more or less since its inception. As early as 1890, Francis Galton indicated the need to compare tests with independent measures in order to select the best ones (see Chapter 6). This sounds suspiciously like the test-criterion method, which in 1921 was the only methodology available for the assessment of test validity. This "new" idea of validity was, then, really putting old wine in new bottles. To the extent that we have already established that the test-criterion method sanctions measurement without definition, it remains that the field was still committed to this approach after the introduction of validity.

SOME ELABORATIONS OF VALIDITY

A number of important issues emerged as the test-criterion method and validity became more firmly established in the methodological canons of the testing enterprise. Validity and the test-criterion method became the centerpieces of a rather complex and sophisticated **theory of measurement,** which represented a synthesis of the ideas and practices that guided the development of tests for the next half century and beyond.

Criterion-Related Validity

Over time, assessing validity using the test-criterion method became known as **criterion-related validity.** Any procedure that uses the assessment of the degree of relationship with outside, independent measures to validate a test falls under this general rubric of validity. Inherent in almost all these approaches is the **validity coefficient,** which is the measure of relatedness between the test and the criterion. In most applications, this index is the Pearson product-moment correlation. The validity of a test is thought to be proportional to the size of the validity coefficient in cases where appropriate criteria and respondents are employed.

A reasonable question to ask is how big the coefficient has to be before it can be interpreted as demonstrating validity for the test. This is a complex question because the size of the correlation, and the amount of fluctuation that might be expected on the basis of chance, is a function of the number of pairs of observations that go into calculating it. The greater the number of observations, the more robust the index of correlation becomes. For example, if 100 pairs of observations are used to calculate a correlation, statistical reasoning tells us that a value of .25 is considered significantly greater than 0, with a probability of .01 or less.[5] In other words, a correlation larger than this would only be found 1 in 100 times if random data were used. It seems a safe bet, then, that a correlation this size or higher does represent a significant finding. Thus, for 100 pairs, the value of .25 represents the **critical value** above which a correlation may be considered to be significantly different from 0, or, in our context, as indicative of a degree of validity for the test. If, however, there are only 10 pairs of observations used to calculate the correlation, the same statistical reasoning indicates that the critical value becomes .66. In other words, with 10 pairs of observations making up the correlation, it would be necessary to demonstrate a value of .66 to prove that the size of the relationship is meaningfully different from 0. This greater value is due to the possibility of there being proportionally much more error with fewer observations; thus, it is necessary to have a higher critical value.

The testing enterprise has accepted a convention for determining if a given correlation is meaningful. The assumption is made that it is possible to repeat, or replicate, a given statistical test on equivalent data a large number of times. If the chances of attaining a correlation the size of the one found on the extant sample exceeds a given probability level, the correlation is said to have **significance**. That is, the probability of obtaining a correlation of a critical size by chance is thought to be beyond a reasonable level if a correlation is significant. In the testing enterprise, probability levels of .05 (1 chance in 20) and .01 (1 chance in 100) have been adopted as conventional levels for considering a given correlation to be significant. The more conservative .01 level is the safer one if researchers wish to avoid labeling a correlation as significant when in actuality it is due to chance factors such as random error.

Figure 8-1 shows the relationship between numbers of pairs of observations making up a correlation coefficient and the size of the critical correlation value for probabilities of .01 and .05. Validity coefficients that exceed the critical values shown in this figure can be interpreted as providing evidence for the validity of the test. Values that fall below the critical value do not provide this evidence. Appendix B presents a more detailed version of these values, along with detailed instructions on its use.

One difficulty with this approach to significance is that the critical value of the correlation becomes ridiculously low as the number of pairs becomes high. For example, extending Figure 8-1 out to 1000 observations would reveal that a correlation of .08 would be significantly different from 0 at $p < .01$. Even though this is a significant correlation, how good would the prediction of criterion status be from test score? Not particularly good, to be sure. Because many of the testing applications involve large numbers of respondents (for example, the army testing program), this is a very real concern.[6] The eventual solution to this problem was to

---

[5] The actual calculation of this value, although not overly complicated, is beyond what we need to know now. If you want details, see Ferguson (1966, pp. 184–187, 413).

[6] Because of this concern, a number of different approaches to establishing the usefulness of tests, apart from considering the size of the validity coefficient, has evolved. Some of these are discussed in Chapters 11, 13, and 19.

Figure 8-1   Critical values of the correlation coefficient as a function of the number of pairs of observations involved in the calculation of the coefficient.

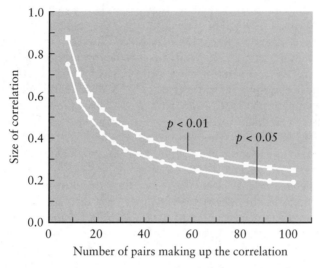

(SOURCE: Based on Ferguson, 1966, p. 413.)

consider alternate types of indexes of relationship focusing on the numbers of correct and incorrect predictions that would be made (see, for example, Chapter 11).

The answer to the question "How big does a validity coefficient have to be?" is "It depends." There is no absolute answer here; it is contingent not only on various aspects of the manner in which the data were collected (for example, number of observations) but also on the particular situation. Sometimes collecting needed data is too expensive, or ethical constraints deny its collection. Hence, the evaluation of validity information must be conducted in a thorough case-by-case basis. What is important is that the idea of validity and the test-criterion method provide a clear and concise set of questions that must be answered before a test can be considered valid. Although there may be variability in the size of correlations necessary to support this contention, the introduction of the idea provided a definite schema for attacking this most important question.

Conditions Affecting the Size of Validity Coefficients

The preceding discussion makes it clear that the number of pairs of observations that go into the calculation of a validity coefficient is an important contributor to the size of the validity coefficient. Some other, equally important, aspects, however, should be mentioned. The nature of the group used to generate the coefficient is critical. If the group has a narrow range of scores on the criterion measure, the validity coefficient is likely to be lower. For example, if academic performance was being used as a criterion and the particular sample used to calculate a validity coefficient received grades between 75% and 80%, the likelihood of finding a high coefficient is seriously reduced, particularly in comparison with a group with grades ranging between, say, 40% and 95%. Thus, it is important that the sample used have a reasonable degree of **heterogeneity**, or variability, on the criterion and on the test.

Another possible problem is **preselection.** As an example, in many validity studies in industry, a test is administered to all newly hired employees. When it comes time to generate the criterion measure, some of these employees have already left the job—meaning that the obtained estimate of validity is compromised because some workers, perhaps those who were not doing well, have not been included in the validation sample. Preselection of this type tends to restrict the range of both criterion and test scores and can seriously affect the size of the obtained coefficient—typically lowering it.

Other possible group characteristics can affect the size of the obtained validity coefficient, with sample variability and preselection being two of the more frequent types of difficulties. The apparently simple idea of the test-criterion method is clearly more complex than it seemed at first. Attempts to deal with these types of problems led to the emergence of a rather sophisticated set of methods and concerns within the testing field—all of which stem directly from the test-criterion methodology and its realization in the concept of criterion-related validity.

Criterion Contamination

Another important methodological consideration to emerge in the early days of validity was the issue of independence between the test and the criterion. If there was the possibility that those assigning criterion status were aware of the test scores, the entire validation exercise is deeply compromised. This possibility, called **criterion contamination,** would have the effect of elevating the validity coefficient because test scores would possibly affect criterion status. For example, if a teacher made intelligence ratings being aware of how pupils had scored on the Stanford–Binet, the obtained validity coefficient would be a gross overestimate of the validity of the test. This signaled the need for researchers to be very careful about the manner in which they gathered their data and the detail they reported.[7]

Subtypes of Criterion-Related Validity

Another elaboration of validity involved the adaptation of the older concepts of prognostic and diagnostic value to the new language. Prognostic value, which involved criteria collected after the test was administered, became known as **predictive validity**. A test had predictive validity in proportion to the extent that it was possible to use the test score to forecast criterion status. This subtype of validity is particularly important if tests are being used to select or place employees within an organization because the concern is with how people will perform in the future.

---

[7]The various factors shown here to affect the size of the *validity* coefficient apply to **reliability coefficients** as well. These factors have been discussed in the context of validity simply because it is the more important concept.

Predictive validity would be relevant if tests are being used to help decide which candidates will fare best in training programs (such as professional schools or as military officers) or to screen out persons who will not perform adequately in some task (such as determining the likelihood of a soldier suffering from shell shock). Predictive validity, then, became the basic concern for tests used in many different situations to forecast performance in the future. Clearly, this is a particularly important evaluative criterion when tests are adapted to solve many social problems.

The older notion of diagnostic value was eventually replaced by the idea of **concurrent validity**—the extent that a test provides an accurate measurement of a person's present status. For example, it would be of concern if a test was being used to determine if a given individual was suffering from depression *at the time of testing*. The major gain of tests demonstrating concurrent validity is that they provide inexpensive, simpler, and frequently quick means of determining present status when compared with other nontest methods.

A given test could have *both* predictive and concurrent validity. For example, an achievement test might be used to indicate how much a person knows about a specific school subject at the time of testing (a concern of concurrent validity) and to predict how well the pupil will do with more complex materials (a predictive validity concern). Thus, the type of validity that must be demonstrated is a function of the uses to which the test is put. The correct type of validity must be demonstrated, of course, to justify the particular use of the test. For example, using a test with only demonstrated concurrent validity to make predictions about performance is unjustified. To make forecasts about performance, evidence of predictive validity must be clear, else the test is being misused.

Common Criteria

Only the imagination of the investigator limits the choice of which criteria to use to demonstrate test validity. Demonstrating validity for every specific use of the test is necessary, thus indicating the diversity of criteria that might be employed. The guiding principle in the selection of criteria is their relevance to the task that the test is intended to address.

For intelligence tests, one of the most popular classes of criteria are indexes of academic achievement such as grade point average, promotion to the next grade, achievement of special honors, teacher ratings, amount of education attained, and a wide variety of other possible measures of school-related performance. These could be drawn from all levels of the school system, from preschool to graduate work, pending the goals of the test being validated.

With tests intended to measure special aptitudes, criteria typically relate to performance in specialized training. A test of artistic aptitude, for example, might be validated against a criterion of performance in art school. Indeed, any test intended to select the best candidates for jobs or training would typically be validated using criteria of performance in a training program. Many examples in professional schools and the military attest to the popularity of this approach (see, for example, Chapter 12). The actual criteria employed could involve grades obtained during

Figure 8-2   Approximate dates of the emergence of the notion of validity up to about 1925.

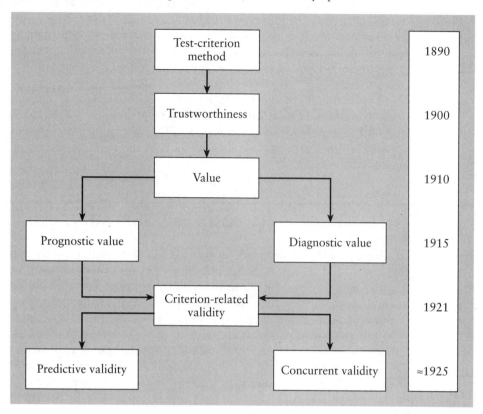

training, instructors' ratings, ratings of performance during training, and elimination from the program, to name a few.

Predicting training may not necessarily predict posttraining performance. For example, candidates who fare well in a graduate program may not necessarily do well as professionals after graduation. The ultimate criterion in this case would be posttraining performance that might be measured in terms of actual job performance using supervisor ratings, productivity indexes, promotion records, and other measures.

In the domain of personality tests, a wide variety of criteria can be used. If the concern is with diagnosis, a useful criterion is the patient categorization and ratings of severity of the disorder provided by professionals. If the concern is to use a test to predict how well someone will do in therapy, then therapeutic outcome measures such as physician ratings or patient self-ratings, time to completion of treatment, and remission might be appropriate. Personality tests can also be validated against a wide range of ratings such as roommate or spousal indications of the characteristic the test purports to measure. An even better type of criterion would relate to actual behavioral observations of what the tested person does in a specific situation.

An almost endless number of possibilities to the selection of the criteria can be used to validate a specific test. The test user *must* be able to demonstrate that the test being used does indeed have demonstrated validity for the use to which the test is being put. It is *not* sufficient to use a test to predict job performance when the only validation data available are related to performance in school. In other words, a test must have demonstrated validity for the specific application in which it is being used.

By the middle of the 1920s, a whole set of conceptual and methodological ideas had surfaced in relation to the emergent notion of validity. This idea had indeed become the centerpiece for an entire theory of measurement. Figure 8-2 shows the development of validity, along with the approximate dates of the emergence of the other ideas.

AN EMERGING THEORY OF MEASUREMENT

During this time, the foundations for a specific approach to psychological measurement were laid. This was in the form of a series of statements and practices regarding the best way to proceed in developing the tests. The elaborations of validity were a component of this emerging theory of measurement, but there were other aspects as well. For example, one major aspect of this theory is the manner in which it sanctioned measurement without definition. Several other assumptions are embedded in this theory as well, including (1) the testing experience should be as short and inexpensive as possible, (2) levels of motivation are constant for all respondents, (3) the influences of learning on test scores are thought to be minimal, and (4) respondents are being honest in their approach to the test. Each assumption has important implications for the manner in which the domain of psychological testing developed from here on.

Relationship Between Reliability and Validity

Once accepted into the lexicon of the testing movement, validity was related to some of the other extant terms. For example, researchers were quick to note a relationship between reliability and validity. Reliability, as estimated by the test/retest method, reflects the amount of error-free variance in a test score. Certainly, the error in a score could not enter meaningfully into a validity coefficient. This suggested that a test could never be more valid than it was reliable. That is, reliability sets an upper limit on the validity. If validity coefficients exceed reliability estimates, something is clearly wrong.

Parallel-Form Reliability

There was also some elaboration of the idea of reliability. With tests of intelligence, gathering true estimates of the test's reliability became somewhat problematic. Even if the researcher waited 3 weeks before retesting for a reliability estimate, the respondents would still remember some of the questions. This is a problem because it could be argued that the second score represented the effects of both intelligence and memory. This, of course, would have an unpredictable effect on the obtained reliability coefficient, making it less useful. If test developers waited for a longer period before retesting, to combat the issue of memory, they would run the risk of gaining a lower reliability estimate than warranted because respondents' status on the variable being assessed could have changed. Thus, regardless of the time span between testings, the obtained reliability coefficient from the test/retest method was less than perfect.

One of the first attempts to solve this problem involved developing different versions of various tests. These are called *parallel forms* and were constructed to be identical except that the content of the items was different between the two versions. To calculate a better reliability estimate, the test developers would administer one version (say, Form A) to a group and the second version (say, Form B) a few days later. Another group would get Form B first. The correlation between scores obtained on the first and second testings would be a reliability estimate from which the effects of memory for answers to specific questions had been removed. This type of reliability was called **parallel-form reliability** and should be carefully differentiated from the test/retest variety, although they both require two test administrations.

It is exceedingly important that the two forms be developed to ensure that they are truly comparable, else the reliability coefficient would be lower than warranted. Parallel forms should have the same number of items, the same response format, and cover the same content—albeit with different items. They should also be equally difficult, use the same instructions, have the same time limits if relevant, and be equivalent in all possible ways. The content of the items should be the *only* difference between the two forms. Such forms are not only useful to estimate reliability independent of memory for specific items but can also be very useful in cases where there is a need to do a follow-up assessment, say, to evaluate the effect of a treatment program.

Parallel-form reliability did not solve all the problems of developing a good reliability estimate. Two problems warrant mention at this time: (1) For characteristics that are expected to change as time passes (for example, depression, happiness, satisfaction), the parallel-form estimate of reliability is not particularly appropriate because this naturally occurring change would become part of the estimated error. Having to administer a test (parallel-form or not) on two separate occasions is a problem for tests of these types of **ephemeral characteristics.** (2) Even with the content changed between the two forms, practice effects are still likely to occur on the second administration of the test. Familiarity with the instructions, having learned how to solve the types of problems on the test, lessened anxiety because of reduced uncertainty about the testing experience, and a host of other factors can contribute to enhanced performance in the second testing session. These, of course, would amplify score differences on the two sessions and thereby affect the reliability estimate. It would seem that the need to administer a test twice to estimate reliability creates some significant problems for gaining a truly effective estimate of reliability. Nevertheless, reliability remained as a highly significant aspect of the prevailing approach to evaluating the goodness of psychological tests.

Speed and Power Tests

Another procedural wrinkle emerged, almost unnoticed, during this critical time in the development of the testing enterprise. On tests such as the Stanford–Binet and the Alpha, some subtests were administered with a strict time limit, with eventual performance being dictated by how fast the respondent could work through the items. These types of subtests have become known as **speed tests.** In the extreme case, a pure speed test would involve relatively simple items such as proofreading, with performance being strictly a function of speed. In most of the tests of the 1920s, speed was an element underlying performance in some subtests, but not in the sense of a pure speed test.

Speed tests contrast to those with no time limit, which are often called **power tests.** In this situation, respondents are given enough time to demonstrate the maximal level of performance of which they are capable—being allowed to demonstrate their full "power" with the test items. Almost all voluntary tests of the kinds you might find in personality or social psychology are power tests, having no time limits imposed on them.

Speed and power tests tap different aspects of performance and, as such, are differentially useful in test development. Speed tests are relevant only if speed is a significant aspect of the characteristic being measured by the test. If effective procedures of assessing validity are put in place, the issue of power-versus-speed tests can be resolved on the basis of the effectiveness with which the test predicts criterion status.

The Norm Group

Another development during this time was the realization that test scores, in and of themselves, convey no information. Saying that an individual obtained a score of 77 on the ABC intelligence test does not tell us anything useful. For this score to have any meaning, we must relate it to something. Usually, this "something" is a specific group of individuals, called a **norm group,** who have taken the test. In the case of the Stanford–Binet, this group was 2300 pupils (see Terman, 1916, Chapter 4). The scale units (IQ points) were determined with reference to this norm group, and the eventual scores reflect the comparison of an individual with reference to this specific group.

It emerged that the norm group must be representative of the population being discussed if test scores were to have useful meaning. The term **population** is meant to include all possible individuals to whom the test is relevant. For example, if the original Stanford–Binet norm group included too many intelligent children, then the test would produce artificially lower scores when used with other groups. Thus, the representativeness of the norm group emerged as a critical aspect of the usefulness of a psychological test.

Ideally, the entire population should be included in the norm group, but this is impractical. It becomes necessary to create a **sample,** or subset, of respondents that is a fair representation of the population and use this as the norm group. In technical terms, the respondents in the norm group should be a **random sample** from the entire population of respondents for whom the test is intended. Each individual in the population should have an equal probability of selection in the norm group if this condition were met. The following Close Up outlines some of the factors that should be considered in developing a good norm group.

CLOSE-UP | **Issues in the Determination of a Norm Group**

The establishment of a norm group is an arduous and expensive task. Because of this, test developers sometimes make decisions of convenience that have major implications on test-score meaning. For example, schools, mental hospitals, and prisons provide opportunities for easy gathering of test protocols. This convenience, however, can lead to subtle biases in the norm group, and these must be examined with considerable care—particularly if one is contemplating using a specific test. Some of the important issues are the following:

Size. The norm group must be large enough to provide stable estimates of the values. There is no set formula for determining sample size, but selection of a test with a larger norm group would appear to be appropriate if it came to choosing between two tests that were equal on all other aspects.

Geographic representation. The norm group should contain individuals from all geographic regions of relevance to the test. For example, if a test is marketed for use all across the United States, then the norm group should contain individuals who are representative of all regions of the country. Failure to do this leaves open the possibility of a regional bias in the eventual scores.

Socioeconomic level. If a norm group consisted of excessive numbers of children from wealthy, upper-class families, the representativeness of the obtained scores would be highly suspect, particularly if the test were used in another class context. Thus, matching the norm group with the prevailing socioeconomic levels in the population that the test is intended to address is necessary. Failure to do this leaves the test open to a number of critical difficulties.

Ethnic composition. The exclusion of specific ethnic groups (for example, Blacks) from a norm group can create all kinds of interpretive difficulties. If, for any reason, test performance of a minority group was lower, then the use of an ethnically nonrepresentative norm group is blatantly unfair. If the test is administered to members of the minority group, they will obtain lower scores than would be expected from a representative norm group.

The construction of a truly representative norm group is an obviously difficult task. Because of this, it is exceedingly important for test users to be very knowledgeable about the nature of the norm group, else they are open to making significant interpretive errors. If there is one safe way of proceeding here, it involves developing local, regional norm groups that are representative of the specific subpopulations being assessed. Using locally generated norms brings the sample closer to the actual group of persons on whom the test will be used, thereby increasing the possibility that the test scores have been derived from the relevant population.

At this point in our narrative of the testing enterprise, a specific set of criteria of excellence for tests has been developed. Represented by the dual idea of reliability

Figure 8-3   Schema for evaluating psychological tests around 1925.

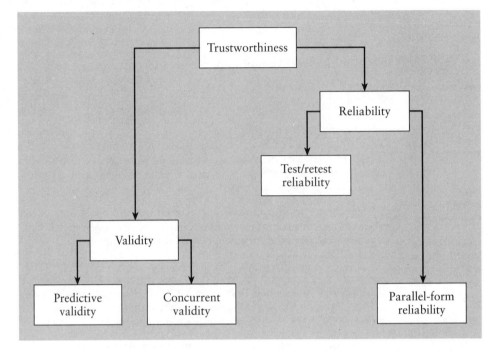

and validity, each with specific subtypes, testers of the mid-1920s had a useful arsenal of concepts at their disposal, which they could use to select, develop, and evaluate the burgeoning numbers of tests appearing in the marketplace. Figure 8-3 shows this evaluative schema.

The emergence of this systematic and powerful methodology for evaluating psychological tests occurred with considerable speed, given that it was not until 1890 that tests were even being discussed in America. A mere 35 years later, we find a systematic and complex network of evaluative concepts in place. Virtually everyone working in the field was aware of these basic ideas and their methodological and procedural implications. The development of this schema, along with the theory of measurement that they imply, is testimony to the rapid development of the testing enterprise, particularly between 1910 and 1925.

SOME NEW DIRECTIONS

Even more significant development occurred during this time with the types of tests being published and the topics with which they dealt, showing radical growth. The developing approach to measurement was extended in a number of different directions and subjected to several interesting challenges: projective testing, testing for university admission, and tests of physical-motor development.

Projective Testing

The mid-1920s saw the importing of a radically different approach to measurement from Germany. Robert Woodworth's introduction of personality assessment during World War I had focused on structured self-report. Respondents were given a standard set of questions to which they were to respond yes or no, and these answers were used to make inferences about various psychological states such as emotional stability. In the mid-1920s, an alternative to this, known under the generic name of **projective testing,** was introduced to the United States. The approach involves showing respondents intentionally vague or ambiguous stimuli (for example, inkblots, visually degraded pictures, incomplete sentences, cloud pictures) and asking respondents to tell stories about them or to indicate what they see in the stimuli. The underlying rationale of this method is that respondents will project, or impose, their enduring propensities or, at the very least, their current mood onto these vague stimuli. For example, a person whose personality is dominated by the need to achieve will interpret the projective stimuli as reflecting this need, revealed in interpretations that show consistent themes demonstrating this aspect of his or her personality. Interpretation of a person's responses, then, involves searching for themes that appear to dominate the interpretations. There is considerable subjectivity in the scoring process, which signals some problems it will encounter in the American context with its valuing of objectivity in the assessment enterprise. The projective technique is firmly grounded in psychoanalytic theory, with **projection** being one of **Sigmund Freud**'s original defense mechanisms.

Without doubt, the best known projective test is the **Rorschach Inkblot Test,** the target of more than 50% of the research dealing with projective techniques. Several different versions have emerged in the literature, but the original set of inkblots still remains the traditional instrument. The most important paper introducing the Rorschach to the United States was Rorschach and Oberholzer (1924). During the next decade, the test proliferated, with scattered references throughout the literature. In 1937 a comprehensive manual was published in English, but the test was introduced and the foundations were laid for its eventual acceptance (or lack thereof) into the field during the late 1920s.

CLOSE UP | **The Rorschach Inkblot Test**

The Rorschach Inkblot Test consists of ten stimuli mounted on cards. These inkblots are symmetric about the vertical axis and highly ambiguous. The cards are presented one at a time to a respondent who is told

> You will be given a series of cards, one by one. The cards have on them designs made up out of inkblots. Look at each card, and tell the examiner what you see on each card, or anything that might be represented there. Look at each card as long as you like; only be sure to tell the examiner everything that you see on the card as you look at it. When you have finished with a card, give it to the examiner as a sign that you are through with it. [Horrocks, 1964, p. 625]

Virtually no constraints are placed on a respondent, and no guidelines about expected types of responses are provided. Time taken on each card is recorded by the examiner. If the respondent returns the card after a single answer, he or she is prompted for further interpretations. The examiner records the interpretations using a prelearned shorthand, writing them down on a score sheet that contains a reduced copy of the inkblots for reference. Figure 8-4 shows a hypothetical localization chart used for scoring.

After going through all ten cards, the examiner returns them, one by one, and queries the various interpretations offered by the respondent. The goal here is to allow the examiner an opportunity to clarify exactly what it was that determined the given response. Of particular importance here is whether location, color, form, movement, or content were part of the obtained interpretation. For example, if a respondent indicated seeing a bat on a specific card, the examiner might ask to have the bat pointed out in order to be certain of the response. New interpretations provided during the query period are not recorded.

Scoring. In the original Rorschach, each response was scored for three things: location, determinant, and content. Although some alternative scoring schemes have been presented in the literature since then, what follows is drawn from Beck (1950), which is close to the original schema proposed by Rorschach.

Location scoring is concerned with the degree to which the respondent uses the entire card or focuses on specific details of it. A response is considered whole (coded W) when the respondent reacts to the entire card as a unit. For example, a person seeing an entire card V as a bat would be scored with a W. A detail response (coded D) is assigned when an examinee bases the interpretation on specified subparts of the card. After an examiner has administered the test to a number of people, a sense of common or rare details emerges. If a respondent provides an unusual detailed response, it is coded Dd. Responses based on white space within a card are also considered detailed responses (coded s).

Determinant scoring involves the response to form, color, shading, and movement in the inkblots. Interpretations that center on the form of the inkblot are cate-

---

Figure 8-4
Localization chart of several hypothetical Rorschach inkblots.

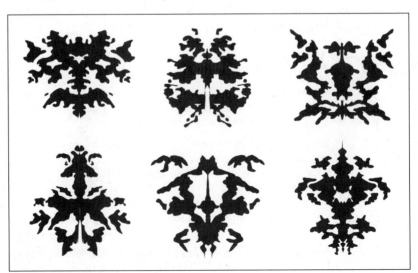

Table 8-1

Meanings accorded specific response categories on the Rorschach Inkblot Test

Category	Explanation	Meaning
Location		
Whole (W)	Uses entire card	Intelligence
Details (D)	Uses only part of card	Concern for practical
Rare D (Dd)	Unusual response	Obsessive/compulsive
Space (s)	Uses white space	Negativistic tendencies
Determinant		
Form (F)	F+ good form	Ego-strength
	F– poor form	Ego-weakness
Color (C)	Projection of color	Affect and emotionality
Chiaroscuro (ch)	Use of shading	Affective adaptability
Content		
Human movement (M)	Sees animate human	Creativity
Human detail (Hd)	Sees part of human	Anxious, unintelligent
Animal (A)	Sees whole animal	Stereotyped thinking

SOURCE: Based on Horrocks (1964, 631–635).

gorized as either good (coded F+) or bad (coded F–) form, with reference to a set of criteria learned by the examiner. Color responses (coded C) are scored when the examinee implies the existence of color in the interpretation of a card. The inkblots have shading on them, and responses based on this region of a card are called *chiaroscuro* (coded ch). Combinations of F, C, and ch are also noted by putting both letters together with the predominant determinant first (for example, F+ch, if good form predominated with a shading response). Movement is recorded in several ways. For example, the object moving can be human (coded M), animal (coded FM), or a nonliving object (coded m).

Content scoring is based on the label the respondent attaches to the object of the interpretation. Included here are entire humans (coded H), animals (coded A), parts of animals (coded Ad), parts of humans (coded Hd), inanimate objects (coded Obj), plants (coded Pl), anatomy (coded At), sexual objects (coded Sex), blood (coded Bl), clouds (coded Cl), and X rays (coded Sym). In addition, based on previous experience, the examiner will rate whether specific content is popular (coded P) or original (coded O).

There are many other scoring categories. These have been presented just to provide a sense of the manner in which the Rorschach interpretations are coded by the examiner. Considerable training is required before a person is competent to administer and score this test.

Interpretation. Based on extensive experience with the cards, certain characteristics are attributed to persons who show frequent numbers of responses in scored specific categories. It is beyond the scope of the text to provide an exhaustive list of these interpretations, but Table 8-1 indicates some of the interpretations of response categories noted earlier.

This is but a very coarse summary of some interpretations of Rorschach protocols. However, it is possible to see that specific classes of psychological characteristics are attributed to specific classes of Rorschach interpretations, which are highly
complex. For the most part, the scoring is based on interactive patterns observed
between the various categories of responses.

The Rorschach, for a number of reasons, was not well received by the North
American academic establishment. When the tools of the evolving technology of
testing (for example, validity, reliability) were applied to projective techniques,
they failed miserably (for the Rorschach, see McCall, 1959). Validity and reliability
are exceedingly low in large numbers of research papers. Yet the test persisted, particularly in its apparent utility in clinical assessment. This is an intriguing aspect of
psychological measurement, but to understand the reasons between the conflict
surrounding projective techniques, we must continue our story of the development
of the testing enterprise. The important point here is that projective techniques
were introduced to North America in the mid-1920s when the emerging enterprise
was formulating a set of rigorous and explicit criteria for the evaluation of psychological tests.

Testing for University Admission

In 1926 the **College Entrance Examination Board** was formed. Consisting of a
number of universities as members, its principal mandate involved the development
and use of tests for the admission, placement, and counseling of college students.
This represented a major excursion into social decision making for the testing
enterprise because tests were being used to help make very important decisions
about whom should receive the benefits of higher education. The **Scholastic
Aptitude Test (SAT)** is a particularly illuminating example of the tests that the
Board has developed.

CLOSE UP **The Scholastic Aptitude Test**

Ever since its introduction in 1926, the SAT has undergone constant revision and
upgrading. Typically, several new forms are prepared each year. Today the major
goal of the test is to provide information about the respondent's *current readiness*
for college work.

The test is divided into two sections, Verbal and Mathematical, with a separate score being provided for each section. Figure 8-5 presents some sample items.
Considerable care and attention to the technical details of these tests have characterized the College Board's work over the years. In general, the parallel-form reliabilities range from .86 to .90 for both the Verbal and Mathematical scores. The
cumulated knowledge of over 2000 studies conducted by 685 colleges have gone
into the development of this technology. When the Verbal and Mathematical
scores were combined into one composite score for this impressive data set, the
composite correlated .42, with freshman grade point average (GPA). When the

Figure 8-5

Illustrative examples of the Scholastic Aptitude Test.

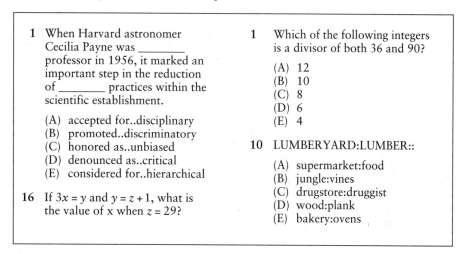

1 When Harvard astronomer Cecilia Payne was _____ professor in 1956, it marked an important step in the reduction of _____ practices within the scientific establishment.

   (A) accepted for..disciplinary
   (B) promoted..discriminatory
   (C) honored as..unbiased
   (D) denounced as..critical
   (E) considered for..hierarchical

16 If $3x = y$ and $y = z + 1$, what is the value of x when $z = 29$?

1 Which of the following integers is a divisor of both 36 and 90?

   (A) 12
   (B) 10
   (C) 8
   (D) 6
   (E) 4

10 LUMBERYARD:LUMBER::

   (A) supermarket:food
   (B) jungle:vines
   (C) drugstore:druggist
   (D) wood:plank
   (E) bakery:ovens

SAT questions selected from *Introducing the New SAT,* College Entrance Examinations Board (1993). Reprinted by permission of Educational Testing Service, the copyright owner of the test questions. Permission to reprint the above material does not constitute review or endorsement by Educational Testing Service or the college board of this publication as a whole or of any other questions or testing information it may contain.

SAT score was combined with high school GPA, the correlation with freshman grades rose to .55, indicating a reasonable degree of predictive validity.

The pervasiveness of this application of testing is revealed in the emergence of several other services. Notable here is the American College Testing Program that provides a set of work samples of college work in the following domains: English Usage, Mathematics Usage, Social Studies Reading, and Natural Sciences Reading.

These testing programs have moved up a level in the educational system with the emergence of a series of tests for admission to graduate and professional schools. This extension emerged in 1936, just 10 years after the College Board was established. The Graduate Record Examination (GRE), currently conducted by Educational Testing Service, is the best known example of this approach.

These tests are not intended to act as *substitutes* for grades, either at the high school or undergraduate levels. Grades predict subsequent performance as well, or better, than the tests do.[8] It is when the tests and the grades are used in combination that a gain is observed. Tests, then, can be useful *adjuncts* to grades when it comes to making predictions about academic success at the university level.

---

[8] Recalling Wissler's results (see Chapter 6) reminds us that this should not be particularly surprising.

Get the inside story on SAT® I and II

For most students, answering the test questions that appear in the free booklets *Taking the SAT I* and *Taking the SAT II* is enough. But if you want more preparation, here are two books that contain actual, complete tests.

Introducing the New SAT
The College Board's Official Guide

Here is the only official guide to the new SAT I: Reasoning Test. *Introducing the New SAT* is designed to help you prepare more effectively and confidently for the test. Written in a clear and lively style, the *Guide* provides expert advice and helpful test-taking strategies and includes more than 80 practice questions plus one complete practice test.

1993, 260 pages, $12.

The Official Guide to SAT II: Subject Tests

This is *the* authoritative preparation guide if you will be taking the SAT II: Subject Tests. The *Guide* includes full-length practice tests, along with answer sheets, answer keys, and scoring instructions for:

- Writing
- Literature
- American History
- World History
- Math I

- Math IIC
- Biology
- Chemistry
- Physics

Also provides minitests in French (reading only), German (reading only), Italian, Latin, Modern Hebrew, and Spanish. Includes descriptions of all five SAT II Language Tests with Listening, and samples of the new Writing Test.

1994, approx. 380 pages, $15

The publications are also available in bookstores and most school libraries.

A considerable amount of pre-test material is available for the Scholastic Aptitude Test (SAT).

The excursion of the testing enterprise into college-level admission and beyond was effective from the university's perspective. This family of tests provided the administration with information that was tailor-made for the kinds of decisions they had to make. The extent to which these programs were viewed as successes by the test takers is a matter for consideration later on.

Tests of Physical-Motor Development

Another postwar application of the emerging test theory involved the notion of developmental maturation. At that time, evidence suggested that the earlier an intellectual problem was detected, the better the opportunity to take corrective action. The standard IQ tests, however, could only deal with a child of 2 years or older. There appeared to be a need for a downward extension of the tests that could be applied to prelinguistic children and infants.

Developmental schedules emerged during this postwar period as efforts to provide the needed downward extension of human performance measures. Based on numerous observations of healthy infants as they grew up, developing age benchmarks at which the normal child would perform specific acts such as holding a rattle, rolling over, and walking became possible, thus allowing a psychologist or a physician to determine if an infant was developing at a normal rate. The best known of these developmental schedules was the Gesell, which was started at Yale University in 1927.

CLOSE UP: | **The Gesell Developmental Schedules**

Initial research for the **Gesell Developmental Schedules (GDS)** began at Yale University (see Gesell & Amatruda, 1956). A group of 107 normal infants were observed at the ages of 4, 6, and 8 weeks and at 4-week intervals thereafter until they were 56 months old. Systematic observations on various structured tasks were taken during these periods. These tasks ranged from very simple (for example, stares at surroundings) to rather complex (for example, gives full name and gender), selected to represent the range of normal activities of a developing child during the first 4½ years of life. As Figure 8-6 shows, each task has an associated age with it. To facilitate scoring, behaviors were sorted into four categories (Table 8-2) that are thought to develop at different rates, as shown in Figure 8-7.

Each task in the schedule is associated with a given age zone representing the age at which the normally developing child attains the specific behavior. Scoring involves giving a + if the child shows the behavior, a ++ if a more advanced behavior is demonstrated and a − if the child fails to show the behavior. In any of the four categories, the child's *maturity level* is the point where the aggregate of − scores changes to +. At first, the GDS did not supply a single score but suggested an approximate developmental level (in months) for each of the four behavior categories. These levels are related to the chronological age to determine if there is a lag relative to the expected sequence. Gesell eventually did suggest a **developmental quotient (DQ)**, which involved dividing the average developmental age over the four categories by chronological age and multiplying by 100. DQs less than 100 would indicate a degree of developmental lag, whereas DQs greater than 100 would indicate acceleration relative to the average.

Validity of the GDS. One of the earliest questions that was asked of the GDS (and several other schedules that emerged shortly thereafter) was whether or not maturational speed predicted later scores on the standard IQ tests. Are the faster developing infants likely to attain higher scores on the IQ tests? The answer to this question was a clear no. Correlations between the GDS and subsequent Stanford–Binet scores were virtually zero. Variability in the rate of infant development was so great that it was virtually impossible to establish any predictive validity for such tests. Infants change too fast and too abruptly for scales such as the GDS to be able to predict subsequent IQ test performance (for an extensive retrospective analysis of this point, see McCall, Hogarty, & Hurlburt, 1972).

Figure 8-6
Samples of various Infant Test Tasks for selected key ages from the Gesell Developmental Schedules.

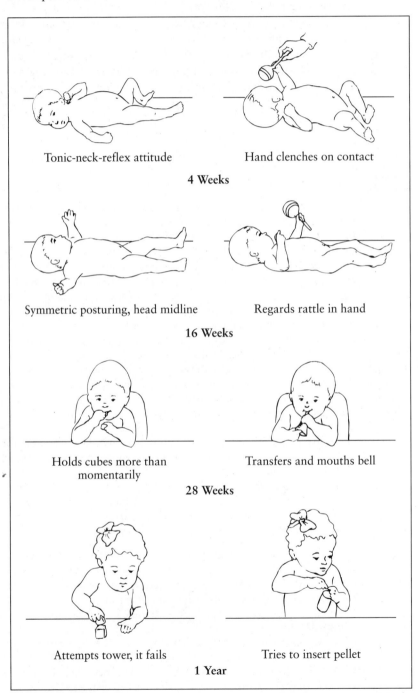

Tonic-neck-reflex attitude   Hand clenches on contact

4 Weeks

Symmetric posturing, head midline   Regards rattle in hand

16 Weeks

Holds cubes more than momentarily   Transfers and mouths bell

28 Weeks

Attempts tower, it fails   Tries to insert pellet

1 Year

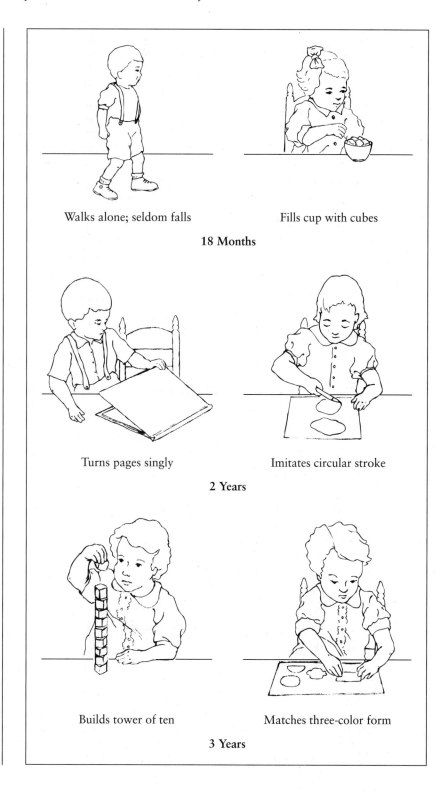

Walks alone; seldom falls

Fills cup with cubes

18 Months

Turns pages singly

Imitates circular stroke

2 Years

Builds tower of ten

Matches three-color form

3 Years

Table 8-2
Categories of behaviors employed in the GDS

Category	Description and Examples*
Motor behavior	Gross and fine-motor coordination including postural reactions, head balance, crawling, walking, and related motor skills. *Examples*: Head erect, sits leaning forward, pulls to feet, walks well alone, runs, rides tricycle.
Adaptive behavior	Developing patterns of resourcefulness dealing with finer sensorimotor adjustments to objects. Includes hand/eye coordination and the use of motor system to solve practical problems. *Examples*: Brief eye following, puts cube into cup, makes a tower of four cubes, draws a cross.
Language behavior	All visible and audible forms of communication including both mimicry and comprehension of the communications of others. *Examples*: Coos, M-m sound, says "dada" or "mama," responds to "give it to me," ten-word vocabulary, sentences, gives full name.
Personal/social	Development of relationships and competence in dealing with others. Bladder and bowel control is included here because it is thought to reflect social, cultural practice. *Examples*: Spontaneous social smile, feeding self, cooperates in dressing, carries and hugs dolls, puts on socks.

*Examples are ordered from younger to older.
SOURCE: Adapted from Gesell and Amatruda (1956, p. 407).

This failure to demonstrate validity, in a sense, made these tests less desirable in the testing enterprise. Because the primary criterion of test validity was the demonstration of high test-criterion correlations, the developmental schedules could be seen as having lessened value. However, they do retain their utility as preliminary diagnostic instruments. The GDS allows for the detection of developmental lags early in development, and this, in some cases, can be very useful in suggesting further testing and exploration that may have benefits for the child.

Of particular import for this aspect of developmental schedules is the very strong caution that should be exercised in the interpretation of the GDS and related tests, particularly those demonstrating moderate acceleration or lag. Parents who create very high intellectual expectations for their children because they learn to talk or walk early may not be doing them a favor. Research indicates that these are *not* predictive of subsequent intellectual development, and parents may be creating a failure-bound context for the child. Parents who begin to fret excessively because their child is several months slow in learning to walk, for example, may be creating difficulty for the child. Children develop in radically different ways—some progress gradually, and others are faster—and tests such as the GDS do not take this into account. Extreme lags, however, should be taken seriously.

Figure 8-7

The development of behavior as postulated by Gesell in the four major fields.

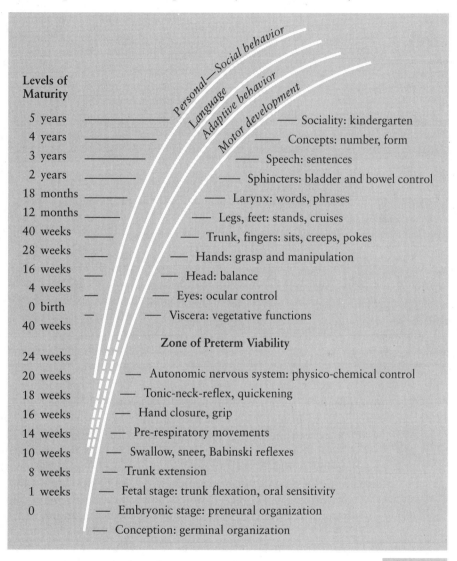

Levels of Maturity

5 years	— Sociality: kindergarten
4 years	— Concepts: number, form
3 years	— Speech: sentences
2 years	— Sphincters: bladder and bowel control
18 months	— Larynx: words, phrases
12 months	— Legs, feet: stands, cruises
40 weeks	— Trunk, fingers: sits, creeps, pokes
28 weeks	— Hands: grasp and manipulation
16 weeks	— Head: balance
4 weeks	— Eyes: ocular control
0 birth	— Viscera: vegetative functions
40 weeks	

Zone of Preterm Viability

24 weeks	
20 weeks	— Autonomic nervous system: physico-chemical control
18 weeks	— Tonic-neck-reflex, quickening
16 weeks	— Hand closure, grip
14 weeks	— Pre-respiratory movements
10 weeks	— Swallow, sneer, Babinski reflexes
8 weeks	— Trunk extension
1 weeks	— Fetal stage: trunk flexation, oral sensitivity
0	— Embryonic stage: preneural organization
	— Conception: germinal organization

Personal—Social behavior
Language behavior
Adaptive behavior
Motor development

Summary

As the Roaring 20s came to a close, the psychological testing enterprise had established beachheads in a number of important domains. Work was continuing apace with group and individual measures of intelligence. Personality assessment, both structured and projective, was proliferating. New developments in abilities and

Figure 8-8 Domains to which the new testing methods and theory were being applied in the mid-1920s.

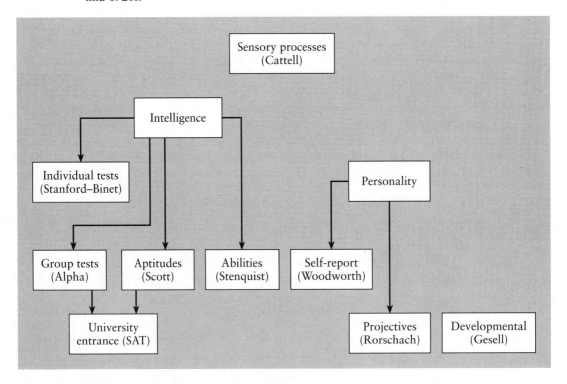

aptitudes had been achieved. Infant development had been subjected to the new approach to psychological measurement. A new theory of measurement, with validity as its touchstone, had emerged. These developments were remarkably rapid, given that the first major demonstration of testing's practical worth had only been during World War I, a mere 15 years earlier. Figure 8-8 shows the spreading influence of testing during this critical period of its development.

The chronological order in which these various areas were addressed by the testing enterprise is represented on the vertical plane in this figure, with the earliest efforts being closest to the top. As can be seen, testing's theory of measurement expanded rapidly, particularly during and after World War I. The swift acceptance and spread of the testing enterprise was clear testimony that North American society was ready and willing to embrace this scientific approach to making important social decisions.

Glossary

College Entrance Examination Board An organization, consisting of many universities as members, that was charged with applying testing technology to the selection, placement, and counseling of would-be university students. The Scholastic Aptitude Test (SAT) is the best known of their accomplishments.

concurrent validity   A variant of criterion-related validity where the criterion is measured while testing takes place. Tests with concurrent validity provide accurate estimates of current criterion status such as might be required in a test used for diagnosing mental health at the time of testing.

criterion   An independent, nontest variable that is used to demonstrate the value (and later, criterion-related validity) of a test using the test-criterion method. For example, with measures of intelligence, teacher ratings of intelligence were frequently used as criteria during the 1920s.

criterion contamination   The situation in which the person assigning criterion status is aware of test results (or vice versa), which leads to a false inflation of (criterion-related) validity coefficients.

criterion-related validity   A family of approaches to establishing whether a test measures what it purports to measure by assessing relationships between the test and relevant criteria. This form of validity, which involves the application of the test-criterion method, has two subtypes: predictive and concurrent validity.

critical value   The size that a correlation must be before it can be thought of as being significantly different from zero. Critical values are a function of the number of pairs of observations that go into calculating the index and are typically given with a known probability such as .01 or .05. (See Figure 8-1.)

developmental quotient (DQ)   An estimate of level of advancement from the Gesell Developmental Schedule. It is calculated by dividing developmental by chronological age and multiplying by 100.

developmental schedule   A set of behaviors appropriate to growing children that is, by reference to a norm group, associated with specific ages. Performance on these tests can be used as benchmarks to determine if a child is ahead or behind normal development.

diagnostic value   The extent to which a test predicts criterion status at the time of testing. This idea was subsequently replaced by the notion of concurrent validity.

Downey Will Temperament Tests   A series of tests involving activities such as handwriting and speech, which purported to be effective measures of temperament. These were the first tests to be subjected to the criteria expected of the new idea of validity and did not fare particularly well.

ephemeral characteristic   A psychological attribute that is expected to change as a function of the passage of time. Depression, satisfaction, and happiness are ephemeral in this sense. Estimates of reliability that require tests be administered twice (for example, test/retest and parallel-form) are not appropriate for estimating the reliability for such characteristics because the observed change between the two testing sessions is thought to reflect unreliability.

Freud, Sigmund   An Austrian physician who pioneered the theories and practices of psychoanalysis. One of the defense mechanisms formulated by Freud, projection, is the basic rationale underlying the Rorschach Inkblot Test.

Gesell Developmental Schedules (GDS)   The first developmental schedule, it provides indexes in the areas of motor, adaptive, language, and personal/social behaviors.

heterogeneity   The characteristic of being highly variable or mixed.

homogeneity   The characteristic of being very similar or demonstrating a lack of variability.

measurement without definition   Developing tests for which an adequate definition of what is being measured is not provided. Early testing such as the Stanford–Binet and the Army Alpha are examples of this in their failure to provide a detailed and specified definition of what they were assessing. The test-criterion method and (criterion-related) validity emerged in the service of this approach.

norm group   A carefully chosen set of test respondents selected to maximally represent the population to which test results will be generalized. Test results are compared to the performance of this group, using techniques such as the z score. Adequate representativeness and size of the norm group are essential for test scores to have utility.

parallel-form reliability   Developing two equivalent versions of the same test so that reliability can be assessed with two different tests on two occasions. The correlation between these is an index of reliability that solves the problem of memory for specific responses that serves to complicate test/retest reliability estimates.

population   The universe of all possible persons to whom a particular test is relevant.

power test   A test that does not have a time limit, thereby giving the respondent an opportunity to demonstrate optimal performance.

predictive validity   A variant of criterion-related validity where the criterion is measured a meaningful period of time after testing takes place. Tests with predictive validity can forecast criterion status in a situation when the criterion has yet to be measured.

preselection   The situation in attempting to demonstrate predictive validity when some of the respondents drop out of the study prior to criterion measurement, thereby confounding the validity estimate because the range of scores has been affected.

prognostic value   The extent to which a test predicts criterion status when the criterion is assessed subsequent to testing. This idea was subsequently replaced by the notion of predictive validity.

projection   One of the defense mechanisms proposed by Sigmund Freud, wherein a person transfers an anxiety-arousing, internal impulse onto some external aspect of the environment.

projective testing   A test where the respondent is presented with intentionally ambiguous stimuli and asked to react to them. Responses are scored in terms of the themes that emerge, based on how respondents have imposed (projected) their personalities on the stimuli.

random sampling   The selection of a smaller subset of individuals from a larger pool such that each individual has an equal probability of being chosen.

reliability coefficient   The actual correlation derived from either test/retest or parallel-form approaches to estimating reliability.

Rorschach Inkblot Test   A projective test using stimuli made of highly abstract inkblots. Responses are scored in terms of location, determinant, and content of images seen within the inkblots. The best known projective test, it continues to have considerable popularity despite its failure to conform to many of the criteria expected of psychological tests.

sample A subset drawn from a population. The adequacy of choosing the sample from the population is particularly important for determining the adequacy of a norm group for a psychological test.

Scholastic Aptitude Test (SAT) A testing program developed by the College Entrance Examination Board to select, place, and counsel applicants to university. Consisting of Verbal and Mathematical scales, the SAT is constantly revised and changed, with several new forms being created each year.

significance A statistics term indicating that a given correlation (or other statistic) is sufficiently large to believe that it is not due to chance factors—that is, that the result reflected by the statistic is meaningful. Probability levels of .05 and .01 have been (arbitrarily) selected as cutoffs for considering given statistics to be significant.

speed test A test that has a time limit.

temperament An early term for characteristics of individuals not subsumed under the rubric of intelligence—that is, nonintellective components of individual differences. Today the term *personality* includes what the earlier researchers meant by temperament.

test-criterion method The methodology of administering a test to a group of individuals, as well as measuring them on some nontest, independent variable thought to reveal the characteristic being measured by the test (the criterion). Calculating the correlation between test scores and criterion status provides an index of whether the test measures what it says it does.

theory of measurement A set of recommended procedures, assumptions, and criteria for the development and evaluation of psychological tests.

trustworthiness An early criterion of the goodness of tests. Trustworthy tests were those in which the user could have faith that the numbers it generated were reasonably accurate and useful. It included both of the contemporary ideas of validity and reliability.

validity The extent to which a test measures what it purports to measure. During the 1920s, the only way of assessing validity was using the test-criterion method, which today is called criterion-related validity.

validity coefficient A Pearson product-moment correlation between test scores and criteria. The size of this coefficient is thought to reveal the validity of the test.

value As used in its technical sense, value was an earlier name for the concept that was eventually called validity. Depending on the criteria used to determine the value of a test, this idea was divided into two subtypes: prognostic and diagnostic value.

Suggested Further Reading

Danziger, K. (1990). *Constructing the subject: Historical origins of psychological research*. Cambridge, Eng.: Cambridge University Press.

This book provides a wonderfully developed argument regarding the manner in which experimental psychologists negotiated or constructed their approach to generating and analyzing data. Of particular importance from our perspective is the impact Francis Galton had in the emergence of North American experimental psychology. The processes involved in coming to a consensus within the experimental community, as indicated by Danziger, is very much like the negotiation processes suggested in the emergence of criteria of excellence for tests, making this book excellent support reading for this chapter of *The Enterprise.*

Ghiselli, E. E., Campbell. J. P., & Zedeck, S. (1981). *Measurement theory for the behavioral sciences.* San Francisco: Freeman.

This book provides a fine overview of the contemporary version of the theory of measurement. Being well presented and slightly more mathematical than what appears in *The Enterprise,* those who want to gain a sense of how this theory eventually was transformed to meet modern demands will be well served by reading this book. The section on validity (Chapter 10) is particularly useful.

Groth-Marant, G. (1990). *Handbook of psychological assessment* (2nd ed.). New York: Wiley-Interscience.

This book contains several chapters that are of direct relevance to projective testing. Chapter 9 provides a good overview of the Rorschach, including a list of recommended readings, which is useful. Chapter 11 provides a review of another projective approach that involves having patients draw specific objects. In combination, these chapters provide an examination of the current technology of projective methodology.

Kelley, T. L. (1927). *Interpretation of educational measurements.* New York: World Book.

This textbook emerged as the classic treatment of the measurement theory and practices that evolved during this period. Working through this book provides a wonderful sense of the manner in which the worldview inherent in the practices was elaborated and extended to a wide variety of topics and issues that emerged as tests were proliferating. It is the best primary source for a deep understanding of the thinking at the time.

Meisels, S. J., & Provence, S. (1989). *Screening and assessment: Guidelines for identifying young disabled and developmentally vulnerable children and their families.* Washington, D.C.: National Center for Clinical Infant Programs.

This report provides a wide-ranging discussion of the more modern verisons of the challenge originally tackled by the Gesell Developmental Schedules. Here you find a wonderfully rich presentation of contemporary ideas and thoughts concerning the assessment of children's developmental levels as they are practiced today. This provides a great index of the manner in which this domain of the testing enterprise has grown from its early beginnings.

von Mayrhauser, R. T. (1992). The mental testing community and validity: A prehistory. *American Psychologist, 47,* 244–253.

This paper presents an analysis of the wider institutional context into which validity was born. It provides insight into a number of important methodological and conceptual conflicts that emerged during this time in its explicit consideration of the idea of *accuracy.* It nicely complements the present analysis by approaching it from a slightly different perspective.

Discussion Questions

1. Analysis of criteria of excellence, as presented in this chapter, can be difficult because we can sometimes get so busy deciding what is good or bad that we forget to explicitly examine the criteria we are using. Discuss this possibility with respect to the criteria you use to decide which musical group or artist is your favorite.

2. Discuss whether you think there is still room for the concept of trustworthiness once validity and reliability have been formulated. (In other words, is there anything left to trustworthiness once we remove validity and reliability?)

3. You have been asked to develop a measure of university/college teacher effectiveness using the test-criterion method. List all possible criteria that you might use to validate this test. Which one would be the most important? Why?

4. With respect to your discussions in Question 3, indicate why you think prognostic or diagnostic value would be the most important consideration.

5. Discuss whether the notion of measurement without definition would better be considered as measurement without *explicit* definition.

6. Suggest four reasons why researchers had so much trouble generating a consensual definition of intelligence.

7. With respect to two other disciplines, debate the contention that measurement without definition is a necessary starting place for the development of technology but that it should not last very long.

8. Outline the social pressures in the early 1920s that facilitated the emergence of the notion of validity. Which of these do you think was the most influential? Why?

9. In the Close Up entitled "The Negotiation of Validity," only one line of evidence was presented—namely, the manner in which the word was used in the literature. Describe as many other approaches to this issue that you can think of. Which of these would be the best? Why?

10. Discuss the contention that Mark May's criticism of the Downey Will Temperament Test resulted in the premature abandonment of this approach to assessing nonintellective factors.

11. Design a test-criterion study that would result in an optimally artificially inflated validity coefficient.

12. Discuss the strengths and weaknesses of adopting a criterion of significance of $p < .05$.

13. You have been asked to discuss testing on a radio talk show, and someone who knows very little about tests asks you how big a validity coefficient has to be in order to establish the validity of a test. Sketch out the answer you would give this person.

14. With reference to a specific example, discuss the possibility that there might be some situations in which homogeneity of a sample could result in an inflated validity coefficient.

15. If the Alphonse Bureau Test of Intelligence demonstrated a correlation of .42 with teacher ratings based on a sample size of 15, would you use the test? Why, or why not?

16. You have been hired by your college to help them select the best first-year students. Assume that the research literature reported a validity coefficient of .24 between GPA and SAT performance, based on a sample of 100 students from your college. Would you recommend using the test to your employer? Why, or why not.

17. Prepare a list of all factors that can affect the size of a reliability coefficient.

18. Discuss as many procedures as you can think of that would make it almost impossible for criterion contamination to occur.

19. Design a study that would demonstrate the predictive and concurrent validity of the Rorschach Inkblot Test.

20. Provide a list of the factors that should go into the selection of a criterion.

21. List all terms you would find in the theory of measurement around 1925.

22. You are trying to select a measuring device for a research project in childhood personality, and you encounter a measure that states its concurrent validity is a remarkably high .87. Later on in the test manual, you find that its test/retest validity is .77. Assuming the samples on which these statistics were gathered were large and appropriate, would you use this measure? Why, or why not?

23. Discuss the memory factors that parallel-form reliability does not resolve.

24. Outline a method that might be appropriate to estimate the reliability of tests of ephemeral characteristics.

25. Outline a situation in which it might be appropriate to use a speed test as a measure of personality.

26. Describe the best possible norm group you could use if you were developing a test to measure degree of cultural adaptation of Hispanic immigrants.

27. What strikes you as the most unusual in the summary of the development of criteria of excellence for tests shown in Figure 8-3. Why?

28. If you are familiar with Sigmund Freud, suggest one defense mechanism other than projection that might be adaptable to a method of measurement.

29. Discuss the strengths and weaknesses of the Rorschach Inkblot Test using the criteria of excellence presented in the chapter.

30. Even though developmental schedules do not appear to have predictive validity, are they entirely invalid? Why, or why not?

31. With respect to the summary of the areas in which tests have been published, shown in Figure 8-8, where do you expect that the next major developments are apt to occur?

32. Discuss anything you think might be missing in the criteria of excellence for tests presented in this chapter.

Part IV

The Golden Age

With foundational ideas such as validity and reliability well established, testing entered a time of exceptional growth. Its influence spread to a wide variety of social issues, and its toolbox began to expand, although the basic idea of criterion-related validity remained as the singularly most important evaluative criterion of tests. This part of the text provides a summary of the developments during this tremendous growth period for testing, which lasted (roughly) from 1930 until World War II.

In Chapter 9, we encounter yet another important social event that had an influence on testing—the Great Depression. Even though opportunities for the growing testing enterprise were reduced during the economic upheaval of the 1930s, ideas and innovations did continue. For example, during this time a number of very important ideas (for example, operationism) and tests (for example, the MMPI) were developed, and these are chronicled in this chapter.

Another debate emerged during the 1930s. As summarized in Chapter 10, theoretical ideas about the nature of intelligence began to diverge. In North America, a movement toward viewing intelligence as a number of independent abilities came to the fore, in contrast to the British view of intelligence being a single entity. The American position fostered the emergence of the statistical technique of factor analysis which spawned an alternative view of intellect as comprised of multiple abilities rather than one over-arching entity. Chapter 10 also includes discussion of a compromise between the multiple and single views of intelligence initiated by David Wechsler. The progeny of the tests he developed are, today, considered to be "state of the art" measures of intellectual ability.

Chapter 11 provides a snapshot of some of the new ideas in testing which were added during this "Golden Age" of testing. Included here are: the introduction of a family of internal consistency measures which were new approaches to the estimation of reliability, formulation of the idea of content validity concerned with how fairly the items in a test represents the domain the test purports to measure, and a number of conceptions about how to select the best possible items for inclusion in a test.

The Golden Age of testing saw the introduction of a wide variety of new tests and ideas. All of these followed directly from the notions discussed in the previous parts of the text, representing a continuation of a coherent story of the emergence of tests in our culture. By the time this era was terminated by World War II, testing had emerged as a full-blown and sophisticated domain of inquiry and social practice.

Spreading the Word
Operationism and the MMPI

MOVING AHEAD

The next phase of development in the rapidly expanding testing enterprise was characterized by the rapid spread of the new methods and ideas to a number of different domains, as well as to the improvement of some of those that had already received extensive treatment. In addition, a new and highly sophisticated way of thinking about both psychology and testing emerged during this time. When we add to this mix a catastrophic social event, the Great Depression, we find the 1930s to have been an exceedingly interesting time.

The recent chapters of this text have been concerned, more or less, with events that have occurred within the discipline of psychology. Although there has been some reference to the impact of society on the testing enterprise and vice versa (for example, the Lippmann critique in Chapter 7), most of the story being told is from a perspective of inside the discipline. The eminent historian Herbert Butterfield (1951) describes such histories as Whig histories—where emphasis is on an internalist interpretation of events (that is, the world as psychologists see it). Of course, important events were happening outside the halls of psychology departments in U.S. universities, and these also had significant impact on the emerging story of psychological testing.

OTHER DEVELOPMENTS IN THE ACADEMY

Just across the campus, in physics departments, an incredibly important drama was being acted out. In 1903 Albert Einstein induced a major philosophical crisis with the publication of his special theory of relativity. This event represented the result of a number of decades of philosophical unease with scientists' understanding of the fundamental nature of their endeavor.

Prior to Einstein, many scientists held to a view that can be described as **mechanistic materialism,** a very simple doctrine that suggested everything could be explained in mechanical terms. It was assumed that a single, real, and objective world existed independently of the observer and that good science involved making new discoveries in this objective world: "Science ... gradually establishes the fact that ... existence obeys, in its origin, life, and decay, *mechanical laws inherent in things themselves* [italics added], discarding every kind of super-naturalism and idealism in the exploration of natural events. There is no force without matter; no matter without force" (Buchner, 1855, cited in Passmore, 1957). According to this doctrine, science presents a picture of the world firmly based on empirical inquiry, rather than on philosophical speculation. There was no doubt that a real, objective world existed independently of perceivers, and science was considered to be the discovery of the mechanisms in this objective world. Everything was concrete; everything was mechanical. All that remained was for the scientist to discover these things and the laws that governed them.

Albert Einstein and the Demise of Mechanical Materialism

By the late 1800s, there was an emerging dissatisfaction with this view. For example, von Helmholtz demonstrated the need to consider the actively thinking observer as part of the process of science. Mechanistic materialism could not entertain the idea that there was an intermediary between the products of science and the external world, as von Helmholtz suggested. Soon a full-blown debate was in progress. Einstein's proof of the relative nature of matter and time dealt a death blow to the purely mechanistic approaches to science, and a major crisis was under way. If the very fundamental building blocks of nature, time, and matter, are not absolute but subject to vicissitudes of context, how is it possible to build a science in the vision held by the mechanistic materialists? A considerable amount of soul-searching ensued within the intellectual community as the implications of this argument clarified (for a review, see Suppe, 1974).

Rising from the Ashes: Logical Positivism

Mechanistic materialism was eventually replaced by another view of science. The first systematic version was published by Rudolph Carnap (1923), but it was based on several decades of analysis—mostly in Germany. In very general terms, the new philosophy retained the old belief in the possibility of positive knowledge but also made room for the addition of theoretical or logical terms. Rather than assuming that everything we need to know about nature can be found in nature herself, this position made allowance for theoretical terms that represented abstractions or explanatory devices distinct from the empirical world. This amalgam was called **logical positivism.**

Logical positivism argued that all scientific formulations ought to have a specific form. The world was thought to consist of two basic types of terms: (1) **theoretical terms,** which were best formulated mathematically, and (2) **observational statements,** which represented sentences describing the empirical status of the world. A third set of concepts linked the theoretical terms to the observational statements. These were called **correspondence rules.** According to logical positivism, all terms within a scientific theory can be classified as theoretical terms, observational statements, or correspondence rules.

Of particular concern for this view was the fear that theorizing might get out of hand and science might return to the old days of unrestrained rational or idealistic analysis. If this happened, the gains of the scientific method would be lost. To combat this fear, a fairly stringent set of rules about the kinds of theoretical terms that could be admitted was part-and-parcel of logical positivism. In a sense, this philosophy of science allowed for theory but only in very specific and structured ways.

An example will help here. Let's suppose we are interested in developing a scientific theory of learning, defined as relatively permanent changes in behavior that can be attributed to the environment. We might, as part of this endeavor, create the notion of *habit* in our theory, in that we believe that individuals who habitually do certain things are more likely to behave in consonance with this tendency. Further, we might evoke the notion of *drive,* suggesting that organisms that are highly motivated are more likely to react to environmental conditions. Finally, we might postulate that individuals can have varying degrees of *readiness to respond,* which are a joint function of habit and motivation. These three terms—*habit, motivation,* and *readiness to respond*—are our theoretical terms in that they are concepts invented by the theorist to try to make sense of the phenomenon of interest.[1]

In a proper theory, according to logical positivism, the relationships between theoretical terms will be explicitly formulated, preferably in mathematical terms. Equation 9-1 presents a possible manner of specifying this for our minitheory of learning:

$$_sE_r = {_sH_r} \times D \tag{9-1}$$

where

$_sE_r$ = readiness to respond (reaction potential)

$_sH_r$ = habit (habit strength)

D = drive

---

[1]For those who are interested in history, this theory is derived from Hull (1943).

Readiness to respond is a multiplicative function of drive and habit. Thus, we have a set of theoretical terms with the nature of their interrelationships specified mathematically. At this point, however, our theory is merely an idea; it is not the least bit scientific.

To proceed scientifically, we must have a way of bringing the theoretical terms into contact with the empirical, observable world. We do this by developing correspondence rules that allow us to translate the theoretical terms into observational statements. For example, we might formulate the correspondence rule that organisms deprived of food for a long period of time will be highly motivated if obtaining food is the outcome of the learning situation (for example, chow is presented at the end of a maze). Thus, we can formally specify drive by manipulating hours of deprivation with increasing hours without food increasing drive. Our correspondence rule for drive, then, involves monitoring the hours of deprivation from food. This correspondence rule allows us to rewrite our theoretical term as an observable sentence because it provides a means for us to manipulate the theoretical term *drive* in the real world of observables. We have brought our theory into the real world with our correspondence rule.

We might also formulate a correspondence rule for habit, suggesting that the greater the number of times the organism has been in a similar situation previously, the stronger the habit will be. Again, the correspondence rule for habit translates the theoretical term into an observable and manipulatable conception.

Once we have our two correspondence rules, we can actually test our theory. In a laboratory experiment using a maze, we might, for example, deprive one group of subjects for 3 hours and another group for 1 day. If our theory is correct (Equation 9-1) and all other things are equal (habit is the same in both groups), the 1-day deprived animals should show increased readiness to respond compared with the 3-hour group. Of course, we would need a correspondence rule to reveal readiness to respond. Perhaps speed through the maze would be appropriate. Our theory then predicts that the 1-day deprived rats will run faster through the maze than the 3-hour group. If this observable prediction is confirmed (which, incidentally, it usually is), then we have positive evidence that our theory is tenable. The results of this experiment can be written as an observable sentence of the form: "Under like conditions of habit, highly deprived animals run a maze faster than satiated animals." A whole series of such experiments could be conducted to determine if the mathematical relationship proposed in Equation 9-1 holds. We could also test other propositions logically derived from this minitheory.

This example, although representing a gross oversimplification of a classic learning theory, does contain the nub of the notion of logical positivism. We have theoretical terms (*habit, drive, readiness*), each related mathematically (Equation 9-1); correspondence rules tying the theoretical to observable terms (hours of deprivation corresponding to drive); and an observational sentence derived from the former considerations (under like conditions of habit, highly deprived animals run a maze faster than satiated animals). These are the essential terms in the logical positivistic analysis of scientific theory.

Figure 9-1 illustrates this analysis of scientific theory. Theoretical terms are entered to the left of the vertical line, observational statements to the right. The

Figure 9-1   Graphical representation of our simplified learning theory.

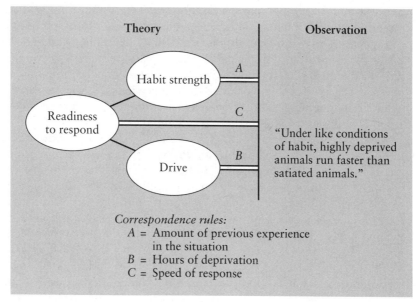

three theoretical terms are circled and joined with single lines indicating the mathematical (logical) relationships between them. All three theoretical terms are linked to the observational realm with correspondence rules, which are indicated with double lines and defined in the boxed legend. Finally, the observational sentence derived from one of many possible experiments is presented in quotes in the observational side of the representation.

This graphical approach to describing theory development is merely a shorthand used to help communicate the view of science that directed psychology during this time. Drawn from Margeneau (1950), there is no suggestion intended here that researchers of the time were busily drawing pictures like Figure 9-1 to decide how to embellish their theories. This is simply a convenient way of demonstrating the fundamental ideas of science that were guiding their efforts.[2]

A large part of the program of logical positivism involved demonstrating the manner in which major breakthroughs in the natural sciences were associated with the kind of system presented in Figure 9-1. Be it optics, astronomy, or natural selection, successful scientific theories appeared to be prototypical examples of the logical positivistic way of approaching science. Example after example of major scientific accomplishments were analyzed to the point that people began to believe that logical positivism was the only possible way of doing good science. On the basis of these analyses, it emerged that more highly mathematized theories were better.

---

[2]This graphical approach will also be used in Chapters 13, 15, and 20.

Part of the logical positivist position was the **doctrine of cognitive significance,** which suggested that theories that could not be described using the terms outlined above were scientifically questionable. Figure 9-2 presents a theoretical addition to our example, which would be unacceptable according to the doctrine. The addition of *expectancy* to the theory, although rationally plausible, would not be acceptable under the original view of logical positivism because there is no way of linking the term to the observable world.[3] There is no correspondence rule for expectancy. In rejecting this type of theoretical term, early versions of logical positivism made the assumption that all theoretical meaning is captured in the correspondence rules and other superfluous ideas should not be admitted.

Figure 9-3 demonstrates another possible violation of the doctrine of cognitive significance. Here a theoretical term, *divine purpose,* has been added to our example. Notice how this addition is not logically attached to any of the other theoretical terms. In addition, this new term does not have a correspondence rule linking it to the world of observables and no relationship to the theoretical structure. It violates the doctrine of cognitive significance in two ways, and a logical positivist would reject it. This rejection is not related to the content of the added term but to the fact that it is not linked to observables and other theoretical terms.

The system presented in Figure 9-3 may, on the surface, seem so absurd that it seems unnecessary to mention it. However, from a logical positivist perspective, a good many of the popular theories during the 1920s and 1930s could be classified in this manner. Perhaps the most obvious example was Freud's psychoanalytic theory. The interrelationships between theoretical terms were, at best, vaguely logical and certainly nonmathematical. Additionally, the correspondence rules linking Freud's theoretical terms to observables were highly suspect for a number of reasons. For example, recall the difficulties of reliability and validity with projective techniques (Chapter 8), which suggest that the theory does not contact the observable world particularly well. Thus, from the perspective of the logical positivist, theories like Freud's were seen as strong examples of how *not* to go about theory building in science.

Logical Positivism and Psychology

The young upstart discipline of psychology, flushed with its apparent successes during the war and aspiring to scientific legitimacy, was quick to note that the kind of thinking associated with logical positivism appeared to offer a "royal road" to scientific credibility. In a sense, logical positivism provided the discipline with a charter of how to go about attaining scientific respectability. All that was required was to follow the canons of this philosophical system. This realization turned out to be a particularly important milestone in the development of the psychological testing enterprise.

Many of the developments in psychology during this period were not *directly* driven by logical positivism per se. That is, psychologists were not avidly reading

---

[3]This point is true of the original, or so-called **received view of logical positivism.** As we will see later on, this aspect of the philosophy changed over time. For now, though, it is important to remember that the original view was most adamant that all theoretical terms be tied to observables.

Figure 9-2   Graphical representation of our simplified learning theory, showing an inappropriate
theoretical term because it does not have a correspondence rule.

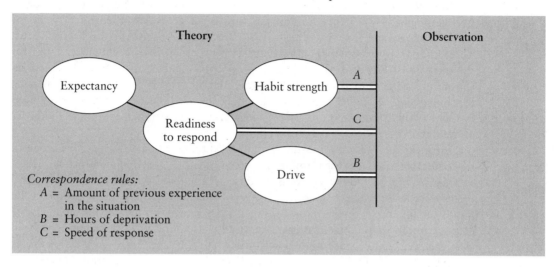

Figure 9-3   Graphical representation of our simplified learning theory, showing an inappropriate
theoretical term because it has neither a correspondence rule nor an explicit link to the
other theoretical terms.

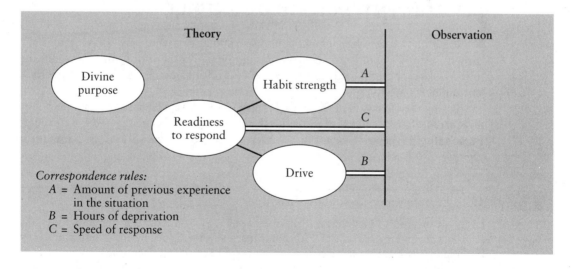

Carnap and applying his ideas to their work—indeed, very few psychologists were
even aware of Carnap's system. In their efforts to develop workable solutions to
the problems they were facing, many North American psychologists developed
their own perspectives, many of which in hindsight are remarkably similar to the
logical positivist position (see Smith, 1986). What remains, however, is the

observation that the ideas of logical positivism serve as relatively accurate descriptions of what psychologists actually did during this important time.[4]

In psychology it was not long before the idea underlying the doctrine of cognitive significance was being brandished with great zeal. Any theoretical term for which correspondence rules could not be specified should be thrown out. Throughout the halls of psychology departments, there was a widespread call for the purging of any and all subjectivist concepts—that is, those for which correspondence rules and proper theoretical interrelationships were not available. Psychology was going to become a legitimate science, and there was a strong need to rid it of any "nonscientific" ideas. Logical positivist thinking became the order of the day.

With the lack of a consensual definition, intelligence should have been one of the primary candidates for purging. It was impossible to articulate a proper correspondence rule for intelligence tests because an adequate theoretical definition and model of the idea had not been presented. There was, however, a problem: To purge intelligence from psychology would rob the discipline of its most visible demonstration of practical utility. The young discipline was in a conundrum—if tests were rejected because of their scientific problems, so too would it be necessary to reject the practical benefits they had wrought for the discipline. There was clearly the need for a creative solution that would allow psychology to retain its positivist position but at the same time legitimate the mental test.

DEVELOPMENTS IN TESTING CONTINUE

While all of this was happening, testing psychologists were busy developing their inventories and the technology surrounding them. The Stanford–Binet was still the most frequently mentioned test in the literature, followed closely by the Rorschach (see Sundberg, 1954).

Personality assessment was developing apace. A representative example of the new breed of personality inventories emerging during this time was the **Bernreuter Personality Inventory** (Bernreuter, 1931). The following Close Up provides a glimpse of this test.

CLOSE UP   The Bernreuter Personality Inventory

This inventory, introduced in Bernreuter (1931), contains 125 items such as "Do you daydream frequently?" Respondents answer yes, no, or ? to these and, using multiple-scoring stencils, are given scores on six scales: Neurotic Tendency, Self-sufficiency, Introversion/Extraversion, Dominance/Submission, Self-confidence,

---

[4]We sometimes forget that philosophies of science, such as logical positivism, do not spontaneously arise as ideas about how to do science. They are usually (post hoc) summaries of how researchers are working at a specific time. The value of philosophical analysis here is to find out if there are logical inconsistencies within these systems.

and Sociability. The inventory is intended for use with adolescents and adults with percentile norms provided for each gender at high school, college, and adult levels.

The scales were developed using a somewhat unusual criterion—namely, performance on other personality inventories. Respondents were placed in groups, depending on their answers to several inventories. A set of items adapted from the older inventories by Bernreuter was then administered to the same respondents. Items that differentiated between the classification groups were selected to make up the new scales. The keys were arranged with weights between −3 and +3, meaning that the same item response could contribute to all six scale scores.

The test/retest reliabilities for the scales range between .75 to .91, being described as "rather low to warrant use with individuals" (Mosier, 1941, p. 81). Correlating the scales with the inventories used during the development of the schedule established the validity of the inventory. Thus, the report of reasonably high correlations between tests (around .70) does not constitute validity information in the strictest sense because the validities of the original tests were not that high (around .25). The Neurotic Tendency and Introversion scales were found to be so highly correlated with each other ($r = .95$) that Bernreuter suggested that only one scale be used. Newcomb (1941) demonstrated how these high intercorrelations were an artifact of the manner in which the scales were keyed because each item contributed to each scale score. Thus, he argued against the use of the Bernreuter in any application.

The Bernreuter Personality Inventory did not pass the more-or-less standard tests of the emerging test theory. Both its reliability and validity were low, and internal properties were suspect (for example, exceedingly high scale intercorrelations). Yet it was a reasonably popular inventory in the 1930s. More than anything, the Bernreuter indicated that there was room for considerable improvement in the technology of developing measures of the abstract characteristics of personality. Such improvements were not far off, as we will see later in this chapter.

Along with the proliferation of personality tests, several other testing domains continued development during this time. For example, the trend initiated by the Stenquist, examining specific abilities, was extended. A number of tests for specialized abilities emerged during this time, with the most popular being the **Seashore Measures of Musical Talent** (Sundberg, 1954). As the 1920s wound down, the testing enterprise was flourishing, with the publication of many new and interesting tests covering an ever-widening sphere of psychological domains with increasingly greater detail.

THE GREAT DEPRESSION

In 1929 a major calamity intervened in our story. An overoptimistic view of the economic security of North America, in combination with several other factors, caused the stock market to crash. Within months the continent was thrown into the numbing **Depression**, which sapped its resources and suspended many human

In the West, depression dust storms caused great hardship and poor crops.

activities. Research activity slowed and psychology's quest for scientific legitimacy and practical utility was at a standstill at the start of the 1930s.

The Great Depression also had a major effect on the opportunities available for the psychological testing enterprise to demonstrate its utility. Budgets in educational institutions were slashed, and testing programs were one of the first items to fall under some very deep fiscal cutbacks. To give you an idea of the seriousness of the problems in schools during this time, teachers were not paid in cash in some western communities but were issued IOUs by the government (Douglas, 1979). The economic disaster of the 1930s caused many of the resources to dry up, particularly those on which the practical wing of testing was based. The opportunities for the young discipline to demonstrate its worth diminished greatly during this time, and there was an increasing concern about the future of the testing movement. As in the past, what was needed was some kind of dramatic action or conceptual breakthrough that would see the testing enterprise through these difficult times.

Psychiatry and the Testing Enterprise

One manner in which the Great Depression directly affected the testing enterprise was the emergence of **paramedical personnel** in mental-health settings. Being relatively short-staffed, the discipline of **psychiatry** had welcomed the addition of psychologists to their multidisciplinary teams prior to the Great Depression. The **psychiatric case conference**, initiated by William Healy around 1917, was a team approach positing that a complete view of the person, including physical, mental, and social realms, should be considered in a proper psychiatric orientation. The team, which might include "psychologists, social workers, educational specialists, nurses, dietitians and anyone else who might be helpful" (Burnham, 1974, p. 97), was a natural outgrowth of this view. In the team setting, psychologists with their tests were most welcome:

> The psychologists were particularly useful because they could administer and interpret mental tests. ... Like psychiatrists, psychologists gained recognition in the war period and after, and mental testing and the IQ enjoyed much favorable publicity. At first useful primarily in identifying the mentally deficient, clinical psychologists were beginning to introduce personality tests and tests for psychopathology. [Burnham, 1974, p. 101]

This popularity was short-lived, however, when the resources available for psychiatric practice became competitive. In combination with a desire for increased professionalization (and therefore autonomy) within the psychiatric community, a distinct change of heart came about, and soon the paramedical members of the former team were the brunt of considerable criticism from their former hosts. For example, the eminent psychiatrist **James V. May** of Boston, president of the American Psychiatric Association in 1932, "denounced psychologists who 'invaded the clinical field and are now laying down rules intended to guide those who are interested in the actual treatment of the abnormal'" (Burnham, 1974, p. 102). Before long, psychologists were *persona non grata* in the psychiatric community.

Psychiatrists initiated a twofold attack to regain lost territory: (1) They made the hospital the center of practice so that they could control all nonmedical professionals (Grob, 1966a); (2) they attacked the scientific foundations of the paramedical disciplines. This latter point is particularly important because it signals an increased need for scientific legitimacy on the part of the testing psychologists. If they were to survive the attacks of the scientific foundations of their activity, some form of scientific legitimacy was needed.

In a very real sense then, the Great Depression cut off one of psychology's most useful contacts in the medical community. The economic downturn created an atmosphere of competition that drove the medical practitioners to capture back the territory they had willingly relinquished to paramedical personnel like clinical psychologists when times were better. In so doing, mental health treatment was reestablished in the sanctity of the hospital where the medical profession could retain control, and the need for strong scientific rationalization of the testing enterprise became evident.

Changes in the Wind

By 1935 the stage had been set for the emergence of change in the testing enterprise. To summarize the foregoing, the following factors were involved:

1. Testing, which had emerged as psychology's most visible exemplar of its practical worth, was under critical attack.

2. No consensual definition of intelligence had emerged, which was somewhat of an embarrassment particularly for those who desired to demonstrate that psychology was a science.

3. A sophisticated theory of measurement had evolved that endorsed measurement without definition.

4. Pressures for demonstrable scientific legitimacy were being felt within the discipline in continual calls for the purging of subjectivist concepts. Psychology was in a quandary with intelligence because the failure to have a consensual definition made it a candidate for purging, but to do so would be to disavow the discipline's practical utility.

5. Several rounds of controversy in the public press had demonstrated the need for stronger argument.

6. With the adoption of restrictive immigration legislation and the economic disaster of the 1930s, the social needs being served by the testing enterprise were changing.

7. The Great Depression had severely restricted the resources available to support the kind of social decision making to which the testing enterprise was dedicated (particularly in the educational and medical fields), thereby causing concern for the future of the area.

These factors prompted many researchers to start searching for alternatives, creating a climate ready for virtually any kind of "new deal." All of this combined to create a context that was primed and ready for change.

OPERATIONISM

Change did come. The most important change in the testing movement during the 1930s was undoubtedly the advent of a philosophical position called **operationism.** This position resolved a goodly number of the prevailing problems in the assessment area and stimulated the emergence of several of the most important tests yet to be published. The lingering problems of the tension between practical and academic approaches to testing were resolved, and the future of the testing movement seemed ensured.

Touted as the "revolution that will put an end to the possibility of revolutions" (Stevens, 1935, p. 323), operationism emerged in psychology in 1935. This approach to the scientific definition of concepts offered promise of long overdue housecleaning of subjectivist concepts from the discipline and further showed the potential of bringing the discipline into even closer line with the natural sciences. As you might expect, the logical positivist style of thinking was at the heart of this movement.

The foundational idea of operationism was that the meaning of a theoretical concept was identical to the operations that go into measuring it—nothing more, nothing less. An examination of the nature of measurement helps illustrate this position. Virtually any measurement involves five things: (1) the characteristic being measured (length), (2) an object being measured (a piece of string), (3) an arbitrary unit of measurement (centimeter), (4) an operation (counting the number of centimeters in the string), and (5) an outcome ("the string is 5.89 centimeters long"). In terms of logical positivism outlined earlier, (1) is the theoretical term, (4) is the correspondence rule, and (5) is the observational sentence. The unique aspect of operationism was the manner in which it was made explicit that the meaning of theoretical terms was *identical* to the operation. That is, the measurement operation specifies the entire meaning of the theoretical term—there is nothing else involved. Although this view was implicit in the original view of logical positivism, operationism made it explicit and developed a philosophical system that emphasized this (radical) reading of logical positivism. The operation of measurement contained all of the meaning of the theoretical term.

How Operationism Emerged in Psychology

The manner in which operationism was introduced in psychology gives us a good glimpse at the manner in which it represented a creative solution to some of psychology's pressing problems being experienced in the 1930s. Because operationism was developed by physicist Percy Bridgman (1927), it carried considerable status for psychology with its aspirations to scientific legitimacy. The first explicitly operational analysis in psychology occurred in B. F. Skinner's 1931 doctoral dissertation (Skinner, 1945).

Four years later, **S. S. Stevens** (1935) presented what appears to be the first readily available treatise on operationism in psychology. He stayed relatively close to Bridgman's original position, which argued that

> The concept of length is ... fixed when the operations by which length is measured are fixed: that is, the concept of length involves as much and nothing more than the set of operations by which length is determined. In general, we mean by any concept nothing more than a set of operations; the concept is synonymous with the corresponding set of operations. [Bridgman, 1927, p. 5]

Theoretical meaning, then, is totally defined by the operations of measurement. According to this position, the operation of measuring something was the correspondence rule that uniquely tied an observational statement to a theoretical term. This operation, in turn, specified the complete meaning of the theoretical term.

In his adaptation for psychology, Stevens (1935) defined an operation as "the performance which we execute in order to make known a concept" (p. 323). For example, the idea of the "length of an object is that the ends of the object coincide with certain marks on the measuring rod" (p. 324). His was a relatively strong version of operationism because he indicated that length measured by two different sets of operations (for example, a measuring rod and triangulation) represented two different concepts of length—the two measures "cannot be considered identical" (p. 324). The main virtue of an operational approach, according to Stevens, was that it "insures us against hazy, ambiguous and contradictory notions and provides the rigor of definition which silences useless controversy" (p. 323). He concluded his introduction of operationism to mainstream psychology by suggesting that

> The course for psychology is clear. We must examine and sift the meanings of its concepts in accordance with operational procedure ... we must expect to still maintain constant vigil against the human tendency to read into a concept more than is contained in the operations by which it is determined ... only then are we fortified against meaningless concepts. [p. 330]

Within months this new philosophical position was applied to such topical concepts as learning (McGeoch, 1935), temporal perception (Boring, 1936), identity and numerical quality (McGregor, 1935), and drive (Tolman, 1936). McGregor (1935) aptly captures the fervor of the operational revolution of 1935, wherein this position is thought to have resolved the **mind/body problem**:

> Psychological measurement, understood in operational terms, is a fait accompli. It is physical measurement. It has always been. And the psychologist, now aware that he is using no mysteriously unique scientific instrument (the observer), can, secure in his new self-knowledge, proceed with his measurement, unimpeded by the hampering difficulties of the Cartesian dichotomy between mind and body. [pp. 265–266]

The immediate and uncritical adoption of operationism was astounding (see Leahey, 1980; Rogers, 1987). The philosophical position was firmly established by 1939—a truly significant change.

Operationism and the Testing Enterprise

The application of operationism to the testing enterprise was deceptively simple. If a theoretical term is defined by the operations that go into measuring it, then it is possible to argue that the theoretical meaning of a test is defined simply by the test itself. Simply put, personality is what a personality test measures—nothing more, nothing less. Mechanical aptitude is what a mechanical-aptitude test measures—nothing more, nothing less. With the operationist position, there is no need to get caught up in endless debates about what tests measure—they are simply **operational definitions** of the theoretical terms. This was a wonderfully simple solution to an incredibly complex set of problems.

In one bold stroke, the operationist philosophy provided solutions to the most vexing problems being experienced in the assessment domain. By this view, there was no need to define what a test measures—its meaning was specified by the operation of administering the test. This high-status philosophical position, which was borrowed from physics, the most revered natural science, completely justified the prevailing measurement theory, particularly its adherence to measurement without definition. Defining intelligence as what the Stanford–Binet measures was highly liberating for the testing enterprise because it meant that there was no need to get caught up in endless debates and hassles about the underlying meaning of the test scores. Psychology's most visible demonstration of its practical worth had been salvaged from scientific obscurity by operationism because it was now possible to defend the test as an operational procedure in keeping with the prevailing canons of contemporary science. Once viewed in operational terms, the lack of a consensual definition of intelligence (and other constructs measured by various other tests) was no longer a problem because the theoretical terms were simply the application of standardized operational procedures—intelligence was what an intelligence test measures. The need for debates about definition no longer existed. This, of course, rationalized measurement without definition. By simply defining intelligence (or any theoretical term) as the operation of applying a given test to a given subject, the prevailing measurement theory was completely justified; there was virtually no need to define what one was measuring. The received view of logical positivism, as adapted by Bridgman and Stevens via operationism, provided a high-status, post hoc justification for the measurement theory. This emancipated intelligence from the list of subjectivist concepts that should be purged from the discipline. It was now safely a member of the scientific community.

The acceptance of operationism added even more strength to the rhetoric surrounding testing because associating the field with philosophical positions acknowledged in the natural sciences was now possible. Testing was also brought into the academic fold within psychology because the problems of definition, which had proven problematic, no longer existed. Operationism also appeared to have a sense of newness that fulfilled the search for alternatives that was so much a part of life in the United States during the Great Depression.

In sum, operationism was an incredibly useful solution to a number of very important problems that were impinging on the field of psychological testing. It rationalized a whole series of practices and beliefs that had been in place since the emergence of the mental test. It was a great solution to a number of very vexing problems.

Not as New as Advertised

The ideas underlying operationism were presented in the testing literature well before Stevens's 1935 article. In the mid-1920s, the fundamental ideas underlying Bridgman's position were being discussed in the context of intelligence. In an article in the *New Republic,* E. E. Boring (1923) presented a discussion of intelligence that clearly presages an operational view of the construct.[5] He started out listing a series of "observational facts of the psychology of intelligence" such as the consistency of individual differences and the peaking of performance in the second decade of life. In discussing the meaning of these facts, Boring stated "They mean in the first place that intelligence as a measurable capacity must at the start be defined as the capacity to do well in an intelligence test. *Intelligence is what the tests test* [italics added]"

[5]Interestingly, this article appeared at the time Walter Lippmann was presenting, in the same magazine, his set of six papers highly critical of testing (see Chapter 7). An editorial note in the *New Republic* indicates that Boring's essay had been received prior to Lippman's articles being written.

(p. 35). This is a clear statement of an operational approach where the theoretical entity is equated with the measurement procedure. Boring went on to suggest that this would best be considered a "point of departure" and ended his presentation with a call for more research before becoming embroiled in debates about the intelligence of minorities and other controversial issues.

A view very similar to operationism was clearly part of the testing area 4 years before Bridgman published his seminal work (and 12 years before Stevens's introduction of operationism to psychology). When the formal statement of operationism did arrive, it served to validate a series of ideas that were already in place in the field. It is small wonder that the position enjoyed such immediate acceptance. Operationism, then, was not the revolution that Stevens would have us believe but the restatement (and legitimation) of ideas and practices that were more or less in place since the ascendance of tests in North America.

The decade following Stevens's 1935 introduction of operationism saw numerous articles discussing the strengths and weaknesses of the position. In large measure, operationism received favorable reviews because it was extrapolated to include numerous theoretical terms and methods. Two particularly important extrapolations from this position deserve consideration. The first is the development of what remains today the most important testing device for measuring **psychopathology**. The second is the development of an influential measure of vocational interests.

THE MINNESOTA MULTIPHASIC PERSONALITY INVENTORY

The fundamental philosophical position underlying operationism was interpreted in a number of different ways throughout North America. In Minnesota it emerged as what has been called **Dust Bowl empiricism**. In this approach to psychology, emphasis was placed on empirical data with little concern for the theoretical underpinnings of the science. This version of logical positivism had a great impact on testing because several important technological developments occurred under the aegis of this philosophical position. In the discussion that follows, it will be implied that the operational and Minnesota versions of logical positivism were fundamentally the same thing at one level of analysis, but there were differences as well. Perhaps, more than anything else, what unites these two views of psychology is the manner in which they both accepted and promoted measurement without definition. This is clearly revealed in the emergence of a seminal psychological test—the **Minnesota Multiphasic Personality Inventory (MMPI)**.

The Backdrop

Since Woodworth's publication of the first personality inventory, the domain of personality assessment had shown considerable development. By the mid-1930s, a considerable number of inventories had emerged, but so had much criticism (see, for example, the Close Up on the Bernreuter). The following are some representative quotations from the critical literature of the time:

> Investigation fairly consistently confirms the low worth of the most widely publicized instruments. [Watson, 1938, p. 270]

> Since the scales in current use have not been adequately validated, studies employing them as measuring instruments and accepting the derived scores as measures, cannot be considered as particularly meaningful. [Mosier, 1938, p. 10]

> There are some 500 personality tests, most of which are of little or no value as measurement devices. A few, probably not more than a dozen, could be recommended for experimental use in a testing program. [Kornhauser, 1945, p. 9]

Personality assessment was clearly under siege. Several reasons were suggested. In keeping with the prevailing positivistic dogma, one of the leading candidates for fault was theory. At a general level, the discipline was expressing the need for less emphasis on theory:

> The outstanding weakness of modern psychology is a scarcity of fact and an oversupply of theory. Heidbreder, for example, in a recent summary of seven so-called "schools of psychology" makes the disturbing statement that "there is not enough fact in the whole science of psychology to make a single solid system." [Ross, 1936, p. 197]

This desire to deemphasize theory was part-and-parcel of the logical positivist position and its operational variant.

In relation to personality assessment, **Paul Meehl** argued that the basic problem was the use of **a priori assumptions** to construct personality inventories. By this Meehl meant theoretical expectations about the universe of content being addressed by the inventory. For example, Woodworth's Personal Data sheet had been constructed using the author's "intuitions" about how the items related to shell shock. Meehl thought that this reliance on theoretical expectations was the prime problem in personality assessment:

> Associated with this approach to structured personality tests is the construction of items and their assembling into scales upon an *a priori basis,* requiring the assumption that the psychologist building the test has sufficient insight into the dynamics of verbal behavior and its relation to the inner core of personality that he is able to predict beforehand what certain sorts of people will say about themselves. The fallacious character of this procedure has been shown by the empirical results.... It is suggested tentatively that the relative uselessness of most structured personality tests is due more to a priori item construction than to the fact of their being structured. [Meehl, 1945, p. 297]

This criticism did not come out of a vacuum but was launched from a strong operationist position that favored the use of empirical means to assign items to subscales and that argued for an empirical rather than a theoretical approach to doing psychology. The MMPI can be seen as a direct outgrowth of the operationist philosophy. The clever use of empirical methodology finessed the need to define the constructs that the test measures; thus, operationism justified and sustained the development of this inventory.

The Test

The problem faced by the test developers, Hathaway and McKinley (1943), was to construct an inventory that would detect the presence of psychopathological states such as **schizophrenia** and **depression.** (For biographical details of Hathaway, see Thompson, 1978.) The solution, which became known as **empirical criterion keying,** was deceptively simple. A series of statements relating to a wide range of psychopathological states was gathered from contemporary textbooks. These statements were rewritten as first-person singular sentences such as

I am concerned about sex matters.

Some of my family have habits that bother me very much.

It takes a lot of argument to convince most people that they are wrong.

I wish I were not as shy as I am.

There were 550 sentences like these, and respondents were to answer these questions either "true," "false," or "cannot say." Initially, cards with the item printed on them were sorted into three boxes marked by the response alternatives, but eventually it took the more familiar structured format.

In the development stage, the items were administered to a specific psychopathological group, such as depressive patients. These respondents were placed in the group because they were diagnosed as such by psychiatrists. The inventory was also administered to a group of "normal" people. Five hundred and fifty statistical tests, one for each item, were conducted to determine if the responses of the target group were meaningfully different from the normal group. In the case of depressive patients, 60 of the 550 items showed meaningful differences. On these items, the depressives answered differently from the normals. Figure 9-4 lists hypothetical examples of the kinds of items found on the MMPI Depression scale.

For the first three of these items, the depressive patients tended to answer "true," whereas normal people said "false." These are called **true-keyed items** because a true response is indicative of membership in the depressive category. The second three items in Figure 9-4 tended to be answered false by the depressives and

Figure 9-4   Hypothetical items from the Minnesota Multiphasic Personality Inventory Depression (d) scale.

True-keyed items:
I am easily awakened by noises outside of my home.
I seldom get a good night's sleep.
I am considered to be a brooding person.

False-keyed items:
My daily life is full of things that keep me fascinated.
My memory seems to be fine.
I believe I am no more anxious than most others.

true by the normals. These are **false-keyed items** because a false response is a sign that the respondent should be categorized as depressive. A Depression score is calculated by adding up the number of times a respondent answers an item in the keyed direction.

The scores are related to a normative sample using a z score that is then transformed, using Equation 9-2, into a **T score,** which has a mean of 50 and a standard deviation of 10:

$$T = 50 + (10 \times z) \tag{9-2}$$

where

T = T score (mean = 50; standard deviation = 10)

z = z score (mean = 0; standard deviation = 1; see Equation 4-1)

The T score is an arbitrary transformation of the z score, intended to make it easier to understand the numbers. In standard practice, a T score greater than 70 (that is, 2 SDs above the mean) is considered the cutoff point for the identification of membership in the diagnostic group addressed by the scale. Thus, a person obtaining a Depression-scale score of 74 would be considered depressed, whereas a person with a score of 65 would not. A similar procedure was used to develop scales for a number of forms of psychopathology (see Figure 9-5).

The ten clinical scales in Figure 9-5 represented the current categories of psychopathology. The scales were thought to be *unipolar* in that they ran from normal to extreme cases of the diagnostic category of concern. Additionally, the scales were treated conceptually as though they were independent of each other. In other words, a person's status on one scale was thought not to affect their status on another. Finally, not all items were involved in all scales—the only items that were included on a specific scale were those that reliably differentiated the criterion group from people in general.

Besides the standard clinical scales, a number of validity scales were included, which were checks for misunderstanding of the instructions, **honest responding, careless responding,** or **test-taking defensiveness** (Figure 9-6).

The MMPI provided the clinician with a particularly useful tool. The clinical scales provided a broadband measure of the dimensions of psychopathology current at the time. The validity scales provided a means of checking whether the assumptions underlying the testing process (for example, careful responding, defensiveness) had been met. In very general terms, this test was a particularly powerful addition to the psychologist's toolbox and rapidly gained acceptance in the field. Test results are typically reported in the form of a profile such as those shown in Figures 9-7 through 9-9.

To facilitate the interpretation of the profiles, a numerical system was developed that allowed the user to reference an obtained profile to a **cookbook,** which then offered an interpretation (see Butcher & Keller, 1984; Hathaway & Meehl, 1951). The coded profiles involve, among other things, listing the most extreme scale numbers at the beginning. For example, the code for Figure 9-9 begins with the numbers 86, which represent the Schizophrenia and Paranoia scales,

Figure 9-5   Descriptions and items of the type used in the clinical scales of the Minnesota Multiphasic Personality Inventory. Some early versions of the Minnesota Multiphasic Personality Inventory did not contain all of these scales.

Hypochondriasis (Hs):	Persons scoring high on this scale show abnormal concern for bodily function. Worries and preoccupations with physical symptoms typically persist in the face of strong evidence against any valid physical problem. (33 items)
	HYPOTHETICAL ITEMS:
	I have a great deal of trouble with digestion. (true keyed)
	I wake up rested most mornings. (false keyed)
Depression (D):	A mood state characterized by pessimism of outlook on life and the future, feelings of hopelessness or worthlessness, slowing of thought and action, and frequently by preoccupation with death and suicide. (60 items)
	HYPOTHETICAL ITEMS:
	I seldom get a good night's sleep. (true keyed)
	My daily life is full of things that keep me fascinated. (false keyed)
Hysteria (Hy):	High scorer uses physical symptoms as a means of solving difficult conflicts or avoiding mature responsibilities. Will appear normal between (usually stress-induced) episodes (60 items)
	HYPOTHETICAL ITEMS:
	Often I feel as if there is a steel band around my head. (true keyed)
	Often I can't understand why I have been so upset. (false keyed)
Psychopathic deviate (Pd):	A personality pattern that includes repeated and flagrant disregard for social customs and mores, an inability to profit from punishing experiences as shown in repeated difficulties of the same kind, and an emotional shallowness in relation to others. (50 items)
	HYPOTHETICAL ITEMS:
	My family does not like the work I do. (true keyed)
	It does not bother me what others think of me. (false keyed)
Masculinity/femininity (Mf):	To identify the personality associated with male sexual inversion; tendency to engage in homoerotic practices; shows many feminine characteristics such as expression, speech, interests and styles. (60 items)
	HYPOTHETICAL ITEMS:
	If I were an artist I would like to sculpt flowers. (true keyed)
	If I were a newspaper writer I would very much like to write about sports. (false keyed)

Paranoia (Pa):	Delusional beliefs, frequently including delusions of reference, influence and grandeur. (40 items)
	HYPOTHETICAL ITEMS:
	I believe that someone is following me. (true keyed) I have no enemies who wish me harm. (false keyed)
Psychasthenia (Pt):	Neurotic pattern of personality often referred to as the obsessive/compulsive syndrome; obsessive ruminations and obsessive behavioral rituals; some forms of abnormal fears, worrying, difficulties in concentrating, guilt feelings, and excessive vacillation in making decisions. (48 items)
	HYPOTHETICAL ITEMS:
	I have to stop and think before I act. (true keyed) I seem to be about as intelligent as others around me. (false keyed)
Schizophrenia (Sc):	Bizarre and unusual thoughts and/or behavior; described as constrained, cold, apathetic, and indifferent; delusions of varying degrees of organization, hallucinations, either persistent or fleeting, and considerable disorientation. (77 items)
	HYPOTHETICAL ITEMS:
	Almost every day something happens that scares me. (true keyed) My memory is good. (false keyed)
Hypomania (Ma):	The manic portion of manic/depressive cycles, characterized by overactivity, emotional excitement, and flight of ideas. Mood varies between good-humored euphoria and irritability and temper outbursts (46 items)
	HYPOTHETICAL ITEMS:
	At times I feel that I can make decisions very easily. (true keyed) My speech never changes in speed. (false keyed)
Social introversion (Si):	Withdraws from social contacts and responsibilities; displays little real interest in people. (70 items)
	HYPOTHETICAL ITEMS:
	I am considered to be a brooding person. (true keyed) I like to tease members of the opposite sex. (false keyed)

Reproduced by permission of the University of Minnesota Press.

respectively. In the cookbook, profiles beginning with these two numbers would be categorized as paranoid schizophrenia, a specific subtype of the disorder. These cookbooks were particularly important components of the MMPI technology. They provided a clear means of rendering the test interpretations as objective as possible because they ensured that interpreters would agree on the reading of a given profile. This apparent objectivity was seen as one of the major strengths of this technology.

Apart from individual diagnosis, the MMPI can also be used to assess group characteristics. For example, Figure 9-10 presents the group-average profiles of 47 teenagers admitted to a drug-abuse treatment center before and after treatment.

Structural Characteristics of the MMPI

It is an interesting empirical question to explore the characteristics of the scales emerging from the MMPI. In a sense, the nature of the scales determined in this empirical fashion provides useful information about the domain being measured.

Figure 9-6 Validity scales from the Minnesota Multiphasic Personality Inventory. Some early versions of the Minnesota Multiphasic Personality Inventory did not contain all of these scales.

Cannot Say (?) Score:	The number of items that the respondent marks ?, indicating they are unable to answer. The median score is 1, with high scores suggesting an invalid protocol.
The L Scale:	The extent to which the respondent is being honest in responding. High scores suggest profile should be regarded "with suspicion." (15 items)
	HYPOTHETICAL ITEMS:
	Once in a while, I put off things that I ought to do now. (false keyed)
	I prefer winning games. (false keyed)
The F Scale:	The number of items answered in the exceedingly unpopular direction, suggesting sloppiness in responding or a very unusual response pattern. (63 items)
	HYPOTHETICAL ITEMS:
	My spirit sometimes leaves my body. (true keyed)
	I believe in traffic laws. (false keyed)
The K Scale:	Test-taking defensiveness. Developed by comparing responses of clinically classified defensive respondents to people in general. (30 items)
	HYPOTHETICAL ITEMS:
	At times I feel like cursing. (false keyed)
	It makes me impatient to have people ask for my opinion when I am working on something important. (false keyed)
	Clinical scales can be "K-corrected" to adjust for the tendency to be defensive.

Reproduced by permission of the University of Minnesota Press.

Figure 9-7   Minnesota Multiphasic Personality Inventory profile of a normal respondant.

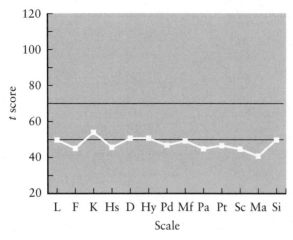

Data used by permission of the University of Minnesota Press.

Figure 9-8   Minnesota Multiphasic Personality Inventory profile of an alcoholic patient.

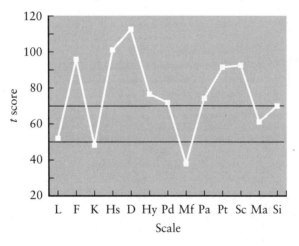

Data used by permission of the University of Minnesota Press.

As well, several characteristics of the MMPI presage a number of developments in the testing enterprise and thereby warrant mention at this point.

Subtle items. With empirical item selection, the possibility exists that an item will be selected that bears no conceptual resemblance whatsoever to the characteristic being measured. For example, an item like "I sometimes tease animals" could

Figure 9-9   Minnesota Multiphasic Personality Inventory profile of a schizophrenic patient.

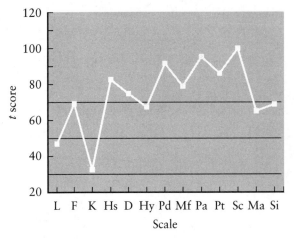

Data used by permission of the University of Minnesota Press.

Figure 9-10 Average Minnesota Multiphasic Personality Inventory of a group of substance abusers.

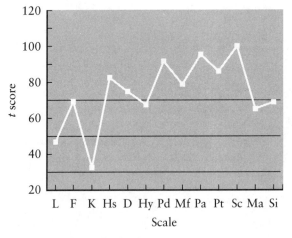

(SOURCE: Brook & Whitehead, 1980.)

emerge as a false-keyed item on the D scale. Deriving a conceptual link between this **subtle item** and depression is somewhat difficult. Such items did not pose a problem for the MMPI because they were simply viewed as bits of verbal behavior with empirically demonstrated links to the diagnostic category. These links had been established because the item had been selected using empirical criterion keying.

Unbalanced scales. A second characteristic of the test development strategy is the finding that the proportions of true- and false-keyed items varied, creating **unbal-**

anced scales. For example, 23 of the 60 items (38%) on the D scale were true-keyed, whereas 28 of 40 (70%) of the Pa scale items were true-keyed. Although this was not considered problematic at the time, it turned out to be an important characteristic of the MMPI in later years.[6]

Item overlap. A third aspect of the MMPI, which derives directly from the item-selection strategy, is the tendency for certain items to occur on more than one scale. For example, one item appeared on the D, Hy, Pd, Pt, Sc, and Si scales. This meant that the various scale scores were not independent of each other. People responding in the keyed direction on this item would automatically increment their scores on all six scales of which this item is a member. If it should turn out that scale independence is important, the item-selection strategy associated with the MMPI will definitely prove to be a problem because of this **item overlap.**[7]

Seeing things that are not there. Another feature of the MMPI scales is the tendency, in some cases, for scales to suggest psychopathology when it really does not exist. Perhaps the most obvious example is the Schizophrenia scale, which contains a number of items about hallucinations. Were the inventory administered to a group of drug-abusers, they would likely endorse the hallucination items in the keyed direction, even though they may not necessarily be schizophrenic. The data in Figure 9-10 suggest that this may be the case, even though there appears to be an indication of schizophrenic tendencies as well. This indicates, then, that the MMPI scales may well find aspects of personality that do not automatically implicate the pathology measured by the scale, even though they might be interpreted as such.

Changing horses in midstream. The MMPI was designed to make a categorical decision. It was developed using a nominal criterion and would appear to be restricted to making nominal decisions. A given clinical scale tells us whether or not a respondent belongs to a specific diagnostic category; either the person is depressed or not—nothing more, nothing less. We might get a bit brave and suggest that the higher the score, the higher the probability a person belongs to the diagnostic category, but such an inference would require empirical data that are not inherent in the scale-construction strategy. This use of the test to make probabilistic statements would require new normative information.

However, in typical usage, an even greater interpretive leap was made. Essentially, people began to think in terms of a linear model underlying the MMPI scales, wherein the size of the scale score indicated "how much" of the characteristic the respondent possessed. In other words, users began to assume that the MMPI was an ordinal, and perhaps even an interval, scale. For example, a very high D-scale score was soon being interpreted as indicating that the respondent was "very depressed." Users began to assume that the MMPI scales were linear indexes of the amount of the characteristic possessed by the respondent—the higher the score, the

---

[6]The implications of this point are discussed in Chapter 16.

[7]The implications of this point are discussed in Chapter 16.

more of the characteristic the respondent has. This interpretation is totally unjustified from the scale-construction technique used because the criterion made absolutely no discrimination about the degree of disease in the diagnostic categories. The imposition of a linear model onto the MMPI scales signals the realization that aspects of the inventory did not fulfill the needs of the clinicians because they were working in a context demanding linear, not nominal, scales.

You name it, I'll measure it. Perhaps the most clear and astounding implication of the strategy underlying the MMPI is the fact that this technique permits the measurement of virtually anything. If it is possible to put people into two groups, then it is a very simple technological task to develop a scale that will predict group membership. Simply give the MMPI to the two groups, empirically determine which items differentiate them, and use these to construct a scale. In a very real sense, the MMPI strategy opens the door to the measurement of virtually anything.

This observation did not escape the attention of the field because one of the first things to happen to the MMPI was an incredible proliferation of scales to measure characteristics as wide ranging as anxiety, the authoritarian personality, ego-strength, prejudice, and social status. In fact, there are over 400 MMPI scales available, each developed using fundamentally the same approach as the original MMPI, borrowing the item pool developed by Hathaway and McKinley.

This "you name it, I'll measure it" quality of the measurement field is possible because of the inherent sanctioning of measurement without definition, which is so firmly embedded in the MMPI and related instruments. All that is needed is a group of people assigned to specific categories and a set of items that need not even relate directly to the decision being made. Once these are in hand, the development of a scale is the simple enactment of an easy technology. At no point during this process is it necessary to define exactly what the scale is measuring. Given the operationist context that sired the MMPI, it emerged as a sophisticated means of sanctioning the prevailing view that devalued the theoretical meaning of the ideas underlying the test.

Reliability

In general terms, the reliabilities of the MMPI scales were disappointing. Test/retest correlations range from .46 to .93, over periods of 2 days to 1 year. The averages seem to be somewhere around .76 (see Horrocks, 1964, p. 550). Such reliabilities might be acceptable in research contexts, but the level of measurement error revealed in these data might be too high to justify the use of the test for making an important social decision such as admission to mental hospitals.

Validity

Of particular concern with the MMPI was the manner in which the inventory discriminated between various criterion groups. How accurate is the test in placing individuals into specific categories? Calvin and McConnell (1953) surveyed 80 studies in which the MMPI was used to place people in specific criterion groups and found that 89% (71) of these showed significant validity coefficients. However, Ellis (1959) surveyed twice the number of studies several years later and found that only 64% showed significant discriminations. This figure is somewhat better than other personality inventories, which come in around 55%. However, values in the range of 65% are still relatively low, particularly if important social decisions are being made. It would seem that the MMPI was more valid than its competitors, but in absolute terms its criterion-related validity remained in doubt.

Several other problems have been noted with the MMPI. For example, the normal group, which was used in the development of the scales, was recruited from among visitors to the hospital that housed the patients in the diagnostic group. Although clearly convenient, this procedure introduced some problems into the scales because the normal group may not have been representative of the population. To the extent that psychopathology "runs in families," this method of recruiting the norm group is deeply problematic. Despite this difficulty and several others, the MMPI emerged as a particularly important scale representing an important development in the assessment of personality.

A Creative Solution to a Difficult Problem

The association of the MMPI with state-of-the-art approaches to science (for example, logical positivism, operationism) was one of the major factors that made the MMPI immensely popular in clinical work. Recall that psychiatry, in its zest for professional status and the recapture of territory given out to paraprofessionals in earlier times, attempted to purge psychology from the mental-health field. This was accomplished by assailing the scientific basis of the discipline and reestablishing the hospital as the center of mental-health practice. The MMPI can be seen as a direct response to this attack because it took the psychiatrists' view as given. That is, the starting point for the development of the MMPI was the psychiatrists' categorizations of membership in various diagnostic groups. Hathaway and McKinley developed a system that would permit making these decisions more efficiently (that is, less expensively)—offering psychiatrists potentially great savings in money and time by releasing them from diagnostic work to spend more time on therapy. In addition, the MMPI, by virtue of its contact with the prevailing version of logical positivism, offered a strong buttress against attempts to criticize the scientific base of the discipline and the instrument. In its time, the MMPI was a truly creative solution to a number of vexing problems within the psychological community—it was a timely arrival. Indeed, it was such an effective solution that the test remained untouched until 1989 when it was finally upgraded (the revision is discussed in Chapter 16).

THE STRONG VOCATIONAL INTEREST BLANK

A second area where the operationist approach was revealed is in the domain of vocational interests. Social decisions about the role a young person should play in a society are fairly important. Recall Mishi, the young Ojibway boy, who underwent an important ritual in the interests of negotiating his place in the social structure of the tribe. Clearly, these kinds of placement decisions are important in any society, and we should expect to find considerable activity in most cultures addressing this problem.

With this in mind, it should not seem surprising that the assessment of vocational interests was one of the first areas to which psychological testers turned their attention, once the breakthrough by Binet was made known. In fact, as early as 1912 (the same year Terman and Childs published the Americanized Binet), work on the measurement of interests was appearing in psychology journals (see Dubois, 1974, pp. 77–79). The emergence of a formalized test of vocational preferences, however, was considerably longer in coming. One reason for the delay was that measurement theory and technology were not yet ready to handle a topic as complicated as vocational interests. The essential problem was to develop a means of measuring adolescents' current interests and relating these, in a meaningful way, to various professions that these interests may sustain. This is further complicated by the realization that the interaction between interests and abilities is most perplexing and that the nature of occupations is in a continual state of flux as new technologies and approaches to the work place emerge. This was not an easy problem to solve.

The first major instrument that emerged in this area was constructed by **Edward K. Strong, Jr.** and was published in 1927 as the **Strong Vocational Interest Blank (SVIB)**. The fundamental strategy Strong used involved identifying people who were satisfied with their jobs. They were administered a set of interest items, and those that differentiated satisfied occupational members from people-in-general made up the scale for the specific occupation. For example, interest items checked significantly differently by satisfied physicians from people-in-general were selected for the Doctor scale on the SVIB. This is an excellent example of empirical criterion keying, much like the technique used with the MMPI.

The SVIB, with its empirical criterion keying, predates the MMPI by almost 15 years. It emerged well before the "operationist revolution." However, the initial version of the test did not fare very well in the psychological and counseling communities. It was not until 1938, with the publication of the first revision, that the SVIB began to be accepted, partly because the prevailing philosophy legitimated Strong's approach.

The Inventory

Strong taught at the Carnegie Institute of Technology from 1919 through 1923. In the context of a graduate seminar during that time, he (along with graduate student Karl Chowdery) developed a 1000 item pool of interest items. Chowdery's doctoral dissertation demonstrated that responses to these items could be used to discriminate which professions respondents entered. In 1927 Strong added some items to those found useful in Chowdery's research and published the SVIB. Described as incredibly compulsive, organized, and dedicated, Strong developed, revised, and promoted his test for the remainder of his career.

Strong's fundamental approach involved the comparison of responses of specific occupational groups with those of people-in-general. Like the MMPI, the preference items were administered to the two groups, and those statements showing a meaningful difference between the two groups were selected as indexes of preferences for the occupation. For example, members of the artist group may have indicated a greater preference for attending symphony concerts than did people-in-general. This item would then become part of the Artist scale. Items not differentiating the two groups were not included in the scale.

The occupational groups were selected to represent the major occupational titles of the time, and only members who had been in the occupation for 3 years or more and indicated they were satisfied with their jobs were included. The people-in-general group was a bit more problematic because Strong's research revealed that different items would emerge for the scales as a function of the makeup of this group. For example, the use of a people-in-general group made up mostly of skilled workers would yield different scales compared with a more professionally oriented group. Strong chose to bias his general group toward the professional occupational titles because his basic goal was differentiation among the business and professional occupations. The SVIB was revised in 1938 and 1946.

A more contemporary version of the SVIB was constructed after Strong died in 1963. Revised by **David Campbell** in 1974, it was called the **Strong–Campbell Interest Inventory (SCII)**, and it was revised in 1985 (Strong, Hansen, & Campbell, 1985). A new version, the Strong Interest Inventory (SII) was published in 1994. The SII consists of 317 items covering occupations, school subjects, work-related activities, hobbies, types of people, preferences between different activities, personal characteristics, and work preferences. Respondents mark like, indifferent, or dislike beside items such as

Operating machinery	_____
Forest ranger	_____
Chemistry	_____
Doing research work	_____
Magazines about art or music	_____
Contributing to charities	_____
People who assume leadership	_____

A number of different types of scales are obtained from these responses. The occupational scales were developed using the methodology outlined above. In addition, there are several other types of scores provided with the SII.

Occupational scales. These are the oldest scales of the SII—designed to provide information about the degree of similarity between the respondent's interests and those of various occupations. The long tradition of research initiated by Strong has led to the number of such scales being large, with 211 occupational scales representing 109 different occupations. All but seven of these have separate female and male criterion groups and therefore provide gender-differentiated scores. Thus, the people-in-general group has been divided into gender groups. The 1994 revision has additional scales for both professional and non-professional occupations.

Administrative indexes. Besides the occupational scales, several validity scales (for example, counting infrequent or sloppy responses) can be used to determine if the respondent approached the inventory with care.

Personal style scales. There are several special scales related to general aspects of interest. These include measures of work style, learning environment, leadership style, and risk taking.

General occupational themes. Because of the continually changing nature of occupations, it became necessary to develop a higher-order manner of scale organization that would permit the designation of the classes of occupations to which a respondent might consider orienting. Campbell adopted a system developed by Holland (1973), which divides occupations into six themes. For example, people who score high on the R-Theme are typically described as rugged, robust, practical, and physically strong. They frequently have good physical skills and like to work outdoors, with tools, and with their hands. Occasionally, high scorers on the R-Theme demonstrate difficulty expressing themselves, preferring to deal with things rather than with ideas or people. These theme scales of the SII provide a score on each of the six general occupational themes that can be used to direct the respondent into various classes of occupations.

Basic interest scales. These 25 scales provide information about the likes and dislikes of the respondent. The scores are based on the accumulation of items endorsed in the keyed direction for various activities. For example, the public speaking scale would obtain a high score if the respondent indicated preference for activities such as "making a speech," and "expressing judgments publicly regardless of what others say." All 25 scales are accompanied with male and female norms drawn from the general population.

The wide range of scales available from the SII provide vocational counselors with a considerable amount of information that can help direct people to various occupations. Figure 9-11 presents a portion of a sample profile. A wide diversity of information is available with varying levels of generality that provide a truly complex interplay of ideas and suggestions that have use in the counseling situation. The SVIB emerged as a major tool in the vocational counseling situation and remains so today in the form of the SII.

The SVIB has also been adapted to the selection situation, arguing that job satisfaction (reflected in a match between interests and job characteristics) is an important component of the hiring process. This latter application, however, is somewhat controversial.

Psychometric characteristics. Test/retest reliabilities of the SII scales are in the high .80s and low .90s. The intervals reported in the literature vary between 2

Figure 9-11 A sample profile sheet from the Strong Vocational Interest Blank–Strong–Campbell Interest Inventory.

STRONG INTEREST INVENTORY

Profile report for ROBIN BYRD
ID:
Age: 24
Gender: Female

Date tested: 04/11/94
Date scored: 04/15/94

Page 1 of 6

SNAPSHOT: A SUMMARY OF RESULTS FOR ROBIN BYRD

GENERAL OCCUPATIONAL THEMES

The General Occupational Themes describe interests in six very broad areas, including interest in work and leisure activities, kinds of people, and work settings. Your interests in each area are shown at the right in rank order. Note that each Theme has a code, represented by the first letter of the Theme name.

You can use your Theme code, printed below your results, to identify school subjects, part-time jobs, college majors, leisure activities, or careers that you might find interesting. See the back of this Profile for suggestions on how to use your Theme code.

Theme Code	Theme	Very Little Interest	Little Interest	Average Interest	High Interest	Very High Interest	Typical Interests
A	ARTISTIC				✓		Creating or enjoying art
C	CONVENTIONAL			✓			Accounting, processing data
S	SOCIAL			✓			Helping, instructing
R	REALISTIC			✓			Building, repairing
I	INVESTIGATIVE		✓				Researching, analyzing
E	ENTERPRISING		✓				Selling, managing

Your Theme code is ACS—(see explanation at left).
You might explore occupations with codes that contain any combination of these letters.

BASIC INTEREST SCALES

The Basic Interest Scales measure your interests in 25 specific areas or activities. Only those 5 areas in which you show the *most* interest are listed at the right in rank order. Your results on all 25 Basic Interest Scales are found on page 2.

To the left of each scale is a letter that shows which of the six General Occupational Themes this activity is most closely related to. These codes can help you to identify other activities that you may enjoy.

Theme Code	Basic Interests	Very Little Interest	Little Interest	Average Interest	High Interest	Very High Interest	Typical Interests
A	WRITING					✓	Reading or writing
S	RELIGIOUS ACTIVITIES				✓		Participating in spiritual activities
A	ART				✓		Appreciating or creating art
A	CULINARY ARTS				✓		Cooking or entertaining
R	AGRICULTURE				✓		Working outdoors

OCCUPATIONAL SCALES

The Occupational Scales measure how similar your interests are to the interests of people who are satisfied working in those occupations. Only the 10 scales on which your interests are *most* similar to those of these people are listed at the right in rank order. Your results on all 211 of the Occupational Scales are found on pages 3, 4, and 5.

The letters to the left of each scale identify the Theme or Themes that most closely describe the interests of people working in that occupation. You can use these letters to find additional, related occupations that you might find interesting. After reviewing your results on all six pages of this Profile, see the back of page 5 for tips on finding other occupations in the Theme or Themes that interest you the most.

Theme Code	Occupation	Very Dissimilar	Dissimilar	Mid-Range	Similar	Very Similar
A	LIBRARIAN					✓
AIR	TECHNICAL WRITER					✓
A	LAWYER				✓	
A	TRANSLATOR				✓	
CE	PARALEGAL				✓	
SA	SOCIAL WORKER				✓	
AES	CORPORATE TRAINER				✓	
AE	ADVERTISING EXECUTIVE			✓		
ASE	ENGLISH TEACHER			✓		
SEA	SOCIAL SCIENCE TEACHER			✓		

***PERSONAL STYLE SCALES** measure your levels of comfort regarding Work Style, Learning Environment, Leadership Style, and Risk Taking/Adventure. This information may help you make decisions about particular work environments, educational settings, and types of activities you would find satisfying. Your results on these four scales are on page 6.*

CPP CONSULTING PSYCHOLOGISTS PRESS, INC. • 3803 E. Bayshore Road, Palo Alto, CA 94303 weeks and 3 years. A review of the validity coefficients reflecting the accuracy with which it can discriminate between people in different occupations reveals that its validity is reasonable (Campbell & Hansen, 1981). The inventory has remained contemporary because of the extensive revisions through which it has gone since its introduction in 1927.

Summary

Both the MMPI and the SVIB were highly significant tests arising from the operationist era of the testing enterprise. Both tests have been subjected to revision since then, but both are still important. The events of the Great Depression were critical to the evolution of the testing enterprise and these two tests. It provided a context in which instruments could demonstrate increasing sophistication in design and construction. At the same time, it freed testers from becoming embroiled in debates about the underlying theoretical terms in their instruments. The impact of those times remains with us not only in the tests but also in some of the underlying philosophical considerations that were so much a part of the 1930s.

Glossary

a priori assumptions A term used by Paul Meehl to refer to the unsubstantiated theoretical claims used by test constructors to rationally construct and select items for their personality inventories.

Bernreuter Personality Inventory One of many personality inventories published during the 1930s. This 125-item inventory provided measures of neurotic tendency, self-sufficiency, introversion/extraversion, dominance/submission, self-confidence, and sociability.

Campbell, David A student of Edward Strong's who revised the Strong Vocation Interest Blank, eventually producing the Campbell–Strong Interest Inventory.

careless responding The extent to which an individual is showing attention to the nature of the items and response alternatives while answering a self-report inventory. The F scale of the MMPI provides an index of carelessness.

cookbook A set of MMPI profiles that can be used to look up the personality descriptions, etiologies, prognoses, and so on for various patterns of scores. Such cookbooks are derived empirically from scores of persons with specific diagnoses who have taken the MMPI previously.

correspondence rules A set of procedures that allows the logical positivist to link theoretical terms with observational sentences. Operationism rendered the correspondence rules identical to the meaning of the theoretical terms.

criterion keying *See* empirical criterion keying.

Depression (1) The period of economic hard times from 1929 up to World War II, during which the lack of financial resources severely limited the growth of psychology, testing, and many other service-oriented professions. (2) A scale on the MMPI to measure a state of pessimism and hopelessness.

doctrine of cognitive significance An aspect of logical positivism that indicated the only acceptable theoretical terms were those that were tied directly to observational sentences using explicit correspondence rules.

Dust Bowl empiricism A nickname for a variant of logical positivism developed in Minnesota that deemphasized theoretical terms in favor of documented empirical relationships. The MMPI emerged from this perspective.

empirical criterion keying Developing scales in psychological tests by selecting only items that empirically differentiate a criterion group from a reference group. The MMPI and SVIB were developed this way.

false-keyed item A personality item to which a false response is indicative of presence of the characteristic assessed by the item and/or to which a true response is indicative of a denial of the presence of the characteristic.

honest responding The extent to which a respondent is being truthful on a self-report inventory. The L scale of the MMPI provides an index of honesty in responding.

item overlap The instance when one item is represented on a number of different scales. Characteristic of the MMPI, item overlap creates unduly high intercorrelations between the clinical scales.

logical positivism The dominant philosophy of science during the 1920s through the 1950s that added under several strict conditions theoretical (logical) terms to the strong positivist position. Mathematical formulations were seen as the most desirable types of formulations within this position.

mechanistic materialism An early philosophy of science that assumed (1) the existence of a single, knowable reality that existed in material fact and (2) all explanations of scientific events could be made mechanistically. This view could not deal with the possibility that there was a human intermediary between the real world and scientific propositions.

Meehl, Paul An influential figure in the testing field who, among other things, provided a strong rationale for empirical criterion keying in his critique of a priori assumptions in personality assessment.

mind/body problem A long-standing philosophical problem regarding the relationships between the duality of mind and body. This problem has resisted persuasive philosophical resolution since its inception.

Minnesota Multiphasic Personality Inventory (MMPI) A self-report inventory developed by Hathaway and McKinley to differentiate among various psychopathological states such as depression, schizophrenia, and paranoia. Consisting of 550 items that are answered either true, false, or cannot say, the MMPI became the standard for tests of psychopathology.

observational statement A term in a logical positivist scheme that is based on sensory information. "The sky is blue" would be such a sentence. Observational sentences represent the fundamental empiricist heart of logical positivism.

operational definition A description of the procedures that are used to make known a specific theoretical concept. In the testing context, administration of the MMPI Depression scale can be seen as an operational definition of depression.

operationism A variant of the logical positivist position, wherein the meaning of a theoretical term is said to be totally contained in the operations used to measure the term. This confirmed the suggestion that "intelligence is what the intelligence tests test."

paramedical personnel Nonphysicians in the mental-health field such as social workers, nurses, nutritionists, and psychologists.

psychiatric case conference A multidisciplinary team of medical doctors and paramedical personnel who treated mental patients prior to the Great Depression.

psychiatry The branch of medicine involved with the treatment of mental illness. It is important to differentiate psychiatrists from psychologists because the latter do not have medical degrees and thereby have less power within the mental-health system.

psychopathology Literally means "sickness within the psyche," or what today we would call mental disorder or psychological dysfunction.

rationally developed scale A test developed from the a priori assumptions of the test constructor.

received view (of logical positivism) The original view of logical positivism as formulated by Rudolph Carnap in 1926. Because this position has changed significantly, the term *received view* has been used to differentiate the original from later variants.

schizophrenia A type of mental disorder characterized by dissociation between intellectual and emotional processes.

Seashore Measures of Musical Talent A multiple set of tests developed to measure musical talent using tasks such as repeating rhythms, assessing pitch differentiation, and a variety of other music-related performances.

Stevens, S. S. An American psychologist who led the introduction of operationism to mainstream psychology.

Strong–Campbell Interest Inventory (SCII) A 1974 revision and update of the Strong Vocational Interest Inventory that provides feedback on occupational, administrative, theme, and basic interest scales. It was revised again in 1985.

Strong, Edward K. The developer and proponent of the Strong Vocational Interest Blank.

Strong Vocational Interest Blank (SVIB) A self-report inventory that provides indications of occupations that match the stated interests of the respondents. Developed in 1926 using empirical criterion keying, the SVIB became the flagship of testing in vocational counseling.

subtle item An item for which there is no clear rational link to the characteristic it purports to reflect but empirical evidence suggests that it is an appropriate item. Several MMPI items were very subtle in this sense.

test-taking defensiveness The extent to which an individual is censoring or shielding personality-item responses. The K scale of the MMPI provides a measure of test-taking defensiveness, which can be used to adjust the clinical scales to take this into account.

theoretical term A proposition in a logical positivist scheme which is not an observational sentence. Examples would include ideas such as learning, intelligence, and personality.

true-keyed item A personality item to which a true response is indicative of presence of the characteristic assessed by the item and/or to which a false response is indicative of a denial of the presence of the characteristic.

T score A variant of the *z* score that, instead of having a mean of 0 and a standard deviation of 1, has an average of 50 and a standard deviation of 10. (See Equation 9-2.) The output of the MMPI is in *T* scores.

unbalanced scale A scale that has a significantly greater number of true- or false-keyed items.

Suggested Further Reading

Boring, E. G. (1923). Intelligence as the tests test it. *New Republic, 35*, 35–37.

> This short article is the source of the famous epithet "intelligence is what the intelligence tests test." It is worth reading because it indicates clearly that Boring's intention was to view this idea as a place to start, not as an end state. Interestingly, Boring himself was not too enamored of applied psychology such as tests but did defend them here in his role as a senior member of the psychology community.

Dahlstrom, W. G., & Welsh, G. S. (1960). *An MMPI handbook: A guide to use in clinical practice and research*. Minneapolis: University of Minnesota Press.

> Everything you ever wanted to know about the MMPI (and more!) can be found in the volume. Sections on administration, interpretation, and clinical applications, along with numerous appendixes, make this a highly authoritative source for gaining a sense of MMPI technology.

Leahey, T. H. (1992). *A history of psychology* (3rd ed.). Englewood Cliffs, N.J.: Prentice Hall.

> This book contains a fine presentation of the "golden age" of behaviorism. The section entitled "The Rise of Behavioralism" provides great contextual information regarding the manner in which the general discipline of psychology developed during the period discussed in this chapter of *The Enterprise*.

Smith, L. (1986). *Behaviorism and logical positivism*. Palo Alto, Calif.: Stanford University Press.

> The less-than-clear relationship between behaviorism and logical positivism is discussed in this enlightening book. It is highly recommended for those who want to explore the manner in which these two schools of thought are interrelated or constitute parallel play.

Stevens, S. S. (1935). The operational basis of psychology. *American Journal of Psychology, 47*, 323–330.

> This article introduced operationism to mainstream psychology. A great primary source, it gives a sense of the fervor of this "new" view. The strong rhetoric that accompanied its introduction is also clear in this short piece.

Suppe, F. (Ed.). (1974). *The structure of scientific theories*. Urbana: University of Illinois Press.

> The first section of this edited work, authored by Suppe himself, is a highly technical presentation of logical positivism that documents prelogical positivist thinking, the

received view, how it has changed, and a detailed philosophical criticism of the position and those that have been proposed to replace it. Although aspects of this presentation are slow reading, it remains a definitive presentation that should be consulted if further details are desired.

Tzeng, O. C. S. (1987). Strong–Campbell Interest Inventory. In D. J. Keyser & R. C. Sweetland (Eds.), *Test critiques compendium.* Kansas City, Mo.: Test Corporation of America.

One of the most recent critiques of the SCII, this provides a sense of the current status of this instrument.

Discussion Questions

1. Indicate the strengths and weaknesses of Whig history using the emic/etic distinction provided in Chapter 1.

2. Evaluate this statement: The version of science presented in high school is incorrect because it presupposes the mechanistic materialist position. What really happens in science is nothing like what is taught in grades 10–12.

3. Outline the manner in which realizing the existence of an active observer undermined mechanistic materialism. Suggest several other ideas, which we have now, that pose equal problems for this position.

4. Analyze a scientific theory from another course you have taken, using the logical positivist perspective.

5. Define the doctrine of cognitive significance. Outline its major implications for the testing enterprise.

6. Suggest as many reasons as you can why the ideas underlying logical positivism would be favorably received by psychologists in the mid-1930s.

7. Critically evaluate the criteria that were used by Bernreuter to establish the validity of his personality inventory.

8. Outline the major impact of the Great Depression on the testing enterprise as it was being practiced in industry in 1929.

9. Even today the psychiatric case conference seems like an effective approach for mental-health professionals. Discuss why you think this has not become the most popular means of dealing with these important problems.

10. Develop a checklist of the pressures that were facing the testing enterprise around 1935. Beside each entry, indicate how operationism appeared to provide a solution. In a third column, indicate whether you think this was an effective solution.

11. Clearly specify the characteristic, object, unit, operation, and outcome implied when you give someone the MMPI to determine if they are schizophrenic or not.

12. Generate an example that indicates there is more to a theoretical term than what is conveyed in the operations that go into measuring it.

13. S. S. Stevens suggested that length measured by a ruler is different from length defined by triangulation. Outline a critical response to this idea. How do you think Stevens might counter your argument?

14. What is wrong with the idea that intelligence is what an intelligence test tests?

15. Discuss the similarities between the test-criterion method, validity, and operationism.

16. How can you account for the observation that operational thinking appeared to exist in the testing enterprise 12 years before the formal idea of operationism was introduced to mainstream psychology?

17. Debate the contention that operationism was a "revolution to put an end to all revolutions."

18. In the chapter, it was noted that personality assessment was the brunt of criticism, particularly when contrasted with intelligence testing. Why do you think this might have been the case?

19. You have been hired by a department store chain, and they have asked you to construct a test that will help them identify employees who will steal from the company. How would you do this using a rational approach (for example, a priori considerations)?

20. Given the same situation outlined in Question 19, how would you proceed using empirical criterion keying?

21. Indicate which of the two methods you used in Questions 19 and 20 would produce the superior test. Why?

22. Generate three true-keyed and three false-keyed items that might be useful to develop a measure of aggressiveness.

23. Using the rationale embedded in Equation 9-2, generate a score called the CEEB, which has a mean of 500 and a standard deviation of 100.

24. Discuss the advantages and disadvantages of the *T* score.

25. Suggest aspects of responding to personality items, other than those addressed in the MMPI, that could (and perhaps should) be analyzed by developing validity scales.

26. Do the data presented in Figure 9-10 indicate that the drug-treatment program was a success? Why, or why not?

27. Discuss the advantages of having subtle items in an inventory such as the MMPI that measures socially undesirable characteristics.

28. What effect would item overlap have on MMPI scales? Discuss several situations in which this might prove to be a problem.

29. Outline an empirical criterion keying strategy that you could use to develop a measure of schizophrenia that would give proper indications of the severity of the disease being suffered (that is, a test that would culminate in an interval scale of schizophrenia).

30. The evaluation of university instructors' teaching effectiveness is a complex topic. Suggest how you might develop a measure of this using empirical criterion keying. Do you think this would produce a good scale? Why, or why not?

31. Summarize the validity and reliability of the MMPI.

32. If you were a vocational counselor, what would you say to someone who shows an extremely high score on Artist? How would you reasonably respond if this person asked "Does this mean I should become an artist?"? Discuss how confident you would be of this answer.

Chapter 10

Intelligence Dismantled...
Sort Of
Factor Analysis and IQ Tests

ANOTHER COUNTRY HEARD FROM

While the testing enterprise was evolving in America, a somewhat different course of development was taking place in Britain. Recalling that Francis Galton had pioneered testing in England, it should not be surprising to find that developments flowed directly from his intellectual heritage. It was under the agency of **Charles Spearman** that aspects of Galton's program were elaborated, emerging in a strong theoretical position endorsing the existence of a "general" intelligence.

SPEARMAN'S *g*: A GLOBAL, UNITARY VIEW OF INTELLIGENCE

Spearman started out with the empirical observation that diverse measures of performance tend to be highly correlated with each other. For example, let's suppose that 50 students took five tests:

1. Opposites, which involve specifying antonyms to a set of 30 words
2. Completions, wherein the student provides proper endings to 20 sentence frames
3. Memory, which is the digit span with 15 trials of ascending length
4. Discrimination, which involves the number of times, in 100 trials, the student correctly tells which of two closely similar weights is heavier
5. Cancellation, which involves crossing out a set of specified words in a long paragraph, with 20 being the maximal number the student could get correct

The data can be summarized in a **data matrix** such as that shown in Table 10-1, where Student 1 obtained a score of 15 on Opposites, 11 on Completion, 9 on Memory, 66 on Discrimination, and 10 on Cancellation.

Calculating the correlations between the tests is the first step in examining the relationships between the five tests represented in these data. As Table 10-2 shows, the correlation between Opposites and Completion was found to be .80, revealing a strong relationship. A somewhat lower relationship was found between Opposites and Memory, with a correlation of .60. Notice how the upper-right triangular and lower-left triangular portions of Table 10-2 are redundant. The correlation between Opposites and Completion is exactly the same as the correlation between Completion and Opposites and so on. No new information is contained in the lower triangular portion of the **matrix**. As well, the correlations in the diagonals (for example, between Completion and Completion) are 1.00 and do not carry any interesting information.[1] Because of this, the traditional method of presenting a **correlation matrix** is to show only the upper triangular portion, as has been done in Table 10-3. This is simply a conventional method of formatting correlation matrices, designed to minimize the amount of nonessential information that is presented.

Early on, Spearman noted that correlation matrices between these types of tests tended to look like the one presented in Table 10-3 (see, for example, Spearman, 1904). Spearman noted that such matrices showed correlations that were almost always positive in direction, which seemed a curious empirical finding. It appears that a person who scores high on one test typically scores high on the others—else how could the correlations be so consistently positive? Similarly, persons obtaining low scores on one test tend to gain low scores on the others if the matrix demonstrates overall positive correlations. Thus, performance on these types of tests seems to be dictated by one general characteristic—persons who score high on all the tests have a lot of this characteristic, whereas those scoring low do

---

[1] In some applications, the reliabilities are presented in the diagonal.

Table 10-1 Hypothetical data from the administration of five tests to 50 students

Student	Opposites	Completion	Memory	Discrimination	Cancellation
1	15	11	9	66	10
2	20	14	11	81	17
3	16	13	11	70	12
4	5	15	5	51	3
.	.	.	.	.	.
.	.	.	.	.	.
.	.	.	.	.	.
.	.	.	.	.	.
50	22	17	13	89	19

Table 10-2 Matrix of intercorrelations between our sample tests*

	Opposites	Comp	Memory	Disc	Cancel
Opposites	1.00	.80	.60	.30	.30
Completion (Comp)	.80	1.00	.48	.24	.24
Memory	.60	.48	1.00	.18	.18
Discrimination (Disc)	.30	.24	.81	1.00	.09
Cancellation (Cancel)	.30	.24	.18	.09	1.00

*$n = 50$.
(SOURCE: Spearman, 1927, p. 74).

Table 10-3 Matrix of intercorrelations between our sample tests presented in the conventional triangular form

	Opposites	Comp	Memory	Disc	Cancel
Opposites		.80	.60	.30	.30
Completion (Comp)			.48	.24	.24
Memory				.18	.18
Discrimination (Disc)					.09
Cancellation (Cancel)					

not have as much. Spearman (1904) interpreted this as follows: "Whenever branches of intellectual activity are at all dissimilar, then their correlations with one another appear wholly due to their all being variously saturated with some common fundamental function" (p. 202). He called this fundamental function a general factor, which he subsequently shortened to *g*. Thus, **Spearman's g** became the symbol for the expectation that human performance is determined in large measure by a general, single characteristic. The consistent observation of correlation matrices, such as the one shown in Table 10-3, was seen as confirmation of this basic proposition.

To account for the less-than-perfect correlations between various tests, Spearman postulated the existence of **task-specific factors,** which he labeled *s*. For example, the finding that Opposites and Memory are correlated only .60 is due to the existence of a specific factor necessary for performance in Opposites and another *s* associated with Memory. The two *s*'s are independent of each other (that is, uncorrelated) and uniquely associated with performance on the specific test. Thus, Spearman's is a **two-factor theory of intelligence** because performance on intellectual tasks is seen as due to two factors: (1) a general factor, *g*, and (2) skills specific to the given task, *s*.

Spearman equated *g* with mental energy, suggesting that there is continual competition for mental resources revealed in the continuity of psychological existence. This is caused by a constant flow of mental energy, and the amount of this energy available to a person is measured by *g*. However, *g* does not occur in a vacuum, but it drives "mental engines," which are the *s*'s. These are neural, mental structures that are primed and serviced by *g*.

A second characteristic of correlation matrices between test scores also caught Spearman's eye. He noted how it is possible to arrange correlation matrices among measures of intellect so that the size of the correlations generally decrease as you move from left to right along the rows and from top to bottom along the columns of the matrix. For example, notice how the correlations in Table 10-3 get smaller as you move from left to right in the Opposites row (.80 to .60 to .30 to .30) or down the Cancellation column (.30 to .24 to .18 to .09). This suggested a kind of **hierarchical ordering** within the correlation matrix. Spearman noted that almost all correlation matrices among intellectual activities could be hierarchically ordered and attributed special meaning to this finding. Tests that are highly correlated with each other (for example, Opposites and Completion in Table 10-2) share something in common—*g*. As you move to the right of the correlation matrix, the amount of this *g* shared by the tests decreases (for example, in Table 10-3, Opposites shares considerably less *g* with Cancellation than it does with Opposites). This suggests that tests vary in the amount of *g* they reveal (in Table 10-3, the tests at the left, Opposites and Completion contain more *g* than the ones at the right, Discrimination and Cancellation). Spearman called this aspect of tests their **saturation** with *g*. In other words, when a correlation matrix is hierarchically ordered, the tests with the greatest saturation in *g* appear in the left columns of the matrix, and the lesser saturated tests occur on the right. This conclusion holds only if all the intercorrelations are positive *and* if the hierarchical criterion is met.

Spearman (1927) offered a mathematical means of testing the hierarchical nature of a correlation matrix, which provided the field with a degree of precision unrivaled in the testing domain. Partitioning the correlation matrix into sets of interrelationships between four tests provides a submatrix such as that shown in Table 10-4. Spearman (1927) demonstrated that the difference of the products of the diagonals of this type of submatrix tended to equal 0 if the overall correlation

Table 10-4 A submatrix of Table 10-2 showing the intercorrelations between four tests

	Opposites	Memory
Completion	.80	.48
Discrimination	.30	.18

Table 10-5 Test intercorrelations*

	1	2	3	4	5	6	7	8	9	10	11	12	13	14
1. Completion	.98	.94	.79	.62	.91	.71	.54	.78	.88	.55	.42	.33	.25	
2. Hard Opposites		.84	.80	.64	.81	.79	.70	.73	.74	.52	.43	.26	.25	
3. Memory Words			.62	.55	.82	.49	.56	.73	.71	.53	.40	.28	.21	
4. Easy Opposites				.57	.52	.68	.53	.42	.56	.45	.20	.38	.48	
5. "A" Test					.53	.54	.73	.39	.51	.39	.59	.25	.22	
6. Memory Pass						.53	.57	.59	.66	.54	.31	.28	.19	
7. Adding							.45	.39	.47	.51	.57	.17	.25	
8. Geometry Forms								.35	.49	.34	.56	.25	.25	
9. Learning Pairs									.69	.36	.29	.26	.09	
10. Recognized Forms										.44	.37	.34	.28	
11. Scroll											.31	.19	.27	
12. Completed Words												.21	.07	
13. Estimated Lengths													.24	
14. Drawing Length														

*$n = 37$.

SOURCE: Simpson (1912).

matrix was hierarchical. This figure is called the **tetrad difference**.[2] For example, in Table 10-4 the tetrad difference is $(.80 \times .18) - (.48 \times .30) = .14 - .14 = .00$. If you were to calculate all possible tetrad differences from the Table 10-2 matrix, you would find that most of them are very close to 0. Thus, the tetrads provide an empirical method of determining if a matrix is hierarchical and is thereby explainable by Spearman's two-factor theory. If the tetrad differences are basically 0, the two-factor theory is supported.

Spearman applied this criterion to a large number of data sets and found that almost all of them fulfilled his criterion of hierarchical ordering. For example, he reanalyzed some data from Simpson (1912), which involved the intercorrelations of 14 tests given to 37 respondents. Simpson's data generated the correlation matrix shown in Table 10-5. Spearman then calculated all possible tetrad

---

[2]If you are familiar with matrix algebra, you will note a striking similarity between the tetrad and the determinant of a matrix.

Figure 10-1 Distribution of tetrad differences for the correlations from Simpson (1912).

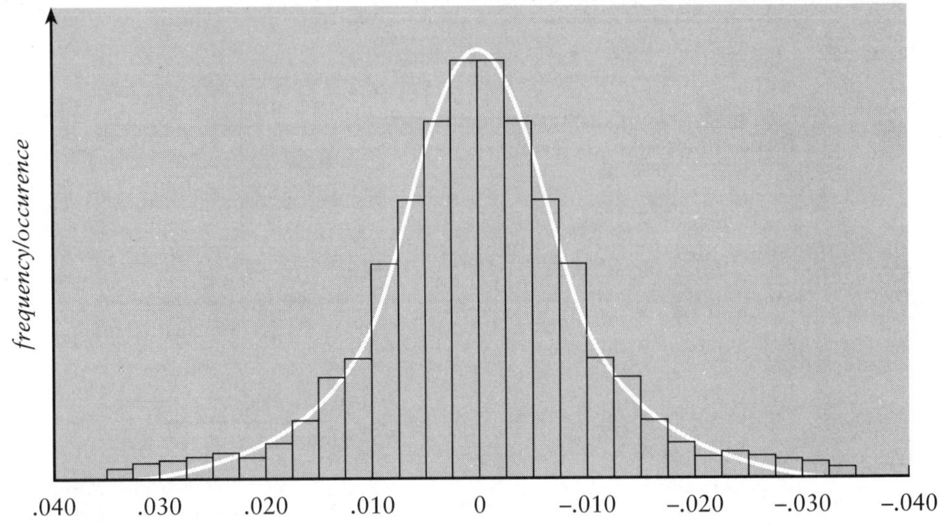

(SOURCE: Spearman, 1927, p. 146.)

differences (*n* = 3003) in this matrix and found a median value of .062. This mean value, because of its closeness to 0, led Spearman to consider that Simpson's matrix was hierarchically ordered. Spearman also plotted the frequency distribution of the tetrads, which is shown as the bars in Figure 10-1.

The distribution of the tetrads is normal, with a relatively small standard deviation. The smooth curve shown in Figure 10-1 represents Spearman's theoretical expectations derived from the hypothesis that the matrix was hierarchically ordered. Spearman (1927) described this fit between the expected and observed distribution of tetrad differences as "one of the most striking agreements between theory and observation ever recorded in psychology. Indeed, it would not easily be matched in any other science" (p. 146). There is a degree of mathematical rigor and sophistication to demonstrations such as these that makes it almost impossible to question the existence of *g*.

CLOSE UP **The Theorem of the Indifference of the Indicator**

One of the tremendous advantages of developing a theory mathematically is the possibility of deriving hypotheses and theorems from the basic formulation. One such derivation from Spearman's theory, the **theorem of the indifference of the indicator,** resulted in the counterintuitive idea that under some conditions any test is as good as any other as a measure of *g*. In other words, if this theorem is correct, virtually any aspect of human intellectual performance can be seen as a measure of *g*.

Spearman presented the following formula as his final version of the two-factor theory:

$$x_{ij} = (r_{jg} \times g_i) + (r_{js} \times s_{ij}) \tag{10-1}$$

where

x_{ij} = score of person i on test j

r_{jg} = saturation of test j on g

g_i = the amount of g possessed by person i

r_{js} = saturation of s in test j

s_{ij} = the amount of s for test j possessed by person i

Spearman suggested that there can be considerable variation in r_{jg} for different tests. For example, the proportion of g to s for Classics is 15 to 1, whereas for Musical Aptitude it is 1 to 4. That is, g is implicated in varying amounts in the performance of certain tasks. The involvement of g in test performance is estimated by the size of r_{jg}, with numbers closer to 1.00 indicating higher saturation.

If Equation 10-1 is true, it is possible to gain an accurate estimate of g_i, which could be useful for a number of applications. The simplest case is when $r_{js} = 0$ and $r_{jg} = 1.00$, as in this case: Equation 10-1 simplifies to $x_{ij} = g_i$. That is, the obtained test score x_{ij} would be the best estimate of g_i from Equation 10-1.

However, any test is as good an indicator of g_i as long as r_{jg} is *not* equal to 0. If we know x_{ij}, r_{jg}, r_{js}, and s_{ij}, we can calculate g_i from Equation 10-1—no matter the size of r_{jg}. This is the theorem of the indifference of the indicator, which states that any measure whatsoever is as good an estimate of g as any other as long as precise values for the remaining four terms in Equation 10-1 were available.

This theorem conveys the sense of precision that was emerging in the testing field under Spearman. The sophisticated mathematical derivations provided an incredibly complex rationalization for the existence of a general intelligence factor as underlying test-score performance.

Partly as a result of Spearman's ideas, partly because it matched researchers' current intuitions, and partly because it fed into the prevailing biological/hereditarian ideology, the notion of intelligence as a single thing was dominant during the 1930s in both Britain and America. The Stanford–Binet culminated in a single number describing a child's intellect. Spearman, with his idea of g, had offered a theory and an apparent empirical proof that intelligence was indeed **univariate**. In the late 1930s, the prevailing and relatively unquestioned view was that intelligence could be adequately represented as a single number and characterized as a one-dimensional continuum.

In 1938 a test was introduced that offered a quick, easy, and purportedly culture-free measure of Spearman's g. The Raven Progressive Matrices was introduced in Britain and was soon adopted as the kind of test that persons holding to a **unitary view of intelligence** could cite as an appropriate operational definition of g.

CLOSE UP   **The Raven Progressive Matrices**

The **Raven Progressive Matrices** is a nonverbal test of general intelligence that was specifically designed to measure Spearman's g (Raven, 1938). The test involves highly abstract material that is foreign to classroom activities and everyday experience. This differentiates it from some of the more familiar intelligence tests we have encountered thus far, which effectively were samples of classroom-type performance.

There are both black-and-white and colored forms of the test, which can be administered either individually or in groups. The first (black-and-white) versions were issued in 1938, with subsequent revisions being published in 1947, 1950, 1952, and 1956. The colored form was published in 1947, with revision in 1956.

The black-and-white form consists of 60 items, each of which is made up of a 3×3 matrix of geometric forms. The form in the bottom right corner of this matrix is missing, and the respondent must indicate which of several alternatives (6 or 8) belongs in the missing spot. The hypothetical examples presented in Figure 10-2 have only four alternatives, but these are sufficient to give you a sense of the task demanded in the Raven. The 60 items are presented as five sets of 12, each

Figure 10-2

Item of the type used in the Raven Progressive Matrices. (a) Correct answer is B; (b) correct answer is D.

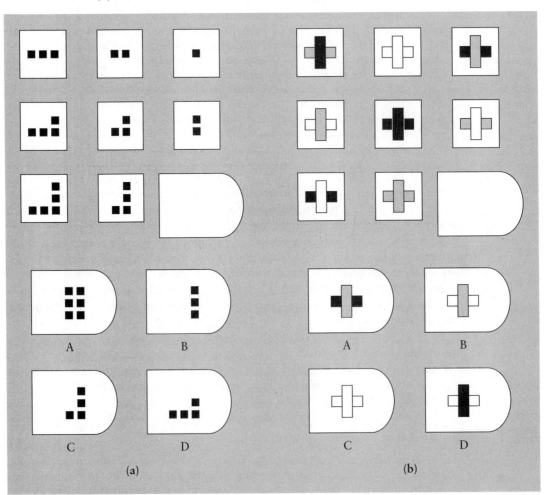

relating to a different theme in the original set. The examples in Figure 10-2 show one of each theme. Within each set, the items are arranged in order of difficulty established using a norm group. A second set of 48 items, called Set II or the Advanced Progressive Matrices, is available for use with persons of more-than-average intellectual ability. It is based on the same basic principles as the latter (more difficult) items of the original set. The colored matrices were developed for ages 5 through 11 and are based on the easier items from the original set. They are particularly useful for persons with disabilities such as deafness, partial paralysis, defective speech, or mental impairment. None of the forms is timed.

The first large-scale application of the Raven was for screening British naval candidates. Analyses of these data demonstrated test/retest reliabilities in the range of .88. In terms of validity, Westby (1953) indicated that, based on the Navy data, the Raven functioned as an almost pure *g* test. As well, Westby indicated that the matrices test provided a valid means of measuring the capacity for clear thinking and accurate intellectual work. Without doubt, the Raven emerged as one of the strongest candidates to be a measure of *g* in the sense originally defined by Spearman. The norms for the test are inadequate (see Horrocks, 1964, pp. 277–278), but the Raven remains one of the best exemplars of *g*, giving us a sense of the British approach to the concept of intelligence as a global, or unitary, entity.

PROBLEMS WITH THE GLOBAL VIEW

With a well-designed test such as the Raven in hand and the bulk of opinion in the field supporting a unitary view of intelligence, it seemed likely that the **global** (univariate) **view of intelligence** would dominate the field. Several important factors, however, argued for breaking down this monolith into smaller components. First, the unitary view seemed to have difficulty keeping out of trouble. No sooner would a study be published but another round of controversy (usually relating to the nature/nurture issue) would emerge in the public press. After all, a unitary view of intelligence was highly compatible with the Galtonian perspective, with all of its inherent biological and genetic assumptions. In an analysis, Gould (1981) indicates that "Spearman's *g*, and its attendant claim that intelligence is a single, measurable entity, provided the only promising theoretical justification that the hereditarian theories of IQ ever had" (p. 264).[3] This association of *g* with the hereditarian perspective meant that researchers who wished to reject the fundamental hereditarian views in favor of more environmental explanations needed an alternative to *g*. This need stimulated, in part, an effort to dismantle the global conception of intelligence into smaller pieces.

A second factor favoring the breakup of intelligence was a tendency in the natural sciences toward **reductionism.** It seemed that the typical path of progress in the hard sciences was to move from large, or molar, units of analysis down to

[3]Gould's analysis is highly critical of this particular approach to intelligence. It is highly recommended reading to complement this section of the text.

smaller, or molecular, levels. This kind of divide-and-conquer strategy appeared to be producing dividends in other disciplines—why shouldn't it work in psychology?

A third line of attack on the unitary status of intelligence came from a series of arguments that suggested Spearman's proofs of the existence of *g* were not as airtight as Spearman would have us believe. The strongest statement of this view came from Godfrey Thomson, a British scholar who entered into a ferocious debate with Spearman. Thomson challenged the proposition that hierarchical order in a correlation matrix *necessarily* confirmed Spearman's two-factor theory (see Brown & Thomson, 1940). Using a technique known today as **Monte Carlo simulation,** he showed how it was possible to generate a correlation matrix with hierarchical order (that is, near 0 mean tetrad differences) *from a situation in which there was no general factor*. He generated his correlation matrices, assuming the existence of several nongeneral factors:

> ... It is possible, by means of dice throws or in other ways, to make artificial experiments on correlation.... Working on these lines, one of us (Thomson, 1914) made a set of imitation "mental tests" [dice throws of a complicated kind], which were known to contain no General Factor.... These imitation mental tests, containing no General Factor, gave however a set of correlation coefficients in excellent hierarchical order. [Brown & Thomson, 1940, p. 174]

While not necessarily invalidating Spearman's notion of *g*, this demonstration (and a number of others presented in Brown & Thomson, 1940) clearly laid significant doubt about the validity of Spearman's claim that hierarchical ordering of correlation matrices was substantive proof of his own theoretical position—it could just as easily be proof of an alternative view of intellect. (For further discussion of this issue, see Evans & Waites, 1981, pp. 180–183.)

COMMON-FACTOR ANALYSIS

The outcome of these factors favoring the dismantling of intelligence was the development of some new, highly sophisticated statistical techniques that facilitated the demonstration of the multidimensionality of complex ideas. The technique is called **common-** or **group-factor analysis,** which was invented as part of a program to dismember the unitary view of intelligence.

The fundamental argument for breaking down intelligence into smaller components was actually simple. Suppose we are interested in measuring a person's size and have decided that we want to state the result of our measurement as a single number. To squeeze every aspect of size (weight, height, breadth, density, reach, bone size, shoe size, length of hair, and so on) into a single measure, we would have to develop an elaborate and artificial measurement technique. Perhaps we would have to submerge a person completely in a full tank of water and measure the volume of water that the person displaces (or some such equally ridiculous procedure). After a number of unsuccessful experiences of trying to sell our water tank to doc-

HERMAN®

"You're exactly the same size as me."

tor's offices and department stores, we might begin to think that our initial assumption that size could be represented as a single number is a bit of a problem. Indeed, we would soon realize that what we ought to be doing is trying to isolate the components of size and measure, each of them separately. Perhaps three separate measurements such as height, weight, and bone structure would give us all the information we needed. These components would be much easier to measure and would probably fit better with whatever practical applications we had in mind for our measurement in the first place. This type of argument was applied to intelligence, suggesting that trying to measure intelligence with a single test is as ridiculous as trying to measure size using water displacement. If a scale of measurement encompasses a great range of things (such as height and breadth in the measurement of body size), then a single number is not appropriate. Such inappropriate usages of numbers can lead to some major misrepresentations of the state of the world.

The major difficulty with this argument is how to determine the number and nature of the components we should use. Are three measures sufficient to represent a person's size, or should we have 4, or 6, or 17? Are we missing anything important in using, say, 3 measures? Perhaps, a skeptic could argue, the 3 measures are really all measures of the same thing (for example, we all know that height and weight are highly correlated, so measuring them both is a waste of time). The researchers hoping to challenge the unitary view of intellect had a clearly difficult task ahead of them.

LEON THURSTONE AND THE PRIMARY MENTAL ABILITIES

The leader of the movement to dismantle intelligence was the American psychologist **Leon L. Thurstone.** His interest in intellectual functioning was spurred by a series of studies exploring ability in telegraphy during World War I (Thurstone, 1919). Based on the results of 165 men drafted into the services, he developed a battery of tests that permitted reasonably accurate predictions of a person's eventual ability to use the telegraph. These included some of the Army Alpha tests as well as some he designed himself, such as a rhythm exercise. He also developed a test battery for the measurement of clerical skills. Although these studies were not remarkable, being part of the movement toward aptitude measurement outlined earlier, they did serve to stimulate Thurstone's interest in looking at discrete measures of intellectual functioning in contrast to more unitary or overarching views.

After World War I, Thurstone became actively engaged in the testing enterprise and eventually made some highly significant contributions to the field. For our purposes, his major contribution emerged in a monograph entitled "Primary Mental Abilities" (Thurstone, 1938). In this large-scale study, he administered 56 different tests of intellectual functioning to 240 college students. The 56 tests represented a wide range of specific abilities that students would need to be successful. Figure 10-3 presents representative examples of the items he used. These indicate a wide spectrum of cognitive tasks.

Having collected the responses of his 240 students to the 56 tests, he asked if there were a number of basic components underlying performance on the tests. Could he find a smaller set of factors that would capture the essence of the intellectual skills demanded of these tasks? Would he need more than one factor (g) to account for test performance?

The approach he used to ask the last, particularly difficult question is interesting. Let's assume, for the sake of this discussion, that he administered two scales, Spelling (SP) and Verbal Fluency (VF), and found they were correlated .90. Using the idea of the correlation matrix presented earlier, we could represent this finding as

	SP	VF
SP		.90
VF		

Looking at this matrix, if we know several persons' scores on SP, we can make a substantial prediction about what their scores will be on VF because of the high intercorrelation of the two tests. In a very real sense, this matrix represents only one thing because the two variables are so highly correlated with each other. Because of the correlation of .90, the two variables are redundant, and we only need to know one of them to capture most of the information in the matrix.

Let's also assume that Thurstone administered a third test, Folded Boxes (FB), and found that it was correlated .00 with SP. This could be represented as

	SP	FB
SP		.00
FB		

Now, in this case, we cannot make a prediction about FB knowing a person's score on SP because of the .00 correlation. To represent the information in this matrix, we will have to know two bits of information—the person's scores on SP and FB. In other words, we will need to know two different numbers if we want to be able to describe the data accurately.[4]

Figure 10-3 Items of the type used by Thurstone (1938).

(a) **Subtraction:**   1543 − 657 = _____
                        4567 − 987 = _____

(b) **Flags** (48 items):

Look at the two flag pictures below. They represent opposite faces of the same flag. A minus sign (−) has been placed in the square to indicate that the pictures show opposite faces of the flag.

Now compare the next two pictures. If they represent the same face of the flag, mark them plus (+). If they represent opposite faces of the same flag, mark them minus (−).

The two pictures show the same face of the flag, so a plus sign (+) should be written in the square.

Mark in this way each of the following pairs of flag pictures. If the two pictures show the same face of the flag, write a plus sign (+) in the square. If the two pictures show opposite faces of the flag, write a minus sign (−) in the square. Go right ahead. Do not wait for any signal.

continued

[4]Another reason for a correlation of .00 would be that one of the tests has a reliability of .00. For this example, let's assume that all tests have substantial reliabilities.

Figure 10-3 Items of the type used by Thurstone (1938) *(continued)*.

(c) **Identitical forms** (60 items):

The first figure in each line below is exactly the same as one of the five numbered figures following. In the blank space at the right of each line, write the number of the figure which is exactly the same as the first figure in the line. The first two blank spaces have been filled in correctly. You fill in the other three. Go right ahead.

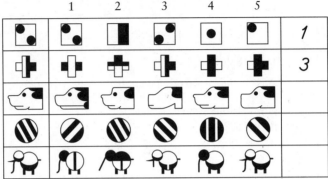

(d) **Syllogisms** (32 items):

Read carefully: You will be shown a list of arguments, each followed by a conclusion. Some of the conclusions are right, others are wrong.

On the line after each argument, make a plus sign (+) if the conclusion is right; make a minus sign (–) if the conclusion is wrong.

The three following examples are marked correctly.

Jones is younger than Brown.
Brown is younger than Smith.
Therefore Smith is younger than Jones. ____ –

Smith is older than Jones.
Jones is older than Brown.
Therefore Brown is younger than Smith. ____ +

Smith is older than Jones.
Smith is younger than Brown.
Therefore Brown is older than Jones. ____ +

Answer the following practice problems in the same way.

Brown is older than Jones.
Jones is older than Smith.
Therefore Brown is older
  than Smith. ____

Smith is younger than Jones.
Brown is older than Jones.
Therefore Smith is older
  than Brown. ____

Jones is younger than Brown.
Smith is younger than Jones.
Therefore Smith is older
  than Brown. ____

Smith is older than Jones.
Smith is younger than Brown.
Therefore Brown is younger
  than Jones. ____

Brown is older than Smith.
Jones is younger than Smith.
Therefore Jones is older
  than Brown. ____

Brown is younger than Smith.
Brown is older than Jones.
Therefore Jones is younger
  than Smith. ____

Figure 10-3 Items of the type used by Thurstone (1938) *(continued).*

(e) **Completion** (39 items):

There is one word missing in each of the following sentences. The first letter of the missing word is shown in the parentheses.

A contest of speed is a .... (r) ___*race*___

In order to complete the sentence we have written the word race in the blank space. The two sentences below are completed correctly.

A fluid used in writing is .... (i) ___*ink*___
A short sleep or doze is a .... (n) ___*nap*___

Complete the following sentences in the same way. The word you use must begin with the letter shown in parentheses.

A person licensed to practice medicine is a .... (d)
A cap used in sewing to protect the finger when pushing
the needle is a .... (t) _____
The red fluid that circulates in the veins and
arteries of man is .... (b) _____
The part of the day between noon and evening is .... (a) _____
A head covering is called a .... (h) _____
_____

(f) **Word/number paired associate learning:**

Word-Number was prepared as a test involving memorizing. The subject memorizes a set of paired associates. Each stimulus word is to be associated with a response number. In the recall the subject is given the stimulus word, and he is asked to write the corresponding response number. The test is arranged with instructions and a fore-exercise followed by a recall. A second fore-exercise, which is longer, is then given. It is followed by a recall. The test proper with twenty words and associated numbers is then presented. This is followed by the recall. The test really consists of three sections with a presentation and recall in each section. This was done in order to make sure that the subjects understood the nature of the task.

(g) **Number series** (22 items):

The numbers in each row of this test follow one another according to some rule. You are to find the rule and fill in the blanks to fit the rule.

In the example below each number can be obtained from the one before it by the rule *add 2*. The blanks have been filled in accordingly.

2	4	6	8	10	*12*	*14*

Find the rule in the series below and fill in the blanks. You may use addition, subtraction, multiplication, division, or any combination of these.

10	8	11	___	12	___	13

The above series goes by alternate steps of subtracting 2 and adding 3. You should have written 9 and 10 in the blanks.

Find the rule in each series below and write the numbers in the blanks accordingly. There is a different rule for each line. Go right ahead. Do not wait for any signal.

19	18	17	___	15	14	___
8	11	14	___	20	___	
27	___	23	23	19	19	___

Now let's put these two matrices together, assuming that the correlation between VF and FB is also .00:

	SP	VF	FB
SP		.90	.00
VF			.00
FB			

What can we say about this matrix? In this case, SP and VF show high correlation and make up one "thing" while FB stands alone. Thus, to describe the matrix properly, we have to know: (1) a score that represents SP and VF and (2) a score that represents FB alone. In other words, even though there are three variables in this matrix (SP, VF, and FB), we only have to know two things to capture the essence of the information in the matrix—we have saved one variable because of the high correlation (redundancy) between SP and VF.

Let's carry on and assume that a fourth test score, Picture Memory (PM), was available, and it was correlated with SP, VF, and FB, yielding this matrix:

	SP	VF	FB	PM
SP		.90	.00	.00
VF			.00	.00
FB				.90
PM				

How many "things" are going on here?[5] How about if the result was this?[6]

	SP	VF	FB	PM
SP		.90	.00	.00
VF			.00	.00
FB				.00
PM				

This demonstration is an intuitive introduction to the ideas underlying **factor analysis.** In essence, the technique, which was pioneered by Thurstone, involves trying to determine the number of things that are needed to capture the essence of the information in a correlation matrix. The things are called **factors,** and the technique is concerned with discovering the number and nature of the underlying factors that can be used to describe the information in a correlation matrix. The quest is for the minimum number of factors that can describe most of the information in the matrix.[7] The emergence of more than one factor in analyses such as these, however, would pose a serious challenge to the global, or unitary, view of intelligence.

---

[5]The answer is two because SP and VF show high correlation, as do FB and PM, and each thing is uncorrelated with the other one.

[6]The answer here is three because SP and VF are together, but FB is all by itself, as is PM. As well, FB and PM are unrelated to each other, so there are three things going on here—SP/VF, FB, and PM.

[7]The technical terms here are that the minimum number of factors are sought to explain the maximal **proportion of variance** in the correlation matrix.

CLOSE UP **An Example of Factor Analysis in Action**

Before looking in detail at the results of Thurstone's (1938) factor analysis, we will work through a simple example of the technique to provide some insight into the way it functions. Let's examine a subset of Thurstone's data by looking at five tests from his series:

1. Flags (see Figure 10-3)
2. Number Series (see Figure 10-3)
3. Cubes, which involves determining if it is possible to rotate a given cube to be identical with a specified target (Thurstone, 1938, pp. 31–32)
4. Tabular Completion, which involves looking at an incomplete table of figures and figuring out what the missing entries should be
5. Figure Classification, which involves abstracting the rule relating a series of simple figures and using this to select which of four items would come next. These are a bit like one-line Raven Progressive Matrices items (Thurstone, 1938, pp. 210–226).

The data matrix. For purposes of demonstration, let's assume we have administered these five tests to 100 students, yielding a data matrix containing five observations for each of our 100 students—500 pieces of data all told.

The correlation matrix. We then calculate the correlations between each of our five variables and obtain the correlation matrix presented in Table 10-6. Inspection of this correlation matrix indicates several interesting properties. First, there is a substantial correlation between Flags and Cubes ($r = .77$). Second, Number Series and Tabular Completion are highly correlated ($r = .65$). Third, all the correlations with Figure Classification are moderately high ($r = .50, .48, .52,$ and $.47$). Finally, the remaining correlations are relatively low. This pattern of correlations suggests that there might be two factors underlying the five tests: one associated with Flags and Cubes and the other associated with Number Series and Tabular Completion. Figure Classification would appear to be involved in both of them to some degree. Factor analysis of this matrix of correlations would allow us to determine if these expectations are met.

The factor matrix. The output of the factor analytic process is a matrix of values called **factor loadings**. They can be thought of as correlations between the various

Table 10-6

Correlations between our five tests*

	Flags	Num	Cubes	Tab	Fig
Flags		.22	.77	.20	.50
Number Series (Num)			.21	.65	.48
Cubes				.19	.52
Tabular Completion (Tab)					.47
Figure Classification (Fig)					

*$n = 100$.

Table 10-7
Factor matrix underlying the
intercorrelations of our five tests

	Factors	
	I	II
Flags	.92	.10
Number Series	.11	.89
Cubes	.93	.09
Tabular Completion	.09	.89
Figure Classification	.59	.57

tests and the factor said to underly the correlation matrix.[8] The loadings represent the degree of association between the test and the factor; like correlations, values close to 1 indicate a strong degree of relationship, whereas values near .00 indicate no meaningful relationships between the test and the factor. Table 10-7 presents the **factor matrix** derived from Table 10-6. As can be seen, our expectation of two factors underlying the five tests represented in Table 10-6 was met. These two factors have been arbitrarily labeled with the roman numerals I and II.

Interpreting the factors. Factor I shows very high loadings for Flags (.92) and Cubes (.93). These high loadings on the first factor give us a clue to its nature. Both tests involve spatial manipulation of pictorial stimuli, and this aspect of the items has undoubtedly had a great influence on the emergence of this factor. Figure Classification involves some spatial manipulation because it also loaded Factor I, albeit somewhat moderately (.59). On the basis of this pattern of results, it would be reasonable to identify the first factor in Table 10-7 as Spatial Manipulation.

Factor II is deeply associated with Number Series and Tabular Completion (loadings of .89). These two tests both require the student to demonstrate reasoning by figuring out a specific rule and using this rule to solve a problem. Thus, it would seem appropriate to label this factor Reasoning. Note, as well, that Figure Classification involves an element of reasoning and thus is moderately loaded on this factor.

In sum then, the factor analysis of our subset of five of Thurstone's tasks reveals two factors as underlying test performance—Spatial Manipulation and Reasoning. Both factors have relatively clear representatives (Flags and Cubes for Spatial Manipulation; Number Series and Tabular Completion for Reasoning), as well as one test that is saturated in both factors (Figure Classification). Tests that show high loadings for one and only one factor are said to be **pure indicators of a factor.** Thus, in Table 10-7, the top four variables are pure measures of their appropriate factors, whereas Figure Classification is not.

How good is our solution? Factor analytic solutions can vary in the degree to which they represent the correlation matrix. There are several ways of assessing

---

[8]In some situations, they are not technically correlations, but they are sufficiently similar conceptually that, for our introductory purposes, thinking of them as correlations does not cause any problems.

Table 10-8
Complete factor matrix underlying the intercorrelations of our five tests

	Factors		
	I	II	h^2
Flags	.92	.10	.86
Number Series	.11	.89	.80
Cubes	.93	.09	.87
Tabular Completion	.09	.89	.80
Figure Classification	.59	.57	.67
Eigen value	2.08	1.93	
Total variance (%)	41.6	38.6	

this. For one, it is possible to derive an index of how much of the variance in each test has been captured in the obtained solution. This is accomplished by means of a statistic called **communality**, represented as h^2. It is calculated by summing the squared factor loadings separately for each test. For example, the communality for Flags is $(.92)^2 + (.10)^2 = .86$.[9] If this figure was 1.00, it would indicate that all the variance in the Flags test had been picked up in the factor solution. If h^2 was equal to 0.00, it would indicate that none of the variance in the test had been captured in the solution. Table 10-8 shows the communalities for all five tests.

In Table 10-8, substantial proportions of variance for the first four tests have been accounted for, but Figure Classification has not done so well ($h^2 = .67$). This tells us that the solution failed to pick up some of the variance in this latter test. If the communalities were consistently low in a specific factor analysis, it would be reasonable to doubt that it was a good solution. As well, if we were concerned with accounting for as much variance as possible in our solution, we might be tempted to extract a third factor from the correlation matrix. Thus, concerns about the proportions of variance accounted for also implicate the numbers of factors we might choose to extract.

A second way of determining how good a solution we have is to estimate what proportion of the total variance has been captured. This is accomplished by the use of a statistic called the **eigen value**. In simple cases such as that shown in Table 10-8, the eigen value can be estimated by summing the squared factor loadings across tests. For example, the eigen value for Factor I in Table 10-8 is $(.92)^2 + (.11)^2 + (.93)^2 + (.09)^2 + (.59)^2 = 2.08$. By the same process, the eigen value for Factor II is 1.93. In some cases such as that represented in Table 10-8, the factor analysis is conducted by assuming that the total variance for each test is equal to 1.00. Thus, with five tests, the total variance in the correlation matrix is 5.00. The eigen value tells how much of this total variance is accounted for in the solution. The proportion of the total variance in Factor I is calculated by dividing the eigen

---

[9]This calculation assumes that the factors are uncorrelated.

value (2.08) by 5.00, yielding a figure of .416. This is 41.6% of the total variance, as indicated in Table 10-8. Factor II accounts for 38.6% of the total variance, and together the two factors account for 80.2% of the total variance. This is a reasonably high proportion of the variance to have captured with a factor solution. Judging from the communalities, we can see that a good proportion of the lost variance (the unaccounted for 19.8%) is associated with the Figure Classification test.

There is yet a third way of deciding if an obtained factor analysis is a good one. Although this approach is not used extensively in practice, it provides a useful way of exploring the meaning and implications of the technique of factor analysis. The basic theorem of factor analysis is that the maximal amount of information in the correlation matrix is represented in the factor solution. We can gain a direct estimate of this by reconstructing the correlation matrix from the factor matrix. If the reconstructed matrix is nearly identical to the original, we have a strong indicator that our factor analysis fully represents the original information. In other words, we will have lost little or no information in the factor analysis if the reconstructed matrix is similar to the original.

Reconstructing the correlation matrix from the factor matrix is achieved by summing the cross products of the factor loadings across factors. For example, the correlation between Flags and Number Series, as estimated from the factor matrix, is $(.92 \times .11) + (.10 \times .89) = .101 + .089 = .19$. For Cubes and Figure Classification, the **reconstructed correlation** is $(.93 \times .59) + (.09 \times .57) = .60$. Table 10-9 shows the correlations reconstructed from the loadings in Table 10-8, using this method.[10] Inspection of this matrix reveals fundamentally the same pattern of interrelationships demonstrated in Table 10-6. The high correlations between Flags and Cubes as well as Number Series and Tabular Completion remain, as do the moderate correlations of all tests with Figure Classification.

Table 10-9

Reconstructed correlation matrix for our five tests

	Flags	Num	Cubes	Tab	Fig
Flags		.19	.87	.17	.60
Number Series (Num)			.18	.80	.54
Cubes				.16	.60
Tabular Completion (Tab)					.52
Figure Classification (Fig)					

We can be more precise with this by calculating the differences between the original and reconstructed correlations. These are called **residuals**. For Flags the residual is $.22 - .19 = .03$. The residual represents the unique variance left over in the test after the influences of the factors have been removed. A good factor solution would yield small residuals throughout, meaning that very little information has been lost in the factor solution. Table 10-10 presents the matrix of residuals

---

[10]For those of you familiar with matrix algebra, this is the equivalent of postmultiplying the factor matrix by its transpose. The matrix obtained will be the reconstructed correlation matrix.

Table 10-10
Residuals between reconstructed and original correlations for our
five tests

	Flags	Num	Cubes	Tab	Fig
Flags		.03	−.10	.03	−.10
Number Series (Num)			.03	−.15	−.06
Cubes				.03	−.08
Tabular Completion (Tab)					.05
Figure Classification (Fig)					

for our five-test example. The average absolute residual in this matrix is .07, indicating that it is possible to reconstruct the original correlations from the factor matrix with considerable accuracy. We have captured a goodly percentage of the variance in the original matrix with our factor solution.

In sum, we have noted three different methods of assessing the goodness of a particular factor analytic solution: (1) proportions of variance in each test accounted for using communality; (2) proportions of total variance attributable to each factor using the eigen values, which implicate how many factors will result; and (3) examination of the residuals obtained by reconstructing the original correlations from the factor matrix. In practice, factor analysts make a series of decisions about which of these aspects they want to optimize, and then a computer is programmed to seek the best solution fulfilling these criteria by iterating through a series of solutions.

The importance of factor analysis to the debate about whether intelligence is unitary or multidimensional should be clear. If Spearman is correct in his assertion that all aspects of human intellectual performance are saturated with a unitary intelligence, factor analysis should reveal one large factor plus a clutch of specific ones. If, on the other hand, it is more appropriate to view intelligence as a set of smaller variables, some factors ought to emerge that combine some but not all the tests making up the matrix. In other words, there should be clusters of tests that go together but that do not combine with each and every test in the battery.

Thurstone's Solution

Recalling that Thurstone administered 56 tests to 240 college students, you could anticipate that the first thing he did was construct a correlation matrix. It would be large (56 × 56) with 1540 correlations computed.[11] It is hard to grasp the amount

---

[11]The number of correlations derived from a data matrix is obtained by the equation $n = [k(k-1)]/2$, where k is the number of variables.

of work involved here because computers were not available—it was all done manually. The computational work here required over 20 clerical workers over a period of 1 year (Gulliksen, 1974). Thurstone then subjected the matrix to factor analysis.

Seven group factors emerged from this analysis. Thurstone's landmark result indicated that a multidimensional view of intellect was appropriate. After an examination of the factor matrix, Thurstone identified the **Primary Mental Abilities** (PMA) listed in Table 10-11. This list of abilities is a radically different way of construing intelligence. Instead of representing intellectual functioning as a single number, Thurstone's work revealed the necessity of presenting it as a profile, where each person would be represented by seven scores, not just one. Intelligence, by this view, is best seen as a **multivariate** profile.

Table 10-11 The Primary Mental Abilities

Numerical Ability	The speed and accuracy of working with numbers. Tests that involved reasoning with numbers were not associated with this factor. A speeded arithmetic test would be a good example of this factor—see Figure 10-3(a).
Spatial Ability	The ability to manipulate pictorial stimuli and solve problems dealing with them. The Flags test from Figure 10-3(b) is a good example of the kinds of tasks on this factor.
Perceptual Speed and Functioning	The ability to make fine and fast distinctions among pictorial stimuli and to reason using them. Picture recall and the recognition of identical forms are examples—see Figure 10-3(c).
Verbal Reasoning	The ability to think when the problems are presented verbally. Analogies such as star : rats :: radar : ?* would qualify here—see Figure 10-3(d).
Word Fluency	The speed and accuracy of dealing with words, in contrast to reasoning with them. Tasks such as anagrams and spelling were included here—see Figure 10-3(e).
Memory	An estimate of the memory capacity of the individual. Involved traditional tasks of memory performance such as digit span—see Figure 10-3(f).
Inductive Reasoning	The ability to abstract relationships and generalize these to the solution of problems. The Number Series task shown in Figure 10-3(g) is a good example of the tests loading on this factor.

*The correct answer is *radar* because *rats* spells *star* backward and *radar* spells *radar* backward.
SOURCE: Thurstone (1938).

While they appeared almost a decade after the publication of "Primary Mental Abilities," several tests that incorporated Thurstone's findings were developed. One test is the Differential Aptitude Test Battery, intended for use with high school students and incorporated into many vocational counseling programs. The underlying theory and the scales are drawn directly from Thurstone's work.

CLOSE UP   **The Differential Aptitude Test Battery**

The **Differential Aptitude Test (DAT)** was first introduced in 1947 and has been revised several times since (see Bennett, Seashore, & Wesman, 1974). A battery of tests directly stemming from Thurstone's PMA, it is intended for use with students in grades 8–12. Table 10-12 lists the subtests of the DAT.

Table 10-12
Subtests of the DAT

Numerical Ability	Involves basic computational skills and understanding of numerical relationships.
Space Relations	Taps the student's ability to visualize and manipulate simple pictorial stimuli.
Clerical Speed and Accuracy	Involves mostly speeded alphabetizing and coding tasks.
Verbal Reasoning	Consists of a series of analogies much like those described in Table 10-11, except that they are double-ended. The format of these questions is _____ is to end, as appetizer is to _____ 1. beginning, dessert 2. ending, appetizing 3. sunset, dusk 4. final, midterm 5. fruit cup, open bar
Abstract Reasoning	Involves the determination of which of several alternative figures would logically be in the next part of the series. This is much like the Figure Classification test described in the section on factor analysis.
Spelling	Taps the student's ability to recognize whether words are correctly spelled.
Language Usage	Consists of basic language skills such as grammar, punctuation, and the like.
Mechanical Reasoning	Examines understandings of basic principles of Newtonian physics using pictures and a multiple-choice format.

SOURCE: Adapted from Bennett el al. (1974).

DAT subtests Numerical Ability, Space Relations, Clerical Speed and Accuracy, Verbal Reasoning, and Abstract Reasoning all have direct counterparts in the PMA. Spelling and Language Usage in the DAT share part of the PMA Word Fluency scale, whereas Mechanical Reasoning is an addition. The PMA Memory scale has been dropped in the DAT. The degree of overlap between the PMA and DAT leaves no doubt about the genesis of the latter test.

This test is generally oriented toward vocational counseling with a computer-assisted "Career Planning Program" being included with the 1972 revision. This interpretive aid uses a supplementary questionnaire that helps in the assessment of interests, educational goals, and preferences, which, when combined with the DAT scores, provides an extensive career-planning package.

The norm group for the DAT is impressive, being greater than 64,000 high school students. A wide range of types of school districts (rural and urban) is represented. Norms are stratified by grade, gender, socioeconomic status, type of school, and minority representation. Separate male and female profiles are generated because gender differences have been found with females scoring, on average, higher on the Spelling, Language Usage, and Clerical Speed and Accuracy scales and lower on the Mechanical Reasoning and Space Relations scales.

Psychometric characteristics. Reliability estimates are on average higher than .90. The availability of parallel forms (S and T in the 1974 revision) permits calculation of parallel-form reliabilities that range from .77 to .93, with the mode around .80. The scales themselves are relatively uncorrelated, which justifies the use of a profile in the presentation of results. The manual provides extensive evidence for the criterion-related validity of the DAT. For example, the median correlation between Verbal Reasoning scores and high school science grades calculated on 25 different samples (representing a total of 2393 students) was .55, indicating that the test clearly measures aspects of high school science performance (Bennett, Seashore, & Wesman, 1966). There is an impressive range of such data in the manual.

The availability of Thurstone's method of factor analysis and the tests it has spawned appears to provide a clear way of testing which of the global or multivariate views of intelligence is correct. Very simply, the univariate view (for example, Spearman's theory) predicts a factor matrix like the one shown on the left side of Table 10-13, and the multivariate view predicts the one shown on the right.

In the univariate case, it is expected that all tests will be saturated in varying degrees with a general factor (noted on the left with loadings of .7 and .8). Notice how such a factor matrix reveals a very large first factor when its eigen values are tabulated. Additionally, a series of specific factors—one for each test—will also appear in the univariate solution. In the multivariate case, group factors are expected to emerge that show some high *and* some .0 loadings. These .0 loadings (particularly on the first factor) are a critical point of difference between the univariate and multivariate views of intelligence because there is a clear expectation of finding tests that have no involvement in the first factor. It would seem a simple matter, then, to examine a wide range of correlation matrices with this criterion in mind and resolve the debate between these conflicting views of intelligence.

Table 10-13 Factor matrices expected of the univariate and multivariate views of intelligence

Tests	General Factor	Specific Factors						Group Factors	
A	.8	.5	.0	.0	.0	.0	.0	.7	.0
B	.7	.0	.4	.0	.0	.0	.0	.8	.0
C	.8	.0	.0	.4	.0	.0	.0	.8	.0
D	.8	.0	.0	.0	.5	.0	.0	.0	.7
E	.7	.0	.0	.0	.0	.4	.0	.0	.8
F	.7	.0	.0	.0	.0	.0	.4	.0	.7

(Univariate (Spearman) spans the General Factor and Specific Factors columns; Multivariate (Thurstone) spans the Group Factors columns.)

However, matters are not quite as simple as they seem, and verifying one or the other view of intelligence using the factor analytic method becomes almost impossible. As with most complicated statistical techniques, there are a number of judgment calls that the user must make to perform an analysis. In the case of factor analysis, these judgment calls are exceedingly important in determining the type of solution that is eventually found. The following Close Up briefly discusses some of these issues as they pertain to the factor analytic methodology. None of the issues invalidate factor analysis as a statistical and research technique. They do reveal, however, the complexity of the technique and illustrate the reasons why it has not resulted in a definitive test of the univariate versus multivariate views of intelligence.

CLOSE UP **Some Judgment Calls in Using Factor Analysis**

How many factors? There is no set way of determining the number of factors to extract from a correlation matrix. The number of factors removed is related to the proportions of variance accounted for because more factors will capture more variance. The question of how many factors to keep then becomes a matter of making a decision about the proportions of variance the researcher wants. This indicates that the decision about how many factors to extract is deeply tied up in the overall goals of the analysis. If the objective is to account for as much variance as possible, then the researcher is likely to extract a large number of factors. If, on the other hand, the goal is to test a theoretical position, the proportions of variance extracted will likely be sacrificed to demonstrate the desired theoretical result. Thus, any effort to use factor analysis to verify a specific theory must be evaluated carefully with respect to the researchers' judgments about the number of factors extracted and the proportions of variance accounted for.

The literature has suggested several approaches to deciding on the number of factors. For example, in some cases, it is reasonable to consider only factors with eigen values greater than 1.00 because the remaining factors would account for less variance than one single variable. In other cases, the eigen values are plotted, and the point where there is a clear jump in the sizes of the values is selected as the place to stop extracting factors. Each method imposes certain assumptions on the eventual solution and should only be used if these assumptions are congenial to the intention of the analysis.

Interpreting factors. There is no hard-and-fast way of naming factors. More often than not, factors are identified using researchers' intuitions. This poses a very serious problem if one is trying to use the nature of extracted factors to buttress a theoretical position because other researchers frequently arrive at alternate interpretations. Often the very propositions being verified go into labeling the factors that makes the process vulnerable to a criticism of circularity.

Rotation. A convenient way of representing a factor solution is to plot the location of each test as a function of its loadings on the various factors. Figure 10-4 shows such a plot for the factor analysis shown in Table 10-8. Notice how the location of the point for Figure Classification in the plot is the intersect of projections drawn from .59 on the Factor I axis and .57 on the Factor II axis. These two figures (.59 and .57) are the loadings of the Figure Classification test on Factors I and II, respectively from Table 10-8. Thus, each test is represented as a point in the two-dimensional space described by the factors. If it were a three-factor solution, the plot would be three dimensional and so on.[12]

One of the most convenient aspects of this kind of geometric representation of a factor solution is that the degree of correlation between any two tests in the space defined by the factors is a direct function of the proximity of the two points. Variables that are highly and positively correlated with each other tend to be close together in the plot. Notice how Cubes and Flags, which are correlated .77 from Table 10-6, are very close to each other, whereas Flags and Number Series are far apart and correlated .22. Indeed, the distance between the points in factor space is an index of their correlation.

This turns out to be important because the position of the axes in the factor space has no effect on the intertest correlations. In other words, the axes can be placed anywhere, and the interrelationships between the tests (their distances from each other) will be preserved. The only restriction here is that the origin (the point where the axes intersect) remains in the same place. Thus, rotating the axes to any position without losing any information about interrelations between the tests is possible.

The issue of interpreting exactly what a given factor represents is well served by this mathematical property because positioning the axes to maximize interpretability is possible. This process is called **rotation**—the axes are placed to make the factors as interpretable as possible. There are quite a few approaches to rotation, with the best known being called **Varimax**. Here the intent is to position the axes so that there is a maximal number of 0 and 1 loadings because these would be representative of the most pure measures of a given factor. The axis position that maximizes the variance of the loadings (hence the name Varimax) produces this result.

It should be clear, though, that rotation is highly judgmental. Decisions about whether to rotate at all, which approach to use, and whether to keep the axes at right

---

[12]Although a bit difficult to visualize, there is no reason why we could not consider a four- or five-dimensional space. Indeed, Thurstone's Primary Mental Abilities would be represented in a seven-dimensional space. These higher dimensional situations are called *hyperspaces.*

Figure 10-4
Plot of factor matrix shown in Table 10-8.

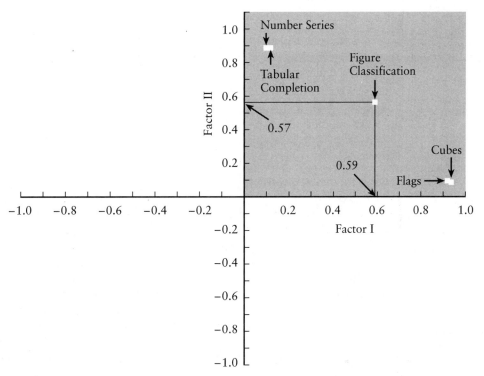

angles to each other (which is not necessary to preserve the test intercorrelations)[13] are all highly significant and have meaningful influences on the final solution.

Issues of context. The set of tests included in any factor analysis has a great effect on the obtained solution. Using a series of tests with similar characteristics (for example, all involving pictures and answered in a multiple-choice format) would produce a very large first factor because of the test similarities. On the other hand, selecting tests to be maximally different from each other would produce a factor solution showing a large number of different factors. Thus, the sampling of tests to be included in a factor analysis is exceedingly important because these choices can deeply influence the nature of the obtained factors. A similar argument can be advanced if similar subjects are used in the analysis.

Summary. Each judgment call indicates that a large number of important decisions go into the performance of a factor analysis and that these decisions can have a significant effect on the obtained solution. A considerable degree of expertise is necessary to be able to use this technique properly.

---

[13]Techniques that do not keep the axes at right angles to each other are called *oblique rotations*

The controversiality attending some of these judgment calls is captured in the following ditty:[14]

"God Bless You Merry Factorers"

God Bless you merry factorers
I'm glad you've come our way!

Your data are so mountainous
We don't know what they say!

We can't rebut your eigen cut
Nor ken your vast array!

So tell me: What, then, do all these factors mean?
What do they mean?

Oh tell me, then, what do all those factors mean?

These judgment calls are only one set of reasons why factor analysis has not resolved the multivariate/univariate debate in intelligence. In addition, certain aspects of the data initially used by Spearman and Thurstone contributed to the controversy. Spearman tended to use highly mixed groups of respondents, with a highly mixed variety of tests. Thurstone, on the other hand, used highly homogeneous university-student samples. These differences, in and of themselves, add complexities to the emergent ideas of intelligence because they contribute in several ways to the factor structures that were documented, with Spearman's data being more likely to demonstrate a large first factor compared with Thurstone's. It is not unreasonable, as well, to remention the ideological differences between the two camps, with the British univariate approach being so firmly associated with the Galtonian view and the multivariate perspective being congenial to the Mill-like egalitarian position. These differences induce a context in which the complexities of understanding intellectual performance might be unintentionally shaded in one direction or the other, pending the prevailing worldview.

OTHER VARIETIES OF FACTOR ANALYSIS

Factor analytic methodology has not been restricted to issues of the multivariate/univariate nature of intelligence, despite the fact that it was developed in the service of this topic. This technique has since been applied in a number of different ways in a wide variety of other domains. It has been used extensively in personality research (for details see Chapter 16) and has found applications in other disciplines as disparate as biology, geology, and political science.

Perhaps the simplest use of factor analysis is to break down a complex set of scores into their constituent, algebraic components. This is accomplished using a

---

[14]Sung to the tune of "God Rest Ye Merry Gentlemen"; from McGrath, nd

variant of factor analysis called **principal components analysis,** and the only concern is the development of mathematical factors that account for the maximal proportions of variance. In this case, no effort is made to interpret the factors—they are just simple algebraic components of a larger set of values. This can be a very useful way of rendering large, complex domains into simpler parts for subsequent analysis. Some researchers argue that this is the only legitimate application of the factor analytic methodology because it minimizes the amount of interpretation involved and guards against unwarranted "psychologizing."

As Thurstone did, however, factor analysis can be used to try and identify underlying psychological attributes rather than being restricted to algebraic solutions. This use of factor analysis is aptly captured in the title of one of Thurstone's (1935) many books, *Vectors of the Mind.* Here concern is to identify a latent subset of psychological characteristics or factors that underlie a specific domain, with PMA being a prime example. Such studies use **exploratory factor analysis,** attempting to document the psychological characteristics of a specific domain. Factors are sought out and interpreted as psychological entities. Common-factor analysis, as described in this chapter, is a good example of the methodology that can be used in this situation.

A third variant of factor analysis involves explicit attempts to test theoretical propositions regarding the structure of a domain. For example, if a researcher thought that there were two types of personalities—one associated with introversion and one linked to neuroticism—it is possible to actually test this theoretical expectation by factor analyzing a matrix of intercorrelations of personality measures, expecting to find two factors that lined up per the expected introversion/neuroticism distinction. A number of highly sophisticated methods of actually testing hypotheses using factor analysis, known collectively as **confirmatory factor analysis,** has been presented to facilitate this use of the technique. (A detailed example is presented in Chapter 16.)

Finally, factor analysis need not be restricted to correlations between test scores. For example, if we had a series of test scores on a set of persons, it is possible to calculate a correlation between *people* by adding up the cross products of the z scores over tests rather than over persons as is usually done. In this case, a high correlation would indicate that two persons' sets of scores were very similar (that is, you could predict one person's scores from the other's). Factor analysis of such a matrix of people correlations would identify groups of people who go together. This variant of factor analysis is called the **Q-technique** and is but one of a number of novel applications of the technology that could be developed (see Cattell, 1952; 1978, pp. 321–376).

Even this very brief summary of different applications of factor analysis indicates that the technology has had substantive application in psychology and beyond. Many creative uses of this technique have followed from Thurstone's initial documentation of its utility in exploring the nature of intelligence. Apart from the tests themselves, factor analysis represents one of the most important ideas that has emerged from this domain of inquiry, offering to the research community an impressive arsenal of techniques that can be applied to the solution of a wide variety of different problems.

COMPROMISING THE UNIVARIATE AND
MULTIDIMENSIONAL VIEWS OF INTELLIGENCE

Despite the apparently overwhelming implications of Thurstone's work, the unitary view of intelligence did not go away. In part, this was due to the inability of factor analysis to decide decisively which of the two views of intelligence was correct. As well, the univariate view matched most people's intuitions of the underlying structure of intelligence.[15] As noted earlier, the Stanford–Binet, in all its univariate glory, was still the most popular intelligence test available. Thurstone did not dismantle intelligence, but he did present an alternative formulation that testers could adopt or not adopt, pending the practical decisions for which they were using tests. Thurstone, however, did have an impact on the new generation of intelligence tests. In fact, just as "Primary Mental Abilities" was being published, David Wechsler was beginning a program that would result in state-of-the-art tests, which are, in a very real sense, a compromise between the hard-line unitary view and one that considers components most important.

David Wechsler was born in Romania in 1896 and came to the United States in 1902. After obtaining a B.A. from New York City College in 1916, he enrolled as a graduate student at Columbia. When World War I erupted, he became part of Yerkes's army, being actively involved in the testing program. His job was to administer the Stanford–Binet to recruits who had done poorly on the Alpha and Beta. Through this experience, he realized the need to develop a test that properly measured the intelligence of adults.

Upon graduation from Columbia, Wechsler worked in private practice. In 1932 he was appointed chief psychologist to New York's large Bellevue Hospital where he was responsible for testing thousands of mental patients. Many of the patients in this hospital came from multilingual, multinational, and multicultural backgrounds, which provided significant difficulties for the existing tests. As well, Wechsler's doubts about the existing intelligence tests had grown. He determined to develop his own test to take into account the weaknesses and problems he had identified in his 15 years of testing experience.

The first test he published was called the **Wechsler–Bellevue Intelligence Scale** (W–B) (Wechsler, 1939). He drew inspiration for his items from a wide range of previously published tests including, among others, the Army Beta. However, he introduced a degree of rigor and careful attention to detail that rendered the W–B a much better test than the original army version. The W–B was designed specifically for adults, being differentiated from the Stanford–Binet in several important ways. First, it was based upon the *point-scale* method of assessment, with each subtest having items intended for all age groups. Second, the content of the items was oriented toward adults. Third, because older persons do not tend to work as rapidly as children, minimal emphasis was placed on speed although a number of the sub-

---

[15]These intuitions were shaped by the current intelligence tests and their surrounding rhetoric. Hanson (1993) has developed this point into a strong critical analysis of testing practice.

tests were timed. Finally, Wechsler included a significant nonverbal component (what we earlier called pictorial content) in the scale.

The Wechsler Adult Intelligence Scales

Several difficulties with the W–B were identified as it was put to use. Problems with the original standardization sample, poor internal reliabilities of several subscales, a lack of adequate range of item difficulty in some subscales, and ambiguous scoring criteria plagued the early version. The W–B was replaced in 1955 by the **Wechsler Adult Intelligence Scale** (**WAIS**) (Wechsler, 1955, 1958). Over one-half of the original W–B items was retained in this new test. The WAIS soon emerged as the most widely used adult intelligence test (Matarazzo, 1972). A revised version, known as the **WAIS–R**, which provided a more contemporary norm group, was published in 1981.

Particularly noteworthy in the Wechsler series is the presentation of two basic intelligence scales—one based on predominantly verbal tasks and another derived from performance tasks using pictorial content such as matching block designs or doing jigsaw-puzzle-like items. These two scales culminate in separate IQ scores called **verbal IQ** and **performance IQ**. A **full-scale IQ,** based on a combination of the verbal and performance scores, was also provided. Here we find the essence of Wechsler's compromise between the univariate and multivariate views of intelligence. The full-scale score represents the univariate view, and the two sub-IQs (verbal and performance) present a componential version of intellect. It would seem the Wechsler series allowed testers to have their cake and eat it too, with both views of intelligence being represented in a single test. Table 10-14 (page 348) presents brief descriptions of the 11 subtests that make up the WAIS–R.

The WAIS–R is administered strictly on an individual level by a highly trained psychologist. Verbal and Performance subtests are administered alternately. Within each subtest, items are arranged in order of difficulty, starting with the easiest. Administration order of the items is based on respondent performance, with easier items being skipped (and assumed correctly answered) if the respondent shows little difficulty with similar items. If the respondent is laboring with items at a specific level of difficulty, administration of the subtest is terminated, moving on to another. The goal here is to maximize respondent interest. The test administrator keeps detailed notes during the testing sessions and does not attempt to interpret the results until after the testing session (which typically takes 45–90 minutes) is completed.

Scoring is fairly straightforward for some subtests (for example, Arithmetic, Block Design), with the number correct representing the raw score for the subtest. However, the open-ended subtests (for example, Information, Vocabulary, Comprehension, Similarities) require informed professional judgment to translate the responses into raw scores. The manual is most helpful in providing direction in the proper scoring of these subtests.

The WAIS–R test manual provides tables that transform the raw scores into *standardized scores,* which are variants of the *z* score (see Chapter 6). As Equation 10-2 shows, these subtest scores have a mean of 10 and a standard deviation of 3.

Table 10-14 Subtests of the WAIS–R

Verbal Scale

Information	Covers knowledge of general information, reflecting facts that the normally functioning adult could reasonably be expected to acquire in our culture. (29 items)
Digit Span	A measure of short-term memory designed to discover memory capacity for numbers, both backward and forward.
Vocabulary	Defining or explaining each of 35 words presented orally and in writing.
Arithmetic	A set of simple arithmetic problems that can be solved mentally. This test is typically considered a measure of reasoning rather than arithmetic ability. (14 items)
Comprehension	Explaining why certain things should be done or what might do in specific situations. Scoring is in terms of the amount of insight revealed in the answers. (16 items)
Similarities	Indicating how two things are alike. (14 items)

Performance Scale

Picture Completion	Respondents are shown a series of pictures in which a critical detail is missing. They must locate the missing detail.
Picture Arrangement	Respondents are shown a series of pictures like cartoon frames and have to place them into the proper order to tell a story.
Block Design	After being given a set of red and white blocks, duplicating a design shown on a card. (9 items)
Object Assembly	Assembling cutup pictures of common objects (like a jigsaw puzzle) into their original form. (4 items)
Digit Symbol	After being given a code to match symbols to digits and on presentation of a series of digits, substituting the correct symbol. This subtest is timed, with the number correct in 90 seconds being the raw score.

$$W_{S_{ij}} = 10 + (3 \times z_{ij}) \tag{10-2}$$

where

$W_{S_{ij}}$ = Wechsler standardized score of person i on subtest j

z_{ij} = z score for person i on subtest j

The tables used to calculate the standardized scores are based on a sample of 1880 White and non-White Americans stratified by age, gender, race, geographic region, occupation, education, and urban/rural residence to match the 1970 U.S. census. These standardized scores permit comparison of performance on the 11 subtests, indicating that Wechsler's compartmentalization of intelligence is extensive—he suggests 11 components by this procedure. The verbal, performance, and full-scale IQ scores are tabulated by summing the standard scores on the relevant subtests and consulting a table in the manual. These three IQs are presented as variants of z scores, with a mean of 100 and a standard deviation of 15.

This approach to defining performance on an intelligence test is called a **deviation IQ** because the resultant number, although retaining a mean value of 100, has been modified so that all groups have equal standard deviations (that is, 15). Per our earlier reasoning (see Chapter 4), we can readily transform deviation IQ scores to percentiles, which is an aid to interpretation. This form of IQ score contrasts with the old ratio IQ (see Chapter 6), which could result in differing standard deviations at various age groups. Later revisions of the Stanford–Binet adopted the deviation IQ as well (using a value of 16) because of the problems of interpretation caused by having different variances associated with different ages. Notice how this approach obviates the problem of having to use chronological age in the actual calculation of the IQ score, thus making this type of score appropriate to the target adult population.

Psychometric characteristics. The norms are good. Reliability is excellent, with the full-score IQ reliability being higher than .95. The Verbal and Performance scales have reliabilities in the range of .90 to .95. The reliabilities of individual subtests are a bit lower, being in the range of .80. Because the smaller subtest scores consist of fewer items, these lower reliabilities are to be expected.

Matarazzo (1972), in his review of the criterion-related validity of the WAIS, indicates significant correlations with a number of criteria such as academic performance, life success, grades, measures of work performance, and occupational level. Of note is the finding that WAIS validity coefficients tend to be lower than those found for the Stanford–Binet. This would appear to be because intelligence is a more important source of individual differences in children than it is in adults.

Content validity of the WAIS is reasonable. The subtest items represent a fairly wide range of cognitive tasks (see Table 10-14). Factor analytic studies have confirmed the division of the full-scale IQ into its two components (Cohen, 1957).

A new interpretive aid for the WAIS–R is computer-assisted systems. The respondent's raw scores are entered and a printout is produced, which includes (1) raw, scaled, and percentile scores for each subtest; (2) all three IQ scores and percentiles; (3) a profile; (4) confidence intervals, which provide a window of values within which a person's score could be expected to fall with a given probability; and (5) a narrative report focusing on any discrepancies observed between the Verbal and Performance components of test performance.

The Wechsler Intelligence Scales for Children

The success of the W–B soon prompted Wechsler to extend the age ranges associated with this adaptation of the point scale for the individual assessment of intelligence. The first extension involved the development of a very similar test for children in 1949. The **Wechsler Intelligence Scale for Children (WISC)**, and its revision, the **WISC–R,** released in 1974, followed the same basic format as the WAIS, with the norm group being children from 6 ½ to 16 ½ years old. A third revision, the **WISC–III,** was released in 1991. Examination of Table 10-15, which lists the subtests of the WISC–R, indicates the similarities between the child and adult versions of the Wechsler series. As can be seen, a significant overlap exists between the subtests of the WISC–R and WAIS–R (see Table 10-14). The item content and stimuli have been changed, of course, to make the items more appropriate for younger respondents. The instructions for the WISC–R have also been modified to be more understandable to children.

The WISC–R is administered in a similar fashion to the WAIS–R, alternating between Verbal and Performance subtests. Subject responses and estimated intellectual performance are used to determine if all subtest items are administered, with subtest administration being terminated after a specified number of failures. Like the WAIS–R, subtest raw scores are converted to standard scores (mean = 10, standard deviation = 3), and the three IQ estimates (verbal, performance, and full-scale) are generated to have a mean of 100 and standard deviation of 15. The WISC–R norm group on which these raw scores are transformed is, like the WAIS–R, well constructed, being based on 2200 cases stratified with respect to the 1970 census. One of the main reasons behind the development of the WISC–R was the lack of non-White representation in the original WISC norm group.

Table 10-15 Subtests of the WISC–R

Verbal Scale

Information

Similarities

Arithmetic

Vocabulary

Comprehension

Digit Span (an alternate test for the Verbal scale in the event of the misadministration of one of the other five subtests)

Performance Scale

Picture Completion

Picture Arrangement

Block Assembly

Object Assembly

Coding

Mazes (solving a series of paper-and-pencil mazes within a time limit; an alternate test for the Performance scale in the event of the misadministration of one of the other five subtests)

Testing materials for the WISC–III

WISC–R reliabilities are excellent. Test/retest reliabilities of the IQ scores are consistently above .90, and subtest reliabilities are almost always higher than .70. Factor analyses have supported the use of the two scores (see Cohen, 1959; Gutkin & Reynolds, 1981; Kaufman, 1975), although a third factor related to distractibility also emerges on occasion (see Silverstein, 1977; Van Hagen & Kaufman, 1975). Concurrent validity is good with the WISC full-scale IQ and Stanford–Binet IQ showing correlations around .80 in most studies. Full-scale IQ correlations with criteria such as academic achievement are typically in the region of .55 (see Kaufman, 1975, for a review). For example, Covin and Lubimiv (1976) found correlations of .68, .35, and .58 between a standardized reading test and the verbal, performance, and full-scale WISC–R IQ scores, respectively, based on a sample of 51 children aged 12 to 14 years. In general terms, the WISC and WISC–R are excellent individual measures of children's intelligence, emerging as the most widely used tests of this type.

The Wechsler Preschool and Primary Scales of Intelligence

A third member of the Wechsler series grew out of the WAIS/WISC tradition. Here concern was with a downward extension of age from the WISC to include children between the ages of 4 and 6 ½ years. The **Wechsler Preschool and Primary Scale of Intelligence (WPPSI**—pronounced "whipsy") was released in 1968. A revised version, the **WPPSI–R,** was released in 1990. As Table 10-16 shows, all but three of the WPPSI subtests are the same as those of the WISC. Indeed, many of the WISC items are repeated in the version for younger respondents.

Table 10-16 Subtests of the WPPSI

Verbal Scale

Information

Vocabulary

Arithmetic

Similarities

Comprehension

Sentences (same as Digit Span, except that the stimuli are sentences the child must repeat after having heard them; used as an alternate Verbal subtest)

Performance Scale

Animal House (an Orwellian-sounding subtest very much like the Digit Symbol task of the WAIS, except that colored pictures of animals are the stimuli)

Picture Completion

Mazes

Geometric Design (copying a series of geometric designs using pencil and paper)

Block Design

Administration of the test mirrors the previous Wechsler tests, with alternation between Verbal and Performance subtests. The scores obtained from the test are identical to those for the WISC and WAIS. There are special demands on the administrator to ensure that the child is engaged throughout the entire testing period.

Perhaps the major advantage of the WPPSI is its well-conceived norm group. It was based on a national sample of 1200 preschool children, with 100 each in six half-year age groups between the ages 4 and 6 ½ years. It was stratified to match the 1960 U.S. census.

Reliabilities for the WPPSI IQ scores are in the .90 range, and subtest reliabilities are around .80—higher than those found with the other two tests. Factor analyses indicate that the expected two factors underlie performance on the test (see Carlson & Reynolds, 1981). Concurrent validity is mixed, with correlations between the WPPSI full-scale IQ and Stanford–Binet ranging between .44 (Ruschival & Way, 1971) and .92 (Austin, 1970) with a median around .80. Very few criterion-related validity studies are reported in the WPPSI manual.

Summary. By 1968 Wechsler had published IQ tests to span from preschool through to old age. Figure 10-5 shows the evolution of this family of tests. The organization of subtests into Verbal and Performance scales facilitated the generation of hypotheses and the clinical utility of the tests. The clarity of instructions for administration of all three tests is exemplary, although it requires substantial training to become an effective administrator. The extensive and representative norm groups associated with these tests are perhaps their greatest strength. The demon-

Figure 10-5 The family tree of Wechsler tests.

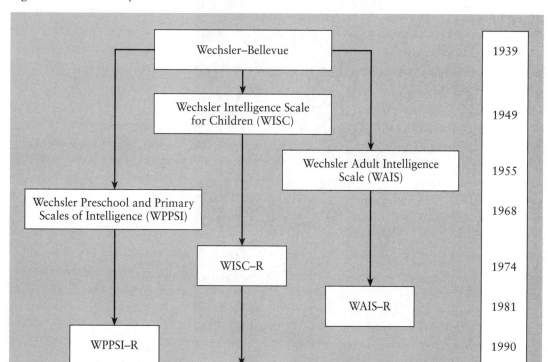

strated psychometric strengths of the tests make them among the most important models for the testing enterprise.

The literature has noted several limitations to these tests:

1. There is some concern about the subjectivity inherent in scoring the open-ended items.

2. The norm groups failed explicitly to consider socioeconomic status, and there are several gaps in the norms for the WISC–R.

3. The variable standard deviations on subtests place limits on the range of possible scaled scores for some subtests.

4. The relative lack of validity data published with the tests themselves is a bit disconcerting.

The WISC–III was formulated, in part, to rectify these limitations as well as to update the item content. In today's testing enterprise, the Wechsler tests are excellent examples of contemporary testing methodology.

Administering the Block Design subtest of the WISC

Based as they are on a compromise between the univariate and multivariate views of intelligence, the Wechsler tests represent the current technology in the individual assessment of intelligence. They are clearly the most widely used tests in the enterprise.

Summary

In this chapter, we outlined the early research and theory dealing with the structure of intelligence. (Figure 10-6 summarizes the developments in intelligence.) The prevailing unitary view was presented, and it was challenged for several reasons, including problems emerging with the univariate approach, the move toward reductionism, and the development of factor analysis. The eventual multivariate view had a number of advantages including the ease with which it could be applied to important social decisions such as vocational counseling.

However, there were also disadvantages. For example, it became increasingly difficult to communicate to the general public the idea of multiple intelligences.

Figure 10-6 The unfolding of intelligence as it occurred in the testing enterprise.

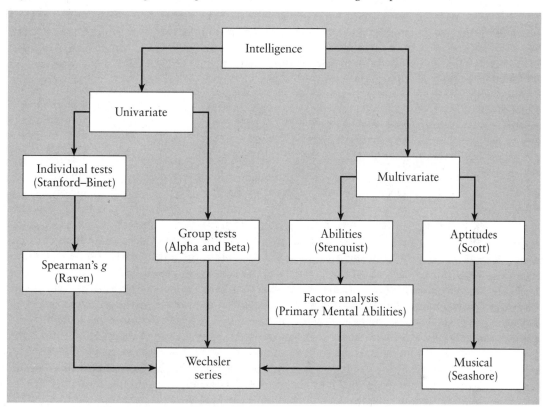

Because the society had been educated for several decades about the unitary nature of intelligence, the multivariate view posed problems. In a sense, society wanted a single intelligence because it was easier to understand and appeared to have a greater relevance to solving social problems. In addition, the unitary view remained because of the availability of tests such as the Stanford–Binet and Raven Progressive Matrices. These tests, as technological devices, had become an important part of the toolbox of social decision makers such as teachers and psychologists and to abandon them, because the underlying ideas about the structure of intelligence were no longer tenable, was not a consideration. The pragmatic utility of the tests, despite their being based on a contentious model of intelligence, carried the day, and the unitary view survived this attack on its empirical foundation. Again, pragmatics held sway.

The solution to this dilemma involved disassociating the multivariate approach from the univariate one, by labeling the latter domain as concerned with abilities or aptitudes. In most presentations of the time, intelligence and abilities would be discussed as though they were entirely different things. Separate chapters would be given to each in textbooks, and very little "cross talk" between the two approaches would occur. Each went merrily on its way, paying little heed to the developments in the other camp.

David Wechsler did present an important compromise when he determined that there should be two basic types of intelligence: performance and verbal. However, he provided the tester with a single score (the full-scale IQ) as well. Wechsler divided intelligence on the basis of the types of cognitive processes and stimuli used in the test rather than on the kind of factor analytic work stemming from Thurstone's research program. Another important contribution for Wechsler was the extension of age both downward (WPPSI) and upward (WAIS) from the Stanford–Binet. The Wechsler series provided an incredibly wide-ranging and useful set of tests that adhered to the unitary view and that could also be used to make several types of multivariate decisions. Without doubt, the Wechsler series is the most used and important set of individual measures of intelligence available today.

The Wechsler series was initiated in the late 1930s, during the halcyon days of operationism. As revealed in the last two chapters, there were a number of highly significant contributions to the testing enterprise during this era. A new philosophy of science was introduced and accepted, and the factor analytic paradigm emerged to address some of the pressing problems within the testing enterprise. Tests proliferated, and the industry had begun significant development in America.

It is important, at this point, to realize that the debate between the univariate and multivariate perspectives was focused on the notion of the *structure* of intelligence. That is, the debate was concerned with the best (or most ideologically congenial) way of construing the form of intellect. Was it one thing? Or was it a series of smaller things? The issue of the actual content of intelligence or the processes that were responsible for its realization were not being considered at this point—all that was "up for grabs" in this argument was its structure. In this sense, the field of intelligence was still courting the notion of measurement without definition. The structural debate addressed the number of "things" needed but the actual definition of these, and indeed the definition of the psychological domain that was or was not being parsed into parts, remained unclarified. To be certain, the operational doctrine was playing well in this debate.

Glossary

common-factor analysis   A mathematical technique used to determine the number and nature of dimensions underlying a set of empirical observations such as test scores. Pioneered by Leon Thurstone in his efforts to dismantle intelligence, this technique has become a mainstay of testing methodology because it permits breaking down complex domains into simpler, more efficient sets of variables.

communality (h^2)   An index of the proportion of variance in a given test that is accounted for in a factor solution.

confirmatory factor analysis   A variant of factor analysis where the goal is to test specific theoretical expectations about the structure of a set of measures.

correlation matrix   An array of correlation coefficients that represents all possible relationships among a set of tests. The correlation matrix is triangular in shape. (See Table 10-3.)

data matrix   A rectangular array of empirical observations organized such that each element in the array is a score on a specific test obtained by a specific individual. (See Table 10-1.)

deviation IQ   An IQ score that has been transformed to have a mean of 100 and a constant standard deviation across all age groups. In the Wechsler series, the standard deviation is 15, whereas in later versions of the Stanford–Binet it is 16. This form of IQ score replaced the earlier ratio IQ, which had difficulties associated with variable standard deviations across ages.

Differential Aptitude Test Battery (DAT)   For use with high school students, a battery of tests that was based on Leon Thurstone's Primary Mental Abilities.

eigen value   An indication of the amount of variance attributable to a factor in a factor solution.

exploratory factor analysis   A variant of factor analysis where the goal is to determine the number and nature of the psychological variables that underlie a set of measures.

factor   A dimension found to underlie performance on a set of test scores, using the technique of factor analysis.

factor analysis   A mathematical technique used to determine the number and nature of dimensions underlying a set of empirical observations such as test scores. There are various types of factor analyses, with common-factor analysis being the one discussed in most detail in this chapter.

factor loading   An index of the saturation of a specific test by a specific factor. Conceptually similar to a correlation between the test and the factor, higher loadings indicate that the test performance is more highly determined by the factor.

factor matrix   A rectangular array with the elements being factor loadings. (See Table 10-7.) Being the primary output from factor analysis, this matrix is used to interpret the meanings of the factors.

full-scale IQ   One of three IQs derived from the Wechsler series. This IQ, which conforms to the unitary view of intelligence, is calculated by taking into account performance on all subtests and has been standardized to have a mean of 100 and a standard deviation of 15.

g   A shorthand for representing general intelligence introduced by Charles Spearman.

global view of intelligence   *See* unitary view.

group-factor analysis   *See* common-factor analysis.

hierarchical ordering   An arrangement in a correlation matrix where the coefficients decrease in order of magnitude as one moves down or across the matrix. Considered to be characteristic of matrices permeated with *g*, it can be estimated by inspection or by calculating tetrad equations.

matrix   A rectangular array of mathematical elements such as data points or correlation coefficients.

Monte Carlo simulation   Using random numbers to test various mathematical propositions.

multivariate   Relating to multiple variables. Leon Thurstone's is a multivariate view of intelligence.

performance IQ   One of three IQ scores obtained from the Wechsler series. It is based on subtests with pictorial content such as Picture Completion, Picture Arrangement, Block Design, Object Assembly, and Digit Symbol.

Primary Mental Abilities   A set of seven abilities found by Leon Thurstone, using common factor analysis, to underlie intelligence.

principal components analysis   A variant of factor analysis where the goal is to break down a complex set of measures into a smaller set of algebraic variables.

proportion of variance   A technical term that relates to the percentage of the variability in a given domain (for example, a test of a factor solution) that has been accounted for or explained.

pure indicator of a factor   A test with a very high loading on a given factor. Because of the high loading, such a test is thought to be a good index of whatever it is that the factor represents.

Q-technique   A variant of factor analysis where the goal is to isolate groups or types of people that go together.

Raven Progressive Matrices   A nonverbal British test that was developed to be an effective measure of *g*.

reconstructed correlation   A correlation between two variables derived from a factor matrix that contains the two tests. The similarity of this correlation to the original correlation serves as an indication of the goodness of a given factor solution.

reductionism   The use of smaller and smaller units of analysis in exploring scientific phenomena. Reductionism appears to be an indication of progress within a scientific enterprise.

residual   The difference between reconstructed and original correlations, with lower values being indicative of better factor solutions.

rotation   A procedure of realigning the axes in the space defined by factors to maximize the interpretability of the obtained factors. Rotation does not affect the size of the residuals.

s   A shorthand for representing specific factors introduced by Charles Spearman. Specific factors were likened to "mental engines" that were driven by *g*.

saturation   A technical term in factor analysis that reflects the extent to which a given test score is determined by a specific factor. A test that obtains a high loading on a factor is said to be saturated with this factor.

Spearman, Charles   A British psychologist who introduced the idea of reliability and who formulated the notion of general intelligence (*g*) and the two-factor theory of intelligence.

Spearman's *g*   Per Charles Spearman, defining intelligence as a single entity. Seen as a kind of "mental energy," Spearman elaborated *g* using sophisticated mathematical methods. This view of intelligence permeated almost all thinking about intelligence prior to Leon Thurstone's work.

task-specific factors (*s*)   Postulated by Charles Spearman in his two-factor theory of intelligence to be unique dimensions underlying performance on specific tests.

tetrad difference   A mathematical device that involves calculating the cross products of a 2×2 submatrix from a correlation matrix. According to Charles Spearman, matrices determined by *g* should show average tetrads near 0.

theorem of the indifference of the indicator   A derivation from Charles Spearman's two-factor theory of intelligence stating that any measure of human performance is a good estimate of intelligence as long as the person's and test's status on *s* is known, as well as the saturation of the test in *g*.

Thurstone, Leon L.   An American psychologist who pioneered common-factor analysis and who dismantled *g* by providing evidence for the Primary Mental Abilities.

two-factor theory of intelligence   Charles Spearman's view that performance on a test was a joint function of *g* and *s*, which was developed into a sophisticated mathematic formulation.

unitary view of intelligence   Conceiving of intelligence as a single or univariate entity, such as Spearman's *g* or as implied in the Stanford–Binet.

univariate   Relating to a single variable. Thus, Spearman's *g* is a univariate view of intelligence.

Varimax rotation   A formalized procedure of rotation that maximizes the variance in the factor loadings, thus enhancing the possibility of interpreting the factor.

verbal IQ   One of three IQ scores obtained from the Wechsler series of intelligence tests. It is based on subtests with semantic content such as Information, Digit Span, Vocabulary, Arithmetic, Comprehension, and Similarities.

WAIS–R   The 1981 revision of the Wechsler Adult Intelligence Scale.

Wechsler Adult Intelligence Scale (WAIS)   David Wechsler's 1955 individual test of intelligence for use with individuals older than age 16 years.

Wechsler–Bellevue Intelligence Scale   David Wechsler's first attempt to develop an intelligence test for adults around 1939.

Wechsler, David   An American psychologist responsible for development of the entire Wechsler series of intelligence tests.

Wechsler Intelligence Scale for Children (WISC)   David Wechsler's 1949 intelligence test for children aged 6 ½ through 16 ½ years.

Wechsler Preschool and Primary Scale of Intelligence (WPPSI)   David Wechsler's 1968 intelligence for children aged 4 through 6 ½ years.

WISC–R   The 1972 revision of the Wechsler Intelligence Scale for Children.

WISC–III   The 1992 revision of the Wechsler Intelligence Scale for Children.

WPPSI–R   The 1990 revision of the Wechsler Preschool and Primary Scale of Intelligence.

Suggested Further Reading

Comrey, A. L. (1973). *First course in factor analysis*. New York: Academic Press.

This book's major strength lies in the manner in which it presents various aspects of factor analysis from a number of different perspectives such as matrix algebra, ordinary algebra, and geometric presentations. Although quite advanced, this book can be very helpful to someone who is looking for a more sophisticated treatment of the technique than is presented here.

Edwards, A. J. (1971). *Individual mental testing Part I: History and theories*. Scranton, Ohio: Intext Educational Publishers.

This is a highly readable presentation of much of the material presented in this chapter of *The Enterprise*. Of particular note are the discussions of the work of Spearman, Thurstone, and Wechsler in Chapters 6 through 8, respectively, which provide more detail and a slightly different perspective regarding these ideas.

Frank, G. (1983). *The Wechsler enterprise: An assessment of the development, structure, and use of the Wechsler tests of intelligence*. Oxford, Eng.: Pergamon.

As the title suggests, this is a thorough evaluation of the Wechsler tests. Focus is on the clinical utility of the tests, and it presents a provocative, critical review. This book is good reading for anyone who is looking for information about the effectiveness of using the Wechsler tests in a variety of different situations.

Gorsuch, R. L. (1983). *Factor analysis* (2nd ed.). Hillsdale, N.J.: Erlbaum.

Of the many texts dealing with factor analysis, I have found this one to be the most approachable. The mathematics are not overwhelming in the presentation, but there is sufficient detail to help out the reader who wants to move to the next level of complexity in this topic.

Gould, S. J. (1981). *The mismeasure of man*. New York: Norton.

This critical analysis of the univariate notion of intelligence, especially pp. 256–272, should be considered required reading for a complete understanding of the implications of this perspective. Gould clearly articulates the real human costs inherent in the univariate view.

Matarazzo, J. D. (1972). *Wechsler's measurement and appraisal of adult intelligence*. Baltimore: Williams & Wilkins.

Everything you ever wanted to know about the WAIS can be found in this invaluable resource. It provides extensive detail about the WAIS, drawing on decades of research and work with it.

Spearman, C. (1927). *The abilities of man: Their nature and measurement*. New York: Macmillan.

This is an excellent primary source to gain an insight into Spearman's thinking. Although it presents a great amount of detail, it is still readable, particularly in the manner in which he presents his theoretical ideas.

Thurstone, L. L. (1938). Primary mental abilities. *Psychometric Monographs, 1* [entire issue].

Here you will find the entire idea underlying the PMA exceedingly well presented. This monograph is a particularly good primary source because Thurstone has presented many details of the tests that he used and his final factor solution, permitting the reader to gain a real sense of the ideas developed by this important contributor to the testing enterprise.

Wechsler, D. (1958). *The measurement and appraisal of adult intelligence.* Baltimore: Williams & Wilkins.

This is a very thorough presentation of the Wechsler adult test. It is recommended primary material because it provides great insight into the detailed aspects of the thinking and techniques for assessing adult intelligence that Wechsler developed.

Discussion Questions

1. Draw examples of correlation matrices that do and do not support Charles Spearman's ideas about *g*.

2. Create a hierarchically ordered correlation matrix involving four tests. Calculate all possible tetrads for this matrix, plot them, and discuss the appropriateness of Spearman's assertions that the tetrad is a good way of supporting his theory.

3. Critically evaluate Spearman's two-factor theory of intelligence.

4. Outline a condition under which Spearman's theorem of the indifference of the indicator is not true. Does this have any implications for Spearman's overall theory? Why, or why not?

5. Discuss whether or not you think the Raven Progressive Matrices is truly a culture-fair test.

6. List as many problems with the univariate view of intelligence as you can. Which one is the most important? Why?

7. With reference to a science other than psychology, indicate the manner in which reductionism appears to be associated with progress.

8. Outline the manner in which a contemporary feminist might take umbrage with the notion of reductionism.

9. Generate an example of a context (other than intelligence) in which a univariate approach to measurement is clearly inappropriate. Suggest a multivariate alternative.

10. Discuss whether or not you are surprised that attempts to dismantle intelligence began in America.

11. From the examples given in Figure 10-3, what aspects of intellectual performance did Leon Thurstone omit?

12. Draw five correlation matrices involving five tests that, if factor-analyzed, would reveal one, two, three, four, and five factors, respectively.

13. Indicate the factor matrix you might find if you factor-analyzed the two-factor matrix you generated in Question 12. Calculate the following for this matrix: communalities for all tests, eigen values, proportions of total variance accounted for, and the reconstructed correlation between the first and second test.

14. You have factor-analyzed six different tests and found three factors. Draw the factor matrix you would expect to find if there were pure measures for each factor.

15. You have collected a series of 50 cardboard boxes of all different sizes, from several intended to hold jewelry to the box in which your refrigerator arrived. You

then set about making all possible measurements of each box: length, height, the long diagonal, volume, weight, and so on, up to a total of 31 different measurements for each box. If you intercorrelated these 31 measurements and subjected them to factor analysis, how many factors would you obtain? What would they be? Explain.

16. Discuss the possible relationship between reliability and communality.

17. What would be your appraisal of a factor solution if you found that all the residuals were greater than .30 and negative?

18. Using the description of the Primary Mental Abilities given in Table 10-11, draw your own personal ability profile, based on your subjective estimates of the amounts of the various abilities you think you possess. (HINT: You might find it useful to use a score like the z score to represent your estimated performance.)

19. Looking at your answer to Question 18 and assuming that your univariate IQ was 120, which of these two approaches to intelligence seems the most useful to you? Why?

20. Draw a correlation matrix that would support Thurstone.

21. Which of the judgment calls outlined in the chapter appears to be the most important in terms of producing equivocal results in a factor analysis? Why?

22. Suggest several alternatives to Varimax as a means of placing axes to enhance the interpretability of factors.

23. Suggest three possible uses of factor analysis in disciplines other than psychology.

24. Would you have reservations about the MMPI if you learned that factor analysis of the ten clinical scales consistently produced two factor solutions that accounted for over 80% of the total variance? Why, or why not?

25. Discuss the importance of any omission you can note in the cognitive activities covered by the Wechsler scales.

26. Discuss the relative advantages and disadvantages of ratio versus deviation IQs.

27. Is the Wechsler series of IQ tests culture-fair? Why, or why not?

28. Discuss the possible psychological consequences of the technique of assessment in the Wechsler series that almost invariably ends with the respondent failing several of the items.

29. Indicate the factor matrix you would expect to obtain if you factor-analyzed the intercorrelations between the subtests of the WAIS–R (Table 10-14) if David Wechsler's contention of three different IQ scores was tenable.

30. Based on the materials presented in the chapter, suggest a less expensive alternative to the WISC series that would produce approximately equivalent information.

31. Indicate why or why not you would feel comfortable if your child's WISC score was used to make a decision about whether he or she should be admitted to a prestigious private school.

Chapter 11

New Developments
Content Validity, Internal Consistency, Item Analysis, and More

In This Chapter

ON INCREASED EMIC UNDERSTANDING

The last few chapters of *The Enterprise* have begun to show a change in narrative flow. The stories are taking on a different flavor, and the amount of propositional knowledge is clearly on the increase. As noted in Chapter 1, this was to be expected as we became more familiar with the in-group ideas and concepts of the testing field. We are becoming more emic in our understanding of the testing enterprise, and the shift in narrative flow is a result of this. Indeed, the amount of propositional knowledge in the enterprise was on the increase at this time, so finding increased propositional knowledge in the text is not unexpected.

We have retained, however, the narrative metaphor. The topics are being presented in chronological order, but there is a deeper level at which we are still being narrative—despite the increase in propositional content. Each topic is being presented in the context of a specific solution to a specific problem. For example, factor analysis was presented as a solution to the problem of "dismantling" intelligence. The problem addressed in these solutions is clearly located in the narrative that we are following. Thus, even though propositional content is increasing, it is still firmly embedded in the chronological sequence of events that occurred in the enterprise. In other words, it is still narrative.

The major gain of this approach emerges when we see that old solutions to old problems are offered as solutions to new problems. For example, factor analysis has been applied to the dismantling of personality (details are presented in Chapter 16). Having seen the original solution in action, we are in a strong position to examine the appropriateness of this new application. This allows us to ask questions such as "Is the new problem appropriate for enactment of this old solution?" and "What are the limitations of the old solution?" Being able to ask these kinds of questions is the major gain of the narrative approach.

Chapter 11 is perhaps the most propositional of the chapters so far. In it you will be introduced to a number of ideas that form the very heart of the measurement theory of the testing enterprise. All developments presented in this chapter were sired in a context that valued the use of empirical and objective evidence as a significant part of both the development and evaluation of psychological tests, and the solutions clearly reflect this. Yet all of them have flowed directly from developments that were documented earlier in the text. Here we see a number of interesting solutions to a number of problems relating to issues of access to information about tests, reliability, validity, utility, and the construction of the "best possible" tests.

ONWARD AND UPWARD

The psychological testing enterprise was rapidly growing by the late 1930s. With its high-status philosophy in hand, several applied successes, and numerous published tests being available, the foundations of the contemporary testing field had been laid. A significant compendium of published tests, the *Mental Measurements Yearbook (MMY)*, emerged during this time (Buros, 1938). This comprehensive listing of tests marked a critical development within the testing enterprise, representing the beginning of a thorough source of documentation that could be consulted to evaluate the usefulness of published instruments. In a sense, the publication of the *MMY* was the formalized beginning of the testing enterprise because its products were now being presented clearly and visibly within the reference sections of most university libraries.

THE FIRST *MENTAL MEASUREMENTS YEARBOOK*

Starting in 1933, **Oscar Buros** had published a yearly series of listings of available psychological tests. He was responding to the tremendous proliferation of tests during this time, noting the need for systematic cataloging of these new instruments as they became available. The lists were circulated yearly between 1933 and 1936 by Rutgers University as technical reports under the name *Educational, Psychological, and Personality Tests.* Responses to these lists was favorable, but the field wanted more:

> Since ninety out of every hundred tests published in the United States should be withdrawn because they have never been satisfactorily validated and standardized, Professor Buros's annual publication would be made much more useful if he would mark with a prominent star those which were valid, reliable, and had satisfactory norms. Then busy workers could neglect the rest, or if they wasted their money on "gold bricks," the fault would be their own. [Sandiford, 1938, p. 200]

In response to these concerns, Buros decided to institute a review policy along with the descriptions of tests that were part of the earlier series of publications—hence the emergence of the format of the *MMY.*

The label *mental measurements* was coined to represent the "generic term which includes the more specific terms such as aptitude, educational, intelligence, personality and psychological tests, questionnaires, and rating scales" (Buros, 1938, p. xiii). This indicates that the *MMY* was casting a very wide net indeed because a large number of different types of tests would fall under this definition.

A sense of the size of the testing enterprise in 1938 can be gathered from the observation that 868 different tests had been listed in the earlier technical reports, and an additional 211 were presented in Buros (1938), for a total of 1179 published psychological tests! For each of the tests listed in the *MMY* and the earlier reports, the following information was presented:

1. Title of the test
2. Description of the group for which the test was constructed
3. Date of copyright or publication
4. Individual or group test
5. Number and nature of forms
6. Cost
7. Time required to administer
8. Author(s)
9. Publisher
10. References regarding the construction, validation, and use of the test

Selected tests were also reviewed in Buros (1938), with frequent evaluative commentaries about the norms, validity, and reliability.

Besides the test listings, a total of 522 books on measurement, statistics, and research were listed (with some reviews) in the first edition of the *MMY.* The following appendixes were also included: (1) a list of periodicals cited in the references, (2) a directory of test publishers (along with their addresses), (3) an index of test titles, and (4) an index of persons cited in the book. These appendixes and book listings rounded out a very thorough and useful information package about the testing enterprise.

The 1938 *MMY* offered test consumers a tremendous amount of information. Now, assembled under one cover, the current state of the measurement arts could be accessed. The popularity of the MMY format remains today because this book has undergone ten revisions, with the latest being published in 1992. The following Close Up outlines the current state of these reference publications. This information will prove useful if you want to find information about a specific test.

CLOSE UP   **Information About Tests: The 1990s Version**

You want to find out something about a specific psychological test, or, as part of a project, you need a test to measure something that is integral to your research. Where do you look? What kind of information is available? How good is the test you eventually choose? These, and many more related queries, are the kinds of questions researchers and students frequently ask. In part, because of the efforts initiated by Buros in the mid-1930s, these are relatively easy research problems because a number of very useful resources are available. The needed information can be found in a variety of places in a university library. Of particular note are the *MMY*s, several speciality publications dedicated specifically to testing, manuals published with the tests, books of readings, textbooks in the field, the open psychology literature, and test users themselves. Most of this material should be available in your university library. The following outlines some of these sources of information.

The Mental Measurements Yearbook *series.* Buros (1938) was the editor of the first yearbooks. For the most part, the original format has been retained throughout the series. The second yearbook was published in 1940, followed by subsequent editions in the years 1949, 1953, 1959, 1965, 1972, 1978, 1985, 1989, and 1992. The seventh through ninth editions contain two volumes, with the ninth and tenth having supplements as well. The *MMY* is designed to help test users in education, industry, psychiatry, and psychology to locate and select standardized tests of all types. Bibliographies of tests published in English-speaking countries, critical test reviews, excerpts from reviews of tests, and references from the literature for specific tests are included.

The *Eleventh MMY* (Kramer & Conoley, 1992) lists 477 tests, with a total of 703 reviews (by 412 different authors). The indexes in this edition include (1) test titles, (2) classified subject index, (3) publisher directory, (4) index of authors (of tests and reviews), (5) abbreviations (for example, MMPI) because many tests are known by these and not their full titles, and (6) a score index, which is an alphabetic listing of the scores available for all the tests included in the edition.

It should be noted that the *MMY* is not, in the strictest sense, cumulative. That is, not every available test is included in the eleventh edition; the focus is on those that have been published or significantly revised since the tenth edition. This means that you have to have a rough idea of when a specific test or revision was published to be able to access reviews and the like. However, sometimes reviews do appear in editions subsequent to the initial one in which it was included, so a careful search of the various indexes of subsequent editions of the *MMY* can on occasion prove useful.

To help you use the *MMY*, Appendix C of this text presents a list of important psychological tests from the contemporary testing enterprise. It is organized using the categorization scheme presented in the *Eleventh MMY*. Publishers and their mailing addresses are included. A bonus of this listing is referral to the most contemporary *MMY* listing/review of each test in this appendix. This provides you with ready access to detailed information and reviews for a wide range of contemporary tests.

All of the materials in the *MMY* since the seventh edition (1972) are presently available as an on-line computer database. This means that you can access these materials using a computerized terminal via phone lines. Updated monthly, it is possible to interrogate the database using a wide variety of search terms. This can prove particularly helpful if the hard-copy version is not readily available.[1]

Tests in Print. The listing of published tests, without the evaluative commentaries, has been taken over by another series of reference books by the publisher of the *MMY*. These three volumes, **Tests in Print,** consists of descriptive listings and references, without reviews, of commercially published tests that are in print and available for purchase. It also serves as a comprehensive index to the contents of the *MMY*s published to date. *Tests in Print III* (Mitchell, 1983) includes entries for 2672 tests arranged alphabetically by test title.

Other speciality publications. Sweetland and Keyser (1983) have published a book that is a quick reference guide to over 3000 tests. The main sections—Psychology, Education, and Business—are divided into relevant subgroups. There are title, author, and subject indexes. This volume does not include bibliographies or information concerning the validity of the test and the like—it is simply a listing.

The series **Test Critiques** (Keyser & Sweetland, 1984) has been designed to supplement Sweetland and Keyser's (1983) listings. Here we find three volumes that provide scholarly, in-depth reviews of selected tests. Each review offers a short history of the test, practical applications, technical aspects, and a critique of the test. Bibliographic references are included at the end of each review.

The annual series, **Tests in Microfiche,** provides an annotated index of unpublished tests. Published by Educational Testing Service, it serves an important role in trying to discover newer tests or those that have not achieved publication in the major compendia.

Test manuals. **Test manuals** are another invaluable source of information. When available, these manuals provide extensive information about the test, which are absolutely necessary to evaluate and use a given test. (Considerable discussion of the standards and expectations for test manuals will be presented in Chapter 12.)

Books of readings. Often specific books are published that contain detailed reviews of specific tests. For example, Taulbee and Clark (1982) provide extensive reviews of the Short Form of the MMPI, plus several other tests. Newmark (1985) provides detailed information about the MMPI and Rorschach, among a number of other important tests. These books can sometimes be located through the library catalog.

Textbooks are another quite useful source of information. As you are already aware, all kinds of useful data are spotted throughout this text. In addition, some other texts may prove useful in providing general information about some specific tests not covered in *The Enterprise.* Included here are Aiken (1988); Anastasi (1988); Cohen, Montague, Nathanson, and Swerdlik (1988); Cronbach (1990); Gregory (1992); Kaplan and Saccuzzo (1989); Murphy and Davidshofer (1988); and Walsh and Betz (1990).

---

[1]For information about access and costs, contact your university library or BRS Databases, 8000 Westpark Dr., McLean, VA 22102, USA; (800)955–0906. The database has the title MMYD.

The open literature. Information about tests is often published in psychology and education journals. The most effective mechanism for accessing this information is **Psychological Abstracts,** which lists everything published in a given year within the discipline. A fairly elaborate system of cross-referencing makes it relatively easy to find articles on specific topics.

All issues of *Psychological Abstracts* dating from 1974 have been released on a computerized system called the **PsychInfo CD-ROM** (compact disc: read-only memory). If your library has this facility, you may sit at a terminal and interrogate *Psychological Abstracts*. It is a very efficient and helpful way to gain information about specific tests. Another useful database available in the CD-ROM format is called **ERIC (Educational Resource Information Catalog).** It contains many applications of various tests in educational situations.

Test users. Perhaps the most valuable—and hardest to find—information about tests can be gained by chatting with people who actually use a particular test in their day-to-day work. If you know of someone who works in a social service setting that employs tests, you may well have access to a font of knowledge that is virtually invaluable.

This Close Up has provided you with a short tour through some of the resource information that is presently available on psychological tests. In general, the information support in this domain is excellent. If you work your way through any of these materials, you will find out very quickly that the testing enterprise is indeed gigantic. There is no way anyone could gain a complete understanding of the entire field because of the tremendous amount of information that is available in these sources. Hopefully, this Close Up will give you enough information to allow you to approach, as efficiently as possible, any test-related research you may have to do. Through the miracle of modern technology and the hard work of many editors and librarians, it is indeed astounding that you can find your way around this incredibly large field with a minimum of difficulty.

With the publication of the *MMY* and tests such as the MMPI and Strong entering the market and providing useful adjuncts to the solution of some important social needs, the theory underlying the assessment enterprise was also changing. The basic idea of reliability was undergoing significant revision, validity was undergoing some major changes with the postulation of a number of different "types," the notion of utility was being embellished, and technologies associated with the empirical analysis and selection of items were advancing. An examination of these changes provides a particularly interesting perspective on the manner in which the enterprise was beginning to take on its modern shape.

INTERNAL CONSISTENCY: NEW DEVELOPMENTS IN ESTIMATING RELIABILITY

As the operational doctrine was being established in the testing area, the pursuit of solutions to some of the problems confronting the test developers was continuing.

One of these involved the traditional notion of reliability, which demanded some revision in order to be applicable to certain types of variables.

Test/retest and parallel-form reliabilities had been well established (see Chapters 6 and 8), but there were still some problems. This became particularly evident with tests of characteristics that were supposed to change over time. For example, how would it be possible to assess the reliability of a measure of happiness? Test/retest estimates are useless for two reasons: (1) Memory is a contaminating factor, and (2) it is entirely possible that respondents' status on the variable could change between testings—for example, happiness is expected to show relatively short-term variability. A test/retest reliability coefficient for such a test would treat the valid variability associated with real change as error! This second problem also applies to parallel-form reliability. In other words, measures demanding two administrations of an instrument are not appropriate to establish the reliability of measures of variables that are expected to show variation. Characteristics like happiness, which change as a function of the passage of time, are called **ephemeral variables.**

Split-Half Reliability

The solution to this problem emerged by suggesting that it might be possible to gain an estimate of reliability from one administration of a test. For example, it is possible to develop two **half scores,** one based on the first half of the test and another on the second half of the test. The correlation between these two half scores would be technically the same as parallel-form reliability with virtually no interval between testings. This became known as **split-half reliability,** which soon became an important part of establishing the reliability of measures of ephemeral characteristics. Now the issues of time between testings was no longer a problem, and reliability could be estimated easily and efficiently. In effect, split-half reliability is the functional equivalent of the parallel-form approach with no time interval between the two forms. This observation also demands that the two half tests be, in effect, parallel.

One problem, however, emerged here. Each of the half scores would be based on one-half the number of items of the total scale. As the number of items decreases, so too does the reliability of the scale. Thus, the split-half reliability estimate is actually an underestimate of the test's reliability. Several corrections were offered for this, with the most popular known as the **Spearman–Brown Formula:**

$$R_{xx} = \frac{2r_{xx}}{1 + r_{xx}} \tag{11-1}$$

where

R_{xx} = the corrected split-half reliability estimate

r_{xx} = the obtained split-half correlation

For example, let's assume we have a test with 40 items. Each half score is then based on 20 items. If the obtained split-half correlation between the two scores is

.82, applying Equation 11-1 reveals that this correlation would be .90 [(2 × .82)/(1 + .82) = 1.64/1.82 = .90)] if it were possible to generate half scores based on the same number of items making up the original score.

Odd/Even Reliability

One disadvantage of the split half is that it produces a poor estimate if performance is expected to change as the test is being administered. For example, if respondents tend to tire as they work through the test, the second half score will be more greatly affected; hence, the split half would produce a less-than-perfect value. A simple way around this is to use the odd-numbered items to generate one half score and the even-numbered items for the other. The correlation between the two half scores generated in this way is called the **odd/even reliability** estimate. This index is more appropriate for scales in which fatigue or interference play a part. Such performance deficits would be approximately equal across the pairs of items making up the two half tests. Like the split-half reliability, though, it is necessary to correct the estimate using the Spearman-Brown Formula or some equivalent.

Other half-score reliabilities. As you might expect, there are many different ways in which half scores could be generated to develop various indexes of this general type of **half-score reliability estimate.** For example, it is possible to create the half scores by selecting items of equal difficulty or popularity, basing this classification on respondents' performance levels on the items. This would produce roughly parallel forms for the half scores. Assigning alternate blocks of items to create the half scores is also possible, as is random assignment of items to the half scores. Thus, a wide variety of specific indexes could be used here. The decision about which one to use should be dictated by careful attention to the exact nature of the measurement problem being addressed, recognizing that whatever method is used has both strengths and weaknesses.

Measures of Internal Consistency

The ultimate in reliability based on one administration of a test emerged in 1937 with the introduction of a method for estimating the average of all possible half-score reliabilities of a test. Although it is possible to arrange test items into every conceivable configuration to provide the maximal number of half scores and then to calculate the average correlations between these, Kuder and Richardson (1937) derived a way of estimating this average directly from the response data. In their original article, Kuder and Richardson numbered the formulas they used in proving their derivation. The 20th formula in this paper was the one that proved most useful for data that were answered in a dichotomous format. Because of this, the estimate of **internal consistency** has become known as **Kuder–Richardson Formula 20**—shortened to **KR20.** The mathematical way of calculating the KR20 is presented in Equation 11-2:

$$KR20 = \left[\frac{n}{n-1} \right] \left[\frac{SD^2 - \Sigma pq}{SD^2} \right] \qquad (11\text{-}2)$$

where

KR20 = Kuder–Richardson Formula 20 measure of internal
consistency

n = number of items

SD = the standard deviation of the test scores

p = proportion of respondents who got an item correct

q = $1 - p$, the proportion who got the item wrong

Σpq = sum of the products of p and q over items

As can be seen from Equation 11-2, all researchers have to know is the standard deviation of the test scores, the number of items in the test, and the proportion correct for each separate item in order to calculate the KR20. In cases of personality items answered true or false, the proportion responding true to an item becomes p.

Table 11-1 presents an example of the manner in which the KR20 is calculated for a 22-item test. For this test, which is actually a course quiz, the mean score was 16.1, and the standard deviation was 3.5. The number produced by this procedure varies between 0 and 1, with higher values indicating greater internal consistency or reliability. That is, in the example, the average of all possible half-score correlations is .75. The data shown in Table 11-1, then, has moderate internal consistency. The KR20 is considered to be the ultimate in measures of internal consistency, which is the most appropriate estimate of reliability of ephemeral variables.

Cronbach (1951) introduced a variant of the KR20 that was intended to be used when items were answered in formats with more than two alternatives. The most popular version of a multiple alternative style is called the **Likert format,** where respondents indicate their reactions to items on a numbered scale such as the following:

Strongly Disagree	*Disagree*	*Neutral*	*Agree*	*Strongly Agree*
1	2	3	4	5

In this situation, Cronbach's **Coefficient Alpha** is used as a measure of internal consistency. We can calculate the standard deviation of responses separately for each item in such cases because each item has a range of possible values. These item-specific standard deviations (squared) replace the p and q in Equation 11-2 to give alpha (α).[2] Thus, the formula becomes

$$\alpha = \left[\frac{n}{n-1} \right] \left[\frac{SD^2 - \Sigma \text{var}(i)}{SD^2} \right] \qquad (11\text{-}3)$$

where

α = Cronbach's Coefficient Alpha

n = number of items

---

[2]In the dichotomous case, $p \times q$ is the standard deviation.

Table 11-1 Calculating the KR20 for a 22-item test

Item	p	q	$p \times q$
1	.65	.35	.23
2	.98	.02	.02
3	.69	.31	.21
4	.88	.12	.11
5	.50	.50	.25
6	.98	.02	.02
7	.68	.32	.22
8	.94	.06	.06
9	.79	.21	.17
10	.75	.25	.19
11	.51	.49	.25
12	.23	.77	.18
13	.95	.05	.05
14	.65	.35	.23
15	.59	.41	.24
16	.76	.24	.18
17	.97	.03	.03
18	.45	.55	.25
19	.93	.07	.07
20	.66	.34	.22
21	.87	.13	.11
22	.55	.45	.25
Total			3.54

Mean = 16.1, standard deviation = 3.5, variance = $3.5 \times 3.5 = 12.25$

From Equation 11-2:

$$KR_{20} = \frac{22}{21} \times \frac{(12.25 - 3.54)}{12.25} = 1.05 \times \frac{8.71}{12.25} = 1.05 \times .71 = .75$$

SD = the standard deviation of the test scores

$\Sigma \text{var}(i)$ = sum of the separate variances for each item

Like the KR20, this formula produces numbers that range between 0 and 1, with higher numbers indicating greater degrees of internal consistency.

CLOSE UP   **Speed Kills: Difficulties in Estimating the Reliability of Speed Tests**

A pure **speed test** is one in which the final score depends entirely on how fast the respondent works. Such tests typically consist of relatively easy items, within the ability range of the test taker, and a time limit is set such that no one can finish all items. A test that required individuals to solve as many addition problems as they can in 5 minutes would be an example of a speed test. The existence of a time limit

A time limit is a clue that a test is speeded, but the important issue is the extent to which test performance depends on speed.

for a test is a hint that the test is speeded, but this does not guarantee that it is. For example, if the time limit was exceedingly liberal, allowing everyone to attempt all items, it would not be a speed test. The important point is the extent to which performance in the test is dictated by speed of work.

Pure speed tests contrast with pure **power tests,** which permit adequate time for the respondents to attempt all items. Power tests typically contain some items that are exceedingly difficult, under the expectation that very few, if any, respondents will get perfect scores. Administering the Raven Progressive Matrices (see Chapter 10) without a time limit (as is recommended in the manual) would be an example of a pure power test.

In practice, the distinction between speed and power is one of degree, with performance being dictated by both attributes. For example, the Block Design items on the WISC have time limits, and they contain some very difficult items toward the end; thus, there are elements of both speed and power involved in performance on this subtest. The eventual scale score on this subtest results from a combination of variability attributable to speed *and* power. Such mixed power/speed tests are relatively frequent in the objective/testing domain. Unfortunately, estimating the amount of variability attributable to speed or power on mixed tests is difficult because respondents sometimes adopt differing strategies while answering the questions. Known in cognitive psychology as the **speed/accuracy trade-off,** adopting a strategy of working fast can cause more errors, whereas working carefully can result in attempting fewer items but requiring more time in a mixed context. Of course, the amount that speed or power effects the final score will be dictated in large measure by the strategy adopted by the test taker. Thus, the issue of speed versus power tests presents a number of complexities to the test maker.

However, the real difficulty with speed tests emerges when we want to estimate their reliability. Estimates of reliability based on one test administration (for example, odd/even, split-half, KR20) are inapplicable to speed tests because they produce spurious values. The clearest example is odd/even reliability. If a person scores 76 on a 100-item pure speed test, the odd-numbered half score will be 38, as will the even-numbered half score, because the respondent will receive credit for the first 76 items on the test. A person who scores 88 will obtain 44 on both halves and so on. If this is repeated over a number of different individuals, the odd/even correlation will be +1.00—inordinately high and not reflective of the actual reliability of the test. If, on the other hand, the split-half correlation is used, the first half score will be exceedingly high, whereas the second half score will be much lower because many more items in the second half of the test would not have been attempted. The split-half correlation will spuriously reflect this aspect of performance and be indeterminant as an estimate of reliability. The more general measures of internal consistency such as KR20 are equally unmeaningful in the pure speed test.

Even in the case of mixed speed/power tests, these one-administration estimates of reliability are problematic. Although the odd/even estimate would drop below +1.00 in this situation, it would still be inordinately high in proportion to the amount of variability in the scores due to speed. Similar arguments render the other single-administration approaches to reliability of mixed tests uninterpretable.

In some cases, estimates of reliability based on two test administrations (for example, test/retest and parallel forms) are appropriate for speed tests. If, for example, memory for previous performance is not an issue (as in the addition test described above or the Coding subtest of the WISC), the use of test/retest methods is justifiable; parallel forms could also be useful if they were available. However, if the first administration has effects that carry over to the second administration, this family of reliability estimates proves problematic. For example, the first time a child takes the Block Design subtest of the WISC, a significant element of performance is figuring out that the blocks with diagonal lines can be used to construct the oblique aspects of the design. This insight, gained at some expense of time during the first administration, will be more readily enacted on the second administration, thereby adding spurious variability to the reliability estimate based on two administrations. Hence, there are some situations in which it appears that neither the one- nor the two-administration versions of reliability estimation can be used.

There is a solution, though, in the case of highly speeded tests. Here it is possible to use **separately timed half scores**. For example, you can administer half tests, each with its own time limit. The performance on each half is tabulated, and the correlation between the two scores is calculated. Each half score reflects the speeded performance adequately, and this estimate is not artificially affected. Like the more traditional split-half estimates, the correlation between the two half scores would have to be adjusted to take into account the fact that the half scores are based on fewer items (see Equation 11-1).

Data from an updated version of the Primary Mental Abilities can be used to demonstrate the differences between reliabilities based on odd/even and separately timed half scores (Anastasi & Drake, 1954). On four subtests, the odd/even reliability estimates were .94, .96, .90, and .92. Split-half reliabilities based on separately timed half scores were .90, .87, .75, and .83, respectively, indicating the extent to which the inappropriate use of the odd/even estimate inflates reliability estimates. Notice that the drops in reliability estimates in these data are *not* the same for each of the four subtests. This reflects the differential amount of speed involved in the subtests, with the third test involving speed to the greatest extent because of the greater difference between the two reliability estimates. The difference between these two reliability estimates can be used to index the degree of speed involved in test performance.

In summary, the estimation of reliability for speed tests is complex. Particularly in light of the observation that most objective tests are a mix between speed and power, developing an appropriate method of reliability estimation is difficult. For the student, at this point, the major lesson is to pay very close attention to the manner in which reliability coefficients reported in the literature have been calculated. In more than one case, finding odd/even reliabilities inappropriately reported for partially speeded tests will be possible. Careful evaluation of methodology is the watchword when evaluating the reliability of psychological tests, particularly if there is a speed component involved.

The family of estimates of internal consistency such as the split half and KR20 provided an important new methodology for the testing enterprise. The advantages of these techniques were many, including the following:

1. They solved the problem of estimating reliability for ephemeral characteristics because a given test need be administered only once.

2. They introduced a relatively cost-effective and convenient way of estimating reliability because of the single test administration that was required.

3. They eliminated the need to deal with the problem of the optimal amount of time between testing that was a continual difficulty with the two test–administration approaches.

4. They helped reduce the memory confounds on test performance associated with the test/retest and parallel-form approaches because the estimate was based on only one administration of the test.

In all, this new orientation toward reliability was a definite step forward for the testing enterprise.

It is worth noting that there is a relationship between factor analysis and internal consistency. If the matrix of intercorrelations between the items of an internally consistent scale is factor-analyzed, the result will be one large first factor, plus a number of other small ones. This follows when we realize that internal consistency demands that the item intercorrelations must be high. If they are not high, all internal consistency measures will be low. Thus, factor analysis of items from an internally consistent scale will have to lead to one large factor.

The internal consistency, or one test–administration, approaches to reliability still have some problems, rendering them inappropriate for some situations:

1. These indexes of reliability have great limitations when applied to speed tests.

2. Because they are based on one testing session, these estimates of internal consistency tend to consider such transient effects as level of motivation, mood, luck in guessing, and so on, as part of the reliable, or nonerror, variability, producing slightly inflated estimates if these are relevant considerations.

3. The introduction of measures of internal consistency began to create some confusion about the differences between reliability and validity. For a test to demonstrate high internal consistency, virtually all items on the test must be measuring the same thing. It is fairly easy to lapse into thinking about this as an aspect of a test's validity, rather than reliability.

Despite these limitations, this approach to reliability began to gain considerable favor.

Figure 11-1 shows the manner in which the means of estimating reliability had been developed when Kuder and Richardson published their measure of internal consistency.

The emergence of this relatively complex set of methods of estimating reliability, each with its strengths and weaknesses, signals the need to be very careful

Figure 11-1 Estimates of reliability incorporating the newer ideas of internal consistency.

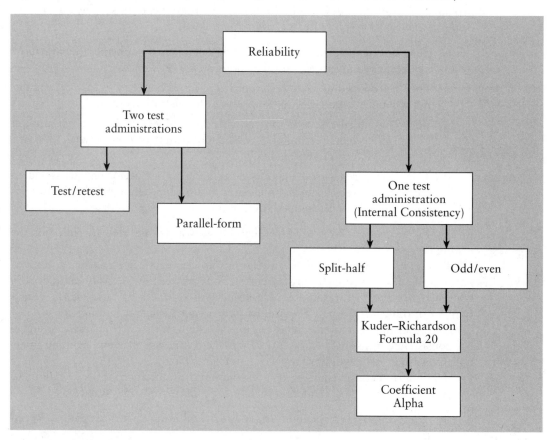

about the method employed in a specific situation. There is no single, universal way of determining reliability—the choice of method has to be dictated by the goals of the exercise. The generic idea of reliability as the error-free component of a test score remains, but the numerous methods of empirical estimation show considerable variation.

CLOSE UP | **Enhancing Reliability**

Reliability is clearly a highly desirable characteristic for measures that will be used to make important social decisions. After all, we cannot direct someone's future using error variance. An understanding of reliability, along with a good dose of common sense, generates several suggestions that will produce measures showing a greater chance of being reliable in the long run. Some of these considerations are presented below to give you a sense of some of the controllable factors that can be used to enhance the chances of decent reliability.

Increasing the number of observations. As indicated above, reliability increases as the number of items making up a test increases (see Equation 11-1). It follows, then, that numerous replications of your observations are best if reliability is a concern. This could entail increasing the number of items within a test or administering several tests and generating a composite score based on these. However, many measurement contexts are constrained by time available, and often the number of observations possible is less than optimal because of this. As well, long testing sessions demanded by a large number of items sometimes lead to respondents withdrawing full cooperation and effort. The gains in reliability of including many items have to be weighed against the possible losses in respondent cooperation and the impact these might have on validity and utility.

Practicing good administration. The fundamental idea of standardization is to ensure that all respondents are treated in exactly the same way so that variability in tests scores can be attributed to individual differences. Anything interfering with this "first principle of test administration" will lead to unreliability. It follows, then, that careful attention to the details of administration will produce more reliable measures. Included here are the following:

1. With speed tests, timing should be as precise as available technology allows.
2. Lighting, ventilation, and physical comfort should be optimal and consistent across all administrations.
3. Instructions should be clearly communicated to respondents.
4. Details of the actual administration procedures, as indicated in the test manual, should be consistently followed.

These are just several of the important considerations of test administration that can help produce more reliable measures.

Scoring carefully. The mechanical procedures of scoring tests are often boring and uninteresting. Yet any slip up with these procedures can add a significant degree of unreliability to the eventual test score. The scoring procedures presented in the test manual should be followed consistently and carefully. Considerable care should be exercised when referring to norm tables and/or transforming the raw score to a standardized score. Frequent checks to ensure that all computations are accurate are recommended.

Using better items. Confusing, incoherent, and convoluted items will produce error in the eventual test score because responses will be dictated by any number of factors—some of which will undoubtedly contribute to unreliability. Hence, items should minimize incoherence. Avoid using the following item characteristics as much as possible:

1. Double-barreled items (for example, "I am sometimes lonely and anxious") are problematic because different respondents are likely to respond to different aspects of the item, thus compromising the reliability of the answer.
2. Negations ("I never feel I don't like not going downtown") cause processing errors that can contribute to unreliability.
3. Item content unknown to the respondent ("I am a xenoglossopheliac") will produce fundamentally random guesses and thereby create unreliability.
4. Complex grammatical structure reflected in convoluted sentence structures, use of the passive voice, exceedingly long items, and so on can cause processing errors.
5. Mixed-response formats within a set of questions can cause transformation and processing errors that will add to unreliability.

When using a published test, you do not have any control over the quality of the items so this may seem like less-than-useful advice. However, you do have control over the decision to use the test in the first place. If reliability is a concern, an examination of the items, looking for the kinds of attributes outlined above, can help select tests with better potential reliability. However, consideration of the published validity and reliability figures should enter foremost into this decision. Of course, if you are in a situation of creating your own test, it is readily possible to create items that show optimal chances of producing reliable test scores.

There is an extensive technology of item selection. using a number of useful statistical techniques to cull a larger set of items to choose the best ones. The final section of this chapter discusses some of these methods. In combination with the common sense presented in this Close Up, these empirical item-evaluation techniques provide considerable wisdom regarding the manner in which it is possible to develop tests with optimal reliability.

CONTENT VALIDITY: A NEW IDEA

Developments in the testing enterprise during the 1930s were not restricted to reliability. The notion of validity received significant elaboration during this time as well. Thus far, consideration of validity has been restricted to criterion-related methodologies. Here the validity of a test varies directly with the size of the correlation between a test score and a relevant criterion. If the criterion relates to future performance, this type of validity is called *predictive validity*. If the criterion relates to an individual's current status (at the time of testing), then this is called *concurrent validity*.

Another strand of our story has also been unfolding during this time. As indicated earlier, one of the historical antecedents of psychological testing was the university examination. To differentiate these kinds of tests from the others discussed so far, they will be called **achievement tests,** which focus on assessing how much of a subject a person knows at the time of testing. Such tests are used to make decisions about whether respondents should be given credit for having mastered a given amount of material. In addition, achievement tests are sometimes used to decide whether students should be admitted to the next level of an educational system.

As you might expect, the criteria of goodness of measurements emerging in the psychological testing area were soon applied to this kind of situation. The notions of reliability and validity have clear relevance to decisions about the fairness, usefulness, and accuracy of achievement tests. For example, tests of low reliability should not be used to make important social decisions such as admission to college.

One important test characteristic in achievement tests, however, was not addressed by the notions of validity and reliability. A test could be valid as an achievement test (for example, predict performance in the next year of school) and highly reliable but nonrepresentative of the content that was supposed to be mastered. In other words, it might be possible to develop reliable and valid achievement tests that did not fully cover all the material that was supposed to be mastered—hence, the test would not be fair. Some manner of establishing whether an achievement test actually covered all relevant material was needed.

An example of a test that fails to be representative would be a final examination for this course that was based on only the material covered in Chapter 3. Most of you would be quite upset with such an exam—with justification. You would consider that the test was unjust because it failed to represent all the material you had been asked to master. You probably also would not be particularly impressed with an argument that the test was reliable and valid. The unfairness of the test, by its failure to represent the entire domain of knowledge, would remain, even in the face of evidence of predictive validity and reliability. Some kind of reminder of the need for representativeness is necessary to ensure proper coverage of the relevant domain.

A technical term for this type of representativeness emerged as **content validity** in the 1930s (Long & Sandiford, 1935; Odell, 1930).[3] Content validity is the degree to which the test items reflect the entirety of content to which the test will be generalized. In the case of the final exam in a university course, the test would have content validity to the extent that each item of the assigned curriculum had an equal opportunity of appearing on the exam. In this case, the representativeness of the material on the exam would be adequate.

Providing a simple index of a test's content validity is a bit difficult. Unlike its criterion-related cousins, which can be represented as a correlation, content validity cannot be expressed as a single number. Rather, a detailed discussion of the manner in which the items were selected and an assessment of the extent to which they represent the totality of the relevant content are required.

---

[3]When originally introduced, this idea was called **curricular validity,** indicating its genesis in the educational field. However, in later years, it was renamed *content validity* and was applied to other domains. To reduce confusion, the newer name will be used throughout.

The first order of business in establishing content validity is to fully describe the domain under consideration. This should be done prior to the development of the test. For example, to establish the content validity of an examination for this chapter of *The Enterprise*, listing all aspects of the content of the chapter that should be mastered would be necessary. The "Glossary" at the end of the chapter provides a beginning for this, as do the "Discussion Questions." However, numerous other aspects would also have to be included, such as degree of understanding the implications of the content and the ability to solve specific puzzles involving the ideas. Once the complete chapter has been documented in this manner, we have defined the **content universe,** which represents all curriculum that should be mastered.

The evaluation of the content validity of an examination of this material involves determination of whether the examination fairly represents the content universe. The simplest method of proceeding here is to randomly sample from the universe, such that each element in it has an equal opportunity of appearing on the test. If this can be demonstrated, strong evidence for the content validity of the examination has been provided. This is not a trivial exercise in terms of the time required. The specification of a content universe is very time-consuming, requiring a considerable amount of detailed and painstaking work (for an explicit example of this, see Chapter 17).

The determination of content validity involves a careful evaluation of the manner in which the test was developed. For published tests, this information should be available in the test manual, and, if it is not, the content validity of the test should be queried. Information about the content areas involved, the skills needed, the instructional objectives covered in the test, and a clear indication of how the items in the test relate to these constitute minimum expectations if content validity is to be demonstrated (see Chapter 17 for an example). In many published achievement tests, experts in the curriculum involved help define the content universe and function as item writers. The test manual should clearly indicate the qualifications of such experts so that the test user can evaluate their appropriateness for the intended use of the test.

Several cautions should be considered in the evaluation of content validity. Sometimes we can get fooled into overgeneralizing the domain to which our test applies. For example, performance on a test that asks respondents to recognize whether words are spelled correctly can easily be interpreted as an index of spelling mastery. However, this test is actually mute about whether respondents can *produce* correctly spelled words. Overgeneralization of the content of the test to include production could lead to incorrect statements about a student's spelling mastery. It is important, then, to pay careful attention to the exact content universe and the manner in which it is tested in assessing content validity. As well, factors can turn up in tests that are irrelevant to the content universe. For example, test items that require extensive intelligence to understand may not be appropriate to a measure of the mastery of a specific curriculum unit.

Because content validity evolved from the achievement-test domain, it is appropriate, at this point, to consider some of the developments in this field. The following Close Up presents one of the best examples of an achievement test, which was started during the 1930s—the Metropolitan Achievement Test.

The Metropolitan Achievement Test

The Metropolitan Achievement Test (MAT) was first published in the early 1930s and has undergone considerable revision since then. As you might expect, periodic revision is necessary for tests of this type because the curricula they represent change continually. The most recent revision was in 1978, with an extensive renorming project reported in 1985. The current version of the MAT consists of eight batteries of tests that extend, with considerable overlap, from kindergarten to grade 12. For example, the Elementary Level, which spans grades 3.5–4.9, is made up of the following tests:

Reading
    Vocabulary
    Word Recognition Skills
    Reading Comprehension
Mathematics
    Concepts (numeration, geometry, and the like)
    Problem Solving
    Computation
Science
Social Studies

Five scores are provided (Reading, Mathematics, Language, Science, and Social Studies), which offer the teacher comparative information about the student's level of performance. There is also a Research Skills score based on material

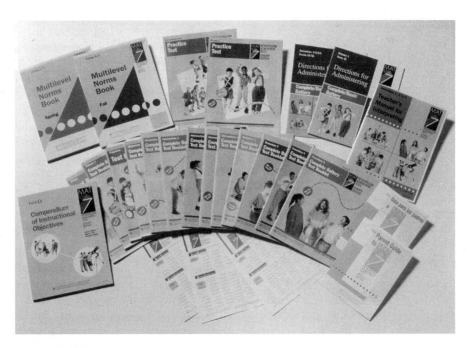

Test materials for the MAT.

in all ten of the subtests. Several types of scores are computed (for example, percentile ranks and grade equivalents), and norms for both fall and spring administrations are available. All eight batteries have parallel forms. The standardization sample was revised in 1985, consisting of 250,000 million students sampled in a highly systematic and representative manner.

This particular test is very time-consuming, requiring eight different sittings varying from 35 to 50 minutes each. The KR20s for the battery are most impressive with a figure of .98 reported for the Elementary version and others generally in the .90s.

Content validity was established by examining current textbooks and other curricular sources to develop sets of instructional objectives for each subject and level. Items were then constructed and tested on a national sample, with continual concern that the identified objectives were properly represented throughout all batteries. In keeping with contemporary concerns in the assessment field, the more recent revisions have also been reviewed by a panel of minority educators to identify any possible gender or cultural biases that might have crept into the test.

The MAT is a fine example of the manner in which standardized achievement testing has evolved over the years. The notion of content validity is perhaps the most important with tests such as these. In the 1930s, the conventional wisdom was that content validity should be restricted to the domain of achievement tests. There was concern that the use of this evaluative criterion with voluntary tests such as personality inventories would serve to sanction the use of a priori or nonempirical strategies, a move that would be interpreted as retrogressive.

By the late 1930s then, the generic notion of validity as the extent to which a test measures what it purports to measure had been elaborated into two basic variations: criterion-related and content. Not unlike reliability, the idea of validity was receiving elaboration and development as the testing enterprise evolved. Figure 11-2 shows this developmental sequence. When combined with the complex and evolving structure of reliability (see Figure 11-1), the evolving schemata for evaluating the goodness of tests were showing significant elaboration and growth—a true sign of progress. However, one piece in the puzzle was yet to fall into place, and we discuss this next.

THE TAYLOR–RUSSELL TABLES: BEYOND RELIABILITY AND VALIDITY

The developments in both reliability and validity documented in this chapter are testimony to the rapid and complex development of the testing enterprise during the 1930s. Clearly, the more reliable and valid the test, the better it is. Efforts oriented toward maximizing these characteristics of tests were well worth the investment because social decision makers would have increased confidence in the decisions they made. Yet, the entire story regarding the effectiveness of tests has yet

Figure 11-2 The structure of validity around 1938.

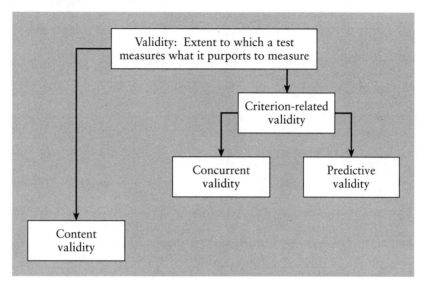

to be told. In the late 1930s, a somewhat different approach to examining tests, as they are used in specific situations, began to emerge. We now turn our attention to this way of thinking about tests.

It is not automatic that a highly reliable and valid test will provide useful information for making social decisions. For example, let's assume an employer wants to use a test to select employees. No matter how reliable or valid a test is, if there are only as many applicants as there are available positions, the test will not make a meaningful contribution to the hiring decision. Indeed, using the test will have negative impact because the money used to develop, administer, score, and interpret the test would have been wasted because everyone who applied would be hired. Thus, something other than reliability and validity needs to be involved in deciding if a test is useful.

Another concern being voiced at the time was that the efficiency of tests in making actual decisions was not particularly good, given that test-criterion correlations tended to hover in the range of .20–.50. This follows when we realize that the effectiveness of a test in predicting a criterion falls off rather sharply, in fact geometrically, as the validity coefficient dips below 1. According to the standard means of estimating efficiency available at the time (for example, the **index of forecasting efficiency;** Kelley, 1923), a validity coefficient of .50 would predict only 13% better than chance (for details, see Taylor & Russell, 1939, p. 565). A validity coefficient of .20 would predict but 2% better than chance. This prompted "considerable pessimism with regard to the validity coefficients which are ordinarily available when tests are tried out in the employment office of a business or industry or in an educational institution" (Taylor & Russell, 1939, p. 566).

In an influential paper, H. C. Taylor and J. C. Russell (1939), who were employees of the Western Electric Company, offered an interesting set of arguments that would set the tone for the explicit consideration of the usefulness of a test for predicting criterion status. Here concern was with the number of correct predictions a test would make, rather than some abstract measure of effectiveness based on the correlation coefficient. For purposes of presenting their ideas, let's assume that we have an employee-screening test that has been validated on a performance rating of how satisfactory a selected worker has been after 6 months on the job. We are interested in the implications of using this test to select a second set of job applicants to optimize the numbers who would perform satisfactorily. Taylor and Russell (1939) started out by presenting a scatter plot of the test and criterion data, where each point represents one individual in the original sample of employees for whom both test and criterion information was available. The scatter plot was then divided into four segments by introducing criterion- and test-score cutoff lines, as shown in Figure 11-3.

All persons who score above the criterion cutoff (those in areas A and D, designated as A + D) were deemed to perform satisfactorily on the job, whereas those below this line (C + B) were not. Although Taylor and Russell did not use this term, this has since been labeled **base rate,** defined as the proportion of unselected individuals who fall in a specific category of a criterion group. In the example presented in Figure 11-3, base rate for satisfactory performance is calculated as $(A + D)/(A + B + C + D)$.

A second consideration, shown in Figure 11-3, is the test-score cutoff. The position of this line will be dictated by the employment situation. If there were twice as many applicants as vacancies, this line would be placed at the median of the test score, with persons scoring above the median being selected. The location of the line, then, is a function of the proportion of vacancies to the number of applicants, which is called the **selection ratio.** In Figure 11-3, all individuals below (to the left of) the test-score cutoff line (C + D) are rejected, whereas those above the line (A + B) are selected. The selection ratio is calculated as $(A + B)/(A + B + C + D)$ representing the proportion of applicants who are selected. The sum of all four quadrants $(A + B + C + D)$ equals the total number of applicants, whereas A + B represents the number who were chosen.

The best-case scenario would be if all cases fell in areas A and C. In this situation, there would be absolutely no prediction errors, and the test would be exceedingly useful. However, as the number of cases falling in areas B and D increases, the usefulness of the test begins to taper off. Taylor and Russell's (1939) concern was the relationship between the test-criterion validity coefficient and the number of prediction errors.

Taylor and Russell argued that A/(A + B) was a good indicator of the effectiveness of a test. This is the proportion of selected employees who would perform satisfactorily if the test were used on a second sample of applicants with the test-score cutoff enacted. Individuals falling in area B of Figure 11-3 would be those who were selected on the basis of the test but who subsequently attained an unsatisfactory criterion score—in other words, area B contains the selection errors. If the test were perfect, no cases would fall in area B. In this perfect case, A/(A + B) would equal 1.00 [A/(A + B) = A/(A + 0) = A/A = 1.00], indicating that no selection errors had occurred. Taylor and Russell's statistic A/(A + B) represents the **proportion of**

Figure 11-3 A scatter plot representing various prediction zones for a typical test-criterion relationship.

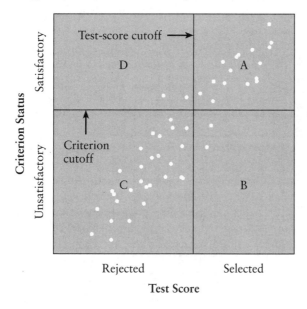

correct predictions that would be made if the test was used to select employees with values approaching 1.00 being most desirable.

However, perfection is seldom the case in real-life applications. Taylor and Russell noted that as the number of cases in areas A and D increases, the value of the statistic A/(A + B) would decrease. For Taylor and Russell, the concern was the effect that the size of the validity coefficient had on the numbers of selected individuals who would be classified correctly. In other words, they wanted to know the nature of the relationship between A/(A + B) and the validity coefficient.

Here is an example of how they addressed this concern. Let us assume that half of the present employee group is considered satisfactory [(A + D)/(A + B + C + D) = base rate for satisfactory performance = .50]. The criterion cutoff would be placed at the median in this case, as Figure 11-4 (page 386) shows. Further assume that we have 334 applicants for 100 positions, thus making the selection ratio .30 (100/334 = .30). We would locate the test-score cutoff such that 30% of the cases fall above (to the right of) it. Now let's assume that the validity coefficient for our test predicting the criterion is .50. Under these conditions, it turns out that 74 cases *must* fall in area A. The distribution of applicants in all four quadrants in this specific situation (*n* = 334; base rate = .50; selection ratio = .3; test validity = .50) is shown in Figure 11-4. This must be the distribution of cases if the conditions of this specific example are true. In this specific situation, the proportion of correct predictions would be .74 [74/(74 + 26) = 74/100 = .74]. That is, if we used the test, we would be correct 74% of the time.

If the validity coefficient was 0, the number of correct predictions would be at a chance level—the equivalent of rolling dice. That is, 50 of the 100 selected

Figure 11-4 A scatter plot representing a test-criterion correlation of .50, with a selection ratio of .3, in which 50% of the employees are considered satisfactory.

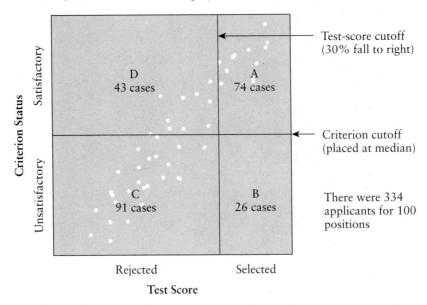

candidates would perform satisfactorily. It follows that the lowest proportion of correct predictions (in this case) would be .50 [50/(50 + 50) = 50/100 = .50]. In the best-case scenario of a perfect test, 100% of the predictions would be correct making the proportion of correct predictions equal to 1.00. Thus, the proportion correct can, in this case, vary between .50 and 1.00, with the size of the value being dictated by the size of the validity coefficient. In our specific case, the value was found to be .74.

Taylor and Russell (1939) were able to demonstrate the interrelationships between base rate, selection ratio, proportion of correct predictions, and validity coefficient. For example, Figure 11-5 shows what happens to the proportion of correct predictions as a function of the selection ratio for our example (base rate = .50; validity coefficient = .50). The point on this graph directly above .30 is the exact example outlined in Figure 11-4 (proportion of correct predictions = .74). As can be seen, the proportion correct is maximal when the selection ratio is very low. The highest proportions of correct predictions occur when very few of the best candidates are selected. If it were possible to select the best one out of ten (selection ratio = .10), the proportion satisfactory becomes .84. Using the test in this situation would result in being right with 84% of our predictions! This is a far cry from the pessimistic comments about 13% predictive accuracy that were in circulation when Taylor and Russell published their tables.

Taylor and Russell (1939) presented a series of tables that show the proportion of correct predictions for all possible combinations of (1) validity coefficients from .00 to 1.00 (in steps of .05), (2) selection ratio from .05 to .95, and (3) base rate from .05 to .95. Figure 11-6, which shows the proportion of correct responses as a function of the validity coefficient and the selection ratio for a situation in which the base rate is .50, presents a graphed example of the obtained values. As can be

Figure 11-5 The relationship between the proportion of correct predictions and the selection ratio for a situation with a base rate of .50 and a test with a validity coefficient of .50.

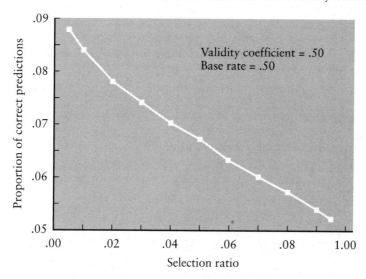

Figure 11-6 The proportion of correct predictions as a function of the selection ratio and validity coefficient for the situation in which base rate is equal to .50.

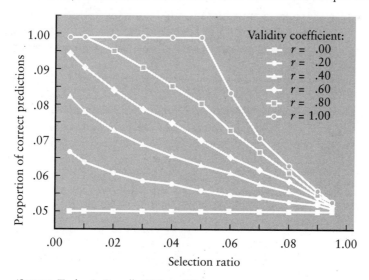

(SOURCE: Taylor & Russell, 1939, p. 575.)

seen, the proportion of correct predictions is indeed a function of the validity coefficient. However, it is equally clear from Figure 11-6 that the selection ratio is important. And, as we will find out later on, when these ideas were elaborated, the base rate turns out to be exceedingly important too. The Taylor–Russell tables serve to indicate that the situation in which a test is used is a significant contributor to the numbers of prediction errors that will be made. It is not sufficient merely to select the most reliable and valid test available and assume thereby that the attending predictions will be maximally useful. It is also important to consider situational factors such as the selection ratio and the base rate when determining how useful a given test is. From the Taylor–Russell tables, it is possible to construct situations in which a less valid test could make fewer prediction errors! However, all else being equal, the most valid test will make the least number of prediction errors.

Tables such as the Taylor–Russell can be used to determine beforehand the number of prediction errors that will be made if a test is used in a specific situation. For example, an industrial psychologist can say how many more prediction errors will be made by his or her test if the number of applicants for a particular position is considerably less than previously. This is a much more concrete way of representing **predictive efficiency** than reference to validity coefficients or related transformations. The strength of this approach is the manner in which it permits abstract ideas such as correlation coefficients to be translated into bottom-line arguments (that is, how many mistakes will I make?). This line of attack clearly indicates that the criteria of what constitutes a good testing event transcend the more traditional indicators such as test validity and reliability, adding significantly to the conceptual tools that can be used to determine if a given test is making a significant contribution.

The Taylor–Russell tables are just the beginning of an approach to testing that goes beyond the technical aspects of the test itself. In a later chapter, we will see how these ideas have been embellished into a complex and sophisticated notion of **utility,** which relates to the costs and benefits of using a test in a specific situation. For the present, Taylor and Russell have laid the foundations for a very important aspect of the testing enterprise.

It should be noted here that all of this argumentation has been developed from the point of view of the organization doing the testing. The errors discussed are those for the company, not those for the applicants. In other words, this technology does not apply to considering the costs of errors to specific individuals who are either rejected or accepted by this strategy. The odds are being calculated from the perspective of the organization, not the individual. It will be worthwhile to keep this observation in mind when we come back to discuss the notion of utility in more detail in Chapters 14 and 19 and discuss the institutional-friendly nature of testing in Chapter 20.

ITEM ANALYSIS

Large numbers of new tests were being introduced during this period, and the point-scale approach with a structured response format was clearly becoming the norm. This trend in test development paved the way for the emergence of a number of interesting methods that were oriented toward determination of the best possible items for inclusion in a test. This general concern of those developing tests eventually became known as **item analysis,** which emerged as an important subfield of the testing enterprise. Here we find a set of techniques and practices that helps determine which items from a larger set will best serve the particular goals of the test developer.

The contemporary field of item analysis is immensely complex. Detailed and sophisticated mathematical, statistical, and conceptual approaches abound (some are discussed in Chapter 19), and the computer makes it possible to calculate many item statistics at the press of a button. Because of this, what follows is but a very elementary presentation of item analysis. The goal here is to provide enough background to help you understand the reasoning used in the testing enterprise when it attempts to develop the best possible tests.

We have seen the beginnings of item analysis in the presentation of both the MMPI and SVIB in Chapter 10. In this approach to selecting items, called **empirical criterion keying,** focus was on enhancing criterion-related validity by the use of a specific strategy. Items that were answered differently by people-in-general and a specific criterion group were selected from among a larger pool of possible items, thus creating a scale with optimal validity. Developments in the domain of item analysis in the late 1930s can be seen as part of this tradition, introducing a number of clever mathematical variations on this basic theme. Of particular note is a number of interesting applications of the correlation coefficient to the task of item selection, which added considerable sophistication and power to emerging psychological tests.

Item Difficulty

The simplest index that we can use to decide if we want to keep an item is to examine how well a representative group of respondents performs on it. In objective domains, this is relatively easy by simply determining the proportion of respondents who answer the item correctly. Called the *p*-value, this statistic is calculated by dividing the number of respondents who answered the item correctly by the total number of respondents who took the test. The example shown in Table 11-2 (page 390) is for a 30-item multiple-choice quiz that was taken by 46 students. Only a portion of the data matrix is shown here for purposes of illustration. If the student answered an item correctly it was coded 1, and incorrect responses were coded as 0 (for example, respondent 1 answered item 2 correctly and item 6 incorrectly).

To calculate *p*-values from Table 11-2, the number of correct responses for each item was tabulated (for example, 17 of the 46 students answered item 2 correctly).[4] A separate *p*-value for each item was then calculated by dividing each of the number of correct figures by 46 (the *p*-value for item 5 is 37/46 = .80). One *p*-value is calculated for each item on the test. Notice that *easier items* have *higher p*-values by this method of calculation (item 1, $p = .70$, is easier than item 2, $p = .37$). Thus *p*-value varies inversely as **item difficulty.**

In voluntary domains that use dichotomous response formats (for example, the MMPI), we can also calculate a *p*-value by determining the proportion of respon-

---

[4]Coding the answers as 1 for correct and 0 for incorrect is convenient because the number of correct responses for an item can be calculated simply by calculating the sum of the column containing the item data.

Table 11-2 Calculation of *p*-values for a 30-item multiple-choice quiz taken by 46 students

Respondent	Items							
	1	2	3	4	5	6	...	30
1	0*	0	1	1	1	0	...	1
2	1	1	1	0	1	1	...	1
3	0	0	0	0	0	1	...	0
4	1	0	1	0	1	0	...	1
⋮	⋮	⋮	⋮	⋮	⋮	⋮		⋮
46	1	1	0	1	1	0	...	1
Number of correct answers	32	17	35	21	37	25	...	42
p-value:	.70	.37	.76	.46	.80	.54	...	.91

*0 = incorrect response; 1 = correct response.

dents who selected a specific response alternative (for example, the *p*-value for an MMPI item would be the proportion of respondents who responded true to it).

The *p*-value statistic can be quite useful in deciding which items to select from a larger set. If the goal of the test is to maximally discriminate between respondents taking the test, then items with extreme *p*-values are not particularly useful. For example, if everyone correctly answered a given objective item ($p = 1.00$), it would not provide any information about the relative performance of individuals within the group who took the test. Conversely, items with extremely low *p*-values (for example, $p < .05$) do not provide very much, if any, differential information. In the example in Table 11-2, item 30 ($p = .91$) would have questionable discriminative powers because so many of the students answered it correctly. It turns out that the best possible item in this situation is one with a *p*-value at or near .50. From this perspective, items 4 and 6 in Table 11-2 would be the best. When the *p*-value is at or near .50, the amount of information about the relative standing of a specific respondent is maximal. In practice, this translates to selecting items with *p*-values between .30 and .70 when the goal is to optimize differentiation among respondents.

It should be noted, though, that the manner in which *p*-value is used to select items is a function of the goals of the test. If a test were intended to provide an index of how well a specific curriculum had been mastered, it might turn out that items with extreme *p*-values were very useful. High *p*-values would indicate which parts of the curriculum had been well learned, whereas low *p*-values would point toward content that for one reason or another had not been mastered. All else being equal, in this situation selecting items solely on the basis of middle-range *p*-values would be inappropriate, indicating that statistics such as the *p*-value should be used very carefully, always bearing in mind the goals of the test.

Another place where the *p*-value can be useful is in the determination of order for the presentation of objective items. If the tester wants to start a test with easy items and gradually increase the difficulty, the *p*-value provides a ready means of doing this simply by presenting the items in reverse order of *p*-value, such that the items passed by most respondents are presented first and so on.

Item Discrimination

Another concern of a number of tests is the extent to which an item performs satisfactorily relative to the test in total—that is, **item discrimination**. Again, using an example of objective tests, if an item is passed by most of the respondents who did well on the total test, it would appear to be a better item than one that equal numbers of high and low total tests scorers answered correctly. In other words, better items are those that, in a sense, predict the total score.

Perhaps the simplest index for use here involves dividing the group of respondents who took the test into three groups on the basis of total test performance: high scorers, middle-range performers, and low scorers. Kelley (1939) suggested that this should be accomplished by placing those in the 0th through 27th percentile in the low group and those in the 73rd through 100th percentile in the high group. In practice, it appears that selecting cutoffs anywhere between 25% and 33% of the extreme scoring respondents (Kelley selected 27%) seems reasonable (for example, Allen & Yen, 1979). The *p*-values for the high (pH) and the low (pL) scoring groups are then calculated. The **item-discrimination index** (*d*) is generated by subtracting pL from pH.

Returning to the 30-item multiple-choice quiz (*n* = 46) presented in Table 11-2, the first step in calculating *d* involves tabulating the total score for each student, which is the number of questions to which the respondent gave the correct answer. Table 11-3 shows this for some of the data.[5]

Table 11-3 Calculating the total score for each of the 46 students who took the 30-item multiple-choice quiz

Respondent	Items								Total Score
	1	2	3	4	5	6	...	30	
1	0*	0	1	1	1	0	...	1	15
2	1	1	1	0	1	1	...	1	28
3	0	0	0	0	0	1	...	0	5
4	1	0	1	0	1	0	...	1	17
⋮	⋮	⋮	⋮	⋮	⋮	⋮		⋮	⋮
46	1	1	0	1	1	0	...	1	13

*0 = incorrect response; 1 = correct response.

[5]Again, coding correct answers as 1 and incorrect answers as 0 is used here because all that has to be done is to add up the row for each respondent to generate the number-correct value

Table 11-4 Calculating *p*-values for the low- and high-scoring groups on a 30-item multiple-choice quiz taken by 46 students

	Respondent	Items								Total Score
		1	2	3	4	5	6	...	30	
	3	0*	0	0	0	0	1	...	0	5
	6	0	0	1	0	1	1	...	0	11
Low Scorers	15	0	0	0	0	0	1	...	0	9
(*n* = 12)	22	1	0	1	0	0	0	...	1	10
	⋮	⋮	⋮	⋮	⋮	⋮	⋮		⋮	⋮
	46	1	1	0	1	1	0	...	1	13
Number of correct answers		5	7	6	6	6	8	...	7	
pL†		.42	.58	.50	.50	.50	.67	...	.58	

	Respondent	Items								Total Score
		1	2	3	4	5	6	...	30	
	2	1	1	1	0	1	1	...	1	28
	8	1	1	1	0	1	1	...	1	29
High Scorers	17	1	1	1	1	1	1	...	1	30
(*n* = 12)	24	1	0	1	1	1	0	...	1	26
	⋮	⋮	⋮	⋮	⋮	⋮	⋮		⋮	⋮
	45	1	1	0	1	1	0	...	1	25
Number of correct answers		11	8	10	6	10	11	...	11	
pH‡		.91	.67	.83	.50	.83	.91	...	.91	

*0 = incorrect response; 1 = correct response.

†pL = *p*-value for the low-scoring group. This value was calculated by dividing number of correct answers by 12 because 12 individuals were in each group.

‡pL = *p*-value for the high-scoring group. This value was calculated by dividing number of correct answers by 12 because 12 individuals were in each group.

Students were then divided into three groups based on their total scores—the 12 receiving the lowest total scores, which we will call the low group; the 12 receiving the highest total scores, which we will call the high group; and the remaining 22 who made up the middle group. (These divisions are close to Kelley's suggested criterion because they are at the 26th percentile.) The *p*-values were then tabulated separately for the high and low groups. Table 11-4 shows this for some of the demonstration data. Notice that *p*-values are very different in the two groups. For example, the *p*-value for item 1 in the low-scoring group is .42, whereas it is .91 in the high-scoring group.

The *d* statistic was then calculated by subtracting, separately for each item, the two sets of *p*-values (pH − pL), as shown in Table 11-5. Item 1 shows a high value of *d*, whereas item 4's value is very low. In the ideal case, where all high scorers answered the item correctly and all low scorers answered it wrong, *d* would equal 1.00 ($d =$ pH − pL $= 1.00 - .00 = 1.00$). The questionable item, that which equal numbers of high and low scorers answered correctly, would culminate in $d = .00$ (for example, item 4 in Table 11-5). Thus, items with *d* close to 1.00 would be the best discriminators. In the example presented in Table 11-5, items 1, 3, 5, and 30 are discriminating fairly well by this reasoning. Items with values of *d* around .00 would not discriminate the total score very well; items 2 and 4 are doing rather poorly. Items with negative values of *d*, although providing information, are clear indicators of problems because the high scorers are answering the item incorrectly, whereas the low scorers are answering it correctly. Such items would be seen as deeply problematic in an objective context. No such items are shown in Table 11-5. If the goal is to maximize discrimination, then items with *d* closest to +1.00 should be selected.

The item-discrimination index is one of a number of possible item statistics that can be used to select the best from a pool of possible items. It provides the test maker with an easily calculated indication of the extent to which the item will place respondents into the same groupings that the total score does.

Table 11-5 Calculating *d* for each item in our 30-item multiple-choice quiz ($n = 46$)

Item	pH	pL	*d**
1	.91	.42	.49
2	.67	.58	.09
3	.83	.50	.33
4	.50	.50	.00
5	.83	.50	.33
6	.91	.67	.24
⋮	⋮	⋮	⋮
30	.91	.58	.33

*$d =$ pH − pL.

Item-Total Correlation

The *d* statistic can be seen as a special case of a more general approach to item analysis. Essentially, the goal of *d* is to determine if performance on a specific item predicts the total test score—if a person does well on an item with a high *d*, we can predict that he or she will do well on the overall test. Putting it in this language suggests that the correlation coefficient might be helpful here because it is concerned with prediction of this sort. Indeed, a statistic that will let us know the degree of relationship between performance on one item and the total test score would be particularly helpful. In theory all we have to do is calculate the correlation between performance on the item and the total score, what is known as the **item-total correlation,** to give us this index. Items with high item-total correlations are the better items if our concern is with how well it discriminates. Items with high positive item-total correlations would under most conditions have high *d* values, suggesting that the *d* statistic is a special case of the item-total correlation.

The practicalities of calculating the item-total correlation introduce some complexities into the picture. In Table 11-6, the item-total correlations have been calculated for the same data that we used to demonstrate the *p*-value and *d*. The item-total correlation for item 1 is the correlation between the column of 1s and 0s beneath item 1 and the total score that would be based on 46 pairs of observations. There would be 30 such correlations—one for each item. Because one of the variables in this computation is dichotomous (item performance is either right or wrong), we cannot use Pearson's index of correlation. Rather, per Chapter 5, it is reasonable to use the biserial correlation because we have arbitrarily divided item performance into two categories of response. The obtained item-total biserial correlations are presented in the bottom row of Table 11-6.

Table 11-6 Data for calculating item-total correlations for a multiple-choice examination

Respondent	Items								Total Score
	1	2	3	4	5	6	...	30	
1	0	0	1	1	1	0	...	1	15
2	1	1	1	0	1	1	...	1	28
3	0	0	0	0	0	1	...	0	5
4	1	0	1	0	1	0	...	1	17
:	:	:	:	:	:	:		:	:
46	1	1	0	1	1	0	...	1	13
p-value:	.69	.38	.77	.45	.81	.55	...	.92	
Item-total correlation	.33	.46	.59	.03	.47	.29	...	.23	

It is advisable to remove the item for which you are calculating an item-total correlation from the computation of the total score. Failure to do so will inflate the size of the obtained coefficient. This is particularly important if small numbers of items are involved or if alternatives are involved in the item responses.

Item-total correlations are particularly useful for selecting items from a larger set and in evaluating them. Adapting our reasoning with a correlation, the size of the item-total correlation reflects the extent to which it is possible to predict the total score from performance on the single item. If our goal was to generate a new but shorter test based on these data, the best strategy would be to select the items with the highest item-total correlations (for example, items 3 and 5 of those shown). These would maximize the chances of the new scale being comparable to the older, longer one. We should recognize, however, per the earlier discussion in this chapter, that the overall reliability of the test would decrease if we used fewer items. Should an item-total correlation be 0, we would have pause about including it in a revised test because there is no relationship between item performance and the total score. And, like the *d* statistic, negative values would indicate the possibility of substantive problems with the item.

The item-total correlation is a helpful statistic for gaining a sense of how well an item predicts the total score of the test. It can be adapted to voluntary tests in a number of ways as well, but these are beyond what we have to know now (see Chapter 13 for some examples). There are some practical problems with biserial correlations, particularly if *p*-values are extreme, which suggests the need to be fairly cautious in interpreting item-total correlations. As well, individual item performance tends to be unreliable relative to aggregated measures such as total scores, and this can have a significant effect on the sizes and robustness of item-total correlations. Finally, because a large number of such correlations are often calculated, the number of significant values that are due to chance is likely to be quite high. All of this indicates that considerable caution should be exercised here; but within these practical constraints, the item-total correlation is a useful tool.

Item-Validity Index

Thus far we have only applied the item-level correlation to the prediction of the total test score. If we are developing a test and want to maximize criterion-related validity, we can employ a variant of the item-total correlation to great advantage. Suppose that we want to develop an improved multiple-choice exam based on the data in Table 11-6 and that our basic concern for this new test was to make the best possible prediction about how well students are doing in their other courses. In other words, we want to develop a test with maximal concurrent validity where our criterion is grade point average (GPA) in other courses. We could start by gathering our criterion measures. Then we could calculate the correlation between item performance *and* criterion status (for example, GPA in other courses). This correlation, called an **item-validity index,** is a clear indication of which items are useful in predicting criterion status. Those with high positive values are the best items for predicting the criterion, whereas those with 0 values are not. Selection of the subset of items with the highest values of this correlation would produce a scale with optimal validity! Again, reduction in the number of items in the test would reduce reliability and hence validity, but our new test would optimize validity within these constraints. If we were selecting a relatively large set of items from an exceedingly large pool, this would not be so much of a problem. Note that this approach is in reality very similar to MMPI-style empirical criterion keying because items are selected to optimize the manner in which they predict criterion status. With item-validity indexes, though, it is possible to employ continuous criterion measures.

Item-Reliability Index

Another variant of this approach is to maximize reliability. Again referring to Table 11-6, assume that we want to design the most reliable test possible. If we developed a parallel form of our test and administered it to our respondents, we could then calculate the correlation between item performance on the first test and total score on the parallel form. Called an **item-reliability index,** this correlation would let us know which items contributed the most to the reliability of the first test, and selecting the items with the highest values would result in a maximally reliable test. Many other variations in developing item-reliability indexes are possible here—limited only by the creativity of the test developer.

The three examples of item-level correlations provided here (item-total correlation, item-validity index, and item-reliability indexes) are but examples of what could be an infinite number of possible statistics that could be used to select and evaluate items. Careful consideration of the goals of the test, combined with a well-thought-out application of item-level correlations, provides a vast arsenal of very useful tools and techniques for test development. The examples here just skim the surface of what is possible. This family of item-level correlations is a direct extension of the reasoning behind the correlation coefficient. They can be applied, with great effect, to the solution of problems such as the establishment of reliability and validity. These extensions of Pearson's index represent an interesting amalgamation between the correlation technologies and the criteria of goodness of tests which were so much of a part of the enterprise during its formative years.

Cross-Validation

All item statistics discussed here (as well as any others) must be viewed as tentative until such time as the results are confirmed by administering the new, revised test to a second group of representative respondents. If all has gone well, the results should replicate on this second group, and the item-level findings are said to have been cross-validated. Partly because of the notorious unreliability of single responses (compared to aggregated total scores), **cross-validation** is exceedingly important in the item-analytic domain. In many instances, correlations that were very promising in the first sample simply disappear in the second, creating all kinds of problems and disappointments for test developers. Correlations of all kinds tend to become lower the second time around because of the operation of chance factors. This is called **shrinkage** and is especially prominent in item-level correlations. Caution and replication must be the watchwords in this domain.

The gains in sophistication that accrued from the application of this methodology, however, were tremendous. Now, rather than people deciding which items belong on a scale solely on the basis of their a priori notions, a powerful and useful technology had emerged that allowed for empirical determination of the place of an item in the context of a given scale. This is a far cry from the early years of testing and can be seen as one sign of the progress enjoyed by the fledgling testing enterprise as it began to mature.

Summary

The 1930s ushered in some highly important developments for the testing enterprise. The toolbox available for the evaluation and development of tests was significantly augmented during this important time. Detailed and comprehensive reference sources such as the *Mental Measurements Yearbook* emerged during this time. Internal consistency measures of reliability, with their attending complexities and strengths, were introduced. Content validity became part of the structure of validity. The beginnings of the concept of utility surfaced. A number of developments in the domain of item analysis provided strong methodologies for the design and refinement of tests.

Testing was "on a roll" as the 1930s ended—only to have yet another international disaster affect its progress. Economic conditions in Europe and the South Pacific, combined with the emergence of some charismatic political leaders, created a context primed for war. And war did come—with a vengeance. While the United States tried to distance itself from the conflict as much as possible, by the early 1940s involvement seemed unavoidable, and the major mobilization of the American people to fight World War II induced yet even greater change for the testing enterprise.

Glossary

achievement test A psychological test designed to discover how much of a subject, or curriculum, an individual has mastered at the time of testing.

base rate The proportion of unselected individuals who fall in a specific category of a criterion.

Buros, Oscar A psychologist who began compilation of the *Mental Measurements Yearbook*.

Coefficient Alpha A specific measure of internal consistency for use with items that are answered using a Likert format. Introduced by Lee Cronbach, the statistic represents the average of all possible half-score reliability estimates.

content universe The complete curriculum to be mastered in an achievement test. This must be defined in order to determine if a given test has content validity.

content validity The degree to which items in a test reflect the content universe to which the test will be generalized.

cross-validation   Replicating an item analysis on a second group of respondents to ensure that the obtained results of the first analysis were not due to chance. In more general terms, cross-validation refers to the process of checking out any validity estimate on a second group of respondents to establish the robustness of the findings.

curricular validity   An earlier name for content validity.

empirical criterion keying   A means of assigning items to scales in which only those items that are answered (significantly) differently by a criterion group and people-in-general are assigned to a specific scale. This method was used in developing both the Strong Vocational Interest Blank and the Minnesota Multiphasic Personality Inventory.

ephemeral variables   A psychological characteristic that is expected to change as a function of the passage of time. Happiness, job satisfaction, and mood are examples. The reliability of such a variable has to be estimated using measures of internal consistency.

ERIC (Educational Resource Information Catalog)   A CD-ROM database containing abstracts of published articles dealing with educational topics. It is a good source of information about educational tests.

half score   A score generated by using only one-half of the items in a test. Such scores are used in the calculation of reliability from one test administration, such as split half and odd/even.

half-score reliability estimates   A family of methods for estimating reliability that involves generating scores on half of the items (divided by various means) and calculating the correlation between the half scores. Such reliability estimates, which include split half and odd/even, have to be adjusted by using the Spearman–Brown Formula.

index of forecasting efficiency   An early index of test usefulness (Kelley, 1923) that reflected how well a test would predict compared to random guesses.

internal consistency   A measure of the extent to which items in a test are correlated with each other. Statistics such as the KR20 and Coefficient Alpha are indexes of internal consistency.

item analysis   A series of techniques oriented toward selecting the best items from a larger pool.

item difficulty   An empirical estimate of how many respondents passed or failed a specific item. (*See* p-value.)

item discrimination   An empirical index of the extent to which an item predicts the total score. (*See* item-discrimination index; item-total correlation.)

item-discrimination index (d)   An item statistic that is the difference in p-values for answers of an extreme low- versus high-scoring respondents. High positive values of this difference indicate items that predict the total score on the test.

item-reliability index   The (biserial) correlation between performance on a specific item and a parallel-form total score. Higher item-reliability indexes indicate more reliable items.

item-total correlation   The (biserial) correlation between performance on a specific item and the total score on the test. Higher item-total correlations indicate items that predict the total score.

item-validity index   The (biserial) correlation between performance on a specific item and criterion status. Higher item-validity indexes indicate items that predict the criterion.

Kuder–Richardson Formula 20 (KR20)   A specific measure of internal consistency for use with items that are answered using a dichotomous format. The statistic represents the average of all possible half-score reliability estimates.

Likert format   A structured response format that consists of a number of graded response alternatives such as strongly disagree, disagree, and so on.

Mental Measurements Yearbook (MMY)   A set of reference books that provides bibliographies, reviews, descriptions, and references for most published psychological tests. Started in 1938, eleven editions of the *MMY* have been published, with the most recent in 1992.

Metropolitan Achievement Test (MAT)   A set of standardized achievement tests for kindergarten through grade 12. Tests of Reading, Mathematics, Science, and Social Studies are available in the most recent revision.

odd/even reliability   A means of estimating test reliability by dividing the test into two halves, using the odd-numbered items for one half and the even-numbered items for the other. The correlation between the two half scores is an index of test reliability. The Spearman–Brown Formula (Equation 11-1) has to be applied to compensate for the fact that the half scores are not based on as many items as the total score.

power test   A psychological test in which all respondents have an opportunity to attempt all items.

predictive efficiency   A pre-1937 statistic, based on the validity coefficient, that purported to be an index of how well a test could predict a criterion. Taylor and Russell rendered this notion more concrete by providing tables that allowed testers to determine the proportion of correct predictions that tests of varying validity would make in various situations.

proportion of correct predictions   A statistic used by Taylor and Russell to reflect the accuracy with which a test will predict criterion status.

PsychInfo CD-ROM   A computer-tied system that allows for the retrieval of massive amounts of information, which is stored on a compact disc, of all issues of *Psychological Abstracts* dating from 1974.

Psychological Abstracts   A publication that contains summaries of all articles published in major psychological journals. It also contains much detailed cross-referencing and many indexes that help locate psychological research on specific topics.

p-value   The proportion of respondents who answered an objective item correctly. In voluntary domains, the *p*-value represents the proportion of respondents choosing a particular response alternative.

selection ratio   The proportion of applicants for whom there are positions in a selection situation.

separately timed half scores   The generation of half scores for a test by providing each half with its own time limit. This is a necessary procedure for establishing the reliability of speed tests.

shrinkage   The amount that the size of a correlation changes when calculated using a second group of respondents. Chance fluctuations almost always deflate correlations when calculating them on a second sample.

Spearman–Brown Formula   A means of estimating what the reliability of a test would be if the number of items making it up was increased. (See Equation (11-1.)

speed/accuracy trade-off   The dilemma in which increased speed of work will create more errors but is offset by the converse tendency that increased accuracy or care will result in less work being done. This is an important concept in understanding the problems associated with mixed speed and power tests.

speed test   A psychological test in which the final score depends on how rapidly the respondent works through the items. Such tests are typically designed so no one can finish all items.

split-half reliability   A means of estimating test reliability by dividing the test into the first and second half and generating two scores. The correlation between the two half scores is an index of test reliability. The Spearman–Brown Formula (Equation 11-1) has to be applied to compensate for the fact that the half scores are not based on as many items as the total score.

Taylor–Russell tables   A series of matrices of values of proportions of correct predictions that would be made using tests of varying validities, in situations with differing selection ratios and base rates.

Test Critiques   A book that includes in-depth, scholarly reviews of selected psychological tests.

test manual   The documentation that comes with a test and contains instructions for administration, scoring, and interpretation, as well as other necessary information to use the test properly.

Tests in Microfiche   An annotated index of unpublished psychological tests produced by Educational Testing Service.

Tests in Print   A set of volumes that lists published tests but does not provide reviews and evaluative commentary.

utility   A measure of the costs and benefits of using a psychological test in a specific situation.

Suggested Further Reading

Conoley, J. C., & Kramer, J. J. (Eds.). (1989). *The tenth mental measurements yearbook*. Lincoln: University of Nebraska Press.

The introduction to this latest edition of the *MMY* is worth reading for anyone who thinks they might be using this important reference source. It provides a good sense of the breadth of coverage of the listings. I also recommend that you read the section on the sixth revision of the Metropolitan Achievement Test (pp. 503–519). Here you will find a detailed description of the most recent version of the MAT, a total of 44 different references to relevant materials, and two detailed reviews, one by A. J. Nitko and one by B. G. Rogers. This provides an excellent opportunity to get a sense of the kind of information available in the *MMY* and to see how the MAT developed from its beginnings. A sense of more recent developments can be attained by examining the eleventh edition as well (Kramer & Conoley, 1992).

Crocker, L., & Aligna, J. (1986). *Introduction to classical and modern test theory*. Fort Worth, Tex.: Harcourt Brace Jovanovich.

Chapter 14 of this book presents item analysis in more detail than has been done in this chapter of *The Enterprise*. It is not overly mathematical in its orientation but does offer sufficient mathematical material to permit movement beyond the really basic level presented here.

Cronbach, L. J., & Gleser, G. C. (1965). *Psychological tests and personnel decisions*. Urbana: University of Illinois Press.

If you are the type who reads the last chapter of a mystery novel first, so you don't have to wait and see "whodunnit," this book is for you. Basically, this volume presents the modern idea of utility as it eventually evolved from the preliminary thinking of the likes of Taylor and Russell. Quite sophisticated and mathematical in tone, the position presented by Cronbach and Gleser involves adapting the complex domain of mathematical decision theory to the determination of utility of psychological testing. Some of the details of the presentation will be discussed further in Chapter 14 of *The Enterprise*.

Ghiselli, E. E., Campbell, J. P., & Zedeck, S. (1981). *Measurement theory for the behavioral sciences*. San Francisco: Freeman.

Chapters 8 and 9 of this book provide a very detailed discussion of the fundamental ideas surrounding reliability, including theoretical and practical issues. The chapters are readable and present current thinking about this aspect of psychological test scores.

Helmstadter, G. C. (1964). *Principles of psychological measurement*. New York: Appleton-Century-Crofts.

Chapter 4 of this book, entitled "Evaluation of Tests—Content Validity," is a wonderfully detailed presentation of the basic notion of content validity. It presents many of the subdivisions of this basic idea that have emerged since its introduction and shows some of the broader implications of this type of validity.

Discussion Questions

1. Indicate as many reasons as you can why the *Mental Measurement Yearbook* emerged when it did.

2. Considering the sources of information about tests presented in the chapter, draw a flowchart that would indicate the optimal sequence of order that you would use to find detailed information about a specific test.

3. Outline the weaknesses that stem from the *MMY* not being cumulative.

4. Prepare a list of all materials that you think should be included in a test manual.

5. Compare the information available about psychological tests to reference materials available in another discipline.

6. List as many ephemeral variables as you can. Apart from the fact that they are

expected to change over time, what other common characteristics do they have? Place these in "families" (of the type that might emerge if the set was factor-analyzed).

7. List all strengths and weaknesses of split-half reliability.

8. Evaluate this suggestion: The Spearman–Brown Formula for reliability as a function of the number of items in a test is cheating because it makes correlations larger than they ever could be in reality.

9. Outline all strengths and weaknesses of odd/even reliability.

10. List four different approaches to reliability estimates based on half scores. Indicate one appropriate use for each method.

11. Discuss the relative merits of KR20 and split-half estimates of reliability.

12. By comparing the two formulas, indicate the relationship between the KR20 (Equation 11-2) and Coefficient Alpha (Equation 11-3).

13. With reference to a test that involves locating as many misspelled words as possible in 2 minutes, indicate the problems that emerge due to the speed/accuracy trade-off. How do these restrict the meanings you can attribute to test scores?

14. Using the list from your answer to Question 10, indicate how each half-score method is inappropriate for a pure speed test.

15. Outline the strengths and weaknesses of using half scores based on separately timed half scores to estimate the reliability of speed tests.

16. List the strengths and weaknesses of the internal consistency approach to estimating reliability.

17. Under what conditions can the idea of luck be a problem for measures of internal consistency? What are the implications of this for the determination of the reliability of tests?

18. Outline a situation in which excessive concern for reliability might have negative effects on validity.

19. Thinking back on your experience with multiple-choice examinations, generate a list of "thou shalt nots" associated with creating this type of question. Provide examples of items that demonstrate these aspects of poor item writing. Indicate whether there is reason to suspect that each of these item characteristics would reduce reliability.

20. Define the content universe for the section on content validity in this chapter.

21. Evaluate the content validity of the Raven Progressive Matrices.

22. Discuss the possible relationships between content and criterion-related validity.

23. List the possible applications of the MAT that a school superintendent might use.

24. Here are some data for a test-criterion relationship, with the entries in each cell indicating the number of employees falling in each segment of the contingency table:

| | | *Test Score* | |
		Reject	*Select*
	Satisfactory	20	45
Criterion Status			
	Unsatisfactory	56	9

Calculate the base rate, selection ratio, and proportion of correct predictions for these data. Draw the contingency table that would be expected if the test were perfectly valid. Draw the contingency table that would be expected if the test-criterion correlation was .00. Using Figure 11-6, (roughly) what is the value of the validity coefficient?

25. Using the data in Table 11-1, construct an 11-item test that would be equally difficult compared with the 22-item version presented in the table. If the reliability of the shorter version is .88, what value would you expect for the longer version?

26. In what sense is the item-discrimination index (d) a special case of the item-total correlation?

27. If you administered a quiz in a class and found that all of the item-total correlations were uniformly high, how many factors would you get if you factor-analyzed the matrix of correlations between the items? Why?

28. In what ways are the item-validity index and empirical criterion keying the same? How are they different?

29. You have been hired by the ABC Oil Company to develop a test to select rig workers. You tell your boss that the preliminary item analyses indicate that the test looks good but that you want to cross-validate it to be sure. Your boss doesn't want to spend the money to do this. Develop a strong argument to convince him that you *have* to do it.

30. Evaluate the possibility that all approaches to estimating reliability presented in this chapter indicate that reliability is an index of the average intercorrelation between the test items.

31. Debate the assertion that all measures of reliability based on half scores are circular and thereby of little use in determining the goodness of a psychological test.

Part V

The Modern Era

Several critical developments during World War II framed the emergence of psychology as an important member of the helping professions. During this evolution, which occurred (roughly) from 1940 to 1970, a number of innovations and some negative reactions to testing surfaced. These are documented in this part of the text.

Chapter 12 provides a brief sketch of the involvement of testing in World War II. Spawned in part by large numbers of returning war veterans, the postwar era saw a strong push toward the professionalization of psychology. By the mid-1950s, the discipline had adopted all the trappings of a professional institution, including the acceptance of ethical codes as well as standards for acceptable tests and testing practices. These are documented in Chapter 12.

The most significant change in test theory since the introduction of validity occurred in the mid-1950s. Driven by scientific and pragmatic concerns, a new type of validity, called construct, was introduced. As shown in Chapter 13, construct validity focused on the extent to which a test served as a measure of a substantiated scientific theory. This new variety of validity served to end the operationist approach to testing and paved the way for a number of novel and significant innovations and tests.

All was not calm and quiet on the testing front, however. Driven by increased concerns about individual freedom that were part of the 1960s, a number of intellectual and political forces converged to create an antitest movement. Chapter 14 outlines the criticisms of tests and testing practices that emerged during this time. In addition, the manners in which the field responded to these criticisms are presented to underscore the impact that negative reactions to testing had on the traditions in the domain.

By the late 1960s, testing had emerged as a mature and sophisticated component of the psychologist's toolbox. Its professional house was in order, it had adopted a state-of-the-art philosophy of science (construct validity), and it had endured a major critical assault by changing some of its practices and procedures. Without doubt, testing as we know it today had been fully framed and elaborated by the end of this important era.

Chapter 12

On Becoming a Profession
Ethics, Training, and Standards

In This Chapter

A Profession Evolves

Testing During World War II

Professionalization of Psychology After the War

The Emergence of Formal Guidelines for Tests

Testing in the Early 1950s

True-Score Test Theory

Projective Testing Continues Apace

Summary

A PROFESSION EVOLVES

As the 1930s ended, the testing enterprise had made significant strides in developing a set of methods, a worldview, and an approach to solving problems that held promise of a great contribution to the solutions of social problems. Numerous tests measuring an incredible variety of psychological characteristics were available. With the evaluative criteria of validity (both criterion-related and content), reliability, and an emerging notion of utility in hand, the basic conceptual apparatus for determining the goodness of a given test in a given situation had been mapped out. Many of the practical aspects of testing had been developed and fared quite well. A new technology, which promised untold pragmatic benefits, was available and was soon to be used across a wide variety of situations with considerable success.

One part of the equation, however, was yet to fall into place. What was missing was the development of the institutional context into which this technology and the practices it generated would be placed. As the testing enterprise became larger and began to take on more responsibility for making social decisions, it became increasingly necessary for psychology, in general, and testing, in particular, to develop explicit rules of conduct that could be used to monitor the manner in which this new technology would be applied. It was important to protect the ideas from interlopers, and it was critical that uses and developments within the testing field were properly constructed so as to contribute to the overall goals of the emerging profession of psychology. A particularly interesting chapter of the testing enterprise emerged in response to these concerns. This was a time during which the institutional framework that supports the testing enterprise was created, explicated, fine-tuned, and eventually accepted as the proper way of doing things within the field. Psychology, as a formal, practical profession, was about to emerge.

Not unlike earlier developments in testing, opportunities afforded by a wartime environment contributed significantly to emergence of the modern profession of psychology. Some technical developments during World War II, combined with several changes in the workforce wrought by the return of many soldiers from the fronts, created a context that was tailor-made for the emergence of a formalized profession of psychology. We now turn to some of these developments that set the framework for the emergence of the modern concept of professional psychology.

TESTING DURING WORLD WAR II

As early as 1939, U.S. involvement in the war seemed likely. In anticipation, the Anthropology and Psychology Section of the National Research Council (NRC) established a Committee on Selection and Training of Aircraft Pilots. Funded by the Civil Aeronautics Administration as part of its program for training civilian pilots, the research conducted at this time laid the foundation for work in both the army and navy air forces (see Hunter, 1946).[1] In 1940 the War Department asked the NRC to set up an advisory committee on personnel problems and, later in that year, an NRC Emergency Committee in Psychology. These developments were followed shortly by the creation of a number of research initiatives in which psychologists dedicated their skill and knowledge to the war effort. These included (1) an army general staff panel to study the problems of psychological warfare; (2) pilot, bombardier, and navigator selection (Flanagan, 1948); (3) morale studies in the Division of Special Services in the army; (4) important extensions and developments of clinical and social psychology to the military context; and (5) **human factors** work associated with technological developments such as sonar, fire control (for example, antiaircraft gunnery), acoustics, and optics. Other initiatives also emerged including the development of psychiatric screening programs (see Star, 1950). In 1943 the Office of Strategic Services (OSS) adapted various aspects of prevailing testing technology to select agents (for a summary, see Wiggins, 1973, pp. 519–539). Clearly, war had provided psychology with yet another forum to demonstrate the varied ways in which it could contribute to American society.

---

[1]The U.S. Air Force did not emerge until after the war.

Table 12-1 Percentage of psychologists involved in the war effort in the various branches of the U.S. armed forces

Branch of Military Service	Percentage of Psychologists
Army	41.3*
Air Forces	27.2
Navy	25.0
WAVE	2.2
Marines	1.0
U.S. Public Health Service	1.0
WAC	0.9
Merchant marines	0.8
Coast Guard	0.5
SPAR	0.1

*Based on a sample of 1168 psychologists surveyed after the war.

SOURCE: Andrews and Dreese (1948, p. 534).

Psychologists flocked into the armed forces to support the war effort. Some simply joined up to be assigned to various units that would use their training, whereas others were directly commissioned to perform specific duties. Table 12-1 lists the percentages of the total number of psychologists involved in the war effort as a function of the service in which they served. The major services (army, navy, and air forces) were clearly the greatest users of psychological skills. Interestingly, the marines did not use as many psychologists as the other combat branches, but they did use services provided by the navy.

As you might expect from the experience of World War I, **selection** and **classification** of recruits were the major foci of concern for most of the testing applications. This does not deny a number of very important developments such as studies of night vision, fire control, and communications (Hunter, 1946). However, for our purposes, we will consider the selection applications because these were the ones that involved the testing enterprise to the greatest extent.

In the army, it was estimated that over 9 million recruits were tested using the **Army General Classification Test (AGCT)**, which was devised as a modern version of the Alpha. Initially, this test battery yielded a single number considered to be a classification score, not a measure of global intelligence. In keeping with the trend toward the dismantling of intelligence (see Chapter 10), the AGCT was soon expanded to include component scores: reading/vocabulary, arithmetic computation, arithmetic reasoning, and spatial relations (Dubois, 1970). Numerous specialty tests were also added as the needs emerged. To give you a sense of the amount of psychological research carried out under this program, it is estimated that over 600 research papers (mostly technical reports) were published by the Adjuntant General's Office during this time (Hunter, 1946).

It is almost impossible to provide a summary of the incredible amount of work that emerged surrounding the testing programs during this period. Rather than attempt a review, we will examine one fairly representative case study that provides a glimpse of the highly technical and sophisticated systems of personnel classification and selection that were pioneered during World War II. The prediction task to be considered was the selection of pilots, navigators, bombardiers, and other highly trained air crew members for the various air forces. The following Close Up provides some details of this program.

CLOSE UP   Selection in the Army Air Force

A fine example of a testing application can be seen in the program for selection of pilots and other highly trained personnel for the Army Air Force (AAF). Would-be AAF pilots began a rather arduous selection procedure by applying to a local Aviation Cadet Examining Board (for a history of this program, see Staff, 1944). The decision about which recruits should be trained as part of an air crew is immensely complex. Not only are a diversity of physical, cognitive, and learning skills required, but a significant cost is also involved. Thus, considerable effort, and not a little technological sophistication, was dedicated to determining which of the many young men wanting to become combat pilots should be trained.

The eventual program that emerged was a **successive hurdles approach** that involved a number of decision-making branches at which would-be pilots could be either passed on for further examination or routed to another service role. Basic credentials were assessed using a file-review procedure. An interview to determine if the recruit was officer material was included, as was a physical examination. In addition, a number of psychological tests were employed to make the optimal decision. Figure 12-1 shows the manner in which these were organized. Although clearly a costly procedure, the gains from implementimg this strategy far outweighed the costs associated with the interviewing and testing.

There are clearly a number of assessment devices incorporated into this program, but the **Aviation Cadet Qualifying Examination (ACQE)** is particularly noteworthy. It was especially developed to facilitate decision making about suitability for advanced training in various roles of an air crew such as navigator, bombardier, or pilot. It consisted of a series of questions, such as those shown in Figure 12-2 (page 412), which were framed using a military/aviation content. The ACQE was a nonspeed test described as "a carefully standardized sample of the man's ability to do some of the kinds of things which an Aviation Cadet must be able to do in the training schools" (Flanagan, 1942, p. 232). The items were clearly related to the content of the training that the test had been designed to predict. There were 150 such items, and an applicant had to answer at least 90 of them correctly to pass on to the next hurdle.

Empirical data regarding the item performance as a function of success in pilot training were used to select the items for the ACQE. Table 12-2 (page 413) presents the keyed response and performance data for the three items presented in Figure 12-2. The size of the difference in percentage correct between the passing and failing groups was used to select items, thereby optimizing predictive validity. This is clearly a variant of the *d* statistic presented in Chapter 11.

After a period of basic training and college-level class work, all applicants who passed the ACQE were given a complete physical examination and their prefer-

Figure 12-1

A schematic representation of the pilot-selection system that incorporated the Aviation Cadet Qualifying Examination along with a number of other psychological tests and assessments to provide the Pilot Aptitude Score.

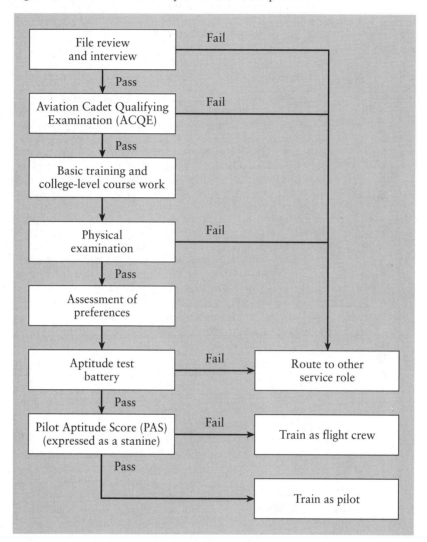

ences for various roles within the aviation sector (for example, pilot, bombardier, navigator) were assessed. In addition, the cadet took a comprehensive battery of aptitude tests that required several hours to complete. On the basis of extensive research, using success in pilot school as a criterion, the cadet was given a **Pilot Aptitude Score (PAS)** that was converted to a **stanine**, which is a standardized score that can take on a value of 1 through 9. Higher values of this test were thought to be associated with a higher probability of success during the training program.

Figure 12-2
Questions of the type found on the Aviation Cadet Qualifying Examination.

1. A simulated airdrome is one which is:
   a. hidden.
   b. exposed.
   c. feigned.
   d. camouflaged.
   e. occupied.

2. When a balloon rises through a layer of clouds and ascends into the sunshine above, the superheat generated by the sun's rays will cause the balloon to rise unless its ascent is stopped by valving gas through the appendix. On descending, the descent may be made slowly until the clouds are reached, but as soon as the balloon enters the clouds and the sun becomes obscured, the gas contracts and increases the descending forces. This descending force accumulates until counteracted by the discharging of ballast. If the balloon has descended through a layer of clouds and the earth is immediately below, a considerable amount of ballast must be discharged to compensate for loss of lift due to contraction of the gas. If the pilot waits too long before discharging the ballast, the amount thrown is very much larger than if he checks his descent by discharging ballast gradually as the gas contracts.

   The most advisable procedure to follow when descending through clouds is to discharge it:
   a. rapidly when entering the clouds.
   b. gradually as gas is released from the appendix.
   c. slowly as the balloon tends to gain momentum.
   d. only during the last part of the descent.
   e. immediately after the balloon emerges from the clouds.

3. Bombing attacks are usually made at night chiefly because:
   a. pursuit planes have great difficulty locating the bombers.
   b. radio detection devices do not work well at night.
   c. fires started by the bombs can be used as targets.
   d. they prevent the enemy population from obtaining rest.
   e. they are as effective as daylight attacks but are less dangerous.

The stanine, which is an acronym for *stan*dard *nine*, is an interesting score that was developed to minimize the amount of clerical work necessary to keep track of the mountains of data generated by such testing/selection programs. Keeping the score down to one digit was particularly helpful here, meaning that less time was needed in recording the test score. Additionally, single-digit scores were amenable to being represented as holes in cards, making it possible to effectively sort and select individuals on the basis of their test scores. Table 12-3 shows the relationship between percentages of cases in each category and stanines as developed during this time.

The stanine is a variant of the *z* score, with a mean of 5 and an approximate standard deviation of 2. Interestingly, Hollerith, one of the the researchers who helped pioneer this approach, was instrumental in developing the computer punch card, which later became the main method of entering data into computers in the 1960s.

The original sample tested under the PAS program included 152,933 cases. The potential utility of the PAS for identifying those who would succeed in training can be determined by calculating the percentage of recruits failing training as a function of PAS score. Table 12-4 presents these data.

The AAF training program was clearly rigorous, with one in four of the applicants (39,818/152,933 = .26) not completing training. The vast majority of training

Table 12-2
Item-performance statistics for the sample Aviation Cadet Qualifying Examination items

Item	Answer	Percentage Correct of Those Who Passed Aviation Training	Percentage Correct of Those Who Failed Aviation Training
1	C	76	29
2	C	71	30
3	A	78	50

Source: Flanagan (1942, p. 234).

Table 12-3
The relationship between stanines and percentages of cases in each category

Stanine	1	2	3	4	5	6	7	8	9
Percentage of Cases	4	7	12	17	20	17	12	7	4

Table 12-4
Failure during army air force pilot training as a function of the Pilot Aptitude Score

PAS (stanine)	Number of Applicants	Failure Rate (%)	Number who Failed
1	904	78	705
2	2239	68	1523
3	11,471	55	6309
4	22,827	42	9587
5	31,091	32	9949
6	30,066	21	6314
7	24,367	13	3168
8	15,286	10	1529
9	14,682	5	734
Total	152,933		39,818

Source: Hunter (1946) and Staff (1945).

failures were because of flying deficiency, but some were because of "fear or at own request" (Hunter, 1946, p. 489).

As can be seen by comparing the PAS score and failure-rate columns, there is a systematic relationship between stanine and training failure, with higher test scorers tending to fare better. In fact, there is a substantive linear relationship, with the correlation between PAS and failure rate being amazingly high ($r = .99$, $p < .001$, $n = 9$). This does not mean the PAS score is perfectly valid but indicates that **failure rate** is a linear function of test score. Despite this strong relationship, there is still considerable predictive noise within each stanine level. For example, the probability of a person scoring 3 on the test-failing training is .55, indicating that, at this score level, the prediction of training failure is random. The effective use of the test involved determining a **cutoff score** that minimized failure rate as well as ensuring that the AAF graduated a sufficient number of pilots to staff its needs. Hunter (1946) indicates that a minimum qualifying score of 6 was eventually instituted.

Based on the data presented in Table 12-4, the institution of a cutoff score of 6 would reduce the failure rate from .26 to .14.[2] This latter figure was calculated by dividing the total number of applicants who failed, 11,745, by the number who received a score of 6 or greater, 84,401. The savings in money, suffering brought on by failure, and teaching efficiency appear to be substantial—all based on the institution of this testing program. Although the predictive validity of the PAS is not perfect, the use of the stanine score to make a "best guess" about good pilot candidates appears to be justifiable.

It should be noted that this research is mute about the performance in the field; it relates only to how well the candidate will do during training. Apart from the assumption that a well-trained pilot is apt to do better than a poorly trained one under combat conditions, the research does not permit predictions about combat under fire. However, in the sense that the goal of the program was to help make the best guess possible about who will complete training, the testing data have clear import for the solution of military personnel problems.

The AAF selection program is but one of a number of examples from World War II in which psychological testing was able to make a significant contribution. Several other examples are provided in the suggested readings at the end of this chapter. The particular example of the AAF air crew–selection program conveys the sense of efficiency and fiscal savings that psychologists were able to generate during this time. Of particular note in most of these applications is the complete and total dominance of the tenets of criterion-related validity in both the development and evaluation of the various programs. Although considerable sophistication in optimizing the predictiveness of scales had been demonstrated during this gigantic research effort, the fundamental idea driving the effort was to predict criterion status. This remained as it had prior to the war. In times of crisis such as World War II, focus on the immediate prediction of socially meaningful criteria is clearly a highly successful strategy.

---

[2]This conclusion is based on the assumption that things did not change between the initial and implementation phases of the testing program. As will be indicated later on, this may not be a tenable assumption, but it was the best guess that could be made at the time.

Administration of a classification test to female recruits at the Boston Induction Center, 1943.

This strategy paid dividends because postwar evaluations of psychology's contributions were generally positive. For example, Hunter (1946) quotes a "distinguished Naval officer" as indicating

> As a result of such scientific applications of psychology in the selection and training of personnel, we have killed more submarines, have used radar better, have better gunners, better engineers, better communications both by voice and code, have been shooting down more airplanes because our rangefinder operators were selected and trained better. [p. 480]

In evaluating the success of a shakedown cruise for the battleship USS *New Jersey*, the officer in command of its 2600 men indicated that

> The initial placement of personnel [using various testing programs] has definitely contributed to the apparent extraordinary rapid progress made during the shakedown period by the crew of this vessel. By this method, the following benefits were derived:
>
> 1. Obviously unsuited personnel were eliminated from the start without waste of training effort.
> 2. Transfers between divisions and departments were kept at a minimum due to proper placement prior to the training period.
> 3. There was a reduction in the number of men failing to profit by training due to the reduction of malplacements. [Hunter, 1946, pp. 480–481; entry in brackets added]

In this case, tests had contributed to the allocation of sailors to appropriate roles on shipboard. This is an example of using tests to facilitate **placement** decisions that involve determination of the most effective activity for a specific individual within an organization. To be sure, the psychological testing enterprise had made a meaningful contribution to World War II.

If the number of people tested during World War II is a criterion of success, then the testing enterprise exceeded even its own expectations. Looking at the year 1944 alone, the following numbers of tests were administered in the military (Wolfle, 1947):

Army: 5 million tests to 2.3 million people

Army air force: 10 million tests to .4 million people

Navy: 9 million tests to 1.2 million people

Bureau of Medicine and Surgery: .24 million tests to .08 million people

Over 24 million tests were administered over the period of just 1 year—a truly remarkable accomplishment.

Not all was positive, however. Miller (1970) comments that a secondary, unintended consequence of the selection system for air crew was to put less competent individuals in command. This happened because the pilot, who may not necessarily have all cognitive skills of other aviation crew members such as navigators, was the ranking officer, and leaders were subsequently chosen from among the higher-ranking individuals:

> It is a debatable point, of course, but I believe that many of the cadets who were admitted to this pool of pilots were too low in verbal and mathematical aptitudes to qualify as navigators. In short, a case can be made that the subsequent selection of Air Force generals from a sample drawn in this way [using the PAS program] was probably not in the best interests of the nation. [Miller, 1970, p. 993; entry in brackets added]

Taken in total, though, particularly at the time they were instituted, it seems clear that the various applications of testing during World War II made significant contributions to the war effort. Although World War II may not have put psychology "on the map" in the same sense that World War I was said to have, the psychological testing enterprise clearly contributed to this most important and trying time.

Clinical Psychology and World War II

Of particular note during the war was the manner in which clinical psychology emerged as a strong professional force. It is here that we begin to see the emergence of the modern-day profession of psychology.

In October 1944, the first clinical psychologists were commissioned in the army. By 1946, 50 were in place, with most being associated with the larger medical installations. The major activities of this group of pioneer clinicians were tied more or less directly to testing, with their primary functions being the administration and interpretation of individual tests (Hutt & Milton, 1947). As in World War I, the majority of tests administered related to the assessment of intellectual status. According to Hutt and Milton (1947), 44.58% of the tests administered related to intelligence.[3] However, these tests were used somewhat differently in World War II than they had been under the Yerkes program in 1917. Although there was some concern with the measurement of current level of intellectual functioning, the intelligence tests were "used almost as often for **differential diagnosis** [emphasis added], which is based upon scatter analysis, qualitative evaluation of the content of responses, evaluation of modes of intellectual functioning, and an evaluation of specific mental abilities and disabilities" (Hutt & Milton, 1947, p. 54). This tendency toward qualitative interpretations is noteworthy because it begins to signal some difficulties with the prevailing view of testing that focused on measurement operations that culminated in objective, numerical data—not subjective interpretations.

The movement away from objective assessment is also revealed in the large numbers of personality tests administered by the army clinical psychologists. Over 40% of all tests administered were measures of personality, with 82% of these being projectives (Hutt & Milton, 1947). The Rorschach accounted for over one-half of these, although other tests such as the Thematic Apperception Test (which is described in detail later on in this chapter) were also used frequently. These wartime applications of projective tests are clear testimony to the emerging application of projective tests in the clinical sphere and hint that the more objective, structured forms of tests may have limited utility in the clinical realm.

PROFESSIONALIZATION OF PSYCHOLOGY AFTER THE WAR

Perhaps one of the most interesting trends in wartime clinical psychology was a definite increase in the amount of time that clinicians spent doing therapy. In their survey, Hutt and Milton (1947) documented a continual increase in estimated percentages of time that army clinicians spent in guidance and therapy as the war proceeded. In the early phases of the war, time spent in therapy was estimated to be 12%. By the end of the conflagration, this had more than doubled, being listed as 29.6% in the last third of 1945. Although the need for such services would undoubtedly increase as more and more casualties and veterans returned from the fronts, this increase appears to be signaling an important change in clinical psychology. These data suggest a movement toward recovering some of the territory lost during the Great Depression, when the psychiatric profession retrenched its position (see Chapter 9).

---

[3]This figure includes 35.08% intelligence tests, plus an additional 9.5% for tests of "intellectual deficiency."

It was during this upswing in the fortunes of clinical psychology that World War II ended with the dropping of two atomic bombs over Japan. The world, quite unprepared, entered the atomic age. The redistribution of power deriving from the various treaties and accords set the U.S.S.R and the United States on a course that would shape the cold war and have an enduring effect on the nature of American society.

The psychological testing enterprise, like everything else during this time, was swept up into the changes and adjustments of the new postwar era. Perhaps the most notable feature of this period in North American psychology was a major movement toward professionalization within the psychological community. Psychology was ready to join the professions with a new exuberance born of its successes and victories during the war. Journal pages in the 1940s and early 1950s were filled with references to all sorts of issues attending the emergence of psychology as a strong and significant clinical profession. Issues of how best to train new professionals, images of professionalism, protective legislation, relationships with other professions, and the development of an explicit code of ethics all surfaced during this critical time.

Images

Numerous articles discussing "psychology as a profession" appeared during this period (for example, Armstrong, 1947; Hunt, 1951). In several cases, these concerns emerged in some rather self-conscious examinations of the manner in which the public viewed psychology. For example, Blake (1948) analyzed the manner in which *Time* magazine had portrayed psychology in the decade since 1937. Comparing the frequency of topics covered in *Psychological Abstracts* with *Time,* Blake concluded

> *Time*'s emphasis in presenting psychology roughly parallels the work done in the various fields, as measured by the number of articles appearing in *Psychological Abstracts*.... While *Time*'s reports are terse and well-written, they lack background and contextual material. This lack probably makes it difficult for the average reader to fit these reports into any very meaningful framework, and constitutes the chief limitation in *Time*'s handling of psychological work. [p. 132]

Guest (1948) conducted a survey to determine, more directly, what people thought of psychology. His results showed a considerable degree of confusion and inaccuracy about the things psychologists do, prompting the observation that there is a need to

> ... publicize the variety of duties that psychologists perform. Indeed, there is a need to inform the public regarding sources where they will be likely to find a reputable psychologist.... Changing undesirable attitudes and implanting more knowledge of the work of psychologists will not be easy, but this area is one in which psychologists are well qualified to function. [p. 139]

Constructive suggestions about how to improve psychology's image followed (for example, Blakeslee, 1952). The literature of the late 1940s and early 1950s showed a clear and consistent concern with the image of psychology as a profession. This was a definite indication of a self-conscious orientation toward the problems being faced in the postwar era.

Relationships with Medicine and Psychiatry

One fundamental issue underlying professionalization was the manner in which psychology was going to interact with the medical profession. In the clinical realm, initial concerns surfaced in surveys revealing that most medical schools did not include psychology in their curricula (Page & Passey, 1949). An article by the eminent psychiatrist W. C. Menninger (1950) set the tone for the interchange between the two professions. He argued that psychologists had a meaningful contribution to make in the testing of mental patients, but he had severe reservations about their role in therapy. An article with the provocative title "Are Psychologists Afraid of Therapy?" (Seard, 1950) argued for psychology's role in treatment and reflected the increasing desire of the clinical psychology community to be known as more than mere testers in clinical settings. New, clearly psychological, therapeutic techniques were becoming available (for example, Rogers, 1946), and it seemed reasonable that psychologists should assume a role in the treatment, as well as testing, of mental patients. This issue became so important that the APA created an "ad hoc Committee on Relations Between Psychology and the Medical Profession" (APA, 1952), but this did not stem the relatively negative view of psychology held by the medical profession (Huston, 1953; Jenkins, 1954).

An important observation in relation to the testing enterprise was the realization that clinical psychology was beginning to branch out in ways that imply a loss of influence for testing. As long as clinicians were locked in to being testers, the enterprise would flourish. However, as clinical psychology began to reach out for other kinds of activities such as therapy, testing's stranglehold on the clinicians would be weakened. This trend emerged in the postwar era and is still being played out in the 1990s as clinical psychology continues along the path of increasing the numbers of contributions it can make to the mental-health field.

Issues of Training

During this time, there was considerable concern about how the profession might best go about training its graduate students (for example, APA, 1947). Recommended program descriptions for clinical psychology mentioned considerable need for training in testing as well as a number of other activities that would complete the clinical psychologist's toolbox.

Of particular concern was the relative balance between practical and scientific skills in Ph.D. programs training clinical psychologists. On the one extreme, it would be possible to train **clinical technicians** who had acquired a set of specific skills such as test administration and interpretation, certain types of therapies, and so on. Such technicians would lack the scientific background on which their profession was based. On the other extreme was the possibility of training clinicians as full-blown scientists, arguing that they would be able to work their way into the clinical world once they had demonstrated their competence in research. In a landmark conference in Colorado, the **Boulder model** emerged as a compromise between these two extremes (Raimy, 1950). This training model defined the clinical psychologist as a **scientist/practitioner,** viewing basic scientific competence as a requisite to effective clinical practice but noting the need for extensive training in specific clinical skills *as well.* Clinical psychology then emerged as a very rigorous program of study because clinical skills had to be acquired as "add ons" to the standard scientific training. The add ons were to be accomplished by the use of **internships** or **practica** that involved supervised placements in specific clinical settings (see Foster, Benton, & Rabin, 1952).

The field of educational psychology, which was also emerging as a major consumer of the products of the testing enterprise, also debated issues regarding the most effective training models that might be employed (Burnham et al., 1951). Equally certain was the emerging professionalization for industrial psychologists. Those fields in which testing was a significant component were all moving toward increasing professionalization during this critical time in their development.

The place of the non-Ph.D. in the emerging profession also gained considerable attention, with emphasis on the relegation of master's-level people to technological positions such as administering tests but not interpreting them (Black, 1949; McTeer, 1952). Training concerns also surfaced in considerable discussion of the manner in which to teach undergraduate psychology (Pressey, 1949).

Legislation

Perhaps the major issue in psychology's move toward professional status was legislation oriented toward legal definition and protection of the psychological community. The desiderata of introducing legal constraints on the profession was hotly debated (see Heiser, 1950; Jacobsen, 1950; Kelly, 1950; MacFarlane, 1950; Peatman, 1950; Saffir, 1950; Wendt, 1950; Wolfle, 1950). Before long, however, legislation defining and protecting the profession of psychology began to emerge in scattered locations. In some jurisdictions, the Ph.D. degree was considered necessary for **certification,** whereas some other districts demanded only a master's degree.

The current ramification of this movement toward legislation is the institution of mechanisms by which psychologists earn **registration** as acceptable professionals. Much like most other professions, state or provincial examinations, which are typically taken after training is completed, are used to determine if a given individual is properly trained to practice. If these exams are passed, the individual is said to be registered or certified and has the right to practice as a professional psychologist. This provided a solution to concerns about improperly trained practitioners (Lebo, 1953) and the detection of "phonies," or charlatans (David, 1954; David & Springfield, 1958). Because of the certification process and its attending legal standing, nonregistered or noncertified persons practicing within the profession would be acting illegally, thus protecting the profession. As well, members of the profession who act contrary to the prevailing accepted standards of practice could be "unregistered," providing the profession with a mechanism of control over its constituents.

The benefits of legal status also meant that it would be possible for a recipient of bad psychological services to pursue legal damages in the courts. This raised the need for **malpractice insurance** (see Appleman, 1953) and the formation of an APA committee to examine the issue (APA, 1952), which reported its recommendations several years later (APA, 1955). Both the issue of charlatans and the need for malpractice insurance are clear indicators of the emergence of psychology as a major and well-established profession within North American society.

Ethics

Another aspect of the movement toward professionalization is shown by the beginnings of concerns for the development of a set of ethics to guide the behavior of psychologists working in the community. The first explicit mention of this was Hobbs (1948), with a preliminary progress report being published by a new APA Committee on Ethical Standards for Psychology the next year (APA, 1949).

The APA Committee on Ethical Standards was very busy in 1951 publishing standards dealing with a wide range of professional issues such as clinical and consulting relationships, research, writing/publishing, public responsibility, and teaching (see *American Psychologist,* 1951, for details of these standards).

The first set of **Ethical Principles of Psychologists** was approved and adopted in 1952 (APA, 1953), and a monitoring committee was established, which published reports of current ethical cases being discussed (for example, APA, 1954). The requisite periodic revisions of the standards were instituted at this time. By the end of the 1950s, psychology's professional house had been put in order with a wide range of ethical standards intended to guide the conduct of its members in ways which would ensure the emerging profession would continue to grow and prosper.

Of course, times and ethical codes change. Indeed, nine major revisions or republications with significant amendments to the Ethical Principles have been published between 1953 and 1992. What follows is a summary of the most recent APA ethical statement (APA, 1992) because it is most relevant for our purposes. Of note is that the movement toward formalized ethical principles started during the movement toward professionalization after World War II.

CLOSE UP   The Ethical Principles of Psychologists (1992)

Any ethical code is apt to be a complex document. The number of possible concerns about and manifestations of ethical or unethical behavior is astounding in a situation as complicated as the provision of psychological services. Because of this, much detail has been included in this Close Up. The intent here is not to intimidate you by presenting all kinds of memory-work material but to indicate the level of thinking that has gone into the most recent ethical code for psychologists. Four components of the code will be discussed: (1) the preamble, which sets the ground rules; (2) six general principles thought to apply to all situations; (3) a listing of the eight categories of specific ethical standards, including detailed presentation of the ones of particular relevance to testing; and (4) a brief discussion of a new set of rules and procedures to be enacted in the event that a complaint of unethical conduct is lodged.

Preamble. Setting the general tone of the documentation that follows, the APA ethical code begins with a preamble:

> Psychologists work to develop a valid and reliable body of scientific knowledge based on research. They may apply that knowledge to human behavior in a variety of contexts. In doing so, they perform many roles, such as researcher, educator, diagnostician, therapist, supervisor, consultant, administrator, social interventionist, and expert witness. Their goal is to broaden knowledge of behavior and, where appropriate, to apply it pragmatically to improve the condition of both the individual and society. Psychologists respect the central importance of freedom of inquiry and expression in research, teaching, and publication. They also strive to help the public in developing informed judgments and choices concerning human behavior. This Ethics Code provides a common set of values upon which psychologists build their professional and scientific work.
>
> This Code is intended to provide both the general principles and the decision rules to cover most situations encountered by psychologists. It has as its primary goal the welfare and protection of the individuals and groups with whom psychologists work. It is the individual responsibility of each psychologist to aspire to the highest possible standards of conduct. Psychologists respect and protect human and civil rights, and do not knowingly participate in or condone unfair discriminatory practices.
>
> The development of a dynamic set of ethical standards for a psychologist's work-related conduct requires a personal commitment to a lifelong effort to act ethically; to encourage ethical behavior by students, supervisees, employees, and colleagues, as appropriate; and to consult with others, as needed, concerning ethical problems. Each psychologist supplements, but does not violate, the Ethics Code's values and rules on the basis of guidance drawn from personal values, culture, and experience.

The discussion of the goals of psychology ("to develop a valid and reliable body of scientific knowledge") is clearly articulated, as is the desirability of applying this to "improve the condition of the individual and society." Ethical conduct is seen as requiring a lifelong effort, indicating the significance placed on this aspect of professional behavior.

General principles. The next entry in the 1992 Ethical Principles is a set of six general principles related to almost all aspects of professional and scientific conduct.

Principle A: Competence

Psychologists strive to maintain high standards of competence in their work. They recognize the boundaries of their particular competencies and the limitations of their expertise. They provide only those services and use only those techniques for which they are qualified by education, training, or experience. Psychologists are cognizant of the fact that the competencies required in serving, teaching, and/or studying groups of people vary with the distinctive characteristics of those groups. In those areas in which recognized professional standards do not yet exist, psychologists exercise careful judgment and take appropriate precautions to protect the welfare of those with whom they work.

They maintain knowledge of relevant scientific and professional information related to the services they render, and they recognize the need for ongoing education. Psychologists make appropriate use of scientific, professional, technical, and administrative resources.

Principle B: Integrity

Psychologists seek to promote integrity in the science, teaching, and practice of psychology. In these activities psychologists are honest, fair, and respectful of others. In describing or reporting their qualifications, services, products, fees, research, or teaching, they do not make statements that are false, misleading, or deceptive. Psychologists strive to be aware of their own belief systems, values, needs, and limitations and the effect of these on their work. To the extent feasible, they attempt to clarify for relevant parties the roles they are performing and to function appropriately in accordance with those roles. Psychologists avoid improper and potentially harmful dual relationships.

Principle C: Professional and Scientific Responsibility

Psychologists uphold professional standards of conduct, clarify their professional roles and obligations, accept appropriate responsibility for their behavior, and adapt their methods to the needs of different populations. Psychologists consult with, refer to, or cooperate with other professionals and institutions to the extent needed to serve the best interests of their patients, clients, or other recipients of their services. Psychologists' moral standards and conduct are personal matters to the same degree as is true for any other person, except as psychologists' conduct may compromise their professional responsibilities or reduce the public's trust in psychology and psychologists. Psychologists are concerned about the ethical compliance of their colleagues' scientific and professional conduct. When appropriate, they consult with colleagues in order to prevent or avoid unethical conduct.

Principle D: Respect for People's Rights and Dignity

Psychologists accord appropriate respect to the fundamental rights, dignity, and worth of all people. They respect the rights of individuals to privacy, confidentiality, self-determination, and autonomy, mindful that legal and other obligations may lead to inconsistency and conflict with the exercise of these rights. Psychologists are aware of cultural, individual, and role differences, including those due to age, gender, race, ethnicity, national origin, religion, sexual orientation, disability, language, and socioeconomic status. Psychologists try to eliminate the effect on their work of biases based on those factors, and they do not knowingly participate in or condone unfair discriminatory practices.

Principle E: Concern for Others' Welfare

Psychologists seek to contribute to the welfare of those with whom they interact professionally. In their professional actions, psychologists weigh the welfare and rights of their patients or clients, students, supervisees, human research participants, and other affected persons, and the welfare of animal subjects of research. When conflicts occur among psychologists' obligations or concerns, they attempt to resolve these conflicts and to perform their roles in a responsible fashion that avoids or minimizes harm. Psychologists are sensitive to real and ascribed differences in power between themselves and others, and they do not exploit or mislead other people during or after professional relationships.

Principle F: Social Responsibility

Psychologists are aware of their professional and scientific responsibilities to the community and the society in which they work and live. They apply and make public their knowledge of psychology in order to contribute to human welfare. Psychologists are concerned about and work to mitigate the causes of human suffering. When undertaking research, they strive to advance human welfare and the science of psychology. Psychologists try to avoid misuse of their work. Psychologists comply with the law and encourage the development of law and social policy that serve the interests of their patients and clients and the public. They are encouraged to contribute a portion of their professional time for little or no personal advantage.

These six general principles are a more detailed articulation of the basic premises outlined in the preamble. Here we find a more precise statement of the fundamental concerns driving the Ethical Principles. A careful reading of these principles indicates that it would be no easy task to adhere to all desiderata that are mentioned.

Ethical standards. The next level of specificity in the 1992 code is a set of eight ethical standards. Each contains a number of subtopics indicating that they are more precise and situational than the general principles.

1. *General Standards.* Discussion of 27 topics including the maintenance of competence (1.05), sexual harassment (1.11), misuse of influence (1.15), and fees and financial arrangements (1.25).
2. *Evaluation, Assessment, or Intervention* (discussed below).
3. *Advertising and Other Public Statements.* Discussion of six topics including avoidance of deceptive statements (3.03) and media presentations (3.04).
4. *Therapy.* Discussion of nine topics such as sexual intimacies (4.04–4.07) and termination of services (4.09).
5. *Privacy and Confidentiality.* Discussion of 11 topics. This aspect of ethics will be discussed in Chapter 14.
6. *Teaching, Training Supervision, Research, and Publishing.* Discussion of 26 topics such as design of training programs (6.01), assessing student performance (6.05), informed consent in research (6.11), and plagiarism (6.22).
7. *Forensic Activities.* Discussion of six topics on the use of various aspects of psychology in the legal system, including forensic assessments (7.02) and truthfulness and candor (7.04).
8. *Resolving Ethical Issues.* Discussion of seven topics including the necessity of being familiar with the ethical code (8.01) and reporting ethical violations (8.05).

Each category contains a considerable amount of information. The topics are wide-ranging and deal with myriad concerns for the psychologist.

Ethical standards directly relevant to testing. Of the eight categories in the ethical standards, the second set—Evaluation, Assessment, or Intervention—are by far the most directly relevant to the testing enterprise. The ten topics covered in this section of the code highlight the basic concerns of the testing community. Notice that the genesis of all these test-related standards flow directly from the considerations that we have been discussing in the last few chapters of *The Enterprise*.

2. *Evaluation, Assessment, or Intervention*

2.01 Evaluation, Diagnosis, and Interventions in Professional Context
   a. Psychologists perform evaluations, diagnostic services, or interventions only within the context of a defined professional relationship.
   b. Psychologists' assessments, recommendations, reports, and psychological diagnostic or evaluative statements are based on information and techniques (including personal interviews of the individual when appropriate) sufficient to provide appropriate substantiation for their findings.

2.02 Competence and Appropriate Use of Assessments and Interventions
   a. Psychologists who develop, administer, score, interpret, or use psychological assessment techniques, interviews, tests, or instruments do so in a manner and for purposes that are appropriate in light of the research on or evidence of the usefulness and proper application of the techniques.
   b. Psychologists refrain from misuse of assessment techniques, interventions, results, and interpretations and take reasonable steps to prevent others from misusing the information these techniques provide. This includes refraining from releasing raw test results or raw data to persons, other than to patients or clients as appropriate, who are not qualified to use such information.

2.03 Test Construction
   Psychologists who develop and conduct research with tests and other assessment techniques use scientific procedures and current professional knowledge for test design, standardization, validation, reduction or elimination of bias, and recommendations for use.

2.04 Use of Assessment in General and with Special Populations
   a. Psychologists who perform interventions or administer, score, interpret, or use assessment techniques are familiar with the reliability, validation, and related standardization or outcome studies of, and proper applications and uses of, the techniques they use.
   b. Psychologists recognize limits to the certainty with which diagnoses, judgments, or predictions can be made about individuals.
   c. Psychologists attempt to identify situations in which particular interventions or assessment techniques or norms may not be applicable or may require adjustment in administration or interpretation because of factors such as individuals' gender, age, race, ethnicity, national origin, religion, sexual orientation, disability, language, or socioeconomic status.

2.05 Interpreting Assessment Results
   When interpreting assessment results, including automated interpretations, psychologists take into account the various test factors and characteristics of the person being assessed that might affect psychologists'

judgments or reduce the accuracy of their interpretations. They indicate any significant reservations they have about the accuracy or limitations of their interpretations.

2.06   Unqualified Persons
Psychologists do not promote the use of psychological assessment techniques by unqualified persons.

2.07   Obsolete Tests and Outdated Test Results
a. Psychologists do not base their assessment or intervention decisions or recommendations on data or test results that are outdated for the current purpose.
b. Similarly, psychologists do not base such decisions or recommendations on tests and measures that are obsolete and not useful for the current purpose.

2.08   Test Scoring and Interpretation Services
a. Psychologists who offer assessment or scoring procedures to other professionals accurately describe the purpose, norms, validity, reliability, and applications of the procedures and any special qualifications applicable to their use.
b. Psychologists select scoring and interpretation services (including automated services) on the basis of evidence of the validity of the program and procedures as well as on other appropriate considerations.
c. Psychologists retain appropriate responsibility for the appropriate application, interpretation, and use of assessment instruments, whether they score and interpret such tests themselves or use automated or other services.

2.09   Explaining Assessment Results
Unless the nature of the relationship is clearly explained to the person being assessed in advance and precludes provision of an explanation of results (such as in some organizational consulting, preemployment or security screenings, and forensic evaluations), psychologists ensure that an explanation of the results is provided using language that is reasonably understandable to the person assessed or to another legally authorized person on behalf of the client. Regardless of whether the scoring and interpretation are done by the psychologist, by assistants, or by automated or other outside services, psychologists take reasonable steps to ensure that appropriate explanations of results are given.

2.10   Maintaining Test Security
Psychologists make reasonable efforts to maintain the integrity and security of tests and other assessment techniques consistent with law, contractual obligations, and in a manner that permits compliance with the requirements of this Ethics Code.

This listing of concerns related to testing provides you with a sense of the detail included in the ethical code. A considerable amount of thought has gone into this description of professional test-related behavior. Most of the points raised here flow directly from an approach to testing that carefully considers the needs of the test taker. For example, 2.09 indicates that assessment results must be understandable to the respondent under most circumstances (this point will be discussed more fully in

Chapter 14). The onus is clearly on the test user to provide evidence that a given assessment and its interpretation is appropriate to the situation in which it is used (for example, 2.01, 2.04, 2.08). The points related to competence (2.02, 2.06), proper use of tests (2.04), and up-to-date testing materials (2.07) are clear indications of the desire to maintain optimal quality standards within the testing enterprise. The topic related to test security (2.10) will be discussed in detail in Chapter 14.

Rules and procedures. A new addition to the 1992 ethical code is a detailed set of rules to be used in the event that formal charges of ethical misconduct are lodged. The incredibly detailed procedures map out the appropriate course of action, such as the makeup of committees, issues of confidentiality of proceedings, record keeping, time limits, and reopening cases. The legal-sounding tone of these rules is clear testimony to the increased concerned with legal process that appears to be part of the contemporary professional climate.

Overall, the 1992 ethical code is a very substantial document. In it we find a combination of wisdom born of experience, attempts to consider the various stakeholders in the enterprise, and a concerted effort to induce the highest possible standards of conduct within the profession. This document is clearly a lineal ancestor of the 1950s concerns for professionalism and the first explicit code of ethics (APA, 1953).

Despite the level of detail and concern in all versions of the APA ethical code and the clear relevance of many of the points to the testing enterprise, some very important points were still missing. The 1953 ethical code, for example, did not come close to providing enough direction to serve as a useful charter for the development and monitoring of tests.[4] Much more detail was required. Interestingly, this emerged in the form of two distinct documents created within the testing field: an ethical code associated with the distribution of tests and a set of technical guidelines that provided great detail about the kinds of supporting information necessary to consider a test acceptable.

THE EMERGENCE OF FORMAL GUIDELINES FOR TESTS

The first domain in psychology to adopt an explicit ethical code was the testing enterprise. Leading the adoption of an ethical code for the entire profession by 3 years, the testing enterprise began considering the important issues in 1949. There was considerable concern within the profession that the potential lucrative profits attending the sale of tests and **diagnostic aids** could lead to some problems. The stakes were very high; for example, it was estimated that over 60 million psychological tests were administered in 1944 alone (Wolfle, 1947). A **royalty** rate of even 1 cent per administration indicates that considerable amounts of money were involved for both the test developers and publishers. It was clearly in their best interests to sell as many tests as possible. This state of affairs signaled the need for

---

[4]The same observation holds for the 1992 code presented in the Close Up. However, several other documents have evolved over the years to fill in these missing points.

policies surrounding the sale, distribution, and marketing of tests because the potential for abuse was legion. Based on the experience of APA members, a wide range of potential problems was cited to indicate the need for an ethical code. Table 12-5 gives examples of these problems to provide you a sense of the concerns stimulating the eventual ethical code.

Table 12-5 Vignettes citing a need for ethical standards in the distribution of tests and diagnostic aids

Regarding Qualifications of Test Users	A personnel man employed by a medium-sized steel company called for advice on a teaching problem. He had given a battery of well-known tests to candidates, had scored them, and wanted to be told over the telephone what he should use as a passing score. He had made no validating studies and had no idea that they should be made (p. 621).
Regarding Qualified Psychologists Supervising Testing Programs	A large institute selects personnel for commercial and industrial concerns by means of psychological tests. Some of the psychologists connected with this institute are reputable and even outstanding. Procedures include self-administration of a battery of tests at home by the client; return of these by mail and scoring by clerical workers; and automatic interpretation by relatively untrained workers, utilizing charts and tables. It is common place for friends and family to cooperate with the client in filling in responses (p. 623).
Regarding Salespersons	A test salesmen, asked by a school superintendent (who admitted he knew little about guidance) to draw up a guidance program for his school, thereupon gave him a "complete program" by checking items in his catalog (p. 624).
Regarding Test Publishers	A publisher of other types of supplies announced publication of a personality inventory, making it available to any would-be purchaser. The manual is excellent, although nontechnically written, and the questionnaire well constructed. But anyone may buy it and interpret it (p. 624).
Regarding the Readiness of a Test for Release	A nonprofessional person approached an industrial psychologist with extreme claims for a "temperament" test of his own devising. He claimed approval for it by university faculty members and local businessmen and manufacturers; he produced unorthodox "validation" statistics. Retest reliability turned out to be about zero (p. 625).
Regarding the Test Manual	A book on administrative ability gives the impression that the author's test of "administrative ability" is well validated. Investigation showed that the author had no data that could be examined either in raw or in analyzed form, the ostensible reason being their confidential nature (p. 626).

SOURCE: APA (1950).

As can be seen from these vignettes, the issues regarding test distribution are both complex and highly important. The potential damage to individuals, institutions, and the profession of psychology embedded in these incidents is great. These stories give a sense of the need for control being felt within the emerging profession and provide a clear indication of why the testing enterprise was the first explicitly to adopt an ethical code.

The Test Distribution Sub-Committee of the APA Ethics Committee published a preliminary set of recommendations for comment (APA, 1949), and the revised version of these standards, **Ethical Standards for the Distribution of Psychological Tests and Diagnostic Aids** was adopted in the next year (APA, 1950). The following Close Up presents an overview of the standards presented in this important document.

CLOSE UP   **Ethical Standards for the Distribution of Psychological Tests and Diagnostic Aids (1950)**

Qualifications of test users. The basic issue was the need to restrict the distribution of certain tests to ensure that the professional **qualifications of test users** to administer and interpret the test without causing harm to individuals, institutions, and the profession were established. The standards involved developing three levels of tests that varied in how much training a person had to have in order to be able to purchase them. Level A tests are those that anyone could administer and interpret properly with the aid of the manual. Level B tests where those that required some technical knowledge of test construction and use and a smattering of training in statistics, individual differences, guidance, and the like. The onus is on purchasers to demonstrate to the publisher that they have the required knowledge. Tests in the highest level, C, require substantial understanding of testing and supporting psychological subjects, together with supervised experience in the use of these devices. Again, the demonstration of adequate credentials was demanded before Level C tests would be sold.

There were other recommendations in this section relating to the need to demonstrate qualification in the specific area addressed by the test and the notion that anyone releasing a test to an "ignorant user" has committed a breach of ethics.

Psychologists sponsoring test activities. In some cases, qualified psychologists supervise testing operations, and this category of recommendation related to the responsibilities of such supervisors. Recommendations included the need for the psychologist to be actively involved in the program, the supervisors' responsibilities to ensure the security of test materials, and the need to ensure that all users are adequately qualified.

Test salespersons. There was concern that salespersons would have a tendency to overestimate the quality of tests in the interests of selling them. The recommendations suggested that tests should be ordered on the basis of facts in the technical literature, not salesperson's rhetoric. It was also suggested that salespersons without adequate technical knowledge should restrict their activities to distribution and not pose as consultants. Even qualified publisher representatives should be very clear about their affiliation with the publisher if they are involved in marketing.

Choice of distributor. Sometimes tests are published by firms who do not possess sufficient technical knowledge to market the test with proper restrictions and the like. The standard in the section indicated that tests should only be published by firms who are demonstrably familiar with testing procedures and problems.

Readiness of a test for release. The desire to gain recognition, praise, and income can place pressures on test developers to publish too early in the developmental sequence. The standards indicated the need for the availability of adequate reliability and validity data prior to any publication. Any early publications should be clearly indicated with conspicuous labels such as "for experimental use only."

Test manuals. It is possible to present overly selected or misrepresentative data in a test **manual** to make the test look better than it really is. To remedy this, the standards indicated that manuals must summarize the exact method of construction and standardizing and include detailed presentations of all validity studies. The need for constant revision of manuals, clear definitions of test purpose, and standardization samples was also indicated.

This set of ethical standards for the distribution of tests has addressed what appear to be some of the major issues surrounding the professionalization of psychology, in general, and the testing enterprise, in particular. The interaction between society and the testing enterprise has continually been difficult, and it is not the least bit surprising to find that the enterprise was the first to propose the kind of internal policing that is oriented toward reducing the number of difficulties that may arise.

Of particular note here is the failure of the APA to provide any mechanism for the enforcement of these ethical standards. Although adopted by the APA, they were published merely "for the guidance of members of the American Psychological Association" (1950, p. 620). For some reason, the APA did not volunteer to publish a register of tests and distributors that adhered to the standards. This appears to be a major weakness of the efforts of the APA to police the testing enterprise.

Another difficulty with these standards also emerged. The guidelines were not complete: "No attempt is made to cover the ethics or standards of test construction, or test application, although the distinctions are at times difficult to make" (APA, 1950, p. 620). What was missing in the 1950 standards was a discussion of expectations about the level and kind of technical information needed before a potential test user has enough information to make an informed choice of which test to use. What kinds of validity were required for a test to be acceptable? What is a minimal level of reliability acceptable to a specific domain? How much of this information should be included in the test manual? How much detail should be included about the proper use and interpretation of test scores? What about the details of administration, scoring, scales, and norms? All these questions were left unanswered by the 1950 ethical recommendations. Although commentary about some of these issues was published (for example, Stuit, 1951), a major gap remained in the standards attending the testing enterprise.

In the early 1950s, the APA created a committee to develop a set of technical recommendations that would address the omissions in the 1950 ethical statement. The committee consisted of **Lee J. Cronbach** (chair), E. S. Bordin, R. C. Callman, H. S. Conrad, Lloyd G. Humphreys, Paul E. Meehl, and Donald E. Super—all experts in the assessment field. In 1952 this group published a preliminary set of guidelines, asking for feedback from members (APA, 1952). Two years later, a set of revised recommendations was published (APA, 1954). The following Close Up presents these important **Technical Recommendations for Psychological Tests and Diagnostic Aids.**

CLOSE UP   **Summary of the 1954 Technical Recommendations for Psychological Tests and Diagnostic Aids**

These recommendations indicated that, although the testing enterprise had been careful in the manner in which tests were developed, the time was ripe for a formalized set of standards that would help ensure "a high degree of quality and usefulness" (p. 210). The need for a guide that articulated "a consensus as to what information is most helpful to the test consumer" (p. 210) was noted, as was the concern that such guidelines "not stifle growth" (p. 210). The focus of this document was on the test manual: "The essential principle that sets the tone for this document is that a test manual should carry information sufficient to enable any qualified user to make sound judgments regarding the usefulness and interpretation of the test" (p. 202).

Three levels of recommendation were presented: (1) *Essential* recommendations are defined as "the consensus of present-day thinking as to what is normally required for operational use of a test" (p. 205). Information listed as essential was thought to be "genuinely needed" for most tests. (2) *Very desirable* recommendations are those "which contribute greatly to the user's understanding of the test" (p. 205). (3) The third category of recommendation, *desirable,* includes information that would be helpful but less so than the *very desirable* category. The following summarizes the broad categories of the recommendations. Each category contains subpoints that provide greater detail and some discussion.

A. Dissemination of information

1. When a test is published for operational use, it should be accompanied by a manual that takes cognizance of the detailed recommendations in this report. (*Essential*)
2. The manual should be up-to-date and should be revised at appropriate intervals. (*Essential*)

B. Interpretation

1. Insofar as possible, the test, the manual, record forms, and other accompanying material should help users make correct interpretations of the test results. (*Essential*)
2. The test manual should state explicitly the purposes and applications for which the test is recommended. (*Essential*)
3. The test manual should indicate the professional qualifications required to administer and interpret the test properly. (*Essential*)
4. When a test is issued in revised form, the nature and extent of any revision and the comparability of data for the revised and old test data should be explicitly stated. (*Essential*)
5. Statements in the manual reporting relationships are by implication quantitative and should be stated as precisely as the data permit. If

data to support such a statement have not been collected, that fact should be made clear. (*Essential*)

C. Validity

1. When validity is reported, the manual should indicate clearly what type of validity is referred to. The unqualified term *validity* should be avoided unless its meaning is clear from the context. (*Essential*)

2. The manual should report the validity of each type of inference for which a test is recommended. If validity of some recommended interpretation has not been tested, that fact should be made clear. (*Essential*)

3. Findings based on logical analysis should be carefully distinguished from conclusions established by correlation of test behavior with criterion behavior. (*Essential*)

4. If a test performance is to be interpreted as a sample of performance in some universe of situations, the manual should indicate clearly what universe is represented and how adequate sampling is. (*Essential*)

5. When predictive validity is determined by statistical analysis, the analysis should be reported in a form from which the reader can determine confidence limits of estimates regarding individuals or the probability of misclassification of the individual on the criterion. (*Essential*)

6. All measures of criteria should be described accurately and in detail. The manual should evaluate the adequacy of the criterion. It should draw attention to significant aspects of performance that the criterion measure does not reflect and to the irrelevant factors that may reflect. (*Essential*)

7. The reliability of the criterion should be reported if it can be determined. If such evidence is not available, the author should discuss the probable reliability as judged from indirect evidence. (*Very desirable*)

8. The dates when validation data were gathered should be reported. (*Essential*)

9. The criterion score of a person should be determined independently of his or her test score. The manual should describe precautions taken to avoid contamination of the criterion or should warn the reader of any possible contamination. (*Essential*)

10. Test scores to be used in validation should be determined independently of criterion scores. (*Essential*)

11. When items are selected or a scoring key is established empirically on the basis of evidence gathered on a particular sample, the manual should not report validity coefficients computed on this sample or on a group that includes any of this sample. The reported validity coefficients should be based on a cross-validation sample. (*Essential*)

12. If the manual recommends that interpretation be based on the test profile, evidence should be provided that the shape of the profile is a valid predictor. (*Very desirable*)

13. The validation sample should be described sufficiently for the user to know whether the persons he tests may properly be regarded as represented by the sample on which validation was based. (*Essential*)

14. The author should base validation studies on samples comparable, in terms of selection of cases and conditions of testing, to the groups to whom the manual recommends that the test be applied. (*Very desirable*)

15. If the validity of the test can reasonably be expected to be different in subgroups that can be identified when the test is given, the manual should report the validity for each group separately or should report that no difference was found. (*Very desirable*)

16. Reports of validation studies should describe any conditions likely to affect the motivation of subjects for taking the test. (*Essential*)

17. Reports of concurrent validity should be so described that the reader will not regard them as establishing predictive validity. (*Essential*)

18. The manual should report all available information that will assist the user in determining what psychological attributes account for variance in test scores. (*Essential*)

D. Reliability

1. The test manual should report such evidence of reliability as would permit the reader to judge whether scores are sufficiently dependable for the recommended uses of the test. If any of the necessary evidence has not been collected, the absence of such information should be noted. (*Essential*)

2. The manual should avoid any implication that reliability measures demonstrate the predictive or concurrent validity of the test. (*Essential*)

3. In reports of reliability, procedures and sample should be described sufficiently for the reader to judge whether the evidence applies to the persons and problem with which he or she is concerned. (*Essential*)

4. If two forms of a test are made available, with both forms intended for possible use with the same subjects, the correlation between forms and information as to the equivalence of the scores on the two forms should be reported. If the necessary evidence is not provided, the manual should warn the reader against assuming comparability. (*Essential*)

5. If the manual suggests that a score is a measure of a generalized, homogeneous trait, evidence on internal consistency should be reported. (*Essential*)

6. Coefficients of internal consistency should be determined by the split-half method or methods of the Kuder–Richardson type, if these can properly be used on the data under examination. Any other measure of internal consistency that the author wishes to report in addition should be carefully explained. (*Essential*)

7. The manual should indicate what degree of stability of scores may be expected if a test is repeated after time has elapsed. If such evidence is not presented, the absence of information regarding stability should be noted. (*Essential*)

E. Administration and scoring

1. The directions for administration should be presented with sufficient clarity that the test user can duplicate the administrative conditions

under which the norms and data on reliability and validity were obtained. (*Essential*)

2. Where subjective processes enter into the scoring of the test, evidence on degree of agreement between independent scorings should be presented. If such evidence is not provided, the manual should draw attention to scorer error as a possible error of measurement. (This recommendation was not assigned a level.)

F. Scales and norms

1. Scales used for reporting scores should be such as to increase the likelihood of accurate interpretation and emphasis by test interpreter and subject. (*Essential*)

2. Where there is no compelling advantage to be obtained by reporting scores in some other form, the manual should suggest reporting scores in terms of percentile equivalents or standard scores. (*Very desirable*)

3. Standard scores obtained so that they have a normal distribution and a fixed mean and standard deviation should in general be used in preference to other derived measures. For some tests, there may be a substantial reason to choose some other type of derived score. (*Very desirable*)

4. Local norms are more important for many uses than published norms. In such cases, the manual should suggest appropriate emphasis on local norms. (*Very desirable*)

5. Except where the primary use is to compare individuals with their own local group, norms should be published at the time of release of the tests for operational use. (*Essential*)

6. Norms should report the distribution of scores on an appropriate reference group or groups. (*Essential*)

7. Norms should refer to defined and clearly described populations. These populations should be the groups to whom users of the test will ordinarily wish to compare the persons tested. (*Essential*)

This set of recommendations provides a concise review of the theory of measurement underlying the 1950s view of psychological testing. There is considerable emphasis on the clear communication of the intent of the test (for example, A.1, A.2, E.1), the scientific nature of the enterprise (C.2, C.3, E.2), and the use of prevailing statistical techniques (C.5, D.6, F.3).

Of particular note in these recommendations is the emphasis on validity (with 18 subrecommendations, whereas reliability received only 7). This signals the importance of validity to the measurement theory underlying the testing enterprise.

The 1954 recommendations were almost immediately adopted by the **National Education Association (NEA)** and, in retrospect, have been described as "...a monumental achievement. They [the 1954 recommendations] had pervasive influence on test reviews, textbooks, test manuals, and published research" (Novick, 1981, p. 1042). However, the document was also a "somewhat tentative, almost defensive statement that clearly was presented as an aid to, rather than a monitor of, professional activity" (Novick, 1981, p. 1042). According to the committee chair Lee Cronbach, "The drafting committee was opposed from the outset to the idea of dividing tests into classes of acceptable and unacceptable tests and was greatly concerned lest a perfectionist approach would inhibit the development of tests" (Cronbach, 1979). So the guidelines were just that—guidelines. No mechanism of enforcement was proposed, and the policing of the testing enterprise was left to the individuals developing and using the tests.

Not unlike the ethical code, the Technical Recommendations for Psychological Tests and Diagnostic Aids has undergone revision and change. The most recent version was published in 1985. To give you a sense of these changes, Appendix D provides a discussion of some of the points that have emerged in the Technical Recommendations since the 1954 version. This update provides an interesting glimpse to the manners in which the testing enterprise has changed since the first Technical Recommendations were published.

Thus, by 1954 the areas of psychology that involved tests were demonstrating considerable professionalism. This was clearly reflected in various developments such as standards for training (the Boulder model), legislation protecting the profession, a series of ethical documents intended to act as rules of conduct for members of the profession, and the emergence of a set of technical guidelines for psychological tests. Without doubt, the institutional component of the psychological testing enterprise had been well articulated and formalized by the mid-1950s. This context had set rather rigorous standards for becoming credentialed as a member and served the purpose of ensuring that only competent individuals would practice psychology.

TESTING IN THE EARLY 1950s

Throughout the postwar activities associated with the professionalization of psychology, the testing enterprise was continuing its growth at a rapid rate. By the end of the 1940s, the foundations for the modern psychological testing enterprise had been laid. Stemming from beginnings established in the previous three decades, tests were being developed and improved in the following areas: individual measures of intelligence, group tests of intelligence, abilities, special aptitudes, developmental schedules, personality, achievement, psychiatric diagnosis, and vocational interests. All the contemporary major areas of assessment were established and growing apace by 1950. The testing enterprise had inserted itself into a number of exceedingly important social decision-making contexts, with contributions being particularly noteworthy in the education, military, and the medical communities. It appears that testing had succeeded in providing the discipline with dramatic action to verify its worth and had emerged as a particularly successful social enterprise, serving society's needs with the accuracy and efficiency of science.

An examination of the tests that were being most frequently discussed in the literature of the time provides a snapshot of the testing enterprise in 1951.

Table 12-6 Publications concerning the 12 leading tests in 1951

Test	Number of Publications	Rank
Rorschach	1219	1
Stanford–Binet	493	2
Wechsler–Bellevue	371	3
TAT	299	4
MMPI	283	5
ACE	276	6
SVIB	273	7
Bernreuter	259	8
Kuder Preference	208	9
Bell Adjustment Inventory	119	10
Seashore (Musical Talent)	117	11
Primary Mental Abilities (PMA)	102	12

SOURCE: Sundberg (1954).

Sundberg (1954) reported such data, which includes information up to and including 1951; Table 12-6 summarizes these. The most "talked about" test in 1951 was the Rorschach, accounting for an average of 2.7 publications per week during the reporting period! The ten famous inkblots were generating considerable print with the press being both negative and positive. The Thematic Apperception Test (TAT), another projective test, had also entered the top ten. In addition, individual measures of intelligence (Stanford–Binet, Wechsler–Bellevue, PMA), personality inventories (MMPI, Bernreuter, Bell), college admission (ACE), vocational interests (SVIB, Kuder), and the Seashore Test of Musical Talent round out the most discussed tests within the enterprise. These data indicate the domains of concern and development within the testing enterprise during this time.

While all of this was going on, the enterprise had also developed a relatively sophisticated theory of measurement. The critical term in this theory was *validity*, with especial emphasis on the criterion-related variation of this concept. The meaning of a test score was determined by correlating the test with some outside criterion. Cases where the correlation was high indicated that the test and criterion had shared variance and allowed inferences about what the test measures (for example, a high correlation of IQ with scholastic achievement indicated that IQ tests measured scholastic achievement). Cases where the correlation was low or 0 would be used to suggest areas that the test did not measure (for example, a 0 correlation between IQ and impulsivity indicated that impulsivity was not part of the domain of behaviors associated with intelligence). This theory of measurement was radically empirical and neither admitted nor needed a definition of the entity being measured. Statements of theory about the intent of the scale were not important in this theory of assessment. A pragmatic and empirical philosophy of science carried the day.

TRUE-SCORE TEST THEORY

In 1950 **Harold Gulliksen** published a book that articulated the prevailing theory of measurement. The roots of this presentation went back as far as the mid-1920s (for example, Kelley, 1923), but Gulliksen's exposition, which emerged as a classic, integrated a number of strands of thinking into a coherent position.

The basic approach involved defining the observed test score as a joint function of the respondent's true score and random error (Gulliksen, 1950b). A person's **true score** represents "the actual ability of the person a quantity which will be relatively stable from test to test as long as the tests are measuring the same thing" (Gulliksen, 1950b, pp. 4–5). The **random error** component of a given test score is "due to the various factors that may cause a person sometimes to answer correctly an item that he does not know, and sometimes to answer incorrectly an item he does know" (p. 5).[5] Equation 12-1 represents the starting point:

$$X_i = T_i + E_i \tag{12-1}$$

where

X_i = the observed score on test X for person i

T_i = the true score on test X for person i, representing the actual ability that is stable from test to test, assuming the tests measure the same thing

E_i = the error represented in the score on test X for person i

T_i is a hypothetical idea because we cannot gain a direct estimate of its value from Equation 12-1—there are too many unknowns. Perhaps the easiest way to conceptualize true score is to consider the clearly idealized situation of administering a given test to the same person a number of times—say, 100.[6] Even if the respondent did not get bored and did not remember the items across these many administrations, we would still expect the scores to show some variation over the 100 administrations. Indeed, with what we know about the normal curve and its applicability to human measurement (see Chapter 4), we might expect these 100 scores to be normally distributed as illustrated in Figure 12-3. (This distribution is *not* the more standard normal distribution of scores of multiple persons on one administration of the test.)

According to Gulliksen, the true score would be the mean of this distribution. Such a distribution would have a standard deviation, which proves to be an interesting statistic. If the test was perfectly reliable, we would expect the standard

---

[5]The use of masculine pronouns in this quote (and many of the historical quotations in the text) reflects the linguistic (and presumably political) conventions of the day. To change them to fit today's gender-sensitive conventions is tempting but has been resisted in the interests of keeping close to the original materials.

[6]Gulliksen's derivations were based on an infinite number of administrations. The number 100 has been used here to provide a more concrete example.

Figure 12-3 The hypothetical frequency distribution of test scores obtained from administering the same test 100 times to one person.

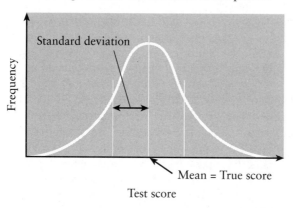

deviation of this distribution to be 0. That is, in the perfectly reliable case, all observations would be equal to the true score. It follows that the size of the standard deviation is a direct function of test reliability, with the spread of the distribution being inversely related to test reliability.

Gulliksen (1950b) added the assumptions that the average amount of **error** and the correlation between T_i and E_i are both equal to 0 and derived an estimate of the size of the standard deviation of distributions such as the one shown in Figure 12-3. This statistic is called the **standard error of measurement** and is calculated using Equation 12-2:

$$s_e = s_X \sqrt{1 - r_{XX}}$$ (12-2)

where

s_e = the standard error of measurement of test X

s_X = the standard deviation of the scores on test X

r_{XX} = the reliability of test x

According to this formula, a perfectly reliable test ($r_{XX} = 1.00$) would have a standard error of measurement of 0. Tests with lower reliabilities would obtain larger standard errors of measurement. The standard error of measurement, then, is an alternative way of describing the reliability of a test.

This statistic is particularly useful when interpreting individual scores. For example, if we are dealing with a WISC subscale score that has a standard deviation of 3 (see Chapter 10) and this subscale has a reliability of .73, we can calculate the standard error of measurement using Equation 12-2. In this case, $s_e = 3\sqrt{(1 - .73)} = 3\sqrt{.27} = 3 \times .52 = 1.56$. This means that the standard deviation of the distribution shown in Figure 12-3 for a WISC subtest with a reliability of .73 is 1.56.

Now let's apply what we know about the normal curve to the interpretation of the standard error of measurement. Recall that roughly two-thirds of the cases in a normal distribution fall between ±1 SD of the mean. Let's go back to our intrepid test taker who had to sit through 100 administrations of a test—say, the WISC subtest described above—and that the true score (the mean test score of these 100 administrations) was 12. We now know that two-thirds of the time this respondent's observed score will fall within 1 SD of the mean or between the values of 10.44 and 13.56 (12 ± 1.56). That is, for all persons with true scores of 12, we expect the observed score to fall between 10.44 and 13.56 about two-thirds of the time. This provides us with an expected range of test scores for a test with given reliability.

We could be more precise with our range specification and argue that we should use a more stringent criterion than two-thirds. For example, in a normal curve, 95% of the cases fall between ±1.96 SDs of the mean (see Table 4-6 and Appendix A). In our WISC example, this means that 95% of the time the observed score for a person with a true score of 12 will fall between 8.94 [12 − (1.96 × 1.56)] and 15.06 [12 + (1.96 × 1.56)]. If our intrepid test taker did indeed take the test 100 times, we would expect the observed score to fall outside of the range of 8.94 through 15.06 only five times.[7]

In actual practice, we do not know a person's true score—only the score obtained on one administration. However, as a convenient shorthand, we can apply the above reasoning in reverse. If an obtained score is within ±1.96 s_e of the true score 95% of the time, then we can argue that the true score will fall within ±1.96 s_e of the obtained score 95% of the time. That is, we can create a **confidence limit** for an observed score that reflects the probabilistic certainty that a person's true score falls within specified limits based on their observed score and the s_e. For example, for persons who obtain a score of 8 on our WISC subtest with a reliability of .73, we can say with 95% certainty that their true scores fall between 4.94 and 11.06 [8 ± (1.96 × 1.56)].

This demonstrates rather vividly how careful we have to be in the interpretation of a single test score. For example, observing a score of 8 on a WISC subtest with a reliability of .73 tells us that a person's true score may fall anywhere between (roughly) 5 and 11. This is a fairly wide range. Not only that, even if this wide range is acceptable, *we will be wrong 1 in 20 times*. That is, the true score will fall outside of this range .05 of the time because it represents a 95% confidence limit. This line of reasoning provides a convenient way of understanding the limits that should be placed on the interpretation of individual tests score. It also demonstrates, in a rather striking fashion, the effect of unreliability on individual test scores, revealing how important reliability is in the confidence we can place in a single test score as the standard error of measurement (see Equation 12-2).

---

[7]Earlier, the equivalent statistic to the standard error of measurement was calculated to include 50% of the observations (rather than 95% as outlined above), resulting in many of the formulas in early test theory containing the constant 0.6745 because the area between *z* values of −.6745 and +.6745 contains one-half of the cases in a normal distribution (see Stout, 1987, pp. 212–221).

Gulliksen (1950b) used **true-score theory** to provide a series of mathematical derivations that nicely captured the essence of the prevailing measurement theory. In addition to standard error of measurement, he provided discussions of the effect of test length on validity and reliability (which were, in essence, mathematical rationalizations of the earlier Spearman–Brown Formula), the impact of group heterogeneity on reliability and validity, speed and power tests, standardizing and item analysis—many of the ideas that have been presented in previous chapters. All of this provided an impressively sophisticated and highly mathematical presentation of prevailing **test theory** within the single cover of Gulliksen's text.

PROJECTIVE TESTING CONTINUES APACE

Despite the the introduction of a rigorous and sophisticated mathematical formulation of test theory, projective testing still remained a significant aspect of clinical assessment. Projective testing with its inherent subjectivity seemed to fly in the face of the emerging movement toward objective tests and mathematical elaborations—yet it continued to gain momentum during the postwar period.

Without doubt the most important new projective test came from the Harvard Psychological Clinic under the creativity of personality theorist Henry Murray. While the test was initially published in the mid-1930s (Morgan & Murray, 1935), it was not until the arrival of systematic scoring manuals (for example, Murray, 1943) and reviews (for example, Stein, 1955; Tompkins, 1947) that the test began to really catch on. By the mid-1950s, Murray's *Thematic Apperception Test* had become a highly popular projective test, second only to the Rorschach in reported usage and published commentary.[8] The following Close Up provides some details of this test.

CLOSE UP   The Thematic Apperception Test

The purpose of the **Thematic Apperception Test (TAT)** is to explore dominant drives, emotions, sentiments, complexes, and conflicts of a personality (Murray, 1943). The general view is that the TAT is particularly useful in identifying underlying, inhibited tendencies that people are unable to admit either because they do not want to do so or because they have repressed them. In contrast to the Rorschach, which emphasizes personality structure, the TAT focuses on the content of personality.

The TAT stimulus materials consist of 30 cards containing pictures plus 1 blank card. The pictures are black-and-white drawings of ambiguous scenes. Ten of these cards plus the blank card are intended for all respondents, whereas the remainder was developed variously for use with children and older people. Card 12F from the TAT is shown in Figure 12-4.

Table 12-7 presents brief descriptions of the 10 basic cards.

---

[8]In the *Fifth Mental Measurements Yearbook* (Buros, 1959) the TAT showed 610 bibliographical entries.

Figure 12-4
Card 12F of the Thematic Apperception Test

Reprinted by permission of the publishers from Henry A. Murray,
Thematic Apperception Test, Cambridge, Mass.: Harvard
University Press, Copyright © 1943 by the President and Fellows
of Harvard College, © 1971 by Henry A. Murray.

The following instructions are read to respondents:

> This is a test of imagination, one form of intelligence. I am going to show you
> some pictures, one at a time; and your task will be to make up as dramatic a
> story as you can for each. Tell what has led up to the event shown in the pic-
> ture, describe what is happening at the moment, what the characters are think-
> ing and feeling; and then give the outcome. Speak the thoughts as they come to
> your mind. Do you understand? Since you have 50 minutes for 10 pictures,
> you can devote about five minutes to each picture. Here is the first picture.
> [Horrocks, 1964, p. 641]

Successive cards are then handed to respondents, who dictate the pace of the session.
    If at all possible, a complete transcript of respondents' stories is taken. Pending
feasibility, subsequent sessions are scheduled in which respondents are instructed
to "give freer rein to their imaginations." A third session can involve asking
respondents to indicate the sources of their stories: Were they from their personal
past? Did they read the story somewhere?

Table 12-7
Description of the Thematic Apperception Test cards intended for all respondents

Card Number	Description
1	A young boy looking at a violin on a table in front of him.
2	A rural scene featuring a man working in a field, a woman standing in the foreground holding two books, and another woman leaning against a tree.
4	A woman holding the shoulders of a man who is looking away from her and appears to be pulling away.
5	An older woman opening a door and looking into a room, only a portion of which is shown in the picture.
10	A male and a female head in close juxtaposition.
11	A road between high cliffs, with an ambiguous figure and a bridge in the background. The head and neck of a dragon are seen protruding from a cliff on one side.
14	Silhouette of a human figure against a lighted window. Most of this card is black.
15	A thin man in a coat standing among gravestones clasping his hands before him.
19	Halloween-type picture of ambiguous formations overhanging a snow-covered cabin.
20	Relatively ambiguous figure (gender unclear) leaning against a lamppost during the nighttime.

SOURCE: Adapted from Horrocks (1964, p. 638).

Interpretation of the obtained stories is, of course, quite subjective. Murray suggested that any interpretations of TAT stories should be regarded as working hypotheses that demand verification by other methods. The fundamental agents of analysis are (1) the concept of **hero**, as the protagonist in the stories; (2) an analysis of the environmental forces involved in the narratives; and (3) the manner in which the two combine or interact.

Locating the *hero* in a story is sometimes difficult because it can shift even within a given story. Once the heros are identified, the examiner must then characterize them. This is typically done with reference to Murray's theory of personality in which he postulates a series of **needs** as motivating behavior. Murray's theory includes 28 different needs, some of which are shown in Table 12-8. Each need is rated on a 5-point scale with reference to intensity, duration, frequency, and importance in the story plot.

Murray calls an environmental force a **press**. Table 12-9 presents several examples typical of the press from Murray's theory. As with needs, each press is evaluated on a 5-point scale against criteria of intensity, duration, frequency, and general significance to the plot.

Table 12-8

Some of Murray's 28 needs used in interpreting the heros in Thematic
Apperception Test stories

Need	Description
Abasement	To submit to coercion or restraint in order to avoid blame, punishment, pain, or death; to suffer an insult, injury, or defeat without opposition; to confess, apologize, promise to do better, atone, reform; to resign oneself passively to unbearable conditions; masochism
Achievement	To work at something important with energy and persistence; to strive to accomplish something creditable; to get ahead in business, to persuade or lead a group, to create something; ambition manifested in action
Nurturance	To express sympathy in action; to be kind and considerate to the feelings of others, to encourage, pity, and console; to aid, protect, defend, or rescue

Table 12-9

Several examples typical of Murray's press

Press	Description
Affiliation-Associative	The hero has one or more friends or sociable companions or is a member of a congenial group.
Affiliation-Emotional	A person (parent, relative, lover) is affectionately devoted to the hero. The hero has a love affair (requited) or gets married.
Dominance-Coercion	Someone tries to force the hero to do something. Story involves hero's exposure to commands, orders, or forceful arguments.
Dominance-Restraint	A person tires to influence the hero, resulting in restraint or imprisonment.
Dominance-Inducement	A person tries to influence the hero to do something by gentle persuasion, encouragement, clever strategy, or seduction.
Physical Danger-Active	The hero is exposed to active physical dangers from nonhuman forces such as animals, accidents, lightning, and storms.
Physical Danger-Insupport	The hero is exposed to the danger of falling or drowning through accidents, shipwrecks, or by being on the edge of a cliff.

The final stage in the analysis involves determination of the comparative strengths of the forces deriving from the hero and from the environment. From this a series of important **themes** is extracted. These are where the forces of the hero and press interact or fuse. Themae, considered in terms of their importance of the corpus of stories told of the TAT cards, represent the primary content of personality.

Considerable research relating to frequent response characteristics for each card has been published to aid in interpretation. Included here is normative information about how cards are perceived, typical themes and roles assigned to the characters, emotional tone, response latency, and average story length (see Atkinson, 1958; Murstein, 1972). Most clinicians use these norms, along with their own experience with the cards, in interpreting the TAT. Because of the costs of administering this test, it has been adapted to written and group administrations.

Psychometric characteristics. Interrater reliabilities of TAT interpretations are surprisingly high, particularly if the raters are well trained. Freidman (1957) reports interjudge reliabilities ranging from .32 to .94, while Jensen (1959) notes an average of .71. Test/retest reliabilities are also reasonable. For example, Child (1956) reports an average correlation of .89 between two sets of TAT protocols gathered from college students 6 months apart. Tompkins (1947) reports that test/retest reliabilities are between .80 and .90, pending time between testings and the competence of the examiners.

Validity coefficients have shown considerable range, with the norm appearing to be in the vicinity of .60 (see Horrocks, 1964, p. 646). However, a number of reports have demonstrated significantly lower coefficients, leading to continued questioning of the validity of this test (for example, Meyer & Tolman, 1955; Saxe, 1950; Winch & Moore, 1956). For example, Atkinson (1958) shows that ephemeral characteristics such as hunger and the recent experience of failure significantly affect TAT responses.

McClelland and his colleagues (for example, McClelland, 1985) provide substantive validity information related to one specific aspect of the TAT—the measurement of achievement motivation (see Table 12-8). In this case, two TAT cards (along with two others) have been analyzed in great detail with respect to the expression of need for achievement. With the kind of focus and in-depth analysis carried out in this program, the validity of the TAT seems much more justifiable than more global applications. An example of the utility of this detailed approach can be found in McClelland (1976) in which the role of need for achievement was related to the rise and fall of societies.

The controversy surrounding projective tests remains. On the one hand, it is possible to cull the literature and find strong data to support the validity of these procedures; on the other hand, numbers of studies with very poor results can be found. The popularity of projective technology was on the rise at this point because Horrocks (1964) reported 41 different projective techniques he found in the literature. Yet the complex issues of validity remained unresolved, despite massive amounts of research.

CLOSE UP   Projective-Test Lore

Jokes and humor poked at specific objects in a subculture are indicative of some anxiety associated with the brunt of the humor (see Rogers, 1987). One particularly amusing TAT joke has been in circulation for some time now. The last card of the TAT is what might be considered the ultimate in projective technology—it is completely blank.

The story goes that a psychologist was administering the TAT to a particularly bright young man. When the doctor came to the last, blank card, the patient responded almost immediately: "Why, it's a picture of a cow eating grass."

The psychologist was somewhat amazed at the speed of this answer because response latency is one of the key factors in the interpretation of projective protocols. He looked carefully at the card to be certain that it was the blank one and queried "Are you sure you see a cow eating grass on this card?"

"For sure," responded the young man.

Looking again at the blank card the psychiatrist said "I don't see any cow on here."

"Well, the cow isn't any fool, you know—she left."

"Left," said the psychiatrist, realizing he'd been outwitted. To recover his position and composure, he then said "Yeah, well the cow may have left, but I sure don't see any grass either."

Quietly, with no theatrics, the young man replied "Yeah, there's no grass in the picture because the cow ate it all—that's why she left."

This little bit of projective-test humor captures, in a sense, the discomfort that many researchers in the testing domain felt (and continue to feel) with projective technology. The subjectivity of response interpretation is seen as a major problem for those wishing to demonstrate the legitimacy of the testing enterprise. Because projectives do not culminate in simple numbers, it was impossible to demonstrate any of the classical forms of validity that were expected of psychological tests during this postwar period. Projective tests became the "bad guys" of the assessment field, and several later developments in the manner in which test theory was developed were directed precisely at projective tests, with the goal of ridding the area of these nonscientific instruments.

Summary

In this chapter, we examined the manner in which World War II had an impact on the testing enterprise. Several military applications of tests were noted, revealing increasing precision and technological sophistication underlying tests. The postwar period showed the development of the institutional component of professional psychology. The development of training standards and the emergence of ethical guidelines and technical recommendations for tests were clear indicators of this movement toward professional status for the domains of psychology involved with testing. The integration of extant test theory within the covers of Gulliksen's mathematical treatise and the continued popularity of projective tests were also shown during this time.

Yet, there appeared to be something missing in the testing enterprise. Measurement without definition still persisted. Most of the new professions emerging within psychology were making efforts to move away from sole reliance on testing being their basic activity. There was a sense that things were not progressing in the cumulative way associated with other sciences. As the testing enterprise entered the 1950s, there was a very real sense of a need for change, and it was soon to come.

Glossary

Army General Classification Test (AGCT)   A wide-ranging test that was administered to over 9 million army recruits during World War II. It provided an overall classification score and a number of component scores.

Aviation Cadet Qualifying Examination (ACQE)   A nonspeed test that was used to evaluate an air force recruit's ability to do the kinds of things required of an aviation cadet. This test, along with other service-related variants, was a primary selection and placement device during World War II.

Boulder model   A 1950s approach to training clinical psychologists that emphasizes *both* the scientific and practical training of the student. This approach has become the norm within programs sanctioned by the Canadian and American Psychological Associations.

certification   The process of credentialing clinical psychologists in which their qualifications are reviewed, exams written, and decisions taken about their suitability to be a member of the profession. An adequately trained psychologist in good standing who has undergone this process is said to be *certified*. In some jurisdictions, the term *registered* is used.

classification   The use of psychological tests to place already-accepted applicants into activities that best suit their abilities.

clinical technician   A psychological worker who has not obtained a Ph.D. degree but who possesses useful, practical skills. This term was used extensively during the debates about training and professionalization during the 1950s.

confidence limit   A range, or window, of score values into which a true score falls with a given probability.

Cronbach, Lee J.   Chair of the APA committee that formulated the 1954 Technical Recommendations for Psychological Tests and Diagnostic Aids.

cutoff score   A test score that is used to make selection decisions. For example, aviation candidates obtaining a PAS of less than 6 were not accepted into aviation school—6 is a cutoff score.

diagnostic aid   A psychological test that is used to classify respondents into diagnostic categories. Emphasis of such instruments is traditionally on concurrent validity.

differential diagnosis   A qualitative interpretation of structured tests by the use of techniques such as scatter analysis and other interpretive approaches.

error   The factor that causes an observed score to deviate from an individual's true score.

Ethical Principles of Psychologists   An evolving set of guidelines formulated by the American Psychological Association, intended to counsel psychologists on the proper course of action, particularly in applied situations. Originally approved in 1952, the most recent version came out in 1992.

Ethical Standards for the Distribution of Psychological Tests and Diagnostic Aids   A 1950 set of recommendations regarding activities surrounding the use of tests, including qualifications of users, distribution, and test manuals.

failure rate   The proportion of people entering a program who do not successfully complete it.

Gulliksen, Harold   Author of the 1950 classic book *Theory of Mental Tests,* which presented true-score test theory in a coherent, mathematical way.

hero   As used in interpreting the TAT, the main protagonist of a story given to a TAT card.

human factors   Empirical investigation of the interaction between people and machines, such as the design of instrument panels and studies of perceptual effects of various control displays. Currently called *ergonomics,* methods of experimental psychology are frequently used in this domain.

internship   A period during which a student clinical psychologist is trained in specific clinical skills. Typically, internships are highly supervised and conducted outside the university in hospitals and related service-delivery institutions.

malpractice insurance   Held by health-service deliverers, insurance that covers them in the event they make a mistake. There was considerable discussion of malpractice insurance for clinical psychologists during the debates about professionalization during the 1950s.

manual   The book that accompanies a test in which instructions for administration, interpretation, data regarding validity and reliability, norming information, and a plethora of other information is presented.

National Education Association (NEA)   A major body representing educators that adopted the APA Technical Recommendations for Tests and Diagnostic Aids in 1954.

need   As used in Henry Murray's personality theory, a psychological entity thought to motivate behavior. (For several examples, see Table 12-8.)

Pilot Aptitude Score (PAS)   A composite score, including among other things the ACQE, that reflected a best guess about how well an aviation cadet would perform in aviation school.

placement   The use of psychological tests to decide into which activity within an organization an applicant would best fit.

practica   Periods during which a clinical psychology student is trained in specific clinical skills. These are typically conducted outside the university in actual clinical settings. (The singular of *practica* is *practicum.*)

press   As used in Henry Murray's personality theory, an environmental force that has an important effect on behavior. (For several examples, see Table 12-9.)

qualifications of test users   Part of the Ethical Standards for the Distribution of Psychological Tests and Diagnostic Aids that indicates tests should be classified in terms of the amount of training necessary before a psychologist can purchase and use them.

random error   The factor that causes an observed score to deviate from an individual's true score.

registration   The process of credentialing clinical psychologists in which their qualifications are reviewed, exams written, and decisions taken about their suitability to be a member of the profession. An adequately trained psychologist in good standing who has undergone this process is said to be *registered*. In some jurisdictions, the term *certified* is used.

royalty   A fee paid to the creator of a work by those who use it. Many tests have royalties that are paid to test constructors.

scientist/practitioner   The product of a training program directed by the Boulder model in which the psychologist has a combination of scientific *and* practical skills.

selection   The use of psychological tests to choose which applicants from a larger number would be the best candidates for further training or employment.

standard error of measurement   An alternative form of reliability from true-score test theory (see Equation 12-2). Provides a range into which a person's true score will fall with a given probability.

stanine   A form of standardized score that ranges between the values 1 and 9 (see Table 12-3), with a mean of 5 and an approximate standard deviation of 2. Used with tests such as the ACQE, the stanine was developed by the army to be convenient from a clerical perspective because it required only one number to be entered onto personnel files.

successive hurdles approach   An approach to designing a selection program in which a series of tests is administered in sequence, with candidates not performing adequately at any one point being rejected or routed on to other activities. The AAF selection program is an example of such an approach.

Technical Recommendations for Psychological Tests and Diagnostic Aids   A set of guidelines outlining the information that is necessary before a test should be considered for applied use. Originally published in 1954, and most recently revised in 1985, it includes detailed recommendations regarding the content of the test manual, interpreting scores, validity, reliability, administration and scoring, scales, and norms.

test theory   A set of propositions formulated to guide the construction, development, and evaluation of psychological tests. A number of variants of this theory exist with true-score theory being the classical treatment.

Thematic Apperception Test (TAT)   A projective test in which respondents tell stories about intentionally vague drawings. Protocols are evaluated in terms of the themes consistently demonstrated in the responses.

theme   The primary idea used to interpret TAT protocols that involves a combination of the needs and presses shown with greatest frequency and intensity in the stories given by respondents. (The plural of *theme* is *themae* in Henry Murray's work.)

true score A hypothetical idea that suggests for any given test and individual there exists an actual, error-free value of his or her score. Deviations from the true score are thought to be due to error.

true-score theory A test theory built on the assumption that an observed test score is the sum of a true score plus error. Harold Gulliksen's 1950 book presented this theory in an integrated fashion.

Suggested Further Reading

Groth-Marnat, G. (1990). *Handbook of psychological assessment* (2nd ed.). New York: Wiley.

> Chapter 10 of this book provides a very readable review of the Thematic Apperception Test. Sections on the history of the test, Murray's theory of personality, assets and limitations of the instrument, and discussions about interpretation provide detailed and rich information about this test.

Gulliksen, H. (1950). *Theory of mental tests*. New York: Wiley.

> This is recommended primary-source reading if you wish to gain a deeper appreciation of true-score theory than is presented in this chapter of *The Enterprise*. Although a degree of mathematical understanding is necessary to follow the arguments, those who work their way through sections of the book will soon come to know how persuasive the general formulation is. It is particularly interesting to see how the basically simple tenets of true-score theory can be elaborated into a rich and sophisticated approach to understanding test scores.

Nietzel, M. T., Bernstein, D. A., & Milich, R. (1991). *Introduction to clinical psychology* (3rd ed.). Englewood Cliffs, N.J.: Prentice Hall.

> The last chapter (13) of this introductory text provides a good overview of the current issues in professional clinical psychology. The manner in which the issues introduced in this chapter of *The Enterprise* have evolved in the profession of clinical psychology is nicely presented in the sections dealing with training, regulation, ethics, and independence. A short section on the perils of professionalism is also worth reading.

Sarason, S. B. (1985). *Caring and compassion in clinical practice*. San Francisco: Jossey-Bass.

> Sociologists of knowledge have continually emphasized the importance of institutional context on the kinds of knowledge that are created within its confines. This book presents a particularly relevant and powerful dissertation on the impact of institutionalization on clinical psychology practice. It provides a good sense of "what happened" once the institutional framework, shown to evolve in this chapter of *The Enterprise*, was fully realized.

Star, S. A. (1950). The screening of psychoneurotics in the army: Technical development of tests. In S. A. Stouffer, L Guttman, E. A. Suchman, P. F. Lazarsfeld, S. A. Star, & J. A. Clausen (Eds.), *The American soldier, volume IV: Measurement and prediction* (pp. 486–567). New York: Wiley.

> This is a particularly readable presentation of another testing application during World War II. Here the task was to flag recruits who warranted psychiatric scrutiny

because of neurotic tendencies. The distinctly MMPI-like strategy used here, in combination with some of the item-analytic procedures presented in Chapter 11 of *The Enterprise,* makes this a particularly interesting example of how testing was used during this time.

Wiggins, J. S. (1973). *Personality and prediction: Principles of personality assessment.* Reading, Mass.: Addison-Wesley.

Chapter 11 of this fine book, especially the latter part, provides some wonderful detail on various testing applications involving personality. Of particular note for this chapter of *The Enterprise* is the section on the Office of Strategic Services (OSS) selection program, which began during World War II and afterward was taken over by the Institute of Personality Research (IPAR). Wiggins renders these complex and interesting programs very accessible on pp. 519–553.

Discussion Questions

1. Compare the impact psychology had during World Wars I and II.

2. List as many factors as you can think of that led to the emergence of concerns about professionalism in psychology, starting around 1940.

3. Indicate how the eventual form of the Army General Classification Test (AGCT) recapitulated developments in the measurement of intelligence that have been outlined in previous chapters.

4. You have been put in charge of developing a system to admit students into medical school. Design a successive hurdles approach that you might implement to do this chore using GPA, MCAT scores, letters of reference, and interviews.

5. How would you go about demonstrating the utility of the system you developed in Question 4?

6. What are the advantages and disadvantages associated with making the ACQE a nonspeed test?

7. What is the *z* score for a person who obtains a stanine score of 7? (HINT: You will need to use the information in Table 12-3.)

8. What effect do you think the restriction of score values inherent in the stanine had on the usefulness of the tests represented with this type of score?

9. Evaluate the utility of the PAS system if a cutoff score of 7 were employed.

10. What problems, other than the unintended selection of less-able generals, do you think were created by the PAS system?

11. Define and evaluate the notion of differential diagnosis.

12. Debate the contention that testing actually impeded clinical psychology from making optimal contributions to the solution to contemporary social problems.

13. Reflect for a moment on your impressions about the nature of psychology that you held prior to taking any psychology courses. In what sense are these impressions similar to those discussed in the psychology professionalization literature of the 1950s? In what ways have your impressions been changed?

14. Discuss the implications of psychology adopting a professionalization model that is very much like that employed in medicine.

15. Evaluate the strengths and weaknesses of the Boulder model. What aspects of this training model would you find the most offensive if you wanted to become a clinical psychologist? Why?

16. The concept of registering clinical psychologists has a number of important implications. Outline these and indicate what you think are the major strengths and weaknesses of this approach to policing the profession.

17. With reference to recent events in the news, indicate the importance of ridding professional psychology of charlatans.

18. It can be argued that codes of ethics are unnecessary because they apply only to a very small proportion of individuals within a profession—being for the very few rotten apples in the barrel. Debate the pros and cons of this assertion.

19. Critically analyze the institution of qualifications of test users as articulated in the Ethical Standards for the Distribution of Psychological Tests and Diagnostic Aids.

20. Outline the basic omissions from the Ethical Standards for the Distribution of Psychological Tests and Diagnostic Aids.

21. List the strengths and weaknesses of the Technical Recommendations for Tests and Diagnostic Aids.

22. Using the technical recommendations presented in the chapter, prepare a list of everything that you think should be included in a test manual before you would consider using the test to help make important decisions.

23. Prepare a counterargument to Lee Cronbach's assertion that the "dividing of tests into classes of acceptable and unacceptable tests ... would inhibit the development of tests."

24. Given that reliability is a necessary prerequisite of validity, why do you think the testing enterprise of the mid-1950s placed so much emphasis on validity (as revealed in the tremendous number of recommendations relating to validity)?

25. Using Equation 12-2, draw a graph that relates test reliability to standard error of measurement.

26. Why do you think projective tests such as the TAT continue to survive, despite the difficulties test developers have in demonstrating the validity of such measures?

27. Using the descriptions presented in Tables 12-7 through 12-9, create a brief TAT response to card 11 that would suggest achievement in an affiliative-associative context.

Construct Validity
A Major Shift

TEST THEORY UNDER PRESSURE

The Technical Recommendations for Psychological Tests and Diagnostic Aids (APA, 1954) were more than a list of desiderata for tests. Indeed, in one section of these guidelines, there was a recipe for major change within the testing enterprise. The seeds for a major and highly significant shift were sown with the publication of this document. To understand the nature and importance of this change, however, examining some of the problems that were being faced by the testing enterprise during the early 1950s is necessary. A number of difficulties stemmed from philosophical considerations, but concern that the approach was limiting the utility of aspects of the testing enterprise was equally significant. The notion of validity, which lay at the very heart of the field, also began to show signs of wear, prompting some significant revision. These major challenges, which were occurring, not coincidentally, as psychology was undergoing major professionalization, set the scene for some important changes to the testing enterprise.

Philosophical Considerations

A number of important concerns with the philosophy underlying the testing enterprise surfaced in debates surrounding the operationist position, wherein some logical difficulties were noted. Philosophers first began to notice problems, and soon these were appearing in the psychology journals as well. Of particular note is an article by Israel and Goldstein (1944) who focused on two points. First, they clearly indicated how operationism, as applied in psychology, was a shortcut to the definitional process associated with usual scientific procedure: "As a method in science, the operationism of the psychologists attempts to abbreviate, by omitting the usual process of definition, the series of operations involved in scientific procedure" (p. 185). This observation signals an emerging awareness that definitional process ought not be ignored in the pursuit of science. This is one of the first explicit statements of discomfort with the foundational idea of measurement without definition. The unease of the kind felt by these authors eventually spawned major changes in the measurement field.

In addition, Israel and Goldstein demonstrated how the nature of operationism had changed since its 1935 introduction into psychology. They observed how Bridgman had originally intended the position to serve as an adjunct to scientific approaches by facilitating methodological clarity. But as psychologists adapted the position to their own needs, it became much more than an adjunct: "Operationism in psychology constitutes an entirely new method in science—a method designed to supersede, rather than to supplement and improve, the familiar method of science" (Israel & Goldstein, 1944, p. 185). Rather than being considered correspondence rules between observable and theoretical terms in a scientific formulation, operationism was interpreted by some psychologists as a means of "specifying the operations necessary to *produce* phenomena for which a concept stands" (p. 183). This is a far cry from the originally modest proposals of Bridgman, who was in the process of disassociating himself from operationism (see Bridgman, 1945).

Israel and Goldstein's critical comments prompted a symposium on operationism, which made up an entire issue of *Psychological Review* (Langfeld, 1945). Participants in the symposium were asked to address, among others, the following issue:

> Some radical operationists assert that the meaning of a quantitative concept lies exclusively in the set of measuring operations which determine the application of the concept. (E.g.: "Intelligence is what the intelligence test tests.") But how can we then know what it is we are after in constructing tests; and what possible meaning is there in talking about improving or revising tests and measurements if there are no criteria outside the chosen test methods? [p. 242]

The fact that editor Langfeld raised this issue signals a sense of unease with the operational doctrine as originally proposed by Stevens and adopted in the testing enterprise. The responses of the participants indicate rather clearly that operationism had indeed undergone major revision in the 10 years since its introduction. For example, Edwin Boring indicated that "Operationism is not opposed to the validation or extension of a concept. If intelligence is what the tests test, it is still possible to ask whether what tests test is neural speed or normal education or something else" (Langfeld, 1945, p. 244). Rather than having the operation specify uniquely the theoretical meaning of a term, Boring is suggesting that other components (for example, neural speed) can be evoked. This is clearly at variance with the original propositions regarding operationism. Another participant, Herbert Feigl, stated

> Out-and-out operationists have often resorted to such easy and dogmatic quips as: "Intelligence is what intelligence tests test.". . . Statements of this sort may be intended to intimidate inquirers of a somewhat mystical or metaphysical bent. But they do not even begin to give an adequate account of the meaning of concept formation in the sciences. [Langfeld, 1945, p. 255]

Here we find tacit acknowledgment of nonoperational meaning as an integral part of science, as well as a suggestion that "hard" operationism is more a tactic of intimidation than a substantive approach to science. Finally, B. F. Skinner, apparently recognizing the latitude with which operationism had been applied in psychology, talked about the **operational attitude** rather than in terms of the formal requirements as set down by Bridgman (Langfeld, 1945, p. 271). These changes in the position signaled an emerging discomfort with old-school operationism, which guided some significant revisions in the next decade. Clearly, some sort of change might be in the wind.

Limitations of Operationism

The prevailing notion of validity suggested that the only way of assigning meaning to a test score was to correlate it with a criterion (or perhaps some other test) and use the results to infer the nature of what the test is measuring. To the extent that this view finessed the need to define what a test was measuring, a problem emerged when the practitioner wanted to apply the test to another context. For example, suppose a clinician wanted to use the scores on the MMPI Depression (D) scale to decide which patients would benefit from a brand new therapy such as **electroconvulsive shock therapy (ECT)**. Because no definition of depression was associated with the MMPI, it was impossible to have any certainty that this would be a proper application of the scale. The only thing the clinician could do would be to run a series of studies to determine if patients with varying D scores show differential effects of ECT treatment. This would be a reasonable and appropriate way to proceed if you were a researcher and had unlimited resources and access to patients.

Clinicians, however, were not in this position. Dealing with large caseloads and many pressing human problems, the last thing in the world they had time for was to do the kind of empirical studies demanded by the positivist position. Despite the disciplinary commitment to the science/practitioner model (Raimy, 1950), the reality of clinical practice made it increasingly difficult to conduct the research necessary to investigate every possible new application of an extant test. What clinicians wanted were measures that they could use to confirm or disconfirm their clinical wisdom and theoretical expectations about various forms of mental illness. Put another way, the lack of a theoretical definition of what the D scale was measuring was severely debilitating for clinicians. It restricted the use of tests such as the MMPI to situations in which relevant and comparable empirical data were available. This created untold frustrations for clinical workers who did not have the time to seek out or conduct this requisite research.

Clearly, the positivistic position was interfering with the conduct of clinical work, and the pragmatic concerns were again at the forefront. So either the approach had to be changed, or clinicians would proceed using the MMPI in opposition to the philosophical position that had sustained it. For example, it would have been very tempting to assume that the MMPI D scale represented the clinician's idea of depression and to assume that very high-scoring patients (for example, T score > 80) would benefit from ECT. The manner in which the MMPI was developed did not permit inferences of this nature because it was designed as a nominal, not an interval, scale. Because of the demands for their time, clinicians were tempted to misuse the test in order to incorporate it into their toolboxes.

This is just one example of the kinds of difficulties that the assessment field was encountering because of its old-school philosophy. Similar restrictive problems can be found in educational and industrial applications. In the absence of a specific definition of what the test was measuring, the situation was ripe for test users to project their own view of test-score meaning onto it. In other words, the failure to define clearly the constructs being measured opened the door to people interpreting test scores exactly the way they wanted, not the way they were intended. The potential for real problems was looming—it was just a question of time before someone would misinterpret a test score to serve an inappropriate end and jeopardize the professional credibility of the discipline. There was an increasing sense of the need for control of the testing enterprise, which undoubtedly played an important role in the emergence of the APA guidelines for testing. But despite the guidelines, the underlying philosophical and pragmatic problems remained, and it seemed imminent that wholesale revision would emerge.

Problems with Validity

A third challenge to the accepted approach to testing surfaced when researchers began to encounter problems with the classical notion of validity. The experience of World War II stimulated a number of questions that bore directly on this concept. These are summarized in a paper by John Jenkins of the Navy Department entitled "Validity for What?" (Jenkins, 1946).

Jenkins started out by indicating the extent to which the requirement for test validity had been accepted. He noted how researchers in the field had developed considerable expertise in learning how to validate tests. However, he suggested, the field was lax when it came to validating the criterion: "Prior to the war—if the publications in our journals are any indication—psychologists in general tended to accept the tacit assumption that criteria were either given of God or just to be found lying about" (p. 93). This tacit assumption was found to be inadequate when confronted with the task of selecting men for the war effort: "Psychologists working in Naval Aviation in World War II soon found that their criterion was not 'given'. Asked to help in forwarding to the combat areas as many 'good' pilots as possible, they began to inspect and to discuss the whole problem of obtaining adequate criteria" (p. 94).

Jenkins went on to indicate how the criterion was highly susceptible to both reliability and validity problems. He suggested that a criterion could emerge as invalid if

1. It lacked adequate representation of the total field performance desired.
2. Performance in training did not **predict** performance in the field.
3. There were major changes in the training program because of an apparent problem, in extrinsic pressures such as the tides of war shifting, or in the field performance itself (for example, the introduction of new technology that required new skills).

This is an impressive list. What worried Jenkins more than anything was that many of the factors involved were beyond the control of the psychologists doing the validity studies.

Validity, then, was not simply a property of the test—it was also embedded in the criterion. And the criterion was prone to change and modification as a function of uncontrollable external pressures:

> Flight training during the war proved to be particularly fluid, involving changes both in the items taught and the method of appraisal. Such changes always held the threat that we might be predicting what the sponsor desired yesterday rather than what he desired today. Finally as the nature of the war changed from defensive, through defensive-holding, to all-out offensive, there was real reason to believe that the qualities desirable in combat aviators were themselves subject to change. [Jenkins, 1946, p. 97]

Jenkins concluded by suggesting that "the same may hold true in industry" and that "validation is not a simple technical problem—the criterion itself may present the psychologist with as great a technical challenge as the procedures incident to the assembly of good predictors" (p. 98). The fundamental point here is the realization that validity is not solely a function of a test, but that it is situation-specific. Tests, then, would have as many validities as situations in which they were used. Because the situations can change and shift quite rapidly and uncontrollably, the utility of the notion of validity was diminishing.

The impact of this critique was brought home quite dramatically in a paper by Meehl and Rosen (1955). They argued that any application of a psychological test in a selection context must be evaluated against the frequency of occurrence of the criterion in the relevant population. This naturally occurring frequency, called the **base rate,** is absolutely critical to the demonstration of the **predictive efficiency** of a test. The following Close Up demonstrates Meehl and Rosen's logic as applied to the army air force pilot-selection data outlined in Chapter 12 (see Table 12-4).

CLOSE UP **The Predictive Efficiency of the Army Air Force Pilot Aptitude Score**

Recall from the Close Up in Chapter 12, entitled "Selection in the Army Air Force," that 152,933 applicants were tested in the AAF program using the Pilot Aptitude Score (PAS). Of these 113,115 completed training, providing a base rate for the criterion of training success of .74 (113,115/152,933). The data led the

AAF to recommend a cutoff stanine of 6 on the test, with those receiving 6 or greater being admitted to training, reassigning the remainder to other duties such as ground crew. Table 13-1 shows the numbers of cadets above and below the cutoff score (see data in Table 12-4).

Let's first examine how well the PAS does in predicting failure in pilot training. If all of those receiving a stanine of 5 or less were not admitted to pilot school, 68,532 cadets would be eliminated. Of these, 28,073, or .41 (28,073/68,532), would actually drop out, whereas the decisions for 40,459, or .59 (40,459/68,532), of those screened out would be incorrect. If we did not use the test, .26 of our admission decisions would be wrong, so the test actually *inflates* the **error rate** by .33 (.59 – .26).

How about the efficiency of predicting all cases? If we made a prediction for every man, using the PAS, we would be correct 100,730 times (28,073 + 72,656). This represents .66 of the cases (100,729/152,933). Without the PAS, though, every man would be predicted to pass, and 113,115, or .74 (113,115/152,933), of our decisions would be correct. Thus, the use of the test *reduces* our predictive accuracy by .08 (.74 – .66).

At this point, we have to wonder if using the PAS is justifiable because it is clearly enhancing errors—by 26% in predicting failure and by 8% in predicting all cases.

The one place where the PAS "beats the base rates" is in predicting training success. If only those men predicted by the PAS to pass training are accepted, 84,401 would enter training. Of these 72,656, or .86 (72,656/84,401), would complete pilot school. If we accepted everyone, our success rate would be .74 (113,115/152,933). Thus, the test actually *increases* our training success rate by .12 (from .74 to .86). Of course, whether this gain offsets the losses outlined above is a function of the particular situation in which the test is being used.

In summary, the PAS actually increases error when predicting failure and all cases. The only place where the test has any utility, and this is not particularly spectacular (a gain of .12), is in the prediction of success in training. Although this may be reasonable for the selection of candidates to an expensive and popular training program, it seems clear that the demonstration of predictive efficiency is a somewhat complex yet subtle undertaking. If, for any reason, the base rates changed as the program was in progress, so too would the predictive utility of the

Table 13-1

Numbers of AAF cadets who passed or failed training as detected by the Pilot Aptitude Score stanine using a cutoff value of 6

		Actual Performance				
		Fail		Pass		Total
		(*n*)	(proportion)	(*n*)	(proportion)	(*n*)
Predicted	Fail	28,073	.71	40,459	.36	68,532
performance	Pass	11,745	.29	72,656	.64	84,401
	Total	39,818	1.00	113,115	1.00	152,933

Source: Data from Hunter (1946).

test. For example, if the numbers of applicants increased faster than the number of required pilots, before long the .12 gain shown for the pilot-aptitude test would be obliterated. In the rapidly changing context of wartime theaters, this is quite likely, indicating a major problem for the notion of predictive validity.

This base-rate analysis of the PAS demonstrates the situational nature of predictive efficiency and criterion-related validity. It turns out that predictive efficiency falls radically as the base rate deviates from .5 (see Meehl & Rosen, 1955). Of note here is the realization that base rate is a function of external variables over which the psychologist has no control. For example, the number of people applying for training and the number of available vacancies fluctuate independently of the testing program, being dictated by the available personnel pool and the needs of the training unit. Yet, as shown by Meehl and Rosen, these factors have a radical effect on the utility of the test. In other words, external factors actually dictate the utility of tests in a selection context. This provided a fundamental challenge to the idea that predictive validity could remain as the sine qua non of the measurement theory underlying psychological tests.

Proliferation of subtypes of validity. The issue of external factors on test validity was one of a barrage of critical attacks on the notion of criterion-related validity that emerged in the postwar era. In the main, these attacks took the form of pointing out deficiencies with the classical criterion-referenced type of validity and proposing subtypes of validity to rectify the omission. For example, Guilford (1946) proposed the idea of **factorial validity** to evaluate whether the results of factor analyses could be thought of as having significance. Other additions to the stable of validity subtypes were **logical** and **empirical validity** (Cronbach, 1949) and **intrinsic validity** (Gulliksen, 1950a). Validity was proliferating and fractionating at a spectacular rate.

One of the many subtypes of validity warrants special mention at this point. During this time, it was argued that respondents' reactions to a test were an important part of how they answer it. Respondents answering tests come into the situation with expectations about what they will encounter. If these expectations are not met, it is likely that they will answer differently than if they are. For example, if respondents are in a situation expecting to take a personality test and the items focused on arithmetic, their responses would likely be affected in a way that would undoubtedly effect the subsequent test-criterion correlations. This suggested that the respondents' view of the test was important and had a bearing on the eventual criterion-referenced validity that would be established. **Face validity** was introduced to describe respondents' reactions to the test, and it was added to the growing list of validity subtypes (see Mosier, 1947, for a detailed discussion).

Summary. The foregoing reveals a number of important factors priming change in the testing enterprise. The version of logical positivism that had sustained operationism was under attack. As well, this philosophical position was beginning to inhibit the pragmatic utility of tests. Equally important was the demonstration that criterion-related validity had a number of weaknesses including dependence on external factors and a degree of ambiguity of meaning associated with the introduction of numerous subtypes of the notion. When combined with the near zealous movement toward professionalization within psychology outlined earlier, these factors indicate that the time was ripe for a major change in the testing enterprise.

READMITTING THEORY: CONSTRUCT VALIDITY

The factors priming change in the testing enterprise converged on the very same committee that formulated the APA Technical Recommendations for Psychological Tests and Diagnostic Aids outlined in Chapter 12. Indeed, a major revision of the underlying philosophy was presented at exactly the same time—in the same publication—as the APA technical recommendations for tests. The APA guidelines, then, were not only a set of recommendations but also contained the essence of what was to be a major change in the testing field. This shift emerged in the form of a new type of validity, called **construct validity**, which was a very creative solution to the problems being experienced in the testing field.

The traditional notions of validity were discussed and defined in the preamble to Section C of the APA recommendations (APA, 1954). In keeping with the material we have covered so far, the report contained discussions of content, predictive, and concurrent validity. But there was also a new kid on the block:

> *Construct validity* [italics added] is evaluated by investigating what psychological qualities a test measures, i.e., by demonstrating that certain explanatory constructs account to some degree for performance on the test. To examine construct validity requires both logical and empirical attack. Essentially, in studies of construct validity we are validating the theory underlying the test. [APA, 1954, p. 214]

This definition was followed by an exceedingly brief discussion of how one might go about evaluating construct validity. These methods involve both correlational and experimental techniques.

This is a somewhat surprising turn of events—an entirely new variety of validity, clearly thought to be on a par with criterion-related and content, was proposed by the APA—seemingly with no justification. Where did it come from? Why was it added? This was the first time the words *construct validity* were used in print, although it is possible to locate isolated instances of people discussing the same basic idea prior to the 1954 recommendations (for example, Peak, 1953).

As if the introduction of a new variety of validity out of nowhere was not enough, there was a real surprise in the notion of construct validity. An entirely new vision of measurement was introduced—one that totally changed the prevailing operationist-based views. The recommendations suggest that construct validity is appropriate when no criterion is involved: "Construct validity is ordinarily studied when the tester has no definitive criterion measure of the quality with which he is concerned, and must use indirect measures to validate the theory" (APA, 1954,

P. E. Meehl   Lee J. Cronbach

p. 214). Note the last part of this quote that indicates that a focal concern is the *validation of a theory*. This is not compatible with earlier positions such as operationism that suggest theoretical propositions are completely contained in measurement operations. The APA is suggesting that there is something beyond operationism, which they have called *theory*. Just so there could be no doubt that construct validity was intended to replace the operationist position, the authors stated "It is one thing to insist that in order to be admissible, a complex psychological construct must have some relevance to behavioral indicators; it is quite another thing to require that any admissible psychological construct must be equivalent to any direct operational behavioral measure" (APA, 1954, p. 215). Clearly, the operation is seen as something different from a **theoretical construct**—the measurement operations now only partially define theoretical terms. This is a radical departure from the operationist dogma. So in one very brief, two-page addition to the APA recommendations, an entirely new approach to understanding psychological measurement was proposed.

If you are wondering what all of this meant, you are not alone. Many members of the psychological community were confused by this very cryptic addition to the recommendations. Partly in response to this, two committee members published a detailed presentation of construct validity, which is considered the definitive exposition of the idea (Cronbach & Meehl, 1955).

Cronbach and Meehl acknowledged that there were problems with the conventional notion of validity but argued that the elaboration of different types of validity was not the best solution: "Writers on validity during the preceding decade had shown a great deal of dissatisfaction with conventional notions of validity, and introduced new terms and ideas, but the resulting aggregation of types of validity seems only to have stirred the muddy waters" (p. 281). They argued that the solution to the problem involved the explicit recognition of the role of theory in testing. The fundamental tenet of construct validity is that a test is valid in proportion to the extent to which the measure is an effective definition of an explicit theoretical statement about what the test is intended to measure. The term *construct* refers to a theoretical term. Thus, the **construct** underlying a test of depression is the theory of depression from which the test was derived and which the test scores are thought to reflect. A test, then, has construct validity to the extent it is an effective measure of the theoretical entity.

Let's examine, in detail, a case history of how Cronbach and Meehl (1955) suggested establishing the construct validity of a test. Once done, we will be able to focus more directly on the intended meaning of the term and its impact for the testing enterprise. The example used here is adapted from the version presented in Cronbach and Meehl (1955) using the construct of anxiety. In what follows, the original example has been embellished to provide a sense of the kinds of approaches that might be used to establish the construct validity of an anxiety test. The following data have been gathered from students who participated in a series of pilot studies in our lab.

The Unadorned Anxiety Test

Most of us have experienced that somewhat painful and unpleasant feeling of uneasiness just prior to a specific event such as an examination or athletic contest. It is as though the body is sending us a danger signal, telling us to beware that things could get a bit messy. Most of us, too, have been in a situation where these feelings continued to grow and finally got to the point where it was difficult to concentrate. Indeed, when this happened, performance in the anticipated event was sometimes disrupted. For purposes of this example, we will call this feeling-state **anxiety**.

Let's assume that we are interested in developing a psychological test, which we will call the **Unadorned Anxiety Test (UAT)**, to measure this thing called anxiety and that we are particularly keen to demonstrate that this scale has construct validity. How would we go about it?

First, we would have to develop a theoretical idea of our specific view of the characteristic. On the basis of a detailed search of the relevant literature, we may decide that anxiety is a constellation of specific characteristics. Additionally, we may come to believe that some people have chronic experiences of anxiety, across numerous situations and with considerable intensity. For our theoretical purposes, let's assume such highly anxious respondents show specific attributes such as those indicated in Table 13-2.

This list of characteristics of a highly anxious person provides a starting place for the development of a test. At this point, our view of anxiety is fundamentally descriptive in nature, but it does represent a beginning theoretical statement about the characteristic or construct we hope to measure. With this description of the highly anxious person in hand, generating a series of test items that can make up our anxiety scale becomes possible. Table 13-3 lists some items we could use. The

Table 13-2 Attributes of highly anxious persons as articulated by our theory of anxiety

1. *Self-perceptions* such as
   a. Fearfulness
   b. Unhappiness
   c. Being high strung
   d. Being a "choker"
   e. Nervousness
   f. Self-consciousness
   g. Lack of self-confidence

2. *Behaviors* such as
   a. Continual restlessness or agitation
   b. Fear of situations that involve being in front of groups
   c. An inability to work for extended periods
   d. Difficulties performing under threat or competition

3. *Physiological reactions* including
   a. A tendency to blush
   b. Sleep loss
   c. Excessive perspiration
   d. Feelings of nausea
   e. Bowel problems (for example, diarrhea)

4. *Cognitive patterns* such as
   a. Compulsive worry about numerous things
   b. An inability to focus attention
   c. Excessive sensitivity to personal feedback

Table 13-3 Items for the Unadorned Anxiety Test*

1. I freeze up in competitive situations. (+)
2. I worry about my mental health more than most people do. (+)
3. I am a high-strung person. (+)
4. I am as happy as most others seem to be. (−)
5. I never worry about my social adjustment. (−)
6. I hardly ever blush. (−)
7. When I have to talk to a group, I get very anxious. (+)
8. I am usually calm. (−)
9. I perspire a lot when I am with a group of strangers. (+)
10. I sometimes get so excited I have trouble getting to sleep. (+)
11. I am generally pretty easy going. (−)
12. There are times when I have lost sleep over worry. (+)
13. I have been afraid of things or people that I know could not hurt me. (+)
14. It is very hard to embarrass me. (−)
15. I can sit in a chair and read for hours on end. (−)

*Items marked + are agree-keyed, and items marked − are disagree-keyed.
SOURCE: Adapted from Sarason (1972, p. 385).

items are answered on a 5-point Likert scale, with the alternatives of strongly disagree, disagree, neutral, agree, and strongly agree. Items marked with + are positively keyed, which means that a strongly agree response will be coded as 5, agree as 4, and so on, such that a higher number is indicative of higher anxiety status. Items marked with a − are negatively keyed, meaning that a strongly disagree response is coded as 5, disagree as 4, and so on, such that a higher number is also indicative of higher anxiety status. In this way, for all items, higher numbers indicate greater anxiety. To generate a scale score, we simply add up the values for the 15 items, yielding an anxiety score varying between 15 and 75.

At this point in the development of the UAT, we have a theoretical construct of anxiety as well as a correspondence rule that allows us to translate our theoretical notion into an observational statement. The correspondence rule is the proper administration and scoring of the UAT culminating in a specific number. Figure 13-1 graphically represents this beginning phase of our research program, using the same conventions we used in Chapter 9. In this figure, which is based on Margeneau (1950), the correspondence rule is indicated by a double line. Now that we have a scale and a theoretical description, how do we go about demonstrating its construct validity?

A correlational study. One place to start is to conduct a study using the **correlational method** to explore some of the predictions that emerge from our theory of anxiety. For example, one aspect of our theory is that states of high anxiety are associated with **physiological arousal** (for example, blushing, perspiring, nausea). If our theory of anxiety has any merit, it should be possible to demonstrate a relationship between degree of arousal and UAT scores. There is a relatively easy way to measure how much people perspire by placing electrodes on the palms of their hands and measuring the amount of electrical conductance between the electrodes. This measure of perspiration is called **palmar sweating (PS)**. For simplicity, the conductance figures are transformed such that higher numbers indicate greater amounts of perspiration.

Our theory tells us that people with a high score on our test *should* demonstrate a greater amount of PS using our electrode measuring technique, particularly if the situation is stressful. We could run a study in which we measure PS in a situation where we tell university students that they have done poorly on an examination. We would also have them fill in the UAT. Results of this study make it possible to determine whether our theory has survived this empirical test—if the correlation is meaningfully high, our theory has been confirmed; if it is low or 0, it has not. The correlation, based on 23 respondents, was .43, which is significantly greater than 0 ($p < .05$). Hence, our theory and the UAT have survived the empirical test. We have one piece of evidence in favor of the construct validity of the UAT.

Figure 13-2 illustrates the current state of our research program. The single line between "physiological arousal" and "anxiety" indicates that the link is a rational one. The observational result ($r = .43$) is represented with a bracket on the right side of the figure.

Figure 13-1 A graphical representation of the Unadorned Anxiety Test as a correspondence rule.

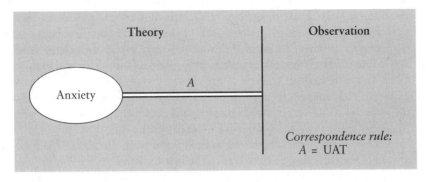

Figure 13-2 Diagram of the Unadorned Anxiety Test, with the addition of "physiological arousal."

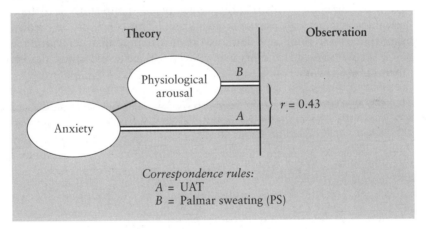

It should be noted, at this point, that this correlational study is not that different from the standard criterion-related validity study. Basically, we have correlated our test (the UAT) with a criterion (PS) and found concurrent validity in the significant correlation. However, and this is what makes the introduction of construct validity so important, *the reasons for selecting the specific criterion are explicitly and precisely framed in terms of the theoretical concerns underlying the test.* In other words, even in the criterion-related validity case, the readmission of theory via construct validity clarifies our research procedures, rendering the previously hidden assumptions about criteria visible.

A group-difference study. Now we have to continue to develop a stronger case for the construct validity of the UAT—one simple demonstration is not adequate. A second study could involve a simple experiment to test yet another deduction from the theory. Highly anxious people are, according to our theory, quite susceptible to performance breakdowns, particularly if there is pressure involved in the task. One way to manipulate this would be to conduct a **group-difference study,** using two sets of instructions for a difficult learning task. One set of instructions, given to a randomly selected half of the participants, would be very neutral—saying, for example, that the results are just for curiosity. A second set of instructions, given to the other half of the respondents, would indicate that people who perform well on this learning task also do well in university courses and that the task is being considered as a graduate school entrance requirement. Presumably, these instructions would mobilize a degree of threat in the respondents.

One hundred and ten students were administered the UAT. From this group, we chose the 20 highest and the 20 lowest scorers and ran them in the learning task, with 10 under each instructional condition. Our theory predicts a greater performance deficit for the high scorers than the low scorers under the threatening instructions. Table 13-4 shows the results. Statistical analysis indicated that there was no effect of instructions in the low group, but that high-scoring respondents given the threatening instructions remembered significantly less than high scorers run under the neutral instruction condition.[1] This confirms the prediction from our theory and adds another demonstration of the construct validity of the UAT. Figure 13-3 indicates the manner in which this second study has elaborated our theoretical network.

Correlation matrices and factor analysis. We can now pursue the construct validity of the UAT in a number of ways. For example, several other anxiety tests may be available in the literature. Some of these may reflect a construct similar to our theoretical ideas, whereas others may be radically different. For example, there may be tests that focus on anxiety as involved in the fear of specific objects (such as snakes).

Table 13-4 Mean number of correct responses on the learning task as a function of instructional condition and the Unadorned Anxiety Test score

	Instructional Condition	
	Neutral	Threatening
High UAT scorers	17.2	12.1
Low UAT scorers	18.9	18.0

[1] These results would emerge as a statistically significant **interaction** between UAT group and instructional condition in an analysis of variance of the data. The difference within the threatening condition would have to be confirmed using an appropriate post hoc test.

Figure 13-3 The growing theoretical network with the addition of "threat."

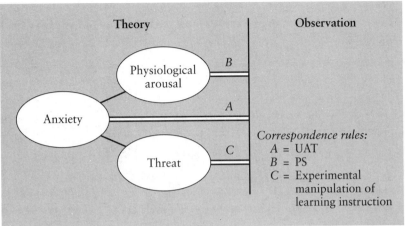

Considering our theory, there is no reason to expect substantially high correlations between this type of test and the UAT. Why not give a whole battery of such tests, along with the UAT, to a group of respondents? Once we have done this, we could calculate the correlation matrix of these measures and examine it to determine if the theoretically expected pattern of results emerges. In our example, this might involve finding that the fear-oriented anxiety scales would show lower intercorrelations with the UAT than we found with scales focusing on self-perceptions, behaviors, and cognitions. Of course, if we are aware of other developments in testing, we might factor-analyze our correlation matrix to determine if there was evidence of several "types" of anxiety in our battery of tests. Indeed, if we are really astute, we could test our theoretical hypotheses using confirmatory factor analysis. Note that there is a fundamental difference in this suggested approach, compared to some of the pre–construct validity work because *the entire exercise is theory-driven.*

Another way we might approach establishing the construct validity of the UAT is to determine the manner in which it correlates with tests designed to measure fundamentally the same thing. For example, the Manifest Anxiety Scale (MAS) (Taylor, 1953) was derived using MMPI items, assuming that variation in the **drive** level of individuals is related to "degree of internal anxiety and emotionality" (p. 285). At a theoretical level, given that we have included a physiological arousal component in our view of anxiety, it seems rational to consider that there should be a reasonable relationship between the MAS and the UAT. Based on 110 respondents, the correlation was .71, thereby confirming our prediction.

Figure 13-4 (page 468) presents the current version of our theory and data set.

Studies of internal structure. Yet another approach we could use to demonstrate the construct validity of the UAT would be to examine the **internal structure** of the scale itself. Thus far we have been discussing anxiety as though it were a single thing. That is, the UAT is built on the assumption that anxiety is a singular,

Figure 13-4 "Drive" and the "MAS" are added to the network.

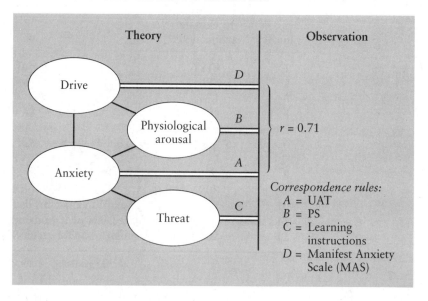

bipolar dimension and that it is meaningful to assign people numbers that represent the degree to which they demonstrate anxiety along this continuum. We can test this aspect of our theory of anxiety in a number of ways. Perhaps the simplest is to determine the extent to which all UAT items measure the same thing. Presumably, if our theory is correct, the correlations between our items should be uniformly high. This can be accomplished by calculating the intercorrelations between the items. Our theory predicts that these correlations should be approximately equal. Finding a mean correlation of .41 with a standard deviation of .06 certainly confirms this expectation (based on $n = 110$). Thus, we have yet another piece of evidence in favor of the construct validity of the UAT. Figure 13-5 shows the new version of our theoretical network.

Studies of change over occasions. We could use several other techniques in our relentless pursuit of construct validity for the UAT. One involves exploring the manner in which UAT scores change over time. Again, from our theoretical model, we have no reason to expect that UAT scores should change simply because of the passage of time. Our model treats anxiety as though it were a stable trait of the individual and makes no allowance for ephemeral variations. This is relatively easy to confirm using a repeated-measures design in which we administer the test a number of times over a specified time frame. Our theory predicts that we should observe little variation in scores in such a study.

Studies of process. Perhaps one of the best ways to establish construct validity is to move beyond the basically descriptive construct such as underlies the UAT and attempt to uncover the actual mechanisms involved in anxiety. A simple example

Figure 13-5 The theoretical network with the addition of structural considerations.

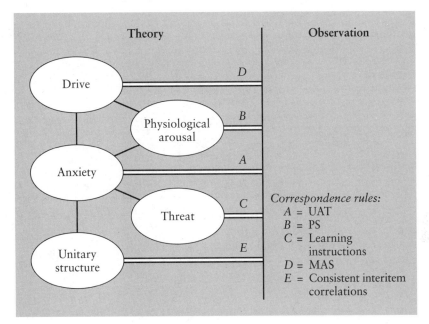

might be to have a close look at the physiological components of our theoretical definition of anxiety and notice how they appear to be related to the action of the **sympathetic nervous system (SNS)**, which is that part of the human nervous system associated with emotional excitement or arousal. Perhaps the processes being tapped by the UAT are related to excessive stimulation of this part of the nervous system. Once we include this idea into our theoretical network, we are in a position to begin a whole new set of studies in which we investigate the psychological processes responsible for anxiety. Perhaps there are biochemical correlates of SNS arousal that we can isolate in high UAT scorers, which will provide a mechanism for a very strong test of our theoretical proposition.

Figure 13-6 (page 470) demonstrates this possibility. Of particular note in this figure is the possibility of entering theoretical terms, such as "SNS activity," which do not have a direct tie to observation. In Figure 13-6, there is no double line linking SNS directly to observation. Such entries in the theoretical net are called **partially defined theoretical terms.** The acceptance of theoretical terms not directly tied to observation is perhaps the most significant aspect of the new vision of measurement carried forth by construct validity. Rather than being hamstrung by the strictures of operationism, the researcher is now free to pursue ideas. However, any term in the theoretical network should have the *potential* of being tied to observational terms at some point. This is clearly the case for SNS activity in Figure 13-6 because there are any number of indexes that could be used.

Figure 13-6 Adding "Sympathetic Nervous System activity" to the emerging network.

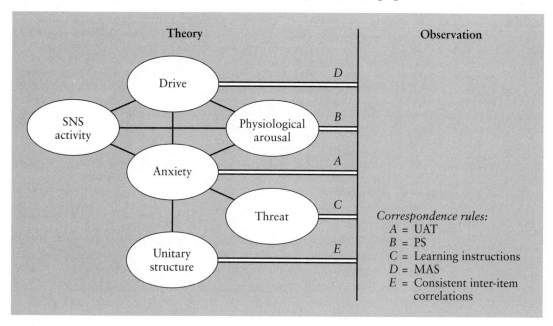

One other point relates to the possibility of including other terms in our theory, which are in a sense promissory of future research. For example, if you return to Table 13-2, which lists high-anxiety characteristics, you will notice that the fourth category relates to cognitive patterns. Clearly, it would be appropriate to add constructs related to cognitive processes to our theoretical network, even though we have not established correspondence rules. Figure 13-7 presents one such possibility. These additions would serve to describe the proposed research program and indicate the future developments of the theory and its associated test. As before, though, the researcher must be prepared to indicate how correspondence rules will be generated when the research is eventually conducted.

Summary. As can be seen from this example of the UAT, the number of possible approaches to establishing construct validity is legion. Indeed, we are limited only by our creativity. The list of available techniques maps exceedingly well into a basic text in psychological research methodology—virtually any of the procedures available to the research community can be used in construct validation studies. Included here are simple correlational studies, experiments in group differences, factor analysis, analyses of internal structure, studies of change over occasions, and considerations of underlying processes. Although none of the techniques are new, the inclusion of such a broad set of acceptable approaches certainly is. Under the aegis of construct validity, testing has been liberated from the 60-year-old tyranny of the test-criterion correlation as the preeminent method of establishing test-score meaning.

Figure 13-7 Including some proposed constructs about the cognitive aspects of anxiety to the theoretical network.

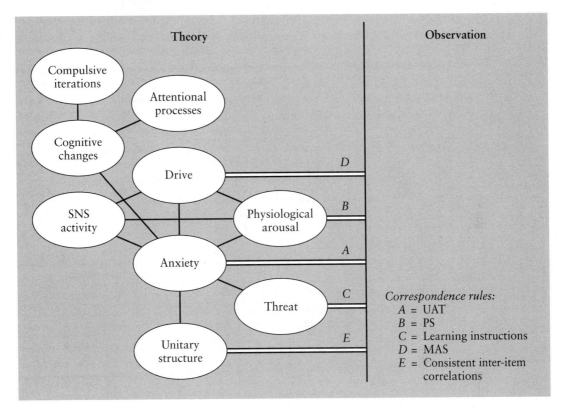

The Nomological Network

An important aspect of Cronbach and Meehl's (1955) discourse on construct validity involved the introduction of the **nomological network.** This idea described the contemporary view of how to do science, which itself is firmly embedded in the prevailing version of logical positivism. Any scientific proposition, according to Cronbach and Meehl, is made up of an "interlocking system of laws," which they labeled the nomological network. The laws therein are of three types:

Those that relate observable properties or quantities to each other (intraobservational laws)

Those that relate theoretical constructs to observables (correspondence rules)

Those that relate theoretical constructs to each other (intratheoretical laws)

Figures 13-1 through 13-7 are examples of the evolution of a nomological network, which conforms to this definition. Note how Figure 13-7 resembles a net indicating the source of the term. As noted earlier, theoretical constructs that do not contact data directly are permissible in the new liberalized system being proposed by Cronbach and Meehl (1955). Now theoretical terms need only be partially defined by the measurement operations—their total meaning is not bound up in the manner in which they are measured. This revised version of logical positivism, sometimes called *logical empiricism,* legitimates the explicit inclusion of laws and relational statements that do not have direct operational definitions.

Almost apologetically, Cronbach and Meehl (1955) were very quick to point out that this formulation was not a return to the preoperationist days where theory seemed to exist independently of data: "A necessary condition for a construct to be scientifically admissible is that it occur in a nomological net, at least some of whose laws involve observables. ... The construct is not reduced to the observations, but only combined with other constructs in the net to make predictions about observables" (p. 290). Clearly, the fundamental goal was to introduce theory into consideration of psychological testing but with the strict provision that contact with the empirical realm be maintained. Another aspect of this was the requirement that all chains of inference linking theoretical terms to each other must be public, such that anyone can follow the logic underlying the reason why a specific intratheoretical relationship is thought to exist.

The ideas underlying construct validity represent a significant change in the manner in which the testing enterprise is to be conceived. The explicit acknowledgment of theory, combined with the scientific legitimacy of the idea, provided very persuasive argument for this new validity. Cronbach and Meehl (1955) concluded their important paper by stating

> Without in the least advocating construct validity as preferable to the other three kinds (concurrent, predictive, content) we do believe it imperative that psychologists make a place for it in their methodological thinking, so that its rationale, its scientific legitimacy, and its dangers may become explicit and familiar. This would be preferable to the widespread current tendency to engage in what actually amounts to construct validation research and use of constructs in practical testing, while taking an "operational" methodology which, if adopted, would force research into a mold it does not fit. [p. 300]

In essence, they were arguing that the field had been using theory all along—even during the radical operationist days—and construct validity provided a vehicle that acknowledges this fact and allowed the field to proceed with an approach that is much more compatible with actual practice.

IMPLICATIONS OF CONSTRUCT VALIDITY

It is difficult to articulate fully the impact of this new validity. Suggesting that the worth of a psychological test was a function of the validity of its underlying theory was a radical departure from both the historical and pragmatic antecedents. The introduction of construct validity can be seen as the singlemost significant change in the testing enterprise since Binet's invention of the intelligence test! It brought with it a number of important implications that were to shape the testing enterprise in significant ways up to and including the present time. These are discussed next.

Banishing Measurement Without Definition

Perhaps the most important implication of construct validity was the manner in which it literally eliminated the age-old testing bugaboo of measurement without definition. Simply, the theoretical construct thought to underlie performance on a test score would function as the definition of whatever it was that the test was supposed to measure. For example, for an intelligence test to have construct validity, an explicit theory of intelligence must be articulated. *This theory, and its surrounding nomological network, will serve as a definition of whatever it is that the test measures.* Thus, the criterion of construct validity can be seen as directly challenging measurement without definition: Tests that have failed to define what they are measuring can now be discounted because they are not valid (that is, they have no *construct* validity). So in one stroke construct validity challenged and banished the idea that it was possible to develop tests without paying attention to the definition of what they actually were intended to measure. Sixty years of testing tradition, from Galton, through operationism, into the early 1950s, was radically changed by the introduction of this new type of validity. Measurement without definition was gone.[2]

Bringing Testing into the Mainstream

The introduction of construct validity elevated the testing enterprise from its status as a mere technology to a scientifically legitimate enterprise, fully integrated into the prevailing approach to doing psychological science. This is nicely revealed in a review article published several years after its introduction: "As this review has pointed out, the work of construct validation is arduous but rewarding to the test developer interested in being part of the main stream of the philosophy of science and behavioral sciences" (Clark, 1959, p. 100).

The new view of testing implied by construct validity was in actuality a sophisticated statement of the current view of logical positivism being debated in philosophical circles in the mid-1950s. The admission of partially defined theoretical terms, as sanctioned by construct validity, was being proposed in a number of philosophy departments as a means of countering the critique that the older (received) version of positivism was too restrictive and bore little resemblance to what researchers actually did in their laboratories (for details, see Suppe, 1974). By adopting a more liberal view, the testing enterprise could now boast of having a highly sophisticated philosophy of science. This provided a much needed boost to the testing enterprise.

Besides providing a strong philosophical justification, construct validity served to expand the methodological horizons of testing. Prior to construct validity, testers were typically restricted to the use of correlations to demonstrate the worth

---

[2]Whether measurement without definition was in actuality banished by construct validity is a matter for considerable debate, some of which will be picked up in Chapters 15 and 20. The main point here is that the idea of construct validity was clearly in the service of attempting to eliminate this older practice.

of a test. For example, the most important type of validity involved the correlation of test scores with criteria of some sort or another (that is, predictive and concurrent validity).

To the extent that the only mandated methodology of establishing validity was correlational (including, of course, factor analysis), testers were second-class citizens in scientific circles because correlational methodology was seen as inferior to experimental technology. According to the received wisdom of the time, the only possible way to infer **cause** was by the use of experiments. Correlations allowed for a description of relationships among responses, and the finding of lawful regularities between responses (called by some—for example, Spence, 1944— **response/response,** or **RR laws**) was simply descriptive of the nature of things. In the typical test-validation situation, one response (for example, performance on the WISC) was used to predict a criterion (for example, teacher ratings), indicating that testing was restricted to RR laws.

The basic difficulty here is that it was thought that causal inferences cannot be made from RR laws. For example, observing that the barometer falls every time it rains (an RR law) cannot be used to suggest that falling barometers *cause* rain (or vice versa). All we can say is that this relation holds with a given probability. Causal statements cannot be extrapolated from the RR situation with any certainty.

What is needed is a methodology that allows us to observe variables embedded in time; then it might be possible to infer cause. For example, if we find that massive volumes of hot, wet air rise *prior* to it raining *and* that the barometer also falls *prior* to it raining, we might be in a position to make causal inferences (the falling barometer and the falling rain have been caused jointly by the rising of hot, wet air). Both observations in an RR law may be caused by some third underlying variable. However, to get to this point, we need a methodology other than the correlation.

In the mainstream psychology of the 1950s, the technique of choice for establishing causality was the **experimental method.** Here it was possible to embed observations in time by documenting a relationship between a specific environmental condition and a specific antecedent response. Under conditions of proper experimental design (for example, the use of control groups), it was possible to formulate **stimulus/response (SR) laws,** which have the potential of being causal. During this time, the experiment was seen as the preeminent method because of its potential for causal inference.

By the late 1950s, there was clear evidence that the experimental (SR) and correlational (RR) approaches to psychology were isolated from each other—what Cronbach (1957) called the **two disciplines of scientific psychology.** Furthermore, there was a sense that the experimental camp was the more legitimate of the two. The introduction of construct validity liberated the testing enterprise from this second-class citizenship born of its exclusively correlational methodology because, within the framework of the nomological network, using experiments and eventually converging on causal statements became possible. For example, the study using threatening instructions in a learning situation outlined in our anxiety example is clearly experimental in nature, yielding the possibility of SR laws and their attending causal powers. Thus, construct validity brought a major gain for the testing enterprise, allowing it to partake more vigorously in the ongoing scientific debates of the time.

In addition, the revaluing of theory inherent in construct validity was liberating for testing because discussing tests and what they measure in concert with contemporary theoretical dialogs became possible. Construct validity did indeed promise testing a place with the current leaders of psychological theory and research. It was a truly emancipatory idea for the testing enterprise, bringing it into the scientific fold.

Helping Clinicians

One factor priming the introduction of construct validity was the manner in which the older views of testing made it exceedingly difficult for clinicians to use tests as part of their **intuitive theoretical networks** surrounding human behavior. This was cited as an important limitation of test theory prior to the introduction of construct validity. The reintroduction of theory into the testing enterprise and the acceptance of partially defined theoretical terms provided clinicians with some flexibility. It now became possible to use tests as part of a theoretical system and to extrapolate beyond situations in which specific test-criterion data were available. Tests could now be thought of as indexes of theoretical entities, rather than restricted to situations where empirical test-criterion correlations had been demonstrated.

For example, if a test of depression had demonstrated construct validity associated with a cognitive theory of the disease, the clinician could make many more useful inferences from the response protocol. If the theory stated that depression was associated with consistent and systematic negative biases in self-perception, the clinician could use the test to explore whether a certain type of therapeutic process would be appropriate. The reintroduction of theory into the assessment domain was highly emancipatory for clinicians because it allowed them to use tests to tap into their years of clinical wisdom and knowledge. It freed test users and designers from the restrictive tenets of what Cronbach (1960) has since called **exhaustive definitional operationism.**

Acceptance of the Theory on Which the Test Is Based

There is one particularly important implication of the inclusion of theory into psychological measurement. If tests user do not accept the theory underlying the test, they ought not use it! To quote Cronbach and Meehl (1955) about this issue,

> Unless substantially the same nomological net is accepted by the several users of the construct, public validation is impossible. If A uses aggressiveness to mean overt assault on others, and B's usage includes repressed hostile reactions, evidence which convinces B that a test measures aggressiveness convinces A that the test does not. Hence, the investigator who proposes to establish a test as a measure of a construct must specify his network or theory sufficiently clearly that others can accept or reject it. *A consumer of a test who rejects the author's theory cannot accept the author's validation* [italics added]. He must validate the test for himself, if he wishes to show that it represents the construct as he defines it. [p. 291]

Thus, the acceptability of a test now becomes a function of the acceptability of the theory underlying it.

Perhaps an example will help here. If test users do not hold to a univariate theory of intelligence (do not agree with, say, Terman's idea of global intelligence), then they should not use the Stanford–Binet. This is important because it begins to suggest that it is inappropriate just to grab a test from the shelf. Rather, test users must now make themselves familiar with the theory underlying the test and use it only in the context of that specific theory, else they will be misusing the test. This is a very subtle yet important implication of the notion of construct validity.

More Rigorous Standards

The philosophical, methodological, and pragmatic gains of construct validity outlined thus far brought another advantage. Specifically, by adopting a state-of-the-art view of validity, the testing enterprise demonstrated very explicitly the manner in which it was moving toward increasingly rigorous standards. In a time characterized by escalating professionalization in clinical, educational, counseling, and industrial applications, the reaffirmation of diligent criteria for self-policing of testing was timely. Indeed, as will be seen in Chapter 14, social forces were beginning to stir that would challenge the testing enterprise, and the availability of rigorous standards for tests would end up being quite important.

Validation as an Ongoing Process

Another implication of construct validity was the manner in which it characterized the exercise of validating a test. As was demonstrated with the example of anxiety and the UAT, the process of demonstrating construct validity is never-ending. There are no set rules about when a test developer can stop elaborating the nomological network surrounding the test and its underlying construct—rather, it goes on forever (or until absolute truth is discovered, whichever comes first). This is a somewhat different view of validity compared with the older visions. The validation of a test is never finished—it is a dynamic, perpetual process, and arguments saying that a test is thoroughly validated must now be viewed with suspicion. This, of course, characterizes the validation of a test as an onerous (say, lifetime) endeavor.

What Do We Do with the Old Tests?

The pragmatic utility of psychological tests remains as perhaps their most important characteristic. Instruments such as the Stanford–Binet, MMPI, and SVIB retained their position of importance with each time they were used acting as testimony to psychology's practical worth. Yet there were problems. These early tests were not developed in a context demanding explicit recognition of the role of theory. In fact, most were sired in a period where such issues were thought to be irrelevant at the least and a waste of time at the worst. This, of course, created a problem—how will it be possible to rationalize tests developed before the introduction of construct validity? Do we have to throw them all away? If the testing enterprise was serious about the importance of theory in test construction, it would seem inappropriate to somehow exempt the grand old tests from this consideration. To do so would be to send a poorly timed message to the testing community, implying that the criterion of construct validity really was not that important. But to force the field to throw out the old tests would be tantamount to abandoning the powerful position that the applied field earned after years of strenuous effort. In addition, failure to apply construct validity to the old tests would penalize the newer tests by imposing an additional burden of validation. Some kind of compromise was needed that would allow the domain to retain the grand old tests (because of their pragmatic utility), while bringing them into contact with the brand new philosophical position.

Cronbach and Meehl (1955) anticipated this problem and proposed the **bootstraps effect** as one means of rationalizing established tests. Basically, this argument suggests that a test developed under the old criterion-oriented view could become a criterion in its own right. They offered an example involving the Stanford–Binet and teacher ratings. A brief history of the empirical relationship between these two variables was presented:

> ...the Binet scale was first valued because children's scores tended to agree with judgments by school teachers. If it had not shown this agreement, it would have been discarded long ago with reaction time and the other measures of ability previously tried. Teacher judgments once constituted the criterion against which the individual intelligence test was validated. [Cronbach & Meehl, 1955, pp. 286–287]

They then go on to indicate that the test has, over time and with the accumulation of empirical evidence, become so well established that it can become a criterion against which either the old criterion or new tests can be validated:

> But if today a child's IQ is 135 and three of his teachers complain about how stupid he is, we do not conclude that the test has failed. Quite to the contrary, if no error in test procedure can be argued, we treat the test score as a valid statement about an important quality, and define our task as that of finding out what other variables—personality, study skills, etc.—modify achievement or distort teacher judgment. [p. 287]

Thus, it is possible to consider Stanford–Binet performance as a criterion against which other measurement devices (and criteria) can be validated. This saves the older tests from the garbage can because they have a legitimate place, even in the context of the post–construct validity era.

METHODS OF ESTIMATING CONSTRUCT VALIDITY

Another problem remained to be solved. As indicated earlier, Cronbach and Meehl (1955) suggested that the standard practices of scientific methodology were appropriate to the establishment of construct validity. Disconcertingly, there is no set way of going about scientific inquiry. Thus, no iron-clad rules of how to establish construct validity were presented. This was a problem for the field that wanted a set of clear-cut methodological statements about the establishment of construct validity.

The Multitrait/Multimethod Matrix

One of the first attempts to provide such explicit methodological guidelines emerged in an article entitled "Convergent and Discriminant Validation by the

Multitrait-Multimethod Matrix" (Campbell & Fiske, 1959). They suggested that in order to establish construct validity two important types of validity had to be demonstrated: (1) convergent validity that involves "confirmation by independent measurement procedures" (p. 81) and (2) discriminant validity that refers to the extent to which a new test is independent of other established tests—"tests can be invalidated by too high correlations with other tests from which they were intended to differ" (p. 81).

This is best demonstrated with reference to an example. Let's assume that we want to demonstrate the construct validity of a short personality inventory that provides measurements of three traits: (1) achievement (Ach: the extent to which persons want to get ahead and accomplish things), (2) dominance (Dom: the extent to which persons wish to exert their will over others), and (3) nurturance (Nur: the extent to which persons want to look after other people). Each scale, made up of 20 items, is measured by a self-report (true/false) questionnaire. Let's further assume that there is an acceptable theoretical statement about the intended meaning of each of the three traits.

The three personal characteristics (Ach, Dom, and Nur) constitute the *multitrait* component of Campbell and Fiske's proposed matrix. To fill out the complete matrix, we must measure each of these characteristics using a number of different methods. This is the *multimethod* component of the matrix. We already have one method in hand—namely, the true/false, three-scale personality inventory. To this we will add two others, resulting in three methods.

1. Self-report measures (Self). During the construct-validation phase for our three-scale personality inventory, we might run a study where 100 respondents answer the inventory. Three scores for each respondent would be available, ranging from 0 to 20 because there are 20 items making up each scale score.

2. Peer ratings (Peer). In addition, we could have the roommates of our 100 respondents rate their roomies on the three characteristics. We might use a 5-point Likert scale (with a value of 1, which represents very little of the characteristic, through 5, which means a great deal of the characteristic). Thus, we would have three scale ratings for each respondent.

3. Projective measures (Proj). Finally, we could also have our 100 respondents tell stories about pictures showing ambiguous scenes (not unlike Murray's Thematic Apperception Test discussed in Chapter 12). We would carefully examine the responses for evidence of themes relating to achievement, dominance, and nurturance and assign each respondent a number from 1 through 10 for each trait, with 10 indicating that the stories revealed a considerable amount of the trait. As with the peer and self-report measures, we would have three scores for each of our 100 respondents.

By the time we have gathered all our data, we would have nine scores for each of 100 respondents. Table 13-5 shows the matrix for these data. Note in this matrix that we have scores for each of several traits measured by several different methods. These multiple methods for multiple traits make up what Campbell and

Table 13-5 Hypothetical data matrix for the multitrait/multimethod matrix

Trait	Ach			Dom			Nur		
Method	Self	Peer	Proj	Self	Peer	Proj	Self	Peer	Proj
Respondent 1	19	4	9	10	3	7	3	2	0
Respondent 2	10	3	6	2	1	3	15	4	7
⋮	⋮	⋮	⋮	⋮	⋮	⋮	⋮	⋮	⋮
Respondent 100	3	1	4	10	4	6	18	5	9

Table 13-6 Intercorrelations in a hypothetical multitrait/multimethod matrix

		Ach			Dom			Nur		
		Self	Peer	Proj	Self	Peer	Proj	Self	Peer	Proj
	Self		.87	.77	.06	.10	.09	.11	−.01	−.13
Ach	Peer			.89	.11	.00	−.06	.06	.22	−.04
	Proj				.10	−.00	−.09	.10	−.04	.06
	Self					.76	.91	.00	.08	−.03
Dom	Peer						.54	.05	−.07	−.11
	Proj							.17	−.07	.00
	Self								.77	.89
Nur	Peer									.76
	Proj									

Fiske (1959) called the **multitrait/multimethod matrix.** However, their concern was not so much with the raw-data matrix like that given in Table 13-5, but with the correlation matrix that emerges when the nine variables are intercorrelated. This is shown in Table 13-6. The .87 in the upper-left entry in this matrix represents the correlation between the Achievement self-report score and the roommate ratings of Achievement. All correlations in this matrix are based on $n = 100$.

The notion of **convergent validity** relates to the extent to which different measures of a given construct appear to measure the same thing. For example, if we measured the length of a set of randomly selected lines using a ruler and then also did the same thing using a method of triangulation, we would expect to find a pretty high relationship between the two measures. Such measures of the same theoretical entity (length) would be said to converge if the correlation was particularly high. If, on the other hand, our two measures of the same thing were not highly correlated, we might begin to have concerns about either our theory or our measurement technique. In our

Table 13-7 Interrelationships between all measures of each trait, with highlighting indicating where in the matrix convergent validity is demonstrated

		Ach			Dom			Nur		
		Self	Peer	Proj	Self	Peer	Proj	Self	Peer	Proj
Ach	Self		.87	.77	.06	.10	.09	.11	−.01	−.13
	Peer			.89	.11	.00	−.06	.06	.22	−.04
	Proj				.10	−.00	−.09	.10	−.04	.06
Dom	Self				.76	.91		.00	.08	−.03
	Peer					.54		.05	−.07	−.11
	Proj							.17	−.07	.00
Nur	Self								.77	.89
	Peer									.76
	Proj									

example, we can see that the three different measures of Achievement are indeed highly correlated (.87, .77, and .89). This would be evidence for the convergent validity of our achievement measures. As Table 13-7 shows, the Dominance and Nurturance scales are also demonstrating convergent validity.

Thus, in the context of the multitrait/multimethod matrix, we begin to see a method for estimating convergent validity. The demonstration of convergent validity indicates, in a relatively simple way, whether or not a given set of measures is measuring the same fundamental construct. Failure to demonstrate this type of validity indicates that one cannot claim construct validity because either the theory or the measures are not functioning the way they should.

The matrix is also useful for estimating another important component of construct validity. One problem with scientific work is the possibility that sometimes the same constructs can masquerade under different names. Admitting a new construct, which in reality is just another one with a different name, would not be a positive step in the development of the science. The notion of discriminant validity emerged to signal the importance of this consideration.

Perhaps one of the best examples of the importance of discriminant validity is the notion of social intelligence (SI). A rather sophisticated theory involving this construct was proposed in the literature, and a number of studies showed SI to be effective at predicting aspects of social behavior. Everything seemed to be in place for the admission of SI as a viable and important construct. However, subsequent research revealed that there was a high and substantial relationship between SI and the more standard measures of global intelligence. This meant that there really was not an acceptable reason for considering SI as a construct on its own. Rather, scores on the SI scale were merely reflections of the already well-researched notion of global intelligence. Thus, it seems important for a variable to show a degree of independence from other constructs if it is to be a candidate for a viable construct and a useful addition to the family of scientifically meaningful variables.

The need for a construct to show relative independence from other, already existing variables, is known as **discriminant validity,** which also can be estimated from a multitrait/multimethod matrix. Looking back to our example, note that the correlations between measures of the different constructs, no matter the method of measurement, are low. For example, all correlations between the various measures of Ach and Dom are basically 0. The regions of the multitrait/multimethod matrix that reflect discriminant validity are highlighted in Table 13-8. The highlighted correlations should be low or 0 if discriminant validity is in evidence.

Thus, the matrix in Table 13-6 demonstrates evidence of both convergent and discriminant validity, which in turn is evidence for the construct validity of the inventory. The multitrait/multimethod matrix provided the field with a particularly sophisticated way of demonstrating construct validity. The presence of both convergent and discriminant validity in such a matrix was seen as necessary to demonstrate the new validity. Campbell and Fiske's (1959) proposal provided the area with a set procedure for assessing construct validity, leading to the methodology being accepted rather rapidly into the field.

Preliminary Concerns About How People Respond to Tests

One special case of the multitrait/multimethod matrix deserves note at this point. The matrix shown in Table 13-9 (page 482) is exactly the same as the one in Table 13-6, except for the highlighted changes.

Inspection of the relevant submatrices indicates that the inventory and other measures are showing reasonable convergent validity. The square submatrices are also showing signs of discriminant validity, except that the entries in the diagonals of each square submatrix seem a bit high. For example, the correlation between the Ach and Dom self-rating scores is .76. If you look carefully at this matrix, you will

Table 13-8 Interrelationships between the measures of different traits, measured by all methods, highlighted to show where in the matrix discriminant validity would be demonstrated

		Ach			Dom			Nur		
		Self	Peer	Proj	Self	Peer	Proj	Self	Peer	Proj
Ach	Self		.87	.77	.06	.10	.09	.11	−.01	−.13
	Peer			.89	.11	.00	−.06	.06	.22	−.04
	Proj				.10	−.00	−.09	.10	−.04	.06
Dom	Self					.76	.91	.00	.08	−.03
	Peer						.54	.05	−.07	−.11
	Proj							.17	−.07	.00
Nur	Self								.77	.89
	Peer									.76
	Proj									

Table 13-9 Hypothetical multitrait/multimethod matrix highlighted to show method variance.

		Ach			Dom			Nur		
		Self	Peer	Proj	Self	Peer	Proj	Self	Peer	Proj
Ach	Self		.87	.77	.76	.10	.09	.91	−.01	−.13
	Peer			.89	.11	.80	−.06	.06	.82	−.04
	Proj				.10	−.00	−.79	.10	−.04	.76
Dom	Self					.76	.91	.60	.08	−.03
	Peer						.54	.05	−.77	−.11
	Proj							.17	−.07	.80
Nur	Self								.77	.89
	Peer									.76
	Proj									

see that in all cases when the same method of measurement is being used, the correlations tend to be high, regardless of what scale is involved.

Results such as these suggest that the same people are all scoring high (or low) on the measures gathered by the same method of measurement—no matter what is being measured. For example, respondents who obtain a high score on self-report Ach also obtain high scores on self-report Dom and on self-report Nur. It would appear that, in this matrix, some people score high on the self-report measure, regardless of what is being measured. The technical term for this phenomenon is **method variance.** The method of measurement is contributing substantial amounts of variance to the correlations between the variables. In other words, the correlations observed in this particular matrix are due to the method of measurement. What might be going on here?

One explanation follows if we assume that all items in the three self-report scales are true-keyed. That is, for all items in the scale, a true response is indication of possessing whatever characteristic the item is thought to measure. Let's assume, even further, that some respondents just plain like to say false a lot. Such a responding habit (or what is known as a **response style**) would have quite an effect on inventory scores. Persons who like to say false will always obtain a low score on completely true-keyed inventory scales because the only way they could obtain a high score would be to say true frequently. Respondents who have a bias to say true most of the time would typically obtain high scores on all three scales of this inventory. Individual differences in the tendency to say true is called **acquiescence**—one of many response styles proposed during this time. The acquiescence style predicts substantially high intercorrelations between scale scores no matter what the scale is measuring. The presence of variance associated with response habits or styles has been picked up in the multitrait/multimethod matrix. Clearly then, evidence of convergent and discriminant validity must be complemented by an indication of reasonably low interscale correlations within each method of measurement—else a response-style hypothesis can be used to suggest that the scales do not have construct validity (for an extended discussion, see Berg, 1967).

CLOSE UP   **Content Versus Style on the MMPI**

The issue of response styles and the manner in which people respond to personality items surfaced in the mid-1960s in the form of a heated debate that involved the factor structure of the MMPI. One of the more disturbing aspects of the MMPI is that factor analysis of the clinical scales typically reveals two or three large factors (for example, Messick & Jackson, 1961). If the MMPI were behaving as expected—that is, measuring ten different aspects of psychopathology—more than three factors would be expected. That the same items appear on several scales (item overlap) is one contributor to this lack of discriminant validity. The question of the nature of these two or three factors, however, remains important, and an interesting controversy erupted surrounding the interpretation of these two "grand" dimensions that underlay MMPI responding.

The content hypothesis. One group of researchers (for example, see Block, 1965; Rorer, 1965) argued that MMPI responses were due to **content responding,** considered to be "variation in test response that may be attributed to a postulated characteristic of people, commonly called a 'personality construct'" (Wiggins, 1968, p. 308). Numerous researchers interpreted the first two MMPI factors as reflecting actual content of psychopathology. In these studies, the more-or-less standard approaches to interpreting factors were used. The first factor has been variously identified as anxiety, psychoticism, general maladjustment, or ego resiliency (for a review, see Block, 1965, Chapter 8). The second factor has been described as repression, introversion, overcontrol and undercontrol (see Block, 1965, Chapter 8). These interpretations appear to suggest two grand content dimensions of psychology that are revealed in MMPI **protocols.**

The stylistic hypothesis. The other side of the debate viewed MMPI responses as attributable to **stylistic responding,** defined as

> ... expressive consistencies in the behavior of respondents which are relatively enduring over time, with some degree of generality beyond a particular test performance to responses both in other tests and non-test behavior, and usually reflected in assessment situations in consistencies in response to item characteristics other than specific content. [Jackson & Messick, 1962, p. 134]

Response styles such as acquiescence (individual differences in the tendency to respond true), **desirability** (individual differences in the extent to which a person answers in the socially expected direction), and **deviation** (individual differences in the extent to which persons respond atypically) reflect some of the possible sources of stylistic responding.

Jackson and Messick (1961) suggest that the two major MMPI factors were acquiescence and desirability, not the kinds of psychopathology suggested by other researchers. To demonstrate acquiescence, they divided each MMPI clinical scale into two subscales: one made up of the true-keyed items and the other made up of the false-keyed items. If acquiescence is involved, the correlations between the true- and false-keyed subscales should be negative; if content is determining the responses, the subscales should be positively correlated. Using several different samples, they showed that the first MMPI factor was clearly associated with true- and false-keyed subtests, with all true-keyed subtests receiving positive loadings and the false-keyed subscales attaining negative loadings. This indicated that the true and false subscales were negatively correlated with each other—exactly what would be expected if acquiescence was involved. Individuals who tend to respond true would attain high scores on all true-keyed subscales and low scores on the false-keyed ones, predicting the observed negative correlations between the sub-scale scores. Thus, the first MMPI factor appears to be due, in part at least, to acquiescence.

Jackson and Messick (1961) demonstrated the nature of the second MMPI factor by using a set of independent judgments of the social desirability of a true response to each item. Using these ratings, developing an average desirability level for each MMPI subscale was possible. The factor loadings obtained on the second MMPI factor were very highly correlated with these average desirability levels, indicating that desirability is a significant aspect of the second factor.

Taken in total, the acquiescence and desirability data appear to challenge the validity of the MMPI. The vast majority of the variability in MMPI scores appears, by Jackson and Messick's reasoning, to be attributable to responding habits associated with true responding and desirability—thus calling into question its effectiveness as a measure of psychopatholgy.

The content-style debate was never satisfactorily resolved. Both sides were able to show problems in the other's methods, and both were able to present persuasive data to support their own position. In the final analysis, the benefit of this debate was the realization that test constructors should take all steps possible to minimize the potential influence of stylistic responding. If the MMPI had been designed to minimize the chances of stylistic responding, the controversy would not have emerged. Selecting items to minimize the effects of desirability, developing scales with equal numbers of true and false items, eliminating item overlap, and a number of other practices have since become more-or-less standard within the field. To the extent that the long-term goal is to maximize content responding, all steps taken in this direction will prove beneficial.

The multitrait/multimethod matrix was an important addition to the tools available to the post–construct validity theory of assessment. It provided researchers with a mechanism that could be used to explore this new type of validity with considerable sophistication. In addition, the problem of response styles, as revealed in the multitrait/multimethod matrix, was drawn to test developer's attention, forcing some major changes in the manner in which various inventories were developed.

Summary. Construct validity was indeed a major shift in the testing enterprise. Nine major implications of this new validity were noted:

1. Measurement without definition had been banished.

2. Testing had been brought into the mainstream of psychological and philosophical thought.

3. Clinicians and other applied psychologists had more freedom to use their intuitive theories.

4. Test users were explicitly warned that they must accept the test developer's theory.

5. More rigorous standards for tests had been introduced.

6. Validation was recast as a continual, ongoing process.

7. The bootstraps effect had been proposed to salvage the old tests.

8. Construct validity did not culminate in a single number, and approaches such as the multitrait/multimethod matrix had emerged to provide a relevant technology.

9. Some preliminary concerns about the manner in which people respond to tests were noted in the form of response styles.

This considerable number of implications signals the truly significant impact of construct validity in the testing enterprise. It was a new vision of measurement that had an important effect.

THE IMMEDIATE ACCEPTANCE OF CONSTRUCT VALIDITY

The acceptance of construct validity was rapid, rivaling operationism for the speed with which a major change was taken to the bosom of the testing field. Loevinger (1957) published a long dissertation dealing with several of the implications of the idea. She thought that the other forms of validity (criterion-related and content) were essentially ad hoc, leading to the conclusion that "construct validity is the whole of validity from a scientific point of view" (p. 641). So within 2 years of the Cronbach and Meehl paper, construct validity was being touted as the preeminent form of validity.

By 1960, a mere 5 years after its introduction, construct validity had become an expected part of the testing enterprise. For example, Clark (1959) lists studies examining the construct validity of eight current tests. She also mentions seven areas of psychological inquiry as involved in construct validity work. In 1960, "Validity/construct" became a heading in *Psychological Abstracts,* and in 1961 eight tests were listed. In sum, the notion of construct validity was rapidly accepted in the assessment field and very soon became an important and fundamental concept for researchers and practitioners alike. It remains so today.

SOME NEW TESTS DESIGNED TO MAXIMIZE CONSTRUCT VALIDITY

Although they took a while to arrive, some new tests were developed with the goal of maximizing construct validity. As indicated earlier, the renewed concern with theory created a series of different foci for the test constructor. Issues of bringing a

Donald Fiske

Douglas N. Jackson

test into contact with a nomological network, response styles, relationships with the older tests, and a number of other technical developments all combined to foster a new and sophisticated approach to test construction. This is perhaps most ably reflected in a series of tests developed by **Douglas N. Jackson** at the University of Western Ontario. The following Close Up provides a brief description of the concerns that guided the development of Jackson's first test, called the Personality Research Form (PRF).

CLOSE UP   **The Personality Research Form**

The **Personality Research Form (PRF)** (Jackson, 1967) is a self-report inventory that yields scores for personality characteristics of normal individuals considered across a wide variety of situations. It is particularly appropriate for the university-student population. The constructs cover a wide range of dimensions, taking as their starting point Murray's (1938) system of traits. Table 13-10 lists the content scales of the PRF. These scales provide a wide-ranging conceptual framework that serves as the theoretical foundation for the PRF.

Each scale is accompanied by a detailed description of high scorers on each of the traits. For example, a high scorer on the PRF Autonomy scale is described as a person who "tries to break away from restraints, confinement, or restrictions of any kind; enjoys being unattached, free, not tied to people, places, or obligations; may be rebellious when faced with restraints" (Jackson, 1967, p. 6). Additionally, a series of trait adjectives is associated with each scale. For high scorers on the PRF Autonomy scale, these are unmanageable, free, self-reliant, independent, autonomous, rebellious, unconstrained, individualistic, ungovernable, self-determined, nonconforming, uncompliant, undominated, resistant, lone-wolf (Jackson, 1967, p. 6). These descriptions, when combined with the wide range of characteristics listed in Table 13-10, provide a rich nomological network on which the construct validity of the PRF can be established.

Table 13-10

Content scales of the Personality Research Form

Scale	Abbreviation	PRF Form*
Abasement	Ab	AA, BB, E, G
Achievement	Ac	A, B, AA, BB, E, G
Affiliation	Af	A, B, AA, BB, E, G
Aggression	Ag	A, B, AA, BB, E, G
Autonomy	Au	A, B, AA, BB, E, G
Change	Ch	AA, BB, E, G
Cognitive Structure	Cs	AA, BB, E, G
Defendence	De	AA, BB, E, G
Dominance	Do	A, B, AA, BB, E, G
Endurance	En	A, B, AA, BB, E, G
Exhibition	Ex	A, B, AA, BB, E, G
Harmavoidance	Ha	A, B, AA, BB, E, G
Impulsivity	Im	A, B, AA, BB, E, G
Nurturance	Nu	A, B, AA, BB, E, G
Order	Or	A, B, AA, BB, E, G
Play	Pl	A, B, AA, BB, E, G
Sentience	Se	AA, BB, E, G
Social Recognition	Sr	A, B, AA, BB, E, G
Succorance	Su	AA, BB, E, G
Understanding	Un	A, B, AA, BB, E, G

*The scales in Forms A, AA, B, and BB are based on 20 true/false items each, whereas those in Forms E and G are based on 16 items each. Note that Forms AA and BB are significantly longer than the others.

Source: Jackson (1967).

The PRF scales were developed explicitly to bring the measures into contact with the nomological network, using a combined rational and empirical approach. Every step of the process of scale development was oriented toward enhancing the construct validity of the inventory. In addition, a number of important concerns regarding the manner in which respondents answer the inventory were included: (1) an **Infrequency scale** was used to detect careless or noncompliant responding; (2) a **Desirability scale** was used to measure the extent to which respondents present favorable pictures of themselves; (3) item selection was conducted to minimize the relationships between responding and desirability; and (4) half of the items were true-keyed to eliminate interpretive problems attending acquiescence response style.

The shorter forms of the PRF (A, B, E, and G) take between 30 and 45 minutes to answer, with the two extended versions (Forms AA and BB) requiring 40–70 minutes. Hand scoring is relatively easy, culminating in a gender-specific profile sheet that is based on a large and geographically disparate university-student norm group ($n > 2000$ for all forms). Normative information for a number of other groups is also presented.

Developing the scales. The most important feature of the PRF is the manner in which the entire scale-construction procedure is oriented toward enhancing the construct validity of the inventory. It represents one of the first large-scale attempts to operationalize the recommendations regarding construct validity introduced by the APA in 1954. An understanding of the manner in which the PRF was constructed, then, not only provides insight into this inventory but also allows us to glimpse the true working nature of the ideas underlying construct validity.

The first stage of scale development involved the generation of detailed and thorough scale descriptions. This was conducted with reference to current empirical literature in personality, and considerable care was taken to minimize redundancy between scales. Item writing was done separately for each scale, with sole reference to the scale definitions. Thus, each item demonstrated a clear and explicit relationship to its construct. Several of the items of the type in the Autonomy scale are presented in Table 13-11 to demonstrate this point. Notice how the keyed response to each item makes sense in terms of the construct definition presented earlier. For example, it seems reasonable that people who like rules because they guide them (the fifth item in Table 13-11) would be relatively low in autonomy.

During the scale-development stage, a large number of possible items for each scale was generated and edited—in some cases as many as 140! These provisional items were administered to university students along with similar items from several other scales and a desirability scale. A provisional scale score for each trait was determined by adding up the number of times respondents answered in the keyed direction. Thus, a number of provisional scale scores on the traits and a desirability score were available for each respondent in this preliminary stage.

Item-total correlations were calculated for each item using item response and the provisional score. A high item-total correlation revealed that the single item was predictive of the scale score. Selecting items with high item-total correlations, as was done by Jackson, would enhance the internal consistency of the scale.

As well, it was possible to compare the sizes of the correlations of the item with the scale score to which it was supposed to belong with the other scores included in the test booklet. If an item was more highly correlated with one of the other scale scores than it was with the scale to which it was supposed to belong, there was clear evidence that the item was problematic. Such items were rejected because their discriminant validity would be low.

The correlation between item responses and the desirability score was also calculated. In this case, the ideal item would be one with no relationship with desirability, so items with high correlations with desirability were rejected.

Statements that showed maximal relationship with the trait to which they belonged and minimal relationship to the desirability scale were selected for inclusion in the final scale. For example, if an autonomy item was more highly correlated with the desirability scale than it was with the provisional autonomy score, it was discarded. Indeed, it became possible to select items that showed the minimum correlation with desirability. In addition, an autonomy item that correlated more highly with one of the other provisional scores would be discarded. Of the items passing this test, those with the greatest correlation with the provisional score would be selected. Once items had been chosen, they were culled to ensure minimal content overlap, and scales were constructed with equal numbers of true- and false-keyed items.

The final inventory. This manner of construction provided a set of scales that conform very nicely to the criteria of a good inventory embedded in the APA standards

---

Table 13-11
Several hypothetical Personality Research Form Autonomy items demonstrating the manner in which the items are rationally linked with the construct

---

I would like to wander freely around Europe. (true-keyed)
I always wanted to be independent. (true-keyed)
If I have a problem, I prefer to work it out by myself. (true-keyed)
I am frightened if I have to go out on my own. (false-keyed)
I respect rules because they counsel me. (false-keyed)
I do my best work when I am encouraged by other people. (false-keyed)

---

for psychological tests. This can be seen from an examination of a number of the properties of the scales that were developed using the techniques outlined above.

The PRF-construction technique resulted in scales with maximal scale homogeneity. For example, the final PRF Autonomy scale showed a KR20 ($n = 71$) of .78 (Jackson, 1967, p. 41), which reveals a reasonable degree of scale homogeneity. In Jackson (1967), all PRF scales showed decent internal consistency, indicating the success of the construction strategy.

Discriminant validity was enhanced by this construction process. In examining the intercorrelations among the eventual PRF-scale scores, Jackson (1967) commented: "An examination of these matrices reveals that correlations between PRF scales are generally low or moderate, indicating that each possesses substantial unique variance" (p. 8). Table 13-12 shows the levels of scale interrelationship for the Autonomy scale, using the original normative sample. Although there is some evidence of redundancy between some of the scales in Table 13-12 (for example, Autonomy with Affiliation, Harmavoidance, Social Recognition, Succorance), the overall pattern is quite reasonable. Factor analyses of the PRF typically reveal seven or eight factors (Siess & Jackson, 1971; Stricker, 1974), indicating that there is a degree of descriptive redundancy within the entire set of PRF traits. However, this redundancy is minimal and does not detract from the manner in which the PRF interfaces with the theoretical domain of which it is intended to be a measure.

The PRF scales correlate well with peer ratings (see Jackson, 1967). For example, the relationship between the PRF Autonomy-scale score and roommate ratings was significant ($r = .57$; $p < .01$; $n = 92$). Indeed, meaningful correlations with peer ratings were found for all PRF scales in this study (mean $r = .52$), demonstrating good convergent properties of the scales. Correlations with self-ratings are also reasonable (for Autonomy, $r = .44$; $p < .01$; $n = 204$). An examination of the PRF in a multitrait/multimethod form indicates that the scales have acceptable degrees of convergent and discriminant validity, hence providing some evidence of construct validity (see, for example, Jackson & Guthrie, 1968).

In summary, the PRF emerges as one of the first inventories developed with the explicit goal of establishing construct validity. The scales that emerged show impressive psychometric properties, in addition to a well-elaborated nomological network based on generations of personality theory. The PRF represented the current technology in the post–construct validity era of psychological testing. With tests like the PRF emerging, the psychological testing enterprise was truly entering the modern era.

Table 13-12
Personality Research Form scale correlations with Autonomy

Scale	Females ($n = 1002$)	Males ($n = 1029$)
Abasement	−.05	−.05
Achievement	.13	−.02
Affiliation	−.45	−.37
Aggression	.17	.05
Change	.33	.28
Cognitive Structure	−.29	−.23
Defendence	.18	.10
Dominance	.12	.00
Endurance	.16	.04
Exhibition	.01	−.05
Harmavoidance	−.40	−.30
Impulsivity	.17	.17
Nurturance	−.31	−.23
Order	−.21	−.20
Play	−.12	−.06
Sentience	.09	−.04
Social Recognition	−.47	−.36
Succorance	−.63	−.50
Understanding	.26	.16
Infrequency	.18	.15
Desirability	−.11	−.12

SOURCE: From Jackson (1967, p. 22).

Summary

Problems with the old theory of measurement began to surface as the testing enterprise entered the 1950s. Included here were philosophical difficulties, applied limitations, and several important problems with the notion of validity. In response to these pressures, a new form of validity emerged. Construct validity was concerned with the manner in which a psychological test was integrated into a valid theoretical statement about the entity thought to underlie performance on the test. This new idea heralded a major shift in the testing enterprise, causing significant revision to the fundamental notion of validity. It provided a whole new toolbox for test developers, banished measurement without definition, provided flexibility for

Figure 13-8 The structure of validity around 1955.

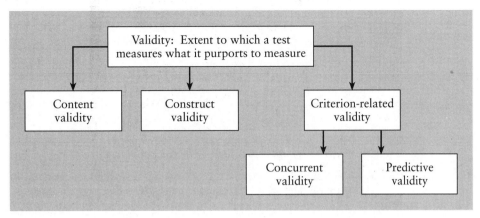

clinicians and other applied workers, and highlighted the idea that validation was a never-ending process. This was a truly astounding change. The Personality Research Form, developed with the exclusive goal of maximizing construct validity, was also introduced to help explicate this new validity.

As the testing enterprise entered the 1960s, it did so with a new and revised version of validity in hand, which is diagrammed in Figure 13-8. The increasing prosperity of North America combined with increased activity within the testing field promised that the coming decade would be one of considerable growth and development.

Glossary

acquiescence   A response style that postulates individual differences in the tendency to respond true to dichotomously formatted personality items.

anxiety   A feeling-state associated with somewhat painful and unpleasant feelings of uneasiness experienced just prior to specific events. Anxiety was used in this chapter as an example for demonstrating the establishment of construct validity.

base rate   The naturally occurring frequency of occurrence of a specific outcome. In this chapter, the success rate during aviation school was defined as the base rate for success of the program.

bootstraps effect   Using one test as a criterion for the validation of another. Derived from computer science, this idea was evoked to permit the continuance of the pre–construct validity tests once this new form of validity had been introduced.

cause One event (say, A) is said to cause another (say, B) if and only if it can be demonstrated that preoccurrence of A is invariably associated with the occurrence of B. Experimental methods are thought to have a corner on the demonstration of this form of causality. This is not the only possible approach to causality, but it is the one that directed much of the thinking in the 1940s and 1950s.

construct A theoretical term of the type one would find in a logical positivist analysis of a scientific formulation and/or in a nomological network.

construct validity The extent to which a test may be said to measure a theoretical construct or trait.

content responding Variation in test responses that may be attributed to a postulated characteristic of people, commonly called a *personality construct.*

convergent validity The extent to which several tests all purporting to be measures of the same theoretical construct are correlated (converge) with each other.

correlational method A research method that employs the correlation coefficient. Includes, among other things, test-criterion studies and factor analysis.

desirability response style A response style that postulates individual differences in the extent to which a person answers personality items in the socially expected direction.

Desirability scale A scale that provides an estimate of desirability responding. Jackson used such a scale to select PRF items to minimize the extent to which they are affected by desirability responding.

deviation response style Individual differences in the extent to which persons respond atypically.

discriminant validity The extent to which a set of tests thought to measure different theoretical constructs are *not* correlated with each other.

drive A heightened motivational state relating to the degree of internal anxiety and emotionality experienced by an individual.

electroconvulsive shock therapy (ECT) A treatment for depression that involves delivering significant shocks to the brain of the depressive person.

empirical validity An estimate of validity based on actual data (from Lee Cronbach).

error rate The proportion of individuals who are placed in the wrong category (relative to an actual criterion), using a psychological test.

exhaustive definitional operationism A term used by Lee Cronbach to describe the aspect of operationism that denied the possibility of partially/defined theoretical terms.

experimental method A group of research methods that, by virtue of embedding the investigation in real time, offer promise of causal inference.

face validity The extent to which a test appears (to the respondent) to measure what it purports to measure.

factorial validity An estimate of the significance of a given factor that emerges from a factor analysis.

group-difference study A research method that involves selecting people to groups based on their test scores and then testing theoretical expectations by examining the performance of the groups on theory-related tasks.

Infrequency scale A measure from the PRF that estimates carelessness in responding, by asking a number of questions that virtually everyone would answer in a given direction. For example, very few would respond true to the item "I make all of my own clothes." Several such infrequent responses suggest that care should be exercised in interpreting the protocol.

interaction A statistical term indicating that two variables combine in a manner that exceeds the expectations derived from examination of the two variables in isolation. In this chapter, statistical interactions were theoretical predictions derived from the anxiety theory used to demonstrate construct validity.

internal structure Relating to the internal consistency of a measure. Assessment of internal structure is one of many methods that can be used to assess construct validity.

intrinsic validity One of the many variants of validity proposed prior to the introduction of construct validity. This notion, proposed by Harold Gulliksen, was an elaboration of content validity.

intuitive theoretical network The informal nomological network used by clinicians. Typically based on clinical experience and wisdom, this network differs from the more formal nomological network discussed in the text in that it is not typically based on research results but on more experiential sources.

Jackson, Douglas N. A psychologist who pioneered the development of various tests (for example, the PRF) with the explicit intent of maximizing construct validity.

logical validity An evaluation of the extent to which a test measures what it purports to measure as estimated using rational procedures. Derived by Lee Cronbach in the early 1950s, this form of validity presaged the concern with theory heralded by construct validity.

method variance Variability in test scores that is due to the methodology used to generate the score. For example, if a test uses a Likert format, method variance relates to the amount of variability in the obtained scores that can be attributed to this format.

multitrait/multimethod matrix A matrix of correlations representing all possible relationships between a set of constructs, each measured by the same set of methods. This matrix is one of many methods that can be used to evaluate construct validity by demonstrating both convergent and discriminant validity.

nomological network The complex set of interconnections that emerges when a scientific formulation is analyzed in terms of the relationships between and among the various theoretical and observational terms. In the text, the nomological network is frequently diagrammed (see Figure 13-7) and serves to indicate the manner in which the new vision of logical positivism inherent in construct validity acknowledges the manner in which theoretical terms are embedded in a matrix of other theoretical ideas.

operational attitude Approaching the analysis of psychological phenomena from a frame of reference guided by operationism. This term was used by B. F. Skinner to characterize the manner in which operationism had become more of a generalized approach than a static philosophy of science.

palmar sweating (PS)   An index of physiological arousal that involves measuring the amount of electricity that passes across the palm of a person's hand. Aroused peoples' hands perspire, thus increasing the amount of electricity that will flow.

partially defined theoretical term   A term in a nomological network that does not have a direct correspondence rule to translate it into an observational sentence. Construct validity was an advance over the received view of logical positivism in that it permitted this type of term, under the condition that there was the potential for developing a correspondence rule.

Personality Research Form (PRF)   A personality inventory designed by Douglas. Jackson, based on the theory of Henry Murray, to maximize construct validity.

physiological arousal   A bodily reaction to the experience of anxiety, such as blushing, perspiring, and nausea.

prediction   An expectation of empirical results derived rationally from a theory.

predictive efficiency   The proportion of individuals placed in the correct category (relative to an actual criterion) using a psychological test.

protocol   An individual's actual responses to test items.

response/response (RR) law   A regularity in behavior that involves the occurrence of one response contiguously with another. Typically thought of as descriptive, RR laws are associated with correlational methods. The classic test-criterion study involves the demonstration of an RR law.

response style   A habit employed while responding to a psychological test. Response tendencies such as saying true very frequently or fashioning responses to match social expectations are examples of response styles that detract from the construct validity of a test.

stimulus/response (SR) law   The meaningful relationship between an antecedent environmental situation and a subsequent behavior. Such laws were highly valued within research psychology of the 1950s and were thought to be most easily demonstrated by the use of experimental methodologies.

stylistic responding   An expressive consistency in the behavior of a respondent that is relatively enduring over time, usually reflected in assessment situations by the consistency in response to item characteristics other than specific content.

sympathetic nervous system (SNS)   A segment of the human nervous system associated with emotional excitement or arousal. It controls such functions as heart rate, perspiration, and a number of other anxiety-related responses.

theoretical construct   A theoretical term of the type one would find in a nomological network.

two disciplines of scientific psychology   The term used by Lee Cronbach to refer to the separation between experimental and correlational methods and the types of laws (SR and RR, respectively) that underlie them.

Unadorned Anxiety Test (UAT)   A sample test used in this chapter to demonstrate the establishment of construct validity.

Suggested Further Reading

Bechtoldt, H. P. (1959). Construct validity: A critique. *American Psychologist, 14,* 619–629.

> Lest you think that construct validity was unanimously accepted as a constructive addition to the field, you should read this paper. Bechtoldt indicates the manner in which construct validity is really nothing new relative to extant practices in psychological research. The clear link between construct validity and logical empiricism as practiced in the experimental field is clear in this critical piece, which provides a bit of a balanced view of the nature of the revolution stimulated by construct validity.

Cronbach, L. J., & Meehl, P. E. (1955). Construct validity in psychological tests. *Psychological Bulletin, 52,* 281–302.

> This paper is absolutely mandatory reading for anyone interested in construct validity. It is the most important and definitive exposition of the concept. This critical primary article is as close to any you will find in psychology that represents a paradigm shift, or a major revolution, in how researchers approach the solution of problems within their various domains.

Jackson, D. N. (1970). A sequential system for personality scale development. In C. D. Speilberger (Ed.), *Current topics in clinical and community psychology* (Vol. 2), (pp. 61–96). Orlando, Fla.: Academic Press

> This paper provides a very detailed description of the manner in which the Personality Research Form was developed. If you are ever in the position of having to develop a test, this presentation will give you a very good place to start. It is worth noting some of the clever applications of the item-total correlation that are used throughout the development of this inventory.

Loevinger, J. (1957). Objective tests as instruments of psychological theory. *Psychological Reports, 3,* 635–694.

> This monograph contains an extended discussion of construct validity that draws out a number of the important implications of the idea as presented by Cronbach and Meehl (1955). It represents the second major presentation of construct validity, showing how the concept was quickly and effectively extended and embellished.

Williams, E. B. (Ed.). (1980). *Construct validity in psychological measurement: Proceedings of a colloquium on theory and application in education and employment.* Princeton, N.J.: Educational Testing Service.

> This is a set of papers and ensuing discussions conducted at Educational Testing Service in 1979, which included many of the Who's Who of the testing field. The focus of this conference was construct validity, and in the papers and conversations, you can get an excellent sense of the manner in which the idea of construct validity has had profound effects in a number of different areas. Of particular note is John Carrol's chapter on abilities constructs (p. 23) and D. N. Jackson's on personality and vocational interests (p. 79). The conversations following each paper are very revealing of the impact of construct validity.

Discussion Questions

1. Outline as many criticisms of operationism as you can that stimulated the emergence of construct validity.

2. Describe what you think would constitute the basic notions of B. F. Skinner's operational attitude.

3. In what ways would the discussion of limitations of operationism in the text apply to industrial psychology? (Discuss with respect to a specific situation, such as selection for a job).

4. In what way did the idea of construct validity solve the problem of shifting criteria articulated by John Jenkins?

5. If the validity of a test is a function of both the test and the situation in which it is used, how is it possible to justify the idea of a generic validity being associated with a specific test?

6. From the following data, evaluate the efficiency of Test A for predicting performance in basic training.

| | | \multicolumn{5}{c}{Actual Performance} | |
| | | Poor | | Good | | |
		(*n*)	(%)	(*n*)	(%)	*Total*
Predicted	Poor	275	55	1805	19	2080
performance	Good	225	45	7695	81	7920
	Total	500	100	9500	100	10,000

7. Discuss the relationship between selection ratio (Chapter 11) and base rate.

8. Define and critically evaluate the notion of face validity.

9. Define and critically evaluate the notion of construct validity.

10. Roughly sketch out how you might go about demonstrating the construct validity of a scale intended to measure the cognitive aspects of depression.

11. Indicate how you might go about developing correspondence rules for the terms in Figure 13-7 that do not already have them.

12. Outline the major differences between (the received view of) logical positivism (Chapter 9) and the version implied in construct validity.

13. List the major implications of construct validity. If you can think of any other implications, briefly discuss them.

14. Indicate an approach that you might be able to use to allow for the combination of RR and SR laws.

15. Critically evaluate the approach to causality outlined in this chapter.

16. What are the implications of viewing the establishment of construct validity as neverending for the marketing of tests?

17. Define and critically appraise the notion of the bootstraps effect.

18. In what sense did the idea of the bootstraps effect serve to retain measurement without definition, rather than banish it?

19. Evaluate the convergent, discriminant, and construct validity of the measures in this multitrait/multimethod matrix. (The variables are explained in the text.)

		Ach			Dom			Nur		
		Self	Peer	Proj	Self	Peer	Proj	Self	Peer	Proj
	Self		.07	.17	.66	.50	.49	.41	−.51	−.63
Ach	Peer			.29	.91	.70	−.86	.76	.82	−.94
	Proj				.50	−.90	−.69	.80	−.74	.66
	Self					.16	.21	.50	.68	−.73
Dom	Peer						.04	.85	−.77	−.61
	Proj							.57	−.47	.50
	Self								.17	.29
Nur	Peer									.36
	Proj									

20. Evaluate the convergent, discriminant, and construct validity of the measures in this multitrait/multimethod matrix. (The variables are explained in the text).

		Ach			Dom			Nur		
		Self	Peer	Proj	Self	Peer	Proj	Self	Peer	Proj
	Self		.87	.77	.56	.60	.79	.81	−.71	−.63
Ach	Peer			.89	.81	.70	−.66	.56	.42	−.34
	Proj				.50	−.40	−.39	.40	−.54	.66
	Self					.76	.91	.70	.88	−.73
Dom	Peer						.54	.65	−.57	−.41
	Proj							.37	−.47	.50
	Self								.77	.89
Nur	Peer									.76
	Proj									

21. Evaluate the convergent, discriminant, and construct validity of the measures in this multitrait/multimethod matrix. (The variables are explained in the text).

		Ach			Dom			Nur		
		Self	Peer	Proj	Self	Peer	Proj	Self	Peer	Proj
Ach	Self		.07	.17	.06	.10	.09	.11	−.01	−.13
	Peer			.09	.11	.00	−.06	.06	.22	−.04
	Proj				.10	−.00	−.09	.10	−.04	.06
Dom	Self					.16	.01	.00	.08	−.03
	Peer						.14	.05	−.07	−.11
	Proj							.17	−.07	.00
Nur	Self								.07	.19
	Peer									.16
	Proj									

22. Discuss the relationship between method variance and construct validity.

23. Why was construct validity so rapidly accepted in the testing enterprise?

24. Draw a flowchart of the scale-construction method used by Douglas Jackson to develop the Personality Research Form.

25. Evaluate the validity of the PRF.

26. It has been argued that construct validity was not really new—rather, it simply made explicit the methods people had been using to develop and validate tests all along. Do you agree with this? Why, or why not?

27. Debate whether or not you agree with the assertion that the introduction of construct validity was the most important development in the testing enterprise since Binet and Simon's tests were developed. (If you disagree, which concept is more important, and why do you think it was?)

Chapter 14

The Antitest Movement

In This Chapter

THE TESTING ENTERPRISE ENTERS THE 1960s

North America was entering a time of great prosperity as the 1950s came to a close. Material wealth abounded, and people felt that life was going to get even better during the 1960s. It was a time of great energy and enthusiasm as American society prepared to enter one of its richest and most exciting decades. This sense of vigor was clearly evident in the halls of psychology departments across the country. Social forces promised considerable progress for the discipline in its relentless pursuit of social worth. Indeed, the most powerful man on the continent took up a challenge that was to have an important effect on the profession of psychology.

Mustering his best rhetoric and New England charm, President John F. Kennedy addressed the U.S. Congress in February 1963 on a subject of great concern:

It is my intention to send shortly to the Congress a message pertaining to this Nation's most urgent needs in the area of health improvement. But two health problems—because they are of such critical size and tragic impact, and because their susceptibility to public attention is so much greater than the attention they

499

have received—are deserving of a wholly new national approach and a separate message to Congress. These twin problems are mental illness and mental retardation. [Kennedy, 1963, p. 280]

He argued for a "bold new approach" to these crippling problems and outlined a highly ambitious National Program for Mental Health. At the heart of this proposal was the creation of comprehensive **community mental-health centers** to replace the antiquated and ineffective state-run custodial **asylums**. Diagnosis, treatment, and rehabilitation were to become local concerns, and the federal government was willing to pour significant financial resources into this new orientation. Of particular concern for the psychological community was the president's observation regarding the need for trained mental-health workers:

At present manpower shortages exist in virtually every field of the key professional and auxiliary personnel categories—psychiatrists, clinical psychologists, social workers, and psychiatric nurses. To achieve success, the current supply of professional manpower in these fields must be sharply increased—from the 45,000 in 1960 to approximately 85,000 by 1970. [p. 284]

The president was also willing to back up this argument with significant financial resources:

To help toward this goal I recommend the appropriation of $66 million for training of personnel, an increase of $17 million over the current fiscal year. ... It is essential to the success of our new national mental health program that Congress enact legislation authorizing aid to train more physicians and related mental health personnel. [p. 284]

The emerging personnel shortage was identified in a report of the Joint Commission on Mental Illness and Health, published several years before Kennedy's plan (Joint Commission, 1961). This report recommended that one fully staffed, full-time mental-health clinic should be in place for every 50,000 people. Using even conservative estimates of population statistics, 2500 *additional* psychologists would be needed to staff these clinics by 1965 (Albee, 1963). Only slightly more than 18,000 members belonged to the American Psychological Association (APA) in 1960, indicating the extent of this new demand. The universities were soon filled to overflowing with graduate students pursuing careers as clinical psychologists.

The Kennedy plan was perhaps the strongest endorsement the discipline of psychology had ever received from its sponsoring society. More than ever, psychology had a highly visible demonstration of its practical worth to society. Doubtless, this boded well for the futures of the discipline in general and the testing enterprise in particular. Psychology entered the decade of the 1960s with considerable optimism and enthusiasm for its newfound social value.

With psychology poised for a period of considerable growth and increasing social importance, the testing enterprise was anxious to do its part in this new initiative. Indeed, in the early 1960s, testing was deeply involved in the day-to-day activities of the psychological profession in unprecedented numbers. According to a survey of over 9000 APA members, testing flourished as an important tool in five relatively distinct subfields. Serving as an initial impetus to the formation of the

Table 14-1 Percentages of APA members indicating primary affiliation with test-related subfields in psychology

Subfield	Total Number	Percentage
Clinical	3441	36.1
Educational	1364	14.3
Counseling	1000	10.5
Industrial	866	9.1
Psychometrics	248	2.6
Other subfields*	2602	27.4
Total	9521	

*The most frequently selected "other" subfield was experimental, which accounted for 12.7% of the sample.

SOURCE: Lockman (1964, p. 647).

areas and remaining a critical part of the methodologies of the domains, testing was highly influential in clinical, counseling, industrial, and educational contexts. All four of these areas underwent significant growth in the period following World War II, and by 1960 were showing signs of considerable professionalization. In addition, the academic study of testing, typically called **psychometrics**, had emerged as a significant area of specialization within the general discipline of psychology. Table 14-1 presents the proportions of 1961 APA members who described themselves as belonging to these five basic areas, which relied most heavily on testing. These data indicate that testing-related subfields occupied a significant place in the discipline of psychology. These approximate proportions are also revealed in analyses of the numbers of Ph.D. degrees being awarded in U.S. universities at this time (Ross & Lockman, 1964).

Figure 14-1, which presents the activities in which members of the various subfields were involved, reveals that testing was not the only activity of these subfields. In some cases, testing activity was relatively light. Assessment, however, undoubtedly represented one of the *fundamental activities* within each of these fields. In terms of historical precedent in defining the field and current practice, testing was an important activity of over 70% of APA members in this sample.

Personality (which includes projectives), vocational interests, and intelligence have remained the major topics of the testing enterprise. Tests dealing with school subjects (English, mathematics, reading, science, and social studies), however, are exceedingly important, with 417 (34.2%) of the instruments listed being clearly related to school curricula. The development of new tests dealing with foreign languages, vocations, and sensorimotor processes was also on the upswing.

With tests being used with such frequency, the general level of activity of the testing enterprise was on the upswing, which the *Sixth Mental Measurements*

Figure 14-1 Clinical, counseling, educational, industrial, and psychometric psychology subgroups (activities that involve mostly testing are highlighted).

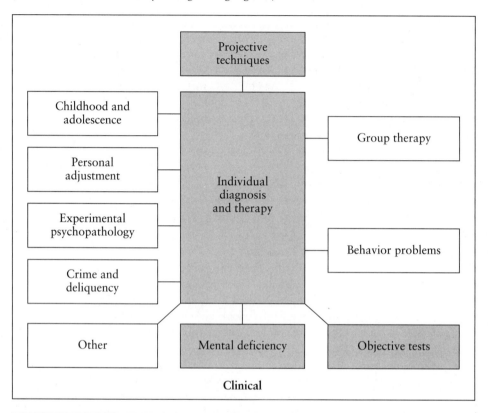

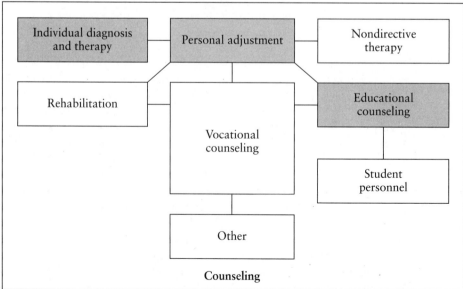

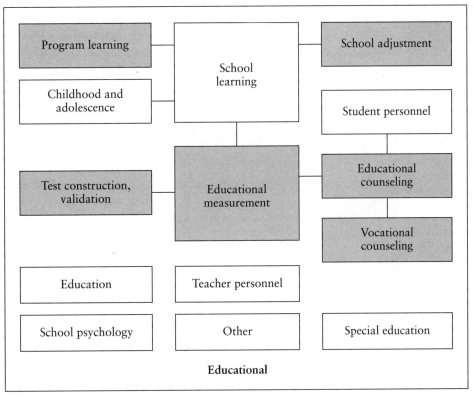

Educational

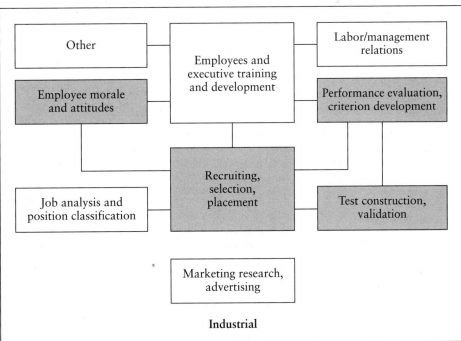

Industrial

Figure 14-1 Clinical, counseling, educational, industrial, and psychometric psychology subgroups (activities that involve mostly testing are highlighted). *Continued*

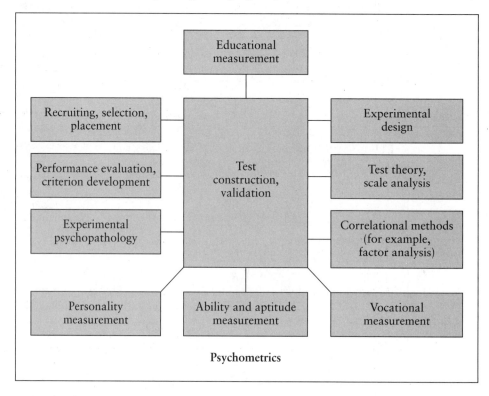

(SOURCE: Lockman, 1964.)

Yearbook (Buros, 1965) confirms. The number of tests listed in the sixth edition had increased 27.4% since the publication of the fifth edition 6 years earlier. The sixth edition listed 1291 tests along with 795 critical reviews, which included a total of 8001 references. Table 14-2 shows the classifications of these tests.

A snapshot of the manner in which these tests were being used can be found in the clinical area where it was estimated that over 7000 clinical psychologists were seeing 1 million people every year, and, of these, psychological tests were administered to 700,000 people (Sundberg, 1961). If one factors in the testing done in the other subfields, the number of tests administered per year would be astronomical.

Let's have a brief look at which tests were being used in clinical psychology. Table 14-3 lists the instruments mentioned most often in a survey conducted on 185 clinical agencies (Sundberg, 1961). Compared with similar data from 1951 (see Chapter 12), projective tests (for example, Rorschach, Thematic Apperception Test) had maintained their positions in the top five. Use of the Wechsler–Bellevue was down, but the newer Wechsler tests (WAIS, WISC) were picking up the slack. The MMPI remained in roughly the same position. Several classic personality inventories (for example, Bernreuter, Bell) had been replaced by pictorial production tests with fundamentally interpretive-scoring systems (for example, **Draw-a-**

Table 14-2 Classifications of tests from the *Sixth Mental Measurement Yearbook*

Classification	Number	Percentage
Personality	196	16.1
Vocations	179	14.7
Intelligence	131	10.7
Miscellaneous	108	8.9
English	99	8.1
Mathematics	96	7.9
Reading	87	7.1
Foreign languages	77	6.3
Science	74	6.1
Social studies	61	5.0
Business education	29	2.4
Achievement batteries	28	2.3
Sensorimotor	27	2.2
Multiaptitude	16	1.3
Fine arts	11	.9
Total	1219	100.0

SOURCE: Buros (1965).

Table 14-3 Tests used most frequently in clinical psychology around 1959

Test	Total Mentions	Rank Order
Rorschach	170	1
Draw-a-Person	160	2.5
Thematic Apperception Test (TAT)	160	2.5
Bender–Gestalt	158	4
Stanford–Binet	146	5
WAIS	132	6
MMPI	123	7.5
Wechsler–Bellevue	123	7.5
Draw-a-Man	119	9
WISC	114	10

SOURCE: Sundberg (1961, p. 80).

Person, Bender–Gestalt, Draw-a-Man). These data suggest a movement away from objective and standardized measures. However, testing remained a significant aspect of the prevailing clinical practice.

Testing was clearly a critical aspect of a wide range of psychological research and practice at the beginning of the 1960s. Additionally, the enterprise was exceedingly busy formulating new tests and revising the old ones. With the emergence of presidential support for activities encompassing most of the test-related subfields, even the most conservative "futurologist" of the time would have predicted exponential growth and gain for the testing enterprise as the decade unfolded. However, this was not to happen—at least at the rate projected in the early 1960s. Several developments within American society began to challenge the testing enterprise in a most interesting and consequential way.

EMERGING DISCONTENT WITH TESTING

The success of the testing enterprise in becoming part of the social decision-making processes of American society brought with it a number of risks. If tests emerged as an integral part of making important decisions, it would seem inevitable that they would come under considerable scrutiny. Indeed, as we saw earlier, this was the case immediately following World War I when Walter Lippmann, among others, initiated stinging critical attacks against testing (see Chapter 7). The 1960s saw a resurgence of an **antitest movement** driven in large part by an emerging awareness of civil rights and their importance to the overall goals of American society.

Starting in the 1950s, a number of events began to highlight increased discomfort with testing—a discomfort that would have a profound effect on the practices of the testing enterprise. Beginning with the publication of a book about the use of tests in industry, followed by several instances of public outcry, the testing enterprise was soon to find itself in the vortex of an intense and volatile controversy that was to shape its entire future.

The Organization Man

One of the first signs of discontent emerged in the form of a popular book by William Whyte, a student of American culture and editor of *Fortune* magazine. This book (Whyte, 1956), a study of American corporate culture, expressed concern about the manner in which individuals' rights and freedoms were being subordinated, ever so subtly, to the needs of the company. Whyte's concept of the social ethic emerged from the analysis. The **social ethic** was

> . . . a body of thought which makes morally legitimate the pressures of society against the individual. Its major propositions are three: a belief in the group as the source of creativity; a belief in "belongingness" as the ultimate need of the individual; and a belief in the application of science to achieve the belongingness. [p. 7]

The personality test, and its pervasive use in industry, was singled out as one of the most transparent exemplars of this social ethic because it represented the application of scientific methodology to the maintenance of conformity. Test scores were used to select, promote, and fire many members of the corporate sector and, according to Whyte, represented an important component of the shifting power from the individual to the organization. But more than a critique of contemporary practice, Whyte offered a proactive option:

> I hope to redress the balance of power between the individual and The Organization. When an individual is commanded by an organization to reveal his innermost feelings, he has a duty to himself to give answers that serve his self-interest rather than that of The Organization. In a word, he should cheat. [p. 179]

He then proceeded to an exposé of personality tests wherein he presented a series of examples and indicated how they were scored and how respondents would best answer the items if they wanted to survive in the corporate world. For example, Whyte suggested,

> When in doubt, however, there are two general rules you can follow: (1) When asked for word associations or comments about the world give the most conventional run-of-the-mill pedestrian answer possible. (2) To settle on the most beneficial answer to any question, repeat to yourself:
> a. I loved my father and my mother, but my father a little bit more.
> b. I like things pretty much the way they are.
> c. I never worry much about anything.
> d. I don't care for books or music much.
> e. I love my wife and children.
> f. I don't let them get in the way of company work. [p. 405]

He counseled readers to cheat in the following ways: (1) to respond consistently as opposed to candidly, (2) to figure out the values of the test maker and reflect these in their responses, (3) to be selective about which neuroses were admitted, (4) to be submissive, (5) to incline toward conservatism, (6) to not split hairs, and (7) to anticipate what the company wanted to hear and reflect this in their responses.

Although these comments seemed harmless enough, they signaled a number of anxieties being felt about the testing enterprise in the corporate sector. Whyte's book foreshadowed a change in attitude toward testing, which was soon to be felt throughout the entire psychological testing enterprise.

CLOSE UP | **The Barnum Effect in Industrial Psychology**

The discomfort being felt with personality testing in industry was even demonstrated empirically. Stagner (1958) had a group of 68 personnel managers take a published personality inventory. He then provided a report of results. Each manager then rated the accuracy of their individual feedback on a 5-point scale labeled amazingly accurate, rather good, about half and half, more wrong than right, and almost entirely wrong. Fifty percent of the group rated the report as amazingly accurate, 40% as rather good, and 10% about half and half. It would appear that the inventory was very sensitive and valid.

However, Stagner had tampered a bit with the report given to the managers. Each individual had received exactly the same report. The items in this report were drawn from dream books and astrology charts representing statements that were true of almost everyone. The statements are presented below:

You have a great need for other people to like and admire you.

You have a tendency to be critical of yourself.

You have a great deal of unused capacity which you have not turned to your advantage.

While you have some personality weaknesses, you are generally able to compensate for them.

Your sexual adjustment has presented problems for you.

Disciplined and self-controlled outside, you tend to be worrisome and insecure inside.

At times you have serious doubts as to whether you have made the right decision or done the right thing.

You prefer a certain amount of change and variety and become dissatisfied when hemmed in by restrictions and limitations.

You pride yourself as an independent thinker and do not accept others' statements without satisfactory proof.

You have found it unwise to be too frank in revealing yourself to others.

At times you are extraverted, affable, sociable, while at other times you are introverted, wary, reserved.

Some of your aspirations are pretty unrealistic.

Security is one of your major goals in life. [Stagner, 1958]

The feedback provided to the personnel managers, then, was bogus—representing a set of statements with virtually no discriminatory power at all. Yet the personnel managers had rated the reports as amazingly accurate! This indicates that the shrewd salesperson could easily dupe a would-be test user, by demonstrating the "amazing accuracy" of a test report. Paul Meehl dubbed this phenomenon the **Barnum Effect** to draw attention to the deceptive effect of these glittering generalities incorporated into test reports.

In technical terms, the Barnum Effect is a demonstration of the problems inherent in the notion of face validity. In this particular case, respondents' reactions to the test interpretation convey no validity information whatsoever. More important, though, these results point to the possibility of serious misuse of tests and testing that was at the heart of the emerging social discontent with the testing enterprise.

Test Burning in Texas

In June 1959, the board of the Houston Independent School District, one of the largest in the nation, voted five to one to have over 5000 test-answer sheets burned (see Nettler, 1959). The symbolic impact of ordering these data burned is a clear indication of society's discomfort with the manner in which the testing enterprise was serving social needs. Book burnings have long been associated with attempts to control information in true Orwellian fashion, with such activities being associated with most totalitarian regimes. The Houston **test-burning** incident foreshadowed some trying times for the testing enterprise.

The incinerated data had been collected as part of a national talent-discovery project being conducted by a number of psychologists. Some of the items in the tests were the following:

I enjoy soaking in the bathtub.

A girl who gets into trouble on a date has no one to blame but herself.

If you don't drink in our gang they make you feel like a sissy.

Sometimes I tell dirty jokes when I would rather not.

Dad always seemed too busy to pal around with me. [Nettler, 1959]

The incident was sparked by a number of phone calls from concerned parents who believed the questions could serve no useful function in a talent search, would undermine moral character, and would yield some answers that would be of interest to Communists (for example, those relating to family income). News items and exchanges in the letter-to-the-editor sections of local newspapers preceded the test burning by about 2 weeks. Indeed, within 24 hours of a planned televised meeting, which would have resulted in a restraining order regarding the use of the test data, the Houston school board destroyed the answer sheets.

The cold war between the United States and the USSR was at a high point during this time. A very real fear of communism was rampant throughout the country, with politicians such as Senator Joseph McCarthy scouring the ranks of the intelligentsia for "Commies" and "traitors." The fear of nuclear war, the perception of the USSR as a power-hungry force wanting to take over the world, and the sense of technological inferiority brought on by the Russians launching the first successful orbiting satellite (*Sputnik I* in 1957) contributed to a defensive climate that was primed for the kind of antitest sentiments that were revealed by the test-burning incident.

The Texas episode was the first of a number of such occurrences (see also Berdie, 1964; Eron and Waller, 1961). Rather unexpectedly for the testing enterprise, national bodies were interested in attacking psychology. The emergence of such incidents indicated that the enterprise had failed in its attempts to explain the role of tests. The enterprise also became aware of the difficulties of explaining the rationale underlying tests to journalists and laypeople. The need for careful public relations management for testing programs was identified, as was the underlying ethnocentric assumption of most members of the testing enterprise that everyone agreed with their specific ethic. These well-intentioned efforts of the discipline to change its public image, however, were not sufficient to stem the accelerating discontent about testing being voiced in the United States.

Myart v. Motorola

The test burning led to even greater problems—problems that were to involve the legal system. In the summer of 1963, the first mention of psychological testing practices in the courts was heard, *Myart v. Motorola*. Leon Myart, a Black man, applied for employment as a "television phaser" with Motorola, Inc., at its

Franklin Park, Illinois, plant (Ash, 1966). As part of the job-selection process, he was administered an ability test known internally in Motorola as Test No. 10. Myart did not receive the job even though the company continued to advertise the position. He filed a complaint with the Illinois Fair Employment Practices Commission in which he alleged he had passed the test and was rejected because of his race.

A hearing was held before examiner Robert Bryant. Motorola testified that Myart was not offered employment because he had failed Test No. 10. The company, however, refused to produce Myart's test sheet. In fact, all Motorola presented was a witness who testified that he believed the test was "color blind." The eventual ruling (handed down in February 1964) favored Myart. The hearing examiner was persuaded that the availability of the test, Myart's responses, the key, and normative information would have been unfavorable to Motorola. Bryant, however, went further suggesting that the test "does not lend itself to equal opportunity to qualify for the hitherto culturally deprived and disadvantaged groups" and was "obsolete in light of today's knowledge" because "its norm was derived from standardization on advantaged groups" (Ash, 1966, p. 798). In this case, "advantaged groups" denoted the White Anglo norming sample on which Test No. 10 had been based. Bryant directed Motorola to stop using Test No. 10 and suggested that any test used to replace it should "reflect and equate any inequalities and environmental factors among the disadvantaged and culturally deprived groups" (Ash, 1966, p. 798).

This was a landmark judgment because the right of a company to use psychological tests in its hiring processes had been legally challenged and was found unsuitable. If Bryant's ruling was to be applied across the board, it would be necessary to demonstrate that all tests used in industrial selection did not unfairly discriminate against people from disadvantaged and culturally deprived groups. Clearly, this would be an exceedingly difficult if not impossible task, particularly if the job demanded skills affected by the cited cultural deprivation and disadvantage (for example, verbal aptitude).

The Civil Rights Act of 1964

This concern with unfair employment practice soon snowballed, becoming part of a highly significant debate in the U.S. Congress—namely, the **Civil Rights Act of 1964**. This act addressed **discrimination** across a broad spectrum of contexts, speaking specifically against discrimination on the basis of race, color, religion, gender, and national origin. The act consisted of 12 titles dealing with various aspects of discrimination.

Title VII was concerned with employment and hiring practices. In this title the following actions were defined as "unlawful employment practices:

Hiring or admitting to training facilities on the basis of race, color, religion, gender, and national origin

Discrimination with respect to compensation, terms, conditions, and privileges based on race, color, religion, gender, and national origin

Limitation or segregation of employees based on race, color, religion, gender, and national origin to the disadvantage of the individual

Indication of a preference based on race, color, religion, gender, and national origin in employment ads

This title clearly represented a major challenge to the testing enterprise because a wide range of employment practices using psychological tests would fall under these new federal laws.

There was some discomfort with Title VII—even within political circles. In the debate surrounding the act, Senator Everett Dirksen asked whether the bill would make it unlawful for an employer to use qualification tests based on verbal skills and other factors that may be related to the environmental experiences of the applicant. After some debate on this issue, Senator John Tower introduced an amendment that would forestall the possibility of qualification tests becoming illegal under the Civil Rights Act. In part, the **Tower Amendment** read

> Notwithstanding any other provision of [the act], it shall not be . . . an unlawful employment practice for an employer to give and to act upon the results of any professionally developed employment test, provided that such test, its administration or action upon the results is not designed, intended, or used to discriminate because of race, color, religion, sex, or national origin. [Ash, 1966, p. 797]

This amendment gave "professionally developed employment tests" special status in the Act, exempting them under some conditions. Debate surrounding this amendment focused on its apparent redundancy with other clauses of the act. Indeed, Senator Hubert Humphrey stated "These tests are legal. They do not need to be legalized a second time" (Ash, 1966, p. 799). The amendment, as originally posed, was defeated by a vote of 49 to 38. However, a slightly revised version (presented above) was resubmitted, and it was carried by voice vote on June 13, 1964. The Tower Amendment, protecting qualification tests in industry, was passed into law, and the psychological testing enterprise had survived its first major test by the lawmakers of the land.

The basic legal touchstone adopted in enacting the Civil Right Acts was to consider discrimination like murder—an intentional act. Thus, demonstration of discrimination would depend on proving intent. However, like murder, intention need not be demonstrated directly but can be shown by circumstantial evidence. In time, the following conditions of test use were thought to discriminate in the sense forbidden by the Civil Rights Act:

1. When scores on the test tend to differentiate between identifiable subgroups, where the subgrouping itself is not a relevant selection factor. [*Example*: Finding black/white differences on an IQ test used for selection when IQ does not predict subsequent job performance for one group.]

2. When scores for the lower group improperly predict performance on the job *when the standards of the upper group* are applied. [*Example*: Finding a test that uniformly assigns higher predicted criterion status to one group; for details, see *intercept bias* in the Close Up, "Test Bias and Fairness," later in this chapter.]

3. When scores on the test do not predict job performance for either group. [*Example*: Finding that an ability test being used for selection does not predict job performance.] [Ash, 1966, p. 800]

This third point meant that tests showing criterion-related validity where the criterion was of *direct* relevance to the job would not be deemed discriminatory under the Civil Rights Act and the Tower Amendment. At this point, it might seem that the testing enterprise had successfully defended itself against the increasing intensity and vigor of antitest sentiment. But the unrest of the 1960s and the wholesale social changes being wrought during this turbulent time were not to be satisfied with this proposed solution.

More Critical Appraisals

Even before the the drama of the Tower Amendment was being acted out in Washington, a number of authors were busily constructing strong and vigorous attacks on the testing enterprise (for example, Alexander, 1965; Black, 1963; Gross, 1962; Hoffman, 1962; Packard, 1964). A representative example of these critiques was entitled *The Brain Watchers* (Gross, 1962). Here, not unlike Whyte (1956), the principal concern was the use of personality inventories in the selection of executives for industry. M. L. Gross, a journalist, raised a number of issues that appeared to call into question the utility of prevailing practice. Interspersed with numerous anecdotes, Gross noted the following:

1. The inventories were often scored as though there was a "correct" answer (in contradiction to the instructions for these voluntary tests).
2. There was a questionable link between item content and the scale to which it purported to belong.
3. The inventories could be faked.
4. Many of the tests relied on strictly empirical test-construction techniques.
5. The testing process imposed conformity.
6. Personnel workers were susceptible to the Barnum Effect.
7. There were poor relationships between test items and job requirements (particularly with projectives).
8. The ethics of requiring (or appearing to require) that employees and applicants submit to testing were questionable.
9. Unqualified persons were often interpreting the tests.
10. There appeared to be some inconsistencies in the research literature.
11. There were inherent difficulties in establishing reliable criteria in executive placement.

The MMPI, Bernreuter, and Rorschach were singled out for special critical attention—including the publication of specific sample items for a number of tests. The flavor of Gross's commentary can be seen in this excerpt from the concluding chapter of *The Brain Watchers*: "The moral implications of personality testing lie not only in its inaccuracy but [also in] its approach to group statistical guilt. A man is accused and convicted not for any unsocial act or behavior, but for his *variance,* either from a norm or a projective tester's highly imaginative criteria" (Gross, 1962, p. 277).

Not unlike Walter Lippmann 40 years earlier, Gross offered a critical appraisal, which, though it may have lacked the stylistic and sanctioned language expected by members of the testing enterprise, signaled significant social concern about testing. Interestingly, creating a sense of déjà vu for the Lippmann incident, the testing enterprise's response was, in some quarters, very like the condescending response attempted by Terman four decades earlier:

> The attack was not particularly original; it did, however, stimulate a high degree of adrenal activity in many of you if the number and tone of the letters I received about *The Brain Watchers* (Gross, 1962) is a valid index of this kind of glandular function. [McGehee, 1964, p. 799]

> What will be the impact of the book on the general public? It is certainly likely to raise questions about the utility and value of tests. Some people may without further evidence discontinue testing. More sophisticated readers are likely to discern axe-grinding in the diatribe. [Crissey, 1963, p. 229]

But there were some important points embedded in critiques such as Gross's. A well-reasoned and careful appraisal of the critical issues being raised in the public press was needed. However, events in American society did not afford the time to prepare this much-needed analysis. Rather, the attacks escalated, eventuating in psychological testing becoming the subject of special attention of a congressional investigation by Senate and House committees, accompanied by directives from the government either banning or severely restricting the use of tests in some contexts.

A Congressional Inquiry

It was not long before the controversy surrounding testing came to the attention of elected officials. Indeed, Senator Barry Goldwater, a right-wing politician, branded tests as an "indirect inquisition into your most personal affairs" (cited in Amrine, 1964, p. 216). Slowly but surely, tests were mentioned more frequently on Capitol Hill.

Things came to a head when Senator Samuel J. Ervin expressed considerable concern about the extent to which personality tests were being used in selecting government employees. The Peace Corps employed the Minnesota Multiphasic Personality Inventory (MMPI), and considerable use of this test (or similar types) in other departments was reported. Ervin's Constitutional Rights subcommittee had received numerous complaints about these procedures. He determined that tests could constitute an invasion of privacy and that they also could present serious **due process issues,** which involved the possibility of persons being accused or labeled on the basis of test performance without having the opportunity to rebut the assertion. As a result, Ervin's subcommittee held hearings between June 7 and 10, 1965, with the stated purpose to examine

1. The content of psychological tests administered by the Government and the extent to which the questions asked constituted an unjustified invasion of the individual's psyche and private life,

2. Whether tests were scientifically valid, and

3. The procedural and use process issues involved in the administration of the tests, including the employee's right to confront his accusers when his emotional stability and mental competency are questioned. [Ervin, 1965, p. 880]

Similar concerns were expressed by Representative Cornelius Gallagher, Chairman, Special Inquiry, House Government Operations Committee, who convened a series of hearings starting on June 2. He argued that

The American people would rise in great protest if the Government of the United States conducted a physical search of public employees as a condition of employment.... Yet the Federal Government has been engaged in a much more insidious type of search than going through someone's home, mail, or personal papers. It has been searching the minds of Federal employees and job applicants through personality testing.... The means [testing], in my view, violates the Fourth Amendment to the Constitution and perhaps the First, Fifth, Ninth, and Fourteenth Amendments as well. [Gallagher, 1965, p. 881]

The antitest sentiments of the American people had become very focused, and the testing enterprise was about to undergo its closest public scrutiny ever.

The hearings became a media event in Washington—described by some as a circus. For example, John Macy, the chairman of the U.S. Civil Service

Pickets at American Psychological Association during congressional hearings.

Commission (USCSC) clarified the existing policy of his unit in his testimony to Gallagher's subcommittee. In essence, the USCSC had always taken a very cautious position regarding personality tests for selection. However, in cases where mental stability was deemed a significant aspect of the job, the commission did use tests under qualified professional guidance (see Macy, 1965, for elaboration). Two headlines, which described this statement of (existing) policy, read "Civil Service Bans the Use of Personality Testing" (*Washington Post*) and "Personality Tests Out for U.S. Job Seekers" (*Washington Star*). The headlines implied that the commission had banned testing, when in actuality the testimony referred only to a statement of extant policy. Of Macy's testimony, Representative Gallagher said "Everyone in our Civil Service owes you a debt of gratitude" and predicted that this order would also influence private industry and "be helpful to everyone who has to work for a living" (Amrine, 1965, p. 863). It would seem that the need to demonstrate some kind of progress due to the hearings was more important than the actual observation that all Macy had done was to describe existing policies.

The issue of using the MMPI in the Peace Corps was clarified as well (Shriver, 1965). The goals of this organization, which sent volunteer workers to various underdeveloped regions, were to help interested countries meet their personnel needs as well as to increase Americans' understanding of foreign peoples and vice versa. The MMPI was used to select out persons whose mental makeup would prevent them from meeting the exacting demands of this work. The MMPI was a small part of a complex selection process. Shriver, the director of the Corps, indicated that "The Peace Corps will continue to make full use of psychologists and psychological tests. But, as our psychologists have always been quick to point out, the prediction of future performance is still a 'chancy' business. Our own research efforts point the way towards greater predictability of overseas performance" (Shriver, 1965, p. 877).

As the testimony rolled in and the media continued to feed on it, it became increasingly clear that a significant part of the furor was caused by misunderstandings between the major parties (see Clopton, 1965). Most observers agreed that the investigation did not find widespread misuse of the MMPI or similar tests. Nor was it established that the uses to which tests were being put in government constituted an invasion of privacy. Further, in terms of the numbers of people involved, the hearings did not uncover substantial numbers of due process issues. The final determination of the hearings was the creation of a task force on testing that would report on the usefulness of tests. By the time this report was finished, the storm had blown over. Today there is general consensus that the practices of the testing enterprise have remained pretty much the same as before the congressional hearings—with psychologists becoming a bit more cautious in their forays into the community.

The public mistrust of testing, however, persisted. Tests were still seen as an invasion of privacy. It remained that tests were thought of as "silent accusers," offering the respondent no opportunity to challenge the results. The triviality of some items, and the seemingly magic relationships these bear to what the scale was measuring, remained a source of discomfort. Tests were seen to foster rigid and mechanistic decision making, and concerns about the fairness of tests to

"You've Been Deciding Who's All Right And Who Isn't?"

A newspaper cartoon regarding the use of tests to select government workers.

From *The Herblock Gallery* (Simon and Schuster, 1968). Reproduced by permission.

disadvantaged groups persisted. These issues remained a significant part of the public perception of the testing enterprise despite it surviving its first major test case at the hands of a government inquiry.

CLOSE UP **A 1960s Personality Inventory**

During the heat of public outcry against testing, humor became an effective weapon. For example, in circulation at the time was a fake personality inventory meant to spoof personality assessment (from Amrine, 1965, p. 990). The following are some of the items from this satirical piece:

1. When I was younger, I used to tease vegetables.
2. Sometimes I am unable to prevent clean thoughts from entering my mind.
3. I am not unwilling to work for a jackass.
4. I would enjoy the work of a chicken flicker.
5. I think beavers work too hard.
6. It is important to wash your hands before you wash your hands.

7. It is hard for me to say the right thing when I find myself in a room full of mice.
8. I use shoe polish to excess.
9. It makes me furious to see an innocent man escape the chair.
10. As a child, I used to wet the ceiling.
11. The sight of blood no longer excites me.
12. I am aroused by persons of the opposite sexes.
13. I believe I smell as good as most people.
14. When I was a child, I was an imaginary playmate.

Syndicated columnist Art Buchwald suggested an interesting intrepretive scheme for items such as these:

> If you had more true than false [responses], you should work for the Labor Department. If more false than true, you should go to the Peace Corps. If you were evenly divided true and false, you should apply for work with the Voice of America. If you held your hand over the questions while you answered them, you should go with the FBI, and if you refused to answer some of the questions, you might work for the White House. [Cited in Amrine, 1965, p. 989]

Some of these items are parodies of MMPI statements. Spoofs such as these, though amusing in their own right, have an edge in that they signal the very real discomfort felt about the secrecy and apparent magic of the activities of the testing enterprise.

Legal Difficulties

It did not end here either. Since 1965 there has been a number of landmark legal cases involving psychological measurement that are indicative of even greater difficulties. Three areas of activity have shown much legal analysis of psychological testing:

1. Test use in educational settings where cultural bias has been alleged (typically, disadvantaging Blacks was at issue)

2. The validity of employment tests, with, again, considerable involvement of Blacks

3. Several important issues regarding disclosure of test materials (see Bersoff, 1981)

An examination of this experience is useful because it portends some important changes in the testing enterprise.

With respect to legal involvement in the use of tests for placement in educational programs, the cases have emerged as "challenges to practices perceived as attempts to continue, more subtly, the racial and ethnic separation that school systems imposed more blatantly in the 1950s and 1960s" (Bersoff, 1981, p. 1049). In large measure, the challenges were based upon the 1964 Civil Rights Act.

A celebrated case involved *Larry P. v. California State Department of Education (CSDE)* in 1979. At issue was the use of standardized tests to identify children for placement in **educable mentally retarded** (EMR) classes. Blacks were highly overrepresented in the classes and scored lower than Whites on these tests. It was argued that this disparity in scores was evidence of cultural bias in the tests. In the *Larry P. v. CSDE* case, Judge Peckham ruled in favor of Larry P., thereby supporting the contention of cultural bias. Furthermore, the court permanently prevented the department "from utilizing, permitting the use of, or approving the use of any standardized tests . . . for the identification of black EMR children or their placement into EMR classes, without first securing approval of this court" (cited in Bersoff, 1981, p. 1048). This was and continues to be an exceedingly important ruling because it is a direct affront to the entire program of the testing movement. Standardized testing had been banned in California! In a very real sense, the *Larry P. v. CSDE* ruling is a clear indication that society, which the movement is supposed to be serving, is not satisfied with the manner in which it is proceeding.

The ruling went even further because it imposed a very arduous set of standards before it would permit the use of intelligence scales:

1. Tests would have to yield the same pattern of scores when administered to different groups of students.

2. Tests would have to yield approximately equal means for all subgroups in the standardization sample.

3. Tests would have to be correlated with relevant criterion measures; that is, IQ scores of black children would have to be correlated with classroom performance. [Cited in Bersoff, 1981, p. 1048]

These criteria make it virtually impossible to use any of the extant tests because they were not developed to meet these stringent criteria. The whole storehouse of experience developed over almost a century of psychological research was rendered socially ineffective in this one ruling.[1]

However, as is often the case in law, another state court ruled in exactly the opposite manner. The ruling in *Parents in Action in Special Education (PASE) v. Hannon* in Illinois was that "the WISC, WISC–R and Stanford–Binet tests, when used in conjunction with the statutorily mandated criteria for determining an appropriate educational program for a child do not discriminate against black children" (Judge Grady's ruling—cited in Bersoff, 1981, p. 1048). Clearly, there were regional variations in the United States regarding the usefulness of tests in making educational decisions. However, the issue remains that there was an enhanced level of legal involvement in the testing field, which was symptomatic of some substantive problems with the testing enterprise serving its social mandate. It could be that since the 1960s there has been a general increase in the numbers of people who turn to the courts to solve various disputes, and psychological testing has just been caught in this trend. However, because psychological tests have been singled out for this kind of action, they represent a very real issue in today's cultural context and probably will continue to be so.

Equally confusing and contradictory rulings have been made in the use of tests for employment decisions (see Bersoff, 1981, for a summary).

Test developers have long held to the position that the content of items on tests is privileged information. The reason for this is the fear that, if the examination

---

[1] For an update on these developments, see Turkington, 1992.

items were known, it would be possible to coach respondents and thereby invalidate the test. This policy of the testing enterprise came under fire with the passage of the **Family Education Rights and Privacy Act** in 1974. The focus of this legislation was that educational programs receiving funds under various departments of education must allow parents access to records directly related to their children. This meant that parents have legal access to test information as well as to the testing materials. In several cases, the provision has been upheld, breaking the test developer's monopoly on access to test items. Interestingly, Judge Grady in the *PASE v. Hannon* case publicized WISC and Stanford–Binet items in making his judgment about these tests not being culturally biased. Again, the needs of contemporary society were not being met by the testing enterprise, thereby forcing a legal challenge to aspects of the testing enterprise.

Although this is only a brief look at the legal scrutiny of psychological testing, it makes it clear that such confrontations are likely to continue to occur. At least three lessons for the testing enterprise have emerged from this enhanced scrutiny:

1. It has made the testing enterprise, and society in general, more sensitive to cultural and racial differences, indicating how apparently benign practices can (unintentionally or otherwise) foster discrimination.

2. It has alerted the testing movement that it will have to be accountable for all of its actions and policies (even in cases of unintended effects).

3. It has also begun to create a context in which there is an increased search for alternatives that will withstand the definitely "hard" standards that the courts are setting for the enterprise. [Bersoff, 1981, p. 1055]

LOOKING AT THE CRITIQUES

There are two sides to every story. So far in this chapter, most of the discussion has been about the antitest side of the debate, without giving the testing enterprise a chance to respond to the various allegations outlined in the previous section. The sections that follow outline the kinds of responses and actions that stemmed from the critical assaults during this time. The manner in which the enterprise reacted to the criticisms has had a profound effect on current testing practices. We will also see that the psychological testing enterprise actually anticipated a number of the critical issues but failed to defend itself well when the public furor mounted.

As the antitest movement was gaining in force, psychologists were busy formulating counterarguments. Some of the responses were acrimonious, some were defensive, and some chose to ignore the issues being raised. However, many responses to the criticisms were well-thought-out and carefully considered attempts to understand the nature of the comments being made. Additionally, after carefully considering the points being raised, psychologists often made genuine efforts to change the matter of concern if it was warranted. In most cases, these changes emerged in the form of recommendations that were eventually incorporated into the evolving ethical code and testing practices.

Invasion of Privacy

Most of the concern that tests constitute an **invasion of privacy** was focused on personality tests. Here the fundamental apprehension related to the right of the test administrator to interrogate respondents on topics thought to be of such a private nature that to ask the question was a violation of their constitutional rights. It could be argued, though, that virtually any kind of test—intelligence, interest, or ability—could, under some circumstances, be considered an intrusion on human rights. But so too could the traditional employment interview, or the therapeutic session, or the vocational-counseling encounter. Thus, this aspect of the controversy surrounding testing is part-and-parcel of a much larger issue in the conduct of human affairs: To what extent and under what circumstances is it permissible to ask penetrating personal questions, whether formulated in terms of a structured test or in any other format?

No amount of effort to formulate general guidelines defining acceptable situations for asking probing personal questions will produce adequate protection of individual rights. The diverse variation in the situations in which this type of information is gathered and the numerous reasons for its collection render the possibility of finding a suitable broadband solution to the problem intractable. The issue really comes down to a detailed consideration of the specific case being considered (Anastasi, 1967; Messick, 1965). However, three classes of situations in which tests are used lead to a number of conclusions about invasion of privacy: counseling or psychotherapy, research studies, and selection or promotion.

In the case of counseling or psychotherapy, where assessment is conducted for the benefit of the client, the then-current APA ethical standards were clearly relevant:

> The psychologist informs this prospective client of the important aspects of the potential relationship that might affect the client's decisions to enter the relationship. [APA, 1963, Principle 8, p. 58]

> The psychologist who asks that an individual reveal personal information in the course of interviewing, testing, or evaluation, or who allows such information to be divulged to him, does so only after making certain that the responsible person is fully aware of the purposes of the interview, testing, or evaluation and of the ways in which the information may be used. [APA, 1963, Principle 7d, p. 57]

The key point is that the client, in this type of situation, must enter the relationship aware of the possibility and implications of divulging personal information. This is the principle of **informed consent**.[2] Under this doctrine, the client offers personal data voluntarily, and, as such, there is no invasion of privacy—only a willing revelation of it. Written contracts that clearly articulated the need, nature, and use of the testing data, signed prior to the therapeutic encounter, were recommended (see Lovell, 1967).

Research studies are another class of situations in which tests are used. In these situations, information is being obtained for scientific purposes and is only

---

[2]Informed consent has become a standard part of *all* versions of the APA ethical code since 1963 (see Chapter 12).

revealed in such a manner that the individual cannot be identified. Here, the onus falls on the psychologist to ensure that no link between test data and the individual respondent is possible. To the extent these assurances are in place, there can be no invasion of privacy.

The most controversial class of testing situations is assessment for selection or promotion. Here test information is gathered to help the sponsoring institution make a decision about an individual's acceptability or promotability. In many cases, test takers never see their results, nor are they aware of how the test data enter into the decision making. In many cases, test takers do not have the opportunity to challenge the decisions that are made. This constitutes a very real threat to individual rights—one that cannot be ignored. There is a hard-line response to these suggestions. Here the argument is that the respondent is captive because the institution seems to have the right to ask for any information it wants. Failure to comply would result in an incomplete application and decisions made on that basis. However, this is not a solution because it implies, among other things, that the right to privacy has to be purchased at the expense of giving up one's opportunity to apply for gainful employment. The observation that many people do comply to institutional demands for test data—in some cases, applicants actually bear the testing costs—is more testimony to the coercive nature of this practice than it is evidence that the applicants "don't mind" (see Hanson, 1993, for an extended discussion of this point). Testing for selection and placement constitute very problematic situations when the right to privacy is an issue. The conflict of values between the institution and the individual appear to come into full relief in this situation. (This point is discussed further in Chapter 20.)

These three classes of testing situations (counseling, research, and selection) do not exhaust the contexts in which testing occurs but represent some of the *major* situations in which one might raise privacy issues. For our purposes, the most important observation is this: A blanket assertion that tests constitute an invasion of privacy is *not* tenable. They may invade privacy in some situations and may not in others. A careful evaluation of the specific situation in which privacy concerns are raised is absolutely necessary.

The best protection against invasion of privacy is to ensure that any use of tests is being conducted by properly trained and qualified psychologists who, by virtue of their professional status, are committed to the ethical code of the relevant association. Under these conditions, in almost all cases, any invasion of privacy will also constitute a breach of ethics on the part of the practitioner.

Cronbach (1960) presents a discussion of these issues that predates the controversy in the press by almost 5 years—as does the APA code of ethics (see Chapter 12). The point is that the testing enterprise had been active prior to the emergence of the antitest movement in the public eye. Most of the issues surrounding invasion of privacy that were to emerge in the 1960s had been anticipated by more forward-looking members of the psychological community. The problem was the inability of psychology to make its points clearly as the controversy unfolded (see Clopton, 1965). In part, this was because psychologists did not have the opportunity to rebut the assertions in public, but there was a failure in psychological circles to fully appreciate the potential gravity of the situation.

Confidentiality

The very existence of personal information in the form of responses to structured tests is a threat to the individual. Once in concrete form, this information is potentially available to outsiders, either through malicious intent, carelessness, or even legal demands for the information. Despite the assurances of counselors, clinicians, researchers, and industrial psychologists (and their well-intended ethical code), the possibility of test data becoming available to other parties is very real and should not be underestimated. This was identified as a significant problem in the congressional hearings and remains a critical issue in the testing enterprise today.[3] Simply put, there is no ironclad way of ensuring **confidentiality** of test data—once it exists, it is potentially available to others.

Another aspect of the confidentiality issue was also discussed during this time: the manner in which test performance was to be communicated to others. Three issues are embedded here. First, respondents have the fundamental right to see their own test results. One of the major objections to testing raised in the congressional hearings was the possibility of persons being accused or labeled on the basis of test performance without having the opportunity to rebut the assertion—that is, due process concerns. Although the inquiry could not document substantial numbers of such problems, they remain important. Clearly, the best solution to this was to *ensure that individuals have the right to see their own test results*. Situations where this was not the case were to be viewed with suspicion. In cases of children or respondents with intellectual disabilities, it was deemed appropriate that the parent or guardian would have the right to see the results.

The second issue is who else should see the results—parents, teachers, supervisors, prospective employers, and so on. The major reason for concern here, apart from the breach of confidence, was some emerging literature on **self-fulfilling prophecies**. For example, some data suggested that knowledge of test scores by teachers sometimes had an effect on pupils' intellectual development. A student identified as subnormal on a test may, through differential treatment by the teacher, begin to actualize this (potentially false) characterization. Self-fulfilling prophecies were one of several lines of argument that highlighted the need for restrictions in access to test data. The eventual resolution of this problem was to indicate that *results can be shown to others if and only if respondents are told at the outset what use is going to be made of the results*. Ideally, this should include a list of actual people who will have access to the data. Any change in this plan would have to be cleared with respondents (or their parents or guardians).

Third, the nature of the feedback is also an important issue. There would seem little point in suggesting that respondents have access to their actual behavioral responses because the important aspect of the testing process is the interpretation of the data, not the actual responses. Most respondents, however, do not have the technical training to properly evaluate a professional interpretation. The possibilities of misinterpretation are legion. Contemporary discussion suggested that the

---

[3]The emergence of powerful database technologies and the attending threats to the confidentiality of electronically represented data posed by hackers and the like make this an even greater problem in the 1990s than it was in the 1960s.

psychologist is obligated to present the results of tests to the respondent *in a manner that is compatible with the respondent's level of understanding of the process* (for example, Anastasi, 1967).

Confidentiality emerged as an obviously complex issue. Like invasion of privacy, there was no single solution, but each situation demands careful evaluation in its own right. The fundamental possibility of a breach of confidentiality of test data remains as one of the major difficulties in the testing enterprise. Any resolution of uncertainty surrounding this issue rests on the development and actualization of trust between respondents and testers. Without this, the very foundation of testing is on shaky ground.

Test-Item Content

Much of the critical literature during this time focused on questioning what a specific item was supposed to demonstrate. What did it mean, some asked, to respond true to the item "I sometimes get headaches" as part of a selection interview? Does this imply that a true responder should not be hired as a drafter, or a nurse, or a pilot? Should job applicants answer it false because it might be a critical item for deciding their occupational fate? Indeed, a sizable proportion of the popular critiques (for example, Gross, 1962; Whyte, 1956) emphasized the apparent lack of relationship between actual item content and the decisions being made on the basis of responses to it. This line of critique can be very effective when applied to subtle items where the relationship between the item and scale is not the least bit obvious (see Chapter 9).

For the psychologist, this line of argument represents a very real challenge. As students of testing, we know that psychological test scores are based on the aggregation of a large number of indicators, or signs, of the construct being measured. Thus, a true response to the item "I occasionally have headaches" may, on the basis of substantial research and data collection, be 1 of 60 putative signs of the presence of hypochondriasis. In other words, it represents, at an absolute maximum, one-sixtieth of an obtained scale score. Persons scoring in the 90th percentile on the scale may *or* may not respond true to this item (although the odds are they would). Thus, asking what a single item means is not a particularly answerable question; about all we can say is that, with a slight probability, hypochondriacs tend to say true to the item. This answer is deeply troubling to many. How, some might ask, is it possible to base important social decisions on items with such low response probabilities? Is there that much error in the system? Indeed, this answer probably creates more problems than it answers.

From the previous chapters, we know that the aggregated total score is relatively reliable and that inferences from a single item are unreasonable. But how do we communicate this to someone who has not had the benefit of training in testing? This was one of the fundamental challenges to the testing enterprise as it began to interact with an increasingly skeptical public. There were a number of strategies that could be taken to this problem:

1. The enterprise could choose to ignore the question; however, this would result in increased distrust and suspicion.

2. It might suggest that questions of this type should be left to the "experts," asking for trust from the general public. Both historically (remember Terman's attempt to rebut Lippmann) and logically this is not an effective solution if the experts and their tests are already under fire.

3. It might try to educate the public in test theory so it could appreciate the inappropriateness of inferences from single-item responses. However, restricted space in the media and a certain unwillingness to learn new concepts (particularly if you already disagree with the proposition being defended) argue against the viability of this strategy.

4. It might restrict access to test items so that only those with adequate training would ever be able to see the actual items. Then anyone asking this kind of question could be declared "out of line" because they should not have access to the item. This would be one way of diffusing the criticism. However, respondents see the items when they respond (and may remember them), and increased secrecy surrounding the testing enterprise implied by this solution would in all likelihood increase the intensity of the critique, not reduce it.

5. It might change items so that their relevance to the construct being measured was obvious, thereby reducing the chances of this type of criticism. This would bring a number of problems, particularly if the test was trying to measure something that was not socially desirable (for example, lying, psychopathology).

None of these strategies is a totally effective way of dealing with the problem. Indeed, this line of attack on the testing enterprise poses a very difficult problem. The very nature of the testing enterprise and the manner it has chosen to go about its business make it highly vulnerable to this type of criticism from the outside.

Concerns Relating to the Uses of Testing

One category of criticism during this time related more to the manner in which tests were used than to the tests themselves. For example, there was considerable concern about the rigid use of tests that failed to make allowance for possible changes on the part of the respondent (Brim, 1965). It was also felt that tests encouraged mechanical, impersonal evaluations (Messick, 1965). Finally, a number of people felt that tests had a pervasive effect on the kind of talent selected because those constructs that were easy to measure became more valued than were subtle and complex phenomena such as creativity (Brim, 1965; Messick, 1965).

Each criticism focuses on the manner in which tests have been applied to social decision making. There is nothing in the tests themselves that *cause* such problems to emerge; the problem exists in the application of the instrument to social decision making. This, of course, does not exonerate testing from these criticisms but draws our attention to the fact that the only reasonable response to such criticisms lies in considering the specific situation in which tests are being faulted.

One way to make sense of these issues is to consider testing relative to alternatives. In other words, to address this category of criticism, evaluating the utility of tests in comparison to some other strategy becomes necessary—that is, are tests better or worse than something else? Only if phrased in this manner is it possible to develop a rational strategy for dealing with this category of concern about the testing enterprise. The simplest comparison is to contrast using tests with not using them. The issue of rigidity in test use, then, can be rephrased as a problem of whether using tests will result in better decisions than *not* using them. This question can only be answered by systematic research.

Ideas such as the index of forecasting efficiency, the Taylor–Russell tables, and base rates, which were presented earlier, set the background for the emergence of a sophisticated approach to this issue. This involved the postulation of the notion of **utility**, which relates to the payoff that accrues to an institution when an individual is accepted as an employee, trainee, or student. Several very elegant methodologies for determining the effectiveness of tests for making decisions evolved during the 1960s, and one of these is outlined briefly in the following Close Up.

CLOSE UP   **Testing and Decision Theory**

For testing, the important thing is to demonstrate that utility is enhanced by the inclusion of a test. From Cronbach and Gleser (1965), the gain in utility from the use of a test can be represented as

$$\Delta U = s_c r_{yc} E(y') - C_y \tag{14-1}$$

where

$$\Delta U = \text{the gain in utility}$$
$$s_c = \text{the standard deviation of the criterion}$$
$$r_{yc} = \text{the test-criterion correlation (validity)}$$
$$y' = \text{cutting score to generate the appropriate } \textbf{selection ratio}$$
$$E(y') = \text{the ordinate of the normal curve at the cutting point}[4]$$
$$C_y = \text{the average cost of testing one person}$$

Notice how this formula includes many more terms than the earlier conceptualizations. As before, test validity (r_{yc}) and selection ratio ($E(y')$) are explicitly considered. Additionally, however, Cronbach and Gleser have included the variability of the criterion measure (s_c) as well as the cost of testing (C_y). Clearly, this is a more inclusive conceptualization than the views presented in Chapters 11 and 13.

At a very general level, Equation 14-1 defines **utility** as a joint function of the costs and benefits of testing. In most applications of a **cost/benefit analysis**, both the costs and benefits are determined from the perspective of the institution doing the testing and decision making. Thus, the costs to applicants of taking the test (for example, taking off work, transportation, wages lost if they hold another job) do not enter into this formulation, as neither are the costs and benefits of being either

---

[4]For example, if the selection ratio was .5, $E(y')$ would equal the height of the normal curve at the cutoff score that divides the applicants into two equal halves. This would be the mean ($z = 0$) in a true normal distribution. From tables of the normal curve, the ordinate when $z = 0$ equals .3989, which would be the value of $E(y')$ for this particular example. Ordinates for the normal curve can be found in Appendix A.

selected or rejected. This is a particularly clear example of the manner in which psychological assessment is typically evaluated from the perspective of the sponsoring agency. This does not preclude, however, the possiblity that utility from the individual view could not be incorporated into such a formulation.

To illustrate Equation 14-1, Figure 14-2 shows the graphical representation of the relationship between selection ratio and the gain in utility for tests of varying degrees of validity. Costs and criterion variability are assumed constant for all three levels of validity. Notice the inverted U shape of this function, with negative gains (losses) being associated with tests of low validity and at extreme selection ratios. In other words, there are cases where the use of a test actually decreases the institutional payoff because the costs outweigh the benefits. In addition, notice how the optimal gain in utility occurs when the selection ratio is .5, regardless of the validity of the test.

Equation 14-1 can be elaborated to include cases where more than one test is used. For example, consider three ways in which two tests (A and B) could be used:

1. **Battery:** Give both A and B to all applicants and use the optimally weighted composite score as a single cutoff.[5]
2. **Single-screen test:** Use only the most valid of A or B alone.
3. **Sequential-testing program:** Give A and on the basis of the scores divide the applicants into three categories:
   a. Accept immediately
   b. Reject immediately
   c. Administer B
      In (c), the optimally weighted score using both A and B would be used to select which applicants would be accepted.

An extension of Equation 14-1 allows a priori evaluation of which method would be the most effective under varying conditions. For example, Figure 14-3 demon-

Figure 14-2

Change in utility as a function of the selection ratio.

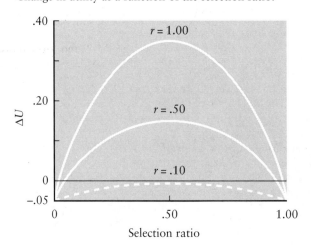

SOURCE: based on Cronbach and Gleser, 1965, p. 38

[5]This would be achieved using multiple regression.

Figure 14-3

Gain in utility with sequential, single-screen, and battery strategies.

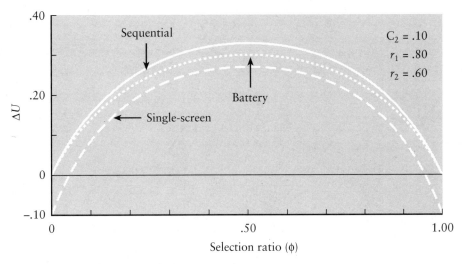

SOURCE: based on Cronbach and Gleser, 1965, p. 38

strates the gains in utility for these three strategies as a function of selection ratio when the validities of A and B are .8 and .6, respectively, and test B costs $.10 per administration. The cost of test A and criterion variability are assumed constant across all conditions in this figure. Notice how the sequential strategy is superior throughout the range of selection ratio, but the gain in utility is nil at extreme selection ratios. The negative gain shown at extreme selection ratios for the battery strategy is due to the necessity of administering both tests to all applicants.

Clearly, the **decision-theory** approach permits detailed appraisals of the manner in which tests can enter into decision making. There are many other derivations possible from this formulation, with Figures 14-2 and 14-3 representing only a small sample (see Cronbach & Gleser, 1965, for many examples and an extended discussion). These examples, however, provide a sense of the solutions that can be derived from the application of decision theory to problems such as selection.

The foregoing Close Up indicates that the issue of test use is highly complex, at best. This indicates that a considerable amount of systematic research is necessary to design and evaluate a specific testing application. Figure 14-4 (page 528) represents the manner in which the notion of utility evolved over the course of the developing testing enterprise. The key concept used to evaluate the utility of a test in a specific situation started out simply as a test-criterion correlation and evolved in complexity until it finally culminated in the notion of utility. The boxes to the right of each major contribution indicate the terms that are used to estimate the specific key terms.

The preceding criticisms relating to the use of tests emerge when testing becomes the sole driving force in the entire decision-making system. Under these

Figure 14-4 The evolution of utility.

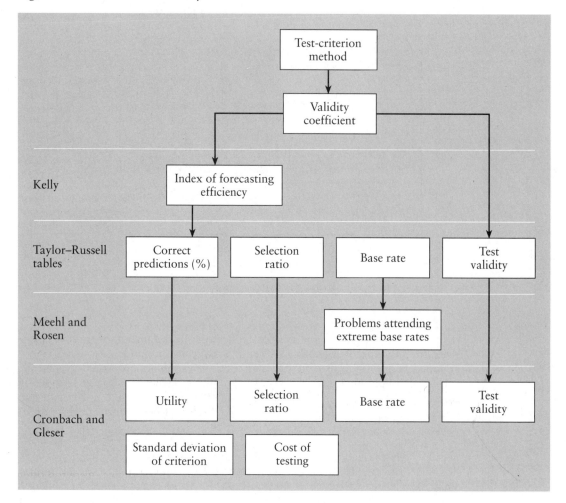

conditions, there is a very real possibility of rigidity, mechanistic interpretation, and the inhibition of creativity. However, tests typically play a relatively small role in most social decision-making contexts. For example, selection programs usually involve a series of **hurdles** over which job applicants must jump. From the previous Close Up, the most efficient strategy for such programs involves two factors: (1) The situation should be arranged so that (roughly) 50% of the applicants are accepted at each hurdle (see Cronbach & Gleser, 1965), and (2) the least expensive hurdle should be placed first, saving the more expensive selection processes (for example, interviewing) until the latter part of the process when there are fewer candidates. Testing, by virtue of being relatively inexpensive (compared, say, with an interview or probationary job training), tends to appear at the earlier stages of selection programs. In the main then, tests serve to narrow down the field of applicants so the more subtle and complicated aspects of the decision-making processes can be brought to bear. In this type of situation, the chances of testing driving the entire decision-making program are slight because the important decisions are not being made by the tests. In other words, a well-designed selection program will not be driven by tests in any sense of the word, and fears about rigidity, mechanical evaluations, and inhibiting creativity are unfounded. This line of reasoning, however, rests on the demonstration that a specific selection program is well designed and researched.

Criticisms about the uses and abuses of testing are exceedingly important because the future of the testing enterprise rests on their resolution. Blanket assertions that tests inhibit creativity or force mechanistic decision making are *not* tenable; the specific context in which the test is being used must be considered. Equally certain, though, is that tests are sometimes used badly—very badly. There can be no doubt that they have been misapplied in numerous situations, both prior to the antitest movement and after it. In an important way, the very existence of tests creates a climate where it is tempting to lapse into rigid and mechanistic ways of thinking about human issues. The fundamental challenge is to construct situations in which we can have the best of both worlds where tests can contribute in constructive and worthwhile ways to the complex and agonizing task of making important social decisions. Tests appear to have a place in today's world as relatively inexpensive and efficient *adjuncts* to social decision making.

Fairness to Minorities

With the 1964 Civil Rights Bill and the Tower Amendment in hand, suggestions that tests did not show **fairness to minorities** would seem to rest on shaky legal ground. The legal definitions, however, did little to stem concern that social inequities were supported by the testing movement. Indeed, some aspects of the emerging test data were cited as evidence that tests were unfair to minority groups:

> Conventional instruments of mental testing, experience had shown, were too often fashioned to fit the intellectual and social ways of middle-class children with the result that minority group children were being excluded from opportunities for training because of the accident of what has come to be called "cultural deprivation." [Deutsch, Fishman, Kogan, North, & Whiteman, 1964, p. 127]

The fundamental concern was that, although tests may not legally discriminate, they do have an immense impact on the opportunities afforded those who, by no fault of their own, do not score well. Three principal difficulties with standardized tests were identified. First, tests appeared to be differentially reliable across the entire range of scores, with reliability being lower in the scores obtained by minority groups. Second, the predictive validity for minority groups may be quite different from that of the original validation subjects. Third, the validity of the interpretation of a test score is strongly dependent on an adequate understanding of the cultural background of the group being tested. Each of these points reveals potential problems within the testing enterprise, which could lead to **unfairness**.

CLOSE UP   Test Bias and Fairness

The issue of fairness of tests turns out to be more complicated than first supposed. There is an extensive literature on the mathematical and empirical analysis of **bias,** which is much too large to review here. However, we can touch on some of the more important features of the manner in which tests may be evaluated for bias in the interests of promoting fairness.

Ideally, bias concerns should be integrated into the strategies used to construct tests, using every method possible to minimize or eliminate all potential problems. This is not always possible, however, because sometimes older tests are used and sometimes a test originally developed as unbiased for several groups will be used with another population—requiring a reexamination. Social issues and programs change so rapidly that it is not possible to anticipate all potential concerns. Thus, a post hoc approach to detecting and eliminating bias is often required. We will examine one such approach because it provides a sense of some of the more important components of contemporary thinking in the area.

We will assume that a bias and/or unfairness concern about a specific test has been raised. It involves the suggestion that a test is biased with one group of persons (called Group A) achieving differential results relative to another (called Group B). The person responsible for the test has to troubleshoot to determine if bias exists. And, if it is present, this person must take steps to eliminate it. How might she proceed?

Berk (1982) generated a useful sequential approach, which can be used in this situation. Figure 14-5 presents this model, which is an idealization of how best to proceed. Our discussion of test bias is organized around this figure, touching on some of the more important issues emerging in contemporary considerations and methods involved in the assessment of test fairness and bias.

Clarify and define bias and/or unfairness. First, it is necessary to distinguish between bias that is associated with the test itself and unfairness in the use of the test. Some tests, by virtue of specific characteristics of the items or response format, may disadvantage one group over another. For example, a paper-and-pencil test that demands reading skills may result in a well-educated group obtaining higher scores. If it should turn out that performance was equivalent between groups with differential amounts of education when the test was administered verbally, the paper-and-pencil verison of the test may be said to be biased.

However, even if a test were completely unbiased, it could still produce unfairness. For example, an unbiased selection test might predict job performance quite well for all groups but lead to an underrepresentation of a minority group. If it were demonstrated that a 2-week training program altered the pattern of job performance, the use of (the perfectly unbiased) test would still be unfair. It is important to clearly identify and clarify the exact nature of a specific fairness or bias concern because the methods of remediating the problem will vary substantially.

Once the nature of the problem has been clarified, we can move to the next step in our troubleshooting model.

Level of bias. The simplest level of analysis that can be used to identify bias involves examination of specific items in a test. **Item bias** would *not* exist if, for all individuals who obtained the same score on a homogeneous subtest containing the item, equal proportions of individuals in the groups being considered get the item correct. Any number of statistical methods (such as those reviewed under "Item

Figure 14-5
A sequential model of procedures available for troubleshooting test bias.

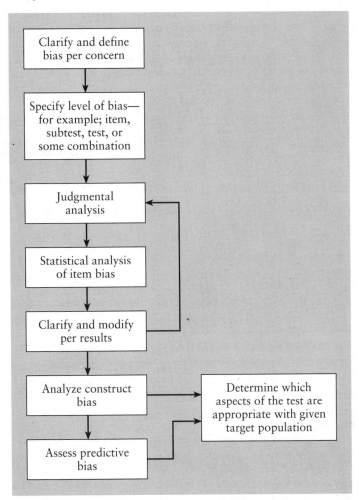

(SOURCE: Based on Berk, 1982, p. 6.)

Analysis" in Chapter 11) can be applied to determine this aspect of bias (for details, see Angoff, 1982). However, this is only part of the story. Bias has to be examined in terms of any aggregated subscores that are used because these could produce nonequivalent score distributions for various subgroups. This would be **subtest bias**. **Test bias** would be demonstrated if there were major inequalities across groups in the distributions of obtained total scores. Bias could exist at any of these three levels or a combination of them, regardless of the status of the other levels. Thus, identifying the exact level at which bias is evident is important. Once done, it becomes possible to move to the next stage in Berk's formulation.

Judgmental analysis. **Judgmental analysis** involves an entire family of methods that has the major goal of evaluating, from a rational perspective, if bias is present (for a review, see Tittle, 1982). One approach brings together representatives of the various groups on which a given test is used, and they determine if, from their perspective, they perceive any stereotyping, misrepresentation, and/or content unfamiliarity. Various types of experts can also be used in this process, which can vary from casual evaluations to highly systematic rating procedures. Once the various experts and group members are satisfied that there is no bias, it is possible to move to the next stage.

Statistical analysis of item bias. A wide variety of methods can be used to document the presence of item bias between various groups (see Angoff, 1982). Perhaps the simplest involves plotting various item statistics into a two-dimensional space—one axis associated with a given group (say, Group A) and the other with another group (say, Group B). Each item would be represented as a point in this space. The perfectly unbiased item would line up on the diagonal of this space because the statistics would then be identical for both groups. Deviation from the diagonal would indicate biased items, with greater distances revealing greater bias. This is a convenient and simple method of detecting bias at the item level. Comparison of various item-discrimination indexes (see Chapter 11) is possible using this procedure as well, with the selection of index being dictated by the intentions of the demonstration. In addition, a wide range of other approaches, such as the use of various experimental methods, can also be applied here (see Berk, 1982, Chapters 3–7).

If item bias is detected, either eliminating or reworking the offending items becomes necessary. After such steps are taken, it might be necessary to recycle the test through the judgmental and statistical analyses to ensure that the modifications have indeed rectified the problem.

Construct bias. The next stage involves determining if the test measures different constructs for different groups or if it measures the same construct but with varying degrees of accuracy. These possibilities are considered under the label **construct bias.** The fundamental concern here is whether or not the psychological mechanisms underlying test performance are adequately tapped by the test in the various groups for which fairness concerns have been raised. As you might expect from our discussions in Chapter 13, virtually any methodology—factor analysis, experimental approaches, or change over occasions, to name but a few—could be used here. Reynolds (1982) provides a good review of several of these applications in the bias context. If construct bias is ruled out, we can move to the next stage of Berk's system.

Predictive bias. One source of bias, called **predictive bias,** lies in the possibility that a specific test is differentially valid for different groups. For example, an aptitude test might be highly valid for selecting Group A applicants but invalid for Group B. This would emerge as meaningfully different test-criterion correlations for Group A as compared with Group B. Such differential predictability is called **slope bias** because it would also result in significantly different slopes of the regression lines relating the test-criterion values for each group. Figure 14-6 illustrates this situation.

The use of such a test would yield unfair predictions in the sense that individuals selected from the group with the higher validity coefficient would, on average, fare better at the criterion task than the low-validity group. This would enhance the numbers of inappropriate candidates selected from the low-validity group. Clearly, this would have a heavy impact on both the institution using the test and the individuals concerned.

Figure 14-6
Regression lines showing differential slopes between two groups, illustrating the problem of slope bias.

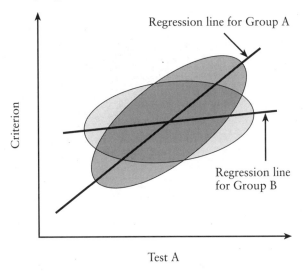

There have been quite a few empirical attempts to demonstrate the presence of slope bias in test-criterion data (for reviews, see Hunter, Schmidt, & Hunter, 1979; Schmidt, Berner, & Hunter, 1973). Unfortunately, methodological problems such as sample size have rendered the results of these studies inconclusive. However, three very large studies in varying contexts have failed to document significant differences in predictive validity (Breland, 1979; Campbell, Crooks, Mahoney, & Rock, 1973; Maier & Fuchs, 1973). Thus, slope bias may not be a major problem, but it is necessary to be continually aware of its possibility.

Even if the validities are the same for both groups (the slopes of the regression lines were parallel), the possibility of another type of bias exists. Specifically, it could emerge that a given test or subtest score is associated with different levels of criterion performance for each of two groups. Figure 14-7 (page 534) shows this possibility. In this case, there is a regression line for Group A as well as one for Group B. These regression lines are parallel, revealing the absence of slope bias. However, the two regression lines would intersect with the criterion axis at different points, thus indicating an important difference between the two groups. Because the regression lines meet the criterion axis at different points, this form of bias is called **intercept bias**.

The thin regression line in the middle of Figure 14-7 is that which would be generated if the data for the two groups (A and B) were combined to create a single sample—which is the typical manner in which such test data would be used. Using the common regression line results in a bias that works against the group with the higher mean criterion score (Group B in Figure 14-7). Looking at the figure, for a person who scores x_i on the test, the common regression line predicts a criterion status of y_c. This predicted score (y_c) overestimates how well members of Group A will perform and underestimates the criterion performance of Group B, revealing the possibility of considerable unfairness. Like slope bias, though, empirical documentation of intercept bias has been hard to secure (Breland, 1979; Hunter, Schmidt, & Rauschenberger, 1984; Linn, 1975).

Figure 14-7

Regression lines with equal slopes and differing intercepts, indicating the presence of intercept bias.

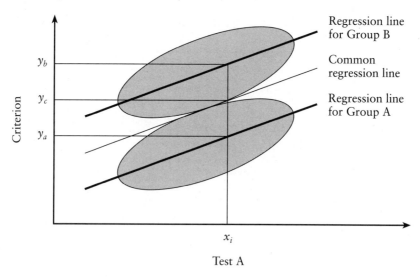

Test A

Predictive bias could also involve the criterion. For example, a work sample used as a criterion measure could tap only those characteristics demonstrated by the members of a specific group. Such a situation can be considered **criterion bias**, which is an aspect of predictive bias. Analysis of the criterion should be as rigorous as the analyses of the test.

If a given test to be used in a given situation has survived Berk's sequential model to this point (there is clear evidence of successful passing of the judgmental, construct, and predictive analyses), there is reason to suspect that bias does not exist in this situation. The extent to which various test publishers have employed these techniques and their successes in achieving nonbiased results are documented in Chapter 9 of Berk (1982).

Even if a test survived Berk's model, social inequities could still be wrought by the use of test data, indicating that a constant guard must be held up against the misuse of tests. In the contemporary climate of **equal opportunity**, one approach to selection involves a **top-down strategy** where the highest scorers are selected from each group of concern. By this method, controlling the proportions of accepted candidates from each group is possible, and predictions within each group will be maximal, assuming the test has a modicum of validity. This technique tends to yield acceptable results (Hunter & Hunter, 1984).

In general terms, the issue of test bias and fairness is complex. This Close Up has only scratched the surface of an exceedingly sophisticated methodology. Of particular importance for our purposes is to notice the extensive amount of effort that the testing enterprise has invested in its efforts to minimize the bias inherent in its tests and the manner in which they are used. Tests surviving Berk's methods do not guarantee the absence of bias, but they do endeavor to minimize the chances that it will occur.

In 1964 the common wisdom within the testing enterprise was to realize these limitations of tests and to go forward with sensitivity and compassion: "The task of the conscientious educator is to ponder what lies behind the test scores. Rather than accepting test scores as indicating fixed levels of either performance or potential, educators should plan remedial activities which will free the child from as many of his handicaps as possible" (Deutsch et al., 1964, p. 143). The challenge to the testing enterprise was clear in Deutsch et al.'s (1964) guidelines for the testing of minority children:

> Many comparisons depend upon tests, but they also depend upon *our* intelligence, our good will and our sense of responsibility to make the proper comparison at the proper time and to undertake proper remedial and compensatory action as a result.... Their [tests] proper use is a sign of professional and personal maturity. [Deutsch et al., 1964, p. 144]

The issues of unfairness, then, are seen as solvable with sensitive and compassionate interpretations of test scores. Intelligent appraisals of performance on mental tests would forestall difficulties the testing enterprise might encounter when the unfairness critiques were voiced.

BEING A BIT MORE HUMAN

One outcome of the antitest movement was an increased concern with the human aspects of the testing experience. A wide range of issues was raised that related to the actual psychological aspects of being tested and the possibilities that these might produce unfairness. The underlying rationale of this work was to determine if specific aspects of the testing situation cause performance decrements that were unfair to various subgroups of respondents. Typically, these emerged in the form of empirical studies dealing with physical and psychological factors of testing, the effects of anxiety, and the impact of coaching and test sophistication. Brief descriptions of some of the findings from this research are presented below to provide a sense of how the testing enterprise began to consider, even more deeply, the human side of testing.

Physical Aspects of the Testing Process

In the 1960s, there was increased research oriented toward teasing out the effects that the conditions of testing had on the obtained results. A wide variety of examples could be cited here, including Bell, Hoff, and Hoyt (1964), who showed that the type of answer sheet used had an effect on test scores; Cashen and Ramseyer (1969), who noted that the use of a separate answer sheet lowered test scores with younger children; and Kirchner (1966), who, in a typing test, demonstrated that group testing decreased performance speed. These and a wide variety of other physical attributes were shown to affect test scores, suggesting that unfairness could result if testing conditions were not carefully considered in interpreting results.

Poor testing conditions putting test taker at an obvious disadvantage.

Psychological Aspects of the Testing Process

A wide variety of examiner characteristics were suggested to affect test performance. Age, gender, ethnicity, socioeconomic status, professional qualifications, experience, personality characteristics, and appearance, as well as interactions among them, have all been singled out as influencing respondent performance (for a review, see Sattler, 1970). Other aspects of the psychological character of the testing situation were also mentioned. Exner (1966) demonstrated that a "warm" relationship between tester and respondent produced elevated WISC scores compared with a "cold" one. The effect of self-fullfilling prophecies has also been documented, wherein tester expectations are confirmed in subsequent test performance (Masling, 1965). Even the experience of failure just prior to being tested produces performance decrements (Davis, 1969).

In large part, empirical evaluations of these psychological factors have been equivocal because of the complexity of the actual testing event. Numerous effects are often confounded in attempts to demonstrate simple effects. The influence of these factors is generally greater with unstructured tests such as projective tests. This wide variety of potential examiner and situational effects indicates the need to be exceedingly careful when interpreting tests results if fairness is a concern.

Test Anxiety

The variable of anxiety, as described in Chapter 13, was applied to the actual testing situation during the 1960s. A number of research instruments, not unlike the Unadorned Anxiety Test (UAT) but written to deal with specific aspects of the testing situation, were developed. In general, a negative correlation was found between scores on such test-anxiety instruments and performance on achievement and intelligence tests—higher anxiety being associated with lower scores and vice versa

(Sarason, 1961). This finding holds up in longitudinal designs as well (Hill & Sarason, 1966). Whether this correlation is a cause or an effect of **test anxiety** cannot be determined from such results.

The critical question here is the extent to which test anxiety interferes with the ability of individuals to perform at their best on a test. If anxiety does cause performance to degenerate, then the testing experience is patently unfair because there are individual differences in the variable. French (1962) addressed this concern by administering parallel forms of the Scholastic Aptitude Test (SAT) under both competitive and relaxed instructions—assuming that the former condition would mobilize test anxiety to a greater degree. Results indicated no differences in average SAT scores between the two instructional conditions. As well, the concurrent validity of the instrument remained constant regardless of instructional condition. Thus, it appears that anxiety concerns may not translate into the direct performance decrements initially feared—yet those using tests must be aware of the potential for such effects to affect the utility of test scores for specific individuals.

Coaching and Test Sophistication

A natural spin-off of the kinds of human concerns outlined above is the impact of coaching, or practice, on test performance. **Coaching,** in contrast to education, is involved when a person is trained on skills and/or item content specific to a particular test and when this training elevates a test score without affecting the behaviors that the test is intended to measure (see Anastasi, 1981). By this definition, coaching does not only produce unfairness (if it is available to only some respondents) but also undermines the validity of the test.

As might be expected, the amount of improvement possible with coaching is highly variable, depending on the abilities and education of the respondent. As well, greater performance gains are expected if there is a close resemblance between the test and coaching materials. In several carefully controlled studies involving the SAT, it was found that a variety of coaching methods using a wide range of respondent populations seldomly produced meaningful gains in test-score performance (for examples, see Donlon, 1984; Messick, 1980), suggesting that coaching might not be as critical a concern as might be expected.

Respondents' degree of exposure to testing per se, called **test sophistication,** has also been suggested to have an effect on obtained scores. There is a tendency for test performance to improve on successive administrations of parallel forms. As well, persons with extensive experience with testing, regardless of the type of test, have an advantage over more naive peers. One way to correct for the unfairness associated with test sophistication is to provide orientation sessions that cancel out any advantage the test-wise taker might have (see Wahlstrom & Boersman, 1968). Of note here are publications associated with a number of achievement tests that are miniorientation programs providing suggestions for effective test taking, illustrations of items, and sample tests (for example, College Board, 1984, for the SAT and various publications associated with the Graduate Record Examination). Some familiarization programs involve slides, films, and video cassettes.

Summary

The aspects of testing outlined above (physical and psychological factors, anxiety, and coaching) are all testimony to some of the ways in which the testing enterprise reacted to fairness concerns regarding testing. The very fact that this research was conducted and that the results, if conclusive, were applied to testing practice is testimony to the importance of the antitesting movement. The field made many efforts to deal with the concerns that were raised and, in so doing, strengthened its practices and the contributions that it could make to the solution of significant social problems.

DECREASING OPTIMISM

This chapter began by providing a sketch of the testing enterprise in the early 1960s. An outline of the chronology of a large and vocal antitesting movement was then presented to provide a sense of the difficulties that the testing enterprise began to encounter during this turbulent time. The manners in which the testing enterprise addressed the critical appraisals encountered during this time were then offered. In some cases, the APA code of ethics was revised and clarified (for example, in response to problems of invasion of privacy and confidentiality). Criticisms of the uses of psychological testing were addressed by noting the need for careful analysis of the specific situations involved and the introduction of some novel technology (Cronbach & Gleser, 1965). Issues of unfairness to minorities were elaborated (for example, test bias) and deferred to internal control within the discipline (Deutsch et al., 1964). New domains of research dealing with the human component of testing were initiated and applied to testing practice. Yet the fundamental issue of privacy in some situations, confidentiality, and the manner in which psychologists could respond to queries about the meaning of specific items remained.

At this point, dismissing the significance of the issues raised by the antitest movement would be relatively easy. At one level, it does appear that the testing enterprise has reacted responsibly and with sensitivity to the issues. That being said, it is tempting to move ahead with no further consideration of these important issues—assuming they have been resolved. But this would be a mistake. The substantive human issues underlying the conflicts still remain. Situations still emerge in which testing practice is an affront to privacy and confidentiality. Test bias still exists. Some testing practices are still coercive. The "progress" over the past several decades is really an enhanced awareness of these problems, not their solution. We have witnessed the emergence of several procedures oriented toward correcting such issues should they emerge, but it remains that the issues must be raised continually and vocally, else inappropriate practices will surface in increased numbers. Subgroups of the psychological community itself, such as the Society for the Psychological Study of Social Issues, have adopted advocacy positions surrounding issues such as test use. Clearly there is an important place for informed critique from educated test takers. Perhaps if you find yourself being angered or perturbed by this discussion of these issues, your voice could be added to this important component of public discourse.

Through all of this, it is becoming clearer and clearer that the controversy reflected in the antitest movement is really a dialog between conflicting values. The testing enterprise was, as it always had been, committed to facilitating social decision making from an institutional perspective. When this perspective conflicts with the values of the individual, there is an inevitable clash of values. Indeed, the antitest movement of the 1960s is an excellent demonstration of this conflict, which has been part-and-parcel of the testing enterprise since its inception. The 1960s brought this conflict into stark relief, making it more visible and thereby forcing significant change. The fundamental values of American society were changing rapidly during the 1960s. Whether discussed in terms of the turmoil surrounding the Vietnam War, or political change of the times, or even in the rebellion of the popular music of the period, this decade was a time of great social change. The old ways were constantly being challenged and, by virtue of being associated with mainstream American life, so too was the testing enterprise.

The testing enterprise was not the only domain of social science that was affected by these tumultuous times. For example, a massive research program, which was described as the "largest single integrated project in the entire history of social science" (Amrine, 1966, p. 401), not only received public criticism but also was actually canceled as a result of public furor. **Project Camelot** was a research program for measuring and forecasting the causes of revolutions in underdeveloped nations. Sponsored by the U.S. Army, Camelot was intended to provide a social science database that could be used to track the emergence of a wide range of social phenomena. Protests and a congressional hearing eventually resulted in the cancelation of all funding for this project—dealing social science research in America a severe blow (see Horowitz, 1966, for a history). The distemper of the 1960s and the value clashes it represented were indeed significant forces, shaping a number of important events in the academy. Not the least of these was the testing enterprise.

Once the antitest movement and other protest movements of the time are viewed in terms of value conflicts, it becomes clear that "there are no *correct* answers; there are only opinions as to what some *good* answers might be" (Messick, 1965, p. 141). More than at any point in its past, this statement is particularly true of the testing enterprise today.

A SHIFT AWAY FROM TESTING

Within psychology the role of tests was undergoing considerable change. In almost all subfields, there was a clear indication of a continuing and growing tendency to de-emphasize testing activities. In part, this was fueled by the antitest movement, but in the main it represented continued professional growth. Although testing remained important, discussions surrounding the domains and the manner in which new recruits were to be trained indicated that it was losing its foothold as a primary professional activity.

Clinical Psychology

As indicated earlier, the post–World War II development of clinical psychology was characterized by an increased movement toward practitioners becoming more involved in therapy and less in testing. This is revealed in descriptions of the field, such as this one summarizing the results of an important conference on training clinicians: "... clinical psychology includes the following broad functions: psychological analysis and assessment for decision-making purposes; psychotherapy and other forms of behavior modification; psychological investigation (research and evaluation); training and education; consultation; administration" (Hoch, Ross, & Winder, 1966, p. 50). Testing had clearly evolved to become only one of a series of techniques in the clinician's toolbox, rather than being the preeminent method. Additionally, some of the newer theoretical and therapeutic ideas were not positively disposed toward testing. For example, a major thesis of **Carl Rogers**'s **nondirective therapy** was that diagnosis via testing was neither necessary nor desirable (see Schofield, 1966). As well, the adaptation of behaviorist technologies to the clinical sphere (for example, behavior therapy, behavior modification) imported a series of assumptions about the utility of traditional testing, suggesting that the standard tests were not particularly useful (more about this in Chapter 17). The continued popularity of psychoanalysis also contributed to the trend toward de-emphasizing structured and objective testing, with the attendant effect of increasing the use of projective tests (Sundberg, 1961).

Another major change that affected the role of testing in clinical psychology involved the discovery of some important drugs that had an impact on psychotic symptoms. The implications of this important discovery for the practice of clinical psychology is outlined in the following Close Up.

CLOSE UP   **The Impact of Antipsychotic Drugs on Testing and Clinical Psychology**

The major event in this story occurred in 1952. Prior to this time, it had been suggested that psychoses such as **schizophrenia** were the result of brain malfunction. Some early research indicating that ingestion of selected drugs (for example, atropine) could produce behavior that looked distinctly **psychotic** was used to reinforce this proposition. The data, however, were not even close to sufficient to make this case clearly.

In 1952 several French physicians observed that a drug used prior to surgical anesthesia seemed to have a tranquilizing effect on patients. This chemical agent, **chlorpromazine**, was then tried on psychotic patients with somewhat spectacular results. Psychotic symptoms totally disappeared in a number of cases. By 1955 chlorpromazine was in wide use in North America, creating a revolution in the mental-health field. Figure 14-8 indicates the effect that the introduction of psychopharmaceuticals had on the number of patients in mental institutions in the United States.

From these early discoveries, a whole new method of treating psychotic patients emerged. Rather than having all patients housed in mental hospitals, it became possible to develop many more outpatient-treatment programs where, after brief periods in the hospital, patients were allowed to return home because the drugs had alleviated their symptoms. Indeed, the Kennedy initiative mentioned at the beginning of this chapter was spurred in part by these developments. However,

---

Figure 14-8

Numbers of resident patients in state and local government mental hospitals in the United States from 1946 through 1970.

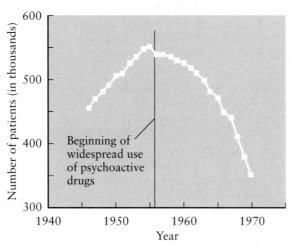

(SOURCE: Kolb & Whishaw, 1985, p. 58.)

with fewer patients housed in mental institutions, the need for continual testing diminished. As well, the drug therapies firmly established the medical practitioners as the kingpins of the treatment community because only they could write prescriptions for the new "wonder" drugs.

The emergence of drug treatments, however, actually provided a new avenue for the testing enterprise to pursue. The new drugs were not effective for all patients. It would be very helpful to be able to identify which ones would benefit from which drug (and how much of it) prior to developing an individual therapeutic program. Testing, defined as systematic observations of behavior, has a very definite contribution to make in providing information to psychiatrists as they design drug-treatment regimens for their patients.

As early as 1960, the implications of the movement away from testing for the new generation of clinical psychologists was clearly articulated by Meehl (1960):

My advice to fledgling clinical psychologists is to construct their self-concept mainly around "I am a researcher" or "I am a psychotherapist," because one whose self-concept is mainly "I am a (test oriented) psychodiagnostician" may have to maintain his professional security over the next few years by not reading the research literature, a maneuver which has apparently proved quite successful already for some clinicians. [p. 26]

Slowly but surely, testing was being assigned a lower priority. The public furor generated by the antitest movement undoubtedly helped accelerate the gradual slide in the popularity of testing within clinical psychology.

Counseling Psychology

This subfield of psychology started out addressing the fundamental issues surrounding vocational choice. It gained its main impetus from the development of instruments for assessment of students such as the Strong Vocational Interest Blank (SVIB). Very much like clinical psychology, the need to counsel numerous veterans following World War II created a context from which a professional community emerged. Its frame of reference expanded somewhat with the realization that proper counseling must also involve the emotional side of the person, so the subfield began to take on a kinship with clinical psychology (see Schofield, 1966, for a discussion). In the 1960s, a trend toward the devaluation of testing was a primary activity of counselors, which in some quarters was more extreme than the clinical case: "In brief, an atmosphere within post World-War-II psychiatry and a specific point of view within counseling psychology have encouraged ... counselors to be neglectful if not actually hostile to the diagnostic process" (Schofield, 1966, p. 124). So, in concert with clinical psychology, we see a movement away from testing within counseling offices. Tests were still part of the arsenal of techniques used by counselors, but their use was declining.

Industrial Psychology

Developments within industrial psychology also suggested decreasing popularity for testing. The critiques of Whyte (1956), Stagner (1959), and Gross (1962) undoubtedly had effects on personnel workers' enthusiasm for tests. However, like clinical psychology, forces from within the subfield were pointing toward a lessened value for tests. In a survey of 89 executives, it was found that most would-be employers of psychologists felt that testing for selection and promotion was the service they would most likely use (Feinberg & Lefkowitz, 1962). However, this view misrepresented the kinds of contributions that industrial psychologists could make: "It would seem that education is needed to help industry view more favorably the role of an industrial psychologist as a general problem solver in market studies, advertising, and broadly gauged, more imaginatively conceived industrial research" (Feinberg & Lefkowitz, 1962, p. 110). A similar call for an extension of the contribution of industrial psychology emerged in discussions of industrial psychology as an academic discipline. Guion (1965) suggested that education in testing for selection went well beyond the technological aspects of testing:

> For example, a common topic in industrial psychology deals with selection testing. The significant human situation to which selection relates includes the problems of maximum employment, and of the optimal utilization of society's manpower resources. A course in industrial psychology which stops with cutting scores and the Taylor–Russell tables is unlikely to face these problems and, therefore, does not contribute significant knowledge. [p. 820]

Not unlike developments in clinical psychology, the 1960s was a period during which testing was not emphasized in industrial psychology. This does not deny the importance of testing to industrial applications but reveals the manner in which the subfield was moving away from this one particular technique being its fundamental contribution.

Educational Psychology

Of the four test-related subfields, educational psychology showed the least reduction of interest in testing during the 1960s. The introduction of new technology such as **teaching machines** occupied the field and drew some attention away from intelligence, aptitude, and achievement tests. Assessment, however, remained an important part of the field (see Glover & Ronning, 1987). It is interesting to speculate whether this might have been, in part, because intelligence tests were more or less left alone by the antitest movement in the early 1960s.[6]

Clearly, testing was on a decline toward the end of the 1960s. This was reflected not only within the relevant professional communities but also in the training programs. Both graduate and undergraduate programs were teaching less and less testing (Anderson, 1970; Holt, 1970). There appears to be a significant correlation between the decline in popularity of testing and the antitest movement of the 1960s. This is particularly evident in clinical, counseling, and industrial psychology. As with any correlation, of course, it is important that no causal inferences be made from this observation. It cannot be argued that the antitest movement *caused* the decrease in popularity (or vice versa). The most likely interpretation is that developments within the professional subfields would have continued the way they did even without the furor of the 1960s. Perhaps the antitest movement accelerated aspects of this development, but it would have happened nonetheless. For our purposes, the most important point to note here is that testing was becoming less and less the *primary* activity of practitioners in these professional subfields. Other activities were emerging that competed for the professional psychologist's time.

It is instructive to return, for a moment, to the beginning of this chapter where the president of the United States was making policy statements that appeared to promise untold gains for psychology in general and the testing enterprise in particular. Clearly these gains did not emerge. From the foregoing, it can be seen that there were a number of factors that inhibited the fulfillment of Kennedy's promise. Included here are (1) the antitest movement, which reflected the distemper of the times; (2) internal developments within the test-related subfields; and (3) an emerging sense that the testing enterprise was not keeping pace with the rapid changes in the society it was servicing. Each factor, and no doubt others, left the testing enterprise in a weaker position than it had been at the beginning of the decade.

Summary

The 1960s was a turbulent time for the testing enterprise. A strong antitest movement emerged in concert with increasing concerns for civil rights and personal freedom. In this chapter, we examined the critical appraisals of this time and then outlined the manner in which the enterprise adjusted to take these new concerns into account. We looked at changes in testing practice and ethics relating to invasion of privacy, confidentially, test use, and fairness. As well, we discussed adjustments intended to increase the humanity of testing practice. These changes aside, a

---

[6]As will be discussed in Chapter 15, this hiatus for educational psychology did not last for long.

general decrease in the importance of testing for a wide variety of applications was noted as new and varied ideas and technology began to offer alternative approaches to psychometric methodologies.

Glossary

antitest movement   A fairly generalized attitude, and subsequent critical school of thought, that had considerable concern about the negative influence of tests. This movement was particularly active during the 1960s but is still active today.

asylum   An institution for housing mental patients. Typically very large and located outside of major urban areas, they were highly criticized and replaced by community mental-health centers in the 1960s.

Barnum Effect   The demonstration that people react positively to nonindividualized personal feedback that has been constructed to be virtually true for everyone.

battery   As used in selection and classification, a set of tests that are administered to all applicants for a position, from which a single composite score is derived and used to make decisions.

Bender–Gestalt   A psychological test in which respondents reproduce simple drawings. It was originally designed to measure individual differences and various perceptual skills but was later generalized to a number of other uses. (See Chapter 18.)

bias   The finding of unequal consequences for different groups of test takers that are caused by aspects of a psychological test. This contrasts to unfairness, which relates to the use of the test.

chlorpromazine   A drug discovered in the 1950s that alleviated schizophrenic symptoms in many patients. This drug, and several others that affected other disorders, stimulated many significant changes in the mental-health field, which in turn spawned changes in testing.

Civil Rights Act   A landmark 1964 legislation that addressed discrimination on the basis of race, color, religion, gender, and national origin across a broad spectrum of contexts. Title VII related specifically to employment practices, thereby implicating the testing enterprise.

coaching   To train a person in skills or test-specific content when the training does not alter behaviors that the test is intended to measure. Contrasts to education that should affect both test and criterion performance.

community mental-health center s   Small, local clinics for the treatment of mental illness that were proposed to replace asylums in the National Program for Mental Health.

confidentiality   A general term in testing dealing with concerns about whom should see test results and interpretations. The norm in the field is that only the test interpreter and respondent will see the results unless negotiated otherwise prior to testing. In research contexts, confidentiality is typically guaranteed by making it impossible for anyone but the experimenter to associate a given response protocol with a specific individual.

construct bias   A type of bias that is demonstrated if the same test measures different psychological characteristics in different populations.

cost/benefit analysis   A mathematical approach from decision theory that rationalizes the relative gains and losses attending a particular activity.

criterion bias   A type of bias that is demonstrated if a criterion measures entities that tap only those characteristics demonstrated by members of a specific group.

decision theory   A branch of mathematics dealing with models to determine the gains and losses associated with various activities.

discrimination   An intentional act that results in members of various races, colors, religions, genders, and national origins not having an equal opportunity to participate in society. In legal terms, proof of discrimination depends on the demonstration of intent on the part of the discriminator.

Draw-a-Man Test   Popular in the late 1950s, a subjectively scored test in which a respondent's drawings of various people are evaluated in terms of detail and affective tone.

Draw-a-Person Test   A subjectively scored test in which a respondent's drawings of various people are evaluated in terms of detail and affective tone.

due process issue   A 1960s concern that tests were being misused and constituted a violation of individual's civil rights. The major concern here was that persons were branded by tests without having the opportunity to rebut the assertions.

educable mentally retarded   A person classified as mentally retarded (handicapped in today's nosology) but in the upper range of intellectual abilities for the classification. Such people are thought to have the potential of benefiting from special educational programs.

equal opportunity   The act of providing individuals of all races, colors, genders, religions, and national origins with comparable chances to gain employment and the like. This term was part of the 1964 Civil Rights Act and seen as necessary for the act to be realized in social practice.

fairness to minorities   Associated with the Civil Rights Act of 1964, proper testing procedures should provide equal, nonbiased opportunities to all applicants for jobs and so on, particularly those who do not come from the majority groups of the culture.

Family Education Rights and Privacy Act   1974 legislation that gave parents legal access to all information regarding their child's education. This included psychological test scores, creating some difficulties for psychologists, because it implied that test-item content should be revealed.

hurdles   An approach to designing selection programs that entails having candidates take a sequential set of tests, interviews, and so on and using the results of each activity to make decisions such as accept, reject, or continue testing.

informed consent   The procedure of ensuring that an individual is aware of the nature, implications, uses, and distribution of test results prior to testing. This helps guard against misuses of test associated with invasion of privacy and confidentiality.

intercept bias   A type of bias that is demonstrated when a given test score is associated with different levels of criterion performance for two groups. The dual meaning of test scores in this situation creates the possibility of significant inequities in test interpretation.

invasion of privacy The occurrence of an activity that is a violation of individuals' constitutional rights. In testing, the most frequent concern is that items solicit deeply personal and private information that is beyond what should be expected.

item bias A type of bias that is demonstrated when an item produces unequal proportions of individuals from varying groups who all score at the same level on a homogeneous test containing the item.

judgmental analysis A family of procedures used in troubleshooting for bias in which rational judgments of the content and style of items in a test are made.

Larry P. v. California State Department of Education (CDSE) A landmark 1979 legal case in which the use of tests was banned to select participants in classes for educably mentally retarded children.

Myart v. Motorola A 1963 legal case in which the Motorola Corporation was told to stop using an employee-selection test because it was ruled to discriminate against Blacks.

nondirective therapy An approach to treating clinical patients, derived from Carl Rogers's theory of personality that emphasized growth and the gaining of self-knowledge.

Parents in Action in Special Education (PASE) v. Hannon An Illinois legal case in which the use of psychological tests was supported.

predictive bias A type of bias that is demonstrated if a specific test is differentially valid for different groups.

Project Camelot A huge social sciences project to measure and forecast revolutions in underdeveloped nations. Project Camelot was canceled in 1966 on the basis of numerous protests.

psychometrics A subdiscipline of psychology concerned with the development and evaluation of psychological tests.

psychotic A class of mental illness involving serious cognitive and affective disturbances (for example, schizophrenia), which prior to 1950 almost inevitably led to incarceration of the patient. Psychoses are generally thought to be more serious and problematic than neuroses.

Rogers, Carl An American psychologist who developed client-centered therapy and a humanist theory of personality.

schizophrenia A psychosis, commonly and erroneously called "split personality," characterized by the patient being split off from reality. There are a number of variants of this serious disorder (for example, paranoid, hebephrenic), and most of these have hallucinations associated with them.

selection ratio The proportion of candidates who will be chosen relative to the number who have applied.

self-fulfilling prophecy A conclusion based on and conforming to previous assertions. For example, in educational testing, a self-fulfilling prophecy was that knowledge of test scores by teachers would affect the manner in which children were treated. This was seen as a potential source of bias due directly to tests.

sequential-testing program　An approach to selection or classification in which one test is given and the decision to reject, accept, or test with another test is made on the basis of the results of the first test. In the case of those tested twice, a composite score of the two tests is used to make an accept/reject decision.

single-screen test　The use of one maximally valid test in a selection or classification program.

slope bias　A type of bias that is demonstrated when one test is differentially valid for two different groups, thereby imparting systematic inequity to the decisions made by the test.

social ethic　A body of thought that legitimates the pressures of society as having precedence over those of the individual. Coined by William Whyte, this term was part of his attack on personality tests.

subtest bias　A type of bias that is demonstrated when a subtest produces nonequivalent score distributions across varying groups.

teaching machine　An instrument used to instruct specific curricula, using the ideas from B. F. Skinner's operant conditioning paradigm (for example, reinforcement).

test anxiety　A feeling-state associated with somewhat painful and unpleasant feelings of uneasiness experienced just prior to and during psychological testing.

test bias　A type of bias that is demonstrated when a test produces nonequivalent score distributions across varying groups.

test burning　A series of incidents around 1960 in which concerned citizens forced the destruction of psychological test data because of a perceived threat to national security. Details of the Houston, Texas, incident are provided in the text.

test sophistication　A generalized tendency of persons who have been tested many times to do well on tests because of their familiarity with the activity. Test-orientation programs are thought to minimize the effect of this variable.

Title VII (of the 1964 Civil Rights Bill)　The portion of the act relating to unlawful employment practices in which there was some concern that psychological tests might become illegal. The Tower Amendment addressed these concerns.

top-down strategy　An approach thought to minimize test unfairness where the best candidates from both a majority and minority group are selected in a specified proportion by working downward from the highest scores separately in each group.

Tower Amendment　Legislation that acknowledged the lawfulness of the use of employment tests, notwithstanding any other provisions of the Title VII of the Civil Rights Act.

unfairness　As used in the context of test bias, the finding of unequal consequences wrought by the use of tests. This contrasts to bias, which refers to inequities in the tests themselves.

utility   (1) A technical term from decision theory that relates to the outcome of mathematical formulations attempting to demonstrate the relative advantage of one approach over another; (2) a generic term used to reflect the outcome of a cost/benefit analysis where utility is the gain or loss associated with a specific treatment such as a testing program.

Suggested Further Reading

Amrine, M. (Ed.). (1965). The 1965 congressional inquiry into testing. *American Psychologist, 20,* 858–991.

> This special issue of the *American Psychologist* provides all kinds of rich and intriguing detail regarding a highly active period of the antitest movement. It contains articles documenting the manner in which the controversies were reported in the newspapers; a number of great photos of protest marches against testing; invited comments from journalists, politicians, and civil servants; and verbatim transcripts of the actual hearing. This issue provides a wonderful view of the interchanges that are described in the chapter.

Berk, R. A. (Ed.). (1982). *Handbook of methods for detecting test bias.* Baltimore: Johns Hopkins University Press.

> This primary source provides considerable elaboration of the troubleshooting model for bias described in the chapter. Readers looking for greater detail about these various techniques and some "how to" information will find this book very useful. The sections at the end in which various major test publishers discuss their strategies to reduce or eliminate bias are also very instructive.

Bersoff, D. N. (1981). Testing and the law. *American Psychologist, 36,* 1047–1056.

> This article provides a wonderfully detailed discussion of a number of important legal cases involving the psychological testing enterprise. It is a very readable summary and commentary on this aspect of the enterprise and highly recommended if you wish to discover more about the interactions between testing and the law.

Cronbach, L. J. & Gleser, G. C. (1965). *Psychological tests and personnel decisions* (2nd ed.). Urbana: University of Illinois Press.

> This book provides great detail about the decision-theory model to utility presented in the chapter. Although very mathematical, the text is well enough written to give you a good understanding of the methods—even if you are math phobic. This is an excellent piece of primary reading because it enlightens the reader about the complexities and subtleties of the selection process.

Glasscote, R. M., Sussex, J. N., Cumming, E., & Smith, L. E. (1969). *The community mental health center: An interim appraisal.* Washington, D.C.: American Psychiatric Association.

> This book contains an excellent description of the community mental-health center and the reasons for its introduction. As an added bonus, you will find a detailed appraisal of the progress around 1968 in establishing these centers as part of Kennedy's initiative. The volume also includes case histories of several clinics, outlining the successes and failures that they encountered.

Discussion Questions

1. With reference to your local community, indicate the extent to which community mental-health centers have emerged as the primary source for the provision of mental-health services. Why has your community developed in the way it did?

2. With reference to Figure 14-1 and the chapter text, prepare a list of activities in which clinicians are engaged that do *not* involve psychological tests. Discuss the implications of this for the psychological testing enterprise.

3. Compare the testing enterprise in the late 1960s with the 1950s (Chapter 12), noting the most important differences and similarities.

4. Discuss two examples that illustrate the extent to which William Whyte's *social ethic* is still alive and well today.

5. Evaluate the extent to which Whyte's advice about cheating on personality tests being used in industry is still appropriate.

6. Describe as many situations as you can where you have encountered the equivalent of the Barnum Effect in action. Evaluate the ethicality of these practices.

7. Prepare a 1-minute "sound bite" (about 300 words) for public radio in which you defend the use of subtle items in personality assessment.

8. Outline the strengths and weaknesses of Title VII of the 1964 Civil Rights Act.

9. Prepare a summary of the reasons for the congressional and Senate hearings into testing. Were these concerns warranted?

10. If you were a judge, which of the two decisions, *Larry P. v. CDSE* or *PACE v. Hannon,* would you favor? Why?

11. Under what conditions does informed consent provide protection against invasion of privacy? When doesn't it work?

12. Discuss the situations in which a written contract between the tester and the respondent would be very useful in reducing testing problems.

13. Describe a situation in which testing could cause mechanistic and rigid decisions. How could this be avoided?

14. According to Equation 14-1, larger values of the standard deviation of the criterion increase the gain in utility of a test. Why do you think this is so?

15. Differentiate between *test bias* and *unfairness.*

16. The procedures used in the judgmental analysis stage of troubleshooting for bias sound suspiciously like those used for the establishment of content validity. Suggest why this might be more than a coincidence.

17. Discuss the implications of construct bias for researchers who wish to use tests developed in one culture to measure in another cultural context.

18. Draw a graph to indicate a test that has both slope and intercept bias. Draw the regression line expected if the two groups are combined. Discuss the unfairness inherent in using this combined regression line to make selection decisions.

19. Discuss the strengths and weaknesses of the top-down strategy to selection outlined in the chapter.

20. Prepare a complete list of physical aspects of the testing process that could lead to unfairness.

21. Generate a complete compendium of psychological aspects of the testing process that might lead to unfairness.

22. With reference to your personal experience, evaluate the importance of test anxiety in the fairness debate.

23. Using a specific example, indicate the manner in which coaching undermines the criterion-related validity of a test.

24. Discuss whether you think that the familiarization and practice booklets regarding tests like the SAT actually compensate for a lack of test sophistication.

Part VI

Contemporary Developments

This part of the text provides summaries of a number of domains of current testing practice and procedure. Developments in intelligence, personality, behavioral assessment, and neuropsychological measurement are provided, not so much to discuss test involvement in the 1990s but to give samplers of the manners in which testing is involved in important social decision-making contexts.

Chapter 15 continues our narrative of intelligence by introducing several complex theories of intellect that evolved from the earlier ideas. We also encounter a specific debate in which the foundational concern of nature/nurture creates a number of significant controversies. Finally, we explore the impact that the cognitive "revolution" in psychology has had on theories and tests on intellectual functioning.

Interestingly, developments in personality testing mirrored those in intelligence in a number of very important ways. Chapter 16 outlines this sequence and shows the similarities between the two areas. In following this evolution, we encounter a number of new tests and ideas related to the complex and intriguing notion of personality.

Chapter 17 documents the emergence of a major alternative to traditional psychological testing. Previously, most approaches to testing had endorsed the notion that the response to an item on a test was a sign of some underlying characteristic such as intelligence or personality. The new view challenged this and argued that tests are best viewed as samples of specific behavior. As shown in Chapter 17, when this idea is generalized to include areas such as school learning, performance in complex jobs, and progress in clinical therapy, a new vision of testing emerges. This new vision has a number of exciting implications for the future of the testing enterprise.

In the mid-1980s, there was an impressive increase in research and knowledge related to the human brain. Perhaps not surprisingly, the testing enterprise soon was suggesting that standardized psychological tests could profitably be applied to this field. Chapter 18 documents these developments by examining some of the earlier work and by reviewing some of the newer approaches to neuropsychological assessment.

This part of the text provides you with a broad-based sampler of current applications of testing in a number of fields. No claim is being made that all possible fields have been included. Indeed, the sampling of four areas (intelligence, personality, behavioral assessment, and neuropsychology) is woefully un- der-representative of the totality of domains in which testing can be found. But the four samplers do give you understandings of the manner in which testing is practiced and rationalized in our own specific cultural context.

Chapter 15

The Construct of Intelligence
Structure, Challenges, and New Directions

INTELLIGENCE RECONSIDERED

Most of the 1960s furor surrounding the testing enterprise mentioned in Chapter 14 centered around personality tests and their applications to various important social decision-making contexts. Intelligence tests, though mentioned in some of the critical work, were in the main left alone by this critical barrage. This situation did not last long because intelligence tests and their underlying assumptions were about to come under very close critical scrutiny—both from within and outside the discipline of psychology. In this chapter, we will chronicle some of these developments. Of particular import for us is the extent to which these critical appraisals have resulted in significant changes to the domain of intelligence testing.

From within the discipline of psychology, the introduction of construct validity had finally sounded the death knell of measurement without definition. It now became appropriate to consider the theoretical nature of the construct of intelligence as meaning more than what the tests measured. A starting place for this exercise was the examination of the volumes of research that had been published using these tests and then the attempt to infer what it was they were measuring. This involved exploring the criterion-related validity of the tests in an effort to get a sense of the constructs underlying performance on them. This is a somewhat backward attempt to understand the nature of intelligence because what is really being explored is what the tests themselves measure, rather than a direct examination of intelligence per se. Thus, what follows rests on the assumption that intelligence is, in a sense, what the tests measure. Nonetheless, this work does provide a starting point for proceeding with an examination of the construct of intelligence.

WHAT THE CRITERION-RELATED VALIDITY STUDIES TELL US

A detailed review of the tremendous amount of correlational research using intelligence (IQ) tests culminates in the conclusion that they primarily measure **scholastic aptitude** (see, for example, Tyler, 1965, pp. 72–81). Those who score high on these tests tend to do well in school, and low scorers tend to have difficulties in academic settings. This should not come as a surprise because the entire domain, from Binet on, had been concerned with school performance. As well, the tasks selected for IQ tests were typically sampled from the kinds of activities underlying school performance. The criteria that the tests best predict are related to academic performance.

Intelligence tests, however, are by no means perfect indicators of scholastic aptitude. Correlations between school grades and IQ-test performance tend to be somewhere between .4 and .6 across a wide range of school settings from first grade through graduate school. There are caveats on this generalization; for example, verbal tests produce higher correlations than do those that emphasize performance. In addition, predictive validity is higher if the interval between test and criterion performance is shorter. Despite these local perturbations, the robustness of this general finding is impressive.

Correlations of this magnitude do not permit us to make exact predictions about school performance for individuals. Application of the standard error of measurement makes it clear that correlations in the .4–.6 range do not permit precise predictions of criterion status for individual cases. This is revealed in the data shown in Table 15-1, which represents performance on the Ohio Psychological Examination (measured in stanines) and grade point average (GPA) in first-year university that are correlated .43—roughly the size of the the typical test-criterion correlation in the intelligence domain.

Making somewhat accurate predictions for students who score at the extremities of the IQ test may be possible, but it is impossible for those in the middle. Some of those in the midrange on the test show good GPAs while others do not. For example, respondents scoring in the sixth stanine received GPAs anywhere between 0.00 and 3.50. As well, even at the extremes, there is a wide range of possible scores (for example, for the ninth stanine, the range of GPA is 0.50 to 3.50,

Table 15-1 Data demonstrating the relation between an IQ test and school performance, where the two variables are correlated .43

		Stanine Rating on Intelligence Test								
		1	2	3	4	5	6	7	8	9
	4.00								1	
	3.50						1	3	4	2
	3.00				5	15	16	14	11	9
Grade	2.50		2	4	22	30	17	28	11	6
Point	2.00	5	9	22	42	45	42	25	9	2
Average	1.50	1	6	20	30	29	20	13		
(GPA)	1.00	6	2	5	9	7	6	3		
	0.50	1	3	5	6	0	1	0		1
	0.00		2		2	1	1	1		

SOURCE: Tyler (1965, p. 74.)

although the 0.50 could be an outlier). Thus, it is important to realize that the correlational literature does not translate as readily to individual cases as we might have hoped. Rather, the discussions of the meaning of IQ-test scores appear to focus on groups of individuals with inferences to specific persons being suspect because of the sizes of the obtained validity and reliability coefficients.

A major source of support for the educational aptitude hypothesis is the finding of consistent, long-term correlations between test scores and academic achievement. IQ tests predict, fairly well, how far up the academic ladder a student will progress, with low scorers dropping out of the educational stream sooner. This predicts, among other things, that the average scores on IQ tests should increase with higher levels of education because the low scorers would be dropping out. This indeed appears to be the case (Embree, 1948; Plant & Richardson, 1958; Wrenn, 1949). However, in all cases, the variability within a specific level of the educational system was considerable, again indicating the cautions that must be applied in dealing with the individual case.

As would also be expected, IQ-test scores vary with occupational level, with average scores being higher for occupations requiring more education (Ball, 1938; see Kaufman, 1990, for a review and Matarrazo & Herman, 1984, for a specific example). However, IQ tests do not predict success within a specific organizational category (for an example, see Wells, Williams, & Fowler, 1938), reinforcing the cautious attitude that must be taken in extrapolating this general research to individual cases. With these caveats in mind, the research does suggest that IQ tests are best characterized as measures of scholastic aptitude.

We can explore which aspects of the general idea of scholastic aptitude are tapped by IQ tests. To be certain, IQ tests do *not* tap the *rapidity* with which a person improves with practice on the same task (see Woodrow, 1940). A considerable amount of research during the 1960s using IQ tests to predict performance on teaching machines also converged on the idea that the rate at which material was acquired was not predictable from test scores (for a detailed discussion, see Stolurow, 1960).

However, there do appear to be some qualitative differences between high and low scorers on IQ tests. For example, under properly controlled conditions, IQ tests appear to predict the **readiness** of a person to grasp new and more complex ideas (Tilton, 1949). By this view, low scorers would be characterized as slow developers, taking more time than their high-scoring peers to be ready to move to the next level of complexity in an ordered curriculum such as mathematics. In other words, it is not the speed with which students work through information that is tapped by these tests but the speed with which they become ready to move to the next level of complexity.

There is also some evidence of qualitative differences in the manner in which high and low IQ-test scorers learn new concepts. For example, Osler and Fivel (1961) found more **sudden learners** on a concept-formation task in a high-IQ group. This suggested that the high scorers were actively testing hypotheses during the learning task more so than the low scorers.

Even this very brief review of the research attempting to induce the nature of intelligence reveals that there is no simple way to characterize the relationship between test-score performance and learning ability. Rapidity of learning is not a factor, whereas readiness to learn new and more complex concepts does appear to be involved. Some evidence also suggests that high scorers employ different learning strategies in some situations (for example, active hypothesis testing). These observations drawn from the previous four decades of correlational research on IQ tests provide a background against which it is now possible to begin active consideration of the construct of intelligence as mandated by the notion of construct validity.

Carroll (1979) labels the attempt to determine the nature of constructs underlying a specific assessment device as a **bottom-up strategy** for establishing construct validity. In this case "the problem is to determine what construct or constructs, if any, this measurement procedure measures" (p. 25). Of course, any results deriving from this kind of work are constrained by the nature of the test itself. That is, any view of intelligence emerging from, say, a bottom-up examination of the Stanford–Binet is severely limited by the original assumptions and item-selection procedures of the test developers. Such a view of intelligence is highly dependent on the nature of the test itself—representing a sense of intelligence as the developers of the Stanford–Binet saw it.

An alternative to this procedure is a **top-down strategy** of establishing construct validity (Carroll, 1979). This involves defining the construct *first* and then embellishing the nomological network and theoretical schema directly and explicitly from this beginning. A test is then developed to maximally reflect the totality of the intended construct. The advantage of this procedure is that the eventual theory is not constrained by the original device.

It seems reasonable to look at bottom-up approaches as less useful than top-down strategies because of the manner in which the latter are more congenial to the emergence of theory-driven tests (those with good construct validity). If a theory is well articulated first and then tests derived to completely reflect and represent the theory, the probability of demonstrating adequate theory-to-test links is significantly enhanced. This would demand the use of a top-down strategy. In what follows, several examples of researchers who adopted variations of the top-down strategy will be outlined. We will examine several approaches to describing the structure of intelligence. These will be followed by two explicitly top-down research programs that culminated in new, cognitive tests of intelligence.

FACTOR ANALYSIS AND EXPLORING THE STRUCTURE OF INTELLIGENCE

During the 1960s, one focal problem addressed by researchers in the field involved the structure of intelligence. Any effort to explore the construct demanded the clarification of the manner in which intelligence was organized. As you will recall, there were previously two competing views on this problem. British thinking continued to embrace the Spearman orientation of a single intelligence, whereas the American school leaned toward viewing intellect in terms of a number of specific abilities. New developments in factor analysis, combined with a desire to resolve the tensions between these two positions, resulted in several distinct approaches to describing the factor structure associated with intellectual tasks. Each position provides purchase on the fundamental nature of the psychological processes underlying performance on IQ-type tests and, as such, can be seen as part of an effort to articulate the construct of intelligence. Ideally, tests deriving from these positions would eventually demonstrate better construct validity than the older tests.

Hierarchical Models

Thurstone's original work on the Primary Mental Abilities (PMA) (see Chapter 10) was extended and elaborated in a number of ways after its introduction. For example, Thurstone and Thurstone (1941) replicated the PMA study using over 700 younger respondents (14-year-olds) and found roughly the same factor structure as the original PMA. One difference did emerge, though. In this sample and in most others, the PMA scores tended to be positively correlated with each other. This was a bit surprising because the original factors had been extracted to be uncorrelated (or **orthogonal**, to use the contemporary term).

British psychologists such as Spearman, Burt, and Vernon were quick to point out that these PMA-scale intercorrelations were problematic for the Thurstone position. Indeed, it was suggested that the PMA scores themselves could be intercorrelated and factor-analyzed just as Thurstone had done with his original set of 54 tests. If there were positive correlations between the PMA scores, the resulting factor solution would reveal a general factor very much like Spearman's *g*. This approach to factor-analyzing factor matrices became known as **higher-order factor analysis.**[1]

As an example, assume six of the PMA tests selected from the Differential Aptitude Test battery were correlated as shown in Table 15-2. A factor analysis of this matrix would yield evidence of a large single factor, generating the factor matrix shown in Table 15-3.

This matrix is compatible with the notion of a general factor as underlying the PMA battery. In this case, the general factor accounts for 36% $[(2.14/6) \times 100]$ of the total variance in the PMA-test scores. It would seem then, that to the extent scales obtained from the PMA are themselves intercorrelated, they can be seen as

Table 15-2 Intercorrelations of Primary Mental Abilities–based test scores

	N	S	P	V	W	I
Numerical Ability (N)		.33	.38	.37	.35	.42
Spatial Ability (S)			.32	.31	.29	.35
Perceptual Functioning (P)				.36	.34	.41
Verbal Reasoning (V)					.32	.40
Word Fluency (W)						.37
Induction (I)						

Table 15-3 Higher-order factor matrix of Primary Mental Abilities–based test scores

	I
Numerical Ability (N)	.63
Spatial Ability (S)	.52
Perceptual Functioning (P)	.61
Verbal Reasoning (V)	.59
Word Fluency (W)	.55
Induction (I)	.67
Eigen value*	2.14

*See Chapter 10.

[1]Higher-order factor analysis is more complex than is suggested here. One of the complexities relates to the manner in which the axes are placed in the factor space. To conduct higher-order analyses, the axes of the primary analyses are not rotated at right angles to each other as we have discussed previously. Such an **oblique rotation** permits the emergence of higher-order factors on a subsequent analysis of the obtained matrix.

saturated by a common underlying function (which, if we still believe in Spearman, we would probably like to call *g*). In this example, the PMA tests would be considered **first-order factors,** and the *g*-like factor would be called a **second-order factor.** In discussing this issue, **Philip E. Vernon** (1960) notes:

> Since they [PMA scores] correlate with one another moderately highly, they themselves can be analyzed in the same way as tests are analyzed, and they usually reveal a kind of super-factor, or what Thurstone calls a second-order general factor. Though he does not go so far as to identify this with *g*, he admits that it constitutes a bridge between his own and Spearman's viewpoints. He now describes primary factors as "facilities" in the mind, or "media of expression," and regards second-order factors as more central. This theory is strongly reminiscent of Spearman's general energy and specific engines. [p. 21]

This apparent crisis for the Thurstonian, or American, approach to intelligence resulted in the formulation of a number of **hierarchical models** of intellectual functioning, which eventually resolved the controversy. Simply, it was thought that human intellect was arranged in a highly ordered manner with *g* (or some such general variable) at the top. This general factor breaks down into a number of broad-group factors at the next level, which in turn break down into a series of narrow-group factors at the next level. The whole process may end, perhaps, with a fourth level that reflected the tests themselves. Figure 15-1 illustrates this model.

This hierarchical model can be likened to a tree. Working from the top, the main trunk branches into several roots, and these in turn branch out until a final point, which represents the thinnest roots on the tree. Each root can be traced back to the main trunk. In the case of the hierarchical model, the thin roots are the specific tests, the trunk is *g*, and the tracing back is accomplished by the use of higher-order factor analysis. Figure 15-2 (page 568) presents a specific example of such a hierarchical model.

This model shows *g* at the top and two major group factors (verbal : educational and perceptual : psychomotor) beneath it. These spread into a number of minor group factors (for example, verbal, mechanical information), which lead to specific tests. Although there are a number of different ways of proceeding (see, for example, Humphries, 1962, and Vernon, 1965), the general notion of a hierarchy

Figure 15-1 A three-stage hierarchy.

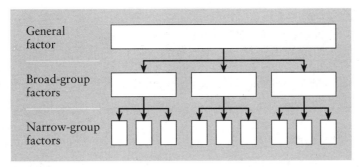

(SOURCE: Adapted from Humphries, 1962, p. 479.)

Figure 15-2 A hierarchical model of human abilities.

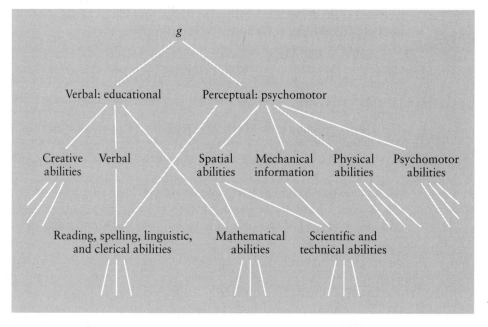

(SOURCE: Adapted from Vernon, 1965, p. 725.)

is congenial to contemporary views of intelligence. This structure, which can be based on the test scores of large numbers of subjects, provides a means for accommodating the diverse views about the structure of human intelligence. The issue of multiple versus global intelligence is strictly a function of the level at which one enters the hierarchy.

J. P. GUILFORD'S STRUCTURE OF INTELLECT MODEL

An alternative view of intellect emerged from a long-term factor analytic program initiated by **J. P. Guilford** in the late 1950s (see Guilford, 1959, 1967). He suggests that the factors identified by factor analysis can themselves be classified because they resemble each other in certain ways. Guilford's **structure of intellect model** relies on an examination of the kinds of stimuli, processes, and products involved in performing any intellectual activity.

Stimuli, or Content

Guilford suggests, for example, that the abilities discovered so far in the factor analytic pursuit of intelligence can be classified in terms of the nature of the stimuli making up the tests. These vary from simple pictures through to complex verbal and behavioral inputs, with four specific classes of **content**:

1. *Figural content* involves concrete material as perceived through the senses such as pictures (*Example:* The Picture Completion subtest of the WISC).

2. *Symbolic content* are tasks that involve letters, digits, or other conventional signs (*Example:* An anagram task in which the respondent is asked to indicate what word can be spelled from the letters *A, C,* and *E*).

3. *Semantic content* involves tasks where the stimuli are words (*Example:* Standard word analogies such as "Cow is to calf as horse is to ?" and items from the Comprehension subtest of the WISC).

4. *Behavioral content* focuses on tasks that involve the interactions of people (*Example:* A question asking what is the best thing to do if two friends are feuding).

Processes, or Operations

No matter what type of stimulus is involved, the processes used in obtaining a solution to a test item can also vary. Here Guilford suggests that the factor analytic literature has uncovered five different classes of **operations** or processes:

1. *Cognition* relates to the discovery, rediscovery, or recognition of what is known (*Example:* Asking a person to put vowels in the blanks to produce words:

   P __ W __ R
   M __ RV __ L
   C __ RT __ N

   Here focus is on the rediscovery of specific cognitive units).

2. *Memory* involves the more-or-less standard recall tasks (*Example:* The Digit Span subtest of the WISC).

3. *Divergent thinking* involves the production of a variety of responses. In keeping with a trend of the times to consider the creative aspects of behavior (for example, Harlow, Miller, & Newcomb, 1962; MacKinnon, 1962), this factor is somewhat different from what has gone before (*Example:* The Alternate Uses task in which the respondent is asked to name as many different uses for an object, such as a brick, as possible. Good answers involve demonstrating a wide variety of creative responses).

4. *Convergent thinking,* which contrasts with divergent thinking, focuses on the production of a single, correct answer (*Example:* Arithmetic tasks because there is but one correct response).[2]

---

[2]These are the same operations that were labeled as *objective* in Chapter 2.

5. *Evaluation* involves decisions about goodness, suitability, or adequacy of what a person knows, remembers, or generates in productive thinking (*Example*: Decisions about which of two paintings is the best).

The four types of content and the five operations are thought to be independent of each other such that it is possible to have tasks that represent any combination of content and operation. Indeed, Guilford's model can be thought of as a 4×5 matrix of tasks in which it is possible to derive tasks for any of the possible 20 cells. Figure 15-3 shows this matrix.

Any intellectual task can fit into this matrix. Here are four examples:

1. Asking a person to recognize the silhouettes of famous persons would be placed in the upper-left corner of the matrix because it represents the cognition of figural content.
2. A standard word-definition task (for example, "gravity" means _____) would fall into the semantic:cognition cell of the matrix.
3. An arithmetic test would be considered symbolic:convergent thinking.
4. Asking a person "What is the best thing to do if you cut your finger?" (as is asked on the WISC) would be an example of semantic:evaluation.

This part of Guilford's model is a taxonomy of intellectual tasks that divides the domain into 20 different cells on the basis of the stimulus of the item and the operation applied to it.

Products, or Outputs

Guilford goes even further with his model. He suggests a third aspect of intellectual tasks must also be considered in order to map the domain properly. This general category of task is defined to be its **product**. Products relate to the way or form in which any information occurs. In essence, Guilford has built a hierarchical model of information requirements of intellectual tasks that vary from very simple "chunks" through to drawing extensive implications from a set of precepts. The notion of products in Guilford's model brings with it an explicit attempt to consider the manner in which information is involved in the solution of intellectual tasks and is an index of the informational burden demanded by the task. Perhaps the term *conception* is more appropriate here because it also connotes ways of knowing or understanding that Guilford intended to capture in this third dimension of his model (see Guilford, 1967, p. 63).

Guilford identifies six products in his model:

1. Information can be conceived of in the form of *units*—separate entities segregated as "bits" or "chunks."
2. *Classes* relate to sets of units that are joined to each other in some specifiable form.
3. *Relations* involve some kind of connection between two things—a bridge or link that has its own character.

Figure 15-3 The matrix generated from consideration of the content and operation of intellectual tasks.

		Operation				
		Cognition	Memory	Divergent thinking	Convergent thinking	Evaluation
Content	Figural					
	Symbolic					
	Semantic					
	Behavioral					

(SOURCE: Adapted from Guilford, 1959.)

Figure 15-4 Illustrations of the six kinds of products using figural examples.

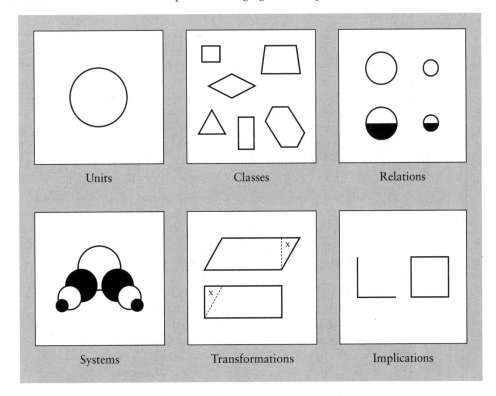

Units   Classes   Relations

Systems   Transformations   Implications

(SOURCE: Guilford, 1967, p. 64.)

4. *Systems* are complexes, patterns, or organizations, of interdependent or interacting parts.

5. *Transformations* are changes, redefinitions, or modifications by which one product moves into another.

6. *Implications* are expected, anticipated, or predicted products.

Figure 15-4 presents examples of each of these six products as they relate to figural content.

The six products are considered to be independent of content and operation, so the final version of Guilford's model is a three-dimensional matrix ($4 \times 5 \times 6$), as shown in Figure 15-5. This model consists of six matrices like the one shown in Figure 15-3—one for each product. Each intellectual task can be placed into its minicube within the model. For example, the convergent production of relations using semantic content (shortened NMR in reference to Figure 15-5) could involve a task called Inventive Verbal Relations. The respondent is told what the relation is between two words and then asked to fill in an analogy. A sample item (Guilford, 1967, p. 175) is the following:

(a) is the opposite to (b)

(a) black is to (b) _____ as (a) strong is to (b) _____

(Answers: white, weak)

In this task, the content is semantic, and the operation is convergent thinking (because there is a correct answer). The information demand of the task involves determining a relationship between the cognized units, hence, this task is representative of the NMR minicube in the model. If the stimuli in the sample item were pictures, the task would be the convergent production of relations using figural content, or NFR.

A total of 120 different classifications of intellectual tasks is possible with Guilford's model. This is a far cry from Spearman's original idea that intelligence could be captured in terms of a single general factor. Guilford's model postulates more types of intellectual tasks than Thurstone had tests in the development of the Primary Mental Abilities! Of particular note, though, is the inclusion of divergent thinking that brings the notion of creativity into the intellectual fold. Additionally, Guilford's model represented a valiant attempt to bring some of the emerging thinking about cognitive processes into play in the consideration of psychological test performance. Guilford's program was clearly compatible with the idea of construct validity.

Surprisingly, Guilford did not design tests for each of the 120 cells of his model. He viewed his theory as an heuristic device that could not only describe current intellectual tasks but also provide directions for future work. Thus, the failure to fill in each cell was not really a weakness of his theory. By implication, the model was an indication that contemporary tests had failed to sample the entire domain of intellectual performance. Models such as Guilford's provided a long-

Figure 15-5 Guilford's structure of intellect model.

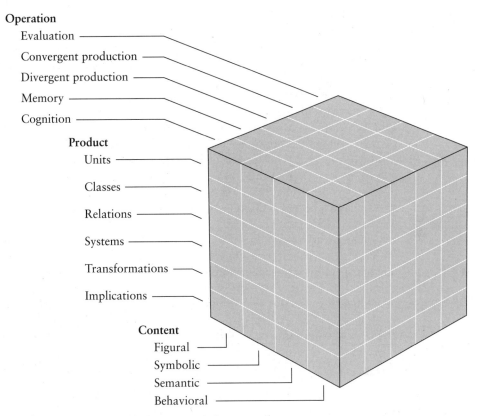

Operation
- Evaluation
- Convergent production
- Divergent production
- Memory
- Cognition

    Product
- Units
- Classes
- Relations
- Systems
- Transformations
- Implications

    Content
- Figural
- Symbolic
- Semantic
- Behavioral

(SOURCE: Adapted from Guilford, 1967, inside front cover.)

term plan of research action that had the potential of correcting some of the biases inherent in the classic IQ tests with their focus on convergent thinking and simpler informational products.

PHILOSOPHICAL CONSIDERATIONS

The use of factor analysis to develop megamodels of intellectual functioning represented an interesting elaboration of the basic logical positivist stance, which continued to be the bedrock of psychology during the 1960s. These factor-based theories can be seen as logical extensions of the movement toward construct validity chronicled in Chapter 13.

Perhaps the simplest way of demonstrating the place of factors in the positivist scheme of things is to return to the notion of nomological network introduced in Chapter 13. Figure 15-6 demonstrates a very simple nomological network, which involves three types of constructs. Those marked C and labeled **primary constructs** are mapped, via a correspondence rule (for example, a psychological test), into observable terms. The links are indicated by thick lines between the observable plane and the construct. Constructs marked C′ bear a formal, or logical, relationship to other constructs but are not mapped directly into observables. These C′ terms are partially defined theoretical terms that were a part of construct validity and the more liberalized view of logical positivism (see Chapter 13). The farther a C′ is from its observation-tied C construct, the more it is said to be formally weak (Margeneau, 1950). In keeping with earlier discussions, the optimal link between constructs is mathematical. The one construct marked X is insular and scientifically meaningless because it fails to contact either the observational plane or another construct. (This reflects the doctrine of cognitive significance discussed in Chapter 9.)

Royce (1963) suggests that, although the vision of science imparted in Figure 15-6 may be appropriate to the physical sciences, it is not a fair representation of the current state of psychology. In many cases, the linkages between theoretical terms in psychological theory are loose and weak. Royce thought that the net diagrammed in Figure 15-7 was more accurate. In this case, the thin lines, labeled **weak logical links**, are verbal and relatively loose. These contrast to **strong links** such as would be expected in a mathematical theory. According to Royce, the degree of formalization of the theory diagrammed in Figure 15-7 is questionable. The complex of constructs marked C′ have no strong, **formal link** to the primary C-type constructs. That is, they are not robustly associated with terms that are

Figure 15-6 A simple, physical science-type nomological network.

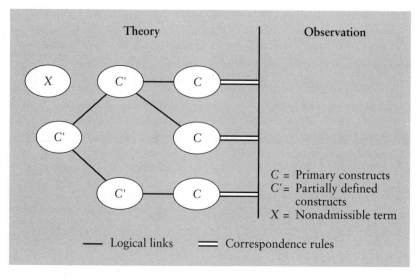

(SOURCE: Adapted from Royce, 1963, p. 524.)

Figure 15-7 A nomological network more compatible with current psychological theory.

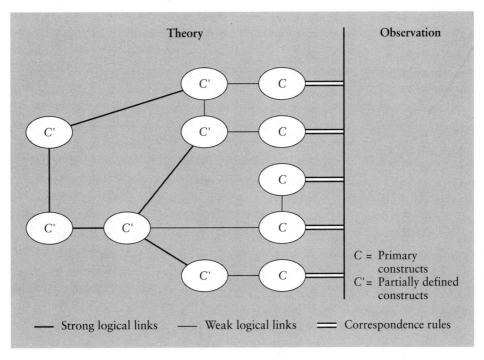

(SOURCE: Adapted from Royce, 1963, p. 524.)

directly tied to the observational world. The obvious conclusion from this state of affairs is to note the need for psychology to stay closer to the observational plane if it hopes to become a good science and for it to institute properly strong, mathematical links between and among theoretical terms.

According to Royce (1963), factors provide a way out of this problem. Simply, they constitute bona fide constructs that are tied *directly* and *strongly* to observational terms. In other words, by virtue of their formal properties, factors deserve to be considered true C-type constructs. They provide a clear and mathematical correspondence between theory and observation. But it goes even further than this. If one conducts a higher-order factor analysis on the C-type constructs (as, indeed, Vernon and Guilford have done), the resultant factors are mathematically related to the lower-level ones. Therefore, they constitute formally defined constructs in the positivist scheme. Then it is possible to do a **third-order factor** analysis and obtain yet another set of formally acceptable constructs and so on. Figure 15-8 (page 568) demonstrates the results of this line of argument.

In presenting this strong argument for factor analysis as conforming to the expected rules of psychological theory, Royce (1963) concludes:

> First-order factors, being close to the observable data, are seen as intervening, descriptive variables. They do an excellent job of summarizing masses of con-

Figure 15-8 The nomological network derived from higher-order factor analysis.

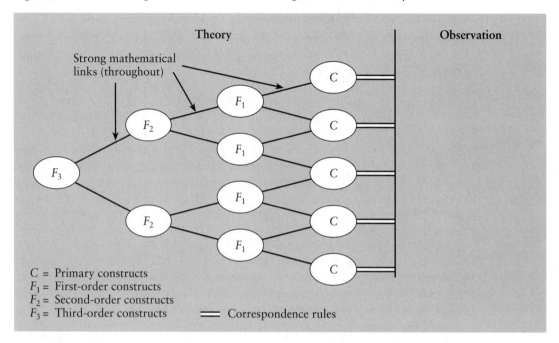

(SOURCE: Adapted from Royce, 1963, p. 525.)

fusedly interrelated observations. Higher-order factors, which are further from the data, are seen as hypothetical constructs. They carry the potential of providing broad and penetrating explanations on the basis of a relatively small number of constructs. [p. 527]

The manner in which all factors are mathematically defined makes them prime candidates for entry into properly formal nomological networks (see also Carroll, 1979).

In terms of providing grand theoretical visions of the nature of intellect and as viable exemplars of a properly mathematical approach to science, the factor analytic models made a strong contribution to psychology. The 1960s can be thought of as the golden age of factor analysis, wherein this mathematical technique was assuming a role of considerable importance. There was a sense that it was just a matter of time before the true nature of intelligence would reveal itself through this incredibly powerful technology. Perhaps, at last, the long tradition of measurement without definition would be banished forever, as the factor analysts closed in on the fundamental nature of intellect.

Other Approaches to the Structure of Intelligence

Factor analysis is not the *only* method that has been used to examine the structure of intelligence; several other orientations have been offered. For example, Gardner (1983) reviewed extensive research evidence in a wide variety of domains such as studies of prodigies, gifted people, brain-damaged patients, experts in specific lines of work, and individuals from a variety of cultures. On the basis of this research, he generated a set of six natural intelligences, which he suggested were relatively independent and autonomous. Gardner demonstrated that each intelligence existed in relative isolation in certain populations such as individuals with special abilities or disabled persons with specific deficits. His six intelligences are linguistic, logical/mathematical, spatial, bodily/kinesthetic, personal, and musical. The first three of these are typically represented on the more-or-less standard IQ tests, whereas the other three are not. Gardner (1983) offers a rather convincing case for his view of **multiple intelligences**, representing an approach to analyzing the structure of factor analysis without relying on factor analytic methodology.

Regardless of the method used, analysis of the structure of intelligence has emerged as one of the most well-developed facets of this complex and important construct. Yet, as we will see in the next section, this progress was offset by the maintenance of some of the older, pre–construct validity notions. Indeed, some older ideas were about come back to haunt the field as the 1970s arrived.

OPERATIONISM'S LAST STAND

Despite the introduction of construct validity and the attending movement toward scientific exploration of the nature of intelligence, the operationist view that intelligence is what intelligence tests test did persist in some quarters. This was clearly demonstrated in a highly controversial debate that surfaced in the late 1960s. A number of researchers accepted the operationist view of intellect, added a sprig of hereditarian argument, and then proceeded to apply their conclusions to several highly significant areas of educational practice—with explosive results. These debates and the new ideas emerging from them were exceedingly significant in the development of contemporary psychological testing. What follows is a presentation of these debates, followed by a description of some of the ideas that changed as a function of the issues being discussed.

Arthur Jensen and Compensatory Education

This incident began when the editors of a graduate student publication, the *Harvard Educational Review*, asked Berkeley psychologist **Arthur Jensen** to write an article addressing the question of how much it might be possible to boost IQ and **scholastic achievement** by the use of special and intensive education programs. The editors' intent was to have a number of eminent researchers comment on Jensen's paper, making the whole series a discussion piece for consideration of several important issues. Jensen gladly accepted this opportunity to present his views, and his 123-page paper was published in the winter 1969 issue of the *Review* (Jensen, 1969). The commentaries were published in the next two issues of the journal.

Because Jensen has been described as the most frequently quoted and infrequently read author since Karl Marx, we shall examine this article in some detail. This examination is not intended to reify, or support, Jensen's fundamental

Head Start was one of several compensatory education programs discussed by Jensen in his "Boosting IQ" paper.

argument but is offered in the interest of coming to an understanding of the basic issues and their eventual impact on the testing enterprise.

The operationist nature of Jensen's arguments was clear from the outset. In discussing the nature of intelligence, he stated

> Disagreements and arguments can perhaps be forestalled if we take an operational stance. First of all, this means that probably the most important fact about intelligence is that we can measure it. . . . There is no point in arguing the question to which there is no answer, the question of what intelligence *really* is. [pp. 5-6]

Clearly, this is a rather faithful recapitulation of the measurement-without-definition view outlined earlier in the text. Jensen even cites Boring's classic 1923 operationist definition of intelligence (p. 8). The research strategy endorsed by Jensen was clear in its blind empirical assault on intelligence.

> The best we can do is to obtain measurements of certain kinds of behavior and look at their relationships to other phenomena and see if these relationships make any kind of sense and order. It is from these orderly relationships that we can gain some understanding of the phenomena. [1969, p. 6]

He appeared to have been aware of some of the potential difficulties with this position: "The trouble comes only when we attribute more to intelligence and to our measurements of it than do the psychologists who use the concept in its proper sense" (p. 8). The next part of his argument involved coming down on the Spearman (unitary) side of the structural debate. He then reviewed the literature involving univariate tests of intelligence in a manner similar to the sketch presented at the beginning of this chapter, but with some significant additions. For example, he concluded his review by commenting on the social importance of intelligence and stated that the construct was "a biological reality and not just a figment of social convention" (p. 20). It is here that we begin to see the leading edge of what was to follow.

After discussing the nature of the distribution of IQ scores, Jensen introduced the concept of heritability. Citing British psychologist Sir Cyril Burt as "the most distinguished exponent of the application of these methods to the study of intelligence" (p. 33), he provided a detailed mathematical definition of heritability, using an analysis of variance model. Basically, **heritability** (*H*) was considered to be the correlation between a specific manifest characteristic of an individual (the **phenotype**) and its genetic basis (the **genotype**). A high degree of heritability would indicate that there was very little variance associated with environmental influences in the characteristic, and this would be revealed by a value of *H* that approaches 1.00. Low heritability, indexed by near-0 values of *H*, would indicate that environmental influences played a major part in the emergence of the characteristic. Jensen was at pains to point out that *H* is a population statistic and has no relevance to the individual case.

Empirical estimate of *H* is highly complicated, involving the detailed examination of correlations between individuals of varying kinship (for example, see Huntley, 1966). To do this properly, large samples of persons of different relationships to each other—such as identical twins, fraternal twins, siblings, parents/children, and cousins—are needed. The data involving identical twins who were separated at birth and reared apart is especially important in estimating *H* because this is the one case where genetically identical individuals experience different environments.

Jensen reviewed the available literature and concluded that the "best single estimate of the heritability of measured intelligence" was .77 (p. 51). This suggests that a substantial proportion of the variance in IQ is heritable, leaving very little for environmental influences and various genetic/environmental interactions. This conclusion, however, was based solely on data from White Anglo populations.

To this point in Jensen's paper, there is little to suggest that a major storm was brewing. He had espoused an older view of the nature of intelligence, and he also presented the notion of heritability—both done with considerable cautiousness regarding the kinds of interpretations that could be drawn from these domains. Indeed, his scholarship and care in presenting his material, to this point, was good. However, things changed abruptly on page 78 in a subsection entitled "Race Differences." What followed was an extensive review of the research revealing that, on average, Blacks score 1 SD, or 15 points, lower than Whites on standard IQ tests.[3] If **socioeconomic status** (SES) is controlled, this difference reduces to 11

---

[3]Recall a similar observation from the World War I Army data (see Figure 7-2).

points (Shuey, 1966). Not surprisingly, recalling the correlation between IQ and scholastic aptitude, similar levels of lower performance for Blacks in academic settings were noted. He concluded this review by stating

> There is an increasing realization among students of the psychology of the disadvantaged that the discrepancy in their average performance cannot be completely or directly attributed to discrimination or inequalities in education. It seems not unreasonable, in view of the fact that intelligence variation has a large genetic component, to hypothesize that genetic factors may play a part in this picture. [p. 82]

To buttress his conclusion, Jensen then proceeded to critique the current research, noting the ways in which the present literature did not provide direct support for the competing hypothesis that the IQ and scholastic differences between Whites and Blacks were due to environmental differences (pp. 82–88). Discrediting the opposing view in this way appeared to create a strong case for his hereditarian argument.

Jensen then turned to a review of the literature dealing with major **compensatory education programs**. He noted the failure of mammoth programs such as Head Start to produce meaningful (or, at least, statistically significant) gains in either IQ or scholastic performance. Some smaller, focused, programs did appear to produce spectacular gains, but Jensen offered a series of arguments to suggest that these gains were illusory, not reflective of real change.

The conclusions Jensen drew from this massive paper warrant summary at this point because they probably constitute one of the least read parts of his dissertation. Here, perhaps surprisingly, we find a very positive and forward-looking view of education and a fairly negative appraisal of IQ tests. The major points made at the end of the paper were:

1. Compensatory education programs should emphasize teaching basic skills directly, as opposed to trying to increase general concepts such as IQ. Indeed, Jensen recommended de-emphasis of IQ tests as a measure of program gain (p. 108).

2. He strongly criticized the univariate concept of intelligence, indicating that emphasis ought to be placed on stable differences in the patterns of abilities across various groups (p. 109).[4]

3. He indicated that traditional classroom methods were directed toward capitalizing upon the kinds of abilities measured in IQ tests (what he called **level II learning**). He urged that educators "must discover and devise teaching methods that capitalize on existing abilities" (p. 117) rather than trying to force everyone into the same (level II) mold.

His final two sentences deserve quotation:

> Diversity rather than conformity of approaches and aims would seem to be the key to making education rewarding for children of different patterns of ability. The

---

[4]This conclusion appeared to contradict his earlier endorsement of *g*.

reality of individual differences thus need not mean educational rewards for some children and frustration and defeat for others. [p. 117]

Viewed in hindsight, Jensen's major conclusions do not appear to be overly controversial. Indeed, the rebuttals of his paper, which were published in the next two issues of the *Harvard Educational Review,* were described as "generally temperate in tone, and not overly damaging to Jensen's case" (Fancher, 1985, p. 198).

But other opinions were voiced. Indeed, the more-or-less standard interpretation of Jensen's argument was "there is no use in trying to remove the difference in IQ [between Blacks and Whites] by education since it arises chiefly from genetic causes and the best thing that can be done for black children is to capitalize on those skills for which they are biologically adapted" (Lewontin, 1970). This reading of Jensen's argument was so clearly at odds with the prevailing egalitarian view favoring equal opportunity and equal rights that it is not surprising that controversy erupted almost immediately on publication of Jensen's article. The *Review* was attacked by Harvard's Black and liberal communities for publishing a "racist" article. In a panic, the editors denied they had invited the paper and left Jensen "out to dry" as the furor mounted. The Society for the Psychological Study of Social Issues, a division of APA, urged members to write local newspapers in opposition. Calls for Jensen's immediate dismissal from Berkeley resounded, and even other academic disciplines such as anthropology joined in the anti-Jensen movement. The term **Jensenism** was coined as a synonym for *racism.* Signs like "Jensen must perish" and "Kill Jensen" appeared on campus, and Jensen received a sufficient number of threats to his life that the university had to hire bodyguards for him. Jensen had undoubtedly touched an exposed nerve of the American community.

Several other dissertations dealing with these issues were published after Jensen's. Each of these received equally vehement reactions. William Shockly, a Nobel Prize laureate for physics, was harassed openly when he used Jensen's article to support his thesis about the genetic inferiority of Blacks. Jensen's former academic mentor, Hans Eysenck, developed Jensen's thesis from his hereditarian perspective (see Eysenck, 1971) and was physically assaulted at a lecture. Harvard psychologist Richard Herrnstein, who supported Jensen's genetic but not his racial hypotheses in an article in the *Atlantic Monthly* (Herrnstein, 1971) also received grievous treatment. Some responses to Herrnstein's article were thoughtful and interesting, but many were not. Pamphlets entitled "Fight Harvard Prof's Facist Lies" were soon on the streets, rabble-rousers were planted in Herrnstein's classes, posters with his picture containing the caption "Wanted for Racism" appeared, and threats to his life ensued. All in all, the issues raised by Jensen were receiving widespread rejection from segments of the community, creating a situation where rational and considered response to the fundamental issues was in large measure missing.

A Closer Look

The Jensen debate raised a large number of exceedingly important issues that warrant discussion. It would be impossible to touch on all the critical appraisals, rebuttals, and commentaries that have emerged since the publication of the "boosting

IQ" paper. For our purposes, the most important reactions are those that speak directly to the testing enterprise: (1) the use of measurement without definition, despite the current discussion of construct validity; (2) issues of convergent validity; and (3) Jensen's use of stable measures to measure change. These three test-related points will be the focus of the following discussion, although some other issues will also be mentioned. Emphasis will also be on the points raised by Jensen, not touching on the subsequent papers by Herrnstein (1971) and Eysenck (1971). Critical appraisals of these two presentations can be found in Scarr-Salapatek (1976).

Measurement without definition. One of the major contributing factors to the debate lurks in the historical traditions of the testing enterprise. As we have seen in earlier chapters, the idea of measuring something without knowing what it is (measurement without definition) emerged very early as testing developed. Since that time, a number of sophisticated mathematical techniques (for example, correlational methodologies) and an elaborate philosophical rationalization (for example, operationism) were created that sanctioned this view of measurement in general and intelligence in particular. While this approach provides wide-ranging intellectual freedom to the domain, it has a major downside. In the absence of a clear and concise definition of intelligence, the situation was ripe for interpretation of the extant data in virtually any way. Without a concise definition, there was no independent way of checking the accuracy of the interpretations of the empirical test data because there were no limiting conditions on what the test scores meant. The operationist position allowed researchers to "smuggle in" their hidden assumptions and beliefs because there was no independent means of uncovering or checking them. Even though the logical positivist schema evolved to check a no-holds-barred approach to science, the operationist version of this position—particularly as applied to IQ tests—opened the door to this possibility. In other words, the weaknesses of measurement without definition came home to roost in the Jensen debate.

   As an example, consider Jensen's assertion that IQ-test performance is a "biological reality" (Jensen, 1969, p. 20). This conclusion emerged from the examination of data dealing with the distribution of IQ scores that had a distinctly normal shape. He also noted some minor deviations from normality that seemed congenial to his thesis. As well, Jensen borrowed heavily from the univariate intelligence literature to support his conclusion. While these data are *compatible* with the possibility that IQ-test performance is a biological reality, there is nothing in either the data or the argument presented by Jensen that clearly demonstrated it. In other words, the assertion of biological reality in this case was not confirmed by the data, even though a plausible case could be presented in favor of this interpretation.[5] Nor was there a concisely formulated theoretical argument that indicated IQ tests had or had not been designed to capture a biological reality. Indeed, if we read Binet's caveats carefully (see Chapter 6), we realize that the original tests were *not* designed to capture biological variance at all. In the absence of a clear, theoretical, conceptual definition of what underlie IQ-test performance and specified

---

[5]An equally plausible argument that IQ was not a biological reality could be made relatively easily—and was.

boundary conditions on justifiable meaning attributable to test scores, inserting any number of unwarranted propositions becomes possible. Jensen did just this. Whether knowingly or not, the hereditarian view was smuggled into his argument because the notion of intelligence and its measurement had not been fully defined and elaborated. There was enough "noise" in the conceptual apparatus surrounding intelligence to permit this to happen. Jensen used the unwarranted assertion of the biological reality of IQ scores to introduce his discussion of heritability, which then led to the major controversy once he introduced his racial thesis.

This point is particularly significant in light of the testing enterprise's efforts to repair the weaknesses of the operationist position by introducing construct validity in 1954. As indicated earlier, it was exactly the problematic nature of operationism that led the field to propose that a theoretical definition of the construct underlying performance on a test is a necessary part of validity. Jensen chose to ignore these strictures on tests in his clear adoption of a pre–construct validity theory of measurement. Said differently, Jensen (and others) erred in their acceptance of an outdated and clearly flawed theory of measurement. Perhaps, more than any other, this observation underscores the importance of construct validity.

When we recall that the bifurcation of hereditarian and environmental views of individual differences predates the invention of the IQ test by several hundred years (for example, the Locke–Reid debate outlined in Chapter 5), we begin to realize the extent of the value systems underlying the Jensen controversy. As well, the whole intellectual tradition underlying the testing enterprise was sired from within an hereditarian perspective (see Chapter 5). It should not be surprising, then, to find that the hereditarian pole of the argument emerged in this debate. A whole intellectual tradition conspired to reinforce the hereditarian view. Once the basic premise of an undefined IQ was accepted and the correlational technology surrounding it was embellished, it was an apparently logical and reasonable jump to an hereditarian view. In a sense, Jensen was the unwitting victim of decisions made almost a century ago when Francis Galton and his followers laid the intellectual foundations for the testing enterprise. This set of events can be likened to a slippery slope that, once the fundamental assumptions have been made, lead to a number of inescapable outcomes such as those articulated by Jensen.

Assuming convergent validity. Another test-related point in the Jensen controversy involves the indiscriminant use of all kinds of tests as measures of intelligence. In his review, and most of those that followed, an assortment of specific measurement devices was used to generate data to estimate heritability and support various claims. The Raven Progressive Matrices, the Stanford–Binet, the Wechsler series (in various forms of revision), vocabulary tests, and a wide range of other instruments were indiscriminately grouped together as measures of intelligence, implicitly assuming that these tests all measured exactly the same thing. In other words, Jensen *assumed* the existence of convergent validity among all measures of intelligence. The justification for this procedure rested on the observation of high correlations (~.50 to .70) between the various measures. Although the tests were related, this correlation was not perfect—even taking into account the reliabilities of the measures. Thus, there was no justification for assuming that they all measure *exactly* the same thing. Again, we find the lack of a definition of intelligence critical because it permitted the wholesale amalgamation of various instruments under the label "intelligence"—an unjustified procedure given the lack of perfect correlations between the tests. This calls into question the basic data on which Jensen based his claims.

Stable measures to assess change.   One final test-related point involves consideration of the appropriateness of Jensen using measures that were developed to be maximally stable as indicators of the change wrought by compensatory education programs. Intelligence tests are typically developed to yield indexes that do not show change over time, demonstrating a distinct valuing of measures that yield stable values. To be sure, the research record indicates considerable stability in these scores over the life span (for a review, see Tyler, 1965). How is it justifiable, then, to use an inherently *stable* measure when the goal is to document *change* as a function of a specific program such as Head Start? In a very real sense, Jensen's choice to use IQ tests to evaluate compensatory education programs stacked the cards against demonstrating any meaningful change because of the inherent stability of the measures. To be fair, Jensen did suggest this critique in the latter part of his paper, but it is still necessary to ponder why he did it—particularly if he was aware of the potential problem.

Some other critiques.   The three test-related critiques outlined above (problems with measurement without definition, accepting all tests of intelligence as measuring the same thing, and the inappropriateness of using measures constructed to minimize change to evaluate change) indicate clear problems with Jensen's argument. However, Jensen also made a number of other assumptions and assertions that must be mentioned in any treatment of the debate surrounding his work:

1. The data on which he based his estimates of *H* were derived from White Anglo groups. The extrapolation to Blacks was clearly unwarranted.

2. Jensen himself described the data on the failure of compensatory education as scanty, indicating that his conclusion regarding the ineffectiveness of these programs was not conclusive. He should have been more temperate in making assertions based on this research.

3. In a number of places, Jensen fell into the trap of pitting hereditarian *against* environmental views. This strategy is inappropriate because an interactional view is more plausible. Although Jensen paid lip service to **interactionism** in several places, his general style of argumentation continually focused on the **main effects** of the two major sources of variance.[6]

4. It is possible to generate scenarios wherein heritability estimates of 0 and 1.00 can be generated from assumptions of complete genetic or complete

---

[6]To be fair to Jensen, it should be noted that he did provide estimates of the proportions of variance attributable to interactional factors in his paper (Jensen, 1969, p. 47), and these were pretty small (for example, 5.9%). This might appear to justify his tendency to ignore interactions, but the points already made about the data on which these estimates were based (see item 1 in this list) mitigate against this conclusion.

environmental sources of variance (see Lewontin, 1975). This calls into question the types of inferences Jensen drew from his literature review and (among other things) has led to a "growing disillusionment with the concept of heritability" (Scarr-Salapatek, 1976, p. 126).

5. Geneticists have indicated that there is a **range of reaction** that would be normally expected for a given genotype. That is, there is considerable variability in the manner in which a given genotype will unfold. Hirsch (1976) indicates that the range of reaction is not predictable in advance *and* that "different genotypes should not be expected to have the same norm [range] of reaction" (p. 163). Thus, even if Jensen were correct in his assertion of high heritability of IQ in Black populations, it would say nothing about potential sensitivity to educational treatment programs of this group because they may have different ranges of reaction. Jensen would have to demonstrate that the range of reaction was nil in the Black population to justify his point. He did not do this. To quote Hirsch (1976), "High or low heritability tells us absolutely nothing about how a given individual might have developed under conditions different from those in which he actually did develop. Heritability provides no information about norm of reaction" (pp. 172–173).

These five points, although not inclusive of the volumes of commentary both scientific and public that followed Jensen's paper, do give a sense of the flawed nature of Jensen's argument.

Showing Jensen's hereditarian argument to be flawed does not automatically support or verify an environmental position. Making this assertion renders one vulnerable to the criticism noted in item 3 of the preceding list. An entirely different type of data and argument would have to be presented to assess the viability of a radical environmental position.

One final point should be made before moving on. It would be unfair to condemn all of Jensen's contributions based solely on one of many papers that he published. Jensen has, throughout his career, made many important and useful contributions to the testing enterprise. For example, he has been a major player in developing some of the issues of test bias discussed in Chapter 14 (for example, Jensen, 1980). Although he is likely to be remembered historically for his "boosting IQ" paper, we should not forget that he was an active and important contributor in other issues as well as this one.

Sir Cyril Burt and His Twins

One research finding does stand out above the rest as providing promise of an empirical resolution to the nature/nurture problem. As indicated previously, identical twins reared apart provide purchase on the possible contribution of heritability to IQ because it represents a situation in which two identical genotypes are raised in different environments. Presumably, finding substantive relationships between tests scores of such twins would support the genetic nature of intelligence.

Monozygotic twins raised separately are difficult to find. The most extensive collection of this kind of data was published by British psychologist **Cyril Burt**, and his results entered significantly into the nature/nurture debate. They were key data in the estimation of heritability of intelligence.

By virtue of his extensive testing program in London, Burt (1943) noted that the correlation of IQs for 62 pairs of unseparated, identical twins was .86. He also noted another 15 cases where the monozygotic twins had been raised separately, and the correlation was .77. No details were offered regarding these data, and Burt made very little of the results in this early article. He did, however, cite them in Burt (1955) in the context of defending his views against critical assault. Burt also indicated that an associate of his, J. Conway, had collected an additional 6 pairs of identicals reared separately, bringing the total to 21. A correlation of .771 was reported between these twins on a group test of intelligence. In Burt (1958), the number had risen to 30, and later that same year Conway (1958) reported 42. The correlation between IQ scores for these twins was stable at .771. Burt (1966) indicated that his sample had been increased to 53 pairs of identicals reared separately. As before, the correlation between IQ scores for these twins was .771. This was the most extensive data set for the evaluation of heritability of intelligence available at that time. Of particular note for these data was Burt's demonstration that there was no correlation between the IQs of the adoptive parents and the childrens' IQs. In other words, not only was this a reasonably large sample, but adoption placement was random. Because of this, Burt's data became the cornerstone of hereditarian arguments during the time of the Jensen debate.

Burt's data, however, seemed just too good to be true. Kamin (1974) noted the incredible consistency of the correlation for the twins (at a value of .771) for samples ranging from $n = 15$ through to 53, a most unlikely coincidence. Indeed, once raised, researchers and journalists began to question the veracity of Burt's data and one of the greatest scandals in the history of science soon erupted. The following Close Up provides a glimpse at this turbulent time.

CLOSE UP   The Burt Controversy

> The following strange advertisement appeared in the *London Times* of October 16, 1976: "Sir Cyril Burt. Could Margaret Howard or J. Conway who helped Sir Cyril in studies of the intelligence of twins or anyone else who knows them telephone (reverse charges) Oliver Gillie, 01-485 8953." Oliver Gillie was the medical correspondent of the *Times*. On October 24, 1976 the headline "Crucial Data was Faked by Eminent Psychologist" appeared, along with a photograph of Burt. Gillie's article began:
>
> > The most sensational charge of scientific fraud this century is being levelled against the late Sir Cyril Burt, father of British educational psychology. Leading scientists are convinced that Burt published false data and invented crucial facts to support his controversial theory that intelligence is largely inherited.
>
> Four main charges were leveled against Burt in this article:
>
> 1. Burt often only estimated parents' IQs and then presented these guesses as hard scientific data.

2. The two women, Margaret Howard and J. Conway, who were reported to have helped him in his twin studies, appeared to have never existed.
3. The strangely consistent correlation of .771 between IQ scores for monozygotic twins reared apart was suspect and probably fudged.
4. Burt made up data to fit the predictions of his favored genetic theories.

To the extent that these (faked) data were essential to the nurture side of the nature/nurture debate and that this debate had significant social implications, these were grave charges indeed. In the *Times* of the next day, it was announced that "Theories of I.Q. Pioneer Completely Discredited." This, of course, cast a pale of doubt on the rest of Burt's work and set the scene for one of the most sensational cases of scientific fraud ever witnessed.

Actually there was nothing really new in the Gillie article except the explicit charge of fraud. Gillie's charge regarding the "missing ladies" was directly derived from Tizard. The issue of "guesses" about parents' IQs to establish independence between the IQs of the children and adopted parents had been published previously. Kamin had documented the problem with the important correlations. Gillie exposed and sensationalized the already extant problems: "Gillie's article made public, and added substance to, things that a number of psychologists had been saying for some years, though in more circumspect language" (Tizard, 1977, p. 4).

Some came to Burt's defense. John Cohen of Manchester University described his former supervisor as "meticulous, thorough and painstaking," and rejecting the fraud charge "lock, stock and barrel" (Cohen, 1977). Hans Eysenck insisted that there was no evidence that would support anything other than the charge that Burt made errors of estimation and calculation. Jensen and others suggested that if Burt had tried to fake his data he would have made a much better job of it.

But the anti-Burt faction stepped up its campaign. Clarke, Clarke, and McAskie (1976) noted that Burt's errors were always in a direction that supported his views. Kamin (1976) hardened his stand indicating that "the charges of scientific fraud clearly have some substantial basis." In a letter to *Science,* a most prestigious natural science journal, he clearly implied that Burt's work was unsatisfactory (Kamin, 1977).

In a fairly balanced review, Wade (1976) suggested that "it would be of some historical interest to know whether the flaws [in Burt's data] resulted from systematic fraud, mere carelessness, or something in between. The facts so far available do not allow any of these explanations to be ruled out." In the final analysis, it is unknown whether Burt was an active fraud or whether he was just a victim of overzealous belief in his theories. His real motivations will never be known, but the incident remains as one of the most sensational cases of scientific fraud ever.

Thus, the cornerstone of the hereditarian argument, Burt's twin data, was discredited and along with it any thoughts that there might be a tractable, empirical solution to the nature/nurture debate. In retrospect, it appears that even with the incredibly sophisticated and elegant statistical techniques and the considerable amount of kinship data available today, the nature/nurture debate remains at roughly the same place as we encountered it in the debates between John Stuart Mill and Francis Galton. The evidence remains ambiguous, and there is enough room for intelligent people to interpret it differently.

As you might expect, throughout all of this controversy, the stock of the classical IQ test began to wane. Following this particular round of the nature/nurture debate, the numbers of researchers, journalists, and educators espousing strong antitest views increased. The testing enterprise had strayed from its initial effort to serve social needs. Changes were clearly demanded, and these have begun to occur—albeit somewhat slowly.

Today the general view is that emphasis in educational settings should be on academic achievement rather than intelligence. In using tests to select job applicants, the only case in which IQ tests should be used is when there is a strong and documented correlation between test performance and *posttraining* performance on the specific job. In clinical applications, emphasis has been moving away from the use of the obtained scores toward viewing the tests as standardized behavior samples. These provide the clinician with invaluable comparative data, although there is concern about this application (for example, Frank, 1983). The possibility of using the tests to help identify hidden intellectual strengths is also noteworthy. Individual IQ tests can be effective in discovering intellectual functioning problems and useful in the design of programs to help deal with these. Group IQ tests have a place in research settings where focus is on developing a theory of intellect. In some settings, they can also be useful as premeasures to ensure equivalence of participants in various training programs.

These contemporary applications of IQ tests are a far cry from the original enterprise as sketched by the likes of Terman and Yerkes (see Chapter 7). Today there is a much more modest and carefully considered role for IQ tests. The entire shape of the testing enterprise and its relationship to the sponsoring society had changed in ways that were designed to protect and enhance the individual. Perhaps it is here that the debates such as Jensen's have made a significant contribution, by alerting us to the potential difficulties and problems underlying inappropriate extrapolations from test data. It should be mentioned that the Burt incident is not closed. A number of researchers have continued to come to Burt's defense (for example, Fletcher, 1991), and the issue underlying the Burt scandal is far from resolved (see Chapter 20).

These changes to the testing enterprise were just the beginning. With the introduction of construct validity, it was really only a matter of time before intensified research into intelligence would emerge. Indeed, in other areas of psychology, several important events had already occurred prior to the Jensen debate, which were to shape the current approach to intellectual assessment.

THE COGNITIVE "REVOLUTION"

On September 11, 1956, those attending a symposium at the Massachusetts Institute of Technology heard a series of papers that laid the foundation for a major shift in psychology. Allen Newell and Herbert Simon presented the first complete proof of a theorem ever carried out on a computing machine. Noam Chomksy read a paper that promised realization of long-held hope that language could be effectively described using mathematics. And George Miller introduced his notion that human short-term memory was limited to seven pieces of information. Taken in isolation, each of these papers would not be sufficient to create a "revolution," but in combination they were devastating. Taken ensemble, the ideas conveyed in these papers provided workers with an immensely powerful set of tools—namely, the computer, mathematics, and information theory. This set of ideas was soon to be applied to the age-old problem of understanding the human mind—with spectacular results (for a detailed discussion of this **cognitive "revolution,"**[7] see Gardner, 1985).

As the 1960s unfolded, research sired from this new perspective increased geometrically. Ulrich Neisser's book *Cognitive Psychology* (1967) marked the true debut of this new view. An immensely popular book, it soon became the unquestioned manifesto of a new order of psychological thought. Replacing the older view that the human organism was relatively passive, caught in the web of environmental control, the new **cognitive psychology** viewed the human as an active, hypothesis-testing agent. All cognition from perception onward was considered to involve inventive, analytic, and synthetic processes. This was radically different from the older view that cast the human as a puppet of the environment. The new perspective construed the person as a constructive, creative organism full of ideas, rules, and images. Equally importantly, the human was seen to be imminently understandable, using the electronic computer as the fundamental metaphor. Before long, models of cognitive processes involving executive processes, temporary sensory input buffers, network models of memory, preprogrammed output sequences, and many other representational notions were filling the technical literature. A major shift in thinking about the human mind had occurred. This shift has created the fundamental core of the manner in which we study the human mind in the 1990s.

This shift from a passive to active view ushered in by the cognitive "revolution" was to provide a major challenge to the testing enterprise—a challenge that is still in the process of working itself out today. Prior to the 1960s, characteristics such as intelligence and personality, the foundational notions of the testing enterprise, were seen as relatively static characteristics of individuals. In a sense, these constructs embraced the older passive conception. There was no mechanism for accommodating the dynamic and active nature of human cognition in the older descriptive models of intellect such as those held by Terman, Thurstone, and Wechsler. Change was typically thought to represent "unreliability" of measurement. Not unlike eye color or height at maturity, these psychological constructs were considered to be static and unchanging. Yet the cognitive "revolution" was saying something else about these constructs—they were continually in a state of flux, being directed by an active and enterprising organism reacting to a constantly changing environment. This new perspective was particularly relevant in the domain of intellectual performance, but it also had its place in the consideration of personality variables. Although not denying the possibility of upper limits, the new cognitive view began to push test developers closer and closer to a major

---

[7]The word "revolution" has been placed in quotation marks throughout this section because there is some concern that the cognitivization of psychology is not really a revolution in the traditional sense. Revolutions involve throwing out the old order, replacing it with another. Many observers of psychology feel that this has not happened—at least not as yet. Hence, the cautionary quotation marks in this section.

reconceptualization of their field—one that would be more sympathetic to the active, constructive nature of the human. Rather than view intellectual performance as unchanging, the need for a more active and dynamic view began to surface.

Another factor had an impact here—namely, the introduction of construct validity (see Chapter 13).[8] Prior to the mid-1950s, tests of intelligence had, for the most part, been developed under the old atheoretical program sanctioned by criterion-related validity and operationism. Once the APA announced its view that tests ought to be tied explicitly to theoretical ideas, the need for formal consideration of theories of intellectual functioning emerged—else new tests would not be able to demonstrate construct validity. A likely source for theoretical inspiration in the testing enterprise was the cognitive domain because these researchers were tackling, with apparent success, exactly these problems.

This movement from the old tests to ones incorporating the new vision of the human mind has been relatively slow, being in a clear state of transition at the present time. It has occurred in three ways:

1. In some cases, efforts have been made to update the older tests and provide them with post hoc theoretical interpretation. Revisions to the WISC (Wechsler, 1974) and WAIS (Wechsler, 1981) are good examples of this approach (for detailed reviews, see LaGreca & Stringer, 1985, for the WISC–R; House & Lewis, 1985, for the WAIS–R).

2. A number of important developments from cognitive psychology have been applied to the IQ-testing domain in an effort to articulate further the fundamental nature of intellect. Of particular note here is a research program initiated by Robert Sternberg around 1977 and some process-oriented research into several classic tests. These are discussed in the next section.

3. Some new tests have been developed explicitly to bring assessment and cognition together. Perhaps the most noteworthy of these is the Kaufman Assessment Battery for Children (K–ABC), which will be discussed later in this chapter.

Although the movement toward embracing the new cognitive view of the human in the testing enterprise has really only begun, it seems safe to say that it is one of the directions of the future. More and more tests will be forced to rationalize themselves against the criterion of existing scientific knowledge, and the movement to include cognitive psychology into the testing enterprise is both timely and significant.

Robert Sternberg's The Triarchic Mind

In 1977 Yale psychologist **Robert Sternberg** published a book entitled *Intelligence, Information Processing, and Analogical Reasoning: The Componential Analysis of Human Abilities*. This book signaled what would become a major research effort directed at applying the resources of the cognitive domain to the study of intelli-

---

[8]It's worth noting the relative closeness of the dates suggested to have begun the cognitive "revolution" (1956) and the introduction of construct validity (1954–1955).

gence. Sternberg's goals in this volume were to discuss the optimal form that a theory of intelligence ought to attain; to present his view, what he called a "componential theory"; and to discuss how this laid the groundwork for a theory of intelligence. Roughly a decade later, Sternberg (1988) presented a fully blown **triarchic theory of intelligence** (*The Triarchic Mind*), which represents the present state of the art of this important development in the testing enterprise.

A fine example of the manner in which Sternberg has adapted the cognitive literature to redress the notion of intelligence is in an excerpt entitled "Looking for Smarts in All the Wrong Places" (Sternberg, 1988). He points out four fallacies that appear to have guided the development of many IQ tests:

1. To be "quick" is to be "smart."

2. The person with excellent verbal skills reads everything with great care and comprehension.

3. Vocabulary size is a good index of smartness.

4. Intelligent people solve problems in the same way as less intelligent—but better.

From your knowledge of IQ testing, you should have no difficulty finding examples of how specific intelligence tests are guided by these assumptions (for example, the WISC vocabulary subtest assumes item 3, and the Raven Progressive Matrices assumes item 4.

Sternberg shows quite clearly how research in the cognitive area challenges the validity of each of these fallacies. Certainly the work by Wissler (1903) (see Chapter 6) challenges fallacy (1), but even more telling is the idea that **speed selection**—knowing when to be fast and when to be slow and careful—is much more important in conceptualizing intelligence. Considerable research in the cognitive domain has indicated that some situations demand quick, immediate responses, whereas others are better served by a slow, careful strategy (for example, Baron, 1982). That the classic IQ tests do not consider this possibility is clear evidence that the cognitive perspective has something to offer the domain of intelligence.

Sternberg's componential theory of intelligence incorporates a wide range of literature and theory from the cognitive domain. The triarchic part of the name comes from the suggestion that there are three classes of cognitive processes (or what Sternberg calls **components**) underlying intelligent behavior. These are (1) **metacomponents**, which are the executive processes used to plan, monitor, and evaluate problem solving;[9] (2) **performance components**, which are the lower-order processes used to implement the commands of the metacomponents; and (3) **knowledge-acquisition components**, which are the processes used to seek out the information needed to fulfill the plans and so on of the metacomponents. Intelligent behavior is seen as the joint functioning of these three classes of cognitive processes.

Perhaps one of Sternberg's examples will help here. In writing a term paper for a course such as this one, all three classes of cognitive processes are active.

---

[9]Speed selection, mentioned above, is a good example of a metacomponent

1. Metacomponents are involved when you decide on a topic, plan the paper, monitor your writing, and evaluate how well you think you might do when it is handed back.
2. Performance components are involved in the actual writing.
3. The actual conducting of research, such as going to the library and using the computerized search service or scouring the stacks for useful information, reflect the activity of the knowledge-acquisition components.

Thus, a given act is a combination of all three classes of cognitive processes.

In virtually any meaningful cognitive situation, all three classes of processes are demanded and are highly interdependent, with the results of one set of processes having major effects on the other. For example, returning to our paper-writing example, the planning aspects of the metacomponents may have to change if the knowledge-acquisition components reveal that a necessary reference book is not available in the library. The monitoring functions will also have to change if during performance attempts to write do not go well. Under these conditions, it might be necessary to plan a different style of writing or to try to reevaluate the approach that will be taken. Thus, the three components are highly interdependent. Figure 15-9 shows the nature of this interaction; the metacomponents serve as the overall executive function, while the other two components "report back" to them.

But matters are even more complex than this. The manner in which the three components are applied in a given situation is a function of the novelty of the situation. When you have very little experience with a specific task, no matter which component is involved, it demands a considerable amount of attention. You might recall the first time you tried to hit a golf ball, or to use a new piece of computer software, or to drive a car. In all of these cases, the initial task seemed almost overwhelming, acting to use up all of your attention in coping with basic details. Over time, though, it becomes possible to *automatize* some of the processes, and performance improves dramatically. This capacity to deal with novel tasks and subsequently to render aspects of performance automatic are important aspects of Sternberg's theory as well.

There are several layers of "threeness" in Sternberg's triarchic theory of intelligence because another level of activity in the theory has three entries. These are (1) the componential aspect (outlined above and consisting of three components itself), (2) the **experiential aspect** (described above in terms of novelty and automatization); and (3) the **contextual aspect**. This latter facet of the theory is concerned with the manner in which intelligence is applied to the work-a-day world, thereby shaping the context in which the individual is functioning. In keeping with his threeness, Sternberg suggests the following functions: (1) adapting to existing environments, (2) selecting new environments, and (3) shaping existing environments into new ones. Thus, the contextual aspect of the theory is concerned with the manner in which the first two aspects (components and experience) affect our own cognitive world in the sense that they shape the context in which we exist. In his writing, Sternberg focuses upon what he calls **practical intelligence**, or what might be called "street smarts," to characterize successful activity in this contextual domain.

Figure 15-9 The relationships among metacomponents, performance components, and knowledge-acquisition components. Metacomponents activate the other two kinds of components, which in turn provide feedback to the metacomponents.

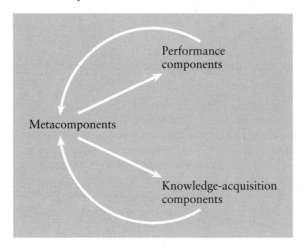

All three of these aspects (and their associated subaspects) interact in complex ways to produce an overall picture of the intelligently functioning cognitive machine. This interaction is diagrammed in Figure 15-10.

This complex interaction reveals that intelligence should be examined in three separate ways if any kind of representativeness of the cognitive domain is desired. First, the components of intelligence and their interrelationships must be examined. Second, it is necessary to take into account the effects of experience as they relate to novelty and automatization. Third, the manner in which the first two aspects of intelligence shape the external world of the individual, as revealed in practical skills, must be considered.

Sternberg suggests that what have traditionally been viewed as individual differences in intelligence can be more aptly described as differences in the manner in which the specific aspects of intelligence are combined in a specific context. The relative energy invested in the components, experience, and contextual aspects of a person's cognitive machine provides an interesting alternative to the more traditional perspectives of intelligence. Such a view spawns a radically different approach to IQ testing than we have seen thus far. A univariate view would be useless for Sternberg because it masks all the important components and aspects outlined above. So too would the more traditional ability profile (for example, Thurstone's Primary Mental Abilities; see Chapter 10) be ineffective because of its failure to consider such things as metacomponents, experience, and context. Even the overinclusive view of Guilford with his 120 different intelligences is inadequate to cover the range of cognitive activities sketched out in Sternberg's triarchic theory.

Figure 15-10 Relationships among the various aspects of the triarchic theory of human intelligence.

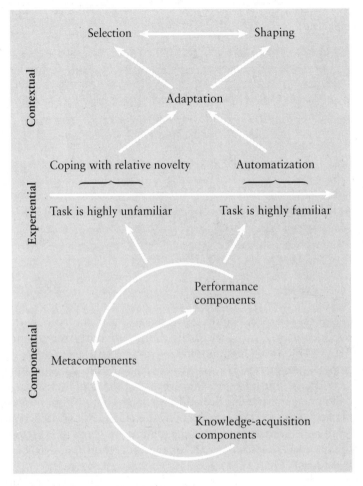

Source: based on Sternberg, 1988, p. 68

Where, for example, do metacomponents fall in Guilford's scheme? Clearly, some other kind of tests will be required to fulfill this theory.

Sternberg is currently working on a triarchic test of intelligence. It will be called the **Sternberg Multidimensional Abilities Test (SMAT)** and designed for people as young as 5 years of age and as old as senior citizens. The SMAT will provide separate scores for each of the three main parts of the triarchic theory: components of intelligence, coping with novelty and automatization (two separate subscores), and practical intelligence. As currently planned, the SMAT will be a paper-and-pencil, multiple-choice test suitable for group administration. Two parallel forms will be available. The fundamental assumption underlying the SMAT is that intelligence is malleable, not fixed, because scores could change as a function of changed

Table 15-4 Several sample items from the Sternberg Multidimensional Abilities Test

Componential	The concern here is the ability to pick up information from relevant context. For grades 10–12, this item is representative:
	The Depression did not happen suddenly with the 1929 stock market crash, although the *laz* that preceded it seemed carefree and spendthrift. The twenties saw homeless workers beginning to wend their way across the country, and small businesses going bankrupt.
	Laz most likely means: (a) economy, (b) years, (c) history, (d) lifestyles.
Coping with Novelty	The ability to think in relatively novel ways is tapped by items such as this one of grades 8–9:
	If dogs laid eggs, which of these would most likely be true? a. Dogs would fly. b. Puppies would have feathers. c. Eggs would have tails. d. Puppies would hatch. e. Chickens would bark.
Automatization	All items here are highly speeded in which respondents must make rapid decisions. *Example:* In one test, respondents have to decide if both letters of a pair are vowels or consonants or a mix of the two.
Practical	These items involve everyday inferential reasoning such as this item for grades 8–9:
	Johnson's Service Station makes good on its claim that "We will not be undersold." Which of these is most likely to be true? a. Garcia's Station charges more than Johnson's Service Station. b. No other garage charges less than Johnson's Service Station. c. The owner of Johnson's Service Station has a good head for business. d. Johnson's Service Station is the busiest garage in town.

SOURCE: Sternberg (1990).

experience or in a different context. Table 15-4 presents several examples of verbal items from the SMAT; there are also figural and quantitative items.

Critical appraisal. Sternberg has mapped out an exciting future for the study of intelligence. It offers the challenge of a new and vibrant conceptualization of intelligence—one that perhaps can answer some of the criticisms being heaped on the more traditional conceptions. However, the triarchic view is not a panacea; it has its own difficulties as well. Some of these difficulties include the following:

1. In the tradition of the pragmatic values of the testing enterprise, acceptability of the theory will depend on the success of the SMAT, which will require quite a few years to determine.

2. Paper-and-pencil tests are often of doubtful relevance to the real world, and the SMAT and its underlying theory will have to demonstrate that this is not the case.

3. Even with its inclusion of contextual factors, Sternberg's theory runs the risk of devaluing the incredible significance of the interface between intelligence and the context in which it is exercised. Many psychologists and anthropologists doubt whether it is possible to fully understand intelligence except in relation to the context in which it develops and is exercised (see, for example, Berry, 1974, 1981, 1982; Charlesworth, 1976, 1979; Dewey, 1957; Keating, 1984; Laboratory of Comparative Human Cognition, 1982, 1983; Neisser, 1976; Sternberg, 1984; Sternberg & Salter, 1982), thus calling into question the feasibility of Sternberg's overall project.

In summary, Sternberg's triarchic theory offers an exceedingly promising alternative to the more traditional IQ tests. By virtue of attending to the cognitive processes underlying performance on the test, the strength of the emerging theory and test will be its construct validity. The work described thus far provides a good sense of just what researchers on human abilities (particularly researchers of **information processing**) have accomplished and of what they have yet to accomplish. The cognitive vision of intelligence will be highly significant in the near future of IQ testing. To conclude then, theories of intelligence have progressed well over the years, but they still suffer from areas of weaknesses that need strengthening.

Cognitive Analysis of Test-Item Responding

A fascinating example of the interaction between the testing enterprise and the cognitive approach to understanding human intellectual functioning can be found in some recent work with the Raven Progressive Matrices (see Chapter 10 for details of the test). Incorporating a wide range of experimental measures such as verbal reports, eye fixations, and error patterns, Carpenter, Just, and Shell (1990) developed simulation models for moderately and highly successful Raven performance in a college sample. These models are not only interesting in their own right but also provide some useful ideas about the nature of individual differences and testing when viewed through the cognitive perspective.

Carpenter et al. (1990) began by developing a taxonomy of rules used in the solution of Raven items. These are shown in Table 15-5, with reference to the sample items shown in Figure 15-11 (page 590).

The Raven (Advanced Series I and II) was then administered to determine the numbers and kinds of errors that college students made. Conditions were arranged so that it was possible to track the nature of eye fixations demonstrated while solving the problems. Respondents' verbal comments while solving the problems were also encouraged and recorded.

These data revealed that error rates increased geometrically with the number of rules required to attain a correct solution. In addition, the eye-fixation data and the verbal reports indicated a markedly incremental process was involved—respondents decomposed problems into successively smaller subproblems and then solved

Table 15-5 Rules used in the solution of Raven items

Quantitative Pairwise Progression	There is a quantitative increment or decrement between adjacent entries including size, position, or number of elements. *Example:* In Figure 15-11(a), the number of black squares in each entry increases in a row from 1 to 2 to 3.
Constant in a Row	The same value occurs throughout a row but changes down the column. *Example:* In Figure 15-11(b), the location of the dark component is constant within each row being in the upper half in row 1, the lower half in row 2, and both halves in row 3.
Figure Addition or Subtraction	A figure from one column is added to (juxtaposed or superimposed) or subtracted from another figure to produce a third. *Example:* In Figure 15-11(b), the dark triangle in column 1 is added to the one in column 2 to produce the larger triangle in column 3.
Distribution of Two Values	Two values of a categorical attribute are distributed through a row, and the third value is nil. *Example:* In Figure 15-11(c), the V appears in two of the three boxes in each row and not in the third.
Distribution of Three Values	Three values from a categorical attribute (such as figure type) are distributed through a row. *Example:* In Figure 15-11(d), one of a triangle, diamond, or square appears in each row.

SOURCE: Carpenter et al. (1990, p. 408).

these. The processes used were incremental both in addressing one rule at a time and in the pairwise approach to comparing elements. This incremental character of the cognitive processes involved suggested the need to consider some mechanism for keeping track of subproblem solutions and redefining the problem, on line, to take this into account.

Once this glimpse of the cognitive processes needed to solve Raven items was in hand, it became possible to write a computer program that could account for the kinds of results observed in the earlier experiments. **FAIRAVEN** was developed to account for the performance of moderately successful students and was based on the incremental ideas generated from the earlier work (considerable detail is presented in Carpenter et al., 1990, pp. 417–418). However, FAIRAVEN only incorporated four rules, excluding distribution of two values. As well, it did not incorporate a mechanism for keeping track of subproblem solutions.

When the program was run, it solved 23 of the 34 problems—the same performance level demonstrated on average by the student group. Performance also showed the same distribution of *p*-values, and the error patterns were roughly similar to human respondents. Performance breakdowns for this model were associated with failures of bookkeeping, or keeping-track, operations, indicating that a model for superior performance would have to incorporate these aspects of the problem.

Figure 15-11 Problems of the type found on the Raven Progressive Matrices, illustrating the rules shown in Table 15-5.

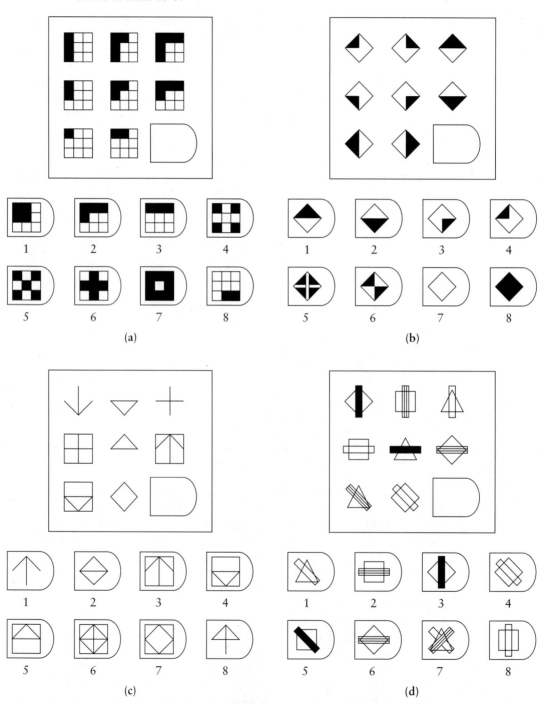

(SOURCE: Carpenter et al., 1990, p. 409.)

BETTERAVEN was developed by adding several components to the earlier model. It contained a *goal monitor,* which set subgoals and kept a record of the attained results. Backtracking to previous subproblems was also permitted. Rule application was serial in the advanced model, being controlled by the goal monitor. Based on the earlier observations, the order of rule application was the following:

First rule applied

1. Constant in a row
2. Quantitative pairwise progression
3. Distribution of three values
4. Figure addition of subtraction
5. Distribution of two values

Last rule applied

Notice that BETTERAVEN incorporates all five rules, which constitute another addition to the previous simulation. BETTERAVEN solved 32 of the 34 problems, reflecting the performance of the best respondent in the earlier empirical tests.

At this point, Carpenter et al. had developed models for average and superior Raven performance. Individual differences could then be examined by systematically degrading BETTERAVEN to find out what kinds of effects emerge if specific components of the model are removed or inhibited. Two such degradations were examined: (1) lesioning the ability to induce rules and (2) interfering with the goal-management mechanism. A middle-range model, which failed to solve 9 of the 34 problems, emerged when the rule stack for BETTERAVEN was reduced to four by eliminating the distribution-of-two-values rule. If limits were placed on the number of rules that could be applied in a given situation (effectively limiting memory), performance showed systematic decrements. These experiments suggest an interesting explanation of individual differences in Raven performance: Failure to induce the fifth rule and limitations in the numbers of rules that can be used in a specific problem are two of the factors underlying differential performance on this task.

This approach to examining test-item performance is a natural outcome of the cognitive "revolution." Here we see a great concern with the processes underlying test-item performance. Although this particular example suffers from its use of a bottom-up strategy (it is constrained by the original items selected by Raven), it does illustrate the promise of a cognitive- and process-oriented approach.

Perhaps, more than any other orientation, the cognitive metaphor sensitizes us to the incredible complexity of what goes on in the mind when we ask respondents to answer items on an IQ test. By the time it is possible to simulate processes as (relatively) simple as answering Raven items, it is necessary to develop computer programs filled with numerous complex subroutines, executive processes, and not a small number of assumptions about the nature of the human information-processing system. Perhaps, then, it should not come as a surprise to discover that simplistic models of human performance reflected in notions such as the univariate conception of intelligence have little or nothing to do with what actually happens in the human brain. Such simple ideas are convenient constructions that exist, not because they reflect some kind of scientific reality, but because they have provided useful and functional devices to aid in the solution of social problems.

The Kaufman Assessment Battery for Children

Sternberg's approach is a wholesale revision of the construct of intelligence and represents a major challenge to the testing enterprise. In a sense, the radically cognitive approach embodied in the triarchic theory of mind has created an immense gulf between the cognitive theorists and the more traditional members of the testing enterprise. Of particular note is the need for standardized assessment batteries that solve specific measurement problems. This stems from the need of the community to contribute to the solution of social problems and is a highly significant part of the activities of the testing enterprise. Sternberg's theory—at its current level of articulation—does not provide this practical utility, although the future promises some significant developments along this line.

The Kaufman Assessment Battery for Children (K–ABC) is an important contribution to the cognitivization of the testing enterprise because it presents a compromise between the more traditional approaches and the newer vision of the human mind. It is kind of a midway point between the extremes represented in the cognition/psychometric debate. The K–ABC is relatively new, being published in 1983. It incorporates a considerable amount of cognitive theory and research. The main theoretical idea embodied in the test is the distinction between sequential and simultaneous mental processes. Tests have been designed specifically to capture this distinction and are presented as separate subscores. Like the Wechsler series, an overall intelligence score, called the *Mental Processing Composite (MPC)*, is provided. The following Close Up provides you with some details on this test. A measure of intellectual achievement is also included.

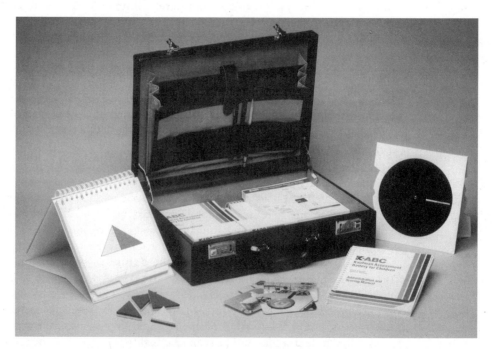

Testing materials for the Kaufman Assessment Battery for Children (K-ABC).

CLOSE UP **The Kaufman Assessment Battery for Children**

The **Kaufman Assessment Battery for Children (K–ABC)** (Kaufman & Kaufman, 1983) is an individually administered measure of intelligence and achievement for ages 2½ through 12½ years. Its major theoretical claims focus on the distinction between sequential and simultaneous mental processes. **Sequential tasks** involve the solution of problems by mentally arranging input into serial order. A prototypical sequential task would be alphabetizing a set of words, where the task is to place items into a proper order on the basis of some previous learning. **Simultaneous tasks** involve ability to synthesize information in order to solve the problem. Standard arithmetic problems would be examples because they demand bringing together information from a number of different spheres to derive the solution of a given problem. Sequential and simultaneous skills combine in very complex ways in most problem-solving situations. Although one or the other skill may be primary in a given problem, almost all scholastic contexts demand a combination of the two. The K–ABC also includes an **Achievement scale**, which focuses on the actual knowledge that a child has acquired. Table 15-6 (pages 594-595) presents the subtests of the K–ABC.

Administration. Each subtest consists of a series of items ranked from easy to hard and graded for age. Because the K–ABC uses a tabletop easel of flip cards, it can be administered across the corner of a table rather than across its width, making it easier to interact with the respondent during test administration.

For ages 2½ through 4 years, administration begins with the Magic Window. For ages 5 through 12½ years, testing begins with Hand Movements. Testing then continues on through the appropriately ordered items and tests. The K–ABC takes, on average, 35 minutes for 3-year-olds, 50–60 minutes for 5-year-olds, and 75–85 minutes for children ages 7 and up.

Scoring. Every item on the K–ABC is scored dichotomously, with correct responses scored 1 and incorrect responses 0. Subtest scores are simply the number of items scored as correct. Raw scores are then converted to standard scores (mean = 10; SD = 3—just like the WISC) using the "Administration and Scoring Manual." Separate simultaneous, sequential, and achievement scores are generated and converted using the manual. The manual also contains separate tables for global-scale standard scores, expected windows of variability (per the standard of error of measurement discussed earlier), and a number of national percentile scores. These scores are based on a norming sample of 2000 children designed to be representative of the U.S. population around 1980, stratified at each age group by gender, race, socioeconomic status, geographic region, and community size. Tables in the manual present a number of scores relative to this group, including sociocultural percentiles; age equivalents; grade equivalents for Arithmetic, Reading/Decoding, and Reading/Understanding; and global-scale comparisons. The **Mental Processing Composite (MPC)**, which is the combination of the sequential and simultaneous processing scales, represents the integration of the two processing styles.

The K–ABC also has a special **Non-Verbal scale** designed to assess the intelligence of hearing-impaired and limited English–proficient children. Consisting of subtests that can be administered in pantomime and responded to motorically, it includes Face Recognition, Hand Movements, Triangles, Matrix Analogies, Spatial Memory, and Photo Series subtests.

Psychometric properties. The test authors have reported satisfactory estimates of test/retest and split-half reliability estimates for the overall scores at each age level.

Table 15-6
Subtests of the Kaufman Assessment Battery for Children

Sequential Processing Subtests

Number Recall	Measures the child's ability to repeat—in sequence—a series of numbers spoken by the examiner. *Ages:* 2 years, 6 months (2-6), through 12 years, 5 months (12-5).
Hand Movements	Measures the child's ability to copy the precise sequence of taps on the table with the fist, palm, or side of the hand as performed by the examiner. *Ages:* 2-6 through 12-5.
Word Order	Measures the child's ability (both with and without an interference task) to point to silhouettes of common objects in the same order as these objects were named by the examiner. *Ages:* 4-0 through 12-5.

Simultaneous Processing Subtests

Magic Window	Measures the child's ability to identify and name an object whose picture is rotated behind a narrow slit so that the picture is only partially exposed at any point. *Ages:* 2-6 through 4-11.
Face Recognition	Measures the child's ability to attend closely to one or two faces whose photographs are exposed briefly, and then to select the correct face(s) shown in group photograph. *Ages:* 2-6 through 4-11.
Gestalt Closure	Measures the child's ability to mentally fill in the gaps in a partially completed inkblot drawing and requires naming or describing that drawing. *Ages:* 2-6 through 12-5.
Triangles	Measures the child's ability to assemble several identical rubber triangles (blue on one side, yellow on the other) to match a picture of an abstract design. *Ages:* 4-0 through 12-5.
Matrix Analogies	Measures the child's ability to select the picture or design that best completes a 2-inch-square visual analogy. *Ages:* 5-0 through 12-5.
Spatial Memory	Measures the child's ability to recall the locations of pictures arranged randomly on a page. *Ages:* 5-0 through 12-5.
Photo Series	Measures the child's ability to organize a randomly arranged array of photographs illustrating an event and then to order them in their proper time sequence. *Ages:* 6-0 through 12-5.

Achievement Subtests

Expressive Vocabulary	Measures the child's ability to name the object pictured in a photograph. *Ages:* 2-0 through 4-11.

Faces and Places	Measures the child's ability to name well-known people, fictional characters, or places pictured in photographs. *Ages:* 2-0 through 12-5.
Arithmetic	Measures the child's ability to demonstrate knowledge of numbers, mathematical concepts, counting and computing skills, and other school-type abilities. *Ages:* 3-0 through 12-5.
Riddles	Measures the child's ability to name the concrete or abstract object or idea from a list of characteristics. *Ages:* 3-0 through 12-5.
Reading/Decoding	Measures the child's ability to identify letters and reading of words. *Ages:* 5-0 through 12-5.
Reading/Understanding	Measures reading comprehension by how well the child responds to commands given in sentences. *Ages:* 7-0 through 12-5.

For example, the *sequential* score demonstrates a median reliability of .89 for all age groups. Achievement subtest reliability coefficients range from .91 to .97.

Construct validity of the K–ABC was evaluated using factor analysis to determine if the expected two-factor structure (simultaneous and sequential) emerged. Such factors appeared at every age group for the standardization sample, providing one piece of evidence for the construct validity of the K–ABC. The convergent validity of the K–ABC is revealed in a correlation between the MPC and WISC–R Full Scale of .70 ($n = 182$) and .61 with the Stanford–Binet IQ ($n = 121$). In addition, considerable effort has gone into minimizing bias in the test, using some of the procedures outlined in Chapter 14.

Evaluation. The K–ABC provides an articulated and up-to-date theoretical foundation, as well as completely separate Intelligence and Achievement scales. It provides a fairer assessment of preschoolers, minority children, and various exceptional populations, in part because of the colorful items and in part because of the Non-Verbal scale. The 1980 census-based norm sample is excellent. However, the reliability of the sequential tasks is a bit low. High verbal children are not rewarded with exceptionally high scores as they are in most other IQ tests. In general, the K–ABC is a promising alternative to some of the more classic IQ tests, particularly with its construct validity orientation.

Summary

In this chapter, we have traced the arduous changes that have been wrought on the construct of intelligence. Explorations of the factor structure of intelligence provided a base on which it was possible to begin consideration of the construct of intelligence from a scientific perspective. A case history in the problems inherent in measurement without definition was highlighted in the context of the Jensen debate. Issues of misinterpretation and data fudging were noted, with a clear movement away from IQ tests being shown in the 1970s. Reactions to this change, particularly by incorporating emerging cognitive theory, were then documented.

As the testing enterprise enters the mid-1990s, it seems clear that the cognitive "revolution" will continue to have a profound effect. Our reviews of Robert Sternberg's triarchic theory of intelligence, a cognitive approach to the Raven, and the K–ABC begin to provide a sense of the directions that the field will take. When you take this course in assessment 15 years from now (which I'm sure you are already lining up to do), you will undoubtedly find an enhanced degree of cognitivization of the enterprise. This is a natural outcome of the current developments in psychology in general and the testing field in particular. It anticipates the manner in which the enterprise will accommodate the cognitive shift that is so prominent in mainstream psychology. We can look forward to an increasing dialog between the cognitive sciences and the testing enterprise as a major factor in the future directions of the measurement field.

Glossary

Achievement scale   A score based on a series of subtests from the Kaufman Assessment Battery for Children that provides an index of the child's current level of acquired knowledge.

BETTERAVEN   A computer simulation of performance on the Raven Progressive Matrices, designed to explain the performance of superior college students taking the test.

bottom-up strategy   An approach to establishing the construct validity of a test by examining carefully what an extant test measures and attempting to develop a post hoc theoretical explanation of test performance.

boundary condition   The limit of meaning and applicability associated with a given theoretical term. In this chapter, the failure to specify boundary conditions for intelligence was argued to be instrumental in the Jensen controversy.

Burt, Cyril   A British psychologist who was a strong proponent of the univariate view of intelligence and its genetic characteristics. His twin data purporting to demonstrate high heritability of intelligence was found to be fraudulent in the mid-1970s.

cognitive psychology   The study of processes associated with human thinking that has emerged as the major activity of experimental research psychology since the mid-1960s.

cognitive "revolution"   A major change in thinking in psychology that framed the individual as an active, hypothesis-testing agent, rather than as a passive recipient. This "revolution" continues to pose a challenge to contemporary discussions of IQ tests and intelligence.

compensatory education program   A school program intended to provide extra opportunities and help for individuals from disadvantaged environments. There were a large number of such programs (for example, Head Start) started in the 1960s.

components (of intelligence)   The mental processes involved in intellectual performance as articulated in Robert Sternberg's triarchic model of intellect. Subcategories of components are metacomponents, performance, and knowledge-acquisition components. These components act in combination with experiential and contextual aspects to produce specific behaviors.

content   One of three classes of intellectual tasks proposed by J. P. Guilford that relate to the nature of the stimulus in the task. Subclassifications of content are figural, symbolic, semantic, and behavioral.

contextual aspect (of intelligence)   The extent to which specific task characteristics affect the intellectual demands of a cognitive task as articulated in Robert Sternberg's triarchic model of intellect. Factors relating to selection, adaptation, and shaping are involved in this aspect of Sternberg's theory. These components act in combination with experiential and componential aspects to produce specific behaviors.

experiential aspect (of intelligence)   The manner in which intellectual performance varies as a function of practice with a specific intellectual task as articulated in Robert Sternberg's triarchic model of intellect. Novel tasks are performed significantly differently from those for which an automatic process has been learned. These components act in combination with componential and contextual aspects to produce specific behaviors.

FAIRAVEN   A computer simulation of performance on the Raven Progressive Matrices, designed to explain the performance of average college students taking the test.

first-order factor   A factor obtained from the factor analysis of the intercorrelations of specific test scores.

formal link   A connection between terms in a nomological network that is mathematized.

genotype   The genetic representation of a specific individual.

Guilford, J. P.   An American psychologist and factor analyst who developed the structure of intellect model that implied there were 120 different intelligences.

heritability (H)   The correlation between the phenotype and genotype of a given characteristic. High values of H were thought to indicate that the genetic component of the characteristic is very high and that environmental treatments can have little effect. This concept is not particularly popular now.

hierarchical model   A theory of intellect that postulates varying levels of generality, with g at the top and specific tasks at the bottom. Higher-order factor analytic models are examples.

higher-order factor analysis   Factor-analyzing the factors from a previous analysis in order to discover more general (higher-order) factors associated with the original analysis.

information processing   One of the approaches associated with cognitive psychology that examines the various transformations of information occurring between the activation of the organism by an external event and the eventual behavior.

interactionism   A theoretical position indicating that emphasis ought to be placed on the manner in which two characteristics work together to produce specific effects rather than focusing on the two characteristics separately. An interactional position has been suggested as a solution to the nature/nurture dilemma.

Jensen, Arthur   An American educational psychologist who became embroiled in the nature/nurture controversy around 1969 with the publication of his "boosting IQ" paper. He also has made many positive contributions to the testing enterprise, such as his work on test bias.

Jensenism   From the Jensen controversy, a synonym for *racism*.

Kaufman Assessment Battery for Children (K–ABC)   A 1983 IQ test based on the distinction between simultaneous and sequential cognitive processes. It is intended for children between the ages of 2 ½ years and 12 ½ years.

knowledge-acquisition component   The aspect of intelligence responsible for gathering information from the environment, as articulated in Robert Sternberg's triarchic model of intellect.

level II learning   The categories of learning that are picked up in classic IQ tests, with special emphasis on verbal skills. Jensen used this term in his "boosting IQ" paper.

main effect   A term from the analysis of variance that relates to the proportion of variance that can be attributed to an experimental factor in and of itself. It contrasts with interactions, which consider the joint or combined effects of variables.

Mental Processing Composite (MPC)   The estimate of general intelligence provided by the Kaufman Assessment Battery for Children.

metacomponent   The aspect of intelligence responsible for selecting the strategy to be used in the solution of a specific task, as articulated in Robert Sternberg's triarchic model of intellect.

multiple intelligences   A term coined by Howard Gardner to describe his nonfactor analytic model of the structure of intelligence that suggested the existence of six relatively independent intelligences.

Non-Verbal scale   A composite score from the Kaufman Assessment Battery for Children that provides an intelligence estimate for hearing-impaired and limited English–proficient children.

oblique rotation   A rotation in factor analysis that does not require the axes to be perpendicular to each other. Generally, it is necessary to perform oblique (rather than orthogonal) rotations to conduct higher-order factor analyses.

operations   One of three classes of intellectual tasks proposed by J. P. Guilford that related to the processes involved in task performance. Subcategories of operations are cognition, memory, divergent thinking, convergent thinking, and evaluations.

orthogonal   A technical term relating to the placement of axes in a two-dimensional factor space perpendicular to each other. Such axis placement implies that the factors are thought to be uncorrelated with or independent of each other.

performance component   The aspect of intelligence related to the execution of specific plans and strategies, as articulated in Robert Sternberg's triarchic model of intellect.

phenotype   The specific, outward manifestation of a specific genotype.

practical intelligence   From Robert Sternberg's view, involving everyday "street smarts" in adapting successfully to a given context.

primary construct   A first-order theoretical term that is connected directly to the observational plane with a correspondence rule (which is usually a psychological test in this chapter).

products   One of three classes of intellectual tasks proposed by J. P. Guilford that related to the nature of the output unit demanded of the task. Subcategories of products are units, classes, relations, systems, transformations, and implications.

range of reaction The variability expected in the manner in which an individual genotype will develop. It cannot be predicted in advance and varies across genotypes, thus calling into question any simple inferences from notions such as heritability.

readiness The preparedness of an individual to grasp more complex ideas. Seen as an important component of what classic IQ tests measure.

scholastic achievement The demonstrated performance in school-related tasks.

scholastic aptitude The ability or capacity to perform school-related tasks. Found to be the best descriptor of what classical IQ tests measure.

second-order factor A factor obtained from the higher-order factor analysis of first-order factors.

sequential task A task requiring that input be arranged into specific orders. Typically timed, such a task represents one class of subtests on the Kaufman Assessment Battery for Children.

simultaneous task A task requiring the synthesis of information and implies the ability to examine all the information concurrently. This is one class of subtests on the Kaufman Assessment Battery for Children.

socioeconomic status An index of the quality of the environment in which an individual lives, based on various economic indicators such as family income and education received.

speed selection The skill in knowing when to be fast and when to be slow and careful in executing intellectual tasks. Speed selection is an example of Robert Sternberg's metacomponents.

Sternberg Multidimensional Abilities Test (SMAT) A test based on Robert Sternberg's triarchic theory of intellect and currently under development.

Sternberg, Robert An American psychologist who, among other things, developed the triarchic theory of intelligence.

strong link A connection between terms in a nomological network that is mathematized or at least highly formalized.

structure of intellect model J. P. Guilford's three-dimensional model of intellect that focuses on the content, operation, and product of intellectual tasks. Derived from factor analytic studies, this model suggests the need for 120 different measures to capture the totality of human intelligence.

sudden learner An individual who shows abrupt transitions in the grasp and understanding of various materials. Seen to be characteristic of high scorers on IQ tests.

third-order factor A factor derived from the higher-order factor analysis of a set of second-order factors.

top-down strategy An approach to establishing the construct validity of a test by first elaborating a theory of intellect and then developing a test to reflect this theory.

triarchic theory of intelligence Robert Sternberg's cognitively oriented theory of intellect that suggests human intellectual performance is based on componential, experiential, and contextual factors.

Vernon, Philip E.   A British (then Canadian) psychologist who developed extensive hierarchical models of intelligence.

weak logical link   A connection between theoretical terms in a nomological network that is loosely and verbally formulated. Clear and mathematical links are said to be strong, or formal, links.

Suggested Further Reading

Gould, S. J. (1981). *The mismeasure of man*. New York: Norton.

This book contains much background that is helpful in understanding the idea of higher-order factor analysis (see especially Chapter 6), as well as some commentary on both the Burt and Jensen incidents. This book is highly critical of the psychometric tradition, showing several other "skeletons in the testers' closet" as well.

Guilford, J. P. (1967). *The nature of human intelligence*. New York: McGraw-Hill.

This is the best primary source for gaining a more detailed sense of Guilford's structure of intellect model. In this volume, you will find a considerable amount of detail about the empirical studies and factor analyses that led to the emergence of Guilford's model.

Jensen, A. R. (1969). How much can we boost IQ and scholastic achievement? *Harvard Educational Review, 39*, 1–123.

I have done my best to provide a fair summary of this controversial paper in the chapter. However, if you are intending to discuss the paper in any context, you should go back and read the original.

Matarazzo, J. D. (1972). *Wechsler's measurement and appraisal of adult intelligence* (5th ed.). Baltimore: Williams & Wilkins.

This very thorough volume contains all kinds of information related to the correlates of IQ-test scores in the adult population. It is an invaluable source of information about the WAIS, providing considerably more detail about the meanings of WAIS scores than could be presented in this chapter.

Scarr-Salapatek, S. (1976). Unknowns in the IQ equation. In N. J. Block & G. Dworkin (Eds.), *The IQ controversy: Critical readings*. New York: Pantheon.

This article contains an extensive collection of critical discussions of the nature/ nurture controversy. It is exceedingly important reading for anyone who wants to move beyond the level of analysis presented in this chapter.

Sternberg, R. J. (1988). *The triarchic mind: A new theory of human intelligence*. New York: Viking.

This is the best introduction and elaboration to Sternberg's theory. It is a good read and communicates a great sense of the dynamic nature of his model.

Discussion Questions

1. Outline the manner in which construct validity sounded the death knell of measurement without definition in the domain of intelligence.

2. Discuss whether or not the bottom-up validation studies provide any justification whatsoever for using IQ tests such as the WISC outside of educational contexts.

3. You are teaching an introductory course in testing and want to caution students against making inferences about individuals from group-based correlations. Briefly outline the arguments that you would use.

4. Critically evaluate the use of a bottom-up strategy to gain an understanding of intelligence as measured by the Stanford–Binet.

5. Derive a hypothetical higher-order factor analysis of the Personality Research Form (see Chapter 13).

6. Draw the hierarchical model of intellect that is presumed to exist in the Wechsler series of IQ tests.

7. Locate the following tests in J. P. Guilford's cubic structure of intellect model: (a) MMPI, (b) Rorschach Inkblot Test, (c) the Army Alpha, (d) SVIB, and (e) a multiple-choice exam given in this course.

8. Discuss how Guilford's idea of divergent thinking adds a new dimension to the concept of intelligence.

9. Discuss the extent to which you feel Guilford was out of line to suggest 120 different intelligences and then not provide 120 tests to assess them.

10. If you have studied the developmental psychology of Jean Piaget, discuss the possible relationships between this view and that of Guilford.

11. Critically evaluate Royce's contention that factors are the best possible means of developing nomological networks.

12. Which approach to the structure of intelligence, Gardner's or Guilford's, do you think is the best? Why?

13. Discuss whether you think that a heritability of .77 suggests that the environmental component of intelligence is minimal.

14. With reference to the Arthur Jensen affair, critically evaluate the idea of measurement without definition.

15. In the text it was suggested that Jensen was on a slippery slope and that once he bought in to the testing enterprise it was not unreasonable for him to end up where he did. Starting with Thomas Reid's commonsense psychology, draw an historical chart that documents the nature of this slippery slope.

16. Prepare an argument to reject the assertion in the text that Jensen made mistakes regarding the convergent validity of the IQ tests used to generate indexes of heritability.

17. Indicate how you might develop a reasonable measure of intellectual *change* that would have been an improvement over the one used by Jensen. How would you demonstrate the reliability of this measure?

18. Outline the substance of the range of reaction criticism of Jensen's arguments. Discuss whether you agree with the chapter that this is a highly devastating argument for Jensen's position.

19. Write an unbiased summary of the Cyril Burt affair.

20. Outline the major differences between the Terman/Yerkes vision of IQ tests and the contemporary one.

21. List and briefly describe all the trilogies in Robert Sternberg's theory.

22. It can be argued that knowing when to delve into detail is an important part of being intelligent. Indicate how this idea might be integrated into Sternberg's triarchic theory.

23. Discuss in Sternberg's terms the act of developing an historical dramatic screenplay for TV.

24. From your own experience, indicate the effects of automatization in the acquisition of a specific skill.

25. With reference to two people who you know, differentiate between the componential and practical aspects of intellect per Sternberg's theory.

26. Compare and contrast the strengths and weaknesses of Guilford's and Sternberg's vision of intellect.

27. Develop a new set of rules for solving the Raven Progressive Matrices that assume vertical rather than horizontal processing.

28. To what extent do you think that the kinds of computer simulation demonstrated for the Raven will eventually produce viable theories of individual differences?

29. Evaluate the similarities of the (implied) theoretical model underlying the WISC and the explicit one provided for the K–ABC.

30. Which of the three cognitive applications presented in the chapter (Sternberg, the Raven simulations, or the K–ABC) do you think will have the greatest positive influence in making social decisions. Why?

Chapter 16

Testing Personality
Normal and Abnormal

DÉJÀ VU ALL OVER AGAIN

The concept of personality has surfaced in a number of different places in our narrative treatment of the testing enterprise. In the early years, personality was thought to involve all nonintellective factors that contributed to individual differences. Types of people, body builds, physiological characteristics, habitual ways of reacting to the environment, character traits, and a wide variety of other individual variables have, at varying times, been considered to be part of personality. Over time, the definition of this complex construct has gone through a number of transformations, with the current view being that **personality** reflects the stable factors that make a person's behavior consistent from one time to another or different from the behavior other people would manifest in comparable situations. Personality is typically thought of as *stable* over time—yet it may change over the long term, and a person may well behave differently in different situations. Personality, then, refers to long-lasting and important characteristics of an individual that exert a strong influence on behavior.

One of the traditional units of analysis in the domain is a **trait**, defined as the predisposition to respond in a particular way to persons, objects, or situations. At root this conception assumes that consistencies in behavior are due to some entity, or trait, that resides *inside* the individual. By this view, measurement of a person's status on these various variables, or traits, constitutes an important key to understanding personality.

Starting with Robert Woodworth's invention of the structured personality inventory, work in this field has played a significant part in the story of testing. Figure 16-1 presents an overview of the major domains of work that have been treated thus far in the text. Structured approaches such as the Minnesota Multiphasic Personality Inventory (MMPI) and Personality Research Form (PRF) can readily be contrasted with unstructured, projective techniques such as the

Figure 16-1 An outline of the emergence of personality assessment as revealed in the earlier chapters of *The Enterprise.*

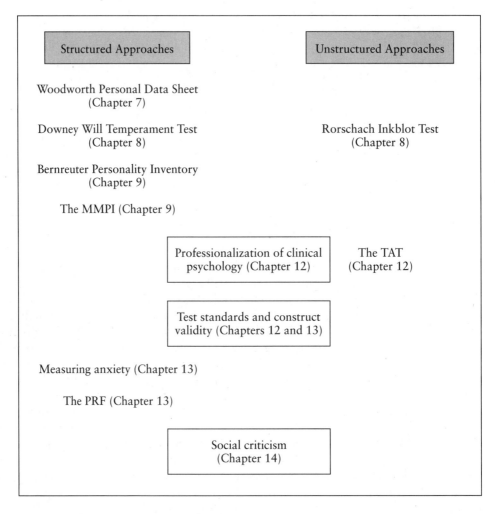

Rorschach and Thematic Aperception Test (TAT). In addition, several important developments in the general testing enterprise have also been noted in this figure, such as the movement toward professionalization, the introduction of construct validity, and the emergence of considerable social criticism.

The topics shown in Figure 16-1 have been highly selected from among many other possibilities, to demonstrate specific points about the emerging testing enterprise. As such, they do not represent a complete historical overview of the field of personality. Indeed, tremendous numbers of tests have been published during this time frame, and only a very small number of these have been mentioned. It would take a text easily as large as this one just to present descriptions of all these tests! As well, a wide range of theoretical analyses of personality have been presented. The variety of such theories is hard to communicate because almost every idea known to humanity has been applied to try to make sense of individual differences in personality. Finally, a whole collection of methods associated with the measurement of personality has evolved. It has been an active (and sometimes controversial) field of inquiry since its introduction during World War I.

One of the more intriguing observations is the surprising similarity between the stories associated with this domain and intelligence. The sameness of the plot lines of these two stories is almost scary—creating a definite sense of déjà vu. Like intelligence, early British researchers in personality determined to develop models with minimal numbers of constructs. The work of Hans Eysenck and the three-scale inventory he developed is a clear example of this orientation. North American personality researchers, on the other hand, seemed bent on breaking down the domain into a large number of facets—harkening back to Thurstone's program in intelligence. The work of factor analytic pioneer Raymond Cattell[1] and his inventory of 20 scales is a clear example of this perspective. Since then, again mirroring the work in intelligence, considerable research has been oriented toward the development of hierarchical models of personality where the differing number of proposed personality constructs is a function of the level of entry in the hierarchy. Research documenting the so-called Big Five dimensions of personality and the inventory it has inspired instantiates this point. Again ringing with familiarity, critical appraisals of personality, such as that of Walter Mischel, forced significant changes to theory and practice in the personality domain. Finally, as if to ensure the near identical nature of these two plot lines, a considerable amount of work has been done in the attempt to develop a cognitive basis for aspects of personality. Some of these are also reviewed in this chapter. In all, the narratives of intelligence and personality appear to share a common plot line. Given that personality and the constructs evoked to describe it are radically different from intelligence, this turn of events is somewhat surprising.

For us, though, the similarity of the two stories provides a useful way of approaching the study of the complex domain of personality. We already have the skeleton of our story in place—all we have to do now is to fill in some of the details. Let's now turn to this task.

---

[1] Raymond B. and James McKeen Cattell are not related to each other. For the remainder of this chapter, all references to Cattell will be to R. B. However, mentions of either of these psychologists later on will always be prefaced by their initials.

THE BRITISH FACTOR ANALYTIC TRADITION

The domain of personality, because of its incredible complexity, was a natural place to apply the techniques of factor analysis. By intercorrelating empirical test data and conducting appropriate factor analyses, discovering the fundamental dimensions or traits that underlie the human personality should be possible. To illustrate the British orientation to this problem, we will examine the program of **Hans Eysenck** who began his research into personality in the mid-1940s and continued to develop his position into the early 1990s. This research culminated in the publication of the Eysenck Personality Questionnaire in 1975.

Hans Eysenck's Theory of Personality

Hans Eysenck's approach to personality was highly theory-driven. He began with a consideration of the classical typologies of people that appeared across a wide variety of intellectual traditions. One such view was presented earlier—namely, Galen's typology, which suggested four types of people: melancholic, choleric, sanguine, and phlegmatic (see Table 3-1). Eysenck took such positions and added the assumption that it was more effective to think in terms of dimensions underlying these types rather than considering types per se. People could be located anywhere along a dimension rather than being restricted to the all-or-none concept of types. Eysenck's idea was to use factor analysis to isolate the best dimensions for use in describing the classical typologies as well as personality in general.

In his early work, Eysenck thought that only two factors were necessary to capture the essence of personality. The first related to **introversion/extraversion,** a dimension drawn for Jung's classical distinction. Extreme extraverts focus their energy outward and are sociable people who thrive on human company and seek out exciting activities. They are traditionally described as restless, optimistic, and impulsive. Extreme introverts, on the other hand, focus their energies inward and prefer the company of books or computers to people. They are often described by adjectives such as orderly, serious, and restrained.

Eysenck's second dimension was called **neuroticism/stability.** A person high on neuroticism would show a variety of somatic and interpersonal difficulties associated with tension and anxiety. The normal, or stable, person would not show these characteristics.

An example of how this dimensional characterization of personality encompasses the typological considerations of earlier views is demonstrated in Figure 16-2, which indicates the manner in which Eysenck's two dimensions describe Galen's four types. As well, descriptors of individuals falling in various places in Eysenck's two-dimensional space are included in the figure.

Inward (introverted) people who are high on the neurotic dimension would fall into Galen's melancholic type, whereas stable extraverts would be classified as sanguine. Those who direct their emotional responses outward (choleric types) would be high on extraversion and neuroticism, whereas seemingly distant, emotionally cold persons (phlegmatic types) would be stable introverts.

Figure 16-2 The manner in which Eysenck's proposed dimensions of personality encompass Galen's earlier typological view.

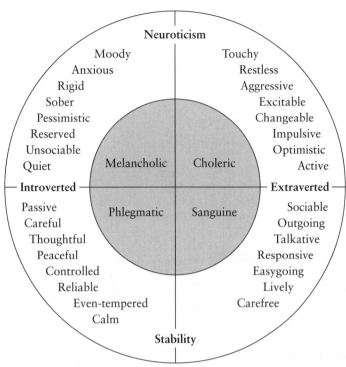

In his earlier work, Eysenck tested this theoretical idea using abnormal patients. He gathered 39 personality and demographic ratings from 700 patients in a military hospital and factored them (Eysenck, 1944). He found two main factors to underlie the intercorrelations of these ratings and was able to identify these as neuroticism/stability and introversion/extraversion. Some of the rating scales that loaded highly on the neuroticism factor were badly organized personality, dependence, and low-energy level. The other factor was clearly bipolar, with the introversion factor showing high loadings for ratings such as anxiety, depression, obsessional tendencies, and degraded work history. The neuroticism factor was associated with severity of a person's illness, whereas the introversion factor distinguished between two major forms of neurosis: anxiety (high introverts) and hysteria (high extraverts).

Eysenck then had psychiatrists rate the disorders of the patients and determined if his factors matched their judgments. The factors matched, and Eysenck had one of a large number of pieces of evidence to support the validity of his two-factor structure. Since then he has extended the samples involved and replicated these findings in a wide range of situations (for a review, see Eysenck & Eysenck, 1985).

One aspect of personality, however, was missing—namely, the characterization of persons who were suffering from the more severe mental illnesses associated with psychoses. In his desire to include this component of individual differences,

Figure 16-3 Eysenck's three-dimensional factor space.

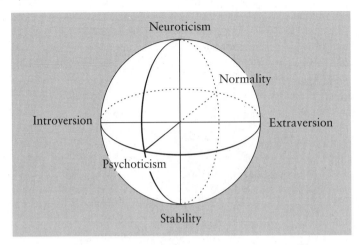

Eysenck added a third dimension to his factor structure called **psychoticism/normality** (Eysenck & Eysenck, 1968). High scorers on the psychoticism dimension had not necessarily experienced a psychotic episode but were predisposed toward such catastrophic breakdowns. Like the earlier work, large numbers of empirical research and factor analytic studies were offered in support of this third factor.

The third factor was added to the earlier structure to suggest that personality could be adequately described in the three-dimensional space shown in Figure 16-3. In this case, the third factor (psychoticism) can be thought of as coming out from the page, being at right angles to the older dimensions.

Like his theory, the tests that Eysenck has developed have shown some sequential growth. One of the first attempts, the **Eysenck Personality Inventory (EPI)**, included only measures of neuroticism and extraversion/introversion. Eysenck and Eysenck (1975) added the psychoticism dimension, and this revised instrument has become known as the **Eysenck Personality Questionnaire (EPQ)**. The following Close Up provides some details of this test.

CLOSE UP   The Eysenck Personality Questionnaire

There are two versions of the EPQ—one designed for persons age 16 and up and another, called the **Junior EPQ**, that is suitable for children from age 7 through 15. Both versions of the EPQ provide measures of Eysenck's three major factors of personality: Psychoticism (P), Extraversion (E), and Neuroticism (N). In addition, a Lie (L) scale is used to assess the validity of a respondent's answers. It contains 90 items formatted as second-person questions that are answered either yes or no. Table 16-1 presents several items of the type found on the various EPQ scales.

Psychoticism. Persons who score high on P are aggressive, hostile, and impulsive; show a preference for unusual things; and are poor at showing empathy. Persons with a predisposition toward schizophrenia and those demonstrating antisocial personalities often score highly on this scale. Low scorers demonstrate empathy and interpersonal sensitivity.

Table 16-1
Items of the type found on the Eysenck Personality Questionnaire

---

Psychoticism	1. Would being in debt worry you?*
	2. Do you believe that insurance schemes are a good idea?*
	3. Do you prefer to go your own way rather than act by the rules?
	4. Do good manners and cleanliness matter much to you?*
	5. Do you enjoy cooperating with others?*
Extraversion	6. Are you rather lively?
	7. Do you enjoy meeting new people?
	8. Do you like going out a lot?
	9. Would you call yourself happy-go-lucky?
	10. Are you mostly quiet when you are with other people?*
Neuroticism	11. Does your mood often go up and down?
	12. Do you feel "just miserable" for no reason?
	13. Are you an irritable person?
	14. Do you often feel "fed-up"?
	15. Are you often troubled about feelings of guilt?

---

*Signifies no-keyed items, in which a no response is interpreted as a sign of possessing the factor to which the scale belongs. All of the remaining items are yes-keyed.

Extraversion/Introversion. High scorers on the E scale are described as loud, gregarious, outgoing, and fun-loving. Of a high E scorer, the authors say

> The typical extravert is sociable, likes parties, has many friends, needs to have people to talk to, and does not like reading or studying by himself. He craves excitement, takes chances, often sticks his neck out, acts on the spur of the moment, and is generally an impulsive individual.

Low scorers on the E scale show preference for solitude and quiet activities and are generally inward:

> The typical introvert is a quiet, retiring sort of person, introspective, fond of books rather than people, he is reserved and distant except to intimate friends. He tends to plan ahead, "looks before he leaps," and mistrusts the impulse of the moment.

Neuroticism. Emotionality is the essential nature of the N scale. This can range from nervous, maladjusted, and over-emotional for high scorers through to stable and confident for low scorers.

Psychometric properties. EPQ reliability is good. For example, 1-month test/retest correlations are .78, .89, .86, and .84 for the P, E, N, and L scales, respectively. Internal consistency reliability estimates are in the .80s for the three major scales.

A wide variety of validation studies have been reported in the literature (for a review, see Aiken, 1988). For example, it has been found that introverts are more vigilant in watch keeping and tend to perform better in signal attention tasks that involved paying attention for extended periods of time. They are also less tolerant of pain. Extraverts are more readily conditioned using stimuli associated with sexual arousal and demonstrate a greater need for external stimulation. Indeed, the construct validity of the EPQ is impressive, given the life-long research enterprise on which it is based (see Friedman, 1987, for a review). A particularly noteworthy feature of the constructs underlying Eysenck's tests is the amount of effort that has gone into attempting to relate the three variables to physiological and biological processes, indicating a definite effort to map personality into the physical structures that support it (see Hampson, 1988, pp. 53–58, for a brief introduction to this aspect of Eysenck's work).

The overall technical quality of the EPQ is good, comparing favorably to most other personality inventories. The extensive construct validity of the inventory is also one of its strongest points. Interestingly, the EPQ has not gained a great deal of acceptance in North America because of the preference for inventories that provide a greater variety of measures (such as the MMPI).

THE AMERICAN TRADITION

Factor analysis was used somewhat differently in the North American tradition, at least initially. Many of the early adaptations of this technique in America were concerned with generating inclusive taxonomies that would "cover the waterfront" of the entire domain of personality. Because of this, a number of researchers proposed that personality consisted of large numbers of dimensions. The factor analytic program of **Raymond B. Cattell,** an American personality theorist, resulted in the development of the **Sixteen Personality Factor Questionnaire** (**16PF**), which was originally published in 1949 but was revised and fine-tuned well into the 1970s. Besides demonstrating the American approach to personality structure, Cattell's work also reveals an important interaction between theoretical and empirical concerns, which lies at the heart of the notion of construct validity.

Raymond Cattell's Personality Theory

Cattell started out with a relatively atheoretical approach to the study of personality. He chose to use factor analysis, initially at least, in an exploratory fashion to discover what the factors underlying personality actually were. The final result of his work was a personality structure involving as many as 20 traits and a wide range of other characteristics such as motivation, emotion, and learning.

Because Cattell wanted to map out the entire domain of personality, he was very careful to be as inclusive as possible in the selection of items and constructs for factoring. He started considering the entire domain of English-language words that could be used to describe people. This lexicon numbers over 18,000 entries (see Allport & Oldbert, 1936). By carefully examining this list, removing redundant entries, and including only those used exclusively to describe people, 160 trait terms were finally selected. In addition, he added 11 other traits from the psychological literature, for a total of 171 terms that were thought to cover the area of personality in the English language.

To make this list workable, Cattell further reduced it by examining the research literature. If previous research studies showed that some of the 171 terms tended to be correlated in rating studies, he grouped them into clusters. He then selected a single term to represent the cluster. He finally ended up with 35 terms, which he felt encompassed personality.

Cattell then assembled groups of people (up to a maximum number of 16 persons) who knew each other well. Each member of the group rated each other member on the 35 characteristics. During this process, respondents were forced to distribute their ratings over the entire rating scale. Cattell called the ratings **Life (L) data**. The ratings were then intercorrelated and factored. In a number of such studies somewhere in the vicinity of 16 factors emerged; Table 16-2 lists 15 of the more consistent.[2] When it came to labeling the factors, Cattell often invented words rather than using self-explanatory terms. The rationale here was that he did not want to confuse these factors, what he called **source traits**, with the more common characteristics existing in day-to-day language. Source traits are the stable but less visible antecedents of behavior that can be found only by the application of factor analytic technology.

Table 16-2 Factors found in Q and L data

Factor	Description	Data Source	
A	Sizia (reserved) versus Affectia (outgoing)	L	Q
B	Intelligence	L	Q
C	Dissatisfied emotionality versus Ego-strength	L	Q
D	Excitability	L	
E	Submissiveness versus Dominance	L	Q
F	Desurgency versus Surgency	L	Q
G	Superego	L	Q
H	Threctia (shy) versus Parmia (adventurous)	L	Q
I	Harria (tough-minded) versus Premsia (tender-minded)	L	Q
J	Zeppia (zestful) versus Coasthemia (individualistic)	L	
K	Boorishness versus Mature socialization	L	
L	Alexia (trusting) versus Protension (suspicious)	L	Q
M	Praxernia (practical) versus Autia (unconventional)	L	Q
N	Natural forthrightness versus Shrewdness	L	Q
O	Self-confident versus Guilt-prone	L	Q
P	Sanguine casualness		Q
Q1	Conservatism versus Radicalism		Q
Q2	Group dependency versus Self-sufficiency		Q
Q3	Strength of self-sentiment		Q
Q4	Ergic tension		Q

SOURCE: Cattell & Kline (1977, pp. 112–119).

---

[2]The differences in number of factors between Cattell and Eysenck relate to the judgment calls (see Chapter 10) that each researcher made in performing their factor analyses. Differences between the two included issues of how many factors to extract, the proportions of variance that were to be accounted for, the kinds of rotation employed (orthogonal versus oblique), and the content addressed by the items.

To explicate the obtained structure, Cattell then turned to questionnaire approaches, which he called **Questionnaire (Q) data**, to differentiate them from the ratings (L data). Using a wide variety of subjects and item pools, Cattell found that 17 factors were associated with Q data. Table 16-2 lists these factors as Q indicated as the data source. There is significant overlap between the factors derived from the L and Q data.

Cattell developed his theory beyond the chronicling of the structure of personality revealed in Table 16-2. He provided some interesting analyses of motivation and the manner in which it interacts with various goals and environmental events. In the final analysis, based on his factor analytic model, Cattell provided a very rich and comprehensive theory of personality. In addition, he developed an important personality test to provide accessible measures of his various dimensions of personality. This test, the 16PF is the subject of the following Close Up.

CLOSE UP   **The Sixteen Personality Factor Questionnaire**

The 16PF is a personality test intended for high school seniors and adults. It provides measures of the most central constructs identified by Cattell's extensive factor analytic work. The test employs a forced-choice format. Each item contains a declarative stem, and the respondent must select one alternative. Several 16PF-like items are

1. I make decisions based on
   a. Feelings.
   b. Feelings and reason equally.
   c. Reason.
2. Which of the following items is different from the others?
   a. Candle
   b. Star
   c. Light bulb
3. I find it hard to give a speech to strangers.
   a. Yes
   b. Somewhat
   c. No

Notice that the second hypothetical item resembles questions from an intelligence test, indicating Cattell's contention that personality and intellect interact with each other. Indeed, factor B in Cattell's model is intelligence.

Five forms of the 16PF contain between 105 and 187 items. Forms A through D involve three alternative questions (like the ones presented above), whereas Form E has only two alternatives. The major difference between the forms is the reading level required to answer the questionnaire (grades 3 through 7). Any of the forms can be completed in under an hour.

The test yields 16 scores reflecting Cattell's research and the Q-data factors shown in Table 16-2. An additional four indexes provide estimates of second-order factors that Cattell has identified in his research. In total, the inventory provides 20 scores. Table 16-3 lists these, and more easily understood terms replace Cattell's more esoteric names.

The 16PF is a very popular instrument used extensively for vocational guidance. The availability of a mail-in computer scoring and interpretation system is an important reason for this. The report generated is extensive, including a capsule personality description, several score profiles, and summaries of clinical signs, cognitive factors, and need patterns.

Table 16-3
The 20 scales of the Sixteen Personality Factor Questionnaire

Scale Name	Low Scorer	High Scorer
Basic Scales		
Warmth (Factor A)	Reserved, detached, cool, impersonal	Warm, outgoing, likes people
Intelligence (Factor B)	Concrete thinking	Abstract thinking
Emotional Stability (Factor C)	Emotionally less stable, changeable	Emotionally stable, calm, mature
Dominance (Factor E)	Submissive, conforming, mild	Dominant, assertive, competitive
Impulsivity (Factor F)	Serious, prudent, sober taciturn	Enthusiastic, cheerful, heedless
Conformity (Factor G)	Expedient, disregards rules	Conforming, persevering, moralistic
Boldness (Factor H)	Shy, timid, restrained	Bold, uninhibited, spontaneous
Sensitivity (Factor I)	Tough-minded, self-reliant	Tender-minded, sensitive
Suspiciousness (Factor L)	Trusting, adaptable	Suspicious, hard to fool, opinionated
Imagination (Factor M)	Practical, conventional	Impractical, absentminded, unconventional
Shrewdness (Factor N)	Forthright, genuine, unpretentious	Calculating, polished, socially alert
Insecurity (Factor O)	Confident, self-satisfied, secure	Self-blaming, worrying, troubled
Radicalism (Factor Q1)	Conservative, resisting change	Liberal, analytical, innovative
Self-Sufficiency (Factor Q2)	Group-oriented, sociable	Resourceful, self-sufficient
Self-Discipline (Factor Q3)	Undisciplined, impulsive	Compulsive, socially precise
Tension (Factor Q4)	Relaxed, tranquil, low drive	Frustrated, driven, tense

continued

Table 16-3

The 20 scales of the Sixteen Personality Factor Questionnaire *(continued)*

Scale Name	Low Scorer	High Scorer
Second-Order Scales		
Extraversion (Factor QI)	Introversion	Extraversion
Anxiety (Factor QII)	Low anxiety	High anxiety
Tough Poise (Factor QIII)	Sensitivity, emotionalism	Tough poise
Independence (Factor QIV)	Dependence	Independence

Psychometric characteristics. The norm group for the 16PF is not particularly good, being based on data collected in 1970. However, Form E (the most recent) has a more representative norming sample.

Reliabilities are not as high as desirable because each score is based on relatively few items. This is inevitable because there are so many scores to be generated. Split-half reliabilities as low as .54 for the 16 first-order scores have been reported. Test/retest reliabilities for same- or next-day administration range between .70 and .80 but drop off substantially with longer intertest intervals.

The majority of the validity evidence available for the 16PF is concerned with demonstrating how the scales relate to the obtained factor structure. In general, this research indicates a good fit. The care taken in sampling the universe of traits indicates that the content validity of the test is good. A wide variety of published studies provides considerable evidence of criterion-related validity (see Cattell, Eber, & Tatsuoka, 1970).

This outline of Cattell's research program and test reveals that factor analysis has been adapted to personality assessment with some success. A particularly noteworthy aspect of this project is the manner in which theoretical concerns were at the forefront of the test development. Cattell used factor analysis in an exploratory mode (at least initially) and was clear in emphasizing the importance of underlying considerations in developing his test.

RECONCILING THE TWO TRADITIONS

We now find ourselves in the uncomfortable position of being told by one researcher that there are three dimensions of personality (Eysenck) and by another that there are at least 20 (Cattell). Who should we believe? Which test, the EPQ or

16PF, should we use? Again, taking the lead from developments in the domain of measuring intelligence, there might be some middle ground here.

The beginning of this reconciliation appeared in the literature as early as 1949. Fiske (1949) factor-analyzed L data from 21 of Cattell's bipolar scales and determined that they could be effectively represented by *five* factors. Because Cattell's scales had been derived from factor analysis originally, Fiske effectively factor-analyzed factors. In other words, he conducted what we earlier called a higher-order factor analysis (see Chapter 15). Finding five second-order factors suggests a kind of hierarchy in personality, not unlike the one noted for intelligence (see Figures 15-1 and 15-2). These factors, of course, were not the same as the ones suggested in Chapter 15, but they did conform to the general hierarchical model found in that area. A number of other personality researchers began to find similar results (see Digman, 1990, for a complete review). Indeed, the relatively consistent finding of five factors prompted Goldberg (1981) to coin the term the **Big Five** to reflect the factors that appeared to underlie most domains of personality ratings (L data).

The Nature of the Big Five

Interpretation of Dimension I is the most straightforward of the Big Five because it appears to be similar to Eysenck's Extraversion. It is generally labeled Extraversion/Introversion in the literature. Notice how the hierarchical model has already accommodated aspects of the Eysenckian model. Dimension II is a bipolar factor typically labeled Friendliness/Hostility, although some have called it Agreeableness. Characteristics such as altruism, caring, nurturance, and emotional support are at one pole of this dimension, whereas the other end embraces traits such as hostility, self-centeredness, spitefulness, indifference to others, and jealousy. Dimension III is often labeled Conscientiousness, relating to descriptors such as fussy, tidy, responsible, scrupulous, and persevering on the one pole and careless, undependable, unscrupulous, and fickle on the other. The observed relationship between this dimension and educational achievement (high scorers on Conscientiousness perform well in school) has led some to suggest that this could well reflect a "will to achieve" component of personality. Dimension IV is marked at the one pole as Neuroticism and as Emotionally Stable at the other. Again, we see how the Big Five accommodates Eysenck's model because this sounds very much like his Neuroticism factor. The last dimension of the Big Five is frequently called Intellect in the literature. There seems to be an aspect of capacity to accept new experience and fantasy in this dimension as well, so it is sometimes labeled Openness. These five dimensions appear to capture most of the variability observed when people are asked to rate others (L data).

Although these five dimensions are based on L data, they can be seen as a possible reconciliation of two factor analytic traditions outlined earlier in this chapter. The Big Five accommodate Cattell to the extent that they are higher-order factors based on his original 16 factors. They also encompass Eysenck's model because two of the Big Five are very similar to Eysenck's Extraversion and Neuroticism (Dimensions I and IV, respectively) and several have noted that Psychoticism can be seen as a combination of Dimensions II and III (see Eysenck, 1970). Figure 16-4 demonstrates the basic **hierarchical model** suggested by this research, showing four different levels of abstraction from specific behaviors through to traits as described by the Big Five. The similarity of the structure of this model to those presented in Chapter 15 for intelligence is notable.

Figure 16-4 A hierarchical model for the structure of personality from traits to specific behaviors incorporating the Big Five.

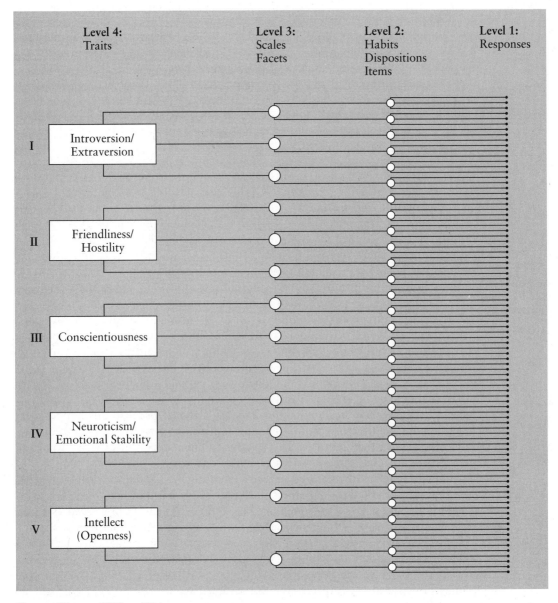

The suggestion that the Big Five might also be useful to describe Q data began to surface in the early 1980s. For example, Birenbaum and Montag (1986) factored the 16PF, along with several other inventories, and obtained a five-factor solution highly reminiscent of the Big Five. Costa and McRae (1985) tackled the problem more directly and actually developed a personality inventory specifically to provide measures of the Big Five. The following Close Up provides some information about this new measurement device.

CLOSE UP | **Measuring the Big Five: The NEO Personality Inventory**

The NEO in the **NEO Personality Inventory (NEO-PI)** is an acronym for three of the "Big Five:" Neuroticism, Extraversion, and Openness. In addition, the authors provide scales to measure Conscientiousness and Agreeableness (their preferred interpretation of Dimension II, often called Friendliness/Hostility). These latter two scales do not provide the level of detail of those captioned in the test name. The test is intended to be a concise measure of the five major dimensions or domains of normal adult personality.

In keeping with the model shown in Figure 16-4 (page 618), total scores for each of the five major dimensions are provided, as well as subscores for six facets thought to underlie the three major traits. This yields the 23 scores, which are listed in Table 16-4.

The inventory consists of 181 items, which are answered using a 5-point Likert format (strongly agree to strongly disagree). Each of the 18 facet scores is based on 8 nonoverlapping items. The total scores for Neuroticism, Extraversion, and Openness, then, are derived from responses to 48 items. The Agreeableness and Conscientiousness scales are based on 18 items each. Item 181 asks respondents to rate how honestly and accurately the items were answered. Initial item construction was based on rational/theoretical considerations, and item selection was directed by internal consistency and factor analytic data (Widiger, 1992).

There are three versions of the NEO-PI: (1) Form S uses self-reports to provide measures of the 23 scales listed in Table 16-4; (2) Form R uses observer ratings to provide the 23 measures; (3) the NEO–FFI (Five Factor Inventory) is an abbreviated, self-report inventory that provides measures on only the Big Five.

Reviewers have noted the following special characteristics of the NEO series:

1. In its search for psychological meaning, the inventory is based on almost 50 years of substantive research, thereby having the potential for good construct validity.
2. The development and validation samples are composed of adult men and women rather than college students or mental patients, thereby enhancing its general applicability.
3. The authors offer data and logical analyses compatible with the view that social desirability does not make test scores ambiguous.
4. Acquiescence is not a problem because all scales contain equal numbers of agree- and disagree-keyed items.
5. Psychometric properties are not compromised by item overlap.

On the other hand, the following shortcomings have been mentioned:

1. Only three of the Big Five scales are fully developed.
2. The representativeness of the normative sample is suspect on a number of fronts (see Hess, 1992; Hogan, 1989).

Table 16-4
Trait and facet scores provided by the
NEO Personality Inventory

Trait (Level 4)
     Facet (Level 3)

Neuroticism (Dimension IV of Big Five)

     Anxiety
     Hostility
     Depression
     Self-Consciousness
     Impulsiveness
     Vulnerability

Extraversion (Dimension I)

     Warmth
     Gregariousness
     Assertiveness
     Activity
     Excitement-Seeking
     Positive Emotions

Openness (Dimension V)

     Fantasy
     Aesthetics
     Feelings
     Actions
     Ideas
     Values

Agreeableness (Dimension II)

Conscientiousness (Dimension III)

---

3. The meaning of the Openness scale is unclear, with it being a mélange of intellect, vulnerability, and culture factors extracted in other factor analytic studies.
4. Because of its newness, validity data for the NEO-PI are not as extensive as would be hoped for in the long run.
5. The NEO-PI does not have adequate validity or dissimulation scales,[3] forcing the user to assume honest responding.

Psychometric characteristics. Internal consistency reliability estimates for the Big Five scales are respectable, being between .86 and .91. These values are a bit lower, in some cases disturbingly so, for the facet scores with a reported range between

---

[3]Item 181 in Forms S and R is a self-report item of honesty in responding. This may provide a warning to the test interpreter, but it is not adequate if the context is such that dishonesty appears appropriate to the respondent. This limits the number of situations in which the test could be used.

.60 and .86. Six-month test/retest reliabilities for the five total scores are decent, being between .86 and .91, and the facet scores show a test/retest reliability range of .66 to .92.

Good convergent and discriminant validity are suggested by the nature of the correlations between the NEO-PI and numerous other tests such as the EPI and MMPI. Correlations between the self-report and rating version, using peers and spouses, are in the range of .50 and .70, showing a very good level of criterion-related validity.

In a sense, the "jury is still out" on the NEO Personality Inventory. It emerges as a promising means of providing numerical estimates of the Big Five. Psychometric characteristics reported to date are generally within acceptable limits, but a wider range of empirical validation would strengthen confidence in this new test.

The Big Five along with its new measure, the NEO-PI, provide researchers and test users with a means of placing individuals within a schema of personality that has a very long history. Here we find a schemata that has more interpretive richness than Eysenck's and less exhaustive detail than Cattell's. As such, it represents a reconciliation between the extreme positions reviewed in the first segment of this chapter. As reflected in Figure 16-4, the structure of this compromise position has much in common with that demonstrated for intelligence in Chapter 15, thus strengthening our observation that the plot lines of the stories of intelligence and personality are similar.

The similarity of the intelligence and personality narratives is enhanced when we discover that the very notion of personality came under strong critical attack. Just like intelligence, a number of important weaknesses in the domain were noted, and the field was forced to make major changes in its conceptualizations and practices because of these. We now turn to these events as they unfolded in personality.

WALTER MISCHEL'S CRITICAL APPRAISAL OF PERSONALITY

The best-known critical analysis of personality was launched by Stanford University psychologist **Walter Mischel** (1968) in his book *Personality and Assessment*. This appraisal had exceedingly important ramifications for the general area of personality, as well as the testing enterprise, resulting in rethinking several very important, foundational ideas. The responses to Mischel's analysis underscore some interesting contemporary work in the domain, particularly the manner in which they relate to the idea of **consistency** in both behavior itself as well as in its relationships to test scores. The points and counterpoints associated with the debate about consistency are chronicled in this section to provide an up-to-date idea of current thinking in the field.

The concept of a trait has much intuitive appeal. To all of us, it seems clear that both our own and other people's behavior is consistent. Our actions, and those of others, appear to be directed in no trivial way by personality characteristics such as achievement, aggression, and extraversion. For example, we can probably all think of a male acquaintance who is boisterous, loud, outspoken, and gregarious in almost every social situation imaginable. Let's call him John. It seems a small jump from our observation of John to invoke the conception of extraversion to describe his behavior. In doing this, we have a useful description or summary of his past actions. But there is more—we can use our knowledge of John's extraverted personality to predict how he will behave in the future. Given a social situation, our extraverted friend will undoubtedly be very active and loud, command considerable attention, and demonstrate the wide variety of other behaviors expected of the extravert (per Figure 16-2). So the concept of a trait offers considerable benefit—it can summarize behavior in an efficient way (for example, John has, in the past, behaved as an extravert) and be used to make some pretty good guesses about what will happen in the future (for example, when John is in a social situation, expect extraverted behavior). By adding a sophisticated measurement technology such as Eysenck's E scale to this mix, trait theory is a highly useful and powerful scientific approach to the study of personality.

Mischel, however, had some severe reservations about this technique of studying persons. His concern was with the *scientific* utility of this approach—was it an effective orientation on which to base a science? Mischel, (1968) set out to examine the scientific track record of the trait approach, and his conclusions were not comforting to those who found traits useful explanatory constructs. He started out by indicating that trait theory focuses on "responses as signs (direct or indirect) of pervasive underlying mental structures" that "assume . . . these underlying inferred dispositions (whether called traits, states, processes, dynamics, motives or labeled in other ways) exert generalized and enduring causal effects on behavior" (p. 8). The trait approach has been dedicated to the search for signs (for example, psychological tests) that are reliable indicators of the hypothetical, underlying dimensions.

Mischel noted one critical factor that must be true in order for trait theory to work; namely, there must be considerable consistency in behavior: "Data that demonstrate strong generality in the behavior of the same person across many situations are critical for trait . . . theories; the construct of personality itself rests on the belief that individual behavioral consistencies exist widely and account for much of the variance in behavior" (p. 13).

As an example, let's return to our extraverted friend John. For our trait-based descriptive and predictive system to work, he must reliably and consistently demonstrate extraverted behavior in almost every social situation. If he is extraverted in one situation and not so in another, the utility of both our descriptions and our predictions is compromised. Thus, the demonstration of behavioral consistency is crucial if we wish to advance trait theory as a useful approach to studying persons.

Mischel's critical appraisal involved detailed examination of the research relating to behavioral consistency from a number of perspectives. The classic studies of Hartshorne and May (1928) dealing with the trait of honesty serve as a good example. If honesty is viable as a trait, a person who is high on the characteristic should behave honestly in a wide variety of situations. Using several thousand children in over 100 situations in which it was possible to act either honestly or dishonestly, Hartshorne and May found very little evidence of consistency. Honesty, it appeared, was a function of situational factors, not due to an underlying personality characteristic. While there has been some controversy surrounding this interpretation (for example, Burton, 1963; Epstein & O'Brien, 1985), it demonstrates that a vital link in trait theory—the empirical demonstration of behavioral consistency—may not be as strong as expected. When Mischel added in a number of other studies, such as the honesty work but dealing with other constructs, he concluded that the evidence for this type of consistency was far from convincing.

Mischel's conclusions regarding the consistency between test scores and nontest behavior was even more condemning than the previous interpretation. He did not challenge the consistency of measures as revealed in the test/retest design or when one questionnaire was related to another, but he was concerned about the poor predictive record when using tests to predict nontest criteria—what we have been discussing as the criterion-related validity of the tests. In reviewing considerable research on this topic, he stated

> Indeed, the phrase "personality coefficient" might be coined to describe the correlation between .20 and .30 which is found persistently when virtually any personality dimension inferred from a questionnaire is related to almost any conceivable external criterion involving responses sampled in a different *medium*—that is, not by another questionnaire. [1968, p. 78]

This low level of consistency between test scores and nontest behavior raises some serious doubts not only about the utility of personality tests but also about the fundamental notion of personality. According to Mischel, the tests just plain do not work very well!

Mischel's attack on the Achilles' heel of personality—consistency—was effective. In the second part of his book, he sketched out an alternative that appeared to hold significant promise of a traitless approach to studying persons. Called **situationism**, this position argued that investigative effort should be focused on the contextual factors that shape behavior. He thought that the situation in which behavior occurred was the most important factor if the desire was to understand behavior. Although this alternative position had considerable impact on the study of personality, it had devastating implications for personality tests. If it was possible to study persons without traits, there was no place for the personality test whatsoever!

This conclusion is clearly at odds with our intuitive idea that traits appear to be useful. It seems inappropriate to abandon the usefulness shown in understanding our extraverted friend John, but Mischel is telling us that we should. And he is telling us that substantive measurement of characteristics like extraversion has minimal scientific utility—certainly a challenge to the testing enterprise.

Responding to Mischel's Challenge

Mischel's critique has been addressed in a number of different ways, both by those in the general area of personality as well as by the testing enterprise. In personality research, a number of provocative ideas have been raised and debated. Of note here are the following:

1. Perhaps the case against consistency has not been adequately made because different types of situations have not been properly studied (Frederiksen, 1972).

2. A class of theoretical positions, called **interactionism**, emphasizing that behavior is a joint function of internal and situational causes has been proposed (Bowers, 1973; Endler & Hunt, 1966), including an interesting process model based on template matching (Bem & Funder, 1978).

3. An examination of sources of consistency has shown some interesting gains (Underwood & Moore, 1981).

4. Considerable work examining why traits have such an intuitive appeal has been launched (Jones & Nisbett, 1971).

Mischel himself has moderated his 1968 radical situationist view to include some individual difference variables, although these variables bear very little resemblance to classical traits, being couched in contemporary cognitive language (Mischel, 1973). However, this evolution is not yet completed (for example, see Wright & Mischel, 1987).

Within the testing enterprise several lines of response to Mischel's critique have been presented. Some of these are discussed next.

Let's not be too hasty. Much of the research reviewed by Mischel was relatively old, being based on tests that were developed using older technologies. Perhaps abandoning traits and their tests would be premature because newer approaches may improve matters. As we have seen in the later chapters of the text, a number of important methodological innovations have been introduced, with construct validity being one of the most important. Although unanswerable at this point, it may well be that the new generations of tests developed under the new technology will fare better than those reviewed by Mischel. This, of course, is an empirical question that will have to await execution of considerable research.

A methodological problem in Mischel's analysis. One of the really telling blows dealt by Mischel was the demonstration of disappointing levels of criterion-related validity for personality tests—in the range of .3, which Mischel called the **personality coefficient**. Epstein (1979) drew attention to a methodological problem that could have a major impact on the observed validity coefficients. It has been known for a long time that a single item in a test will seldom produce a reliable measure. The aggregation of many items to make up a scale score is indeed a necessary condition for producing measures with acceptable levels of reliability. Why, Epstein argued, should not the same be required of criterion measures? Typically, criterion measures are one-shot attempts to provide a measure, and, as such, they must be highly unreliable. Perhaps the poor test-criterion correlations are due to unreliability of the one item criteria that are typically used.[4] Few investigators would be

---

[4]This point is somewhat reminiscent of the arguments presented by Spearman in 1907 in response to Wissler's demonstration of poor test-criterion relationships with the batteries of faculty psychology–inspired tests such as those of J. M. Cattell (see Chapter 6).

impressed with a one-item test, whereas many appear to be willing to correlate test results with single instances of behavior in the development of validity coefficients. To demonstrate this point, Epstein (1979, 1980) calculated correlations between a single-item personality variable measured on two occasions and obtained the traditional value of (roughly) .3. He then calculated similar correlations based on **aggregated data** where behavior had been assessed over several occasions. The obtained correlations were impressive—often greater than .80. He was also able to demonstrate similar gains using the original Hartshorne and May (1928) data (Epstein & O'Brien, 1985). It would appear that the traditionally low test-criterion correlations in the personality domain are due, to some degree at least, to unreliability of the criterion measures.

The issue of aggregation is not as simple as might be expected. For an observation to serve as an aggregation, it must be demonstrably equivalent to any of the other observations that go into forming the aggregated measure. If it is not, the obtained aggregated measure will be unreliable. The establishment of this equivalence prior to conducting an aggregation study is exceedingly important, and failure to do so can lead to all kinds of interpretive problems (for discussions, see Jackson & Paunonen, 1985; Mischel and Peake, 1982). Despite this difficulty, Epstein's work served as a timely reminder that some methodological defects underlying the data were being used to assail trait theory.

Consistency as an individual difference variable. Another approach to rectifying Mischel's observations lies in examining the possibility that different people are consistent on different dimensions. For example, some people may be consistent in their punctuality behavior, whereas others may not. If this were the case, the overall grouping of differentially consistent individuals in a test-criterion study would obscure some very real and important test-criterion relationships.

The generic term for this kind of differential predictability is **moderator variable**. Such a variable can be used to predict if the criterion-related validity of one group will be different from another. For example, if the test-criterion correlation calculated using persons who all score low on an IQ test is substantial, while the same correlation calculated using high IQ test scorers is zero, then IQ is said to be a moderator variable regarding the test-criterion relationship. Bem and Allen (1974) suggest that consistency is a moderator variable for personality test-criterion correlations.

They explored this possibility by gathering a series of test scores and behavior measures of friendliness and conscientiousness from a group of college students. In addition, they asked the respondents to rate how consistent they felt they were on the two characteristics. When all respondents were considered together, the observed test-criterion correlations were in the traditional range of .3. However, when they looked at the respondents who had rated themselves as consistent, the test-criterion correlations were significantly higher. This demonstrates that there are indeed individual differences in consistency and that assertions about the inconsistency of behavior should be tempered by this realization. Unfortunately, this important point has been challenged in an extensive study that failed to replicate Bem and Allen's findings (Chaplin & Goldberg, 1984), leading to the necessity of being skeptical of the idea of individual differences in consistency.

Developing alternative visions of measurement. With trait theory in retreat, it seemed appropriate to begin to explore the possibility of developing measurement technology that did not depend on this particular conception. If it were possible to develop methods of assessment that did not commit the user to trait theory, it might be possible to continue progress within the testing enterprise without having to deal with the contentious issues of behavioral consistency. A number of techniques emerging since Mischel's appraisal of personality assessment have focused on assessing behavior without interpreting it as a sign of underlying predisposition. Because these alternative approaches are so important in the contemporary measurement field, they have had their own, separate chapter dedicated to them. Chapter 17 presents some details of these newer approaches to measurement.

Traits are still important anyway. Even if Mischel's case were ironclad, there are a number of reasons why there is a place for traits and the instruments that measure them. First, traits appear to be an integral part of how people understand their world, so a knowledge of how these work—and their limitations—is exceedingly important. Second, we do not end up in situations randomly. Rather, we are very active in selecting the kinds of situations we enter. Thus, though it may be possible to explain considerable behavioral variance using the situation *once we are in it,* it is still necessary to explain *why we ended up in that situation in the first place.* At this point, traits and other traitlike terms (values, vocational interests, cognitive styles, and so on) are good candidates for such explanations. Third, a number of traitlike terms have particularly important social meaning, and tests measuring them are thereby important. Perhaps most notable here are the personality characteristics associated with abnormality. Although there may be some consistency problems with constructs like depression, schizophrenia, and character disorder (to name but a few), tests that provide quick and efficient assessment of such attributes remain useful, particularly if they are part of a well-designed assessment system (for example, per the examples in Chapter 14). It appears that traits remain important despite Mischel's critique. Indeed, a number of recent positions are beginning to reestablish what might be considered strong trait positions (for example, Buss, 1989; McCrae & Costa, 1990; Tellegen, 1991).

Thus, the generic notion of traits has not been banished entirely by Mischel's critique. Rather, the field has reacted in a number of positive ways to his analysis and has emerged stronger and more diverse since the original critical appraisal. This does not deny the consistency issues raised by Mischel, but it serves to underscore the fact that the field has reacted to the appraisal in some interesting and useful ways.

COGNITION AND PERSONALITY

The final facet of our efforts to document the similarity of developments within the fields of intelligence and personality comes in the demonstration of efforts to "cognitivize" personality. As noted in Chapter 15, the cognitive "revolution" had a profound effect on the manner in which intelligence is conceptualized. This "revolution" also had an impact on personality, albeit in considerably different ways. What follows is a brief sampling of the manner in which the cognitive concerns have emerged in several aspects of the study of personality.

The cognitivization of personality has occurred in the form of a series of dimensions thought to underlie individual differences. These have become known as **cognitive styles**, defined as individual differences in approaches to perceiving, remembering, and thinking. One such style, field dependence, is particularly interesting because not only was it discovered by accident, or serendipitously, but it also provides an intriguing window on the interface between personal attributes and the manners in which individuals interact with their environment. The following Close Up tells the story of this cognitive style.

CLOSE UP | **Field Dependence as an Individual Difference Measure**

Herman Witkin's experimental interests were firmly embedded in the phenomena of perception. In the early 1950s, his particular concern involved studying the role of external cues in the perception of verticality. What effect did almost vertical lines have on the ability to locate the true vertical? To investigate this problem, in the traditional S/R (stimulus/response) framework, Witkin and his co-workers designed a number of clever tests. The **Rod and Frame Test** (**RFT**) involved an illuminated rod inside of an illuminated square frame, which was shown to respondents in a darkened room. Respondents used a lever to move the rod into what they believed to be a true vertical position. When the frame was tilted away from the true vertical, the RFT provided a means of studying the effect of context upon verticality judgments. Figure 16-5 shows several examples of how the rod and frame might be oriented at the beginning of a trial. In all cases, the task of the respondent was to align the rod to the true vertical.

As he began this work, Witkin made a totally unexpected discovery. Some people were able to locate true vertical regardless of the frame orientation. Others, though, were continually influenced by the context created by the frame and

Figure 16-5

Several examples of the starting position of the rod and frame in the Rod and Frame Test. The respondent's task is to orient the rod to the true vertical using a joysticklike device. The test is administered in complete darkness.

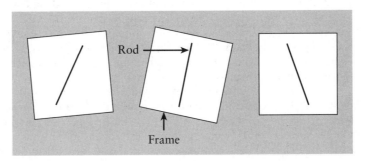

In this approach to examining the cognitive style of field dependence, the chair in which the respondent is seated and the rod and the frame can be rotated off of level to isolate the cues used in locating "true" vertical. The rod and frame are visible in front of the respondent, and the test would be administered in darkness.

oriented the rod to take this into account, producing rod positioning that reflected the orientation of the frame. These individual differences were so pronounced that Witkin had to abandon his S/R project in traditional perception research. The error terms in his analyses, created by the individual variation, were simply too large for any general findings to emerge. However, this experimental program was not a total loss because Witkin and his co-workers began to consider RFT performance as an individual difference variable.

He hypothesized that persons who were readily able to locate true vertical on the RFT were using internal cues in this task. He labeled these people as showing **field independence** because their processing was not affected by the surrounding context or field. Respondents who were influenced by the context provided by the frame emphasized external information in performing the task. Witkin said such people demonstrate **field dependence** because their performance was dictated, in large measure, by the surrounding context or field.

To explore this possibility, Witkin developed some more clever tests. One involved a tilting chair in a room that could itself be tilted. This provided an even clearer delineation of the cues used in assessing verticality because body orientation (an internal cue) could be manipulated. Performance on this task was highly correlated with RFT in the direction expected by the notion of field dependence.

Witkin also developed the **Embedded Figures Test (EFT)** as a measure of his newly discovered individual difference. In this test, respondents must find a relatively simple figure that is hidden in a larger more complex one. Figure 16-6 illustrates several examples of items from this test. Persons who are readily able to find the hidden figures would appear to be uninfluenced by surrounding context and thereby considered to be field-independent. Those who were more context-sensitive would be considered to be field-dependent. EFT and RFT performance was highly correlated in the expected direction, suggesting the existence of a substantive individual difference variable (see Witkin, 1959, for a summary of the earlier work).

Once the robust nature of the field-dependence/independence variable was established, it became possible to conduct a wide variety of research investigations to embellish understanding of this construct. Domains researched include problem solving (for a review, see Witkin, Dyk, Faterson, Goodenough, & Karp, 1974), interpersonal behavior (for a review, see Witkin & Goodenough, 1977), developmental trends (for a review, see Witkin, 1959), and cross-cultural comparisons (for a review,

Figure 16-6

Several items from the Embedded Figures Test. Respondents must locate the simple figure on the left in the complex on the right.

Table 16-5
Some differences between field-dependent and field-independent persons

Field-Dependent	Field-Independent
Score low on EFT	Score high on EFT
Difficulty isolating true vertical on RFT	No difficulty isolating true vertical on RFT
Low on anagrams	High on anagrams
Higher proportion of females	Higher proportion of males
Greater use of social information	Less use of social information
Greater sensitivity about when to use social information	Less sensitive about when to use social information
Pay attention to faces	Ignore faces around them
Ambiguous self/other distinctions	Clear self/other distinctions
Deal with environment holistically	Parse environment into bits
Sensitive to context	Ignore context
Described As	
Popular	Unpopular
Friendly	Ambitious
Considerate	Inconsiderate
Warm	Opportunistic
Clinging vine	Autonomous
Occupations	
Social work	Engineering
Clinical psychology	Architecture
Teaching	Experimental psychology
	Science
Cultures	
Tight, rule-bound (the Temne in Sierra Leone)	loose, individualistic (the Inuit in Northern Canada)

see Witkin & Berry, 1975). A tremendous amount of knowledge has emerged from these studies, with Table 16-5 reflecting some of the documented results.

As Table 16-5 shows, the field-dependence/independence construct has been exceedingly well elaborated in a number of contexts, providing a particularly interesting dimension of individual differences. The style contrasts two approaches to the processing of information: Field dependence emphasizes the role of external cues and context sensitivity, and field independence concentrates on the role of internal cues and fine levels of discrimination in the processing of information.

Several aspects of the field-independence variable make it particularly useful for studying personality. First, using our terminology from Chapter 2, both the RFT and EFT are *objective tests*, meaning that this aspect of personality can be measured without recourse to the *voluntary tests*, which characterize most other approaches to personality. This finesses the need to be concerned about problems associated with response styles and the like, which can pose interpretive problems for traditional personality measures. Second, field dependence is a well-elaborated construct, bringing the idea into close proximity with contemporary research in cognition. This clearly demonstrates that the domains of personality and intellectual functioning are not as separate as we might have expected. Third, the idea of field dependence and its objective measurement provides an interesting alternative to the more traditional trait-based approaches, providing a new and interesting perspective on the study of both personality and its interface with intellect.

A wide variety of cognitive styles, not unlike field dependence, have been postulated and researched. Table 16-6 presents a brief description of some of these cognitive/personality variables. This list of cognitive styles indicates a different approach to the study of personality. Here concern is focused on the manner in which an individual interacts with the environment, under the assumption that personality derives, at least in part, from these various differences. The list of styles in Table 16-6 brings to mind some of the same cognitivization to personality as Robert Sternberg's triarchic of intelligence (see Chapter 15), with ideas like planning, categorization, and impulsivity being mentioned.

Table 16-6 Some cognitive styles discussed in the literature

Abstractness/Concreteness	Those who experience the environment at an abstract level discriminate among situations and adapt their behavior to whatever the situation demands. Those functioning at a concrete level appear to behave in similar ways regardless of situational expectations.
Broad Versus Narrow Categorizing	Broad categorizers prefer fewer, big categories when faced with a task where they have control over the nature of categories in a sorting task. Narrow categorizers prefer a larger number of more precise categories.
Constricted Versus Flexible	Constricted persons are easily distracted by irrelevant details, whereas flexible persons more readily stay focused on the particular task.

continued

Table 16-6 Some cognitive styles discussed in the literature *(continued)*

Impulsive Versus Reflective	Reflective thinkers tend to be slow and accurate in problem-solving situations, whereas impulsive thinkers are quick but often inaccurate in their approach.
Internal Versus External Locus of Control	Internals firmly believe that any rewards which they receive are the result of their own actions. Externals are more apt to attribute success to outside influences such as luck or the actions of others.
Leveling Versus Sharpening	Levelers tend to miss details and attempt to fit new ideas into previously developed memory categories. Sharpeners focus on details and show a strong tendency to differentiate new instances from old ones.
Receptive Versus Perceptive	Perceptive individuals integrate incoming information into their own category systems (see also levelers), whereas receptive people try to minimize the amount of interpretation they employ and deal with sense data in as "raw" a form as possible.
Risk Taking Versus Caution	Risk takers will enter activities with a low probability of high payoff, such as gambling, whereas cautious persons will prefer high probability, low-payoff situations.
Scanning Versus Focusing Strategies	Scanners start with broad categories and then narrow them down as they proceed. Focusers tend to proceed in a trial-and-error basis when they are approaching novel situations.
Systematic Versus Intuitive	Those high on the systematic dimension tend to plan in an orderly, sequential manner. Intuitives are more idea-oriented and tend to move to a holistic level of analysis as soon as possible.
Tolerance Versus Intolerance	The tolerance of concern in this style relates to incongruous or unrealistic experiences. Tolerants embrace new, challenging experiences with little questioning, whereas intolerants demand a great deal of information before they are willing to proceed.

Source: Based on Aiken (1989, pp. 403–407).

The research support for these dimensions, particularly studies regarding the interface with standard personality constructs, varies substantially across these postulated styles. None are as well examined as field dependence, but they all have the potential of providing interesting insights into the nature of individual differences. As well, there is a clear sense that all these postulated dimensions are not necessarily independent of each other (for example, levelers and perceptives appear to be very similar), indicating the need to further map out the domain of cognitive styles. Also, the quality and nature of the various tests proposed to measure these styles vary substantially.

These problems aside, the domain of cognitive styles provides a new and potentially useful alternative to the more traditional trait approach. The main gains here are twofold: (1) The possibility of developing objective measures that can be used as indexes of personality has the potential of great utility, and (2) being able to develop a nomological network using the contemporary language, research, and metaphors of cognition has considerable appeal. Whether cognitive styles become the approach to personality measurement of the future will have to await a considerable amount of further research. Indeed, Cantor and Kihlstrom (1987) have reviewed the area and note a number of significant conceptual and empirical difficulties. Yet, the sense in which the notion of cognitive styles forces the inclusion of interpretive and reasoning processes into the domain of personality represents an important strength of these ideas.

PERSONALITY IN ITS ABNORMAL FORM

To make the stories surrounding "testing personality" tellable, we have to consider two narratives. The first deals with personality of the normally functioning individual. We have examined this in the context of the similarity of developments in the fields of personality and intelligence. The second story deals with a parallel but somewhat separate domain of the measurement of personality in its abnormal form. Both narratives have been shaped by similar methodological developments such as factor analysis and the ascendancy of construct validity, and both have been influenced by events in the discipline of psychology such as the cognitive "revolution." The abnormal personality, however, is qualitatively different from the normal variant, hence the decision to treat these as two parallel yet separate stories. Again, the coverage here is selective, with the material included being carefully chosen to reveal aspects of the manner in which the challenges of measuring personality have contributed to the testing enterprise.

The most visible test in the abnormal area has been the MMPI (see Chapter 9). This particular instrument, however, has been the brunt of considerable criticism. Apart from the expected datedness of a test developed in the early 1940s, the following are some of the more crucial concerns raised:

1. The original sample of people-in-general used to assign the MMPI items to scales was suspect, being made up mostly of relatives of patients who were

visiting the hospital in which the patients were housed. This compromised some aspects of the discriminative power of the test.

2. Categories of psychopathology have undergone significant changes since the original MMPI was published, meaning that the scores provided were poorly related to the ongoing thinking in the area.

3. Issues of item overlap (one item appearing on more than one scale) and unbalanced scales (grossly unequal proportions of true- and false-keyed items across scales) compromised the psychometric properties of the clinical scales.

4. The construct validity of the scales was weak because they had not been developed with theoretical considerations in mind, although some "bottom up validation" had been provided.

With these serious problems, it seems that the MMPI is less than a perfect measure and that changes should be welcomed.

By the mid-1980s, however, this had not happened—the MMPI was still the most used test of psychopathology. There are a number of reasons for this, including the following:

1. Tremendous volumes of research were available concerning use of the test, including cookbooks, which provide detailed interpretations of almost every conceivable score profile. This tome of empirical support for interpreting test scores was unrivaled.

2. The wide-variety scale scores that can be extracted from the item set gave the test considerable interpretive flexibility.

3. Being positioned as the first test of its type brought a sense of familiarity and acceptance.

4. By being in use so long, a considerable amount of clinical wisdom surrounding the test had accumulated, making clinicians reluctant to abandon the test because they would thereby abandon this MMPI-related wisdom.

However, though these points were important, it would seem that the major reason for the staying power of the MMPI was the lack of strong competition. A number of fine tests have been developed over the years, but few, if any, have been able to establish the substantive empirical foundations of the MMPI. For a new test to compete with the MMPI, it would not only have to address the weaknesses of the old test but also provide the kinds of benefits associated with it. Thus, the MMPI persevered.

It was not until 1983 that a possible challenger to the supremacy of the MMPI presented itself. This new test, the **Millon Clinical Multiaxial Inventory (MCMI)**, explicitly addressed most of the weaknesses of the MMPI and began to give the grand old test a run for its money. The following Close Up provides some details of the 1987 revision of the MCMI, dubbed the **MCMI II** (Millon, 1987).

CLOSE UP   **The Revised Millon Clinical Multiaxial Inventory**

The MCMI II is an objective psychodiagnostic instrument intended for use with psychiatric patients who are undergoing clinical evaluation. It consists of 175 items that are answered either true or false. The major feature of this test is the extensive clinical theory on which it is based. All scales relate to prototypes derived from an elaborate theory of personality and psychopathology (see Millon, 1981). In contradistinction to the MMPI then, the MCMI II has been designed from a theoretical position and thereby has the potential for demonstrating strong construct validity.

T. Millon's complex theory of personality is concerned, in part, with the primary source from which individuals gain comfort or satisfaction or attempt to avoid pain and distress, which Millon calls **sources of reinforcement**. He suggests that clinical patients have shown five basic orientations regarding reinforcement: (1) *Detached patients* are those who experience few rewards in life; (2) *dependent patients* are those who measure their reinforcements in terms of other people; (3) *independent patients* evaluate their reinforcements without considering the concerns or needs of others; (4) *discordant patients* are those who reverse negative and positive reinforcements; and (5) *ambivalent patients* are in a state of conflict about whether to attend to their own or others' desires and needs. In addition, there are two **levels of coping** patterns demonstrated in this population: (1) passive patients who seem apathetic, restrained, yielding, and resigned and (2) active patients who seem aroused and attentive.

Reinforcement and coping combine in a 5×2 matrix (Figure 16-7) to create a set of styles of personality functioning basic to Millon's theory. Table 16-7 briefly describes the ten **basic personality patterns** created in the matrix in Figure 16-7.

Figure 16-7

The basic personality patterns in Millon's theory, created by combining the five reinforcement and two coping patterns.

| | | Pattern of Coping Behavior | |
		Passive	Active
Primary Source of Reinforcement	Detached	*Schizoid* Scale 1	*Avoidant* Scale 2
	Dependent	*Dependent* Scale 3	*Histrionic* Scale 4
	Independent	*Narcissistic* Scale 5	*Antisocial* Scale 6A
	Discordant	*Self-defeating* Scale 8B	*Aggressive* Scale 6B
	Ambivalent	*Compulsive* Scale 7	*Negativistic* Scale 8A

Millon considers several additional personality patterns as elaborations of the ten shown in Table 16-7. The maladaptive nature of these three **pathological personality disorders** is significantly greater than the ten basic patterns. Table 16-8 presents the MCMI II scales that measure these three patterns.

Table 16-7
Basic personality pattern scales from the MCMI II

Scale 1:   *Schizoid Personality (Passive/Detached)*
High scorers are characterized by a lack of desire and an inability to experience pleasure or pain deeply. They tend toward apathy and listlessness and appear to be distant. They appear passive and detached from the rewards as well as the demands of human relationships. (35 items)

Scale 2:   *Avoidant Personality (Active/Detached)*
High scorers experience very little positive reinforcement from either themselves or others. They are almost always on guard and try to avoid painful experiences. (40 items)

Scale 3:   *Dependent Personality (Passive/Dependent)*
High scorers have learned to turn to others as their primary source of nurturance and security, as well as to wait passively for others to act. They want to lean on others for affection, safety, and guidance. (37 items)

Scale 4:   *Histronic Personality (Active/Dependent)*
High scorers, like submissives, turn toward others but are much more active in their orientation. They are facile and enterprising in manipulating the attention and favor of others. Characterized by an almost insatiable search for stimulation, they are, under the surface, fearful of independence and need almost constant approval. (40 items)

Scale 5:   *Narcissistic Personality (Passive/Independent)*
High scorers are very self-oriented, experiencing significant pleasure simply by focusing on themselves. They tend to be self-assured and assume that others will recognize their special qualities. (49 items)

Scale 6A: *Antisocial Personality (Active/Independent)*
High scorers anticipate pain and suffering at the hands of others and act to counteract it through duplicitous and illegal behaviors designed to exploit others for their own gain. They have a strong drive toward autonomy and often voice a desire for revenge for past injustices. (45 items)

Scale 6B: *Aggressive Personality (Active/Independent)*
High scorers are not publicly antisocial but tend to abuse and humiliate others. They tend to be generally hostile and combative and are not bothered by the negative consequences of their actions. (45 items)

Scale 7:   *Compulsive Personality (Passive/Ambivalent)*
High scorers have been shaped into accepting the rewards imposed on them by others. Their prudent and perfectionistic ways derive from a conflict between a fear of social disapproval and hostility toward others. They tend to be self-restrained and publicly compliant. (38 items)

Scale 8A: *Negativistic Personality (Active/Ambivalent)*
High scorers struggle between following the rewards offered by others and those desired by themselves. These conflicts remain explicit and

intrude into everyday life. They tend toward being erratic, showing anger in one situation and guilt and contrition in another. (41 items)

Scale 8B: *Self-defeating Personality (Passive/Discordant)*
High scorers are characterized by putting themselves in positions that allow, even encourage, others to take advantage of them. They tend to focus on their worst features, magnify their flaws, and repeatedly recall past misfortunes. (40 items)

SOURCE: Based on Millon & Green (1989).

Table 16-8
Three MCMI II scales measuring pathological personality disorders

Scale S: *Schizotypal Personality*
High scorers are poorly integrated and dysfunctionally detached. They prefer social isolation with minimal personal attachments and obligations. Often cognitively confused, they frequently seem self-absorbed or ruminative. (44 items)

Scale C: *Borderline Personality*
High scorers experience extreme moods with recurring periods of dejection and apathy often interspersed with spells of anger, anxiety, or euphoria. Mood shifts or swings are seen very clearly. (62 items)

Scale P: *Paranoid Personality*
High scorers demonstrate active mistrust of others and a defensiveness against imagined or anticipated criticism and deception. Often irritable, suspicious they tend to resist external influences (44 items)

Besides these 13 scales of personality functioning, the MCMI II provides measures of a series of **clinical syndromes**. Theoretically, these syndromes are embedded in the patient's basic personality pattern and emerge during stressful situations. In effect, the syndromes are amplifications of the basic personality patterns. There are nine syndrome scales on the MCMI II, with three being considered as significantly more severe than the others. You will notice that the descriptions of the MCMI II scales that measure these syndromes, shown in Table 16-9 (page 636), bear a degree of similarity to the MMPI clinical scales discussed in Chapter 9. Finally, there are a number of scales intended to facilitate the interpretability of a given patient profile. Table 16-10 (page 636) briefly describes these.

As can be seen, the MCMI II provides a wide range of scores, all of which relate directly to Millon's theory of personality. This newer test has clearly made significant strides in incorporating theory, thus addressing one of the foundational criticisms of the MMPI.

A second criticism of the MMPI relates to the dated nature of the diagnostic categories revealed in the obtained clinical scales. The American Psychiatric Association has, for a number of years now, attempted to standardize the labels given to various mental illnesses in its periodically revised ***Diagnostic and Statistical Manual (DSM)***. This volume documents current thinking about categories of mental illness and has to date gone through three major revisions with a

Table 16-9
Clinical syndrome scales from the MCMI II

Clinical Syndrome Disorders (Moderate Severity)

Scale A: Anxiety	Acute feelings of apprehensiveness. (25 items)
Scale H: Somatoform	Recurrent, multiple somatic complaints, best described as hypochondriacal.
Scale N: Bipolar/Manic	Periods of restless overactivity and distractibility, flights of ideas, labile shifts of mood. (37 items)
Scale D: Dysthymia	Acute feelings of discouragement, guilt, lack of initiative, apathy, low self-esteem, and many self-deprecatory comments. (36 items)
Scale B: Alcohol Dependency	(46 items)
Scale T: Drug Dependence	(58 items)

Clinical Syndrome Disorders (Marked Severity)

Scale SS: Thought Disorder	Usually classified as schizophrenic, with a number of possible behavioral manifestations. (33 items)
Scale CC: Major Depression	(24 items)
Scale PP: Delusional Disorder	Typically, acute paranoia. (23 items)

Table 16-10
Modifier and correction scales from the MCMI II

Validity Index	Indicates careless, confused, or random responding. (4 items)
Scale X: Disclosure Level	Extent to which patients are willing to reveal themselves. Like the MMPI K scale, various of the scale scores (for example, scales 4, 5, 7) can be adjusted to take disclosure level into account.
Scale Y: Desirability Gauge	Extent to which the patient wants to appear socially attractive, morally virtuous, and/or emotionally well composed. Again, corrections to scale scores are possible with this scale.
Scale Z: Debasement Measure	Extent to which patients depreciate or devalue themselves. Corrections to scale scores can be made using this scale as well.

fourth about to emerge. Every revision has presented new labels, thinking, and nosological systems. Clearly a 1940s vocabulary, as used in the MMPI clinical scales, is behind the times. The MCMI II and its underlying theory have been developed to be compatible with the revised third edition, the *DSM III–R*

Table 16-11
MCMI II scales, Millon's theoretical personality patterns, and their Axis II
DSM III–R equivalents

Scale	Theoretical Pattern	*DSM* III–R Classification
1	Passive/detached	Schizoid personality
2	Active/detached	Avoidant personality
3	Passive/dependent	Dependent personality
4	Active/dependent	Histrionic personality
5	Passive/independent	Narcissistic personality
6A	Active/independent	Antisocial personality
6B	Active/discordant	Aggressive (sadistic) personality
7	Passive/ambivalent	Compulsive personality
8A	Active/ambivalent	Passive/aggressive personality
8B	Passive/discordant	Self-defeating personality

(American Psychiatric Association, 1987). In the *Manual,* basic personality patterns are given the label **Axis II**. As Table 16-11 shows, Million's ten basic personality patterns map very neatly into the *DSM* III–R Axis II categories.

In the *DSM* III–R, clinical syndromes such as depression and schizophrenia are described as belonging to **Axis I**. Again, the MCMI II maps well into this domain because the Clinical Syndrome scales (see Table 16-9) are compatible with the categories indicated in the *DSM.* Indeed, the very name of the MCMI II, specifically the word *multiaxial,* derives from Millon's efforts to map his test into *DSM* categories. Millon's commitment to keeping the MCMI II in line with current thinking is clearly revealed in the revision of the test. The original inventory (MCMI) was designed to map into the *DSM* III, whereas the revision (MCMI II) was made explicitly to render it compatible with the 1987 system revealed in the *DSM* III–R.[5] To the extent that Millon continues to keep his test compatible with current thinking and labels, the MCMI II can be seen as an improvement over the MMPI.

It should be noted, however, that the MCMI II scales were developed from Millon's theory, not directly from the *DSM.* Thus, suggestions that the MCMI II provides measures of *DSM* categories should be made with caution. Specific research directed at determining the effectiveness of MCMI II scales as measures of the *DSM* categories must be conducted before any such assertions are justifiable (for a discussion, see Widiger, Williams, Spitzer, & Frances, 1985; for a rejoinder, see Millon, 1985).

Besides providing a strong theoretical rationale for the MCMI II, Millon employed a wide variety of the newest techniques in developing his test. Item selection and scale development were carefully undertaken to maximize construct validity. An initial pool of 3500 items was carefully written to reflect the constructs in his theory. Then they were subjected to extensive internal evaluation, using some

---

[5]The MCMI II also involved some other changes intended to improve the instrument. Included here were the rewording and replacement of a number of items, increasing the number of scales, and the introduction of a complex item-weighting system. For a discussion of the MCMI relative to the MCMI II, see Streiner and Miller, 1989.

variations of item-total correlations outlined in Chapter 11. The goal here was to optimize internal properties (for example, reliability) of the test. Finally, items were selected in terms of the manner in which they differentiated between the scale category and an undifferentiated criterion group of psychiatric patients. Using this patient group, rather than people-in-general, sharpened the discriminative power of the test relative to the MMPI. Subsequent cross-validation, the development of effective cutting scores that optimize predictive efficiency considering base rates, and a considerable amount of validity data have been presented (for a review, see Millon & Green, 1989). Research to support profile analysis of the various patterns of MCMI II scores has also been presented (Millon & Green, 1989). Automated computerized scoring systems are available.

Evaluation. The MCMI II is a relatively new test, and final assessments of its psychometric properties will have to await further research and experience with the test (for reviews, see Overholser, 1990; Widiger, 1985). Validity studies, to date, suggest a mixed record for the MCMI II, with some studies indicating problems with specific scales (Goldberg, Shaw, & Segal, 1987) and indications of some weaknesses in the computer-scoring reports (DeWolfe, Larsen, & Ryan, 1985). At this point, it seems inappropriate to suggest that this newcomer should replace the MMPI. Indeed, Millon (1984) himself suggests that the test should be used jointly with other instruments, especially the MMPI. One difficulty with the MCMI II is the presence of significant item overlap in the scales. This, of course, compromises the discriminant validity of the scale scores because the same items can, in some cases, contribute to different scale scores, thereby increasing the sizes of scale intercorrelations. These difficulties aside, the MCMI II represents a bold effort to use modern technology to develop an improved instrument to determine psychopathology.

With the MCMI beginning to demonstrate a degree of clinical utility and the critical appraisals of the MMPI continuing to escalate (for a review, see Butcher & Pope, 1992), it seemed only a matter of time before it would become necessary to subject the grand old test to substantive revision. Indeed, it was as early as 1982 that an extensive restandardization of the MMPI was begun.

The guiding premise of these efforts to update the MMPI was to answer as many of the criticisms as possible while retaining the original format and intent of the test so that the last 50 years of research would still be applicable to the new version. This latter point cannot be overemphasized because the MMPI has been the subject of over an estimated 8000 published reports (Groth-Marnat, 1990, p. 179)! It was exceedingly important that the new version of the MMPI not force the abandonment of this invaluable corpus of knowledge and wisdom. The specific goals of the revision involved the following:

1. Development of a representative normative sample
2. Modernization of the item pool by the deletion of objectionable items and the addition of items related to contemporary clinical problems (for example, drug problems, suicide)
3. Maintenance of the continuity of the original clinical and validity scales

4. Development of new norms that would better reflect current clinical problems

5. Collection of new data to evaluate all changes

6. Development of new scales to address further clinical problems

7. Development of a new form that was suitable for adolescents (Butcher & Pope, 1992)

The main revision has become known as the **MMPI-2**, and the adolescent version (ages 14–18) is the **MMPI-A**. The following Close Up provides a sense of the major revision that emerged from these considerations.

CLOSE UP The MMPI-2

The restandardization committee published the revised MMPI in 1989 (Butcher, Dahlstrom, Graham, Tellegen, & Kaemmer, 1989). The approach employed to develop the test can best be described as conservative because efforts were made to minimize the numbers of changes to the original test to enhance equivalence of the two forms.

An experimental booklet (**Form AX**) was prepared and included the 550 unique items from the original MMPI plus 154 new questions deemed to reflect important new clinical content. Eighty-two of the original MMPI items were rewritten. Fifteen involved elimination of specific reference to gender (for example, the original item "Any man who is willing to work hard has a good chance of succeeding" was changed to "Anyone who is willing to work hard has a good chance of succeeding"). Obsolete expressions were changed to more contemporary wordings ("cutting up" was replaced with "bad behavior"). Dated references were modified ("sleeping powder" became "sleeping pills"), and items that implied a cultural or subcultural bias were changed ("I go to church almost every week" was changed to "I attend religious services almost every week"). The grammar of some items was clarified, and some of the more convoluted items were simplified. These minor wording changes were shown to have no significant effect on item-endorsement patterns (Ben-Porath & Butcher, 1989).

After substantial amounts of data collection and analysis based on a variety of additional subject groups, 567 items from Form AX were retained to make up the MMPI-2. An indication of the similarity of the new and old versions of the test is presented in Table 16-12 (page 640), which shows the changes made to the traditional clinical and validity scales. The order of items was changed in the MMPI-2 so that the traditional validity and clinical scales could be generated from the first 370 items, with the remaining 197 providing supplementary content.

An additional set of 15 new **content scales** was also introduced with the MMPI-2 (Butcher, Graham, Williams, & Ben-Porath, 1990). These were developed using both rational and statistical procedures and were added to measure important personality factors. Table 16-13 (page 640) lists these content scales.

Several new validity scales were also introduced with the MMPI-2. Included here are (1) Back-Page Infrequency (Fb), which is the equivalent of the F scale garnered from items later on in the test booklet; (2) Variable Response Inconsistency (VRIN), which is an index of the number of times respondents contradict themselves when answering items with similar content; and (3) True Response

Table 16-12
Item changes and deletions in the basic validity and clinical scale in MMPI-2

	Numbers of Items			Types of Changes*			
	Deleted	Left	Changed	A	B	C	D
Validity Scales							
Lie (L)	0	15	2	1	1	0	0
Infrequency (F)	4	60	12	1	5	0	0
Defensiveness (K)	0	30	1	0	1	0	0
Clinical Scales							
Hypochondriasis (Hs)	1	32	5	0	1	3	1
Depression (D)	3	57	2	1	1	0	0
Hysteria (Hy)	1	32	5	0	1	3	1
Psychopathic Deviate (Pd)	0	50	4	0	2	1	1
Masculinity-Femininity (Mf)	4	56	6	1	2	1	2
Paranoia (Pa)	0	40	2	1	0	0	1
Psychasthenia (Pt)	0	48	2	0	0	1	1
Schizophrenia (Sc)	0	78	13	0	1	7	5
Hypomania (Ma)	0	46	7	4	2	1	0
Social Introversion (Si)	1	69	6	0	3	2	1

*Types of changes: A = elimination of sexist wording; B = modernization; C = grammatical clarification; D = simplification.
SOURCE: Reproduced by permission of the University of Minnesota Press.

Table 16-13
New content scales introduced with the MMPI-2

Anxiety	Bizarre Mentation	Low Self-Esteem
Fears	Anger	Social Discomfort
Obsessiveness	Cynicism	Family Problems
Depression	Antisocial Practices	Work Interference
Health Concerns	Type A	Negative Treatment Indicators

Inconsistency (TRIN), which is the number of times people respond with two false or two true responses to items that are opposite in content. Elevated values of these validity scales suggest potential invalidity problems for the specific protocol.

The normative sample for the MMPI-2 consisted of 1138 males and 1462 females selected to match the population parameters of the 1980 U.S. census. In relation to the original norm sample, this one was balanced for demographic variables and demonstrated a higher educational level (as would be expected given educational trends since 1940). This would appear to be one of the major improvements of the MMPI-2 over the original test. Considering the major scales, *T* scores generated from this sample were not as deviant as the original. Practically, this translated into the need to use a *T* score of 65 (compared with 70 of the original test) to indicate clinical significance.

Some psychometric data. Test/retest reliabilities of the major scales ranged between .67 and .89 for males and .58 to .91 for females. Moderate validity coefficients have been reported (Butcher et al., 1989). Many issues of validity have been addressed in the context of the congruence between the original and revised versions. To the extent that the vast majority of the clinical scales contain the same items, validity between the two forms is said to be comparable (for a review, see Butcher & Pope, 1992).

A number of basic psychometric concerns have not been addressed by the revision:

1. Item overlap remains a concern.
2. Some items are false-keyed on one clinical scale and true-keyed on another, meaning that *any* response is indicative of psychopathology (see Fekken, 1992).
3. Scales are still unbalanced regarding the numbers of true- and false-keyed responses, indicating potential problems regarding response styles (see Chapter 13) even though new validity scales have been added to address these concerns (for example, VRIN, TRIN).
4. The comparability of the rewritten items to the originals *could* affect the membership of a specific item on a specific scale.

Ben-Porath and Butcher (1989) demonstrated that item-endorsement frequencies (*p*-values) were not affected by the rewriting, but these data are mute on the issue of whether the new items would empirically discriminate the criteria in exactly the same way as the 1940s sample. All these concerns combine to indicate that a number of substantive issues have not been addressed by the revised MMPI, leading to the need for caution in accepting the new test.

It is a bit early to make determinations about the utility of the new MMPI. Much more research and practical experience is needed before any firm evaluations can be made. However, some early indications show that the MMPI-2 may not be gaining universal approval. For example, Adler (1990) interviewed a number of practitioners and received a relatively negative response. Alan Friedman (Northwestern University) was quoted as suggesting that the test "let test-users have a choice much like classic Coke and and new Coke." While indicating that much more research was needed, Irving Gottesman (University of Virginia) hazarded the guess that "the consumers will say they prefer classic Coke." But, like all taste tests, it will take some time before a final decision is taken. Hopefully, when a final decision is taken, the domain will be able to say "You have chosen wisely."

The emergence of both the MCMI II and the MMPI-2 indicate that the testing enterprise is still very active in the domain of assessing psychopathology. The MCMI-II brings with it a number of sophisticated psychometric improvements, which remedy some of the age-old criticisms of the MMPI. However, the complexity of the theoretical/interpretive system underlying the MCMI II and the comparative lack of empirical support data have detracted from its immediate clinical utility. The MMPI-2, by virtue of its conservative approach, has not addressed some of the major criticisms of the old test. Therefore, it has failed to provide as new an alternative as many might have wished. Additionally, a number of substantive concerns about the new test have led to early indications that it may not replace the original version. Some progress has been made in this most important domain of activity, but there is still room for considerable improvement. The directions that these modifications and changes take over the next several decades will be most interesting because they will reveal the future of the testing enterprise's involvement in the assessment of the abnormal personality.

Summary

The goal of this chapter was to provide a sense of the contemporary domain of measuring personality. The chapter serves to write a conclusion for the story begun with the various early developments in personality measurement sketched out in the earlier chapters (see Figure 16-1). Developments in the structure of personality, along with the different tests these spawned were noted (for example, EPI, 16PF, and NEO-PI). The discussion of Walter Mischel's critical appraisal of personality and its assessment, and the manners in which the field reacted to these, provided a window on some of the major controversies in the field. The cognitivization of personality in the postulation of cognitive styles provided some evidence for the manner in which the field was influenced by the cognitive "revolution." Finally, a review of contemporary developments in the measurement of psychopathology provided a sense of where this aspect of personality measurement is headed.

Again, I must emphasize that the inclusion of the tests discussed in this chapter was highly selective. Many fine and important tests have not been discussed, including a number of alternate factorial and structural models of personality. Many critical developments in the domain of personality have not been addressed. To be inclusive with a field of this magnitude is clearly impossible in a single chapter. The topics presented in this chapter give you a sense of the important developments in personality because they related to the testing enterprise but are by no means inclusive. Several sources for more inclusive treatments of personality are mentioned in "Suggested Further Reading" at the end of the chapter.

Despite the selectivity, this chapter has demonstrated that the field of personality assessment is an active and controversial one. Probably no amount of research and debate will resolve the foundational concerns that were highlighted. Perhaps this is to be expected. After all, the domain of personality is immensely complex, and it is necessary to make a number of simplifying assumptions in order to proceed. The very necessity of having to simplify things sets the stage for significant controversy because something important is likely to be omitted. These disagreements and controversies will most likely remain with the field for the foreseeable future. There is a sense, however, that the field is moving toward deeper understandings of this most important domain of inquiry.

Glossary

aggregated data Measures based on a series of observations or items. The phrase was coined by S. Epstein in his arguments that the use of multiple-measured criteria produced significantly higher personality coefficients.

Axis I A series of severe clinical syndromes, such as schizophrenia and paranoia, listed in the *Diagnostic and Statistical Manual.*

Axis II A series of basic personality patterns, such as avoidant personality and self-defeating personality, listed in the *Diagnostic and Statistical Manual.*

basic personality patterns Ten patterns of personality created by combining T. Millon's five sources of reinforcement with two levels of coping. (See Table 16-7.) These are measured in the MCMI II and considered Axis II variables using *DSM* categories.

Big Five A factor structure that appears to underlie a wide range of observer ratings and questionnaire data. The five factors are Extraversion/Introversion, Friendliness/Hostility, Conscientiousness, Neuroticism/Emotional Stability, and Intellect. The NEO Personality Inventory (NEO-PI) provides measures on these factors.

Cattell, Raymond B. A factor analyst who developed a major theory of personality that contained 16 source traits as well as 4 second-order traits. The Sixteen Personality Factor Questionnaire (16PF) provides measures on these dimensions. (R. B. is not related to James McKeen.)

clinical syndrome A stress-related aberration of a basic personality pattern that is considered to be very maladaptive. There are nine such syndromes measured by the MCMI II. These are considered Axis I variables using *DSM* categories.

cognitive style Individual differences in approaches to perceiving, remembering, and thinking. There are a number of different examples of such styles, with field dependence/independence being treated in detail in the chapter. (A list of other possibilities is provided in Table 16-6.)

consistency The extent to which personality data do not change as a function of time and situation. Walter Mischel examined behavioral consistency and consistency between test scores and nontest criteria, among others, in his critical appraisal of personality.

content scales A series of new personality scales added to the MMPI in the revised MMPI-2. (See Table 16-13.)

Diagnostic and Statistical Manual (DSM) A publication of the American Psychiatric Association that contains definitions of contemporary forms of mental disorders. It exists in several revisions, with the most recent being the revised third edition known as *DSM* III–R.

DSM III The third revision of the *Diagnostic and Statistical Manual.*

DSM III–R The third, revised version of the *Diagnostic and Statistical Manual.* Scales from the MCMI II are said to be compatible with the categories in *DSM* III–R.

Embedded Figures Test (EFT)   A test of field dependence/independence in which respondents have to locate a simple figure in a more complex one. (See Figure 16-6.) Persons who have difficulty finding the simple figure are said to be field-dependent.

Eysenck, Hans   A British psychologist who formulated a three-factor theory of personality (extraversion, neuroticism, psychoticism) along with significant supporting data and who developed the Eysenck Personality Questionnaire (EPQ) as a measure of this theory.

Eysenck Personality Inventory (EPI)   An early test developed by Hans Eysenck that measured only Extraversion and Neuroticism. It was replaced by the EPQ.

Eysenck Personality Questionnaire (EPQ)   The most recent test developed by Hans Eysenck that provides measures of extraversion, neuroticism, and psychoticism, as well as a Lie scale.

field dependence/independence   A cognitive style associated with a person's ability to extract information from complex contexts. Field-independent persons can process information without being affected by the surrounding context, whereas the surrounding context strongly influences the performance of field-dependent persons. Many other personality characteristics are associated with this dimension. (See Table 16-5.)

Form AX   A 704-item experimental version of the MMPI that was used to develop the MMPI-2.

hierarchical model   A model of the structure of personality that views behaviors, items, facets, and traits as part of a multilevel system in which factor analytic results are determined by the level of entry. (See Figure 16-4.)

interactionism   A theoretical position that argues that the joint impact of both the situation and personality direct behavior.

introversion/extraversion   One of the three dimensions in Eysenck's factor analytic theory of personality. Extraverts focus their energy outward and are sociable people who thrive on human company. Introverts focus energy inward and prefer being alone. This dimension is measured in the Eysenck Personality Questionnaire (EPQ).

Junior EPQ   A version of the EPQ suitable for children ages 7 through 15 years.

level of coping   As used in T. Millon's theory of personality, the manner in which a person adapts to day-to-day stresses. According to Millon, people tend to be either active or passive in their coping level.

Life (L) data   Personality observations gathered from the use of various types of ratings by people who know the target rates. Raymond Cattell used this type of data to develop his set of 16 source traits.

MCMI II   See Millon Clinical Multiaxial Inventory.

Millon Clinical Multiaxial Inventory (MCMI)   A test for the objective classification of psychiatric patients that is based on T. Millon's theory of personality and provides scales compatible with *DSM* III categories. The revised version, which is compatible with *DSM* III–R, is called the MCMI II.

Millon, T. A psychologist who developed a complex theory of personality and who designed the Millon Clinical Multiaxial Inventory (MCMI) and its revision (MCMI II) to measure his theory.

Mischel, Walter A Stanford University psychologist who, among other things, launched a strong critical attack on the notion of personality by focusing on the poor demonstrated levels of consistency in personality data.

MMPI-A A 1989 version of the MMPI intended for adolescents (ages 14–18).

MMPI-2 A 1989 revision of the MMPI in which items were rewritten and a new norm group used.

moderator variable A third variable in the traditional test-criterion correlation dyad that predicts predictability. For example, if a test predicts criterion performance better for females than for males, gender is then said to be a moderator variable. Bem and Allen demonstrated that self-rated degree of consistency functioned as a moderator variable in several situations.

NEO Personality Inventory (NEO-PI) A measure of personality developed by Costa and McCrae that provides measures on the Big Five as well as estimates of facets of three of these major dimensions.

neuroticism/stability One of the three dimensions in Hans Eysenck's factor analytic theory of personality. Neurotics show a variety of somatic and interpersonal difficulties associated with tension and anxiety, whereas stable persons do not. This dimension is measured in the Eysenck Personality Questionnaire (EPQ).

pathological personality disorders Three highly maladaptive personality patterns formulated by T. Millon. (See Table 16-8.) These are measured by the MCMI II.

personality The stable factors that make a person's behavior consistent from one time to another or different from the behavior other people would manifest in comparable situations.

personality coefficient A term coined by Walter Mischel to describe the typical test-criterion correlation in personality that is usually in the range of .3.

psychoticism/normality One of the three dimensions in Hans Eysenck's factor analytic theory of personality. High scorers on psychoticism are predisposed toward major catastrophic breakdowns, whereas normal scorers are not. This dimension is measured in the Eysenck Personality Questionnaire (EPQ).

Questionnaire (Q) data Personality observations gathered from the use of questionnaires. Raymond Cattell used this type of data to develop the 16PF.

Rod and Frame Test (RFT) A test of field dependence/independence in which respondents are shown, in a darkened room, an illuminated rod surrounded by an illuminated square frame. Both the rod and frame may be off level at the beginning of the trial (see Figure 16-5), with the respondent's task being to rotate the rod to true vertical. Persons who easily locate true vertical, regardless of the orientation of the frame, are said to be field-independent.

situationism A theoretical position that argued the context in which behavior occurs is the most important contributor to understanding why specific behaviors occur. Walter Mischel proposed a radical version of situationism as an alternative to trait theory.

Sixteen Personality Factor Questionnaire (16PF) An inventory developed by Raymond Cattell to measures his 16 source traits and his 4 second-order traits.

source of reinforcement As used in T. Millon's theory of personality, the primary source from which individuals gain comfort or satisfaction or attempt to avoid pain and distress. According to Millon, there are five basic reinforcement orientations: detached, dependent, independent, discordant, and ambivalent.

source traits From Raymond Cattell's theory of personality, a stable but less visible antecedent of behavior that can be discovered only through the application of factor analytic technology. (See Table 16-2.)

trait An individual difference variable in personality that reflects a person's predisposition to respond in a particular way to persons, objects, or situations.

Suggested Further Reading

Aiken, L. R. (1989). *Assessment of personality.* Needham Heights, Mass.: Allyn and Bacon.

> This book provides more detail on the measurement of personality and is recommended if you wish to investigate this area more fully than was possible in this chapter. Sections on ratings, inventories, projective techniques, and a variety of other approaches and issues make this text a good next step in coming to know this domain.

Cattell, R. B., Eber, H. W., & Tatsuoka, M. M. (1970). *Handbook for the Sixteen Personality Factor Questionnaire (16 PF).* Champaign, Ill.: Institute for Personality and Ability Testing.

> Everything you ever wanted to know about the 16PF can be found in this handbook. Chapter discussions include the utilities of the test, how it was designed and constructed, psychometric properties, tremendous amounts of criterion-related validity research, and several other important topics.

Graham, J. R. (1990). *MMPI-2: Assessing personality and psychopathology.* Oxford, Eng.: Oxford University Press.

> Tremendous detail about the development of the revised MMPI, scale descriptions, profile configurations, the new content scales, other supplementary scales, psychometric properties, intepretive information, and a wide variety of other topics are discussed in this most important book. Anyone wishing further details regarding the MMPI-2 would be well advised to consult this book.

Hampson, S. E. (1988). *The construction of personality: An introduction* (2nd ed.). London: Routledge.

> This book provides excellent follow-up presentations of three of the topics in this chapter. Chapter 2 provides a more detailed review of the cognitive style of field dependence/independence, replete with many references that can be followed up if you wish to know more about this interesting individual difference variable. Chapter

3 contains a good summary of Eysenck's personality theory, and Chapter 4 is a fine analytic presentation of the consistency issue.

Kenrick, D. T., & Funder, D. C. (1988). Profiting from controversy: Lessons from the person–situation debate. *American Psychologist, 43,* 23–34.

This article presents a very constructive and fair appraisal of the person/situation debate described in this chapter of *The Enterprise.* A paper that takes an even-handed approach in exploring the implications of a highly controversial topic such as this one is rare and deserves reading by anyone interested in learning more about this topic.

Millon, T. (1981). *Disorders of personality: DSM-III: Axis II.* New York: Wiley.

This book presents the theoretical model underlying the MCMI basic personality scales exceedingly well. It provides the reader with a very rich and detailed presentation of the complex theory that led to the emergence of the MCMI.

Mischel, W. (1968). *Personality and assessment.* New York: Wiley.

This book is required reading if you want to develop a further understanding of the consistency issue. You will find a very coherent and well-argued critical appraisal of trait theory, as well as an impassioned argument for a radical situationist position. To the extent that the entire person/situation debate was framed by this book, it is important primary reading.

Mischel, W. (1993). *Introduction to personality* (5th ed.). New York: Harcourt Brace Jovanovich.

This contemporary text provides a good overview of the current area of personality. Presentations of various theoretical perspectives, methodological issues, and emerging domains of research make this an excellent source if you are looking for more detail about personality considered generally.

Discussion Questions

1. In the chapter, it was never asserted that traits *cause* behavior. Develop an argument either pro or con based on the material presented.

2. Evaluate the relative merits of traits versus types.

3. With respect to Figure 16-2, indicate how you think Hans Eysenck might argue his way out of the finding of a person who was both controlled and optimistic.

4. Suggest several other dimensions, other than Eysenck's three, that you think should be included in a complete theory of personality.

5. Evaluate the potential clinical utility of the EPQ.

6. Outline the strengths and weaknesses of Raymond Cattell's decision to use uncommon names (for example, Sizia, Zeppia) as labels for his source traits.

7. Discuss the extent to which Cattell's four second-order factors and Eysenck's three theoretical dimensions are same same thing.

8. You are a vocational counselor and decide to use a personality test as part of a program for a client. Would you use the EPQ or the 16PF? Why?

9. Compare and contrast the psychometric properties of the EPQ and 16PF.

10. Outline the strengths and weaknesses of the hierarchical model of personality presented in Figure 16-4.

11. Using the definitions of the Big Five, draw a profile that indicates your personality. Evaluate the usefulness of this profile for making social decisions.

12. Outline three possible studies that could be used to strengthen claims for the validity of the NEO Personality Inventory.

13. With reference to someone you know, indicate how traits can function both as descriptors and predictors of behavior.

14. Discuss why the usual personality coefficient is about .3, whereas the typical intelligence coefficient (IQ test-criterion correlation) is about .5 (see Chapter 15).

15. To what extent do you think that more modern tests would produce higher degrees of consistency than the older tests?

16. Outline the similarities between S. Epstein's idea of aggregation and Charles Spearman's notion of correction for attenuation (see Chapter 6).

17. List and describe the effects of four variables that you think would serve as moderators to test-criterion correlations in the personality sphere.

18. Outline as many reasons as you can think of why the idea of traits should be retained in personality.

19. Outline as many reasons as you can think of why the idea of traits should be banished from the realm of personality.

20. Discuss the possible relationships between cognitive and response styles.

21. Using your understanding of field dependence/independence, suggest a means other than the EFT, tilting room, and RFT that might be used to measure it.

22. Design a task in which field-independent people would perform poorly.

23. Table 16-5 notes that males tend to be more field-independent than females. Discuss the implications of this finding as they relate to current feminist concerns.

24. Debate whether you think field-dependent or field-independent persons would make better scientists.

25. Rate yourself on the amount of each of the cognitive styles presented in Table 16-6 that you think you possess. Using these ratings, develop an optimal strategy for studying university course material.

26. Discuss whether objective measures of personality are better than voluntary ones.

27. Outline the response you would have if you found out that a relative had been administered the old MMPI during an intake procedure in a psychiatric unit of a hospital in 1993.

28. You are a clinician and can use only one test to assess psychopathology. Would you use the EPQ, MCMI II, or MMPI-2? Why?

29. Indicate whether or not you would feel confident using the MCMI II to indicate whether a person should be assigned a *DSM* Axis I diagnosis.

30. Prepare a list of the weaknesses of the old MMPI and indicate whether the MCMI II is an improvement over these.

31. Discuss your views about the conservative approach taken in developing the MMPI-2.

32. Evaluate the strengths and weaknesses of the MMPI-2.

Chapter 17

The Neobehavioral Alternative

RESPONDING TO THE CRITIQUES

In Chapter 15, we encountered a period of turmoil and scandal within the domain of intelligence and its testing. Developments stemming from these conflicts were also outlined, paying particular attention to emerging theories of intellect and some newer tests. In Chapter 16, Walter Mischel's critique of personality was presented, along with a number of responses that were made to this formulation. Both chapters demonstrated significant change in the testing enterprise—changes that have been important in shaping the contemporary field of testing. The changes, however, were, in a sense, formulated from *within* the testing enterprise. That is, to this point, we have examined the manner in which the field itself adjusted to the tumultuous times of the 1960s and 1970s. The general tenor of these changes was "let's continue doing what we've been doing all along—but strive to do it better." Although there can be no doubt that this approach has merit, some researchers began to explore the possibility of wider-ranging changes than those noted in Chapters 15 and 16. Indeed, some of these newer developments cut a wide swath and posed serious challenges to age-old conceptions in the field, such as validity and reliability. In this chapter, we will examine a number of such changes. Here we will encounter several different arguments and test-related developments that begin to outline the alternative positions to what might be considered the classical psychometric approach to measurement.

Of particular note for this chapter is the manner in which a new approach to measurement, called here the *neobehavioral alternative,* emerged in response to critiques such as those of Mischel. In this orientation toward assessment, conscious efforts were made to eliminate or at least minimize the necessity of recourse to concepts such as traits, abilities, or aptitudes when interpreting the results of measurement procedures. The goal of this orientation is to provide accurate measures of actual behavior rather than collect signs or indicators of underlying predispositions. This view posed some serious challenges to several important traditions within the testing enterprise.

During this period, many changes were occurring. The 1970s ushered in a series of important political events, social trends, and changes to the cultural landscape. These factors influenced the introduction of the new approaches to measurement, albeit it somewhat indirectly. This period saw what became known as the **information explosion**. The amount of knowledge that was becoming available to decision makers was growing exponentially with the availability of cheaper computer technology and large databases. The increasing amounts of information reflected the emerging complexity of life during these times. Many decision makers faced the overwhelming task of trying to maintain control of increasingly complex and sophisticated organizations and situations. Because of this, there was a constant search for relatively simple solutions to incredibly complex problems.

BREAKING UP THINGS INTO LITTLE PIECES

One popular 1970s strategy for solving these problems of complexity involved partitioning a problem into smaller bits, thereby gaining a sense of control of the "bigger picture." For example, this was the era of **management by objectives** where executives would break down an organization's total activity into a set of goals. Management would then be directed by efforts to fulfill these objectives. This provided managers with a ready-made way of reducing the complexity of the work environment, giving them a sense of focus and permitting them to make decisions in the face of the massive complexity of the emerging workplace. This generalized style of problem solving—breaking down problems into smaller bits to gain control of them—emerged in a number of important areas and affected, in no small way, the testing enterprise.

The information explosion.

Another aspect of the information explosion was the manner in which it prompted a tendency to protect or shelter already extant ideas and information. Many people found themselves highly vulnerable in the face of a continual onslaught of new concepts and technology. Being assaulted by wave after wave of newness began to provide the "already known" with special status. Many people began to retrench in the face of such massive change and adopt what might be called a *conservative posture*. This involved holding on to the old ways with much more vigor than might have occurred, say, two decades earlier. This tendency was mirrored in a number of political events that profoundly changed the character of North American life. In 1974 Richard Nixon resigned as president of the United States. A year later, the Vietnam War ended, followed shortly by the election of Jimmy Carter as president. During the Carter, era there was a gradual swing from the fundamentally liberal perspective that had guided American thinking during the 1960s to a more conservative view. Defense budgets began to swell, the cold war heated up, and a sense of intellectual retrenchment followed. This trend climaxed in the election of Ronald Reagan as president in 1980. Conservative policies and thinking, where big business was the primary driving force, became the order of the day. This general trend toward conservatism framed the manner in which the testing enterprise was to develop during the 1970s and 1980s.

An inkling of the directions that the new approaches to assessment would take can be found in a paper by Alexander Wesman, one of the developers of the Differential Aptitude Test battery, entitled "Intelligent Testing" (Wesman, 1968). His fundamental argument was that intelligence, no matter how defined, is the "summation of the learning experiences of the individual" (p. 267). From this view then, there are no meaningful differences between any and all measures of ability: "All ability tests—intelligence, aptitude, and achievement—measure what the individual *has* learned—and they often measure with similar content and similar process" (p. 269).

It follows that the challenge for test developers is to sample from a relevant domain of previous learnings in the interests of predicting some future learnings (that is, criteria). What differentiates the various domains of ability testing is the criterion that the test user wishes to predict. If concern is with highly specialized and homogeneous criteria, then sampling directly relevant previous learnings—called **narrow-bandwidth testing**—is appropriate. For example, if the the criterion relates to the performance of specific skills—such as the ability to use a specific computer program—narrow-bandwidth testing would be involved because sampling previous learning of the computer application would be possible.

However, if we are interested in a wide range of relatively undifferentiated criteria, selecting a general measure such as a Wechsler test is more appropriate. This is called **wide-bandwidth testing**. For example, if the criterion involves performance of an undifferentiated criterion such as "performance in graduate school," wide-bandwidth testing would be involved, and recourse to the more traditional tests for the purpose (for example, the Graduate Record Examination) would be appropriate.

Thus, the decision about which test to use is directed by the nature of the criteria, but previous learning is being assessed in all cases. For Wesman, the critical point is which approach to ability measurement "provides the most useful information for the various purposes we wish the test to serve" (1968, pp. 273–274).

The reasoning underlying narrow-bandwidth testing is of particular significance in Wesman's argument. In this case, concern is with predicting specialized, homogeneous criteria. An example might be skill in the use of a highly technical machine such as a computerized surveying station—a machine surveyors use to help map out the exact locations of specific geographic features. In predicting who would be the best candidate to acquire skill with this instrument, testing can involve sampling candidates' abilities to perform specific, highly structured skills that are part of the overall criterion. This could involve familiarity with computer technology, understanding of surveying principles, previous history of mastery of similar instruments, and a wide range of other related skills and knowledge required to master the machine. In other words, the most effective predictive strategy is to sample from the domain of content demanded by the criterion when dealing with narrow-bandwidth contexts.

This should have a familiar ring to it. Eighty-five years previously, Alfred Binet solved a riddle that had been plaguing the neophyte testing enterprise since its birth. He argued that the best way to predict success in school was to measure success in school (see Chapter 6). By designing minisituations that allowed pupils to demonstrate their scholastic knowledge, he developed a long-sought-after means of making predictions about proper educational placement. Of particular note here was that all Binet was doing was sampling the criterion activities—vocabulary, figure copying, general knowledge, and so on—that are required to advance in the school curriculum. If you recall his caveats, Binet was adamant that the scores derived from his test were merely practical devices and did not buttress any theory of intellect. Generations of subsequent research have confirmed Binet's essential view—the best way to predict anything is to examine performance on that thing (for example, Fulkerson & Barry, 1961). For example, previous grades are the best index of future grades. From this perspective then, the best possible testing is *criterion sampling*. Simply develop a representative sample of the criterion activities and have people show how well they can do on it. Performance in this minisituation can then be used to predict future performance. Detailed criterion analysis is needed here, as is care that all relevant aspects of performance are included in the minisituation or test. An effective test, by this view, would be one that is demonstrably representative of the target activity.

CRITERION-REFERENCED TESTING

Perhaps the clearest example of this generic approach can be found in the educational field under the label **criterion-referenced testing**. Here concern is with the comparison of test performance with a specified set of criterion skills (for reviews, see Ebel, 1972; Glaser, 1963; Gronlund, 1973). For example, a criterion-referenced test in arithmetic would involve determination of whether the respondent had mastered certain types of operations (for example, ability to multiply three-digit by two-digit numbers or to compute square roots of four-digit numbers). All comparisons are made with respect to predetermined levels of performance. That is, the outcome of the test is whether or not a specific individual has performed up to standard, or demonstrated **mastery** of the material being tested.

This contrasts with the more traditional approach that might be called **norm-referenced testing**, where comparisons are made with some kind of group, or normative, population (for example, the respondent scored in the 90th percentile on an arithmetic test). Almost all tests covered so far in *The Enterprise* have been norm-referenced in this sense. Concern has been to isolate dimensions of individual differences by comparing a person's performance with that of a given norm group. In the criterion-referenced case, emphasis is on how well individuals have mastered a predetermined curriculum, not on how well they have performed relative to another group.

The following Close Up, which is adapted from Gronlund (1973), provides an example of the manner in which a criterion-referenced test can be developed. While you are examining this exemplar, notice there is no mention of higher-order constructs such as intelligence or scholastic aptitude.

CLOSE UP   Developing a Criterion-Referenced Test

Let's assume we are interested in developing a test to assess the extent of understanding of weather maps in an elementary school science class. The first step involves carefully delimiting the domain to be tested. Typically, this involves specifying the general instructional **objectives** of the unit, followed by the definition of a representative sample of the types of behaviors the students are expected to demonstrate at the completion of the unit. Table 17-1 lists the objectives and expected behaviors for our weather map example. Notice how emphasis is placed on specific (and readily measurable) learning behaviors in this table.

The next step involves preparing a **content outline**, which includes the actual material that will be instructed during the unit. Table 17-2 (page 656) presents this outline for the weather map unit. Of course, we could develop a much more elaborate outline that contains the exact terms to be used (nimbus clouds, cold fronts, and so on).

The next step in the development of a criterion-referenced test for the unit involves constructing an **objectives-by-content matrix**, which shows the intersect of each objective with each content category. Decisions about the numbers of items for each combination of objective and content area are then made and added to this matrix. Table 17-3 (page 657) presents the resultant matrix for the weather

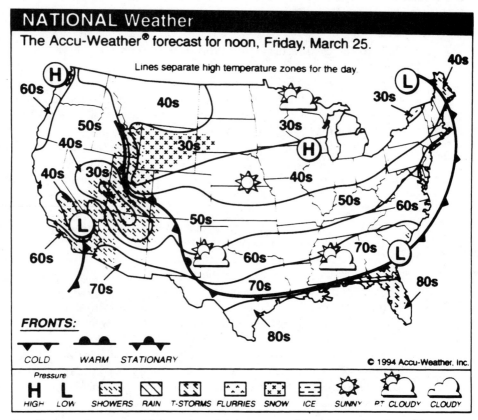

A typical weather map with legend explaining some of the conventional markings.

Table 17-1
Objectives and learning behaviors for a unit on weather maps

Objective 1:   **Knows Basic Terms**

    a. Writes a definition of each term.
    b. Identifies the term that represents each weather element.
    c. Identifies the term that best fits a given weather description.
    d. Matches the term to a picture of the concept.
    e. Distinguishes between correct and incorrect uses of the term.

Objective 2:   **Knows Map Symbols**

    a. Matches each symbol with the name of the weather it represents.
    b. Draws the symbol for each weather element.
    c. Identifies the meaning of each symbol on a weather map.

Objective 3:   **Knows Specific Facts**

    a. Lists the characteristics of a given weather condition.
    b. Identifies the elements affecting a given weather condition.
    c. Names the instrument used for measuring each weather element.
    d. Identifies the unit of measurement used in reporting each weather element on a weather map.
    e. Distinguishes between correct and incorrect procedures for determining each weather element.
    f. Matches the name of each cloud type with a description of its characteristics.
    g. Identifies weather conditions associated with each type of front.

Objective 4:   **Interprets Weather Maps**

    a. Describes the weather for a given locality.
    b. Identifies the different types of fronts shown on a weather map.
    c. Describes the weather conditions surrounding each front shown on a weather map.
    d. Identifies the direction of movement for each front shown on a weather map.

Source: Gronlund (1973, p. 25).

map unit. The variable number of items in each element of the matrix in Table 17-3 indicates the instructor's view of the importance of the particular combination of objective and content area.

The next step involves setting standards for adequate performance on the test. In essence, this is a determination of the numbers of correct items expected before the unit is considered to be mastered. This is a complex decision that requires considerable attention to instructional objectives and consideration of levels of performance necessary to proceed to a more complex unit. As a simple example, it might be determined that 85% of the specific-fact items should be answered correctly in order to accept that a student has mastered this objective. To set these standards, the instructor estimates the difficulty and importance of the various elements in the matrix.

Table 17-2
Content outline for the unit of weather maps

---

1. Air pressure
   a. Measuring and reporting air pressure
   b. Factors affecting air pressure
   c. Relation to weather changes

2. Air temperature
   a. Measuring and reporting air temperature
   b. Factors affecting air temperature
   c. Relation to weather formations

3. Humidity and precipitation
   a. Measuring and reporting humidity
   b. Factors affecting humidity
   c. Forms of precipitation
   d. Measuring and reporting precipitation

4. Wind
   a. Measuring and reporting air speed and direction
   b. Factors affecting speed and direction
   c. Symbols for reporting speed and directions

5. Clouds
   a. Types of clouds
   b. Characteristics of cloud types
   c. Factors causing cloud formations
   d. Relation to weather conditions
   e. Symbols for cloud types

6. Fronts
   a. Types of fronts
   b. Formation of fronts
   c. Weather related to fronts
   d. Symbols for fronts

SOURCE: Gronlund (1973, p. 26).

Items are then written to fill in all elements in the matrix shown in Table 17-3. For example, a question for the "Knows Specific Facts" by "Clouds" element might be a true/false question such as "Seeing nimbus clouds indicates that thundershowers are on the way." Table 17-4 presents sample items of the type that might be constructed to fill out the matrix. The choice of item format is based on consideration of the learning objectives being assessed. For example, the more complex objectives (for example, interpretation) could tend toward less structured formats (open ended), whereas the more fact-oriented material (units of measurement) could be measured using more structured formats (multiple choice).

Grading and interpreting the test is relatively straightforward with the structured items. The numbers of items correct as a function of objective and content domain are counted. Grading unstructured questions requires more interpretation but can be reliably accomplished by considering the objectives underlying the question in conjunction with the specific content being interrogated. Performance of a specific student is then compared to the preset mastery standards. Any students

Table 17-3

A matrix demonstrating the intersect of objectives and content for the weather map unit. Entries in the matix are the number of items to be included in a test.

| | Instructional Objectives | | | | |
Content	Knows Basic Terms	Knows Map Symbols	Knows Specific Facts	Interprets Weather Maps	Total Items
Air pressure	2	2	2	2	8
Air temperature	2	2	2	2	8
Humidity and precipitation	2	2	3	3	10
Wind	2	3	3	4	12
Clouds	3	2	3	2	10
Fronts	3	3	3	3	12
Total items	14	14	16	16	60

SOURCE: Gronlund (1973, p. 27).

Table 17-4

Items constructed to assess mastery of the weather map unit

Short-Answer Item
  Write a one-sentence definition of the term *humidity.*

Multiple-Choice Item
  U.S. weather maps indicate air pressure in
  a. inches.
  b. feet.
  c. pounds.
  d. millibars.

Matching Items
  Match the terms in the two columns by drawing lines to join the terms that belong together.
  1. Air pressure   a. Anemometer
  2. Air temperature   b. Barometer
  3. Humidity   c. Hygrometer
  4. Wind velocity   d. Rain gauge
                         e. Thermometer
                         f. Wind vane

Open-Ended Item
  Provide the student with a weather map and ask for a specific interpretation.

SOURCE: Gronlund (1973, p. 28–30).

who fall below the criterion are given specific remedial training to get them up to standard. Notice how the test results themselves signal the aspects of the unit that need remediation. For example, the remedial strategy for a student falling below mastery on knowledge of specific facts, but above on the rest, would be clear—teach the student the meanings of the specific terms. Once the unit is mastered, the student may then move on to the next unit in the curriculum, such as world weather patterns, which presumes mastery of the weather map unit.

Criterion-referenced testing is particularly compatible with computerized-teaching technology because students who demonstrate early mastery of a unit can move ahead at their own pace rather than having to wait for their peers.

Perhaps the most significant characteristic of criterion-referenced testing is the simple nature of the inferential network underlying test interpretation. Low performance on such a test indicates that more teaching is required. Deficiencies in specific domains of the criterion, which are identified by the test itself, can be addressed by remedial teaching. Such tests, by virtue of their mapping into the criterion are ready for remedial action, with the test results directing the next stage in the learning process. In this sense, criterion-referenced testing does not involve the extensive inferential networks (for example, nomological networks) demanded by more traditional approaches to testing.

Criterion-referenced testing is radically different from more classical views because its ultimate goal is the *elimination* of individual differences! That is, the eventual objective of a criterion-referenced program is to get all students up to standard and thereby have everyone demonstrate the same level of performance.[1] This is a very different focus compared with the more traditional view of testing, which is concerned with the measurement of enduring individual differences rather than their elimination. Norm-referenced testing would be concerned with issues of how rapidly or efficiently (or if) we might expect a student to get up to standard, whereas the criterion-referenced approach is concerned with whether or not individuals had actually attained mastery. Clearly, both approaches have their strengths, but there are important differences between them.[2]

The issue of mastery is not as simple as the foregoing section implies. This aspect of criterion-referenced testing involves placing students into one of two categories (for example, master or nonmaster) on the basis of a predetermined cutoff score (for example, answering 85% of the definitional items about weather maps correctly). The complexity arises when we realize that performance itself is clearly graded, or continuous. That is, the learning of a specific curriculum unit does not occur in an all-or-none fashion but proceeds in a cumulative and continuous fash-

---

[1] In practical applications, "up to standard" typically means some minimal level of performance that reveals that the individual is ready to proceed to a more complex unit of material.

[2] This difference between classical and criterion-referenced testing reflects the two grand intellectual traditions outlined in Chapter 5. The criterion-referenced approach seems to be more compatible with the egalitarian perspective because it is concerned with providing equal opportunities for educational programs. Norm-referenced testing can be seen as concerned with the selection of individuals for special educational treatments based on comparisons with groups of individuals.

ion. Thus, the setting of the cutoff for defining mastery involves making an important decision that has serious implications for the effectiveness of the entire testing/teaching program (see Shepard, 1984, for a discussion). For example, setting the cutoff score too low can result in students being advanced to subsequent curriculum units unprepared for the challenges to follow. Setting the cutoff score too high can result in frustration and poor use of time. Thus, decisions about placement of the cutoff between mastery and non-mastery are much more complex and important than we might have expected. Proper placement of cutoff scores requires considerable research. Although some sophisticated methods of resolving this issue have been proposed (for example, Hambleton, 1984), they typically involve considerably more research and time than are available in the day-to-day applications for which criterion-referenced testing is intended.

The issue of mastery aside, however, criterion-referenced testing does supply a new vision for the testing enterprise. It provides a means of tying the measurement process directly to action, unmediated by extensive inferential networks associated with more traditional constructs such as intelligence and personality. Viewed as a response to the extensive critiques of traditional testing resounding in the late 1960s and 1970s, this approach to measurement has considerable appeal and potential utility.

CRITERION SAMPLING

Another assessment application that demonstrates the same spirit as criterion-referenced testing was discussed under the rubric of **criterion sampling**. A provocative paper by David McClelland (1973) sketched out the rough outlines of this approach. His proposed solutions to several problems in the domain of job selection bear a striking resemblance to the approach outlined in the previous section, but with some differences.

McClelland started out by questioning the relationships between school performance and various **life-success measures**. Although intelligence tests do predict scholastic performance with some accuracy (see Chapter 15), he noted that "researchers have . . . had great difficulty demonstrating that grades in school are related to any other behaviors of importance—other than doing well on aptitude tests" (p. 2). This is a grave observation because it suggests that the testing enterprise is caught up in a vicious circle where the only thing it predicts is itself, not a useful indicator of subsequent performance. For example, he noted that Thorndike and Hagen (1959) found that the number of meaningful correlations between test performance and measures of later job success "did not exceed what would be expected by chance" (p. 3). McClelland (1973) also dissected a number of the larger studies that purported to demonstrate correlations between test performance and occupational success (for example, Ghiselli, 1966; Terman & Oden, 1947), noting that the conclusion of significant relationships was suspect. Thus, according to McClelland, neither the tests nor the school grades have much power to predict competence in real-life contexts.

Having painted a rather bleak portrait of testing, McClelland then asked the question "Where do we go from here?" His first answer to this query was the suggestion that "the best testing is criterion sampling" (1973, p. 7). He urged testers to get out into the field and analyze performance in important life situations into their behavioral components. The next step involved measuring how well an individual performed on the various components of the criterion. This sampling of criterion behaviors can then be used as a "test" that will have built-in predictive efficiency. Again, we see the evocation of narrow-bandwidth ideas as part-and-parcel of an alternative perspective on testing.

An example will help here. Suppose the goal of an assessment project is to select police officers. The first stage in developing a criterion-sampling test involves following officers around and finding out exactly what they do on a day-to-day basis. This stage is called a **task analysis** (for a contemporary discussion, see Harvey, 1991). An eventual list of police officer activities might include the following:

Driving an automobile under numerous situations ranging from normal traffic through to high-speed chases

Doing paperwork (writing accident reports, filling in various forms, and so on)

Communicating with members of the community under varying degrees of duress (for example, postaccident interviews, giving tickets, case investigations)

Emergency first-aid treatment

Disciplined radio communication

Maintaining attention under monotonous conditions (for example, at stake-outs, various security functions)

Considerable interaction with colleagues and supervisors

Court appearances

Firearm discharge

Physical confrontations

Varying types of social interactions (maintaining contact with merchants while on a beat, getting to know students in a local school, and so on).

These activities can form the basis of a testing approach that will have built-in predictive validity. All the tester has to do is develop measures of how well a person is able to perform the target activities. Driving, for example, can be assessed with a road test under specified conditions. Paperwork skills can readily be determined by developing a set of forms and asking the candidate to fill them out. It is possible to develop a rather simple and effective technique for assessing each of the component activities. In combination, this sampling of the required criterion behaviors can serve as a very effective means of selecting police officers, with those performing well on the samples being selected. This is the basic approach suggested by criterion sampling. Rather than test wide-bandwidth constructs such as intelligence or personality, McClelland suggests that assessment should be based on the criterion we are hoping to predict.

The criterion-sampling approach is not as new as suggested here. For example, in 1927 German military psychologist J. B. Rieffert convinced his superiors that the

Disciplined radio communication is one of a number of activities expected of police officers, which could be incorporated into a criterion sampling approach to selection.

selection of officer candidates would be well served by simulating some features of real military life. Candidates performing well in these simulations would be selected. Rieffert developed a number of situations in which would-be officers had to perform complex tasks under severe stress, as well as others in which they had to function as leaders.[3] Performance was evaluated in terms of how well the candidates demonstrated desired qualities of character, such as expressive behaviors of voice quality, facial expression, and movement. This approach to officer selection was very successful, with many psychologists gaining employment in the German military complex (for a review, see Danziger, 1990, pp. 165–171). So the tradition of criterion sampling is not as new as we might have thought. However, this orientation did emerge with increased popularity in America as the more traditional approaches to measurement were coming under increased scrutiny.

One of the best examples of the criterion-sampling approach is the **In-Basket Test,** which involves placing candidates for high-level management positions into a

---

[3]Interestingly, the testers in Rieffert's situations were not the passive observers we are used to in the Anglo American tradition; the German testers functioned actively and interactively to increase the stress of the situation.

situation that forces them to make decisions based on material presented to them. This form of simulation is a particularly good example of criterion sampling, and a specific example is outlined in the following Close Up.

CLOSE UP   ### The In-Basket Test

The In-Basket Test is oriented toward selection of people who would make the best administrative officers at the higher levels of an organization. This is a very challenging area of measurement because a wide variety of complex skills contribute to effective functioning at this level. Included here is the ability to organize information, to discover problems hidden within a given situation, to anticipate events that may arise, and to make proper decisions based on many considerations. Because the possibility of developing separate tests in the traditional mold to measure this wide diversity of skills and abilities would be difficult (and expensive), some other alternative was needed.

The test. The In-Basket Test consists of putting candidates into a realistic situation that demands the appropriate action with the types of materials executives might find on their desks at the start of the day. The first presentation of this test was in the context of selecting officer candidates for the U. S. Air Force (Frederiksen, Saunders, & Wand, 1957). This version of the test consisted of four sessions of 2 hours each in which candidates assumed four different roles related to air force functioning. The in-baskets for each test contained incoming letters, memos, staff studies, letters prepared for signature, and the like. In addition, a considerable amount of background information was included by being appended to the in-basket materials. This information was never complete because it typically never is in real-life situations, but there was sufficient data to allow the candidate to select an appropriate course of action.

The Director of Personnel Sub-Test. One of the four subtests, the **Director of Personnel Sub-Test,** involved the candidate assuming the position of a personnel manager. The accompanying story for this subtest was the following:

> Today you are asked to take the role of Director of Personnel of the 71st Composite Wing. The previous Director of Personnel, Lt. Col. Hart, was killed in an auto accident and you have been assigned to take his place. A manila envelope on your desk contains the materials which have collected in Hart's in-basket together with additional material placed there for your guidance. Your job is to read your mail and take appropriate action as though you were actually on the job. Write the appropriate notes, memos, letters, or directives. Take as much action as you can with the information available to you. You are limited in that no more information can be obtained during the next few hours and you can communicate only in writing. [Frederiksen et al., 1957, p. 5]

Items like the following were in the manila envelope: (1) a letter for the policy file that draws attention to an emerging public relations problem because of conflicts between service personnel and civilians; (2) a letter indicating that one airman needed a good "talking to" because of his aggressive behavior while on duty; (3) a note demanding the writing of policy to deal with hardship and bad-conduct discharges, along with information about several recent cases; and (4) a letter of grievance from some civilians who lived in a town near the base. Other types of executive problems were also placed in the envelope. The following series of letters is representative of the types of problems that occur in the test.

Communication 1: A Letter to the Director of Personnel from a Local Citizen

Dear Colonel,

Two weeks ago, two soldiers stationed at your base bought a used car from me for $400. The soldiers were Sgts. M. Jones and H. Snyder. They each gave me a cheque for $203.98 drawn on the Second Bank, with the story that these were their pay cheques for May. The cheques have been returned marked "Depositor Unknown." They asked me not to report that they were out of uniform, although this was true.

The car has since been sold to Sgt. H. Dinger, according to the State Registrar of Motor Vehicles. Sgts. Jones and Snyder have been sent overseas according to reports given me by soldiers still living in their quarters.

I wish you would do something about this. Either Sgt. Dinger should return the car to me, or pay for it. Jones and Snyder should be brought back to stand trial for bad cheque passing.

Signed: D. East

Communication 2: A Memo to the Legal Officer from the Personnel Director

Please draft an appropriate reply to this letter for my signature.

Communication 3: A Letter Drafted by the Legal Officer for the Signature of the Personnel Director

Dear Mr. East,

Your letter criticizing the actions of three airmen of this command has been referred to my legal officer for consideration. We are sorry to learn of your experiences with them.

However, we are powerless to be of any assistance to you in this matter. Sgt. Dinger's title to the car is evidently clear since the State Registrar of Motor Vehicles has accepted it. He cannot be expected to pay for the same car twice.

Although we did send a Sgt M. Jones and a Sgt. H. Snyder overseas last week, there is no proof that they were not impersonated. Sgt. Dinger tells us that he conducted all of his negotiations by long distance telephone the day after they left here for overseas. He wired them their money to Seattle, and they mailed him his title. While this is a highly unusual way to do business, the story checks in every detail except for the positive identification of Jones and Snyder.

Signed: Lt. Col. Hart

The specific materials included in the test demanded that the candidate take some kind of action. The test is unstructured in that no specific options are provided. Rather, the respondent must initiate some form of action, and the decisions taken here are thought to reveal officer potential. In the car example, the candidate has a number of options, which include (1) simply signing the letter, (2) initiating further inquiry into the records of the two principals, (3) referring the issue to his superior, (4) searching for some budgetary resources in order to enter negotiations with Mr. East, or (5) turning the issue over to civil authorities. The candidates indicated what action they would take either by signing the letter or by writing a memo to initiate one of the other alternatives.

The problems included in the In-Basket Test were derived from a wide range of interviews and written essays by accomplished officers in the role being assessed. They were validated by other members of the services to ensure that the tests had

Table 17-5
Behavior categories and sample behaviors used in interpreting the
In-Basket Test

Behavior	Car Example
Efficient use of routines	Refrains from making inappropriate requests to other administrative units.
Flexibility	Able to make changes to accommodate the unusual nature of the purported crime.
Foresight	Anticipates the problems inherent in taking the "hard line" suggested by the legal officer.
Effective data evaluation	Recognizes the important issues of the incident in relation to the goals of the base.

content and face validity. Although face validity is not important in terms of evaluating the In-Basket Test, it is an exceedingly important consideration in the design and execution of the process because the simulation must be as realistic as possible.

Scoring the test. The responses of the candidates were then sorted into categories representing the various types of responses possible. Categories included such things as "concurring with a recommendation" or "referring the problem to a higher authority" and so on. Table 17-5 lists some of the categories and some sample behaviors observed in the test. Expert judges rank-ordered the importance of the various response categories, and candidate responses were then assigned a numerical value based on this ranking. Interjudge reliabilities ranged from .47 through .91 for three judges across eight problems, with an average interjudge reliability of .73. When judges were more carefully trained, the reliabilities converged on a value of .90 (Frederiksen et al., 1957, p. 12). Split-half reliabilities are not as impressive, showing median values in the range of .55 (see Schippmann, Prien, & Katz, 1990, for a review).

The In-Basket Test was not developed primarily to demonstrate predictive validity but was intended to measure achievement of the candidates. Despite this it was found to correlate .25 with some of the achievement tests traditionally used to select officers and .15 with performance in an officer-training course. Attitudes of the candidates toward the examination were favorable, and the Frederiksen et al. report ended with a recommendation to continue test development. Subsequent reports elaborated the factors underlying test performance (Frederiksen, 1962) and relationships of these factors with subsequent administrative performance (Frederiksen, 1966).

In a careful review of In-Basket Test performance, Schippmann et al. (1990) note a tendency to confuse face and content validity in the research supporting the In-Basket. Face validity relates to the extent to which participants see the test as effective, whereas content validity relates to the degree to which all of the required job-related tasks are included in the exercise. Schippmann et al. indicate that evidence for content validity was relatively sparse in the literature. Equally sparse was evidence of construct validity. Very few examples of using the In-Basket in concert with an explicit theory of job performance were uncovered in the literature. However, some of the emerging research appeared to be offering a degree of promise. Schippmann et al. (1990) conclude their review by indicating that, to this point, only modest support of the usefulness of the In-Basket procedure was available in the literature.

In its purest form, criterion sampling is appropriate only in situations where experienced workers will be hired or when it is expected that applicants will have already mastered some of the prerequisite job components. For example, returning to our police officer–selection example, if disciplined radio communication skills are part of the criterion activity set, only those with previous experience with radio communication (which, incidentally, is strongly regulated) will fare well in a criterion test. To resolve this issue, Guion (1974) suggests that it might be possible to develop employment tests that are *predictors* of criterion performance, rather than measures of it. Thus, it might be possible to develop a test that predicts whether an inexperienced candidate would be able to master disciplined radio communication. In such cases, concern should focus on the hypothesis that a given skill is predictive of the eventual posttraining job-criterion activity. As you might expect, the similarity of the predictor test to the criterion will dictate the tenability of such an hypothesis (Fulkerson & Barry, 1961). In other words, even in cases of selecting inexperienced candidates, the fidelity of the test to the criterion being predicted is exceedingly important. Like before, there is no need to evoke wide-bandwidth constructs such as intelligence, personality, or teachability to develop such predictive tests.

A more contemporary application that incorporates some of the reasoning behind criterion sampling is known as the **assessment center technique** (for an introduction, see Bray, 1982). A small group of candidates for management or administrative positions are assembled for 2 or 3 days, during which time they are subjected to multiple measurement techniques including interviews and a variety of standard personality tests, as well as a number of situational tests such as the In-Basket. Most assessment center programs involve extensive job simulations, role playing, group problem solving, and various games. Much of the material generated in assessment centers can be considered criterion-sampling in the sense outlined above, but with the addition of some of the more traditional approaches as well. The validation of these techniques is highly situation-specific, with some of the more careful studies revealing promise (see Thornton & Byham, 1982).

Perhaps the greatest problem with this style of testing is the manner in which the tests are completely tied to a specific situation. A criterion-sampling test battery for one occupational group will not be appropriate for use with another. For example, a criterion-sampling test for police officers is of no use in selecting research scientists, or accountants, or teachers. Thus, the criterion-sampling approach is expensive because separate tests are needed for each occupation.

Criterion-sampling tests also have limited applicability within a given organization. For example, the police officer–selection test is not necessarily useful for placing candidates as detectives, street officers, or administrators once they are accepted. A whole new battery of tests would have to be developed to make these decisions. Again, this approach becomes expensive.

As well, there may be geographic and cultural constraints on the utility of a particular test battery. For example, job requirements for police officers vary as a function of geographic region (for example, rural *versus* urban), suggesting the need to develop different tests for each geographic region. In the final analysis, it would appear necessary to develop a new criterion-sampling test battery for every specific situation! Economically and practically, this is a very real difficulty with the criterion-sampling approach.

Despite this difficulty, criterion-sampling emerges as a powerful alternative to the more traditional approaches to measurement. Here we find an effective means of ensuring that an assessment enterprise will have social utility. To the extent that the criterion activity we are measuring is related directly to the performance of socially valued activities, our test will *automatically* have social worth. Drawing on the wisdom of Alfred Binet, this orientation provided a compelling option, particularly in a time when the more established domains were under tremendous critical attack.

NEOBEHAVIORISM

The criterion-referenced and criterion-sampling approaches to testing are clearly compatible with each other in their focus on measurable, explicit samples of the criterion. In addition, both modes of measurement appear to shun extensive and elaborate inferential leaps by providing a direct link between measurement and subsequent action. These communalities determined the title of this chapter: "The Neobehavioral Alternative." Both of these orientations are part-and-parcel of a much larger movement within psychology—behaviorism. To understand this linkage and some of the developments that have since emerged from it, we must step back for a moment and examine the antecedents of this most important perspective in psychology.

During the heyday of the new psychology at the beginning of the century (see Chapter 6), **introspection** was the method of choice for the development of the emerging science. Subjects would reflect on the kinds of processes they thought they were enacting while thinking and remembering, and psychology was based on these introspective reports. Watson (1913) offered a major challenge to this view in his suggestion of a psychology *without* introspection. He argued that the only proper road to a science of psychology was to follow the lead of the natural sciences and restrict consideration to entities that were public and observable. He argued that what a subject *did* was public, whereas what a subject *thought* was not; thus, the subject matter for a scientific psychology should be these public, documentable events of what subjects did. Watson called these observable events **behaviors**. This behavioristic orientation avoided the use of introspection and led to the development of a whole school of thought about optimal approaches to doing psychology.

It is difficult to overestimate the impact this argument had and continues to have on the discipline of psychology. Before long, behaviorism had spawned a language for describing human activity, which is with us today. The term **stimulus** (S) came to represent a whole class of documentable antecedent conditions, while the term **response** (R) came to represent a class of observable outcomes (that is, behaviors). Once formulated in this manner, the challenge for scientific psychology became the explanation of the links between these stimuli and responses—what came to be known as **S/R psychology**. Numerous mechanisms were proposed to underlie the S/R links, including the notions of operant conditioning formulated by Skinner (1938) and those incorporating cognitive variables thought to mediate between the stimulus and the response (Tolman, 1932). During the 1930s through the 1950s, scientific psychologists formulated many theories and constructs thought to join stimulus and response. As well, incredible mountains of data were collected to buttress these various theoretical accounts.

Viewed in hindsight, the debates about which account of S/R links is correct do not seem as important as the incredibly useful language that emerged. The division of the world into stimuli and responses—both being observable and thereby scientifically admissable—was a truly effective way of reducing the complexity of human behavior to a place where it might be possible to proceed scientifically without being overwhelmed by the incredible complexity of human thought and action. This fundamental language has become the operating metaphor for the vast majority of North American psychologists.

In this text, **behaviorism** (without the *neo*) refers to specific theoretical positions regarding the nature of S/R links (see Tolman, 1932; Watson, 1913). The *neo* in neobehaviorism refers to the generalized style of thought that places emphasis on the analysis of human behavior in terms of stimuli and responses. **Neobehaviorism**, then, is intended to indicate clearly that we are dealing with a generalized language about human conduct, not the specific theoretical accounts of S/R links. This language chooses to use the ideas of stimuli and responses as starting points in developing an analysis of human activity. In a sense, neobehaviorism refers to a *basic attitude* adopted by most North American psychologists in their attempts to solve important problems within the discipline.

It is exactly this neobehavioristic attitude that unites criterion-referenced and criterion-sampling testing outlined earlier. In both cases, the approach involved defining a set of discrete, observable entities. Indeed, both approaches involved gathering *samples of behavior*. Thus, criterion-referenced testing and criterion sampling both subscribe to the neobehavioristic attitude. The behavior samples are used as data to inform subsequent social judgments such as suitability to proceed in an ordered curriculum or the identification of the best job candidate.

Notice that there has been an important shift in this application of the neobehavioristic attitude. In the classical experimental case, such as Skinner, the emphasis was on developing accounts of S/R links. In the assessment case, the fundamental approach involves using one set of responses (the criterion sample) to predict performance on another, albeit closely related, set of responses (the criterion). Thus, in the testing enterprise, the search is for relationships between sets of responses. If experimentalists are concerned with finding **S/R laws**, it can be argued that testers are searching for **R/R laws**.

BEHAVIORAL ASSESSMENT

The most direct example of this neobehavioristic approach to measurement emerged in the mid-1970s under the label of **behavioral assessment**. Here we find an interesting mix of methods, as well as some substantial challenges to classical psychometric theory. When viewed in the context of the movement away from classical testing documented in the previous chapters, this alternative approach to assessment emerges as a particularly important and significant shift in the testing enterprise.

The fundamental goal of behavioral assessment is to facilitate clinical treatment. Thus, the measurement procedures are driven, in no small way, by therapeutic goals. The primary purposes of a behaviorally oriented clinical treatment are to identify problems and to develop behavioral interventions for the problem domain (see Barrios, 1988). For example, behavior modification involves the application of Skinnerian learning paradigms to the solution of some clinical problems (for example, Bandura, 1969). In this approach to therapy, undesirable behaviors are thought to be maintained by particular variables that reinforce, or strengthen, their performance. For example, a young child's tantrums in the classroom may be maintained by the attention that the child elicits from the teacher. To test this assertion, a miniexperiment is performed in which the teacher ignores the child's tantrums. If the frequency of tantrums decreases under this condition, then attention can be said to be the reinforcer of the behavior. Having established this, it becomes possible to develop a therapy program that will reduce and hopefully eliminate the tantrum behavior by severing the contingency between teacher attention and the undesirable behavior.[4]

Of particular note in this example, and in behavior therapies in general, is the fundamental importance of measurement for the actualization of the therapy. Behavior modification depends heavily on adequate assessment of both the specific behaviors needing modification and the reinforcers maintaining them. In the tantrum example, failure to properly assess specific events as tantrums will seriously affect the chances of demonstrating therapeutic effectiveness. The failure to properly measure teacher attention toward the child will also result in the failure to demonstrate success. Without adequate assessment, the entire therapeutic enterprise is intractable. This realization led researchers in the late 1960s and on to voice increased concern about measurement issues within the behavior modification paradigm (Kanfer & Saslow, 1969). Although some early attempts were made to force the more traditional approaches to measurement into this mold (Greenspoon & Gersten,1967), it soon became evident that the basic assumptions underlying classic psychometrics were not appropriate. Calls for new approaches were sounded: "Just as the behavioral framework has been used to generate new therapeutic procedures, it would seem advantageous to use this orientation for the construction of new assessment techniques as well" (Goldfried & Kent, 1972, p.

---

[4]Establishing a definite S/R link in situations such as this is more difficult than suggested here. Often there is no appropriate comparison group, so it is not possible to be certain that the reinforcer causes the behavior. Reintroduction of the reinforcer with a concomitant increase in the target behavior can be used effectively in this situation. For discussions, see Bandura (1969).

409). This approach to assessment is revealed in the following Close Up, which is adapted from Neitzel, Bernstein, and Russell (1988, pp. 302–305).

CLOSE UP | **A Trip to the Dentist**

Even though he was 38-years-old, Alan had never been able to shake his fear of going to the dentist. Indeed, he had avoided even a simple dental examination for over 13 years. Just the thought of making an appointment caused him acute anxiety. The added stress of feeling that his negligence might be creating serious dental problems, however, began to play on his mind, making the whole situation very difficult. He finally acceded to an examination but found the situation to be so stressful that he failed to return for the much-needed treatment. His dentist recommended that Alan enroll in a fear-reduction program, which might make him sufficiently comfortable to allow him to follow the prescribed dental treatment. He agreed to participate but refused to enter treatment unless he felt very relaxed about the situation.

A number of measures were administered to Alan in the first session with the behavioral therapist. He filled in a Dental Fear Scale and an inventory entitled Conceptions of Dentistry. He was also given another checklist that asked about his fear of other specific objects and situations in which he felt comparable amounts of distress.

Several interviews followed. Alan revealed that his fear of dentistry stemmed from very unhappy childhood experiences in the hands of a "rough, unsympathetic" dentist. These were compounded by some oral surgery during his 20s, in which Alan had not been adequately anesthetized. In all, his fear showed considerable specificity and a clear pattern of increasing intensity and growing avoidance—all suggestive of a learning process being active.

The next stage of the treatment was the most difficult. Alan had to undergo another dental examination during which a number of different measures were taken. He was told that this was necessary to provide a level of discomfort against which his performance after therapy could be compared. The therapist called this

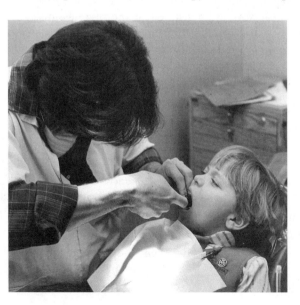

Fears associated with dentistry can be approached using behavior therapy and its allied tool of behavioral assessment.

pretreatment assessment the **baseline** measure. He filled in a short inventory called the **Anxiety Differential** while sitting in the dental chair prior to the exam. His physiological arousal was measured using Palmar Sweating (PS) (see Chapter 13) before, during, and after the examination. In addition, the therapist was in the room, observing Alan's behavioral responses using an observational system called the Dental Operatory Rating Scale (DORS). As you might expect, results of the Anxiety Differential were compatible with the PS measures, revealing considerable physiological arousal and discomfort.

Alan then participated in several treatment sessions. These included teaching him some relaxation techniques and practicing them in a dental chair in the therapist's office. He also watched a number of videotaped scenes of dental treatment (for details of the therapy, see Kleinknecht & Bernstein, 1979). A number of different measures was taken continuously during these sessions, with Alan's level of comfort being used to pace the presentation of the feared stimuli.

Finally, Alan underwent a second oral examination during which all pretherapy measures were collected again. The posttreatment Anxiety Differential score dropped to the same level documented in a relaxed, nondental setting. The PS, while still elevated relative to readings while relaxed, were meaningfully lower than the baseline levels. Although there were no pre- and postbehavior differences on the DORS, Alan was able to enter a dental-treatment program (including major oral surgery), which he had continued with minimal difficulties as noted in a 3-month follow-up assessment session.

For our purposes, the most important aspect of this Close Up is the extensive and virtually continuous processes of measurement involved. Indeed, this is one of the most distinctive features of the therapy-driven approach called behavioral assessment.

We can draw several distinctions among the multiple and frequent measures employed in behavioral assessment. For example, a number of different types of measures are typically employed. These include (1) self-reports of specific behaviors (the Dental Fear scale administered in the first session), (2) structured interviews (documenting the genesis of Alan's fear through a personal history), (3) physiological indexes (PS), and (4) behavior ratings (DORS).

As well, these measures were gathered to serve a number of different functions in the therapeutic process, including the following:

1. Documentation of the extent of the problem, including baseline measures, which can be used to evaluate treatment effectiveness

2. Determination of the specificity of the problem, which can be used to decide if a generalized or behavior-specific strategy should be employed

3. Identification of antecedent consequences that may have caused the problem and may, in turn, suggest a specific therapeutic approach

4. Isolation of agents that may be reinforcing or maintaining the problematic behavior, which can be used to design an effective treatment

5. Evaluation of the state of the client during treatment, which can be used to check if the therapy is progressing as planned and to pace delivery of the treatment

6. Assessment of therapeutic outcomes, which when compared with the baseline provide measures of treatment effectiveness[5]

7. Follow-up measures, which are particularly useful in tracking the long-term effectiveness of a treatment.

This represents a wide range of possible functions of measurements in the behavioral assessment context.

Even with this diversity of types and functions of measurement, all the various assessments in the neobehavioral category have a number of points in common. When considered collectively, these communalities clearly indicate the distinctiveness of behavioral assessment when compared to the more classic psychometrically derived measures discussed in earlier chapters.

Scope of Assessment

Behavioral assessment (as well as criterion-referenced and criterion-sampling orientations) takes a highly specific approach to the measurement act. Emphasis is on the here-and-now of actual behavior (or criterion performance), making every effort to restrict considerations to narrow-bandwidth contexts. Efforts are made to have the assessment as direct and self-explanatory as possible. This contrasts with the more traditional approaches that tend to examine global, or wide-bandwidth, characteristics. The specificity of behavioral assessment has the advantage of clarity of interpretation. However, this is purchased at the expense of generality of findings and applications of the various measurement devices emerging in the field.

Level of Inference

Like criterion-referenced and criterion-sampling approaches, behavioral assessment tends toward a rather low level of inference. That is, the nomological network underlying behavioral assessment is made as small as possible because measurements are direct observations of specific behaviors. It is not necessary, then, to create an elaborate theoretical network to make sense of what the particular measurement means. This simplification and movement away from elaborate inferential systems is an important indicator of the manner in which the behavioral assessment domain can be seen as a reaction against the more traditional approaches that value extensive nomological networks (see Chapter 13).

Frequency of Assessment

As noted in the Close Up, behavioral assessments are made very frequently before, during, and after therapy. Baseline measures, many and varied observations during treatment, and a number of follow-ups are more or less standard. This contrasts

---

[5]Ideally, a comparison group or case could be employed to strengthen conclusions about any observed changes actually being due to the treatment rather than, say, simply the passage of time or some other threat to internal validity.

with the traditional psychometric approach where multiple measurements are typically less frequent.

Making many observations on the same individual brings with it a new wrinkle. Rather than comparing an individual with a set of norms (what is called **nomothetic** testing), it becomes possible to make comparisons *within* a person. This **idiographic** approach to measurement facilitates tracking the progress of a specific individual over the course of a treatment regimen or a set of test scores. Here, then, we find a major distinction between behavioral assessment and the more traditional forms, with the former placing considerably more emphasis on idiographic, or within-subject, treatment of test scores.[6]

Emphasis on What a Person Does

Goldfried and Kent (1972) note that most classical personality inventories have been designed to provide information about underlying personality structure. Theoretical constructs such as motives, needs, drives, defenses, and traits are at the heart of nomological networks underlying these instruments. The driving metaphor within these classic tests, called **psychic determinism**, is the idea that the measured psychological states drive an individual's behavior. For example, a person's aggressive and assertive action in the workplace could be interpreted as due to a high need for achievement. People's actions, then, are seen as due to internal psychological states such as traits and drives, which motivate them to act in the way they do. In contrast to psychic determinism, behavioral assessment places emphasis on what an individual actually does in various situations. Human action, by this view, is thought to be determined by the person's previous social learning, current environmental events, and the perceived consequences of ongoing behavior, not by some deep-seated psychic construct. By this perspective, personality is seen more as a function of what a person actually does rather than as due to some underlying predisposition (see Wallace, 1966). Behavioral assessment, then, focuses on observable behaviors, not inferred constructs.

Signs Versus Samples

The difference between the traditional approach and behavioral assessment is clearly noticeable in the domain of personality assessment. In the traditional case, the response to a particular item is viewed as a **sign** of an underlying construct. For example, a response in the keyed direction to an item from the D scale of the MMPI is interpreted as a sign, or indicator, of the presence of depression. The number of such signs are added up to produce a measure of the construct. In the behavioral assessment case, the response to a particular item is thought to be a **sample** of behavior that is directly related to the criterion of interest.[7] Following from the neobehaviorist tradition, behavioral assessment focuses on specific acts

---

[6]Idiographic approaches to measurement are not that new (see Allport, 1937); under the behavioral assessment regime, however, they attained a higher degree of popularity and importance.

[7]This sign/sample differentiation can be traced to Goodenough (1949).

that the respondent does or does not do. Following our depression example, it might be possible to observe unobtrusively whether a person withdraws in several types of social situations—an aspect of classic depression. If these behaviors are demonstrated, the clinician then has the solution to two important problems: (1) A measure of the problem of concern is in hand, and (2) a ready-made beginning for fixing the difficulty is available (for example, if social withdrawal is present, facilitating social engagement may prove to be an efficient treatment). Although clearly much more complex than this example, emphasis on observable acts is the foundation on which behavioral assessment rests. In this case, all measurements are viewed as indicators of what individuals *do*, not as indexes of underlying theoretical constructs.

Locating the Cause of Behavior

Besides the major differences in their approaches to measurement, the traditional and behavioral assessment domains differ in the kinds of attributions about the causes of behavior that they value. In the extreme, the psychic determinism of the traditional perspective implies that behavior is caused by some agent (or construct) *within* the individual—for example, violent behavior is caused by being aggressive. By contrast, again in the extreme, the neobehavioristic perspective places the cause of behavior *outside* the individual—for example, violent behavior is caused by a set of extrinsic or environmental factors, what we called radical situationism in Chapter 16. These two approaches to measurement, then, carry with them a number of different assumptions about what causes behavior, with the behavioral assessment orientation being much more willing to attribute causal powers to the situation in which behavior occurs.

The debate surrounding the internal versus external origin of behavior has led many researchers to search for middle ground between the extreme positions. From this search has emerged a number of provocative ideas that in varying ways have attempted to reconcile the internal/external debate. Of note here is a class of theoretical positions that emphasizes behavior is a joint, or interactive, function of internal and external causes (Bowers, 1973; Endler & Hunt, 1966). Although these issues are far from resolved (see Wright & Mischel, 1987), they do highlight some of the major debates surrounding the internal versus external causes of behavior.

BEHAVIORAL ASSESSMENT AS A DISTINCT APPROACH TO MEASUREMENT

In the measurement domain, the debates surrounding the interaction between internal and external causes of behavior have had the unfortunate effect of blurring the distinctions drawn earlier between traditional and behavioral assessment. To the extent that researchers accept an interactional position that incorporates both extremes, there will be little sympathy for the argument that two measurement approaches, which themselves derive from the extremes, need to be considered separately. That is, many researchers consider traditional and behavioral assessment as basic variations on a single theme, rather than as distinct measurement orientations. This implies, among other things, that these two approaches to measurement ought to be evaluated using the same standards or yardstick—namely, the classical notions of validity and reliability.

However, this may be a mistake. Considering both the historical and theoretical underpinnings of these two approaches to measurement, they are radically different from each other. They are *not* variations on a single theme but represent extremely different ways of approaching the act of measurement—so different, in fact, that they must be considered separately. Fundamental and immutable differences need to be taken into account as we begin to explore the critical question about the schemata we should use when evaluating the effectiveness of a behavioral assessment.

EVALUATING BEHAVIORAL ASSESSMENTS

Initially, it seems appropriate to suggest that the age-old criteria of reliability and validity are adequate to determine if a given behavioral assessment is effective. Clinicians would not be content with a set of measurements that were demonstrably *unreliable* and *invalid* because they are dealing with issues of significant human importance. From this view, initial attempts to discuss explicitly the quality of behavioral assessment argued that application of the traditional notions of validity and reliability was both necessary and desirable (Cone, 1978; Curran and Mariotto, 1980). Indeed, early attempts to gauge progress in the field voiced disappointment because these classic psychometric criteria were not being met (Mash, 1979; Goldfried, 1979).

However, the notions of validity and reliability, as demonstrated by the historical analysis in this text, were developed in the service of the traditional/classical psychometric perspective on measurement. Perhaps these age-old evaluative criteria for tests are not appropriate to this new domain that is actively trying to disassociate itself from the more traditional approach. This argument can be developed from a number of different perspectives.

Test/Retest Reliability

From the traditional view, a test score is considered good if it represents an enduring, stable characteristic. Tests fulfilling this criterion demonstrate substantive reliability measured by the test/retest family of procedures. Such measures are thought to be less contaminated by error and to have a high proportion of true-score variance.

Behavioral assessment, however, does not assume that behavior is necessarily stable and enduring. Inconsistency in measurement *may* be due to imprecise measurement, but it may also be due to *actual changes* in behavior. Finding an unreliable (unstable) measure in the behavioral assessment context is indeterminant because it may be due to the measure or to the behavior being measured. To throw out a behavioral measure because it fails to demonstrate test/retest reliability may be throwing out the baby with the bathwater; the measurement could be perfect, and it is the behavior that is changing. Instead of assuming that low reliability reflects bad measurement, the behavioral assessment domain would address the question about what is causing the observed inconsistency (see Hayes, Nelson, & Jarrett, 1986 for a discussion). This argument presents a strong challenge to the more or less traditional notion of reliability: "Since behavior is assumed to be modifiable (often rapidly so), test–retest reliability should not be expected. . . . Thus, when inconsistency across situations, responses, or time is found, it is not necessarily a statement about the quality of behavior assessment. It is, instead, an empirical fact requiring explanation" (Hayes et al., 1986, p. 472).

Internal Consistency

Perhaps it is possible to adapt the Kuder–Richardson and Coefficient Alpha approaches to reliability in this context. These procedures, which are different from the test/retest family, permit evaluation of reliability by administering a test only once (see Chapter 11). However, these procedures also require that a number of different items or exemplars be used to generate a score. For example, it is necessary to have a number of items converging on a specific measure in order to calculate the KR20. This requirement of internal consistency measures is problematic for the behavioral assessment domain because it implies that the separate items are indicators, or signs, of some underlying construct. As noted above, this interpretation is not compatible with the behavioral assessment domain, which chooses to view test responses as samples of behavior—not signs of some underlying construct.

Practical problems also loom large with measures of internal consistency. To the extent that a behavioral researcher is trying to keep the nomological network underlying the behavior measurement and the assessment itself as simple as possible, there is a desire to minimize the number of items that are used to gauge specific behaviors. Thus, it becomes very difficult to develop the appropriate data needed to calculate a measure of internal consistency (see Rogers, 1990, for a discussion of this in the health-care context). The necessity of measuring the same behavior a number of times to calculate a measure of internal consistency is deeply limiting and typically not desirable in the behavioral assessment context.

It seems that both the test/retest and internal consistency approaches to reliability are problematic in the behavioral assessment situation. To be practical and sensitive to change, behavioral measures cannot be selected using these indexes of reliability, else the risk of failing to observe meaningful change is enhanced. It would seem that other evaluative criteria are necessary in contexts that emphasize simple, practical, and behaviorally oriented measurements. This is not to say that the generic concept of reliability (using optimally consistent measures) is not desired or demanded in the behavioral assessment context. Rather, the classic evaluative criterion of reliability and especially the methods of measuring it, which were developed to solve nonbehavioral problems, are not particularly useful in the behavioral domain. Several new developments regarding the idea of reliability, especially generalizability theory (discussed in Chapter 19), speak directly to this issue.

Criterion-Related Validity

Whether a behavioral measure predicts (is correlated with) something else is typically of little concern in behavioral assessment. As indicated previously, the focus is on what a person does, not how it is possible to use one response to predict something else. Thus, selecting behavioral measures on the basis of their concurrent or predictive validity seems inappropriate. We have already identified problems inherent in the notion of reliability, one of which is that it sets the upper limit on criterion-related validity (see Chapter 8). That is, if behavioral measures have inherently low test/retest reliabilities, there is virtually no chance of demonstrating correlations with other criteria. These factors all contribute to the inappropriateness of selecting behavioral measures to maximize correlations with outside criteria (criterion-related validity) or evaluating their utility on the basis of such correlations.

Construct Validity

Construct validity is not an important concern in behavioral assessment because every attempt is made to minimize the nomological network attending a behavioral measurement. Simply, this criterion of acceptability of a test is irrelevant for the behavioral domain.

Content Validity

The one traditional form of validity that has relevance for the behavioral domain as well as for criterion-referenced and criterion-sampling approaches outlined earlier is content validity. The extent to which a given measure represents the domain of content to which the researcher or clinician wishes to generalize is exceedingly important because failure to include all aspects of the target criterion or behavior will result in ineffective measurement. In criterion-referenced testing, if the entire curriculum of interest is not included, the inferences about mastery would be suspect. Should an important aspect of job performance not be included in a criterion-sampling approach (for example, failure to consider paperwork skills for police officers), selection decisions would result in inappropriate recruitment. In the behavioral assessment domain, it is important to consider all aspects of the target behavior, else the assessments will not have utility. We can identify three response systems that should be addressed to establish content validity in the behavioral assessment context. This **triple-response system** (Lang, 1968) involves motor, physiological, and cognitive aspects of behavior. Under conditions of behavior change, these systems can show asynchrony, with change in one or the other systems preceding change in others. Thus, the failure to assess all three components of a behavior could result in missing an actual change—thereby resulting in poor measurement. It is necessary to tap into each of these three systems before, during, and after therapy, else the chances of missing real change are legion. Content validity, defined as the representativeness of the specific behavioral measurement, emerges as an important idea in the evaluation of these types of measures.

Of the major forms of validity, the only one with direct relevance to the neobehavioral domain appears to be content validity. This does not deny the importance of the generic notion of validity—the extent to which a test measures what it purports to measure. Clearly, at a very general level, neobehavioral assessments should conform to this consideration. The problem arises when we attempt to apply methods of estimating validity that imply the existence of ideas such as traits and predispositions in this new domain. Because most of the traditional methods of estimating validity have evolved in the service of concepts such as traits and predispositions, many of the current conceptualizations and methods of determining validity pose problems for the neobehavioral domain.

Summary

The classical methods of evaluating tests—reliability and validity—are not particularly appropriate for the domain of behavioral measurement. The primacy and intuitive appeal of these classic notions make this a difficult point to accept. Ever since the emergence of the psychological test, these two foundational ideas have been the yardstick against which measurement devices have been gauged. Yet, we are arguing here that these are not entirely appropriate in neobehavioral approaches. To apply these criteria in the neobehavioral context is to force an inappropriate model onto these measurement techniques. This lesson is apt to be hard-won because there is an inevitable tendency toward accepting the first and seemingly most authoritative ideas that we encounter (see Reis & Trout, 1986).

Separating traditional from behavioral measures in this way does not imply that they cannot be used together in a specific applied situation. The foregoing relates to the manner in which we choose to select or evaluate specific tests, not to the manner in which they can be used in specific situations. Presumably, the pragmatic result of using such instruments, be they traditional or behavioral, is the touchstone we should bear in mind.

TREATMENT UTILITY AS A CRITERION FOR BEHAVIORAL ASSESSMENT

The critical question now becomes "What criteria should we use for behavioral assessment?" The answer resides in careful consideration of the purposes to which the measurements are being put. In most applications, there are two goals of behavioral assessment: (1) selecting and measuring target behaviors for modification and (2) selecting and monitoring appropriate treatment to change these behaviors. If appropriate target behaviors are chosen, clients should improve more than if inappropriate ones are chosen. If appropriate treatment is selected, then clients should improve more than if an inappropriate one is used. Thus, if the two goals are fulfilled, proper or good behavioral assessment will have contributed to improved treatment outcome. That is, the functional criterion defining a good behavioral assessment in this situation is **treatment utility**, defined as the extent to which the therapy is able to induce meaningful change in the target behaviors (see Hayes et al., 1986, for an extended discussion). Basically, considerations of reliability and validity aside, the most important concern for behavioral assessment is the extent to which measurement contributes to the overall therapeutic enterprise. If the therapy is a failure, so too is the measurement. If the therapy is successful, so too is the measurement. This deeply pragmatic criterion makes it clear that the utility of a measurement is embedded in the practical applications to which the device is put. Among other things, this suggests that the evaluation of a specific behavioral device is situational. The search for overarching criteria of good measurements is not an appropriate strategy in this particular domain. Rather, the usefulness of a behavioral assessment resides in the manner in which it facilitates desired behavior change.

Perhaps the major gain from the neobehavioral orientation is the reduction of theoretical apparatus necessary to establish the meaning of a test score. In criterion-referenced testing, there is no need for theories of academic achievement or intelligence to make sense of an obtained test score; all the teacher has to know are the areas of content deficiency and reinstruct appropriately. With criterion sampling, there is no need for a sophisticated theory of vocational choice and competence; all that is done is to sample whether the candidate can perform job-related behaviors. And in behavioral assessment, there is little or no need for an extensive nomological network underlying the test score; all one is doing is measuring therapy-related behaviors. The neobehavioral alternatives appear to undercut the necessity of demonstrating construct validity, freeing the domain from the need to consider extensive theoretical propositions as underlying test scores. In a time when the very theoretical networks underlying traditional tests are under significant critical fire (see Chapters 15 and 16), this is clearly a desirable end to achieve. The neobehavioral approaches emerge as timely solutions to important problems facing the testing enterprise.

This apparent lack of theory in the neobehavioral perspective, however, is illusory. Though it may not be evident at first, the neobehaviorist *does* employ a substantive theoretical apparatus that has a significant impact on the measurement process. This theory emerges when the test developer decides how the world will be broken down into smaller pieces. That is, the very way a neobehavioral tester chooses to divide the world into behaviors constitutes a significant theoretical enterprise. There are an infinite number of ways in which it might be possible to package units of human action into behaviors. Some may choose to focus on physiological, or bodily, reactions; some will emphasize verbal processes; some will be concerned with overt motor responses; and some may concern themselves with affective, or emotional, behaviors. There is no intuitively obvious, clearly consensual, or theoretically neutral way of defining behaviors. The very act of deciding to call something a "behavior" is to employ a theoretical belief about the nature of the world. It is here that the theoretical enterprise underlying the neobehavioral perspective becomes evident. The neobehavioral approach has simply moved the theoretical activity to another place in the measurement paradigm. Rather than having the theory underlie test-score interpretations, as is the case for the traditional perspective, neobehaviorists have their theories active in the manner in which they choose to divide the world into units. This line of argument does not imply that this family of measurement methods is useless or somehow dishonest. Rather, it indicates that one of the apparent gains of the neobehavioral approach, its seeming lack of theory, is not really the case. It is more a question of where researchers, clinicians, and/or test users wish to put their theory—up front in their definitional processes or as part of the nomological network used to interpret test scores.

It follows, then, that any attempt to develop a yardstick for the evaluation of neobehavioral tests must explicitly consider the theoretical system that has gone into determining the labeling and selection of the implied units. This involves, among other things, explicit consideration of (1) how one labels curriculum materials as units, (2) the manner in which specific behaviors are chosen as good indicators of job potential, and (3) the ways in which selection of specific behavioral measures are directed by theoretical expectations.

Thus, rather than being theoretically neutral or atheoretical, the neobehavioral position does have a significant theoretical component. For the purposes of the testing enterprise, the critical question is whether the devices, no matter their theoretical biases, can be seen to facilitate social decision making.

Summary

In this chapter, we outlined a number of different measurement approaches that can be viewed as reactions against the more traditional psychometric orientation toward assessment. Included here were criterion-referenced testing, criterion sampling, and behavioral assessment. Each mode is compatible with the generalized canons of neobehaviorism in that they all attempt to divide aspects of the world into small, readily measurable units of analysis. Whether talking about breaking down a teaching curriculum into small bits and objectives, creating opportunities for job candidates to demonstrate specific job-related behaviors, or tying the measurement process to a therapeutic endeavor, all three approaches subscribe to the reductionism inherent in the neobehavioral attitude. In this sense, they are all variations on a single theme—even though the domains to which they are applied are incredibly diverse.

The neobehavioral approaches provide an effective solution to the issues of increasing complexity, which were mentioned earlier in the chapter. The need to find a way to break down complex systems into manageable pieces in order to control them is well served by these measurement techniques. They provide a highly practical way of dividing up the world into manageable units. Indeed, the neobehavioristic attitude was a significant contributor to the emerging technology of reducing complexity to manageability by virtue of the explicit methodologies it presented to the world.

These new approaches to measurement pose a significant challenge to the traditional methods of evaluating a test. For the most part, the age-old notions of reliability and validity have to be significantly revised to provide workers in the field with an appropriate yardstick to use in determining the goodness of measures derived from these newer orientations. The single, most important criterion throughout this approach to measurement is content validity—the degree to which the measure represents the domain to which the test user wants to generalize.

Beyond that, the more traditional standards may not be particularly appropriate. These reconsiderations and reformulations (some of which will be discussed in Chapter 19) are still under way in the 1990s, revealing that there is no simple answer to the question of evaluative standards for neobehavioral tests.

Behavioral assessment and the family of methods it so ably represents emerged during a time when many researchers were attempting to move away from general, inferential characteristics such as are found in the classical IQ and personality tests. Because of this, they employed a methodology and metatheory that are very different from the more traditional approach. It remains a debate for the future whether the evaluative schemata that were derived from the earlier period of test development (for example, validity, reliability) are useful in the emerging neobehavioral domain. For the present, these newer approaches clearly provide a major challenge to the classical notions of test theory, and we can but await the directions that this debate may take.

Glossary

Anxiety Differential   A relatively wide-bandwidth measure of anxiety (not unlike the UAT presented in Chapter 13) that was used in the behavioral assessment example.

assessment center technique   An approach to job selection in which candidates are brought into a situation for several days and subjected to multiple measures (including various situational tests such as the In-Basket). Performance in this situation is carefully monitored, and employment decisions are made based on these observations.

baseline   A measure of behavior, taken prior to the introduction of treatment, that is necessary to ascertain whether a treatment has produced change.

behavior   An overt, observable act on which John Watson (1913) argued it was possible to develop a true science of psychology.

behavioral assessment   An approach to measurement in the clinical/therapeutic realm that incorporates a wide variety of techniques all oriented toward the documentation and modification of specific behaviors. Behavioral approaches are radically different from the more traditional psychometric approaches.

behaviorism   The explicit mechanistic accounts of the links between stimuli and response, such as those proposed and researched by Skinner, Tolman, and Hull.

content outline   From criterion-referenced testing, a listing of the actual material that will be instructed in a specific curriculum unit. (See Table 17-2.)

criterion-referenced testing   A neobehavioral approach for test development from education. Criterion performance is carefully articulated, and tests are developed to determine the extent to which students have mastered these.

criterion sampling   An approach to testing in which criterion activities are documented and a person's ability to deal with these aspects of performance are assessed to predict how well the individual will do in the overall criterion. This approach is particularly useful in narrow-bandwidth contexts.

Director of Personnel Sub-Test One of several subtests in the U.S. Air Force version of the In-Basket Test. The applicant must adopt the role of a personnel director and process a series of items dealing with this activity.

idiographic An approach to interpreting test scores that involves the comparison of an individual's score on one test with those obtained by the same individual on other tests. An idiographic orientation involves the search for unique patterns of test scores *within* an individual.

In-Basket Test A representative criterion-sampling test in which job applicants are given a series of items related to the job for which they are applying and asked to act on these. The effectiveness of their decisions are used as an indicator of job suitability.

information explosion A term given to the tremendous amounts of knowledge and information that have emerged particularly in the last three decades. The overwhelming amounts of information available have forced us to adopt new strategies for accepting and valuing new data.

introspection The act of trying to determine the nature of ongoing psychological processes by reflecting inward on what appears to be occurring while tasks are being performed. John Watson's behaviorism was explicit in its formulation of a psychology without introspection.

life-success measure An indicator that reflects how well persons are contributing to society and/or to the actualization of their own abilities. David McClelland notes that correlations between these measures and tests of wide-bandwidth constructs such as intelligence are not particularly high.

management by objectives A strategy adopted in business wherein management decisions are made in terms of the stated goals and aspirations of the unit. The manner in which this process integrates with financial planning and the facility it gave managers in breaking down complex organizational systems into manageable units renders this a particularly popular approach. This strategy is compatible with the neobehavioral attitude.

mastery A preset standard of performance on a criterion-referenced test that will communicate to a teacher that a student has adequately understood the instructed materials and is ready to move on to a more complex unit. Setting mastery standards is an important, difficult, and complex aspect of criterion-referenced testing.

narrow-bandwidth testing A testing situation in which the criterion being predicted is highly specialized, specific, and homogeneous. Criterion-sampling is thought to be the most effective approach to measurement in such contexts, which contrasts with wide-bandwidth testing.

neobehaviorism A generalized attitude toward the solution of psychological problems that involves breaking down stimuli and responses into small units (often called behaviors) in order to reduce complexity and to gain a lever for their scientific investigation.

nomothetic An approach to interpreting test scores that involves the comparison of an individual's score on one test with the scores of a relevant sample of other individuals. A nomothetic orientation involves the search for test score variability *between* individuals.

norm-referenced testing   An approach to testing where scores are interpreted by making comparisons with some kind of group or normative population. Most of the testing applications covered in *The Enterprise* are norm-referenced, with criterion-referenced testing in this chapter being an exception.

objective   A stated goal. In criterion-referenced testing, objectives are stated in terms of the learning performances and content knowledge expected if a curriculum unit has been mastered.

objectives-by-content matrix   A table representing the intersect of learning objectives and instructional content from which it is possible to develop a criterion-referenced test that fairly represents the entire curriculum to be mastered. (See Table 17-3.)

psychic determinism   A position that suggests internal states such as traits and drives cause behavior.

response   A documentable, observable, and external action performed by an organism.

R/R laws   A regularity demonstrated in the relationships between one class of responses and another. Typically associated with correlational approaches (for example, test-criterion relationships), R/R laws were suggested to be an aspect of how the neobehavioral attitude emerged in the testing enterprise.

sample   The manner in which behavioral assessors tend to view test-item responses as actual indicators of human action rather than as signs of some underlying construct.

sign   The manner in which test-item responses are interpreted as evidence for the presence of an underlying construct such as a trait or intelligence. This contrasts with behavioral assessment that views test-item responses as samples of behavior.

S/R laws   A regularity demonstrated in the relationships between stimuli and responses.

S/R psychology   An approach to developing a science of behavior that focuses on developing explanations of the links between stimuli and responses.

stimulus   A documentable, observable, and external event that occurs in the environment.

task analysis   Breaking down a specific job into a series of activities that must be performed in order to be successful. This is an important first step in the development of criterion-sampling tests.

treatment utility   A general term that relates to an evaluative judgment about whether a given behavioral treatment was effective. The quality of a given behavioral assessment is said to be dictated by overall treatment utility.

triple-response system   A convenient division of behavior into motor, physiological, and cognitive components. This idea serves as a check for the behavioral assessor to ensure that all aspects of a given behavior are included in a given context.

wide-bandwidth testing   A testing situation in which the criteria are general and relatively undifferentiated. In such contexts, the more traditional psychometric tests such as general measures of intelligence are more appropriate. This contrasts with narrow-bandwidth testing.

Suggested Further Reading

Bellack, A. S., & Hersen, M. (Eds.). (1988). *Behavioral assessment: A practical handbook* (3rd ed.). New York: Pergamon.

This is one of two highly useful handbooks that provide considerable detail and updating to the domain of behavioral assessment (see also Ciminero et al., below). The discussion of fundamental issues underlying this approach to measurement in Chapter 1 is very useful, as is the presentation on psychometric issues in Chapter 2. There is an interesting section relating behavioral assessment to *DSM* III (Chapter 3) and an excellent discussion of future directions in this growing field.

Berk, R. A. (Ed.). (1984). *A guide to criterion-referenced test construction.* Baltimore: Johns Hopkins University Press.

Perhaps one of the best ways to gain a sense of the evolving area of criterion-referenced testing is to look at a state-of-the-art presentation of the "how to's" of the domain. Berk's guide is exactly this, providing the reader with a rich sense of the very fabric of the criterion-referenced approach. It is highly recommended if you want to pursue this area at greater depth than is presented here.

Ciminero, A. R., Calhoun, K. S., & Adams, H. E. (Eds.). (1986). *Handbook of behavioral assessment* (2nd ed.). New York: Wiley.

Part 2 of this book provides very nice detail on the various approaches possible in the complex and expanding domain of behavioral assessment. Part 3 contains chapters on a number of specific applications such as the behavioral assessment of anxiety, depression, and social skills. For the student interested in exploring possible applications of behavioral assessment, this book is highly recommended.

Harvey, R. J. (1991). Job analysis. In M. D. Dunette & L. M. Hough (Eds.), *Handbook of industrial and organizational psychology* (2nd ed.). Palo Alto, Calif.: Consulting Psychologists Press.

This chapter provides a wonderfully rich review of many contemporary developments in the area introduced as criterion-sampling in this chapter of *The Enterprise*. Here you find a detailed and thorough review of the emerging literature associated with the isolation of job characteristics, the manner in which these can be matched to individuals, and the attending predictive issues.

Leahey, T. H. (1992). *A history of psychology: Main currents in psychological thought* (3rd ed.). Englewood Cliffs, N.J.: Prentice Hall.

This book provides, among other things, a wonderfully argued history of the emergence of behaviorism, which is particularly relevant for the discussion of behavioral assessment in the present chapter. After sketching some of the background factors, Leahey introduces the emergence of behaviorism in Part 3. He then considers developments in this position after World War II and traces the emergence of a number of challenges to the behaviorist perspective (Chapter 14). For the forward-looking student, the latter part of the book provides some interesting insights into contemporary issues. Leahey is fine support reading for the present chapter.

Discussion Questions

1. Discuss two examples of the neobehavioral attitude based on some experiences that you have had.

2. Debate the advantages and disadvantages of the information explosion as they have emerged in the last several years in our culture.

3. Using some of the concepts discussed at the end of the chapter, develop a critical position regarding management by objectives.

4. If you are familiar with the feminist critique, offer an appraisal of the neobehavioral attitude as defined in the chapter.

5. Develop a clear link between Alexander Wesman's idea of intelligent testing and Alfred Binet's time-honored approach.

6. Discuss the strengths and weaknesses of narrow- versus wide-bandwidth testing.

7. In information processing, there is a problem called the *bandwidth-fidelity dilemma*—the narrower the bandwidth, the more faithful information transmission. Suggest how this idea might be used to provide an understanding of some of the measurement difficulties outlined in the chapter.

8. Outline a criterion-reference approach to developing a test to assess mastery of the material in this present chapter.

9. Would you be happy with the test developed in Question 8 above? Why, or why not?

10. Briefly discuss four different situations in which the criterion-referenced approach appears to have particularly good application. Defend your choices.

11. Delineate the fundamental difficulties attending the decision to adopt a specific criterion of mastery in a criterion-referenced situation.

12. Discuss whether you think it is true that more complex learning objectives cannot be addressed using structured questions, requiring more open-ended formats. If this is true, what can you say about a course that is evaluated solely using multiple-choice questions?

13. Do you see the possibility of developing a complete approach to testing that has the fundamental goal of eliminating individual differences? What would it look like?

14. In the early German military application of criterion-sampling discussed in the text, the test administrators were very active during the testing situation, ensuring that it was stressful and combatlike. Outline the strengths and weaknesses of this procedure.

15. Discuss your view of the importance of David McClelland's observation that tests do not predict life-success measures very well.

16. Do a task analysis for being a successful student at your level of study.

17. Looking at your answer to Question 16, develop a method of predicting success at your level of study without recourse to wide-bandwidth constructs such as intelligence and personality.

18. Sketch a rough outline of how you might adapt the In-Basket Test to selecting candidates to be hired for the job you most recently held (or presently hold).

19. Discuss the importance of face validity in situational tests such as the In-Basket.

20. Clearly differentiate between face validity and content validity in situational tests.

21. You are approached by an executive from MacDonald's who wants to develop a means of selecting individuals to become franchisees in their fast-food chain. Would you consider using the assessment center technique? Why, or why not?

22. Outline a contemporary line of thought that is patently *not* neobehavioristic in its fundamental orientation.

23. Outline a behavioral assessment program that might be helpful for a colleague who is experiencing significant test anxiety.

24. Suggest as many strengths and weaknesses as you can surrounding the high degree of frequency of administration associated with behavioral assessments.

25. Clearly indicate the relationship between the notion of psychic determinism as discussed in this chapter and some of the issues discussed in Chapter 16.

26. Outline an alternative to the classic ideas of reliability that might be useful for evaluating behavioral assessments.

27. Indicate why the triple-response system is *not* a sufficient check to ensure that a behavioral assessment has content validity.

28. Critically evaluate the notion of treatment utility as a means of determining the effectiveness of behavioral assessments.

29. With reference to a specific example, indicate exactly how the action of categorizing a piece of human action as a "behavior" is theoretically driven.

Chapter 18

Neuropsychological Testing

In This Chapter

INCREASED INTEREST IN BRAIN RESEARCH

By the early 1980s, a great movement toward conservatism was in full swing in North America. Within social service agencies and allied research enterprises, this trend emerged as continual fiscal attacks that forced rationalization of their organizations to an increasingly skeptical and cost-conscious public. A particularly good indicator of the times was demonstrated in the tremendous media coverage attending the attempted assassination of President Reagan by John Hinkley, Jr., in 1981. Hinkley's defense rested fundamentally on an insanity plea arguing that he was mentally deranged when the crime was committed. The insanity plea had been a viable defense since 1954 by virtue of the **Durham Rule** wherein an accused is blameless if the crime was the result of mental disease or mental deficit. The major activity of the highly publicized trial involved psychiatrists for the defense, arguing insanity, and other psychiatrists for the prosecution, arguing the opposite view. These proceedings were described as a three-ring circus, where it became clear that the mental-health disciplines disagreed within themselves and could not provide the kind of conclusive evidence demanded by the courts in this most important case.[1] In a watershed decision, the Durham Rule was overturned, prompting many to suggest that the insanity plea, not Hinkley, had been on trial and that it had lost. The trial received massive television coverage, as did the apparent weaknesses of the mental-health professions.

The Hinkley trial is just one incident of many that supported increasing skepticism about the mental-health field during this time. Before long, many social programs were experiencing budget cuts, all under the banner of increased fiscal accountability and financial belt-tightening. As part of the overall policies of the time, the educational, clinical, and counseling domains, three of testing's major areas of activity, faced increasing financial woes.

A particularly important trend emerged during this gradual shift in the American mainstream. Slowly but surely, the intelligentsia began to embrace a more physicalist perspective in its attempts to understand the human condition. Physiological approaches that focused on the brain and brain functioning appeared to offer less controversial and perhaps more tractable perspectives on human problems. The impressive earlier successes of innovations such as drug therapies to alleviate psychotic symptoms (see Chapter 14) helped sustain this gradual shift. Television and radio shows documenting ongoing research exploring the brain became popular. The emergence of new technologies like computerized transaxial tomography (CT scans), positive-emission tomography (PET scans), and nuclear magnetic resonance measurement (NMR) in hospitals across North America contributed to the sense that brain research was on the cutting edge of current scientific progress. Established brain researchers such as Roger Sperry won Nobel Prizes. Indeed, some incredible breakthroughs were occurring. The genetic sources of diseases such as Huntington's chorea were unraveled. The neurochemical basis of Parkinson's disease came to light. Genetic duplication of life (cloning) was demonstrated. The actual manipulation of genes became possible. These and myriad other incredible developments gradually strengthened the swing toward physical, biological explanations of human phenomena.

Brain research, however, had been ongoing for centuries; the historical roots of this endeavor can be traced back to the Greeks (see Churchland, 1986). Since then, countless numbers of researchers have been toiling away in their laboratories sketching out the foundations of brain science. In more recent times, the interaction between these classic brain sciences and the discipline of psychology has become known as **neuropsychology**. What changed during the 1980s was the popularity of this subdiscipline and the general perception of its importance for solving important human problems.

---

[1]In fairness, the mental-health professions were not designed to fit into the confrontational approach on which legal proceedings are based. This debate was really played out on an uneven field where the rules favored the creation of an image of psychiatry as being in a state of disarray and confusion.

High tech methods of observing the brain have contributed to the popularity of this approach.

Perhaps it should not come as a surprise, then, to find that the testing enterprise became increasingly involved in neuropsychology during the 1980s. An indication of this can be found by examining various editions of the *Mental Measurements Yearbook (MMY)*. In the eighth edition (Buros, 1978), neuropsychological tests were not considered to be a major classification, even though some relevant tests were reviewed in both this edition and several of the earlier ones. However, by the ninth edition of the *MMY* (Mitchell, 1985), neuropsychological tests had become a major classification entry. This yearbook indicated that there were 14 neuropsychological tests accounting for 1% of the total 1409 listed. All 14 tests were listed as new, and 20 reviews of 12 of the tests were included. It would appear, then, that neuropsychological tests emerged somewhere around 1980 as far as the testing enterprise is concerned. This does not deny the long tradition of research dealing with the topics of neuropsychology but indicates that published batteries of tests deriving from this perspective have only recently achieved major status within the testing enterprise. Indeed, many different neuropsychological tests were being developed prior to 1985, but most of these were not being published or actively promoted.

EARLY NEUROPSYCHOLOGICAL TESTS

Prior to the 1980s, several tests had been proposed to facilitate clinical practice within the framework of neuropsychology. In large measure, these tests were concerned with attempting to make a gross evaluation about whether a presenting clinical symptom was due to brain damage (described as an **organic deficit**). In clinical practice this distinction is important because the therapy selected will be determined, to a great degree, by the organicity of the problem. These earlier tests, though gaining some popularity in the field, were often adapted to neuropsychological applications from elsewhere, with the original test being developed to serve some other purpose. The best known of these early tests was the Bender–Gestalt Test, which is outlined in the following Close Up that will give you a sense of some of the problems confronting efforts to design tests that can facilitate the job of the clinical neuropsychologist.

CLOSE UP   The Bender–Gestalt Test

The **Bender Visual-Motor Gestalt Test** has received extensive clinical use since its introduction in the late 1930s (Bender, 1938). It involves nine simple designs, like the ones shown in Figure 18-1, asking patients to copy each one as best they can. The original test was intended to examine the responses of children and adults to visual stimuli. Bender was interested in the extent to which they saw the designs as integrated, or whole, perceptual experiences. However, it was not long before the test was being used to make other kinds of decisions. Indeed, over time, at least five major methods of scoring, all of which involved departure from Bender's original ideas, have been proposed (see Canter, 1985). For example, Pascal and Suttell (1951) developed a complex interpretive schema that results in a score said to identify patients "in need of psychiatric help." As well, Bender's figures have been used as stimuli for a projective test (Hutt, 1977).

From a neuropsychological perspective, Hain (1964) developed a scoring system (the **Hain scoring system of the Bender–Gestalt Test**) based on the types of errors made by organic and nonorganic patients in copying the Bender patterns. For example, he noted that organic patients tended to rotate the designs when they reproduced them more than did nonorganics. Eighteen types of errors made more frequently by organics were identified, and a scoring system that assigned varying weights to each sign was developed. For example, a rotation was given a weight of 4, and a significant omission was worth 2. This process results in a number that can vary between 0 and 42 (multiple instances of the same error are scored only once). A cutoff score was established for discriminating organic from nonorganic patients.

Initially, the Hain scoring system for the Bender appeared to be an impressive indicator of organicity. Original research indicated that the test was between 60% and 90% correct in placing patients into the organic category (see Bigler & Ehrfurth, 1981, for a review); however, there were some problems. Table 18-1 presents results from one of the less favorable validity studies for the Hain system. These data show the accuracy of the Hain system for differentiating between a group of 21 brain-damaged and 21 nonorganic, psychiatric control patients (Hain, 1964). The cutoff point used with Bender in this table was >8, the optimal point

Figure 18-1
Designs of the type used in the Bender–Gestalt Test.

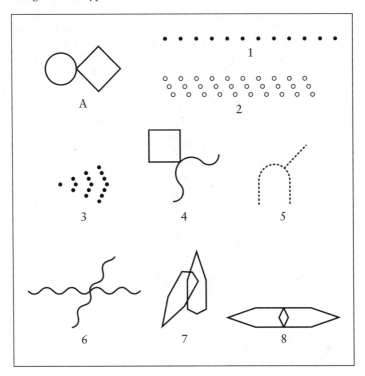

Table 18-1
Validation data for the Bender–Gestalt

| | | Patient type (Based on Confirmed Diagnosis) | | |
		Brain-Damaged	Psychiatric Control	Total
Predictions from	Nonorganic	10	15	25
the Bender	Organic	11	6	17
	Total	21	21	42

Source: Hain, (1964).

derived from another sample of 58 patients from the same population presented in Table 18-1.

These data can be understood using the same approach employed with the army air force tests described in Chapter 12. First, how well does the test do in predicting nonorganic status? If all patients predicted to be nonorganic by the test were treated as such, a total of 25 patients would be selected. Of these, 15 patients (that is, 60%) would be correctly classified. This represents a 10% gain over not using the test (that is, calling everyone nonorganic). Second, how does it predict organicity? Of the 17 patients whom the test predicts to be organic, 11 (65%) would have been correctly classified. This is a 15% gain over not using the test (calling everyone organic). Finally, considering all predictions, the test accurately identifies 11 + 15 = 26 of the 42 patients (62% correct). This is 12% greater than the base rate. By this analysis, the Hain system for scoring the Bender appears to "beat the base rates."[2]

There is more to evaluating a test, however, than beating the base rates. Significant problems loom for the Bender as an indicator of organicity when we realize that classification errors can have horrendous therapeutic implications. For example, the error of labeling people "organic" when they are not could result in the decision to perform a permanent and invasive therapy (such as surgery) when it is not warranted. Thus, examining the significance of the different types of errors that the test makes before considering the Bender to be an acceptable test becomes necessary. Of particular interest here is the performance of the test with true brain-damaged patients. Looking at only the organic cases in Table 18-1, the test is not particularly accurate because 10 of the 21 diagnosed brain-damaged patients (48%) are *misclassified* using the test. That is, the test functions at a chance level when dealing with diagnosed brain-damaged patients. This is deeply problematic because the therapeutic implications of missing a true organic case (which happens 48% of the time) are highly significant. Though less significant in terms of the numbers, the implications of misclassifying a nonorganic patient as brain damaged (which happens 6/21, or 29%, of the time) can be equally devastating—particularly, as indicated earlier, if permanent and invasive (surgical) therapy is involved.

So in the hard light of important decision making, the generally poor level of accuracy of the Hain system for interpreting the Bender indicates that it ought not be used (see Bigler & Ehrfurth, 1981, for detailed argumentation). The Bender might be able to contribute as part of a larger battery, but such an application would require extensive empirical analysis of the kinds of unique variance the test can contribute to such a battery. Such empirical analyses are not available. Another very important point is that the clinical utility of a gross differentiation between organic and nonorganic is questionable. It would seem more appropriate to focus concern on tests that provide more detailed and precise information than the crude (and not overly accurate) label of organic versus nonorganic.

The experience with the Bender–Gestalt and other similar earlier tests begins to hint at the incredible range of problems facing researchers who hope to develop tests that might make meaningful contributions to clinical neuropsychology. This is exacerbated by the incredible complexity of the basic organ at the root of this domain—the human brain.

---

[2]Hain (1964) selected the sample in Table 18-1 such that the base rate for organicity was .5. Recall from Chapter 12 that these are the conditions under which a test will show optimal discriminative power. In other words, the data in Table 18-1 are the best-case scenario for the Bender. It is an empirical question whether this is a fair test of the test—perhaps the base rates in the real world are significantly deviant from .5, which would soon consume the gains over the base rates demonstrated above.

THE COMPLEXITY OF THE HUMAN BRAIN

On average the brain occupies about 1300 cubic centimeters (cm³), just a bit larger than a softball. There are, of course, individual differences with human brain volume, revealing a range between (roughly) 1000 and 2000 cm³ across individuals. An incredible array of differing types of cells is packed into this rather small package. The basic building block of the human nervous system is a family of cells called **neurons**. These are like most other cells observed in nature—with nuclei, cell bodies, DNA, and so on—except that they are specialized for the transmission of **impulses**, which makes up the major activity of the system. It is estimated that the human **central nervous system (CNS)**, which includes the spinal cord and major sensory nerves as well as the brain, contains over 20 billion (20×10^9) neurons! In addition, there is a whole family of support units, called **glial cells**, of which (roughly) 10 exist for each neuron. Thus, on average, the CNS contains somewhere in the vicinity of 20×10^{10} cells—an astronomical number of individual units.

You might think that all of this is really not that complex—after all, if each neuron is attached to one another, there would be only 10^9 connections between these cells in the brain. These connections are called **synapses** and transmit impulses between cells by means of highly sophisticated chemical reactions between substances secreted by the stimulated neurons (called **neurotransmitters**). Life, however, is not that simple. For example, one class of neuron in the brain, called a **Purkinje cell**, can connect with as many as 100,000 other neurons. Can you imagine the almost infinite numbers of possible connections between neurons within the CNS under these conditions? Even if each neuron contacted a mere 100 others, the emergent network would be staggering in size. Viewed in terms of the number of potential nodes within a neuronal network, the size of the human brain is absolutely mind-boggling (forgive the pun).

From this perspective, it seems somewhat of a miracle that a sense of order and organization emerges from this virtually infinite network of neurons and synapses. Perhaps even more miraculous is that this immense complexity supports the sense of self and self-related experience that drives our phenomenological world. It turns out that, based on generations of brain research, many impressive consistencies in organizational patterns have emerged. These consistencies, and some of the basic research exploring how they are affected by various types of damage, provide the foundation for attempts to develop useful neuropsychological tests.

Perhaps an example will help here. Research in brain function has, for some time now, documented that damage to specific regions of the brain may produce discrete and measurable behavioral changes. For example, a lesion in **Broca's area** (a small region in the left frontal section of the brain[3]) produces a condition in which a person cannot speak but can understand what others say; this is called **aphasia** (Figure 18.2, page 694).

One approach to neuropsychological testing is to work backward from this type of finding by suggesting that the documentation of specific behavioral changes

---

[3]In some left-handed persons, Broca's area is in the right frontal region.

Figure 18-2 Schematic of human brain: top, from above; bottom, the left hemisphere from the left side of a right-handed person.

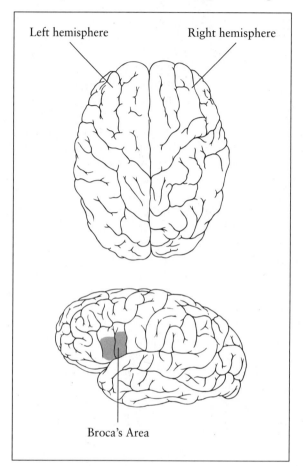

Left hemisphere   Right hemisphere

Broca's Area

can be used to localize the affected area of the brain. For example, finding a patient who can understand what others say, but who cannot speak would seem to suggest damage to Broca's area. In the interests of remediating the problem to the greatest extent possible, some tests provide a sophisticated means of assessing behavior in order to permit inferences about the site of possible brain damage. One possible criterion for validating these tests is the accuracy with which the predicted locus of brain damage agrees with the actual area involved. Thus, neuropsychological tests emerge as systematic behavioral observations that can be used to provide a relatively convenient indicator of the locus of brain damage. This knowledge can be particularly useful in helping professionals explore the possible area of damage and monitor the effects of whatever therapeutic interventions are undertaken to treat the complaint.

INDIVIDUAL DIFFERENCES IN NEUROLOGICAL ORGANIZATION

In practice, though, matters are not as simple as our Broca's area example might suggest. Without doubt, the major difficulty in successful application of neuropsychology in the testing enterprise is the problem of individual differences. Most research in neuropsychology attempts to find consistent relationships between brain function and behavior. In the tradition of the experimental or S/R psychology outlined in Chapter 17, these researchers are searching for generalizable, universal laws relating the brain to behavior.

In the practice of neuropsychological assessment, however, these relations vary considerably from person to person. The brief glimpse of the immense complexity of the CNS is a good hint that we might expect substantive variation in the manner in which the networks evolve for different individuals. For example, there is clear evidence that neurological organization is different in left- and right-handed persons (for details, see Springer & Deutsch, 1989). Left-handers also have a number of possible different modes of organization. The fundamental issue is that no two human brains are alike. Substantive variations in the distribution of various types of cells, blood vessels, neurochemistry, and various other factors are the rule in this domain, indicating that generalizations from the experimental literature to individual cases must be made with considerable caution.

But there is more. The largest part of the human brain, called the **cerebrum**, is made up of two half brains called **cerebral hemispheres** (Figure 18.2). These sit on the left or right of a major fissure and, except for a large tract of fibers called the **corpus callosum**, are totally separate from each other. Another dimension of individual differences emerges when it becomes clear that the two cerebral hemispheres within a given brain are themselves different from each other in terms of size, the nature of the major folds on the brain surface (called **fissures**), organization, distribution of neurotransmitters, and a wide range of other variables (see Geschwind & Levitsky, 1968). This finding of differences between the two half brains is called **cerebral asymmetry**. Generations of neuropsychological research have revealed a wide range of **functional asymmetry** also associated with the two hemispheres. That is, not only are the two half brains different in size, but they also appear to control different aspects of various psychological functions. Indeed, the example of Broca's area and aphasia reveals that one hemisphere appears to be more deeply implicated in certain linguistic processes than the other.

The implications of these findings for neuropsychological testing are legion. In such an individuated environment, neuropsychological principles derived from research must be applied to specific cases carefully and conservatively to avoid serious errors. Here neuropsychological testers find themselves in the onerous position of having to be experts not only in assessment but also in the fundamentals of all aspects of neuroscience, else the chances of misanalysis of data are great. There is no such thing as a part-time neuropsychological tester; persons involved in this domain of testing, because of the inherent complexity of the domain, must be competent in neuropsychology *and* testing. The idea of pulling a test like the Bender off the shelf and generating a viable assessment result by following the instructions is *not* acceptable practice in this domain.

A number of other factors also complicate the picture, including the following:

1. Patients involved in research are highly selected for specific types of (researchable) disorders, thus attenuating the generalizability of the research literature.

2. The effects of smaller brain injuries can be highly subtle and ephemeral, demanding considerable sensitivity from the tests.

3. In some cases, the brain is wonderfully creative at compensating for brain injury, making the task of using behavioral indicators very challenging— particularly with younger patients.

4. Current neuropsychological assessment procedures cannot easily discriminate between people with extensive brain damage and people with gross cerebral dysfunction such as occurs in schizophrenia.

Each of these difficulties reveals that neuropsychological testing is a highly challenging and sophisticated enterprise.

With these caveats in mind, let us now examine the manner in which contemporary neuropsychological testing works. In the following Close Up, we will examine a specific case, followed by a detailed discussion of the tests used in this example.

CLOSE UP   **Ron Paints the House**

It was on one of those blue-skyed September days when Ron realized that he should paint the trim on the house before winter set in. He had always enjoyed painting because it was such a diversion from his work as a corporate tax attorney. On Saturday morning, he busily set about his work, renting a ladder and purchasing paint. By 10:00 his foot hit the first rung of the ladder, and his day of diversion had begun.

He was working on the soffit under the garage, trying to avoid covering himself completely in paint, when the ladder collapsed, throwing him awkwardly onto the driveway. He hit his head and collapsed into a heap as the paint ran slowly down the driveway toward the street.

His wife said it was at least 10 minutes before he regained consciousness. She immediately took him to the emergency room at the general hospital. He had a massive headache, and his pupils were slightly dilated—signs of head injury. His speech seemed relatively normal, but he did have some difficulty finding words when talking—a condition the medical staff called dysnomia. An X-ray series was negative, but the attending physician admitted Ron for further tests. An **EEG** and a CT scan revealed no abnormalities. The next day his symptomatology abated, so he was released.

Six weeks later, Ron returned for a follow-up exam. Since his fall, he had regularly suffered from headaches and had experienced frequent periods of dizziness. The dysnomia had returned, and he was experiencing deep feelings of anxiety and depression. What worried him most was a loss of memory abilities, which was causing him considerable difficulty at work. His wife indicated that his personality had changed, with her usually well-controlled husband showing frequent signs of anger and loss of temper at the smallest incident. There was now a real sense of concern that Ron's injury may have been worse than originally thought.

He was admitted to the hospital again, but, as before, the standard diagnostic tests (EEG and CT scan) were within normal limits. In addition, though, Ron was referred to the neuropsychological assessment center at the hospital. According to his physician, the reason for this referral was to delineate the cognitive and behavioral aspects of his problem, with an eye to developing a proper treatment.

This Close Up presents the details of a specific case of head injury, which culminated in the referral of 32 year-old Ron to a neuropsychological testing center. The goal of this section of the text is to provide a broad level of understanding of the manner in which the testing enterprise can contribute to cases such as this one. Before returning to Ron's case history, it will be necessary to explore several important ideas underlying neuropsychological assessment and to examine the battery of tests that Ron took as part of the efforts to help him through his trauma.

CONTEMPORARY NEUROPSYCHOLOGICAL TESTING

Most neuropsychological assessments for adults begin with standard IQ tests such as the WAIS–R. They provide invaluable information about the base level of cognitive functioning, which is very important for tracking recovery. These tests are also useful diagnostic tools in themselves because of the separate verbal and performance measures they provide. A difference of more than 10 points between the verbal and performance scores is usually taken to be clinically significant, although statistically this interpretation is somewhat questionable.[4] Research has shown that well-defined left-hemisphere lesions produce a relatively low-verbal IQ, whereas well-defined right-hemisphere lesions produce a relatively low-performance IQ.[5] Diffuse damage, on the other hand, tends to produce a low-performance IQ, complicating the issue somewhat.

To be thorough, though, a neuropsychological assessment requires a series of different tests covering a wide range of different cognitive skills. Failure to do this could result in missing an important aspect of the presenting symptomology. Hence, some neuropsychological batteries have been developed to "cover the cognitive waterfront." Such batteries provide the neuropsychologist with a wide range of useful measures.

---

[4] Recall the example about the impact of standard error on the interpretation of Wechsler subscale scores outlined in Chapter 12.

[5] In this discussion, left and right are used with respect to normal right-handed persons who tend to have verbal skills represented in the left hemisphere.

The following Close Up describes one of the best known of such neuropsychological test batteries, the **Halstead–Reitan Neuropsychological Test Battery**. Based on a series of tests originally devised by Ward Halstead in the late 1940s, it has since been expanded and molded into a useful set of tools for neuropsychological assessment.

CLOSE UP   The Halstead–Reitan Battery

Halstead's original research program involved an exploration of what he called "biological intelligence" (Halstead, 1947). In the course of this research, he developed a series of tests that served as the foundation for the development of the battery bearing his name.

By the application of factor analytic procedures, Halstead identified eight tests thought to measure biological intelligence (Russell, Neuringer, & Goldstein, 1970). These tests included the following cognitive activities—categorization of visual stimuli, rhythm duplication, perception of speech sounds, tactual (tactile) performance, fine-motor behavior, and two measures of the perception of movement when viewing a series of rapidly presented pictures (critical flicker frequency and critical flicker fusion)—and a test of time estimation.

One of Halstead's students, Ralph Reitan, added to this research by applying the tests to a variety of neurologically impaired patients, attempting to discover if their performance would allow discrimination from normal subjects (see Reitan & Davison, 1974). Results indicated what was considered acceptable predictive validity.

With the passage of time and considerable research, three of Halstead's original eight tests were dropped, with five being kept to form part of the Halstead–Reitan Battery. Table 18-2 describes the five original tests. A number of new tests were then added to the five survivors of Halstead's original battery. Table 18-3 (page 700) describes these.

Table 18-2
The five original tests included in the Halstead–Reitan Battery

Halstead Category Test	This test is made up of 208 slides of geometric figures (divided into seven sets), which are projected onto an opaque screen. Patients are instructed to watch the slides and to determine which number between 1 and 4 is suggested by each slide. Responses are indicated by pressing an appropriately labeled button, with the correctness of responses being indicated by auditory feedback. One of the slide sets begins with a square. Patients can respond either 1 (because there is one object) or 4 (because the figure has four sides). The patient's task is to figure out which aspect of the stimulus is the effective cue by taking into account the auditory feedback. The sets get progressively more difficult as the test progresses. Scoring is simple for this test and requires only a record of the total number of errors (range = 0 – 208).

Speech–Sounds Perception Test	This test involves a taped presentation of 60 nonsense words, all of which contain the "ee" sound. Patients must select which of 4 printed words on an answer sheet matches a spoken word. Only 1 of 4 words on the answer sheet is correct. The scoring for this test is the total number of errors (range = 0 – 60).
Seashore Rhythm Test	This test requires patients to indicate whether the members of a pair of rhythmic patterns are the same or different. Using a tape recorder, 30 such pairs are presented, with patients indicating their answers on a sheet, which is provided. The score for this test is the number of correct responses (range = 0 – 30), which is traditionally converted to a score that can vary between 1 and 10 using a table provided in the manual.
Tactual Performance Test	This test involves the blindfolded respondent placing ten different shaped blocks (for example, square, circle, triangle) into like-shaped holes in a form board. The first trial involves the use of the dominant hand, a second trial has the patient use the other hand, and a third trial uses both hands. All three trials are timed. The form board and blocks are then removed, and the patient is asked to draw the board and the blocks. There are six scores for this test: (1) time for dominant hand; (2) time for nondominant hand; (3) time for both hands; (4) total time for all three trials; (5) memory, based on the drawing, the number of blocks correctly drawn; (6) localization, the number of blocks located in their correct order on the drawn form board.
Finger Oscillation Test	In this test, patients quickly tap a lever with their index fingers. This lever is connected to a mechanical counter, which provides the scores. Separate 10-second trials for both the dominant and nondominant hand are used, and an elaborate procedure of retesting is initiated if there is a five-tap difference between the two hands. Scoring is the number of taps per 10 seconds for each hand.

Besides the eight tests described in Tables 18-2 and 18-3, both the WAIS–R and the MMPI are typically considered part of the overall testing program. Other allied procedures are often added as well, including (1) strength of grip test (hand dynamometer),[6] (2) academic-achievement testing, (3) **Wechsler Memory Scale**, and

---

[6]Recall that this was one of J. M. Cattell's original ten basic tests (see Chapter 6).

(4) an assessment of hemispheric dominance.[7] This battery covers a significant number of functions and can be useful in several aspects of clinical neuropsychological work.

Neuropsychological assessment with the Halstead–Reitan Battery demands a high level of technical expertise. To permit focus on patient behavior, instructions must be memorized, and tests such as the Sensory-Perceptual Examination require extensive training and experience to administer properly.

The Halstead–Reitan Battery provides a wide range of quantitative and qualitative data that can be used in a number of ways to facilitate the processes of the clinical neuropsychologist. In large measure, the interpretation of the entire range of battery scores is based on an impressionistic analysis of the overall pattern of

Table 18-3
Newer tests in the Halstead–Reitan Battery

Trail Making Test

This test is a variation of follow the dots. In the first part, called Trail Making A, the patient joins in sequence 25 circles, each of which contains a number between 1 and 25. In the second part, Trail Making B, patients must join 25 circles containing either letters (A to L) or numbers (1 to 13) in the order 1, A, 2, B, 3, C, 4, D, and so on. The four scores are the time in seconds needed to complete the tasks and the number of errors made.

Halstead–Wepman Aphasia Screening Test

In this test, the patient is asked to follow 32 relatively simple commands such as copying a square, naming pictures such as a drawing of a fork, writing phrases, reading letters, explaining the meanings of phrases, simple mathematical computations, and following commands associated with sequential movement of body parts (for example, lift your hand and then touch your head). This test does not culminate in a score but is used for a qualitative estimate of gross communication deficits and language-processing problems.

Sensory-Perceptual Examination (Reitan–Klove)

This test, which is similar to the perceptual component of the standard neurological examination, consists of six subtests oriented toward discovering the nature of any perceptual problems that the patient might be experiencing. The six domains tested are (1) tactual, (2) auditory, (3) peripheral vision, (4) finger agnosia, (5) fingertip-writing perception, and (6) tactual-form recognition. For example, the finger agnosia subtest requires the blindfolded patient to indicate which finger on either hand has been lightly touched by the tester. Each of the six subtests culminates in scores reflecting the number of errors made by the patient. In some clinical applications, these scores are summarized under categories such as sensory suppressions or unilateral sensory errors (that is, those made consistently with one hand). The tactual form–recognition scores (one for each hand) are sometimes considered by themselves as indicators of cerebral dysfunction.

---

[7]Handedness is an aspect of hemispheric dominance, but a proper evaluation involves a careful examination of the degree of handedness (for example, does a "lefty" use his or her left hand for everything or just some things?) as well as the investigation of historical variables such as handedness of parents.

Table 18-4
Halstead's cutoff scores for calculation of the Halstead
Impairment Index

Test	Impaired Range
Category	51 or more errors
Speech–Sounds Perception	8 or more errors
Seashore Rhythm (rank score)	6 or more rank scores
Tactual Performance	
Total time	15.7 or more minutes
Memory	5 or fewer memories
Localization	4 or fewer localizations
Finger Oscillation	50 or fewer taps (dominant hand)

SOURCE: Reitan (n.d.)

Table 18-5
Conversion of impaired test scores to the
Halstead Impairment Index

Number of Tests in the Impaired Range	Impairment Index Score
0	0.0
1	0.1
2	0.3
3	0.4
4	0.6
5	0.7
6	0.9
7	1.0

SOURCE: Barth & Macciocchi (1985)

results. The actual scores are important and indeed constitute the primary observations on which judgments are based. Experience is a key ingredient to the successful interpretation of the battery data.

At a descriptive level, the scores on the battery are combined to form the **Halstead Impairment Index**, which is said to reflect the general level of brain dysfunction. Table 18-4 presents the ranges of the seven scores used to calculate this index. These values were derived from consideration of a large number of cases. On the basis of extensive experience with the battery, the number of tests observed in the impaired range is then used to provide the Impairment Index per Table 18-5. As this table shows, the greater the number of test scores falling in the impaired range, the higher the Impairment Index. An Impairment Index less than or equal to 0.3 is considered to reflect normal functioning to mild cognitive impairment, 0.3 to 0.6 reveals mild to moderate deficits, and greater than 0.6 is thought to indicate moderate to severe impairment.

Beyond the Impairment Index, the major issues addressed in the interpretation of the Halstead–Reitan are (1) the description of the psychological strengths and weaknesses of the patient, (2) implications of these for everyday life, and (3) suggested treatment or rehabilitation. These can be addressed by examining three aspects of the test results, all of which should be considered.

1. *Level of performance.* Actual test scores can be compared to normative and pathological populations (Boll, 1981) to provide a sense of where the patient falls relative to specific groups. The Impairment Index is a first cut at this, but it is also possible to make normative comparisons with specific tests.
2. *Pattern of performance.* The relationships between and within scores can provide clues about the nature of a given neurological problem. For example, a detailed comparison of the dominant/nondominant hand scores for the various tests can be very revealing of specific cerebral problems.
3. *Pathagnomic signs.* A **pathagnomic sign** is a clear indicator of a specific disorder that can emerge in a number of the tests in the battery. For example, labeling the picture of the fork as a spoon indicates a type of aphasia called **dysnomia**.

In addition, patient demographic data can be integrated as part of the interpretive process. Included here are documentation of present circumstances, academic history, family situation, developmental history, and any recent psychological changes.

The final integration of all these data is a highly complex and experience-driven process. A tremendous amount of training and wisdom is necessary to permit adequate interpretation of the Halstead–Reitan Battery. However, because the battery provides a fairly wide-ranging observational base on which an experienced clinician can base an effective interpretation, the Halstead–Reitan is a useful instrument.

The battery is most often criticized for its lack of extensive age norms, its lengthy administration time (about 6 hours), and cost. Better age norms are certainly necessary because it is sometimes difficult to determine if a given level of performance reveals pathology or is simply a natural consequence of normal aging. The construct validity of the battery is suspect because the instrument has not been developed on the basis of an explicit theory of brain function.

The best way of demonstrating the usefulness of the Halstead–Reitan Battery is to pick up our earlier story of Ron, the 32-year-old tax attorney who sustained a head injury while painting his house. Let's examine the manner in which the test battery helped him.

CLOSE UP **Ron and the Halstead–Reitan Battery**

Upon referral to the neuropsychological assessment center, Ron was administered the Halstead–Reitan. He was extremely cooperative throughout the test procedures, producing maximum effort, and was genuinely concerned about his test results. He informed the examiners that he was worried about the strange symptoms he was having because they were disrupting his work and family life. He clearly wanted to know what was wrong with him and how to correct it. Figures 18–3 and 18–4 show his neuropsychological results.

Figure 18-3 Halstead–Reitan summary sheet for Ron, a 32-year-old man who sustained a head injury.

Summary Data Sheet
Results of Neuropsychological Examination

Case Number: _001_ Age: _32_ Sex: _M_ Education: _20+_ Handedness: _R_

Name: _____Ron_____ Employment: __Attorney__ Impairment Index: _0.3_ *

WAIS (or WAIS-R)

VIQ	1 1 4
PIQ	1 1 2
FS IQ	

Scaled Scores

Information	1 5
Comprehension	1 5
Digit Span	1 0
Arithmetic	1 4
Similarities	1 4
Vocabulary	1 5
Picture Arrangement	1 0
Picture Completion	1 4
Block Design	1 0
Object Assembly	1 4
Digit Symbol	1 0

Minnesota Multiphasic Personality Inventory
(t scores)

?	0 0 0
L	0 4 0
F	0 5 2
K	0 6 9
Ms	0 6 5
D	0 7 0
Hy	0 5 6
Pd	0 6 2
Mf	0 5 1
Pa	0 6 4
Pt	0 6 8
Sc	0 5 1
Ma	0 6 9
St	0 5 3

Category Test 0 5 4 *

Tactual Performance Test

	Time	# of Blks. In
Dominant hand:	5 . 2	– 1 0
Nondominant hand:	3 . 1	– 1 0
Both hands:	2 . 6	– 1 0

Total Time:	1 0 9 *
Memory:	0 7 *
Localization:	0 4 *

Trail Making Test

Part A: 0 2 8 seconds 0 0 errors
Part B: 1 0 7 seconds 0 0 errors

Seashore Rhythm Test (correct)
Raw Score: 2 8   Rank: 0 2 *

Speech-sounds Perception Test
Errors: 0 2 *

Finger Oscillation Test

Dominant hand:	5 2 . 5 *
Nondominant hand:	4 7 . 2

Unilateral Sensory Errors

Dominant hand:	0 0
Nondominant hand:	0 0

Sensory Suppressions

Dominant hand:	0 0
Nondominant hand:	0 1

Reitan–Klove Tactile Form Recognition

	Errors	Seconds
Dominant hand:	0	0 0
Nondominant hand:	0	0 1

Aphasia Signs: Mild dysnomia

Strength of Grip

Dominant hand:	4 7 kilograms
Nondominant hand:	4 2 kilograms

(SOURCE: From "The Halstead-Reitan Neuropsychological Test Battery," by J. T. Barth and S. N. Macciocchi, 1985, *Major Psychological Assessment Instruments,* edited by Charles S. Newmark, p. 409. Copyright ©1985 by Allyn and Bacon. Reprinted by permission.)

Figure 18-4

Ron's results on the Aphasia Screening Test.

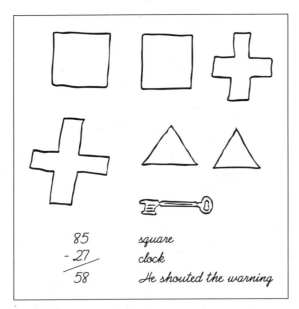

Ron's Halstead's Impairment Index was 0.3, placing him in the normal to mildly impaired range of adaptive cognitive abilities. His Category score of 54 errors, Tactual Performance Test localization of 4, and Trail Making B of 107 seconds all suggested mildly impaired functioning. However, there were no indications of severe impairment in his scores. The most troublesome score was his 54 errors in the Category Test, which is well above what would be expected from a bright, well-educated lawyer.

There were no **lateralized deficits** on the tests, and the Sensory-Perceptual Examination is unremarkable. WAIS Verbal and Performance IQ scores were 12 points apart, with the Performance subtest scores being generally lower and more variable. This could indicate right-hemisphere problems, but more data would be necessary to confirm this because these differences could reflect pretrauma levels of performance.

Ron did well on the Aphasia Screening Test (see Figure 18-4). There was a hint of dysnomia (for example, he first called the "cross" a "plus sign"), and he showed some mild difficulty repeating several complicated phrases. These findings were not normal for an individual with Ron's education and were consistent with data shown by other mild-to-moderate closed head injuries. The following results were also congenial to the diagnosis of mild-to-moderate closed-head injury: (1) the lower Performance subtest scores on the WAIS–R, (2) impaired functioning levels on the Category Test, and (3) poor performance on the Trail Making Test, given that testing had not revealed any major motor and sensory deficits. The findings, then, were consistent with the medical history—Ron's present problems appear to be related to his recent accident combined with his reaction to the associated cognitive difficulties.

Ron's MMPI indicated a mild yet clinically significant level of depression that is typical of closed-head trauma.

The results of Ron's assessment, although indicating generally moderate deficits, do reveal problems that were significantly disruptive for his day-to-day existence. His job as a tax attorney demanded a high level of concentration and cognitive flexibility, which appeared to be affected by his injury. He would undoubtedly experience a drop in his office efficiency, which would in turn increase his level of frustration. In all likelihood, his reported personality change and lowered tolerance of frustration stemmed from these factors.

Having established that Ron's difficulties were the result of a moderate closed-head trauma with no other severe implications, it became possible to counsel him and his family about the expected course of recovery. According to the literature, the typical recovery for this type of injury ranges from 6 to 18 months. It would be reasonable to inform Ron and his family that his symptoms were normal and that he should enjoy significant recovery over the next several months. He should also be counseled that his specific deficits, although relatively mild, can become frustrating. By proper education about what to expect, Ron's adjustment during the recovery period can be helped, and his family and employer can make appropriate adjustments. Finally, a follow-up neurological examination should be scheduled to ensure that the expected recovery does indeed take place.

As can be seen, neuropsychological testing served a very important role in Ron's treatment. On the basis of the documentation of a mild degree of impairment attributable to his fall, it became possible to counsel Ron, his wife, and his employer about what to expect. It allowed everyone concerned to have a well-reasoned approach about expectations, particularly in light of the anticipated recovery period. The fears and anxieties that were affecting Ron were readily understood through this analysis, providing him with a very effective understanding of his current plight. These contributions are of no small moment in contributing to Ron's recovery. Although the eventual decision about Ron's problems was based on the test scores, these in and of themselves were only a small part of the overall clinical process. Extensive knowledge of the domain of head injury and general neuropsychology were a requisite part of the overall decision making that went into this case. This demonstrates the necessity of extensive and substantial training for neuropsychological assessment.

In more severe cases, such testing can be very useful in developing and monitoring rehabilitation techniques and related constructive approaches to adjusting to head injury.

Clearly demonstrating administration, scoring, and interpretation of a complex and comprehensive set of neuropsychological assessment procedures in one section of a general text such as this one is impossible. The goal of this section has been to provide a sense of clinical neuropsychology as well as introduce the Halstead–Reitan Battery. Extensive training is necessary if one is to develop a proficiency with these procedures and begin to understand brain/behavior relationships.

OTHER APPROACHES

Several other neuropsychological test batteries are available. Of particular note is the **Luria–Nebraska Neuropsychological Battery** (Christensen, 1975; Golden, 1981). These other batteries vary in the breadth and depth of coverage of various aspects of relevance to neuropsychology.

The exhaustive batteries bring several problems with them. Of particular note is the considerable amount of time in administering the entire battery. In many cases, patients cannot dedicate up to 6 hours of high concentration time because of their injury. When it turns out that some of the tests may not prove useful in the overall evaluation, the utility of the comprehensive battery becomes somewhat suspect.

A second and related difficulty emerges if we consider the construct validity of the Halstead–Reitan. This battery provides a wide sampling of a number of cognitive and sensory activities that have, over the years, been shown to provide behavioral evidence of use to the neuropsychologist. However, no wide-ranging theory of brain functioning underlies this battery. The Halstead–Reitan can be seen as the equivalent of the Stanford–Binet in its failure to provide a clear and explicit theory of exactly what psychological phenomena lead to specific test scores. This lack of theoretical underpinning has a number of implications for the use of this type of battery.

Foremost here is that without a theoretical base it becomes necessary to administer all the subtests, in a sort of shotgun manner, because there are no explicit theoretical grounds on which to pick and choose among the various subtests. If an effective theory of brain function undergirded the battery, entering into a sequential testing strategy where the results of a specific test could be used to test given theoretical expectations and to determine the course of subsequent testing would be possible. Under these conditions, it could emerge that considerably less testing would be necessary. For example, if an initial theoretical hypothesis about a given patient were verified early in the testing (and with considerable certainty), it would not be necessary to carry on with the rest of the tests—thus saving considerable clinical time for both the tester and the patient. However, an explicit and effective theoretical formulation would have to be in place before this advantage could be garnered. It is in this sense that the lack of construct validity of batteries such as the Halstead–Reitan takes on considerable practical importance.

THEORY-DRIVEN BATTERIES

The problems attending this lack of theory are solved in some clinical practices by explicit inclusion of a formulation of a theory of brain functioning into the assessment program. Kolb and Whishaw (1985) call such a theory-driven approach an **informal composite battery.** Many researchers have developed specific tests to reflect particular aspects of brain functioning. In the course of this work, evidence for the utility of a given test as an index of a particular condition is presented.

Many of these tests are inappropriate for clinical use, but some of them have demonstrated considerable utility, permitting the research/practitioner to test specific hypotheses quickly and efficiently. From this model, we begin to find the emergence of a set of tests with construct validity, which can, in some circumstances, be highly useful in clinical work.

One of the better known sets of tests, which can be thought of as a theory-driven battery, derives from decades of research at the Montreal Neurological Institute. Table 18-6 presents this battery. These tests are based for the most part on research with patients who have had surgery for various types of brain tumors. Extensive use of the specific tests in pre-, post-, and follow-up designs has led to masses of information about expected test performance as a function of the locus

---

Table 18-6 A theory-driven battery based on work at the Montreal Neurological Institute

---

1. Determination of speech lateralization
   a. Handedness questionnaire: Determines dominant hand by examining a number of activities and family history.
   b. Dichotic digits or words: After different sounds or words are played to each ear via stereo headphones, respondents state what they hear.

2. General intelligence: WAIS–R

3. Visuoperceptual
   a. McGill Picture Anomalies: After a series of pictures, each containing something unusual, is presented, respondents point out the oddity in each picture.
   b. Mooney Faces: Respondents identify the gender and age of drawings of human faces with exaggerated shadows.
   c. Rey Complex Figures (copy): Respondents copy or recall a complex geometric figure.

4. Memory
   a. Wechsler Memory Scale
   b. Rey Complex Figures (delayed recall)
   c. Delayed recall of stories, paired-associates learning, and drawings
   d. Corsi Block Span: The tester taps a sequence of blocks (for example, third, sixth, ninth), and the respondent reproduces the sequence. This is a visual/kinesthetic version of the digit-span task.

5. Spatial
   a. Right-Left Differentiation: Respondents answer a series of questions asking to note left and right sides of various objects, including own body.
   b. Semmes Body-Placing Test: Respondents touch parts of their bodies as illustrated in a diagram.

6. Somatosensory
   a. Passive movement
   b. Point localization
   c. Two-point discrimination
   d. Simultaneous extinction

---

continued

Table 18-6 A theory-driven battery based on work at the Montreal Neurological Institute
(*continued*)

7. Language
   a. Object naming
   b. Chapman–Cook Speed of Reading Test
   c. Spelling
   d. Phonetic discrimination
   e. Token Test: After a series of tokens that consist of various shapes and colors is shown, respondents indicate specific examples (for example, "Touch the white circle").

8. Hippocampal function (the hippocampus is a neural structure sometimes implicated in certain kinds of brain injury)
   a. Corsi Recurring Blocks: This is the same as the Corsi Block Span except that a particular sequence is repeated every three trials. Certain types of brain damage render respondents incapable of profiting from the repetitions, with their performance demonstrating no gain on the repeated sequence.
   b. Hebb Recurring Digits: This is a standard digit-span task except that every third trial a particular sequence of digits is repeated. Certain types of brain-damaged patients cannot learn this repeated sequence.

9. Frontal lobe
   a. Wisconsin Card-Sorting Test: The respondent sorts cards that bear designs that differ in form, color, and number of elements. Subjects make a sort and are told whether they are right or wrong. They must infer the basis of correctness in sorting from their correct or incorrect responses. At first the sorting must be done on the basis of color; then without warning, the rules change, and the sort must be made on the basis of form and number of elements. Some patients are unable to switch.
   b. Chicago Word Fluency Test: Respondents write as many words beginning with a specific letter as they can during a timed interval.

10. Motor function
   a. Dynamometer: Measures strength of squeeze; weakness is often associated with damage to the contralateral cerebral hemisphere.
   b. Kimura Box Test: Respondents make three consecutive movements of pushing a button three times with the index finger, pulling a handle with four fingers, and pressing a bar with the thumb. Certain types of neuropsychological patients are unable to execute these simple sequences.
   c. Complex arm and facial movement copying

SOURCE: Kolb & Wishaw (1985, p. 681).

and extent of brain injury. As well, over time, tests that do not demonstrate predictive and concurrent validity have been eliminated. Table 18-6 lists the survivors of a highly rigorous and extensive research program dealing with hundreds of patients with known brain injury and thus provides a substantive basis for the clinical neuropsychologist. This research provides the foundation for the construct validity of the battery because the physiological antecedents of test performance are known. One advantage here is that it permits selection from among the various tests in the battery based on knowledge of the nature of the putative brain injury and the problems being reported by the patient. Having such a battery of tests at their disposal, neuropsychologists can focus on the problems of concern. For example, if language difficulties are the presenting problem, it is possible to select from several of the test categories shown in Table 18-6 and explore these difficulties with considerable precision and detail.

Other systems of theory-driven orientations toward neurological assessment are also available. Perhaps the best known is the **Boston process approach** (Milberg, Hebben, & Kaplan, 1986). Here a finite list of tests are used to converge on various aspects of brain functioning.

It must be pointed out here, though, that the development of a substantive theory of human brain function is a long way away. The literature has some fine theoretical analyses, however, they are highly tentative and demand considerably more research. Every year thousands of published research papers provide new data and technologies that must be folded into an emerging theory of how the human brain works, particularly when it is injured. Thus, the development of the strategy underlying informal, theory-driven test batteries is an ever-changing process. Familiarity with the ongoing literature and knowledge of the fundamentals of brain science are absolute prerequisites to realizing the potential gains from this approach to assessment.

Another problem with this approach is that the tests are often poorly validated. Because many of the instruments are clinical and experimental in nature, often aspects of the tests' psychometric properties have not been particularly well researched. Such work and data collection are costly, time-consuming, and not particularly exciting. However, effective informal composite batteries will, in the long run, depend on detailed investigation of the psychometric properties of the specific instruments included in the theory of brain function being touted by the specific clinical neuropsychologist.

The relatively late emergence of neuropsychological test batteries noted earlier in this chapter is really due to the late emergence of wide-range, comprehensive batteries such as the Halstead–Reitan. For decades the tests included in informal composite batteries, such as those listed in Table 18-6, have been available and under investigation; but, in the context of experimental work in neuropsychology, these tests have, for the most part, not been formally published or considered as part of the psychological testing enterprise. However, they constitute a very important aspect of the ongoing development of the science of neuropsychology and the manner in which this field can be applied to clinical work.

LEARNING DISABILITIES

This chapter started off describing an increased acceptance of biological analyses of human behavior in the 1980s—hence the heightened popularity of neuropsychological testing during this decade. Another aspect of this movement toward biological analyses occurred in the context of developmental and educational psychology. During the 1970s, educators began to forge a new language for dealing with children and adults demonstrating difficulties in school-related tasks such as reading and writing. This new language, which was actually an operating metaphor, cast the poorly performing individual as having a **learning disability**—describing them in the same way as someone with a physical disability might be described. Thus, poor performance was viewed as the result of some kind of disability rather than a lack of a general entity such as intelligence. Terms such as *minimal brain dysfunction*, **dyslexia**, *hyperactivity*, and *developmental aphasia* began to appear in both the technical and popular literatures. This new language, which was actually mandated by the federal government as Public Law 94-142, provided a much more specific way of dealing with the low-performance individual because it provided a new set of labels with some implied treatment and management possibilities.

Learning disability is an umbrella term applied to a wide range of cognitive problems. To provide a sense of the breadth of this concept, Table 18-7 presents a brief listing of the subtypes of learning disabilities demonstrated in adults. This list shows considerable emphasis on verbal/writing skills, with a smattering of concerns regarding nonverbal and organizational processes. A key assumption here is that an individual would be demonstrating normal performance were it not for the specific deficit. In other words, the individuals concerned all had an equal opportunity to learn, but for some reason adequate performance has not been achieved.

The actual definition of a learning disability is fairly complex because it is necessary to exclude certain general disabling conditions (for example, mental retardation) as well as to demonstrate considerable specificity in the presenting problem. This combines to form a four-part definition. To qualify as a learning disability, the individual's performance (1) must *not* be due to other general conditions such as mental retardation, emotional disturbance, visual or hearing impairment, or some form of cultural/social disadvantage; (2) must demonstrate a discrepancy between specific performance and general ability indicating that the problem is unique to a delimited domain of cognitive functioning;[8] (3) must readily fall into one of the subtypes of the sort shown in Table 18-7; and (4) have a definite developmental component (that is, has been evident, in one form or another, since early childhood).

Individuals with learning disabilities often experience social and emotional difficulties. These can emerge either because of or in response to their disability. Feelings of frustration, tendencies to act before thinking, low self-confidence, shyness, and control of emotional expression are frequent in this population (for details, see Hoffman, Sheldon, & Minskoff, 1987). The social and emotional problems are often the presenting complaint, making the diagnosis of learning disabilities a challenge.

The relevance of the notion of learning disability to neuropsychological testing becomes clear when you consider the possible reasons behind these disorders. Most contemporary thinking views these disabilities as biological and/or neurological in origin. Cruikshank (1984) aptly reveals this in his discussion where he argues that

---

[8]The size of this discrepancy must be sufficient to interfere with successful performance. In practice, an informal rule of thumb states that there should be at least a 1-SD difference between general ability (say, IQ) and demonstrated performance in the target domain (say, as measured by a standardized achievement test).

Table 18-7 Subtypes of learning disabilities

Disorders of Organization, Planning, and Attention	Such individuals show poor self-monitoring and planning skills that interfere with their ability to actualize their potential. They are typically bright and show good reading skills.
Expressive Language Comprehension Disorders	These individuals have good nonverbal skills but serious problems with oral-language comprehension, leading to poor verbal expression, reading comprehension, writing skills, and mathematical reasoning.
Expressive Language, Reading, and Writing Disorders	These individuals demonstrate significant reading problems as well as poor spelling and major problems with writing.
Generalized Meaning Problems	These individuals demonstrate difficulty with the acquisition and meaning of concepts. They can memorize well but cannot generalize to new contexts.
Nonverbal Conceptual Disorders	These individuals have difficulty with tasks that require abstraction of meaning from observation. Because of this, there is often an associated deficit in social skills that are developed using such processes.
Nonverbal, Visual/Spatial, and Quantitative Disorders	These individuals demonstrate problems with handwriting, arithmetic, and everyday living skills. They generally are good verbal problem solvers but have problems with mechanical, or visual/ spatial, skills.
Primary Spelling and Written-Language Disorders	These individuals show good language skills but falter in written expression and spelling.
Reading (Decoding) and Spelling Disorders	These individuals are traditional dyslexics who demonstrate significant difficulties with sequencing and auditory analysis. This is most often demonstrated as persistent transposition of letters while spelling words.

SOURCE: Johnson & Blalock (1987).

"learning disabilities are the result of perceptual processing deficits." He goes on to suggest that "perception is neurological . . . an inherent function of the neurology of the organism" (Cruikshank, 1984). Thus, the genesis of learning disabilities is seen to be in the neurology, or "hardware," of the individual. Although this conclusion can be debated from a number of different perspectives, it certainly reflects the tendency toward biological explanations outlined at the beginning of this chapter.

Most approaches to assessing learning disabilities adopt a strongly multi-method approach using a wide range of tests. To estimate general levels of functioning, standard IQ tests (for example, the Wechsler series) can be used. In addition, specific IQ subtests that are related to the presenting problem can be employed to sharpen diagnostic focus (for example, the Wechsler Digit Span to explore possible memory problems). Standardized achievement tests such as the Metropolitan series can be informative of specific deficits, as can tests designed to measure specific aspects of cognitive functioning. Indication of a learning disability would be signaled by finding a discrepancy between the general and at least one specific measure. Personality inventories such as the Eysenck Personality Questionnaire can be useful in teasing out the social/emotional component of disabilities, while a wide range of available standardized reading- and language-skill tests can be used to explore specific components of verbal performance. Indeed, almost any of the tests discussed in the text can, in one way or another, be brought to bear on the assessment of learning disabilities.

Perhaps the major gain of the disability metaphor is the manner in which it becomes possible to talk about underachievement in terms of specific psychological components, rather than suggesting that a person is unintelligent or some related generalized term. This is a more human and useful approach than branding a person as "dumb" or somesuch. By bringing increased specificity (or, using our earlier term, *narrower bandwidth*) to the analysis of performance problems, the notion of a learning disability provides clinical and educational workers with an alternate perspective. The extent to which it is possible to develop effective rehabilitation strategies based on the narrow-bandwidth analysis of cognitive problems is an active and important area of research and development.

ATTENTION-DEFICIT HYPERACTIVITY DISORDER

Another class of disorder that sometimes co-occurs with learning disabilities is known to the general public as **hyperactivity**. Such children are often very fidgety, have difficulty remaining seated, are easily distracted, have difficulty waiting their turn in games, seem unable to complete tasks, cannot pay attention for long periods of time, tend to be noisy and highly talkative, interrupt others, seem not to hear what is said to them, and frequently lose things. Evident before the age of 7 years, a severe case would demonstrate all of the above characteristics in the extreme relative to normal children of a comparable age. Such individuals demonstrate significant academic underachievement and are frequently referred for assessment of learning disabilities.

In the revised third edition of the *Diagnostic and Statistical Manual of Mental Disorders* (*DSM III–R*) (American Psychiatric Association, 1987) the term **attention-deficit hyperactivity disorder** (ADHD) was introduced to describe this syndrome. The new, longer name served to provide some much-needed precision in the use of this diagnostic category. In addition, it signaled that the activity problems, while being the major problem for adults having to deal with these children, were apparently a function of attentional processes.

The more-or-less standard approach to diagnosing ADHD involves the use of rating scales or checklists that allow users to estimate the frequency with which hyperactive and related behaviors are observed in a specific child. For example, Connors (1990) produced a set of rating scales for teachers and for parents (or parent-surrogates). The following items are the kind that can be found on the **Connors' Rating Scales:**

	Not at All	*Just a Little*	*Pretty Much*	*Very Much*
Cries easily	0	1	2	3
Restless and fidgety	0	1	2	3
Acts without thinking	0	1	2	3
Gets into trouble	0	1	2	3
Talks excessively	0	1	2	3

Both the teacher and parent forms come in a short and a long version, yielding hyperactivity scores along with a number of other indexes that are helpful in exploring the nature of a child's problems. The norm groups are small but representative. The internal consistencies of these scales is good with, for example, the hyperactivity scale on the long teacher form being .94 (see Trites, Blouin, & LaPrade, 1982).

Issues of Construct Validity

There is a problem here, however. In both the learning disability and ADHD contexts, the tests make no reference to a theory undergirding performance on the instrument itself. In other words, the tests mentioned so far (and in the domains generally) suffer from a lack of construct validity. Although the instruments may show reasonable content and criterion-related validity, as well as a degree of reliability, they do not pass muster when it comes to construct validity. It is here that the biological and neurological underpinnings of both learning disabilities and ADHD emerge as paramount. If we believe the arguments of Cruikshank (1984) and others, any theory of these disorders will, in the long run, have to be based on the neurology of the individual. This is a tough requirement because the scientific understanding of these disorders is only now beginning to emerge. Perhaps we should view the development of instruments to assess learning disabilities and ADHD that possess construct validity as an expectation of what we might expect in the future.

One brief example of some exciting work in ADHD will provide a sense of the manner in which this work is proceeding. Michael Posner and his co-workers (for example, Posner, 1988) have done a considerable amount of research developing a neurological model that can account for aspects of attention in human performance. Based on extensive experimentation and integrative work, they have identified two attentional systems, each with different neurological loci. The **posterior attentional system**, located (roughly) in the back part of the brain, appears to be involved in *covert shifts* of attention, which occur early on during the processing of information. Tasks that require orientation toward various parts of a stimulus field could be used to explore this system. The **anterior attentional system**, located in the more frontal regions of the brain, has been implicated in *overt shifts* in attention, which occur later on during information processing. Tasks requiring sustained or directed attention over a longer time period could be used to explore this system. Both systems, each of which is best thought of as a complex network of connections, are necessary for the demonstration of normal attention.

In one study, Swanson et al. (1991) employed a cued reaction-time test to explore the nature of the attentional deficit in ADHD children. Respondents were carefully chosen using *DSM* III–R criteria, and a normal, matched comparison group was used. Their data indicate that ADHD children show no difference from normal children in performance of the early, posterior system. However, abnormalities in the later, anterior attentional system were observed. These findings were interpreted to indicate that the fundamental problem with ADHD children lies in the domain of directed, or focused, attention. In other words, the neurological deficit underlying ADHD occurs in the neurological loci identified by the anterior attentional system.

Swanson et al. (1991) conclude their paper by indicating that considerable further investigation of the anterior attentional system and its relationship to ADHD attentional deficits will be necessary. However, these data begin to point toward the gains in knowledge that are being garnered as experimental psychology and neurology begin to come together. Perhaps it will not be too long before this increased understanding of neurological process will begin to influence theories of hyperactivity and eventually be reflected in the kinds of tests that are made available. Such promising developments portend of an interesting and fruitful future for the psychological testing enterprise as it moves ahead into the 21st century.

Summary

This chapter has introduced some of the issues surrounding neuropsychological assessment. We examined the Bender–Gestalt as an early example of a neuropsychological instrument and found it to be inadequate for contemporary needs. Then we looked at the Halstead–Reitan Battery as an atheoretical, shotgun approach to neuropsychological assessment, noting both its strengths and weaknesses. The emergence of theory-driven test batteries was noted in the context of the Montreal Neurological Institute research program. The advantages of this orientation were highlighted. Discussion then shifted to learning disabilities and attention-deficit hyperactivity disorder. It was noted that the construct validity of the current tests was weak but that it might be necessary to await further progress in the scientific exploration of brain/behavior relationships before strong neurological theory can be proposed. One example of emerging work with ADHD was briefly outlined to indicate the promise of this approach.

The most important message to glean from this chapter on neuropsychological assessment is a respect for the astounding complexity of the field. The brain itself is incredibly complicated. When we begin to investigate dysfunction of this organ, matters get very involved. Because of this, years and years of training are necessary before one should venture into neuropsychological assessment. Although it may be possible to take several workshops on a specific test, this does not provide the necessary background and knowledge to interpret and understand test findings. It is critical that anyone venturing into this field be aware of current research in the general field of neurosciences, which is a not an easy task given the volumes of research currently under way. Failure to have an understanding of the basic organ of interest in this work will undoubtedly lead to improper inferences and interpretations. Once this fundamental knowledge is obtained, the neuropsychological component of the testing enterprise holds great potential for the future.

Glossary

anterior attentional system A neural network that is involved in overt shifts of attention, as might occur later on in a processing sequence. It is thought to lie in the frontal portions of the brain.

aphasia A condition in which a person cannot speak but can understand what others say. Damage to Broca's area is typically associated with this condition.

attention-deficit hyperactivity disorder (ADHD) A *DSM* III–R diagnostic category applied to children who are very fidgety, have difficulty remaining seated, are easily distracted, have difficulty waiting their turn in games, seem unable to complete tasks, cannot pay attention for long periods of time, tend to be noisy and highly talkative, interrupt others, seem not to hear what is said to them, and frequently lose things.

Bender Visual-Motor Gestalt Test A 1930s test of perception in which respondents must copy a series of simple designs. Originally intended to examine aspects of perception, the test was adapted by Hain to provide a measure of organicity.

Boston process approach A system of neuropsychological assessment that uses a preset group of tests to explore various hypotheses about brain dysfunction in individuals.

Broca's area A small region in the left frontal section of the brain. Damage to this area results in aphasia.

central nervous system (CNS) The collective name for all neurons found in the brain, spinal cord, and major sensory nerves.

cerebrum The largest part of the human brain, sometimes called the cerebral cortex.

cerebral assymetry The finding of various differences such as size between the two cerebral hemispheres.

cerebral hemispheres The two half brains into which the cerebrum is divided—one on the left side and one on the right. These two hemispheres are separate from each other except that they are joined by the corpus callosum.

Connors Rating Scales A series of scales used to facilitate the diagnosis of ADHD. There are long and short forms for both teachers and parents.

corpus callosum A large band of neural tracts that joins the left and right cerebral hemispheres.

Durham Rule A legal precedent wherein individuals will not be found guilty for crimes committed by them if it can be proven that they were mentally deranged at the time. The rule was overturned in the trial of John Hinkley, Jr.

dyslexia A disorder that is characterized by difficulties in sequencing such as transposing the order of letters when spelling or writing words.

dysnomia A neurological disorder in which patients make persistent errors in naming common objects.

EEG The abbreviation for electroencephalograph, which is a technique for measuring electrical activity at the surface of the brain.

fissures The folds on the exterior of the cerebrum.

functional assymetry The finding that various psychological processes appear to be differentially located in the two cerebral hemispheres. For example, in right-handed persons, most components of verbal skill reside in the left hemisphere.

glial cell A cell that co-occurs with neurons. It is thought to serve a support role in the CNS.

Hain scoring system of the Bender–Gestalt Test A method of scoring the Bender–Gestalt, based on the types of errors made by the respondent. Certain types of errors were thought to indicate the presence of an organic deficit.

Halstead Impairment Index A summary score from the Halstead–Reitan Neuropsychological Test Battery that reflects general level of brain dysfunction.

Halstead–Reitan Neuropsychological Test Battery A battery of eight psychological tests designed primarily to provide information relevant to clinicians concerned with brain injury and related difficulties.

hyperactivity *See* attention-deficit hyperactivity disorder.

impulse As used in the context of neuropsychology, the major activity of neurons in which an electrical charge is transmitted the length of the cell to another neuron or neurons as part of the functioning of the central nervous system.

informal composite battery A collection of psychological tests that have been assembled to permit clinicians to test specific hypotheses (theoretical expectations) about various aspects of brain dysfunction.

lateralized deficit A situation in which there is a substantial difference between performance by one side of the body compared with the other.

learning disability A domain-specific cognitive performance deficit that is not due to general disabling conditions and that shows a clear developmental etiology.

Luria–Nebraska Neuropsychological Battery A popular test battery with goals similar to the Halstead–Reitan.

neuron A cell that is the basic building block of the human nervous system. Specialized for the transmission of impulses, neurons come in a wide assortment of shapes and forms, pending their function in the system.

neuropsychology The subdiscipline that involves the interaction between the classic field of neurology and the discipline of psychology.

neurotransmitter A complex chemical that is responsible for conducting impulses across the synapse.

organic deficit An earlier technical term applied to a performance decrement that can be attributed to a physical cause such as brain injury.

pathagnomic sign   A specific behavior that is clearly related to a specific neurological disorder.

posterior attentional system   A neural network that is involved in covert shifts of attention that occur early on in a processing sequence. It is thought to lie in the back part of the brain.

Purkinje cell   A neuron that can readily become associated with many other nearby neurons.

synapse   The location where the end brushes of different neurons, which are not physically joined to each other at the synapse, come together. A synapse has a small gap over which impulses cross via various chemical substances.

Wechsler Memory Scale   A test developed by Wechsler to measure memory for a number of different types of stimuli examining a number of different kinds of memory tasks.

Suggested Further Reading

Churchland, P. S. (1986). *Neurophilosophy: Toward a unified science of the mind/brain.* Cambridge, Mass.: MIT Press.

> It might seem a bit strange to be recommending a philosophy book in this chapter, but there is a good reason. The first two chapters of this book contain a very readable historical introduction to the field of neuropsychology. In addition, the next three chapters provide summaries of some of the more recent thinking. If you feel venturesome, you can move beyond there and examine Churchland's claims for a radically biological psychology.

Kolb, B., & Whishaw, I. Q. (1990). *Fundamentals of human neuropsychology* (3rd ed.). New York: Freeman.

> This text is a fine introduction to and elaboration of a number of points developed in this chapter. The background section provides some good contextual information for anyone interested in gaining further information, and sections on basic neurology and brain function are exceedingly useful. There is a good treatment of neuropsychological testing, including some detailed information about learning disabilities and dyslexia in the last section on applied neuropsychology.

Lezak, M. D. (1983). *Neuropsychological assessment* (2nd ed.). New York: Oxford University Press.

> This book provides considerable detail regarding numerous aspects of neurological assessment. It is recommended for students who wish to further explore this intriguing domain. Lezak is accessible, although some basic neurophysiological background (as can be found in Kolb and Wishaw mentioned above) is recommended.

Pirozzolo, F. J., & Harrell, W. (1985). The neuropsychology of learning disabilities. In L. C. Hartlage & C. F. Telzrow (Eds.), *The neuropsychology of individual differences: A developmental perspective*, pp. 183–202. New York: Plenum,.

> This is a fine introduction to some detailed thinking about the biological bases of learning disabilities. It provides a good overview of the major neurological considerations underlying these disabilities.

Springer, S. P., & Deutsch, G. (1989). *Left brain, right brain* (3rd ed.). New York: Freeman.

This book is a great introduction to some of the subtleties associated with functional assymetry in the human nervous system. It is well written and can be easily read by students with little formal background in neuropsychology.

Discussion Questions

1. Discuss several recent events from your university community that demonstrate the kinds of fiscal attacks on social services and allied activities suggested to be part of the context of the 1980s and 1990s.

2. Debate the virtues and difficulties associated with the Durham Rule.

3. Suggest as many reasons as you can to support the contention that a shift to physicalist (for example, biological) explanations of human behavior can be attributed to the cultural context of the 1980s and 1990s. Do you agree with this? Why, or why not?

4. In Chapter 9, an economic reason for the earlier strained relations between medicine and psychology was given. In this chapter, an economic reason was given for the adoption of a physicalist perspective. Are these two explanations contradictory? Why, or why not?

5. Outline the problems attending the construct of organic versus nonorganic categories in neuropsychological testing.

6. Would you be happy with using the Hain scoring system for the Bender–Gestalt if the following validity data were offered (instead of those presented in Table 18-1)? Why, or why not?

		Patient type (Based on Confirmed Diagnosis)		
		Brain-Damaged	Psychiatric Control	Total
Predictions from	Nonorganic	5	18	23
the Bender	Organic	16	3	19
	Total	21	21	42

7. Draw a contingency table like the one in Question 6 that would be necessary for you to accept the use of the Hain scoring system for the Bender–Gestalt as a measure of organicity. Indicate why the data you present would be sufficient to justify your use of the system.

8. If each Purkinje cell were capable of linking up with 50,000 others and there were 5 billion such cells in the human cortex, calculate the number of possible connections that could occur. What are the major implications of this figure?

9. Outline the limitations of the strategy of working backward from observed behavioral deficits to making statements about damage to specific regions of the brain.

10. Francis Galton was the first to suggest that everyone's fingerprints were unique. On the basis of the discussions in the chapter, discuss whether it seems reasonable to make the same supposition about human brains. What are the implications of this?

11. Why do you think our species developed to have two half brains?

12. What are the evolutionary implications of functional assymetry?

13. What do you believe are the major benefits of using the Wechsler series of intelligence tests as part of a neuropsychological testing program?

14. In what sense is the Halstead–Reitan Neuropsychological Test Battery atheoretical?

15. Evaluate the strengths and weaknesses of the Halstead Impairment Index.

16. Outline the difficulties that would emerge if a dysnomic became involved in the popular television advertisement for Campbell's Chunky Soup that is concerned with the proper eating utensil used to consume the product.

17. With reference to three specific subtests, indicate why there is a need for better age norms for the Halstead–Reitan.

18. If a very close friend sustained a head injury like Ron's, would you recommend that the Halstead–Reitan be used? Why, or why not?

19. Suggest how the Halstead–Reitan might be used as part of a rehabilitation program for a patient who has sustained major brain injury.

20. Discuss the relative strengths and weakness of atheoretical versus theory-driven neuropsychlogical test batteries. Which would you use if you had a choice? Why?

21. Discuss the problems of generalizing from data based on research patients who have received very discrete surgical brain lesions (like the Montreal Neurological Institute cases discussed in the chapter) to patients who have sustained brain injury through some form of trauma (say, an auto accident). What are the implications of this for the utility of informal composite test batteries?

22. Outline the patient benefits that accrue from the relabeling of certain educational problems as learning disabilities.

23. In Table 18-7, which lists the various subtypes of learning disabilities, there is a distinct bias toward verbal processing. Discuss whether you feel this is reasonable.

24. Outline as many psychometric problems as you can associated with the four-part definition of learning disabilities presented in the chapter.

25. Debate the pros and cons of considering that learning disabilities are solely biological in origin.

26. In what senses are the contemporary approaches to identifying learning disorders atheoretical? What are the implications of this for the validity of the approaches?

27. Write a scene for a screenplay in which the viewer comes into contact with an ADHD child.

28. The Connors Rating Scales are fundamentally descriptive in nature, although it is possible for both parents and teachers to use long and short forms. What are the implications of this for the development of theory and therapeutic measures to resolve ADHD?

Part VII

The Postmodern Era

We have now come to the end of our narrative of testing. What remains is to conclude several of the substories that have emerged, as well as to take a tentative glimpse into what the future might hold for testing in our culture.

Chapter 19 provides summaries of several state-of-the-art developments in testing. Included here are the application of computers to testing, new ideas in item analysis and reliability, and a discussion of a new, integrated view of validity. This emerging perspective on validity, which suggests that the establishment of validity is actually hypothesis testing, serves to define the fundamental perspective that will direct the immediate future of the field.

This new version of validity, however, does not resolve all the tensions being experienced in the testing field. Indeed, it may even be seen to create some. To explore this, in Chapter 20, we will look at a number of the recurring and important anxieties that are part of the domain. The tensions between nature and nurture, individuals and institutions, science and art, and positivistic and alternative approaches to science are discussed as a means of framing some of the future concerns that will confront the field. An appeal for increased democraticization of our testing practices and policies is offered as a means of pushing us closer to resolution of these important tensions.

And with this appeal for increased consideration of all voices involved in the testing enterprise, we conclude our narrative of psychological testing.

Chapter 19

Recent Developments in Testing

TYING UP SOME LOOSE ENDS

We are now entering a part of our narrative of testing that is difficult to organize. Previous sections have, for the most part, been able to maintain a chronological flow, mostly because sufficient time had passed to allow the story to unfold. Hence organization was relatively straightforward. However, as we move into a chapter that deals with contemporary developments, we do not have the luxury of hindsight to permit organization of the emerging story. In a sense, we have a disparate and unrelated set of topics whose story is yet to unfold.

This chapter contains discussions of four topics, each of which is clearly an elaboration of ideas introduced earlier. The computer and testing will be discussed as a natural extension of the observation made earlier that technology is a significant part of social decision making in any culture (see Chapter 3). The discussion of item analysis presented in Chapter 11 will be updated, providing a sense of contemporary thinking in the field. Finally, sections dealing with current views of reliability and validity will be presented to bring these two seminal concepts up to date. We have seen both of these ideas evolving since their introductions very early in the history of the testing enterprise. Thus, this chapter ties up a number of loose ends in the interests of bringing our understanding closer to contemporary concerns.

The topics covered here do not exhaust the possibilities of all new developments in testing. Every time a new issue of a journal or a new test catalog is published, myriad new ideas and technologies are offered. The few new developments selected for this chapter have been chosen from among the many available because they represent particularly significant modifications to older traditions in the testing enterprise. It is by examining these that we can begin to get a good sense of the manner in which the field is changing and adapting to the times. Thus, there is a clear element of selection in this chapter. This sampler of recent thinking will hopefully give you a feel for the testing enterprise as it exists today.

THE COMPUTER AND TESTING

While developments within the testing enterprise were continuing apace, numerous scientists busy in labs all around the world were developing what might be considered the "mechanical brain." The emergence of the computer, particularly smaller and cheaper models with incredible power, has been the most significant technological development during the last decade. From huge mainframe machines in the 1970s, computers have continued to grow in power with an associated decrease in size and price. By the mid-1980s, personal computers with amazing power were becoming available at highly reasonable prices. These important technological developments are beginning to have a significant impact on the testing enterprise, and it is to these we now turn.

As indicated earlier, technology inevitably has an impact on social decision making. Recall the manner in which the invention of paper radically changed the nature of university examinations (see Chapter 3). Not surprisingly, the computer has had and will continue to have a profound effect on the field of psychological testing (for a review and discussion, see Butcher, 1987).

Computers as Electronic Clerks

The major developments with computers have involved the development, administration, scoring, and interpretation of tests. In many of these contexts, computers serve as electronic clerks and thereby save considerable time and money.

A reading of the current trade literature reveals an impressive array of constructs that have been computerized in one way or another. Table 19-1 presents a selective list of tests and constructs that are presently adapted to computers. This list was derived by searching the intersect of the terms *computer* and *testing* in the computerized version of *Psychological Abstracts* for 1986 and 1987. This is a very clear indication of the receptivity of the testing enterprise to computerization. The range of constructs being adapted to the computer is impressive, and a geometric increase in this domain can be anticipated.

Table 19-1 A sample list of computerized constructs

Abstract problem solving (head injured)
Abstract reasoning (for example, Raven Progressive Matrices)
Academic skills
Achievement tests
Attention span (for example, WAIS Digit Span)
Attitudes
Categorization (for example, Wisconsin Card Sorting)
Career guidance
Color discrimination
Dementia (Alzheimer's disease symptomatology)
Draw-a-Person Test
Handedness
Intelligence (for example, Wechsler series)
Language skills (for example, DAT)
Matching figures
Mechanical aptitude (for example, DAT)
Personality (for example, MMPI, EPQ)
Vocabulary
Spatial ability
Spelling (for example, DAT)
Visual memory
Vocabulary (for example, Mill Hill)

For these constructs, the computer has been applied to virtually every stage of the measurement process. The computer has been used to facilitate (1) constructing tests, (2) presenting items to respondents, (3) providing a response medium, (4) recording responses directly, (5) adjusting which items are presented as a function of previous responses, (6) scoring, (7) norming, (8) generating written reports, and (9) doing analyses to aid in interpretation. Figure 19-1 (page 726) shows a flowchart of the overall procedure of assessment, with the arrows indicating the direction of movement within the chart. At virtually every step in this chart, the computer either has or could have significant effects on testing. The savings in time and the possibility of more reliable and efficient assessments are legion at every phase.

This flowchart considers only the eventual output from the testing process in that it ends at the stage labeled "generate written report." The basic output of the overall assessment process is a complex of test-based information combined with observational data, which is then used to feed into social decision making. Information regarding legal status, current social standards, political matters, individual biographic detail, local variations in the collective context, and a large number of other concerns are factored into the eventual social decision-making process, with the weight accorded the test data varying considerably as a function of the use to which the test is being put. It is not even necessary that the test data

Figure 19-1 The major steps of the assessment process in which the computer can be useful.

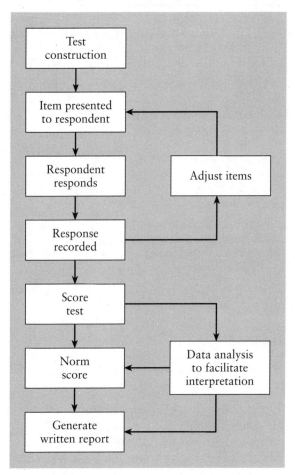

be represented as a formal written report (it could be in the form of testimony at a legal proceeding). For our purposes, the flowchart has been constructed to indicate the basic stages that can be enhanced by the use of a computer. There is no intent to imply that social decision making ends with the generation of a written report. The discussion that follows includes a presentation of computer applications in each of the stages noted in the diagram.

Test construction. Perhaps the first place where computers had an impact on the testing enterprise was the manner in which they made it possible to analyze tremendous amounts of data in increasingly complex ways. Recall that Thurstone did the factor analyses that derived the Primary Mental Abilities by hand and that it took a number of months to do it. Today, such an analysis would require a trivial amount of time on a mainframe computer. This advance opened the door to a massive increase in the feasibility of doing these types of analyses. Indeed, the complexities, sophistication, and sample sizes of analyses observed in the testing enterprise have grown significantly over the past several decades.

The availability of high-speed computers has also added considerable sophistication to the ways in which tests can be developed. The emergence of the complex approaches to inventory construction shown in, for example, the Personality Research Form (see Chapter 13) are due to the availability of the technology that permitted the rapid and efficient computation of myriad intercorrelations and related statistics.

Presenting items to respondents. The computer screen is a particularly powerful medium for the presentation of test items to respondents. If properly created, computerized stimulus displays can be attractive, providing an interesting and motivating alternative to the usual paper-and-pencil format. In addition, the computer screen provides a previously unattainable degree of stimulus control because items can be displayed for intervals timed to the nearest millisecond if the assessment context demands it. As well, very tight control of the content and duration of interitem intervals is possible.

At first it might seem that the administration of a test via a computer is dehumanizing—taking the person out of the entire process. However, the data thus far appear to indicate that respondents react favorably to computerized presentation. In our work here at the University of Calgary, opinions have routinely favored computerized administration (see also, Burke & Normand, 1987). This favorable response undoubtedly increases motivation during the testing procedure, which is a great benefit. Of particular note is some work we are doing with hospitalized depressive patients who are reacting favorably to the Macintosh applications we have designed in our laboratory.

In a comparison of computer, face-to-face, and self-report measures, Skinner and Allen (1983) found that the computer was seen as less friendly, shorter, more relaxing, and more interesting than the other two formats. Reliabilities for the three modes of presentation were comparable. The computerized version was most acceptable to respondents with good visual/motor skills and least preferred by better educated and defensive individuals.

Another area where initial impressions proved a bit problematic was the use of computers with elderly patients. Some early work indicates that the computer contributed to heightened anxiety levels with older clients (Carr, Ghosh, & Ancil, 1983). However, other research indicates that anxiety associated with computer testing is short-lived (Luschene, O'Neil, & Dunn, 1974), is typically the result of poorly designed procedures (Hedl, O'Neil, & Hansen, 1973), and is easily correctable with minimal training (say, 1 hour of tutoring; see Johnson & White, 1980).

First impressions aside, the research appears to offer promise of considerable utility for computerized testing. Of note is the tremendous saving in clerical time supervising the testing session once things have been adapted to the computer.

Collecting responses. The next place where computers have had an impact on the testing enterprise is the manner in which they have facilitated responding. The respondent can answer questions to items presented on a computer terminal using a number of input devices. Current applications have mentioned the following "manipulanda," which respondents can use to signal their response to the computer: (1) a keyboard especially designed for the test or adapted from the standard typewriter key set; (2) a mouse, a small hand-held box controlling a cursor on the screen, allowing respondents to indicate which of several alternatives they wish to select by moving the cursor into a response box on the screen; (3) a touch screen, which records where on the computer screen respondents place their finger, allowing for the immediate selection from among a number of alternatives; (4) a light pen, which can be used to signal a response location either on the computer screen or on a graphics tablet; and (5) various joysticks and roller balls, which control the position of a cursor on the screen. The recent revolution in personal computers, which have the power to present the items as well as collect the responses, makes these particularly attractive options. This application provides the benefit of having respondents enter their data directly, thus saving clerical costs and errors.

Recording responses. Prior to computers, the testing process was highly laden with clerical work where responses had to be tallied using answer keys and the like. These clerical activities were costly. The computer changed this by providing a means by which item responses could be transferred directly into a computer. One of the first large-scale computer applications in the testing enterprise involved the use of machines that read responses directly from the answer sheet. These *optical scanners* provide a quick and relatively inexpensive means of collecting item-response data. They are particularly appropriate for contexts in which large numbers of items and/or respondents are involved. For example, the multiple-choice section of the examinations in most large university courses are read using such systems. Many classical tests are marketed with optical-scoring sheets indicating the popularity of this application. The main gain is a considerable saving in clerical time.

The "mouse" in the respondent's right hand is one of the input devices that facilitates computerized testing.

If adapted to a computer, using one of the devices outlined in item 3 above, response recording is a trivial programming task, with the observed behavior moved directly into storage. There is minimal opportunity for respondent or clerical error in this recording process. These applications are particularly effective if the program has an option that allows the respondent to review and change previous responses.

Adjusting items. Another gain from a system that both presents the items and records the responses is **computerized adaptive testing**—that is, adapting the items shown to respondents as a function of their answers to previous questions. For example, if a respondent has failed to answer the last several questions correctly on an achievement exam, the computer could be programmed to terminate testing or to move to an easier set of questions.[1] The gains of such a procedure are numerous:

1. Because the person's ability is monitored a number of times during the test, the probability of a more reliable score estimate is enhanced, as is the potential for greater validity.
2. Testing time, boredom, and fatigue are minimized because only critical items are presented.
3. Considerable time and money can be saved by having "walk-in" testing stations for inventories that are not restricted.
5. Research indicates that adaptive testing is considerably less expensive than paper-and-pencil tests, even considering the costs of the hardware. (Greist & Klein, 1980; Neihaus, 1979; Space, 1981).

One problem with adapting tests to the computer is the complexity of attempting to validate them. One fundamental tenet of the prevailing measurement theory is that everyone should receive fundamentally the same stimuli when taking a test. If this is not the case, then differences between scores could be due to stimulus variations, not the characteristic being measured. Yet in adaptive testing, everyone does *not* receive the same stimuli; the stimuli presented are different for different respondents, with these differences being a function of the attribute being measured. Thus, normative (between-person) comparisons are confounded with stimulus differences (see Weiss, 1982, 1985 for discussion). This is a major challenge to the prevailing measurement theory that, if applied strictly, would have to reject the utility of adaptive testing, thereby denying the potential gains outlined above.

Scoring the test. Once the respondent has answered questions on a test, the programming to calculate a raw score is trivial. All that is usually required is adding up the number of correct or keyed responses made by the respondent. This means that the score can be fed back to the respondent (or the clinician if warranted)

---

[1]This procedure is not new; Terman's 1916 Stanford–Binet incorporated an adaptive strategy in that older children never saw the easier items and testing was terminated on a specified number of incorrect answers. What the computer allows is the use of much more sophisticated and standardized on-line decision making than was possible previously.

immediately, a major gain in terms of the utility of computerized testing. Another potential gain is the possibility of entertaining more complex (less linear) scoring systems than are presently in evidence in the field. For example, there may be cases where a complex statistic requiring substantial multivariate data reduction provides a better score than the sum that is the modal response summary currently in use. Such scoring schemes would have to be based on extensive research to justify their use over the more traditional and accepted linear scoring systems.

Norming the score. Another trivial programming exercise is converting a raw score to some form of scaled score by relating it to a data set stored in memory. The gains in speed are legion here. This frees the tester to spend time explaining the meaning of the score to the respondent rather than being caught up in looking up various values in sets of tables.

Generating a report. Once the scale scores have been calculated, it is (again) a relatively trivial programming task to have the machine interpret the obtained scores. This could involve the presentation of a verbal text that describes the characteristics of persons who have obtained similar scores or profiles in the past, selecting these from a stored library of interpretations keyed to specific test profiles. Minor programming adjustments also permit the generation of personalized reports by inserting the respondent's name in appropriate places.

Perhaps the most popular application of computer technology today is the generation of actuarial interpretations of tests. A written, textual interpretation of test performance is prepared by these programs, which are available in a number of computer environments. In the January through March 1986 *APA Monitor* (the monthly newsletter of the American Psychological Association), interpretive programs for the tests listed in Table 19-2 were advertised. There were also single mentions of several other tests over this 3-month period. Clearly, the interpretive program has gained considerable popularity within the enterprise (see also Butcher,

Table 19-2 Interpretive test programs advertised in the APA Monitor

Test	Number of Advertisements
MMPI	21
WAIS–R	8
WISC–R	7
Sixteen Personality Factor Questionnaire	6
Beck Depression Inventory	3
WPPSI	3
Wechsler Memory Scale	3
Bender–Gestalt	3
California Personality Inventory	2
Halstead–Reitan Battery	2
Luria–Nebraska Neuropsychological Battery	2
High School Personality Inventory	2

1987). This is not surprising because comparative studies indicate that in general computerized interpretations are either equally or more valid than clinical judgments (see LaBeck, Johnson, & Harris, 1983). However, the relative newness of these applications means that caution should be exercised because of the relatively small amount of data that is available (see Matarazzo, 1986).

Data analyses to facilitate further interpretation. Because the item responses are already in the computer environment, it becomes relatively easy to use the data to update norms and the like, to permit better norming and interpretation. In addition, the replication of analyses (such as the determination of reliability and validity) can be done almost immediately as new data become available. These benefits promise substantial utility in enabling the testing enterprise to keep up with changing times.

Several other possibilities. The computer environment is amenable to expanding the types of observations that can be made during the assessment process. Measuring response time during the responding process is possible, and such a measure could prove to be a very useful adjunct to the more traditional measures obtained from a scale. For example, it may be that items on which a respondent spends significant time are indicative of sensitive content. Research will be necessary to document the utility of such adjunctive information in the testing context.

Another benefit is the assistance that the computer can lend to individuals with visual, auditory, and physical limitations. Properly designed computer interfaces can greatly expand the potential of testing for such respondents (see Sampson, 1983; Wilson, 1987).

Summary. In a report to the APA Scientific Affairs Office, Jackson (1986) outlined the following advantages for computerized testing:

1. It is economical, particularly in the saving of expensive professional time.
2. Training technical assistants to supervise administration permits considerable savings.
3. The reduction of time between administration and interpretation speeds feedback to the client or patient.
4. Virtually all clerical errors are eliminated.
5. There is a considerable gain in reliability of interpretation by using preset rules consistently.
6. There is considerable potential for the systematic gathering of normative information because data recording is inexpensive and accurate.
7. Complex (nonlinear) scoring procedures are much more feasible in the computer environment.
8. Proper human-factors concerns will permit a move to special populations, some of whom are unserviced by the testing field.

This reveals a sizable list of gains that flow from the adaptation of computer technology to the testing enterprise. Computerization *is* the wave of the future.

Some Issues and Problems

Several persistent problems have presented themselves, and these demand consideration before assuming that computerized testing will solve all problems of the future.

Equivalence between paper-and-pencil and computerized tests. One problem associated with the application of computers to tests is the need to demonstrate comparability between the paper-and-pencil and computerized versions of a specific instrument. Failure to do this when an extant test is adapted to the computer is totally unacceptable according to the APA guidelines. As well, the demonstration of **equivalence** is particularly important if there is any possibility of an interaction between the medium of administration and the characteristic being assessed. For example, some preliminary research indicates that people tend to respond more honestly to a computer than they do in an interview (Carr, Ghosh, & Ancil, 1983). This suggests that computerized versions may obtain different scores for different types of constructs. Only proper equivalence research would solve the problem.

The demonstration of equivalence, however, is a complex problem, requiring a considerable amount of research (see Angoff, 1971; Hofer & Green, 1985; Lord, 1980; Marco, 1981). For example, the minimal experimental design required to demonstrate equivalence of paper-and-pencil and computerized versions of the same test involves using four groups with respondents assigned randomly. The groups would receive the (1) paper-and-pencil version twice; (2) the paper-and-pencil version first, followed by the computerized version; (3) the computerized version first, followed by the paper-and-pencil form; and (4) the computerized version twice. The times between testings would have to be the same across all groups. Equivalence would be demonstrated if the changes between the first and second testings were the same for all four groups, and various standard psychometric statistics (for example, test/retest reliability, internal consistency, validity coefficients) were comparable. The demonstration of equivalence in validity would involve a whole set of new studies treating the test as if it were brand new; the adaptation of a test to the computer obliges the adaptor to act as though it is a new test and to start from scratch. Because this is highly time-consuming and expensive (and not particularly interesting research), a great deal of this work has not emerged (see Burke & Normand, 1987).

Resistance in applied settings. One major obstacle to the adoption of computerized testing appears to be applied workers. The research indicates considerable potential gains, as well as debunking most major concerns, but the general finding is that computerized testing has not been widely accepted (Burke & Normand, 1987). Several researchers note a gain in acceptability of computerized testing following systematic training (Klonoff & Clark, 1975), but implementation is still relatively low. Perhaps the poor record of implementation of computerized testing lies in poor consideration of the human-factors elements of the testing process (Tomeski & Lazarus, 1975). Some of the earlier systems were indeed cumbersome and involved the use of very poorly conceived input media such as unwieldy keypads and adapted keyboards. However, the availability of the mouse and touch screen as input media and the tremendous human-factors gains associated with them render this an untenable hypothesis.

Perhaps one major reason for the apparent underutilization of computerized tests is that they eliminate one of the most important components of the testing exercise—namely, qualitative observations of respondent behavior during the testing session. If the respondent is alone in a small room or off in a corner filling out a test on a computer, the tester does not have the opportunity to observe the subtle aspects of behavior and motivation that are often important clues to the present status. Of course, if the respondent typically fills out the test in a testing room anyway (as is often the case with structured tests like the MMPI), this objection is not important. Many testing situations, however, require factoring in these impressions and observations as part of the testing process. It is these contexts in which computerized applications are not likely to be met with favor, and perhaps this is one aspect of the apparent underutilization of computer technology in assessment.

The possibility of circumventing professional expertise. When tests are administered, scored, and interpreted by a computer, the possibility of respondents receiving feedback in the absence of proper human and professional contact is increased. As well, many of the available computerized interpretation systems lack the necessary technical information to permit informed evaluation of their suitability to important social decision-making situations (see Lanyon, 1984; Tallent, 1987). This leads to a situation in which it becomes possible for tests to be used in unprofessional and unacceptable ways. In response to these matters, widespread concern about computerized test interpretation has been voiced (Moreland, 1985).

To rectify this situation, the APA (1986) has prepared a set of guidelines for the evaluation and use of computerized test-interpretation systems. This document articulates the nature of the information required to properly evaluate a test-interpretation service. Included here is information about the procedures used to develop the interpretations. These could be in the form of a technical manual or in other published reports. Detail must be sufficient to permit users to make an informed decision about the utility of the interpretations for their specific applications. Here is an example of the kinds of guideline included in APA (1986):

> The extent to which statements in an interpretive report are based on quantitative research versus expert clinical opinion should be delineated. When statements in an interpretive report are based on expert clinical opinion, users should be provided with information that will allow them to weigh the credibility of such opinion. [Cited in Butcher, 1987, Appendix B]

Besides the requirement of technical information, the APA guidelines discuss the need to specify the qualifications of the test-interpretation system producers, publishers, and users. As an example, the guidelines indicate that the user of such services should be adequately trained to evaluate the service. Users should also have sufficient qualifications to allow them to combine, in a professionally responsible manner, the computerized report with other sources of assessment information. This means, among other things, that the user of such tests should have extensive training in *assessment*. In most cases, this implies that users of these computerized systems should have high degrees of professional training.

Whether the APA's efforts at self-regulation revealed in its 1986 guidelines for computerized testing will prevent misuses of these applications of testing is unknown. Although many of those involved with computerized assessment have demonstrated considerable concern about the practice, the possiblity of misuse is still real.

Replicating errors. Although effort is continually invested to ensure that all aspects of the measurement process are accurate and proper, significant errors may be built into any assessment device. These could range from simple miskeying of items through to grand misconceptions about the constructs being measured. Once a test containing such mistakes is computerized, these errors will be replicated and amplified, creating a situation where the computer can actually contribute to error variance, rather than decrease it. Clearly, the onus of accuracy lies with the programmer, and this becomes a particularly important responsibility of the test publisher.

A related issue is the manner in which a computerized test serves to create an impression of it being a "final" version. The appearance of a test on a computer screen has an air of permanence that is difficult to deny. Because the test-development process, particularly the demonstration of construct validity, is ongoing, this sense of constancy can interfere with proper incremental development of tests, particularly because casual users do not have the resources to modify the program in the event they perceive the need for specific change.

Despite these problems, the gains from computerization of the testing enterprise appear to be great. Genuine savings in time and money are only a small part of the potential benefits that accrue from integrating the computer into the testing enterprise. The potential for development of more sophisticated methods of administration, scoring, and interpretation are certainly worth mentioning. In all, it is not surprising that the implementation of computers is emerging apace.

CONTEMPORARY DEVELOPMENTS IN ITEM ANALYSIS

The availability of high-speed computers with their extensive number-crunching capacities paved the way for a number of important developments in test construction and evaluation. Starting in the late 1960s, a series of mathematical models added considerable sophistication to the analysis of items. Initially, this family of methods was known as **latent-trait models** because they were concerned with the probability that a person of a given ability level (or latent trait) would succeed on a given item with known difficulty level (see Lord & Novick, 1968). However, in these models, the notion of latent trait was a statistical abstraction, not a reference to a construct that exists in any physical or psychological sense or to an entity proposed to "cause" behavior. This specialized use of the term *trait* created a number of communication difficulties, and eventually this approach to item analysis became known as **item-response theory (IRT)** (see Lord, 1980).

The Item-Characteristic Curve

IRT represents a natural extension of the item analytic procedures discussed in Chapter 11. The starting point involves creating an **item-characteristic curve (ICC)**,

Table 19-3 Proportion of correct responses on selected items on a 12-question, short-answer quiz as a function of total number of items correct

Total Score	Item Number 4	5	7	8
0	.00	.00	.00	.00
1	.00	.50	.00	.17
2	.03	.61	.00	.18
3	.06	.19	.00	.22
4	.08	.30	.03	.31
5	.23	.89	.06	.40
6	.31	.31	.08	.43
7	.70	.79	.23	.57
8	.77	.20	.31	.61
9	.82	.52	.70	.72
10	.99	.59	.77	.82
11	1.00	.31	.82	.83
12	1.00	.70	.99	.85

Figure 19-2 The item-characteristic curve for item 4 in Table 19-3.

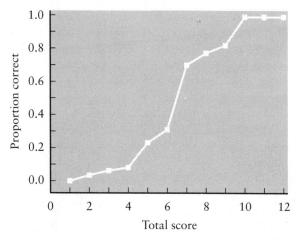

which relates the proportion of persons who get an item correct to their total test score. Table 19-3 presents some hypothetical data of this type based on a 12-item short-answer quiz. Each item was scored as either correct or incorrect, and a person's total score was the number of items answered correctly. In this table, for example, 23% of those who obtained a total score of 5 on the quiz passed item number 4.

Figure 19-3 The item-characteristic curve for an item that discriminates perfectly.

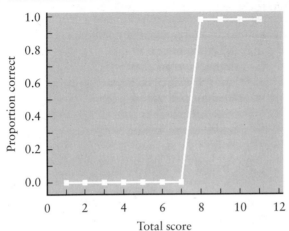

The ICC is constructed by plotting the proportions correct as a function of total score, drawing one separate curve for each item. Figure 19-2 demonstrates this for item 4. Notice how the proportions of correct responses on the ICC for item 4 gradually increase with greater total scores, indicating that a higher score on the quiz is associated with a stronger probability of answering item 4 correctly.

There are several old friends embedded in this ICC. For example, if everyone answered the item correctly, the ICC would be a horizontal line across the top of the curve through a proportion correct of 1.00. This would translate to a p-value of 1.00 for such an item (see Chapter 11). If everyone answered an item wrong ($p = .00$), the ICC would be a horizontal line across the graph going through 0.0. As you might have guessed, the p-value is a linear function of the area under the ICC—the greater the area under the curve, the higher the p-value, indicating that the ICC is a graphical representation of p-value (among a number of other things).

Now let's consider, for a moment, what the ICC for a particularly good item might look like. From a test developer's perspective, the best possible item would be one where everyone below a specific score answered the item wrong, while everyone above the same score answered it correctly. In this case, the item would be providing perfect discrimination. Figure 19-3 illustrates such a perfectly discriminating item.

The shape of this ICC can best be described as a **step function** because of the abrupt transition between proportions correct of 0 and 1.00, which occurs between total scores of 7 and 8. It is not difficult to visualize the possibility of items that vary as a function of where the *step* in the step function occurs, with some occurring at a low total score and others at a higher one. Figure 19-4 shows two examples of empirical ICCs that vary in terms of their location along the horizontal axis. These ICCs are for items 4 and 7 from Table 19-3. In this case, item 7 is located to the right of item 4, but they are both the same shape.

Drawing a horizontal line from the proportion correct of .5 leads to an intersection with the ICCs. In Figure 19-4, this intersection occurs directly above a total score of 6.5 for item 4. The intersection occurs at the total score 8.5 for item 7. The value of this intersection has become known as the **threshold** because it represents the turning point for the item. Persons who obtain a total score below this point have a lower than chance probability of answering the item correctly, whereas those above are more likely to succeed on the particular item. This suggests that item performance is related to the amount of ability possessed by the individual taking the test.

Figure 19-5 shows two examples of ICCs for items that do not discriminate the total score very well. Item 5 shows no systematic relationship between proportion correct and total score, indicating that the item is not functioning particularly well. The "hypothetical poor item" in Figure 19-5 shows the extreme case of an item where the probability of answering it correctly is the same for all levels of total score.

Figure 19-4 The item-characteristic curves for items 4 and 7 from Table 19-3, showing differential location on the horizontal axis.

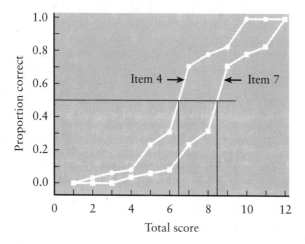

Figure 19-5 The item-characteristic curves for two poor items, one hypothetical and the other drawn from Table 19-3.

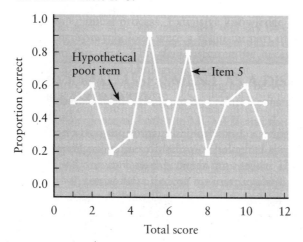

Figure 19-6 The item-characteristic curves for two items with identical thresholds but different shapes (from Table 19-3).

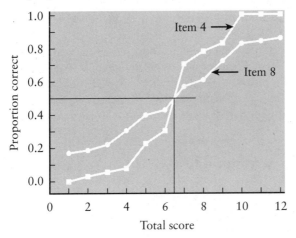

As you might expect, true ICCs typically exist somewhere between the two extremes shown in Figures 19-3 and 19-5. The closer to a step function an ICC is, the better the item—in terms of predicting the total score. This should remind you of another old friend from Chapter 11. It turns out mathematically that items with ICCs shaped like step functions have high item-total correlations. ICCs like those in Figure 19-5 have item-total correlations around 0. This suggests that the shape of the curve is a direct function of the item-total correlation, with higher values being associated with steplike ICCs.

So far we have suggested two different parameters underlying ICC—threshold and shape. These two parameters are independent of each other. For example, Figure 19-6 shows ICCs for two items of varying shape but with the same threshold. These curves, again drawn from Table 19-3, show that item 4 is closer to a step function than item 8, even though they have identical thresholds.

Item-Response Theory

The foregoing serves as an introduction to IRT. This theory is concerned with mathematizing some of the ideas discussed above to solve several important problems in the testing enterprise. The first step in IRT involves determining the underlying mathematical shape of the ICCs. Here an effort is made to fit the best possible mathematical curve to the ICC.[2] Figure 19-7 shows an example of what this might look like for item 4 in our sample data.

Once the curve has been fitted, it becomes possible to derive the parameters such as threshold and shape. For example, the total score associated with a propor-

---

[2]In many versions of IRT, this is achieved by finding the curve that minimizes the squared distances between it and the observed data. This is often called the *least-squares best fit.*

Figure 19-7 A mathematical fitting of the item-characteristic curve for item 4 from Table 19-3.

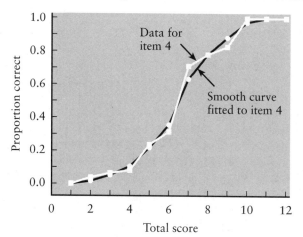

tion correct of .5 for the fitted curve would be the threshold. An estimate of the **shape parameter** can also be derived from the smoothed curve.

Most applications of IRT have found that *three* different values are needed to properly describe ICCs:

1. The shape parameter, called a_i for item i, which indicates the shape of the curve, with high values suggesting a more steplike structure;

2. The threshold parameter, called b_i for item i

3. The **chance parameter** to adjust for the probability of obtaining a correct response by guessing, called c_i for item i

This third parameter would be necessary in situations such as multiple-choice exams where there is a chance that a person with very low ability will answer some of the questions correctly just by randomly selecting an alternative.

Parameters are estimated by a complex process that involves making a good guess (for example, by using the item-total correlation as an initial estimate of the shape parameter, a) and then going through a series of successive approximations or iterations until the values of the parameters stabilize. The three values, a_i, b_i, and c_i, then, are mathematical parameters derived from the idealized or smoothed ICC.

Figure 19-8 (page 740) presents smoothed curves for three different hypothetical items. Items y and z have the same shape parameter ($a_y = a_z$) but different thresholds. Items x and y share the same values of the b parameter but have different values of the shape parameter. Item x requires a guessing parameter, c_x, because a small proportion of persons of no ability have answered the item correctly.

The smoothed curves and their associated parameters, a_i, b_i, and c_i, provide a number of benefits. For example, they provide sophisticated measures of item difficulty and discrimination. As well, it is possible to select the best items from a set

Figure 19-8 Hypothetical IRT-generated item-characteristic curves for three items.

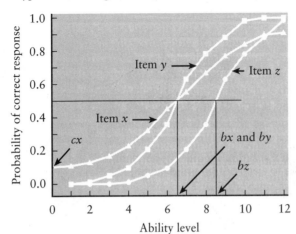

using **item-information functions,** which consider all aspects of an item's performance rather than restricting considerations to just one characteristic.

Variations of the three-parameter model exist, with some suggesting that the guessing estimate is not necessary, thereby reducing consideration to two estimates. Even a one-parameter model, using the threshold alone, has been proposed. The results from this family of models appear to be relatively unaffected by violations of underlying assumptions, although empirical checks are always necessary under such conditions.

Perhaps the greatest claim of IRT comes under the austere sounding name of **invariance of item parameters.** A basic supposition of this modeling technique is that the item parameters derived from the smoothed curves should not change as a function of the group taking the test. That is, the threshold, or b parameter, for a given item should be the same regardless of the ability level of the group on whom the item is used. The a and c parameters should also remain constant. This suggests the possibility of developing a uniform measurement scale. In a situation where ability levels are highly variable, such as achievement tests for overlapping grades, IRT appears to provide a means of calibrating items so they are comparable across samples. By using **anchor items** in varying groups, we can calibrate them such that any subset can be administered to any group and the scores will be comparable (for a discussion, see Thissen, Steinberg, & Wainer, 1988). Of course, empirical verification of this comparability is always advisable.

If the item parameters from IRT are indeed invariant, a number of the difficulties attending computerized adaptive testing mentioned in the previous section become less problematic as well. For example, concerns that item properties might change because each individual receives a different set of items are assuaged if IRT item parameters are invariant.

IRT models provide an elegant and sophisticated solution to a number of significant problems faced by the testing enterprise. However, they are far from universally accepted within the field—considerable debate remains. One problem is that the three-parameter model assumes that the **latent-ability continuum** is unidimensional. This is a difficult assumption to sustain, particularly if persons of varying experiences or at different levels of mastery are involved. Generalization to a multidimensional continuum set is possible, but the resulting model is ponderous. Another limitation is the need for tremendous amounts of data to be able to conduct an IRT analysis. To fill in all of the cells of the starting data matrix (such as Table 19-3), large numbers of respondents must be tested. This may not be a problem for some of the major testing programs, but it does pose problems for the use of IRT in other situations. These limitations aside, it seems clear that IRT is the wave of the future for item analytic procedures.

CONTEMPORARY VIEWS OF RELIABILITY

We now move to consideration of several of the seminal concepts within the testing enterprise. The first to be discussed is reliability. The manner in which this aspect of test performance is estimated from test scores remains pretty much the same in the 1990s as it was in the 1940s. As Figure 19-9 (page 742) shows, test/retest, parallel-form, and the family of internal consistency measures remain as the basic methods of estimating a test's consistency, or error-freeness. True-score test theory, which views the extent to which a score deviates from a true or population value as unreliability, still remains the major theoretical interpretation of reliability (see Chapter 11).

However, beginning in the 1950s, an alternate view of reliability began to surface. This new view challenged true-score test theory and today represents a major alternative to the older view. Tyron (1957) laid the foundations for a new perspective on reliability when he noted that there were a number of important similarities between the various approaches to estimating test-score consistency: "The welter of different 'methods' of calculating the reliability coefficients commonly employed are either different computational forms that yield the same correct value, or they refer to various empirical designs devised to estimate this value" (p. 229). For example, Tyron indicated that, if concern was with measuring a particular construct, say X, the usual test score (X_t) would be calculated as

$$X_t = X_1 + X_2 + \cdots + X_n \qquad (19\text{-}1)$$

where $X_1, X_2 \ldots X_n$ represent items in the test transformed to keyed or correct responses. There could also be a second test score designed to assess X, X'_t, defined as

$$X'_t = X'_1 + X'_2 + \cdots + X'_n \qquad (19\text{-}2)$$

The reliability estimate could, according to Tyron, be defined as the correlation between X_t and X'_t, or $R_{X_t X'_t}$. In the case of test/retest reliability, X_t and X'_t would be the administration of the same test on two different occasions; with parallel forms, the two scores would be based on two different sets of comparable items. In the case of split-half reliability, X_t and X'_t would be based on the items making up the first and second halves of the test, respectively, and so on. Tyron demonstrated that all of the formulas used in the methods of estimating reliability empirically

Figure 19-9 Summary of the approaches to estimating reliability from test scores (from Chapter 11).

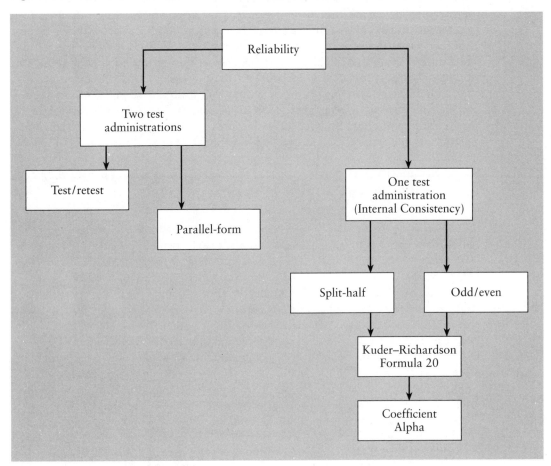

(that is, those shown in Figure 19-9) reduce to the same fundamental mathematical proposition. Because of this, he suggested that "a statistic that is more meaningful than the reliability coefficient is the correlation of X_t with a score on a *domain* of composites comparable to X_t. A **domain score** [emphasis added] of an individual would be the best criterion of his status in the property X, as operationally defined" (1957, p. 237). He termed this theoretical approach to reliability **behavior domain sampling,** which emphasizes the manner in which the items on a test converged on the construct X as being the essential component of reliability.

Generalizability Theory

This reinterpretation of reliability suggests that an important concern is the extent to which it is possible to generalize from the observed test score to the domain of concern. This start has since been picked up by a number of authors who have developed several strong interpretive positions that might be considered the "new" ideas of reliability. Perhaps the best known of these is **generalizability theory** (Cronbach, Gleser, Nanda, & Rajaratnam, 1972; Feldt & Brennan, 1989). This position begins by acknowledging that when test developers design a measure, they typically have a domain, or universe of behaviors, in mind. For instance, in designing a measure of aggression, the test developer might conceptualize the domain as an almost infinite number of different behaviors—each of which would signal the presence of the trait. In practical terms, though, we can only use a small number of the actual behaviors as items. This being the case, the focal concern becomes the extent to which it is possible to *generalize* from the smaller item set to the universe thought to underlie the trait being measured. In other words, does our small, finite sample of behavior allow us to make meaningful statements about the universe of behaviors underlying our construct? This is the nub of generalizability theory.

Of course, we could envision a **universe score**, which would represent a person's score on all possible manifestations of a trait. Conceptually, this would be very similar to the traditional idea of the true score. As well, the (hypothetical) correlation of observed scores with universe scores would be an indication of what we typically think of as reliability. High correlations would indicate good reliability. This correlation between the observed and universe score also represents the extent to which we can generalize from the small to the universal set of behavior, with higher correlations revealing better generalizability. So both the true score and generalizability views provide different points of view on the idea traditionally known as reliability.

The major gain of the generalizability interpretation is that it sensitizes us to the possibility that there may be several alternate but acceptable universes of generalization for a given construct. For example, in one case, we might be interested in how aggressive a person is under stress, so we would employ a stressful situation while measuring the trait, acknowledging that variability due to stress is considered reliable, nonerror variance. In another case, though, we might be interested in assessing aggression under normal conditions. In this situation, because we wish to generalize to nonstressful conditions, measuring aggression under stress would add error variance. Thus, the presence or absence of error is, in part, a function of the universe to which we wish to generalize.

We also have to be careful about the manner in which we estimate reliability or generalizability, continually bearing in mind the domain to which we wish to generalize. From these arguments, it follows that error is not solely a property of a test, but it also is the result of the uses to which we choose to put it.[3]

Classical true-score theory is still the dominant interpretation of reliability in the 1990s. However, the generalizability notion does provide a useful alternative perspective that draws attention to some components of error that the traditional perspective can overlook. Of particular note is the manner in which this newer view promotes the understanding of all individual sources of variance that contribute to a given test score.

---

[3]You might recognize this fundamentally contextual argument because Jenkins (1946) made a very similar point regarding criterion-related validity (see Chapter 13).

CONTEMPORARY VIEWS OF VALIDITY

Three developments regarding the idea of validity will be presented in this section. First, we will examine the issue of whether validity coefficients generalize across different situations and examine a technology that has evolved to determine this. Second, we will discuss the ascendance of construct validity to become the whole of validity. Third, we will investigate the interaction of validity with issues of value-ladenness and social consequences.

Validity Generalization

One benefit of the relatively long history of using psychological tests in various applied situations is the availability of an extensive amount of accumulated data on test use. For example, well over 500 separate research literatures that provide estimates of test- and job-performance correlations in employment selection have been documented (see Schmidt, 1988). If we were able, somehow, to combine studies within one of these literatures, we might be able to make some very strong statements about the nature of the *true* relationships between the variables of interest. These estimates would be robust because they would be based on an incredibly large data set. An emerging technique in statistical psychology, called **meta-analysis**, has begun to provide a means of combining various research studies to provide such robust estimates of effect size. In this domain, individual research studies are examined, and, considering issues such as sample size, measurement error, range restriction, and other possible sources of error such as computational mistakes, an estimate of the "population" value of the effect size is calculated. The increased power that these meta-analytic methods provide makes them potentially powerful techniques.

In the domain of criterion-related validity, meta-analytic techniques have been applied in a number of different ways (see Glass, McGaw, & Smith, 1981; Hedges, 1988; Hunter, Schmidt, & Jackson, 1982). Perhaps the best known of these applications has become known as **validity generalization** in which the goal is to gain estimates of the *true* size of test-criterion correlations within a given domain. This is a particularly important issue because the received wisdom of the field suggests that a test should be validated separately for each situation in which it is used (see Albright, Glennon, & Smith, 1963; Lawshe, 1948). If meta-analysis provided a robust estimate of the size of the true correlation between test and job performance, this need could, at least in theory, be obviated.

The simplest approach to meta-analysis of criterion-related validity involves deriving an estimate of the average size of the correlation between the test and criterion. This is not adequate, however, because it fails to take into account a number of important issues such as sample size and makeup, measurement error in both the test and the criterion, and a wide range of other potentially confounding sources of variability. For example, the test-criterion correlation reported in one study might be significantly deflated because there was a restriction of range in the criterion scores. Statistical adjustments must be made to the estimate to account for these sources of error and any other confounding influences on the correlation.

It also becomes necessary to gain some kind of estimate of the variability of the adjusted test-criterion correlations around the grand average of all the estimates. If this variability is low, then considerable confidence can be placed in the estimate of the average size of the correlation. If, however, the correlations demonstrate significant variability across studies, particularly when issues of sampling error, measurement error, restriction of range, and the like are taken into account,[4] generalization about the nature of test-criterion correlations must be made with considerable caution.

As an example, Pearlman, Schmidt, and Hunter (1980) used this technique to explore the relationship between quantitative ability and overall performance in clerical jobs. They identified 453 research studies that presented useful correlations between scores on various quantitative tests and a variety of clerical job-performance measures. In total, the scores of 39,584 individuals were involved in this meta-analysis. The mean size of the test-criterion correlations, adjusted for various artifacts was .47, whereas the variability of the observed test-criterion correlations was very small, prompting Schmidt (1988) to state that the "integration of this massive amount of data leads to the general and generalizable principle that the correlation between quantitative ability and clerical performance is .47, with very little, if any, true variation around this value" (p. 176). This is useful information because it indicates that anyone faced with the task of selecting clerical workers would do well to include a measure of quantitative ability and that a test-criterion coefficient of .47 is what might be expected.

This meta-analytic finding, and the many others in the literature, however, do not free the test user from having to demonstrate the utility of the tests in the specific situation in which they are being used. The average estimate of test-criterion correlation derived from these meta-analyses represents an estimated population value, and any single case could deviate substantially from this average. Because Schmidt and his colleague's estimates are corrected for errors, much like Spearman's original correction for attenuation (see Chapter 6), they represent a hypothetical state of affairs—in a sense, the correlation expected if all else was equal. But can we be sure that all else is indeed equal in a given testing situation? The answer here is a qualified no, indicating that the safest and most effective way of proceeding is to calculate the actual test-criterion correlation for the specific case. Then it is possible to be certain that the testing program is working effectively *and* to examine the comparability of the obtained data with the meta-analytic results. Meta-analyses provide very useful information about which tests to include in a testing program, but they do not free the test user from the obligation of demonstrating that the tests are performing as expected.

---

[4]The techniques of adjusting observed test-criterion correlations for the effects of sample size, measurement error, and so on are complicated. The techniques themselves are not presented here because they are beyond the scope of this text. This section is intended only to give you a sense of the overall orientation of these techniques. If you are looking for specific methodological procedures, consider sources such as Hunter et al. (1982)

Construct Validity as the Whole of Validity

Investigating the generic notion of validity has not been static either. Since its introduction in 1954, construct validity has, slowly but surely emerged as the preeminent form of validity. For example, construct validity is now a central part of experimental design, where various approaches to designing experiments are evaluated in terms of this idea (for examples, see Cook & Campbell, 1979, pp. 59–70; Kidder & Judd, 1986, pp. 65–68). A fundamental concern with experimental designs has become known as **external validity**, which refers to the extent to which an experimental situation can be generalized to the real world. This type of validity has been subsumed under the general framework of construct validity in a number of places, indicating the manner in which construct validity has spread to other areas of the discipline. Validity has also been applied in other social science disciplines such as sociology (see Bailey, 1988; Heise & Bohrnstedt, 1970, pp. 1–16; Zeller & Carmines, 1980, Chapter 4).

In addition, construct validity is gaining increasing importance in the more recent literature. Like Cronbach and Meehl before them, several authors have bemoaned the compartmentalization of validity into various subtypes such as content, criterion-related, and construct. One major problem with this proliferation of validities is that it allows the test developer to be selective about the kind of validity demonstrated, thereby creating a shortcut to publishing "valid" tests. Guion (1980) suggests that the major subtypes of validity (criterion-related, content, and construct) were "something of a Holy Trinity representing three roads to psychometric salvation. If you can't demonstrate one kind of validity, you've got two more chances" (p. 398). The problem, according to Messick (1980), was that referring to the various concepts underlying the subtypes of validity by the same name blunted their distinctiveness, creating the possibility that "any one of these so-

Table 19-4 Suggested renaming of various types of validity

Validity Designation	Descriptive Designation
Content validity	Content relevance—domain specifications
	Content coverage—domain representativeness
Criterion validity	Criterion relatedness
Predictive validity	Predictive utility
Concurrent validity	Diagnostic utility
	Substitutability
Construct validity	Interpretive meaningfulness
Convergent validity	Convergent coherence
Discriminant validity	Discriminant distinctiveness
Nomological validity	Nomological relatedness
Factorial validity	Factorial composition
External validity	External relatedness

Source: Messick (1980).

Figure 19-10 The current structure of validity showing that construct validity has become the whole of validity.

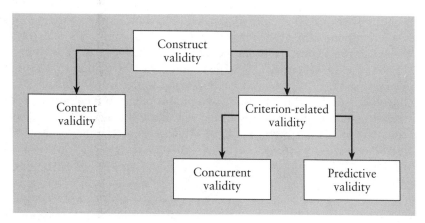

called validities, or a small set of them, might be treated as the whole of validity, while the entire collection to date might not still exhaust the essence of the whole" (p. 1014). He goes on to suggest that it would be more effective to relabel the subtypes of validity with names more closely representing their character and intent. For example, content validity would be better labeled as representativeness. Criterion-related validity would benefit from being renamed criterion relatedness or predictive utility. Messick (1980) presents a table that provides alternate descriptors for 15 types of validity referenced in the literature. Table 19-4 is a subset of this table, which includes the types of validity mentioned earlier in this text. As this table shows, virtually all the classical concepts considered to be part of validity have been renamed without using the term *validity*. This is a major change, given the historical importance of word.

In one sense, Table 19-4 can be interpreted as semantic quibbling (for example, what is the real difference between *discriminant validity* and *discriminant distinctiveness*?). However, Messick has a very important reason for suggesting these changes. One exception to this renaming program is noted—construct validity— which, according to Messick, is the only one that deserves "to bear the name 'validity' and wear the mantle of all that name implies" (1980, p. 1015). He then shows how the other forms of validity can all be reduced to considerations of construct validity. For example, he shows how the standard test-criterion study involves a number of theoretical propositions about the relevance of the test to the criterion, which imply the existence of a theory in the selection of the criterion. Clearly, then, criterion-related validity is a special case of construct validity. The possibility of demonstrating content validity similarly presumes the existence of a comprehensive theoretical definition of the domain, thereby indicating that content validity too is a subtype of construct validity. By 1980 then, construct validity had indeed become the "queen bee" of validities. From its initial introduction as adjunctive to the criterion-related subtypes (see Figure 13-8), construct validity had become the whole of validity. Figure 19-10 demonstrates the current structure of validity.

Validity as hypothesis testing. Once construct validity assumed its ascendant position, it became necessary to reconsider the exact nature of validity. This emerged as the gradual realization that Cronbach and Meehl's original ideas about construct validity were fundamentally views about the nature of science. More specifically, several authors have argued that construct validation is, at root, *hypothesis testing.* For example, Landy (1986) argues that "the validity analyst is carrying out traditional hypothesis testing" (p. 1186). Messick (1988) amplifies this suggestion by proposing that "test validation in the construct framework is integrated with hypothesis testing and with all of the philosophical and empirical means by which scientific theories are evaluated" (p. 41). Recapitulating the list of approaches to construct validation proposed originally by Cronbach and Meehl (1955), Messick (1988) states that:

> Construct validation embraces all of the statistical, experimental, rational, and rhetorical methods of marshalling evidence to support the inference that observed consistency in test performance has circumscribed meaning. With respect to the generality of process, the development of evidence to support an inferential leap from an observed consistency to a construct or theory that accounts for that consistency is a concern of all science. [p. 41]

Going even further, Hogan and Nicholson (1988) argue that test validation *is* experimental research. All of this indicates that there has been a shift in interpretation of validity. Initially viewed as "the extent to which a test measures what it purports to measure," validity is now viewed as a scientifically driven process of hypothesis testing. This is a significant and important change.

Viewing construct validation as hypothesis testing is compatible with the presentation of construct validity presented in Chapter 13. Recall the example of the Unadorned Anxiety Test, which served as an exemplar of how to establish construct validity. Throughout this example, there was constant reference to testing various hypotheses derived from anxiety theory and thereby extending the nomological network underlying the test. More than anything, this recent stress on hypothesis testing recognizes the fundamental scientific nature of the validation process, giving it greater emphasis than had been evident earlier. Without doubt, viewing construct validation as hypothesis testing strengthens the position of logical empiricism (with partially defined correspondence rules tolerated) as the fundamental metatheory in the contemporary testing enterprise. At this point in our story, we can rest assured that the construct validity–oriented testing enterprise rests on a firm scientific footing and that progress in the field is inevitable because this footing has provided so many remarkable achievements in the past.

Consequential Bases of Validity

Perhaps the most important development in rethinking the notion of validity comes from efforts to bring the idea into contact with the value-laden situations in which tests are used. Messick (1988) provides an interesting framework for pursuing this important point. He suggests that the construct interpretation of a given test score contributes to the **evidential basis for test interpretation**. This includes all the standard data regarding validity (and reliability) that would be part of the supporting documentation for a given test. Equally important, though, are the judgmental appraisals associated with construct interpretations. These value-laden assumptions bring into focus what Messick calls the **consequential basis for test interpretation.** Included here are a wide range of concerns regarding the social implications of proposing a specific test-score interpretation. For example, the decision to interpret IQ-test scores as reflecting genetic propensity (even if the evidence supports it) has a number of serious value consequences, which researchers and testers ignore at their peril (see Chapter 15).

When a test is used in a specific situation, evidential concern shifts to utility. Here data are presented to justify a specific use of a test in the specific situation (see Chapter 14). This might be considered the **evidential basis for test use** in which both the notions of utility and construct validity are involved. Additionally, though, considering the social consequences of using a test in a specific situation is important. For example, a selection officer might employ a test with an undocumented gender bias that, perhaps inadvertently, contributes to significant gender unfairness in that specific situation. Such concerns can be considered the **consequential basis for test use.**

Messick (1988) indicates that these evidential and consequential bases of test interpretation and use can be summarized in the matrix shown in Figure 19-11. This figure summarizes what is emerging as a **unified view of validity.** Here we find the more-or-less standard ideas of validity and utility being crossed with considerations of the consequential and value implications of test interpretation and use. All four facets outlined in Figure 19-11 should be considered within the framework of evaluating the usefulness of a test in a specific situation.

This unified view of validity sensitizes us to the fact that test use is fundamentally a local issue. That is, the sociopolitical context into which a test is placed is likely to vary with the location and time of its use. This indicates that test use must be carefully evaluated in situ. Although there may be a degree of universality to the evidential bases of a test, the same cannot be said for the consequential bases because they are so locally driven. This means that the test user inherits the ethical responsibility for actual test use because the user is in the "best position to evaluate the meaning of individual scores under local circumstances" (Messick, 1988, p. 43).

Figure 19-11 The facets of validity.

	Test interpretation	Test use
Evidential basis	Construct validity	Construct validity + Utility
Consequential basis	Value implications	Social consequences

(SOURCE: Messick, 1980.)

Test developers do their best to provide maximal evidence for the proposed interpretation of a test, but that is not enough—the consequential issues must be addressed as well. The test user must go a step further and elaborate and eliminate the possible contaminants that might be operating in the local situation: "Thus, the test user bears not only a heavy ethical burden but a heavy interpretive burden. And that interpretation entails responsibility for its value consequences" (Messick, 1988, p. 43). Here we find an explicit statement of the kinds of responsibilities that fall onto anyone who chooses to use a test in a specific situation. Purely and simply, when it comes to morally reasonable test use, *it is not enough to be able to demonstrate the reliability, validity, and utility of a test, but it is also necessary to take into account the consequential bases—implicit, explicit, and local—associated with the use of the instrument.* Failure to do this decreases the possibility of tests making a positive contribution to social decision making.

It is interesting to compare this unified conception of validity with the most recent set of test standards (APA, 1985). A description of this set of standards is presented in Appendix E. Of particular interest is Part II of the 1985 *Standards* entitled "Professional Standards for Test Use." Here we find a number of concerns that reflect Messick's consequential basis of test interpretation and use, such as consideration of unintended consequences (Standard 6.5) and clear delineation of the rationale underlying the use of a specific cutting score (Standard 6.9). It seems, then, that the unified view of validity reflects current thinking to the extent that components of this view have emerged in the APA *Standards*. The advantage of Messick's view, though, is that it makes the consequences of testing much more visible than do the APA *Standards*.

Summary

These three developments, validity generalization, construct validity as the whole of validity, and the consideration of consequential bases, indicate that the notion of validity has evolved significantly since its formal introduction in 1921. Although validity remains as the most important aspect of the evaluation of a test, all these developments point to the necessity of expanding concern beyond the simple test-criterion design that was the methodological bedrock of the testing enterprise more or less since its inception. By the mid-1990s, it has become clear that the development of tests demands substantive scientific support *and* that moral and ethical issues must be part-and-parcel of this development. The decision to use a test in a specific situation must similarly employ the maximal amount of available scientific information in the interests of empirically demonstrating utility. In addition, the use of a test must be rationalized within the context of prevailing local values and with sensitivity to potential consequential effects. The decision to use a test is not simply going to the "test cupboard" and pulling out the one that seems to give the most useful data; the decision to use a specific test demands a unique combination of scientific and moral judgment. The potential of the testing enterprise to contribute meaningfully to social decision-making hinges, in no small way, on the effectiveness and sensitivity with which these important judgments—both scientific and moral—are made.

Summary

This chapter summarized a number of contemporary developments in the testing enterprise. The use of computers in testing, item-response theory, and new perspectives on both reliability and validity were presented. Through all of this, we can see some gradual and important shifts in the enterprise as it adjusts to the 1990s. For example, there is a clear movement toward the incorporation of new technology in the explicit use of the computer to administer, score, and interpret tests. The emerging popularity of sophisticated mathematical and theoretical analyses has also been stimulated by the computer because it is now possible to readily analyze mountains of test data to provide information about individuals, items, and a wide range of other concerns. Continued technological impact and mathematization is likely to be a significant part of the 21st-century testing enterprise.

The testing enterprise also has shown some movement toward consideration of the moral and ethical implications of its practices. The institution of ethical standards and guidelines for testing (Chapter 12) as well as a number of reactions to social criticisms of testing (see Chapter 14) have been followed up by recent concerns about incorporating ethical and moral issues into the very notion of validity itself (for example, consequential issues). A heightened awareness of the significance of these concerns is likely to be an important part of the future of testing as our culture enters the postmodern era.

There is one area, however, in which the testing enterprise has not shown a great deal of movement. This relates to the fundamental approach to science that undergirds the entire field. Simply put, the practices and values of the field appear to be holding onto a specific vision of science and measurement. This vision, which we earlier labeled the liberalized version of logical positivism, remains the fundamental view of the world reflected in the proceedings of the testing enterprise. The ascendance of construct validity as the whole of validity is clear testimony to this because this idea is an almost literal translation of the doctrine of logical empiricism. The popularity of emerging topics such as validity generalization, item-response theory, and generalizability theory also serve to strengthen this worldview because they are firmly embedded within it. Logical positivism, in its contemporary form, lies at the very heart of today's psychological testing enterprise.

It is important, at this point, to ask whether this positivistic view of the world will provide the testing enterprise with the resources it will need over the next few decades. There can be little doubt that the economic, political, and intellectual turmoil that confronts us today will continue. This will undoubtedly force some significant changes to society at large and, in turn, to the testing enterprise. Will the current positivistic view of the world be sufficient to meet these emerging challenges? It is to these concerns that we now turn.

Glossary

anchor item An item administered to a wide variety of respondents that can then be used, in conjunction with IRT, to calibrate tests across diverse populations.

behavior domain sampling   From Tyron, the idea that the manner in which items represent the entire behavioral universe of a characteristic is akin to the test's reliability.

chance parameter   A value used to adjust ICCs to take into account the probability of obtaining a correct response on the basis of chance. Estimates of this parameter, c, are part of IRT.

computerized adaptive testing   An approach to using the computer in testing in which a person's responses to specific items are used to select the ensuing items.

consequential basis for test interpretation   Implications of value-laden assumptions that are part-and-parcel of accepting a specific interpretation of a test score. Local in nature, these concerns must be considered in the unified view of validity.

consequential basis for test use   Social and moral implications of value-laden assumptions that are part-and-parcel of using a specific test (and its interpretation) in a specific situation. Local in nature, these concerns must be considered in the unified view of validity.

domain score   From Tyron, the hypothetical score a person would obtain on all possible manifestations of a given psychological characteristic.

equivalence   The complex and time-consuming process of demonstrating that a computerized version of a test performs in exactly the same way as a paper-and-pencil version.

evidential basis for test interpretation   The empirical data and supporting theoretical evidence that are used to make a case for a specific interpretation of a test score. Includes all properties associated with construct validity.

evidential basis for test use   The empirical data and supporting arguments that are used to make a case for the utility of a psychological test in a specific situation. Conventional notions of construct validity and utility are involved here.

external validity   An estimate of the extent to which it is possible to make statements about the real world, based on a specific experimental result.

generalizability theory   A theoretical interpretation of reliability that focuses on the extent to which it is possible to make effective statements about the universe of a specific construct, based on the small sample of items used in a specific test.

invariance of item parameters   An expectation of IRT estimates of item properties (for example, a, b, and c) that these specific values will not change as a function of the group of respondents who are taking a specific test.

item-characteristic curve (ICC)   A graphical representation between the probability of obtaining a correct response on an individual item and the total score on the test. (See Figure 19-2.)

item-information function   A mathematical function derived from IRT that provides a sophisticated summary of numerous aspects of item performance.

item-response theory (IRT)   A class of models dealing with mathematical aspects of item-characteristic curves and other aspects of psychological test items.

latent-ability continuum   The unitary dimension thought to underlie the ability being addressed in a specific IRT analysis.

latent-trait models The early name given to a class of mathematical models of item-response characteristics. More recently, these models have come to be known under the label *item-response theory*.

meta-analysis A family of statistical procedures that allows the combination of separate empirical studies on a specific topic to provide a more robust estimate of the effect sizes documented in the research. Validity generalization is a specific type of meta-analysis.

shape parameter An estimate of the shape of an ICC. For example, the item-total correlation is one version of a shape parameter. Estimates of ICC shape are one of the parameters, *a*, in IRT.

step function A term used to describe a perfectly differentiating ICC wherein the probability of a correct response shows an abrupt change from 0 to 1.0 at a specific total score. (See Figure 19-3.)

threshold The point on an ICC where the probability of a correct response changes from being below chance to being above chance. Estimates of this point are one of the parameters, *b*, in IRT.

unified view of validity A perspective on validity that considers both the evidential *and* consequential bases of test interpretation *and* use. This unified view sensitizes us to the need to consider test use and interpretation carefully in local context as part of the assessment of the validity of the test.

universe score The hypothetical score that an individual would obtain if tested on all manifestations of a given construct. Akin to true score, the universe score is an aspect of the generalizability theory interpretation of reliability.

validity generalization A specific form of meta-analysis in which it is possible to gain an estimate of the true value of a test-criterion correlation by combining numbers of separate empirical estimates.

Suggested Further Reading

Baker, F. B. (1977). Advances in item analysis. *Review of Educational Research, 47,* 151–178.

> This is a fine introduction to the methodology surrounding item-response theory. It is a good next step for the reader who wishes to become more familiar with this sophisticated technology.

Butcher, J. N. (Ed.). (1987). *Computerized psychological assessment.* New York: Basic Books.

> This edited book provides considerable detail regarding current developments in the application of computers to testing. The APA guidelines for computerized testing are provided in this volume, along with a number of discussions of ongoing developments in the field.

Cronbach, L. J. (1988). Five perspectives on the validity argument. In H. Wainer & H. I. Braun (Eds.), *Test validity.* Hillsdale, N.J.: Erlbaum.

> This is an excellent overview of the various perspectives that can be taken regarding the idea of validity. It provides some good historical links with material we covered earlier

and culminates in an interesting set of arguments for the importance of construct valid-ity. It is highly recommended if you want to gain a sense of the current thinking in the domain.

Cronbach, L. J., Gleser, G. C., Nanda, H., & Rajaratnam, N. (1972). *The dependabil-ity of behavioral measurements: Theory of generalizability for scores and profiles.* New York: Wiley.

This primary source is tough reading, but it is well worth it if you want to gain a full sense of generalizability theory. The introduction provided in *The Enterprise* has, out of necessity, barely touched the surface of this theoretical perspective, and refer-ring interested students to "the" source is appropriate here.

Green, B. F. (1988). Construct validity of computer-based tests. In H. Wainer & H. I. Braun (Eds.), *Test validity.* Hillsdale, N.J.: Erlbaum.

This short chapter provides a relatively recent overview of the major issues sur-rounding computer-based testing. In keeping with the message of this chapter of *The Enterprise*, this article is useful in its emphasis on construct validity. It is recom-mended initial reading for anyone who wishes to gain a quick grasp of current thinking in this domain.

Hedges, L. V. (1988). The meta-analysis of test validity studies: Some new approaches. In H. Wainer & H. I. Braun (Eds.), *Test validity.* Hillsdale, N.J.: Erlbaum.

This chapter provides a detailed overview of a number of different approaches that are being taken to meta-analysis of criterion-related validity studies. It provides a more general orientation than in the chapter, which has selected one version (Hunter and Schmidt's) of this approach. It also includes a number of current references, which will prove helpful for readers wishing to read further in this domain.

Loevinger, J. (1957). Objective tests as instruments of psychological theory. *Psychological Reports, 3,* 635–694.

The idea that construct validity is the whole of validity is not as new as implied in this chapter. Indeed, a very articulate exposition on this topic can be found in Loevinger's monograph, which came out shortly after construct validity arrived on the scene. What has changed is the popularity and acceptability of this idea in the 1990s. Reading an early argument about the importance of construct validity is par-ticularly enlightening, knowing that these ideas are now part-and-parcel of the domain.

Messick, S. (1988). The once and future issues of validity: Assessing the meaning and consequences of measurement. In H. Wainer & H. I. Braun (Eds.), *Test validity.* Hillsdale, N.J.: Erlbaum.

This should be considered primary material, and thereby important reading, if you want more details regarding the issues of the consequential basis of test interpreta-tion and use as formulated in the chapter. This is a readable presentation that places the arguments for a unified view of validity into context and sheds light on a num-ber of implications of this argument.

Discussion Questions

1. List the advantages and disadvantages of using computers as electronic clerks in the testing enterprise. Discuss what you believe to be the greatest disadvantage.

2. By consulting with *Psychological Abstracts*, prepare an up-to-date list of constructs that have been computerized. Compare this list with the one presented in Table 19-1 and discuss the changes that you observe.

3. Discuss the uses of the computer in testing and assessment. Indicate the important differences that the computer forces on this distinction.

4. Discuss the advantages of using a computer screen to present items to respondents.

5. Outline a research study that you could conduct to determine if respondents felt that computerized testing was dehumanizing.

6. Discuss the problems you would expect to encounter if you attempted to test elderly patients using a computer. Indicate how you might solve these problems.

7. Draw a flowchart that reveals the programming stages you would have to go through to develop a computerized testing version of the Raven Progressive Matrices.

8. Outline as many advantages of computerized adaptive testing as you can.

9. Why do you think that, despite the facility of doing so with computers, the use of complex, nonlinear scoring systems for psychological tests has not become popular?

10. What are the disadvantages and limitations of computer-generated written interpretations of psychological test scores?

11. Provide some detailed suggestions about how computerized test administration could be of use to a visually disabled person.

12. Given the problems and expense of demonstrating comparability between paper-and-pencil and computerized versions of the same test, why do you think that the testing enterprise is still attempting to adapt the old tests to the computer?

13. You have been hired by a clinical psychology firm to present an argument in favor of introducing computerized testing. Outline the argument you would present. As well, indicate the kinds of problems you think the clinicians in the firm might raise.

14. You are the instructor in this course in testing. Would you consider conducting the examinations on a computer? Why, or why not?

15. Draw an ICC for an item that negatively discriminates the total score (that is, high scorers answered it wrong, and low scorers answered it correctly.) Evaluate the utility of this item.

16. Generate data and ICCs that demonstrate the assertion that *p*-value is a direct function of the area under the ICC.

17. Draw an ICC for a four-choice multiple-choice item that perfectly discriminates the total score on the test.

18. Discuss the similarities and differences between ICCs as discussed in the chapter and Alfred Binet's approach to item selection outlined in Chapter 6.

19. Evaluate the usefulness of the idea of invariance of item parameters, which is part of IRT.

20. Some have argued that the difference between the true-score and generalizability interpretations of reliability is just semantic because both lead to assessing reliability using the same procedures. Do you agree? Why, or why not?

21. The generalizability interpretation of reliability focuses on the extent to which it is possible to generalize to the universe from the small item set used in the test. In what sense is this different from content validity? Do you think this touches on an important problem?

22. Evaluate the strengths and weaknesses of validity generalization.

23. You are an administrator in a company. Your personnel officer introduces a selection program, arguing that, because the known predictive validity of IQ tests to predict job success, using meta-analysis, is .35, it is unnecessary to validate the specific test being proposed. How would you respond to your personnel officer? Would you accept the proposal? Why, or why not?

24. Discuss whether it is possible to have content validity without construct validity.

25. Was Messick right in reserving the word *validity* for construct validity? Why, or why not?

26. Discuss the advantages and disadvantages of describing validating a test as hypothesis testing.

27. Evaluate the consequential basis of test interpretation of (inappropriately) arguing that a vocational-interest test, such as the JVIS, indicates a person's ability to do well in a given profession identified by the test.

28. Describe in detail a (hypothetical) situation in which evidential bases for test use and interpretation are satisfactory, as is the consequential basis of test interpretation, but the consequential basis of test use is not.

29. Develop a credo for test users that takes into account the necessity to consider local conditions in evaluating the consequential basis of test use.

Looking Toward the Future

THE TENSIONS OF TESTING

In Chapter 2, we examined a snapshot of the contemporary testing enterprise. We encountered the ten-word definition of a test as "an objective and standardized measure of a sample of behavior." The source of this definition can now be seen as rooted in the historical traditions of psychology. The concern with *objectivity* is generated from the adoption of a natural science perspective to solving human problems. It seems to allow test users to throw off the veil of subjectivity and value-ladenness that infiltrates other approaches to understanding human action. To the extent that one of the fundamental pragmatic goals of testing was to make normative comparisons among persons, the concern with *standardization* is understandable. Simply, if tests are not standardized, comparisons among people are compromised. That tests culminate in a number or categorical judgment can be seen as part-and-parcel of the high priority accorded mathematical analyses of natural phenomena dating back to the early foundations of science itself. The term *sample of behavior* is clearly embedded in the behaviorist traditions of the discipline, reflecting the prevailing metatheory of positivism—particularly the manner in which it was demonstrated in Chapter 17. All of this indicates that our ten-word definition includes a fairly strong prescription regarding the best way to study the human being, revealing a set of values that has a long and illustrious history within the discipline of psychology and the testing enterprise.

The approach embedded in our deceptively simple, ten-word definition has been a success. Tests have been inserted into the very social fabric of our culture by virtue of the promise of positivistic solutions to pressing human problems. From this has emerged the tremendous variety in both tests themselves and the situations in which they are used. The impressive business portfolio revealed in the wide variety of stakeholders involved in testing is even further testimony to the success of the testing enterprise.

However, both from within the testing enterprise itself and among the various stakeholders involved, a number of important tensions remain. There are conflicts of values between stakeholder groups, which are perhaps inevitable but nevertheless exceedingly important to consider in the final chapter of our narrative of testing. There are also controversies and disagreements within the various stakeholder groups. It is possible to find rabid anti- *and* pro-testers within the test-taker group—some holding diametrically opposed views that defy resolution. A controversy also surrounds tests used to evaluate educational practice. On the one hand, there is escalating criticism of testing; on the other, there is an increasingly loud call for national testing programs to monitor educational systems. Within the academy, many are campaigning for a moratorium, or outright ban, on testing, and an equal number are arguing for more and more use of psychological tests. There appears to be a love/hate relationship in many sectors of the testing enterprise. Despite its apparent successes, controversy remains. Like our ten-word definition, the source of such controversies lies in the historical traditions of the enterprise. It is to these tensions that we now turn. Future developments in the testing enterprise will likely be shaped, in no small way, by these conflicts and controversies, so examining them provides us with a window on the next few decades of testing in our culture.

For convenience, these **tensions of testing** have been sorted into four categories:

1. The issue of biological versus social explanations of behavior, treated earlier as the nature/nurture controversy, is still an important source of disagreement in the testing field.

2. The age-old conflict between the individual and the institution is still being played out in the testing enterprise, particularly as economic pressures are placing considerable pressure on our institutional frameworks.

3. Within the testing enterprise, there is a significant conflict between "tests as science" and "tests as art," which is still being played out.

4. The very bedrock of testing, positivism, is being challenged from a number of perspectives. The outcomes of debates between the traditional positivists and a new generation of scholars will undoubtedly have a great impact on the future of the testing enterprise.

This final chapter of the text is dedicated to a discussion of these tensions as a means of framing consideration of the future of testing.

The four tensions noted above are not necessarily mutually exclusive. For example, some of the current dissatisfaction with positivism has its intellectual roots in the desire to give more power to the individual, thus bringing the tensions labeled as "individual versus institution" and "positivism versus alternatives" together. As well, there is no suggestion here that there are four, and only four, conflicts within the testing enterprise. Depending on how you wish to "cut the cake," selecting either one or an almost infinite number of tensions as involved is possible. Four just seems to be a good number.

In what follows, the tensions will be voiced in a confrontational language—for example, nature versus nurture. This has been done intentionally to signal that these are very deep-rooted concerns and that, in most instances, readers will have to make a decision about their own personal position on the tension in order to come to grips with the implications involved. When it comes to these important issues, remaining neutral or eclectic is almost impossible. This is not to suggest, however, that it might not emerge in the future that the two poles of a given tension could come together. Rather, the choice of a confrontational language reflects the current state of the art. In no small way, the future of the testing enterprise, and indeed of many of our current cultural practices, will be determined by the manner in which these tensions are played out.

TENSION 1: NATURE VERSUS NURTURE

This tension would have been easy to write about 10 years ago. Simply, the nurture side of the debate had, more or less, prevailed in the enterprise, with most testing practice and thinking in the field being framed within a family of environmental positions. Ethical and practical guidelines had been constructed to ensure that every possible environmental manifestation of human ability would have an opportunity to unfold. Indeed, the nurture side of the debate remains the most politically correct, even in today's intellectual climate.

However, increasing evidence indicates a swing back to the nature side of this perpetual tension. Recent moves to resurrect Sir Cyril Burt's reputation (for example, Fletcher, 1991), a new cycle of theories making reference to Spearman's *g* with all of its genetic implications, and several public outcries against proponents of biological positions (for example, Phillipe Rushton) deeply reminiscent of the Jensen incident (see Chapter 15) are testimony to a reemergence of the biological arm of this controversy.

The traditional approach within psychology to managing this controversy is to adopt an interactional position by arguing that behavior is the result of *both* nature and nurture. By this view, the nature/nurture controversy does not exist because human action is caused by both the environment and genetic materials working jointly together, and any attempt to promote one over the other is a foolish waste of time. The real problem, then, becomes determining the mechanisms by which these interactions take place and developing an understanding of the different situations in which one or the other is ascendant.

In a sense, though, the interactional argument is problematic: It takes the very split between nature and nurture as given. This simplistic division of sources of behavior into environmental and genetic may lie at the heart of the tension. This can be argued from a number of perspectives. Perhaps the simplest is to consider the **social utility** of the category system that assigns causal properties to two classes of variables: those associated with the biology of the organism and those related to its environmental experience. After over a century of research into the nature/nurture issue, it seems we have not come any closer to a resolution than we were when Francis Galton first coined the term (see Chapter 5). There has to come a time when a thinking person begins to ask if it is worth continuing a search if, after 100 years of trying, the problem has remained intractable. Perhaps we have been asking the wrong question all along, and, to the extent that answers do not appear to be forthcoming, we might do well to abandon this question and begin to ask others.[1] This certainly is food for thought.

For the time being, however, the realization that the nature/nurture problem has not been resolved tells us that we should be very wary of anyone who argues as if it has been. More important, it is critical to resist any attempts to introduce social policies that are framed from one of the other perspectives that use "scientific proof" as part of their rhetoric. It is possible to cite research studies that confirm a biological position, but it is equally possible to find other studies, which are just as well done, that support an environmental view. The issue remains moot at this point. Until such time as the scientific community can present an airtight case for the resolution of the tension (which is a long way away), querying any effort that uses this distinction as part of its argument remains exceedingly important. Failure to do so will inevitably lead to misrepresentation and carries great potential for the introduction of unjustifiable social practice.

TENSION 2: THE INDIVIDUAL VERSUS THE INSTITUTION

The psychological testing enterprise was created to serve the needs of social institutions. Galton's original position (see Chapter 5) was clearly in the service of society, with some negative implications for individuals (particularly those who were not blessed as being "eminent"). The first major "success" of testing, Robert Yerkes's enactment of the Army Alpha (see Chapter 7), was definitely shaded toward the interests of the military institution, with a number of significant negative implications for individuals. In discussing research during the time the testing enterprise was being created, Danziger (1990) indicates that "the primary consumers of the

---

[1]This strong statement is being framed in the context of using nature/nurture data and theorizing as part of the argument for the introduction of new and/or the justification of existing social policies. The simplistic nature/nurture distinction may well spawn important breakthroughs in scientists' labs at some point; but, until it is resolved, the argument here suggests that it may not be a useful distinction for the enactment of social policy.

results of such research were those whose controlling position made the results potentially useful to them, not those who participated in the research as subjects" (p. 104). This created a "growing preference for a type of research practice that was capable of yielding the kind of data that could be perceived as relevant to the interests of administrators" (Danziger, 1990, p. 105). The psychological test, with its built-in statistical character and its efficient means of categorizing individuals, was just what the bureaucrats wanted. Indeed, the success of the testing enterprise can be attributed to the effectiveness with which it furnishes a technology to representatives of the social institutions, be they schools to determine suitability for admission or promotion, businesses to find the best job candidate, hospitals to diagnose mental difficulties, or counseling centers to route persons to the "best" occupational path. The historical roots of the testing enterprise bias it toward the institutional side of the individual/institutional tension, exacting some significant negative consequences from individuals.

This aspect of the testing enterprise's history has a number of implications when we begin to consider the tensions between individuals and institutions that are part of today's context. To the extent that the testing enterprise is servicing the needs of the institution, an inevitable conflict will arise between it and individuals, and this indeed appears to be the case. Reflected in a long-standing tradition of antitest argument (for example, the Lippmann critique in Chapter 7, the antitest movement in Chapter 14, and the outcry against Jensen in Chapter 15), the conflict between persons and organizations can be seen as substantial.

A recent contribution to this tradition of antitest critique can be found in a book called *Testing Testing: Social Consequences of the Examined Life* by anthropologist Allan Hanson (1993). In an effort to bring the institutionally friendly aspect of testing into focus, Hanson offers an alternative definition of the test, defining it as a "representational technique applied by an agency to an individual with the intention of gathering information" (p. 42). The phrase "applied by an agency to an individual" signals the importance of the institutional/individual tension as part-and-parcel of the activity of testing. Interestingly, our ten-word definition is mute about this aspect of tests.

In discussing tests that culminate in a decision about socially important categorizations such as "this person is honest," what he calls **authenticity tests**, Hanson (1993) argues quite convincingly that "authenticity testing has been unmasked here as a technique for maintaining people under surveillance and insidiously transforming them into docile and unwitting subjects of an expanding disciplinary technology of power" (p. 310). In other words, he sees tests as important vehicles for the maintenance and enactment of the power of the institution over the individual. He further notes how the parties who are under this exercise of power, the test takers, readily acquiesce to the practice, documenting several cases where groups of individuals have actually requested authenticity testing in the *absence* of any individualized suspicion. Hanson interprets this as evidence for the effectiveness of tests as vehicles of power in that the actual "victims" of the practice have been duped into volunteering for it—indeed, in some cases, they actually bear the costs of testing.

This analysis of testing from an anti-institutional perspective is fine as far as it goes. However, it does overlook some aspects of the social institution of testing. In the data we have collected here in Calgary (some of which are presented in Chapter 2), there is very little negative student reaction against testing as they have experienced it in their lives. Most students view testing as a means of gaining entry to the institution giving the test. In other words, they are asking to become part of the institution by participating in what they view as institutional requirements. Our data do not paint the portrait of "docility and unwitting submission to power" described by Hanson. Rather, we see an active and intentional effort to take advantage of it. Indeed, students have been able to transform what may well be an oppressive practice into one of many possible vehicles that can be used to their advantage. Although students as test takers are only one of a number of possible stakeholder groups involved in the testing enterprise, this example indicates that the analysis of the individual/institutional tension requires a consideration of everyone's perspective if a full understanding is hoped for. This indicates that, though it may be possible to mount a critical appraisal of testing as a pro-institutional practice, we must also consider that it serves the needs of the other principal stakeholders in diverse, unanticipated, and sometimes useful ways.

None of this serves to eliminate the tension between individuals and institutions. This conflict is an inevitable part of the testing enterprise. To be sure, times will change and the power that either individuals or institutions have will change with them. Under current economic pressures, power will likely shift more into the hands of institutions as competition for jobs, placements in graduate and professional schools, hospital beds, and other resources increases. This predicts an increased institutional role for tests. The extent to which this is exacted at a cost to individual freedom and choice remains to be seen. Your new-found understanding of psychological testing and its historical foundations will hopefully put you in a position to react appropriately should such increases touch your life or those of your family members.

With the institutional orientation of a large proportion of the testing enterprise, occasions can emerge when individual test takers are clearly at risk in a testing situation. Whether it is you, a friend, or a member of your family, there is always the possibility that a specific testing application will create significant unfairness for the tested individual. What rights do you have when you are in a testing situation? How can you recognize situations in which unfairness is present? How can you protect yourself and your acquaintances from these? What avenues of protest are open to you? These are heady questions that demand careful consideration.

What follows is a kind of consumers' guide to testing. A series of points derived from earlier parts of the text are discussed in the format of a Bill of Rights for Test Takers. Each right is discussed below, and many of the points include references to the relevant ethical statutes (APA, 1992—see Chapter 12) and test standards (see Chapters 12 and 13 and Appendix D). All the appropriate elements articulated in this bill should be in place if the testing situation is being conducted properly. This Bill of Rights is not an APA document but a summary and discussion of selected aspects of APA policy, framed from the individual's perspective. Considerable controversy and much room for debate lie beneath the apparently tranquil set of "rights" articulated below.

| CLOSE UP | **Bill of Rights for Test Takers** |

1. *Respect and Dignity.* Test takers must be treated with dignity and respect.
2. *Fairness.* All tests and uses of test data related to individual test takers must be demonstrably nonbiased and processes associated with testing must be demonstrably fair to the test taker.
3. *Informed Consent.* Test takers must have the explicit opportunity to accede to testing with a clear knowledge of what will happen. They must also have the right to refuse participation.
4. *Explanation of Test Results.* Test takers must receive an appropriate explanation of the outcome of the testing event.
5. *Confidentiality.* Test takers must be guaranteed that their testing results will not be made available, intentionally or otherwise, to other parties, unless they give their explicit permission.
6. *Professional Competence.* Test takers have the right to expect optimal competence on the part of the test users with whom they come into contact.
7. *Least Stigmatizing Labels.* When reporting test results includes assignment of the test taker to categories, the category label with the least negative connotations, consistent with accurate reporting, must be used.
8. *Members of Linguistic Minority Communities.* Test takers from linguistic minority communities, whose proficiency in a majority language is weak, must be tested with instruments whose reliability, validity, or utility are not compromised by majority language performance.
9. *Disabled Persons.* Persons with disabilities must be tested with instruments that have been properly designed and validated on the disabled population to which the test taker belongs.

1. Respect and Dignity. This point follows not only from normative expectations of proper interpersonal and professional conduct but also from the General Principles of the APA Ethical Code, specifically Ethical Principle C (upholding of professional standards), D (respect for people's rights and dignity), E (concern for others' welfare), and F (social responsibility). Of particular concern is the extent to which the failure to accord proper respect and dignity to test takers could inhibit optimal levels of performance in the testing event.

2. Fairness. This right derives from the substantive concerns about test bias and potential unfairness documented in Chapter 14. It is also articulated in Test Standards 1.20 (predictive bias) and 3.10 (item bias). In this case, the onus of proof of nonbias or fairness rests with the test user who must be able explicitly to demonstrate that the tests, interpretations, and recommendations associated with the test data are nonbiased. The techniques presented in Chapter 14 would be expected to come into play in any such demonstration.

The assertion that processes associated with testing must be demonstrably fair relates to the expectation that testing will be carried out considering the best interests of the test taker. This follows directly from General Principle E of the Ethical Code, which is concerned with respect for the welfare of others (for details, see Chapter 12). In practice this should include, at the very least, opportunities for appeal and reevaluation if the test results are detrimental to the test taker. As well, it is expected that the actual processes of test administration and interpretation are sufficiently well documented so that the test taker can determine if the entire process is fair and just.

3. *Informed Consent.* A number of aspects of informed consent must be considered here. First, in a language that they understand, test takers must be made aware of (1) the reasons for testing, (2) the type of tests to be used, (3) the intended use of the test results and interpretations, (4) the range of potential consequences of the intended use, and (5) what testing information will be released and to whom. All of these follow directly from Test Standard 16.1.

Second, it is understood that test takers who give consent (1) have the capacity to consent, (2) have freely and without undue influence expressed consent, and (3) have formally (for example, in writing) given consent. These points follow from the normative notions of informed consent as articulated, for example, in Ethical Standard 4.02 and implied in General Ethical Principles D, E, and F.

Third, in the case of a person who is legally incapable of giving informed consent, the test user must (1) provide an appropriate explanation, (2) obtain the participant's assent, and (3) obtain appropriate permission from legally authorized persons (if permitted by law). These rights follow from normative practices in dealing with human research respondents (for example, Ethical Standard 6.11).

One deeply problematic point, from the test taker's perspective, is that the APA *Test Standards* indicate that informed consent *may* not be explicitly required (1) in situations where testing is mandated by law (for example, state- or provincewide testing programs), (2) as part of regular, ongoing school activities (for example, schoolwide testing programs), or (3) when consent is clearly implied (for example, application for employment or educational admission). These exceptions are noted in Test Standard 16.1 (APA, 1985, p. 85). These exceptions carry the potential of problems for the individual because they can violate the test taker's right to know why testing is taking place. In the comment regarding these exceptions, the APA *Test Standards* do state that "test takers should always be given relevant information about a test" (p. 85) but adds the troubling rider "when it is in their best interests to be informed." Exactly who determines "their best interests" (indeed, whose interests are being referred to) is unclear.

This problematic aspect of the APA *Test Standards* has led to the inclusion of a "right to refuse testing" condition in our test takers' Bill of Rights. This is a clear departure from the dictates of the APA. Following normative practice in other areas such as research with human subjects (for example, Ethical Standard 6.11), our bill insists that the pretesting documentation must inform test takers of the right to refuse participation. As well, the potential consequences of refusal to be tested must be made clear to test takers prior to giving or refusing consent. Although this does not remove the potential violation of individual rights (for example, refusal to be tested could result in not being considered an applicant for a job), it does at least bring the issue into focus. Ideally, in cases where refusal is costly to the individual, the possibility of appeal or challenge to the entire process should be available.

4. *Explanation of Test Results.* Test takers must receive explanations of (1) the actual test results, (2) the interpretation of the test results, (3) the recommendations for action, and (4) the extent to which test results determined these recommendations. These points are based on Test Standard 16.2. Such explanations must be in a language appropriate to the test taker and at a conceptual level that is understandable to the test taker. These follow directly from Test Standard 16.2 and

Careful explanation of test results is an exceedingly important part of the overall testing process.

Ethical Standard 2.09. As well, test takers (or their legal representatives) must be able to obtain copies of any and all information related to test scores, interpretations, and recommended actions associated with the testing event (Test Standard 16.4). Another component of this right is that test takers must have the opportunity to have scoring accuracy rechecked when tests are being used in a competitive situation such as selection (Test Standard 15.8).

5. *Confidentiality.* Test results identified by individual names must not be released to any person or institution unless the informed consent of the test taker (or legal representative) has been obtained. If this condition is met, it still remains that this information can only be made available to those with a legitimate, professional interest in specific cases. These points are derived from Test Standard 16.4.

Test results not identified by individual name may be distributed by the test user if prior informed consent to do so has been obtained. The reportage of details in such cases, however, must be sufficiently general that it is impossible to trace the test results back to the specific individual.

Test takers have the right to demand that test users make all possible efforts to maintain the security of test results. Test users must ensure that test data maintained in data files are adequately protected from improper disclosure. These points are based on a reading of Test Standards 2.10, 15.7, and 16.5.

6. *Professional Competence.* Test users must be able to demonstrate to test takers that their assessments, interpretations, and recommendations are based on tests and data that are (1) collected and interpreted under procedures consonant with the test manual and related technical information, (2) current and representative of the best possible test for the specific application, (3) appropriate to the particular situation, and (4) explicitly defensible with reference to the available research literature and, demonstrably nonbiased. These points follow from Ethical Standards 2.01, 2.02, and 2.07 as well as the implications of Ethical Principles A, E, and F.

Another important point, embedded in Ethical Standard 2.06, is that tests must be administered and interpreted by persons with adequate qualifications. Details regarding levels of training necessary for various tests were discussed in Chapter 12. In the event that a psychologist has assigned testing or test interpretation to supervisees, the supervising psychologist assumes *all* responsibility for ensuring that adequate levels of training and competence are possessed by the testers. In other words, if you encounter an instance of unqualified persons administering or interpreting tests under the supervision of someone else, the guilty party is probably the supervisor, not the person being supervised.

7. Least Stigmatizing Labels. This right relates to the potential damage that can be wrought by the assignment of a negative label to the test taker. The intent here is to ensure that psychologists exercise considerable caution in this aspect of testing practice. For example, the use of older terms such as *idiot, imbecile,* or *feeble-minded* to describe individuals who score poorly on IQ tests is unacceptable under this right. Within the constraints of accurate reporting, terms with fewer negative connotations should be employed (Test Standard 16.6).

8. Members of Linguistic Minority Communities. The APA *Test Standards* have an entire section dedicated to "Testing Linguistic Minorities" (APA, 1985, Section 13). This section indicates that test users must be able to demonstrate that a test employed on a linguistic minority is not affected by language (Test Standards 13.1 through 13.4 and 13.6). In competitive situations (for example, selection, licensure), linguistic minority test takers must be tested with instruments that are appropriate to the level of language demanded by the criterion being addressed (Test Standard 13.5). In the event that tests are used to determine linguistic proficiency, such tests must tap a wide range of linguistic skills (Test Standard 13.7).

9. Disabled Persons. Testing disabled persons is a complex business at best. There is a temptation to adapt extant standardized tests to this situation. This test taker's right states that, before the results of such testing are acceptable, it must be explicitly demonstrated that the adapted instrument has reliability, validity, and utility *for the specific disabled population on which it is being used.* Such demonstrations may take the form of judgments by informed experts regarding the suitability of the test (and possible modifications to it), but empirical demonstration of suitability is preferred. These points are made in Test Standards 14.1 through 14.8.

What if you discover a violation of test taker rights? If you encounter a situation in which any of these rights have been violated, you are in a position to "cry foul." Exactly how you choose to proceed should be dictated by your perception of the extent of the negative consequences created by the violation. In cases where the negative consequences are minimal, consulting with the test user (or the user's supervisor) might prove sufficient to rectify the situation. If you are in the position of consulting with a test user regarding a violation of one of your rights, it is recommended that you frame your concerns with explicit reference to the APA ethical and test standards. This Close Up directs you to the most appropriate aspects of the codes to examine.

In cases where the negative consequences are significant, there are a number of options available to you. You can approach the employing institution of the violator, asking for redress. You can contact your local state or provincial psychological association and lodge a formal complaint about an ethical violation. You can use the media to advantage (for example, letters to the editor, phone-in shows). You can even use the court system in some instances. If you go forward with an official complaint, it is highly recommended that you carefully document your claim and make explicit reference to the APA Ethical Code and *Test Standards* as much as possible. Because these are clear statements of expected behavior within the profession, the professional community cannot ignore the documentation of deviations from them.

I hope that this Close Up has provided you with sufficient information to mount a protest should you encounter a violation of test taker rights and that the Bill of Rights for Test Takers will help combat the institutional orientation of much of the testing enterprise.

TENSION 3: SCIENCE VERSUS ART

From the beginning of this text, it has been argued that the vast majority of human societies needs a means of categorizing its members in the interests of assigning them to appropriate roles. The manhood rites of North American indigenous peoples were tests of courage and spiritual preparedness for entry into specific roles. The exceedingly complex set of examinations in early Chinese dynasties to choose the most appropriate leaders is another example, and so on through the history of human civilization. Now the question emerges as to whether this is a fair characterization of the contemporary psychological testing enterprise.

Our examination of the history of the testing enterprise clearly indicates that sociopolitical factors play a highly significant part in mental testing. The narrative approach taken herein indicates that psychological testing has emerged because our society has delegated certain decisions to the psychological community or perhaps, more correctly, because psychologists have actively campaigned to serve this decision-making role. The advocacy of the pioneers of the testing movement noted earlier—Binet, Galton, J. M. Cattell, Terman, Yerkes—is testimony to this point.

In our culture, with its valuing of technology and science, it is not surprising to find that aspects of these kinds of decisions have been delegated to the "scientific community" to be executed using technological devices—namely, psychological tests. This kind of socially sanctioned decision making is the fundamental role of testing.

An important reminder here is that, in contemporary application, tests do not make up the totality of social decision making. They serve in general as adjuncts to the overall process of making social decisions. This could be as part of an intellectual evaluation for the legal system, as part of a diagnostic intake procedure in a psychiatry ward, as part of the design of a curriculum for a learning disadvantaged pupil, or as part of a personnel evaluation for hiring purposes. In virtually all social applications, tests are only one component of the social decision-making system. This harkens back to the distinction between testing and assessment introduced in Chapter 2. Here we are talking about assessment because we are considering the use of the test plus other sources of information to make decisions about individuals in specific contexts.

Yet there is a sense that tests, because of their objectivity and scientific rationalization, are somehow better or more privileged indicators than the more subjective and humanistic sources of information that are part of social decision-making processes. It is from this perspective that we can examine what appears to be a fundamental value conflict between the testing enterprise and the social uses to which its devices are put. Here we find the values of a scientific approach, such as objectivity and standardization, confronting the more social, human values attending service to society. For want of a more precise term and to clearly delineate the two poles of this tension, the latter set of values has been referred to as *art*. This use of the term implies the nonscientific values associated with the human aspects of social decision making.

The conflict between art and science emerges in full relief if we consider the manner in which the testing enterprise is able to react to changes in the fabric of the society sponsoring its activities.

Societies change over time. In North America, one such change was the shift from a relatively passive and accepting view of government policies such as was held in the 1950s to a more radical, critical, and activist position in the 1960s. This and many other changes have occurred since the ascendance of the testing enterprise. It would seem important that the testing enterprise change along with these social changes if it is to serve its social goals effectively.

However, some aspects of contemporary practice in the testing enterprise inhibit change. This becomes clear if we look at some aspects of the philosophy of science, or what has more recently become known as the study of **metatheory**. Thomas Kuhn (1970) examined science from a social perspective and generated some interesting insights, which we can usefully apply to testing and assessment. He defined the **disciplinary matrix** as a complex of generalizations, beliefs, values, and exemplars that direct the normal day-to-day activities of a given scientific group.[2] In our case, we will consider the researchers and test developers as such a collective. The disciplinary matrix for testers contains a wide range of elements that informs the basic view of the world held by members and that in turn drives their activities. The ideas of validity, reliability, and utility; the technologies of test construction; the prevailing ethical standards—all are part of this matrix for the testing community.

Kuhn notes that disciplinary matrices are fundamentally conservative in nature, resisting change for as long as possible. It takes considerable force to change the prevailing matrix, a process Kuhn calls a **scientific revolution**. However, between revolutions things remain pretty much business-as-usual, with the disciplinary matrix guiding and directing activities. The inherent resistance to newness of disciplinary matrices can, in some situations, work against the ability of an enterprise like testing to react to significant social change.

It is here we begin to uncover some interesting observations about testing because aspects of earlier practice were guided by ideas that are for the most part

---

[2]In the first edition of his book, Kuhn (1962) used the term *paradigm* instead of *disciplinary matrix*, and this initial term may be the one with which you are familiar because it became popular in certain fields. However, Kuhn argues persuasively in his second edition that *disciplinary matrix* is a less confusing and more accurate concept—hence, what follows is based on this revision.

no longer appropriate to our current social context. For example, Gordon and Terrell (1981) suggest that

> The psychometric movement developed in a period of concern for quicker and more objective methods for identifying persons most likely to succeed in designated situations or treatments. A part of the original charge to Binet was to develop a procedure by which persons most likely to benefit from schooling—a scarce resource at the time—could be identified. The first large-scale introduction of testing in the United States came during World War I, when it was deemed necessary to screen out incompetents from pools of potential soldiers. [pp. 1167–1168]

It can also be argued that the use of tests in industry, to identify "individuals meriting special attention" also evolved in a time when the resource of concern (special attention) was scarce (Gordon & Terrell, 1981, p. 1168). Such uses of psychological tests were clearly appropriate in a time when these resources were scarce—but what about today? "It may be also argued that such an emphasis [on allocation of resources like education and special attention] is inappropriate to a period such as the latter half of the 20th century, when these resources—in the United States at least—are limited only by the will to allot them" (Gordon & Terrell, 1981, p. 1168). Education is now universally available in North America, so there is very little need to have a set of instruments that determine who should receive this resource. This change in resource availability is a direct function of changes in the social, political, and economic status of America. Since the 1960s, "a commitment to democratic access to human developmental resources and opportunities has been repeatedly voiced; indeed, recent history has been marked by the assertion of a constitutional right to equal opportunity in education and employment" (Gordon & Terrell, 1981, p. 1169).

Clearly, then, a psychological test that has been designed to sort, predict, and select with a view to identifying the "chosen few" who will succeed is no longer of use to the society where concerns have changed to issues of equal opportunity. Almost all of the contemporary debate surrounding testing can be understood from this perspective. The old tests are not up to making the kinds of decisions demanded of today's society, and almost all critical attacks on them are generated from this concern (see Gordon & Terrell, 1981, for an extended discussion). Perhaps even more important, the foundational elements of the disciplinary matrix of the testing enterprise (validity, reliability, and so on), which themselves grew out of these earlier times, may not be appropriate to the contemporary social context. Indeed, they may hamper the testing enterprise's capacity to react to social change.

The basic argument here is that changes in social context ought to force important changes in the testing enterprise. Since the 1960s, our culture has shown an increasing awareness of the many manifestations of human diversity. Enhanced concern with civil rights, equal opportunity, and interracial tolerance are all indicators of this important change in our social context. The emergence of **multiculturalism** in Canada is a particularly fine example of this change. In response to the 1960s decision to make both French and English official languages of Canada, the government dedicated considerable resources to the celebration of the cultures of groups falling outside these two main languages. As such, these "ethnic" communities gained considerable visibility and importance in Canadian society. To the

extent that the testing enterprise is an effort to use a standardized and homogeneous yardstick to measure all persons in the same way, it is clearly out of sync
with this changing cultural milieu. If we value diversity, then should we not adopt
a measurement strategy that incorporates as many dimensions as possible, not one
that tries to fit everyone onto a single continuum? Some of the tensions with testing
are due, in part, to this social change. Some of the major psychological tests we
presently have in hand are inappropriate to making the new kinds of decisions
society wants us to make.

A considerable amount of the current concern with psychological testing
derives from the historical perception that class and ethnic chauvinism contaminated the earlier approaches to testing. Test data were often cited to justify the
exploitation of lower-status groups such as immigrants after World War I and
Blacks since the emergence of complex American society: "Standardized test scores
are thus used to blame the victims of exclusion and to exonerate the complex
processes that maintain the status quo" (Gordon & Terrell, 1981, p. 1168).
Perhaps even more problematic in the contemporary view is the opportunity that
standardized tests provide to maintain the status quo and help keep low-status
groups in their "assigned" positions. More recently, the victims of this abuse of
tests have become increasingly vocal, public opposition to this aspect of testing is
becoming greater, and the disciplinary matrix of the enterprise is under considerable attack.

Testing as Science

If the social functions of testing are so important and the disciplinary matrix is
resistant to pressure for change from without, there appears to be considerable
potential for conflict between the social and scientific aspects of testing. To the
extent that testing practice is driven by social forces (as has been demonstrated in a
number of places in this text), the scientific aspects of the testing enterprise would
appear to be of secondary importance. Viewing psychological testing in context, as
we have been doing, makes it very clear that we are dealing with social decision
making—*not science*—in the development and sustaining of the testing enterprise.
Perhaps the most important and emancipating conclusion that can be drawn from
the material in this text is that psychological testing is not scientific but is part-and-
parcel of the sociopolitical world in which we live. The rhetoric of science is used
to promote testing, but at root the enterprise is social *and* political. The scientific
considerations are secondary.

In a review of the history of social concerns about testing, Haney (1981)
argues that the scientific record is irrelevant to an understanding of the testing
field. He suggests that the prominence accorded testing over the past 70 years is a
reflection of its success as a social enterprise, not its scientific accomplishment. He
argues that testing grew out of a social context that faced problems dealing with
large numbers of individuals. A sevenfold increase in U.S. school enrollments
between 1880 and 1920 (Leary, 1987) and the entry of over 10 million immigrants
to the United States between 1905 and 1915 (Burgess, 1960) is testimony to this
need to deal efficiently with large numbers of people. This growth combined with
the "special place of technology in American society" (Haney, 1981, p. 1029) to

create an accepting climate for testing. According to Haney, an additional factor was a special kind of "number consciousness," which emerged in the United States (see Chapter 4). All of this set the stage for the enthusiastic acceptance of structured assessment with virtually no questions asked.

The upshot of Haney's argument is that the social functions of standardized tests are independent of scientific status. That is, in the final analysis, it will be the social success of the testing enterprise, not its scientific status, that will dictate the acceptance of the testing movement. In a very real sense, social function preempts science in this case.

A hint that this may be the case comes when we examine the characteristics of the tests that have had particular longevity. One of the most remarkable aspects of tests such as the Stanford–Binet, MMPI, and Rorschach is that they are surrounded by complicated interpretive schemata. The obtained score or profile analysis does not flow automatically from the test—there is a need to insert a considerable amount of wisdom and experience between the testing procedure and the final report. In fact, Haney suggests that "standardized tests, for at least some purposes, are valued not as valid and reliable measurement instruments per se, but because they yield information that can be interpreted in numerous different ways" (Haney, 1981, p. 1030). So perhaps the staying power of the old tests is more related to their being amenable to multiple interpretations than it is to their reliability, validity, and other scientific characteristics. In other words, to serve various social functions the best tests are those that permit multiple interpretations. This allows the test to adapt to new social conditions and provides the test interpreter with some power because the interpretation does not flow mechanically from the measurement process.

A particularly illuminating example of how much testers need interpretations that do not flow automatically from the test can be found in the controversy over clinical versus statistical prediction (see Chapter 9). In this debate, there was considerable resistance to the notion that MMPI diagnoses could be effectively generated by reference to a statistical **cookbook**. Many members of the field resisted the possibility of formulaic MMPI interpretations, despite a number of strong empirical and rational arguments that indicated how it strengthened the clinician's position (for a review, see Sawyer, 1966). Thus, flexibility of interpretation seems to be an important aspect of the utility of psychological tests to solve important social problems.

It is appropriate, at this point, to reflect on our earlier analysis of manhood rites in the Ojibway tribe (see Chapter 3). Recall that Mishi underwent the Vision Quest as part of a two-way social negotiation process wherein he was able to enter into a dialog with the tribal elders about his eventual status within the community. An important component of this analysis was the indication that there had to be room to negotiate, even in the case of this relatively simple social system. A social decision-making procedure that does not provide this room for flexibility and discourse is apt to be relatively unsuccessful because it will be too inflexible and will not act to serve the needs of the social system. In the Ojibway case, a significant contribution was to provide the elders with the control they need to govern the social system. In no small way, the mental-testing movement has been a century-long quest for a workable system to serve these needs within the 20th-century North American community.

It is also worth recalling the story that began Chapter 2. The cold, harsh decision implied by the Differential Aptitude Test Battery scores for Jack's university aspirations was deeply hurtful to this young man's dreams. In this case, one of the major sources of pain and anguish was the fact that the hard, cold test scores negated an opportunity for the kind of social negotiation that is so important. This lack of flexibility and room for negotiation is one of the root problems with the current testing enterprise. In its efforts to be a natural science, it has failed to consider the kinds of social needs that are being serviced by the measurement instruments. The necessary humanity and flexibility can be missing.

Perhaps, then, attempts to rationalize testing from a scientific perspective are doomed to failure because the very social needs being served demand exactly the opposite criteria. Science demands empirically verified, consensual analyses, whereas society demands multiple-interpretable ones in many cases.

Clearly, this is a somewhat problematic interpretation for anyone who argues that the testing enterprise is justifiable to the extent that it rests on firm scientific footing. If the major strength of tests is that they permit multiple interpretations and they are being defended with a metatheory that values precision and singularity of interpretation, problems will certainly arise. And this appears to be the case. Concepts such as validity demand consensual, empirical observations, whereas the social role of testing demands multiple, divergent interpretations of the same phenomena. There is an inherent conflict—one that ought to be recognized.

Thus, a fundamental problem appears to be rising out of our analysis of scientific approaches and the social goals of the testing enterprise. The two concerns appear, in some cases, to be incompatible. Scientific criteria demand that psychological tests have a set of characteristics that render them sterile for making social decisions. Social uses demand flexible interpretive schemata that provide the decision maker with latitude to take various nuances of the individual case into account. There also must be room for social negotiation. Scientific applications, on the other hand, demand a singularity of interpretation that renders them weak for social purposes. When the search is for "the" correct answer, there is no room for the kind of social negotiation that has characterized human social decision making since the beginnings of social organization in our species. The two approaches do not seem to work well together and are indeed strange bedfellows.

Perhaps this analysis will help explain why the MMPI, an instrument that has virtually no construct validity, is still the instrument of choice in clinical diagnosis. Perhaps this will help explain why the Rorschach, which has virtually no predictive validity, continues to survive in clinical application and indeed is enjoying a revival. Perhaps this will help explain why a Wechsler test is still the first test that some clinicians grab from the shelf when asked for a measure of intelligence. In applied practice, the goal is to make social decisions, and the scientific integrity of the tools that go into making these decisions is secondary. The grand old tests still continue to be the instruments of choice. It is not because applied test users are somehow tradition-bound and unwilling to change that they use these old tests, but it is because these tests provide them with the kind of freedom they need to do their jobs properly.

Perhaps it should come as no surprise, then, to realize that we have encountered a major tension in testing. This is the value confrontation between science and art as reflected in a conflict between testing defined as a scientific activity and social decision making as it occurs within our culture. Like the two previous tensions, no attempt toward resolution has been attempted here. The goal of this presentation is to make you aware of the conflict that appears to exist between those who wish a scientific/positivistic solution to human problems and those who are uncomfortable with this type of solution. Many of the contemporary debates within the testing enterprise can be deciphered as dialogs between the two sets of values articulated in this section. The shape that the testing enterprise will take over the next several decades will be determined in no trivial manner by the way in which the value differences between science and art are dealt with.

Of course, tests are useful in research settings where the goal is the development of theory and technology conducted in a laboratory environment sheltered from these social factors. In such situations, the limitations of a scientific orientation are not as relevant. Yet it remains that efforts to apply lab-derived knowledge to real-world problems will inevitably encounter the same problems being discussed here.

TENSION 4: POSITIVISM VERSUS ALTERNATIVES

As noted in Chapter 19, contemporary forms of logical positivism continue to undergird the psychological testing enterprise. The psychological test was conceived, nourished, and brought to fruition under the auspices of this fundamental metatheory. The emergence of construct validity as the preeminent evaluative criterion in the testing field is clear testimony to this observation.

In what follows, the word *metatheory* will be used to refer to the generalized philosophy of science or theory of knowledge that underlies a specific field. In the case of testing, the prevailing metatheory is logical empiricism, which is the liberalized view of logical positivism. This includes partially defined theoretical terms, notions such as the nomological network, and the other range of ideas discussed in Chapter 13. As indicated in Chapter 19, construct validity is the single-most clear exemplar of this metatheory.[3]

The conflict labeled positivism versus alternatives reflects the relatively recent emergence of dissatisfaction with the positivist metatheory. It is here that we find a number of interesting intellectual and practical debates, which are of no small concern for gaining a sense of future directions in the field. Our discussion of this tension will begin with an outline of some critical appraisals of logical empiricism and hence construct validity. Following this, some of the rejoinders from the positivist community will be sketched out. Finally, several emerging alternatives will be discussed.

---

[3]The suggestion here that positivism is the underlying metatheory of testing does not automatically mean that everyone in the field goes around spouting the dictates of positivism or that everyone in the field is even aware of acting as though they are positivists. Rather, the positivist assertion is based on the fact that the major criterion of the goodness of a test, construct validity, is clearly and undeniably a positivist position. Even if individuals are not positivists, they are forced to behave as though they are when it comes to establishing the goodness of a test.

Problems with Positivism

A number of influential scholars have indicated some very significant flaws in the dogma of logical empiricism. Included here are some difficulties encountered with the theoretical/observation distinction that lies at the heart of the positivist program, some considerations of the impossibility of ever proving a theory to be true, and a discussion of whether it is ever possible to put a theory to a direct test. All these critiques are central to the prevailing metatheory of the testing enterprise and demand serious consideration.

The theoretical/observational distinction. Perhaps the most telling criticism of the received view of logical positivism in philosophical circles involves the distinction between theoretical and observational terms, which is a foundational assumption of the position (see Chapter 9). On close inspection, virtually any attempt to draw this distinction falls apart, prompting Suppe (1974) to suggest that the **theoretical/observational distinction** is "not philosophically significant." The decision about what to observe, and the interpretation of the perceptual event, is clearly infused with theoretical nuance, hereby calling into question the assumption that there are two distinct types of terms (observational and theoretical) in science.

According to the revised view of logical positivism, the fundamental distinction between theoretical and observational terms is that the latter refer to directly observable entities, whereas the former do not. The problem for the distinction emerges when we consider, with some precision, what is meant by *observable*. A number of scholars have demonstrated that the act of observation involves a considerable amount of selection. Observing involves deciding which of a large number of features one will attend to in the observational field. This selection process is, of course, directed in no trivial manner by the theoretical focus of the observer, suggesting that there is a considerable amount of theoretical nuance in actual observation. Using an example from physics, Suppe (1974) indicates that "I can describe movement through a bubble chamber either as a trace (observation term) or as an alpha-particle emission (theoretical term)" (p. 81), thus indicating the manner in which observation is infused with theoretical information. Polyani (1978) points out that there is no strict psychological boundary between theory and fact. And Lakatos (1978) argues that "there can be no sensations unimpregnated by expectations, and therefore there is no natural demarcation between observational and theoretical propositions" (p. 15). These considerations indicate that the notion of observable involved in drawing the observational/theoretical distinction is problematic. This argument was instrumental in philosophy's declaration of the demise of logical positivism as (1) a useful philosophical position and/or (2) a viable description of what scientists do and/or (3) a prescription about how best to go about doing "good" science (for detailed argumentation, see Suppe, 1974).

Interestingly, construct validity anticipated the observational/theoretical problem in its insistence that theory be integrated into measurement. Viewing the primary observational processes of the study of individual differences (that is, mental tests) as infused with theory rendered visible the inherent problem of trying to draw arbitrary distinctions between theory and observation—a bold stroke, indeed. Apparently, Cronbach and Meehl anticipated what was going to become a major problem with the positivist dogma. Perhaps psychology can take some pride in thinking that it was at the forefront of evolving conceptions of doing science. Such an observation placed the idea of construct validity into a positive light as reflecting state-of-the-art thinking in science in the mid-1950s.

Yet a rather major problem remained—a problem that detracts from the boldness of stroke one might choose to attribute to construct validity. Although Cronbach and Meehl (1955) may have anticipated the eventual integration of theory and observation, they used this very distinction in their development of construct validity. This is clearly evident in their notion of the *nomological network*. The laws in a nomological network may relate (1) observable properties or quantities to each other, (2) theoretical constructs to observables, or (3) different theoretical constructs to one another. The fundamental prescription of construct validity was the following: "A necessary condition for a construct to be scientifically admissible is that it occur in a nomological net, (and) at least some of those laws involve observables" (Cronbach & Meehl, 1955, p. 290). Because a nomological network *assumes* the existence of separate theoretical and observational terms, the very notion of construct validity does so as well. To the extent that this distinction has proven problematic, so too has construct validity.

There is an important point here indicating that, rather than being a forward-looking view of science, the notion of construct validity, to some degree, supported the prevailing view of positivism. The essential problem is that the nomological network hangs on the received-view notion of a workable distinction between theoretical and observational terms. Because this distinction is problematic, so too is the notion of construct validity. In a sense, the critical point that contributed to the eventual demise of logical positivism was clearly embedded in construct validity— yet construct validity embraced the foundational system that the idea eventually destroyed. Tacit acceptance of the theoretical/observational distinction implied in construct validity poses a very real logical problem—one that has yet to be resolved.

Karl Popper's argument. A second family of concerns of direct relevance to construct validity involved consideration of the possibility of ever proving a theory to be true, or valid. To the extent that construct validity demands a valid theory to underlie measurements, this is an important issue for the testing enterprise.

Most scientists would agree that one of their primary functions is to make carefully controlled, meticulous, systematic observations. Having done this for a while, the scientist then starts to formulate general hypotheses that appear to describe the observations. The next step involves trying to confirm these hypotheses by examining them under varying conditions. Once done, a new scientific law has been established, and the process begins anew.

The procedure of basing general statements on accumulated observations of specific instances is called **induction**, which is considered to be the hallmark of science. The presence of systematic induction is often used to distinguish science from nonscience.[4] But there are problems here. No matter how many single observations one uses to confirm a hypothesis, there is always the possibility that one single

---

[4]The inductive processes described herein cannot be found in, for example, religious dogma.

observation will come along and destroy the inductive truth thought to reside in the formulation. This means that there is no way of demonstrating the validity of inductive procedures. This is often referred to as **Hume's problem,** and attempts to solve it have proven elusive. For a scientist, Hume's is a real problem because it suggests that the whole of the scientific endeavor rests on a procedure (that is, induction) whose validity is impossible to demonstrate.[5]

Philosopher Karl Popper offered us some insight into this foundational problem in science. He pointed out the logical asymmetry between **verification** and **falsification.** Although Hume's problem states that we can never properly verify a scientific theory, we can with considerable precision prove one to be wrong. For example, if we observe millions of white swans, the statement "all swans are white" is still not established as truth because one single sighting of a black swan allows us to reject this assertion. Falsity of a theoretical proposition, then, can be firmly established, whereas its truth value cannot. **Popper's argument** is that empirical generalizations are not verifiable but they are falsifiable. This suggests that scientific laws are testable, despite being unprovable.

The implications this has for the basic notion of construct validity are important. If we set out to validate a theory in order to demonstrate the construct validity of our measure, we would be duped by Hume's problem. No matter how many confirming instances of our theory we found, we would never be able to validate the theory; hence, we would never be able to validate the measure because theories are never true. From a Popperian perspective, the notion of construct validity is logically untenable because it tacitly requires the test developer to think in terms of a validated theory—which, of course, is an impossibility.

You might like to argue that if we validated our theory time and time again, then at least the probability of our theory being true is increased; Popper, however, has shown this not to be true using basic arguments from probability theory.

Popper argues that *doubt* is the most important commodity in science (and the general conduct of human affairs). It is only through the active search for falsifying instances that we can begin to progress toward a deeper level of understanding. A verification-oriented view of science seduces us away from the realization that theories are sophisticated statements of ignorance representing highly provisional statements awaiting falsification by someone finding but one false instance. Of course, the legislation of a position that is clearly verification-oriented, such as was imposed by the APA in 1954 (see Chapter 12) and recapitulated in revisions to the *Test Standards* several times since (see Appendix D), is a clear indication that construct validity is not the seemingly neutral, value-free position that it was thought to be. Rather, it represents a very biased way of going about the business of doing science and validating psychological tests.

Although theses deriving from Popper's arguments have not achieved consensus within the philosophical or scientific communities, they do represent important positions. The implicit verificationist stance of construct validity de-emphasizes positions embracing a falsificationist perspective. An important assumption underlying construct validity, then, is a metatheoretic and philosophical bias toward con-

---

[5]Indeed, belief in induction can be seen as fundamentally a leap of faith made by all scientists—perhaps not that far removed, in a philosophical sense, from the leaps made in other dogmas.

firmation. It is unfortunate that such biases have become calcified in the dictates of the APA.

There is some confusion about whether the prevailing theory of measurement is antifalsificationist. Campbell and Fiske's notions of convergent and discriminant validity (see Chapter 13) are interesting cases in point. Discriminant validity is necessary to justify the introduction of a novel construct and involves the documentation of low correlations between measures of different constructs. Messick (1980) argues that "discriminant evidence is particularly critical for discounting plausible counter-hypotheses to the construct interpretation" (p. 1016). He then cites Popper, seeming to imply that discriminant validity is compatible with a falsificationist view. This is not the case. Popper's position does not relate to the determination of which of two alternate hypotheses is correct—discriminant validity does. Popper's concern is with putting a single theoretical statement to strong empirical test with the goal of falsification. Though the dictates of discriminant validity are important and worthwhile, particularly in the case of multitrait inventories, this concept does nothing to dismiss the conformationist bias embedded in construct validity. The methodology is still founded on the assumption that it is possible to prove that the theory underlying the test is true or correct—that is, valid. For the present purposes, Popper has warned us that this strategy may not be in the best interests of a scientific procedure.

Paul Meehl's critique. A third critical appraisal of relevance to construct validity emerged in the context of hypothesis testing and general methodology within the discipline. Paul Meehl (1978) initiated a stinging critique of contemporary psychology by stating "I consider it unnecessary to persuade you that most so-called 'theories' in soft areas of psychology (clinical, counseling, social, personality, community, and school psychology) are scientifically unimpressive and technologically worthless" (p. 806). He notes the "disturbing absence of that cumulative character that is so impressive" (p. 807) in the natural sciences and points the finger of blame squarely at the statistical significance test:

> I believe that the almost universal reliance on merely refuting the **null hypothesis** [emphasis added] as the standard method of corroborating substantive theories in the soft areas is a terrible mistake, is basically unsound, poor scientific strategy, and one of the worst things that ever happened in the history of psychology. [1978, p. 817]

This invective is supported, in part, by recourse to Popper's argument. Meehl suggests that a theory is corroborated to the extent it has been subjected to **risky tests**—the more risky the test, the better corroborated the theory. Meehl also introduces the Quine–Duhem thesis in his critical appraisal of psychological theory. This thesis notes that it is necessary to enact a number of **auxiliary hypotheses** in order to subject a theory to a test. Meehl (1978) provides an example dealing with the effects of social fear on visual perception:

> He [the experimenter] attempts to mobilize anxiety in a sample of adolescent males, chosen by their scores on the Social Introversion [Si] scale of the Minnesota Multiphasic Personality Inventory [MMPI], by employing a research assistant who is a raving beauty, instructing her to wear Chanel No. 5, and adopt a mixed

seductive and castrative manner toward the subjects. An interpretation of a negative empirical result leaves us wondering whether the main substantive theory of
interest concerning social fear and visual perception has been falsified, or whether
only the auxiliary hypotheses that the Si scale is valid for social introversion and
that attractive but hostile female experimenters elicit social fear in introverted
young males have been falsified. Or perhaps even the particular conditions were
not met; that is, she did not consistently act the way she was instructed to or the
MMPI protocols were misscored. [p. 819]

This indicates that any experiment is a test of the joint set of theoretical and
auxiliary hypotheses, not just the theory itself. Demonstrating the null hypothesis
in an experiment does not falsify the theory because it may be the auxiliaries (or
interactions between them and/or the substantive theory) causing the results. The
standard psychology experiment does not subject the substantive theory to true falsification "but only to a rather feeble danger" (Meehl, 1978, p. 821).

This argument has tremendous implications for the traditional notion of construct validity, particularly when viewed as hypothesis testing (see Chapter 19). To
the extent that the construct validity of an instrument hangs on the theory underlying the test, Meehl's demonstration calls into question the possibility of ever having
any construct validity at all! If theories are not subjected to test by the standard
experiment, then how can we possibly rationalize a criterion of validity that
demands a valid theory?

This can be demonstrated by considering a typical construct validity study.
Crowne and Marlowe (1964) introduced a scale that measures need for social
approval, along with a series of construct validity studies using contrasted groups.
One study subjected high and low scorers on the scale to an intentionally dull task,
and their reactions to the chore were subsequently assessed. For example, they were
asked if they had found the dull task enjoyable. The theoretical view suggested that
persons high on the need for social approval (that is, high scorers on the scale) would
say they found the task enjoyable because their orientation was to gain approval
from the experimenters. On the other hand, low scorers would be more candid and
provide a more accurate evaluation of the dull task. In this particular study, the
hypothesis was confirmed and interpreted as evidence in favor of the theory. This
type of experiment was cited as evidence for the construct validity of the scale.

But what if the hypothesis had not been confirmed? Is there anything we can
say about either the theory or the measure in the event of negative results? The
answer is a clear no. Failure to confirm the prediction could be due to any combination of problems with (1) the theory, (2) the measure, (3) the experimental
manipulation of the dull task failing to tap the processes assumed by the theory, (4)
the assessment of reaction to the task being ineffective, and (5) various subject-
selection problems, as well as a large list of other possible reasons. Negative results
are indeterminant in this system because pinpointing the locus of the problem is
not possible. This creates the position where negative results can effectively be
ignored because they do not provide definitive evidence to refute the theory. In no
sense has the theory of need for social approval been subjected to a test—let alone
a risky one—by this procedure.

The only useful information is in the case of confirmatory results. As well,
some authors such as Salmon (1975) have argued that even this is not true because

errors could counteract each other. For example, it is possible that one of the auxiliaries was so strong that it "caused" all the effects and that the positive results are mute about the status of the theory. This argument clearly questions the wisdom of the test-evaluation criterion of construct validity.

In the following Close Up is a discussion of the aspects of auxiliary hypotheses as they relate to construct validity. Based on a discussion in Salmon (1975), it brings into relief some of the very difficult issues that are touched on in Meehl's critique and the Quine–Duhem thesis.

CLOSE UP | **Auxiliary Hypotheses in Psychological Research**

Salmon (1975) argues that empirical results failing to confirm a theory do not automatically establish the falsity of our hypotheses. Rather, negative instances falsify the combined effects of the main hypothesis and the auxiliaries. Without data to the contrary, a negative instance could be simply the failure of one of our auxiliaries and is thereby mute about the status of our theory or our assessment device. This means that we are justified in ignoring negative instances in the construct validity context because no evidence indicates conclusively that either our test or our theory have been falsified.

Salmon takes this a step further when he shows that, under certain conditions, evidence disconfirming a hypothesis plus auxiliaries can nevertheless separately confirm each. Thus, in the standard construct validation context, negative results could conceivably be positive outcomes for our theory. With apologies to Salmon for psychologizing his wonderful example of how this translates into scientific practice, consider this situation:

Dr. Marlowe comes home late at night after a hard day at the lab.

"How did your work go today, dear?" asks his wife.

"Well, you know my need for a social approval hypothesis on which I have staked my entire scientific reputation? And you know the experiment I was running today to test it—the one involving that dull spool-packing task? Well, the results were negative."

"Oh, dear, what a shame! Now you have to give up your hypothesis and watch your entire reputation go down the drain!"

"Not at all. In order to carry out the test, I had to make use of some auxiliary hypotheses."

"Oh, what a relief—saved by Quine–Duhem! Your hypothesis wasn't refuted after all," says the philosophical Mrs. Marlowe.

"Better than that," Marlowe continues. "I actually confirmed the need for a social approval hypothesis."

"Why, that's wonderful dear," replies Mrs. Marlowe. "You found you could reject an auxiliary hypothesis, and that in doing so, you could establish the fact that the test actually confirmed your hypothesis? How ingenious!"

"No," Marlowe continues, "it's even better. I found that I had confirmed the auxiliary hypotheses as well."

The critical point here is that virtually any outcome from a construct validation study is indeterminant. Such studies shed conclusive evidence on neither the status of the theory nor the assessment device once we admit the existence of auxiliary hypotheses.

The three critiques outlined above (theoretical/observational distinction, Popper, and auxiliaries) direct an incredibly powerful "triple whammy" toward the rationality of the procedures of science and, by implication, at the processes of construct validation. The intersect of auxiliary hypotheses and falsification suggests that negative empirical results can never decisively refute a theory because it is always possible to cite an auxiliary hypothesis as the reason for the empirical failure—theories, then, are untestable! The Popperian position shows that the establishment of the truth of a theory is impossible. The realization that observation is directed by theory informs us that any attempt to falsify a theory is problematic because the observational basis of the refutation is itself permeated by theory, thus making the entire enterprise theoretical. This, of course, is inacceptable in a scientific context. In all, the cumulative character of these three critical appraisals is devastating, suggesting that the standard procedures of psychological science (and those legislated by the APA for developing construct validity) cannot be defended on rational grounds.

Examining the Critiques

Many members of the testing enterprise are aware of these difficulties. Numerous debates and interchanges have been initiated in efforts to address these foundational concerns. Several interesting responses to these arguments have emerged. These ideas, which provide a newer vision of science and psychology, are the focus of this next section. These concerns have not been explicitly tied to the testing enterprise, but the observation that construct validity is clearly a version of logical empiricism makes these points highly relevant to the future directions the field will take.

Is that what we really do? In examining the Popper–Meehl argument, it seems that a strict falsification argument may not reflect the reality of how scientists actually work in their laboratories. Popper's falsification argument does not account for the tenacity with which theories are held by scientists in the face of apparently strong disconfirmation. Indeed, a number of important breakthroughs have occurred precisely because a researcher ignored mounds of seemingly contradictory evidence. Discussion with almost all practicing scientists will reveal that they function as though they believe their theories are true and that most of their activity is directed toward the verification of this belief. Either Popper is wrong, or virtually all scientists are dishonest in the falsificationist sense sketched out by Popper.

According to Imre Lakatos, the main problem here is the failure to distinguish between *criticism* of a theory and its *abandonment*. Just because a theory is subject to criticism, or some empirical anomalies exist, is not sufficient to force automatic refutation of the theory. Rather, the abandonment of a given theory should be taken very seriously and only under some specific conditions. Serlin and Lapsley (1985) suggest, for example, that there must be a rival research program that accounts for all of the facts of an earlier program before considering abandonment of the latter in favor of the former. As well, the new program should anticipate new observations—some of which have been corroborated. Thus, refutation of a theory is not an all-or-none event predicated on the observation of one dissonant result as the earlier falsification argument suggested. Instead, the decision to refute a theory has to be considered carefully in light of currently available alternatives. In particular, there must be a powerful *other theory* in place before refutation is warranted.

The good-enough principle. This line of argument led Serlin and Lapsley (1985) to formulate their **good-enough principle.** Basically, the practicing scientist makes a decision beforehand about the "standards that indicate what kinds of experimental outcomes are 'good enough'" (p. 79) to be considered an affirmation of a theory (or *bad enough* to constitute a refutation). In other words, scientists have a range of results that they will interpret as a falsifying incident.

Theories, then, survive because they are good enough in the sense that there are no better candidates around *and* because they have survived a number of empirical tests articulated within a framework of good-enough qualifiers. These theories may still be literally false, but they are the best we have at this point.

Meehl (1990) extends this line of argument even further by discussing how it might be possible to withdraw gracefully in the face of accepted falsifiers of a given theory. Meehl calls this a **Lakatosian defense,** which is a strategic retreat conducted in the interests of saving the core ideas of a theory from premature abandonment. This retreat determines if various types of auxiliary hypotheses and other adjunctive aspects of the theory embedded in the empirical demonstration are at fault. Included here is detailed examination of (1) instrumental auxiliaries related to measurement processes, (2) systematic factors that are not comparable across all experimental conditions,[6] (3) auxiliary hypotheses used in the derivation of the major hypothesis being tested, and (4) a revision of the intended domain to which the theory is thought to apply. This entire set of concerns is called the **protective belt** of the theory. **Degeneration** of a given theory occurs if a considerable amount of ad hoc, or after-the-fact, explanation (what Meehl calls **ad hockery**) is consistently necessary to salvage the theory from falsification. If adjustments made in the protective belt lead to increasingly successful empirical demonstrations of the theory, the research program is said to be *progressive.* Thus, theories are effective to the extent they demonstrate this progressive character, and a theory that shows consistent degeneration should be considered weak and suspect. This distinction appears a much better characterization of the way scientists actually think about their theories than does the strict falsificationist formulation. The implications of the irrationality of scientific endeavors are also put to rest by this more sophisticated approach to falsification.

Money in the bank. In revising his position, Meehl (1990) suggests two subcomponents of the good-enough principle that provide a sense of how it is possible to avoid the implications of the strict falsificationist arguments. Knowing that in psychology our theories are imperfect and incomplete, it seems clear that we should not equate good enough with the idea that there is sufficient evidence to continue believing the theory is true. Rather, the concern should focus on whether the theory has sufficient promise to warrant continued tinkering with its auxiliaries and protecting

---

[6]These are called *ceteris paribus* clauses, translated literally from the Latin as "all else being equal."

its core from falsification. A sense of whether a theory warrants this care can be derived from examining the track record of the formulation. If a theory has accumulated considerable credit by strong successes in the past—that is, the theory has lots of **money in the bank**—it seems reasonable to defend it in the face of apparent empirical falsification. In other words, a previously successful theory should be fit with a sufficiently robust protective belt to protect it from hasty refutation.

Risky tests and damned strange coincidences. A second issue underlying the good-enough principle relates to how a theory accumulates money in the bank. As indicated earlier, the simplest way of accumulating a bank balance in the world of theory involves making successful and risky predictions. The more such successful risky predictions are made, the better. The more stringent the limits of acceptable theoretical performance are set (for example, the narrower the good-enough belt), the better. If a theory is good enough to make specific numerical predictions, which are confirmed within previously set good-enough limits, its bank balance is significantly enhanced (see Meehl, 1990, for detailed argumentation).

As well, money in the bank can be achieved by predicting facts that, without the theory, are unexpected. These are Salmon's (1984) **damned strange coincidences.** The goal here is to make low-probability predictions (a priori) that are successfully realized. Even a near miss in this low-probability context can be interpreted as support of the theory. In other words, a theory that allows us to make unexpected predictions has a better bank balance than one that does not.

Summary. In sum then, the decision about whether a theory warrants continued attention is much more complex than the strict falsificationist perspective would have us believe. A given instance of falsification may simply be a matter of one of a number of auxiliary hypotheses being false. Careful examination of this possibility, and subsequent research trying to correct the problem, is a reasonable course of action to follow in such instances. However, if continued tinkering with the auxiliaries fails to produce a progressive formulation, questions about the theory should arise. Even in the face of apparently "valid" falsifications, theories with good track records of previous successes (particularly in risky situations) and those that are able to sustain low-probability predictions warrant the use of the protective belt to ward off abandonment of the theory, at least for a while. The decision to abandon a theory, then, is one that ought not to be taken lightly, particularly if there is no alternative theory waiting in the wings to take over.

Initially, reviews of the theoretical/observational distinction, Popper's strict falsification position, and the Quine–Duhem thesis about auxiliaries appeared to indicate clear and substantive problems underlying the notion of construct validity—the mainstay of the contemporary disciplinary matrix of the testing enterprise. However, consideration of the manner in which scientists actually conceptualize theory in their day-to-day work appears to indicate that the critical appraisals should be tempered a bit. The strict falsificationist perspective does not appear to be a justifiable criticism when the ideas of Lakatos are brought to bear. The issues underlying auxiliary hypotheses are also rendered tractable when we consider the notion of a strategic retreat from negative empirical evidence. Because theory and data are seen to exist in a large interactive network in which the terms are intermixed in many ways (for example, see the discussion of auxiliaries), the force of the breakdown of the theoretical/observational distinction is blunted. In sum, the critical appraisals may not paint as bleak a picture for construct validity as initially thought.

The fundamental problems, however, are far from solved. There are clear disagreements in the field about some of these issues (for examples, see the commentaries surrounding Meehl, 1990). As well, there are a number of places where the emerging positions need work. For example, exactly how much money in the bank is necessary before proceeding on a systematic retreat? When does a theory actually become degenerative? What level of a priori probability is acceptable to consider something a damned strange coincidence? What is the status of a new theory that accommodates only a part of the predictive orbit of an extant theory? These and many other questions await further work. Even with these disagreements, though, a fair reading of the situation is that the metatheory underlying the contemporary testing enterprise appears to have survived some fairly heavy critical onslaughts. Whether ad hoc adjustments to the positivist metatheory captured in terms such as the *good-enough principle, money in the bank*, a *Lakatosian defense*, and *damned strange coincidences* constitute sufficient ad hockery to consider the metatheoretic position to be degenerative will await further elaboration of the position.

Even if the positivist metatheory were found to be degenerative, however, the fundamental idea of construct validity, and its formulation as hypothesis testing, will likely continue to hold sway within the testing enterprise. Positivism represents a number of unquestioned assumptions that workers have to make in order to proceed with their normal problem-solving activities within the testing domain. The metatheory is a set of working assumptions about the nature of the world that facilitates research and test development. It follows that challenges to the belief system, such as the criticisms outlined earlier, will not have a devastating effect on workers. Meehl's (1990) comments on the apparent lack of impact of the critical appraisals are most revealing here. While discussing an edited book by Morrison and Henkel (1970) that examined the types of critical appraisals outlined above, but with reference to significance testing, Meehl (1990) states that

> This excellent book should by rights be called "epoch-making" or "path-breaking," but, regrettably, it was not. I do not know how well it sold, but it is rarely cited; and I find that the majority of psychology students in my department have never heard of it, let alone been urged by their professors to read it. Judging from published research in current soft psychology, the PhD orals I serve on, and colloquium lectures by job candidates, the book has had negligible influence. . . . Our graduate students typically plan and write their doctoral dissertations in blissful ignorance that "the significance test controversy" even exists, or can have a bearing on their research problems. [p. 108]

This strange state of affairs can be understood with reference to the pragmatic stance of most researchers and test developers. Metatheories are challenged and changed, not by inconsistencies within the system, but when numbers of significant problems begin to resist solution (for a detailed discussion, see Kuhn, 1970). As long as the metatheory continues to produce effective solutions to problems deemed as important within the discipline (for example, the production of useful tests), change is unlikely. In this sense, the philosophical critiques of construct validity are irrelevant as long as the matrix continues to function.

This point is strengthened when we reflect for a moment on the content of the metatheory. Here the emphasis is on the positivist approach to the world, which draws its support from empirical demonstration. That is, within the matrix, the here-and-now of empirical demonstration is more significant than rational analysis. In general, within the testing enterprise matrix, philosophical appraisals are not seen as important as hard data. The historical information presented earlier in the text, which noted that psychology emerged from philosophy departments because it favored empirical, positivist dogma, is germane here as well, suggesting a tendency for psychologists to devalue rational criticism. In sum, despite the difficulties within the belief system noted earlier, the disciplinary matrix of the testing enterprise appears to be robust and thriving.

Possible Alternatives

These critical appraisals are accompanied by some movement looking for alternatives to the positivist position. Perhaps another set of ideas about what constitutes a good psychological test can address some of the difficulties noted above. At present, the disciplinary matrix hangs on a positivistic view of the world and all of the symbolic generalizations, beliefs, values, and exemplars this implies. In what follows, some alternative views will be discussed, with an eye to sketching out some of the possible future developments of the enterprise.

Some clinical psychologists provide a place to begin this consideration. Korchin and Schuldberg (1981) suggest that clinical testing "has fallen from its former high estate" because of a confluence of professional, social, and economic problems. They also identify a renewed vitality, signaled by several trends: (1) the development of more focused tests with greater psychometric purity, (2) movement to lower-level interpretations of tests, (3) greater sensitivity to situational and environmental concerns, (4) more respect for the client's views, and (5) fuller acceptance of the inevitable role of clinical judgment (Korchin & Schuldberg, 1981, p. 1156). There can be little doubt that traditional approaches to testing can be brought to bear on the first two of these trends. However, the latter three are more problematic. In a scientific metatheory that searches for general, noncontextual explanations such as is presently embraced by the testing enterprise, accommodating situational variables, client's perceptions, and clinical intuition is difficult. An alternative theory of measurement may prove useful in this search for renewed vitality. What follows is a tentative suggestion about directions such alternatives may take.

Tests as talk. Perhaps an evaluative schema for tests that focuses directly on their integration into social practice would be useful. Rather than viewing tests as science, why not look at them as part-and-parcel of the manner in which we function in our society? Some work from anthropology is suggestive here.

If we examine a wide variety of cultures—sophisticated literate ones like ours through to "primitive" cultures such as those romanticized by Margaret Mead— several almost universal characteristics emerge. One feature that seems to be observed constantly in ethnographic work is the presence of certain **rituals**. Van Gennep (1909/1960) documented and analyzed the presence of **rites of passage** in a number of exotic cultures. These rituals mark the transition of members of the culture from one stage of life to another, such as from youth to adult. They occur at times of "anxiety" or stress when a person is ready to move from one social role (child) to another (adult). The anthropological research clearly indicates that such rituals have a definite form and have since been documented in all cultures—including our own. For example, rites such as hazing and initiation for new members of occupational groups, athletic teams, fraternities, and Ph.D. candidates have been well documented in the anthropological literature. These rites show the same structural and functional characteristics as those viewed in other societies.

A number of levels can be used to understand this human penchant for celebrating rites of passage, but it is beyond the scope of this text to review the various accounts that have been presented in the anthropological literature. However, one aspect of these rites is particularly relevant to our discussion: Virtually all rites of passage involve the use of cultural resources to maximize the common good. In the case of the passage from child to adult, social resources are used to make decisions about how neophytes can be best integrated into the community to maximize their contributions. The rite involves bringing novitiates into the fold, ensuring they are brought under society's control, and assigning them a role within the society that maximizes the common good. The example of Mishi presented in Chapter 3 is a clear example of this. In this case, there was a period of *isolation* where the novitiate was alone; a period of *liminality* where the youngster was marginal to society, being at the cusp of two different roles; and a period of *incorporation* when he was admitted to his new place in society. The Ojibway example relates to the change from child to adult, but there are many others, each with their own rituals—for example, bachelor to married (wedding), active to retired (gold-watch party), or material to spiritual (funeral). The fundamental structure and functions of these rituals appear to be constant across cultures. They are natural indispensable aspects of culture.

In relation to the testing enterprise, I would like to suggest that it is worthwhile to view testing as part-and-parcel of this kind of social activity. That is, testing has emerged in our culture to serve some of the same functions accorded rituals in other societies. Just like rites of passage, almost all testing occurs at times of angst just prior to a major change in social role. These include (1) scholastic-achievement tests as part of the transition from high school to university; (2) vocational-interest surveys as part of the transition from general to specialized student or from student to working member of the culture; (3) measures of psychopathology in cases of a transition between normality and special, mentally ill status; (4) IQ tests as part of the movement from regular to special educational programs; and (5) personality tests in industry as part of the change between being unemployed and becoming a contributing member of the society. Although we do not send our adolescent youths off to a sacred area to have visitations with Manitou, we do send them to a small room and have them fill in the Differential Aptitude Test Battery. We may not have rituals conducted by a shaman to exorcise an evil spirit, but we do sit suffering people down and ask them to fill in the MMPI or free-associate to inkblots. We do not have crash courses on tribal lore held in a bush school like the Poro, but we do have people aspiring to positions of power take exams such as the

SAT, MCAT, GRE, and/or a plethora of civil service examinations. This is an intriguing thought: Perhaps testing has emerged in our culture as the modern-day equivalent of the various rituals associated with other cultures. They occur at the same times, serve the same functions, and are all concerned with maximizing the common good.

This argument does not imply that tests *are* rituals, although this might be possible in some cases. That is, the youngster answering the Differential Aptitude Test Battery is not thought to be off participating in a ritual in the same sense that the young Ojibway was. Rather, the argument is that tests have evolved in *our* culture to serve the same fundamental functions as rituals do in other cultures. Tests can be seen as the first part of a complex social negotiation process of vocational placement, not unlike the Vision Quest was for the Ojibway.

Careful ethnographic analysis of rituals such as rites of passage reveals that participants in these activities are not stupid, as an outsider might think. In large measure, anthropological analyses in the more modern era demonstrate that ritual participants often have a great understanding of exactly what is going on. They are not unthinking puppets, although this may seem to be the case to the outsider. Members actively participate in the rites, seeking and getting as much information about the role for which they have applied. Indeed, effective rituals are ones where **communication** between the novitiate and the elder is maximized. Elders make their expectations known to novitiates, who in turn make their needs and aspirations known to the elders. Although this communication is clearly symbolic in the case of rites in some cultures, the sharing of information is an essential component. Good rituals, then, are those that enhance communication between the decision maker and the novitiate.

Using our metaphor of test as ritual, enhancing communication now becomes a potential criterion for evaluating psychological tests. From this view, the better test would be the one that enhances communication between the respondent and the party sponsoring the assessment and decision making. Rather than focusing on the traditional ideas of reliability and validity, emphasis here would be on the manner in which the test facilitates rapport and information exchange between the two parties.

Perhaps an example will help here. The **Jackson Vocational Interest Survey (JVIS)** (Jackson, 1977) has emerged to help young people in our culture make decisions about which occupations they might like to pursue. Typically, high school students will take this inventory, and the scores are interpreted to highlight certain occupations that fit with their interests. The communication function of tests like the JVIS emerges when we realize that many high school students do not have detailed information about exactly what workers in specific occupations actually do in their day-to-day lives. Students may have views about the status, prestige, and acceptability of various occupations, but in general their specific knowledge about what is involved in these careers is not great. The JVIS has been designed to have students indicate the activities they like. These activities are then keyed to the occupational scales of the JVIS. Thus, "liking to remove warts" is keyed on the Medical Service scale, based on a careful sampling of the day-to-day activities of members of the occupation. Thus, students indicate their preferences for doing specific things, and the JVIS keying sorts these responses into the occupations associated with the various activities. The eventual interpretation of the scale score is

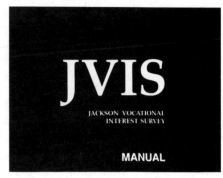

Test materials for Jackson Vocational Interest Survey.

that the student has indicated preference for participating in the kinds of activities associated with a specific class of occupations. Thus, the JVIS serves an important communication function by providing a means for students to "talk" with society about the kinds of occupations associated with the kinds of activities they prefer.

The important thing here is that exactly the same end could have been achieved by sitting down with students and informing them of the activities associated with each occupational group and then having them select which of the groups they prefer. In other words, the JVIS is a substitute for a specific communication event—the disclosure of the relationship between preferred activities and specific occupational groups. It follows that a particularly effective way of deciding whether the JVIS is a good test is to consider if the test-as-communication event is as effective as some other communication medium. Is it more efficient than classroom lectures? Is it less expensive? Is the same information conveyed? Is it as useful as films that teach various occupations? Asking directly about the communication effectiveness of a test is a highly useful question if our goal is to maximize the social utility of our tests.

The communication-based questions are very different from those that flow from the current disciplinary matrix. From the traditional view, we wonder about the validity and reliability of the test. The present argument indicates that it is appropriate to evaluate tests in terms of their effectiveness as communication devices, rather than in terms of their validity or reliability. The following questions might be considered: How well does a test facilitate real communication between the parties involved? Is a test cost-effective when compared to other forms of communication? Are there unintended negative effects on communication enacted by the test? Is the communication medium created by a test appropriate to the intended message of the communication? Can communication be better served by more expensive, face-to-face methods? Are there aspects of communication that are enhanced by the test, compared to other methods? These and a wide range of other questions are suggested once we begin to look at tests as talk.

A communication criterion for tests is incredibly rich in the manner in which it generates novel ideas and considerations into testing. Several of these are:

1. Communication demands common ground between the two parties, so any analysis of tests as communication devices forces consideration of the shared language and values of the tester and the client.

2. All communication involves intent, and the most frequent goal of communicating is to persuade (rhetoric). Thus, proper application of the communication criterion would force testers to clarify the exact nature of the messages inherent in the testing device and being exchanged in the testing session.

3. Communication always occurs in a specific context, and the communication criterion would force the field to take context into account more than it does now.

4. The invocation of the communication criterion provides access to some very exciting new theories of rhetoric, discourse analysis, and social construction (for a selection of these see Stam, Rogers, & Gergen, 1987).

5. By implication, testing processes that result in the tabulation of a number, or profile, or computerized output without using this as part of a larger-scale communication effort are not likely to show social utility—even though the test involved may be exceedingly valid.

The foregoing is only a hand-waving summary of the gains that accrue from considering psychological tests as communication events. It provides a novel way of examining the utility of tests—a way that brings to the fore the social aspects of testing. After all, if testing is fundamentally a social activity, then why not evaluate it directly in those same terms? The major bonus of this view is that tests that fulfill this "new" criterion would have maximal social utility.

In one sense, this communication criterion is not really that new. Conversations with clinicians typically reveal that they frequently use tests as shortcut procedures for facilitating communication. In effect, the test results are employed to help establish rapport and/or to start the therapeutic process. Some recent interviews with vocational counselors conducted by Nancy Johnson Smith in Calgary have revealed consistently that tests are viewed strictly as the starting point for a dialog about career aspirations. It would seem that in order for a social decision-making procedure to work, there has to be a mechanism for two-way dialog, and this idea of viewing tests as communication devices is simply a way of stating this and incorporating the effectiveness with which it serves this role into the evaluation of a test.

This line of argument has been developed in the domain of projective tests. Several researchers suggest that the Rorschach is better viewed as "a clinical inter-

The Rorschach, as seen being administered here, can be seen as an interview in which two persons initiate important talk.

view with emphasis on the content elicited" (Reznikoff, 1972, p. 446). Reznikoff suggests that "a far more productive approach to the Rorschach is to regard it as essentially a standardized interview and to focus, therefore, primarily on content. With this orientation the Rorschach emerges as an exceedingly flexible technique that can be utilized in some diverse and innovative ways" (p. 449). Essentially, the interview interpretation of the Rorschach involves viewing the test as a relatively standardized situation in which the interaction of a patient and therapist can be studied as "they endeavor to arrive at a mutually agreeable Rorschach precept" (Reznikoff, 1972, p. 447). This is an application that treats the test as a communication device rather than as an agent of psychological theory as standard psychometrics would have us do. The jury may still be out as far as the utility of this approach to projective tests, but it suggests that alternative criteria of test utility may be more useful than the current set.

Clearly, a great deal of research will have to be done to explore the communications aspects of testing. For the present, this intriguing possibility has been mentioned to point, ever so tentatively, at a direction toward which the enterprise may move as it continues its quest for social responsiveness.

Tests as rhetoric. A second possible alternative to the traditional evaluative criteria of tests lies in the manner in which they facilitate the persuasion inherent in any communication event. Tests have long been an important part of the psychologist's toolbox and have become an expected part of the therapeutic process (particularly with psychologically sophisticated clients). This suggests that tests can be viewed as agents of **rhetoric**, where they are being used as part of a program to convince clients that the helping process will work and that they would be well served by adhering to the recommended therapeutic regimen. Clearly, tests used in this way would be better evaluated in terms of their convincingness, or effectiveness, in persuasion. The key questions in this orientation relate to how rhetoric is employed in the overall assessment context. This involves determination of the common grounds, or topics, that are necessary for rhetorical process to be effective, as well as an assessment of the manner in which tests contribute to the rhetoric of helping others. The goal of such a project would be the explication of criteria for evaluating tests that explicitly incorporate the rhetorical component.

Toward Democratization

These discussions of tests as rituals, tests as communication, and tests as rhetoric are only three of a wide variety of newer positions that could be taken to help us develop a useful evaluative schema for psychological tests. These examples are only a subset of a much grander movement within the intellectual life of North America. They reflect, for want of a better name, what might be considered a **postmodern** perspective. Across the entire continent, there is an emerging body of thought and associated political action that, probably more than anything else, will direct the immediate future of the testing enterprise. Let's briefly examine this family of ideas as a means of concluding our glimpse into the future for the testing enterprise.

One of the historical events reviewed extensively in this text was the professionalization of psychology. In Chapter 12, we encountered the development of numerous aspects of the formalized profession of psychology—credentialing debates and legislation, technical recommendations for tests, ethical codes, varied associations taking increasingly political and exclusionary positions, and so on. Viewed in social context as they were, these developments were not only justified but also necessary (see Chapters 14 and 15). One implication of these developments, however, was to make a very clear distinction between the *producer* and *consumer* of psychological knowledge. Some people, by virtue of their professional status, were allowed to create and apply psychological knowledge, whereas others were not. This divorce of the consumer from the producer is one of the major characteristics of what might be considered the *modern* era.[7]

In the testing enterprise, as revealed in the earlier chapters of this book, the emergence of this split between the producer and consumer was the outcome of a long and arduous process beginning at the turn of the century with the inventions of Galton, Binet, and other pioneers and brought to fruition by legions of other scholars and entrepreneurs. The professional status of psychologists and their tests in the 1950s merely served to cap this long history. The current disciplinary matrix of the testing enterprise emerged from this evolutionary process, and this matrix incorporated almost all aspects of a modern worldview, including sanctification of the divorce between producer and consumer.

One consequence of the split between consumer and producer is the emergence of a kind of antidemocratic posture. Consider this example taken from psychology:

If I was a credentialed member of the psychological profession and you were not, then, somehow, my words have greater credibility than yours—after all I

---

[7]An interesting presentation of the implications of this divorce between producer and consumer can be found in Toffler (1980), who uses the terms *second wave* to refer to the modern era and *third wave* to refer to the more postmodern perspectives where attempts are made to undivorce (remarry?) the two.

am the expert! This makes your words less worthy than mine and provides me with power over you. Your voice does not equal mine in this case.

From this humble concern about equality, a number of important ideas have emerged, particularly in disciplines concerned with the nature and meaning of human experience. E. E. Sampson (1991) has coined the term **experiential democracy** to capture the essence of these concerns. He sees the communalities among these emerging ideas as "an effort to democratize the bases of human self-understanding by establishing a greater equality of 'voice' in setting forth the very terms by which human experience, knowledge and meaning are understood" (p. 1). In other words, these newer positions want to accord more legitimacy to alternative perspectives on important psychological ideas such as personhood and identity, incorporating them into mainstream thinking rather than relegating these alternative voices to the fringes.

Sampson points to several current intellectual debates that can be seen as instances of the quest for experiential **democratization**, including the following:

1. In the domain of literary criticism, the primacy of the author's (or anyone else's univocal) interpretation of a text has been questioned (Derrida, 1981). The current wisdom suggests that the interpretation of text is multivocal and thereby continually shifting. Thus, the expert's voice is not accorded special status.

2. In several domains of social science, increased emphasis is being placed on attempting to understand the world in terms defined by the members of the society rather than by experts (Garfinkel, 1967; Geertz, 1973). This questions the role of the professional expert, according the participant's voice greater import than is evident in much traditional scholarship.

3. The feminist movement has raised a number of critical questions that pose serious challenges to the domination of the patriarchical view of the world in shaping the bases for self-understanding (Gilligan, 1982).

All these grand intellectual movements, and numerous others, are united in their desire to grant voice, authority, control, and legitimacy to many and different worldviews. All are united in their desire to replace the single, univocal view that characterizes the modern perspective.

It is in this emerging desire to grant legitimacy to other voices that we begin to gain a glimmer of what may be in store for the psychological testing enterprise. From the beginning, psychological tests have been concerned with standardization:

> . . . hiring procedures as well as work were increasingly standardized. Standardized tests were used to identify and weed out the supposedly unfit, especially in the civil service. Pay scales were standardized throughout whole industries, along with fringe benefits, lunch hours, holidays, and grievance procedures. To prepare youth for the job market, educators designed standardized curricula. Men like Binet and Terman devised standardized intelligence tests. School grading policies, admission procedures, and accreditation rules were similarly standardized. The multiple-choice test came into its own. [Toffler, 1980, pp. 63–64].

All of this, and in particular psychological tests, serve to reinforce the idea of the single-voiced expert, which is so much a part of the modern worldview.

To the extent that forces are afoot that are challenging this hegemony, such as the movement toward experiential democratization, it seems clear that the greatest challenge to be faced by the testing enterprise will be to adjust to these concerns. Many and varied changes are likely to emerge as this movement gains momentum. Test development may increasingly begin to reflect the cultural reality experienced by those being tested, rather than revealing the cultural experiences of the test makers. Theoretical constructs may be developed that are integrated into the ongoing cultural context of the group being tested. Tests may be developed to facilitate the manner in which members of a given group can articulate the nature of their problems and concerns *in their own language*, rather than that of the professional. A metatheory that embraces the manner in which the social community defines personhood and the experience of reality may be worked out and translated into an effective disciplinary matrix. Methodologies that permit the subtle exploration of cultural variations in experience will have to be strengthened. These, and many other, changes may be evidenced if the testing enterprise joins the quest for experiential democracy, which appears to be blossoming on our continent.

We can hope that psychology and its favorite tool, the psychological test, will begin to develop the capacity for viewing alternatives in a constructive and fresh manner, rather than trying to ram them unthinkingly into the preexisting disciplinary matrix. Should this happen, the psychological test may have an important part to play in the emerging social fabric of our continent. It could, then, be an agent of revolution providing new ideas, new self-understandings, and opening new vistas of human awareness.

THE LAST WORD ... SORT OF

This brings our story to a close. We started out way back in the history of civilization, with early manhood rites from the first nations, progressed up through the Chinese and Greeks, endured the Dark Ages, and eventually entered the age of science. Once scientific progress began, we traced the intriguing story of how it was slowly and surely applied to the domain of social decision making and how the psychological testing enterprise, as we know it today, emerged from this. We discovered a treasure trove of technology, new ideas, and evaluative schemata that evolved as part of this enterprise. We also found some problems in the field, concluding with the hope that most of the difficulties could be resolved. But substantive change also appears needed.

So the time comes for the moral of our story. Any story is told with a particular value statement in mind—else why tell it? It is reasonable to ask, then, what is the moral underlying our narrative of the psychological testing enterprise?

For me, the major moral of our story lies in documenting the perils of excess. By this I mean that the mistakes made in the enterprise have, for the most part, been born of the *excessive* application of methodological, metatheoretical, and/or political dogma. The difficulties that have been noted throughout the enterprise can all be traced to contexts in which the actors felt they had "the" answer. With this came a reluctance to explore alternatives, and the system became closed to different views. If you agree with me that measurement without definition was a contributing cause of many of the problems in the early enterprise, it is exactly because this position was adopted in the extreme, without concern for alternatives. If you agree with me that construct validity is one of the major reasons why the testing enterprise is having difficulty being socially reactive, it is exactly because this idea was legislated by the APA as "the" way of doing things, without concern for alternatives. If you agree with me that IQ tests can serve as instruments of social-class maintenance, it is exactly because this was viewed as the "only" way, without concern for alternative ideologies. Indeed, the basic problem is this sense of certainty that we know "the" answer.

This is a particularly difficult thing to deal with because we live our lives continually searching for a sense of certainty and correctness. The media continually give us an oversimplified version of what things are like, and sometimes we begin to think that we should be living our lives in this way. Our churches continually preach that they know "the" only way to salvation. Our scientific establishments continually try to convince us that they have "the" answer to fundamental problems. When someone comes along who has "the" answer, we are all too ready to accept it and exclude alternatives. This is exacerbated because so much information is available these days that we seem to need, more and more, this sense of certainty. In this certainty, however, lies grief.

What we need is an intelligent, critical, and informed approach to topics such as the testing enterprise—intelligent in the sense that it is well-grounded in rational deliberation, critical in the sense that it searches for weaknesses without (necessarily) trying to destroy, and informed in the sense that it is based on knowledge of the domain. I sincerely hope that this text has fulfilled these criteria and demonstrated that this modernist world has room for well-conceived rational analysis.

One problem with formulating this text in a narrative format is that by the time we come to the end of it, the expectation has been created that the story has ended too. But in the case of the psychological testing enterprise, the story is far from over. I expect that the next decade will be pivotal for the domain—and the last few chapters of the story have yet to unfold. Perhaps in 10 years, the enterprise will have changed and found ways to resolve its current problems. Perhaps in 10 years, the psychological testing enterprise will have receded into the pages of history, to join the likes of classical learning theory and phrenology. Perhaps in 10 years, things will be exactly the same . . . who knows?

Glossary

ad hockery After-the-fact explanations of negative results obtained when putting a theory to test.

authenticity test A psychological test that culminates in decisions about whether an individual demonstrates important characteristics such as honesty.

auxiliary hypothesis   The secondary assumptions that must be made (and assumed to be true) when one attempts to put a theoretical hypothesis to test. Any test of a theory is a test of the combined theoretical and auxiliary hypotheses, not simply the theory itself.

communication   A system in which meanings are exchanged between individuals through a common set of symbols.

cookbook   A set of profiles for tests, such as the MMPI, that provides interpretations for particular classes of obtained scale scores on a multiscale inventory.

damned strange coincidence   An unexpected or low-probability prediction from a theory that is subsequently empirically confirmed.

degeneration (of a theory)   If a theory demands a significant amount of after-the-fact explanation of negative results it is said to degenerate.

democraticization   The process of granting greater equality of voice and power to the various communities that make up a given cultural context.

disciplinary matrix   From Thomas Kuhn, a complex of generalizations, beliefs, values, and how-to exemplars that direct the day-to-day activities of a given community of scholars. Positivism is a significant component of the disciplinary matrix of the testing enterprise.

experiential democracy   The establishment of greater equality of voice and power to the various communities that make up a given cultural context.

falsification   The effort to prove that a given theoretical statement is not true.

good-enough principle   The development of standards or limits that determine if a given attempt to verify a theory is sufficiently strong to warrant accepting it. These limits should be set prior to efforts to test the theory.

Hume's problem   The realization that it is never possible to demonstrate the truth of an inductive statement because one false instance could arise at any moment and destroy it.

induction   Generation of a general statement based on the accumulation of specific instances.

Jackson Vocational Interest Survey (JVIS)   A structured test that asks respondents to indicate preferences for specific activities. These activities are keyed to specific occupational categories, providing feedback on the kinds of careers that the respondent might find enjoyable.

Lakatosian defense   A strategic withdrawal in the face of finding disconfirming evidence that can, in some cases, save the researcher from having to abandon the theory.

metatheory   Formerly known as philosophy of science, the theoretical claims that individuals make about the nature of theory.

money in the bank   An expression describing a theory that has survived many risky tests in the past and for which there is evidence of some damned strange coincidences. Such a theory is less likely to be abandoned in the face of negative results than one that has a low bank balance.

multiculturalism   The official position of the Canadian government that accords recognition and voice to the diverse, multiple cultures that make up the country.

null hypothesis The experimentalist's tactic of assuming an hypothesis is false (null) and then looking for evidence to reject this hypothesis. Rejecting the null hypothesis is typically assumed to be the same as verifying the theory.

Popper's argument The idea that theoretical terms are not verifiable but they are falsifiable.

postmodern A family of intellectual movements oriented toward according alternate and multiple perspectives, meanings, and interpretations a legitimate place in intellectual discourse.

protective belt The various types of auxiliary hypotheses that provide fuel for ad hockery. Included here are instrumental auxiliaries due to measurement processes, systematic factors that vary across contexts, hypotheses used to generate hypotheses, and the evocation of boundary conditions on a theory's domain.

rhetoric An attempt to persuade individuals to adopt a specific course of action.

risky test An attempt to prove a theory false that puts the formulation to a very tough or stringent evaluation. Risky tests are thought to be highly desirable in the development of a theory.

rite of passage A social ritual that marks the transition of a group member from one role to another. Psychological testing, as used in many situations, can be seen as a rite of passage.

ritual A socially defined and sanctioned activity that takes place as part of an important social event such as changing roles.

scientific revolution From Thomas Kuhn, a radical change in the disciplinary matrix of a given community of scientists. Such revolutions are typically created by the emergence of problems that persistently resist solution using the prerevolutionary disciplinary matrix.

social utility The usefulness that a given idea has for the solution of meaningful social problems.

tensions of testing Four fundamental value positions that undergird the testing enterprise. Very deep seated in nature, these tensions relate to conflicts associated with nature/nurture, individual/institutional, science/art, and positivism/alternatives.

theoretical/observational distinction A characteristic of positivism that divides the world into two separate types of terms—those associated with empirical observation and those of a theoretical (nonempirical) nature. This distinction is difficult to maintain because the act of observation involves theoretical assertions.

verification The effort to prove that a given theoretical statement is true.

Suggested Further Reading

Fancher, R. E. (1985). *The intelligence men: Makers of the IQ controversy.* New York: Norton.

This book provides a fine historical introduction to the nature/nurture controversy. Of note for the present chapter is the concluding essay that places this ever-present controversy into contemporary context. It is fine reading for a student who wishes to gain a framework for consideration of the future of this tension.

Hanson, F. A. (1993). *Testing testing: Social consequences of the examined life.* Berkeley: University of California Press.

> This book is a fine treatment of the individual end of what was labeled the institutional/individual tension in the chapter. Continuing the long line of anthropological criticism of testing, this book provides a very insightful analysis into the impact of testing on our daily lives. Dealing with a broader concept of tests than *The Enterprise* does (for example, includes lie detector and drug tests), this dissertation provides great food for thought for anyone interested in gaining a balanced view of the place of testing in our contemporary culture.

Irvine, S. H., & Berry, J. W. (1983). *Human assessment and cultural factors.* New York: Plenum.

> This book contains a number of chapters that discuss aspects of testing when viewed from a cross-cultural perspective. It is important for the present chapter because the movement toward democraticization implies, among other things, that careful consideration of the impact of testing practice on other cultures must be considered in depth. This book is a fine place to begin these considerations.

Lips, H. M. (1988). *Sex and gender: An introduction* (2nd ed.). Mountain View, Calif.: Mayfield.

> As indicated in the chapter, feminist theory is providing one of the strongest alternative views to positivism. This text provides a good introduction to the major issues that are part of this intellectual movement. Of note is the second chapter on theoretical perspectives on sex and gender that articulates the manner in which mainstream psychology has tended to demean the female voice in a number of significant ways.

Meehl, P. E. (1990). Appraising and amending theories: The strategy of Lakatosian defense and two principles that warrant it. *Psychological Inquiry, 1,* 108–141.

> This is probably the most accessible presentation of the metatheoretical issues discussed in the chapter. It consists of a well-written dissertation by Meehl, followed by discussions of a number of other authors. Although heavy reading, it does provide a wonderfully detailed and useful presentation of the important philosophical issues that are confronting the testing enterprise.

Sampson, E. E. (1991). The democratization of psychology. *Theory and Psychology, 1,* 275–298.

> This article is the cornerstone of the perspective articulated in the present chapter. It is very readable and offers the student a passionate introduction to what appears to be emerging as a viable alternative to positivistic thinking. Although this article does not deal directly with testing, it is clearly relevant in its plea for hearing and according power to other voices.

Sarason, S. B. (1985). *Caring and compassion in clinical practice: Issues in the selection, training, and behavior of helping professionals.* San Francisco: Jossey-Bass.

> This book provides a wonderful treatment of the impact that the institutional organization has on the delivery of services in the health professions. It is of particular relevance for the present chapter because it provides insight into some of the reasons underlying the tension labeled in the text as science versus art. Sarason's proposed solutions are clearly in keeping with what could be considered the art pole of this important tension.

Wilkinson, S. (Ed.). (1986). *Feminist social psychology: Developing theory and practice*. Milton Keynes, Eng.: Open University Press.

> This book of readings provides a good introduction to one of the major alternate voices, which are beginning to affect mainstream psychology. Feminist psychology provides a wonderfully rich critical perspective that opens a number of interesting alternatives to the current positivist worldview of the testing enterprise. Unfortunately, a full-blown feminist critical appraisal of testing is not yet available, so reading books like Wilkinson provides a perspective on what such a critique might look like.

Discussion Questions

1. Discuss the extent to which our ten-word definition of the psychological test is clearly committed to the approach to measurement outlined in Chapter 17 as the neobehavioral alternative.

2. In what sense does the ten-word definition of a test deflect attention away from considering the social implications of testing practices?

3. Develop an argument to support the positive side of the assertion "psychological tests have been a great boon to North American society."

4. Develop an argument to support the negative side of the assertion "psychological tests have been a great boon to North American society."

5. Clearly indicate your personal positions on the four tensions outlined in the chapter (nature/nurture, individual/institutional, art/science, positivism/alternatives).

6. Of the four tensions outlined in the chapter, which one do you believe creates the greatest problems for the testing enterprise? Justify your selection with reference to the materials discussed in the chapter.

7. Do you think it is appropriate to voice the tensions of testing in a confrontational language (for example, science versus art)? Why, or why not?

8. List and discuss three undesirable consequences that have emerged from an acceptance of the nature end of the nature/nurture tension.

9. Critically appraise the interactional position that suggests behavior is the joint result of environmental and genetic causes.

10. List and discuss three undesirable consequences that have emerged from an acceptance of the institutional end of the individual/institutional tension.

11. With reference to examinations you have experienced in recent years, indicate which of your test-taker rights have been least considered. Discuss the implications of this.

12. Develop an argument *against* the position that the only time test results should be used is if they are favorable to the test taker.

13. Develop an argument in *favor* of the position that the only time test results should be used is if they are favorable to the test taker.

14. Critically evaluate the notion of implied consent as discussed in the Close Up on test-taker rights.

15. To what extent do you agree with Allan Hanson's assertion that students, as test takers, are demonstrating docile and unwitting submission to power.

16. List and discuss three undesirable consequences that have emerged from an acceptance of the science end of the science/art tension.

17. Prepare a list of the critical ideas in the disciplinary matrix of the testing enterprise.

18. List and discuss as many functions of the disciplinary matrix as you can think of.

19. What do you think has been the most important social change we have experienced in the last 10 years? Suggest how this might affect the testing enterprise were it to adjust to this change.

20. Suggest ways in which psychological tests can be thought to mute the voices of persons from other cultures.

21. Suppose you had to debate Haney regarding his assertion that scientific concerns were secondary when it comes to evaluating the testing enterprise. What points would you make to challenge his view?

22. Do you think it is reasonable that a test like the Rorschach, which has very little demonstrated validity, should be used in clinical practice? Why, or why not?

23. Develop an argument to link the need for interpretive flexibility of tests to the observation from Chapter 19 that the computerization of tests was not proceeding as fast as one might have expected.

24. List and discuss three undesirable consequences that have emerged from an acceptance of the positivism end of the positivism/alternatives tension.

25. Which of the three critical appraisals of positivism (the theoretical/observational distinction, Popper's point, or Meehl's argument) do you think is the most critical for the testing enterprise? Why?

26. One way of escaping the problems wrought by finding that the theoretical/observational distinction is problematic in positivism is to omit the idea of the nomological network from consideration. Would this resolve the difficulty completely? Why, or why not?

27. Defend the assertion that the leap of faith that a scientist must make to believe in induction is as great as the leap that a person has to make to believe in a god as part of a religious perspective.

28. Discuss the problems associated with the verification-oriented approach to theory testing that appears to represent the current perspective in psychology.

29. Using a psychological experiment with which you are familiar, list all the possible auxiliary hypotheses that have to be assumed to be true. Outline the implications of this list for deciding whether the major theory being tested has or has not been falsified.

30. Outline how it might be possible to develop a risky test of the theory of anxiety presented in Chapter 13.

31. Does the assertion that scientists work in their labs acting as though they believe their theories to be true constitute an adequate rebuttal of Popper's argument? Why, or why not?

32. Critically evaluate the good-enough principle.

33. Develop an argument to prove that the metatheory of positivism is degenerative.

34. Using your knowledge of psychology or other sciences, describe a good example of a damned strange coincidence (DSC). In your view, does this DSC increase the money in the bank for the underlying theory? Why, or why not?

35. With reference to an example from your own experience, indicate the manner in which a psychological test serves as a rite of passage.

36. Would it be possible to find an invalid test to be a good test using the communications criterion? Discuss the implications of your view on this for the testing enterprise.

37. Critically evaluate E. E. Sampson's argument for democraticization.

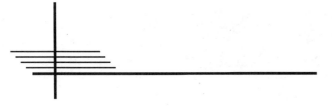

Appendixes

Appendix A

Relating z Scores to Percentiles and Ordinates of the Normal Curve

The left-most column of the table that follows is the absolute value of z scores (see Equation 4-3 regarding the computation). These are presented in steps of .01, providing much greater precision than Table 4-6.

The second column of the table is the percentiles for given z scores if the z scores are *positive*. If an obtained z score is greater than (>) 0 it must also be higher than the mean. Thus, the person with the positive z score must be, at the very least, in the 50th percentile. This is reflected in the values presented in the second column of the table.

The third column is the percentiles for given z scores if the z score is *negative*. In such cases when z is less than (<) 0, a person has scored below the mean (M) and will thereby obtain a percentile of less than 50. This is revealed in the figures in the third column of the table.

The information in columns 2 and 3 of the table can also be considered to relate to the percentages of cases that fall to the left of the z score in a normal curve. For example, the value of 93.32 beside +1.50 indicates that 93.32% of the cases fall below a z score of +1.50 if the distribution is normal.

When $z = +1.96$, the percentile value is 97.50—meaning that 2.5% of the cases are higher than this value. For −1.96, the percentile is 2.50. This means that 5% of the cases in a normal curve (2.5 + 2.5 = 5%) fall *outside* of ±1.96 SDs from the mean. In many cases of psychological research (for example, see standard error of measurement in Chapter 11), discussion of a *confidence interval* with a probability of .05 is mentioned. This is typically generated by using the (seemingly magical) figure of ±1.96 SDs. You can now see where this figure comes from because, if the entity being discussed is normally distributed, 95% of the cases *must* fall within ±1.96 SDs.

The fourth column of the table is the ordinates, or heights, of the normal curve as a function of the z score. These numbers may look a bit strange, but they follow directly from the formula that Gauss developed. The equation for the normal curve with standardized or z scores (that is, M = 0, SD = 1) is:

$$y = \frac{1}{\sqrt{2\pi}} e^{-z^2/2} \tag{A-1}$$

where

y = the height, or ordinate, of the normal curve at point z

π (pi) = 3.1416

e = 2.7183 (e represents Euler's number, the base of Naperian logarithms)

z = the z score for which the height is desired

If $z = 0$, then Equation A-1 becomes

$$y = \frac{1}{\sqrt{2\pi}} = .3989 \quad \text{(because } e^0 = 1) \quad \text{(A-2)}$$

When $z = 0$, the normal curve is at its apex; hence, the maximal height of the curve is .3989 units. This is noted in the right-most column of the table in the case where $z = 0$. Equation A-1 is fairly difficult to use; thus, for convenience the table presents the solution of y for z scores ranging from 0 to ±3.00 in steps of .01. The

obtained values are presented in the fouth column of the table. Because the normal curve is symmetric (you can fold it along the projection from the apex to the place where $z = 0$, and the two half curves will be on top of each other), the values of the ordinates are good for negative z scores as well as positive ones. As the absolute values of the z scores become greater, the curve flattens out. Ordinates of the normal curve were discussed in Chapter 14 as part of the mathematical procedures for determining utility (see Equation 14-1).

z Score	Percentile if $z > 0$	Percentile if $z < 0$	Ordinate	z Score	Percentile if $z > 0$	Percentile if $z < 0$	Ordinate
.00	50.00	50.00	.3989	.35	63.68	36.32	.3752
.01	50.40	49.60	.3989	.36	64.06	35.94	.3739
.02	50.80	49.20	.3989	.37	64.43	35.57	.3725
.03	51.20	48.80	.3988	.38	64.80	35.20	.3712
.04	51.60	48.40	.3986	.39	65.17	34.83	.3697
.05	51.99	48.01	.3984	.40	65.54	34.46	.3683
.06	52.39	47.61	.3982	.41	65.91	34.09	.3668
.07	52.79	47.21	.3980	.42	66.28	33.72	.3653
.08	53.19	46.81	.3977	.43	66.64	33.36	.3637
.09	53.59	46.41	.3973	.44	67.00	33.00	.3621
.10	53.98	46.02	.3970	.45	67.36	32.64	.3605
.11	54.38	45.62	.3965	.46	67.72	32.28	.3589
.12	54.78	45.22	.3961	.47	68.08	31.92	.3572
.13	55.17	44.83	.3956	.48	68.44	31.56	.3555
.14	55.57	44.43	.3951	.49	68.79	31.21	.3538
.15	55.96	44.04	.3945	.50	69.15	30.85	.3521
.16	56.36	43.64	.3939	.51	69.50	30.50	.3503
.17	56.75	43.25	.3932	.52	69.85	30.15	.3485
.18	57.14	42.86	.3925	.53	70.19	29.81	.3467
.19	57.53	42.47	.3918	.54	70.54	29.46	.3448
.20	57.93	42.07	.3910	.55	70.88	29.12	.3429
.21	58.32	41.68	.3902	.56	71.23	28.77	.3410
.22	58.71	41.29	.3894	.57	71.57	28.43	.3391
.23	59.10	40.90	.3885	.58	71.90	28.10	.3372
.24	59.48	40.52	.3876	.59	72.24	27.76	.3352
.25	59.87	40.13	.3867	.60	72.57	27.43	.3332
.26	60.26	39.74	.3857	.61	72.91	27.09	.3312
.27	60.64	39.36	.3847	.62	73.24	26.76	.3292
.28	61.03	38.97	.3836	.63	73.57	26.43	.3271
.29	61.41	38.59	.3825	.64	73.89	26.11	.3251
.30	61.79	38.21	.3814	.65	74.22	25.78	.3230
.31	62.17	37.83	.3802	.66	74.54	25.46	.3209
.32	62.55	37.45	.3790	.67	74.86	25.14	.3187
.33	62.93	37.07	.3778	.68	75.17	24.83	.3166
.34	63.31	36.69	.3765	.69	75.49	24.51	.3144

z Score	Percentile if z > 0	Percentile if z < 0	Ordinate	z Score	Percentile if z > 0	Percentile if z < 0	Ordinate
.70	75.80	24.20	.3123	1.15	87.49	12.51	.2059
.71	76.11	23.89	.3101	1.16	87.70	12.30	.2036
.72	76.42	23.58	.3079	1.17	87.90	12.10	.2012
.73	76.73	23.27	.3056	1.18	88.10	11.90	.1989
.74	77.03	22.97	.3034	1.19	88.30	11.70	.1965
.75	77.34	22.66	.3011	1.20	88.49	11.51	.1942
.76	77.64	22.36	.2989	1.21	88.69	11.31	.1919
.77	77.94	22.06	.2966	1.22	88.88	11.12	.1895
.78	78.23	21.77	.2943	1.23	89.07	10.93	.1872
.79	78.52	21.48	.2920	1.24	89.25	10.75	.1849
.80	78.81	21.19	.2897	1.25	89.44	10.56	.1826
.81	79.10	20.90	.2874	1.26	89.62	10.38	.1804
.82	79.39	20.61	.2850	1.27	89.80	10.20	.1781
.83	79.67	20.33	.2827	1.28	89.97	10.03	.1758
.84	79.95	20.05	.2803	1.29	90.15	9.85	.1736
.85	80.23	19.77	.2780	1.30	90.32	9.68	.1714
.86	80.51	19.49	.2756	1.31	90.49	9.51	.1691
.87	80.78	19.22	.2732	1.32	90.66	9.34	.1669
.88	81.06	18.94	.2709	1.33	90.82	9.18	.1647
.89	81.33	18.67	.2685	1.34	90.99	9.01	.1626
.90	81.59	18.41	.2661	1.35	91.15	8.85	.1604
.91	81.86	18.14	.2637	1.36	91.31	8.69	.1582
.92	82.12	17.88	.2613	1.37	91.47	8.53	.1561
.93	82.38	17.62	.2589	1.38	91.62	8.38	.1539
.94	82.64	17.36	.2565	1.39	91.77	8.23	.1518
.95	82.89	17.11	.2541	1.40	91.92	8.08	.1497
.96	83.15	16.85	.2516	1.41	92.07	7.93	.1476
.97	83.40	16.60	.2492	1.42	92.22	7.78	.1456
.98	83.65	16.35	.2468	1.43	92.36	7.64	.1435
.99	83.89	16.11	.2444	1.44	92.51	7.49	.1415
1.00	84.13	15.87	.2420	1.45	92.65	7.35	.1394
1.01	84.38	15.62	.2396	1.46	92.79	7.21	.1374
1.02	84.61	15.39	.2371	1.47	92.92	7.08	.1354
1.03	84.85	15.15	.2347	1.48	93.06	6.94	.1334
1.04	85.08	14.92	.2323	1.49	93.19	6.81	.1315
1.05	85.31	14.69	.2299	1.50	93.32	6.68	.1295
1.06	85.54	14.46	.2275	1.51	93.45	6.55	.1276
1.07	85.77	14.23	.2251	1.52	93.57	6.43	.1257
1.08	85.99	14.01	.2227	1.53	93.70	6.30	.1238
1.09	86.21	13.79	.2203	1.54	93.82	6.18	.1219
1.10	86.43	13.57	.2179	1.55	93.94	6.06	.1200
1.11	86.65	13.35	.2155	1.56	94.06	5.94	.1182
1.12	86.86	13.14	.2131	1.57	94.18	5.82	.1163
1.13	87.08	12.92	.2107	1.58	94.29	5.71	.1145
1.14	87.29	12.71	.2083	1.59	94.41	5.59	.1127

z Score	Percentile if z > 0	Percentile if z < 0	Ordinate	z Score	Percentile if z > 0	Percentile if z < 0	Ordinate
1.60	94.52	5.48	.1109	2.05	97.98	2.02	.0488
1.61	94.63	5.37	.1092	2.06	98.03	1.97	.0478
1.62	94.74	5.26	.1074	2.07	98.08	1.92	.0468
1.63	94.84	5.16	.1057	2.08	98.12	1.88	.0459
1.64	94.95	5.05	.1040	2.09	98.17	1.83	.0449
1.65	95.05	4.95	.1023	2.10	98.21	1.79	.0440
1.66	95.15	4.85	.1006	2.11	98.26	1.74	.0431
1.67	95.25	4.75	.0989	2.12	98.30	1.70	.0422
1.68	95.35	4.65	.0973	2.13	98.34	1.66	.0413
1.69	95.45	4.55	.0957	2.14	98.38	1.62	.0404
1.70	95.54	4.46	.0940	2.15	98.42	1.58	.0395
1.71	95.64	4.26	.0925	2.16	98.46	1.54	.0387
1.72	95.73	4.27	.0909	2.17	98.50	1.50	.0379
1.73	95.82	4.18	.0893	2.18	98.54	1.46	.0371
1.74	95.91	4.09	.0878	2.19	98.57	1.43	.0363
1.75	95.99	4.01	.0863	2.20	98.61	1.39	.0355
1.76	96.08	3.92	.0848	2.21	98.64	1.36	.0347
1.77	96.16	3.84	.0833	2.22	98.68	1.32	.0339
1.78	96.25	3.75	.0818	2.23	98.71	1.29	.0332
1.79	96.33	3.67	.0804	2.24	98.75	1.25	.0325
1.80	96.41	3.59	.0790	2.25	98.78	1.22	.0317
1.81	96.49	3.51	.0775	2.26	98.81	1.19	.0310
1.82	96.56	3.44	.0761	2.27	98.84	1.16	.0303
1.83	96.64	3.36	.0748	2.28	98.87	1.13	.0297
1.84	96.71	3.29	.0734	2.29	98.90	1.10	.0290
1.85	96.78	3.22	.0721	2.30	98.93	1.07	.0283
1.86	96.86	3.14	.0707	2.31	98.96	1.04	.0277
1.87	96.93	3.07	.0694	2.32	98.98	1.02	.0270
1.88	96.99	3.01	.0681	2.33	99.01	.99	.0264
1.89	97.06	2.94	.0669	2.34	99.04	.96	.0258
1.90	97.13	2.87	.0656	2.35	99.06	.94	.0252
1.91	97.19	2.81	.0644	2.36	99.09	.91	.0246
1.92	97.26	2.74	.0632	2.37	99.11	.81	.0241
1.93	97.32	2.68	.0620	2.38	99.13	.87	.0235
1.94	97.38	2.62	.0608	2.39	99.16	.84	.0229
1.95	97.44	2.56	.0596	2.40	99.18	.82	.0224
1.96	97.50	2.50	.0584	2.41	99.20	.80	.0219
1.97	97.56	2.44	.0573	2.42	99.22	.78	.0213
1.98	97.61	2.39	.0562	2.43	99.25	.75	.0208
1.99	97.67	2.33	.0551	2.44	99.27	.73	.0203
2.00	97.72	2.28	.0540	2.45	99.29	.71	.0198
2.01	97.78	2.22	.0529	2.46	99.31	.69	.0194
2.02	97.83	2.17	.0519	2.47	99.32	.68	.0189
2.03	97.88	2.12	.0508	2.48	99.34	.66	.0184
2.04	97.93	2.07	.0498	2.49	99.36	.64	.0180

z Score	Percentile if z > 0	Percentile if z < 0	Ordinate	z Score	Percentile if z > 0	Percentile if z < 0	Ordinate
2.50	99.38	.62	.0175	2.75	99.70	.30	.0091
2.51	99.40	.60	.0171	2.76	99.71	.29	.0088
2.52	99.41	.59	.0167	2.77	99.72	.28	.0086
2.53	99.43	.57	.0163	2.78	99.73	.27	.0084
2.54	99.45	.55	.0158	2.79	99.74	.26	.0081
2.55	99.46	.54	.0154	2.80	99.74	.26	.0079
2.56	99.48	.52	.0151	2.81	99.75	.25	.0077
2.57	99.49	.51	.0147	2.82	99.76	.24	.0075
2.58	99.51	.49	.0143	2.83	99.77	.23	.0073
2.59	99.52	.48	.0139	2.84	99.77	.23	.0071
2.60	99.53	.47	.0136	2.85	99.78	.22	.0069
2.61	99.55	.45	.0132	2.86	99.79	.21	.0067
2.62	99.56	.44	.0129	2.87	99.79	.21	.0065
2.63	99.57	.43	.0126	2.88	99.80	.20	.0063
2.64	99.59	.41	.0122	2.89	99.81	.19	.0061
2.65	99.60	.40	.0119	2.90	99.81	.19	.0060
2.66	99.61	.39	.0116	2.91	99.82	.18	.0058
2.67	99.62	.38	.0113	2.92	99.82	.18	.0056
2.68	99.63	.37	.0110	2.93	99.83	.17	.0055
2.69	99.64	.36	.0107	2.94	99.84	.16	.0053
2.70	99.65	.35	.0104	2.95	99.84	.16	.0051
2.71	99.66	.34	.0101	2.96	99.85	.15	.0050
2.72	99.67	.34	.0099	2.97	99.85	.15	.0048
2.73	99.68	.32	.0096	2.98	99.86	.14	.0047
2.74	99.69	.31	.0093	2.99	99.86	.14	.0046
				3.00	99.87	.13	.0044

Critical Values for the
Correlation Coefficient

This table presents the values that a correlation, based on a given number of pairs of observations (*n*), must exceed before it can be considered to reflect a meaningful relationship between two variables. These are the data on which Figure 8-1 is based and can be used to determine if a given correlation coefficient can be considered signficant at a given probability level ($p < .05$ and .01, considering the possiblities of an obtained correlation being either negative or positive—or what is called a *two-tailed test* in statistics).

Notice how the size of the critical correlation becomes smaller as *n* increases. By the time *n* gets greater than 100, it takes a very small correlation to consider it statistically significant. Because many of the data sets in the testing enterprise are based on large sample sizes (norm groups are usually in the thousands), this approach to assigning significance has limited applicability. Concepts such as prediction efficiency and utility (see Chapter 13) become important in these situations.

Number of Pairs of Observations on Which the Correlation Is Based	Critical Value for $p < .05$	Critical Value for $p < .01$	Number of Pairs of Observations on Which the Correlation Is Based	Critical Value for $p < .05$	Critical Value for $p < .01$
3	.997	1.000	16	.497	.623
4	.950	.990	17	.482	.606
5	.878	.959	18	.468	.590
6	.811	.917	19	.456	.575
7	.754	.874	20	.444	.561
8	.707	.834	21	.433	.549
9	.666	.798	22	.423	.537
10	.632	.765	23	.413	.526
11	.602	.735	24	.404	.515
12	.576	.708	25	.396	.505
13	.553	.684	26	.388	.496
14	.532	.661	27	.381	.487
15	.514	.641	28	.374	.479

Number of Pairs of Observations on Which the Correlation Is Based	Critical Value for $p < .05$	Critical Value for $p < .01$	Number of Pairs of Observations on Which the Correlation Is Based	Critical Value for $p < .05$	Critical Value for $p < .01$
29	.367	.471	100	.197	.256
30	.361	.463	125	.176	.230
40	.311	.402	150	.160	.210
50	.279	.361	200	.140	.182
60	.254	.330	400	.098	.129
70	.235	.306	1000	.062	.081
80	.212	.286	2000	.044	.058
			5000	.028	.036

Appendix C

Annotated List of Selected Psychological Tests

Introductory Thoughts

Every time I go to the library and look through a version of the *Mental Measurements Yearbook (MMY)*, I am almost overwhelmed by the amount of information and detail that is available on psychological tests—let alone by the sheer number of tests themselves. Almost every review of a specific test contains detailed descriptions of the various forms and scores available, referrals to previous reviews in the *MMY*, a host of references to the test, and, usually, a number of reviews written by independent experts in the field—a wealth of important information about the quality of the test. When you consider that other sources of information are available in addition to the *MMY* (see the Close Up in Chapter 11), it is clear that the domain of information about tests is massive.

The tests listed in this appendix are those that have received considerable discussion in the testing enterprise over the last several decades. This has been assessed by looking at various lists of tests and extracting the instruments that tend to appear in most of these compendia. Being included in this list does not, somehow, make the test better than some other—it has just been mentioned more frequently. To make decisions about "goodness," you must pay special attention to the *context* in which the test will be used. Hence, you will be referred to the most recent *MMY* review of the test to help you make this judgment.

Because of the size of the testing domain, decisions about which tests to include are clearly arbitrary and exclusionary. There is no way of being fair or inclusive here, else the appendix would become larger than the text! Thus the list does not even pretend to be complete; it is a (very) partial list selected to provide exemplars of some of the major types of tests that you will find in the testing enterprise. It is best viewed as a preliminary place to start looking at the details of other tests.

The review material that is referenced for this partial list is restricted to the *MMY*. This does not deny the existence of other important evaluative information (see the Close Up in Chapter 11), but it reflects an arbitrary decision to use only this material in the interests of efficiency. For all tests listed, the most recent *MMY* review is noted, and, if appropriate, other recent reviews (going only back as far as the eighth *MMY*, 1978) are also mentioned. In some cases, where older tests are involved, information about the listing in *Tests in Print, 2nd edition* (TiPII, 1974) has also been provided. Here it is possible to pick up a "reference trail" to discover evaluative information about these more senior members of the testing fraternity.

The annotations provided are gross descriptions of the tests. If you want more precision, check the cited *MMY* review. Again, there is some arbitrariness here because it is possible to describe and categorize these tests in a wide variety of ways. No effort has been made to put the tests into categories because this again forces classifications that are frequently more confusing than they are enlightening. The list is simply presented alphabetically by test name. To minimize confusion, test-name abbreviations (for example, MMPI, WISC) have not been used throughout this appendix.

Finally, the list of test publishers/distributors that appears at the end relates only to companies mentioned in the appendix. Again, this leaves out many firms. Complete lists are available in the *MMY*.

The following provides you with an indication of the information provided for each test included in this appendix:

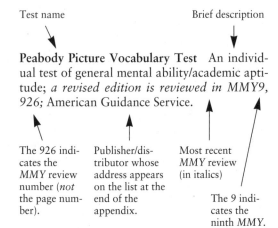

Test name   Brief description

Peabody Picture Vocabulary Test An individual test of general mental ability/academic aptitude; *a revised edition is reviewed in MMY9, 926*; American Guidance Service.

The 926 indicates the *MMY* review number (*not* the page number).

Publisher/distributor whose address appears on the list at the end of the appendix.

Most recent *MMY* review (in italics)

The 9 indicates the ninth *MMY*.

For your information, these are the publication dates of the review sources referenced in this appendix:

Source	Abbreviation Used in Test Entries	Date of Publication
Tests in Print II	*TiPII*	1974
MMY, 8th Edition	*MMY8*	1978
MMY, 9th Edition	*MMY9*	1985
MMY, 9th Supplement	*MMY9s*	1988
MMY, 10th Edition	*MMY10*	1989
MMY, 10th Supplement	*MMY10s*	1990
MMY, 11th Edition	*MMY11*	1992

Partial List of Tests

AAMD Adaptive Behavior Scale A whole series of versions are available for assessing a wide range of mental functioning at the individual level, with applications in the assessment of disabilities and educational risks; *revised edition reviewed in MMY9, 3*; American Association on Mental Deficiency.

ACT American College Testing Assessment A group test battery of general mental ability or development; *the overall battery reviewed in MMY8, 469*; American College Testing Program.

ACT Assessment: Academic Tests Program A whole series of tests dealing with proficiency in a wide range of academic subjects; *the abnormal psychology test reviewed in MMY10, 6; the statistics test reviewed in MMY10, 7*; American College Testing Program.

Adaptive Behavior Inventory An individual test of intelligence/adaptive behavior, with applications in the assessment of disabilities and educational risks in school-age children; *reviewed in MMY10, 9*; The Psychological Corporation.

Adjective Check List A self-report personality inventory for general use; *revised version reviewed in MMY9, 52*; Consulting Psychologists Press.

Advanced Placement Program Examinations A standardized test in a wide range of separate content areas; *a series of reviews of the various content-area tests in MMY8*; Educational Testing Service (for the College Board).

Armed Services Vocational Aptitude Battery A multiple aptitude battery; *reviewed in MMY8, 483; revised edition in MMY9, 81*; U.S. Military Entrance Processing Command.

Arthur Point Scale of Performance Tests An individual measure of intelligence/development, with some utility for the assessment of individual test of intelligence and adaptive behavior; *a basic description plus a listing of some reviews in TiPII*; The Psychological Corporation.

Balthazar Scales of Adaptive Behavior An individual measure of intelligence/development/adaptive behavior; *reviewed in MMY8, 500*; Consulting Psychologists Press.

Bayley Scales of Infant Development   An individual measure of development/adaptive behavior; *revised edition reviewed in MMY10, 26;* The Psychological Corporation.

Beck Depression Inventory   A self-report personality to address Aaron Beck's cognitive theory of depression; *revised version reviewed in MMY11, 31;* The Psychological Corporation.

Bem Sex-Role Inventory   A popular measure of values and attitudes; *reviewed in MMY9, 137;* Consulting Psychologists Press.

Bender Visual-Motor Gestalt Test   A test of perceptual function that has been generalized to other uses such as a performance measure of personality and a measure of neurological status; *various applications of this test reviewed in MMY9, 139, and MMY10, 40;* American Orthopsychiatric Association.

Bennett Mechanical Comprehension Test   A mechanical aptitude test; *revised edition reviewed in MMY10s, 10, and MMY11, 41;* The Psychological Corporation.

Benton Revised Visual Retention Test   A neuropsychological function; *revision reviewed in MMY9, 140;* The Psychological Corporation.

Blind Learning Aptitude Test   An individual test of intelligence/adaptive behavior especially designed for the visually handicapped; *reviewed in MMY8, 320;* University of Illinois Press.

Boehm Test of Basic Concepts   A test for early childhood education; *reviewed in MMY10, 32, and MMY11, 46;* The Psychological Corporation.

Bruininks–Oseretsky Test of Motor Proficiency   An individual test of intelligence and adaptive behavior; *reviewed in MMY9, 174;* American Guidance Service.

California Achievement Tests   An achievement-test battery with a number of specific content specializations; *reviewed in MMY10, 41; Writing Style subtest reviewed in MMY11, 51;* CTB/McGraw-Hill.

California Psychological Inventory   A self-report personality inventory for general use; *revised edition reviewed in MMY9, 182, and MMY11, 45;* Consulting Psychologists Press.

Career Assessment Inventory   A measure of career-related interests; *revision reviewed in MMY10, 43;* National Computer Systems.

Children's Apperception Test   A projective personality test; *revised edition reviewed in MMY9, 219;* C.P.S.

Christensen–Guilford Fluency Tests   Tests of creativity and reasoning for use in early childhood education; *reviewed in MMY8, 237;* Sheridan Psychological Services.

Clerical Abilities Battery   A clerical test; *reviewed in MMY11, 71;* The Psychological Corporation.

Cognitive Abilities Test   A group test of general mental ability/academic aptitude; *Form 4 reviewed in MMY10, 66;* Riverside Publishing.

Columbia Mental Maturity Scale   An individual test of intelligence/adaptive behavior; *reviewed in MMY8, 210;* The Psychological Corporation.

Comprehensive Tests of Basic Skills   A general-achievement battery; *revised edition reviewed in MMY11, 81;* CTB/McGraw-Hill.

Computer Programmer Aptitude Battery   A test of specialized abilities in computer-related activities; *reviewed in MMY11, 85;* Science Research Associates.

Comrey Personality Scales   A self-report personality inventory for general use; *reviewed in MMY9, 261;* Educational and Industrial Testing Service.

Connors Rating Scales   A system for rating behaviors associated with disorders such as ADHD; *reviewed in MMY11, 87;* Multi-Health Systems.

Crawford Small Parts Dexterity Test   A psychomotor performance test; *listed as entry 2223 in TiPII where it is also possible to locate some reviews;* The Psychological Corporation.

Culture Fair Intelligence Test   A group measure of intelligence/academic aptitude; *reviewed in MMY9, 290;* Institute of Personality and Ability Testing.

Diagnosis—An Instructional Aid   A set of diagnostic and prognostic tests including areas such as mathematics and reading; *revision reviewed in MMY9, 332;* Science Research Associates.

Differential Aptitude Tests   A multiple aptitude battery, with a computerized adaptive version, that evolved from the Primary Mental Abilities;

Forms V and W reviewed in MMY9, 352; The Psychological Corporation.

Edwards Personal Preference Schedule   A self-report personality inventory for general use; *reviewed in MMY9, 382;* The Psychological Corporation.

Embedded Figures Test   A group measure of the cognitive style of field dependence/independence that also correlates with elements of personality. There are preschool, children's, and adult versions; *reviewed in MMY9, 382;* Consulting Psychologists Press.

Eysenck Personality Questionnaire   A self-report personality inventory for general use that also has a children's version; *reviewed in MMY9, 406;* Educational and Industrial Testing Service.

Flanagan Aptitude Classification Tests   A multiple aptitude battery; *listed as entry 1072 in TiPII where some references to reviews can be found;* Science Research Associates.

General Aptitude Test Battery   A multiple aptitude battery that grew out of the Primary Mental Abilities; *reviewed in MMY9, 1304;* U.S. Employment Service.

General Clerical Test   A clerical test; *reviewed in MMY8, 1033;* The Psychological Corporation.

Goodenough–Harris Drawing Test   An individual test of intelligence/academic aptitude/adaptive behavior; *reviewed in MMY9, 441;* The Psychological Corporation.

Gordon Personal Inventory   A self-report personality inventory for general use; *reviewed in MMY9, 444, and MMY10, 128;* The Psychological Corporation.

Graduate Record Examinations   A set of tests for facilitating selection decisions to graduate school; *reviewed in MMY9, 448;* Educational Testing Service (for the GRE Board).

Guilford–Zimmerman Temperament Survey   A self-report personality inventory for general use; *reviewed in MMY9, 460;* Sheridan Psychological Services.

Halstead–Reitan Neuropsychological Test Battery   A wide-ranging battery of tests for assessment of neurological function, disabilities, and educational risks; *general review in*

MMY6, 469, and the Category Test reviewed in MMY10s, 77, and MMY11, 361; Reitan Neuropsychology Laboratories.

Hand–Tool Dexterity Test   A psychomotor performance test; *listed as entry 2225 in TiPII where it is possible to find additional references;* The Psychological Corporation.

Henmon–Nelson Tests of Mental Ability   A group-derived measure of intelligence/academic aptitude; *reviewed in MMY8, 190;* Riverside Publishing.

Hiskey–Nebraska Test of Learning Aptitude   An individual test of intelligence and adaptive behavior; *reviewed in MMY8, 217;* Marshal S. Hiskey.

Holtzman Inkblot Technique   A particular scoring and interpretive approach to projective test of personality; *revised system reviewed in MMY9, 480;* The Psychological Corporation.

Iowa Tests of Basic Skills   A series of batteries of tests for the measurement of academic achievement at a number of different levels; *revision reviewed in MMY11, 184;* Riverside Publishing.

Jackson Personality Inventory   A self-report personality inventory for general use; *reviewed in MMY8, 593;* Research Psychologists Press.

Jackson Vocational Interest Survey   An interest inventory; *reviewed in MMY9, 542, and MMY10, 158;* Research Psychologists Press.

Jenkins Activity Survey   A self-report test of relevance to environmental and health psychology; *reviewed in MMY9, 545;* The Psychological Corporation.

Kaufman Assessment Battery for Children   An individual measure of general intelligence/developmental/adaptive behavior; *reviewed in MMY9, 562;* American Guidance Service.

Kaufman Test of Educational Achievement   An individual achievement test with applications in the assessment of disability and educational risk; *reviewed in MMY10, 161;* American Guidance Service.

Kuder General Interest Survey   An interest inventory; *reviewed in MMY8, 1009;* Science Research Associates.

Kuder Occupational Interest Survey An interest inventory; *revised version reviewed in MMY10, 167;* Science Research Associates.

Kuder Preference Record An interest inventory; *reviewed in MMY8, 1011;* Science Research Associates.

Kuhlmann–Anderson Tests of Mental Ability A group measure of intelligence/academic aptitude; *eighth edition reviewed in MMY9, 579;* Scholastic Testing Service.

Law School Admission Test A group test of general mental ability/academic aptitude as related to potential candidacy for law school; *revision reviewed in MMY9, 594;* Law School Admission Council.

Leiter International Performance Scale An individual test of intelligence and adaptive behavior; *listed as item 505 in TiPII where further references can be found;* Stoelting.

Luria–Nebraska Neuropsychological Battery An assessment of neurological function, with application to the determination of disabilities and educational risks; *initial version reviewed in MMY9, 637, with a revised edition reviewed in MMY11, 212; Screening Test reviewed in MMY11, 348, and children's version reviewed in MMY11, 211;* Western Psychological Services.

McCarthy Scale of Children's Abilities An individual measure of intelligence/developmental/adaptive behavior; *reviewed in MMY9, 671;* The Psychological Corporation.

Metropolitan Achievement Tests A series of group tests that include measures of general achievement as well as diagnostic batteries in domains such as language, mathematics, and reading; *eighth edition reviewed in MMY10, 200;* The Psychological Corporation.

Metropolitan Readiness Tests Group tests of general mental ability or development, with applications in early childhood education; *1976 edition reviewed in MMY9, 700;* The Psychological Corporation.

Miller Analogies Test A group test of intelligence/academic aptitude; *reviewed in MMY8, 192;* The Psychological Corporation.

Millon Adolescent Personality Inventory A self-report personality inventory, with primary application in clinical assessment; *reviewed in MMY9, 707;* National Computer Systems.

Millon Clinical Multiaxial Inventory A self-report personality inventory primarily for clinical applications such as screening; *initial version reviewed in MMY9, 709, and the revision (MCMI II) reviewed in MMY11, 239;* National Computer Services.

Minnesota Clerical Test A clerical test; *revised edition reviewed in MMY9, 731;* The Psychological Corporation.

Minnesota Multiphasic Personality Inventory A self-report personality inventory primarily for clinical applications; *original test reviewed in MMY9, 715, and revision (MMPI-2) reviewed in MMY11, 244;* National Computer Systems (for University of Minnesota Press).

Multidimensional Aptitude Battery A group test of general mental ability/academic aptitude; *revised edition reviewed in MMY10, 202;* Research Psychologists Press.

Myers–Briggs Type Indicator A popular self-report personality inventory for use with the general population; *reviewed in MMY10, 206;* Consulting Psychologists Press.

Nelson Reading Skills Test A diagnostic and prognostic test of reading abilities; *Forms 3 and 4 reviewed in MMY9, 747;* Riverside Publishing.

NEO Personality Inventory A measure of the Big Five dimensions thought to underlie the domain of personality; *reviewed in MMY10, 214, and MMY11, 258;* Psychological Assessment Resources.

Objective-Analytic Test Batteries A performance test of personality; *reviewed in MMY9, 848;* Institute for Personality and Ability Testing.

Otis–Lennon School Ability Test A group measure of intelligence/academic aptitude; *sixth edition reviewed in MMY11, 274;* The Psychological Corporation.

Peabody Individual Achievement Test An individual achievement test; *recent revision reviewed in MMY11, 280;* American Guidance Service.

Peabody Picture Vocabulary Test An individual test of general mental ability/development/

academic aptitude; *revised edition reviewed in MMY9, 926;* American Guidance Service.

Personality Inventory for Children   A rating scale/inventory for obtaining evaluations of children's personality; *original reviewed in MMY9, 949, and version with revised format reviewed in MMY10, 281;* Western Psychological Services.

Personality Research Form   A self-report personality inventory for general use; *reviewed in MMY9, 950, and 3rd edition reviewed in MMY10, 282;* Research Psychologists Press.

Planning Career Goals   A series of tests addressing abilities and career counseling; *reviewed in MMY8, 1019;* CTB/McGraw-Hill.

Porch Index of Communicative Abilities in Children   An assessment of learning disabilities, handicaps, and educational risks; *revision reviewed in MMY9, 964;* Consulting Psychologists Press.

Porteus Maze Test   An individual test of general mental ability or development, with some neuropsychological applications; *reviewed in MMY9, 965;* The Psychological Corporation.

Psychological Screening Inventory   A self-report personality inventory primarily for clinical applications; *reviewed in MMY9, 1015;* Research Psychologists Press.

Purdue Pegboard   A psychomotor/dexterity test; *listed as entry 2234 in TiPII where some other references can be found;* Science Research Associates.

Raven Progressive Matrices   A group test of intelligence/general mental ability/academic aptitude; *Advanced set reviewed in MMY8, 200;* The Psychological Corporation (for H. K. Lewis and Co.).

Reading Yardsticks   An achievement test in specific school-related domain, with diagnostic and prognostic applications; *reviewed in MMY9, 1039;* Riverside Publishing.

Revised Minnesota Paper Form Board Test   A group mechanical aptitude test; *reviewed in MMY9; 1045;* The Psychological Corporation.

Rorschach Psychodiagnostic Test   A projective personality test; *reviewed in MMY9, 1059;* Grune & Stratton.

Rosenzweig Picture-Frustration Study   A projective personality test; *reviewed in MMY9, 1060;* Saul Rosenzweig.

Rotter Incomplete Sentences Blank   A projective personality test; *reviewed in MMY8, 663;* The Psychological Corporation.

Schaie–Thurstone Adult Mental Abilities Test   A newly designed multiple aptitude test battery designed as an extension of the Primary Mental Abilities; *reviewed in MMY9s, 67, and MMY10, 322;* Consulting Psychologists Press.

Scholastic Aptitude Test   A group test of general mental ability/academic aptitude, with applications in selection to university undergraduate programs; *revision reviewed in MMY9, 244;* Educational Testing Service (for the College Board).

School and College Ability Tests   A group test of intelligence test/academic aptitude; *Series III reviewed in MMY9, 1075;* Educational Testing Service.

Self-Directed Search   An interest inventory; *1985 revision reviewed in MMY10, 330;* Psychological Assessment Resources.

Senior Apperception Technique   A projective personality test; *reviewed in MMY8; 676;* C.P.S.

Sequential Tests of Educational Progress   A group general-achievement test battery, with versions for many specific subject areas; *in MMY9, reviews of the following tests: Algebra/Geometry (1111), Biology (1112), Chemistry (1113), and Physics (1114), and a general review of Series III in 1115;* CTB/McGraw-Hill.

Sixteen Personality Factor Questionnaire   A self-report personality inventory for general use and also includes a children's version; *reviewed in MMY9, 1136;* Institute for Personality and Ability Testing.

Social Climate Scales   A rating measure for obtaining evaluations of various types of environments; *second edition reviewed in MMY10, 132;* Consulting Psychologists Press.

SRA Achievement Series   A group general-achievement battery; *reviewed in MMY9, 376, along with an evaluation of a revised edition in MMY11, 376;* Science Research Associates.

Stanford–Binet Intelligence Scale An individual test of general mental ability/academic aptitude/adaptive behavior; *fourth edition reviewed in MMY10, 342;* Riverside Publishing.

Stanford Test of Academic Skills A group general-achievement battery; *revised edition reviewed in MMY9, 1182;* The Psychological Corporation.

State-Trait Anxiety Inventory A self-report personality inventory for general use and also includes a children's version; *reviewed in MMY9, 1186;* Consulting Psychologists Press.

Stromberg Dexterity Test A psychomotor/dexterity test; *listed as item 2235 in TiPII where you can locate further references;* The Psychological Corporation.

Strong–Campbell Interest Inventory form of the **Strong Vocational Interest Blank** An interest inventory; *reviewed in MMY9, 1195;* Consulting Psychologists Press (for Stanford University Press).

Study of Values A self-report measure of values for general use; *third edition reviewed in MMY9, 1205;* Riverside Publishing.

Survey of Interpersonal Values A self-report measure of values; *revised edition reviewed in MMY10, 354;* Science Research Associates.

Tests of Achievement and Proficiency A group general-achievement battery; *reviewed in MMY9, 1287;* Riverside Publishing.

Thematic Apperception Test A projective personality test; *reviewed in MMY9, 1827;* Harvard University Press.

T.M.R. School Competency Scales An individual test of intelligence and adaptive behavior; *reviewed in MMY9, 1224;* Consulting Psychologists Press.

Torrance Tests of Creative Thinking Measures of specialized abilities associated with creativity and reasoning; *reviewed in MMY9, 1296;* Scholastic Testing Service.

Vineland Adaptive Behavior Scales An individual test of intelligence and adaptive behavior for use in the assessment of disabilities and educational risks; *revised edition reviewed in MMY10, 381;* American Guidance Service.

Washington University Sentence Completion Test A projective personality measure; *reviewed in MMY8, 708;* Jossey-Bass.

Wechsler Adult Intelligence Scale An individual test of general mental ability/academic aptitude; *revision is reviewed in MMY9, 1348;* The Psychological Corporation.

Wechsler Intelligence Scale for Children An individual test of general mental ability/academic aptitude/adaptive behavior; *revision reviewed in MMY8, 232, and some computerized interpretation systems reviewed in MMY11, 463 and 464; MMY had not reviewed WISC III by its 11th edition;* The Psychological Corporation.

Wechsler Memory Scale A generalized measure of memory, with utility in the assessment of neuropsychological function; *original test reviewed in MMY9, 1355, and revised edition reviewed in MMY11, 465;* The Psychological Corporation

Wechsler Preschool and Primary Scale of Intelligence An individual test of general mental ability/development/adaptive behavior; *revision reviewed in MMY11, 466;* The Psychological Corporation.

Wide Range Achievement Test An individual achievement test; *revised edition is reviewed in MMY10, 389;* Jastak Associates.

Wisconsin Card Sorting Test A neuropsychological test; *reviewed in MMY9, 1372;* Psychological Assessment Resources.

Woodcock–Johnson Psycho-Educational Battery An individual achievement-test battery, with applications to the assessment of disabilities and educational risks; *reviewed in MMY10, 321;* DLM Teaching Resources.

Word Processing Test A computer-related aptitude test; *reviewed in MMY10, 392;* The Psychological Corporation.

Addresses of Publishers/Distributors of the Tests

American Association on Mental Deficiency, 5201 Connecticut Avenue, N.W.,Washington, DC 20015

American College Testing Program, P.O. Box 168, Iowa City, IA 52243

American Guidance Service, Publishers' Building, Circle Pines, MN 55014

American Orthopsychiatric Association, Inc., 49 Sheridan Avenue, Albany, NY 12210

Consulting Psychologists Press, Inc., 577 College Avenue, Palo Alto, CA 94306

C.P.S., Inc., P.O. Box 83, Larchmont, NY 10538

CTB/McGraw-Hill, Del Monte Research Park, Monterey, CA 93940

DLM Teaching Resources, One DLM Park, P.O. Box 4000, Allen, TX 75002

Educational and Industrial Testing Service (EdITS), P.O. Box 7234, San Diego, CA 92107

Educational Testing Service, Princeton, NJ 08541

Grune & Stratton, Inc., 6277 Sea Harbor Drive, Orlando, FL 32887

Harvard University Press, 79 Garden Street, Cambridge, MA 02138

Hiskey, Marshal S., 5640 Baldwin, Lincoln, NE 68507

Institute of Personality and Ability Testing, Inc. (IPAT), P.O. Box 188, Champaign, IL 61820

Jastak Associates, Inc., 1526 Gilpin Avenue, Wilmington, DE 19806

Jossey-Bass, Inc., 615 Montgomery Street, San Francisco, CA 94111

Law School Admission Council, Suite 150, 11 Dupont Circle, N.W., Washington, DC 20036

Multi-Health Systems, Inc., 908 Niagara Falls Boulevard, North Tonawanda, NY 14120–2060

National Computer Systems (NCS), P.O. Box 1416, Minneapolis, MN 55440

Psychological Assessment Resources, Inc. (PAR), P.O. Box 998, Odessa, FL 33556

The Psychological Corporation, 555 Academic Court, San Antonio, TX 78204

Reitan Neuropsychology Laboratories, 1338 East Edison Street, Tucson, AZ 85719

Research Psychologists Press, Inc., Box 984, 1110 Military Street, Port Huron, MI 48061–0984

Riverside Publishing Co., 8420 Bryn Mawr Avenue, Chicago, IL 60631

Rosenzweig, Saul, 8029 Washington Avenue, St. Louis, MO 63114

Scholastic Testing Service, Inc., 480 Meyer Road, P.O. Box 1056, Bensenville, IL 60106

Science Research Associates, Inc., 155 North Wacker Drive, Chicago, IL 60606

Sheridan Psychological Services, Inc., P.O. Box 6101, Orange, CA 92667

Stoelting Co., 1350 South Kostner Avenue, Chicago, IL 60623

University of Illinois Press, Box 5081, Station A, Champaign, IL 61820

U.S. Employment Service, Division of Program Planning and Operations, Employment and Training Administration, U.S. Department of Labor, 601 D Street, N.W., Washington, DC 20213

U.S. Military Entrance Processing Command, Testing Directorate, 2500 Green Bay Road, North Chicago, IL 60064

Western Psychological Services, 12031 Wilshire Boulevard, Los Angeles, CA 90025

Appendix D

The 1985 APA *Standards for Educational and Psychological Testing*

The original 1954 APA *Technical Recommendations*, which were discussed in Chapters 12 and 13, have been revised four times since their introduction. These revisions, which occurred under the auspices of several different organizations, appeared in 1955, 1966, 1977, and 1985. The latest version has been adopted not only by the American Psychological Association but also by the American Educational Research Association and the National Council on Measurement in Education.

The earlier categorization of the standards as essential, highly desirable, and desirable was replaced, in 1985, by primary, secondary, and conditional. *Primary standards* are "those that should be met by all tests before their operational use" (APA, 1985, p. 2). *Secondary standards* are seen as desirable "but are likely to be beyond reasonable expectation in many situations" (APA, 1985, p. 3). *Conditional standards* are those that apply to specific contexts of test use.

Part I: Technical Standards for Test Construction and Evaluation

The first section of the 1985 *Standards* includes most of the information presented in the earlier

versions. These are offered in separate sections dealing with

Validity (25 standards, of which 17 are primary)

Reliability and errors of measurement (12 standards, of which 8 are primary)

Test development and revision (25 standards, of which 12 are primary)

Scaling, norming, score comparability, and equating (9 standards, of which 4 are primary)

Test publication: technical manuals and user's guides (11 standards, of which 7 are primary)

Clear discussions of the various important terms are presented at the beginning of each section (for example, definitions of the major types of validity in Section 1), followed by standards that clearly reveal contemporary measurement wisdom. Many of the standards are followed by a short comment. Here are several examples:

Standard 1.1 Evidence of validity should be presented for the major types of inferences for which the test is recommended. A rationale should be presented to support the particular mix of evidence presented for its intended uses. *(Primary)*

Comment: Whether one or more kinds of validity evidence are appropriate is a function of the particular question being asked and of the context and extent of previous evidence.

Standard 1.12 All criterion measures should be described accurately, and the rationale for choosing them should be made explicit. *(Primary)*

Comment: In the case of interest measures, for example, it is sometimes unclear whether the criterion indicates satisfaction, success, or continuance in the activity under examination. When appropriate, attention should be drawn to significant aspects of performance that the criterion measure does not reflect.

Standard 2.7 Procedures known to yield inflated estimates of reliability for speeded tests should not be used to estimate the reliability of a highly speeded test. *(Primary)*

Comment: For example, split-half coefficients that are obtained from scoring odd and even numbered test items separately yield an inflated estimate for a highly speeded test and are thus inappropriate.

Like the 1954 *Standards*, Part I of the 1985 version provides a wonderful summary of the current thinking regarding the quality of tests. It is a pithy précis of the current technology.

Part II: Professional Standards for Test Use

The second section of the 1985 *Standards*, which contains recommendations not included in the 1954 version, deals with issues of actual test use. Here we find a series of recommendations relating to specific applications of testing. This section of the document begins with a set of recommendations regarding the "General Principles of Test Use." Many of these can be seen as stemming directly from the issues and debates chronicled in Chapters 14 and 20. The standards classified as primary for this section are the following:

Standard 6.1 Test users should evaluate the available written documentation on the validity and reliability of tests for the specific use intended.

Standard 6.2 When a test user makes a substantial change in test format, mode of administration, instructions, language, or content, the user should revalidate the use of the test for the changed conditions or have a rationale supporting the claim that additional validation is not necessary or possible.

Standard 6.3 When a test is to be used for a purpose for which it has not been previously validated, or for which there is no supported claim for validity, the user is responsible for providing evidence of validity.

Standard 6.4 Test users should accurately portray the relevance of a test to the assessment and decision-making process and should not use a test score to justify an evaluation, recommendation, or decision that has been made largely on some other basis.

Standard 6.5 Test users should be alert to probable unintended consequences of test use and should attempt to avoid actions that have unintended negative consequences.

Standard 6.6 Responsibility for test use should be assumed by or delegated only to those individuals who have the training and experience necessary to handle this responsibility in a professional and technically adequate manner. Any special qualifications for test administration or interpretation noted in the manual should be met.

Standard 6.8 When test results are released to the news media, those responsible for releasing the results should provide information to help minimize the possibility of misinterpretation of the test results.

Standard 6.9 When a specific cut score is used to select, classify, or certify test takers, the method and rationale for setting that cut score, including any technical analyses, should be presented in a manual or report. When cut scores are based primarily on professional judgment, the qualifications of the judges should also be documented.

Standard 6.10 In educational, clinical, and counseling applications, test administrators and users should not attempt to evaluate test takers whose special characteristics—ages, handicapping conditions, or linguistic, generational, or cultural backgrounds—are outside the range of their academic training or supervised experience. A test user faced with a request to evaluate a test taker whose special characteristics are not within his or her range of professional experience should seek consultation regarding test selection, necessary modifications of testing procedures, and score interpretation from a professional who has had relevant experience.

Standard 6.12 In school, clinical, and counseling applications, tests developed for screening should be used only for identifying test takers who may need further evaluation. The results of such tests should not be used to characterize a person or to make any decision about a person, other than the decision for referral for further evaluation, unless adequate reliability and validity for these other uses can be demonstrated.

Standard 6.13 Test users should not use interpretations of test results, including computer-interpreted test results, unless they have a manual for that test that includes information on the validities of the interpretations for the intended applications and on the samples on which they were based.

These standards clearly relate to the manner in which tests have been inserted into decision-making contexts. The "General Principles of Test Use" are then followed by a series of application-specific standards under the following topics:

Clinical testing (6 standards, of which 5 are primary)

Educational testing and psychological testing in schools (12 standards, of which 10 are primary)

Test use in counseling (9 standards, of which 8 are primary)

Employment testing (9 standards, of which 5 are primary)

Professional and occupational licensure and certification (5 standards, of which 4 are primary)

Program evaluation (8 standards, of which 6 are primary)

These situational standards represent major additions to the 1954 *Standards* and reflect a concern with the proper and ethical use of tests in real decision-making contexts.

Part III: Standards for Particular Applications

The third section of the 1985 *Standards* contains recommendations for dealing with two important test situations:

Testing linguistic minorities (7 standards, all of which are considered to be primary)

Testing people who have handicapping conditions (8 standards, 4 of which are primary)

These recommendations converge on the general cautious, compassionate, and conservative attitude necessary when using and interpreting test scores gathered in these two situations.

Part IV: Standards for Administrative Practice

The final section of the 1985 *Standards* includes some information from the 1954 *Standards* (for example, recommendations about test administration, scoring, and reporting) and some that is clearly a result of post-1954 revisions to the ethical code as they apply to testing:

Recommendations about test administration, scoring, and reporting (11 standards, of which 9 are primary)

Protecting the rights of test takers (10 standards, of which 9 are primary)

Following the argumentation presented in Chapter 14, test-taker rights are enshrined in standards demanding:

16.1   Informed consent

16.2   Provision of explanations of results and recommendations

16.3   Permission to release results to a third party

16.5   Confidentiality

16.6   The use of least stigmatizing labels

16.7   Cancelation of test results if testing irregularities are evident

16.8 and 16.9   The need for speedy resolution and communication among all parties

in the event of conflicts regarding test scores

16.10   The need to consider all possible sources of information in the event of testing irregularities

If you find yourself in a situation in which any of these rights are not being considered, you have a prefect right to cry "foul" and protest involvement in the exercise.

Clearly, the 1985 *Standards* have evolved from the 1954 version, especially Part I. However, the newer edition shows considerable increase in the concern shown for specific testing contexts (Parts II and III) as well as enhanced awareness of test-taker rights (Part IV). The origins of these new directions can be seen in Chapter 14. It will be interesting to see what gets added to the next revision of the *Standards* because these guidelines appear to function as a barometer of the controversies and debates that the testing enterprise is confronting at a specific time.

References

Abelson, A. R. (1911). The measurement of mental ability of "backward" children. *British Journal of Psychology, 4,* 268–314.

Adler, T. (1990, April). Does the "new" MMPI beat the "classic"? *APA Monitor.*

Aiken, L. R. (1988). *Psychological testing and assessment* (6th ed.). Boston: Allyn and Bacon.

Aiken, L. R. (1989). *Assessment of personality.* Needham Heights: Allyn and Bacon.

Albee, G. W. (1963). American psychology in the sixties. *American Psychologist, 18,* 90–95.

Albright, L. E., Glennon, J. R., & Smith, W. J. (1963). *The use of psychological tests in industry.* Cleveland: Howard Allen.

Alexander, C. (1965). *Personality tests: How to beat them.* New York: Arco.

Allen, M. J., & Yen, W. M. (1979). *Introduction to measurement theory.* Monterey, Calif.: Brooks/Cole.

Allport, G. W. (1937). *Personality: A psychological interpretation.* New York: Holt.

Allport, G. W., & Odbert, H. S. (1936). Trait-names: A psycho-lexical study. *Psychological Monographs, 47* (Whole No. 211).

American Psychiatric Association (1987). *Diagnostic and statistical manual of mental disorders* (3rd ed., rev.) Washington, D.C.: American Psychiatric Association.

Amrine, M. (1964). Psychology in the news. *American Psychologist, 19,* 216–218.

Amrine, M. (Ed.). (1965). The 1965 congressional inquiry into testing. *American Psychologist, 20,* 859–991.

Amrine, M. (1966). "Camelot" and psychological tests: An introductory note. *American Psychologist, 21,* 401–402.

Anastasi, A. (1967). Psychology, psychologists, and psychological testing. *American Psychologist, 22,* 297–306.

Anastasi, A. (1981). Coaching, test sophistication, and developed abilities. *American Psychologist, 36,* 1086–1093.

Anastasi, A. (1988). *Psychological testing* (6th ed.). New York: Macmillan.

Anastasi, A., & Drake, J. (1954). An empirical comparison of certain techniques for estimating the reliability of speeded tests. *Educational and Psychological Measurement, 14,* 529–540.

Anderson, D. R., Sweeney, D. J., & Williams, T. A. (1991). *Introduction to statistics: Concepts and applications* (2nd ed.). New York: West.

Anderson, R. J. (1970). Stability of student interests in general psychology. *American Psychologist, 25,* 630–632.

Andrews, T. G., & Dreese, M. (1948). Military utilization of psychologists during World War II. *American Psychologist, 3,* 533–538.

Angoff, W. H. (1971). Scales, norms, and equivalent scores. In R. L. Thorndike (Ed.), *Educational measurement* (2nd ed.). Washington, D.C.: American Council on Education.

Angoff, W. H. (1982). Use of difficulty and discrimination indices for detecting item bias. In R. A. Berk (Ed.), *Handbook of methods for detecting test bias.* Baltimore: Johns Hopkins University Press.

APA. (1947). Recommended graduate training in clinical psychology. *American Psychologist, 2,* 539–558 (Committee on Training in Clinical Psychology).

APA. (1949a). Developing a code of ethics for psychologists: A first report of progress. *American Psychologist, 4,* 17–20 (Committee on Ethical Standards for Psychology).

APA. (1949b). Ethical standards for the distribution of psychological tests and diagnostic aids. *American Psychologist, 4,* 495–501 (Subcommittee on Test Distribution: Committee on Ethical Standards for Psychology).

APA. (1950). Ethical standards for the distribution of psychological tests and diagnostic aids. *American Psychologist, 5,* 620–626 (Committee on Ethical Standards for Psychology).

APA. (1951) Ethical standards in clinical and consulting relationships. *American Psychologist, 6,* 57–64, 145–146, 427–452 (Committee on Ethical Standards for Psychology).

APA. (1952a). Psychology and its relationships with other professions. *American Psychologist, 7,* 145–152 (Ad Hoc Committee on Relations Between Psychology and the Medical Profession).

APA. (1952b). Technical recommendations for psychological tests and diagnostic techniques: Preliminary proposal. *American Psychologist, 7,* 461–475 (Committee on Test Standards).

APA. (1952c). The case for and against malpractice insurance for psychologists. *American Psychologist, 7,* 677–683 (Committee on Malpractice Insurance).

APA. (1953). *Ethical standards of psychologists.* Washington, D.C.: American Psychological Association.

APA. (1954a). Cases and inquiries before the Committee on Scientific and Professional Ethics and Conduct. *American Psychologist, 9,* 806–807 (Committee on Scientific and Professional Ethics and Conduct).

APA. (1954b). Technical recommendations for psychological tests and diagnostic techniques. *Psychological Bulletin, 51,* 201–238 (Committee on Test Standards).

APA. (1955). Professional liability insurance for psychologists. *American Psychologist, 10,* 243–244 (Committee on Professional Liability Insurance).

APA. (1963). Ethical standards of psychologists. *American Psychologist, 18,* 56–60.

APA. (1985). *Standards for educational and psychological testing.* Washington, D.C.: American Psychological Association.

APA. (1986). *Guidelines for computer-based tests and interpretations.* Washington, D.C.: American Psychological Association (Committee on Professional Standards).

APA. (1992). Ethical principles of psychologists and code of conduct. *American Psychologist, 47,* 1597–1611; Rules and procedures. *American Psychologist, 47,* 1612–1928.

Appleman, J. A. (1953). Professional liability of psychologists. *American Psychologist, 8,* 686–690.

Armstrong, C. P. (1947). On defining psychology as a profession. *American Psychologist, 2,* 446–448.

Ash, P. (1966). The implications of the Civil Rights Act of 1964 for psychological assessment in industry. *American Psychologist, 21,* 797–803.

Atkinson, J. W. (Ed.). (1958). *Motives in fantasy, action, and society.* New York: Van Nostrand.

Austin, J. J. (1970). *Educational and developmental profile.* Muskegon, Mich.: Research Concepts.

Bailey, K. D. (1988). The conceptualization of validity: Current perspectives. *Social Science Research, 17,* 117–136.

Baker, F. B. (1977). Advances in item analysis. *Review of Educational Research, 47,* 151–178.

Ball, R. S. (1938). The predictability of occupational level from intelligence. *Journal of Consulting Psychology, 2,* 184–186.

Bandura, A. (1969). *Principles of behavior modification.* New York: Holt, Rinehart, & Winston.

Baron, J. (1982). Personality and intelligence. In R. J. Sternberg (Ed.), *Handbook of human intelligence.* New York: Cambridge University Press.

Barrios, B. A. (1988). On the changing nature of behavioral assessment. In A. S. Bellack & M. Hersen (Eds.), *Behavioral assessment: A practical handbook* (3rd ed.). New York: Pergamon Press.

Barth, A., & Macciocchi, B. (1985). The Halstead–Reitan Neuropsychological Test Battery. In C. S. Newmark (Ed.), *Major psychological assessment instruments.* Boston: Allyn and Bacon.

Baumeister, R. F. (1987). How the self became a problem: A psychological review of historical research. *Journal of Personality and Social Psychology, 52,* 163–176.

Bechtoldt, H. P. (1959). Construct validity: A critique. *American Psychologist, 14,* 619–629.

Beck, S. J. (1950). *Rorschach's test, Vol.1. Basic processes.* New York: Grune & Stratton.

Bell, F. O., Hoff, A. L., & Hoyt, K. B. (1964). Answer sheets do make a difference. *Personnel Psychology, 17,* 65–71.

Bellack, A. S., & Hersen, M. (Eds.), (1988). *Behavioral assessment: A practical handbook* (3rd ed.). New York: Pergamon Press.

Bem, D. J., & Allen, A. (1974). On predicting some of the people some of the time: The search for cross-situational consistencies in behavior. *Psychological Review, 81,* 506–520.

Bem, D. J., & Funder, D. C. (1978). Predicting more of the people more of the time: Assessing the personality of situations. *Psychological Review, 85,* 485–501.

Bender, L. (1938). *A visual motor test and its clinical use* (American Orthopsychiatric Association Research Monograph No. 3). New York: American Orthopsychiatric Association.

Bennett, G. K., Seashore, H. G., & Wesman, A. G. (1966). *Differential Aptitude Test Manual* (4th ed.). New York: Psychological Corporation.

Bennett, G. K., Seashore, H. G. & Wesman, A. G. (1974). *The fifth edition manual for the Differential Aptitude Tests—Forms S and T.* New York: Psychological Corporation.

Ben-Porath, Y. S., & Butcher, J. N. (1989). The psychometric stability of rewritten MMPI items. *Journal of Personality Assessment, 53,* 645–653.

Berdie, R. F. (1965). The Ad Hoc Committee on social impact of psychological assessment. *American Psychologist, 20,* 143–146.

Berg, I. A. (1967). *Response set in personality assessment.* Chicago: Aldine.

Berk, R. A. (1982). *Handbook of methods for detecting test bias.* Baltimore: Johns Hopkins University Press.

Berk, R. A. (Ed.). (1984). *A guide to criterion-referenced test construction.* Baltimore: Johns Hopkins University Press.

Bernreuter, R. G. (1931). *The personality inventory.* Palo Alto, Calif.: Stanford University Press.

Berry, J. W. (1974). Radical culture relativism and the concept of intelligence. In J. W. Berry & P. R. Dasen (Eds.), *Culture and cognition: Readings in cross-cultural psychology.* London: Methuen.

Berry, J. W. (1981). Cultural systems and cognitive styles. In M. Friedman, J. P. Das, & N. O'Connor (Eds.), *Intelligence and learning.* New York: Plenum.

Berry, J. W. (1982). Ecological analyses for cross-cultural psychology. In N. Warren (Ed.), *Studies in cross-cultural psychology.* London: Academic Press.

Bersoff, D. N. (1981). Testing and the law. *American Psychologist, 36,* 1047–1056.

Bigler, E. D., & Ehrfurth, J. W. (1981). The continued inappropriate use of the Bender Visual Motor Gestalt Test. *Professional Psychology, 12,* 562–569.

Birenbaum, M., & Montag, I. (1986). On the location of the sensation seeking construct in the personality domain. *Multivariate Behavioral Research, 21,* 357–373.

Bjork, D. J. (1983). *The compromised scientist: William James in the development of American psychology.* New York: Columbia University Press.

Black, H. (1963). *They shall not pass.* New York: Morrow.

Black, J. D. (1949). A survey of employment in psychology and the place of personnel without the PhD. *American Psychologist, 4,* 38–42.

Blake, R. R. (1948). Some quantitative aspects of *Time* magazine's presentation of psychology. *American Psychologist, 3,* 124–126, 132.

Blakeslee, A. L. (1952). Psychology and the newspaper man. *American Psychologist, 7,* 91–94.

Block, J. (1965). *The challenge of response sets: Unconfounding meaning, acquiescence, and social desirability in the MMPI.* New York: Appleton-Century-Crofts.

Boll, T. J. (1981). The Halstead–Reitan Neuropsychological Battery. In S. B. Filskov & T. J. Boll (Eds.), *Handbook of clinical neuropsychology.* New York: Wiley.

Boring, E. G. (1923). Intelligence as the tests test it. *New Republic, 35,* 35–37.

Boring, E. G. (1936). Temporal perception and operationism. *American Journal of Psychology, 48,* 519–522.

Boring, E. G. (1957). *A history of experimental psychology.* New York: Appleton-Century-Crofts.

Boulton, T. L. (1891). The growth of memory in school children. *American Journal of Psychology, 4,* 362–380.

Bowers, K. (1973). Situationism in psychology: An analysis and critique. *Psychological Review, 80,* 307–336.

Bray, D. W. (1982). The assessment center and the study of lives. *American Psychologist, 37,* 180–189.

Breland, H. M. (1979). *Population validity and college entrance measures* (College Board Research Monograph No. 8). New York: College Entrance Examination Board.

Bridgman, P. W. (1927). *The logic of modern physics.* New York: Macmillan.

Bridgman, P. W. (1945). Some general principles of operational analysis. *Psychological Review, 52,* 246–249, 281–284.

Brigham, C. C. (1923). *A study of American intelligence.* Princeton, N.J.: Princeton University Press.

Brim, O. G., Jr. (1965). American attitudes toward intelligence tests. *American Psychologist, 20,* 125–130.

Brook, R. C., & Whitehead, P. C. (1980). *Drug-free therapeutic community.* New York: Human Science Press.

Brown, J. (1985). *The semantics of profession: Metaphor and power in the history of psychological testing, 1890–1929.* Unpublished doctoral dissertation, University of Wisconsin–Madison.

Brown, J., & Langer, E. (1990). Mindfulness and intelligence: A comparison. *Educational Psychologist, 25,* 305–335.

Brown, W., & Thomson, G. H. (1940). *The essentials of mental measurement* (4th ed.). Cambridge, Eng.: Cambridge University Press.

Bruner, J. (1986). *Actual minds, possible worlds.* Cambridge, Mass.: Harvard University Press.

Bryk, A. S. (1983). *Stakeholder-based evaluation.* San Francisco: Jossey-Bass.

Burgess, R. W. (1960). *Historical statistics of the United States.* Washington, D.C.: U.S. Department of Commerce, Bureau of the Census.

Burke, M. J., & Normand, J. (1987). Computerized testing: Overview and critique. *Professional Psychology: Research and Practice, 18,* 46–47.

Burnham, J. C. (1974). The struggle between physicians and paramedical personnel in American psychiatry, 1917–41. *Journal of the History of Medicine, 29,* 93–106.

Burnham, P. S., Cutts, N. E., Hovland, C. I., Masy, M. A., Scott, C. W., & Tilton, J. W. (Chair). (1951). Preparation for the work of an educational psychologist. *American Psychologist, 6,* 65–67.

Buros, O. K. (Ed.). (1938). *The nineteen thirty-eight mental measurements yearbook.* New Brunswick, N.J.: Rutgers University Press (reprinted in 1972 by Gryphon, Highland Park, N.J.).

Buros, O. K. (Ed.). (1959). *The fifth mental measurements yearbook.* Highland Park, N.J.: Gryphon.

Buros, O. K. (Ed.). (1965). *The sixth mental measurements yearbook.* Highland Park N.J.: Gryphon.

Buros, O. K. (Ed.). (1978). *The eighth mental measurements yearbook.* Highland Park N.J.: Gryphon.

Burt, C. (1943). Ability and income. *British Journal of Educational Psychology, 13,* 83–98.

Burt, C. (1955). The evidence for the concept of intelligence. *British Journal of Educational Psychology, 25,* 158–177.

Burt, C. (1958). The inheritance of mental ability. *American Psychologist, 13,* 1–15.

Burt, C. (1966). The genetic determination of differences in intelligence: A study of monozygotic twins reared together and apart. *British Journal of Psychology, 57,* 137–153.

Burton, R. V. (1963). Generality of honesty reconsidered. *Psychological Review, 70,* 481–499.

Buss, A. H. (1989). Personality as traits. *American Psychologist, 44,* 1378–1388.

Butcher, J. N. (Ed.). (1987). *Computerized psychological assessment.* New York: Basic Books.

Butcher, J. N., Dahlstrom, W. G., Graham, J. R., Tellegen, A., & Kaemmer, B. (1989). *Manual for administration and scoring: MMPI-2.* Minneapolis: University of Minnesota Press.

Butcher, J. N., Graham, J. R., Williams, C. L., & Ben-Porath, Y. (1990). *Development and use of the MMPI-2 content scales.* Minneapolis: University of Minnesota Press.

Butcher, J. N., & Keller, L. (1984). Objective personality assessment: Present status and future directions. In G. Goldstein & M. Hersen (Eds.), *Handbook of psychological assessment.* New York: Pergamon Press.

Butcher, J. N., & Pope, K. S. (1992). The research base, psychometric properties, and the clinical uses of the MMPI-2 and MMPI-A. *Canadian Psychology/Psychologie Canadienne, 33,* 61–78.

Butterfield, H. (1951). *The whig interpretation of history.* New York: Scribners.

Calvin, A., & McConnell, J. (1953). Ellis on personality inventories. *Journal of Consulting Psychology, 17,* 462–464.

Camfield, T. C. (1973). The professionalization of American psychology. *Journal of the History of the Behavioral Sciences, 9,* 66–75.

Campbell, D. P., & Hansen, J. C. (1981). *Manual for the SVIB-SCII* (3rd ed.). Stanford, Calif.: Stanford University Press.

Campbell, D. T. (1957). A typology of tests, projective and otherwise. *Journal of Consulting Psychology, 21,* 207–210.

Campbell, D. T., & Fiske, D. W. (1959). Convergent and discriminant validation by the multitrait–multimethod matrix. *Psychological Bulletin, 56,* 81–105.

Campbell, J. T., Crooks, L. A., Mahoney, M. H., & Rock, D. A. (1973). *An investigation of sources of bias in the prediction of job performance: A six year study.* Princeton, N.J.: Educational Testing Service.

Cannon, C. J. (1922). American misgivings. *Atlantic Monthly, 129,* 145–157.

Canter, A. (1985). The Bender–Gestalt Test. In C. S. Newmark (Ed.). *Major psychological assessment instruments.* Boston: Allyn and Bacon.

Cantor, N., & Kihlstrom, J. F. (1987). *Personality and social intelligence.* Englewood Cliffs, N.J.: Prentice Hall.

Caplan, A. L. (1978). *The sociobiology debate: Readings on the ethical and scientific issues concerning sociobiology.* New York: Harper & Row.

Carlson, L., & Reynolds, C. R. (1981). Factor structure and specific variance of the WPPSI subtests at six age levels. *Psychology in the Schools, 18,* 48–54.

Carmines, E. G., & Zeller, R. A. (1979). *Reliability and validity assessment.* Newbury Park, Calif.: Sage.

Carnap, R. (1923). Über die Aufgabe der Physik und die Andwendung des Gründsatze der Einfachsheit. *Kant-Studien, 28,* 90–107.

Carpenter, P. A., Just, M. A., & Shell, P. (1990). What one intelligence test measures: A theoretical account in the processing of the Raven Progressive Matrices. *Psychological Review, 97,* 404–431.

Carr, A. C., Ghosh, A., & Ancil, R. J. (1983). Can a computer take a psychiatric history? *Psychological Medicine, 13,* 151–158.

Carroll, J. B. (1979). Measurement of abilities constructs. In Educational Testing Service (Eds.), *Construct validity in psychological measurement: Proceedings of a colloquium on theory and application in education and employment.* Princeton, N.J.: Educational Testing Service.

Cashen, V. M., & Ramseyer, G. C. (1969). The use of separate answer sheets by primary age children. *Educational and Psychological Measurement, 6,* 155–158.

Cattell, J. M. (1890/1973). Mental tests and measurement. *Mind, 15,* 373–381. Reprinted in Poffenberger (1973).

Cattell, J. M. (1922). *The first year of The Psychological Corporation.* Paper read at the annual meeting of The Psychological Corporation. Cited in Samuelson (1977).

Cattell, R. B. (1952). The three basic factor analytic designs—their interrelations and derivatives. *Psychological Bulletin, 49,* 499–520.

Cattell, R. B. (1978). *The scientific use of factor analysis in behavioral and life sciences.* New York: Plenum.

Cattell, R. B., Eber, H. W., & Tatsuoka, M. M. (1970). *Handbook for the Sixteen Personality Factor Questionnaire (16PF).* Champaign, Ill.: Institute for Personality and Ability Testing.

Cattell, R. B., & Kline, P. (1977). *The scientific analysis of personality and motivation.* New York: Academic Press.

Chaplin, W. F., & Goldberg, L. R. (1984). A failure to replicate the Bem and Allen study of individual differences in cross-situational consistency. *Journal of Personality and Social Psychology, 47,* 1074–1090.

Charlesworth, W. R. (1976). Human intelligence as adaptation: An ethological approach. In L. B. Resnick (Ed.), *The nature of intelligence.* Hillsdale, N.J.: Erlbaum.

Charlesworth, W. R. (1979). An ethological approach to studying intelligence. *Human Development, 22,* 212–216.

Child, J. L. (1956). Self-ratings and TAT: Their relations to each other and to early childhood background. *Journal of Personality, 25,* 96–114.

Christensen, A. L. (1975). *Luria's neuropsychological investigation.* New York: Spectrum.

Churchland, P. S. (1986). *Neurophilosophy.* Cambridge, Mass.: Bradford.

Churchland, P. S. (1986). *Neurophilosophy: Toward a unified science of the mind/brain.* Cambridge, Mass.: MIT Press.

Ciminero, A. R., Calhoun, K. S., & Adams, H. E. (Eds.). (1986). *Handbook of behavioral assessment* (2nd ed.). New York: Wiley.

Clagett, M. (1957). *Greek science in antiquity.* London: Abelard-Schuman.

Clark, C. A. (1959). Developments and applications in the area of construct validity. *Review of Educational Research, 29,* 84–105.

Clarke, A. D. B., Clarke, A. M., & McAskie, M. (1976, November 13). *The Times.*

Clopton, W. (1965). If psychologists want understanding.... *American Psychologist, 20,* 875–876.

Cohen, J. A. (1957). The factorial structure of the WAIS between early childhood and old age. *Journal of Consulting Psychology, 21,* 283–290.

Cohen, J. A. (1959). The factorial structure of the WISC at ages 7–6, 10–6, and 13–6. *Journal of Consulting Psychology, 23,* 285–299.

Cohen, J. (1977, March). The detractors. *Encounter,* pp. 86–90.

Cohen, P. C. (1982). *A calculating people: The spread of numeracy in early America.* Chicago: University of Chicago Press.

Cohen, R. J., Montague, P., Nathanson, L. S., & Swerdlik, M. E. (1988). *Psychological testing: An introduction to tests and measurements.* Mountain View, Calif.: Mayfield.

College Board. (1984). *Taking the SAT: A guide to the Scholastic Aptitude Test and the Test of Standard Written English.* New York: College Entrance Examination Board.

Comrey, A. L. (1973). *First course in factor analysis.* New York: Academic Press.

Cone, J. D. (1978). The relevance of reliability and validity for behavioral assessment. *Behavior Therapy, 8,* 411–426.

Connors, C. K. (1990). *Connor's Rating Scales.* Los Angeles: Western Psychological Services.

Conoley, J. C., & Kramer, J. J. (Eds.). (1989). *The tenth mental measurements yearbook.* Lincoln: Buros Institute of Mental Measurements, University of Nebraska.

Conover, W. J. (1980). *Practical nonparametric statistics* (2nd ed.). New York: Wiley.

Conway, J. (1958). The inheritance of intelligence and its social implications. *British Journal of Statistical Psychology, 11,* 171–190.

Cook, T. D., & Campbell, D. T. (1979). *Quasi-experimentation: Design and analysis issues for field settings.* Chicago: Rand McNally.

Costa, P. T., & McCrae, R. R. (1985). *The NEO Personality Inventory manual.* Odessa, Fla: Psychological Assessment Resources.

Courtis, S. (Chair). (1921). Report of the standardization committee. *Journal of Educational Research, 4,* 78–80.

Covin, T. M., & Lubimiv, A. J. (1976). Concurrent validity of the WRAT. *Perceptual and Motor Skills, 43,* 573–574.

Crissey, W. J. E. (1963). Who's watching the watcher of watchers? *Contemporary Psychology, 8,* 228–229.

Crocker, L., & Aligna, J. (1986). *Introduction to classical and modern test theory.* Fort Worth, Tex.: Harcourt Brace Jovanovich.

Cronbach, L. J. (1949). *Essentials of psychological testing.* New York: Harper.

Cronbach, L. J. (1951). Coefficient Alpha and the internal structure of tests. *Psychometrika, 16,* 297–334.

Cronbach, L. J. (1957). The two disciplines of scientific psychology. *American Psychologist, 12,* 671–684.

Cronbach, L. J. (1960). Recommendations for APA test standards regarding construct, trait, or discriminant validity. *American Psychologist, 15,* 546–553.

Cronbach, L. J. (1975). Five decades of public controversy over mental testing. *American Psychologist, 30,* 1–14.

Cronbach, L. J. (1979). Personal communication. Cited in Novick (1981).

Cronbach, L. J. (1988). Five perspectives on the validity argument. In H. Wainer & H. I. Braun (Eds.), *Test validity.* Hillsdale, N.J.: Erlbaum.

Cronbach, L. J. (1990). *Essentials of psychological testing* (5th ed.). Cambridge, Mass.: Harper & Row.

Cronbach, L. J., & Gleser, G. C. (1965). *Psychological tests and personnel decisions* (2nd ed.). Champaign: University of Illinois Press.

Cronbach, L. J., Gleser, G. C., Nanda, H., & Rajaratnam, N. (1972). *The dependability of behavioral measurements: Theory of generalizability for scores and profiles.* New York: Wiley.

Cronbach, L. J., & Meehl, P. E. (1955). Construct validity in psychological tests. *Psychological Bulletin, 52,* 281–302.

Crowne, D. P., & Marlowe, D. (1964). *The approval motive: Studies in evaluative dependence.* New York: Wiley.

Cruikshank, W. M. (1984). Definition: A major issue in the field of learning disabilities. *Journal of Rehabilitation, 50,* 7–18.

Curran, J. P., & Mariotto, M. J. (1980). A conceptual structure for the assessment of social skills. In M. Hersen, R. M. Eisler, & P. M. Miller (Eds.), *Progress in behavior modification* (pp. 1–37). New York: Academic Press.

Dahlstrom W. G., & Welsh, G. S. (1960). *An MMPI handbook: A guide to use in clinical practice and research.* Minneapolis: University of Minnesota Press.

Danziger, K. (1990). *Constructing the subject: Historical origins of psychological research.* Cambridge, Eng.: Cambridge University Press.

Darwin, C. (1859). *On the origin of species.* London: Murray.

Darwin, C. (1871). *The descent of man.* London: Murray.

Darwin, C. (1872). *The expression of the emotions in man and animals.* London: Murray.

David, H. P. (1954). Phones, phonies, and psychologists. *American Psychologist, 9,* 237–240.

David, H. P., & Springfield, F. B. (1958). Phones, phonies, and psychologists II: Four years later. *American Psychologist, 13,* 61–64.

Davis, W. E. (1969). Effect of prior failure on subjects' WAIS arithmetic subtest scores. *Journal of Clinical Psychology, 25,* 72–73.

Derrida, J. (1981). *Dissemination.* Chicago: University of Chicago Press.

Deutsch, M., Fishman, J. A., Kogan, L., North, R., & Whiteman, M. (1964). Guidelines for testing minority group children. *Journal of Social Issues, 2,* 127–145.

Dewey, J. (1957). *Human nature and conduct.* New York: Modern Library.

DeWolfe, A. S., Larson, J. K., & Ryan, J. J. (1985). Diagnostic accuracy of the Millon test computer reports for bipolar affective disorder. *Journal of Psychopathology and Behavioral Assessment, 7,* 185–189.

Digman, J. M. (1990). Personality structure: Emergence of the five-factor model. *Annual Review of Psychology, 41,* 417–440.

Donlon, T. F. (Ed.). (1984). *The College Board technical handbook for the Scholastic Aptitude Test and achievement tests.* New York: College Entrance Examination Board.

Douglas, T. (1979). The highlights of the Dirty Thirties. In D. Francis & H. Ganzevoort (Eds.), *The Dirty Thirties in prairie Canada.* Vancouver, B.C.: Tantalus Research.

Downey, J. E. (1922). The Will-Temperament and its testing. Yonkers, N.Y.: World.

Draper, N., & Smith, H. (1981). *Applied regression analysis* (2nd ed.). New York: Wiley.

Dubois, P. H. (1970). *A history of psychological testing*. Boston: Allyn and Bacon.

Ebel, R. L. (1972). Some limitations of criterion-referenced measurement. In G. H. Bracht, K. D. Hopkins, & J. C. Stanley (Eds.), *Perspectives in educational and psychological measurement*. Englewood Cliffs, N.J.: Prentice Hall.

Edwards, A. J. (1971). *Individual mental testing Part I: History and theories*. Scranton, Ohio: Intext Educational Publishers.

Ellis, A. (1959). The Minnesota Multiphasic Personality Inventory. In O. K. Buros (Ed.), *The fifth mental measurements yearbook*, pp. 166–167. Highland Park, N.J.: Gryphon.

Embree, R. B. (1948). The status of college students in terms of IQ's determined during childhood. *American Psychologist, 3*, 259.

Endler, N. S., & Hunt, J. M. (1966). Generalizability of contributions from sources of variance as measured by the S–R inventories of anxiousness. *Journal of Personality, 37*, 1–24.

Epstein, S. (1979). The stability of behavior: I. On predicting most of the people much of the time. *Journal of Personality and Social Psychology, 37*, 1097–1126.

Epstein, S. (1980). The stability of behavior: II. Implications for psychological research. *American Psychologist, 35*, 790–806.

Epstein, S., & O'Brien, E. J. (1985). The person–situation debate in historical and current perspective. *Psychological Bulletin, 98*, 513–537.

Eron, L. D., & Waller, O. W. (1961). Test burning: II. *American Psychologist, 16*, 237–244.

Ervin, S. J., Jr. (1965). Why Senate hearings on psychological tests in government. *American Psychologist, 20*, 879–880.

Evans, B., & Waites, B. (1981). *IQ and mental testing*. Atlantic Highlands, N.J.: Humanities Press.

Exner, J. L. (1966). Variations in WISC performance as influenced by differences in pretest rapport. *Journal of General Psychology, 74*, 299–306.

Eysenck, H. J. (1944). Types of personality: A factorial study of 700 neurotic soldiers. *Journal of Mental Science, 90*, 851–961.

Eysenck, H. J. (1970). *The structure of human personality* (3rd ed.). London: Methuen.

Eysenck, H. J. (1971). *The IQ argument: Race, intelligence, and education*. New York: Library Press.

Eysenck, H. J. (1979). *The structure and measurement of intelligence*. Berlin: Springer-Verlag.

Eysenck, H. J., & Eysenck, M. W. (1975). *Manual of the Eysenck Personality Questionnaire*. San Diego: Educational and Industrial Testing Service.

Eysenck, H., & Eysenck, S. B. G. (1964). *Manual for the Eysenck Personality Inventory*. San Diego: Educational and Industrial Testing Service.

Eysenck, H. J., & Eysenck, M. W. (1985). *Personality and individual differences: A natural science approach*. New York: Plenum.

Eysenck, H. J., & Eysenck, S. B. G. (1968). A factorial study of psychoticism as a dimension of personality [Special issue]. *Multivariate Behavioural Research*, 15–31.

Fancher, R. E. (1985). *The intelligence men: Makers of the IQ controversy*. New York: Norton.

Feinberg, M. R., & Lefkowitz, J. (1962). Image of industrial psychology among corporate executives. *American Psychologist, 17*, 109–111.

Fekken, G. C. (1992). Ringing in the new: The MMPI–2. *Canadian Psychology/Psychologie Canadienne, 33*, 84–87.

Feldt, L. S., & Brennan, R. L. (1989). Reliability. In R. L. Linn (Ed.), *Educational measurement* (3rd ed.). New York: Macmillan.

Ferguson, G. A. (1966). *Statistical analysis in psychology and education*. New York: McGraw-Hill.

Fernald, G. G. (1912). An achievement capacity test: A preliminary report. *Journal of Educational Psychology, 3*, 331–336.

Fiske, D. W. (1949). Consistency of the factorial structures of personality ratings from different sources. *Journal of Abnormal and Social Psychology, 44*, 329–344.

Flanagan, J. C. (1942). The selection and classification program for aviation cadets. *Journal of Consulting Psychology, 6*, 229–239.

Flanagan, J. C. (Ed.). (1948). *The aviation psychology program in the army air forces, Report 1*. Washington, D.C.: Government Printing Office.

Fletcher, R. (1991). *Science, ideology, and the media: The Cyril Burt scandal*. London: Transaction.

Forman, P. (1991). Independence, not transcendence, for the historian of science. *Isis, 82*, 71–86.

Forrest, D. W. (1974). *Francis Galton: The life and work of a Victorian genius*. London: Paul Elek.

Foster, A., Benton, A. L., & Rabin, A. I. (1952). The internship in clinical psychology: Three alternative plans. *American Psychologist, 7*, 7–13.

Frank, G. (1983). *The Wechsler enterprise: An assessment of the development, structure and use of the Wechsler tests of intelligence*. New York: Pergamon Press.

Frederiksen, N. (1962). Factors in in-basket performance. *Psychological Monographs, 76* (Whole No. 541).

Frederiksen, N. (1966). In-basket tests and factors in administrative performance. In A. Anastasi (Ed.),

Testing problems in perspective. Washington, D.C.: American Council on Education.

Frederiksen, N. (1972). Toward a taxonomy of situations. *American Psychologist, 27*, 114–123.

Frederiksen, N., Saunders, D. R., & Wand, B. (1957). The In-Basket Test. *Psychological Monographs, 71* (Whole No. 438).

Freeman, F. N. (1922). The mental age of adults. *Journal of Educational Research, 6*, 441–444.

Freeman, F. N. (1939). *Mental tests*. Boston: Houghton Mifflin.

Friedman, A. F. (1987). Eysenck Personality Questionnaire. In D. J. Keyser & R. C. Sweetland (Eds.), *Test critiques*. Kansas City, Mo.: Test Corporation of America.

Freidman, I. (1957). Objectifying the subjective: A methodological approach to the TAT. *Journal of Projective Techniques, 21*, 243–247.

French, J. W. (1962). Effect of anxiety on verbal and mathematical examination scores. *Educational and Psychological Measurement, 22*, 553–564.

Fulkerson, S. C., & Barry, J. R. (1961). Methodology and research on the prognostic use of psychological tests. *Psychological Bulletin, 58*, 177–204.

Gallagher, C. E. (1965). Why House hearings on invasion of privacy. *American Psychologist, 20*, 881–882.

Galton, F. (1865). Hereditary talent and character. *Macmillan's Magazine, 12*, 157–166, 318–327.

Galton, F. (1869/1972). *Hereditary genius*. Gloucester, Mass.: Peter Smith.

Galton, F. (1875). The history of twins, as a criterion of the relative powers of nature and nurture. *Journal of the Anthropological Institute Journal, 5*, 391–406.

Galton, F. (1883). *Inquiries into human faculty and its development* (2nd ed.). London: Eugenics Society.

Galton, F. (1908). *Memories of my life*. New York: AMS Press.

Gardner, H. (1983). *Frames of mind: The theory of multiple intelligences*. New York: Basic Books.

Gardner, H. (1985). *The mind's new science: A history of the cognitive revolution*. New York: Basic Books.

Garfinkel, H. (1967). *Studies in ethnomethodology*. Englewood Cliffs, N.J.: Prentice Hall.

Geertz, C. (1973). *The interpretation of cultures*. New York: Basic Books.

Geschwind, N., & Levitsky, W. (1968). Left–right asymetries in temporal speech region. *Science, 161*, 186–187.

Gesell, A., & Amatruda, C. S. (1956). *Developmental diagnosis* (2nd ed.). New York: Hoeber.

Ghiselli, E. E. (1966). *The validity of occupational aptitude tests*. New York: Wiley.

Ghiselli, E. E., Campbell, J. P., & Zedeck, S. (1981). *Measurement theory for the behavioral sciences*. New York: Freeman.

Gilligan, C. (1982). *In a different voice: Psychological theory and women's development*. Cambridge, Mass.: Harvard University Press.

Gladding, S. T. (1992). *Counseling: A comprehensive profession* (2nd ed.). New York: Merrill.

Glaser, R. (1963). Instructional technology and the measurement of learning outcomes. *American Psychologist, 18*, 519–522.

Glass, G. V., McGaw, B., & Smith, M. L. (1981). *Meta-analysis in social research*. Newbury Park, Calif.: Sage.

Glasscote, R. M., Sussex, J. N., Cumming, E., & Smith, L. E. (1969). *The community mental health center: An interim appraisal*. Washington, D.C.: American Psychiatric Association.

Glover, J. A., & Ronning, R. R. (1987). *Historical foundations of educational psychology*. New York: Plenum.

Goddard, H. H. (1908). The Binet and Simon tests of intellectual capacity. *Training School Bulletin, 5*, 3–9.

Goldberg, J. O., Shaw, B. F., & Segal, Z. V. (1987). Concurrent validity of the Millon Clinical Multiaxial Inventory depression scales. *Journal of Consulting and Clinical Psychology, 55*, 785–787.

Goldberg, L. R. (1981). Language and individual differences: The search for universals in personality lexicons. In L. Wheeler (Ed.), *Review of personality and social psychology*. Beverly Hills, Calif.: Sage.

Golden, C. J. (1981). The Luria–Nebraska Neuropsychological Battery: Theory and research. *Advances in Psychological Assessment, 5*, 191–235.

Goldfried, M. R. (1979). Behavioral assessment: Where do we go from here? *Behavioral Assessment, 1*, 19–22.

Goldfried, M. R., & Kent, R. N. (1972). Traditional versus behavioral personality assessment: A comparison of methodological and theoretical assumptions. *Psychological Bulletin, 77*, 409–420.

Goodenough, F. L. (1949). *Mental testing*. New York: Rinehart.

Gordon, E. W., & Terrell, M. D. (1981). The changed social context of testing. *American Psychologist, 36*, 1167–1171.

Gorsuch, R. L. (1983). *Factor analysis* (2nd ed.). Hillsdale, N.J.: Erlbaum.

Gould, S. J. (1977). *Even since Darwin*. New York: Norton.

Gould, S. J. (1981). *The mismeasure of man*. New York: Norton.

Gove, P. B. (Ed.). (1965). *Webster's seventh new collegiate dictionary*. Toronto: Allen.

Graham, J. R. (1990). *MMP–I-2: Assessing personality and psychopathology.* Oxford, Eng.: Oxford University Press.

Green, B. F. (1988). Construct validity of computer-based tests. In H. Wainer & H. I. Braun (Eds.), *Test validity.* Hillsdale, N.J.: Erlbaum.

Greenspoon, J., & Gersten, C. D. (1967). A new look at psychological testing: Psychological testing from the standpoint of a behaviorist. *American Psychologist, 22,* 848–853.

Gregory, R. J. (1992). *Psychological testing: History, principles, and applications.* Boston: Allyn and Bacon.

Greist, J. H., & Klein, M. H. (1980). Computer programs for patients, clinicians, and researchers in psychiatry. In J. B. Sidowski, J. H. Johnson, & T. A. Williams (Eds.), *Technology in mental health care delivery systems.* Norwood, N.J.: Ablex.

Grob, G. N. (1966a). *The state and the mentally ill.* Chapel Hill: University of North Carolina Press.

Grob, G. N. (1966b). The state mental hospital in mid-nineteenth century America: A social analysis. *American Psychologist, 21,* 510–523.

Gronlund, N. E. (1973). *Preparing criterion-referenced tests for classroom instruction.* New York: Macmillan.

Gross, M. L. (1962). *The brain watchers.* New York: Random House.

Groth-Marnat, G. (1990). *Handbook of psychological assessment* (2nd ed.). New York: Wiley-Interscience.

Guba, E. G., & Lincoln, Y. S. (1989). *Fourth generation evaluation.* Newbury Park, Calif.: Sage.

Guest, L. (1948). The public's attitudes toward psychologists. *American Psychologist, 3,* 135–139.

Guilford, J. P. (1946). New standards for test evaluation. *Educational and Psychological Measurement, 6,* 427–439.

Guilford, J. P. (1959). Three faces of intellect. *American Psychologist, 14,* 469–479.

Guilford, J. P. (1967). *The nature of human intelligence.* New York: McGraw-Hill.

Guion, R. M. (1965). Industrial psychology as an academic discipline. *American Psychologist, 20,* 815–821.

Guion, R. M. (1974). Open a new window: Validities and values in psychological measurement. *American Psychologist, 29,* 287–296.

Guion, R. M. (1980). On trinitarian doctrines of validity. *Professional Psychology, 11,* 385–398.

Gulliksen, H. (1950a). Intrinsic validity. *American Psychologist, 5,* 79–94.

Gulliksen, H. (1950b). *Theory of mental tests.* New York: Wiley.

Gulliksen, H. (1974). Looking back and ahead in psychometrics. *American Psychologist, 29,* 251–261.

Gutkin, R. B., & Reynolds, C. R. (1981). Factorial similarity of the WISC–R for White and Black children from the standardization sample. *Journal of Educational Psychology, 73,* 227–231.

Hain, J. D. (1964). The Bender Gestalt Test: A scoring method for identifying brain damage. *Journal of Consulting Psychology, 28,* 34–40.

Halstead, W. C. (1947). *Brain and intelligence: A quantitative study of the frontal lobes.* Chicago: University of Chicago Press.

Hambleton, R. K. (1984). Determining test length. In R. A. Berk (Ed.), *A guide to criterion-referenced test construction.* Baltimore: Johns Hopkins University Press.

Hampson, S. E. (1988). *The construction of personality: An introduction* (2nd ed.). London: Routledge.

Haney, W. (1981). Validity, vaudeville, and values: A short history of social concerns over standardized testing. *American Psychologist, 36,* 1021–1034.

Hanson, F. A. (1993). *Testing testing: Social consequences of the examined life.* Berkeley: University of California Press.

Harlow, H. F., Miller, J. G., & Newcomb, T. M. (1962). Identifying creative talent in psychology. *American Psychologist, 17,* 679–683.

Hartshorn, H., & May, M. A. (1928). *Studies in the nature of character: Studies of deceit* (Vol. 1). New York: Macmillan.

Harvey, R. J. (1991). Job analysis. In M. D. Dunnette and L. M. Hough (Eds.), *Handbook of industrial and organizational psychology* (2nd ed.). Palo Alto, Calif.: Consulting Psychologists Press.

Hathaway, S. R., & McKinley, J. C. (1943). *The Minnesota Multiphasic Personality Inventory* (rev. ed.). Minneapolis: University of Minnesota Press.

Hathaway, S. R., & Meehl, P. E. (1951). *An atlas for the clinical use of the MMPI.* Minneapolis: University of Minnesota Press.

Hayes, S. C., Nelson, R. O., & Jarrett, R. B. (1986). Evaluating the quality of behavioral assessment. In R. O. Nelson & S. C. Hayes (Eds.), *Conceptual foundations of behavioral assessment.* New York: Guilford.

Healy, W. (1914). A pictorial completion test. *Psychological Review, 21,* 189–203.

Hearnshaw, L. S. (1987). *The shaping of modern psychology.* London: Routledge and Kegan.

Hedges, L. V. (1988). The meta-analysis of test validity studies: Some new approaches. In H. Wainer & H. I. Braun (Eds.), *Test validity.* Hillsdale, N.J.: Erlbaum.

Hedl, J. J., O'Neil, H. H., & Hansen, D. N. (1973). Affective reactions toward computer-based intelligence testing. *Journal of Consulting and Clinical Psychology, 40,* 217–222.

Heise, D. R., & Bohrnstedt, G. W. (1970). Validity, invalidity, and reliability. In E. F. Borgatta (Ed.), *Sociological methodology.* San Francisco: Jossey-Bass.

Heiser, K. F. (1950). Survey of departments giving instruction in clinical psychology. *American Psychologist, 5,* 610–619.

Helmstadter, G. C. (1964). *Principles of psychological measurement.* New York: Appleton-Century-Crofts.

Hergenhahn, B. R. (1992). *An introduction to the history of psychology* (2nd ed.). Belmont, Calif.: Wadsworth.

Herrnstein, R. (1971, September). IQ. *Atlantic Monthly,* pp. 44–64.

Hess, A. K. (1992). The NEO Personality Inventory. In J. J. Kramer & J. C. Conoley (Eds.), *The eleventh mental measurements yearbook.* Lincoln, Neb.: Buros Institute of Mental Measurements.

Hilgard, E. (1987). *Psychology in America: A historical survey.* New York: Harcourt Brace Jovanovich.

Hill, K. T., & Sarason, S. B. (1966). The relation of test anxiety and defensiveness to test and school performance over the elementary school years. *Monographs of the Society for Research in Child Development, 31* (2, Serial No. 104).

Hirsch, J. (1976). Behavior–genetic analysis and its biosocial consequences. In N. J. Block & G. Dworkin, G. (Eds.), *The IQ controversy: Critical readings.* New York: Pantheon Books.

Hobbs, N. (1948). The development of a code of ethical standards for psychology. *American Psychologist, 3,* 80–84.

Hoch, E. L., Ross, A. O., & Winder, C. L. (1966). Conference on the professional preparation of clinical psychologists: A summary. *American Psychologist, 21,* 42–51.

Hofer, P. J., & Green, B. F. (1985). The challenge of competence and creativity in computerized psychological testing. *Journal of Consulting and Clinical Psychology, 53,* 826–838.

Hoffman, B. (1962). *The tyranny of testing.* New York: Crowell-Collier.

Hoffman, F. J., Sheldon, K. L., & Minskoff, E. H. (1987). Needs of learning disabled adults. *Journal of Learning Disabilities, 20,* 43–52.

Hogan, R. (1989). The NEO Personality Inventory. In J. C. Conoley & J. J. Kramer (Eds.), *The tenth mental measurements yearbook.* Lincoln: Buros Institute of Mental Measurements, University of Nebraska.

Hogan, R., & Nicholson, R. A. (1988). The meaning of personality test scores. *American Psychologist, 43,* 621–626.

Holland, J. L. (1973). *Making vocational choices.* Englewood Cliffs, N.J.: Prentice Hall.

Holt, R. R. (1970). Yet another look at clinical and statistical prediction *or* is clinical psychology worthwhile? *American Psychologist, 25,* 337–349.

Horowitz, I. L. (1966). The life and death of Project Camelot. *American Psychologist, 21,* 445–454.

Horrocks, J. E. (1964). *Assessment of behavior.* Columbus, Ohio: Merrill.

House, A. E., & Lewis, M. L. (1985). The Wechsler Adult Intelligence Scale–Revised. In C. S. Newmark (Ed.), *Major psychological assessment instruments.* Boston: Allyn and Bacon.

Hull, C. L. (1943). *Principles of behavior.* New York: Appleton-Century-Crofts.

Humphries, L. G. (1962). The organization of human abilities. *American Psychologist, 17,* 475–483.

Hunt, W. A. (1951). Clinical psychology—science or superstition? *American Psychologist, 6,* 683–687.

Hunter, J. E., & Hunter, R. F. (1984). Validity and utility of alternative predictors of job performance. *Psychological Bulletin, 96,* 72–98.

Hunter, J. E., Schmidt, F. L., & Hunter, R. F. (1979). Differential validity of employment tests by race: A comprehensive review and analysis. *Psychological Bulletin, 86,* 721–735.

Hunter, J. E., Schmidt, F. L., & Jackson, G. B. (1982). *Meta-analysis: Cumulating research findings across studies.* Newbury Park, Calif.: Sage.

Hunter, J. E., Schmidt, F. L., & Rauschenberger, J. M. (1984). Methodological, statistical, and ethical issues in the study of test bias. In C. E. Reynolds & R. T. Brown (Eds.), *Perspectives on bias in mental testing.* New York: Plenum.

Hunter, W. S. (1946). Psychology and the war. *American Psychologist, 1,* 479–492.

Huntley, R. M. C. (1966). Heritability of intelligence. In J. E. Meade & A. S. Parker (Eds.), *Genetic and environmental factors in human ability.* New York: Plenum.

Huston, P. E. (1953). Some observations on the orientation of clinical psychology. *American Psychologist, 8,* 191–196.

Hutt, M. L. (1977). *The Hutt adaptation of the Bender–Gestalt Test* (3rd ed.). New York: Grune & Stratton.

Hutt, M. L., & Milton, E. O. (1947). An analysis of duties performed by clinical psychologists in the army. *American Psychologist, 2,* 52–56.

Irvine, S . H., & Berry, J. W. (1983). *Human assessment and cultural factors.* New York: Plenum.

Isreal, H., & Goldstein, B. (1944). Operationism in psychology. *Psychological Review, 51,* 177–188.

Jackson, D. N. (1967). *Personality Research Form manual.* Port Huron, Mich.: Research Psychologists Press.

Jackson, D. N. (1970). A sequential system for personality scale development. In C. D. Speilberger (Ed.), *Current topics in clinical and community psychology* (Vol. 2). Orlando, Fla.: Academic Press.

Jackson, D. N. (1977). *Jackson Vocational Interest Survey manual*. Port Huron, Mich.: Sigma Assessment Systems.

Jackson, D. N. (1986). *Computer-based personality testing*. Washington, D.C.: American Psychological Association.

Jackson, D. N., & Guthrie, G. M. (1968). Multitrait–multimethod evaluation of the Personality Research Form. *Proceedings of the 76th Annual Convention of the American Psychological Association, 3,* 177–178.

Jackson, D. N., & Messick, S. (1961). Acquiescence and desirability as response determinant on the MMPI. *Educational and Psychological Measurement, 21,* 771–790.

Jackson, D. N., & Messick, S. (1962). Response styles and the assessment of psychopathology. In S. Messick, & J. Ross (Eds.), *Measurement in personality and cognition*. New York: Wiley.

Jackson, D. N., & Paunonen, S. V. (1985). Construct validity and the predictability of behavior. *Journal of Personality and Social Psychology, 49,* 554–570.

Jacob, M. C. (1988). *The cultural meaning of the scientific revolution*. New York: Knopf.

Jacobsen, C. F. (1950). Clinical psychology as related to legislative problems. *American Psychologist, 5,* 110–111.

Jastrow, J., Baldwin, J. M., & Cattell, J. M. (1898). Physical and mental tests. *Psychological Review, 5,* 172–179.

Jenkins, J. G. (1946). Validity for what? *Journal of Consulting Psychology, 10,* 93–98.

Jenkins, R. L. (1954). Understanding psychiatrists. *American Psychologist, 9,* 617–620.

Jensen, A. R. (1959). Thematic Apperception Test. In O. K. Buros (Ed.), *The fifth mental measurements yearbook*, pp. 310–313. Highland Park, N.J.: Gryphon.

Jensen, A. R. (1969). How much can we boost IQ and scholastic achievement? *Harvard Educational Review, 39,* 1–123.

Jensen, A. R. (1980). *Bias in mental testing*. New York: Free Press.

Johnson, B. (1982). *Ojibway ceremonies*. Toronto: McClelland & Stewart.

Johnson, D. F., & White, C. B. (1980). Effects of training on computerized test performance in the elderly. *Journal of Applied Psychology, 65,* 357–358.

Johnson, D. J., & Blalock, J. W. (1987). *Adults with learning disabilities: Clinical studies*. New York: Grune & Stratton.

Joint Commission on Mental Illness and Health. (1961). *Action for mental health*. New York: Basic Books.

Joncich, G. (1968). *The same positivist: A biography of Edward L. Thorndike*. Middletown, Conn.: Wesleyan University Press.

Jones, E. E., & Nisbett, R. E. (1971). The actor and the observer: Divergent perceptions of the cause of behavior. In E. E. Jones, D. E. Karouse, H. H. Kelly, R. E. Nisbett, S. Valins, & B. Weiner (Eds.), *Attribution: Perceiving the causes of behavior*. Morristown, N.J.: General Learning Press.

Jones, E. S. (1917). The Woolley test series applied to the detection of ability in telegraphy. *Journal of Educational Psychology, 8,* 27–34.

Jordan, A. M. (1923). The validation of intelligence tests. *Journal of Educational Psychology, 14,* 348–366, 414–428.

Kamin, L. (1974). *The science and politics of IQ*. Hillsdale, N.J.: Erlbaum.

Kamin, L. (1976). The hole in heredity. *New Society, 38,* 460–461.

Kamin, L. (1977). Burt's IQ data. *Science, 195,* 246–248.

Kanfer, F. H., & Saslow, G. (1969). Behavioral diagnosis: In C. M. Franks (Ed.), *Behavior therapy: Appraisal and status*. New York: McGraw-Hill.

Kaplan, R. M., & Saccuzzo, D. P. (1989). *Psychological testing: Principles, applications, and issues* (2nd ed.). Pacific Grove, Calif.: Brooks/Cole.

Kaufman, A. S. (1975). Factor analysis of the WISC-R at eleven age levels between 6½ and 16½ years. *Journal of Counseling and Clinical Psychology, 43,* 135–147.

Kaufman, A. S. (1990). *Assessing adolescent and adult intelligence*. Boston: Allyn and Bacon.

Kaufman, A. S., & Kaufman, N. L. (1983). *K–ABC interpretative manual*. Circle Pines, Minn.: American Guidance Service.

Keating, D. (1984). The emperor's new clothes: The "new look" in intelligence research. In R. J. Sternberg (Ed.), *Advances in the psychology of human intelligence: Vol. 2*. Hillsdale, N.J.: Erlbaum.

Kelley, T. L. (1923). *Statistical method*. New York: Macmillan.

Kelley, T. L. (1927). *Interpretation of educational measurements*. New York: World Book.

Kelley, T. L. (1939). The selection of upper and lower groups for the validation of test items. *Journal of Educational Psychology, 30,* 17–24.

Kelly, G. A. (1950). Single level versus legislation for different levels of psychological training and experience. *American Psychologist, 5,* 109, 111.

Kelves, D. J. (1968). Testing the army's intelligence: Psychologists and the military in World War I. *Journal of American History, 55,* 565–581.

Kennedy, J. F. (1963). Message from the president of the United States relative to mental illness and mental retardation. *American Psychologist, 18,* 280–289.

Kenrick, D. T., & Funder, D. C. (1988). Profiting from controversy: Lessons from the person–situation debate. *American Psychologist, 43,* 23–34.

Kent, C. (1984). A linguist compares narrative and expository prose. *Journal of Reading, 28,* 232–236.

Kerlinger, F. N. (1973). *Foundations of behavioral research* (2nd ed.). New York: Holt.

Keyser, D. J., & Sweetland, R. C. (Eds.). (1984). *Test critiques* (3 vols.). Kansas City, Mo.: Test Corporation of America.

Kidder, L. H., & Judd, C. M. (1986). *Research methods in social relations.* New York: Holt, Rinehart & Winston.

Kirchner, W. K. (1966). A note on the effect of privacy in taking typing tests. *Journal of Applied Psychology, 50,* 373–374.

Kleinknecht, R. A., & Bernstein, D. A. (1979). Short-term treatment of dental avoidance. *Journal of Behavior Therapy and Experimental Psychiatry, 10,* 311–315.

Klonoff, H., & Clark, C. V. (1975). Measuring staff attitudes toward computerization. *Hospital and Community Psychiatry, 26,* 823–825.

Kohn, S. D. (1975). The numbers game: How the testing industry operates. *National Elementary Principal, July–August,* 11–23

Kolb, B., & Whishaw, I. Q. (1985). *Fundamentals of human neuropsychology* (2nd ed.). San Francisco: Freeman.

Kolb, B., & Whishaw, I. Q. (1990). *Fundamentals of human neuropsychology* (3rd ed.). New York: Freeman.

Korchin, S. J., & Schuldberg, D. (1981). The future of clinical assessment. *American Psychologist, 36,* 1147–1158.

Kornhauser, A. (1945). Replies of psychologists to a short questionnaire on mental test developments, personality inventories, and the Rorschach test. *Educational and Psychological Measurement, 5,* 3–15.

Kramer, J. J., & Conoley, J. C. (Eds.). (1992). *The eleventh mental measurements yearbook.* Lincoln, Neb.: Buros Institute of Mental Measurements.

Kuder, G. F., & Richardson, M. W. (1937). The theory of estimation of test reliability. *Psychometrika, 2,* 151–160.

Kuhlmann, F. (1911). Binet and Simon's system for measuring the intelligence of children. *Journal of Psycho-Asthenics, 15,* 76–92.

Kuhn, T. S. (1962). *The structure of scientific revolutions.* Chicago: University of Chicago Press.

Kuhn, T. S. (1970). *The structure of scientific revolutions* (2nd ed.). Chicago: University of Chicago Press.

LaBeck, L. J., Johnson, J. H., & Harris, W. G. (1983). Validity of a computerized on-line MMPI interpretive system. *Journal of Clinical Psychology, 39,* 412–416.

Laboratory of Comparative Human Cognition. (1982). Culture and intelligence. In R. J. Sternberg (Ed.), *Handbook of human intelligence.* New York: Cambridge University Press.

Laboratory of Comparative Human Cognition. (1983). Culture and cognitive development. In W. Kessen (Ed.), *Handbook of child psychology: Vol. 1.* New York: Wiley.

LaGreca, A. M., & Stringer, S. A. (1985). The Wechsler Intelligence Scale for Children–Revised. In C. S. Newmark (Ed.), *Major psychological assessment instruments.* Boston: Allyn and Bacon.

Lakatos, I. (1978). Falsification and the methodology of scientific research programs. In J. Worrall & G. Currie (Eds.), *The methodology of scientific research programs: Vol. 1. Imre Lakatos philosophical papers.* Cambridge, Eng.: Cambridge University Press.

Landau, M. (1986). Trespassing in scientific narrative: Grafton Elliot Smith and *The Temple of Doom.* In T. R. Sarbin (Ed.), *Narrative psychology: The storied nature of human conduct.* New York: Praeger.

Landy, F. J. (1986). Stamp collecting versus science: Validation as hypothesis testing. *American Psychologist, 41,* 1183–1192.

Landy, F. J. (1989). *The psychology of work behavior* (4th ed.). Pacific Grove, Calif.: Brooks/Cole.

Lang, P. J. (1968). Fear reduction and fear behavior: Problems in treating a construct. In J. M. Schlein (Ed.), *Research in psychotherapy: Vol. 3.* Washington, D.C.: American Psychological Association.

Langfeld, H. (Ed.). (1945). Symposium on operationism. *Psychological Review, 52,* 241–294.

Lanyon, R. I. (1984). Personality assessment. *Annual Review of Psychology, 35,* 667–701.

Lawshe, C. H. (1948). *Principles of personnel testing.* New York: McGraw-Hill.

Leahey, T. H. (1980). The myth of operationism. *Journal of Mind and Behavior, 1,* 127–143.

Leahey, T. H. (1992). *A history of psychology: Main currents in psychological thought.* (3rd ed.). Englewood Cliffs, N.J.: Prentice Hall.

Leary, D. E. (1987). Telling likely stories: The rhetoric of the new psychology, 1880–1920. *Journal of the History of the Behavioral Sciences, 32,* 315–331.

Lebo, D. (1953). Degrees for charlatans. *American Psychologist, 8,* 231–234.

Lewontin, R. C. (1970). Race and intelligence. *Bulletin of the Atomic Scientists,* 1–8.

Lezak, M. D. (1983). *Neuropsychological assessment* (2nd ed.). New York: Oxford University Press.

Lindsay, J. (1951). *A short history of science.* Garden City, N.Y.: Doubleday Anchor.

Linn, R. L. (1975). Test bias and the prediction of grades in law school. *Journal of Legal Education, 27,* 293–323.

Lippmann, W. (1922). The mental age of Americans. *New Republic, 32,* 213–215.

Lippmann, W. (1922). The mystery of the "A" men. *New Republic, 32,* 246–248.

Lippmann, W. (1922). The reliability of intelligence tests. *New Republic, 32,* 275–277.

Lippmann, W. (1922). The abuse of tests. *New Republic, 32,* 297–298.

Lippmann, W. (1922). Tests of hereditary intelligence. *New Republic, 32,* 328–330.

Lippmann, W. (1922). A future for tests. *New Republic, 33,* 9–11.

Lips, H. M. (1988). *Sex and gender: An introduction* (2nd ed.). Mountain View, Calif.: Mayfield.

Locke, J. (1690/1975). *Essay concerning human understanding* (P. H. Nidditch, Ed.). Oxford, Eng.: Clarendon.

Lockman, R. F. (1964). An empirical description of the subfields of psychology. *American Psychologist, 19,* 645–653.

Loevinger, J. (1957). Objective tests as instruments of psychological theory. *Psychological Reports, 3,* 635–694.

Long, J. A., & Sandiford, P. (1935). *The validation of test items.* Toronto: University of Toronto.

Lord, F. M. (1980). *Applications of item response theory to practical testing problems.* Hillsdale, N.J.: Erlbaum.

Lord, F. M., & Novick, M. R. (1968). *Statistical theories of mental test scores.* Reading, Mass.: Addison-Wesley.

Lovell, V. R. (1967). The human use of personality tests: A dissenting view. *American Psychologist, 22,* 383–393.

Luschene, R. E., O'Neil, H. H., & Dunn, T. (1974). Equivalent validity of a completely computerized MMPI. *Journal of Personality Assessment, 38,* 353–361.

Lyell, C. (1830–1833). *Principles of geology.* London: Murray.

Lynch, G. C. (1968). *Walter Dill Scott: Pioneer in personnel management.* Austix, Tex.: Bureau of Business Research.

MacFarlane, J. W. (1950). Inter-professional collaboration with medicine and other related fields. *American Psychologist, 5,* 112–114.

MacKinnon, D. W. (1962). The nature and nurture of creative talent. *American Psychologist, 17,* 484–495.

Macy, J. W., Jr. (1965). Psychological testing and the public service. *American Psychologist, 20,* 883–884.

Maier, M. H., & Fuchs, E. F. (1973). *Effectiveness of selection and classification testing* (Research Rep. No. 1179). Alexandria, Va.: U.S. Army Research Institute for the Behavioral and Social Sciences.

Marco, G. L. (1981). Equating tests in an era of test disclosure. In B. F. Green (Ed.), *Issues in testing: Coaching, disclosure, and ethnic bias.* San Francisco: Jossey-Bass.

Margeneau, H. (1950). *The nature of physical reality.* New York: McGraw-Hill.

Mash, E. J. (1979). What is behavioral assessment? *Behavioral Assessment, 1,* 23–29.

Masling, J. (1965). Differential indoctrination of examiners and Rorschach responses. *Journal of Consulting Psychology, 29,* 198–201.

Matarazzo, J. D. (1972). *Wechsler's measurement and appraisal of adult intelligence* (5th ed.). Baltimore: Williams & Wilkins.

Matarazzo, J. D. (1986). Computerized clinical psychologist test interpretations: Unvalidated plus all mean and no sigma. *American Psychologist, 41,* 14–24.

Matarazzo, J. D. (1990). Psychological assessment versus psychological testing: Validation from Binet to the school, clinic, and courtroom. *American Psychologist, 45,* 999–1017.

Matarrazo, J. D., & Herman, D. O. (1984). Relationship of education and IQ in the WAIS–R standardized sample. *Journal of Consulting and Clinical Psychology, 52,* 631–634.

Maxfield, F. N. (1918). Some mathematical aspects of the Binet–Simon tests, *Journal of Educational Psychology, 9,* 1–12.

May, M. A. (1925). The present status of the Will-Temperament tests. *Journal of Applied Psychology, 9,* 29–52.

May, W. W. (1978). A psychologist of many hats: A tribute to Mark Arthur May. *American Psychologist, 33,* 653–663.

McCall, R. B., Hogarty, P. S., & Hurlburt, N. (1972). Transitions in infant sensorimotor development and the prediction of childhood IQ. *American Psychologist, 27,* 728–748.

McCall, R. J. (1959). Rorschach test. In O. K. Buros (Ed.), *The fifth mental measurements yearbook,* pp. 278–285. Highland Park, N.J.: Gryphon Press.

McCall, W. A. (1922). *How to measure in education.* New York: Macmillan.

McClelland, D. C. (1973). Testing for competence rather than for "intelligence." *American Psychologist, 28*, 1–14.

McClelland, D. C. (1976). *The achieving society.* New York: Irvington.

McClelland, D. C. (1985). *Human motivation.* Glenview, Ill.: Scott, Foresman.

McComas, H. C. (1914). Some tests for efficiency in telephone operating. *Journal of Philosophy, Psychology, and Scientific Methodology, 11*, 293–294.

McCrae, R. R., & Costa, R. T., Jr. (1990). *Personality in adulthood.* New York: Guilford.

McGehee, W. (1964). And Esau was an hairy man. *American Psychologist, 19*, 799–804.

McGeoch, J. A. (1935). Learning as an operationally defined concept. *Psychological Bulletin, 32*, 688.

McGrath, J. E. (n.d.). The judgment call follies or research and all that jazz. Unpublished mimeograph.

McGregor, D. (1935). Scientific measurement and psychology. *Psychological Review, 42*, 246–266.

McLoughlin, J. A., & Lewis, R. B. (1992). *Assessing special students* (3rd ed.). Columbus, Ohio: Merrill.

McTeer, W. (1952). A survey of graduate school opinion regarding professional training below the doctorate level. *American Psychologist, 7*, 14–19.

Medina, N. J., & Neill, D. M. (1990). *Fallout from the testing explosion: How 100 million standardized exams undermine equity and excellence in America's public schools* (3rd Ed.). Cambridge, Mass.: FairTest.

Meehl, P. E. (1945). The dynamics of "structured" personality tests. *Journal of Clinical Psychology, 1*, 296–303.

Meehl, P. E. (1960). The cognitive activity of the clinician. *American Psychologist, 15*, 19–27.

Meehl, P. E. (1978). Theoretical risks and tabular asterisks: Sir Karl, Sir Ronald, and the slow progress of soft psychology. *Journal of Consulting and Clinical Psychology, 46*, 806–834.

Meehl, P. E. (1990). Appraising and amending theories: The strategy of Lakatosian defense and two principles that warrant it. *Psychological Inquiry, 1*, 108–141.

Meehl, P. E., & Rosen, A. (1955). Antecedent probability and the efficiency of psychometric signs, patterns or cutting scores. *Psychological Bulletin, 52*, 194.

Meier, N. C. (1923). A study of the Downey test by the method of estimates. *Journal of Educational Psychology, 14*, 385–395.

Meisels, S. J., & Provence, S. (1989). *Screening and assessment: Guidelines for identifying young disabled and developmentally vulnerable children and their families.* Washington, D.C.: National Center for Clinical Infant Programs.

Menninger, W. C. (1950). The relationship of clinical psychology and psychiatry. *American Psychologist, 5*, 3–15.

Messick, S. (1965). Personality measurement and the ethics of assessment. *American Psychologist, 20*, 136–142.

Messick, S. (1980). Test validity and the ethics of assessment. *American Psychologist, 35*, 1012–1027.

Messick, S. (1980). *The effectiveness of coaching for the SAT: Review and reanalysis of research from the fifties to FTC.* Princeton, N.J.: Educational Testing Service.

Messick, S. (1988). The once and future issues of validity: Assessing the meaning and consequences of measurement. In H. Wainer & H. I. Braun (Eds.), *Test validity.* Hillsdale, N.J.: Erlbaum.

Messick, S., & Jackson, D. N. (1961). Acquiescence and the factorial interpretation of the MMPI. *Psychological Bulletin, 58*, 299–304.

Meyer, M. M., & Tolman, R. S. (1955). Correspondence between attitudes and images of parental figures in TAT stories and in therapeutic interviews. *Journal of Consulting Psychology, 19*, 79–82.

Milberg, W. P., Hebben, N., & Kaplan, E. (1986). The Boston process approach to neuropsychological assessment. In I. Grant & K. M. Adams (Eds.), *Assessment of neuropsychiatric disorders.* New York: Oxford University Press.

Mill, J. S. (1843/1973). *A system of logic.* Toronto: University of Toronto Press.

Mill, J. S. (1848/1978). *Principles of political economy.* Toronto: University of Toronto Press.

Mill, J. S. (1909/1971). *Autobiography.* London: Oxford University Press.

Miller, G. A. (1970). Assessment of psychotechnology. *American Psychologist, 25*, 991–1001.

Millon, T. (1981). *Disorders of personality: DSM–III: Axis II.* New York: Wiley.

Millon, T. (1984). Interpretive guide to the Millon Clinical Multiaxial Inventory. In P. McReynolds & G. J. Chelune (Eds.), *Advances in psychological assessment: Vol. 6.* San Francisco: Jossey-Bass.

Millon, T. (1985). The MCMI provides a good assessment of DSM–II disorders: The MCMI–II will prove even better. *Journal of Personality Assessment, 49*, 379–391.

Millon, T. (1987). *Millon Clinical Multiaxial Inventory II manual.* Minneapolis: National Computer Systems.

Millon, T., & Green, C. (1989). Interpretive guide to the Millon Clinical Multiaxial Inventory (MCMI–II). In C. S. Newmark (Ed.), *Major psy-*

chological assessment instruments: Vol. 2. Boston: Allyn and Bacon.

Milton, R. (1992). *The facts of life: Shattering the myth of Darwinism.* London: Fourth Estate.

Miner, J. B. (1914). Correlation. *Psychological Bulletin, 11,* 177–185.

Minton, H. L. (1988). *Lewis M. Terman: Pioneer in psychological testing.* New York: New York University Press.

Mischel, W. (1968). *Personality and assessment.* New York: Wiley.

Mischel, W. (1973). Toward a cognitive social learning reconceptualization of personality. *Psychological Review, 80,* 252–283.

Mischel, W. (1993). *Introduction to personality* (5th ed.). New York: Harcourt Brace Jovanovich.

Mischel, W., & Peake, P. K. (1982). Beyond déjà vu in the search for cross-situational consistency. *Psychological Review, 89,* 730–755.

Mitchell, J. V., Jr. (Ed.). (1983). *Tests in Print III: An index to tests, test reviews, and the literature on specific tests.* Lincoln: Buros Institute of Mental Measurements, University of Nebraska.

Mitchell, J. V., Jr. (Ed.). (1985). *The ninth mental measurements yearbook.* Highland Park, N.J.: Gryphon.

Moede, W. (1926). Kraftfahrer–Eignunsprunfungen beim Deutchen Herr. 1915 bis 1918. *Ind. Psychot., 3,* 23–28.

Monboddo, J. B. (1773). *The origins and progress of language.* Cited in Hearnshaw (1987), pp. 112, 325.

Moreland, K. L. (1985). Validation of computer-based test interpretations: Problems and prospects. *Journal of Consulting and Clinical Psychology, 53,* 816–825.

Morgan, C. D., & Murray, H. A. (1935). A method for investigating fantasies: The Thematic Apperception Test. *Archives of Neurological Psychiatry, 34,* 289–306.

Morrison, D. E., & Henkel, R. E. (Eds.), (1970).*The significance test controversy.* Chicago: Aldine.

Mosier, C. I. (1938). On the validity of neurotic questionnaires. *Journal of Social Psychology, 9,* 3–16.

Mosier, C. I. (1941). Bernreuter Personality Inventory. In O. K. Buros (Ed.), *The 1940 mental measurements yearbook* (pp. 81–82). Highland Park, N.J.: Gryphon.

Mosier, C. I. (1947). A critical examination of the concepts of face validity. *Educational and Psychological Measurement, 7,* 191–205.

Munsterberg, H. (1913). *Psychology and industrial efficiency.* Boston: Houghton Mifflin.

Murphy, K. R., & Davidshofer, C. O. (1988). *Psychological testing: Principles and applications.* Englewood Cliffs, N.J.: Prentice Hall.

Murray, H. A. (1938). *Explorations in personality.* Cambridge, Mass.: Harvard University Press.

Murray, H. A. (1943). *Thematic Apperception Test manual.* Cambridge, Mass.: Harvard University Press.

Murstein, B. I. (1972). Normative written TAT responses for a college sample. *Journal of Personality Assessment, 36,* 213–217.

Neisser, U. (1967). *Cognitive psychology.* New York: Appleton-Century-Crofts.

Neisser, U. (1976). *Cognition and reality: Principles and implications of cognitive psychology.* San Francisco: Freeman.

Neitzel, M. T., Bernstein, D. A., & Milich, R. (1991). *Introduction to clinical psychology* (3rd ed.). Englewood Cliffs, N.J.: Prentice Hall.

Neitzel, M. T., Bernstein, D. A., & Russell, R. L. (1988). Assessment of anxiety and fear. In A. S. Bellack & M. Hersen (Eds.), *Behavioral assessment: A practical handbook* (3rd ed.). New York: Pergamon Press.

Nettler, B. (1959). Test burning in Texas. *American Psychologist, 14,* 682–683.

Newcomb, T. (1941). Bernreuter Personality Inventory. In O. K. Buros (Ed.), *The 1940 Mental Measurements Yearbook,* (pp. 82–83). Highland Park, N.J.: Gryphon.

Newmark, C. S. (Ed.). (1985). *Major psychological assessment instruments.* Boston: Allyn and Bacon.

Niehaus, R. J. (1979). *Computer-assisted human resources planning.* New York: Wiley.

Norsworthy, N. (1908). The validity of judgments of character. In *Essays philosophical and psychological in honor of William James by his colleagues at Columbia University.* New York: Longmans, Green.

Novick, M. R. (1981). Federal guidelines and professional standards. *American Psychologist, 36,* 1035–1046.

Odell, C. W. (1930). *Educational measurement in high school.* New York: Century.

Osler, S. F., & Fivel, M. W. (1961). Concept attainment: I. The role of age and intelligence in concept attainment by induction. *Journal of Experimental Psychology, 62,* 1–8.

Otis, A. S. (1916). Some logical aspects of the Binet scale. *Psychological Review, 23,* 129–152, 165–179.

Otis, A. S. (1918). An absolute point scale for the group measurement of intelligence. *Journal of Educational Psychology, 9,* 239–261, 333–348.

Overholser, J. C. (1990). Retest reliability of the Millon Clinical Multiaxial Inventory. *Journal of Personality Assessment, 55,* 202–208.

Packard, V. (1964). *The naked society.* New York: McKay.

Page, H. E., & Passey, G. E. (1949). The role of psychology in medical education. *American Psychologist, 4,* 405–406.

Paivio, A. (1971). *Imagery and verbal processes.* New York: Holt, Rinehart & Winston.

Parker, I. (1992). *Discourse dynamics: Critical analysis for social and individual psychology.* London: Routledge.

Pascal, G. R., & Suttell, B. J. (1951). *The Bender–Gestalt Test: Quantification and validity for adults.* New York: Grune & Stratton.

Passmore, J. (1957). *A hundred years of philosophy.* London: Duckworth.

Pastore, N. (1978). The army intelligence tests and Walter Lippmann. *Journal of the History of the Behavioral Sciences, 14,* 316–327.

Peak, H. (1953). Problems of objective observation. In L. Festinger & D. Katz (Eds.), *Research methods in the behavioral sciences.* New York: Dryden Press.

Pearlman, K., Schmidt, F. L., & Hunter, J. E. (1980). Validity generalization results for tests used to predict job proficiency and training success in clerical occupations. *Journal of Applied Psychology, 65,* 373–406.

Pearson, K. (1896). Mathematical contributions to the theory of evolution: III. Regression, heredity, and panmixia. *Philosophical Transactions of the Royal Society of London, 187* (Series A), 253–318.

Peatman, J. G. (1950). The problem of protecting the public by appropriate legislation for the practice of psychology. *American Psychologist, 5,* 102–103.

Pepper, S. (1942). *World hypotheses.* Berkeley: University of California Press.

Pirozzolo, F. J., & Harrell, W. (1985). The neuropsychology of learning disabilities. In L. C. Hartlage & C. F. Telzrow (Eds.), *The neuropsychology of individual differences: A developmental perspective.* New York: Plenum.

Plant, W. T., & Richardson, H. (1958). The IQ of the average college student. *Journal of Consulting Psychology, 5,* 229–231.

Poffenberger, A. T. (1921). Symposium on intelligence and its measurement. *Psychological Review, 18,* 426–427.

Poffenberger, A. T. (1973). *James McKeen Cattell: Man of science.* New York: Arno Press.

Polyani, M. (1978). *Personal knowledge.* Chicago: University of Chicago Press.

Popenoe, P. (1921). Measuring human intelligence. *Journal of Heredity, 12,* 231–236.

Posner, M. (1988). Structures and functions of selective attention. In T. Boll & D. K. Bryant (Eds.), *Clinical neuropsychology and brain function: Research and practice.* Washington, D.C.: American Psychological Association.

Pressey, S. L. (1949). The place and functions of psychology in undergraduate programs. *American Psychologist, 4,* 148–150.

Pressey, S. L., & Pressey, L. C. (1923). *Introduction to the use of standard tests.* Yonkers-on-Hudson, N.Y.: World Book.

Raimy, V. C. (Ed.). (1950). *Training in clinical psychology.* New York: Prentice Hall.

Ramul, K. (1960). The problem of measurement in the psychology of the eighteenth century. *American Psychologist, 15,* 256–265.

Ramul, K. (1963). Some early measurements and ratings in psychology. *American Psychologist, 18,* 653–659.

Raven, J. C. (1938). *Guide to using the Progressive Matrices.* London: Lewis.

Reed, J. (1987). Robert M. Yerkes and the mental testing movement. In M. M. Sokal (Ed.), *Psychological testing and American society: 1890–1930.* New Brunswick, N.J.: Rutgers University Press.

Reid, T. (1785/1941). *Essays on the intellectual powers of man.* (A. A. Woozley, Ed.). London: Macmillan.

Reid, T. (1788/1846). Essays on the active powers of man. In W. Hamilton (Ed.), *The works of Thomas Reid* (8th ed.). Edinburgh: Thin.

Reitan, R. M. (n.d.). *Manual for the administration of neuropsychological batteries for adults and children.* Seattle: Privately published.

Reitan, R. M., & Davison, L. A. (Eds.). (1974). *Clinical neuropsychology: Current status and applications.* Washington, D.C.: Winston.

Reynolds, C. R. (1982). Methods for detecting construct and predictive bias. In R. A. Berk (Ed.), *Handbook of methods for detecting test bias.* Baltimore: Johns Hopkins University Press.

Reznikoff, M. (1972). Rorschach. In O. K. Buros (Ed.), *Seventh mental measurements yearbook: Vol. 1,* pp. 446–449. Highland Park, N.J.: Gryphon.

Ries, A., & Trout, J. (1986). *Positioning: The battle for your mind* (2nd ed.). New York: McGraw-Hill.

Robinson, D. N. (1981). *An intellectual history of psychology.* New York: Macmillan.

Rogers, C. R. (1946). Significant aspects of client-centered therapy. *American Psychologist, 1,* 415–422.

Rogers, H. W. (1917). Psychological tests for typists and stenographers. *Journal of Applied Psychology, 1,* 268–274.

Rogers, T. B. (1987). Hearing the unsaids: An essay on the role of folkloristics in metapsychology. In H. Stam, T. B. Rogers, & K. J. Gergen (Eds.), *The analysis of psychological theory: Metapsychological perspectives.* New York: Hemisphere.

Rogers, T. B. (1990). The development of a new measuring instrument. In J. Froom (Ed.), *Func-*

tional status measurement in primary care (pp. 27–42). New York: Springer-Verlag.

Rogers, T. B., & Rogers, P. J. (1990). On the origins of "validity" in psychological testing: A conceptual history. Paper presently under review.

Rorer, L. G. (1965). The great response style myth. *Psychological Bulletin, 63,* 129–156.

Rorschach, H., & Oberholzer, E. (1924). The application of the interpretation of form to psychoanalysis. *Journal of Nervous and Mental Disease, 60,* 225–248, 359–379.

Ross, C. C. (1936). A needed emphasis in psychological research. *Psychological Review, 43,* 197–206.

Ross, S., & Lockman, R. F. (1964). Survey of graduate education in psychology: Some trends for the last decade. *American Psychologist, 19,* 623–628.

Royce, J. R. (1963). Factors as theoretical constructs. *American Psychologist, 18,* 522–528.

Ruch, G. M., & Del Manzo, M. C. (1923). The Downey Will-Temperament Group Test: Further analysis of its reliability and validity. *Journal of Applied Psychology, 7,* 64–76.

Rugg, H. O. (Ed.). (1921). Intelligence and its measurement: A symposium. *Journal of Educational Psychology, 10,* 123–147, 195–216, 271–275.

Ruschival, M. L., & Way, J. G. (1971). The WPPSI and the Stanford–Binet Form L–M: A validity and reliability study using gifted preschool children. *Journal of Consulting and Clinical Psychology, 37,* 163.

Russell, E. W., Neuringer, C., & Goldstein, G. (1970). *Assessment of brain damage: A neuropsychological key approach.* New York: Wiley.

Saffir, M. A. (1950). Certification versus licensing legislation. *American Psychologist, 5,* 105–106.

Salmon, W. C. (1975). Confirmation and relevance. In G. Maxwell (Ed.), *Induction, probability, and confirmation.* Minneapolis: University of Minnesota Press.

Salmon, W. C. (1984). *Scientific explanation and the causal structure of the world.* Princeton, N.J.: Princeton University Press.

Sampson, E. E. (1991). The democratization of psychology. *Theory and Psychology, 1,* 275–298.

Sampson, J. P. (1983). Computer-assisted testing and assessment: Current status and implications for the future. *Measurement and Evaluation in Guidance, 5,* 293–299.

Samuelson, F. (1977). World War I intelligence testing and the development of psychology. *Journal of the History of the Behavioral Sciences, 13,* 274–282.

Samuelson, F. (1979). The technological achievement of the army testing program. In A. R. Buss (Ed.), *Psychology in social context.* New York: Irvington.

Samuelson, F. (1987). Was early mental testing: (a) racist inspired; (b) objective science; (c) a technol-

ogy for democracy; (d) the origin of multiple-choice exams; (e) none of the above? (mark the right answer). In M. M. Sokal (Ed.), *Psychological testing and American society: 1890–1930.* New Brunswick, N.J.: Rutgers University Press.

Sandiford, P. (1938). Review of educational, psychological, and personality tests. *American Journal of Psychology, 51,* 200.

Sarason, I. G. (1961). Test anxiety and the intellectual performance of college students. *Journal of Educational Psychology, 52,* 201–206.

Sarason, I. G. (1972). Experimental approaches to test anxiety: Attention and the uses of information. In C. D. Speilberger (Ed.), *Anxiety: Current trends in theory and research.* New York: Academic Press.

Sarason, S. B. (1985). *Caring and compassion in clinical practice: Issues in the selection, training, and behavior of helping professionals.* San Francisco: Jossey-Bass.

Sarbin, T. R. (1986). The narrative as a root metaphor for psychology. In T. R. Sarbin (Ed.), *Narrative psychology: The storied nature of human conduct.* New York: Praeger.

Sattler, J. M. (1970). Racial "experimenter effects" in experimentation, testing, and interviewing. *Psychological Bulletin, 73,* 137–160.

Sawyer, J. (1966). Measurement *and* prediction, clinical *and* statistical. *Psychological Bulletin, 66,* 178–200.

Saxe, C. H. (1950). A quantitative comparison of psychodiagnostic formulations from the TAT and therapeutic contacts. *Journal of Consulting Psychology, 14,* 116–127.

Scarr-Salapatek, S. (1976). Unknowns in the IQ equation. In N. J. Block & G. Dworkin (Eds.), *The IQ controversy: Critical readings.* New York: Pantheon.

Schippmann, J. S., Prien, E. P., & Katz, J. A. (1990). The reliability and validity of in-basket performance measures. *Personnel Psychology, 43,* 837–860.

Schmidt, F. L. (1988). Validity generalization and the future of criterion-related validity. In H. Wainer & H. I. Braun (Eds.), *Test validity.* Hillsdale, N.J.: Erlbaum.

Schmidt, F. L., Berner, J. G., & Hunter, J. E. (1973). Racial differences in validity of employment tests: Reality or illusion? *Journal of Applied Psychology, 58,* 5–9.

Schofield, W. (1966). Clinical and counseling psychology: Some perspectives. *American Psychologist, 21,* 122–131.

Seard, K. (1950). Are psychologists afraid of therapy? *American Psychologist, 5,* 50–54.

Serlin, R. C., & Lapsley, D. K. (1985). Rationality in psychological research: The good enough principle. *American Psychologist, 40,* 73–83.

Sharma, S. L. (1970). A historical background of the development of nosology in psychiatry and psychology. *American Psychologist, 25*, 248–253.

Shephard, L. A. (1984). Setting performance standards. In R. A. Berk (Ed.), *A guide to criterion-referenced test construction*. Baltimore: Johns Hopkins University Press.

Shriver, S. (1965). Suggestions to the American Psychological Association. *American Psychologist, 20*, 876–877.

Shuey, A. M. (1966). *The testing of negro intelligence* (2nd ed.). New York: Social Science Press.

Siess, T. F., & Jackson, D. N. (1971). Vocational interests and personality: Evidence from the Personality Research Form. In P. McReynolds (Ed.), *Advances in psychological assessment: Vol. 2*. Palo Alto, Calif.: Science and Behavior Books.

Silverstein, A. B. (1977). Alternative factor analytic solutions for the Wechsler Intelligence Scale for Children–Revised. *Educational and Psychological Measurement, 37*, 121–124.

Simpson, B. R. (1912). *Correlations of mental abilities* (Teachers College Series no. 53). New York: Columbia University Contributions to Education. (Reprinted in 1972 by AMS Press, New York.)

Skinner, B. F. (1938). *The behavior of organisms: An experimental analysis*. New York: Appleton-Century.

Skinner, B. F. (1945). Symposium on operationism: Rejoinders and second thoughts. *Psychological Review, 52*, 291.

Skinner, H. A., & Allen, B. A. (1983). Does the computer make a difference? Computerized versus face-to-face versus self-report assessment of alcohol, drug, and tobacco use. *Journal of Consulting and Clinical Psychology, 51*, 267–275.

Smith, L. (1986). *Behaviorism and logical positivism*. Palo Alto, Calif.: Stanford University Press.

Snyderman, M., & Herrnstein, R. J. (1983). Intelligence tests and the Immigration Act of 1924. *American Psychologist, 38*, 986–995.

Sokal, M. M. (1981). *An education in psychology: James McKeen Cattell's journal and letters from Germany and England 1880–1888*. Cambridge, Mass.: MIT Press.

Sokal, M. M. (Ed.). (1987). *Psychological testing and American society: 1890–1930*. New Brunswick, N.J.: Rutgers University Press.

Space, L. G. (1981). The computer as psychometrician. *Behavior Research Methods and Instrumentation, 13*, 595–606.

Spearman, C. (1904). General intelligence, objectively determined and measured. *American Journal of Psychology, 15*, 201–293.

Spearman, C. (1927). *The abilities of man: Their nature and measurement*. New York: Macmillan.

Spence, K. W. (1944). The nature of theory construction in contemporary psychology. *Psychological Review, 51*, 47–68.

Springer, S. P., & Deutsch, G. (1989). *Left brain, right brain* (3rd ed.). New York: Freeman.

Staff, Psychological Branch, Office of the Air Surgeon. (1944). The Aviation Cadet Qualifying Examination of the army air forces. *Psychological Bulletin, 41*, 385–394.

Staff, Psychological Section, Office of the Air Surgeon. (1945). Psychological activities in the training command, army air forces. *Psychological Bulletin, 42*, 37–54.

Stagner, R. (1958). The gullibility of personnel managers. *Personnel Psychology, 11*, 347–352.

Stam, H. J., Rogers, T. B., & Gergen, K. J. (1987). *The analysis of psychological theory: Metapsychological perspectives*. New York: Hemisphere.

Star, S. A. (1950). The screening of psychoneurotics in the army: Technical development of tests. In S. A. Stouffer, L. Guttman, E. A. Suchman, P. F. Lazarsfeld, S. A. Star, & J. A. Clausen (Eds.), *The American soldier: Vol. IV. Measurement and prediction*. New York: Wiley.

Starch, D. (1915a). The measurement of achievement in English grammar. *Journal of Educational Psychology, 6*, 615–626.

Starch, D. (1915b). The measurement of efficiency in reading. *Journal of Educational Psychology, 6*, 1–24.

Starch, D. (1915c). The measurement of efficiency in writing. *Journal of Educational Psychology, 6*, 106–114.

Starch, D. (1916). A scale for measuring ability in arithmetic. *Journal of Educational Psychology, 7*, 213–222.

Steele, R. S. (1986). Deconstructing histories: Toward a systematic criticism of psychological narratives. In T. R. Sarbin (Ed.), *Narrative psychology: The storied nature of human conduct*. New York: Praeger.

Stein, M. I. (1955). *The Thematic Apperception Test*. Reading, Mass.: Addison-Wesley.

Stenquist, J. L. (1923). Measurements of mechanical ability. *Contributions to Education, 130*(Whole No.).

Stern, W. (1914). *The psychological method of testing intelligence*. Baltimore: Warwick and York.

Sternberg, R. J. (1977). *Intelligence, information processing, and analogical reasoning: The componential analysis of human abilities*. Hillsdale, N.J.: Erlbaum.

Sternberg, R. J. (1984). Toward a triarchic theory of human intelligence. *Behavioral and Brain Sciences, 7*, 269–287.

Sternberg, R. J. (1988). *The triarchic mind: A new theory of human intelligence*. New York: Viking Press.

Sternberg, R. J., & Salter, W. (1982). Conceptions of intelligence. In R. J. Sternberg (Ed.), *Handbook of human intelligence*. New York: Cambridge University Press.

Stevens, S. S. (1935). The operational basis of psychology. *American Journal of Psychology, 47,* 323–330.

Stevens, S. S. (1951). *Handbook of experimental psychology.* New York: Wiley.

Stolurow, L. M. (1960). Teaching machines and special education. *Educational and Psychological Measurement, 20,* 429–448.

Stout, D. A. (1987). *Statistics in American psychology: The social construction of experimental and correlational psychology, 1900–1930.* Doctoral dissertation, University of Edinburgh, Scotland.

Streiner, D. L., & Miller, H. R. (1989). The MCMI–II: How much better than the MCMI? *Journal of Personality Assessment, 53,* 81–84.

Striker, L. J. (1974). Personality Research Form: Factor structure and response style involvement. *Journal of Consulting and Clinical Psychology, 42,* 529–537.

Strong, E. K., Jr., Hansen, J. C., & Campbell, D. C. (1985). *Strong Vocational Interest Blank: Revised edition of Form T325, Strong–Campbell Interest Inventory.* Stanford, Calif.: Stanford University Press.

Stuit, D. B. (1951). The preparation of a test manual. *American Psychologist, 6,* 167–170.

Sundberg, N. D. (1954). A note concerning the history of testing. *American Psychologist, 9,* 150–151.

Sundberg, N. D. (1961). The practice of psychological testing in clinical services in the United States. *American Psychologist, 16,* 79–83.

Suppe, F. (1974). *The structure of scientific theories.* Urbana: University of Illinois Press.

Swanson, J. M., Posner, M., Potkin, S., Bonforte, S., Youpa, D., Fiore, C., Cantwell, D., & Crinella, F. (1991). Activating tasks for the study of visual–spatial attention in ADHD children: A cognitive anatomic approach. *Journal of Child Neurology, 6* (Suppl.), 119–127.

Sweetland, R. C., & Keyser, D. J. (Eds.). (1991). *Tests: A comprehensive reference for assessments in psychology, education and business.* Kansas City, Mo.: Test Corporation of America.

Tallent, N. (1987). Computer-generated psychological reports: A look at the modern psychometric machine. *Journal of Personality Assessment, 51,* 95–108.

Taulbee, E. S., & Clark, T. L. (1982). *A comprehensive, annotated bibliography of selected psychological tests: Interpersonal Check List, MMPI Short Form, and The Blacky Pictures.* Troy, N.Y.: Whitson.

Taylor, H. C., & Russell, J. T. (1939). The relationship of validity coefficients to the practical effectiveness of tests in selection. *Journal of Applied Psychology, 23,* 565–578.

Taylor, J. A. (1953). A personality scale of manifest anxiety. *Journal of Abnormal and Social Psychology, 48,* 285–290.

Tellegen, A. (1991). *Positive illusions.* New York: Basic Books.

Terman, L. M. (1906). *Genius and stupidity.* Unpublished doctoral dissertation, Clark University, Worchester, Mass.

Terman, L. M. (1916). *The measurement of intelligence.* Boston: Houghton Mifflin.

Terman, L. M. (1922). The great conspiracy or the impulse imperious of intelligence testers, psychoanalyzed and exposed by Mr. Lippmann. *New Republic, 33,* 116–120.

Terman, L. M. (1924). The mental test as a psychological method. *Psychological Review, 31,* 93–117.

Terman, L. M., & Childs, H. G. (1912). A tentative revision and extension of the Binet–Simon measuring scale of intelligence. *Journal of Educational Psychology, 3,* 61–74, 133–143, 198–208, 277–289.

Terman, L. M., & Oden, M. H. (1947). *The gifted child grows up.* Palo Alto, Calif.: Stanford University Press.

Thissen, D., Steinberg, L., & Wainer, H. (1988). Use of item response theory in the study of group differences in trace lines. In H. Wainer & H. I. Braun (Eds.), *Test validity.* Hillsdale, N.J.: Erlbaum.

Thompson, R. F. (1978). Starke R. Hathaway. *American Psychologist, 33,* 63–68.

Thorndike, E. L. (1898). Animal intelligence. *Psychological Review* (Monograph Suppl.) 2.

Thorndike, E. L. (1900). *The human nature club: An introduction to the study of mental life.* Chautauqua, N.Y.: Chautauqua Press.

Thorndike, E. L. (1903). *Educational psychology.* New York: Lemcke and Buechner.

Thorndike, E. L. (1904). *Mental and social measurements.* New York: Science Press.

Thorndike, R. L., & Hagen, E. (1959). *10,000 careers.* New York: Wiley.

Thorndike, R. L., Hagen, E. P., & Sattler, J. M. (1986). *The Stanford–Binet Intelligence Scale: Technical manual* (4th ed.). Chicago: Riverside.

Thornton, G. C., & Byham, W. C. (1982). *Assessment centers and managerial performance.* Orlando, Fla.: Academic Press.

Thurstone, L. L. (1919). Mental tests for prospective telegraphers. *Journal of Applied Psychology, 3,* 110–117.

Thurstone, L. L. (1935). *Vectors of the mind.* Chicago: University of Chicago Press.

Thurstone, L. L. (1938). Primary Mental Abilities. *Psychometric Monographs* (Whole No. 1).

Thurstone, L. L., & Thurstone, T. G. (1941). Factorial studies of intelligence. *Psychometric Monographs, 2,* 1–94.

Tilton, J. W. (1949). Intelligence test scores as indicative of ability to learn. *Educational and Psychological Measurement, 9,* 291–296.

Tittle, C. K. (1982). Use of judgmental methods in item bias studies. In R. A. Berk (Ed.), *Handbook of methods for detecting test bias* (pp. 31–63). Baltimore: Johns Hopkins University Press.

Tizard, J. (1977). The Burt affair. *University of London Bulletin,* No. 41.

Toelken, B. (1979). *The dynamics of folklore.* Boston: Houghton Mifflin.

Tollfer, A. (1980). *The third wave.* New York: Morrow.

Tolman, E. C. (1932). *Purposive behavior in animals and men.* New York: Appleton-Century.

Tolman, E. C. (1936). An operational analysis of "demands." *Erkenntnis, 6,* 383–390.

Tomeski, E. A., & Lazarus, H. (1975). *People-oriented computer systems: The computer in crisis.* New York: Van Nostrand Reinhold.

Tompkins, S. S. (1947). *The Thematic Apperception Test.* New York: Grune & Stratton.

Toops, H. A. (1923). Tests for vocational guidance of children thirteen to sixteen. *Teachers College Contracts in Education, 136*(Whole No.).

Torgerson, W. S. (1958). *Methods of scaling.* New York: Wiley.

Toulmin, S., & Goodfield, J. (1965). *The discovery of time.* London: Hutchinson.

Trites, R. L., Blouin, A. G. A., & LaPrade, K. (1982). Factor analysis of the Connors Teacher Rating Scale based on a large normative sample. *Journal of Consulting and Clinical Psychology, 50,* 615–623.

Turkington, C. (1992, December). Ruling opens door—a crack—to IQ testing some Black kids. *APA Monitor,* pp. 28–29.

Tyler, L. E. (1965). *The psychology of individual differences.* New York: Appleton-Century-Crofts.

Tyron, R. C. (1957). Reliability and behavior domain validity: Reformulation and historical critique. *Psychological Bulletin, 54,* 229–249.

Tzeng, O. C. S. (1987). Strong–Campbell Interest Inventory. In D. J. Keyser & R. C. Sweetland (Eds.), *Test critiques compendium.* Kansas City, Mo.: Test Corporation of America.

Underwood, B., & Moore, B. S. (1981). Sources of behavioral consistency. *Journal of Personality and Social Psychology, 40,* 780–785.

Van Gennep, A. (1909/1960). *The rites of passage.* Chicago: University of Chicago Press.

Van Hagen, J., & Kaufman, A. S. (1975). Factor analysis of the WISC–R for a group of mentally retarded children and adolescents. *Journal of Clinical and Consulting Psychology, 43,* 661–667.

Vernon, P. E. (1960). *The structure of human abilities.* New York: Wiley.

von Mayrhauser, R. T. (1987). The manager, the medic, and the mediator: The clash of professional psychological styles and the wartime origins of group mental testing. In M. M. Sokal (Ed.), *Psychological testing and American society: 1890–1930.* New Brunswick, N.J.: Rutgers University Press.

von Mayrhauser, R. T. (1992). The mental testing community and validity: A prehistory. *American Psychologist, 47,* 244–253.

Wade, N. (1976, November 26). IQ and heredity. *Science, 194* (no. 4268), 919.

Wahlstrom, M., & Boersman, F. J. (1968). The influence of test-wiseness upon achievement. *Educational and Psychological Measurement, 28,* 413–420.

Wainer, H. I., & Braun, H. I.(Eds.). (1988). *Test validity.* Hillsdale, N.J.: Erlbaum.

Wallace, J. (1966). An abilities conception of personality: Some implications for personality measurement. *American Psychologist, 21,* 132–138.

Walsh, W. B., & Betz, N. E. (1990). *Tests and assessment* (2nd ed.). Englewood Cliffs, N.J.: Prentice Hall.

Washburn, S. L. (1960). Tools and human evolution. *Scientific American, 203,* 63–75.

Watson, G. (1938). Personality and character measurement. *Review of Educational Research, 8,* 269–291.

Watson, J. B. (1913). Psychology as the behaviorist views it. *Psychological Review, 20,* 158–177.

Wechsler, D. (1939). *The measurement of adult intelligence.* Baltimore: Williams & Wilkins.

Wechsler, D. (1955). *Manual for the Wechsler Adult Intelligence Scale.* New York: Psychological Corporation.

Wechsler, D. (1958). *The measurement and appraisal of adult intelligence.* Baltimore: Williams & Wilkins.

Weiss, D. J. (1982). Improving measurement quality and efficiency with adaptive testing. *Applied Psychological Measurement, 6,* 473–492.

Weiss, D. J. (1985). Adaptive testing by computer. *Journal of Consulting and Clinical Psychology, 53,* 774–789.

Wells, F. L., Williams, R., & Fowler, P. (1938). One hundred superior men. *Journal of Applied Psychology, 22,* 367–384.

Wendt, G. R. (1950). Legislation for the general practice of psychology versus legislation for specialties within psychology. *American Psychologist, 5*, 107–108.

Wesman, A. G. (1968). Intelligent testing. *American Psychologist, 23*, 267–274.

Westby, G. (1953). Review of the Raven Progressive Matrices. In O. K. Buros (Ed.), *The fourth mental measurements yearbook*. Highland Park, N.J.: Gryphon.

Whyte, W. H., Jr. (1956). *The organization man*. New York: Simon & Schuster.

Widiger, T. A. (1985). Review of Millon Clinical Multiaxial Inventory. In J. V. Mitchell (Ed.). *Ninth mental measurements yearbook*, pp. 986–988: Lincoln: University of Nebraska Press.

Widiger, T. A. (1992). The NEO Personality Inventory. In J. J. Kramer & J. C. Conoley (Eds.), *The eleventh mental measurements yearbook*. Lincoln, Neb.: Buros Institute of Mental Measurements.

Widiger, T. A., Williams, J. B. W., Spitzer, R. L., & Frances, A. (1985). The MCMI as a measure of DSM–III. *Journal of Personality Assessment, 49*, 366–378.

Wiggins, J. S. (1968). Personality structure. *Annual Review of Psychology, 19*, 293–350.

Wiggins, J. S. (1973). *Personality and prediction: Principles of personality assessment*. Reading, Mass.: Addison-Wesley.

Wilkinson, S. (Ed.). (1986). *Feminist social psychology: Developing theory and practice*. Milton Keynes, Eng.: Open University Press.

Williams, E. B. (Ed.). (1980). *Construct validity in psychological measurement: Proceedings of a colloquium on theory and application in education and employment*. Princeton, N.J.: Educational Testing Service.

Wilson, S. L. (1987). The development of an automated test of immediate memory and its evaluation on severely physically disabled adults. *Applied Psychology: An International Review, 36*, 311–327.

Winch, R. F., & Moore, D. M. (1956). Does TAT add information to interviews? *Journal of Clinical Psychology, 12*, 316–321.

Wissler, C. (1903). The correlation of mental and physical tests. *Psychological Review* (Monograph Series), *3*(6).

Witkin, H. A. (1959). The perception of the upright. *Scientific American, 200*, 51–56.

Witkin, H. A., & Berry, J. W. (1975). Psychological differentiation in cross-cultural perspective. *Journal of Cross-Cultural Psychology, 6*, 4–87.

Witkin, H. A., Dyk, R. B., Faterson, H. F., Goodenough, D. R., & Karp, S. A. (1974). *Psychological differentiation: Studies of development*. Hillsdale, N.J.: Erlbaum.

Witkin, H. A., & Goodenough, D. R. (1977). Field dependence and interpersonal behavior. *Psychological Bulletin, 84*, 661–689.

Wolf, T. (1973). *Alfred Binet*. Chicago: University of Chicago Press.

Wolfle, D. (1947). Testing is big business. *American Psychologist, 2*, 26.

Wolfle, D. (1950). Legal control of psychological practice. *American Psychologist, 5*, 651–655.

Wood, B. (1919, September 16). Letter to Truman Kelley. Cited in Samuelson (1977).

Woodrow, H. (1940). Interrelations of measures of learning. *Journal of Psychology, 10*, 49–73.

Woodworth, R. S. (1919). Examination of emotional fitness for warfare. *Psychological Bulletin, 16*, 59–60.

Wrenn, C. G. (1949). Potential research talent in the sciences based on intelligence quotients of Ph.D.'s. *Educational Record, 30*, 5–22.

Wright, J. C., & Mischel, W. (1987). A conditional approach to dispositional constructs: The local predictability of social behavior. *Journal of Personality and Social Psychology, 53*, 1159–1177.

Yerkes, R. M. (1917). The Binet versus the point scale method of measuring intelligence. *Journal of Applied Psychology, 1*, 111–122.

Yerkes, R. M. (Ed.). (1921). Psychological examining in the United States Army. *Memoirs of the National Academy of Sciences, 15*, 1–890.

Yerkes, R. M., Bridges, J. W., & Hardwick, R. S. (1915). *A point scale for measuring mental ability*. Baltimore: Warwick and York.

Zeller, R. A., & Carmines, E. G. (1980). *Measurement in the social sciences: The link between theory and data*. London: Cambridge University Press.

Author Index

Credits

TABLE AND FIGURE CREDITS

Chapter 1

Table 1-2, Comparison of narrative and propositional formats. Based on "A Lingusit Compares Narrative and Expository Prose," by C. Kent, 1984, *Journal of Reading, 28,* 232-236.

Chapter 2

Table 2-1, Major categories of new or significantly revised test in the 10th Mental Measurements Yearbook. From *The Tenth Mental Measurements Yearbook,* by J.C. Conoley and J.J. Kramer (Eds.). Copyright © 1989 The Buros Institute of Mental Measurements. Reprinted by permission.

Chapter 3

Close Up: The Vision Quest of Mishi-Waub-Kalkaik. Reprinted from *Ojibway Ceremonies* by Basil Johnston, by permission of the University of Nebraska Press and the Canadian publisher, McClelland & Stewart, Toronto. Copyright © 1982 by McClelland and Stewart.

Quotes. Excerpts from *A History of Psychological Testing* by P.H. DuBois, pp. 4-10. Copyright © 1970 by P.H. DuBois. Reprinted with permission by the author.

Chapter 4

Table 4-1, Emergence of discussions about measuring mental phenomena. Summarized from "The Problem of Measurement in the Psychology of the Eighteenth Century" by K. Ramul, 1960, *American Psychologist, 15,* 256-265.

Chapter 8

Table 8-1, Meanings accorded specific response categories on the Rorschach Inkblot Test. Based on *Assessment of Behavior* by J.E. Horrocks, 1964, 631-635. Copyright © 1964 by Charles E. Merrill. Used by permission of the author.

Chapter 9

Figure 9-5, Descriptions and items of the type used in the clincal scales of the MMPI. Minnesota Multiphasic Personality Inventory (MMPI). Based on but not quoted directly from *An MMPI Handbook: A Guide to Use in Clinical Practice and Research* by W.G. Dahlstrom and G.S. Welsh, 1972, 100-133. Copyright © 1972 by the University of Minnesota, 1942, 1943 (renewed 1970). Reproduced by permission of the University of Minnesota Press.

Figure 9-6, Validity scales for the MMPI. Minnesota Multiphasic Personality Inventory (MMPI). Based on but not quoted directly from *An MMPI Handbook: A Guide to Use in Clinical Practice and Research* by W.G. Dahlstrom and G.S. Welsh, 1972, pp. 100-133. Copyright © 1972 by the University of Minnesota. Used by permission.

Figure 9-7, Normal MMPI profile. Data based on *An MMPI Handbook: A Guide to Use in Clinical Practice and Research* by W.G. Dahlstrom and G.S. Welsh, 1960, p. 89, Fig. 6. Copyright © 1960 by the University of Minnesota Press. Used by permission.

Figure 9-8, Alcoholic MMPI profile. Data based on *An MMPI Handbook: A Guide to Use in Clinical Practice and Research* by W.G. Dahlstrom and G.S. Welsh, 1960, p. 94, Fig. 12. Copyright © 1960 by the University of Minnesota Press. Used by permission.

Figure 9-9, Schizophrenic MMPI profile. Data based on *An MMPI Handbook: A Guide to Use in Clinical Practice and Research* by W.G. Dahlstrom and G.S. Welsh, 1960, p. 100, Fig. 20. Copyright © 1960 by the University of Minnesota Press. Used by permission.

Figure 9-11, Strong Interest Inventory. Modified and

reproduced by special permission of the Publisher, Consulting Psychologists Press, Inc., Palo Alto, CA 94303 from the Strong Interest Inventory of the Strong Vocational Interest Blanks, Form T317. Copyright © 1994 by The Board of Trustees of the Leland Stanford Junior University. All rights reserved. Printed under license from the Stanford University Press, Stanford, CA 94305. Further reproduction is prohibited without the Publisher's written consent.

Chapter 10

Figure 10-3, Items of the type used by Thurstone. From "Primary Mental Abilities" by L.L. Thurstone, 1938, *Psychometric Monographs, Whole No. 1*, 1-94.

Table 10-11, The primary mental abilities. Based on "Primary Mental Abilities" by L.L. Thurstone, 1938, *Psychometric Monographs, Whole No. 1*.

Chapter 12

Close Up: The ethical principles of psychologists. From "Ethical Principles of Psychologists and Code of Conduct," *American Psychologist, 47*, 1597-1611. Copyright © 1992 by the American Psychological Association. Reprinted by permission.

Table 12-6, Publications concerning the 12 leading tests in 1951. From "A Note Concerning the History of Testing," by N.D. Sundberg, 1954, *American Psychologist, 9*, 150-151.

Chapter 13

Table 13-2, Attributes of highly anxious persons as articulated by our theory of anxiety. Adapted from "Experimental Approaches to Test Anxiety: Attention and the Uses of Information," by I.G. Sarason, 1972, *Anxiety: Current Trends in Theory and Research*, 381-403. Copyright © 1972 by Academic Press. Adapted by permission of Academic Press and the author.

Table 13-3, Items for Unadorned Anxiety Test. Adapted from "Experimental Approaches to Test Anxiety: Attention and the Uses of Information," by I.G. Sarason, 1972, *Anxiety: Current Trends in Theory and Research*, p. 385. Copyright © 1972 by Academic Press. Adapted by permission of Academic Press and the author.

Table 13-10, Content scale of the Personality Research Form. From *Personality Research Form Manual, Third Edition*, by D.N. Jackson, p. 22. Copyright © 1989 Sigma Assessment Systems, Inc. Reprinted by permission.

Table 13-12, PRF scale correlations with autonomy. From *Personality Research Form Manual, Third Edition*, by D.N. Jackson, p. 22. Copyright © 1989 Sigma Assessment Systems, Inc. Reprinted by permission.

Chapter 14

Figure 14-1, Clinical, counseling, educational, industrial, and psychometric psychology subgroups. From "An Empirical Description of the Subfields of Psychology," by R.F. Lockman, 1964, *American Psychologist, 19*, 645-653.

Table 14-1, Percentages of APA members indicating primary affiliation with test-related subfields in psychology. From "An Empirical Description of the Subfields of Psychology," by R.F. Lockman, 1964, *American Psychologist, 19*, 647.

Table 14-2, Classifications of tests from the Sixth Mental Measurement Yearbook. From *The Sixth Mental Measurements Yearbook,* by O.K. Buros (Ed.). Copyright © 1965 The Buros Institute of Mental Measurements. Reprinted by permission.

Figure 14-2, Change in utility as a function of the selection ratio. From *Psychological Tests and Personnel Decisions*, by Lee J. Cronbach and Goldine C. Gleser, p. 38. Copyright © 1965 by the Board of Trustees of the University of Illinois. Reprinted by permission of the University of Illinois Press.

Figure 14-3, Gain in utility with sequential, single-screen, and battery strategies. From *Psychological Tests and Personnel Decisions*, by Lee J. Cronbach and Goldine C. Gleser, p. 78. Copyright © 1965 by the Board of Trustees of the University of Illinois. Reprinted by permission of the University of Illinois Press.

Figure 14-8, Numbers of resident patients in state and local government mental hospitals in the U.S. from 1964 through 1970. From *Fundamentals of Human Neuropsychology, Second Edition*, by Kolb and Witshaw, p. 58. Copyright © 1985 by W.H. Freeman and Company. Reprinted by permission.

Chapter 15

Table 15-1, Data demonstrating the relation between an IQ test and school performance. From *The Psychology of Individual Differences*, by L.E. Tyler, p. 74. Copyright © 1939 by Prentice-Hall, Inc. Reprinted by permission.

Figure 15-4, Illustration of the six kinds of products using figural examples. From *The Nature of Human Intelligence*, by J.P. Guilford, p. 64. Copyright © 1967 by McGraw-Hill Book Company. Reprinted by permission.

Figure 15-5, Guilford's structure of Intellect Model. From *The Nature of Human Intelligence*, by J.P. Guilford, inside front cover. Copyright © 1967 by McGraw-Hill Book Company. Reprinted by permission.

Figure 15-9, The relationships among metacomponents, performance components, and knowledge acquisition. From *The Triarchic Mind*, by Robert J. Sternberg, p. 60. Copyright © 1988 by Robert J. Sternberg. Reprinted by permission of Viking Penguin, a division of Penguin Books USA Inc.

Figure 15-10, Relationships among various aspects of the triarchic theory of human intelligence. From *The Triarchic Mind*, by Robert J. Sternberg, p. 68. Copyright © 1988 by Robert J. Sternberg. Reprinted by permission of Viking Penguin, a division of Penguin Books USA Inc.

Table 15-4, Several sample items from the Sternberg Multidimensional Abilities Test. From "T and T is an Explosive Combination: Technology and Testing," by

R.J. Sternberg, 1990, *Educational Psychologist, 384*, 201-222. Copyright © 1990 by the American Psychological Association. Reprinted by permission.

Table 15-5, Rules used in the solution of Raven items. From "What One Intelligence Test Measures: A Theoretical Account of the Processing in the Raven Progressive Matrices," by P.A. Carpenter, M.A. Just, and P. Shell, 1990, *Psychological Review, 97*, 404-431. Copyright © 1990 by the American Psychological Association. Reprinted by permission of the author.

Figure 15-11, Problems of the type found on the Raven Progressive Matrices. From "What One Intelligence Test Measures: A Theoretical Account of the Processing in the Raven Progressive Matrices," by P.A. Carpenter, M.A. Just, and P. Shell, 1990, *Psychological Review, 97*, 404-431. Copyright © 1990 by the American Psychological Association. Reprinted by permission of the author.

Chapter 16

Figure 16-2, The manner in which Eysenck's proposed dimensions of personality encompass Galen's earlier typological view. From *Manual for the Eysenck Personality Inventory* by H. Eysenck and S.B.G. Eysenck, 1964, p. 27. Copyright © 1964 by Educational and Industrial Testing Service, San Diego, CA. Reprinted by permission.

Table 16-3, The 20 scales of the Sixteen Personality Factor Questionnaire. Based on *Handbook for the Sixteen Personality Factor Questionnaire (16PF)* by R.B. Cattell, H.W. Eber, and M.M. Tatsuoka, 1970.

Figure 16-4, A hierarchical model for the structure of personality from traits to specific behaviors incorporating the "Big Five." From "Personality Structure: Emergence of the Five-Factor Model," by J.M. Digman, 1990, Annual Review of Psychology, 41, p. 421. Copyright © 1990 by the American Psychological Association. Reprinted by permission of the author.

Figure 16-7, The basic personality patterns in Millon's theory. Based on "Interpretive Guide to the Millon Clinical Multiaxial Inventory (MCMI-II)" by T. Millon and C. Green, 1989, *Major Psychological Assessment Instruments, Volume II*, C.S. Newmark (Ed.). Copyright © 1989 by Allyn and Bacon. Used by permission.

Table 16-7, Basic personality scales from the MCMI-II. Based on "Interpretive Guide to the Millon Clinical Multiaxial Inventory (MCMI-II)" by T. Millon and C. Green, 1989, *Major Psychological Assessment Instruments, Volume II*, C.S. Newmark (Ed.). Copyright © 1989 by Allyn and Bacon. Used by permission.

Table 16-8, ThreeMCMI-II scales measuring pathological personality disorders. Based on "Interpretive Guide to the Millon Clinical Multiaxial Inventory (MCMI-II)" by T. Millon and C. Green, 1989, *Major Psychological Assessment Instruments, Volume II*, C.S. Newmark (Ed.). Copyright © 1989 by Allyn and Bacon. Used by permission.

Table 16-9, Clinical syndrome scales from the MCMI-II. Based on "Interpretive Guide to the Millon Clinical

Multiaxial Inventory (MCMI-II)" by T. Millon and C. Green, 1989, *Major Psychological Assessment Instruments, Volume II*, C.S. Newmark (Ed.). Copyright © 1989 by Allyn and Bacon. Used by permission.

Table 16-10, Modifier and correction scales from the MCMI-II. Based on "Interpretive Guide to the Millon Clinical Multiaxial Inventory (MCMI-II)" by T. Millon and C. Green, 1989, *Major Psychological Assessment Instruments, Volume II*, C.S. Newmark (Ed.). Copyright © 1989 by Allyn and Bacon. Used by permission.

Table 16-11, MCMI-II scales, Millon's theoretical personality patterns, and their Axis II DSM-III-R equivalents. Based on "Interpretive Guide to the Millon Clinical Multiaxial Inventory (MCMI-II)" by T. Millon and C. Green, 1989, *Major Psychological Assessment Instruments, Volume II*, C.S. Newmark (Ed.). Copyright © 1989 by Allyn and Bacon. Used by permission.

Table 16-12, Item changes and deletions in the basic validity and clinical scale in MMPI-2. Based on *Minnesota Multiphasic Personality Inventory-2 (MMPI-2): Manual for Administration and Scoring*. Copyright © by the Regents of the University of Minnesota 1942, 1943, 1951, 1967 (renewed 1970), 1989. This manual 1989. All rights reserved. Reproduced by permission of the University of Minnesota Press.

Chapter 18

Table 18-1, Validation data for the Bender-Gestalt. From "The Bender Gestalt Test: A Scoring Method for Identifying Brain Damage," by J.D. Hain, 1964, *Journal of Consulting Psychology, 28*, 34-40. Reprinted by permission.

Table 18-6, A theory-driven battery based on work at the Montreal Neurological Institute. From *Fundamentals of Human Neuropsychology, Second Edition*, by Kolb and Wishaw, p. 681. Copyright © 1985 by W.H. Freeman and Company. Reprinted by permission.

Chapter 19

Table 19-4, Suggested renaming of various types of validity. From "Test Validity and the Ethics of Assessment," by S. Messick, 1980, *American Psychologist, 35*, 1012-1027. Copyright © 1980 by the American Psychological Association. Reprinted by permission.

Figure 19-11, The facets of validity. Summarized from "The Once and Future Issues of Validity: Assessing the Meaning and Consequences of Measurement," by S. Messick, 1988, pp33-48. In *Test Validity*, by H. Wainer and H.I. Braun, Eds. Copyright © 1988 Lawrence Erlbaum Associates, Inc. Reprinted by permission.

PHOTO CREDITS

Page 6, © Michael Siluk. Page 30, © Eric Kroll/Omni Photo Communications, Inc. Page 54, Allen Zak/Meese Photo Research. Page 69, Monkmeyer Press/Merrim. Page 91, Maynard Owen Williams, © National